Obadiah Sforno: Light of the Nations

Maimonides Library for Philosophy and Religion

General Editor

Giuseppe Veltri (*Universität Hamburg*)

Managing Editor

Sarah Wobick-Segev (*Universität Hamburg*)

Editorial Board

Jonathan Garb (*The Hebrew University of Jerusalem*)
Racheli Haliva (*Shandong University*)
Yehuda Halper (*Bar-Ilan University*)
Warren Zev Harvey (*The Hebrew University of Jerusalem, emeritus*)
Christine Hayes (*Yale University, emerita*)
Julie Klein (*Villanova University*)
Yitzhak Y. Melamed (*Johns Hopkins University*)
Stephan Schmid (*Universität Hamburg*)
Josef Stern (*University of Chicago, emeritus*)
Sarah Stroumsa (*The Hebrew University of Jerusalem, emerita*)
Irene E. Zwiep (*Universiteit van Amsterdam*)

VOLUME 5

The titles published in this series are listed at *brill.com/mlpr*

Obadiah Sforno: Light of the Nations

Or ʿAmmim / Lumen Gentium

Edited by

Giuseppe Veltri
Giada Coppola
Florian Dunklau

BRILL

LEIDEN | BOSTON

Cover illustration: Obadiah Sforno, Lumen Gentium, printed by Anselmo Giaccarelli, 1548.

Library of Congress Cataloging-in-Publication Data

Names: Veltri, Giuseppe, editor. | Coppola, Giada, editor. | Dunklau, Florian, editor.
| Sforno, Obadiah ben Jacob, approximately 1470-approximately 1550. Or ʿamim.
| Sforno, Obadiah ben Jacob, approximately 1470-approximately 1550. Or ʿamim.
English. | Sforno, Obadiah ben Jacob, approximately 1470-approximately 1550.
Or ʿamim. Latin.
Title: Obadiah Sforno : light of the nations : Or ʿammim/Lumen gentium / edited
by Giuseppe Veltri, Giada Coppola, Florian Dunklau.
Other titles: Obadiah Sforno : Or ʿammim
Description: Leiden ; Boston : Brill, [2024] | Series: Maimonides library for
philosophy and religion, 2666-8777 ; volume 5 | Includes bibliographical
references and index.
Identifiers: LCCN 2024026414 | ISBN 9789004689718 (hardback) |
ISBN 9789004689725 (ebook)
Subjects: LCSH: Sforno, Obadiah ben Jacob, approximately 1470-approximately
1550. Or ʿamim. | Jewish philosophy. | Philosophy, Medieval.
Classification: LCC B759.S433 O23 2024 | DDC 181/.06–dc23/eng/20240705
LC record available at https://lccn.loc.gov/2024026414

Typeface for the Latin, Greek, and Cyrillic scripts: "Brill". See and download: brill.com/brill-typeface.

ISSN 2666-8777
ISBN 978-90-04-68971-8 (hardback)
ISBN 978-90-04-68972-5 (e-book)
DOI 10.1163/9789004689725

Copyright 2025 by Giuseppe Veltri, Giada Coppola, Florian Dunklau. Published by Koninklijke Brill BV, Leiden, The Netherlands.
Koninklijke Brill BV incorporates the imprints Brill, Brill Nijhoff, Brill Schöningh, Brill Fink, Brill mentis, Brill Wageningen Academic, Vandenhoeck & Ruprecht, Böhlau and V&R unipress.
Koninklijke Brill BV reserves the right to protect this publication against unauthorized use. Requests for re-use and/or translations must be addressed to Koninklijke Brill BV via brill.com or copyright.com.

This book is printed on acid-free paper and produced in a sustainable manner.

Contents

Preface VII

Introduction—Obadiah Sforno: *Light of the Nations* 1
1. The Author 1
2. Manuscripts, Prints, and Editions 3
   2.1 *The Hebrew Version:* Or ʿAmmim 3
   2.2 *The Latin Version:* Lumen Gentium 5
3. Between Two Worlds: Translation and Cultural Transfer 7
   3.1 *Latin-into-Hebrew and Hebrew-into-Latin?* 7
   3.2 *Teaching and Adapting for the Christians* 13
4. Latin Priority? The Question of Translation 16
5. Light of the Nations 19
   5.1 *Intention* 19
   5.2 *Methodology* 20
   5.3 *Structure* 24
   5.4 *Philosophy: God's Anthropocentric Teleology* 26
6. Reception: Elijah of Butrio's Commentary on *Or ʿAmmim* 33
7. Sforno's Philosophy and *Light* in Modern Scholarship 34

Obadiah Sforno: Light of the Nations
Edited and translated by Florian Dunklau (Or ʿAmmim) and Giada Coppola (Lumen Gentium)

Notes on Editions and Translations 39
1. Note on the Hebrew Edition and Its English Translation 39
2. Additional Note on the Latin Edition and Its Translation 40
3. Sigla in the Critical Apparatus 40
4. Modern English Translations Consulted 41

Editions and Translations of *Or ʿAmmim* and *Lumen Gentium* 43
   Florian Dunklau and Giada Coppola
   Epistola dedicatoria – Dedicatory Epistle 44
   אגרת – Epistle 46
   הקדמה – *Prologus* – Introduction 52
1. תנועת ההויה – *De generatione* 78
2. יסודות – *De elementis* 98
3. חומר ראשון – *De materia prima* 114
4. שמים – *De celo* 130
5. תנועה – *De motu* 154
6. בריאה – *De creatione* 170
7. בלתי גשמי – *De incorporeitate* 194
8. אחדות – *De unitate* 204
9. ידיעה – *De scientia* 220
10. רצון – *De voluntate* 244
11. השגחה – *De sollicitudine* 256
12. נפש – *De anima* 274
13. מעשיות – *De moralitate* 326

14 בחיריות – *De arbitraria diligentia* 336
15 תכלית כל גשמי – *De celestibus* 344
   כלל העולה – *Sumarium* – Summary 360
   Imprimatur 396

Edition of MS IOM B 169,3 399

Essay—From Nothing Comes Nothing: The Theory of Primordial Chaos in Sforno's Writings 408
   Giada Coppola
1 The Function of the Prologue and the Fifteen *Quaestiones* 409
2 Sforno's Incompleteness 414
3 Sforno's Sources 415
4 The Account of Genesis in *Light of the Nations* and Sforno's Biblical Commentaries 417
5 Outline of the First Six Disputed Questions 418
6 Creation and Generation 421
7 *Ex nihilo nihil fit* 422
8 Creation as Generation: On the Movement of Generation and Corruption 424
9 Locomotion and the Movement of Generation and Corruption 425
10 Divine Causation 428
11 Agent and Goal 434
12 Generation *in fieri* 442
13 The Elements and Prime Matter 444
14 The Role of Chance in the Sublunary World 457
15 The Movement of Generation and Corruption and the Compound 458
16 Matter, the Elements, and the Movement of Generation and Corruption in Sforno's Exegetical Interpretation 461
17 The Ultimate Goal in Genesis 474

Glossary 483
1 Hebrew–Latin–English 483
2 Latin–Hebrew–English 495
Bibliography 507
Source Index to the Editions and Translations 513
Index of Persons 519

Preface

> And it says (Jeremiah 9:23): 'But only in this should one glory: having understanding and knowing Me,' so that many wise men of the generations, who endeavour to find intellectual arguments for the foundations of the Torah, may hear the voices. [But] insufficient words come from their hearts, like the statements of the adherents of religion. And therefore, they regard as foreign the [intellectual] roots of our Torah, especially regarding the existence of a creator who generates and has providence over all, and others that are not known from clear [examination], but only through a commandment to believe in them, to find pleasure before our God, who [indeed] did not command us anything like this, especially not regarding the theoretical portion [of the Torah]. But He commanded us to know by observing all the pure speech of His justice.
> OBADIAH SFORNO, *Or 'Ammin* (Introduction).

Obadiah Sforno's philosophical treatise *Light of the Nations*, which is published in this volume in its Hebrew and—for the first time—Latin versions together with English translations, is a key text towards achieving a more comprehensive understanding of the work of this sixteenth-century Italian Jewish rabbi, exegete, and philosophical author. Sforno's oeuvre is a vivid example of the biculturalism arising from the two common foundations that shaped medieval and early modern European society—Christian as well as Jewish—no matter how segregated they were by religious, social, and legal boundaries: Jerusalem and Athens; that is, the Hebrew Bible and Greek philosophy, the latter transmitted via Arabic translators and commentators. Obadiah Sforno was well versed in both and was a man "between two worlds."

Today, Sforno is best known as an omnipresent figure in the field of Torah exegesis. Since its first publication in 1567, his rational and philosophical Commentary on the Pentateuch has come to be one of the most referenced works in exegetical literature, and it has been reprinted several times. Sforno's striving for plain, philologically, philosophically, and scientifically backed explanations of the biblical text made him an ideal companion for a modern reader and student of the central books of the Hebrew Bible. It is thus no coincidence that his sole philosophical work in a traditional scholastic style, *Or 'Ammin*, not only preceded his exegetical masterpiece in terms of publication, but—as the most recent research has shown—also predated its compilation, containing interpretations of verses from the Torah, the Psalms, and Job found verbatim in his biblical commentaries.

Sforno was convinced of the heavenly origin of philosophy, following the Humanists' path towards the sources (*ad fontes*) of wisdom, which in his opinion was genuinely rooted in the Torah and given to the whole of mankind. In his view, the final goal of man as created "in the image of God" (Genesis 1:26), which is the divine human intellect, is to seek ethical and intellectual perfection as a striving for *imitatio Dei*. Sforno's *Light of the Nations* serves two purposes: to reveal the rationality of the divine revelations and their indubitable intellectual proofs, and—based on twenty-seven Aristotelian-Averroean propositions—to show the rational conclusiveness of general religious beliefs in both Judaism and Christianity. It was this universalistic mindset that led Sforno to seek the publication of the Latin version as *Lumen Gentium*—a text that fell into near oblivion for centuries.

The "Between Two Worlds ..." project that provided the organisational basis for this publication was initiated in 2015 by Giuseppe Veltri and the editors of this volume, in collaboration with Saverio Campanini, as a research project funded by the Deutsche Forschungsgemeinschaft. We would like to thank the DFG for the generous financial support that made this research on Obadiah Sforno's philosophical work possible. The editors of this volume would like to express their gratitude to Saverio Campanini for his constant help with the project. Many thanks also go to Warren Zev Harvey for his continuous support and advice. We owe a great deal to Daniel Davies, Diana Di Segni, Hanna Gentili, Aleida Paudice, and Gadi Weber for their critical reading and assessment of the texts, editions, and translations. Special thanks go to Sarah Wobick-Segev and Yoav Meyrav for their organisational support and helpful suggestions during the preparation of this volume. The final language and copy editing was carried out by Katharine Handel. To all, we owe many thanks.

Giuseppe Veltri, Florian Dunklau, and Giada Coppola
Hamburg, July 2023

Introduction

1 The Author

Obadiah ben Jacob Sforno[1] is one of the most renowned Jewish biblical exegetes. Born in the mid-1470s in Cesena (Romagna), he was a member of a family of bankers of Catalan origin who came to Bologna in the early fifteenth century.[2] His father Jacob di Rubino Sforno ran a loan bank in Cesena at the time of his son's birth.[3] After receiving a traditional Jewish education from his father, whom he describes as "my honoured teacher and father R. Jacob Sforno" (בכמא״ר יעקב ספורנו זלה״ה) in the introduction to *Or 'Ammim*,[4] Sforno moved to Rome in the 1490s to study medicine, which he concluded with a doctoral degree that was granted to him by the University of Ferrara in 1501.[5] It was during this time that his notable encounter with the German Humanist and Hebraist Johann Reuchlin (1455–1522), who would later write a Latin Hebrew grammar (*De rudimentis hebraicis*; Pforzheim, 1506), took place. It is a testament to Sforno's esteem and erudition at this early age that Reuchlin, who in 1498 was on a diplomatic mission in Rome and who was already well versed in Hebrew from his previous studies, sought his services as a lecturer in Hebrew and also (as Saverio Campanini assumes) an introduction to Maimonidean philosophy.[6]

Sforno was one of the leading personalities of the Roman Jewish community. As such, in 1519, he issued a decision in the case of Donina, the daughter of Samuel Tzarfati (physician to the pope), which had been requested by Israel ben Jehiel Ashkenazi, the chief rabbi of Rome.[7] He was also a member of the delegation that welcomed David Reuveni to Rome in 1524.[8] Following the sack of Rome in 1527, Sforno moved to Bologna, where he practised as a physician

---

1. Note: Transliteration of Hebrew terms and names follows Brill's simple transliteration system (https://brill.com/fileasset/downloads_static/static_fonts_simplehebrewtransliteration.pdf), with the following minor exceptions: א = ' (only transl. if it is a glotal stop or indicates a hiatus (e.g. *Miqra'ot*)). ע = ʻ, ה also when a mater lectionis (e.g. *Torah*). Hebrew names that have a common anglicised form are not transliterated.
2. Samuele and Senton (= Shem Ṭov) "Desforn" are mentioned in Barcelona in 1383 and 1391 (see Isidore Loeb, "Liste nominative des Juifs de Barcelone en 1392," *Revue des études juives* 7 (1882): 59, 62–63). "Samuel figlio di Santo del Forno" came to Bologna, where his son Rubino ran a bank in the Piazza San Stefano, in 1435 (see Elvio Giuditta, *Araldica Ebraica in Italia. Segue parte II: Stemmi esistenti nell'antico cimitero ebraico di Venezia, lettere dalla ralla Z* (Turin: Società italiana di studi araldici, 2007), 92–93).
3. Claudio Riva, "Tracce della presenza del banchiere ebreo bolognese Jacob di Rubino Sforno in Cesena," *Studi romagnoli* 49 (2018): 397–410.
4. §1 (*OA*), p. 2ʳ. In the following, references to paragraphs (§) in the footnotes always refer to our edition of *Light of the Nations*.
5. Vittore Colorni, "Spigolature su Obadià Sforno: La sua laurea a Ferrara e la quasi ignota edizione della sua opera *Or 'Amim* nella versione latina," *La rassegna mensile di Israel* 28, nos. 3/4 (1962): 78–88. His doctoral certificate bears the date 27 April 1501.
6. Saverio Campanini, "Sforno, 'Ovadyah," *Dizionario biografico degli Italiani* 92 (2018), https://www.treccani.it/enciclopedia/ovadyah-sforno_(Dizionario-Biografico). See also Campanini, "Reuchlins jüdische Lehrer aus Italien," in *Reuchlin und Italien*, ed. Gerald Dörner (Stuttgart: Thorbecke, 1999), 69–85.
7. Hermann Vogelstein and Paul Rieger, *Geschichte der Juden in Rom. Band 2: 1420–1870* (Berlin, 1895), 78, 84.
8. Ephraim Finkel, *R. Obadja Sforno als Exeget* (Breslau, 1896), 7.

and established a yeshivah that was particularly open to Jewish students who combined medicine and traditional studies.[9]

Knowledge about Sforno's private life and his considerable material wealth can be gained from his last will and testament (of which there are two versions, dated 1547 and 1549), which was recently published by Andrew Berns.[10] Sforno was married twice, first to Allegra Norsa, who was the mother of his sons Jacob, Florio, and Moses and his daughter Dora, and second to Giulia, daughter of the late Isaac da Pisa, a member of another famous family of bankers.[11] He was survived by his second wife when he died of old age in 1550.[12]

Most of Sforno's literary production was only printed after his death, with the exception of three of his works: (1) his sole philosophical treatise *Or 'Ammim* (Bologna, 1537),[13] (2) a Commentary on *Pirqe Avot* (Bologna, 1540) that was included as part of the Maḥzor of the Roman rite,[14] and (3) the Latin version of *Or 'Ammim*, which was published as *Lumen Gentium* (Bologna, 1548).[15] The publication of his philosophical work prompts us to suggest that Sforno himself considered it to be of significance for the Jewish and Christian public alike. However, to this day, his fame in the Jewish community rests on his Bible commentaries, first and foremost on the Pentateuch (*Be'ur 'al ha-Torah*; Venice, 1567), together with his Commentaries on the Song of Songs and Ecclesiastes[16] and his treatise *Kavvanot ha-Torah*. His Torah commentary was chosen to be part of the Amsterdam *Miqra'ot Gedolot, Qehillat Mosheh* (1724–1728), and it became especially popular among Jews in Eastern Europe, undergoing numerous reprints.[17] His other exegetical writings are Commentaries on Psalms (*Perush Tehillim*; Venice, 1586), Job (*Mishpat Tzedeq*; Venice, 1590, which was printed with Tzemaḥ Duran's Job commentary *Ohev Mishpat*), and Zechariah, Habakkuk, and Jonah (*Liqqute Shoshanim*; Venice, 1602).

As we learn from a mention in an undated letter to his brother Hananel, Sforno also wrote a (lost) Hebrew grammar in Latin for the "Lord of Tosignano," who may be identified as Armaciotto de' Ramazzotti (1464–1539).[18] However,

---

9 Campanini, "Reuchlins jüdische Lehrer," 80.
10 Andrew Berns, "Ovadiah Sforno's Last Will and Testament," *Journal of Jewish Studies* 68 (2017): 1–33.
11 Campanini, "Sforno, 'Ovadyah."
12 Campanini.
13 Obadiah Sforno, *Or 'Ammim* (Bologna, 1537); see below, "2. Manuscripts, Prints, and Editions."
14 Obadiah Sforno, *Maḥzor ke-fi minhag q"q Roma 'im perush Qimḥa de-avshuna* ['a. y. Yoḥanan ben Yosef Ish Ṭrivish] *u-masekhet Avot 'im perush* [...] *ha-Rambam ve-'im perush* [...] *'Ovadyah Sforno* (Bologna, 1540).
15 Obadiah Sforno, *Opusculum nuper editum contra nonnullas Peripateticorum opiniones demonstratiue docens presertim circa creationem & vniuersi nouitatem & diuinam de mortalibus curam & humanarum animarum immortalitatem. Quas ipsi turpiter respuunt religionis penitus irridentes quare illud merito lumen gentium appello* (Bologna, 1548): see below, "2. Manuscripts, Prints, and Editions."
16 Sforno sent a copy of his Commentary on Ecclesiastes with dedications to King Henri II of France (Finkel, *R. Obadja*, 23).
17 To mention only a few here: Dubrowa: s.n., 1804; Lemberg: Grossmann, 1808 (only on the Torah); Berdychiv: S. Isachar Ber, 1817; Warsaw: s.n., 1856; Czernowitz: Eckhardt. 1858 (only on the Torah); Vienna: Zamarski & Dittmarsch, 1859 (*Miqra'ot Gedolot*, ed. Netter); Warsaw: Levensohn, 1860–1866 (*Miqra'ot Gedolot*); and Vilna: s.n, 1876.
18 Campanini, "Sforno, 'Ovadyah"; see Parma, Biblioteca Palatina 2239, fol. 133ʳ; cf. Obadiah Sforno, *Kitve R. 'Ovadyah Sforno*, ed. Ze'ev Gottlieb (Jerusalem: Mossad ha-Rav Kook, 1983), 516.

INTRODUCTION

despite a long period in which it was misattributed to him, he was not the author of an anonymous copy of Moses ibn Ezra's paraphrase of Euclid's *Elements* translated from Arabic (*Be'ur le-Sefer Uqlidas*), which survives in MS Paris, Bibliothèque Nationale hébreu 1007 [MS no. 435], fols. 37^r–65^v.[19]

Three modern editions of Sforno's writings are worth mentioning. Ze'ev (Wolf) Gottlieb edited his Commentary on the Pentateuch and later also his other writings, including *Or 'Ammim* (for the problems with his edition, see part 2.1 below).[20] Rabbi Raphael Pelcovitz provided the first English translation of Sforno's Commentaries on the Pentateuch and *Pirqe Avot*, with lengthy commentaries.[21] Finally, more recent, but still highly important are the editions produced by Rabbi Moshe Kravetz of Bet-Shemesh, who has published some of Sforno's writings from previously unnoticed manuscript sources, including, *inter alia*, the first edition of a pre-editorial recension of his Torah commentary from a manuscript in St. Petersburg[22] and oral Torah lectures noted down by one of his pupils, now known as *Amar ha-Ga'on*.[23]

2 Manuscripts, Prints, and Editions

2.1 *The Hebrew Version:* Or 'Ammim

Obadiah Sforno's philosophical treatise *Light of the Nations* was published by the "partners in silk production" (הצעירים השותפים יצ״ו גם יחד עושים מלאכת המשי) in Bologna in 1537 ([5]297 = עזרך). It appeared in quarto format numbering sixty-four folios. The "silk weavers" ran the only Hebrew printing press in Bologna at that time, and the first for decades following the activity of the Hebrew printing pioneer Abraham ben Ḥayyim "the Dyer" of Pesaro in the city (between 1477 and 1482). The "socii," among them Sforno himself, operated between 1537 and 1541 and published nine books, including the Maḥzor of the Roman rite containing Sforno's aforementioned Commentary on *Pirqe Avot* (1540/41).[24]

Although there are two nearly complete surviving manuscripts of *Or 'Ammim*, they unfortunately do not add to our knowledge about the background of the compilation of the book:

1. MS Paris 1007, fols. 1^r–27^r. This manuscript bears a colophon identifying it as a complete transcript of the printed book that was completed in 1572.[25]

---

19 Obadiah Sforno, *Be'ur 'al ha-Torah*, ed. Ze'ev Gottlieb (Jerusalem: Mossad ha-Rav Kook, 1980), 21 n. 113.
20 Sforno, *Be'ur*; Sforno, *Kitve*.
21 Obadiah Sforno, *Commentary on the Torah*, trans. Raphael Pelcovitz, 2 vols. (New York: Mesorah, 1987–1989); Sforno, *Commentary on Pirkei Avos*, trans. Raphael Pelcovitz (New York: Mesorah, 1996).
22 Obadiah Sforno, *Perush R. 'Ovadyah Sforno ha-mevu'ar: Perush ha-Torah*, ed. Moshe Kravetz (Bet-Shemesh: s.n., 2015); Sforno, *Sifre Yonah, Ḥavaqquq, Zekharyah 'im perush Sforno*, ed. Moshe Kravetz (Bet-Shemesh: s.n., 2015); Sforno, *Shir ha-shirim, Rut 'im perush Sforno*, ed. Moshe Kravetz (Bet-Shemesh: s.n., 2015); Sforno, *Megillat Qohelet 'im perush Sforno*, ed. Moshe Kravetz (Bet-Shemesh: s.n., 2016).
23 Obadiah Sforno, *Amar ha-ga'on. Shi'ure R. 'Ovadyah Sforno mi-ketav yad talmido 'al ha-Torah*, ed. Moshe Kravetz (Bet-Shemesh: s.n., 2017).
24 David Werner Amram, *The Makers of Hebrew Books in Italy: Being Chapters in the History of the Hebrew Printing Press* (Philadephia: Greenstone, 1909), 42, 230–235. Among the other works are Menaḥem de Recanati's *Pisqe Hilkhot* (1538) and Judah he-Ḥasid's *Sefer ha-Ḥasidim* (1538).
25 This manuscript was edited as part of a doctoral thesis by Haïm Harboun, "*Or Ha 'Amim*

2. MS Cincinnati, Hebrew Union College 729, 22 fols. This is also a transcript of the print, which closely resembles it, but omits the summary (*kelal ha-'olah*).

A third manuscript is in the custody of the St. Petersburg-based Institute of Oriental Manuscripts at the Russian Academy of Sciences (signature: MS IOM B 169; fols. 149ʳ–155ᵛ). This is an autograph of an alternate version of the summary and it belongs to a compilation of some of Sforno's major writings, among them his Commentary on the Pentateuch (fols. 1ʳ–128ʳ), *Kavvanot ha-Torah* (fols. 132ʳ–146ʳ), and his Commentaries on Zechariah, Habakkuk, and Jonah (fols. 157ʳ–169ʳ). Until recently, due to Cold War restrictions, this manuscript of *Or 'Ammim* was generally unknown to the Western scholarly world, and it has now been edited for the first time.[26]

Some copies of the *editio princeps* spread beyond the boundaries of the Italian peninsula relatively early after they were purchased by Christian Hebraists and Orientalists (e.g., Johann Albrecht Widmanstetter [d. 1557][27] and Sebastian Tengnagel [1563–1636]),[28] while it is first mentioned in a catalogue of Hebrew works by Johannes Buxtorf the Elder (published 1613), though only in a note as part of the entry for Hasdai Crescas's *Light of the Lord*.[29] Buxtorf translated its Hebrew title as *Lux Populorum* and gave an erroneous year of publication (1550). In the enlarged second edition of his father's catalogue (published 1640), his son, Johannes Buxtorf the Younger, even called it a "medical treatise" (*liber Medicus*), and also retained the wrong date.[30] Another faulty dating (1471!), which was perpetuated by many subsequent bibliographers, was proposed by Cornelius van Beughem.[31] These errors were corrected by the "father of Jewish bibliography" Shabbatai Bass in his *Sifte Yeshenim*,[32] which was the basis for Johann Christoph Wolf's entry in his voluminous *Bibliotheca Hebraea*.[33]

Today, a number of copies are available in national and notable libraries in Europe, Israel, and North America. A copy donated to the National Library of Israel by the Harry Friedenwald Collection in 1951 served as a *Vorlage* for a photo-mechanical reprint in 1970 (Ramat Gan; s.n.), while a mid-nineteenth-century attempt at a reprint made by a publisher named David Slutzqi in Warsaw failed when all copies were lost during the printing process.[34]

In 1983, the chief rabbi of Scotland Ze'ev Gottlieb also published an edition of *Or 'Ammim* in his *Kitve Sforno*.[35] Gottlieb was unacquainted both with Latin

---

de Rabbi Obadia Sforno, XVIe siècle: Édition critique et analyse du manuscrit 435 de la Bibliothèque Nationale" (PhD diss., Aix-Marseille 1, 1994).

26　For its possible relevance to the question of the compilation of the Latin version, see below, part 4.

27　Munich, Bayerische Staatsbibliothek, Res/4 A.hebr. 310.

28　Vienna, Österreichische Nationalbibliothek, 20.K.47.

29　Johannes Buxtorf, *De abbreviaturis Hebraicis liber novus [et] copiosus [...]* (Basileae, 1613), 272.

30　Johannes Buxtorf, *De abbreviaturis Hebraicis liber novus [et] copiosus [...] editione secunda* (Basileae, 1640), 310: "Or Ammim, Lux populorum. Author R. Obadias Medicus Siphonius, Impressus Boloniae anno Christi 1550. Est liber Medicus. Est et alius eiusdem nominis, continens quaestiones quindecim de Deo et Anima."

31　Cornelius van Beughem, *Incunabula typographiae sive catalogus librorum scriptorumque proximis ab inventione typographiae annis, usque ad annum Christi M.D.* (Amstelodami, 1668), 126.

32　Shabbatai Bass, *Sefer Sifte Yeshenim*, vol. 1 (Amsterdam, 1680), 5 (no. 112).

33　Johann Christoph Wolf, *Bibliotheca Hebraea*, vol. 1 (Hamburgi and Lipsiae, 1715), 939.

34　Gottlieb in Sforno, *Be'ur*, 65.

35　Gottlieb in Sforno, *Kitve*, 411–508.

Scholasticism and with philosophy in general, which resulted in severe errors in the Hebrew edition: he obviously consulted the Latin version, but blindly corrected all references to the philosophical writings on which *Or ʿAmmim* and *Lumen Gentium* differ according to the Latin text without checking the original sources. The outcome was a Hebrew edition that inherited many mistakes and typographical errors from its counterpart.[36]

2.2 *The Latin Version:* Lumen Gentium

Ten years after *Or ʿAmmim* was published, Obadiah Sforno published a Latin version of it with the title *Lumen Gentium* (Bologna, 1548). Most unusually, he prepared this version in order to reach a Christian audience. The subtitle of *Lumen Gentium*, which does not appear in the Hebrew version, elucidates the content of the book:

> Against some opinions of Aristotle and demonstrating the doctrines of the creation of the universe from nothing, the providence God has over human beings, and the immortality of the human soul, which they [i.e., Aristotelian philosophers] shamefully reject, deriding religion.[37]

This version was published by Anselmo Giaccarelli, a Bolognian printer who began his activity in the second half of the sixteenth century, between 1547 and 1561. He received an annual subsidy of 200 lire from the local government[38] as his printing press operated for the benefit of the University of Bologna.[39] In light of this information, Sforno's edition must be considered one of the first prints and also one of the few philosophical works to be published by Giaccarelli's printing press.[40] The print consists of 108 folios, which bear page numbers until page 41. From page 41 onwards, the pages are given as *recto-verso* until the end of the book (page 72^v). The print is composed in Bolognese Gothic script—an exceptional instance, according to Vittore Colorni.[41]

There is a single surviving manuscript that was preserved in the monastery de' Minori Osservanti di Reggio (Franciscan order) until 1797 and is now part of the collection of the Panizzi Library in Reggio Emilia (MSS. Vari E. 5). This consists of 166 folios. The copyist's style is clear, with an open and rounded script. Scholars who have turned their attention to this document have concluded that it is a copy that predates the printed editions.[42] This informa-

---

36 E.g., a reference to book 9 of Aristotle's *On the Heavens*, which has only four books in total; see Gottlieb in Sforno, *Kitve*, 419 (seventh proposition).

37 Sforno, *Lumen Gentium*, title page: "Opusculum nuper editum contra nonnullas Peripateticorum opiniones demonstratiue docens presertim circa creationem et vniuersi nouitatem et diuinam de mortalibus curam et humanarum animarum immortalitatem. Quas ipsi turpiter respuunt religionis penitus irridentes quare illud merito lumen gentium appello" (Bologna, 1548), colophon.

38 Pierangelo Bellettini, "La stamperia camerale di Bologna. I. Alessandro e Vittorio Benacci (1587–1629)," *La Bibliofilia* 90 (1988): 26.

39 Guido Zaccagnini, *Storia dello Studio di Bologna durante il rinascimento: Con quarantadue illustrazioni* (Florence: Olschki, 1930), 140.

40 During his printing activities, Anselmo Giaccarelli published around 133 works. Of these, only four, including *Lumen Gentium*, were philosophical or medical books.

41 Colorni, "Spigolature," 83–84.

42 Julius Fürst, *Bibliotheca Judaica: Bibliographisches Handbuch der gesammten jüdischen Literatur mit Einschluss der Schriften über Juden und Judenthum und einer Geschichte der jüdischen Bibliographie nach alfabetischer Ordnung der Verfasser*, vol. 3 (Leipzig, 1863), 319;

tion may be deduced from an entry in De Rossi's *Dizionario storico*, which was also the first bibliography to note the existence of the manuscript.[43] De Rossi suggested that Sforno's Latin translation had not been published and that this manuscript copy was the original document that was intended to be printed.

However, our analysis has clarified that this manuscript was not the *Vorlage* submitted and approved for publication, but that it was more likely copied from the printed edition. The three main pieces of evidence to support this conclusion are as follows:

- In the colophon (fol. 2ʳ), the author's name reads "Servadeus Sphurnus Medicus Hebreus suppliciter." In all printed editions (cf. p. 3), the designation "Hebreus" was added to the printed version and was not present in the original typesetting.
- The manuscript has several omissions, such as on fol. 3ʳ, where the copyist did not include the first two words in the last line, "semper suppliciter" (see p. 3 in the printed version).
- The censor's *imprimatur* is written in the copyist's hand.[44]

The first printed copy of *Lumen Gentium* was discovered in 1926 by Alexander Marx.[45] Before this date, scholars supposed—as mentioned above—that the Latin translation of *Or 'Ammim* had not been published at all. Eight copies of the print have been discovered up to now:[46]

Finkel, *R. Obadja*, 11; Colorni, "Spigolature," 83; Saverio Campanini, "Un intellettuale ebreo del Rinascimento: 'Ovadyah Sforno a Bologna e i suoi rapporti con i christiani," in *Verso l'epilogo di una convivenza: Gli ebrei a Bologna nel XVI secolo*, ed. Maria Giuseppina Muzzarelli (Florence: Giuntina, 1996): 120.

43 Giovanni B. de Rossi, *Dizionario storico degli autori ebrei e delle loro opere* (Parma, 1802), 2:127: "Or 'Ammīm, Luce dei Popoli 4° Bologna 1537. Vi confuta gli epicurei e gli atei che negano la Legge, e disputa filosoficamente dell'anima, di Dio, della sua essenza, unità, onnipotenza e provvidenza. Il Buxtorsio e il Bartoloccio malamente lo dicono stampato nel 1550, e peggio l'Hyde, il Beugem, l'Orlandi, e il Chevillier nel 1471. V, gli Annali nostri del sec. XV pag. 154. Lo Sforno stesso avea fatta una traduzione Latina di questo libro e dedicata al re di Francia, e dalla licenza che v'ha in fine dell'inquisitor di Bologna in data del 1548, si vede ch'egli contava di pubblicarla. Ma restò inedita, e io la vidi ms. nella Biblioteca de' Minori Osservanti di Reggio."

44 *Lumen Gentium* concluded with the censor's imprimatur: "Ego frater Tomasmaria Beccadellus Bononiensis inquisitor consentio ut hic liber possit imprimi" (§ 16.30). Tommaso Maria Beccadelli, who came from an aristocratic Bolognian family, was a censor in Bologna (and Ferrara) between 1543 and 1548 (see Adriano Prosperi, *L'Inquisizione romana: Letture e ricerche* [Rome: Edizioni di storia e letteratura, 2003], 110; Campanini, "Un intellettuale," 123). The sole correction that occurs in the text is found in the header of the epistle to King Henri: "Servadeus Sphurnus Medicus *Hebreus* Suppliciter" (§ 0). *Hebreus* was added a second time to cover another word that was later "scraped away." Colorni suggested that the replacement or addition of *Hebreus* was due to censorship (Colorni, "Spigolature," 84). The addition of the word *Jew* is a correction of a typographical error, which was almost certainly made by the printer Anselmo Giaccarelli; the original text reveals the mistake: "Servadeus Sphurnus Medicus *Suppliciters* Suppliciter" (see Rome, Biblioteca Casanatense, *L[MIN] II 20, p. 3).

45 "Standard for Admission at Theological Seminary Raised, Directors Report," *Jewish Daily Bulletin*, 8 November 1926, 2: "Professor Alexander Marx, Librarian, reported that through the generosity of Mortimer L. Schiff, the Library has been able to obtain three interesting collections of sixteenth century private letters from Italy [...] and two Latin books: One a translation of Isaac Israeli's collected medical and philosophic works, and the other, Servadeus Sphurnus, Lumen Gentium, Bologna 1548, dedicated to King Henry of France."

46 Campanini, "Un intellettuale," 120 n. 3.

1. Rome, Biblioteca Casanatense, *L(MIN) II 20[47]
2. Bologna, Biblioteca Universitaria, A. 5. Tab. 1.F.1 402/3
3. Modena, Biblioteca Estense Universitaria, A 017 G 006
4. Rome, Biblioteca Apostolica Vaticana, R.G. Filos. IV.732
5. Bazzano, Biblioteca provinciale Salvatore Tommasi, CINQ. B 245 / b
6. Paris, Bibliothèque Mazarine, 4° 15228–2 [Res]
7. Jerusalem, National Library of Israel, R8 = FR 889[48]
8. New York, Jewish Theological Seminary, MIC PRINT 484

In *Lumen Gentium*, the author's name is given in Latin. "Obadiah" is rendered as *Servadeus Sphurnus*, the literal Latin translation of his name in a Christian context. Heinrich Graetz's study, which was published in the nineteenth century, was the first to mention Sforno's double name.[49] Scholars referred to Sforno using different names, among them *Ovadia sive Obadias Siphronius*, *Obadia Sephorno*, *Abdias Sphorni*, *Abdia Sphorni*, *Obadia Sporni*, *Obadia Sphorno*, and *Obadia oder Servadeus de Sforno*. It seems possible that these misreadings were the reason why *Lumen Gentium* was not initially recognised as Sforno's work.

3 Between Two Worlds: Translation and Cultural Transfer

3.1 *Latin-into-Hebrew and Hebrew-into-Latin?*

Since *Light of the Nations* was first published in Hebrew and then in a Latin "translation" ten years later, the question arises as to whether Sforno used Hebrew or Latin philosophical sources to compile his treatise. From a comparison of both versions, it quickly emerges that he used Latin sources, which he translated into Hebrew himself for *Or 'Ammim*.

A good example of this is the case of Aristotle's *On the Heavens* 2, text. 45, which is rendered differently every single time it appears in *Or 'Ammim*, while in *Lumen Gentium*, the quotations are identical, except for chapter 9 ("On Divine Unity"), where the author seems to paraphrase:[50]

Dicamus etiam quod si stelle et orbes essent non causati et essent sine causa et agente, non esset omnino necessarium ut orbis esset magnus in omnibus stellis, et motus stella esset in eo velox secundum magnitudinem orbis. Si igitur una stel|a aut due essent huiusmodi non esset inopinabile	נאמר שאם הכוכבים והגלגלים היו בלתי מסובבים ובלתי סבה פועלת לא היה שם הכרח שיהיה הגלגל שומר גודל בכל הכוכבים ושתנועת הכוכב תהיה מהירה כפי גודל הגלגל ואם כוכב אחד או שני כוכבים בלבד היו על זה האופן לא היה כל כך נמנע

---

47 This is the only complete copy.

48 This copy comes from the collection of Dr Harry Friedenwald of Baltimore in Maryland, and he donated it to the Hebrew University of Jerusalem; see also Friedenwald, *Jewish Luminaries in Medical History and a Catalogue of Works Bearing on the Subject of the Jews and Medicine from the Private Library of Harry Friedenwald* (New York: Ktav, 1946), 139.

49 Heinrich Graetz, *History of the Jews, Volume 4: From the Rise of the Kabbala (1270 C.E.) to the Permanent Settlement of the Marranos in Holland (1618 C.E.)*, ed. and trans. Bella Löwy (Philadelphia, 1894), 411 (originally published in German as Graetz, *Geschichte der Juden, Bd. 9: Von der Verbannung der Juden aus Spanien und Portugal bis zur ersten dauernden Ansiedelung der Marranen in Holland (1618)* [Leipzig, 1866]).

50 Sforno's quotes from Averroes's Long Commentary on *On the Heavens* also prove his usage of Latin sources, as the work had not been translated into Hebrew.

tantum, cum autem omnes stelle sint huiusmodi iste sermo est fabulosus[51]	אמנם בהיות הכוכבים כלם בזה האופן הנה זה מאמר בטל
Dicimus etiam quod si stelle et orbes essent non causati et essent sine causa et agente, non esset omnino necessarium ut orbis esset magnus in omnibus stellis, et motus stelle in eo esset velox secundum magnitudinem orbis. Si igitur una stella aut due essent huiusmodi non esset inopinabile tantum, cum autem omnes stelle sint huiusmodi, iste sermo est fabulosus[52]	נאמר גם כן שאם הגלגלים והכוכבים היו בלתי מסובבים והיו בלתי פועל לא היה מן ההכרח שיהיה הגלגל גדול בכל הכוכבים ושתהיה תנועת הכוכב בו מהירה כפי גודל הגלגל. אמנם אם כוכב אחד או שנים היו בזה האופן לא היה כל כך רחוק מן המחשבה. אבל בהיות כל הכוכבים כן הנה דבור בזה הוא כשיחה בטלה
Si igitur una stellarum aut due essent huiusmodi, non esset inopinabile tantum scilicet ut casu et preter agentis intentum contigisset sic esse. Cum autem omnes stelle scilicet planete, sint huiusmodi iste sermo est fabulosus etc.[53]	אם היה על תכונת מה כוכב אחד או שנים בלבד לא היה כל כך נמנע שקרה זה במקרה אבל בהיות כל כוכבי לכת על תכונה אחת הנה זה מאמר בטל.
Si igitur una stella aut due essent huiusmodi non esset inopinabile tantum, cum autem omnes stelle sint huiusmodi iste sermo est fabulosus etc.[54]	אם אולי כוכב אחד או שנים בלבד היו על זה האופן לא היה כל כך רחוק שיהיה מקרה אבל בהיות כל כוכבי לכת על אופן זה. הנה זה המאמר הוא מאמר מתעתע

There is one case where it seems that Sforno may have consulted a Hebrew manuscript. In the introduction, he refers to the beginning of *Metaphysics*, where Aristotle summarised the philosophy of his predecessors, including that of the "Italian" philosophers; namely, Pythagoras and his followers (§ 1.2.1 in our edition). In early printed Latin editions, the so-called Italians are first mentioned in *Metaphysics* A (*primus*), § 2 (987a9 ff.).[55] Sforno apparently refers to this in *Lumen Gentium*:

Quorum primi ut Philosophus **Metaphysicorum, I, 2** narrare videtur fuerunt Itali de quorum numero, ut Commentator ibidem ait fuerunt Anaxagoras, Empedocles et Democritus. Deinde Herculei qui tandem negarunt ut contingat aliquid sciri. Deinde Socrates ...	כפי אשר העיד הפילוסוף **בספר מה שאחר מאמר ב' פרק ה'** היושבים ראשונה במלכות איטאליא מהם פיטאגורס ותלמידיו ואנכסאגורס ואימפידוקליס ודימוקריטוס ואחריהם כת האירקוליאי אשר אמרו היות כל ידיעה נמנעת ואחריהם סוקראטיס אשר ...

---

51 § 2.2.2.
52 § 4.3.2.
53 § 9.6.3.
54 § 15.4.3.
55 Aristotle and Averroes, *Metaphysica*, vol. 3.1 of Aristotle and Averroes, *Opera latine cum commentariis Averrois, recensuit Nicolatus Vernia* ([Venice], 1483), unfoliated.

INTRODUCTION   9

In *Or 'Ammim*, which instead mentions "book 2, paragraph 5," it might seem that he is referring to the Hebrew manuscript tradition in which book A of *Metaphysics* appeared *after* "α" (little alpha) and was counted as book 2 (*ma'amar bet*, following the Arabic tradition). This also perfectly matches the reference to the fifth paragraph (*pereq he*), as it mentions the Italian philosophers (cf. 1.987a29ff.).[56]

However, the influence of Latin culture is also very clear in *Or 'Ammim*, which can be seen in the case of the *Herculei*—meaning "the partisans of Heraclitus"—mentioned in this passage. This faulty reading, which might lead us to think of Hercules rather than Heraclitus, appears in all the Latin prints of Averroes's Commentary on *Metaphysics* A, paragraph 5.[57] In the Arabic edition of Averroes's commentary produced by ʿAbd al-Raḥmān Badawī (1998), the text reads الهرقلين (*'al-hrqlyyn*), and the editor supposed that the (lost) base text for the Latin translation contained a copyist's error.[58] The Hebrew manuscripts that we consulted read הרקליין (*hrqlyyn*)[59] or הרקלייאן (*hrqlyy'n*),[60] which are essentially transcriptions of the Arabic. In the Hebrew version of *Light of the Nations*, Sforno, in contrast to the Hebrew manuscripts, uses האירקוליא״י (*h'yrqwly'y*, likely vocalised as *herqulei*), which looks like a transcription of the Latin *Herculei*. It might well be the case that he used the Latin source to (erroneously) vocalise the name.

Another case in which Sforno introduced a peculiarity from the Latin tradition into his Hebrew version is found in references to book 9 (theta) of *Metaphysics*. A passage from this book is repeatedly referred to as *Contra Gariconem*/נגד גאריקו in Sforno's work.[61] The original Greek name is Μεγαρικοί; that is, the Megarians. At the beginning of book 9, chapter 3, Aristotle affirms: "εἰσὶ δέ τινες οἵ φασιν, οἷον οἱ Μεγαρικοί" ("There are some, such as the members of the Megaric school, etc.").[62] A correct translation into Latin is found, for exam-

---

56   Cf., e.g., the Hebrew manuscript Berlin, Staatsbibliothek, Or. Fol. 1388, fol. 6ᵛ.
57   See Padua: Laurentius Canozius, 1473; Venice: Torresanus/de Blavis, 1483; Venice: Bernadinus Stagninus de Tridino, 1489; Venice: Iohannes et Gregorius de Gregoriis, 1495/96; Venice: Octavianus Scotus, 1516; Aristotle and Averroes, *Metaphysica Aristotelis cum commentariis Averrois* (Lyons, 1529); Aristotle and Averroes, *Aristotelis metaphysicorum libri XIIII cum Averrois cordubensis in eosdem commentariis et epitome, Theophrasti metaphysicorum liber editio Juntina prima*, vol. 8 of *Aristotelis Stagiritae omnia quae extant opera* […] (Venetiis, 1552; revised and republished 1562 and 1574).
58   ʿAbd al-Raḥmān Badawī, *Averroes (Ibn Rushd)* (Paris: Vrin, 1998), 162: "Du même genre est l'autre confusion entre Héraclitéens et Héracléens: elle tient à une faute de copiste, soit dans le texte d'Ibn Rushd, soit dans la traduction arabe dont se servit celui-ci pour son Commentaire. Mais nous croyons que c'est plutôt le texte d'Ibn Rushd sur lequel s'est basée la traduction latine. La preuve c'est qu'Ibn Rushd lui—même cite 7 fois le nom d'Héraclite, rien que dans son grand Commentaire sur la Métaphysique, et une fois dans le grand commentaire sur le De Anima. Ceci prouve qu'Ibn Rushd connut très bien Héraclite, le philosophe présocratique du changement perpétuel et ne le confondit pas avec Hercule. En outre, le mot dans le texte arabe d'Ibn Rushd dans le grand Commentaire de la Métaphysique est ainsi écrit: الهرقلين (pp. 66, 6; 69, 3; 1372, 3—éd. Bouyges)—il ne manque qu'une lettre au milieu pour être juste: الهرقليطين (= partisans d'Héraclite). Cette prétendue confusion, relevée avec tant de clameurs, et de sarcasme de très mauvais gout par Luis Vives, n'est donc qu'une faute de copiste dans le manuscrit arabe du grand commentaire de la Métaphysique sur lequel est basée la traduction latine de celui-ci."
59   Munich, Bayerische Staatsbibliothek, Cod. hebr. 65, fol. 269ᵛ.
60   MS Berlin 1388, fol. 6ᵛ.
61   § I.6 (second proposition); § 1.5.3; § 3.2.3; § 5.3.1 (all references are to *Lumen Gentium*).
62   *Metaph.* 9.3.1046b29.

ple, in the Giunta edition (in the translation by Cardinal Bessarion): "Sunt autem quidam, ut megarici, qui dicunt."[63] A medieval Latin translation traditionally ascribed to Michael Scot and prepared from an Arabic version of the text presents the erroneous reading *garico*,[64] which resembles that found in both versions of *Light of the Nations*,[65] and it seems obvious that Sforno had consulted a print or manuscript with that reading.[66] Hebrew translations prepared from the Arabic contain a similar error, yet contrary to the Latin, the dominant reading in Hebrew manuscripts is עריקון.[67] It seems clear that Sforno was again transliterating from a printed Latin source.

In addition to the abovementioned examples, we also find not only a number of similarities, but also differences between the two versions, which help us to trace Sforno's sources and his *modus operandi* in the compilation of the work. As typographical errors are frequent in book production, these errors are equally frequent in both versions of the text. The editors themselves addressed this problem (especially the confusion of the letters ב and כ) in an annexe to the Hebrew version, in which they list seventy-eight *errata* corrected by Sforno himself (p. 64[r–v]). Numerals (or Hebrew letters used as such) found in references to philosophical source texts (books, parts, chapters, and paragraphs)

---

63 Aristotle, *Aristotelis omnia quae extant opera* [...] (Venice, 1562), vol. 13, fol. 229[r]. The second translation printed in this edition was amended on the basis of Greek sources: "Et quidam ut Megarici etc."

64 Printed, e.g., in: Venice: Torresanus/de Blavis, 1483; Venice: Bernadinus Stagninus de Tridino, 1489; Venice: Octavianus Scotus, 1516; Averroes, *Metaphysica Aristotelis cum commentariis Averrois*.

65 "Et quidam ut Garicon, dicunt" (see also Rome, Biblioteca Apostolica Vaticana, Vat Lat. 2080, fols. 133[v]–134[r] and Vat. Lat. 2081, fol. 100[v]). In the Latin MS Rome, Biblioteca Apostolica Vaticana, Borgh. 306, fols. 90[r]–90[v], the copyist even modifies the text by adjusting the verbal form "et quidam Garico dicit," probably on the assumption that "Garico" was a first name.

66 In Badawi's edition, we find: "ومن الناس مثل غاريقون" (*wa-min an-nās miṯlā ġārīqūn*): see Averroes, *Šarḥ mā baʿd al-ṭabīʿa* (شرح ما بعد الطبيعة); digital copy of Averroes, *Tafsir ma baʿd at-tabiʿat*, ed. Maurice Bouyges, 3 vols. (Beirut: Imprimerie catholique, 1938–1952), available from Cologne's Digital Averroes Research Environment (DARE), 2014: https://dare.uni-koeln.de/app/fulltexts/FT24/section/1120. Sforno apparently did not consult any of the translations of Averroes's works made by his contemporaries during the Renaissance. (For a list of these, see Dag Nikolaus Hasse, *Success and Suppression. Arabic Sciences and Philosophy in the Renaissance* [Cambridge, MA: Harvard University Press, 2016], 69–76.)

67 There are different spellings of the name of the Megaric school in Hebrew manuscripts. MS Berlin 1388, fol. 128[v], presents Aristotle's words as: "מן האנשי(ם) כמו עמקון," likely a mistake for עריקון as Averroes's commentary (fol. 129[r]) reads: "האנשי(ם) כמו עריקון". Rome, Biblioteca Apostolica Vaticana, Vat. Ebr. 336 reads "מן האנשים כמו עריקון" (fol. 143[v]), as do Paris, Bibliothèque Nationale, hebr. 887, fols. 113[v]–114[r], and Paris, Bibliothèque Nationale, hebr. 889, fol. 191[v]. Paris, Bibliothèque Nationale, hebr. 886, fol. 117[r], records another spelling: "עאריקון". In Oxford, Bodleian Library, Mich. 441, fol. 103, the copyist writes: "האנשים כמו גריקון" ("the people like Garicon"). This is the only case in which the name "Garicon" occurs in a Hebrew manuscript. In the Arabic, the name "μεγαρικοί" became غاريقون (*ġārīqūn*). One might suppose that an Arabic copyist, unaware that the name *Megarian* referred to an ancient philosophical school, considered مغاريقون (*maġārīqūn*) an error *tout court* (possibly as a dittography of غغاريقون) and hypercorrected it to غاريقون to fit the root غ-ر-ق. Therefore, the *mem* at the beginning was considered a prefix to the name *ġārīqūn*. This mistake was transferred to the Hebrew text. The Arabic غ (*ġain*), corresponding either to the letters ג (*gimel*) or ע (*ʿayn*), was largely interpreted as the letter (sometimes also followed by an א [*aleph*]) used to render the long vowel ا (*ʾalif*) in Arabic: ע(א)ריקון. The error remained in the philosophical Jewish and Latin Scholastic traditions until the original Greek was translated into Latin.

INTRODUCTION

proved to be a major source of error in both recensions. The following table gives an overview of the most common kinds of mistakes. We can distinguish between at least four categories with regard to the most probable cause of error:

Category of error	Number of cases		Examples: right/(wrong)	Who was responsible?
	Hebrew	Latin		
1. Confusion of a numeral/letter due to similarity in shape in the language concerned	6	16	Hebrew: נ״ח/(פ״ח)[a], כ״ז/(מ״ח)[b], כ״ח/(נ״ח)[c] Latin: 4/(9),[d] 44/(99),[e] 12/(13)[f]	Typesetters
2. Confusion of a numeral/letter due to similarity in shape in a different language	3	2	Hebrew: L: 99, H: מ״ט/(צ״ט [= 49])[g] L:129, H: קב״ד/(קכ״ט [= 124])[h] L: 54/(49), H: מ״ד/(נ״ד [= 44])[i] Latin: H: ט״פ/(כ״ט), L: 89/(59 [= נ״ט])[j] H: מ״ח, L: 48/(45 [= מ״ה])[k]	Author
3. Translation mistake from a source in a different language	2	0	Hebrew: [l]מזמור ק״ב/(ק׳), ק״ד/(ק״ב) = Vulgate: Psalm 101, 103	Author
4. Misreading of source	1	1	Hebrew: [m]הפלת ההפלה מאמר ט׳/(י׳) Latin: *Destructio Destructionum Disputatione* 9/(10)[n]	Author

a *OA* 2ᵛ.
b *OA* 9ᵛ.
c *OA* 10ʳ.
d *LG* 10 (seventh proposition).
e *LG* 30.
f *LG* 11 (twenty-second proposition).
g *LG* 38; *OA* 23ᵛ.
h *LG* 44ʳ; *OA* 28ᵛ.
i *LG* 17; *OA* 16ᵛ.
j *OA* 9ᵛ; *LG* 14.
k *OA* 25ᵛ; *LG* 41ᵛ.
l *OA* 19ᵛ; Vulgate: Psalm 101 and 103; *LG* 32 has "101" and "105" (!).
m *OA* 37ᵛ; see Agostino Nifo, *Destructio destructionum Averroïs cum Agostino Niphi de Sessa expositione* (Venezia, 1497), 98a.
n *LG* 50ᵛ.

In the first category, we find a total of eleven cases of a confusion between 4 and 9 in *Lumen Gentium*, while in *Or 'Ammim*, the similarities between the letters כ and נ, ו and ז, and מ and פ are the main sources of error. This confusion should generally be attributed to the typesetters, whose mistakes Sforno noticed in numerous instances.

Entirely opposite to this category are three cases from the second category in *Or ʿAmmim*. Since it is not likely that the letters ד and ט, מ and צ, or מ and נ would be confused in Hebrew script (print or Italian cursive), but this is fairly possible for the Arabic numerals 4, 5, and 9, it seems conceivable that Sforno made these errors when translating into Hebrew from a drafted Latin text. Nevertheless, there are also instances that show the contrary; that is, that Sforno was translating *Lumen Gentium* from the Hebrew. On p. 9ᵛ, *Or ʿAmmim* reads 29 (כ״ט), which is corrected to 89 (פ״ט) by Sforno himself in the errata, since the typesetters confused פ and כ in the Hebrew version. However, since *Lumen Gentium* reads 59, it seems conceivable that Sforno himself had confused כ (20) and נ (50) when translating from Hebrew into Latin.

The theory regarding a Latin base text is also strengthened by the third category of error, which is of a very specific kind. There are only two occasions in *Or ʿAmmim* where Sforno makes an exact reference to a quotation from the book of Psalms, which occur in close proximity to one another.[68] He states that he is quoting from Psalms 100 (ק) and 102 (ק״ב), but in fact the quotations come from Psalms 102 and 104. This deviation originated because of differences in the enumeration of the Psalms between the Hebrew Masoretic text and the Latin Vulgate. In the Vulgate, the enumeration of Psalms 11–113 and 117–146 is ahead by one in comparison to the Masorah (i.e., the Vulgate's Psalm 10 is the Masorah's Psalm 11). Sforno seems to have been confused by the Vulgate and to have "automatically" corrected the number in the wrong direction by subtracting from rather than adding to it. To resolve the oddity of a renowned Jewish exegete misquoting the Hebrew Bible, we might suggest that he was struggling with the Latin Bible instead.[69]

Last but not least, we can form a fourth category, to which we may add a mistake that resulted from a faulty page header in the 1497 *editio princeps* of *Destructio Destructionum*, Agostino Nifo's Latin edition of Averroes's *Incoherence of the Incoherence*.[70] Instead of the correct chapter 9 ("Nona"), the header reads 10 ("Decima"), which Sforno reproduced in both versions.[71]

There remain a considerable number of errors (twelve in the Hebrew, sixteen in the Latin) that we must leave uncategorised, since they are ambiguous and cannot be easily explained. However, from the other cases, as well as the

---

68 *OA* 19ᵛ. Sforno uses the term *mizmor* instead of *tehillim* for "psalm."

69 The second case is also more confusing in the Latin, since *Lumen Gentium* gives 105 (+ 2), while in *Or ʿAmmim*, the text reads 102 instead of the correct 104.

70 For the editorial history of this edition and the Latin translation of Averroes's *Tahafut al-Tahafut*, see Giovanna Murano, "Il manoscritto della *Destructio destructionum* di Averroè appartenuto a Giovanni Pico della Mirandola (Napoli, Biblioteca Nazionale, VIII E 31)," *Bulletin de philosophie médiévale* 60 (2018): 67–80; Guido Giglioni, "*Haec igitur est nostra lex*. Teologia e filosofia nel commento di Agostino Nifo alla *Destructio destructionum* di Averroè," in *L'averroismo in età moderna*, ed. Giovanni Licata (Macerata: Quodlibet, 2013), 125–144; Heinrich C. Kuhn, "Die Verwandlung der Zerstörung der Zerstörung. Bemerkungen zu Augustinus Niphus' Kommentar zur *Destructio destructionum* des Averroes," in *Averroismus im Mittelalter und in der Renaissance*, ed. Friedrich Niewöhner and Loris Sturlese (Zürich: Spur, 1994), 291–308. A second Latin translation of Averroes's text from the Hebrew was provided by Calo Calonymos in 1527 (cf. Averroes, *Averroes' Destructio destructionum philosophiae Algazelis in the Latin Version of Calo Calonymos*, ed. Beatrice H. Zedler [Milwaukee: Marquette University Press, 1961).

71 Averroes, *Destructio*, 98a (Nifo's edition).

INTRODUCTION 13

emblematic examples of Hebrew transliteration and translations, it becomes clear that Sforno did closely study Latin philosophical sources and traditions for the compilation of *Or ʿAmmim*, making it an example of a Latin-into-Hebrew translatory endeavour.

3.2 Teaching and Adapting for the Christians

Although they are identical to a great extent, as one would expect, the Hebrew and Latin versions differ in a number of passages and instances. Both versions also show a number of peculiarities that demonstrate their status as works compiled "between two worlds," Hebrew and Latin, Jewish and Christian.

Most obvious is the absence of distinctive Jewish sources (religious or philosophical) from *Lumen Gentium*, which likely means that Sforno wanted to avoid any conflict with the Christian authorities and to provide a more universal account. However, in *Or ʿAmmim* too, the only Jewish sources that Sforno explicitly mentions are Maimonides's *Guide of the Perplexed* and *Sefer ha-Maddaʿ* and Samuel ibn Tibbon's *Perush ha-millot ha-zarot*. The latter two are only found in the book's *Iggeret*, which was exclusively intended for Sforno's Jewish readers and was not translated into Latin, and in its introduction (*Haqdamah*).[72] Maimonides's *Guide* is quoted in the introduction (*Guide* 2:22; cf. §1.3.3) and in chapter 4 (*Guide* 3:13; cf. §4.3.1). In the same manner, Sforno also does not refer to rabbinic literature; namely, the Talmud. Only in chapter 12 ("On the Soul") does he paraphrase a quote from Shabbat 152a, introducing the part with the expression *seniorum auctoritate*—the authority of "elderly men,"[73] which is compared to what Aristotle explains in *On the Soul* 3.14 (in both Latin and Hebrew versions).

A special mention is made of biblical references: in the introduction to *Lumen Gentium*, Sforno adds a point to the presentation of his methodological structure, announcing that he will deviate from the traditional Latin translation; that is, Jerome's Vulgate. For him, the Vulgate does not follow the original meaning given in the Hebrew Bible ("rectius apertiusque fulgere patet").[74] The historical setting and the prohibition of translating the Bible into Latin and other vernacular languages should be considered here: the Council of Trent (which was transferred to Bologna between 1547 and 1548) decreed that the Vulgate was the only "authentic" translation of the Holy Scriptures.[75] However,

---

72 §1; §1.4.2 (*OA*).
73 §12.12.2 (*LG*): "Prout habetur Philosophi auctoritate in lib. De Anima III, 14 et idem habetur seniorum auctoritate dicentium, quod idem contingit de beatis animabus et de damnatis. Quod contingit de regalibus vestibus diversis servitoribus a rege traditis quorum quidam illas poliunt et ad ulteriorem ducunt perfectionem."
74 §1.4.1 (*LG*): "Septimo ut Sacrarum Loca ostendamus […] inseruntur sepe etiam eundem [secundum] Latinam translationem que scilicet in plurimis proculdubio deficit, quare omnia in originali Hebreorum textu rectius apertiusque fulgere patet."
75 "The sacred and holy, ecumenical and general Synod of Trent,—lawfully assembled in the Holy Ghost, the same three legates of the Apostolic See presiding therein,—keeping this always in view, that, errors being removed, the purity itself of the Gospel be preserved in the Church. […] But if any one receive not, as sacred and canonical, these same books entire with all their parts, as they have been used to be read in the Catholic Church, and as they are contained in the old Latin vulgate edition; and knowingly and deliberately despise the traditions aforesaid; let him be anathema." In James Waterworth, trans., *Canons and Decrees of the Council of Trent. The Fourth Session Celebrated on the Eighth Day of the Month of April, in the Year 1546* (London, 1848), http://www.bible-researcher.com/trent1.html.

the 1547 edition of *Lumen Gentium* was not deemed to be "dangerous" by the Catholic Church. Even though Sforno's Latin translation is verbatim, his interpretation also recalls his exegetical activities in a Latin context, introducing his Christian audience to details and understandings of Jewish exegesis. One example is the case of the already mentioned central verse in Genesis 1:26: "Et dixit Dominus: 'Faciamus hominem ad imaginem nostram quasi ad similitudinem nostrum.'" In the Vulgate, we find: "Et ait: 'Faciamus hominem ad imaginem et similitudinem nostrum.'" Sforno interprets this verse on the basis of the original Hebrew text: "נעשה אדם בצלמנו כדמותנו." The common translation from the Hebrew is: "Let us make man in our image, *after* our likeness." However, the Vulgate rendered it as "Let us make man in our image, *in* our likeness" or "Let us make man in our image, *according* to our likeness."[76]

In order to understand Sforno's Latin translation, we will refer to his interpretation in *Or ʿAmmim*. In the Hebrew text, Sforno's understanding of the preposition -כ ("as"; "like") in connection with דמות ("image"; "character"; "personality") is rather original:[77] "כדמותנו עם כף הדמיון להורות שההדמות הוא בלתי שלם": "'after Our likeness', together with the [letter] 'Kaf of resemblance,' in order to teach [us] that the likening (הדמות) is not [a] complete [similarity]."[78] The equivalent of -כ in the Latin composition is *quasi*, providing a particular connotation to this significant Bible verse: "quasi ad similitudinem nostram videtur inferre arbitrariam voluntatem";[79] "*quasi* [i.e., 'nearly' or 'almost'] our likeness, which seems to be a reference to the 'arbitrary will' [or free will, in a most radical reading]." In another passage, Sforno explains: "Dicit tamen *quasi* ad similitudinem quia Deus nobilissime homo autem ignobiliter";[80] "Nonetheless, it says 'as our likeness' because God chooses in the noblest way and men [choose] in an ignoble way, as aforementioned."

Another case is the explanation of the (Hebrew) name of God, *Elohim*, which not only denotes a paradigmatic split, but also the exegetical explanation of the name itself:

> Deus Hebraice sub plurali exprimatur dictione divinitus quidem inferri videtur illum quodammodo esse omnia entia sive omnium forma et finis,[81] [...]. Quare in libro Job ubi Gentilium opiniones hec ignorantium narrantur: ly Deus nonnisi sub singulari exprimitur numero.[82]

Sforno's interpretation for the Christian audience is not only a simple grammatical clarification for non-Hebrew readers ("the name of God is given in the plural form"), but also an exegetical interpretation ("He is all beings"); he con-

---

76 E.g., the Italian translation: "E Dio disse: Facciamo l'uomo a nostra immagine, a nostra somiglianza" (C.E.I) or "E Dio disse: 'Facciamo l'uomo a nostra immagine, secondo la nostra somiglianza'" (Bibbia di Gerusalemme).

77 A study of the *imago Dei* is offered by Warren Zev Harvey, "Sforno on Intellectual *Imitatio Dei*," in *The Literary and Philosophical Canon of Obadiah Sforno*, ed. Giuseppe Veltri et al. (Leiden: Brill, 2023).

78 § 12.15.3.

79 § 12.15.3. The corresponding passage in Hebrew is "וזה כי האדם הוא נבדל בפעולותיו בצד יתברך בענין הבחירה. מה מהאל ית׳ עם היותו דומה לאל יתברך" ("and this is so because man, by his actions, is different in a certain way from God—may He be praised—although he is similar to God—may He be praised—with regard to free will").

80 § 16.23.

81 § 8.8.1.

82 § 8.8.2.

tinues his account by saying that the "ignorant" (that is, devoid of knowledge) Gentiles mentioned in the book of Job formulated God's name only in the singular form.

The exegetical *modus operandi* in the Latin translation is carried out according to three different categories that denote the author's approach with respect to a different culture and public. The general references in this section are related to the studies of Eugene Nida,[83] Jean-Claude Margot,[84] and Peter Newmark[85] on linguistic categories resulting from the study of biblical translation, particularly difficulties connected to cultural transfer and adjustment techniques.[86]

The first case can be described as the linguistic phenomenon of adaptation, which means a shift to a different cultural environment. Properly speaking, this is the integration of ideas that do not belong to the Jewish tradition into a Christian context; as Margot stresses, this phenomenon is related to items that are unknown by the target culture. The second category can be described as a phenomenon of altering terms and concepts from Hebrew into Latin; these changes have to be made due to incompatibilities between the two languages because the nature of the signified is naturally altered since the signified is not a *thing*, but rather a mental representation of the *thing*.[87] In the third category, we can put amplifications, meaning an explicative paraphrasing that gives rise to a novel interpretation of the Bible.[88]

To give examples: in his introduction, Sforno changes the commonly used term for the Jewish Bible—*Sacra Scriptura* ("Holy Scriptures")—to *Sacrum Testamentum*,[89] which is perhaps an implicit reference to the New Testament intended for a Christian audience. In the solutions to the disputed questions, which relate to exegetical readings of books of the Torah, Sforno recurrently employs unusual expressions such as *Sacrum Genesis Documentum*, *Sacrum Exodii Documentum*, and *Sacrum Deuteronomii Documentum*.[90] These formulations can be considered *hapax legomena*, since there are no similar designations in other books or sources.

Another example that stresses the idea of "adaptation" to a Christian context is the use of the term *adventus*, which is here applied as a synonym for God's revelation on Mount Sinai instead of the Latin term *revelatio*.[91] Since *adventus* in Christian theology clearly refers to the birth of Jesus Christ and God's word becoming flesh, Sforno has here adopted a Christian term in order to connect with the Christian public by using concepts that were familiar to them.

---

83 Eugene Albert Nida, *Toward a Science of Translating with Special Reference to Principles and Procedures Involved in Bible Translating* (Leiden: Brill, 1964).
84 Jean-Claude Margot, *Traduire sans trahir. La théorie de la traduction et son application aux textes bibliques* (Lausanne: L'Âge d'homme, 1979).
85 Peter Newmark, *A Textbook of Translation* (London: Prentice Hall International, 1988).
86 Nida, *Toward a Science*, 226–240.
87 Roland Barthes, *Elements of Semiology* (New York: Hill and Wang, 1968), 42, and Ferdinand de Saussure, *Cours de linguistique générale* (Paris: Payot, 1949).
88 Newmark, *Textbook of Translation*, 68–94.
89 § 16.13.
90 § 2.6; § 16.17; § 8.8.1.
91 § I.1.2: "Cum autem Divina Revelatio et Sacri Testamenti doctrina eisdem Hebreis preceteris verum in divinis merito per Moysem evenisset, quare Sacra Exodi libri narratio in eiusdem Moysi adventu eosdem Hebreorum nomine appellavit."

4 Latin Priority? The Question of Translation

Although it is *communis opinio* that Sforno translated the Latin version from the Hebrew version, there are indications—as seen above—that allow us to assume that the compilation of the book was more complex, including the possibility that parts of it were drafted in Latin. Saverio Campanini has even suggested that the entire work was "likely composed in Latin."[92]

It seems possible, as Warren Zev Harvey has suggested,[93] that Sforno gave a series of Latin lectures on Averroes for Christian theologians, probably even at the University of Bologna. For this purpose, he would surely have drafted some of the chapters in Latin. Sforno's biography is typical of the upper-class Jews of Renaissance Italy who lived between two worlds, as is amply documented by his doctoral degree and his contacts with the Christian Humanists who approached him for lectures. After 1527, Sforno ran his *Bet ha-midrash* (Jewish academy) in Bologna in close proximity to San Giacomo Maggiore, the monastery of the Augustinian friars,[94] as attested by his epistles addressed to the rabbi of Ferrara[95] and a few *responsa*.[96] He was neither the first nor the only Jew to discuss philosophy with Christians on an academic level and to translate in both directions: others included Elijah Del Medigo (ca. 1458–ca. 1493), who was mostly active in Padua and Venice,[97] and Jacob Mantino (d. 1549), who studied medicine and philosophy at the universities of Padua and Bologna and is well known for his translation activities; indeed, he translated Arabic and Hebrew philosophical and medical texts into Latin for a Christian audience.

There are also some observations about the book that lend more weight to the idea that *Or 'Ammim* was not initially addressed to Jewish/Hebrew readers and that it was only later turned into a book with a foreword, introduction, and summary, following a seemingly stringent plan:

1. As mentioned, all the philosophical quotations and sources that Sforno used are taken from Latin sources and he translated them into Hebrew himself for *Or 'Ammim*, very often with different wordings of the same quotation in different instances (see above, part 3.1). Additionally, there

---

92 Campanini, "Sforno, 'Ovadyah'": "La medesima opera [*Or 'Ammim*], verosimilmente progettata in latino e solo successivamente tradotta in ebraico in vista della pubblicazione, fu poi edita in una versione latina riveduta, con il titolo Lumen gentium, a Bologna, per i tipi di Anselmo Giaccarelli nel 1548."

93 At the Second International Symposium on Sforno entitled "The Philosophical Canon of Obadiah Sforno and His Contemporaries," which was held at the University of Hamburg on 5 and 6 November 2018.

94 Its proximity to the Augustinian monastery should explain Sforno's acquaintance with some of his Christian interlocutors.

95 MS Parma 2399.

96 New York, Columbia University, X 893 T 67; MS Parma 2399. The digitised manuscript is available here: https://www.nli.org.il/en/manuscripts/NNL_ALEPH000078210/NLI#$FL16427991.

97 Del Medigo started to write his Latin Commentary on Averroes's *On the Substance of the Celestial Sphere* in 1485 and translated it into Hebrew soon afterwards. A critical edition is being prepared by Michael Engel and Giovanni Licata. For Elijah Del Medigo, see Engel, *Elijah Del Medigo and Paduan Aristotelianism: Investigating the Human Intellect* (London: Bloomsbury, 2017); Licata, *Secundum Avenroem. Pico della Mirandola, Elia del Medigo e la "seconda rivelazione" di Averroè* (Palermo: Officina di Studi Medievali, 2022).

INTRODUCTION   17

2. are some cases of translation errors in the Hebrew version regarding numerals, as mentioned above, which are best explained by the possibility that he was using a Latin draft manuscript.

2. A lack of specific "Jewishness" has been observed in the main body of the text. Sforno—with one exception—did not mention any Jewish philosophers, thinkers, or literature in *Or 'Ammim* beyond its introduction.[98] While the Hebrew introduction (*Iggeret* and *Haqdamah*) is packed with references to the Bible and the Jewish tradition, there are only a few quotations from rabbinic sources (Talmud) in the fifteen chapters of the main text, all of which only serve to supplement Sforno's biblical exegesis.

3. There is a structural inconsistency between the book's introduction and its chapters. In his introduction, Sforno gives a detailed Scholastic plan presenting twenty-seven propositions (or premises [*hanaḥot*]) that are "regarded as true among the philosophers."[99] Based on these, he wanted to "bring arguments and proofs." However, although he cites Aristotelian and Averroean sources in the course of his book, there is only one instance in *Or 'Ammim* in which he explicitly refers to "proposition no. xy" as such.[100]

These observations do not provide enough of a basis for an unequivocal argument. However, they do at least point to Sforno's deep and consistent interaction and confrontation with the Latin and Scholastic philosophical culture of his Christian interlocutors, which required a more universal approach that was limited to Aristotle and Averroes on the one side and the Bible as a "Holy Scripture" for both disputants on the other. It is intriguing, however, that his very first Jewish readers also noticed the aforementioned points, which can be seen in Elijah of Butrio's[101] efforts to remedy them in his Commentary on *Or 'Ammim* that was written in the 1540s or early 1550s (see below, part 6).

A final argument in favour of a Latin draft text may be derived from the alternate version of the Hebrew summary found in MS IOM B 169.[102] In several places, the text in the manuscript is shorter than it is in the Hebrew print and it also differs in some other respects. As we see in the following example, there is some resemblance between the text of both the manuscript version and *Lumen Gentium*, including the absence of a longer passage that is only extant in *Or 'Ammim*.

---

98 Maimonides (and his *Guide of the Perplexed*) is mentioned three times: twice in the introduction (pp. 2ʳ and 5ᵛ) and once in chapter 4 (p. 17ᵛ). Samuel ibn Tibbon's *Perush ha-millot ha-zarot* is mentioned once (p. 5ᵛ).

99 "אמנם ההנחות אשר נערוך לבאר את החקירות הנזכרות הם הנחות אשר התאמתו אצל הפילוסופים", § 1.5.2 (*OA*), 6ʳ.

100 The only case is in chapter 3 of the book: "... כנזכר לעיל בהנחה השנית והשלישית", § 3.2.3 (*OA*), 15ʳ.

101 Budrio, near Bologna. The town was called "Butrium" in antiquity, and it was only in modern times, in around the eighteenth or nineteenth century, that the spelling changed to "Budrio." Other prominent figures from this town from that age also use the spelling "Butrio." The NLI list him as אליהו בוטריו.

102 MS IOM B 169, fols. 149ʳ–155ᵛ.

Lumen Gentium, p. 69ᵛ (97)	MS IOM B 169, fol. 151ʳ⁻ᵛ	*Or 'Ammim*, p. 60ʳ
Et hoc docet Psalmus 94:9[103] ubi dicit *Qui plantat aurem nonne audiet. Anqui fixit oculum non perspiciat*[104] quasi dicat quod inopinabile est ut ille qui mediate vel immediate tanto artificio formavit mortalium organa. Non habeat de illis cognitionem nedum sollicitudinem, sicut putabant Gentiles, quorum opiniones paulo ante retulit dicens *Et dixerunt non videbit Dominus neque intelligit Deus Jahacob etc.* [Psalm 94:7][105] inferentes quod Deus de mortalium individuis que sensuum tantum videntur esse obiecta nullam habet cognitionem.	וזה אמנם הורה משורר המזמור באמרו: הנוטע אזן הלא ישמע אם יוצר /151ᵛ/ עין הלא יביט; כלומר: מי שכיון לתמונת האוזן והעין אשר בהם תחבולה רבה יראה ממנה תכלית לתועלת הפרטי הלא ישגיח בפרטים הפך מאמר הכופרי(ם) באמרם: לא יראה י(ה) ולא יבין כו׳.	כמו שהורה המשורר באמרו: »הנוטע אזן הלא ישמע אם יוצר עין הלא יביט« (תהלים צ״ד ט׳), כלומר הלא ידע וישגיח. הפך מאמר הכופרים באמרם: »לא יראה יה ולא יבין אלהי יעקב« (שם שם ז׳).
		והוסיף מופת על היותו בהכרח משגיח באישי המין האנושי מצד המוסר והמושכלות הראשונות אשר נמצאו בטבע באישי המין הנזכר באמרו: »היוסר גויים הלא יוכיח המלמד אדם דעת« (שם שם י׳). וזה כי אמנם הם אינם זולתי כלים לשלמות מושכלות נקנות בבחירה אישיית כי במוסר יכסוף לידיעת האמת גם באלהיות הבלתי הכרחית לקבוץ המדיני ובמושכלות הראשונות יהיה איפשר לו זה בבחירה אישיית לא זולתה. ומזה יתחייב שתהיה ההשגחה על הבחירה האישיית.

The additional passage on Psalm 94:10 found in *Or 'Ammim* is also missing from Sforno's discussion of the matter of individual divine providence in the eleventh chapter of the Latin version.[106] Under the assumption that the manuscript was created prior to the Hebrew print,[107] it is conceivable that the differences are due to a shorter Latin *Vorlage*, which seems to have formed the basis for both the Hebrew version and its Latin counterpart.

As shown, translatory activity in both directions played a significant role in the compilation of both versions of the text. It is therefore quite probable that Sforno had developed a Latin version of at least parts of *Light of the Nations*, which he translated, supplemented, and published as *Or 'Ammim*.

---

103 In the original, the Latin text reads "93" in accordance with the numeration in the Vulgate.
104 Sforno had obviously slightly changed the official Vulgate translation: "Qui planta<u>vit</u> aurem <u>non</u> audiet <u>aut</u> qui fi<u>n</u>xit oculum non <u>videbit</u>."
105 Cf. Vulgate: "Et dixerunt non videbit Dominus et non intell<u>eget</u> Deus <u>Iacob</u>."
106 § 11.11.2.
107 The manuscript is undated. Moshe Kravetz assumes that the commentaries in it were written after *Or 'Ammim* and thus that the summary of *Or 'Ammim* that it contains could be an alternate version that Sforno created in order to send a Latin copy of it to a priest (as mentioned in an unpublished letter [Mantua, Comunita Israelitica, MS ebr. 105, 48–49]). It could just as well be the case that the individual parts of MS IOM B 169 were bound together. It seems less probable that Sforno, who, as we have seen, was well versed in Latin, had first prepared a Hebrew text instead of immediately translating (and probably revising) it. See Kravetz, "The Footprints and Influence of *Or 'Ammim* in Sforno's Exegetical Works," in Veltri, *Literary and Philosophical Canon*.

5 Light of the Nations

5.1 *Intention*

Light of the Nations is Sforno's contribution to the central debate on the relationship between reason and religion. Although he has often been described as an opponent of philosophy (see below, part 7), a look at his introduction to *Or 'Ammim* shows that he was not generally opposed to thinking or to rationality, but that he rather sought to demonstrate how the Torah, as divine revelation, was a superior source of divine rationality, leaving its adherents in no doubts, unlike human reason.

In his introduction, Sforno presents a "history" of the development of Gentile philosophy until Aristotle, whom he describes as the thinker who literally "destroyed and broke (*avad ve-shavar*)[108] the foundations of the words of his predecessors [...] and in the natural and divine sciences, he brought to light demonstrations (*moftim*) of and arguments (*re'ayot*) for correct opinions, or [at least] those that were closer to the truth than all the ones before him."[109] Although Aristotle represented the peak of the Gentiles' striving for knowledge (which is a "natural human desire," as he stated at the beginning of *Metaphysics*), he did so without acknowledging a divine creator "in whose light we see the light" (cf. Ps 36:10).[110] The leading idea behind this "genealogy" is based on the concept of *translatio studiorum*, literally the transmission of knowledge from one culture into another. For Sforno, this idea is synonymous with a "loss of wisdom."[111] Since the Torah is the origin of all indisputable science and knowledge, Gentile philosophy is conceived as a kind of corruption of the original wisdom.[112]

Sforno's reservation about Aristotle's teachings is no different from that of any other philosopher of religion before him, since he denied most central doctrines of Judaism (or of any other [mono]theistic religion), including creation *ex nihilo*, God's omniscience, and His providence over particulars and individual human beings.[113] The attitude to Aristotle and his teachings throughout history had therefore been ambivalent in Judaism, Christianity, and Islam alike, involving the greatest scholars such as Moses Maimonides, Thomas Aquinas, and Averroes. Sforno respects the high level of rationality and method in Aristotle's work, but he also criticises the supposed near-total acceptance of all of his teachings among his contemporaries.

The older and superior alternative to Aristotle's reasoning is the tradition transmitted by Eber (*'Ever*), the eponymous forefather of the "Hebrews"

---

108 Cf. Lam 2:9.
109 § I.2.3 (*OA*).
110 § I.1.1 (*OA*).
111 On this topic in general, see Giuseppe Veltri, *Alienated Wisdom: Enquiry into Jewish Philosophy and Scepticism* (Berlin: De Gruyter, 2018).
112 It is worth noting that a copy of *Or 'Ammim* owned by the German theologian and Humanist Johann Albrecht Widmannstetter contains handwritten notes, presumably by Widmannstetter himself. Widmannstetter is also known to have owned a notable collection of manuscripts in Hebrew, Arabic, and Syriac. We cannot exclude the possibility that Reuchlin had recommended that he read or study Sforno's work. Widmannstetter's name is found in the colophon and his commentaries are recorded in the first section of the book, the introduction (fols. 3ʳ–3ᵛ, 4ʳ, and 5ᵛ), in which he noted some similarities with other Jewish thinkers (for example, on fol. 4ʳ, there is a reference to Flavius Josephus, while fol. 5ᵛ refers to Ibn Tibbon's *Iggeret*).
113 § I.2.3.

(*Ivriyim*) and the teacher of Abraham and the patriarchs.[114] Its first and distinctive principle is the existence of a "First Existent" (i.e., God, as the creator), and it is of decisive importance for Sforno that the knowledge of God is a true intellectual "knowledge," not a memorised belief. The Torah instead brings demonstrative proofs for divine commandments as well as for the "roots of the Torah"; that is, the existence of a creator and his attributes (omniscience, providence, etc.). Sforno emphasises this idea by criticising two authorities of Jewish philosophy: Moses Maimonides, who in *Guide* 3:28 had declared some of the Torah's central teachings on God to be "beliefs," and his renowned translator Samuel ibn Tibbon, who was himself a philosopher and one of the fathers of Hebrew scientific and philosophical terminology, for his preference for Aristotle over the account of the book of Genesis in matters of natural science in his *Perush ha-millot ha-zarot*.[115]

Sforno's intention is therefore bifold. On the one hand, he seeks to present inconsistencies in Aristotle's teachings on matters relevant to philosophy and to demonstrate the counter-position from within Aristotle's own system and method. On the other, he acts as an advocate for the intellectual and rational value of the Torah, revealing through exegesis that it provides rational arguments and demonstrations for "beliefs." Despite Sforno's use of harsh expressions such as "the error of those who think that the Holy Scripture teaches many easy answers and doubtful opinions, which is a point of derision for the Philosopher"[116]—which echoes Jewish thinkers such as Judah Halevi[117] and Shem Ṭov Falaquera[118]—behind these layers, his Renaissance spirit is much more reconciliatory thanks to his dialectical method of thesis, antithesis, and finally synthesis.

5.2 Methodology

Due to the methodology employed in *Light of the Nations*, as well as its numerous references to Averroes's commentaries (seemingly as the best representation of Aristotle's philosophical system), Sforno may be defined not only as the last interpreter of "Hebrew Scholasticism," as the late Mauro Zonta called him,[119] but also as the last Jewish Averroist, or an Averroist *malgré lui*.

---

114   Eber, in the Jewish tradition, did not help to build the tower of Babel and was therefore allowed to use the divine Hebrew language. He also ran a *bet ha-midrash* (together with Shem) where the patriarchs learnt about divine wisdom. This is why Sforno makes such prominent mention of him. See Louis Ginzberg, *Legends of the Jews*, trans. Henrietta Szold, 7 vols. (Philadelphia: Jewish Publication Society of America, 1909–1942), vol. 1 (1909), 274–275; vol. 2 (1910), 214; vol. 5 (1925), 205; cf. Wilhelm Bacher, "The Views of Jehuda Halevi Concerning the Hebrew Language," *Hebraica* 8, no. 3 (1892): 136–149.

115   §1 (*OA*), 2ᵛ.

116   §1.4.2 (*LG*).

117   Judah Halevi, *Kuzari*, 1:63: "The Rabbi: There is an excuse for the Philosophers. Being Grecians, science and religion did not come to them as inheritances. They belong to the descendants of Japheth, who inhabited the north, whilst that knowledge coming from Adam, and supported by the divine influence, is only to be found among the progeny of Shem, who represented the successors of Noah and constituted, as it were, his essence. This knowledge has always been connected with this essence, and will always remain so. The Greeks only received it when they became powerful, from Persia. The Persians had it from the Chaldaeans. It was only then that the famous [Greek] Philosophers arose, but as soon as Rome assumed political leadership they produced no philosopher worthy the name." English translation in Halevi, *Kitab al Khazari*, trans. Hartwig Hirschfeld (London: Routledge; New York: Dutton, 1905).

118   Shem Ṭov Falaquera, *Sefer ha-Maʿalot* (Berlin, 1894), 73–74.

119   Mauro Zonta, *Hebrew Scholasticism in the Fifteenth Century: A History and Source Book* (Dordrecht: Springer, 2006), 30.

In *Light*, Sforno embraced the Scholastic tradition by reproducing the *quaestio disputata* (disputed question) in both Hebrew and Latin, which is quite exceptional in the Jewish tradition. The phenomenon of Late Scholasticism affected Judaism in the era of Humanism and the Renaissance in the form of a turn from Arabic to Latin Aristotelianism that took place in Italy and Spain (as testified by the works of Judah Messer Leon, Eli Habillo, Abraham Bibago, and Elijah Del Medigo).

In view of the importance of Averroes in Sforno's work, Elijah Del Medigo should probably not be considered the last "Averroist"[120] of the Jewish tradition. As Josep Puig Montada has noted, the study of Averroes persisted in the Latin world—with its ups and downs—until the Renaissance. A similar phenomenon may be observed in Jewish thought: "Jewish Averroism" is a concept that usually refers to Jewish philosophers who philosophised within the context of Averroes's interpretation of Aristotelian philosophy. Sforno's *modus operandi*, in which only Aristotle and Averroes are quoted since they were still considered the major "authorities" for systematic philosophical thought, is in accordance with what Guido Giglioni describes as the Averroistic tendency in European culture.[121] Sforno's connection to this trend, all the more so given that he decided to write his work in both languages for two different audiences, means that he, not Del Medigo, should be considered the last Jewish Averroist.

The treatise presents itself as a *quaestio disputata* and should be considered a *summa*—namely, a compendium of knowledge in particular fields—in which Sforno develops questions in order to refute Averroes and Aristotle and other Peripatetic doctrines using their own method. The disputed question—the expression *par excellence* of the Christian tradition—became the instrument with which he could refute the Aristotelian errors. In the Renaissance, Aristotelianism was still taught in particular intellectual and scholarly circles,[122] such as the University of Padua, and was represented by professors such as Paul of Venice, Gaetano da Thiene, and Agostino Nifo. The latter's commentaries in his published editions of Averroes's *Incoherence of the Incoherence* (*Destructio Destructionum*; Venice, 1497) and *On the Substance of the Celestial Sphere* (Venice, 1508)[123] had surely not escaped Sforno's eyes when he made use of these sources.[124]

---

120 Cf. Josep Puig Montada: "Eliahu del Medigo, the Last Averroist," in *Exchange and Transmission across Cultural Boundaries: Philosophy, Mysticism and Science in the Mediterranean World*, ed. Haggai Ben-Shammai, Shaul Shaked, and Sarah Stroumsa (Jerusalem: Israel Academy of Sciences and Humanities, 2013), 155–186.

121 Guido Giglioni, "Introduction," in *Renaissance Averroism and Its Aftermath: Arabic Philosophy in Early Modern Europe*, ed. Anna Akasoy and Guido Giglioni (Dordrecht: Springer: 2013), 2: "'Averroistic' refers to the generic cultural label denoting a pronounced rationalistic attitude, of a vaguely Aristotelian ilk, towards questions of philosophical psychology (in particular, the nature of the human mind and its survival after the death of the body), natural determinism and, above all, the relationships between philosophical freedom and dogmatic truths, often of a religious kind."

122 Charles B. Schmitt, "Towards a Reassessment of Renaissance Aristotelianism," *History of Science* 11 (1973): 159–193; Luca Bianchi, "Continuity and Change in the Aristotelian Tradition," in *The Cambridge Companion to Renaissance Philosophy*, ed. James Hankins (Cambridge: Cambridge University Press, 2007), 49–71.

123 Agostino Nifo, *Commentationes in librum Averrois De substantia orbis* (Venitiis, 1508).

124 In his Commentary on *Or 'Ammim* (see below, part 6), Elijah of Butrio, a disciple of Sforno, makes two references to Nifo's commentary on the edition of the *Incoherence of the Incoherence* (MS Parma 2624, fols. 16ᵛ [ch. 4] and 49ʳ [ch. 10]): "ראוי שנדע כי כמו שאין אנו יודעי(ם) ומשיגים השגה ברורה ואמתית על צד החיוב(ב) עצם השמים מהו רק על צד

Jewish authors of the fifteenth and sixteenth centuries composed philosophical treatises in which they discussed the same questions and used the same methods as contemporary Christian philosophers. However, Sforno was yearning for something even more ambitious when he made his *Or 'Ammim* available to a Christian audience. Strikingly, he amended *Lumen Gentium* with particular attention to both terminology and concepts belonging to the Christian tradition such as *gratia*, *benevolentia*, and *diligentia*. His Latin version is therefore not only a translation of a Jewish text, but rather an adaption and interpretation of Christian ideas, which leads us to hypothesise about his close connections to his Christian contemporaries (see above, part 3.2).

Sforno's dialectical methodology follows the traditional approach of medieval Scholastic discussion. He defines the content of each individual *quaestio* in the introduction and discusses each in the classical order: (1) statement of the problem, (2) argument, (3) counterargument, and (4) solution.[125] This structure is extended by a fifth element: Sforno brings an alternative corresponding rational solution from the Tanakh/Old Testament in order to present the truth of divine revelation and reason. Since (even) Aristotle's philosophy proves to be insufficiently equipped to answer the questions without lingering doubts, Sforno unfolds a demonstrative argument by means of his exegesis, resolving the question a second time with complete certainty. Sforno employed expressions such as *in Sacris Dei Scripturis demonstrative probatum*, *demonstrative ostendit*, *demonstrative docere intendens*, *quod demonstrative dicit*, and so on, in order to emphasis the scientific, intellectual, and rational relevance of the Holy Scriptures.

The different parts of the disputed questions are introduced by standard formulae in both Hebrew and Latin:

---

1. Statement of problem

dubitatur utrum [...] *et videtur quod sic* [or: *quod non*]	[...] אם ... ונראה אמנם ש ...

2. Argument

[...] *arguitur*	[...] יתבאר זה

3. Counterargument

ad oppositum arguitur sic	אמנם יתבאר הפך זה

השלילה שאנו נאמ(ר) שהם גשמים לא כבדי(ם) ולא קלים לא בעלי קור וחום לחות ויובש וביוצא כמבוא(ר) בספרם המיוחד כ"ש וכ"ש שלא נשיג מהות רצון האל ית' רק על צד השלילה שנאמ(ר) שאינו פועל טבעי ולא ג"כ רצוני באופן הרצון שבנו והשגת רצונו זה לה לבדו כאשר ביא(ר) הרב המורה ח(לק) א' פרק נ"ח ואחריו בזמננו **הסיסא בביאורו לספר הפלת ההפלה** מאמר י"א חקירת א' ומאמר ג' חקירת א'".

125 John Marenbon, *Later Medieval Philosophy (1150–1350): An Introduction*, paperback ed. (London: Routledge, 1991), 31–34.

(*cont.*)

---

4. Solution

ad dubium ergo respondetur	נשיב אם כן להתיר ספק החקירה
ad argumenta [...] *respondetur*	אמנם לטענות החולק

---

5. Biblical solution (exegesis)

quare Sacrum Documentum docens	ואת כל אלה הודיעה תורת אלהינו

Sforno employs the introductory Latin formula *dubitatur utrum* instead of the classical *quaeritur utrum* or *quaesitum est*, which represents a philological novelty in Jewish Renaissance literature. *Dubia* were a specific part of the *lectiones* in which scholars discussed particularly difficult points.[126] Furthermore, Sforno offers the solution by using the expression *ad dubium ergo respondetur*, which corresponds to the introduction of each question. In the Hebrew, the equivalent of this term is *safeq*, which is a synonym for "objection" in this sense (with reference to the previous arguments) and was first employed by Gersonides in *Wars of the Lord*.[127] In the Renaissance, Isaac Abravanel employed *safeq* to translate the Latin *obiectio* in his *Principles of Faith*,[128] confirming its double function, as did David Messer Leon in his *Tehillah le-David*.[129] Sforno can therefore also be viewed within the context of Jewish scepticism.[130]

---

126   Possibly, Sforno was recalling Paolo Venetus's writings and Agostino Nifo's *Commentaries on Aristotle and Averroes*, in which the Paduan professors preferred *dubia* to *quaestiones*.

127   Levi Gersonides, *Milchamot ha-Schem—Die Kämpfe Gottes* (Leipzig, 1866; repr. Berlin: Lamm, 1923). Cf. Sara Klein-Braslavy, *"Without Any Doubt"—Gersonides on Method and Knowledge*, trans. and ed. Lenn J. Schramm (Leiden: Brill, 2011); Klein-Braslavy, "The Solutions of the Aporias in Gersonides' *Wars of the Lord*" [Hebrew], *Da'at* 50/52 (2003): 499–514, an expansion of "The Solutions of the Aporias in Gersonides' *Wars of the Lord*," a paper presented at the 4th EAJS/ECUTJC Colloquium entitled "Issues in Jewish Philosophy" held at Yarnton Manor, Oxford, 23–25 July 2001, and of the abridged French version thereof published as part of "La méthode diaporématique de Gersonide dans les *Guerres du Seigneur*," in *Les méthodes de travail de Gersonide et le maniement du savoir chez les scolastiques*, ed. Colette Sirat, Sara Klein-Braslavy, and Olga Weijers (Paris: Vrin, 2003), 121–128. In the introduction to the *Wars of the Lord*, Gersonides writes: "Doubts (*sefeqot*) arise on a given matter when we have contrary view concerning it" (Gersonides, *The Wars of the Lord. Book One: Immortality of the Soul*, trans. Seymour Feldman (Philadelphia: Jewish Publication Society of America, 1984), 6 (Hebrew section), 97 (English section)).

128   Isaac Abravanel, *Rosh Amanah*, ed. Menahem Kellner (Ramat-Gan: Bar-Ilan University, 1993). Almost all the questions include the word *safeq*.

129   David ben Yehudah Messer Leon, *Tehillah-le David* (Constantinople, 1577). Messer Leon uses the doubt to introduce a question; cf., e.g., fol. 9.

130   Veltri, *Alienated Wisdom*, 143–144: "The sixteenth and seventeenth centuries are foundational for several aspects connected both with the Jewish consciousness of and attitudes towards scepticism. At the end of the Humanist period and the Renaissance, we can observe the first changes in the perception and formulation of philosophical questions. After some seminal beginnings, mirrored by 'Ovadya Sforno, there could be no hesitation in recognizing that the use of *dubitatur/dubium* and quaestiones *dubitatae* is more than a rhetorical tool. They became a dialectical strategy that played an important role in the Late Renaissance (*Accademia dei Dubbiosi*) and early modern period (*Accademia degli Incogniti*, Simone Luzzatto). The 'doubts' (*dubitationes*) are not primarily a literary instrument to introduce the dogmatic opinion of teachers, masters, or opponents, but a dialectical strategy to introduce very delicate questions that could have dangerous results for the

5.3 Structure

Or ʿAmmim and *Lumen Gentium* have an identical structure, consisting of five different parts. The Hebrew and Latin versions do not appear to offer significant differences in their overall view. The order of the questions and the general approaches to each argument are identical (with very few exceptions).

Something that is unique to *Lumen Gentium* is its opening letter, the dedicatory epistle to the French King Henri II.[131] This can be seen as a preamble to the Latin version parallel to the *Iggeret* (foreword) in the Hebrew version, which Sforno addresses to Jewish readers only,[132] following a scheme from the classical Jewish philosophical tradition, and which also includes a piece of Hebrew poetry incorporating the book's title.[133]

The *prologus/haqdamah* is the first part of the general introduction, in which Sforno presents the genealogy of wisdom and science from biblical times and pre-Socratic philosophy up to Aristotle and his commentators and the idea of divine reason and a loss of wisdom, as described above. The next section is dedicated to explaining the structure and methodology of the book, called the *ordo/seder*.

Following this, Sforno presents a list of twenty-seven propositions (*praesuppositiones/hanaḥot*)[134] that are based on the teachings of Aristotle and Averroes and are fully accepted by the philosophers as evidently true.[135] These presuppositions clearly resemble the twenty-five premises that Maimonides posited at the beginning of book 2 of his *Guide of the Perplexed* that are intended to prove the existence of God, His incorporeality, and His unity, and which, according to his statement there, were also undeniably proved by Aristotle in *Physics* and *Metaphysics*. Sforno refers to the propositions only indirectly by quoting the Aristotelian or Averroean references to them that he had provided. For example, the quotation from Aristotle's *On the Heavens* 1, text. 100 (279a11) mentioned in the ninth proposition occurs in a number of disputed questions in *Light of the Nations*, while only twice in total (*Lumen Gentium*, chapter 6,[136] and *Or ʿAmmim*, chapter 3[137]) does Sforno directly refer to "proposition xy" as such.

Sforno then turns to the disputed questions (*quaestiones/ḥaqirot*), which encompass the major classical philosophical issues of the Middle Ages. These can be grouped into three larger sets, discussing issues of physics, metaphysics, and psychology, each ending with a chapter that forms a bridge to the next part and an additional final question on the relationship between macrocosm (i.e., the celestial bodies) and microcosm (i.e., human beings).

---

majority. The topics handled involve the usual themes of sceptic origins and tradition: authority, morality, theodicy, collective society and individuality, immortality of the soul as a social and moral problem (doctrine of remunerations), etc."

[131] Campanini, "Un intellettuale," 124.
[132] §1 (*OA*), 2ʳ–3ʳ.
[133] The title is taken from Isa 51:4, see part 5.4.
[134] §1.6. While the Latin term *praesuppositiones* is in accordance with common technical terminology, Sforno deviates from the more common Hebrew rendering for *proposition*, which is *haqdamah* or *gezerah*. Cf. "הַקְדָּמָה", in PESHAT in Context—A Thesaurus of Pre-Modern Philosophic and Scientific Hebrew Terminology, ed. Reimund Leicht and Giuseppe Veltri, accessed 2 September 2022, https://peshat.org/display/peshat_lemmas_00001058 and "גְּזֵרָה", https://peshat.org/display/peshat_lemmas_00000543.
[135] §1.5.2.
[136] §6.4.1–3 (*LG*): "in preambuli presuppositorum [...] ratione et auctoritate probatum."
[137] §3.2.3 (*OA*): "כנזכר לעיל בהנחה השנית והשלישית."

INTRODUCTION

Questions 1 to 6 are concerned with the eternity of things: (1) generation and corruption, (2) the elements, (3) prime matter, (4) the heavens, (5) motion, and—after each of these is shown not to be eternal—(6) the existence of a creator who created *ex nihilo*.

1. Utrum motus generationis et corruptionis habuisset esse ab eterno?	ראשונה אם סדר ההויה וההפסד קדמון
2. Utrum corruptibilium elementa habuissent esse ab eterno?	שנית אם היסודות קדמונים
3. Utrum materia prima habuisset esse ab eterno?	שלישית אם החמר הראשון קדמון
4. Utrum celum habuisset esse ab eterno?	רביעית אם השמים קדמונים
5. Utrum motus habuisset esse ab eterno?	חמישית אם התנועה קדמונית
6. Utrum detur creatio qua scilicet tam materia et forma quam totum compositum habuisset esse post merum non esse?	ששית אם יש נמצא קדמון בורא וממציא יש אחר האפיסות המוחלט והוא עשה אינו ישנו

Questions 7 to 11 are concerned with the nature of the divine being/God, regarding (7) His incorporeality, (8) His unity, (9) His omniscience, (10) His will, and (11) His providence over mortal individuals; that is, over human beings individually, which supposes the immortality and divinity of the individual human soul and therefore builds a bridge to the following questions.

7. Utrum data creatione et per consequens Creatore idem Creator sit quid corporeum vel sit quid incorporeum?	שביעית אם הוא גוף או כח בגוף אם אין
8. Utrum unus tantum detur Creator vel plures eque primi dentur creatores?	שמינית אם הוא אחד בלבד אם אין
9. Utrum idem Creator omnia sciat vel econtra?	תשיעית אם הוא יודע כל
10. Utrum idem Creator habeat liberam ad utrumque contrariorum potentiam quorum alterum voluntarie eligat?	עשירית אם יש לו יכולת בשוה על שני ההפכים ובוחר באחד מהם בכונה וברצון
11. Utrum de mortalium individuis habeat sollicitudinem sive curam?	אחת עשרה אם הוא משגיח באישי ההווים ונפסדים

The final group consists of questions on (12) the immortality of the individual human soul, which is by far the longest chapter of the book, (13) the importance of good deeds (i.e., morality) for achieving the perfection of one's soul, and (14) the necessity of free human choice to attain this perfection.

12. Utrum intellectiva individui humani generis anima sit quid immortale vel econverso?	שתים עשרה אם הנפש האנושית השכלית האישיית היא בלתי נפסדת
13. Utrum pia intentio et conatus ad pia opera exequenda concurrat ad eiusdem anime perfectionem?	שלש עשרה אם המעשים הטובים הם מועילים או הכרחיים בהצלחת הנפש השכלית הנזכר
14. Utrum eiusdem intellective anime perfectio per humanam virtutem tantum non autem per naturalem vel divinam acquiri contingat?	ארבע עשרה אם שלמות הנפש יושג בכח אנושי בלבד ולא יושג בכח אלהי או טבעי

The final question (15) deals with the relationship of the celestial bodies to human beings; namely, whether the heavens and the heavenly bodies exist for the sake of the perfection of the human species (i.e., the perfection of the human soul).

15. Utrum celestium horumque motuum finis sit mortalium oportunitas ad humanam perfectionem necessaria?	חמש עשרה אם תכלית המכוון מן השמים וצבאם ומהעולם המוחש בכללו הוא המין האנושי ושלמותו

In the summary (*summarium/kelal ha-ʿolah*) of *Light of the Nations*, we find a *summa* of the arguments discussed in the book. In this section, Sforno makes a clear distinction between the position of Aristotle and the Peripatetic school on the one side and the principles laid down in the reasoning of the divine revelation (the Torah) on the other.

5.4 *Philosophy: God's Anthropocentric Teleology*

Sforno chose a phrase from Isaiah 51:4 as a title for his book: "Listen to me, my people; hear me, my nation: Instruction (*torah*) will go out from me; my justice will become a light to the nations (*or ʿammim*)." The title of the book, which is part of the four-line introductory poem in the Hebrew version, summarises a key feature of Sforno's intellectual and theological programme in his philosophical treatise: *Light of the Nations* is a treatise addressed to Jews and Christians alike and equally. Although Sforno offers no interpretation of the verse in his book, the choice of a title addressing the Nations demonstrates the universalistic nature of its message. This message, as Isaiah presents it, is the Torah, the divine revelation, which was given by God to enlighten not only Israel, but also the rest of mankind.

For Sforno, the core of divinity is presented right at the beginning of the Torah in the account of the creation of man: "Let us make man in our image (בצלמנו), after our likeness (כדמותנו)." This reference to Genesis 1:26–27, describing man as being created in the "image of God" (בצלם אלהים), seems to be the book's central biblical statement, on which Sforno draws both at the beginning[138] and in chapters 12, 13, and 15, as well as the summary.[139] Human beings are made similar to God as they possess a human intellectual soul (signified by the expression צלם אלהים) and free will (signified by the word דמות).[140] This unique nature enables them to willingly follow God's instructions for the sake of the ultimate goal of mankind: the perfection of the individual human intellectual soul through intellectual and practical (i.e., moral or social) efforts in order to become similar to God through *imitatio Dei*.[141]

As man's goal of seeking the perfection of his soul and becoming similar to God is inextricably tied to the divine nature of the human soul and its immortality, it is evident that the question on the immortality of the individual soul is at the heart of Sforno's treatise, and this is by far its lengthiest chapter (chapter 12). Sforno's endeavours to assure his fellow readers about this using both philosophical and biblical demonstrations are not surprising, both due to the general importance of this religious dogma for Jews and Christians alike and in the context of the fierce controversies caused by the publication of Pietro Pomponazzi's *De immortalitate animae* in Venice (1516).[142]

Although Pomponazzi denied the possibility of providing a rational demonstration for the immortality of the soul, he stated that he adhered to faith and the truth of revelation, making it a matter of belief. Sforno condemns a similar position towards central religious teachings presented by Maimonides.[143] His essential ideology in *Light of the Nations* is that the Torah is the ultimate and unquestionable source of knowledge and wisdom, given by an "all-knowing God (lit. God of knowledge)" (אל דעות [1 Sam 2:3])[144] providing "demonstrative proof[s] that accompany each theoretical portion [of His word]."[145] In Sforno's thought, there is no place for a *double truth theory*. *Light of the Nations* therefore shows the same strong intersection of exegesis and philosophy, like all his writings, and the Humanist and Renaissance ideals of going back "to the sources" (Lat. *ad fontes*) in order to search for the most immediate and initial access to ancient wisdom and the struggle to become a *homo universalis* (Hebr. חכם כולל) who attains perfect and comprehensive knowledge are deeply rooted in his work.[146]

---

138 § I.1.2.
139 § 12.8.1; § 12.9; § 12.12.3; § 12.15.1–4; § 13.6; § 15.9; § 16.23.
140 § 16.23 (*OA*).
141 On this, see Harvey, "Sforno on Intellectual *Imitatio Dei*."
142 Pietro Pomponazzi, "On the Immortality of the Soul," trans. William Henry Hay II and John Herman Randall, Jr., in *The Renaissance Philosophy of Man*, ed. Ernst Cassirer, Paul Oskar Kristeller, and John Herman Randall, Jr. (Chicago: University of Chicago Press, 1956), 257–381.
143 Maimonides, *Guide* 3:28.
144 § I (*OA*), 2ᵛ.
145 § I (*OA*), 2ᵛ.
146 Ephraim Finkel suggested that *Or 'Ammim* was probably one of Sforno's earlier works and that it was at least written prior to his Commentary on the Pentateuch (Finkel, *R. Obadja*, 18, n. 4). In a close study of the available manuscripts of the commentary, Moshe Kravetz has recently found plausible hints that support this assumption (Kravetz, "The Footprints and Influence of *Or 'Ammim*"). As we can also see in several places in the oral Torah lessons recorded by one of his students in the margins of a print edition of Gersonides's Commentary on the Bible (Mantua, 1476; see London, Montefiore Library 415 [formerly Montefiore no. 29]), Sforno recommends reading passages of *Or 'Ammim*, and his teachings on the Torah and rabbinical literature also include philosophical issues as a fundamental foundation of the Jewish education.

The structural framework that guides the reader to the heart of Sforno's thought is the literary form of a *summa* of classical questions of religious philosophy,[147] which owes a good part of its structural and content-related inspiration to Maimonides.[148] Although it does not pay reverence to him, every reader of the twenty-seven Aristotelian propositions in the *Light* must have been aware of their resemblance to the twenty-five (respectively twenty-six) propositions given by Maimonides at the beginning of book 2 of the *Guide*. Even the strong criticisms of Maimonides in Sforno's introduction, aimed either directly at statements in the *Guide* or indirectly at a statement from Samuel ibn Tibbon's *Perush ha-millot ha-zarot*, the glossary to his Hebrew translation of the *Guide*, shows the Rambam's exclusive importance in Sforno's work.[149]

From an examination of the general nature of Sforno's dominant philosophical and exegetical arguments in *Light of the Nations*, it is obvious that he seeks to gather teleological arguments from Aristotle's writings or corresponding interpretations by Averroes, which ultimately lead to an anthropocentric position. Although God, the creator, is of course the best and most noble existent, there is not much room to deny that Sforno claims that all of creation, including the celestial spheres, was made so that man may perfect his intellectual soul. This strong anthropocentric position, which is in line with that of Saadia Gaon, Judah Halevi, and Hasdai Crescas,[150] is supported by Sforno's interpretation and selective choice of Aristotelian dicta such as *Politics* 1: "Plants exist for the sake [of animals], and [...] animals exist for the sake of man."[151] The account of finality in natural processes found throughout Aristotle's oeuvre is—as will be seen—a starting point and lever for Sforno to "correct" his errors about the cosmos, the divine, and the human soul and to reconcile him with biblical reason.

Sforno's demonstrations in the first third of the book, arguing against the Aristotelian notion of the eternity of prime matter and motion and for the createdness of the world and the existence of a creator (chapters 1–6), form the basis for the questions on the divine attributes and the nature of the human soul. They do not generally provide new or original ideas, but are based on

---

147 As Julius Fürst put it: "*S. Or 'Ammim* oder eine ausführliche Religionsphilosophie, worin über Gott und dessen Wesen, über Einheit, Allmacht, Vorsehung, über die Seele, über Atheïsten, Epikuräer u. Läugner des Gesetzes u.s.w.: Bologna, 1537, 4. Eine lateinische Uebersetzung dieses Werkes, welche der Verf. selbst verfertigt hatte und dem Könige von Frankreich (Heinr. II) gewidmet, ist unedirt geblieben" (Fürst, *Bibliotheca Judaica*, 319).

148 Alessandro Guetta, "Maimonideanism in the Renaissance," in *Encyclopedia of Renaissance Philosophy*, ed. Marco Sgarbi (Cham: Springer: 2015), https://doi.org/10.1007/978--3--319--02848--4_161--1.

149 An introduction to Maimonides's philosophy might also have been the subject of Sforno's lessons for Reuchlin: see Saverio Campanini, "Roman Holiday: Conjectures on Johann von Reuchlin as a Pupil of Obadiah Sforno," in Veltri, *Literary and Philosophical Canon*: "I am aware of the highly hypothetical nature of this assumption, as well as of the fact that I cannot show proof that Sforno's Hebrew teaching had precisely this philosophical content, but, as Reimund Leicht has pointed out, there is no mention of these three sources, and in particular of Maimonides, in Reuchlin's works before his Roman mission of 1498, and conversely, Maimonides's *Guide* in particular becomes absolutely predominant in Reuchlin's works from that date on to the very end of Reuchlin's life."

150 Saadia Gaon, *Emunot ve-De'ot* 4; Halevi, *Kuzari* 4:15; Crescas, *Or Adonai* 2:6.3. For these and further references, see Yitzhak Melamed, "Teleology in Jewish Philosophy: From the Talmud to Spinoza," in *Teleology: A History*, ed. Jeffrey McDonough (New York: Oxford University Press, 2020), 123–149, https://www.academia.edu/38060851.

151 § 11.9; § 15.6.1.

INTRODUCTION

the principle that assuming the eternity of generation and corruption, the elements, prime matter, the heavens, and motion leads to incongruous and contradictory statements about their nature. It suffices for Sforno to refute them and to present creation *ex nihilo* as the inevitable alternative.

A recurring teleological argument for creation in these chapters, especially chapter 6, goes hand in hand with a statement about the improbability of chance as an explanation for the structure of the cosmos, which is a precursor to the modern-day *fine-tuned universe* arguments:[152] since the heavens need to have a certain (perfectly round) form and measurements that have to fit "by a hair's breadth" in order to enable their rotational movement without hindering each other,[153] and ascertaining, along with Aristotle, that things that happen by chance occur rarely, not regularly,[154] Sforno comes to the conclusion that the entire elaborate hierarchical order of the cosmos, the design of the spheres, and the interconnectedness of all parts of existence are intended for a purpose (מכוין לתכלית) and were thereby arranged by a volitional agent; that is, God.[155] Sforno's explanation of the divine name "אלהים" as signifying God's role as a "governor and arranger of order of existence" (מנהיג ומסדר המציאות)[156] and his exegesis of the verse "Ha-Shem founded the Earth by wisdom" (Prov 3:19) underline his teleological view.[157]

The teleological setting is also detectable in the middle section of the book, in which Sforno discusses divine attributes (chapters 7–11); for example, in the question on the unity (oneness) of the creator (chapter 8): since the world of creation is characterised by the interconnectedness of its parts, behind which Sforno detects purposeful intention for a goal or end, the unity of existence is an argument by analogy for the unity of the creator.[158] Also, in chapter 9 on divine omniscience, which seems to contain influences from Boethius's *Consolation of Philosophy*,[159] and chapter 10 on divine will, half of which consists of direct quotes from Averroes's *Incoherence of the Incoherence* (using Nifo's 1497 *Destructio Destructionum*), Sforno works with similar arguments: a purposeful agent must necessarily know in full detail what he wilfully intends to create,[160] a conclusion that he also finds documented in Isaiah 29:15–16, in an analogy to a potter making a vessel,[161] and in Genesis 1:4–5 in the account of the separation of light and darkness at the beginning of creation.[162]

In the course of chapters 9 and 11, Sforno even introduces further teleological quotations taken from Aristotle that are not actually included among his initial twenty-seven propositions. In his eighth proposition, he mentions *On the Heavens* 2, text. 45, and *Physics* 2, text. 48, which are taken as references for the statement that "everything that [occurs] in many things does not exist by

---

152 See, e.g., Richard Swinburne, "Argument from the Fine-Tuning of the Universe," in *Physical Cosmology and Philosophy*, ed. John Leslie (New York: Collier Macmillan, 1990), 154–173.
153 §4.3.1; §6.4.3 (*OA*).
154 Reference to *Phys.* 2, text. 48, and *De cael.* 2, text. 45, which deal with the rarity of chance and are among the most repeated quotes.
155 §6.5.1–7 (*OA*).
156 §6.9.2 (*OA*).
157 §6.10 (*OA*).
158 §8.3.1–2.
159 Boethius's text (with a commentary by Pseudo-Thomas Aquinas) is also referenced in Elijah of Butrio's Commentary on *Or 'Ammim* (fol. 46r–v); see also below, part 6.
160 §9.7.3–4.
161 §9.12.1–2 (*OA*).
162 §10.8.1–4 (*OA*).

chance." However, to support his arguments for divine omniscience and providence, he also employs *Physics* 2, text. 77 and 86, which he takes as forthright proofs that "naturally generated things necessarily exist for a purpose of an intender" and "an agent, not nature, intends a final purpose."[163]

It is in Sforno's eleventh chapter on the subject of divine providence that the statement that man's soul is superior to the rest of creation as a "separate, incorruptible substance, especially when it is perfected in cognition and action,"[164] is mentioned for the first time (prior to the proof of the soul's incorruptibility [or immortality] in chapter 12). Sforno's argumentation in this chapter bears many parallels to Maimonides's *Guide* 3:17–18, which were also noted by his commentator Elijah of Butrio.[165] The human intellectual soul, as the noblest thing in all of creation, and the human beings, endowed with free will, deserve God's providence. Sforno's exegesis of Psalm 94:9 ("Who planted the ear, shall He not hear? Who formed the eye, shall He not see?") at the end of chapter 11[166] is likewise employed in *Guide* 3:19.

Sforno's twelfth chapter then discusses Aristotle's concept of the human soul in *On the Soul* 3 in close connection to Averroes's commentary. As in the rest of the book and considering its intended brevity, Sforno limits himself to assembling refutations of and contradictions in Aristotle's and Averroes's arguments. One subcase of the arguments against the incorruptibility of the individual human soul that Sforno lists at the beginning of this chapter is Averroes's theory on the unicity of the human intellect. If the soul is a separate substance, then there will either be one soul shared between all human beings (as Averroes said in his Long Commentary on *On the Soul* 3) or as many souls as there are human individuals. If there is one soul shared between all human beings, then it would not be possible for individual human souls to be immortal.[167] To a degree that is at odds with his method, already in this first part, Sforno sees a need to refute this option with a counterargument taken (mediately or immediately) from Thomas Aquinas's *On the Unity of the Intellect against the Averroists* 4:86–91, which states that if there was a single intellect shared between all humans, then this could not explain how humans can think individually, as though—in analogy to this—all human beings were able to see with a single eye.[168]

To develop his own model, Sforno takes up Averroes's postulate of "a fourth kind of being" (*quartum genus essentie*/מן מציאות רביעי) from his Long Commentary on *On the Soul* 3, text. 5,[169] a category to which all separate intellects, including the human material intellect—with the sole exception of the divine agent intellect, which is pure act—belong.[170] For Sforno, the human intellectual soul is a separate substance, unmixed with matter and not individuated by it, like the intellects of the spheres, which are separate from the body of the

---

163 §9.7.3–4; §11.3.5–6.
164 §11.8 (OA).
165 Elijah of Butrio, MS Parma 2624, fol. 51ʳ.
166 §11.11.1.
167 §12.2.3–9.
168 Thomas Aquinas, *On the Unity of the Intellect against the Averroists*, trans. Beatrice H. Zedler (Milwaukee: Marquette University Press, 1968), 59–61.
169 §12.9. For further reading on this, see Symon Foren, "'A Fourth Kind of Being': The Legacy of Averroes in Obadiah Sforno's Theory of the Intellect," in Veltri, *Literary and Philosophical Canon*.
170 Engel, *Elijah Del Medigo*, 61–62.

sphere.¹⁷¹ It is created individually at the moment of its emanation onto a designated substrate (נואש מיוחד),¹⁷² and it retains its individuality since it is created *ex nihilo* and *de novo* to be immortal. Sforno introduces the term *emanation* here and explains the plural in Genesis 1:26 ("Let us make man") as a hint to the separate intellects of the spheres by which the human intellectual soul is mediately created. Plato, via Averroes, is referenced as the source of this idea.¹⁷³ The immaterial and immortal nature of the intellectual soul, which neither wearies nor ages, is also laid down in Sforno's exegetical interpretations of Psalm 1:1–3 and Isaiah 40:29–31 at the end of the chapter.¹⁷⁴

Following this chapter, Sforno seeks to clarify two other aspects related to the perfection of the soul in separate questions, which he had already previously noted. First, in chapter 13, he states that human perfection as *imitatio Dei* can be only attained בעיון ובמעשה ("in cognition and in action") in combination.¹⁷⁵ The synthesis of intellectual and moral perfection is not without tensions, as the debate about Maimonides's model in the *Guide* shows.¹⁷⁶ Sforno identifies the divine commandment regarding sanctification (cf. Lev 11:44: "Sanctify yourselves and be holy, for I am holy") with intellectual and moral perfection.¹⁷⁷ Next to עיון ("cognition"), there is always מעשה ("action"; i.e., good conduct). As Sforno points out, morality and good deeds are useful and necessary for perfecting the human soul.

Second, in the subsequent fourteenth chapter, Sforno clarifies that the perfection of the soul is only attained by human power alone, not by divine or natural powers. Since nature (for the most part, with only a few exceptions due to chance) and God always act perfectly, human perfection should inevitably be achieved, which is in fact not the case.¹⁷⁸ The importance of free choice for human perfection is also demonstrated in his explanation of Leviticus 19:2 ("You shall be holy, for I, ha-Shem, your God, am holy"), since the ability to act out of free choice is a common feature of man and God alone.¹⁷⁹

Finally, Sforno's strong anthropocentric view of creation becomes most obvious in the last chapter (chapter 15), which follows his previous statements about the human soul. Emphasising that the human intellectual soul, by its divine nature, is superior to the celestial bodies, which exist for its perfection, Sforno decisively deviates from Maimonides's position that the heavens, stars, and planets do not exist for the sake of man, but for their own sake, and that anthropocentric teleology obscures the search for ends in nature.¹⁸⁰ He instead inclines towards the positions of Gersonides in *Wars of the Lord* 5.2.3 (based on his astrological views) and Thomas Aquinas in his *Summa contra Gentiles*.¹⁸¹

---

171   §12.8.3–4; 12.10.1.
172   §12.11.2.
173   §12.8.1; §12.15.4.
174   §12.16; §12.17.1–12.18 (*OA*).
175   §11.8; §14.5; §16.24 (*OA*).
176   See Howard Kreisel, "*Imitatio Dei* in Maimonides' *Guide of the Perplexed*," *AJS Review* 19 (1994): 169–211.
177   §13.8 (*OA*).
178   §14.3.1–2. Sforno had already addressed this when speaking about human free will in the course of his explanation of divine providence (see §11.5).
179   §14.8.1.
180   Maimonides, *Guide* 3:13 and 25; see Melamed, "Teleology," 133 ff.
181   Thomas Aquinas, *Summa contra Gentiles* 3:22.7–9: "This the process of generation shows: at the start of generation there is the embryo living with plant life, later with animal life, and finally with human life. After this last type of form, no later and more noble form is

Returning to the book's title, a final remark must be made regarding the universalism in Sforno's philosophy. Sforno, in a very similar manner to Maimonides,[182] did not exclude non-Jews from the achievement of perfection, as he considered all people to be divinely created beings endowed with intellect and freedom of choice. As a key verse, we will look at his interpretation of Exodus 19:5 in his Torah commentary ("And you shall be a treasure (סגולה) for me among all nations"). Sforno writes:

> Even though all types of humans are important to me above all the lower beings, since He is represented only in them, as say Ha[-Rabbanan] z"l: "Humans are beloved because they were created in the Image" (Pirqe Avot)—still, you will be treasured among them. *"Because Mine is all the earth"*—**and the difference between you exists in smaller or bigger amounts, despite the fact that the whole earth is Mine, and the Righteous of the Nations are important to Me without a doubt.**

The Hebrew and Latin versions of *Light of the Nations* nonetheless differ in their choice of biblical references, with the Hebrew version containing explicit references to Israel as the bearer of the divine covenant while only a minority among the Nations are sufficiently righteous to worship God and the rest will do so in messianic times.[183] However, Sforno does not deviate from his abovementioned exegesis that the difference is only in "smaller or larger amounts" and that the Nations are not automatically barred from the goal of the perfection of the soul. He sees no point in not addressing his Christian readers with the same verses as his Jewish co-religionists, such as Leviticus 19:2, "You shall be holy, for I, ha-Shem, your God, am holy."[184] The commandment of *imitatio Dei* is universal. However, the non-Hebrew readers are not fortunate enough to be given the explanation based on Sanhedrin 92a that "absolute holiness" (קדושה בהחלט) is the same as eternal existence (נצחיות).[185]

Although Sforno's brief display of philosophy left many details vague and—especially in the field of psychology—certainly did not resolve the problems that philosophers had been addressing and discussing for centuries, it nevertheless undeniably attained its goal of summarising the main fields of conflict between Aristotelian-Averroean philosophy from the latter's point of view and the rationality, universalism, and Humanism in his biblical exegesis.

---

found in the order of generable and corruptible things. Therefore, the ultimate end of the whole process of generation is the human soul, and matter tends toward it as toward an ultimate form. So, elements exist for the sake of mixed bodies; these latter exist for the sake of living bodies, among which plants exist for animals, and animals for men. Therefore, man is the end of the whole order of generation. [...] So, if the motion of the heavens is ordered to generation, and if the whole of generation is ordered to man as a last end within this genus, it is clear that the end of celestial motion is ordered to man, as to an ultimate end in the genus of generable and mobile beings. Hence the statement in Deuteronomy (4:19) that God made celestial bodies 'for the service of all peoples'" (Aquinas, *Contra Gentiles. Book Three: Providence, Q. 1–83*, trans. Vernon J. Bourke, ed. Joseph Kenny, O.P. [New York: Hanover House, 1955], https://isidore.co/aquinas/ContraGentiles3a.htm).

182 Menachem Kellner, "Maimonides' True Religion: For Jews or All Humanity?", *Me'orot* 7 (2008): 1–24.
183 § 11.8 (*OA*).
184 § 13.7; § 14.8.1.
185 The same interpretation can be found in Sforno's Torah commentary on Lev 11:2.

6 Reception: Elijah of Butrio's Commentary on *Or 'Ammim*

As a concise treatise on basic concepts of religious philosophy built on a Jewish foundation in contrast to Aristotelian and Averroean thought, *Or 'Ammim* gained at least some admirers among Sforno's contemporaries and successive thinkers, although it did not have an impact that was in any way comparable to the greats of Jewish philosophy: Josef Solomon Delmedigo (1591–1655) answered a letter he received from the Karaite Zeraḥ ben Natan of Troki (1578–1657/8), including the latter's theological questions about the existence of God and divine providence (among others), in his *Iggeret Aḥuz*, in which he also recommended a list of works on mathematics, metaphysics, exegesis, and others that reads like a "who's who" of Jewish philosophy, among which he mentions Sforno's *Or 'Ammim*.[186] Nevertheless, probably the earliest and most extensive trace of the book's reception is a commentary on it contained in a manuscript in the Biblioteca Palatina in Parma (MS 2624 [De Rossi 1200]). This was composed at least before 16 December 1555 (as proven by a censors' note by Jacob Geraldini and Caesar Belliosus in Bologna) by an author named Elijah of Butrio (אליה מבוטריו), a disciple of Sforno, better known under the name Elijah ben Joseph di Nola.[187]

The commentary is in large parts also a transcript, or at least a close paraphrase, of Sforno's text. Butrio renamed its chapters and sections using terms designating the parts of the Menorah described in Exodus 25:31.[188] He essentially supplemented Sforno's text with three kinds of comments:

1. References to Jewish philosophers, above all Maimonides,[189] but also Gersonides,[190] Nahmanides,[191] Abraham bar Ḥiyya,[192] and Isaac Arama,[193] thereby illustrating the Jewish philosophical context of *Or 'Ammim*. However, he also adds references to other non-Jewish philosophers (Boethius, Simplicius, [Pseudo-]Thomas Aquinas, and Agostino Nifo), giving insight into what was likely also the wider canon of philosophical literature used by Sforno himself.[194]

---

186 Abraham Geiger, *Melo Chofnajim* (Berlin, 1840), 25 (German section), 19 (Hebrew section).
187 Elijah of Butrio, presumably from Budrio (see n. 114 above), is also known as the author of two elegies on Joseph Karo (*Yivkeh be-mar nefesh*; *La-meqonenot qiru le-'orer qinah*, published by Meir Benayahu in *Sefer Rabbi Yosef Qaro*, ed. Isaac Raphael [Jerusalem: Mossad ha-Rav Kook, 1969], 302–340) and of a now lost Commentary on Proverbs mentioned in Julius Fürst, "Manuscripte in Brody und einzelne Berichte," *Wissenschaftliche Zeitschrift für Jüdische Theologie* 3 (1837): 283, where he is referred to as a physician. His identity with Elijah ben Joseph di Nola has been uncovered by Florian Dunklau and Moshe Kravetz. See Moshe Kravetz, "R. Ovadiah Sforno, his school in Bologna, his disciple R. Elia di Nola, and a study of their relationship through Nola's commentary on the Psalms" (PhD diss., Universität Hamburg, 2023).
188 Namely: קנה (branch), גביע (bowl), כפתור (ornament), פרח (flower).
189 The *Guide of the Perplexed* is found throughout the whole commentary. Butrio also made use of Maimonides's *Commentary on the Mishnah* (Introduction to *Zera'im* [fol. 65ʳ]).
190 There are frequent references to Gersonides's *Wars of the Lord*, which is often criticised (on fols. 12ᵛ and 47ᵛ).
191 Commentary on the Torah (fol. 12ᵛ).
192 *Tzurat ha-Aretz* (on fol. 19ᵛ).
193 Commentary on the Torah (fol. 47ᵛ).
194 Agostino Nifo da Sessa's Commentaries on Averroes's *Incoherence of the Incoherence* (on fol. 50ʳ) and *De anima beatitudine*, which in the commentary is called *Iggeret ha-Hatzlaḥah* (on fol. 32ʳ, probably a translation of the alternative title *Epistola de beatitudine*); Boethius's [*De institutione*] *Arithmetica* (on fol. 56ᵛ), his *Consolation of Philos-*

2. Cross-references throughout the book to the twenty-seven propositions listed in Sforno's introduction, which are only rarely integrated into the rest of the book (see above, part 5.3).
3. Excursions and glosses of philosophical terms and general philosophical concepts, including explanations of the aforementioned twenty-seven propositions.

Elijah of Butrio's commentary therefore both sought to resolve (structural) weaknesses in the book and also attempted to serve the interest of a specifically Jewish reader and philosophical beginner who might require supplementary information in order to understand Sforno's sometimes enigmatic and dense account. It seems probable that the commentary, which includes neither a colophon nor an introduction, might have been written for its first owner, Gershon ben Elisha of Montefiascone ([גרשון בכ״ם אלישע ז״ל ממונטי פיאק]וני), a leading bibliophile rabbi of Rome and Bologna, who was the owner of a copy of *Or 'Ammim* that is today in the custody of the Bibliotheca Casanatense (signature: LL.VIII.33.1).[195]

7 Sforno's Philosophy and *Light* in Modern Scholarship

In the nineteenth century and most of the twentieth century, Sforno the philosopher—in contrast to Sforno the exegete—was widely ignored by scholarship. A review of scholarly opinions of Sforno from the time when Judaism and Jewish literature became a matter of critical academic study during the *Wissenschaft des Judentums* movement may take the historiographer Heinrich Graetz (1817–1891) as an exemplary starting point. Graetz's approach to Jewish history is characterised by a negative attitude towards the epoch of the early modern period and its supposed intellectual and spiritual atmosphere, which he describes in the ninth volume of his *Geschichte der Juden*:

> The refining and civilizing thoughts of Judaism had not yet gained the upper hand. The people were wanting in spirituality, their guides in clearness of mind. Reliance on justification by works and scholastic sophistry were prevalent also among Jews.[196]

For Graetz and others, there was no "Renaissance" taking place for the Jews at that time and even worse, there was also a decline in all fields, especially in philosophy, which had reached its peak by Maimonides's time:

---

ophy accompanied by Pseudo-Thomas Aquinas's commentary on it (on fol. 46^{r-v}), and Pseudo-Boethius's *De unitate et uno* (by Dominicus Gundissalinus; fol. 54^r); Plato's dialogues *Phaedo* (on fol. 10^v) and *Timaeus* (on fol. 40^v), although it is possible that these are only indirect references from Aristotle's or Averroes's texts; Simpicius of Cilicia's Commentary on *On the Heavens* (on fol. 25^v); and the pseudo-Aristotelian *Book of Causes* (on fol. 34^r).

195 Annalisa di Nola, *Le cinquecentine ebraiche—Catalogo* (Milan: Aisthesis, 2001), 167–168.
196 Graetz, *History of the Jews*, 4:477–478; *Geschichte der Juden*, 9:232: "Das Judenthum, seine erhebenden und versittlichenden Gedanken, waren bis dahin nicht zum Durchbruch gekommen; auch hier fehlte beim Volke die Innterlichkeit der Religion und bei den Führern die Klarheit des Geistes. Werkthätigkeit und scholastischer Dunst waren auch unter den Juden heimisch."

Otherwise there was nothing new at this period. Freedom of philosophical inquiry was not favored. Isaac Abrabanel, the transmitter of the old Spanish Hebrew spirit, found in Maimuni's philosophical writings many heresies opposed to Judaism, and he condemned the free-thinking commentators who went beyond tradition. A Portuguese fugitive, Joseph Jaabez laid on philosophy the blame for the expulsion of the Jews from Spain and Portugal. Free-thinking was the sin which had led Israel astray; thereon must the greatest restriction be laid. [...] Similar discomfort with free-thinking was expressed by the physician Obadiah Sforno, Reuchlin's teacher.[197]

The mention of Sforno in this section paved the way for similar unfavourable statements about him and his work. Sforno "was not an expert in Hebrew literature, but saw it through the eyes of Haggadah and Kabbalah."[198] His literary production was designated as "mediocre" (*sehr mittelmäßig*),[199] and as Reuchlin's teacher, he was described as being "not a master" of Hebrew grammar.[200]

An only slightly more positive view of Sforno was presented by Gustav Karpeles in his two-volume 1886 *Geschichte der jüdischen Literatur*. Karpeles called Sforno an "eager adversary of philosophical studies," who "in his treatise 'Or 'Ammim' sought to fight philosophy for the sake of religion."[201] However, he did pay tribute to Sforno's philosophical Commentary on Job, as well as to his "truly cosmopolitan interpretation" of Exodus 19:5–6. ("then out of all nations you will be my treasured possession") in *Or 'Ammim*.[202]

A strong counterpart to Graetz was the first modern study on "R. Obadiah Sforno as an exegete" (*R. Obadja Sforno als Exeget*) written by Ephraim Finkel in 1896. In his detailed doctoral study, Finkel took a stand against the accusations that Sforno was not a kabbalist himself (as seemed to be proven by the near-total absence of kabbalistic exegesis in his Commentary on the Pentateuch) and that there is no proof that he encouraged Reuchlin to study Kabbalah, as Graetz claimed.[203] Instead, he described Sforno as a "calm and logical thinker" (*ruhigen und logischen Denker*)[204] whose *Or 'Ammim* sought proof through "rational demonstrations" (*Vernunftsbeweise*).[205] In his view, Sforno's relationship to philosophy was far more complex, as his Commentary on the Torah was full of "philosophical notions" (*philosophische Gedanken*).[206] However, Finkel's detailed study remained isolated for decades.

---

197 Graetz, *History of the Jews*, 4:479. The final sentence about Sforno is only found in the original German edition (Graetz, *Geschichte der Juden*, 9:235).

198 Graetz, *Geschichte der Juden*, 9:94: "Er war zwar kein feiner Kenner der hebräischen Literatur, sah sie vielmehr durch die Brille der Agada und der Kabbala an aber für Reuchlin wußte er genug."

199 Graetz, 9:50: "Aber so weit die Schriften der so sehr Gepriesenen [Abraham de Balmes, Judah de Blanis and Sforno] der Beurtheilung vorliegen, erweisen sie sich als sehr mittelmäßig." In the third and final edition of his book (1891), Graetz revised this part, confining his verdict to Sforno only: "So weit seine Schriften der Beurteilung vorliegen, erweisen sie sich als sehr mittelmäßig" (ibid., 40).

200 Graetz, 9:192.

201 Gustav Karpeles, *Geschichte der Jüdischen Literatur*, 2 vols. (Berlin, 1886), 2:844 f.

202 Karpeles, *Geschichte der Jüdischen Literatur*, 2:845, 860–861; see *OA* 53^{r-v}.

203 Finkel, *R. Obadja*, 109 n. 6.

204 Finkel, 5.

205 Finkel, 17.

206 Finkel, 19.

A similarly balanced view was taken by Simon Dubnow, who wrote the first Jewish history that sought to base itself on secular and scholarly principles alone and to eschew political and religious dogmatism. Dubnow described Sforno as an "excellent linguist, natural scientist,[207] and philosopher, with a nevertheless conservative attitude,"[208] seeing *Or 'Ammim* as an "apology for faith" that was against Aristotelian religious philosophy and for the "refutation of the Epicurean (free-thinker)."[209]

Among post-Shoah scholars, we must mention Cecil Roth, whose pioneering research on the history of the Jews in the Renaissance (1959) nevertheless only mentions Sforno and *Or 'Ammim* in its chapters on Jewish translators in the context of its translation into Latin. The first extensive study of a chapter of *Or 'Ammim* was presented by Robert Bonfil in his 1976 essay "The Doctrine of the Human Soul and Its Holiness in the Thought of Rabbi Obadiah Seforno."[210] It is thanks to Bonfil's attentive perusal that the original features of Sforno's account were first detected. He pointed out that Sforno was not an adversary of Aristotle or his philosophy *per se*, but that he was rather deeply in tune with the latter's rationalism.

In the last decades, a number of studies, though relatively small in number, have contributed to the understanding of the deep intersection between exegesis and philosophy and between biblically guided rationalism and religious Humanism in Sforno's work.[211] The significance of *Light of the Nations* for the development of the spiritual and philosophical orientation of his oeuvre as a whole has thereby become more visible than ever.

---

207 On the misattribution of a translation of Euclid's *Elements* to Sforno, see above (part 1).
208 Simon Dubnow, *Weltgeschichte des Jüdischen Volkes*, vol. 6 (Berlin: Jüdischer Verlag, 1927), 141.
209 Dubnow, *Weltgeschichte des Jüdischen Volkes*, 6:141.
210 Robert Bonfil, "The Doctrine of the Human Soul and Its Holiness in the Thought of Rabbi Obadiah Seforno" [Hebrew], *Eshel Beer Sheva* 1 (1976): 200–257.
211 In chronological order:
Joseph Walk, "'Ovadyah Sforno ha-Parshan ha-humanist," in *Sefer Neiger; Ma'amarim be ḥeker ha-tanakh le-zekher David Neiger z"l*, ed. Arthur Biram (Jerusalem: Israel Society for Biblical Research, 1959), 277–302; reprinted in *As Yesterday: Essays and Reminiscences* [Hebrew] (Jerusalem: Shasar, 1997), 183–211.
Chaim Shine, "Diyyuno shel Rabbi 'Ovadyah Sforno 'al ha-hashgaḥah," *Pe'amim* 20 (1984): 77–84 (on chapter 11 of *Or 'Ammim*).
Robert Bonfil "Il Rinascimento. La produzione esegetica di O. Servadio Sforno," in *La lettura ebraica delle Scritture*, ed. Sergio J. Sierra (Bologna: Edizioni Dehoniane, 1995), 261–277.
Daniel H. Frank and Oliver Leaman, "Jewish Philosophy in the Renaissance," in *The Jewish Philosophy Reader*, ed. Charles H. Manekin (London: Routledge, 2000), 282–299 (including a partial translation of chapter 13 of *Or 'Ammim*).
Chaim Shine, *Adam, Ḥevrah u-mishpat be-haguto shel R. 'Ovadyah. Sforno* (Tel Aviv: Sha'are Mishpat, 2001).
Eric Dahan, "Philosophie et tradition dans le commentaire de Sforno sur Qohelet," *Yod* 15 (2010): 145–187.
Symon Foren, "Reconciling Philosophy and Scripture in Renaissance Italy: Obadiah Sforno's Hebrew and Latin versions of the *Light of the Nations*" (PhD diss., Oxford University, 2020).

Obadiah Sforno: Light of the Nations

Edited and translated by Florian Dunklau (Hebrew) and Giada Coppola (Latin)

∴

Notes on Editions and Translations

1   Note on the Hebrew Edition and Its English Translation

The present edition of *Or ʿAmmim* (*Light of the Nations*) provides a scientific edition of the Hebrew text based on the first print (Bologna, 1537) and the first-ever complete English translation of the text. The original edition's pagination has been marked by vertical lines. Its punctuation has been retained, but interpreted and supplemented: each paragraph and each line of a list ends with a full stop. "Dots" in the first print have been interpreted either as commas within a sentence or as a full stop at its end. Abbreviated words have been expanded for readability. Common abbreviations (e.g. ז״ל and עכ״ל) have been retained. Plene and defective spellings have also been retained, but in a number of ambiguous instances, we have indicated our understanding by partial vocalisation.

The critical apparatus contains corrections that Sforno made to the text that were originally added in a postscript to the 1537 first edition. Further orthographical or grammatical mistakes have been corrected or (in less obvious cases) conjectured. Emendations have been made on the basis of original sources and the Latin version. A comparison with the Latin version and the work's sources texts (biblical, rabbinical, and philosophical) led to a number of emendations and the correction of further errors that were unnoticed by Sforno (for sigla of sources, see below).

In our edition, direct quotations from biblical, rabbinical, and philosophical sources initiated by the formula באמרו (or similar) have been put into guillemets («…»). If no source reference is given, as is regularly the case for biblical and rabbinical sources, the reference is indicated in-line in brackets. Philosophical, scientific, or theological terms highlighted by Sforno (indicated by נקרא or similar) have been put into single guillemets (‹…›). Headings, subheadings, and the first word of the original paragraphs of the first print are in bold type.

In order to facilitate comparison between the editions and translations, the text has been divided into new paragraphs (§) by the editors, which are parallel in all four columns (Hebrew, Latin, English [2]). The Hebrew edition was chosen as the base text. Since the Latin version differs due to Sforno's revisions of it, differences between the two versions are documented in the following manner: (1) A paragraph number printed in *italics* indicates a considerable difference (pertaining to length, style, or content), though the overall structure and arguments are still parallel in both versions. (2) A paragraph number placed between pointed brackets (⟨…⟩) indicates a missing paragraph in one version. (3) A paragraph number placed between pointed brackets accompanied by an asterisk (⟨…⟩*) indicates that this paragraph's position in the Latin version has been changed. A note indicates its new position, where the paragraph number is placed between asterisks (*…*) and between square brackets in the parallel version.

Sforno's Hebrew style in *Or ʿAmmim* is characterised by simplicity in vocabulary and complexity in syntactical structure. Very often, a single argument is presented in a long hypotactic sentence, which mirrors the book's Latin and Scholastic underpinning. In the English translation, these sentences have been rendered in a more paratactical manner wherever necessary to aid comprehension. Editorial additions and explanations have been added to the text in square brackets.

Sforno translated philosophical sources himself from Latin editions and rendered them differently in various instances. For the translation of quotations from cited sources, we consulted available modern English translations, which are listed below. However, these were often made from Greek (Aristotle) or Arabic (Averroes's *Tahafut al-Tahafut*) sources instead of the Latin texts available to Sforno. The peculiarity of Sforno's sources and the style of his own Hebrew translations have therefore been retained where inevitable and not in conflict with proper understanding. Sforno's references to contemporary Latin printed editions have been supplemented by those according to modern formats if available (in the case of Aristotle, according to Bekker numbering following the editions published in the Loeb Classical Library). Direct quotes from the Bible and Rabbinic literature are noted in in-line references, while allusions to passages integrated into Sforno's text are noted in the footnotes only.

"God" and all names, titles, designations, and personal pronouns referring to the "God of the Bible" (e.g. the Creator, the Holy Spirit etc.) have been capitalised, especially in biblical quotes. This does not apply to philosophical contexts, such as quotations from Aristotle and theoretical arguments in which references are made to the "god of the philosophers" only.

2 Additional Note on the Latin Edition and Its Translation

The innumerable abbreviations, ligatures, and divisions of the 1548 *editio princeps* have been resolved without further notification and have only been retained in a few common cases (cap. = capitulum, lib. = liber, t.c. = textus commenti; Aven R. = Aven Roes).

Original spelling and punctuation have been retained.

In the first Latin print, continuous pagination changes to folio pagination from page 41 onwards. We have provided continuous page numbers to the end of the book in square brackets.

Bible quotations have been set in italic type, with references given in-line in round brackets.

3 Sigla in the Critical Apparatus

a	*Or 'Ammim* (1537)
a^{corr}	the author's corrections in a postscript to the first edition (1537)
b	*Lumen Gentium* (Latin edition [1548])
b^{corr}	the author's corrections in a postscript to the first edition (1548)
A	MS St. Petersburg IOM 169,3
Copp.	Coppola, Giada (editor of *Lumen Gentium*)
DD	*Destructio Destructionum* (Latin edition of Averroes's *Incoherence of the Incoherence* (*Tahafut al-Tahafut*); Agostino Nifo, *Destructio destructionum Averroiis cum Agostino Niphi de Sessa expositione* [Venizia, 1497])
DSO	*De substantia orbis* (Latin edition of Averroes's *De substantia orbis* [translated by Michael Scotus]; revised digital copy of Alvaro de Toledo, *Commentario al "De substantia orbis" de Averroes (Aristote-*

	lismo y Averroismo), edited by Manuel Alonso [Madrid: Bolaños y Aguilar, 1941]; Cologne: Digital Averroes Research Environment (DARE), 2012: http://dare.uni-koeln.de/app/fulltexts/FT2)
Dunk.	Dunklau, Florian (editor of *Or 'Ammim*)
M	Masoretic Text of the Hebrew Bible (based on the Westminster Leningrad Codex and taken from http://sefaria.org)
MN	*Moreh Nevuchim* (Maimonides, translated by Samuel ibn Tibbon, edited by Yehuda Even Shmu'el [Dr. Yehuda Kaufman], 4 vols., Jerusalem: Mossad ha-Rav Kook, 2005)
L	Latin of Aristotle's works and accompanying commentaries by Averroes in the Giunta edition, 11 vols., reprinted and expanded edition (Venice, 1562).
V	The Clementine Vulgate (*Biblia Sacra Vulgatæ editionis, Sixti v Pontificis Maximi jussu recognitaet edita* [1598], with additions by A. Colunga and L. Turrado [Madrid: La Editorial Católica, 1946]: http://vulsearch.sourceforge.net/html).

4 Modern English Translations Consulted

- Translations of Aristotle's works published in the Loeb Classical Library (https://www.loebclassics.com): *Nicomachean Ethics* (73), *Physics* (228, 255), *Politics* (264), *Metaphysics* (271, 287), *On the Soul* (288), *On the Heavens* (338), *Posterior Analytics* (391), *Meteorology* (397), *On Generation and Corruption* [*On Coming-to-be and Passing Away*] (400).
- Averroes. *Averroes (Ibn Rushd) of Cordoba: Long Commentary on the* De anima *of Aristotle*. Translated by Richard C. Taylor. Edited by Therese-Anne Druart. New Haven, CT: Yale University Press, 2009.
- Averroes. *De substantia orbis. Critical Edition of the Hebrew Text with English Translation and Commentary*. Translated by Arthur Hyman. Cambridge, MA: Medieval Academy of America; Jerusalem: Israel Academy of Sciences and Humanities, 1986.
- Averroes. *Ibn Rushd's* Metaphysics: *A Translation with Introduction of Ibn Rushd's Commentary on Aristotle's* Metaphysics, *Book Lām*. Translated by Charles Genequand. Leiden: Brill, 1986.
- Averroes. *Tahafut al Tahafut* (*The Incoherence of the Incoherence*). *Translated from the Arabic, with Introduction*. Translated by Simon van den Bergh. 2 vols. Oxford: University Press, 1954 [reprinted as one volume, 1987].
- Porphyry. *Introduction*. Translated by Jonathan Barnes. Oxford: Clarendon Press, 2003.

Editions and translations of Or ʿAmmim *and* Lumen Gentium

Florian Dunklau (ed. and transl. Or ʿAmmim.*)*
Giada Coppola (ed. and transl. Lumen Gentium.*)*

3 [Epistola dedicatoria]

§ 0 Sacrae et Christianissimae Maestati Domino D. Henrico Gallie ac Gloriosissimo Regi. Servadeus Sphurnus Medicus Hebreus Suppliciter. S. P. D.[a]

Antiqui, quidem, Sacra Maiestas, modernique Aristotelis scilicet opiniones sequentes eiusdem rationibus ducti universum ab eterno et ingenitum esse aperte ferunt. Quare licet dicant illud nonnullam habere causam omnium primam. Reliqua tamen ab ipsa causa seriatim emanantia non voluntarie sed naturaliter tantum ab eadem emanare sequitur, et per consequens licet dicant ipsam primam causam esse substantiarum primam cuius presentia universi partes ordo et colligatio conservantur cum tamen horum esse ab ipsa prima non scilicet voluntarie fiat immo preter eiusdem intentum cum enim[b] sint sibi coeterna semper ergo et eodem modo ab eadem emanare necesse est.

Quare nec minimam universi partem ad libitum mutare procul dubio posset et sic falso diceretur ipsam primam substantiam quam dicunt esse Deum de mortalibus operibus habere curam qua preter naturam[c] merita vel demerita voluntarie retribuat, illud enim suo naturali processui ab eadem substantia necessario emananti penitus repugnaret. Cumque ad huiusmodi Phylosophorum opinionem qua scilicet dicunt universum fuisse ab eterno omnino sequatur ut similiter ab eterno fuisset homo et per consequens infiniti fuerunt homines quare si individue hominum anime ad horum numerum numerabiles essent quid immortale sequeretur ut darentur substantie numero infinite simul tempore existentes quod est falsum et penitus impossibile oportuit eos necessario dicere huiusmodi animas esse quid mortale, et sic sequitur secundum eos ut post hominis mortem nihil meriti vel demeriti dari contingat, quare tota religio piorumque operum cura quid penitus vanum et quodammodo ridiculum esse videretur.

Cumque horum huiusmodi opinionum harumque rationum oppositum in Sacris Dei Scripturis demonstrative probatum esse invenerim hoc edidi opusculum presertim instante Illustrissimo Domino Iulio de Rovero in quo scilicet huiusmodi phylosophorum opiniones harumque rationes diffuse ostenduntur cum citatione locorum ubi talia in suis diversis libris diffusius disputantur quas tamen iactis eorum fundamentis demonstrative redargui, et in Sacris Scripturis oppositum probari aperte docetur. Tue ergo Maiestati tanquam Christianissime; et religionis defensori huiusmodi opus nuper impressum merito presentari curavi cui me semper suppliciter commendo ac penitus trado.

---

[a] Salutem Plurimam Dicit.   [b] enim] b[corr]; omnia b.   [c] preter naturam] b[corr]; propter natura b.

[Dedicatory Epistle]

§ 0 To the holy and the Most Christian King Henri II, king of France, Obadiah Sforno, the Jewish physician, would like to extend warm greetings.

[Your] Sacred Majesty, the opinions of the ancient and modern partisans of Aristotle support the idea that the universe is eternal and uncreated—although they say that there is a first cause, and that everything else was sequentially emanated from this [first] cause and that things come from that one not following a purpose, but naturally. And consequently, they say that the first cause is the first substance from which the parts of the universe are preserved according to order and connection, and since those things are created from that first cause without will, meaning without purpose, therefore things are coeternal, and it is necessary for them that things are emanated from the first cause.

But when they say that an exceedingly small part of the universe can also spontaneously change, they speak falsely. The first substance is God, who takes care of human beings by compensating them according to the nature of their merits or demerits, and this is entirely at odds with the idea that everything is necessarily emanated from a substance. The opinion of the philosophers is that the universe is eternal, and therefore, if the universe was eternal, men would also be eternal, and consequently, there would be an infinite number of men. And if the individual souls of the men, which are countless, were immortal, therefore several infinite substances would exist at the same time, and this is false and impossible. Therefore, the philosophers argue that the soul is mortal and that there is nothing after death and that nothing is given on account of men's merit or demerits, because they [i.e., the philosophers] consider religion and good deeds futile and ridiculous.

However, God's Holy Scripture proves the contrary of these kinds of opinions and ideas by means of demonstration. Therefore, due to the solicitation of the illustrious Giulio della Rovere, I have published this pamphlet, in which the opinions of the philosophers will be exposed by means of quotations discussed in different books, and I will refute their principles by means of demonstration and will prove that the contrary of what is taught in the Holy Scripture. I wish to present this recently published work to your Majesty, the Most Christian as well as the defender of the religion. I commend you suppliantly and wholeheartedly.

[Epistle]

§ 1 This is the *Light of the Nations*[a]
in which He will display [His] glory.
The Living [God] of the [two] Worlds
will shine for us.
For in it, we will understand
the time of Man[na] and the well,
how abundantly *began
Moses to expound*.[b]

The words of Obadiah, the young one—may His rock keep him and grant him life—son of my honoured teacher and father R. Jacob Sforno—his memory is for the life in the world to come—an inhabitant of Bologna, *and the words of the man*[c] *who sees the misery*[d] of the remaining [adherents] of the Holy people; *who stands trembling*[e] as a witness of the fading of the light. And on him is the yoke of *those who turn aside to their crooked ways*,[f] since there are many sages of the nations who have begun to investigate. *How can the thinker stay on his way?*[g] Through the letters of the Bible, the Mishnah, and the Talmud! *Yet they rebelled and grieved*,[h] as it says (Proverbs 20:24): "What does [a man] know about his own way?" And what does a man know who is like this? (2 Samuel 14:19): "Someone who turns to the right or the left." Does he have any reliable proof? *Will he be profitable to God*,[i] *and will he obtain favour from Him*[j] or not? His fear [of God] and his zeal *for the Torah and for the testimony*[k] would be *a commandment taught by man*,[l] which has its foundation in a story passed on from a father to [his] children. And [while] the writings of the first [men] *proclaim the Glory of God*,[m] behold, there are *multitudes upon multitudes*[n] of people who spew venom through [false] stories. *And they turn aside to lies*,[o] *and write oppressive decrees*.[p]

And how will anyone know who it is?[q] Who are those who walk *along the right paths*?[r] Who of us *gives a word*;[s] [who] guides and *has regard for the weak?*[t] [Who] opposes the complainant with proof that *divides between holy and profane*,[u] *and all injustice will shut its mouth?*[v] But there are many now who say that there is a commandment to believe in all the roots of our Torah. And the Rambam [Moses Maimonides]—of blessed memory—is among them, [according] to his book the *Guide* [*of the*

---

[a] Isa 51:4. [b] Deut 1:5. [c] Num 24:3. [d] Lam 3:1. [e] Cf. Dan 10:11. [f] Ps 125:5. [g] Ps 119:9. [h] Isa 63:10. [i] Job 22:2. [j] Prov 8:35. [k] Isa 8:20. [l] Isa 29:13. [m] Ps 19:2. [n] Joel 4:14. [o] Ps 40:5. [p] Isa 10:1. [q] Ex 33:16. [r] Ps 23:3. [s] Ps 68:11. [t] Ps 41:2. [u] *Sukkah* 5:5. [v] Cf. Ps 107:42.

[אגרת]

§ 1 זה אור עמים   בו יתפאר
חי עולמים   לנו יאר
כי בו נשכיל   עת מן ובאר
מה רב הואיל   משה באר

נאם הצעיר עובדיה יצ״ו בכמה״ר יעקב ספורנו זלה״ה מתושבי בולונייא. ונאם הגבר ראה עני שרידי עם קדש עומד מרעיד בעדת מורדי אור ועליו מטה המטים עקלקלות כי ברבים היו חכמי הגוים הבאים לחקור במה יזכה את ארחו ההוגה? באותיות מקרא ומשנה ותלמוד! והמה מרו ועצבו באמרם: «מה יבין דרכו» (משלי כ׳ כ״ד) ומה ידע איש אשר כזה «אם איש להימין ולהשמיל?» (שמואל ב י״ד, י״ט) הלא אין אצלו מופת מודיע? הלאל יסכון ויפיק רצון מאתו אם אין? ותהי יראתו וזריזותו לתורה ולתעודה מצות אנשים מלמדה אשר יסודה בספור אב לבנים ומכתבי ראשונים מספרים כבוד אל. והנה המונים המונים מונים את נפשם בספורים פורים רוש ושטי כזב ומכתבים עמל כתבו.

ובמה יוָדע איפא מי? ומי ההולכים במעגלי צדק? מי משלנו יתן אמר; מורה ומשכיל אל דל? ואל בעל דין חולק במופת מבדיל בין קדש לחול וכל עולה תקפוץ פיה? הן רבים עתה אמרו שמצוה עלינו להאמין כל שרשי תורתנו ומהם הרמב״ם ז״ל בספר המורה מאמר ג׳

EPISTLE – אגרת

Perplexed] 3:28, even though it seems that he departed from what [he says] at the beginning of his *Book of Knowledge*.ᵃ It is as [it says] in these [words]: the heart beats with doubt on the right [side] while it is on the left. And the truth as well as | its contrary are highly doubted among the multitude of our people and among some *who [only] hold [fast to] the Torah*ᵇ by paying lip service. They do not have decisive proof to remove all doubt from the roots of our Torah, such that this kind of belief is not a matter of free choice and is not applicable to a commandment at all, because a man cannot believe absolutely by an act of will, still less if it is commanded, although he will perhaps *open his mouth*ᶜ to please the masses *and speak rashly with his lips*.ᵈ

But *every word of God is purified*ᵉ by a demonstrative proof that accompanies each theoretical portion, as is a rule for every wise man: *declaring from the beginning*ᶠ everything that is concealed, because it is appropriate for him to make it intelligible and to expound his intention with clear arguments. Is this not more appropriate for an *all-knowing God*ᵍ—may He be exalted—the *Guide to Justice*,ʰ *to whom wisdom and power belong*?ⁱ Behold, this is *the joy of His way*ʲ and the wisdom of His order in the existing [world]. He was pleased for His righteousness's sake that it is in the Torah of His Holiness, *and He has withheld nothing from it*.ᵏ For after God made His existence and *the dignity of His kingship*ˡ known to any intelligent person through true intellectual demonstrations, *so that there was no more place*ᵐ for doubt about them, *He gave the world His covenant*ⁿ and His commandments, as the Rabbanan—of blessed memory—said (*Mekhiltah Exodus* 20:3): "They accepted My kingship, and after that, they accepted My decrees as from a king." And therefore, every intelligent person understands that when He commanded love and fear, He was commanding [by this] to contemplate and to know His greatness and His goodness—as far as possible—because with their knowledge [of this], love and fear will be true and without doubt. And without the aforementioned knowledge, or [at least] its transmission by those who know, as God—may He be praised—decreed to His people, love and fear are impossible. And that is what He said, as it says (Deuteronomy 6:4–5): "Hear, O Israel! [...] and you shall love." And therefore, *the wicked man, worthy of being beaten*,ᵒ *will afterwards find grace*ᵖ to know his Lord, if he intends to rebel against Him. Because he will naturally fear Him after he knows Him, as it says

---

ᵃ*Mishneh Torah, Hilkhot Yesode ha-Torah*, ch. 1: "[a commandment] to 'know' that there is a God."   ᵇJer 2:8.   ᶜJob 35:16.   ᵈPs 106:33.   ᵉProv 30:5.   ᶠIsa 46:10.   ᵍ1 Sam 2:3.   ʰCf. Joel 2:23.   ⁱDan 2:20.   ʲJob 8:19.   ᵏCf. Gen 39:9.   ˡEst 1:4.   ᵐIsa 5:8.   ⁿPs 111:9.   ᵒDeut 25:2.   ᵖRuth 2:2.

(Jeremiah 10:7 and 10:6): "Who would not fear You, O King of the nations? For that is Your due, etc. There is none like You!" And what is there to do for us, if a Guide of Justice *completed [His] speech*,[a] *confirming with equity*[b] the foundations of our Torah!? But today, the heads of the people of the [divine] name dedicate all [their time] *to studying Neziqin*.[c] *And we are in our eyes*[d] *like knowers of grace*,[e] *who growl like bears*[f] *to find words of delight*[g] [which are good] enough to answer our inquirer (Song of Songs 5:9): "How is your beloved better than another?" *For His sake are we killed all day long*,[h] and none of us knows for how long.

Surely our weakness is that we do not direct the heart to knowing and the eyes to seeing the miracles from the Torah of our God, by which He made known the power of His deeds for His people through intellectual demonstrations, as it says (Deuteronomy 4:39): "And know therefore this day and keep in mind." For He wrote to teach them and to confirm among them that the world has an innovative forth-bringer who undoubtedly generates all [things], like a bearer who carries it. And He is one, incorporeal, exercising providence over all. He gave man the image of the everlasting God—by Him his heart may live forever! And a huge multitude [of people] fell away from Him into a trap: *an error in study counts as deliberate sin*.[i]

Therefore, I said: *Behold, I come with a book*.[j] I called it *Light of the Nations*, whose goal it is *to set up an everlasting lamp*[k] in front of man and to remove | the dust from the eyes of the wretched among the people of the God of Abraham. *They shall lift up their voices*[l] to open the eyes of all who live on earth *to please Him, who dwelt in the [burning] bush*,[m] *for they all are the work of His hands*.[n] In it, I will call to mind the [world to] come, *with good judgment and knowledge*[o] of the Torah of grace, *enlightening their eyes*[p] as well as others, every single thing in its place. And by it [the Torah], we will know, as we shall answer to the Epicurean [i.e., atheists]: "We give thanks for our portion" (cf. Berakhot 28b), "We exult in our king" (cf. Psalm 149:2), "By His light we see [the] light" (cf. Psalm 36:10), "He, the Most High, will preserve it, and let our eye gaze on Zion, the wonders of His Torah" (Psalm 87:5, Micah 4:11; cf. Psalm 119:18).

---

[a] Cf. Ps 77:8. [b] Cf. Isa 11:4. [c] Cf. *Sanh.* 106b. [d] Num 13:33. [e] Eccl 9:11. [f] Isa 59:11. [g] Eccl 12:10. [h] Ps 44:23. [i] *Avot* 4:13. [j] Ps 40:8. [k] Ex 27:20. [l] Isa 24:14. [m] Deut 33:16. [n] Job 34:19. [o] Ps 119:66. [p] Ps 19:9.

[Introduction]

§ 1.1.1 And therefore, I will begin and say that this is known from experience and from the Philosopher's words in his introduction to *Metaphysics* [1:1]:[a] "Every human being, by his nature, desires to know," *and it is desirable to be knowledgeable*[b] in every science; that is: the intellection of that which is good together with the knowledge of the manner of achieving it. And the intended final purpose of everything is the good that one expects from it, as is explained through clear arguments in *Metaphysics* 2, text. 8,[c] and others. From looking at the Creator's activity, everyone can understand *how awesome He is*[d], just as the globe in relation to the first sphere of the stars is like a dot in [the centre of] a circle *and its inhabitants are like locusts*.[e] [They are] perishable and corruptible vessels since they are far more remote from the rank of the honourable and awesome First One, much more so than the rest of the existents who are remote from Him. Yet this also says something about *all works of the plan*[f] and the wisdom of God—may He be praised—in their particulars. In its appearance, the human species is intended by Him to be *like a vessel which pleases Him*[g] and to be right in His eyes. It is miraculous in the eyes of the Poet, as it says (Psalm 8:5): "What is man that You have been mindful of him?" Is it not worthwhile that we naturally inquire with a yearning heart? *And He gave [the human] intellect*[h] to understand the final purpose intended by God—may He be praised—in the existence of man. But this is only attained after the aforementioned man does what is possible for him: recognising his aforementioned Creator, *by whose light we see light*.[i]

§ 1.1.2 Many wise men from the [first] generations, which have been adherents of the [divine] name ever since, *came and ascended*[j] *to the top level*[k] of scholarship. Among them were Henoch and Noah before the Great Flood, and after the Great Flood Eber and Abraham, who was the "father" of wisdom, the greatest among the Chaldeans. He learned from Eber by oral instruction and stood firm in his opinions, and he is therefore called "Hebrew," as it says (Genesis 14:13): "And he told Abram the Hebrew." And from their

---

[a] *Metaph.* 1.1.980a22. [b] Gen 3:6. [c] *Metaph.* 2.2.994b. [d] Ex 34:10. [e] Isa 40:22. [f] 1 Chr 28:19. [g] Cf. Jer 48:38. [h] Neh 8:8. [i] Cf. Ps 36:10. [j] Ex 7:28. [k] 2 Kings 9:13.

[הקדמה]

§ 1.1.1 ובכן אקדים ואומר כי אמנם מודעת זאת בנסיון ומדברי הפילוסוף בהצעתו בספר מה שאחר: »היות כל אדם בטבעו מתאוה לדעת« ונחמד להשכיל מכל מדע הוא אמנם השכיל הטוב עם ידיעת האופן להשיגו. ובהיות התכלית המכוון בכל דבר הוא הטוב המקווה ממנו כאשר התבאר בראיות ברורות בספר מה שאחר מאמר ב׳ פרק ח׳, וזולתו הנה בהביט כל משכיל אל פועל יוצרו כי נורא הוא עד היות כדור הארץ בערך אל גלגל הכוכבים הראשון כנקֻדה בתוך עגולה ויושביה כחגבים כלים ונפסדים בהיותם רחוקים במדרגה מן הראשון הנכבד והנורא הרבה מאד יותר מאשר רחקו ממנו שאר הנמצאות ואף עם זאת עצמו מספר כל מלאכות התבנית וחכמת האל יתברך בפרטיהם[a] עם הראותו היות המין האנושי מכוון מאתו ככלי חפץ בו ויקר בעיניו היא נפלאת בעיני המשורר באמרו: »מה אנוש כי תזכרנו?« (תהלים ח׳ ה׳) הלא ראוי לנו לחקור בלב נכסף בטבע? ושום שכל לדעת התכלית המכוון מאת האל יתברך במציאות האדם וזה אמנם לא יושג כי אם אחר אשר יעשה האדם הנזכר את האיפשר אצלו להכיר בוראו הנזכר באורו נראה אור.

§ 1.1.2 על אלה עלו ובאו אל גרם מעלת המחקר רבים מחכמי הדורות אשר מעולם אנשי השם מהם קודם המבול חנוך ונח ואחר המבול עבר ואברהם ›אב‹ בחכמה מכל הכשדים אשר למד מפי עבר והחזיק בדעותיו ולכן נקרא ›עברי‹ כמו שנאמר: »ויגד לאברם העברי« (בראשית י״ד י״ג) וכאשר בחקרם נודע להם שיש נמצא

---

[a] בפרשיהם]a[corr]; בפרטיהם a.

[Prologus]

§ I.1.1 Plerique omnes gentilium phylosophi de immortalibus et aliis verbum facientes que ad politicam vitam nihil conferre patet, quamvis nihil tandem invenissent immortalitatis per humanum genus aliquo pacto sperandum cum ad illa contemplanda diversosque libros in his componendos. Tot iam lapsa conteruissent secula nihil inde sperantes non vanam tantam inter homines famam posteris deferendam intendisse. Puto sed potius naturali sciendi desiderio satisfacere, curarunt natura enim vel nature conditor immortalem hominum salutem benigne intendens, huiusmodi desiderium eidem tradidit sicut carnales appetitus comedendi scilicet et coeundi ad individui et generis conservationem eidem tradidisse comperimus.

Sensu enim puto et Phylosophi auctoritate procul dubio patet quod omnes homines natura scire desiderant, scientiarum autem ille videntur prae ceteris cupiende quibus vere bonum noscamus consequendique modum adipisci valeamus. Cum autem cuiuslibet rei finem summum eiusdem esse bonum ratione et Phylosophi auctoritate percipiamus, ingentem ergo universi machinam cuius respectu telluris sphera quasi punctum in magno circulo esse dicatur ibidemque degentia ceteris a primo omnino nobilissimo remotiora corruptioni turpiter subesse. Non ignoremus circa que tamen mirabilem[a] eiusdem nobilissimi curam apparere humanumque genus quasi quid nobile ab eodem nobilissimo sapienter intendi videatur, quod merito miratur Psalmorum octavus dicens: «Quid est homo quod memor es eius?» Finis quidem ab eodem sapiente per humanum genus intenti cognitionem quam non nisi post contemplationem de ipso sapiente non mediocriter factam contingere puto nos naturaliter desiderare; et ardenti cura ad talia scrutanda pro viribus conari opinor deceat.

§ I.1.2 Priscorum ergo sapientes de numero quorum ante magnam orbis Cladem fuerunt Hanoc et Noha prout de illorum perfectione Sacra testatur Scriptura post illam vero fuerunt Heber et Abraham, Caldeorum sapientissimus, eiusdem Heberis doctrinam sequens quare Hebreus dicebatur prout in libro Genesis cap. 14 habetur. Cum scrutan-

---

[a] mirabilem] b[corr]; mirabile b.

[Introduction]

§ I.1.1 It seems that the philosophers among the Gentiles [i.e., the Nations], when speaking about political topics, do not discuss the immortality of the soul, although they would have encountered immortality within the human species [i.e., it would have been natural for the philosophers to end up discussing immortality because it is a natural topic for human beings], because they did not contemplate those things and did not write any books about these topics. Already in generations past, they were terrified of having nothing for which to hope. I do not think that they wanted to abandon such vain fame to posterity. Instead, they took pains to satisfy the natural desire to know.[a] In fact, nature, or the creator of nature, who intended the immortal salvation of men by means of grace, taught his desire in order that we might learn what he has taught for the preservation of individuals and species, to relinquish the carnal and sexual appetites.

Indeed, I think that it is clear from experience and according to the opinion of the Philosopher that "every human being by nature desires to know."[b] Moreover, it is desirable to have knowledge in every science by which we may know the truly good, and consequently, we may achieve the methodology to acquire it, since the Philosopher states that the aim of everything is the highest good. And then we perceive that in relation to the huge machinery of the universe, the earth is like a dot in the centre of a circle, and we say that some perishable things, which are very far from the first and noblest of all beings, are subject to corruption. And we know that the solicitude of this noble being is evident and it seems that human existence might be intended to be something noble by this nobler existent, as Psalm 8 (8:5) discloses: "What is man that You are mindful of him?" Indeed, it is fitting that the aim of the human species that is intended by the wise existent may only be known after the contemplation of this wise existent, [but] not after contemplating an ordinary existent. I think that this is our natural desire and I suppose that we try with all our strength to investigate those things with passionate attention.

§ I.1.2 And there were many ancient wise men before the Great Flood, among them Enoch and Noah, and their perfection is attested in the Holy Scripture. After the Great Flood, there were Heber and Abraham, the wisest man among the Chaldeans, who followed the teaching of Heber, and for this reason, he is called "Hebrew" according to Genesis 14 (14:13). As a result of their investigation, it is

---

[a] Cf. *Metaph.* 1.1.980a22.   [b] *Metaph.* 1.1.980a22.

studies, it became known to them that there was a first existent, which is the principle of all existents, not only with respect to form and final purpose, as was determined by Averroes referring to Aristotle in his Commentary on *Metaphysics* 10, text. 7,[a] but it became clear that He [i.e., God, the first existent] is also a voluntary agent with regard to the final purpose He intends. And from this, it became clear to them that it is | the intended final purpose of the existence of the human species that man shall become similar to his Creator, as far as possible, through morality and intellectual understanding, as He attests it (Genesis 1:26): "Let us make man in our image, after our likeness." They chose to walk in His footsteps and in the ways of His leadership—[how] good is His order in the world!—as far as is possible for them, as Scripture attests about them (Genesis 5:24; 6:9; 24:40; 48:15): "And Enoch walked with God," "Noah walked with God," [Abraham speaks:] "Ha-Shem, whose ways I have followed," [Jacob speaks:] "The God in whose ways my fathers walked."

§ 1.1.3 And although the days of the wise men of the Chaldeans—who are called "fathers" by the Philosopher in *Metaphysics* 12, text. 51,[b] and who studied a great deal in order *to become enlightened with the light of life*[c]—lasted a long time, nevertheless, *their wisdom vanished*.[d] It was lost and was overcome by corruption over time, as happens to all the other [things] that are generated and corruptible, as the aforementioned Philosopher attests in the aforementioned book, text. 50.[e] And then arose the evil of the opinions of the "worshipper of the hosts of the heavens" and the like, and the sect of the Sabaeans and the like, about whom the wise men say (Isaiah 59:15): "The truth has been lacking," also arose. The offspring of Abraham, who are closely linked by His covenant, were excepted [from this], so that the knowledge of the existence of the Creator—may He be exalted—remained among them. He is hidden from the eyes of the Gentiles, ancient as well as modern. They will say (Jeremiah 5:12): "He does not exist." And therefore, He chose His people [to be] knowers of His Name, like a rule, as Moses—our teacher, peace be upon him—explained (Exodus 3:18): "Ha-Shem, the God of the Hebrews"; that is to say, those who are strengthened in Eber's knowledge, which was well-known in those days.

§ 1.1.4 And he [i.e., Moses] gave them His Torah, which He wrote in order to teach them and so that they would remember all these things. What they knew from their fathers about the existence of the Creator—may He be

---

[a] Cf. *Metaph.* 10.1.1052b. [b] *Metaph.* 12.8.1074b. [c] Job 33:30. [d] Jer 49:7. [e] Cf. *Metaph.* 12.8.1074a.

ראשון הוא ראשית לכל הנמצאות לא בלבד צורה ותכלית להם כאשר גזר אבן רשד בשם ארסטוטילו בביאור מה שאחר מאמר עשירי פרק ז׳ אבל התבאר היותו גם כן פועל רצוניי לתכלית מכוון מאתו ועם זה התבאר אצלם היות | התכלית המכוון במציאות המין האנושי הוא שידמה האדם לבוראו כפי האיפשר במדות ובמושכלות כאשר העיד באמרו: »נעשה אדם בצלמנו כדמותנו« (בראשית א׳ כ״ו) בחרו לצאת בעקבותיו וללכת בדרכי הנהגתו וטוב סדרו בעולם כפי האיפשר אצלם כאשר העיד עליהם הכתוב באמרו: »ויתהלך חנוך את האלהים« (בראשית ה׳ כ״ד), »את האלהים התהלך נח« (שם ו׳ ט׳), »ה׳ אשר התהלכתי לפניו« (שם כ״ד מ׳), »האלהים אשר התהלכו אבותי לפניו« (שם מ״ח ט״ו).

§ 1.1.3 **וגם** כי ארכו ימי חכמי הכשדים הנקראים ‹אבות› אצל הפילוסוף בספר מה שאחר מאמר י״ב פרק נ״א אשר הרבו לחקור לאור כאור החיים אמנם נסרחה חכמתם אבדה ונפסדה במשך הזמן על דרך ההיפסד הקורה לשאר ההווים ונפסדים כמו שהעיד הפילוסוף הנזכר במאמר הנזכר פרק נ׳ ועלה באוש דעות ה‹עובדים לצבא השמים› וזולתם וכת אנשי הצבא וזולתם אשר חכמים הגידו: »ותהי האמת נעדרת« (ישעיהו נ״ט ט״ו) זולתי אצל זרע אברהם הדבקים ומחזיקים בבריתו כי אמנם נשארה אצלם ידיעת מציאות הבורא יתעלה אשר נעלם מעיני חכמי הגוים חדשים גם ישנים ויאמרו: »לא הוא« (ירמיהו ה׳ י״ב). ובכן בחר בעמו יודעי שמו כמשפט כאשר באר משה רבינו עליו השלום באמרו: »ה׳ אלהי העברים« (שמות ג׳ י״ח), כלומר המחזיקים בדעות עבר אשר היו אז מפורסמות.

§ 1.1.4 **ונתן** למו את תורתו אשר כתב להורותם ועל כל אזכרתם והנודע אצלם מאבותיהם במציאות הבורא יתעלה הודיעם באותות ובמופתים שכליים שהוא אחד, קדמון, בלתי גוף, יודע כל, בוחר בטוב

tes percepissent nonnullum esse principium omnium primum illudque non modo universi ordinatorem et conservatorem prout phylosophorum nonnulli putarunt verum et agentem finem intendentem esse rationibus sensissent considerantes ut finis de humano genere ab eodem agente intentus merito esset ut homo eidem agenti pro viribus similaretur prout habetur Genesis libro cap 1 [1:26], cum dicit: «Et dixit Dominus: Faciamus hominem ad imaginem no|stram quasi ad similitudinem nostram.» Sapientia ergo et moribus eidem primo assimilari conati eiusdem mores in universi ordinatione eiusque regimine apparentes sanctissimaque eiusdem vestigia pro viribus sequi, decreverunt quare in libro Genesis cap. 5 [5:24], 6 [6:9] et 24 [24:40] de huiusmodi viris verbum faciens illos cum Deo vel in Dei conspectu ambulasse refert.

§ 1.1.3 Cumque Caldeorum cognitio quos Phylosophus Metaphysicorum XII, t.c. 51 patres appellat mortalium more per plura perissent[a] secula prout idem Phylosophus ibidem t.c. 50 refert quod 5. et scientijs contingit quoquomodo corruptio quare Celicolarum et Zabiorum opiniones turpiter successisse priscorum habetur testimonio pristina quidem veritatis cognitio penes Abrahme[b] successores tantum remansisse videtur, qui scilicet prefatam Heberis doctrinam et opiniones sequentes merito Hebreorum nomine appellati sunt.

§ 1.1.4 Cum autem Divina Revelatio et Sacri Testamenti doctrina eisdem Hebreis preceteris verum in divinis opinantibus merito per Moysem evenisset, quare Sacra Exodi

known that there is a first principle of existents, which is not only the ordination and conservation of the universe, as some philosophers [i.e., Aristotle and Averroes] have interpreted, but also the voluntary agent [acting] for a purpose. From these considerations, it is clear that the [intended] purpose of the human species comes from this agent because man, according to his strength, shall become akin to his agent according to Genesis 1 (1:26), in which it says: "And the Lord says: 'Let us make man in our image, | as our likeness.'" And then they [Enoch, Noah, and Heber] chose to follow His manifestations and His most holy wisdom according to their strength, and they tried to adapt their customs to the customs that are seen through His order and through His rule of the universe, as the [holy] book of Genesis 5 (Genesis 5:24), 6 (Genesis 6:9), and 24 (Genesis 24:40) attests when it says that those men walk with God; that is, walk beside God.

§ 1.1.3 And although, after some centuries, the knowledge of the Chaldeans, who are called "fathers" by the Philosopher in *Metaphysics* 12, text. 51,[a] [which was] a human tradition, disappeared. And this also happened to their science by means of corruption, as the Philosopher mentions in the aforementioned book 12, text. 50,[b] and according to the ancient testimony, it seems that the opinions of the "worshippers of the heavens" [lit. *Coelicolarum*] and of the Sabaeans were the continuation of the original knowledge of the truth, which only remains for the offspring of Abraham, who follow the aforementioned teaching of Heber, and for this reason, they are called "Hebrews."

§ 1.1.4 And then, the Divine Revelation and the teaching of the Holy Testament, [whose adherents] believe in the opinion of Heber, was introduced by Moses. According to the Holy Book of Exodus 2 (2:6) and what follows,

---

[a] perissent] coni. Copp.; periissent b. [b] Abrahme] coni. Copp.; Abrahe b.

[a] *Metaph.* 12.8.1074b. [b] *Metaph.* 12.8.1074a.

exalted—was made known to them via the letters [of the Holy Scripture] and via intellectual demonstrations: He is one, eternal, incorporeal, omniscient; He chooses the [absolute] good through intention and will; *from His throne He watches all.*[a] And [they learned that] there is an after[life] and an everlasting hope for the human intellectual soul to gain its immortality. By it, *man will return with joy,*[b] becoming similar—as far as is possible for him—to his Creator and the artisan who made him. He *comes at all times into the Holy Place,*[c] *to walk in all His ways, and hold fast to Him.*[d] *In His pathway there is no death.*[e]

§ 1.2.1 And all of this was hidden from the eyes of the wise men of the Gentiles, who naturally desire knowledge of the truth.[f] They investigated the natural sciences further from generation to generation *to find words of delight.*[g] They turned their faces, their eyes, and their hearts to contemplating [things] like these and others. Were they not *famous men,*[h] as the Philosopher attests in *Metaphysics* 1, text. 5,[i] *who first dwelled in the realm*[j] of Italy? Among them were Pythagoras and his pupils, and Anaxagoras, Empedocles, [and] Democritus, and after them the sect of the Herculeans, who said that all knowledge was impossible. And after them [came] Socrates, who according to the Philosopher's words, ibid., did not produce a [written philosophical] treatise, but taught ethics and politics, *which if man does, he shall live by them.*[k]

§ 1.2.2 *And after some time,*[l] during the highest blossoming of a nation in the cities of Greece, [men] *who were great in the searchings of inner things*[m] appeared |, and in their midst was Plato, who followed the opinions of Pythagoras and the rest of the wise men of Italy. *And he pondered, sought out and set in order*[n] his knowledge of numbers and taught [the] principle that exists in them.

§ 1.2.3 And a man who came after them all was to surpass them. This was Aristotle, the son of Nicomachus. He is the most famous Greek in name and renown among all the nations of the earth, and he arranged his words in a better order than any of his predecessors had, as is appropriate for any successor, because it was important for him to answer with more acceptable and correct words than his predecessors, as the aforementioned Aristotle explains in *On the Heavens* 4, text. 11.[o] *He destroyed and broke*[p] the foundations of the words of his predecessors, which he

---

[a] Cf. Ps 33:14. [b] Cf. Ps 126:6. [c] Lev 16:2. [d] Deut 11:22. [e] Prov 12:28. [f] Cf. *Metaph.* 1.1.980a. [g] Eccl 12:10. [h] Cf. Gen 6:4. [i] Cf. *Metaph.* 2.6.987a29 ff. [j] Est 1:14. [k] Lev 18:5. [l] Neh 13:6. [m] Judg 5:16. [n] Eccl 12:9. [o] *Cael.* 4.1.308a. [p] Lam 2:9.

בכונה ורצון, ממכון שבתו משגיח אל כל, וכי יש אחרית ותקוה נצחית לנפש האנושית השכלית עם אופן השגת נצחיותה, בו יבוא האדם ברנה בהדמותו כפי האיפשר אצלו לבוראו ואומן שעשאו בבואו בכל עת אל הקדש ללכת בדרכיו ולדבקה בו ודרך נתיבו אל מות.

§ 1.2.1 **ובהיות** כל זאת נעלמה מעיני חכמי הגוים המתאוים בטבע לידיעת האמת הבאים לחקור מדור לדור מחקרי ארץ למצוא דברי חפץ שמו פניהם עיניהם ולבם להתבונן בכמו אלה וזולתם הלא הם אנשי השם כפי אשר העיד הפילוסוף בספר מה שאחר מאמר א׳[a] פרק ה׳ היושבים ראשונה במלכות איטאליא? מהם פיטאגורס[b] ותלמידיו ואנכסאגורס[c] ואמפידוקליס ודימוקריטוס ואחריהם כת האירקוליאי אשר אמרו היות כל ידיעה נמנעת ואחריהם סוקראטיס אשר לפי דברי הפילוסוף שם לא עשה מאמר זולתי להורות מדות והנהגות אשר יעשה אותם האדם וחי בהם.

§ 1.2.2 **ולקץ** ימים בפרוח ראשי עם ויציגו מערי יון גדולים חקרי לב | בתוכם אפלטון אשר נמשך אחר דעות פיטאגוראס ויתר חכמי איטאליאה ואזן וחקר תקן דעותיו על ספר מספר ומורה מה שרש דבר נמצא בו.

§ 1.2.3 **ובקום** עליו אדם אחרון מכלם הוא אריסטוטיליס בן ניקומאקו היוני המפורסם לשם ולתהלה בכל עמי הארץ. וכלכל דבריו במשפט יותר מכל הקודמים כראוי לכל אחרון כי לו יאות להשיב אמרים נכוחים וישרים יותר מן הקודמים בזמן כמו שביאר אריסטוטיליס הנזכר בספר השמים והעולם מאמר רביעי פרק י״א. אבד ושבר מוסדי דברי הקדמונים אשר מצא רחוקים מן האמת

---

[a] א] emend. Dunk.; ב a; I L.   [b] פיטאגורס] coni. Dunk.; פיטאגזר a.   [c] ואנכסאגורס] coni. Dunk.; ואנבסאגורס a.

libri narratio in eiusdem Moysi adventu eosdem Hebreorum nomine appellavit prout ibidem cap. 2 [2:6] et sequentibus, habetur non modo habitam de universi agente notitiam eisdem a patribus traditam rationibus docuit quam scilicet Gentilium antiqui modernique Phylosophi creationem respuentes penitus negarunt verum et eiusdem agentis sive creatoris unitatem incorporeitatem scientiam voluntariamque potentiam sollicitudinem sive curam humaneque anime immortalitatem eiusque beatitudinem consequendique modum demonstrative ostendit.

§ I.2.1 Gentilium vero sapientes postea florentes horum scilicet notitia privati naturali tamen sciendi desiderio ducti ad horum quedam scrutanda pro viribus quidem laborasse videtur. Quorum primi ut Phylosophus metha: primo t.c. 5ª narrare videtur fuerunt Itali de quorum numero, ut Commentator ibidem ait fuerunt Anaxagoras, Empedocles et Democritus. Deinde Herculei qui tandem negarunt ut contingat aliquid sciri. Deinde Socrates quod scilicet ut Phylosophus ait moralia tantum edidisse videtur.

§ I.2.2 Cumque post plura secula nonnulli apud Grecos floruissent scrutantes de quorum numero fuit Plato Socratis discipulus prout habetur ab Aven Roy in commento lib. De Celo tertij t. c. 61 Pitagore et aliorum Italorum considerationibus[b] ductus horumque opiniones in quibusdam sequens prout Phylosophus in preallegato loco testatur. Scrutandorum nonnulla diligenter contemplasse librumque circa illa edidisse videtur.

§ I.2.3 Cum autem Aristoteles Stagirita Nichomachi filius natione Grecus his tempore posterior cuius sermo prioribus rectior et acutior non immerito fuit prout idem in lib. De Celo IV t.c. 11 posteriorem decere infert quedam antiquorum dicta invenisset sensu et ratione penitus

Moses, during the revelation [on Sinai], called them "Hebrews." And Moses taught not only what was known from their fathers—namely, the knowledge of the Agent of the universe [God]—but also what the ancient and modern philosophers among the Gentiles [i.e., the Nations] denied concerning creation, and by means of demonstrations, he [Moses] showed the unity of the Agent—namely, the Creator—His incorporeality, His knowledge, His voluntary intention and will, His providence, His solicitude for human beings, the immortality of the soul, and the everlasting hope.

§ I.2.1 The wise men among the Gentiles [i.e., the Nations] flourished after them [the Hebrews]—namely, all of those who were led merely by the most natural desire for knowledge[a]—[as the wise men] seem to have been directed towards the purpose of investigating things. The first among them were Italian, according to the Philosopher in *Metaphysics* 1, text. 5,[b] and according to his commentator, they were Anaxagoras, Empedocles, and Democritus. And after them, there were the Herculeans, who rejected all kinds of knowledge. And after them, there was Socrates, who—according to the Philosopher—seemed to produce only moral treatises.

§ I.2.2 And after some centuries, those who were strong in inquiry prospered among the Greeks. One of them was Plato, a pupil of Socrates, as Averroes explicates in his Commentary on *On the Heavens* 3, text. 61, who was led by the speculations of Pythagoras and other Italian philosophers following their opinions, as the Philosopher shows in the aforementioned book. It seems that he diligently observed some principles behind what he had examined and wrote a book about them.

§ I.2.3 After them, there was Aristotle, the son of Nicomachus, born in the city of Stagira. His speech was more honest and accurate than that of his temporal predecessors, as the said Philosopher explains in *On the Heavens* 4, text. 11.[c] And knowing the position of his predecessors, he found that the words of the Ancients should be completely

---

a   [b] considerationibus] coni. COPP.; cosiderationibus b.

[a] *Metaph.* 1.1.980a22.   [b] *Metaph.* 1.5.987a9 ff.   [c] *Cael.* 4.1.308a.

found to be far-off from the truth, because they introduced arguments that were contrary to sense [perception] and demonstration, as Averroes attests in his Commentary on *Meteorology* 3, text. 2, saying that the words of Aristotle's predecessors are not appropriate, since they are full of doubts, still less [are they appropriate] to be the principles of knowledge of any wisdom. And in the natural and divine sciences, he [Aristotle] brought to light demonstrations of and arguments for correct opinions, or [at least] those that were closer to the truth than all the ones before him.

§ I.2.4 But the aforementioned Aristotle, according to what his commentators understood of him and to what may be deduced from his opinions, denies many noble things. The absence of only one of them would uproot the Torah in its entirety and many of the statutes of all knowers of religion and law. For he denies creation [out of nothing], and the possibility of innovation, and God's knowledge—may He be praised—of the particulars of the existents, and still more of the particulars of the generables and corruptibles. And moreover, he denies His providence over them. And according to most of his pupils' understanding, he also denies the existence of the individual human intellectual soul, and even more its perpetuity [after death]. And he gives very strong arguments for all of his opinions, and also demonstrations for many [of them]. Behold, there is no doubt that they are [technically] perfect, yet many adherents of religion who know the arguments of the aforementioned philosophers regarding the aforementioned opinions *do not have the power*[a] to find contradictions in them, although they bring forth arguments for the contrary and although their tongues also produce *many words that increase the futility*[b] in order to easily reject every difficult issue, *so that they are pleased*[c] *in front of the [ordinary] masses.*[d] But *they lied to Him with their tongues;*[e] *they speak with a doubled heart.*[f]

§ I.2.5 *And how do we justify*[g]—We, people *who came late to contemplating ha-Shem*[h]—neglecting to look at the miracles of His Torah, which tell the errors of the words of the first spectators, who strayed from the intellect's path? [These miracles illustrate the errors] through intellectual arguments for the contrary of their aforementioned [Aristotelian] opinions, *and by confirming with equity*[i] true opinions with intellectual demonstrations *to bring [the] soul back from*[j] darkness, *mire and dirt*[k] to God, who gave it [to them]. *Behold, the voice—the cry*[l] of the prophets of the

---

[a] Deut 28:32. [b] Eccl 6:11. [c] Ex 28:38. [d] 2 Chr 20:12. [e] Ps 78:36. [f] Ps 12:3. [g] Gen 44:16. [h] Isa 54:13. [i] Isa 11:4. [j] Cf. Job 33:30. [k] Isa 57:20. [l] Jer 8:19.

בהביאו ראיות על הפכם מן החוש והמופת כאשר העיד אבן רשד בביאור ספר אותות השמים מאמר ג' פרק ב' עד שאמר היות דברי הקודמים לאריסטוטיליס[a] בלתי ראויים להיות מכלל הספקות כל שכן להיות התחלות לידיעת כל חכמה והוציא לאור בחכמות טבעיות ואלהיות מופתים וראיות על דעות אמתיות או קרובות אל האמת מכל אשר לפניו.

§ I.2.4 **אמנם** בהיות שאריסטוטילו הנזכר לפי מה שהבינו ממנו מפרשיו ולפי הנמשך מדעותיו מכחיש דברים רבים ונכבדים אשר בהעדר אחד מהם תעקר התורה בכללה ורבים ממשפטי כל יודעי דת ודין כי הוא אמנם מכחיש הבריאה ואיפשרות המצאה וידיעת האל יתברך בפרטי הנמצאות ויותר בפרטי ההווים ונפסדים כל שכן שיכחיש[b] השגחתו בהם ולפי המובן מדעתו אצל רבים מתלמידיו הוא מכחיש גם מציאות נפש אנושית שכלית אישיית[c] כל שכן השארותה. ובכל תקף מביא על כל דעותיו אלה ראיות כמופת[d] לרבים הנה אין ספק כי שלמים וכן רבים מבעלי הדתות אשר ידעו ראיות הפילוסופים הנזכרים על דעותיו הנזכרות[e] ואין לאל ידם למצא סתירתם[f] אף כי להביא ראייה על הפכם ואף גם זאת לשונם תהגה דברים הרבה מרבים הבל לדחות בקש כל הדבר הקשה לרצון להם לפני ההמון הם אמנם בלשונם יכזבו לו בלב ולב ידברו.

§ I.2.5 **ומה** נצטדק אנחנו למודי ה' אחרונים בזמן בהתעלם מהביט נפלאות מתורתו המורות שגיאות[g] דברי מעיינים ראשונים תועים מדרך השכל? בראיות שכליות על הפך דעותם הנזכרות ובהוכיח במשור דעות אמתיות במופתים שכליים להשיב נפש ממחשכי רפש וטיט אל האלהים אשר נתנה. הנה קול שועת נביאי הדורות רב מאד על זאת באומרו: «ואת פעל ה' לא הביטו מעשי ידיו לא ראו לכן

---

[a] שיכחיש] שיכחיש a[corr]; לאריסטוטיליס] לאריסטוטילי' a, coni. Dunk.; [b] שיכחיש] שיכחיש a[corr]; [c] אישיית] אישיית a[corr]; [d] כמופת] במופת a[corr]; [e] הנזכרות] הנזכר a, coni. Dunk.; [f] סתירתם] שתירתם a, coni. Dunk.; [g] שגיאות] שגאות a[corr];

6 reprobanda quare Aven | R. in comento lib. Methaurorum tertij t.c. 2 ait: «Illa non digna ut essent dubitationes nedum ut sint sciendorum principia» credibilioribus quidem sermonibus et efficatioribus rationibus veriores nonnullas vel veritati propinquiores edidit sententias. Quare apud plures non immerito Phylosophus absolute appellatur.

§ I.2.4 Cum autem idem Aristoteles licet interdum caute secundum tamen illud quod sui expositores ex suis intelligunt verbis, et ad eiusdem opiniones sequi videtur nonnulla penitus neget quorum uno vere destructoreligionum radices, et ius commune nonnullum turpiter extirpentur ille enim universi creationem, et prime cause de individuis saltem mortalibus cognitionem nedum sollicitudinem sive curam et ut quidem[a] eiusdem Aristotelis sequaces de mente eius inferunt humanarum animarum immortalitatem penitus neget eiusque de premissis opiniones eminentibus rationibus et efficacibus rationibus ostendisse videatur. Nonnulli ergo religionum professores premissarum Aristotelis opinionum harumque rationum non ignari quas quidam solvere nedum redarguere et oppositum probare minime potuerunt. Cum huiusmodi Aristotelis opiniones frivolis subterfugiis respuere et oppositum credere vulgaribus dixerint illos potius fingere quam vere opinari putandum videtur.

⟨§ I.2.5⟩

rejected on the basis of experience and demonstration, in accordance with Averroes's | explication in his Commentary on *Meteorology* 3, text. 2, that [their words] "are not appropriate regarding the principles of knowledge, for they are entirely doubtful." And he [Aristotle] brought forth some true opinions, or those that are closer to the truth than plausible speeches and incisive arguments. For this reason, he was called "the Philosopher." 6

§ I.2.4 Therefore, Aristotle himself, according to what his commentators understood of him and according to what seems to follow from his opinions, denies many things, the destruction of only one of which would uproot the principles of religion and the common law. He denies the creation of the universe and the first cause, the knowledge of particular existents and mortal existents, and also providence or care over them, because those who follow Aristotle state that he denies the immortality of the human soul, and it seems that he showed those aforementioned opinions in notable and plausible arguments. And many adherents of religion also know the aforementioned opinions of Aristotle and these arguments and they try to resolve and confute them, and at least to prove the contrary. They say that the opinions of Aristotle must be rejected as silly subterfuge and they believe what is contrary to common sense. It seems also that thinking to be critical of those things, they taught them.

⟨§ I.2.5⟩

---

[a] quidem] b[corr]; quidam b.

generations—is very loud on this matter, as it says (Isaiah 5:12–13): "But they never give a thought to the plan of ha-Shem, and take no note of what He is designing. Assuredly, my people will suffer exile for a lack of knowledge," as it says (Hosea 4:6): "My people are destroyed because of a lack of knowledge; because you have rejected knowledge. [...] And you have spurned the Torah of your God." And it says (Jeremiah 9:23): "But only in this should one glory: having understanding and knowing Me," so that many wise men of the generations, who endeavour | to find intellectual arguments for the foundations of the Torah, may *hear the voices*.[a] [But] insufficient words come from their hearts, like the statements of the adherents of religion. And therefore, *they regard as foreign*[b] the [intellectual] roots of our Torah, especially regarding the existence of a creator who generates and has providence over all, and others that are not known from clear [examination], but only through a commandment to believe in them, to find pleasure before our God, who [indeed] did not command us anything like this, especially not regarding the theoretical portion [of the Torah]. But He commanded us to know by observing all the pure speech of His justice, as mentioned above. And who is like Him: a guide *who definitively knows*,[c] so that we have no choice but to believe what we want, still less what a commander [would] command [us] to believe? And you will not find anything like this [coming] from Him, as it says (Isaiah 45:19): "I did not say to the stock of Jacob, 'Seek Me in vain.' I am ha-Shem, who foretells reliably." And so the Poet attests, as it says (Psalm 119:172): "For all Your commandments are reliable." Is it not good for us that we return to the Torah and to its testimony and the study of its glory, [turning] it over and over, so that the truth of His truth comes forth like a bright beam, that *by its light we see light*?[d] Is it not so that He, from birth onwards, bestows the grace of the intellect—and the Holy God is well known!—[in order that one may] *cleave unto Him*,[e] and serve Him *with one accord*,[f] *and be sanctified by His glory*?[g] Our Heart rejoices to see the benefactions to our soul, *for You live forever, and do not see corruption*,[h] [but] *grow stronger*,[i] *to open the eyes*[j] of the sons of the living God, *who are caught in a net*[k] of ropes of *lying vanities*,[l] *so that their eyes are shut, unable to see*.[m] And those are the members of the covenant of Abra[ha]m.

---

[a] Ex 20:18. [b] Cf. Hos 8:12. [c] Cf. 1 Sam 26:4. [d] Cf. Ps 36:10. [e] Deut 11:22. [f] Zeph 3:9. [g] Ex 29:43. [h] Cf. Ps 49:10. [i] Job 17:9. [j] Isa 42:7. [k] Eccl 9:12. [l] Jonah 2:9. [m] Isa 44:18.

§ *1.3.1* And due to many words of dispute, [there are] a multitude of difficulties and enough doubts about the statements to frighten an observer. And it is appropriate for every opponent who wishes to disclose the truth that he should arrange his disputant's words and explain his arguments in a better way, to answer *without enmity*,[a] but rather with humility of justice, with love and desire for the examination of the truth.

§ *1.3.2* He will refute the arguments for his [opponent's] opinions by means of intellectual demonstration by showing their contraries, as the Philosopher declares in *On the Heavens* 1, text. 101,[b] and 2, text. 34.[c] Behold, it is fitting for us, so that we may find pleasure before God, *to make known the certainty of the words*[d] of His Torah, that we present the propositions of those *who turn aside to their crooked ways*[e] and their corruptible opinions, which are founded on the basis of conjectures and statements that produce a false sense, and whatever is found in them due to the disruption of [sound] opinion. And this [takes place] via the uncovering of error by means of intellectual demonstrations found in the Holy Scripture. And they are spread *throughout the Scriptures*[f] [and are] *logical to understand*,[g] *given by one shepherd*.[h] Behold, [there is] *a place*[i] [where] every single one them is recorded written in opposition, *so that one can read it easily*[j] in order to find the origin of a word of truth [and] to verify it, *and it enlightens straightaway*.[k]

§ *1.3.3* And Aristotle's words and those of his pupils are very precious in the eyes of many and honourable [people], so that if there is someone among them who opposes Aristotle's words and his aforementioned pupils, he will be [treated] as if he contradicts sense perception or definitive proof. In this manner, the Rambam writes in the *Guide* [*of the Perplexed*] 2:22: "The summary is that everything that Aristotle has said about everything that exists from the sphere of the moon to what is beneath it is true, and no one will deviate from it, except someone who does not understand, or someone who has those preconceived opinions from which he wants to reject every contradiction and defend them, or those opinions lead him to deny obvious things." Therefore, I announced that [I would] bring an argument—to settle any doubt | in each question—[that is derived] from some foundations of the aforementioned Aristotle and [from] his words, his demonstrations, and the sentences from his mouth. And among these [questions], we will not mention the

---

[a] Num 35:22. [b] *Cael.* 1.10.279b. [c] *Cael.* 2.5.288a. [d] Prov 22:21. [e] Ps 125:5. [f] Num 11:26. [g] Prov 8:9. [h] Eccl 12:11. [i] Ex 33:21. [j] Hab 2:2. [k] Ezek 1:12.

§ *1.3.1* **וברבות** דברי ריבות רובי קשת קשיות וספקות בטענות מספיקות להבהיל המתבונן ומן הראוי לכל חולק החפץ לברר האמת שיערוך דברי איש ריבו וראיותיו באר הטב ולהשיב בלא איבה אך בענות[a] צדק עם אהבת ותאות בחינת האמת.

§ *1.3.2* יסתור ראיות דעותיו עם הראות הפכם במופת שכלי כאשר הורה הפילוסוף בספר השמים והעולם מאמר א' פרק ק"א ומאמר ב' פרק ל"ד. הנה ראוי לנו ברצותנו עם אלוהים להודיע קשט אמרי תורתו שנערוך משפטי המטים עקלקלותם ודעות הנפסדות מיוסדות על אדני סברות וטענות נותנות טעם לפגם והנמצא עליהם משבוש הסברא וזה בהראות הפגם[b] במופתים שכליים נמצאים בספרי קדש והמה בכתובים נפרדים נכוחים למבין נתנו מרועה אחד הנה הנה מקום כל אחד מהם רשום בכתב מנגד למען ירוץ קורא למצוא מן מוצא דבר אמת לאמיתו והאיר אל עבר פניו.

§ *1.3.3* ובהיות כי יקרו מאד דברי ארסטו' ותלמידיו בעיני רבים ונכבדים עד היות אצלם מי שיחלוק על אריסטו' ותלמידיו הנזכרים כחולק על החוש או על מופת חותך באופן כי הרמב"ם ז"ל כתב בספר המורה מאמר ב' פרק כ"ב וזה לשונו: »והכלל הוא שכל מה שאמר ארסטו' בכל הנמצא מגלגל הירח ולמטה הוא אמת ולא יטה ממנו אלא מי שלא יבינהו או שקדמו לו דעות ירצה להרחיק[c] מהן[d] כל סותר ולשמרם או שימשכוהו הדעות ההן[e] להכחיש ענין נראה« עד כאן לשונו. על כן אמרתי להביא ראיה בהתר | ספק כל חקירה מקצת יסודות ארסטו' הנזכר ודבריו ומופתיו ומשפטי פיהו ובאלה לא נזכיר חקירות הפילוסוף הנזכר[f] ודעותיו והמון ראיותיו במלין לא יועיל בם

---

[a] בענות] coni. Dunk.; בענוה a. [b] הפגם] coni. Dunk.; הפכם a. [c] להרחיק] a[corr]; להחזיק a. [d] מהן] coni. Dunk.; מהם a. [e] ההן] coni. Dunk.; ההם a. [f] הפילוסוף הנזכר] coni. Dunk.; הפילוסופים הנזכרים a.

PROLOGUS – INTRODUCTION

§ 1.3.1 Nos ergo posteriores et Sacrarum Scripturarum documentis instructos quibus huiusmodi opinionum rationes redarguuntur et ad oppositum demonstrationes nonnullas divinitus inferuntur preceteris quidem veritate pollere decet. Qua scilicet Summi Productoris sive Creatoris intentum sapientius noscamus et ardentes sequamur nosque de felici anime immortalitate certius sperantes letiores reddamus letiusque ad illam consequendam pro viribus procedamus.

§ 1.3.2 Cum autem sicut Phylosophus ait in lib. De Celo primi t.c. 101[a] et eiusdem secundi t.c. 34,[b] duo principaliter iuste opponenti requiruntur. Primo scilicet ut adversarij opiniones eiusque rationes explicite narret. Secundo ut non odiose increpet sed illius rationes verioribus redarguat et oppositum probet. Nobis ergo Sacrarum Scripturarum veritates propalare intendentes illas que[c] saltem Phylosophi opiniones que penitus religioni et nonnulli gentium viri repugnare videntur harumque rationes explicare convenit ut illarum reprobatio Sacrarumque Scripturarum veritates rationibus quidem in processu exprimendis et in eisdem Sacris Scripturis divinitus insertis apertius pateat.

⟨§ 1.3.3⟩

§ 1.3.1 Our predecessors and experts in the Holy Scripture refute the arguments that lead to their opinions and they bring forth some demonstrations of the contraries [that are] in accordance with religion. Indeed, it is necessary to obtain the truth first and foremost. Thanks to the truth, we know more wisely than others the intention of the highest Maker—that is, the Creator—and burning with love, we follow Him and make it possible to trust in the most fortunate manner, having belief in the immortality of the fortunate soul, and we continue until its acquisition [of immortality].

§ 1.3.2 Now, as the Philosopher explains in *On the Heavens* 1, text. 101,[a] and 2, text. 34,[b] we need above all two contrary positions: first, he clearly reports the opinions of the contender and his argument; second, he reproves him kindly, but refutes his arguments in the truest way and proves the contrary. We therefore intend to make public the truths of the Holy Scripture and the opinions of the Philosopher, which seem to be contraries to the religious man and to some of the Gentiles. And it would be better to explain their arguments, because it is clear that their reprobation and the truth of the Holy Scripture comes to light more openly by arguments expressed through the process and inserted by God into the same Holy Scripture.

⟨§ 1.3.3⟩

---

[a] 101] emend. COPP.; 110 b; 101 L.   [b] 34] emend. COPP.; 39 b; 34 L.   [c] illas que] b[corr]; illasque b.

[a] *Cael.* 1.10.279b.   [b] *Cael.* 2.5.288a.

questions of the aforementioned Philosopher and his opinions and his verbose arguments that are of no use for the life of the world [to come]; also, there is neither usefulness nor severe harm to the present life with or without the acquisition of their truth, so they are not mentioned anywhere in the Holy Scripture.

⟨§ I.3.4⟩

§ I.3.5 Are these not his treatises? On the knowledge of the essence of matter and motion and place and time and the elements, and the essence of the celestial bodies and their quality and their movements, which are explained in *Physics*, *Meteorology*, *On the Heavens*, and *On Generation and Corruption*, and his treatises on the [different] kinds of the corruptible soul and its faculties and the senses, and the principles of the generables and corruptibles, and the equivocations and opinions of his predecessors and their statements, [all] together with the arguments of the aforementioned Philosopher against their opinions, which he expanded in extended discourses: in *On the Soul*, *Physics*, *On the Senses and the Sensible*, and *Metaphysics*. Regarding ethics and politics: on these [matters], the aforementioned Philosopher amazes [us] in [*Nicomachean*] *Ethics* and *Politics*, among others. But many *beautiful words*[a] are found in the Holy Scripture, which teaches [us] *great things about righteousness*[b] in ethics and politics in order to improve and orderly arrange *both soul and body*[c] *to turn them towards the [right] way.*[d] But it is *good for those who are pure in heart*[e] to present doubts, *burning arrows*[f] that disturb [us] *and cause sorrow to the soul,*[g] at the beginning of the inquiry and to overwhelm them all *with pure words,*[h] with clear arguments about all that is mysterious. *These [words] are for the life of the world [to come].*[i] *They bring forth justice in truth.*[j] *It shall be told of ha-Shem unto the [next] generation.*[k]

§ I.4.1 **It is therefore appropriate [that]:**

— First: We will present the fundamental questions that we have regarding the knowledge of the existence of a creator who originated everything besides himself, who has providence over everything [and] is incorporeal; and on the issue of the individual human intellectual soul and its immortality, its freedom [of choice], and its reward and punishment.

---

[a] Gen 49:21. [b] Ps 65:6. [c] Isa 10:18. [d] Num 22:23. [e] Ps 73:1. [f] Isa 50:11.
[g] Lev 26:16. [h] Ps 12:7. [i] Dan 12:2. [j] Isa 42:3. [k] Ps 22:31.

לחיי עולם. מבלי אין בהשגת אמתתם וחסרונה תועלת או היזק רב גם לחיי שעה עד אפס מקום לדבר בם בכתבי הקדש.

⟨§ I.3.4⟩

§ I.3.5 הלא המה מאמריו: בידיעת מהות החמר והתנועה והמקום והזמן והיסודות ומהות הגרמים השמימיים ואיכיותם ותנועותם המבואר בספר שמע טבעי ובספר אותות השמים וספר השמים והעולם וספר ההוויה וההפסד ומאמריו במיני הנפש הנפסדת וכחותיה והחושים והתחלות ההווים והנפסדים ושיתופי[a] השמות ודעות הקדמונים וטענותם עם ראיות הפילוסוף הנזכר[b] נגד דעותם אשר בם הרחיב פה האריך לשון בספר הנפש, ובספר שמע טבעי, וספר החוש והמוחש, וספר מה שאחר אמנם במדות ובהנהגת אשר הפליא לדבר בם הפילוסוף הנזכר בספר המדות וספר הנהגת המדינה[c] וזולתם הן רבים אמרי שפר נמצאים בספרי קדש מורים מדות והנהגות נוראות בצדק לתקן ולסדר מנפש ועד בשר להטותם הדרך אך טוב לברי לבב לערוך ספקות מאזרי זיקות מציקות ומדיבות נפש בתחלת העיון ולהכריע את כלם באמרות טהורות עם ראיות ברורות על כל נעלם אלה לחיי עולם לאמת משפט יוציאו יספר לה׳ לדור.

§ I.4.1 **ראוי אם כן:**

— ראשונה שנערוך החקירות העקריות אצלנו בידיעת מציאות בורא מחולל כל מה שזולתו משגיח בכל בלתי גוף. ובענין הנפש האנושית השכלית האישית[d] ונצחיותה ובחירתה וגמולה וענשה.

---

[a] ושותפי] ושיתופי [a corr; הפילוסוף הנזכ׳] הפילוסוף הנזכר [b emend.;] a;
Philosophus b.   [c] המדינית] המדינה [a corr.   [d] האשיית] האישית [coni. DUNK.;
האשיית a.

§ 1.3.4 Cumque hac nostra tempestate tanta sit eiusdem Phylosophi et sequacium fama ut si quis eorum opinionibus contradicerit manifestis et per se notis contradicere procul dubio reputetur eorundem ergo auctoritatum horumque fundamentorum testimonium ad illa que intendimus demonstranda et ad | quedam quodamnodo manifesta approbanda convenire putans horum quidem fundamentorum interdum et sermonum testimonia in singulis pro viribus allegare intendo in hoc scilicet opusculo quo Sacre Scripture documenta nonnulla in humani generis lumen divinitus edita ad Dei reverentiam revelare decrevi. Quare id merito ‹Lumen Gentium› appellare curavi.

§ 1.3.5 Deferentes tamen eiusdem Phylosophi sermones circa illa quorum cogitatio[a] parum nobis prodesse videtur. Quare de illis nihil in Sacris tangitur Scripturis scilicet de quidditate[b] nature et de quidditate[c] motus et loci et temporis celestiumque et elementorum corporum horumque qualitatibus et motibus. De quibus in libris *Physicorum* et *De Celo* et *Metheororum* et *De Generatione* pertractat et illa que intulit de mortalibus anime generibus et de sensibus et de mortalium principijs et nominum equivocationibus antiquorumque opinionibus et harum frivolis rationibus quas idem Phylosophus diffuse oppugnat prout in libris Physicorum et De Sensu et Sensato amplissime edidit illa quoque que de moralibus et polyticis que in libris Ethicorum et Polyticorum et aliis intulit. Quibus prestantiora in Sacris Documentis horumque exemplis rectius docentur.

§ 1.4.1 Convenit ergo:

Primo ut proponamus questiones quarum solutiones humano generi preceteris requiruntur ad hoc ut aliquid Dei cognitionis humaneque anime immortalitatis certiorem consequamur notitiam qua scilicet contemplativam vitam sacrosque mores libentius sequamur.

§ 1.3.4 To this day, the reputation of the Philosopher and his followers is tremendous and if someone irrefutably contradicts their opinions, it is as if he is refuting the proof of their authority and their premises, which we intend to demonstrate and prove clearly. | Thinking that it is sometimes appropriate to choose the proofs of their principles and their speeches, I decided to publish this pamphlet, in which some passages of the Holy Scripture are written following the light of humankind that reveal a reverence for God. And for this reason, I chose to call this pamphlet *Light of the Nations*.

§ 1.3.5 A short reflection concerning what is based on the Philosopher's speeches would seem to be useful for us, because the Holy Scripture makes no reference to the essence of nature or the essence of movement, time, and space or the qualities and motion of the celestial and terrestrial bodies, which are explained in *Physics*, *On the Heavens*, *Meteorology*, *On Generation and Corruption*, and in his treatises on the species of the corruptible soul and their faculties, the senses, the principles of mortal beings, and the equivocations of his predecessors and their opinions that the said Philosopher refutes; for instance, in *Physics* and *On the Senses and the Sensible*. He also wrote about morality and politics in *Ethics*, among others. All of these things are taught in the Holy Scripture, where we find appropriate examples of them.

§ 1.4.1 It is therefore necessary:

First: to present the questions that require specific solutions among humankind because we may [thereby] obtain a more certain acquaintance of the knowledge of God and the immortality of the human soul, by which one may know the contemplative life, and we may more happily follow the sacred ways.

---

[a] cogitatio] coni. COPP.; cogitio b.   [b] quidditate] emend. COPP.; quiditate b.   [c] quidditate] emend. COPP.; quiditate b.

- Second: We will present the propositions that the aforementioned Philosopher brought forth and for which he brought proofs, or [at least] most of them, with references from his books, which we will mention. And we will use the aforementioned propositions to bring arguments and proofs for the intended dispel of doubts about the aforementioned questions. *And You [God] may make an end of the grumblings*[a] of many [people], especially in our time, who think that a person who opposes Aristotle's words is like one who opposes [sense] perception or [rational] demonstration.
- Third: We will present—together with the explanation of every single question—the Philosopher's opinions and those of his followers and their expounded arguments, with references to their books, which we will mention.
- Fourth: For every question, we will bring a demonstration of the contrary of the opinion | of the aforementioned Philosopher regarding that question.
- Fifth: For every question, we will bring a demonstration in favour of an opinion [that is] contrary to the opinion of the aforementioned Philosopher.
- Sixth: For every question, we will refute the arguments that the Philosopher gives in favour of his opinion regarding that question.
- Seventh: For every question, we will give references from the Holy Scripture, teaching a demonstration of the true opinion regarding that question. And some of them will [also] state the opponents' opinions and their statements and refutations.

And after we have completed the explanation of all the aforementioned questions, we will compile a summary, in which we will briefly speak of the philosophers' way and the way of the Torah of our God in the explanation[s] of all the aforementioned questions, so that *they will draw together for judgment*[b] before the reader's eyes, so that he will be able to judge with ease whether this [one] or that [one] is correct, as it is necessary that all contraries are confronted face to face,[c] as the Philosopher testifies in *On the Heavens* 2, text. 40.[d]

§1.4.2 And through these will become clear the error of those who think that there is no word in the Holy Scripture [that can help one] to acquire knowledge, [but] only words that the believer believes, but [by which] he does not know. Every philosopher is amused by this and every denier scoffs at them, so that the sage Rabbi Samuel ibn

---

[a] Num 17:25. [b] Isa 41:1. [c] This is point 8 in the Latin version. [d] *Cael.* 2.6.288b.

Secundo ut quasdam presupponamus sententias a Phylosophis concessas et ut plurimum probatas quibus intenta concludamus citantes loca ubi ab eisdem Phylosophis tractantur et demostrative probantur.

Tertio ut in questionum singula Peripateticorum explicemus opiniones harumque rationes ostendentes loca ubi ab eisdem Phylosophis diffuso pertractantur sermone.

Quarto ut veras sententias huiusmodi opinionibus oppositas demonstrative probemus.

Quinto ut veras sententias inde demonstrative resultantes prefatis Phylosophis oppositas succinte concludamus.

Sexto ut prefatas phylosophorum rationes resolvamus harumque errores pro viribus ostendamus.

Septimo ut Sacrarum Loca ostendamus ubi huiusmodi concluse sententie demonstrative docentur phylosophorumque opiniones nonnulle cum suis rationibus harumque redargutiones divinitus inseruntur sepe etiam secundum[a] Latinam translationem que scilicet in plurimis proculdubio deficit, quare omnia in originali Hebreorum testu rectius apertiusque fulgere patet.

8 Octavo ut diversos phylosophorum et Sacre Scripture processus quibus diversimode ad prefatas questiones solvendas procedunt succincte notemus ut illis iuxta se positis facilius horum verioris fulgeat lumen prout habetur a Phylosopho in lib. De Celo II, t.c. 40.[b]

§1.4.2 Quibus scilicet patebit error putantium ut Sacrarum Scripturarum volumina credulitates tantum frivolasque et penitus dubias doceant sententias a Phylosophis quodammodo deridendas, cuius oppositum docet Sacrum Deuteronomij documentum cap. 4 ubi dicit: «Scito ergo

Second: to propose those opinions that are declared by the Philosopher and to prove most of them according to their intention. We will conclude with the references that are discussed by the same Philosopher and demonstrate [them] by means of reason.

Third: to explain every single question of the Peripatetic philosophers, their opinions, and their arguments, showing the references that are mentioned by the Philosopher.

Fourth: to prove the incoherence of the[se] opinions by means of demonstrations.

Fifth: to conclude in favour of an opinion contrary to the opinions of the above-mentioned Philosopher by means of demonstration.

Sixth: to resolve the aforementioned arguments of the philosophers and show their mistakes.

Seventh: to show the passages in the Holy Scripture, explain the conclusion of the argument by means of demonstration, and include some opinions and arguments of the philosophers and their reproaches, according to the Latin translation, which seems to be lacking in some points that seem to be truer and clearer in the original text of the Hebrew version.

Eighth: to show that the different developments improved by the philosophers and the Holy Scripture are intended to resolve the aforementioned questions and to write some brief remarks to shed light on those that are truer, as the Philosopher explains in *On the Heavens* 2, text. 40.[a]

§1.4.2 And from these becomes obvious the error of those who think that the Holy Scripture teaches many easy answers and doubtful opinions, which is a point of derision for the Philosopher. The contrary of this is taught in Deuteronomy 4 (4:39): "Know therefore this day, and consider it in thine heart, that the Lord He is God in heaven

---
[a] secundum] b[corr]; ecundum b.   [b] 40] emend. COPP.; 90 b; 40 L.

[a] *Cael.* 2.6.288b.

Tibbon wrote under the [Hebrew] letter Ḥet in his *Perush millot ha-zarot* [i.e., *Explanation of Uncommon Terms*], which he authored after he had translated the *Guide of the Perplexed* [by Moses Maimonides]: "Natural science, as the Rabbi—of blessed memory—said, is what our Rabbis—of blessed memory—called 'the work of creation' [*Ma'aseh Bereshit*]." And he further says: "And the principles of the books of that science are the books by Aristotle." And he further says: "And I do not see anything in the [Torah] portion *Bereshit* except the first verses, which are very few [compared] to what is in those books. It is not a hundredth, nor a two-hundredth [of that]." And according to this, the *Guide to Justice*[a] would have been commanding us in vain when He said (Deuteronomy 7:9): "And know therefore that [only] ha-Shem, your God, is God" [and] (Deuteronomy 4:39): "Know therefore this day and keep in mind." And like these, there are many [words] in the Torah and in [the books of] the Prophets that command and stimulate knowledge and understanding. And there is not a [single] commandment [that commands us] to believe. And God—may He be exalted—explains this, as it says (Isaiah 45:19): "I did not say to the stock of Jacob, 'Seek Me in vain.' I am ha-Shem, who foretells reliably; who announces what is true." And this is so, because He did not command [us] to believe in His existence and His might and His providence, because belief is not subordinate to will, as mentioned above, as is clear from experience, and as the Philosopher explains in *On the Soul* 2, text. 153.[b] And if this is so, then it is not subordinate to any commandment, and the commandment concerning it would be invalid. But [it says:] "[I] foretell reliably" (ibid.), [i.e.,] through a description of true knowledge; "[I] announce what is true" (ibid.), [i.e.,] by providing a demonstration for them.

6r §1.5 Now: The fundamental questions, which we mentioned above, are:

First, whether the order of generation and corruption is [pre]eternal.
Second, whether the elements are [pre]eternal.
Third, whether prime matter is [pre]eternal.
Fourth, whether the heavens are [pre]eternal.
Fifth, whether movement is [pre]eternal.
Sixth, whether there is an eternal existent that creates and brings forth being after absolute nothingness and that makes something from nothing.
Seventh, whether it [i.e., that existent] is a body, a power in a body, or neither.

---

[a] Cf. Joel 2:23.   [b] *De an.* 3.3.427b.

hodie et cogitato in corde quod Dominus ipse est Deus in celo sursum et in terra deorsum et non est alius.» Quibus aperte docet quod talia scire non credere tantum convenit. Quorum demonstrationes ibidem et alibi divinitus traduntur prout infra in suis locis Deo dante explicabitur. Et idem videtur esaiam inferre cap. 45:19 ubi dicit: «Non dixi semini Jahacob frustra querite me Ego Dominus loquens iustitiam annuncians recta.» Quasi dicat quod non credula opinione nulla ratione prabata iussit ut ipsum Deum sequeremur illud enim iubere esset quid frustratorium credere enim non est quid nobis arbitrarium ita ut aliquid ad libitum opinemur imaginari enim ad libitum possumus quicquid volumus non autem opinari pro ut experimentum docet et habetur a Phylosopho in lib. De anima II, t.c. 153 immo enuncians iusta et docens recta tantum scilicet rectas assertorum rationes quibus Deum proculdubio noscentes illius vestigia merito sequamur et eundem tantum devote adoremus.

above and upon the earth beneath: there is none else." This means that it is fitting to know those things and not only to believe in them. The demonstration of these things is narrated here and in other passages that will be explained below by God. And it seems that Isaiah said the same in chapter 45 (45:19): "I did not say to the offspring of Jacob, 'Seek me in vain.' I, the Lord, speak the truth; I declare what is right," which means that he did not command [us] to believe in an opinion that has no reasonable proof such that if we were to follow this God, there was a command to believe in something stupid. Indeed, this is not how our will works; namely, that we would by will hold an opinion that we can imagine. Yet we can do whatever we want by will, but [we can]not hold an opinion, as is clear from experience, as the Philosopher explains in *On the Soul* 2, text. 153.[a] On the contrary, by expressing the right ideas and also teaching the right opinions, we follow the said correct arguments by which we can know the ways of God and worship Him with devotion.

§ I.5 Questiones ergo in processu disputande sunt tales sunt:

1. Utrum motus generationis et corruptionis habuisset esse ab eterno.
2. Utrum corruptibilium elementa habuissent esse ab eterno.
3. Utrum materia prima habuisset esse ab eterno.
4. Utrum celum habuisset esse ab eterno.
5. Utrum motus habuisset esse ab eterno.
6. Utrum detur creatio qua scilicet tam materia et forma quam totum compositum habuisset esse post merum non esse.
7. Utrum data creatione et per consequens Creatore idem Creator sit quid corporeum vel sit quid incorporeum.

§ I.5 Now the questions, which we mentioned above, are:

1) Whether the movement of generation and corruption is [pre]eternal.
2) Whether the corruptible elements are [pre]eternal.
3) Whether prime matter is [pre]eternal.
4) Whether the heavens are [pre]eternal.
5) Whether movement is [pre]eternal.
6) Whether there was a creation, meaning a creation in which matter and form, as well the whole composite, came from absolute nothingness.
7) Whether creation—and consequently, a creator—are given, and whether this creator is corporeal or incorporeal.

---

[a] *De an.* 3.3.427b.

Eighth, whether it is only one or not.
Ninth, whether it knows everything.
Tenth, whether it has the equal ability to choose one of two contraries by intention and will.
Eleventh, whether it has providence over the particulars of the generables and corruptibles.
Twelfth, whether the individual human intellectual soul is incorruptible.
Thirteenth, whether good deeds are beneficial or [even] necessary for the success [i.e., perfection] of the aforementioned intellectual soul.
Fourteenth, whether the perfection of the soul is acquired by means of human power only and not by means of divine or natural power.
Fifteenth, whether the human species and its perfection is the intended final purpose of the heavens and of the celestial bodies and of the entirety of the material world.

§ 1.6.1 Now, the propositions that we will present in order to explain the aforementioned questions are premises that are regarded as true among the philosophers, and for them—or at least for their majority—a demonstration exists. And therefore, it will become clear how it befell Aristotle and his followers—who never saw the light of the Torah of our God—that to some of his opinions applies what he [himself] ascribed to Plato in *Physics* 3, text. 61;[a] [namely], that he did not preserve the foundations [i.e., principles] of his opinions. And this is also applicable to what he ascribed to Empedocles in | *On the Heavens* 3, text. 56;[b] namely, that he did not preserve the definition of a thing. And among them there is a proposition that they consider to be not only true, but also self-evident, and this is that according to them, movement is eternal without any doubt. And from this, they give an argument for the eternity of the mover and the object of motion, and the other things that they consider to be eternal. And to them is [also] applicable what they ascribed to the adherents of religion in *Metaphysics* 2, text. 14,[c] and 12, text. 18,[d] which is to deny something necessary and to approve something impossible. And for them, this happens to be the cause of the error that applies to the principles, because indeed, a little bit of error at the beginning of every science is the cause of a much greater error at the end, as Aristotle and Averroes explain in *On the Heavens* 1, text. 33.[e]

---

[a]*Phys.* 3.6.206b.   [b]*Cael.* 3.7.305a.   [c]*Metaph.* 2.2.994b.   [d]*Metaph.* 12.3.1070a.   [e]*Cael.* 1.5.271b.

שמינית אם הוא אחד בלבד אם אין.
תשיעית אם הוא יודע כל.
עשירית אם יש לו יכולת בשוה על שני ההפכים ובוחר באחד מהם בכונה וברצון.
אחת עשרה אם הוא משגיח באישי ההווים ונפסדים.
שתים עשרה אם הנפש האנושית השכלית האישית היא בלתי נפסדת.
שלש עשרה אם המעשים הטובים הם מועילים או הכרחיים בהצלחת הנפש השכלית הנזכר.
ארבע עשרה אם שלמות הנפש יושג בכח אנושי בלבד ולא יושג בכח אלהי או טבעי.
חמש עשרה אם תכלית המכוון מן השמים וצבאם ומהעולם המוחש בכללו הוא המין האנושי ושלמותו.

§ 1.6.1 **אמנם ההנחות אשר נעריך**[a] לבאר את החקירות הנזכרות הם הנחות אשר התאמתו אצל הפילוסופים ובא אצלם מופת עליהם או על רבם ובכן יתבאר איך לארסטו' ולנמשכים אחריו[b] אשר לא ראו אור תורת אלהינו קרה שבקצת דעותיו נפל במה שיחס הוא לאפלטון בספר השמע מאמר ג' פרק ס"א[c] שלא שמר יסודות דעותיו וכמו כן נפל במה שהוא מיחס לאמפידוקליס בספר | השמים מאמר ג' פרק נ"ו[d] שאינו שומר[e] גדר הדבר ובהיות אצלם הנחה אשר חשבו לא בלבד אמתית אבל כמבוארת בעצמה והיא שהתנועה אצלם היא קדמונית בלי ספק וממנה הביאו ראיה על קדמות המניע והמתנועע וזולתם אשר חשבו היותם קדמונים נפלו במה שהם מיחסים לבעלי הדתות בספר מה שאחר מאמר ב' פרק י"ד ובמאמר י"ב פרק י"ח היינו להכחיש קצת ההכרחי ולקיים קצת הנמנע וזה קרה להם לסבת טעות נפל בהתחלות כי אמנם מעט מהטעות בהתחלת כל חכמה הוא סבת טעות רב מאד באחרית כאשר בארו ארסטו' ואבן רשד בספר השמים והעולם מאמר א' פרק ל"ג.[f]

---

[a]הנזכרות] coni. Dunk.; הנזכור a.   [b]אחריו] a^corr; om. a.   [c]ג'] emend. Dunk.; 'ז a; vii b; iii.   [d]נ"ו] emend. Dunk.; נ"ז a; 56 b; 56 L.   [e]שומר] a^corr; om. a.   [f]ל"ג] emend. Dunk.; ל"א a; 35 b; 33 L.

8. Utrum unus tantum detur Creator vel plures eque primi dentur creatores.
9. Utrum idem Creator omnia sciat vel econtra.
10. Utrum idem Creator habeat liberam ad utrumque contrariorum potentiam quorum alterum voluntarie eligat.
11. Utrum de mortalium individuis habeat sollicitudinem sive curam.
12. Utrum intellectiva individui humani generis anima sit quid immortale vel econverso.
13. Utrum pia intentio et conatus ad pia opera exequenda concurrat ad eiusdem anime perfectionem.
14. Utrum eiusdem intellective anime perfectio per humanam virtutem tantum non autem per naturalem vel divinam acquiri contingat.
15. Utrum celestium horumque motuum finis sit mortalium oportunitas ad humanam perfectionem necessaria.

§ I.6.1 Ad prefata autem declaranda quedam ut prefertur videntur presupponenda a Phylosophis concessa[a] et ut plurimum demonstrata;[b] quibus patebit Phylosopho et sequacibus Sacri Documenti lumine carentibus interdum in suis opinionibus contigisse idem quod ipse Phylosophus Platoni imputat Physicorum III t.c. 61[c] scilicet de non observando sua fundamenta, et illud quo Empedoclem et Democritum accusat in lib. De Celo III, t.c. 56 scilicet de non observando rei diffinitionem. Eidem, n. enim, Phylosopho et sequentibus ductis illa propositione quam putarunt non modo veram sed etiam esse necessariam et penitus manifestam; qua scilicet dicitur motum habuisse esse ab eterno per quam processerunt ad eternitatem motoris et mobilis et aliorum que putarunt fuisse ab eterno, contingit idem quod ipsi theologis turpiter imputant *Methaphysicorum* II, t.c. 14 et eiusdem XII, t.c. 18 de negando scilicet quedam necessaria et nonnulla impossibilia approbando; et hoc ratione erroris circa principia contingentis, sicut idem Phylosophus eiusque Comentator asserunt in lib. De Celo primi t.c. 33:[d] «que[e] minimus error in principio est causa maximi in fine.»

8) Whether there is only one creator or there are many creators of equal primary status.
9) Whether the creator knows everything or not.
10) Whether this creator has a will to choose [i.e., the liberty to choose] between two contraries and the power to choose one of them as for a [particular] purpose.
11) Whether he has solicitude or care for mortal individuals.
12) Whether or not the individual intellectual soul of human beings is immortal.
13) Whether good deeds and the effort involved in good deeds are beneficial for the perfection of the intellectual soul.
14) Whether the perfection of this intellectual soul is acquired only through human power or through natural or divine power.
15) Whether the purpose of the celestial bodies and their movement is the benefit required for human perfection.

§ I.6.1 Now we will present the propositions in order to explain the aforementioned questions that are allowed by the philosophers and that are attested by their majority. And therefore, it will become clear how it happened that some of the opinions of the Philosopher and his followers, who never saw the light of the Holy Scripture, may admit of demonstration, as the Philosopher himself says of Plato in *Physics* 3, text. 61;[a] [namely,] that he did not respect his principles. And he also accuses Empedocles and Democritus of not preserving the definition of a thing in *On the Heavens* 3, text. 56.[b] And among the Philosopher and his followers, there is an assumption that they not only consider to be true, but also self-evident, and this is that movement is eternal, and from this, they bring an argument for the eternity of the mover and the object of motion and the other things that they consider to be eternal. And to them is applicable what they ascribe to the adherents of religion in *Metaphysics* 2, text. 14,[c] and 12, text. 18:[d] denying something necessary and approving something impossible. And this happens concerning the cause of the error, as the Philosopher and his Commentator explain in *On the Heavens* 1, text. 33,[e] because a small error at the beginning grows to an enormity at the end.

---

[a] concessa] coni. COPP.; cocessa b. [b] demonstrata] coni. COPP.; demostrata b. [c] III] emend. COPP.; VII b; III L. [d] 33] emend. COPP.; 35 b; 33 L. [e] que] b[corr]; quam b.

[a] *Phys.* 3.6.206b. [b] *Cael.* 3.7.305a. [c] *Metaph.* 2.2.994a. [d] *Metaph.* 12.3.1070a. [e] *Cael.* 1.5.271b.

§ 1.6.2 And therefore, it is appropriate to propose:

1) That the final purpose is the highest good that an agent intends by its activity, and the Philosopher explains this in *Metaphysics* 2, text. 9.[a]

2) That potency is prior in time to the actuality of which it is the potency, and Aristotle explains this in *Metaphysics* 9, text. 5,[b] among his proofs *Against Garicon* [i.e., the Megarians].[c]

3) That the agent is prior in time to its activity, and Averroes explains this in his Commentary on *Metaphysics* 9, text. 13,[d] and his Commentary on *Posterior Analytics* 2, text. 11.[e]

4) That the final purpose in the agent's mind is prior in time to the activity of which it is the purpose, and this will become clear from Aristotle's words and his proofs in *Physics* 2, text. 89,[f] and *Metaphysics* 2, text. 8[g] and 7, text. 23.[h]

5) That the existence of the final purpose provides essential evidence for the existence of the agent, just as motion does for the existence of the mover, and this will be explained by the definition of the "final purpose" that Aristotle explains in *Metaphysics* 2, text. 9,[i] and that Averroes extensively teaches in the *Treatise on the Substance of the Celestial Sphere*, ch. 2.[j]

6) That everything that happens without intention and will is said to happen "by chance," and Aristotle explains this in *Physics* 2, text. 51.[k]

7) That an eternal [thing] truly has no efficient cause [i.e., agent], | and Averroes explains this in *On the Heavens* 4, text. 1.

8) That everything that is in many things is not in them by chance, and this is explained by Aristotle's words in *On the Heavens* 2, text. 45,[l] and in *Physics* 2, text. 48.[m]

9) That there is no time, no space [lit. place], no plenum, and no vacuum beyond the [outmost] heavens, and Aristotle explains this in *On the Heavens* 1, text. 100.[n]

10) That there is no sixth body besides the four elements and the bodies of the spheres, and Aristotle and Averroes prove this in *On the Heavens* 1, text. 23.[o]

---

[a] *Metaph.* 2.2.994b. [b] *Metaph.* 9.3.1047a. [c] See Introduction p. 9–10. [d] Cf. *Metaph.* 9.3.1048a. [e] Cf. *An. post.* 2.11.95a. [f] *Phys.* 2.9.200a. [g] *Metaph.* 2.2.994b. [h] *Metaph.* 7.9.1032b. [i] *Metaph.* 2.2.994b. [j] Cf. Averroes, *De substantia orbis: Critical Edition of the Hebrew Text with English Translation and Commentary*, trans. Arthur Hyman (Cambridge, MA: Medieval Academy of America; Jerusalem Israel Academy of Sciences and Humanities, 1986), 84–85. [k] *Phys.* 2.5.197a. [l] *Cael.* 2.8.289a. [m] *Phys.* 2.4.196b. [n] *Cael.* 1.9.279a. [o] *Cael.* 1.3.270b.

---

§ 1.6.2 ובכן ראוי להניח:

א' שהתכלית הוא הטוב האחרון המכוון מהפועל בפעולתו וזה באר הפילוסוף בספר מה שאחר מאמר ב' פרק ט'.

ב' שהכח קודם בזמן לאותו הפועל אשר הוא כח לו וזה באר ארסטו' בספר מה שאחר מאמר ט' פרק ה' במופתיו נגד גאריקו'.

ג' שהפועל קודם בזמן לפעלו. וזה באר אבן רשד בבאורו לספר מה שאחר מאמר ט' פרק י״ג ובבאור ספר המופת מאמר ב' פרק י״א.

ד' שהתכלית קודם בזמן במחשבת הפועל לפעולה אשר הוא תכליתה. וזה יבואר מדברי ארסטו' ומופתיו בספר השמע מאמר ב' פרק פ״ט ובספר מה שאחר מאמר ב' פרק ח' ומאמר ז' פרק כ״ג.

ה' שמציאות התכלית מורה על מציאות הפועל הוראה עצמית כמו שהתנועה מורה על מציאות המניע וזה יתבאר מגדר ה‹תכלית› אשר באר ארסטו' בספר מה שאחר מאמר ב' פרק ט' ובמאמר רחב הורה זה אבן רשד בספר עצם הגלגל פרק ב'.

ו' שכל מה שנעשה בלתי כונה ורצון יאמר עליו שנעשה במקרה וזה באר ארסטו' בספר השמע מאמר ב' פרק נ״א.

7r ז' שהקדמון אין לו סבה פועלת באמת | וזה באר אבן רשד בספר השמים מאמר ד' פרק א'.

ח' שכל מה שיהיה בדברים רבים לא יפול בהם במקרה, וזה יתבאר מדברי ארסטו' בספר השמים והעולם מאמר ב' פרק מ״ה ובספר השמע מאמר ב' פרק מ״ח.

ט' שאין חוץ לשמים זמן ולא מקום לא מלא ולא ריק וזה באר ארסטו' בספר השמים מאמר א' פרק ק'.

י' שלא ימצא גוף ששי היינו גשם מלבד הד' יסודות והגרמים השמיימיים[b] וזה באר ארסטו' ואבן רשד במופת בספר השמים מאמר א' פרק כ״ג.

---

[a] ב'] emend. Dunk.; ג' a; II L. [b] השמיימים] coni. Dunk.; השממיים a.

§ I.6.2 Propositiones ergo ut prefertur presupponende tales sunt scilicet:

1. Finis est quid ultimum ad quod actiones intenduntur.
Hoc autem habetur a Phylosopho *Methaphysicorum* II, t.c. 9.
2. Potentia est tempore prior ad illum actum cuius est potentia.
Hoc autem habetur ratione et auctoritate Phylosophi *Methaphysicorum* IX, t.c. 5 Contra Gariconem illud negantem.
3. Agens est tempore prior ad suum actum.
Hoc autem habetur ab Aven R. *Methaphysicorum* IX, t.c. 13 et *Posteriorum* II, t.c. 11
4. Finis habet tempore precedere in mente agentis ad illud cuius est finis.
Hoc autem sequitur ad rationes Phylosophi *Metaphysicorum*[a] II, t.c. 8 et eiusdem VII, t.c. 23.
5. Finis significat agentem significatione propria sicut motus significat motorem. |Hoc autem sequitur ad eiusdem finis diffinitionem a Phylosopho traditam *Metaphysicorum* II, t.c. 9 et aperte habetur ab Aven R. in *Tractatu de Substantia Orbis* cap. 2.
6. Quecumque sunt preter voluntatem et cognitionem dicuntur fieri casu.
Hoc autem habetur a Phylosopho *Physicorum* II, t.c. 51.
7. Quicquid habuit esse ab eterno non habuit vere agentem.
Hoc autem habetur ab Aven R. in lib. *De Celo* IV[b] t.c. 1.
8. Quicquid est in pluribus observatum non habet esse casu.
Hoc autem infertur a Phylosopho in lib. *De Celo* II, t.c. 45 et *Physicorum* II, t.c. 48.
9. Extra celum non datur tempus neque locus neque plenus neque vacuus.
Hoc autem habetur a Phylosopho in lib. *De Celo* primi t.c. 100.
10. Non datur sextum corpus quod scilicet sit quid preter quatuor elementorum et preter celestium corpus pro ut habetur *De Celo* I t.c.[c] 23.[d]

§ I.6.2 And therefore, the propositions that will be presented are:

1) That the end is the final purpose for which activities are intended, as the Philosopher explains in *Metaphysics* 2, text. 9.[a]
2) That potency is prior in time to that actualisation of which it is the potency, according to the arguments and authority of the Philosopher in *Metaphysics* 9, text. 5,[b] *Against Garicon*.[c]
3) That an agent is prior in time to its activity, as Averroes explicates in *Metaphysics* 9, text. 13,[d] and *Posterior Analytics* 2, text.11.[e]
4) That the final purpose in the agent's mind is prior to the activity of which is it the purpose, which follows the Philosopher's arguments in *Metaphysics* 2, text. 8,[f] and 7, text. 23.[g]
5) That the final purpose indicates the agent, just as the motion indicates the mover. | And this follows from the Philosopher's definition of the "final purpose" in *Metaphysics* 2, text. 9,[h] as Averroes explicates in his *Treatise on the Substance of the Celestial Sphere*, ch. 2.[i]
6) That whatever happens without intention or knowledge is said to happen "by chance," as the Philosopher explains in *Physics* 2, text. 51.[j]
7) That anything that is eternal does not have an agent [i.e., an efficient cause], as Averroes explicates in *On the Heavens* 4, text. 1.
8) That whatever is observed in many things was not made by chance, as the Philosopher explains in *On the Heavens* 2, text. 45,[k] and *Physics* 2, text. 48.[l]
9) That there is no time, no space, no plenum, and no vacuum beyond the heavens, as the Philosopher explains in *On the Heavens* 1, text. 100.[m]
10) That there is no sixth body besides the four elements and the celestial bodies, as the Philosopher explains in *On the Heavens* 1, text. 23.[n]

---

[a] Metaphysicorum] b[corr]; Physicorum b; ובספר מה שאחר a.   [b] IV] emend. Copp.; IX b; IV L.   [c] pro ut habetur *De Celo* I t.c.] b[corr]; om. b.   [d] 23] emend. Copp.; om. b; כ״ג a.

[a] *Metaph.* 2.2.994b.   [b] *Metaph.* 9.3.1047a.   [c] See Introduction p. 9–10.   [d] Cf. *Metaph.* 9.3.1048a.   [e] Cf. *An. post.* 2.95a.   [f] *Metaph.* 2.2.994b.   [g] *Metaph.* 7.9.1032b.   [h] *Metaph.* 2.2.994b.   [i] Cf. Averroes, *De substantia orbis: Critical Edition of the Hebrew Text with English Translation and Commentary*, trans. Arthur Hyman (Cambridge, MA: Medieval Academy of America; Jerusalem: Israel Academy of Sciences and Humanities, 1986), 84–85.   [j] *Phys.* 2.5.197a.   [k] *Cael.* 2.8.289b.   [l] *Phys.* 2.4.196b.   [m] *Cael.* 1.9.279a.   [n] *Cael.* 1.3.270b.

11) That prime matter was never devoid of form, and the Philosopher explains this in *On Generation and Corruption* 2, text. 6,[a] and it is proved by Averroes in *On the Heavens* 3, text. 29.[b]

12) That no corruptible thing is eternal, and this is proved by Aristotle in *On the Heavens* 1, text. 124.[c]

13) That every single part of an element is in accordance with the whole of it in name and definition, and Aristotle and Averroes explain this in *On the Heavens* 1, text. 19.[d]

14) That there is no part of an element that is incorruptible, and Aristotle explains this in *On the Heavens* 3, text. 52.[e]

15) That none of the elements will ever be completely corrupted, and Averroes explains this in his Commentary on *On Generation and Corruption* 2, text. 37.[f]

16) That it is impossible for any existent to be eternal if there is something that is prior [to it] in time, still less so if it adds to its definition. And this is self-evident, for when a thing comes to be [that is] prior to it in time, there is a compulsive necessity that it did not exist at that time. And if this is so, it is not eternal, as is self-evident from the definition of "eternal," and Aristotle explains this in *On the Heavens* 1, text. 121[g] and 124.[h]

17) That if there were two eternal existents, it would be false [to say] that one preceded the other in time, and this is explained by the previous proposition, because if it was true that one preceded the other in time, then the second one could not be eternal.

18) That it is incongruous that an existent that is essentially one may exist in potentiality and in actuality at one and the same time, insofar as it is essentially one, and this is proved by Averroes in [his Commentary on] *On the Heavens* 3, text. 19. And this is necessary due to the second proposition, which is mentioned above.

19) That every existent that acts without a material instrument is necessarily separate from [and] unmixed with matter, and the Philosopher explains this in *On the Soul* 3, text. 6.[i]

20) That an individual number does not apply to abstract things that are completely equal, and this becomes clear from Aristotle's proof in *Metaphysics* 1, text. 40,[j] and from proofs given by Averroes and al-Ġazālī in *The Incoherence of the Incoherence* 5, second investigation.[k]

---

[a] *Gen. corr.* 2.1.329a. [b] Cf. *Cael.* 3.2.302a. [c] *Cael.* 1.12.282b. [d] *Cael.* 1.3.269b. [e] *Cael.* 3.6.305a. [f] Cf. *Gen. corr.* 2.6.333a. [g] *Cael.* 1.12.282a. [h] *Cael.* 1.12.282b. [i] *De an.* 3.4.429a24–29. [j] *Metaph.* 1.9.992a. [k] Cf. Averroes, *The Incoherence of the Incoherence*, ed. Simon van den Bergh, reprint ed. (Cambridge: E.J.W. Gibb Memorial Trust, 1987), 174–175.

י״א שההחמר הראשון לא היה בשום זמן מופשט מכל צורה. וזה באר הפילוסוף בספר ההויה וההפסד מאמר ב׳ פרק ו׳ והתבאר במופת אבן רשד בספר השמים מאמר ג׳ פרק כ״ט.

י״ב שאין שום דבר נפסד קדמון. וזה התבאר במופת אריסטוטלו בספר השמים והעולם מאמר א׳ פרק קכ״ד.

י״ג שכל אחד מחלקי היסוד מסכים עם הכל שלו בשם ובגדר וזה בארו ארסטוטלוס ואבן רשד בספר השמים מאמר א׳ פרק י״ט.

י״ד שאין שום חלק יסוד שיהיה בלתי נפסד. וזה בארו ארסטוטלו בספר השמים מאמר ג׳ פרק נ״ב.

ט״ו שמעולם לא נפסד אחד מהיסודות בכללו. וזה באר אבן רשד בביאור ספר ההויה וההפסד מאמר שני פרק ל״ז.

ט״ז[a] שכל נמצא שימצא דבר קודם לו בזמן כל שכן שיכנס בגדרו, הוא מן הנמנע שיהיה קדמון. וזה מבואר בעצמו כי בהמצא דבר קודם לו בזמן התתחייב בהכרח שבאיזה זמן לא היה נמצא ואם כן אינו קדמון כמו שהוא מבואר בעצמו מגדר הקדמון ובאר זה ארסטו׳ בספר השמים והעולם מאמר א׳ פרק קכ״א ופרק קכ״ד.

י״ז שאם היו ב׳ נמצאים קדמונים הוא מן השקר שקדם אחד לחברו בזמן. וזה מבואר מן ההנחה הקודמת שאם זה היה אמת שקדם אחד לחברו בזמן הנה אין השני קדמון.

י״ח שהוא מן הנמנע שיהיה נמצא אחד בעצמו בכח ובפעל בזמן אחד כפי יחס אחד בעצמו וזה התבאר במופת אבן רשד בספר השמים והעולם מאמר ג׳ פרק י״ט והתחייב מההנחה השנייה[b] הנזכרת לעיל.

י״ט שכל נמצא שיפעל בלתי כלי חמרי הוא בהכרח נפרד בלתי מעורב עם חומר וזה באר הפילוסוף בספר הנפש מאמר ג׳ פרק ו׳.

כ׳ שלא יפול מספר אישיי על נבדלים דומים לגמרי וזה יתבאר במופת אריסטו׳ בספר מה שאחר מאמר א׳ פרק מ׳ ובמופת אבן רשד ואלגזול בספר הפלת ההפלה מאמר ה׳ חקירה[c] ב׳.

---

[a] י״ו] a. [b] השנייה] השנית coni. Dunk.; a. [c] חקירה] חקירת coni. Dunk.; a.

11. Materia prima nunquam habuit esse denudata a forma.
    Hoc autem habetur a Phylosopho in lib. *De Generatione* II, t.c. 6, et ratione et auctoritate Aven R. in lib. *De Celo* III, t.c. 29.^a
12. Nullum corruptibile habuit esse ab eterno.
    Hoc autem habetur ratione et auctoritate Phylosophi in lib. *De Celo* I, t.c. 124.
13. Cuiuslibet elementi partes conveniunt cum suo toto nomine et diffinitione.
    Hoc autem habetur a Phylosopho et Aven R. in lib. De Celo primi t.c. 19.^b
14. Nulla elementorum pars est incorruptibilis.
    Hoc autem habetur a Phylosopho in lib. *De Celo* III, t.c. 52.
15. Nullum elementorum habuit esse secundum totum corruptum.
    Hoc autem habetur ab Aven R. in lib. *De Generatione* II, t.c. 37.
16. Omne illud ad quod datur quid tempore prius non habuit esse ab eterno.
    Hoc autem per se patet quia ut sic habuit quandoque non esse, et sic non ab eterno habuit esse. Et habetur a Phylosopho in lib. *De Celo* I, t.c. 121 et t.c. 124.
17. Datis pluribus que habuissent esse ab eterno horum nullum habuit esse secundum tempus reliquo prius, et per consequens habuerunt omnia simul tempore esse.
    Hoc autem necessario sequitur ad propositionem precedentem quia si quandoque habuisset horum alterum tantum esse, sequeretur ut reliquum tunc habuisset non esse, et per consequens non habuisset esse ab eterno.
18. Non contingit quid idem simul tempore esse actu et potentia secundum idem.
    Hoc autem habetur ratione et auctoritate Aven R. in comento lib. *De Celo* III, t.c. 19 et sequitur ad secundam propositionem superius positam.
19. Quidquid operatur sine materiali instrumento est necessario quid abstractum sive materie immixtum.
    Hoc autem habetur a Phylosopho in lib. *De Anima* III, t.c. 6.^c
20. Non datur individualis numerus abstractorum omnino equalium sive similium.
    Hoc autem habetur a Phylosopho rationibus^d et auctoritate eiusdem *Metaphysicorum* primi t.c. 40 et Aven R. et Algazelis eiusque ratione in lib. *Destructio Destructionum*, disputatione quinta, dubio 2.

---

^a 29] emend. Copp.; 24 b; 29 L.   ^b 19] emend. Copp.; 14 b; 19 L.   ^c 6] emend. Copp.; 1 b; 6 L.   ^d rationibus] coni. Copp.; rationibus.5. b.

11) That prime matter is never devoid of form, as the Philosopher explains in *On Generation and Corruption* 2, text. 6,[a] and according to the argument and authority of Averroes in *On the Heavens* 3, text. 29.[b]
12) That no corruptible thing is eternal, according to the argument and authority of the Philosopher in *On the Heavens* 1, text. 124.[c]
13) That every single part of a given element is in accordance with the whole of it in name and definition, as the Philosopher and Averroes explain in *On the Heavens* 1, text. 19.[d]
14) That no part of the elements is incorruptible, as the Philosopher explains in *On the Heavens* 3, text. 52.[e]
15) That nothing of the elements will ever be completely corrupted, as Averroes explicates in *On Generation and Corruption* 2, text. 37.[f]
16) That every existent to which something is prior in time is not eternal. And this is evident because if at some point in time it was so, that it did not exist, it therefore would not exist eternally, as the Philosopher explains in *On the Heavens* 1, text. 121[g] and text. 124.[h]
17) That if there were more eternal existents, none of them would precede the other in time, and consequently, they would exist at the same time. And this necessarily follows from the previous proposition, because if at some point in time only one of them existed, then the second one would not exist, and consequently would not be eternal.
18) That it is impossible that an existent may exist in potentiality and in actuality at one and at the same time, according to the argument and authority of Averroes in his Commentary on *On the Heavens* 3, text. 19, and following the second proposition, which is mentioned above.
19) That whatever acts without a material instrument is necessarily separate, or in other words, unmixed with matter, as the Philosopher explains in *On the Soul* 3, text.6.[i]
20) That an individual number is not applicable to abstract things that are completely equal or similar, as the Philosopher explains in *Metaphysics* 1, text. 40,[j] and Averroes and al-Ġazālī explicate in *The Incoherence of the Incoherence* 5, second doubt.[k]

---

[a] *Gen. corr.* 2.1.329a.   [b] Cf. *Cael.* 3.2.302a.   [c] *Cael.* 1.12.282b.   [d] *Cael.* 1.3.269b.   [e] *Cael.* 3.6.305a.   [f] Cf. *Gen. corr.* 2.6.333a.   [g] *Cael.* 1.12.282a.   [h] *Cael.* 1.12.282b.   [i] *De an.* 3.4.429a24–29.   [j] *Metaph.* 1.9.992a.   [k] Cf. Averroes, *The Incoherence of the Incoherence*, ed. Simon van den Bergh, reprint ed. (Cambridge: E.J.W. Gibb Memorial Trust, 1987), 174–175.

21) That the term "knowledge" in "knowledge of God"—may He be praised—and in "human knowledge" may only be said by equivocation, and Averroes explains this in [his Commentary on] *Metaphysics* 12, text. 51,[a] and in *The Incoherence of the Incoherence* 12, second investigation.[b]

22) That "will" means when an agent selects a thing by his own authority, but also knows that it is possible for him to avoid it, and the Philosopher explains this in [*Nicomachean*] *Ethics* 5, text. 13.[c]

23) That locomotion is prior in time to all kinds of movement, and the Philosopher explains this in *Physics* 8, text. 57.[d]

24) That there is necessarily a time between two indivisible instants, and the Philosopher explains this in *Physics* 6, text. 26.[e]

25) That an indivisible instant that is the beginning of future time is itself no part of time, and the Philosopher explains this in *Physics* 6, text. 24.[f]

26) That it is incongruous that any existent may have an infinite number of causes and therefore it follows that one must arrive at a first, uncaused cause. The Philosopher explains this in *Metaphysics* 2, text. 5,[g] and Averroes—quoting Avicenna—in *The Incoherence of the Incoherence* 4, sixth investigation.[h]

27) That there is no material form except in a matter that is designated for it, and this is proved by Averroes in his Commentary on *Physics* 8, text. 46.

---

[a] *Metaph.* 12.8.1074b.   [b] Cf. *Incoherence* 279–281.   [c] *Eth. nic.* 5.8.1135a.
[d] *Phys.* 8.7.260b–261a.   [e] *Phys.* 6.3.234a.   [f] *Phys.* 6.3.233b–234a.
[g] *Metaph.* 2.2.994b.   [h] Cf. *Incoherence* 165–166.

כ״א ששם ה‹ידיעה› יאמר על ‹ידיעת ה׳› יתברך, ועל ‹הידיעה האנושית› בשיתוף השם בלבד וזה ביאר אבן רשד בספר מה שאחר מאמר י״ב פרק נ״א ובספר הפלת ההפלה מאמר י״ב חקירה[a] ב׳.

כ״ב שה‹רצון› הוא כאשר יהיה הפועל ברשות עצמו ויבחר דבר עם שידע שיוכל להמנע ממנו וזה באר הפילוסוף בספר המדות מאמר ה׳ פרק י״ג.[b]

כ״ג שהתנועה המקומית היא קודמת בזמן לכל מיני התנועות וזה ביאר הפילוסוף בספר השמע מאמר ח׳ פרק נ״ז.

כ״ד שבין כל שני רגעים בלתי מתחלקים יפול בהכרח זמן וזה ביאר הפילוסוף בספר השמע מאמר ו׳ פרק כ״ו.

כ״ה שהרגע הבלתי מתחלק הוא ראשית לזמן עתיד ואינו חלק זמן וזה ביאר הפילוסוף בספר השמע מאמר ו׳ פרק כ״ד.

כ״ו שמן הנמנע הוא שימצאו סבות לאיזה נמצא על מספר בלתי בעל תכלית ומזה יתחייב להגיע אל סבה ראשונה בלתי מסובבת וזה באר הפילוסוף בספר מה שאחר[c] מאמר ב׳ פרק ה׳ ואבן רשד ובשם אבן סיני בספר הפלת ההפלה מאמר ד׳ חקירה[d] ו׳.

כ״ז שלא תמצא צורה חמרית זולתי בחמר מיוחד אליה. וזה התבאר במופת אבן רשד בביאור ספר השמע מאמר ח׳ פרק מ״ו.

---

[a] חקירה] coni. Dunk.; חקירת a.   [b] י״ג] emend. Dunk.; י״ב a; 13 b.
[c] שאחר] coni. Dunk.; שאמ׳ a.   [d] חקירה] coni. Dunk.; חקירת a.

21. Equivoce tantum dicitur scientia de divina et humana cognitione.
Hoc autem habetur ab Aven R. *Metaphysicorum* XII, t.c. 51 et in lib. *D[estructio] D[estructionum]*, disputatione XII, dubio 2.
22. Voluntas est illa qua quis in sua potestate existens aliquid eligit sciens se posse aliter facere.
Hoc autem habetur a Phylosopho *Ethicorum* V, t.c. 13.
23. Localis motio est ceteris motibus tempore prior.
Hoc autem habetur a phylosopho *Physicorum* VIII, t.c. 57.
24. Inter quelibet duo instantia datur necessario tempus.
Hoc autem habetur a Phylosopho *Physicorum* VI, t.c. 26.
25. Instans est futuri temporis principium cuius nulla est pars.
Hoc autem habetur a Phylosopho *Physicorum* VI, t.c. 24.[a]
26. Impossibile est in causis procedere ad infinitum, quare necesse est devenire ad quoddam primum nullo pacto causatum.
Hoc autem habetur a Phylosopho *Metaphysicorum* II, t.c. 5 et ab Aven R. et Avicene auctoritate in lib. *Destructio Destructionum*, disputatione IV, dubio 6.
27. Nulla materialis forma datur esse nisi in materia sibi propria.
Hoc autem habetur ratione et auctoritate Aven R. in comento *Physicorum* VIII, t.c. 46.

21) That the term "knowledge" is only said of divine knowledge and human knowledge by equivocation, as Averroes explicates in *Metaphysics* 12, text. 51,[a] and *The Incoherence of the Incoherence* 12, second doubt.[b]
22) That the will is something by which an agent chooses a thing by his own authority, but also knows that it is possible for him to do something else, as the Philosopher explains in *Nicomachean Ethics* 5, text. 13.[c]
23) That locomotion is prior in time to all kinds of movement, as the Philosopher explains in *Physics* 8, text. 57.[d]
24) That between two instants, there is necessarily a [span of] time, as the Philosopher explains in *Physics* 6, text. 26.[e]
25) That the instant that is the beginning of future time is itself no part of time, as the Philosopher explains in *Physics* 6, text. 24.[f]
26) That it is impossible to proceed to an infinite number of causes, and therefore, it has to be [the case] that we will [ultimately] arrive at a first, uncaused cause, as the Philosopher explains in *Metaphysics* 2, text. 5,[g] and Averroes and Avicenna explicate in *The Incoherence of the Incoherence* 4, sixth doubt.[h]
27) That there is no material form except in a matter that is designated for it, according to the argument and authority of Averroes in his *Commentary on Physics* 8, text. 46.[i]

[a] 24] emend. COPP.; 29 b; 24 L.

[a] *Metaph.* 12.8.1074b. [b] Cf. *Incoherence* 279–281. [c] *Eth. nic.* 5.8.1135b. [d] *Phys.* 8.7.260b–261a. [e] *Phys.* 6.3.234a. [f] *Phys.* 6.3.234a. [g] *Metaph.* 2.2.994b. [h] Cf. *Incoherence* 165–166. [i] Cf. *Phys.* 8.6.258b.

§1 And after the introduction of the aforementioned propositions, it is appropriate that we inquire into the fundamental questions for us, as we mentioned above.

8r First:
Whether the movement of generation and corruption is [pre]eternal.

It seems to be that it is [pre]eternal.

§1.1.1 And this is so because we say that the elements are [pre]eternal, as Averroes derives it, as [will be] explained to us below. The movement of generation and corruption necessarily exists because of the existence of the elements. If so, it follows that the movement of generation and corruption is [pre]eternal. The aforementioned consequence is self-evident, and the first [antecedent] premise is proved by Averroes's words in the Commentary on the Philosopher's words in *Metaphysics* 8, text. 12:[a] "And it is appropriate to say that there are immaterial existents." And Averroes explains [Aristotle's] words and says that it was the Philosopher's intention [to say] "that the elements are eternal in respect of the whole and [that they are] generable and corruptible things in respect of the part." And he continues: "Matter only exists in generable and corruptible bodies. But the bodies that are eternal because they have no potentiality for corruption have—if so—no matter, but their substrate is a thing that exists forever in actuality."

§1.1.2 The second [antecedent] premise, which we laid down when we said that the movement of generation and corruption necessarily exists because of the existence of the elements, becomes clear from Aristotle's proof in *On Generation and Corruption* 2, text. 24:[b] "Generation is [a change] into contraries and out of contraries, and all the elements have a mutual contrariety, because their differences are contrary." And Averroes explains these words and says that "every single one of the elements is contrary to every single other one of them. And therefore, it follows that every one of them is generated out of all of the rest of them."

§1.2 Second, it becomes clear that the movement of generation and corruption is eternal from Averroes's proof in his Commentary on *On Generation and Corruption* 2, text. 55,[c] where he says: "It already became clear in *Physics* that locomotion is continuous and eternal. It becomes clear—if so—that the movement of generation and corruption

---

[a] *Metaph.* 8.6.1045a.   [b] *Gen. corr.* 2.4.331a6.   [c] Cf. *Gen. corr.* 2.10.336b.

8r §1 **ואחר** הקדמת ההנחות הנזכרות ראוי שנחקור בחקירות העקריות אצלנו כנזכר לעיל:

8r **ראשונה אם תנועת ההויה וההפסד קדמונית**

נראה שהיא אמנם קדמונית.

§1.1.1 וזה כי באמרנו שהיסודות קדמונים כמו שגזר אבן רשד כמבואר לפנינו ובהמצא היסודות תמצא בהכרח תנועת ההויה וההפסד אם כן יתחייב שתנועת ההויה וההפסד היא קדמונית. הנה חיוב התולדה הנזכרת הוא מבואר בעצמו. וההקדמה הראשונה תתבאר מדברי אבן רשד בביאור דברי הפילוסוף בספר מה שאחר מאמר ח׳ פרק י״ב באמרו שם: «וראוי לומר שיש נמצאות בלתי חומר.» ודבריו אלה אבן רשד ביאר ואמר שכוונת הפילוסוף היא: «שהיסודות קדמונים כפי הכל עם היותם הווים ונפסדים כפי החלק.» והוסיף ואמר כי «אמנם החומר לא ימצא זולתי בגרמים ההווים ונפסדים אבל הגרמים שהם קדמונים מאחר שאין בהם כוחיות על ההפסד אם כן אין להם חומר אבל הנושא שלהם הוא דבר נמצא לעולם בפעל.»

§1.1.2 אמנם ההקדמה השנית שהקדמנו באמרנו שבהמצא היסודות ימצא בהכרח תנועת ההויה וההפסד הנה התבאר במופת ארסטו׳ בספר ההויה וההפסד מאמר ב׳ פרק כ״ד באמרו: «אמנם ההויה תמצא בהפכים מהפכים להם ובכל היסודות נמצא[a] הפכיות קצתם לקצתם כי ההבדלים שלהם הם הפכיים.» ודבריו אלה באר אבן רשד ואמר כי «אמנם כל אחד מהיסודות הפכי לכל אחד מהם ומזה יתחייב שכל אחד מהם יתהוה מכל אחד מהם.»

§1.2 **שנית** יתבאר שתנועת ההויה וההפסד קדמונית בראית אבן רשד בביאורו לספר ההויה וההפסד מאמר ב׳ פרק נ״ה באמרו: «שבהיות שכבר התבאר בספר השמע שהתנועה המקומית היא מתמדת וקדמונית יתבאר אם כן שתנועת ההויה וההפסד היא

---

[a] נמצאו] emend. Dunk.; נמצא a; habent b.

1. DE GENERATIONE

12 **§ 1** Procedentes ergo ad præfatas questiones scrutandas et pro viribus declarandas.

Primo quidem dubitatur
Utrum generationis et corruptionis motus habuisset esse ab eterno;

et videtur quod sic.

§ 1.1.1 Primo scilicet ratione sic arguendo: elementa habuerunt esse ab eterno. Sed datis elementis datur necessario motus generationis et corruptionis, ergo motus generationis et corruptionis habuit esse ab eterno. Consequentia patet et antecedens probatur auctoritate Aven R. de mente Phylosophi *Metaphysicorum* VIII,[a] t.c. 12 ubi Phylosophus dicit: «Et rectum est ut quedam non habeant materiam» et ibidem Aven R. exponens ait: «Quod intelligit de elementis que sunt eterna secundum totum, quamvis sint generabilia et corruptibilia secundum partem» ubi subdit paulo post dicens: «Materia, enim, secundum veritatem cuius esse est in potentia non invenitur nisi in substantijs generabilibus et corruptibilibus. Substantie, enim, eterne quia in eis non est potentia ad corruptionem non est in eis materia, sed materia eorum est aliquid existens in actu.»

§ 1.1.2 Secunda vero antecedentis pars qua scilicet dicitur quod datis elementis datur necessario generatio et corruptio probatur ratione et auctoritate Phylosophi in lib. *De Generatione* II, t.c. 24 ubi dicit: «Generatio enim ex contrarijs in contraria. Elementa autem omnia habent contrarietatem ad invicem, quia differentie sunt contrarie» ubi Aven R. exponens ait: «Cum quodlibet sit contrarium cuilibet necesse est ut omne generetur ex omni.»

§ 1.2 Secundo arguitur ratione et auctoritate Phylosophi et Aven R. in lib. *De Generatione* II, t.c. 55 ubi Aven R. apertius docens ait: «Cum in naturalibus libris declaratum sit quod motus localis sit continuus et eternus, patet quod generatio sit continua et eterna quoniam motus generat

§ 1 Hereafter, the aforementioned disputed questions that 12 are to be examined and evaluated.

First,
it may be inquired whether the movement of
generation and corruption is [pre]eternal.

And it seems to be so [i.e., it is [pre]eternal].

§ 1.1.1 First, I would argue that the elements are [pre]eternal. Given these elements, the movement of generation and corruption necessarily exists, and thus the movement of generation and corruption is [pre]eternal. The consequence is evident, and the antecedent is proved by Averroes in the name of the Philosopher in *Metaphysics* 8, text. 12,[a] where the Philosopher states: "And it is appropriate to say that they have no matter," and Averroes explains: "Because he [Aristotle] distinguishes between elements that are eternal according to the whole, but generable and corruptible according to the part." And he continues: "Matter, according to the truth, which exists in potency, exists only in generable and corruptible substances. Substances, which are eternal according to the truth, since in them there is no potentiality for corruption, do not have matter, but their matter [i.e., substrate] exists in actuality."

§ 1.1.2 The second part of the antecedent in which we said, given these elements, that the movement of generation and corruption necessarily exists, [becomes clear] according to the argument and authority of the Philosopher explicated in *On Generation and Corruption* 2, text. 24:[b] "Generation is a change into contraries and out of contraries, and the elements all involve a contrariety in their mutual relations because their differences [distinctive qualities] are contrary." And Averroes explains: "Since every single one of them [the elements] is contrary to another one of them, it necessarily follows that everything would be generated out of everything."

§ 1.2 Second, I would argue according to the argument and authority of the Philosopher and Averroes in *On Generation and Corruption* 2, text. 55,[c] where Averroes states: "As has been said in the other books about nature [i.e., *Physics*], locomotion is continuous and eternal. It becomes clear that [the movement of] generation [and corruption]

---

[a] VIII] emend. COPP.; quinti b; VIII L.

[a] *Metaph.* 8.6.1045a.   [b] *Gen. corr.* 2.4.331a6.   [c] Cf. *Gen. corr.* 2.10.336b.

is continuous and eternal," for locomotion will happen through the agent's approximation to the affected object. And it is entirely correct that locomotion is prior to every change, as became clear. And it is also already clear that the being moved by this locomotion exists in actuality and that what is generated from its potentiality does not exist in actuality. And the thing existing in actuality is necessarily the cause of what does not yet exist, and a thing that is a continuous existent is the cause of a thing that is not a continuous existent.

§ 1.3 Third, it becomes clear from Aristotle's proof that the movement of generation and corruption is eternal, which Averroes explains in his Commentary on *On Generation and Corruption* 2, text. 59:[a] "And this is what we said: that the movement of generation and corruption | is continuous, which does not only follow because of the material and the efficient cause, but also because of the final cause. And this is so because it already became clear to us that nature is continuously moving to the nobler [being], according to what is possible for every single [being] and according to what every single [being] can receive, and because being is better [i.e., nobler] than non-being, and that which is true is better [i.e., nobler] than that which is untrue, and individual existence is better [i.e., nobler] than existence in species. However, it is impossible that any of these existents will be absolutely noble, since they are remote from the first cause, which possesses essence and nobility, and this is God—may He be praised—who completes the deficiency that occurs in these existents in this way, so that the movement of generation and corruption will be continuous. And by this, a perpetual existence will be possible for these existents."

§ 1.4.1 However, the contrary of this will become clear; namely, that the movement of generation and corruption is necessarily not [pre]eternal. First, because every being to which anything is temporally prior is not [pre]eternal, and this occurs in the actualisation of generation. If it is true that the actualisation of generation is not [pre]eternal, it therefore follows that the movement of generation and corruption is also not [pre]eternal. And this is so because it is necessary that generation is actualised within a finite time. Therefore, it becomes clear that the actualisation of generation is not [pre]eternal. And therefore, it follows that there is a certain actualisation of generation that is prior to all of them, and it also follows that there is a certain movement of generation [that is] prior to all of them, and this is that movement that is prior to the act of that

---

[a] Cf. *Gen. corr.* 2.10.337a.

מתמדת וקדמונית,« כי אמנם התנועה המקומית תהוה בהקריבה הפועל אל המתפעל וזה נכון מצד מה שהתנועה המקומית קודמת לכל השתנות כאשר התבאר[a] ועם זה הנה כבר התבאר שהעצם המתנועע בזאת התנועה המקומית הוא אמנם נמצא בפעל והמתהוה מכחה הוא בלתי נמצא בפעל והדבר שהוא נמצא בפעל ראוי שיהיה סבה לבלתי נמצא ושהדבר שהוא נמצא תמיד יהיה סבה לדבר שאינו נמצא תמיד.

§ 1.3 **שלישית** יתבאר שתנועת ההויה וההפסד קדמונית בראית ארסטו' אשר באר אבן רשד בספר ההויה וההפסד מאמר ב' פרק נ"ט באמרו: »וזה שאמרנו שתנועת ההויה וההפסד היא | תמידית לא יתחייב בלבד מצד הסבה החמרית[b] והפועלת אבל יתחייב גם מצד הסבה התכליתית וזה כי כבר התבאר אצלנו שהטבע יתנועע תמיד אל היותר נכבד כפי מה שיוכל בכל אחד וכפי מה שיקבל כל אחד ואחד ובהיות שהנמצא הוא נכבד מהבלתי נמצא והאמתי הוא נכבד מהבלתי אמתי והנמצא באיש הוא נכבד מהנמצא כפי המין אף על פי שהוא נמנע שיהיה שום נמצא מאלו הנמצאים נכבד בהחלט להיותם רחוקים מן הסבה הראשונה אשר לה המציאות והמעלה והוא האל יתברך הנה מלא את החסרון הקורה לאלו הנמצאות באופן זה שתהיה תנועת ההויה וההפסד מתמדת ובזה אפשר שיהיה מציאות נצחי באלו הנמצאות.«

§ 1.4.1 **אמנם** יתבאר הפך זה רצוני לומר שתנועת ההויה וההפסד היא בהכרח בלתי קדמונית. ראשונה כי כל נמצא אשר קדם לו איזה דבר בזמן הוא בהכרח בלתי קדמון. וזה אמנם יקרה ליציאת ההויה לפועל. אם כן יציאת ההויה לפעל היא בלתי קדמונית ומזה יתחייב שתנועת ההויה וההפסד היא בלתי קדמונית גם כן וזה כי בהיות מן ההכרח שההויה תצא לפעל בזמן בעל תכלית הנה עם זה יתבאר שיציאת ההויה לפעל היא בלתי קדמונית ומזה יתחייב שהיתה איזו יציאת הויה לפעל ראשונה לכלן. יתחייב גם כן שהיתה איזו

---

[a] התמדית a; materiali b. [b] החמרית] a[corr]; התבאר] coni. Dunk.; התבאר a.

faciendo appropinquare generans generato, et hoc rectum est inquantum iste motus est primus omnium transmutationum, ut ostensum est, et etiam apparet quod illud movetur isto motu est ens, et illud quod generatur per ipsum est non ens et quod est maxime ens est causa non entis semper.»

§ 1.3 Tertio arguitur ratione et auctoritate Phylosophi et Aven R. in lib. *De | Generatione* II,[a] t.c. 59[b] ubi Phylosophus ait: «Hoc autem rationabiliter contingit etc.» ubi Aven R. exponens ait: «Et hoc quod diximus quod generatio et corruptio sint continue non tantum sequitur ex causa materiali et agente sed etiam ex causa finali quia iam visum est nobis quod natura semper movetur ad nobilius secundum illud quod potest recipere unumquodque, et quia ens est melius quam non ens, verum quam non verum, individuum quam secundum speciem, quamvis impossibile est aliquod ens in istis rebus esse simpliciter nobile propter remotionem a prima causa habente essentiam et nobilitatem, quia Deus complevit diminutionem in istis contingentem hoc modo secundum quod generatio facta est continua, quare esse potest esse perpetuum in istis rebus.»

§ 1.4.1 Ad oppositum arguitur sic. Nullum ad quod necessario habuit esse quid tempore prius contingit habuisse esse ab eterno. Genitum esse est huiusmodi. Ergo genitum esse non habuit esse ab eterno; et per consequens neque generatio in fieri habuit esse ab eterno; quia cum generatio in fieri sit motus ad generationis actum qui est genitum esse, qui actus ut prefertur non habuit esse ab eterno. Cum scilicet generatio ad quam sequitur sit necessario quid prius, generatio ergo in fieri ad quid tale necessario sequitur, habuit necessario fieri in quodam finito tempore eidem actui conpetenti, et per consequens neque generatio in fieri habuit esse ab eterno, nedum corruptio, ad quam necessario habet generationem secundum tempus prece-

is continuous and eternal, since movement is generated by the approach of the generator and the generated [the coming-to-be]. And this is correct inasmuch as this movement is prior to every change, as was just proven; also, it is clear that what is moved by this motion is being, and what is generated from it is non-being, and the supreme being is the cause of what is always non-being."

§ 1.3 Third, I would argue according to the argument and authority of the Philosopher and Averroes in *On | Generation and Corruption* 2, text. 59,[a] where the Philosopher states: "But this happens in accordance with reason, etc.," and Averroes explains: "Therefore, we say that [the movements of] generation and corruption are continuous, resulting not only from the material and the efficient cause, but also from the final cause. Because it has already become clear to us that nature always moves towards the nobler [being] according to what each individual can receive, and [this is] because existence is better than non-existence, true is better than untrue, and individual is better than species. However, it is impossible that a particular being among these existents may be absolutely noble, since they are far from the first cause, which possesses essence and nobility, and this is God, who completes the deficiency that occurs in these existents in such a way that generation will be continuous and a perpetual existence will be possible in these things."

§ 1.4.1 On the contrary it is to argue: nothing that necessarily has something temporally prior [to it] is [pre]eternal. A generated being has something temporally prior [to it] and therefore, it is not [pre]eternal. Consequently, generation in coming-to-be [the actualisation of generation] is also not [pre]eternal, because generation in coming-to-be is a movement towards the actualisation of generation, which is generated, and which exists in actuality, as previously mentioned. It is not [pre]eternal, which means that if generation is necessarily prior, generation in coming-to-be [the actualisation of generation] is necessarily produced within a finite time due to its specific act. Consequently, neither generation in coming-to-be [the actualisation of generation] nor corruption, which is necessarily preceded

---

[a] II] b[corr]; om. b. [b] 59] emend. Copp.; 19 b; 59 L.

[a] *Gen. corr.* 2.10.337a.

first generation. And by the movement of that generation, the actualisation of the first generation will occur, and this necessarily occurs within a finite time. And therefore, it follows that the movement of generation is not [pre]eternal, still less so the movement of corruption, which is necessarily preceded by the movement of generation by which the corruptible is generated. Therefore, the consequence of the [afore]mentioned syllogism, as we say that it must follow from this that the actualisation of the generation is not [pre]eternal, is self-evident, and so is its first premise. And this is so because the definition of the thing that needs to be temporally preceded by one existent is contrary to the former definition, which says that it follows that there is nothing preceding it.

§ 1.4.2 The second [antecedent] premise, in which we said that it is necessary that something is temporally prior to the actualisation of the generation, is proved by this: the actualisation of generation is necessarily temporally preceded by the movement of generation, without which no generation is actualised, because the actualisation of generation is nothing more than an activity that comes from the prior movement of generation. And therefore, it follows that the actualisation of generation is not [pre]eternal. And if an opponent were to say that the movement of generation and its actualisation of every single [act of generation] was [pre]eternal, it would therefore follow that the existence | of the movement of generation and the existence of the actualisation in prime matter common to the generated things would occur at the same time. In this way, a movement of generation in the common matter would never precede the actualisation of generation, [and] so they would be [pre]eternal. And therefore, it follows that that common matter would be both perfect and imperfect, existing both in potentiality and in actuality at the same time. This is impossible and even inconceivable. And its contrary comes from the proofs of the Philosopher, who states this in *Metaphysics* 9, text. 5,[a] as we mentioned above in the second proposition.

§ 1.5.1 Second, it becomes clear that there is no [pre]eternal movement of generation, because it follows that every activity that is performed for a purpose is necessarily temporally preceded by (1) the existence of the agent, (2) the active and passive disposition, and (3) the existence of the intention of the final purpose in the intending agent, and the movement of generation is an activity performed for a

---

[a] *Metaph.* 9.3.1047a.

1. DE GENERATIONE

dere. Consequentia autem patet qua scilicet dicitur sequi ut genitum esse non habuisset esse ab eterno. Similiter et antecedens quoad primam partem, quia diffinitio eius ad quod necessario habet esse quid tempore prius repugnat eterni diffinitioni[a] ut semper haberet esse, et per consequens nihil habuit esse eo tempore prius.

§ 1.4.2 Quo autem ad secundam partem probatur. Quia ad genitum esse habuit necessario generationem in fieri secundum tempus precedere, sine qua sic precedente non daretur genitum esse, immo genitum esse nil aliud est quam actus ad generationem sequens. Quare patet ut non ab eterno detur genitum esse. Preterea si daretur ut tam generatio quam genitum esse habuissent esse ab eterno, sequeretur ut ab eterno habuissent simul tempore esse generatio in fieri et in facto esse in universali generabilium materia. Itaque numquam habuisset generatio in fieri ad genitum in facto esse secundum tempus precedere cum scilicet ambo habuissent esse ab eterno, et per consequens habuisset ipsa totalis generabilium materia simul tempore esse actu et potentia, sub esse perfecto et imperfecto, quod est quid absurdum implicans contradictionem et penitus inopinabile; et cuius oppositum habetur rationibus et auctoritate Phylosophi *Metaphysicorum* IX, t.c. 5 prout supra in secuda propositione dictum est.

§ 1.5.1 Secundo arguitur sic. Ad quamlibet actionem ad finem factam habuit necessario tam agens quam potentia activa et passiva secundum tempus prece|dere similiter et finis in eiusdem agentis mente generatio est huiusmodi. Ergo ad generationem habuerunt omnia illa secun-

by the generation, is [pre]eternal. The consequence is evident, and we say that a generated being is not [pre]eternal. Similarly, the first part of the antecedent is evident, because the definition of the thing that needs to be preceded by one existent is contradictory to the definition of eternity, which is something that has always existed, and consequently, there is nothing preceding it.

§ 1.4.2 The second part [of the antecedent] is proved because generation in coming-to-be [the actualisation of generation] is necessarily prior to the generated being, without which no generation is actualised, because a generated being is nothing more than an activity that comes from generation. For this reason, it is clear that a generated being is not [pre]eternal. Moreover, if generation and the generated being were [pre]eternal, it would follow that generation in coming-to-be [the actualisation of generation] and completed generation would both be present at the same time in the matter of all generated things; therefore, the generation in coming-to-be [the actualisation of generation] would never precede the completed generation, so both of them would be [pre]eternal. Consequently, the matter of all generated things would be in actuality and in potentiality at the same time, perfect and imperfect. This implies a contradiction and is incongruous. The contrary of this is proven above in the second proposition, in accordance with what the Philosopher states in *Metaphysics* 9, text. 5.[a]

§ 1.5.1 Second, I would argue that every activity that is performed for a purpose is necessarily temporally preceded by the agent and [by] the active and passive disposition. Similarly, the purpose in the mind of this agent [temporally precede] and the generation is an activity performed in order to accomplish a purpose; consequently, all these

---

[a] diffinitioni] coni. COPP.; diffinitioni.5 b.

[a] *Metaph.* 9.3.1047a.

purpose. If so, then it follows that the movement of generation is temporally preceded by all these things. If so, it follows that the movement of generation is not [pre]eternal.

§1.5.2 This consequence is necessarily evident. Now, regarding the first premise, in which we said that potentiality necessarily precedes actuality in time: this became clear from proofs [given] by Aristotle in *Physics* 8, text. 4:[a] "We said: If motion is the action of a thing that is movable insofar as it is movable, then it also follows that it [i.e., motion] exists in things that have the potential to move. And this is so for every single kind of motion—even without this definition: Everyone [naturally] admits that it follows that the only thing that moves is that which is movable. And this is necessarily so in every single kind of movement. And a [comparable] example of this is that the only thing that will alter is that which is capable of altering, and only a thing that is capable of changing place will move from one position to another. If so, it follows that a thing is burnable before it is [actually] burnt, and [that it is capable of] burning before it burns."

§1.5.3 And the same becomes clear in proofs made by Aristotle in *Metaphysics* 9, text. 5,[b] *Against Garicon* [i.e., the Megarians], in which he explains that the disposition to the act necessarily precedes that act in time, and it therefore necessarily follows that the disposition to generation necessarily precedes the movement of generation in time, which is the action of that potential disposition. And in this way, we say that the agent and the purpose are necessarily temporally prior to the activity. This will become clear in this way: because the purpose is indeed the thing on account of which the agent brings a thing forth from potentiality to actuality. If so, the generator will bring forth the thing that is able to be generated from potentiality to actuality for a certain purpose, without which [the generator] would not begin that action, as is self-evident. And according to the Philosopher's words in *Metaphysics* 2, text. 8,[c] it necessarily follows that the same purpose intended at a certain time by the immediately or mediately generating agent is that which gives existence to the beginning of the activity's time. And therefore, Averroes says | in his Commentary on *Physics* 2, text. 89,[d] "the purpose of thought is the beginning of activity." And therefore, it follows that the generator and the purpose of generation are temporally prior at least to the duration of the move-

---

[a] *Phys.* 8.1.251a. [b] *Metaph.* 9.3.1047a. [c] *Metaph.* 2.2.994b.
[d] *Phys.* 2.2.200a.

שלתנועת ההויה קדמו כל אלה בזמן אם כן יתחייב שתנועת ההויה היא בלתי קדמונית.

§1.5.2 הנה חיוב התולדה הוא מבואר. אמנם ההקדמה הראשונה שאמרנו בה שהכחיות יקדם לפעלה בזמן בהכרח. הנה התבאר במופתי אריסטו׳ בספר השמע מאמר ח׳ פרק ד׳ וזה לשונו: «נאמר אם כן שהתנועה היא פעל הדבר המוכן להתנועע מצד מה שהוא מוכן להתנועע אם כן יתחייב שתהיה נמצאת בדברים אשר בהם כוחיות להתנועע. וזה בכל אחד ממיני התנועה ובלעדי הגדר הזה הכל מודים שלא יתחייב שיתנועע אלא הדבר שיוכל להתנועע וזה הוא הכרחי בכל אחד ממיני התנועה. המשל בזה שלא ישתנה אלא הדבר המוכן להשתנות ולא יתנועע ממקום למקום אלא הדבר המוכן להתנועע תנועה מקומית אם כן יתחייב שיהיה הדבר מוכן להשרף קודם שישרף. ולשריף קודם שישרוף» עד כאן לשונו.

§1.5.3 וזה בעצמו יתבאר במופתי אריסטו׳ שעשה נגד גאריקו החולק בספר מה שאחר מאמר ט׳ פרק ה׳ אשר בם באר שההכנה אל הפעל תקדם בזמן לפעל ההוא בהכרח ומזה יתחייב שההתהוות תקדם בזמן בהכרח אל תנועת ההויה אשר הוא פעל אותה ההכנה הכוחיית. וכן מה שאמרנו שהפועל והתכלית קודמים בזמן בהכרח לפעולה הנה יתבאר באופן זה כי אמנם התכלית הוא הדבר אשר בגללו יוציא הפועל את הדבר מן הכח אל הפעל אם כן כשהמהווה מוציא הדבר המוכן להתהוות מן הכח אל הפעל לתכלית מה אשר בלעדיו לא היה מתחיל אותה הפעולה כמו שהוא מבואר בעצמו. ומדברי הפילוסוף בספר מה שאחר מאמר ב׳ פרק ח׳ יתחייב בהכרח שיהיה אותו התכלית מכוון בעת מה אצל המהווה הפועל באמצעי או בלתי אמצעי הנותן מציאות לראשית זמן הפעלה. ולזה אמר אבן רשד | בביאור ספר השמע מאמר ב׳ פרק פ״ט:[a] «שתכלית המחשבה היא[b] ראשית הפעלה.» ומזה יתחייב שהמהווה ותכלית ההויה יקדמו

---

[a] פ״ט] a^{corr}; כ״ט a; 59 b; 89 L. [b] היא] coni. Dunk.; הוא a.

dum tempus precedere; et per consequens ipsa generatio non habuit esse ab eterno, ut supra.

§ 1.5.2 Consequentia patet et antecedens probatur, et primo quoad primam partem qua dicitur quod potentia habet ad actionem secundum tempus precedere rationibus et auctoritate[a] Phylosophi *Physicorum* VIII, t.c. 4 ubi dicit: «Dicamus igitur quod motus est actus eius quod inatum est moveri secundum quod inatum est moveri, necesse est igitur illa esse in quorum potentia est moveri unoquoque motuum et sine hac diffinitione omnes homines concedunt quod non est necesse moveri nisi illud quod post moveri; et hoc necesse est in unoquoque motuum verbi gratia quod non alteratur nisi illud quod natum est alterari nec transfertur nisi illud quod natum est transferri in loco, necesse igitur est quod res sit nata comburi antequam comburatur, et comburere antequam comburat ergo.»

§ 1.5.3 Et idem patet rationibus et auctoritate Phylosophi Contra Gariconem *Metaphysicorum* IX, t.c. 5 quibus aperte demonstrat. Quod habet necessario potentiam ad suum actum secundum tempus precedere, quare habuit generabilitas ad generationem secundum tempus precedere. Cum generatio[b] sit eiusdem generabilitatis actus. Similiter illud quod dicitur de agente et fine probatur per eiusdem finis diffinitionem, qui finis nil aliud esse videtur quam illud intentum gratia cuius agens educit de potentia ad actum. Cum ergo generans educat generabile de potentia ad actum per intento fine sine quo non incepisset suam actionem, prout per se patet. Et habetur a Phylosopho *Methaphysicorum* II, t.c. 8 habuit ergo ipse finis in mente eiusdem generantis mediati vel non mediati actu esse in aliquot instanti, ad hoc ut daretur primum actionis instans. Quare Aven R. in lib. *Physicorum* II, t.c. 89[c] ait: «Quod finis in cogitatione est principum operationis.» Et per consequens tam generans quam finis intentio habent tempore

things [i.e., the agent, the active and passive potency, and the goal in the agent's mind] temporally precede the movement of generation, and consequently, the movement of generation is not [pre]eternal, as mentioned above.

§ 1.5.2 The consequence is evident, and the antecedent is proved, according to the first part, in which we said that "potentiality temporally precedes necessarily actuality," as the Philosopher explicates in *Physics* 8, text. 4,[a] where he states: "Motion, we say, is the action of the movable insofar as it is movable. Each kind of motion, therefore, necessarily involves the presence of the things that have the potential to move. In fact, even apart from the definition of motion, everyone would admit that in each kind of motion it is that which is capable of that motion that is in motion: thus, it is that which is capable of alteration that is altered, and that which is capable of local change that is in locomotion: and so there must be something capable of being burned before there can be a process of being burned, and something capable of burning before there can be a process of burning."

§ 1.5.3 The same becomes clear as the Philosopher explicates in *Metaphysics* 9, text. 5, *Against Garicon*,[b] in which he proves that potentiality temporally precedes its actuality, as the disposition for generation precedes the movement of generation, because the movement of generation is the action of the disposition for generation. Similarly, what we said about the agent and the purpose is proved according to the definition of "purpose," because the purpose is nothing other than the intention by which the agent brings [something] forth from potentiality to actuality, and therefore, the generator will bring forth a generable from potentiality to actuality according to the intention of the final purpose, without which [the generator] cannot begin his activity. As the Philosopher explicates in *Metaphysics* 2, text. 8,[c] the purpose in the mind of its generator acts instantaneously, mediately or immediately, and this gives existence to the first instant of the activity. Therefore, Averroes explains that in *Physics* 2, text. 89,[d] "the purpose in the reasoning is the beginning of the activity." Consequently, the generator and the intended ultimate end are temporally prior at least to the duration of the move-

---

[a] rationibus et auctoritate] coni. Copp.; rationibus.5.7 aucte b.   [b] cum generatio] coni. Copp.; cum.5.generatio b.   [c] 89] emend. Copp.; 59 b; 89 L.

[a] *Phys.* 8.1.252a.   [b] *Metaph.* 9.3.1047a.   [c] *Metaph.* 2.2.994b.   [d] *Phys.* 2.2.200a.

ment of generation, which necessarily occurs in a time that consists of many instants, as the Philosopher explains in *Physics* 6, text. 26.[a]

§ 1.5.4 What we said—that the purpose is an intended thing for whose sake the agent begins the activity—is self-evident and [is derived] from Aristotle's words in *Metaphysics* 2, text. 8:[b] "An agent will not begin a certain activity if he does not intend a certain purpose [by it]." And he explained the same in ibid. [2], text. 9:[c] "The purpose is the intended end." And in [his Commentary on] the same [passage], Averroes explains: "The purpose is the end intended by the activities. Without it, the activity would be in vain."

§ 1.5.5 And apart from these [words], it becomes clear that the agent is temporally prior to his activity from Averroes's words in his Commentary on *Metaphysics* 9, text. 13: "The agent of the thing exists prior to his activity, because the activity would not exist prior to the matter or to the agent, but the agent is temporally prior to the activity." And Averroes continues after that, ibid.: "Every generated thing is moved by a mover prior to it." And he explains the same thing in the *Treatise on the Substance of the Celestial Sphere*, of which he is undoubtedly the author as he stated the same thing in his Commentary on *On the Heavens* 2, text. 8. These are his words in the second chapter of the aforementioned *Treatise on the Substance of the Celestial Sphere*: "There are two kinds of agents. The first is the agent which is prior to his activity in time, and every agent and activity below the sphere of this world is of this kind. And the second is the agent that is prior to [its] activity [both] naturally and temporally, and the sphere is of this kind."[d]

§ 1.5.6 Averroes explains two things from which it follows that the movement of generation is not [pre]eternal. First, he says that every agent below the sphere is temporally prior to his activity, and the generator who enacted the generables and corruptibles and who enacted the movement towards its [act of] generation is of this kind. If so, he will be temporally prior to the movement of generation. Therefore, it follows that the movement of generation is not [pre]eternal.

§ 1.5.7 Second, he says that the sphere is temporally and naturally prior to its activities. The movement of generation coincides with the number of its activities, because it does not happen without the movement of the sphere, as sense perception proves and as becomes clear from the

---

[a]*Phys.* 6.3.234a. [b]*Metaph.* 2.2.994b. [c]*Metaph.* 2.2.994b. [d]Cf. *Sub. orb.* 85–86.

precedere saltem ad generationis processum; in quo plura dantur instantia inter que necessario datur tempus prout habetur a Phylosopho *Physicorum* VI, t.c. 26.

§ 1.5.4 Cum[a] finis habeat esse in mente agentis saltem in eiusdem actionis principio. Quare Phylosophus *Metaphysicorum*[b] II, t.c. 8 ait: «Nihil incepit agere aliquam actionem quemcumque non intendens finem» et idem ibidem, t.c. 9 ait: «Ultimum enim est finis quem intendunt actiones, si non tunc actio esset ociosa.»

§ 1.5.5 Preterea de agente ut habeat secundum tempus precedere ad actionis actum habetur ab Aven R. *Metaphysicorum* IX, t.c. 13[c] ubi dicit: «Et agens aliquid ante actum secundum tempus, actum antecedentem non est ante materiam secundum tempus neque ante agens sed agens est ante actum secundum tempus» subdit paulo post dicens: «Omne, enim, quod generatur movetur a motore in actu ante ipsum» et idem habetur ab eodem in *Tractatu de Substantia Orbis*, quem testatur edidisse in commento lib. *De Celo* II, t.c. 13[d] in quo tractatu cap. 2 aperte dicit: «Sed in genere agentium quoddam est prius tempore, actu, et est omne quod fit in sphera huius mundi et istius | agentis et acti quoddam est prius naturaliter et tempore et est orbis etc.»

§ 1.5.6 Quibus duo docere videtur adque necessario sequitur ut generationes non habuissent esse ab eterno. Primo scilicet cum dicit quod omnes agentes in sphera huius mundi existentes sunt tempore priores suo actu de quorum scilicet numero patet ut sint generantes, qui ut sic habuerunt esse generationibus tempore priores, et per consequens generationes non habuerunt esse ab eterno.

§ 1.5.7 Secundo cum dicit qui orbis est suis actionibus et natura et tempore prior, de cuius actionum numero sunt generationes ad quas suis motibus necessario concurrere videtur, prout sensu percipitur, et habetur a Phylosopho

ment of generation, in which there are many instants, and between them, there is necessarily a [span of] time, as the Philosopher explicates in *Physics* 6, text. 26.[a]

§ 1.5.4 The purpose exists in the mind of the agent, or at least at the principle [beginning] of his activity, as the Philosopher explicates in *Metaphysics* 2, text. 8,[b] where he states: "An agent will not begin any activity if it does not intend an ultimate end." And he explicated the same in *Metaphysics* 2, text. 9:[c] "The purpose is the end intended by the activities; without it, the activity would be in vain."

§ 1.5.5 In addition to this, concerning the agent, it becomes clear that the agent is temporally prior to the act of the activities, as Averroes explicates in *Metaphysics* 9, text. 13,[d] where he states: "The agent is prior to its activity, because the activity cannot be temporally prior to the matter and the agent, but the agent is temporally prior to its activity." Afterwards, he adds: "Every generated thing is moved by a mover prior to it." And the same thing is explained in the *Treatise on the Substance of the Celestial Sphere*, ch. 2[e]— as he also states in the Commentary on *On the Heavens* 2, text. 13—where he says: "But in the class [of things], there is an agent that is temporally prior to that upon which it acts; this applies to all the beings dispersed throughout the sphere of the world. | And there is an agent which acts prior according to nature and to time. This case applies to the celestial sphere, etc."

§ 1.5.6 With these [words], he seems to teach two things from which it would necessarily follow that the movement of generation is not [pre]eternal. First, when he states that "every agent in this sphere of the world is temporally prior" to its activity prior to their multiplicity, and this is clear because they are begotten. And if this is true, then actions are temporally prior to generations, and consequently, generations are not [pre]eternal.

§ 1.5.7 Second, when he states that the sphere is prior to its activity in nature [naturally] and in time [temporally], and then the number of activities are generations that necessarily coincide with their movement, as the senses tes-

---

[a] cum] coni. Copp.; cum.5. b.   [b] Metaphysicorum] b[corr]; Physicorum b; בספר מה שאחר a.   [c] 13] emend. Copp.; 18 b; 13 L.   [d] 13] emend. Copp.; 8 b; 13 L.

---

[a] *Phys.* 6.3.234a.   [b] *Phys.* 6.3.234a.   [c] *Metaph.* 2.2.994b.   [d] *Metaph.* 9.3.1048a.   [e] Cf. *Sub. orb.* 85–86.

Philosopher's words in *Physics* 2, text. 26:[a] "Man is begotten by man and [also] by the sun." And from these [words], if [this is] so, it becomes clear that the sphere is temporally prior to the movement of the [different acts of] generation. And therefore, it follows that the movement of generation is not [pre]eternal. Regarding what we said in the [antecedent] premise, that the movement of generation is for a purpose: this is evident because in every living animal or plant, there are instruments that are necessary for their activities [and] that do not exist by chance. It necessarily follows that they exist for a purpose through the intention of the immediate and mediate intender of the act, | because the things that are done unintentionally are happening by chance, as the Philosopher explains in *Physics* 2, text. 51:[b] "There are causes that take place without intention, and then these are said to be 'by chance.'" Regarding what we said about the instruments that exist in all generated things, they do not exist by chance: this is evident because they exist in all generated things, or at least in most of them, and therefore they cannot exist by chance, as the Philosopher explains in *Physics* 2, text. 48:[c] "Chance is something that happens neither constantly nor in most cases." And the same thing is explained by proofs made by Aristotle, ibid. [2], text. 77 et al.,[d] in which he explains that the naturally generated things necessarily exist for an intended purpose. If so, when the aforementioned Philosopher says in ibid. [2], text. 86,[e] that it is not impossible that a certain thing could be generated for a purpose without the intention of an agent, [then] it will necessarily be understood to be so for an immediate agent. For it is not impossible that either by laws or by order, the first agent acting through an intermediary will generate something that is not intended by the proximate agent, [but] necessarily by the laws or the order of the first intending agent. And Averroes explains this in his Commentary on *Metaphysics* 12, text. 18:[f] "In the kinds of heat that are created from the heat of the stars, which generate the species of living beings, there exist designated ratios of that heat from the quantities of the movements of the stars and their constellations [in relation] to each other by proximity and remoteness. And this measurement exists through the divine intellectual artistry, which is similar to the form of the first artistry, below which there are many arts. And in this way, it is appropriate to understand that nature is acting in perfection and in order, although nature [itself] does not understand. And this [is the case] insofar as it is orderly arranged by active powers nobler than itself, which are called 'separate intellects.'"

10r

---

[a]*Phys.* 2.2.194b.   [b]*Phys.* 2.5.197a.   [c]*Phys.* 2.4.196b.   [d]*Phys.* 2.8.198b.
[e]*Phys.* 2.8.199b.   [f]Cf. *Metaph.* 12.3.1070a.

מאמר ב׳ פרק כ״ו באמרו: »שהאדם מתהוה מן האדם ומן השמש.«
ומאלה אם כן התבאר שהגלגל קודם בזמן לתנועת ההויות.[a] ומזה יתחייב שתנועת ההויה לתכלית היא בלתי קדמונית. אמנם מה שאמרנו בהקדמה שתנועת ההויה לתכלית היא מבואר הנה הוא כי אמנם בכל חי או צומח נמצאו כלים הכרחיים לפעולותיהם אשר בהיותם בלתי מקריים יתחייב בהכרח שהם נמצאים לתכלית בכוונת מכוין הפועל | באמצעי או בלתי אמצעי כי הדברים הנעשים בלתי כוונה נאמר שנעשו במקרה כמו שבאר הפילוסוף בספר השמע מאמר ב׳ פרק נ״א זה לשונו: »יש מהסבות שהן[b] הוות בלי כוונה ואז נאמר שהיו ›במקרה‹« עד כאן לשונו. אמנם מה שאמרנו שהכלים הנמצאים במתהוים הם בלתי מקריים הוא מבואר כי הם נמצאים בכל המתהוים או לפחות ברובם וכזה[c] לא יהיה במקרה כמו שבאר הפילוסוף בספר השמע מאמר ב׳ פרק מ״ח[d] באמרו: »המקרה הוא הדבר אשר אינו תמיד גם לא על הרוב.« וזה בעצמו מבואר במופתי ארסטו׳ שם פרק ע״ז וזולתו אשר בם באר שההויות הטבעיות הם בהכרח לתכלית מכוון אם כן כאשר אמר הפילוסוף הנזכר שם פרק פ״ו שאינו נמנע שיתהוה איזה דבר לתכלית בלתי כוונת פועל יובן בהכרח על פועל בלתי אמצעי כי אמנם אינו נמנע שבמצות או בסדר פועל ראשון הפועל באמצעי יתהוה דבר בלתי מכוון מהפועל הקרוב הפועל בהכרח במצות או בסדר הפועל הראשון המכוין וזה באר אבן רשד בביאורו לספר מה שאחר מאמר י״ב פרק י״ח באמרו וזה לשונו: »במיני החום המתחדשים מחום הכוכבים המהוים מיני הבעלי חיים נמצאו[e] קצבות מיוחדות מאותו החום משעורי תנועות הכוכבים ותכונותיהם זה עם זה מקורבה[f] וריחוק וזה השעור נמצא במלאכה[g] אלהית שכלית דומה לצורת מלאכה ראשית אשר תחתיה מלאכות רבות ובזה האופן ראוי להבין שהטבע אמרנו שהטבע פועל[h] בשלמות ובסדר עם היות הטבע בלתי משכיל וזה מצד היותו מסודר מכחות פעולות נכבדות ממנו הנקראות ›שכלים נבדלים‹.«

10r

---

[a]ההויות] coni. Dunk.; ההויות׳ a.   [b]שהן] coni. Dunk.; שהם a.   [c]וכזה] a^corr; ובזה a.   [d]מ״ח] emend. Dunk.; פ״ח a; 48 b; 48 L.   [e]נמצאו] a^corr; נמצא a; habet b; habent L.   [f]מקורבה] coni. Dunk.; מקירבה a.   [g]במלאכה] a^corr; במלאכת a.   [h]פועל] a^corr; om. a.

Physicorum II, t.c. 26 ubi dicit: «Quod homo generatur ab homine et sole.» Quibus patet quod sol est tempore prior generatione in universali, et per consequens generationes sive generationum motus non habuit esse ab eterno. Quo autem ad secundam antecedentis partem, qua scilicet dicitur quod sunt ad finem facte probatur. Quia in qualibet generatione saltem animatorum facta, sunt organa ad animatorum conservationem horumque actiones necessaria; que cum non contingant esse casu habent fieri per cogitationem ad finem ab agente mediato vel immediato intendente. Illa enim que fiunt preter cogitationem et voluntatem dicuntur fieri casu prout habetur a Phylosopho *Physicorum* II, t.c. 51 ubi dicit ex causis que sunt sine voluntate et precogitatione, et tunc dicitur quod contingunt casu etc. quod autem genitorum organa non contingant casu patet, quia fiunt ut in pluribus sive in maiori parte. Talia autem non dicuntur fieri casu, sicut habetur a Phylosopho *Physicorum* II, t.c. 48 ubi dicit: «Casus non est illud quod est necessarium et semper neque nec illud quod est in maiori parte» et idem habetur rationibus Phylosophi ibidem t.c. 77 et sequentibus, quibus infert quod naturaliter genita habent necessario esse ad intentum finem. Cum ergo Phylosophus ibidem t.c. 86 inferre videatur quod non est inconveniens ut aliquid fiat ad finem preter agentis cogitationem intelligit necessario de agente immediato tantum sicut de natura, non autem de primo et mediato, non, enim, est inconveniens ut medio agentis iussu vel ordine quo scilicet finem intendit, compelletur immediatus agens ad agendum preter eiusdem immediati voluntatem et cogitationem. Quare Aven R. *Metaphysicorum* XII, t.c, 18 hoc docens ait: «Calores generati ex caloribus stellarum generantibus quamlibet speciem animalium, specierum habet mensuras proprias illius caloris ex quantitatibus motuum stellarum et dispositionibus illarum ad invicem in propinquitate et remotione. Et ista mensura provenit ab arte divina intellectuali, que est similis uniforme unius artis principalis sub qua sunt plures artes, secundum hoc igitur est intelligendum quod natura facit aliquid perfecte et ordinate quamvis non intelligat, quasi esse memorata ex virtutibus agentibus nobilioribus ea quae dicuntur intelligentie.»

tify and as the Philosopher explicates in *Physics* 2, text. 26,[a] where he states: "Man is begotten by man and by the sun as well." From these [words], it is clear that the sun is universally prior to the movement of generation, and consequently, generations or the movement of generations are not [pre]eternal. The second part of the antecedent, in which we said that every activity is performed for a purpose, is proved because at least in every generation of living animals, the instruments are made for the conservation of living animals, which are necessary for their activity, and they do not exist by chance. Instruments are mediately or immediately produced by the intention of an intending agent for a purpose. In fact, things produced without intention or will exist by chance, as the Philosopher explicates in *Physics* 2, text. 51,[b] where he states: "Among causes, there are causes that are produced without will or unintentionally, and they are called 'by chance.'" And it is clear that the instruments of the generated things are not produced by chance, because [instruments] exist in all generated things, or in most of them, and for this reason, we cannot say that they are produced by chance, as the Philosopher explicates in *Physics* 2, text. 48,[c] where he states: "Chance is something that happens neither constantly nor in most cases," and the Philosopher explicates the same in *Physics* 2, text. 77,[d] et al., where he states that naturally generated things necessarily exist for the intention of the final purpose. And therefore, in *Physics* 2, text. 86,[e] the Philosopher seems to conclude that it is not absurd that something generated for a purpose, without the intention of an agent, necessarily understands the immediate agent—for instance, nature—but does not understand the first [proximate] and the mediate agent. For this reason, it is not absurd [to state] that a mediate agent's decrees or commands intend the purpose, and it compels the immediate agent to act without will and intention, as Averroes explains in *Metaphysics* 12, text. 18,[f] where he states: "In the heats that are generated from the heat of the stars, which generate the species of animal, there are specific measures of heat from the quantities of the movements of the stars and their dispositions relative to their reciprocal proximity or remoteness. And these measures originate from the divine intellectual artistry, which is similar to the universal form of the first artistry, below which there are many arts. In this way, it is appropriate to understand that nature produces something in perfection and in order, although it does not understand as it is inspired by active powers that are nobler than it, which are called 'intellects.'"

[a] *Phys.* 2.2.194b. [b] *Phys.* 2.5.197a. [c] *Phys.* 2.4.196b. [d] *Phys.* 2.8.198b.
[e] *Phys.* 2.8.199b. [f] Cf. *Metaph.* 12.3.1070a.

§1.6 Third, what we said—namely, that the movement of generation and corruption is not [pre]eternal—becomes clear: because for its existence, it necessarily follows that a substrate that is disposed to be affected by the movement of generation exists prior to it in time. If so, the movement of generation will not be [pre]eternal. The consequence is self-evident and the premise becomes clear in this way: because the movement of generation does not bring the form in the substrate into actuality before it completes the designated kind of disposition for that form in it, as becomes clear from the proof [made] by Averroes in his Commentary on *Physics* 8, text. 46.[a] If so, then it necessarily follows that the disposition of matter for any element is temporally prior [to the movement of generation]. An example of this is the reception of the form of another element by the same matter. It will follow that this disposition will not exist unless there is movement, and the movement will not be there unless there is a certain duration of time that is there some instants before the end of the [afore]mentioned duration of time. It therefore follows that the beginning of the time of the substrate's disposition, and all the more so the substrate itself | in which this movement of disposition will be, precedes the movement of generation in time. If so, then the movement of generation is not [pre]eternal.

§1.7 Fourth, what we said regarding the movement of generation not being [pre]eternal becomes clear in this way: because locomotion necessarily precedes the movement of generation and the other kinds of movement in time. If so, then it follows that the movement of generation is not [pre]eternal. The consequence is necessarily self-evident. The premise becomes clear from Aristotle's proof in *On Generation and Corruption* 2, text. 55:[b] "The movement produces the generation, because it causes the generator to approach and retreat." And Averroes explains these words: "The movement generates the generated things through the agent's approach to the affected thing. And this is correct, insofar as this movement precedes every change." And the agent's approximation to the affected thing is necessarily temporally prior to the movement of generation. And this is so because the approaching will only happen for it [i.e., the agent] if it [takes place] within a duration of time, and until it is completed, the movement of generation will not begin. If so, it is evident that many instants that occur within the time of the aforementioned approaching precede the beginning of the aforementioned movement of generation in time. Therefore, it follows that the move-

[a] Cf. *Phys.* 8.6.258b. [b] *Gen. corr.* 2.10.336b.

§1.6 **שלישית** יתבאר זה שאמרנו שתנועת ההויה וההפסד היא בלתי קדמונית כי אמנם למציאותה יתחייב בהכרח מציאות נושא מוכן להתפעל בתנועת ההויה קודם אליה בזמן אם כן תנועת ההויה היא בלתי קדמונית. הנה חיוב התולדה הוא מבואר בעצמו וההקדמה תתבאר באופן זה כי לא תהיה תנועת ההויה המביאה בפעל הצורה בנושא טרם שישלם בו מין ההכנה המיוחד לאותה הצורה כמו שהתבאר במופת אבן רשד בביאורו לספר השמע מאמר ח' פרק מ"ו ואם כן יתחייב בהכרח שתהיה קודמת בזמן הכנת חומר איזה יסוד דרך משל מיוחדת לקבלת צורת יסוד אחר בחומר ההוא בעצמו. ובהיות שאותה ההכנה לא תהיה כי אם בתנועה והתנועה לא תהיה כי אם במשך זמן מה אשר בו כמה עתות קודמות לסוף משך הזמן הנזכר התחייב אם כן שתחלת זמן הכנת הנושא כל שכן הנושא בעצמו | אשר בו תהיה תנועת ההכנה ההיא קדמו בזמן לתנועת[a] ההויה ואם כן תנועת ההויה היא בלתי קדמונית.

§1.7 **רביעית** יתבאר זה שאמרנו שתנועת ההויה היא בלתי קדמונית באופן זה כי אמנם לתנועת[b] ההויה ושאר מיני התנועות קדמה בזמן בהכרח תנועה מקומית אם כן יתחייב שתנועת ההויה היא בלתי קדמונית הנה חיוב התולדה הוא מבואר בעצמו אמנם ההקדמה תתבאר בראית ארסט' בספר ההויה וההפסד מאמר ב' פרק נ"ה[c] באמרו: "התנועה תעשה ההויה בפעל כי היא מוליכה ומביאה את המהוה." ודבריו אלה באר אבן רשד באמרו: "התנועה אמנם תהוה הויות בהקריבו הפועל אל המתפעל וזה נכון מצד מה שזאת התנועה קודמת לכל השתנות" עכ"ל. ובהיות שהקרבת הפועל אל המתפעל תהיה קודמת בזמן בהכרח לתנועת ההויה וזה כי אמנם ההקרבה לא תהיה כי אם במשך זמן אשר עד שישלם לא תתחיל תנועת ההויה, ואם כן הוא מבואר שהרבה עתות אשר בזמן ההקרבה הנזכרת קדמו בזמן להתחלת תנועת ההויה הנזכרת מזה יתחייב שתנועת ההויה היא בלתי קדמונית וזה בעצמו באר הפילוסוף בספר השמע מאמר ח' פרק

[a] תנועת [לתנועת a[corr]; Dunk.; ט"ו a; 15 b; 55 L. [b] תנועת [לתנועת a[corr]. [c] נ"ה] emend.

§ 1.6 Tertio arguitur sic. Ad generationem requiritur necessario subiectum tempore prius generationi dispositum, ergo non ab eterno habuit esse gene|ratio. Consequentia patet et antecedens probatur, quia nisi expleta subiecti dispositione qua reddatur materia forme propria non daretur generande forme ingressus, prout habetur ratione et auctoritate Aven R. *Physicorum* VIII, t.c. 46. Quare requiritur necessario elementi v.g. dispositio ad hoc ut eiusdem materiam alterius elementi ingrediatur forma. Cumque huiusmodi dispositio non fiat nisi per motum, et per consequens in tempore in quam plura dantur instantia ad eius complementum tempore precedentia, patet ergo ut eiusdem dispositionis principium nedum subiectum in quo fit ipsa dispositione, habeant necessario secundum tempus precedere ad generationem, et per consequens ipsa generatione non habuit esse ab eterno.

§ 1.7 Quarto arguitur sic. Ad generationem et reliqua motuum genera habet necessario localis motus secundum tempus precedere, ergo generationis motus non habuit esse ab eterno, et per consequens non ab eterno habuerunt esse generationes. Consequentia patet et antecedens probatur ratione Phylosophi in lib. *De Generatione* II, t.c. 55[a] ubi dicit: «Latio,[b] enim, faciet generationem actualiter, quia adducit et abducit generans» ubi Aven R. exponens ait: «Quoniam motus generat faciendo appropinquare generans generato, et tunc rectum est inquantum iste motus est primus omnium translationum etc.» Cum autem huiusmodi appropinquatio non fiat nisi in tempore quo non expleto non datur generationis principium, patet quidem quod datur quid tempore prius ad generationem, quia plura instantia in eiusdem appropinquationis tempore occurentia habent necessario secundum tempus precedere ad eiusdem generationis principium, et per consequens generatio non habuit esse ab eterno. Et idem habe-

§ 1.6 Third, I would argue that generation necessarily requires a disposed subject [i.e., substrate] that is temporally prior to it, and therefore the movement of generation is not [pre]eternal. | The consequence is evident, and the antecedent is proved, because nothing is brought forth before the coming of the form into a designated matter. Only a specific disposition of the subject [i.e., substrate] is required to complete the form, according to the argument and authority of Averroes in *Physics* 8, text. 46.[a] For example, elements necessarily require a particular disposition, so that the form of another element may come into the same matter. Therefore, this disposition is generated only by a movement, and consequently in a [span of] time, in which several instants will occur before the end of the duration of that time. It is clear that the principle [i.e., beginning] of this disposition, and even more so the subject [i.e., substate] in which this disposition is generated, necessarily precede the generation, and consequently, generation is not [pre]eternal.

§ 1.7 Fourth, I would argue that locomotion necessarily temporally precedes the movement of generation and the other kinds of movement. Therefore, the movement of generation is not [pre]eternal, and consequently, generations are not [pre]eternal. The consequence is evident and the antecedent is proved, as the Philosopher explicates in *On Generation and Corruption* 2, text. 55,[b] where he states: "For the eternal motion, by causing 'the generator' to approach and retire, will unceasingly produce coming-to-be," while Averroes explains: "Movement generates a generated thing through the approach of the generator, and this is correct because this movement is the first of all changes, etc." The approach will only take place within time [and] before it is not completed, the movement of generation does not have a beginning. And then, it is clear that something temporally precedes the movement of generation, because in the meantime, several instants of the approach temporally precede the beginning of the movement of generation, and consequently, the movement of

---

[a] 55] emend. Copp.; 15 b; 55 L.   [b] Latio] emend. Copp.; illatio b; Latio L.

[a] Cf. *Phys.* 8.6.258b.   [b] Cf. *Gen. corr.* 2.10.336b.

ment of generation is not [pre]eternal. And the Philosopher explains the same in *Physics* 8, text. 57:[a] "Locomotion is temporally prior to the movement of generation and the other kinds of movements."

§ 1.8 Fifth, it becomes clear, as we said, that the movement of generation and corruption is not [pre]eternal in this way: because a designated matter for the form of the generated kind is needed for the movement of generation. And without the matter being designated in this way, the designated form for the generated thing will not be generated in it. It is impossible that the material causes may eternally proceed in a straight line. Therefore, it follows that the thing proceeds [back] to prime matter designated for the form of a kind of the generated individual, because man, for example, is generated only from the semen of man.[b] And this does not proceed to infinity. Indeed, it necessarily follows that the thing proceeds to a first man. And the same thing must follow for every single [being] of the species of existents generated from a designated matter. If so, it follows that the movement of generation by which they are generated is not [pre]eternal. The necessity of this consequence is self-evident, as we said in the premise that a matter designated for the form of the kind of the generated individual is required for the movement of generation. This becomes clear from Averroes's proof in his Commentary on *Physics* 8, text. 46:[c] "If it were possible that man was generated from a non-human being, then it would have to follow that they were called by the name 'man' only by equivocation, because thanks to the diversity of the matter, the form would be diverse. And if this was not true, then there would be no material existents and no designated forms and everything would be generated from everything. And the designated matters would be | void and superfluous."

§ 1.9 Regarding what we said—that it is impossible that this should proceed to infinity—this becomes clear from Aristotle's proof in *Metaphysics* 2, text. 5:[d] "It is clear that everything has a beginning." And he continues, saying: "It is impossible for a thing to be generated from a thing proceeding to infinity." And he continues, ibid. [2], text. 6:[e] "If there was no first thing, it would follow that there would be no cause at all." It is impossible that a designated thing may be generated from a designated thing, and so on [proceeding] to infinity. And [this is so] because if there was no first thing, then things that come from its potential would not exist. [But] it follows that man was not generated, for

---

[a] *Phys.* 8.7.260b–261a. [b] Cf. *Metaph.* 12.3.1070a. [c] Cf. *Phys.* 8.6.258b.
[d] *Metaph.* 2.2.994b. [e] *Metaph.* 2.2.994b.

tur ab eodem Phylosopho *Physicorum* VIII t.c. 57 ubi aperte docet: «Quod motus localis tam motui generationis quam reliquis motuum generibus habet secundum tempus precedere.»

⟨§1.8⟩

⟨§1.9⟩

generation is not [pre]eternal, as the Philosopher explicates in *Physics* 8, text. 57,[a] where he states: "Locomotion temporally precedes the movement of generation and the other kinds of movement."

⟨§1.8⟩

⟨§1.9⟩

---

[a] *Phys.* 8.7.260b.

example, from man in an infinite number. And therefore, it follows that the thing leads to a certain first [being] in man and in the individuals of every single species. And therefore, it follows that the movement of generation by which the species are generated is not [pre]eternal. And this is what we wanted to explain.

§ 1.10 We answer, if so, to dispel [any] doubt about the aforementioned thesis, that the movement of generation is not [pre]eternal: because the agent, the substrate, the intention of the final purpose, and the active and the passive disposition precede it in time, as mentioned above.

§ 1.11 Regarding the opponent's arguments, we answer to the first and second arguments that it does not have to follow that the movement of generation is [pre]eternal, still less so the existence of the generated things, even if someone were to say that the sphere and the elements are [pre]eternal, because the beginning of the movement of generation would not exist if there was no instance prior to it in time in which [there] actually existed (1) the agent and the affected thing prepared with a designated disposition, which does not occur without a duration of time, and (2) the intention of the final purpose of the agent and the agent's disposition for the aforementioned activity.

§ 1.12 And to the third argument, we answer: by the very same argument, it becomes clear that the movement of generation is not [pre]eternal, and this is so because it exists for the intended final purpose of perfecting the deficiency occurring from the movement of corruption, and this is so thanks to the recurrence of the movement of generation. It therefore follows that the intending agent and the intention of the final purpose intended by it precede it in time. And therefore, it becomes clear that the movement of the recurrently generated things is not [pre]eternal.

§ 1.13 And all this becomes clear from the divine wisdom in intellectual proofs at the beginning of the book of Genesis. First, when saying that the existence of the elements temporally precedes the existence of the movement of the things generated from them,[a] and it becomes clear that this is necessarily correct, because the movement of generation only takes place in a substrate that has moved prior [to the movement of generation], as mentioned above. Second, because regarding the existence of every created thing, it says (Genesis 1:4): "And God saw that it was good,"

---

[a] Cf. Gen 1:2.

1. DE GENERATIONE

§ 1.10 Ad dubium ergo respondetur. Quod non ab eterno habuit esse generationis motus immo habuerunt ad illud secundum tempus precedere agens, et subiectum, et finis intentio, et potentia tam activa quam passiva prout supra patuit.

§ 1.11 Ad argumenta vero et primo ad primum et secundum argumentum respondetur. Quod dato licet non concesso ut elementa et orbis habuissent esse ab eterno, non tamen sequeretur ut generationes nedum genita fuissent ab eterno nisi enim daretur processisse aliquod instans in quo habuissent actu esse agens et subiectum in tempore dispositum et finalis intentio in mente agentis existens, et potentia ad actum, non daretur primum generationis instans, prout supra patuit.

§ 1.12 Ad tertium vero argumentum respondetur: Quod immo eadem rationem patet quod non ab eterno habuerunt generationes esse, quia cum habuissent esse ad finem, quo scilicet intenditur ut satisfiat diminutioni per corruptionem contin|genti, sequitur necessario ut habuissent omnia premissa secundum tempus precedere. Cum scilicet ad finem intentum consequendum omnia illa ut prefertur necessario prefuisse requirantur, quare patet quod generationes nedum corruptiones non habuerunt esse ab eterno.

§ 1.13 Hec autem omnia divinitus docet et demonstrative ostendit Sacrum Genesis Documentum cap. primo [1:4]. Ubi ad mortalium generationes narrat precessisse elementorum productio, et in quolibet generabilium tractatu dicit: «et vidit Deus quod esset bonum.» Inferens quod Deus

§ 1.10 To dispel any doubt, I would argue that the movement of generation is not [pre]eternal; on the contrary, the agent, the subject [i.e., substrate], the intention of the final purpose [i.e., intended purpose], and active and passive potentiality [i.e., disposition] temporally precede it, as aforementioned.

§ 1.11 In response to the first and second arguments, I will reply: even if one grants for the sake of argument that the elements and the celestial spheres are [pre]eternal, it would follow that [the movement of] generations and the generated things are [also] [pre]eternal. Because there are several instants in which the agent and the disposed substrate actually exist, the intention of the final purpose in the agent's mind from potentiality to actuality [also exists]. Therefore, there is no first instant of coming-to-be, as mentioned above.

§ 1.12 In response to the third argument, I will reply: the movement of generation is not [pre]eternal, because generations exist for a purpose, which is intended to perfect the deficiency occurring from [the movement of] corruption. | It would then follow that all the aforementioned premises temporally precede it [the movement of generation and corruption]. That means that all the aforementioned things necessarily existed before because they follow the intention of the final purpose, as mentioned above, and therefore it is clear that [the movement of] generation and corruption is not [pre]eternal.

§ 1.13 However, the Holy Book of Genesis, by means of divine teaching and demonstrative explanation, teaches these things in chapter 1, which narrates that the creation of elements was temporally prior to the movement of the mortal beings. And in the account of the creation, it says (Genesis 1:4): "And God saw that it was good," which means in order to convey and teach that everything created by Him is for a final purpose that is an intended "good," which is commonly known and evident in every one of them. And the intention of the aforementioned final purpose of the "good" is necessarily [present] in the creator prior to the [afore]mentioned movement of generation. And therefore, it becomes clear that the movement of generation is | not [pre]eternal, but that the agent and the intention of the final purpose in him and the substrate of the movement of generation necessarily temporally precede it. And it is said (Genesis 1:4): "And God saw." This should not be understood as sensorial seeing, but as intellectual seeing, teaching us that God—may He be praised—also knows the contrary of the existence of the generated [beings] and that this [i.e., their non-existence] is possible for Him.

§ 1.14 He chooses to bring forth what He brings forth because He knows and recognises that it is the "good." And He will scrutinise this [i.e., what He chose to bring forth] with respect to His purpose, because the "good" is His final purpose in every existent, as Aristotle explains in *Metaphysics* 2, text. 8 and text. 9.[a] And therefore, Averroes says in *The Incoherence of the Incoherence* 9, third investigation: "For the philosophers, there is neither quantity nor quality in any existent, except by divine wisdom. And one of two [cases] is inevitable: either that a thing is necessary for the nature of the existence of an existent, or that it is for the sake of a higher 'good.'"[b]

---

[a] *Metaph.* 2.2.994b.   [b] Cf. *Incoherence* 248–249.

להבין ולהורות שכל דבר התחדש מאתו לתכלית שהוא ‹טוב› מכוון אשר הוא מפורסם ונראה בכל אחד מהם. והנה כוונת תכלית ה‹טוב› הנזכר היה בהכרח קודם בזמן אצל המחדש לתנועת ההויה הנזכרת. ומזה התבאר שתנועת ההוייה היא | בלתי קדמונית אבל קדמו לה בזמן בהכרח הפועל וכוונת התכלית אצלו ונושא תנועת ההוייה. ובאמרו: «וירא אלהים» אשר לא יתכן שיובן על ראייה חושיית אבל על ראייה שכלית הורה שעם היות שהאל יתברך ידע הפך מציאות המחודש ויכול עליו.

§ 1.14 הנה בחר להמציא מה שהמציא כי ידע והכיר שזה הוא ה‹טוב›. וזה יבחן מצד תכליתו כי אמנם ה‹טוב› בכל נמצא הוא תכליתו כמו שבאר ארסטו' בספר מה שאחר מאמר ב' פרק ח' ופרק ט'. ולכן אמר אבן רשד בספר הפלת ההפלה מאמר ט' חקירת ג' כי: «אמנם אצל הפילוסופים אין שום כמות ולא שום איכות בשום נמצא זולתי בחכמה אלהית. ומזה[a] לא ימלט מאחת משתים אם שיהיה אותו הדבר הכרחי לטבע מציאות אותו הנמצא. ואם שהיה על צד היותר ‹טוב›.»

---

[a] ומזה] a; ושזה a[corr]; quare b.

illa produxit intendens illud bonum sive illum finem qui in horum singulo sensu apparet, ad quorum bonum sive finem apparentem habuit necessario eiusdem intentio in mente producens secundum tempus precedere, ut supra. Quare sequitur necessario illa non fuisse ab eterno, immo ad illa tempore precessisse agens et finis intentio in eiusdem agentis mente, et horum subiectum, prout idem textus ibidem de facto fuisse testatur per hoc autem quod dicit: «et vidit Deus» [Gen 1:4] quod procul dubio de intellectuali visione tantum non de sensuali intelligi contingit. Videtur inferre quid licet horum oppositum indifferenter scivisset et potuisset.

§ 1.14 Talia tamen sapienter voluisse videns sive noscens illa sic facta esse bona quorum bonitas nonnisi per horum finem consideratur, prout Phylosophus in lib. *Metaphysicorum* II, t.c. 8 inferre videtur. Quare Aven R. in lib. *Destructionis* D., disputatione IX, dubio 3 ait: «Apud enim phylosophos nulla est quantitas neque qualitas in aliquo entium que non sit per eiusdem sapientiam. Quare non evadit quin sit unum duorum videlicet aut quia hoc est necessarium de natura actus illius entis, aut quia est secundum bene esse.»

that God created all beings for an intended good, which is the ultimate end, and this seems to be evident in every single one of them. Concerning their "good," which is their ultimate end, the intention in the creator's mind is temporally prior to them by necessity, as aforementioned, and then it would necessarily follow that the movement of generation is not [pre]eternal. On the contrary, the agent and the intention of the final purpose in the agent's mind and their subject are prior to the movement of generation, as is testified by "and God saw," which means that it is only an intellectual seeing and not a sensorial seeing. This seems to suggest that He knows the contrary [of the existence of the generated beings] indifferently and that it is possible for Him [to know them].

§ 1.14 Nevertheless, He wisely desires those things because He recognises and knows that they are good, because goodness is their ultimate end, as the Philosopher seems to conclude in *Metaphysics* 2, text. 8,[a] [and] as Averroes explicates in *The Incoherence of the Incoherence* 9, third doubt, where he states: "For the philosophers, there is neither quantity nor quality in any existent except by divine wisdom. And one of these two cases is inevitable: either because it is necessary according to the activity of this kind of existent, or because it is according to the good."[b]

[a] *Metaph.* 2.2.994b.   [b] Cf. *Incoherence* 248–249.

§ 2 Second:
We will inquire whether the bodies called "first elements," with regard to the sensible things, are [pre]eternal.

It somewhat seems to be [the case] that they are [pre]eternal.

§ 2.1.1 Because if they were created, His [i.e., the Creator's] creation would either be from a potential being, from an actualised being, or from nothing. And it is not appropriate to say that they were created from nothing, because nothing can come from nothing. And this is self-evident and the Philosopher explains it in *Physics* 1, text. 77:[a] "When something has existence, it does not [have it] from something that does not exist." And aside from this: if the elements were created after absolute nothingness, an impossibility, which the Philosopher explains in *On the Heavens* 3, text. 29,[b] would follow: "It is impossible for a body to be created if there is no vacuum, because the space in which the created body will exist is necessarily void before its generation." We also cannot say that they came to be from another thing existing in actuality before them: if this was correct, then they would not be the first elements, but rather the existent from which they came to be would be the first. And the same doubt would be raised about that existent, and this would proceed to infinity. So, if we say that they were created from an existent in potentiality [and] not in actuality—and this is prime matter—one of two [cases] will be inevitable: (1) either prime matter is prior to them in time, or (2) it is not prior to them at all. It is impossible that it could be prior to them in time, because if so, it would follow that the matter was devoid of all form.

§ 2.1.2 And therefore, two incongruities would follow, as Averroes explains in his Commentary on *On the Heavens* 3, text. 29.[c] First, if prime matter were devoid of all form, then there something outside of the ten categories would exist in actuality. And therefore, it would be in potentiality and in actuality at the same time, and this is impossible.

§ 2.1.3 Second, even if it was possible for it to exist in potentiality only, we would not escape the necessity of the vacuum, which is impossible, since before a composed thing existing in actuality was created from that formless matter, it would be necessary that the space in which the created thing existed after its creation would be void before the creation, because only the [corporeal] quantity existing in

---

[a] *Phys.* 1.8.191a.   [b] *Cael.* 3.2.302a.   [c] Cf. *Cael.* 3.2.302a.

§ 2 שנית נחקור אם הגרמים הנקראים ‹יסודות ראשונות› לכל המוחשים הם קדמונים

והנה נראה קצת שהם קדמונים.

§ 2.1.1 כי אם היו מחודשים היה התחדשותו[a] מאיזה דבר נמצא בכח או בפועל או מלא דבר ואין ראוי לומר שהיה התחדשותם מלא דבר כי אמנם מלא דבר לא יתהווה דבר וזה מבואר בעצמו ובאר אותו הפילוסוף בספר השמע מאמר א׳ פרק ע״ז באמרו: «בהמצא איזה נמצא לא ימצא ממה שהוא בלתי נמצא» עד כאן לשונו. ובלעדי זאת הנה אם היו היסודות מחודשים אחר העדר גמור היה מתחייב אותו הנמנע שבאר הפילוסוף בספר השמים והעולם מאמר ג׳ פרק כ״ט באמרו: «מן הנמנע שיתחדש גשם אם לא ימצא ריקות כי המקום אשר נמצא בו הגשם המחודש היה ריק בהכרח טרם היותו» עד כאן לשונו גם כן לא נוכל לומר שהתחדשו מדבר אחר נמצא בפעל קודם להם שאם כן לא היו הם יסודות ראשונות אבל היה הראשון אותו הנמצא אשר ממנו נתהוו ויפול זה הספק בעצמו על אותו הנמצא וילך הדבר אל בלתי תכלית. אמנם אם נאמר שהתחדשו מאיזה נמצא בכח לא בפעל. וזה היה החומר הראשון אם כן לא ימלט מאחת משתים אם שהיה החומר הראשון קודם להם בזמן או שלא קדם להם כלל אמנם נמנע הוא שהיה קודם להם בזמן שאם כן יתחייב שהיה החומר אז מופשט מכל צורה.

§ 2.1.2 ומזה יתחייבו שתי נמנעות כאשר באר אבן רשד בביאור ספר השמים והעולם מאמר ג׳ פרק כ״ט. ראשונה שאם היה החומר הראשון מופשט מכל צורה | היה אם כן דבר חוץ מהעשרה מאמרות נמצא בפעל ובכן היה בזמן אחד נמצא בכח ונמצא בפעל וזה נמנע.

§ 2.1.3 שנית שגם אם היה זה איפשר שהיה נמצא בכח לבד לא היינו נמלטים מהתחייב הריקות אשר הוא נמנע כי קודם שהתחדש מורכב נמצא בפעל מאותו החומר המפשט התחייב שאותו המקום אשר נמצא בו המחודש אחר התחדשותו היה קודם לכן ריק בהכרח כי לא ימלא את המקום זולתי הכמות הנמצאת בפעל וזה הכמות אמנם

---

[a] התחדשות ‏] a^{corr}; התחדשותו a.

§ 2 Secundo Dubitatur

Utrum prima mortalium elementa habuissent esse ab eterno

et videtur quod ita.

§ 2.1.1 Primo: quia si fuissent genita vel ex nihilo scilicet post purum non esse, vel ex aliquo actu existente, vel saltem potentia ente. Non ex nihilo: quia ex nihilo nihil fit prout per se patet et habetur a Phylosopho *Physicorum* primi t.c. 77 ubi dicit: «Et si igitur aliquod fuerit non ex non ente.» Preterea quia si habuissent esse post purum non esse, sequeretur illud inconveniens quod Phylosophus dicit sequi ad propositionem dicentem corpus fieri post purum non esse in lib. *De Celo* III t.c. 29 ubi dicit: «Impossibile est enim ut aliquod corpus fiat nisi vacuum sit quia locus in quo corpus est, fuit necessario vacuum.» Neque dicendum est secundum ut[a] habuissent esse ex aliquo actu existente; quia ut sic daretur quid prius primis, et eadem surgeret questio de eodem priori et sic fieret processus ad infinitum. Si vero habuissent esse | ex aliquo potentia tantum ente, et talis est materia prima: vel ergo ipsa materia habuit esse prius illis actu a qualibet forma denudata.

§ 2.1.2 Ad quod ut Aven R. ait in lib. *De Celo* III t.c. 29, duo sequerentur inconvenientia. Quorum primum est: quod cum ipsa materia habuisset esse actu a qualibet forma denudata—esset ut sic quid extra decem predicamenta existens et sic simul tempore esset quid potentia et quid actu, quod est quid absurdum.

§ 2.1.3 Secundum inconveniens est: quod non minus sequeretur dari vacuum, quia antequam ex eadem materia fieret quid actu ille quidem locus ubi habet illud actu tandem existere non minus habuisset esse necessario vacuus. Locus, enim, actu existens non datur occupari nisi ab actualibus corporis dimensionibus quales non habuissent

§ 2 Second,

it may be inquired whether the first elements of perishable [i.e., sensible] things are [pre]eternal.

And it seems to be so.

§ 2.1.1 First, I would argue that if they were created, they either come from nothing—that is, from absolute nothingness—or they were created from an actualised being, or at least, from a potential being. [They do] not [come] from nothing, because nothing comes from nothing, and this is clear, as the Philosopher explains in *Physics* 1, text. 77,[a] when he states: "And obviously it could not come out of the non-existent." And aside from this, if [the elements] came to be from absolute nothingness, that same impossibility would follow, as the Philosopher affirms in the book *On the Heavens* 3, text. 29,[b] resulting from the statement according to which a body is created from absolute nothingness, where he says: "It is impossible that a body will be created if there is no vacuum, for the place in which the body is was necessarily void." We cannot say, in accordance with the second [hypothesis], that the elements were created from something existing in actuality, because if this were true, then the existent in actuality would have existed before them, and the same question would arise about their own priority, and the process would proceed to infinity. But if it is true that the elements exist | from a potential being only, such as prime matter, then this matter, which is devoid of all form, will be prior to them in actuality.

§ 2.1.2 And two incongruities would follow, as Averroes explicates in *On the Heavens* 3, text. 29.[c] First: if this matter devoid of all form were to exist in actuality, then something outside of the ten categories would exist, and it would exist in actuality and in potentiality at the same time, and this is impossible.

§ 2.1.3 Second: it would be necessary for there to be a vacuum, because something existing in actuality would be created from this matter, and then it would necessarily be a space in which something in actuality existed, and [this space] would necessarily have been void. Moreover, only something existing in actuality will occupy a space by means of corporeal quantities existing in actuality. Those

---

[a] secundum ut] coni. COPP.; secundum.5.ut.

[a] *Phys.* 1.8.191b.   [b] *Cael.* 3.2.302a.   [c] Cf. *Cael.* 3.2.302a.

actuality would fill the space. And this [corporeal] quantity does not belong to prime matter, which only exists in potentiality, and therefore there is no plenum. Therefore, it would follow that the elements were [formed] from a prime matter that was not prior to them in time. And since prime matter was not created according to Aristotle's explanations in *Physics* 1, text. 82,[a] *On Generation and Corruption* 2, text. 6,[b] and *Metaphysics* 12, text. 12,[c] it follows—if this is correct—that the aforementioned elements were also not created. And therefore, it follows that they are eternal. And Averroes explains this in *Metaphysics* 8, text. 12, in [his] explanation of the Philosopher's words, who says there[d]: "It is true that some existents are without matter." And Averroes explains in his Commentary on this: "Here, the Philosopher's intention was not [to speak] about the celestial bodies, because they are all without matter, but [rather] about the elements, which are eternal according to the whole and corruptible according to the part. This becomes clear from natural things, because true matter, whose existence is potential, is only found in the bodies of the generable and corruptible things." And therefore, it follows that the substrate of the elements is never found in potentiality prior in time to their existence in actuality, but that there is always a part of them in actuality. And therefore, it would follow that the elements would exist in actuality forever. If so, they would be [pre]eternal.

§ 2.2.1 But the contrary of this—namely, that the elements are not [pre]eternal—becomes clear. First, because no generable and corruptible thing is [pre]eternal, and every part of the elements is generable and corruptible. If so, then no part of the elements is [pre]eternal. And therefore, it also follows that their whole is not [pre]eternal, because their whole is nothing other than the composite of all of their parts. And if every part of them is not [pre]eternal, but was created to be generable and corruptible, then there is nothing left to confirm that it [i.e. the whole] is [pre]eternal. The consequence is self-evident and the [antecedent] premise becomes clear, first, when we say that there is no corruptible thing that is [pre]eternal. And this is [found] in the Philosopher's proof in *On the Heavens* 1, text. 124:[e] "We say that everything that is perpetual is not generable and corruptible. And since this is the truth, it becomes clear that a generable and corruptible thing is not perpetual and not eternal. For if this was [the case], it would have the potentiality to [both] exist forever and not exist forever. And this is incongruous."

---

[a]*Phys.* 1.9.192a.   [b]*Gen. corr.* 2.1.329a.   [c]*Metaph.* 12.3.1069b.   [d]*Metaph.* 8.6.1045a.   [e]*Cael.* 1.12.282b.

materie prime inesse cum scilicet essent potentiales tantum; quare non occupassent locum. Restat ergo ut ipsa elementa habuissent esse ex materia prima non tamen eisdem priori secundum tempus. Cumque ipsa materia prima sit quid ingenitum, sicut habetur ratione et auctoritate Phylosophi *Physicorum* primi t.c. 82 et *Metaphysicorum* XII t.c. 12 et *De Generatione* II t.c. 6. Sequitur ergo ut elementa habuissent similiter esse ingenita, et per consequens ab eterno. Et idem videtur inferre Aven R. de mente Phylosophi *Metaphysicorum* VIII t.c. 12 ubi Phylosophus ait: «Et rectum est ut quedam non habeant materiam» ubi Aven R. exponens ait: «Non intendit quedam corporum celestium illa, enim, omnia non habent materiam, sed intendit de elementis que sunt eterna secundum totum, et generabilia et corruptibilia secundum partem, ut dictum est in naturalibus. Materia, enim, secundum veritatem cuius esse est in potentia non invenitur nisi in substantijs generabilibus etc.» Quibus infertur quod elementorum subiectum numquam habuit esse quid potentia tantum ad horum actum precedens, immo horum subiectum habuit semper esse pars eorum actu, per consequens habuerunt elementa esse semper actum, et sic ab eterno.

§ 2.2.1 Ad oppositum arguitur sic nullum generabile et corruptibile habuit esse ab eterno. Quelibet elementorum pars est huiusmodi. Ergo nulla elementorum pars habuit esse ab eterno, et per consequens neque horum totum habuit esse ab eterno, quia cum horum totum nil aliud sit quam omnes partes simul sumpte; de quarum singulis verificatur ut sint genite et corruptibiles, et per consequens non ab eterno. Nullum ergo superest totum sive subiectum cui detur in esse eternitas, sive potentia infinita ad semper esse. Consequentia patet et antecedens probatur et primo quo ad primam partem qua dicitur quod nullum corruptibile habuit esse ab eterno ratione scilicet et auctoritate Phylosophi in lib. *De Celo* I t.c. 124ᵃ ubi dicit: «Et dicamus quod illud quod est semper ens neque est corruptibile. Et cum ita sit, manifestum est quod illud quod est generabile et corruptibile est non ens perpetuum et eternum, si enim esset perpetuum et eternum haberet potentiam ut semper esset ens et semper non ens. Quod est impossibile.»

[corporeal] quantities existing in actuality do not belong to prime matter, because matter exists in potency only. For this reason, they [the corporeal quantities] do not occupy a space. There still remains, therefore, the first [instance]: that these elements exist from prime matter, which is not prior to them in time. Because prime matter is something that is not created, according to the argument and authority of the Philosopher in *Physics* 1, text. 82,[a] *Metaphysics* 12, text. 12,[b] and *On Generation and Corruption* 2, text. 6,[c] it would follow that the elements were also not created, and consequently, they are [pre]eternal. And Averroes explicates [this] in the name of the Philosopher in *Metaphysics* 8, text. 12,[d] where the Philosopher states: "And it is appropriate to say that such a thing has no matter." And Averroes explicates: "Because he [Aristotle] distinguishes between elements that are eternal according to the whole, but which can be generated and corrupted according to the part. That which is only in potency is in truth matter and exists in substances that can be generated and corrupted." With those [words], we can state that the substrate of the elements never exists in potency only, because the substrate precedes them in actuality; on the contrary, there is always a part of their substrate that is in actuality, and consequently, the elements exist forever in actuality, and for this reason, they are [pre]eternal.

§ 2.2.1 On the contrary it is to argue that nothing that can be generated and corrupted is [pre]eternal and that every part of the elements can be generated and corrupted and so no part of the elements is [pre]eternal, and consequently, their whole is not [pre]eternal either, because their whole is nothing more than a composite of all of their parts. This is correct because [the parts] can be generated and corrupted, and consequently, they are not [pre]eternal; there is no whole or substrate in which eternity is given or an infinite potentiality which lasts forever. The consequence is evident, and the first part of the antecedent—in which we say that nothing corruptible is [pre]eternal—is proved, as the Philosopher explains in *On the Heavens* 1, text. 124,[e] where he states: "Everything which is perpetual cannot be generated and corrupted. It is evident that a being that can be generated and corrupted is not perpetual and not eternal, because if it were true that a being that could be generated and corrupted was perpetual and eternal, then this being would have the potentiality to [both] exist forever and not exist forever. And this is incongruous."

---

[a] 124] emend. Copp.; 129 b; 124 L.

[a] *Phys.* 1.9.192a. [b] *Metaph.* 12.3.1069b. [c] *Gen. corr.* 2.1.329a. [d] *Metaph.* 8.6.1045a. [e] *Cael.* 1.12.282b.

12ᵛ §2.2.2 Therefore, | what we said in the [antecedent] premise—that every single part of every element is generable and corruptible—is evident from experience and explained by the Philosopher in *On the Heavens* 3, text. 52:[a] "We said that it is impossible that the elements are eternal, because we see fire and water and all the simple bodies melting and changing." And he continues by saying: "It becomes clear that the elements of the bodies are entirely generable and corruptible." Moreover, these words can perhaps be understood only [to refer] to parts of the elements and not to them as a whole; namely, that it is incongruous that the elements are [pre]eternal in any place. It also becomes clear from this that they are not [pre]eternal as a whole, because there is no part of them that confirms that it is [pre]eternal, but it confirms that it is created without anything being left to confirm that it is [pre]eternal, as mentioned above. And the same thing becomes clear from Aristotle's proofs in *On the Heavens* 1, text. 19:[b] "The place of every element of the earth is the very place where the movement of its parts [occurs]." And he continues, ibid.: "Because what is correct about the whole will be correct about the part." And Averroes explains these words [in his Commentary], ibid.: "The nature of a part of the simple bodies is congruent with the nature of the whole by definition. And since they are congruent in definition, they are congruent in form. And since they are congruent in form, they are congruent in actuality, which follows from that form." And the same thing is explained by Aristotle in the aforementioned book, 2, text. 19:[c] "It is impossible that any one of the elements can be perpetual, because the contraries [inter]act and are affected [by one another]." And since the contraries of the element are in the whole as well as the part, it follows from this very same proof that they as a whole are also not perpetual. And therefore, it follows that it [i.e. the element] [as a whole] is not eternal, as mentioned above. And if the opponent argues and says that the their whole will not differ from its contrary due to the equal proportion of their qualities, by which the whole of them will resist [complete] corruption by the activity of its contrary, as seems to be [clear] from Averroes's words in [his Commentary on] *On Generation and Corruption* 2, text. 37,[d] then it follows that the whole of them would also be corruptible *per se*, but would resist corruption, to which it is disposed. This [would exist] by chance insofar as there is resistance [and] insofar as [there is] an equal proportion of their qualities. And this is incongruous, according to the Philosopher's explanation in *On the Heavens* 1, text. 137:[e]

[a] *Cael.* 3.6.305a.   [b] *Cael.* 1.3.270a.   [c] *Cael.* 2.3.286a.   [d] Cf. *Gen. corr.* 2.6.333a.   [e] *Cael.* 1.12.283b.

2. DE ELEMENTIS

§2.2.2 Quo autem ad secundam antecedentis partem qua scilicet dicitur quod quelibet elementorum pars est generabilis et corruptibilis, patet sensu et Phylosophi auctoritate in lib. *De Celo* III t.c. 52 ubi dicit et impossibile est ut elementa sint eterna, videmus, enim, ignem aquam et omne corpus simplex dissolvi et transmutari ubi subdit dicens Declaratum est igitur quod elementa corporum sunt generabilia et corruptibilia omnino. Et licet ibidem fortasse de partibus tantum intelligat, patet tamen quod idem sit de toto cum nihil sit horum singuli totum quam omnes eiusdem partes simul sumpte, ut supra. Et idem habetur ratione et auctoritate Phylosophi in lib. *De Celo* primi t.c. 19 ubi dicit: «Et locus totius terre idem est cum loco motibus partium eius» ubi subdit dicens: «Sermo, enim, de toto et de parte idem est» ubi Aven R. exponens ait: «Natura enim corporum similium partium eadem est cum natura totius, diffinitione, et cum sint eadem diffinitione, eadem est forma, et si eadem est forma, eadem est actione proveniente ex ipsa forma etc.» etc. et idem patet ratione et auctoritate eiusdem Phylosophi ibidem II t.c. 19 ubi dicit: «Impossibile est ut aliquod elementorum sit semper manens quia contraria agunt et patiuntur.» Cum autem huiusmodi contrarietas non minus insit toti quam partibus eadem ergo ratione sequitur ut neque horum totum habeat semper manere et ut sic non ab eterno ut supra licet enim dicatur quod horum totum non corrumpitur a contrario propter proportionalem qualitatum equalitatem inter ipsa secundum totum observatam; quare fit resistentia ad totalem corruptionem sicut Aven R. inferre videtur in libro *De Generatione* II t.c. 37 non minus tamen sequitur ut per se saltem sint corruptibilia. Quare non datur ut fiant per accidens incorruptibilia,[a] licet fortasse per accidens incorrupta ratione resistentie a proportionali equalitate contingentis et per consequens non habuerunt esse ab eterno; cum scilicet per se seclusa ista resistentia eisdem contingente. Corrumpent se invicem propter horum contrarietatem, et per consequens non habent per se potentiam ut sint semper ens quod eterno requiritur, ut supra. Quare Phylosophus in lib. *De Celo* primi t.c. 137[b] ait:

§2.2.2 Concerning the second part of the antecedent, in which it | says that every part of the elements can be generated and corrupted, this seems to be evident, as the Philosopher explains in *On the Heavens* 3, text. 52,[a] where he states: "It is impossible that the elements can be eternal, because we see fire and water and all the simple bodies melting and changing." And he continues: "It becomes clear that the elements of bodies can be entirely generated and corrupted." And if these words could perhaps be understood to only refer to parts, it is evident that they could also be understood to refer to the whole, because the whole is the composite of all of the parts, as mentioned above, according to the argument and authority of the Philosopher in *On the Heavens* 1, text. 19,[b] where he states: "The place of every element on earth is the same as the place of the movement of its parts," and he continues: "For the same argument applies to the whole and the part." And Averroes explicates: "The nature of a part of a body is congruent with the nature of the whole according to their definition. And since they will be congruent in definition, they are congruent in form. And since they are congruent in form, they are congruent in actuality [lit. activity], which follows from this form, etc.," according to the argument and authority of the Philosopher in the aforementioned book 2, text. 19,[c] where he states: "[With] these four elements, generation clearly is involved, since none of them can be eternal: for contraries interact with one another and destroy one another." Since the contraries are not only in the whole, but also in the parts, it would logically follow that the whole of them does not remain forever, and consequently, it [as a whole] is not eternal, as mentioned above. And then it is possible to assert that they as a whole do not change into [its] contrary, because an equal proportion of their [corporeal] quality is observed in the whole, since there is a resistance against complete corruption, as Averroes explicates in *On Generation and Corruption* 2, text. 37.[d] Nevertheless, it would follow that at least the whole of them will be corruptible *per se*, because it is not possible that corruptible things may be produced by chance—perhaps uncorrupted beings are produced by chance considering the contingent resistance to the equal proportion of quality—and consequently, they [corruptible things] are not [pre]eternal; that is to say, resistance would be contingent to them. Things will corrupt each other because of their contrariety, and consequently, they do not *per se* have the potentiality to always exist, which is necessary for a being that exists eternally, as mentioned above, as the Philosopher explains in *On the Heavens* 1, text. 137,[e] where

---

[a] incorruptibilia] b^corr; corruptibilia b. [b] 137] emend. Copp.; 157 b; 137 L.

[a] *Cael.* 3.6.305a. [b] *Cael.* 1.3.270a. [c] *Cael.* 2.3.286a. [d] Cf. *Gen. corr.* 2.6.333a. [e] *Cael.* 1.12.283b.

"If [this is] so, then according to their words, something would exist that is disposed to corruption that is incorruptible in actuality. And if so, it would be possible that one [and the] same thing would both exist forever and not exist forever." And Averroes explains [in his Commentary], ibid.: "It is impossible that a thing that is eternal will be corruptible in potentiality." And apart from these [words]: if the elements were [pre]eternal, it would therefore follow that there was no [creating] agent for them. And if so, the equal proportion of the qualities of the elements in every single one of them would exist without the intender's intention. And if so, this would have happened by chance, as Aristotle explains in *Physics* 2, | text. 51:[a] "The causes to which no intention and no will is attributed are said to exist by chance." And this is incongruous, because one does not say about a thing that preserves [its] proportion in many existents that this happens by chance. And this is self-evident. And therefore, Aristotle says in *On the Heavens* 2, text. 45:[b] "We say that if the stars and the spheres are not caused and are without an efficient cause, there will be no necessity that the sphere will have a [certain] size with regard to all stars and [no necessity] that the movement of the star will be faster according to the size of the sphere. And if only one or two stars were [moving] in this way, it would be not that impossible. But since all the stars are [moving in] this way, it is an absurd statement."

§ 2.2.3 But regarding what we said, that if the elements were [pre]eternal, it would follow that they had no agent: this is evident because the agent is necessarily prior to its activity in time, as is explained by proof in the previous thesis. And if the elements were [pre]eternal, it would be impossible that anything would be prior to them in time. And therefore, Averroes says in the Commentary on *On the Heavens* 4, text. 1: "The eternal things only have an agent according to a certain likeness." And apart from this, if the elements were [pre]eternal according to the whole, it would therefore follow that a certain part of the elements would also be [pre]eternal. And this [part] would be the part of the [element of] earth that is close to the centre, and the part of the [element of] fire that is within the concave [curvature] of the sphere [of the moon], because corruption never occurs in these two parts. And this would occur in them either by substance or by accident. And if it was by substance, it would follow that for them and for the rest of the parts of the elements, the name of the whole would only be [used] by equivocation. And if this was the

---

[a] *Phys.* 2.5.197a. [b] *Cael.* 2.8.289b.

לשונו: »יהיה אם כן לפי דבריהם דבר מוכן להפסד בלתי נפסד בפעל ואם כן יהיה אפשר שדבר אחד בעצמו יהיה לעולם נמצא ולעולם בלתי נמצא« עכ״ל. ובאר שם אבן רשד ואמר כי: »אמנם מן הנמנע הוא שהדבר אשר היה לעולם יהיה נפסד בכח.« ובלעדי אלה הנה אם היו היסודות קדמונים היה מתחייב מזה שלא היה להם פועל ואם כן היה אותו שווי הנמצא בכמות איכיות היסודות נופל בכל אחד מהם בלתי כוונת מכוין ואם כן היה במקרה כמו שבאר ארסטו' בספר השמע מאמר ב' | פרק נ״א באמרו: »הסבות אשר הם בלתי כוונה ורצון יאמר עליהם שהיו במקרה« עכ״ל. וזה לא יתכן כי הדבר השומר שעור בנמצאים רבים לא יאמר עליו שנפל זה במקרה וזה מבואר בעצמו. ולכן אמר ארסטו' בספר השמים מאמר ב' פרק מ״ה וזה לשונו: »נאמר שאם הכוכבים והגלגלים היו בלתי מסובבים ובלתי סבה פועלת לא היה שם הכרח שיהיה הגלגל שומר גודל בכל הכוכבים ושתנועת הכוכב תהיה מהירה כפי גודל הגלגל ואם כוכב אחד או שני כוכבים בלבד היו על זה האופן לא היה כל כך נמנע אמנם בהיות הכוכבים כלם בזה האופן הנה זה מאמר בטל« עכ״ל.

§ 2.2.3 אמנם מה שאמרנו שאם היו היסודות קדמונים יתחייב שלא היה להם פועל. הוא מבואר כי הפועל הוא בהכרח קודם בזמן לפעולתו כמו שהתבאר במופת בחקירה אשר קודם זאת והנה אם היו היסודות קדמונים לא היה איפשר ששום דבר קדם להם בזמן. ולזה אמר אבן רשד בביאור ספר השמים מאמר ד' פרק א': »הדברים הקדמונים אין להם פועל זולתי כפי דמיון מה« עכ״ל. ובלעדי זאת אם היו היסודות קדמונים כפי הכל הנה יתחייב מזה שאיזה חלק מחלקי היסודות הוא גם כן קדמון והוא חלק הארץ אשר קרוב למרכז וחלק האש אשר במקוער הגלגל כי לאלו שני החלקים לא קרה הפסד מעולם. וזה אמנם יהיה בהם אם בעצם ואם במקרה. ואם היה זה בהם בעצם יתחייב שיאמר עליהם ועל שאר חלקי יסוד שם הכל בשתוף

«Erit ergo corruptibile secundum quod dicunt non corruptum actu. Tunc igitur possibile est ut idem sit semper ens etc.» ubi Aven R. exponens ait: «Impossibile est ut aliquid quod semper fuit habeat potentiam ad corruptionem etc.» Preterea cum horum incorruptio causetur ab equalitatis proportionis resistentia in singulis observata: vel ergo illa equalis proportio habuit esse sic observata preter alicuius intentum et sic habuit esse casu prout habetur a Phylosopho *Physicorum* II t.c. 51 ubi dicit: «Sed ex causis que sunt sine voluntate et sine cogitatione: et tunc dicuntur quod contingunt casu etc.» Et hoc est inconveniens illud, enim, quod in pluribus observatur presertim cum inde sequatur finis quidam inopinabile videtur ut contingat casu. Quare Phylosophus in lib. *De Celo* II t.c. 45 ait: «Dicamus etiam quod si stelle et orbes essent non causati et essent sine causa et agente, non esset omnino necessarium ut orbis esset magnus in omnibus stellis, et motus stelle esset in eo velox secundum magnitudinem orbis. Si igitur una stel|la aut due essent huiusmodi non esset inopinabile tantum, cum autem omnes stelle sint huiusmodi iste sermo est fabulosus.»

§ 2.2.3 Restat ergo secundum: quod scilicet illa proportionalis equalitas in omnibus observata sit a quodam voluntario agente ad finem intenta, et per consequens non habuit esse ab eterno. Agens enim et finis in mente eius intentus habuerunt secundum tempus ad eiusdem actum precedere. Quare Aven R. in comento *De Celo* IV t.c. 1 ait: «Res, enim, eterne non habent agentes nisi secundum similitudinem.» Preterea si elementa essent secundum totum ab eterno, sequeretur ut quedam elementorum partes habuissent similiter esse ab eterno incorrupta quamvis de partibus saltem pateat quod sint corruptibiles, ut supra. Et per consequens non habent potentiam ut sint semper ens quod est inconveniens, ut supra. Quod autem hoc sequatur patet quia ille partes terre, v.g. que sunt in centro terre vel ignis circa orbem lune existens si fuissent quandoque corrupte et in alium elementum converse sequeretur alte-

he states: "According to what they said, it will have the potentiality of something that is not corruptible in actuality, and if this was possible, then this thing would exist forever, etc." And Averroes explains: "It is impossible that a thing that exist forever will be corruptible in potentiality, etc." Moreover, if their incorruptibility is caused by the resistance of the equal proportion observed in each element, then the equal proportion that is observed in each element is without intention. If this is true, then it would be by chance, as the Philosopher explains in *Physics* 2, text. 51,[a] where he states: "But concerning causes in which there is no will or reflection [i.e., intention], we said that they happen by chance, etc." And this is incongruous, especially in this case, because it is observed in many things, and then it would follow that there is a certain purpose and it seems impossible that this would occur by chance. Therefore, the Philosopher explains in *On the Heavens* 2, text. 45:[b] "We say that if the stars and the spheres are not caused and are without an efficient cause, then there will be no necessity that the size of the sphere with regard to all stars and the movement of the star will be faster according to the size of the sphere. If | only one or two stars were [moving] in this way, it would not be that impossible. But since all the stars are [moving] in this way, this statement is absurd."

§ 2.2.3 There remains the second [instance]; that is, that the equal proportions observed in every element proceed from a voluntary agent towards a final purpose, and consequently, it is not eternal. In fact, the agent and the intended purpose in the mind of the agent are necessarily prior in time to its activity, as Averroes explicates in the Commentary on *On the Heavens* 4, text. 1, where he states: "The eternal things only have an agent according to likeness." Moreover, if the elements were [pre]eternal according to the whole, it would follow that any part of these elements would also similarly be incorruptible forever. However, it is evident that parts are corruptible, as mentioned above, and consequently, they do not have the potentiality to always exist, and this is incongruous, as mentioned above. Since it would follow, for example, that if the parts of the earth that are [located] close to the centre of the earth or the fire that is near to the sphere of the moon were corruptible and were combined into one of the other elements, then two different things could happen: either the rest of the elements that are distributed in their parts up to the circumference would be corruptible and they would consequently be combined [with one of the other elements],

---

[a] *Phys.* 2.5.197a. [b] *Cael.* 2.8.289b.

case for them by accident, it would also follow that there was a [pre]eternal thing that was disposed to corruption and potentially corruptible that was not actually corruptible. In this way, it would have the potentiality to [both] exist forever and to not exist forever. And this is incongruous, as mentioned above.

§ 2.2.4 Regarding what we said—that if the elements were [pre]eternal according to the whole, it would follow that the parts of the earth that are attached to the centre and the parts of the fire within the concave [curvature] of the sphere [of the moon] were not subject to corruption—this can be explained in this way: because their change into the quality of the opposite element is impossible for them for one of two reasons. (1) The first [reason] is that [if the change happened], then it would follow that every remainder of the element would change into the form of its opposite. And according to this, it would [then] happen that the form of its whole would be corrupted. From this, it would follow that the elements were not [pre]eternal, and this is what was sought [to prove]. And apart from this, if we said that this [change] happened, we would not know how this element could return to its stability. (2) The second [reason] is that we say, if so, [then it would follow] that these [afore]mentioned parts of the fire and the earth would be outside of their [natural] place during their change and they would change into their opposite by means of a miracle without contact with the opposite into which they would change; and the remainder of the element would still remain in its previous form. And all this is incongruous and does not come to mind.

§ 2.3.1 Second, it becomes clear that the elements are not [pre]eternal in this way: because since | the elements change into one another, it follows that a certain matter is common to all their forms, as proved by Aristotle and Averroes in *On Generation and Corruption* 1, text. 54[a] and 87,[b] and *Metaphysics* 8, text. 14.[c] And since this is correct, one of two [cases] is inevitable: (1) The first is that this matter would be equally disposed to receive the form of every single one of the elements. (2) Alternatively, the second is that it would not be disposed to [receive] them equally. Indeed, it is incongruous that it would be disposed to [receive] every single one of them equally, because the diversity of the forms needs a diversity of matters, as proved by Averroes in the Commentary on *Physics* 8, text. 46[d]. And moreover, because if this was true, no reason would be given [to explain] how it could occur that in any part of matter—

---

[a] *Gen. corr.* 1.7.324a.   [b] *Gen. corr.* 1.10.328a.   [c] *Metaph.* 8.2.1042a–b.   [d] Cf. *Phys.* 8.6.258b.

---

§ 2.2.4 אמנם מה שאמרנו שאם היו היסודות קדמונים כפי הכל היה מתחייב שחלקי הארץ סמוך למרכז וחלק האש אשר במקוער הגלגל לא קרה להם הפסד הנה יתבאר באופן זה, כי אמנם היה נמנע השתנותם באיכות היסוד ההפכי להם אם לא על אחד משני פנים האחד הוא שקרה אז שכל שארית היסוד השתנה לצורת הפכו. ולפי זה קרה לו שצורת כלו נפסד. ומזה יתחייב שהיסודות בלתי קדמונים וזה הוא המבוקש. ובלעדי זאת אם נאמר שקרה זה לא נדע סבה איך אותו היסוד שב לאיתנו. והשני הוא שנאמר אם כן שאותן חלקי האש והארץ הנזכרים היו בהשתנותם חוץ ממקומם ושנשתנו אל הפכם בפלא בלתי מגע הפכי שישינהו ועם זה נשאר שארית היסוד על צורתו הקודמת. וכל זה לא יתכן ולא יעלה על לב.

§ 2.3.1 **שנית** יתבאר שהיסודות הם בלתי קדמונים באופן זה כי בהיות | 13ᵛ
היסודות משתנים קצתם לקצתם יתחייב שיהיה איזה חומר משותף לכל צורותיהם כמבואר במופת ארסטו׳ ואבן רשד בספר ההויה וההפסד מאמר א׳ פרק נ״ד ופ״ז ובספר מה שאחר מאמר ח׳ פרק י״ד ובהיות הדבר כן הנה לא ימלט מאחת משתים האחת היא שיהיה אותו החומר מוכן לקבל צורת כל אחת מהיסודות בשוה או שנית שהוא בלתי מוכן להן בשוה אמנם לא יתכן שיהיה מוכן לכל אחת מהן בשוה כי התחלפות הצורות יתחייב מהתחלפות החומרים כמבואר במופת אבן רשד בביאור ספר השמע מאמר ח׳ פרק מ״ו ועוד כי אם היה זה

rum duorum vel scilicet ut similiter residuum huiusmodi elementi saltem in eiusdem partis directo usque ad circumferentiam fuisset tunc corruptum et conversum: vel ut ipsa pars sic corrupta et in aliud elementum conversa esset tunc in loco sibi non naturali. Quorum utrumque est inconveniens et inauditum. Restat ergo ut huiusmodi centri partes habuissent esse ab eterno incorrupte quamvis in se corruptibiles, et per consequens non habent potentiam ad hoc ut sint semper ens, ut supra quod inconveniens.

⟨§ 2.2.4⟩

§ 2.3.1 Secundo arguitur sic cum elementa in se invicem convertantur. Danda est ergo materia quedam omnibus comunis ratione cuius in se invicem convertantur. Sicut habetur ratione et auctoritate Phylosophi et Aven R. in lib. *De Generatione* primi t.c. 54[a] et 87 et *Metaphysicorum* VIII t.c. 14: vel ergo ipsa materia est his omnibus immediate et eque primo appropriata, vel non. Non primum: quia diversis formis nedum contrarijs diverse requiruntur materie, prout habetur ratione et auctoritate Aven. R. in comento *Physicorum* VIII t.c. 46. Preterea surgeret questio quare quedam eius materie pars habuisset altera illarum

or the part would be corrupted and ut would be combined with another one of the elements in a place that is not natural [for them]. Both of these cases are incongruous and absurd. It remains that the parts of the centre [the parts of the elements located close to the centre] are incorruptible forever, although if they were corruptible in themselves, they would then have no potentiality and would exist forever, as mentioned above, and this is incongruous.

⟨§ 2.2.4⟩

§ 2.3.1 Second, I would argue that since the elements change into one another, there is therefore a matter common to them, which explains why they change from one into another, according to the argument and authority of the Philosopher and Averroes in *On Generation and Corruption* 1, text. 54[a] and text. 87[b] and *Metaphysics* 8, text. 14.[c] And then, either the matter would be immediately and equally disposed for them, or it would not. The first instance is impossible, because different matters are required for different and contrary forms, according to the argument and authority of Averroes in the Commentary on *Physics* 8, text. 46.[d] Moreover, a question arises as to whether part of their matter would be formed from some-

---

[a] 54] emend. COPP.; 59 b; 54 L.

[a] *Gen. corr.* 1.7.324a.   [b] *Gen. corr.* 1.10.328a.   [c] *Metaph.* 8.2.1042a–1042b.
[d] Cf. *Phys.* 8.6.258b.

although [it is] equally disposed to [receive] every single one of the forms of the elements—there would pre-exist one form of them [i.e., of the elements] [that is] more [likely to be contained] in it than its opposite or another.

§ 2.3.2[a] And more wondrous are the words that the Rambam wrote in the *Guide of the Perplexed* 2:19 in order to dispel this doubt. And he answered like a rhetorician, on behalf of Aristotle, saying that the diversity of the elements follows the diversity of the place by its approximation towards and departing motion from the sphere, as if the place is the reason for the existence of the form. And sense [perception] testifies the contrary of this, because when a part of the element changes form into its prevailing opposite, it is [still] in its place, and its place is [only] changed when the form of its opposite comes onto it. This is because the form is the reason for the generation of a composite in a place, and not the other way around. And the air that is around us on the surface of the earth is in water's place [which would be the natural order] and does not change [its] place for the substance of water. And apart from this, it is evident that prime matter, since its existence is only potential, would not be—with regard to its substance—in actuality in any place. And how can its place be a reason for its form?

§ 2.3.3 If so, [only the following second consequence] would remain: that the same common matter of the forms of the elements is not disposed to [receive] all of them equally. And therefore, it follows that every single one of their diverse forms exists in prime matter, not due to the reason that it is common to all of them, but due to the diversity of its change into diverse dispositions [for diverse forms]. And since every movement of change is undoubtedly [taking place] within a duration of time [that is] before that same form comes at the end of the disposition acquired by that movement, it necessarily follows that at least three of the elements are not [pre]eternal.

§ 2.4 We answer, if so, to dispel [any] doubt about the [afore]mentioned thesis, that none of the elements is [pre]eternal, either with respect to the whole or with respect to the part.

§ 2.5.1 Indeed, to the opponent's arguments, first to his saying that nothing can come to be from nothing—and therefore that it would follow that [an existent] would come to be from a thing in actuality, so that this very same doubt

---

[a] Cf. *LG* § 3.4.1–5.

אמת לא נתן סבה איך קרה[a] זה שאיזה חלק מהחומר עם היותו מוכן לכל אחת מצורות היסודות בשוה נמצאת בו מקדם צורה אחת מהן יותר מהפכה או זולתה.

§ 2.3.2 ומה מאד נפלאו דברי הרמב״ם ז״ל שכתב בספר מורה הנבוכים מאמר ב׳ פרק י״ט[b] בהיתר זה הספק והשיב כמליץ בעד ארסטו׳ ואמר כי התחלפות היסודות נמשך להתחלפות המקום בקרבתו ומרחקו מן הגלגל כאלו המקום היה סבת מציאות הצורה והנה על הפך זה יעיד החוש כי בהשתנות חלק יסוד לצורת הפכו הגובר הוא אמנם במקומו וישנה מקומו בבוא אליו צורת הפכו וזה כי הצורה סבת היות המורכב במקום לא הפך זה. והנה האויר אשר אצלנו על שטח הארץ הוא במקום המים ולא ישנהו המקום אל עצם המים. ובלעדי זאת מבואר הוא שהחומר הראשון בהיות מציאותו בכחיי בלבד לא יהיה מצד עצמו בשום מקום בפעל ואיך יהיה מקומו סבה לצורתו?

§ 2.3.3 אם כן ישאר שאותו החומר המשותף לצורות היסודות לא היה מוכן לכלם בשוה ומזה יתחייב שכל אחת מצרותיהם המתחלפות נמצאת בחומר הראשון לא בסבת היותו משותף לכלן אבל בסבת התחלפות השתנותו אל הכנות מתחלפות ובהיות שכל תנועת השתנות תהיה בלי ספק במשך זמן קודם לאותה הצורה אשר תבוא בסוף ההכנה הקנויה באותה התנועה יתחייב בהכרח ששלש מהיסודות לפחות הם בלתי קדמונים.

§ 2.4 **נשיב** אם כן להתיר ספק החקירה הנזכרת שאין שום אחד מהיסודות קדמון לא לפי הכל ולא לפי החלק.

§ 2.5.1 **אמנם** לטענות החולק ראשונה על אמרו שלא יתהוה דבר מלא דבר ובכן יתחייב שנתהוו מאיזה נמצא בפעל ויפול זה הספק

---

[a] קרה] coni.; קרא a. [b] י״ט] emend. Dunk.; ח״י a; 19 MN.

formarum magis quam reliqua informari, cum sit omnibus ab eterno equaliter disposita.

⟨§ 2.3.2⟩

§ 2.3.3 Restat ergo secundum: scilicet ut materia elementis communis non habuisset esse his omnibus immediate uniformiter disposita, et per consequens habuerunt diverse elementorum forme eidem materie, ratione diversorum alterationis modorum successive inesse et per consequens elementa non habuerunt esse ab eterno, alteratio, enim, nonnisi in tempore ad forme ingressum precedente fieri contingit.

§ 2.4 Ad dubium ergo respondetur: quod nullum elementorum habuit esse ab eterno neque secundum totum, neque secundum partem.

§ 2.5.1 Ad argumenta vero et primo quoad primum quo scilicet dicitur: quod cum ex nihilo nihil fiat. Et habuissent elementa tamquam prima a nullo acto ex|istente et tempore precedente fieri, sequitur ut habuissent esse ingenita,

thing that does not belong to their forms or from something that remains in their forms. If this is so, [then the] elements would be equally disposed forever.

⟨§ 2.3.2⟩

§ 2.3.3 There remains the second [instance], that the common matter is not immediately disposed for them and consequently, different forms of the elements have the same matter according to different kinds of alterations [i.e., changes], and consequently, the elements are not [pre]eternal, because the alteration [i.e., change] precedes the form in time.

§ 2.4 To dispel any doubt, I would argue that no element is [pre]eternal, either with respect to the whole or with respect to the part.

§ 2.5.1 In response to the first argument, I will reply: we can postulate the condition that nothing comes from nothing. If the elements, for instance, | were prior in time to an existent in actuality, then it would follow that they were not generated, and then the elements would be [pre]eternal.

about that existent would arise—we answer by saying that the elements are indeed generated from a substrate existing in actuality that has [acquired] its existence through creation, by which that existent was created as composed out of prime matter and first form designated for the aforementioned | prime matter. And in the matter of this compound, all the forms of the elements will potentially exist through change in various ways. And since that existent exists through creation, there will be no doubt regarding from which prior existent it was created, because no substrate was [used] in its creation at all, as is evident from the definition of creation as the bringing-forth of a thing after absolute non-existence, as Averroes explains in [the Commentary] on *Metaphysics* 12, text. 18.[a]

§ 2.5.2 To the second argument, we answer that it does not follow from the creation of the body of the elements or from the substrate that is prior to them after absolute nothingness that the same space in which it now exists was void before them, because before the creation of that body, there was no place there at all, neither a plenum nor a vacuum. In the same way, it is now incorrect [to claim] that there may be a space, either a plenum or a vacuum, outside of the heavens, as Aristotle explains in *On the Heavens* 1, text. 100.[b] And therefore, we answer and say that this space in which they are now was created together with the elements or their substrate. If so, then when the opponent argues and says that nothing comes from nothing—if it is understood from this that nothing comes to be except from another thing—we will answer that this is not correct for anything apart from the activity of generation[s] that are performed [through a change] from [one] form to [another] form. Because in all of these, the generator needs a substrate on which he acts. And therefore, a thing like these [things] can only be generated from another thing that bears two forms, one after the other. But this is not correct for creation, because no substrate is [used] in it, as mentioned above. And this is so because the creator [also] brings forth the substrate and its form. And therefore, Averroes says in [the Commentary on] *Metaphysics* 12, text. 18:[c] "Those who speak of creation say that the agent brings forth every existent from anew. And there is therefore no need for a matter on which he will act, but he creates all." And this is explained by Solomon in his wisdom in Ecclesiastes (11:5): "So you cannot foresee the actions of God, who causes all things to happen."

---

[a] Cf. *Metaph.* 12.3.1070a.   [b] *Cael.* 1.9.279a.   [c] Cf. *Metaph.* 12.3.1070a.

et ab eterno. Respondetur negando: ut a nullo subiecto actu precedente habuissent fieri, immo habuerunt esse ex quoddam primo ex prima materia et prima forma eidem materie immediate competenti composito, quod diversimode alteratum conversum est in ipsa quatuor elementa respective prima que eidem composito potentialiter inerant. Quod scilicet compositum priscorum nonnulli merito confusum sive chaos appellarunt, prout habetur a phylosopho Anaximandri auctoritate *Physicorum* primi t.c. 32 illud autem compositum non ex priori subiecto, sed per meram creationem post purum non esse habuit produci.

§ 2.5.2 Ad secundum vero argumentum respondetur negando consequentiam non, enim, sequitur elementa habuerunt esse post purum non esse, ergo locus ubi nunc sunt habuit prius esse vacuum. Quia ante creationem illorum: vel illius subiecti sive confusi, ex quo producta sunt nullus erat locus neque plenus neque vacuus, sicut nunc extra celum nullus est locus, prout habetur a Phylosopho in lib. *De Celo* primi t.c. 100. Quare simul cum elementis vel composito: ex quo producta sunt, ut supra, creatus est locus in quo habuerunt creata vel producta existere. Illa ergo propositio qua scilicet dicitur quod: ex nihilo nihil fit, intelligendo quidem per ly, ex nihilo, idem quod non ex aliquo, verificatur de illa tantum productione, que fit de forma ad formam per alterationem ad quam requiritur subiectum alterandum. Sed non verificatur de illa productione, que facta est per meram creationem ex non forma ad formam, sive post purum non esse ad quam nullum requiritur subiectum. Quare Aven. R. in cmmento *Metaphysicorum* XII t.c. 18 ait: «Dicentes autem creationem dicunt: quod agens creat totum ens de novo et quod non habet necesse ad hoc ut sit materia in qum agat, sed creat totum.»

We can reply by rejecting this inference: the elements were generated from a substrate existing in actuality, which was prior in time. They are generated from something first that is composed of prime matter and a first form, which is immediately designated for the compound of the matter; this compound is composed out of the first four elements, which were potentially inside [it]. This is what was rightly called a "mixed compound" or "chaos" by the Ancients, as the philosopher Anaximander explicated in *Physics* 1, text. 32.[a] Thus, this composite does not exist before the substrate, but is produced by creation from absolute nothingness.

§ 2.5.2 In response to the second argument, I will reply by rejecting the inference: if the elements came from absolute nothingness, then the place in which they are now was previously void, because before their creation or before the creation of their substrate [i.e., body] from which they are generated, which is also called the mixed compound, there was no place, neither a plenum nor a vacuum, and there is no place outside the heavens, as the Philosopher explains in *On the Heavens* 1, text. 100,[b] and thus they were generated from something at the same time as the elements or the mixed compound, as mentioned above, and the creation was the place in which the created or generated things exist. Then, the proposition in which we said that nothing comes from nothing could be understood as referring to matter generated from another thing. This is only verified for generation from form to form by alteration, for which one needs a substrate that changes. But it is not verified for the creation that is an absolute creation, which is not from form to form, but from absolute nothingness. In this case, one does not need a substrate. Averroes explicates this in the Commentary on *Metaphysics* 12, text. 18,[c] where he states: "Those who speak of creation say that the agent brings forth every existent anew, and there is therefore no need for a matter on which he acts, but he creates all."

---

[a] *Phys.* 1.4.187a. [b] *Cael.* 1.9.279a. [c] *Metaph.* 12.4.1070a.

§ 2.6 And it [i.e., Holy Scripture] explains this with a proof at the beginning of Genesis (1:2):[a] "And the earth was Tohu and Bohu"; that is to say that the created earth was necessarily first a composite of prime matter and its first form designated for it, in substance and at its beginning. And through a change of this composite in various ways, elements with diverse forms were created, as is explained (ibid.): "And darkness was over the surface of the deep and a spirit from God sweeping over the water." And this is so because it was only congruous for prime matter to have one form designated for it, as mentioned above. And this was the form of the first composite called "Tohu," which existed in prime matter called "Bohu," as the prophet testifies (Isaiah 34:11): "A line of Tohu, and weights of Bohu." And it explains that after this, there was (Genesis 1:2) "darkness over the surface of the deep." And this was the air, deprived of light, above the two lower elements [i.e., earth and water], called | "deep." And it continues (ibid.): "A spirit from God sweeping." And this was the mover of the sphere under the command of its Creator (Psalm 104:4): "He makes [the] spirits [or: winds] His messengers," meaning: this mover swept and he moved air deprived of light above the surface of the water. And by that movement, the [afore]mentioned parts of the air that were attached to the sphere were precisely disposed. And by this, the element of fire was generated, as Aristotle explains in *On the Heavens* 2, text. 42.[b] And in saying (Genesis 1:2) "above the surface of the water," a reason is given for the moistness of the air, which was not dried by the heat of the [afore]mentioned movement. And this is so because it is a part [that is] above the surface of the water.

§ 2.7 And perhaps this is what Anaximander and others meant when they said that at first existed a composed and mixed thing. And Aristotle was amused by them in *Physics* 1, text. 32.[c] And Empedocles agreed with Anaximander's opinion, as stated in *On Generation and Corruption* 1, text. 22.[d]

---

[a] Cf. Sforno's Commentary on Gen 1:2. [b] *Cael.* 2.7.289a. [c] *Phys.* 1.4.187a.
[d] *Gen. corr.* 1.3.319a–b.

2. DE ELEMENTIS

§ 2.6 Quare Sacrum Genesis Documentum cap. primo [1:1] docens huiusmodi elementorum productionem, dicit: illa facta esse ex confuso quodam prius creato. Quare dicit: «Deum in principio,» scilicet in instanti, quod scilicet fuit totius temporis tunc futuri principium cuius tamen nulla fuit pars creasse celum et terram. Ubi subdit [Gen 1:2] dicens: «terra autem erat confusum et perplexum.» Quasi dicat: quod per terram huiusmodi creatam, intelligit quid confusum sive chaos cui elementa potentialiter inerant, quamvis interpretes nonnulli ibidem inanis et vacua transtulissent, ex quo confuso diversimode alterato. Producta sunt presentia sensibilium elementa de quibus successive facit mentionem. His ergo: Divinitus solvitur dubium superius tactum: quo scilicet dubitabatur, quomodo contingit, ut materia prima non habens actuales partes, nedum ab invicem diversas, quatuor diversis elementorum formis immediate appropriaretur cum diversis formis diverse requirantur materie eisdem formis immediate appropriate, prout supra patuit ratione et auctoritate Aven R. *Physicorum* VIII t.c. 46 huiusmodi, enim, dubium solvit, prefatum Ge|nesis Documentum dicens quod primum sensibilium ex ipsa materia prima et prima forma eidem propria compositum fuit confusum quoddam cui generabilium elementa potentialiter inerant. Ex quo confuso, Creatoris iussu diversimode alterato, producta sunt elementa, que dicimus prima deinde docet elementalis ignis productionem, per motum, quo aer caluit, sicut et Phylosophus infert in lib. *De Celo* II t.c. 42 et hoc docet cum [Gen 1:2] dicit: «et spiritus Dei circumferebat,» per ly, Spiritus Dei, intelligens illam abstractam substantiam per quam celum moveri videtur. Quare Psalmus 103 [104:4] universi productionem narrans, ait: «fecit angelos suos spiritus.»

§ 2.7 Et idem fortasse sensit Anaximandrus ponens primum confusum sive Chaos, de quo Phylosophus facit verbum *Physicorum* primi t.c. 32.ᵃ

§ 2.6 And the Holy Book of Genesis (1:1), by means of divine teaching and demonstrative explanation, teaches about the generation of the elements: an element was generated from a mixed composite which was previously created. It says: "In the beginning God," which means in the instant that was the beginning of the whole of time as the origin of future time, and then no part of heaven or earth had been created. And then (Genesis 1:2): "And the earth was confused and perplexed,"ᵃ as if when the earth was created, it was a "confusion" or "chaos"ᵇ that contained the elements in potentiality; but some commentators translate it differently, as "void and empty." Then the doubt is divinely resolved. In fact, prime matter does not have different parts in actuality, nor does it belong to the different forms of the four elements, because different forms require different matters that are immediately disposed for their forms, according to the argument and authority of Averroes in *Physics* 8, text. 46,ᶜ as mentioned above. Then the doubt is resolved, thanks to the [Holy] Book of Ge|nesis, where it is explained that the first of all sensible beings was a mixed compound generated from prime matter and the first form that contained the elements in potentiality, out of the mixed compound. By the creator's command, the elements were created by diverse changes, and for that reason, we said that the generation of the first fire was inflamed by the air, by means of motion, as the Philosopher explicates in *On the Heavens* 2, text. 42.ᵈ And this is the same as that which was taught by [the verse]: "The Holy Spirit moves around" (Genesis 1:2), which means that the Holy Spirit is a separate substance by which the heavens are moved. Then Psalm 103 (104:4), concerning the creation of the universe, says: "He makes His angels spirits."

§ 2.7 And perhaps this mixed "confusion" or "chaos" was posited by Anaximander as the first element, as Aristotle mentions in *Physics* 1, text. 32.ᵉ

ᵃ 32] emend. COPP.; 22 b; 32 L.

ᵃ*Perplexum* in Latin.   ᵇCf. Sforno's Commentary on Gen 1:2.   ᶜCf. *Phys.* 8.6.258b.   ᵈ*Cael.* 2.7.289a.   ᵉ*Phys.* 1.4.187a.

§ 3 Third:
We will inquire whether prime matter is [pre]eternal.

And it seems that it is necessarily [pre]eternal.

§ 3.1 And this is so because no substrate from which it can be generated existed prior to it. And since nothing comes from nothing, it follows that prime matter was not created. And therefore, it follows that it is [pre]eternal, as Aristotle explains in *Physics* 1, text. 82:[a] "It is necessary that prime matter is an incorruptible and ungenerated thing, because if it were a created thing, it would require a substrate from which [it had] been generated." And he explains the same thing in *Metaphysics* 12, text. 12:[b] "Everything that changes is a thing that changes from one thing into another, and this proceeds to infinity."

§ 3.2.1 So, the contrary of this becomes clear—namely, that prime matter is not [pre]eternal—in this way: because the actualisation of prime matter was necessarily not [pre]eternal. If so, it would follow that prime matter is not [pre]eternal. Indeed, the consequence is evident, because if prime matter was [pre]eternal and its actualisation was not [pre]eternal, then it would therefore follow that prime matter would have been devoid of all form at a certain time. And this is incongruous, as is evident from Averroes's proof in [the Commentary on] *On the Heavens* 3, text. 29:[c] "And this underlying substrate does not exist in potentiality except insofar as it does not exist in actuality. And insofar as it [i.e., the substrate] does not exist in actuality, it is part of something that exists in actuality, because indeed something that exists in actuality is inevitably either part of an existent in actuality or one of the [ten] categories. But these two [possibilities] do not apply to this substrate. If so, it would not exist in actuality at all. And therefore, it follows that its existence in an existent in actuality, insofar as it is a part of it, will be in potentiality. And if it existed alone, not as a part of any existent, it would not | exist in potentiality, but in actuality." And the summary of his words is: if the prime matter was an existent that existed alone without being part of a composite, it would follow that—insofar as it is prime matter—its existence would be in potentiality only, but—insofar as it existed alone—it would exist in actuality, because every generated and existing existent exists insofar as it [has] its form and it is said of it that it exists in actuality. And therefore, it would follow that one and the same thing [i.e., prime matter] would exist both in potentiality and in actuality at one and the same time, and these words contradict each other.

---

[a] *Phys.* 1.9.192a. [b] *Metaph.* 12.3.1069b. [c] Cf. *Cael.* 3.2.302a.

§3. Tertio Dubitatur
Utrum materia prima habuisset esse ab eterno;

et videtur quod sic.

§3.1 Quia ad materiam primam non datur subiectum ea prius, ex quo habuisset generari, cum[a] dicatur esse subiectorum primum. Cum autem ex nihilo nihil fiat, sequitur ergo: ut sit quid ingenitum, et per consequens ab eterno. Quare Phylosophus *Physicorum* I t.c. 82 ait: «Necesse est, ut sit non corruptibilis neque generabilis, quoniam si fuerit generata indiget subiecto, ex quo generetur res etc.» Et idem infert *Metaphysicorum* XII t.c. 12 ubi dicit: «Neque materia fit neque forma» subdit dicens: «Omne, enim, quod transmutatur ex aliquo in aliquod transmutatur, et sit processus ad infinitum.»

§3.2.1 Ad oppositum arguitur sic materie prime actus non datur fuisse ab eterno. Ergo neque ipsa materia prima habuit esse ab eterno. Consequentia tenet quia si ipsa materia prima habuisset esse ab eterno sine eiusdem actu, sequeretur ut fuisset quandoque a quolibet actu sive forma denudata. Quod est inconveneniens, prout patet ratione et auctoritate Aven R. in cmento lib. *De Celo* III t.c. 29 ubi dicit: «Hoc, enim, subiectum positum non est in potentia, nisi in quantum non est in actu, et in quantum non est in actu, non est pars alicuius quod est in actu, illud, enim, quod est in actu, aut est pars alicuius quod est in actu, aut est unum predicamentorum. Hoc subiectum caret eis ergo non est in actu alicuius omnino, suum ergo esse in ente in actu non est nisi in quantum est pars eius in potentia. Si autem invenirentur per se singulariter non secundum quod est pars alicuius, non esset ens in potentia sed in actu.»

§3 Third,
it may be inquired whether prime matter is [pre]eternal.

It seems to be so.

§3.1 Because no subject from which it would be generated existed prior to it, and for this reason, it is called the first of the subjects. And since "nothing comes from nothing," it would follow that it is ungenerated, and consequently [pre]eternal, as the Philosopher explains in *Physics* 1, text. 82,[a] where he states: "It is necessary that prime matter is an incorruptible and ungenerated thing, because if it was created, it would be in need of a substrate from which it would have been generated, etc." The same [Aristotle] explains this in *Metaphysics* 12, text. 12,[b] where he states: "Neither the matter nor the form comes to be," and he continues: "Because everything changes from one thing into another, and then this process proceeds to infinity."

§3.2.1 On the contrary it is to argue that the actualisation of prime matter is not [pre]eternal, and consequently, prime matter is not [pre]eternal either. The consequence is evident, because if prime matter is [pre]eternal and its actualisation is not [pre]eternal, it would follow that prime matter would, at a certain time, be devoid of all form. And this is incongruous according to the argument and authority of Averroes in *On the Heavens* 3, text. 29,[c] where he states: "And this posited substrate does not exist in potentiality except insofar as it does not exist in actuality. And since it [i.e., the substrate] does not exist in actuality, it is therefore part of a thing existing in actuality, because a thing existing in actuality will inevitably either be a part of an existent in actuality or one of the [ten] categories. If the substrate were to be deprived of these, it would not exist in actuality at all. And therefore, if it exists, it will be in an existent in actuality, only because it is a part of an existent that is in potentiality. And if it existed alone, not as a part of that [existent], there would not be an existent in potentiality, but rather in actuality."

---

[a] cum] coni. Copp.; cum.5. b.

[a] *Phys.* 1.9.192a. [b] *Metaph.* 12.3.1069b. [c] *Cael.* 3.2.302a.

§ 3.2.2 So, regarding what we said about prime matter, that it is potential only and does not exist in actuality: this is evident because a thing that exists in actuality cannot generate a thing *per se* while it is in actuality. And this thing is self-evident, as Aristotle explains in *Metaphysics* 1, text. 17,[a] and 2, text. 7,[b] and in *On Generation and Corruption* 2, text. 6:[c] "We say that there is one matter for all the perceptible bodies, and it is not separate, but is always [accompanied] by contrariety. And from it, the so-called 'elements' come into being." Regarding what we said in the [antecedent] premise, that the actualisation of prime matter is necessarily not [pre]eternal: this is evident because since the matter is a passive thing existing in potentiality only, it is incongruous, insofar as it is so, that it could have been actualised without an active power that actualises it, as is self-evident. And Averroes explains in [the Commentary on] *Physics* 2, text. 48: "A passive thing will not go from potentiality to actuality except through an active potentiality." And [Averroes] explains the same in [the Commentary on] *Metaphysics* 9, text. 13:[d] "The thing that is the first of the potentialities is a thing that is disposed to be an existent in actuality by means of a thing that is an existent in actuality." And since the agent and the potentialities are temporally prior to their actuality, it follows, if so, that the potentialities, the agent who actualises, and the movement of bringing-forth are necessarily temporally prior to every act that actualises.

§ 3.2.3 And therefore, it follows that every actualised existence in matter is not [pre]eternal. Indeed, regarding what we said—namely, that the potentialities and the agent are necessarily temporally prior to their activity—this becomes clear, first, regarding the potentiality, from Aristotle's proof in *Metaphysics* 9, text. 5,[e] *Against Garicon* [i.e., the Megarians], who were opposed to this, and in *Physics* 8, text. 4,[f] as mentioned above. Regarding what we said—namely, that the agent is necessarily temporally prior to its activity—this is evident from Averroes's proof in [the Commentary on] *Metaphysics* 9, text. 13,[g] and from his statement in the *Treatise on the Substance of the Celestial Sphere*, ch. 2,[h] as mentioned above in the second and third propositions.[i] And the same becomes clear from the definition of the agent that the Philosopher explains in *Physics* 2, text. 31:[j] "And in general, the agents are those who exist at the beginning of the change." And since change only exists in time, as the Philosopher explains in *Physics* 4, text.

---

[a] *Metaph.* 1.8.989b. [b] *Metaph.* 2.2.994a. [c] *Gen. corr.* 2.1.329a. [d] Cf. *Metaph.* 9.3.1048b. [e] *Metaph.* 9.3.1047a. [f] *Phys.* 8.1.251a. [g] Cf. *Metaph.* 9.3.1048b. [h] Cf. *Sub. orb.* 85–86. [i] Cf. §1.6. [j] *Phys.* 2.2.195a.

3. DE MATERIA PRIMA

§ 3.2.2 Quibus infertur, quod si daretur materia prima per se existens, preter quam esset alicuius compositi pars, tunc in quantum esset materia prima per se a qualibet forma denudata, esset quid potentiale tantum, et in quantum esset quid per se existens esset quid actu. Quicquid enim actu existit, per suam formam existit, | et dicitur esse quid actu. Quare daretur ut idem simul tempore esset quid actu, et quid potentia tantum sine actu, quod implicat contradictionem. Preterea patet: quod de ratione materie prime sit, ut non sit per se quid actu, quia ex aliquo actu ente sub eadem forma remanente, non datur quid aliud substantialiter fieri, sicut per se patet et habetur a Phylosopho *Metaphysicorum* primi t.c. 17 et eiusdem secundi t.c. 7. Quare idem Phylosophus in *De Generatione* II t.c. 6 ait: «Nos autem dicimus esse aliquam materiam unam corporibus sensibilium, sed hanc non separabilem, sed semper cum contrarietate ex qua generantur vocata elementa etc.» Antecedens vero quo dictum est: quod non datur materie actus fuisse ab eterno, patet quia cum materia sit quid passivum potentia tantum ens, non datum perduci ad actum nisi per virtutem activam ipsam potentialem materiam de potentia ad actum deducentem; prout per se patet, et habetur ab Aven R. in comento *Physicorum* II t.c. 48 ubi dicit: «Passivum non exit ad actum, nisi a potentia activa» et idem docet idem Aven R. *Metaphysicorum* IX t.c. 13 ubi dicit: «Illud enim quod est principium potentie, est illud quod natum est esse actu ab aliquo, quod est in actu.» Cumque ad actum de potentia ductum, habeat necessario ipsa potentia, et agens ad ipsum actum ducens, secundum tempus precedere.

§ 3.2.3 Sequitur ergo, ut non detur ut eiusdem materie actus habuisset esse ab eterno. Quod autem ipsa potentia et agens habeant ad ipsum actum necessario precedere. Probatur: et primo de potentia, ratione[a] et auctoritate Phylosophi *Metaphysicorum* IX t.c. 5 Contra Garicomen, et *Physicorum* VIII t.c. 4, prout supra patuit. De agente vero videtur per se patere, quia agens requiritur in actionis principio, actus vero in eiusdem evenit fine, inter que duo instantia necessario intervenit tempus, prout per se patet, et habetur a Phylosopho *Physicorum* IV[b] t.c. 129 ubi

§ 3.2.2 And the summary of these words is: if prime matter existed *per se* only because it was a part of another composite thing, then prime matter in itself would be devoid of all form, because it would only exist in potency. And if prime matter existed *per se*, then it would exist in actuality. Something that exists in actuality exists according to its form, | and we say that it exists in actuality. And then, if this is so, there would be something existing in actuality and in potentiality without actuality at the same time, and this implies a contradiction. Moreover, this is evident according to the notion of prime matter that it is not something in actuality *per se*, because a substantial thing will not be generated from another being in actuality in which a form remains. This is evident, as the Philosopher explains in *Metaphysics* 1, text. 17,[a] and *Metaphysics* 2, text. 7.[b] In *On Generation and Corruption* 2, text. 6,[c] the Philosopher states: "Our theory is that there is matter for all perceptible bodies, and it is not separable, but is accompanied by contrariety, and it is from this that the so-called elements come into being." The antecedent, in which we said that the actualisation of prime matter is necessarily not [pre]eternal, is proved, because since the matter is a passive being existing in potency only, it would therefore only be actualised by an active power leading this potential matter from potentiality to actuality, as is evident, as Averroes explicates in the Commentary on *Physics* 2, text. 48,[d] where he states: "A passive thing will only be actualised by an active potentiality." And Averroes also explicates this in *Metaphysics* 9, text. 13,[e] where he states: "A thing that is the beginning of potentialities is a thing that naturally exists in actuality by means of another thing that is in actuality." However, if this thing is leading from potentiality to actuality, then there is necessarily a potentiality and an agent who leads [it] to action, which are prior [to it] in time.

§ 3.2.3 It would follow that if this is not possible, then the actualisation in matter will be eternal, and then the potentiality and the agent will necessarily be prior, as proven by the Philosopher's definition of potentiality in *Metaphysics* 9, text. 5, *Against Garicon*,[f] and in *Physics* 8, text. 4,[g] as aforementioned. And this is also evident according to the definition of "agent," because the agent is necessarily [there] at the beginning of activity and an action occurs at the end because time necessarily comes in between two instants, as is evident, and as the Philosopher explains in *Physics* 4, text. 129,[h] where he states: "It is irrefutable that

---

[a] *Metaph.* 1.8.989b.   [b] *Metaph.* 2.2.994b.   [c] *Gen. corr.* 2.1.329a.   [d] *Phys.* 2.4.196b.   [e] Cf. *Metaph.* 9.3.1048b.   [f] Cf. *Metaph.* 9.3.1047a.   [g] *Phys.* 8.1.252a.   [h] *Phys.* 4.14.222b.

---

[a] ratione] coni. COPP.; ratione.5. b.   [b] IV] emend. COPP.; 9 b; IV L.

129,ᵃ "it is evident that every change | and every movement occurs in time," it follows, if so, that the agent, who necessarily exists in actuality at the beginning of that movement by which the passive thing is actualised, is temporally prior to that act, because the act is only found at the end of that movement or change. And Averroes explains the same in [the Commentary on] *Posterior Analytics* 2, text. 11:ᵇ "Things that are [acting] as an efficient cause are things [that are] temporally prior to the effects."

§ 3.3.1 Second, it becomes clear that prime matter is not [pre]eternal in this way: because prime matter is necessarily always a substrate for contraries, as Aristotle explains in *On Generation and Corruption* 2, text. 6.ᶜ If so, it cannot be [pre]eternal. And this consequence becomes clear in this way: if prime matter were [pre]eternal, the contraries in it would also be [pre]eternal, as prime matter is. One of two [cases] would not be prevented:

⟨§ 3.3.2⟩

§ 3.3.3 (1) If we said that prime matter contained differing parts with differing dispositions, in such a manner that every single one of them would be predisposed towards a form that is designated for its disposition, then if so, prime matter itself would forever have an existence in actuality, with a quantity and a quality in actuality by which its parts were separated and differentiated from each other. Therefore, two impossibilities would have to be true. (a) First, that prime matter would have a certain existence in actuality in itself, and this is impossible, because a thing existing in actuality cannot generate another thing while it is in actuality, as Aristotle explains in *Physics* 1, text. 71ᵈ and 75,ᵉ and *Metaphysics* 1, text. 17,ᶠ and 2, text. 7.ᵍ And if any change were to [occur to it], it would follow that there would be another matter that would be prior to it, and this would proceed until infinity. (b) Second, it would therefore follow that the elements were not generated from each other, because this could only happen on [the basis of] them sharing a common matter, as Aristotle explains in *On Generation and Corruption* 1, text. 87:ʰ "The things that change into each other are things that have one [common] matter." And sense [perception] testifies the contrary of this, as Aristotle explains in the [afore]mentioned book, 2, text. 28:ⁱ "Smoke will change into fire, although it [i.e., smoke] is composed of [particles of] earth and air."

ᵃ *Phys.* 4.14.222b.   ᵇ Cf. *An. post.* 2.11.95a.   ᶜ *Gen. corr.* 2.1.329a.   ᵈ *Phys.* 1.8.191a.   ᵉ *Phys.* 1.8.191b.   ᶠ *Metaph.* 1.8.989b.   ᵍ *Metaph.* 2.2.994a.   ʰ *Gen. corr.* 1.10.328a.   ⁱ *Gen. corr.* 2.4.331b.

dicit: «Manifestum est quod omnis transmutatio et omnis motus sit in tempore.» Et idem habetur ratione et auctoritate Aven R. *Metaphysicorum* noni t.c. 13, et eiusdem auctoritate in *Tractatu de Substantia Orbis* cap.2, ut supra. Et idem habetur auctoritate eiusdem in comento *Posteriorum* II t.c. 11 ubi[a] ait: «Quia que sunt secundum viam agentis, sunt res precedentes causata in inventione, et in tempore.»

§ 3.3.1 Secundo arguitur sic materia prima habuit semper esse secundum se totam contrarietatum subiectum, prout habetur a Phylosopho in *De Generatione* II t.c. 6; ergo non habuit esse ab eterno. Consequentia tenet quia si habuisset ab eterno contrarietatibus subijci.

§ 3.3.2 Tunc vel eedem contrarietates habuerunt omnes eidem materie secundum totum inesse, et hoc vel simul tempore, vel successive; aut habuerunt omnes eidem inesse non secundum totum, sed secundum diversas eiusdem partes: simul tempore scilicet vel successive. Si ergo omnes habuissent secundum totum et simul tempore eidem inesse, tunc sequeretur ut idem subiectum numero simul tempore, et substan|tialiter diversis et contrarijs informaretur formis, et per consequens idem numero habuisset simul tempore esse ignis et aqua et reliqua secundum se totum, quod est quid absurdum, et penitus inopinabile. Si vero omnes contrarietates huiusmodi habuerunt eidem materie secundum totum, sed successive tantum inesse. Tunc surgeret questio: utrum ipsa materia prima sit his omnibus immediate et indifferenter appropriata, aut non.

⟨§ 3.3.3⟩*q. v. *infra*

every change and every movement occurs in time," and according to the argument and authority of Averroes in *Metaphysics* 9, text. 13,[a] and the *Treatise on the Substance of the Celestial Sphere*, ch. 2,[b] as mentioned above. And Averroes explicates this in his Commentary on *Posterior Analytics* 2, text. 11,[c] where he states: "Because things that exist in accordance with the way of an agent are prior to the effects in invention and in time."

§ 3.3.1 Second, I would argue that prime matter is always and completely the substrate for contraries, as the Philosopher explains in *On Generation and Corruption* 2, text. 6,[d] and then matter cannot be [pre]eternal. The consequence is evident because if prime matter were [pre]eternal, then the contraries would also be [pre]eternal.

§ 3.3.2 Then, either all the contrarieties would belong to matter according to the whole, either at the same time or at some other time, or all [contrarieties] would not belong to matter according to the whole, but according to different parts, either at the same time or at some other time. And then, if contrarieties belonged to matter according to the whole at the same time, it would follow that at the same time, one substrate | would be formed by different and contrary forms, and consequently, fire and water and the other [elements] would exist in one substrate at the same time according to the whole, and that is incongruous and completely absurd. But if it is true that all contrarieties belong to matter according to the whole but only at different times, then doubt would arise as to whether or not prime matter is immediately and indifferently predisposed to [receive] all of them.

⟨§ 3.3.3⟩*q. v. *infra*

---

[a] ubi] coni. COPP.; ubi.5. b.

---

[a] Cf. *Metaph.* 9.3.1048b.   [b] Cf. *Sub. orb.* 85–86.   [c] Cf. *An. post.* 2.11.95a.
[d] *Gen. corr.* 2.1.329a.

§ 3.3.4 (2) Alternatively, it would follow that the contrary would be said [to be true], that is to say that there would be no parts in prime matter that differed from each other at all. And therefore, it would follow that every single one of the forms of the elements would be in every part of prime matter, without a reason that necessitated the same form for the same part more than [that of] its contrary, unless it was so by chance. And this is incongruous, as Averroes explains in [the Commentary on] *Physics* 8, text. 46[a]: "The form is differentiated by the differentiation of the matter. And if this were not true, there would be no designated matters and no designated forms in existence, and everything would be generated from everything and in everything."

[§ 3.3.3]

§ 3.3.5 What remains, then, is that the elements were generated from an existent prior to them, composed of prime matter and the first form, and that this [generation] came about through the corruption of that existent and its different ways of changing, | every one of which was designated for its form, as mentioned. And since that composite is corruptible, it therefore follows that it is not [pre]eternal, as mentioned above. And it is evident that prime matter is not temporally prior to the existence of that prime subject, because if [this was] so, then it would be devoid of all form, and this is incongruous, as mentioned above. It necessarily follows that prime matter is also not [pre]eternal, as mentioned. And this is what we want to explain.

---

§ 3.3.4 או יתחייב שנאמר הפך זה רצוני לומר שאין בחומר הראשון חלקים מתחלפים זה מזה כלל. ולזה יתחייב שכל אחת מצורות היסודות היה באיזה חלק מהחומר הראשון בלתי סבה מחייבת אותה הצורה לאותו החלק יותר מהפכה אלא שהיה כן במקרה, וזה נמנע כמו שביאר אבן רשד בספר השמע מאמר ח׳ פרק מ״ו באמרו: »בהתחלף החומר תתחלף הצורה. ואם לא היה זה אמת לא היו במציאות חומרים מיוחדים ולא צורות מיוחדות ויתהוה כל דבר מכל דבר ובכל דבר« עכ״ל.

[§ 3.3.3]

§ 3.3.5 ישאר אם כן שנתהוו היסודות מנמצא קודם להם מורכב מחומר ראשון וצורה ראשונה. וזה היה בהפסד אותו הנמצא והשתנותו באופנים מתחלפים | כל אחד מהם מיוחד לצורתו כנזכר ובהיות שאותו המורכב נפסד ומזה יתחייב שלא היה קדמון כנזכר לעיל והוא מבואר שהחומר הראשון לא קדם בזמן למציאות[a] אותו הנושא הראשון כי אם כן היה הוא אז מופשט מכל צורה וזה נמנע כנזכר לעיל בהכרח שהחומר הראשון הוא גם כן בלתי קדמון כנזכר וזה הוא מה שרצינו לבאר.

---

[a] Cf. *Phys.* 8.6.258b.   [a] למציאות] a[corr]; לצאת a.

§ 3.3.4 Si primum: tunc non daretur causa, quare quandoque informaretur altera illarum formarum magis quam reliqua nisi fortasse per diversas alterationes ab alterante tempore precedente, et per consequens non ab eterno. Si vero secundum. Tunc sequeretur: ut illud cuius forme fuisset ipsa materia, magis et immediatus appropriata, fuisset omnium primum, et sic solum illud non reliqua habuit esse ab eterno, et per consequens, illud esset reliquorum principium quare eidem conveniret non fieri ab alijs, sicut habetur a Phylosopho *Physicorum* I t.c. 42, cuius oppositum patet sensu preterea surgeret questio: quando illud primum fuit in alia conversum, et quare tunc et non ante. Si vero omnes huiusmodi contrarietates habuerunt eidem materie secundum diversas eiusdem partes ab eterno inesse. Tunc cum diversas formas diverse et proprie requirantur subiecti dispositiones, prout habetur ratione et auctoritate Aven R. *Physicorum* VIII t.c. 46 ubi dicit: «Quando materia fuerit diversa diversantur forme et si non, non essent hic materie proprie neque forme proprie etc.»

§ 3.3.3 Sequeretur ergo: ut eidem materie diverse inessent partes diversimode disposite, cuius diversitatis ratione, habuisset diversis formis imprimi ad quod duo sequerentur inconvenientia. Quorum unum est: quod cum dispositiones ab invicem diverse, nil aliud sint, quam diverse qualitates ad diversas formas sequentes, sequeretur ut ipsa materia prima ad hoc diversis imprimeretur formis, habuisset esse quid actu, secundum diversas eiusdem partes, diversimode dispositum, non autem quid potentia tantum cuius oppositum patet ratione et auctoritate ut supra. Secundo sequeretur: ut nihil esset materie prime omnibus elementis uniformiter communis, et per consequens non haberent invicem converti,[a] prout habetur a Phylosopho in *De Generatione* I t.c. 87 ubi scilicet dicit: «Hi quidem igitur convertuntur, quorum eadem materia est etc.» Cuius oppositum apparet sensu. Quia sicut Phylosophus ibidem II t.c. 28 ait: «Fumus quidem fit ignis, qui tamen fumus terra est et aer.»

⟨§ 3.3.5⟩

§ 3.3.4 If the first [instance is true], then there is no cause [i.e., it happens by chance], because at a certain time, prime matter will be informed with only one of these forms rather than the others, perhaps because of different variables in a different time that is prior [to them], and consequently, prime matter will not be [pre]eternal. If the second [instance is true], then it would follow that prime matter would be immediately predisposed for one of those forms and that only this one and not the others were [pre]eternal; consequently, the first of them would not have been generated from another one [of them], as the Philosopher explains in *Physics* 1, text. 42.[a] Moreover, the contrary is evident and another question arises: When does the first of them change into the others? The implication is now and not before. But if it is true that all contraries belonging to matter according to its parts are [pre]eternal, then the forms need different and specific dispositions of the substrate, according to the argument and authority of Averroes in *Physics* 8, text. 46,[b] where he states: "When the matter is different, the forms are different. And if this is not true, there would not be a specific matter or a specific form, etc."

§ 3.3.3 It would follow that different matters belong to different parts, because of a difference disposed for different forms. And two incongruities would then follow. The first of them is that dispositions that differ from each other are nothing other than different qualities following different forms. Therefore, it would follow that prime matter, in which different forms are disposed, would be something in actuality according to its parts, which are disposed in different manners, and also in potentiality. But the contrary is proved according to the argument and authority of the Philosopher, as mentioned above. Second incongruity: there is no prime matter [that is] common to all the elements, and consequently, the elements do not change into each other, as the Philosopher explains in *On Generation and Corruption* 1, text. 87,[c] when he states: "The things that change into each other are things that belong to one matter, etc." The senses testify to the contrary, as the Philosopher explains in *On Generation and Corruption* 2, text. 28,[d] where he states: "Smoke becomes fire, although smoke is earth and air."

⟨§ 3.3.5⟩

---

[a] converti] coni. Copp.; covert b.

[a] *Phys.* 1.5.188b.   [b] *Phys.* 8.6.258b.   [c] *Gen. corr.* 1.10.328a.   [d] *Gen. corr.* 2.4.331b.

3. חומר ראשון

⟨§ 3.4.1⟩

⟨§ 3.4.2⟩

⟨§ 3.4.3⟩

⟨§ 3.4.4⟩

⟨§ 3.4.1⟩

⟨§ 3.4.2⟩

⟨§ 3.4.3⟩

⟨§ 3.4.4⟩

§ 3.4.1 Tertio arguitur sic nulla elementorum pars habuit esse ab eterno, quedam eorundem pars habuit simul esse cum materia prima, ergo materia prima non habuit esse ab eterno.

§ 3.4.2 Consequentia patet, et antecedens probatur. Et primo quoad primam partem, qua scilicet dicitur: quod nulla elementorum pars habuit esse ab eterno; sensu, enim, et priscorum testimonio, ut supra patet: quod horum partes sint generabiles et corruptibiles, et per consequens non habuerunt esse ab eterno, prout habetur ratione Phylosophi superius allegata *De Celo* primi t.c. 124[a] ubi scilicet dicit: «Manifestum est, quod illud quod est generabile et corruptibile non est perpetuum et eternum.»

§ 3.4.3 Quo autem ad secundam partem qua scilicet dicitur: quod quedam elementorum pars habuit simul esse cum materia prima, probatur, quia ille partes ignis, que sunt circa orbem lunarem similiter ille partes terre, que sunt in centro vel circa. Non contingit ut fuissent unquam corrupte, nisi totum elementum circumquaque fuisset corruptum, vel saltem in quodam eiusdem latere. Alias enim fuisset pars conversa extra suum naturalem locum. Quod est quid inauditum et inopinabile, quia non videtur dari legitima causa, quare talia quandoque contigissent, et fuissent in pristinum restituta. Cum autem huiusmodi partes nonnisi a materia prima immediate habuissent esse, prout habetur ratione et auctoritate Phylosophi *De Generatione* II t.c. 6.

§ 3.4.4 Sequitur ergo: ut saltem ille partes habuisset esse simul cum materia prima. Cum autem ipse partes tanquam corruptibile non habeant potentiam ad hoc ut sint semper ens, et per consequens non datur ut fuissent ab eterno. Sequitur: ut materia prima ab huiusmodi partium formis nunquam privata, non habuisset esse ab eterno. Non enim videtur dicendum, ut huiusmodi partes centero[b] scilicet vel orbi adherentes differunt a reliquis eorundem elementorum partibus, quo ad corruptibilitatem, quia si sic equivoce diceretur de illis et reliquis terre vel ignis partibus idem nomen, et per consequens daretur sextum corporum natura preter elementorum et celestium.

§ 3.4.1 Third, I would argue that no part of the elements can be [pre]eternal if a certain part of them existed at the same time as prime matter, thus prime matter is not [pre]eternal.

§ 3.4.2 The consequence is evident, and the first part of the antecedent, in which we said that no part of the elements is [pre]eternal, is proved. In fact, it is clear, as the senses and the Ancients testified, as mentioned above, that their parts admit of generation and corruption, and consequently, they are not [pre]eternal, as the Philosopher explains in *On the Heavens* 1, text. 124,[a] where he states: "It is irrefutable that something that admits of generation and corruption is not perpetual and eternal."

§ 3.4.3 The second part of the antecedent, in which we said that a certain part of the elements existed at the same time as prime matter, is proved because the parts of fire that are around the sphere of the moon are similar to the parts of earth that are in the middle or around it. It does not occur at any time that they are corrupted, if not all elements around are corrupted, or at least only on some side of them, because that would be another part that was leaving its natural place. But this is inappropriate and inconceivable, because it seems that there is not a legitimate cause, since such things happen and then are replaced in their original [position]. Nonetheless [this could have occurred] only to the parts that existed immediately in relation to prime matter, according to the argument and authority of the Philosopher in *On Generation and Corruption* 2, text. 6.[b]

§ 3.4.4 It would follow that at least these parts existed at the same time as prime matter. However, these parts, insofar as they are corruptible things, do not have the potentiality to exist forever, and consequently, they are not [pre]eternal. It would follow that prime matter, which is never deprived of the form of its parts, is not [pre]eternal. In fact, it does not seem appropriate to say that the parts of something or the parts adhering to the sphere are separated from the parts of the other elements because of corruptibility. Since one speaks of them by equivocation, the remaining parts of earth or fire have the same name, and consequently, there would be a sixth body in addition to the natural and celestial elements.

---

[a] 124] emend. Copp.; 129 b; 124 L.   [b] centero] b[corr]; cetero b.

[a] *Cael.* 1.12.282b.   [b] *Gen. corr.* 2.1.329a.

⟨§ 3.4.5⟩

§ 3.5 We answer—if this is correct—to dispel [any] doubt about the [afore]mentioned thesis that prime matter is not [pre]eternal, but [that it] was created together with the first composite, which is called "Tohu and Bohu," whose form is first and was designated to prime matter.

§ 3.6 Indeed, to the opponent's arguments, we answer that although it is also absolutely correct [to claim] that nothing will ever come to be from nothing, it is not correct when we say that a thing will only come from another thing—except for the created beings—by means of a movement of change, because the agent needs a substrate for them on which it acts and which is actualised from potentiality to the same actuality for which it has a potentiality, and it will actualise by the change of matter towards a disposition that is designated for the acquired form, as Averroes explains in [the Commentary on] *Metaphysics* 12, text. 18.[a] However, concerning the creation, this is not correct at all; rather, its contrary is true. For the creator acts in his creation and creates not only the form, but also the substrate, as Averroes explains in [the Commentary on] *Metaphysics* 12, text. 18:[b] "Those who say that a thing is already created by means of creation say that the agent creates every existent anew, from nothing. And therefore he needs no matter on which to act, because he creates everything."

---

[a] Cf. *Metaph.* 12.3.1070a.   [b] Cf. *Metaph.* 12.3.1070a.

⟨§ 3.4.5⟩

§ 3.5 נשיב אם כן להתיר ספק החקירה הנזכרת שהחומר הראשון הוא בלתי קדמון אבל נברא יחדיו עם המורכב הראשון אשר נקרא ‹תהו ובהו› (בראשית א׳ ב׳) אשר צורתו היתה ראשונה ומיוחדת לחומר הראשון.

§ 3.6 אמנם לטענות החולק נשיב שגם שיצדק במוחלט שלא יתהוה דבר מלא דבר מכל מקום לא יצדק אמרנו שלא יתהוה דבר כי אם מדבר אחר זולתי בהויות המתחדשות על ידי תנועת ההשתנות כי בהן יצטרך הפועל אל נושא אשר בו יפעל ויוציאהו מן הכח אל אותו הפעל אשר לו כוחיות עליו וזה יפעל בשנותו את החומר אל הכנה מיוחדת לצורה הנקנית כמו שבאר אבן רשד בספר מה שאחר מאמר י״ב פרק י״ח. אבל על הבריאה לא יצדק זה כלל אבל יצדק הפכו כי אמנם הבורא יפעל בבריאתו ויחדש לא הצורה בלבד אבל יחדש גם הנושא כמו שבאר אבן רשד בספר מה שאחר מאמר י״ב פרק י״ח באמרו: »האומרים שכבר התחדש דבר על ידי בריאה אומרים שהפועל בורא כל הנמצא מחדש מאין ולזה לא יצטרך לחומר אשר בו יפעל כי הוא בורא את הכל«.

§ 3.4.5 Cuius oppositum, habetur ratione et auctoritate Phylosophi et Aven R. in lib. *De Celo* primo t.c. 23 ubi Phylosophus ait: «Manifestum est ex hoc quod diximus: quod hec corpora simplicia impossibile est ut sint plura, et diximus quod corporum celestium motus est simplex necessario. Dicimus etiam quod motus simplices sunt duo scilicet circularis et rectus, et quod motus equalis istorum duorum motuum, aut est ad medium aut a medio» ubi Aven R. exponens ait: «Declaratum est sermonibus predictis quod corpora simplicia sunt quinque, quatuor mobilia nutu recto, et unum mobile circulariter. Et cum dixit conclusione dixit propositiones, ex quibus concludebatur etc.» Preterea datis huiusmodi partibus equivoce dictis non minus[a] idem sequeretur argumentum de illis univocis et proprijs terre et ignis partibus, eisdem equivocis propinquioribus.

§ 3.5 Ad dubium ergo respondetur: quod materia prima non habuit esse ab eterno, immo habuit simul cum Chaos, sive primo confuso post purum non esse, Divinitus produci, sive creari.

§ 3.6 Ad argumentum vero respondetur: quod licet absolute sit verum, ut ex nihilo nihil fiat. Propositio tamen dicens: ut non contingat aliquid pro | duci nisi ex aliquo subiecto, non verificatur nisi de factione que fit per transmutationem, qua, scilicet, subiectum transmutatur de forma ad formam. Ad talem, enim, factionem requiritur necessario subiectum in quo agens inferat transmutationem; que, scilicet, est subiecti passio in huiusmodi, enim, actione agens nil aliud facit, nisi quod subiectum transmutando illud ducit ad illum actum, ad quem habuit potentiam, prout habetur ab Aven R. de mente Phylosophi *Methaphysicorum* XII[b] t.c. 18. Sed non verificatur de creatione: ad quam necessario deveniendum est, ut infra patebit; et iam patuit per hoc; quod nihil premissorum habuit esse ab eterno; neque habuerunt esse ab alio prius tempore existente hoc ergo productionis genere; que creatio dicitur Creator quidem totum de novo creat, tam subiectum quam formam. Quare Aven R. ibidem ait: «Dicentes autem creationem, dicunt quod agens creat totum ens de novo ex nihilo, et quod non habet necesse ad hoc ut sit materia in quam agat sed creat totum.»

§ 3.4.5[a] But the contrary is explained according to the argument and authority of the Philosopher and Averroes in *On the Heavens* 1, text. 23,[b] when the Philosopher states: "What we said before is irrefutable as it is impossible that there may be many simple bodies, and we also said that the motion of the celestial bodies is necessarily simple. And we also said that there are two different simple motions, the circular and the straight, and the movement of those two motions is equal, either towards a centre or away from a centre," and Averroes explicates: "As it is said of those discussions, there are five simple bodies, four with a straight motion and one with a circular motion. And as it is said in the conclusion, with reference to those propositions, from which it is possible to arrive at a conclusion, etc." Moreover, one refers to "parts" only by equivocation, and then the argument concerning the parts of earth and fire is also by equivocation.

§ 3.5 To dispel any doubt, I would argue that prime matter is not [pre]eternal. On the contrary, [matter] was divinely generated or created at the same time as the Chaos, which is the first composite brought out of nothingness.

§ 3.6 In response to the first argument, I will reply: it is true that nothing comes from nothing. The statement in which we said that something can | only be produced from another substrate is verified only according to the opinion that [generation] is produced by change, by that means by which a substrate changes from form to form. According to this opinion, one necessarily needs a substrate in which an agent enacts a change—that is, an affection of the substrate in itself—because the agent produces only an activity by changing the substrate, and it leads the substrate to an actuality for which it has potentiality, as Averroes explicates in the name of the Philosopher in *Metaphysics* 12, text. 18.[c] But this is not verified according to the definition of creation that necessarily comes out of nothingness, as is clear below, and now it is evident according to our discussion because nothing of these aforementioned premises [prime matter and the elements] is [pre]eternal. They [prime matter and the elements] exist from another being that existed before, and this kind of production is called "creation," and the creator creates every element anew, matter as well as form. And Averroes, in the aforementioned passage, states: "Creation means that an agent creates all existents anew, from nothing. And therefore, he needs no matter on which to act, because he creates everything."

---

[a] minus] b[corr]; tantum b.   [b] XII] emend. COPP.; II b; XII L.

[a] § 3.4.1–§ 3.4.5; cf. *OA* § 2.3.2.   [b] *Cael.* 1.3.270b.   [c] Cf. *Metaph.* 12.3.1070a.

§ 3.7 And the Torah of our God testifies all these things by saying at the beginning (Genesis 1:1): "In the beginning God created," because the absolute beginning, which was the beginning of time, was an indivisible instant, which was not part of time, as mentioned above. And therefore, this informs [us] that the creation was without time.

§ 3.8.1 And it provides the proof of this (Genesis 1:2): "And the earth was Tohu and Bohu"; that is to say, because the first form was necessarily a form designated for prime matter. The composite of them was called "Tohu and Bohu." And from it, through change in different ways and in different parts of them, darkness, which is air deprived of light (ibid.), was generated "over the surface of the deep," which [i.e., the deep] was the two heavy elements [i.e., earth and water], which were next to the centre. And it continues (ibid.): "A spirit from God sweeping over the water," meaning and teaching elementary fire, which was [generated] by the propulsion of a separate substance that moved and shook the darkness over the water, because the separate substances are called "a spirit from God," as is told in the story of the act of creation (Psalm 104:4): "He makes [the] spirits [or: winds] His messengers." And it testifies that it shook and moved the air over the water. And therefore, part of it became moist through its proximity to the water, and part of it [became] warm and dry, taking on a fiery form through its proximity to the sphere and its motion, as Aristotle explains the cause of elementary fire in *On the Heavens* 2, text. 42.[a]

§ 3.8.2 And the same—namely, the creation of prime matter—seems to be testified and proven by the prophet Isaiah (45:7): "Who forms light and creates darkness, and who makes peace and who creates evil: I ha-Shem make all these things." He meant: "Who creates evil"—that is, prime matter—insofar as its substance is deprived of all form [and] insofar as it is simple potentiality, because the form, insofar as it is the goal of generation in actuality, is called "good." Therefore, prime matter is called "evil" by many of the Ancients, as the Philosopher explains in *Metaphysics* 12, text. 54:[b] "Evil in itself is one of the elements."

---

[a] *Cael.* 2.7.289a. [b] *Metaph.* 12.10.1075a.

§ 3.7 Quare Sacrum Genesis documentum cap. primo [Gen 1:1] docet, creationem fuisse in instanti: ubi scilicet dicit: «In principio creavit Deus etc.» Quasi dicat in principio temporis quod idem est quod instans, ut supra subdit dicens: quod terra quam dicit creasse, erat natura quedam quam confusum sive Chaos aut commixtum appellat, ex prima scilicet materia, primaque forma compositum. Cui illa corpora que nunc elementa nuncupamus, potentialiter inerant, per diversas huiusmodi compositi alterationes ad actum deducenda.

§ 3.8.1 Quare solvitur secundum dubium: quod de materia prima contigit, ut supra, quia cum materia non habeat partes ab invicem diversas, inconveniens videtur: ut immediate quatuor diversis, immo et contrarijs approprietur formis: ut supra. Huiusmodi, enim, dubium solvitur per hoc: quod ex prima materia et prima forma una tantum composita est natura, cuius forme erat ipsa materia prima immediate propria, quam, scilicet, naturam merito Sacrum Genesis Documentum, ut supra, Chaos sive confusum appellat. Ex cuius nature parte per motum celi alterata, factus est aer, de quo aere intelligere videtur cum [Gen 1:2] dicit: «et tenebre super facies abyssi.» Per tenebras, enim, videtur intelligere aerem non illuminatum, per abyssum[a] vero, duo gravia elementa circa centrum iacentia. Subdit ibidem [Gen 1:2] dicens: «et Spiritus Dei circumvehebat super facies aque.» Ubi per Spiritum Dei intelligit: abstractas substantias orbem Dei iussu circumvehentes; quas Dei Spiritum appellat sicut in Psalmo 103 [104:4] ubi dicit: «fecit angelos suos spiritus.» Dicit ergo quod Spiritus Dei tunc circumduxit ipsas tenebras, sive aerem non illuminatum super facies aque, quare factus est idem aer partim humidus aque similis, partimque siccus tanquam per orbis motum in natura igneam conversus. Quibus videtur innuere elementalis ignis productionem, simulque eiusdem cau|sam inferens: quod habuit esse per ipsum motum, cum scilicet tenebrarum, sive aeris partes circa mobilem orbem existentes, habuissent per ipsum motum merito in igneam naturam converti, sicut a Phylosopho habetur in lib. *De Celo* II t.c. 42.

§ 3.8.2 Et de eadem materie creatione, videtur Esaiam verbum facere, cap. 45[b] [45:7] ubi dicit: «faciens pacem et creans malum ego Dominus etc.» Ubi per ly malum videtur intelligere materiam primam, per se bono vel actu privata, quam antiquorum nonnulli malum appellarunt, prout habetur a Phylosopho *Metaphysicorum* XII t.c. 54[c]

§ 3.7 Therefore, the Holy Book of Genesis (1:1) teaches that creation began in an instant, saying: "In the beginning God created etc.," which means "in the beginning of time." That was the instant, as aforementioned. Genesis tells us regarding the creation of the earth that the nature of the earth was "confusion" and "chaos," or what has been called a composite, composed of prime matter and the first form, in which the bodies that are now called the elements were potentially [contained] following different alterations, according to the actualisation.

§ 3.8.1[a] In response to the second argument concerning prime matter, I will reply: matter does not have different parts, as aforementioned. It seems to be incongruous that matter will be immediately disposed for four different and contrary forms, as mentioned above. The doubt is resolved in this way: because there was only one natural compound composed of prime matter and the first form, this prime matter was immediately disposed for its form, which Genesis rightly called "chaos or confusion," as aforementioned. And from it, through the motion of the heavens, the air was created, and Genesis seems to refer to the air, saying (Genesis 1:2): "And darkness was upon the face of the deep," and "darkness" means air without light and "the deep" means the two heavy elements next to the centre. "The Spirit of God was hovering on the surface of the water." "Spirit of God" means the separate substances, which hovered over the sphere by divine will, which is called "the Spirit of God," as in Psalm 103 (104:4), where it says: "He makes his angels spirits." Then it [i.e. Genesis] says that the Spirit of God hovered over the darkness or over the air without light on the surface of the water. Indeed, air is generated from the warm part of water, which is similar to the dry part of water, changed into fire by the motion of the sphere. These things seem to explain the cause of elementary fire, |, which was motion, because the darkness or the part of the air existing near the mobile sphere changed its nature into fire through its motion [sc. of the sphere], as the Philosopher explains in *On the Heavens* 2, text. 42.[b]

§ 3.8.2 And it seems that Isaiah speaks about the creation of [prime] matter in chapter 45 (45:7), where he says: "He who makes peace and who creates evil, the Lord, etc." "Evil" means prime matter deprived of the good in itself or deprived of the activity that is called "evil" by some ancients, as the Philosopher explains in *Metaphysics* 12, text. 54,[c] where he states: "The evil in itself is one of the

---

[a] abyssum] coni. COPP.; abissum b.   [b] 45] emend. COPP.; 98 b; 48 b[corr]; 45 V.   [c] 54] emend. COPP.; 49 b; 54 L.

[a] Cf. *OA* § 1.5.7.   [b] *Cael.* 2.7.289a.   [c] *Metaph.* 12.10.1075a.

And Averroes explains these words: "Many say that there are two principles for all existents, and they are evil and good; namely, the matter and the form." And the prophet explains the nature of prime matter, which is common to every generable and corruptible. And this is with regard to the "peace" that exists between them in the composed things, in which every single one of the contraries changes with regard to the nature of its contrary, because this is made possible only by the nature of a matter [that is] common to all of them, as the Philosopher explains in *On Generation and Corruption* 1, text. 87:[a] "These are [able to] change into each other's nature, since their matter is one." And he continues: "The existents that do not have one and the same matter do not mix [with each other]." And since it is incongruous that one and the same matter could be the substrate for contrary forms, except by means of its change in cases of different dispositions for different forms, then the matter will receive contrary forms [by means of] its change into many aspects [only one after the other]. And this would also be incongruous, unless it is in actuality in a first composite that changes as a whole, as mentioned above. And since this composite is not [pre]eternal, it will be corruptible. And it becomes clear that prime matter is not prior to it in time, because it would then be devoid of all form, which would necessitate that prime matter is not [pre]eternal. And there is no substrate prior to it from which it is generated, from which it is necessarily derived that its existence is by means of creation, as he says (Isaiah 45:7): "And who creates evil," and continues: "I ha-Shem make all these things," which means: "[I made] all parts of the composite, not only the form, like the agents [do], but also the matter."

⟨§ 3.9⟩

אבן רשד באמרו כי רבים אמרו ששתי התחלות הם לכל הנמצאות והם הרע והטוב היינו החומר והצורה עכ״ל והנה באר הנביא את טבע החומר הראשון שהוא אמנם משותף לכל הווה נפסד זה מצד ה׳שלום׳ הנמצא ביניהם במורכבים אשר בהם מתהפך כל אחד מהמהפכים בצד מה אל טבע הפכו כי זה לא יתכן זולתי מטבע חומר משותף לכלם כמו שבאר הפילוסוף בספר הוויה מאמר א׳ פרק פ״ז באמרו: »אלה אמנם יתהפכו זה לטבע זה בהיות החומר שלהם אחד« והוסיף ואמר כי »הנמצאות אשר אין חומרם אחד בעצמו לא יתערבו« עכ״ל. ובהיות כי לא יתכן שיהיה חומר אחד בעצמו נושא לצורות הפכיות זולתי באמצעות השתנותו בפנים מתחלפים מכינים לצורות מתחלפות, הנה אם כן קבל החומר צורות הפכיות בהשתנותו בפנים רבים וזה גם כן לא יתכן זולתי בהיותו בפעל במורכב ראשון אשר נשתנה כלו כנזכר לעיל. ובהיות שאותו המורכב היה בלתי קדמון בהיותו נפסד והתבאר שהחומר הראשון לא קדם בזמן כי אם כן היה מופשט אז מכל צורה יתחייב אם כן שהחומר הראשון הוא בלתי קדמון. ומבלי אין נושא קודם לו אשר ממנו יתהוה יתחייב בהכרח שהיה מציאותו על ידי בריאה באמרו: »ובורא רע« והוסיף ואמר: »אני ה׳ עושה כל אלה« (ישעיהו מ״ה ז׳), כלומר כל חלקי המורכב לא הצורה בלבד כשאר הפועלים אבל גם החומר.

⟨§ 3.9⟩

---

[a] *Gen. corr.* 1.10.328a.

ubi dicit: «Malum, enim, per se est unum elementorum» ubi Aven R. exponens ait: «Quidam ponunt omnibus duo principia, malum, scilicet, bonum que sunt materia et forma.» Ubi videtur propheta probare materie prime creationem, per pacem inter contraria in composito factam qua scilicet in se innicem quoddam modo convertuntur, que scilicet conversio non contingit nisi per naturam materie eisdem communis, sicut per se patet, et habetur a Phylosopho in lib. *De Generatione* primi t.c. 87 ubi dicit: «Hec quidem igitur convertuntur, quorum eadem est materia etc.» Cum autem non contingat huiusmodi communitatem fuisse contrarijis appropriatam, nisi per diversas alterationes eidem, ut supra, contingentes, et per consequens non ab eterno patet fuisse creatam.

§ 3.9 Quod scilicet intelligit dicens et creans malum et de eadem pace fortasse intelligit Empedocles, litem et amicitiam in principia ponens, licet aliter intelligere videatur in *De Generatione* primi t.c. 2.

elements," and Averroes explains: "Many people posit two principles: the evil and the good, that is, the matter and the form." And it seems that the prophet proves the creation of prime matter: through the "peace" that exists between them in the composed things, in which every single one of the contraries changes with regard to the nature of its contrary, because this is only possible from the nature of a matter common to all of them, as is evident and as the Philosopher explains in *On Generation and Corruption* 1, text. 87,[a] where he states: "Those are changed since their matter is one, etc." And then this occurs only if there is a common matter for contraries that is predisposed to different changes, as aforementioned, and consequently, [prime] matter is not [pre]eternal, but rather was created.

§ 3.9 Perhaps this was what Empedocles wanted to explain when he posited strife [evil] and peace as the first principles, as is evident in *On Generation and Corruption* 1, text. 2.[b]

---

[a] *Gen. corr.* 1.10.328a.   [b] *Gen. corr.* 1.2.315a.

§ 4 Fourth:
We will inquire whether the heavens are [pre]eternal.

And it seems at the beginning of the investigation that they are [pre]eternal.

§ 4.1.1 [This is so,] because everything that is incorruptible is [pre]eternal, and the heavens are incorruptible. If so, they are [pre]eternal. This consequence is self-evident and the [antecedent] premise becomes clear from Aristotle's proof, which he explains in *On the Heavens* 1, text. 137:[a] "We also made another statement in which we explained the error of someone who says that it is possible | that there may be a thing that is both uncreated and corruptible, and that there may be a thing that is both incorruptible and created." And he continues: "If it will not corrupt [at any time], it will be [both] disposed to corruption and not disposed to corruption in actuality. And therefore, it follows that it will [both exist] forever and not [exist] forever." From these words, it becomes clear that everything that is incorruptible will exist forever, and therefore it has to be [pre]eternal. What we said—that the heavens are incorruptible—becomes clear from Aristotle's proof in *On the Heavens* 1, text. 20:[b] "We already said that the motion of contraries is contrary. And since this is correct, the first body does not have a contrary, because there is no contrary to a circular motion. It seems good that nature, when it made this body glorious, [made it] uncreated and exempt from contraries, because [the movement of] generation and corruption necessarily exist in contraries."

§ 4.1.2 Second, it becomes clear that the heavens are [pre]eternal from Aristotle's proofs, which he explains in *On the Heavens* 2, text. 1:[c] "We already explained, in sufficient statements and by strong proofs, that the heavens are not composed of [the four] elements and that it is impossible that they may fall under corruption; rather, they are forever perpetual and forever without beginning and without end, and they are the cause of the infinity of time and they contain it." And Averroes explains his words: "Since the sphere is the cause of time, it is like a limiter of time." And therefore, it follows that the time of its existence is infinite. And if so, it is [pre]eternal.

§ 4.2 Third, it becomes clear that the heavens are [pre]eternal from Aristotle's proof in *On the Heavens* 3, text. 29:[d] "It is impossible that a body will be created if there is no vacuum, because indeed, the space in which the created

---

[a] *Cael.* 1.12.283b. [b] *Cael.* 1.3.270a. [c] *Cael.* 2.1.283b. [d] *Cael.* 3.2.302a.

---

§ 4 רביעית נחקור אם השמים הם קדמונים

ונראה בתחלת העיון שהם אמנם קדמונים.

§ 4.1.1 כי כל בלתי נפסד הוא קדמון. והנה השמים הם בלתי נפסדים אם כן הם קדמונים. הנה חיוב התולדה הוא מבואר בעצמו וההקדמה אמנם תתבאר בראיית ארסטו׳ אשר באר בספר השמים והעולם מאמר א׳ פרק קל״ז באמרו: «נאמר גם כן מאמר אחר[a] בו נבאר[b] טעות האומר שאיפשר | שיהיה איזה דבר בלתי[c] מחודש ויהיה עם זה נפסד ושיהיה דבר בלתי נפסד ויהיה עם זה מחודש.» והוסיף ואמר: «כי אם לא יפסד הנה יהיה מוכן אל ההפסד ובלתי מוכן אל ההפסד בפעל. ומזה יתחייב שיהיה דבר נצחי ובלתי נצחי» עכ״ל. הנה התבאר מדבריו אלה שכל דבר שהוא בלתי נפסד הוא נמצא לעולם ומזה יתחייב שהוא קדמון. אמנם מה שאמרנו שהשמים הם בלתי נפסדים הנה התבאר בראיית ארסטו׳ בספר השמים מאמר א׳ פרק כ׳ באמרו: «כבר אמרנו שתנועת ההפכים הם הפכיית ובהיות הדבר כן אין לגשם הראשון שום הפכי כי אין שום הפכי לתנועה הסבובית אם כן היטיב לראות הטבע כאשר עשה זה הגשם מפואר בלתי מחודש והרחיק אותו מן ההפכים כי ההויה וההפסד הם בהכרח בהפכים».

§ 4.1.2 **שנית** יתבאר שהשמים קדמונים בראיית ארסטו׳ אשר באר בספר השמים והעולם מאמר ב׳ פרק א׳ באמרו: «כבר בארנו במאמרים מספיקים ובמופתים חזקים שהשמים אינם מורכבים מיסודות ושהוא נמנע שיפלו תחת הפסד אבל יהיו לעולם נצחיים והיו בלתי התחלה ובלתי סוף לעולמי עד והם סבת הזמן הבלתי בעל תכלית ומחזיקים אותו.» עד כאן לשונו. ודבריו אלה באר אבן רשד באמרו: «בהיות הגלגל סבת הזמן הנה הוא כמו מגביל הזמן.» ומזה יתחייב שיהיה זמן מציאותו בלתי בעל תכלית ואם כן הוא קדמון.

§ 4.2 **שלישית** יתבאר שהשמים קדמונים בראיית ארסטו׳ בספר השמים מאמר ג׳ פרק כ״ט באמרו: «מן הנמנע הוא שיתחדש איזה גוף אם לא ימצא ריקות כי אמנם המקום אשר בו נמצא הגשם המחודש

---

[a] אחר] emend. Dunk.; אחד a; alium b. [b] נבאר] a[corr]; ובאר a. [c] בלתי] emend. Dunk.; om. a; non b; non L.

§4 Quarto

Dubitatur Utrum celi habuissent esse ab eterno,

et videtur quod sic.

§4.1.1 Primo, sic arguendo quodlibet incorruptibile habuit esse ab eterno celum est huiusmodi, ergo celum habuit esse ab eterno. Consequentia patet et antecedens probatur, et primo quoad primam partem, ratione et auctoritate Phylosophi in lib. *De Celo* primi t.c. 137 ubi dicit: Et dicamus etiam alium sermonem, per quem declarabimus errorem dicentes, quod possibile est, ut aliquid sit non generabile et cum hoc sit corruptibile et quod incorruptibile possibile est sit generatum etc.» subdit ibidem dicens: «Quoniam si non corrumpatur erit corruptibile et non corruptibile actu. Tunc ergo possibile est ut idem sit semper ens et non sit semper ens etc.» Ex quibus sequitur: ut quicquid sit incorruptibile, habeat necessario esse quid semper actu existens, et per consequens ab eterno quo autem ad secundam antecedentis partem. Qua scilicet dicitur quod celum est incorruptibile probatur ratione et auctoritate Phyosophi in lib. *De Celo* primi t.c. 20 ubi dicit: «Et iam diximus, quod motus con|trariorum sunt contrarij, et cum ita sit, nullum contrarium habet corpus primum nullum enim contrarium motum habet motus circularis. Consulta igitur bene est natura cumfecit, hoc corpus gloriosum non generabile et removit ipsum a contrarijs generatio enim et corruptio necessario existunt[a] in contrarijs.»

⟨§ 4.1.2⟩

§4.2 Secundo arguitur ratione et auctoritate Phylosophi in lib. *De Celo* III t.c. 29[b] ubi dicit: «Impossibile, enim, est ut aliquod corpus sit nisi vacuum fit quia ille locus in quo cor-

§4 Fourth,

it may be inquired whether the heavens are [pre]eternal.

And it seems to be so.

§4.1.1 First, I would argue that everything incorruptible is [pre]eternal. The heavens are incorruptible, and thus the heavens are [pre]eternal. The consequence is evident, and the first part of the antecedent is proved according to the argument and authority of the Philosopher in *On the Heavens* 1, text. 137,[a] where he states: "We also made a statement in which we explained the error of someone who says that it is possible that something uncreated can be corruptible and that something incorruptible can have been created," and he continues: "If it will not corrupt, it will be [both] disposed to corruption and not disposed to corruption in actuality. And therefore, it would be possible that this thing would [both] exist forever and not exist forever." From these [words], it would follow that an incorruptible thing would necessarily exist forever in actuality, and consequently, it would be eternal. Now, the second part of the antecedent, in which we said that the heavens are incorruptible, is proved according to the argument and authority of the Philosopher in *On the Heavens* 1, text. 20,[b] where he states: "We already said that the motion | of contraries is contrary. And since this is correct, the first body has no contrary, because a circular motion does not have a contrary movement. And if this so, then it seems to be a good thing that nature, when it made this glorious body, did not create it and exempted it from contraries, because [the movement of] generation and corruption exists necessarily in contraries."

⟨§ 4.1.2⟩

§4.2 Second, I would argue according to the argument and authority of the Philosopher in *On the Heavens* 3, text. 29,[c] where he states: "It is impossible that a body will be created if there is no void, because the place where the created

---

[a] existunt] coni. Copp.; sistunt b; existunt L.   [b] III t.c. 29] emend. Copp.; II, 1 b; III, 29 L.

[a] *Cael.* 1.12.283b.   [b] *Cael.* 1.3.270a.   [c] *Cael.* 3.2.302b.

body will exist is necessarily void before that body is created in it." And it is impossible for a vacuum to exist, as was explained by Aristotle's proofs in *Physics* 4, text. 86[a] and 87.[b] And it seems that therefore, it follows that the heavens are a body that was not created. And therefore, it becomes clear that they are [pre]eternal.

§ 4.3.1 But the contrary of this—namely, that the heavens are not [pre]eternal—becomes clear in this way: because for everything for which there is an intended final purpose, it necessarily follows that an agent who intends that final purpose precedes it in time and that the quantity of every single sphere is [designed] for the intended final purpose. If so, an intending agent is necessarily prior to them in time. And therefore, it follows that the aforementioned quantity and the spheres measured by them are all not [pre]eternal. The consequence is necessarily self-evident, and so is the [antecedent] premise, in which we said that an intending agent is necessarily prior to the things that are for an intended final purpose. And this is so when the definition of "final purpose" becomes clear, which is: the thing without which the agent will not begin his activity by which the final purpose will be [achieved]. And this is self-evident | and becomes clear from Aristotle's proofs above. And regarding this, the Rabbi [Moses Maimonides] says in the *Guide* [*of the Perplexed*] 3:13: "The best proof for the creation of the world is what is laid down as proof concerning natural existents, because for each of them there is a final purpose." And he continues: "Intention cannot be imagined unless something is created anew." And therefore, it follows that the existence of the agent and the existence of the intention of the goal in it are prior in time [and] necessarily [prior] to their activity.

§ 4.3.2 Regarding what we spoke about in the [antecedent] premise—that the quantities in the spheres are intended for a final purpose—this becomes clear in this way: because from the quantity of every sphere and their appearance, it follows that there are limited measurements for the final purpose that make it possible in this way, [so] that if there was a transgression in this by [only] a hair's breadth, [either] the spheres would hinder each other from moving or there would be a vacuum between them. And it is impossible that a limitation like this could happen in each of them by chance, without the intention of an intender, because this limitation would not happen by chance as many times as it does. And this is also self-evident. Aristotle explains in *On the Heavens* 2, text. 45,[c] that the speed of

---

[a]*Phys.* 4.9.217b.   [b]*Phys.* 4.10.217b.   [c]*Cael.* 2.8.289b.

היה בהכרח ריק קודם התחדש אותו הגוף בו« עכ״ל. ובהיות מן הנמנע שימצא ריקות כמבואר בראיות ארסטו' בספר השמע מאמר ד'[a] פרק פ״ו ופ״ז נראה שיתחייב מזה שהשמים שהם גוף הם בלתי מחודשים ובכן התבאר שהם קדמונים.

§ 4.3.1 **אמנם** הפך זה רצוני לומר שהשמים בלתי קדמונים הנה יתבאר באופן זה כי לכל דבר אשר הוא לתכלית מכוון יתחייב בהכרח שיקדם בזמן איזה פועל מכוין אותו התכלית והנה שעורי כמות כל גלגל וגלגל הם אמנם לתכלית מכוון אם כן קדם להם בהכרח קדימה זמנית איזה פועל מכוין. ומזה יתחייב שהשיעורים הנזכרים והגלגלים המשוערים בהם הם כלם בלתי קדמונים הנה חיוב התולדה הוא מבואר בעצמו. וכן ההקדמה במה שאמרנו שלדברים אשר הם לתכלית מכוון יקדם בהכרח איזה פועל מכוין. וזה כאשר התבאר גדר ⟨התכלית⟩ שהוא אמנם הדבר אשר בלעדיו לא היה הפועל מתחיל את הפעלה אשר בה יהיה התכלית. וזה מבואר | בעצמו והתבאר בראיית ארסטו' לעיל. ולזה אמר הרב בספר המורה מאמר ג' פרק י״ג וזה לשונו: »הגדולה שבראיות על חדוש העולם הוא מה שיעמוד עליו המופת בנמצאות הטבעיות כי לכל דבר מהם תכלית.« והוסיף ואמר: »ולא יצויר כוונה רק עם התחדשות מחדש« עכ״ל. ומזה יתחייב שמציאות הפועל ומציאות כוונת התכלית אצלו קודמים בזמן ובהכרח לפעלתם.

§ 4.3.2 אמנם מה שאמרנו בהקדמה ששיעורי הכמות בגלגלים הם מכוונים לתכלית הנה יתבאר באופן זה כי אמנם בכמות כל גלגל ובתמונותיהם יתחייב שנמצאו שיעורים מוגבלים בתכלית האיפשר באופן שאם היה בזה חטא נופל כחוט השערה היו הגלגלים מונעים זה[b] את זה מהתנועע או היה נופל ביניהם ריקות. ומן הנמנע הוא שתהיה הגבלה כזאת נופלת בכל אחד מהם במקרה בלתי כוונת מכוֵון כי במקריים לא תקרה הגבלה כזאת נופלת ברבים במספר כאלה, וזה עם היותו מבואר בעצמו בארו ארסטו' בספר השמים והעולם

---

[a]ד׳] emend. Dunk.; ׳ז a, IV b; 4 L.   [b]זה] a[corr]; om. a.

pus est fuit vacuum necessario antequam corpus fuit etc.» Cum autem non detur vacuum, prout habetur rationum et auctoritate Phylosophi *Physicorum* IV t.c. 86, sequi ergo videtur, ut neque corpus celeste fuisset unquam factum, et per consequens habuisset esse ab eterno.

§ *4.3.1* Ad oppositum arguitur sic: ad quodlibet ad finem intentum habet necessario secundum tempus precedere agens huiusmodi finem intendens. Celorum quantitates sunt huiusmodi ergo celorum quantitates non habuerunt esse ab eterno, et per consequens, celum cui huiusmodi quantitates insunt, non habuit esse ab eterno. Consequentia patet, similem et antecedens quoad prima partem per diffinitionem eiusdem finis sine quo non inciperetur intenta actio, prout per se patet, et probatum est superius auctoritate et ratione, prout et in IV habetur propositione quibus necessario sequitur, ut tam agens quam finis in eiusdem agentis mente habeant ad ipsum actum secundum tempus precedere.

§ 4.3.2 Quo autem ad secundam antecedentis partem qua scilicet dicitur quod celi quantitates sunt huiusmodi scilicet quod sunt necessario ad intentum finem ordinate, patet, quia in cuiuslibet orbium quantitate et figura, observatur limitata mensura, sine cuius observatione impedirent se invicem a motu, vel daretur vacuum, huiusmodi autem observatio in omnibus orbibus apparens, inopinabile videtur ut contingat casu. Illa, enim, que casu contingunt, nunquam in tot non punctualiter observatur. Quare Phylosophus in lib. *De Celo* II t.c. 45 ait: «Dicimus etiam

body is would necessarily have been void before the creation of the body, etc.," and then there would be no void, as the Philosopher explicates in *Physics* 4, text. 86.[a] Thus, it seems to follow that the celestial body is not created, and consequently, it is [pre]eternal.

§ *4.3.1* On the contrary it is to argue: an agent who intends a final purpose precedes everything for which the final purpose is intended in time. The quantities of the heavens exist for the intended purpose; therefore, the quantities of the heavens are not [pre]eternal and consequently, the heavens in which such quantities exist will not be [pre]eternal. The consequence is evident, and the first part of the antecedent is proved according to the definition of the final purpose, without which an intended activity could not begin, as is clear from the aforementioned proof in the fourth proposition,[b] from which it would follow that the agent, as well as the final purpose in the agent's mind, are prior to its activity in time.

§ 4.3.2 The second part of the antecedent, in which we said that the quantities of the heavens exist for the intended final purpose, is proved, and [these quantities] are necessarily ordered to an intended final purpose. This is evident because a limited measurement is observed in the quantity of every sphere and in their shape. Without this observation, the spheres would hinder each other in movement or there would be a vacuum. This observation is evident in every sphere and it is impossible that it could happen by chance, because if it happened by chance, it could not be observed in everything, as the Philosopher explains in *On the Heavens* 2, text. 45,[c] where he states: "Then it is clear

---

[a] *Phys.* 4.9.217b. [b] Cf. *Metaph.* 2, text. 8, and 7, text. 23. [c] *Cael.* 2.8.289b.

the motion of a star is necessarily in accordance with the quantity of its sphere, because the star is moving within the motion of its sphere [and does] not have a motion of its own, and it follows that the motion of every single one of the stars is fast or slow relative to the great or small size of its sphere. He says: "We also say that if the spheres and the stars were not caused and had no agent, then it would not necessarily occur that the sphere was great in all stars and that the speed of the motion of the star in it was related to the size of the sphere. And if one or two stars were like this, it would not be that remote from thought. But since all the stars are [doing] so, the speech about this is like absurd talk."

§ 4.3.3 And al-Ġazālī and Averroes seem to have the same opinion in *The Incoherence of the Incoherence* 9, third investigation, especially in Averroes's argument against al-Ġazālī: "We say that the words of this man in this place are very strange, because it is difficult for the philosophers when they say that they are not able to say that there is any agent apart from the celestial body, because they have to answer by one principle, which they refute; namely, that the heavens have a particular size with particular dimensions thanks to a differentiating cause, although it might be possible that they had other quantitative measurements. And that differentiating cause needs to be eternal. And al-Ġazālī errs in this place with what is meant by the term 'differentiation,' because the differentiation to which the philosophers refer is different from the differentiation to which the Mutakallimun [Muslim theologians] refer. For the Mutakallimun [Muslim theologians] understand it as distinguishing between a thing and either a thing similar to it or its contrary, without wisdom being the cause to tend to one above similar things—or one of the stars above its neighbour. But the philosophers understand this as saying that the aforementioned 'differentiation' is wisdom, which bestows upon an existent that which is in it by its nature. And this is the final | cause, because for the philosophers, there is no quantity and no quality in any of the existents which is not [determined] by its [inherent] wisdom." And he continues: "If there was a certain quantity or quality in the created beings which was not generated by wisdom, they would necessarily have attributed something to the first creator which is not [even] appropriate to be attributed to a lower artisan." And he continues: "It becomes clear, then, that it follows that there is an agent, a wise and intelligent artisan, for existence, by whom the order of all the existents exists."[a]

---

[a] Cf. *Incoherence* 248–249.

quod si stelle et orbes essent non causati et essent sine causa et agente, non esset omnino necessarium ut orbis esset magnus in omnibus stellis, et motus stelle in eo esset velox secundum magnitudinem orbis. Si igitur una stella aut due essent huiusmodi non esset inopinabile, tantum cum autem omnes stelle sint huiusmodi, iste sermo est fabulosus.»

that even if the stars were transposed into each others' circles, the one in the larger circle would still be swifter, and the other slower; but in that case, they would possess no motion of their own, but would be carried by the circles. If, on the other hand, this were to have happened by chance, it would nonetheless be equally unlikely that chance should act so that the larger circle would be accompanied by the swifter movement of the star in it in every case. If only one or two stars were [moving] in this way, it would not be that impossible. But since all the stars are [moving] in this way, this statement is absurd."

§ 4.3.3 Et hec videtur quodammodo sentire Algazel et tandem Aven Ro. in libro *Destructio Destructionum*, disputatione IX, dubio 3, ubi contra Algazelem verbum faciens ait: «Dicimus nos, quod verba huius hominis in hoc loco valde sunt admiranda. Ipse, enim, obijcit Phylosophis quodammodo dicens, quod ipsi nequeunt asserere, efficientem preter corpus celeste, quia indigerent responsione cuiusdam radicis, quam ipsi negant. Videlicet quod celi approprianter in proprijs mensuris ratione cause appropriantis licet alias | magnitudines habere possint. Et dicta causa approprians, oportet ut sit antiqua. Unde Algazel erravit in hoc loco in intentione nominis appropriationis, quia appropriatio de qua locuti sunt phylosophi dissimilis est appropriationi loquentium. Loquentes namque intendunt per hoc, quod distinguitur res a suo simili vel a suo contrario, non quod sapientia inclinet unam ipsorum similium vel contrariorum magis quam alium. Sed phylosophi in hoc loco intendunt per dictam appropriationem quod sapientia inferat in effectum id quod habet de sua natura, et hoc est causa finalis. Apud enim phylosophos nulla est quantitas neque qualitas in aliquo entium, que non sit propter suam sapientia etc.» subdit ibidem dicens: «Si enim in creatis esset aliqua quantitas vel qualitas ab illa sapientia non producta sequeretur, ut attribueretur primo Creatori, illud quod non deberet attribui vilissimo artificum materiali» subdit ibidem dicens patet ergo «quod oportet ut mundus habeat unum opificem sagacissimum et sapientissimum, a quo entia cuncta seriatim ministrentur.»

§ 4.3.3 And al-Ġazālī and Averroes explicate this in *The Incoherence of the Incoherence* 9, third doubt, especially in [Averroes's] argument against al-Ġazālī, in which he states: "We say that this man's words about this are astounding, because it is an obstacle for the philosophers, in a way saying that they cannot say that there is an efficient cause other than the celestial body, because they [the philosophers] need to respond on the basis of a principle that they refute: and this principle is that for the heavens, there is a particular size, determined by a cause, although it would have been possible to have other | magnitudes in them. And this determining cause needs to be ancient. And al-Ġazālī errs in this place about the meaning of the term 'differentiation,' because the differentiation to which the philosophers refer is different from the differentiation of the Mutakallimun [Muslim theologians]. For the Mutakallimun [Muslim theologians] understand by this that it is possible to distinguish one thing from a similar thing or from its contrary, not through wisdom, which tends to one of the similar ones, or from a contrary, which is really something else. But the philosophers understand this as saying that differentiation is the wisdom that bestows upon the effect according to its nature, and this is the final cause. For the philosophers, there is no quantity and no quality in any of the existents that does not exist in his wisdom." He continues: "If there is a certain quantity or quality in the existents that is not produced from that wisdom, it would follow that they would attribute to the first creator something that it is not appropriate to attribute to a lower artisan," and he continues: "It becomes clear, if this is correct, that the universe has a wise and intelligent artisan, through whom the order of all the existents exists."[a]

---

[a] Cf. *Incoherence* 248–249.

§ 4.3.4 And Averroes acknowledges the same in the *Treatise on the Substance of the Celestial Sphere*, ch. 2: "Among the kinds of agents, there is an agent [that is] temporally prior to its activity. And every agent within the sphere of this world is of this kind. And there is an[other] agent which is naturally and temporally prior. And the sphere, to which time is subsequent and of which it is an accident, is of this kind. And also [of this kind] is the agent of the sphere; namely, that which brings forth the necessary dispositions to achieve the goal for whose sake it exists. And as it is hidden from the eyes of the many that this is the opinion of Aristotle, they say that Aristotle did not speak of an efficient cause, but only of the moving cause. This is very disgraceful and there is no doubt about it, because its agent is [identical with] its mover, because its mover with the movement designated for it is the same existent that previously bestowed upon it the disposition by which it acquired the movement that is designated for it. And that force is that existent which Aristotle praises in many places in his book *On the Heavens*. And he derives that it is more exalted than the heavens and higher than them."[a] And he explains the same in *The Incoherence of the Incoherence* 3, tenth investigation.[b]

§ 4.4.1 Second, it becomes clear that the heavens are not [pre]eternal in this way: because the order that exists in the stars is necessarily intended by a voluntary agent. And therefore, it follows that it is not [pre]eternal, because the voluntary agent—as Averroes explains in [the Commentary on] *Physics* 8, text. 15[c]—is set in motion before, [by] the thing he wanted or [by] imagining it. And therefore, it follows that the stars are not [pre]eternal. And this consequence is self-evident, because if the stars were [pre]eternal while their order was not [pre]eternal, it would follow that the stars had not been in that order for an infinite duration of time. And doubt would arise about the cause of [their] order, [why it was there] then and not before. And what we said—that the order of the stars undoubtedly occurs thanks to a voluntary, intending arranger of order—becomes clear in this way: because every order would not avoid one of two [cases]: either (1) that there would be something that preserves the natural ranks, or (2) that this would occur through the power of a voluntary arranger of order intending it for a certain final purpose. If so, it would become clear that when the order of the stars does not have someone preserving the natural ranks, it follows that it [i.e., the order] occurs through the power of voluntary arranger of order intending it for a final purpose, as

---

[a] Cf. *Sub. orb.* 85–86.   [b] Cf. *Incoherence* 103–104.   [c] Cf. *Phys.* 8.1.252a.

§ 4.3.4 **וזה** בעצמו הודה אבן רשד בספר עצם הגלגל פרק ב׳ באמרו: »במיני הפועלים יש פועל קדם בזמן לפעולתו ומזה המין הוא כל פועל אשר בכדור זה העולם ויש פועל קודם בטבע ובזמן ומזה המין הוא הגלגל אשר ממנו ימשך הזמן ויקרה לו. וכן פועל הגלגל רצוני לומר אשר המציאו על תכונות הכרחיות לבוא אל התכלית אשר בעבורו נמצא וכאשר נעלם מעיני רבים שזה הוא דעת אריסטו׳ אמרו שאריסטו׳ לא אמר סבה פועלת אבל אמר הסבה המניעה בלבד. זה היה מגונה מאד ואין ספק בזה כי הפועל שלו הוא המניע אותו כי המניע אותו בתנועה המיוחדת אליו הוא בעצמו הנמצא שנתן לו קודם תכונות אשר בהן קנה התנועה המיוחדת לו ואותו הכח הוא אותו הנמצא אשר שבח אריסטו׳ במקומות רבים בחבורו בספר השמים וגזר שהוא יותר נכבד מן השמים ומעולה מהם« עכ״ל. וזה בעצמו באר בספר הפלת ההפלה מאמר ג׳ חקירת י׳.

§ 4.4.1 **שנית** יתבאר זה רצוני לומר שהשמים הם בלתי קדמונים באופן זה, כי אמנם הסדר הנמצא בכוכבים הוא בהכרח מכוון מפועל רצוני, ומזה יתחייב שאינו קדמון. כי אמנם הפועל הרצוני כאשר באר אבן רשד בספר השמע מאמר ח׳ פרק ט״ו הניע אותו קודם לכן אותו הדבר אשר רצה או תמונתו. ומזה יתחייב שהכוכבים הם בלתי קדמונים. הנה חיוב זאת התולדה הוא מבואר בעצמו כי אם היו הכוכבים קדמונים עם היות סדרם בלתי קדמון היה מתחייב שהיו הכוכבים בלתי אותו הסדר במשך זמן בלתי בעל תכלית ויפול ספק מה היה סבת הסדר אז ולא קודם לכן. אמנם מה שאמרנו שסדר הכוכבים בלי ספק היה ממסדר רצוני מכוין יתבאר באופן זה. כי אמנם כל סדר לא ימלט מאחת משתים אם שיהיה שומר מעלות טבעיות או שיהיה מכח מסדר רצוני מכוין לתכלית מה אם כן כאשר יתבאר שסדר הכוכבים הוא בלתי שומר מעלות טבעיות יתחייב היותו מכח מסדר רצוני מכוין

§ 4.3.4 Ei idem habetur ab eodem Aven Ro. in *Tractatu de Substantia Orbis* cap. 2 ubi dicit: «Sed in genere agentium quoddam est prius temporis acto et est omne quod fit in sphera[a] huius mundi, quoddam est prius naturaliter et tempore, et est orbis ad quem sequitur tempus, et cui accidit, ut agens orbem est faciens ipsum in dispositionibus necessarijs, in inveniendo finem propter quem fuit, et cum ignoraverunt hoc quidam de opinione Aristotelis dixerunt ipsum non dicere causam agentem sed causam moventem tantum et illud fuit valde absurdum. Et non est dubium in hoc, quod agens ipsum est movens ipsum, quod enim movet ipsum moto proprio illi, est illud quod largitur illi primo dispositiones, per quas acquirit proprium motum, et illa virtus, est illa quam laudat in multis locis sui libri *De Celo* et indicat ipsam esse celo nobiliorem et altiorem etc.» Et idem aperte habetur ab eodem Aven R. in lib. *Dest. Destruc.*, disputatione III, dubiorum 10.

§ 4.4.1 Secundo arguitur sic: stellarum ordo habuit necessario fieri per voluntarium agentem, sive ordinatorem, ad ipsum ordinem tempore precedentem ergo huiusmodi ordo non habuit esse ab eterno. Consequentia patet, quoad secundam partem, qua scilicet dicitur: quod agens voluntarius habet necessario secundum tempus precedere ad suum actum quia sicut Aven R. Ait, in comento *Physicorum* VIII t.c. 15: «Voluntarius agens habet necessario prius moveri a voluntato[b] vel ab eius imaginatione.» Quo autem ad primam partem qua scilicet dicitur: quod stellarum ordo habuit necessario per voluntarium ordinatorem fieri, probatur quidlibet[c] ordo, vel fit a necessitate nature, vel fit a voluntario ordinatore finem intendente sed sic est quod stellarum ordo non sequitur nature necessitatem

§ 4.3.4 And Averroes explains this in the *Treatise on the Substance of the Celestial Sphere*, ch. 2, where he states: "But among the kinds of agents, one is prior to the activity that is in the spheres of this world and the other is prior in nature [naturally] and time [temporally], which is in the sphere, to which time is subsequent and of which it is an accident. The agent produces the necessary disposition to achieve an end for which it exists. Since people do not know that this is one of Aristotle's opinions, they say that he does not speak of the efficient cause of the universe, but rather of the moving cause. And this is absurd. Because there is no doubt that the efficient cause is the moving cause, because it moves itself according to its motion that is given by the first disposition, through which it acquires the beginning of the movement. And it is this force that he [i.e. Aristotle] praised in many places in his book *On the Heavens* that it is higher than the heavens,"[a] as Averroes explicates in *The Incoherence of the Incoherence* 3, tenth doubt.[b]

§ 4.4.1 Second, I would argue that the order of the stars is necessarily produced by a voluntary agent or by an arranger that is prior to that order in time; therefore, the order is not eternal. The consequence is evident regarding the second part of the antecedent, in which we said that a voluntary agent is necessarily prior to its act in time, as Averroes explicates in the Commentary on *Physics* 8, text. 15,[c] where he states: "A voluntary agent is necessarily moved by will or by its imagination." The first part of the antecedent, in which we said that the order of the stars is necessarily produced by a voluntary arranger, is proved, because every order is either produced by a natural necessity [the necessity of nature] or by a voluntary arranger that intends the final purpose. And if the order of the stars

---

[a] sphera] emend. Copp.; spera b; sphaera DSO.   [b] voluntato] b[corr]; voluntate b.   [c] quidlibet] emend. Copp.; quilibet b[corr]; quia libet b.

[a] Cf. *Sub. orb.* 85–86.   [b] Cf. *Incoherence* 103–104.   [c] Cf. *Phys.* 8.1.252a.

mentioned. What we said—that the order of the stars has no one to preserve the natural ranks—will become clear in this way: because since | the sun is the most exalted among the stars, in light, size, and power of generation, and a giver of life, more so than the rest of the stars, as testified by sense [perception], it is naturally appropriate that it should exist in a more exalted sphere among the spheres, and this is the sphere of the fixed stars. And sense [perception] testifies that the sphere of the sun is lower in place and rank than the [afore]mentioned sphere of the fixed stars. If so, it follows that this is not due to its nature, but thanks to the will of an arranger of order intending it for a final purpose. And perhaps this is what the arrangers of the order of prayers intended [to say] in their order of the blessing of the evening prayer: "[He] who ordered the stars and their positions related to the firmament according to His will."

§ 4.4.2 Regarding what we said, that the sphere of the fixed stars is more exalted than any sphere below it: its place and its potentiality to move the rest of the spheres through its motion and the number of the stars in it testify this, as testified by sense [perception]. And this becomes clear from the Philosopher's words in *On the Heavens* 2, text. 68:[a] "It is appropriate to know that the first sphere is the principle of potentiality and the cause of life for every living being, more so than the rest of the spheres. And therefore, it is the mover of many bodies and every single one of the rest of the spheres moves one star alone." And if the one who says that this is the daily sphere is correct, then it is also more exalted than all the rest [of the spheres] in the speed of its motion. And Aristotle explains the same in *Metaphysics* 12, text. 44:[b] "But that they are substances, and that this is [the] first of them and that this is [the] second, according to the order and motion of the stars, is evident." And Averroes explains his words: "For it is very much evident that this substance, which moves all of them, is more exalted than everything else, because every one of them is intended for this great motion. And if so, it is naturally prior and also prior in place to the rest of the substances, and also prior in size; namely, this substance is prior—due to the precedence of the motion by its potentiality—in place and size and number of stars, and in speed of motion. And all of these things make it prior in rank and in substance, because it is evident that the order of these movers, which begins with a first mover, necessitates that it will be in [its] place according to the order of the spheres and the stars, because their [the spheres] precedence in place and in size makes them prior in rank."

---

[a] *Cael.* 2.12.292b–293a. [b] *Metaph.* 12.8.1073b.

לתכלית כנזכר. אמנם זה שאמרנו שסדר הכוכבים אינו שומר מעלות טבעיות הנה יתבאר באופן זה כי בהיות | זה שהשמש[a] הוא היותר נכבד שבכוכבים וזה באור וגודל וכח הויה ותת החיים יותר מכל שאר הכוכבים כמו שיעיד עליו החוש היה ראוי לו בטבע שיהיה בגלגל היותר נכבד שבגלגלים והוא גלגל הכוכבים הקיימים והנה יעיד החוש שגלגל השמש הוא שפל במקום ובמעלה מגלגל הכוכבים הקיימים הנזכר אם כן יתחייב שלא היה זה מצד טבעו אבל ברצון מסדר מכוין לתכלית ואולי לזה כונו מסדרי התפלות בסדרם בברכת מעריב ערבים: «מסדר את הכוכבים במשמרותיהם ברקיע כרצונו.»

§ 4.4.2 אמנם מה שאמרנו שגלגל הכוכבים הקיימים הוא יותר נכבד מכל אשר תחתיו הנה יעיד עליו מקומו וכחו להניע שאר הגלגלים בתנועתו ומספר הכוכבים בו כמו שיעיד עליו החוש והתבאר מדברי הפילוסוף בספר השמים מאמר ב׳ פרק ס״ח באמרו: «ראוי לדעת שהגלגל הראשון הוא התחלת הכח וסבת החיים לכל חי יותר משאר הגלגלים ולכן הוא מניע גשמים רבים וכל אחד משאר הגלגלים מניע כוכב אחד בלבד» עכ״ל. ואם צדק האומר שהוא הגלגל היומי הוא אם כן נכבד מכל השאר גם במהירות תנועתו וזה בעצמו באר ארסטו׳ בספר מה שאחר מאמר י״ב פרק מ״ד באמרו: «אמנם היות העצמים וזה ראשון מהם וזה שני כפי סדר תנועות הכוכבים הוא מבואר» עכ״ל. ודבריו אלה באר אבן רשד באמרו: «כי אמנם שאותו העצם המניע את כלם הוא נכבד מכלם הוא מבואר מאד כי אמנם כלם מכוונים לתנועה הזאת הגדולה ואם כן הוא קודם בטבע וקודם גם כן במקום לשאר העצמים וקודם גם כן בגודל רצוני לומר שזה העצם הוא קודם מפני קדימת המתנועע מכחו בגודל ומספר כוכבים ומהירות התנועה וכל אלה עושים אותו קודם במעלה ובעצם כי מבואר הוא שסדר אלו המניעים המתחיל מן המניע הראשון צריך שיהיה כפי סדר הגלגלים והכוכבים במקום כי אמנם קדימתם במקום ובגודל עושה אותם קודמים במעלה.» עכ״ל.

---

[a] שהשמש] a^corr; שמש a.

ergo stellarum ordo habuit per voluntarium ordinatorem fieri. Quod autem stellarum ordo non sequatur | earundem naturam patet. Quia cum sol sit stellarum nobilissima lumine scilicet magnitudine producendique virtute et dandi vitam, prout sensu patet eidem ergo naturaliter competeret orbium nobilissimus. Et talis est supremus orbis, sive primum mobile, quod scilicet est ceteris nobilius cuius oppositum patet sensu.

§ 4.4.2 Restat ergo: ut stellarum ordo habuisset esse a voluntario ordinatore finem intendente, quod est intentum. Quod autem primus orbis sit ceteris nobilior, habetur a Phylosopho in lib. *De Celo* II t.c. 68 ubi dicit: «Manifestum igitur est, quod primus orbis principium est potentie et causa in vita cuiuslibet vivi plusquam alij orbes.» Et idem habetur ad eodem Phylosopho *Metaphysicorum* XII t.c. 44[a] ubi dicit: «Quoniam autem substantias esse, et earum hec esse prima hec autem secunda secundum ordinem stellarum motuum, manifestum est» ubi Aven R. exponens ait: «Quod autem illa, scilicet, substantia que omnia movet precedit omnes manifestum est valde, et precise, omnes enim istum motum maximum intendunt. Quapropter prior est naturaliter, et etiam secundum locum, et etiam secundum magnitudinem, et stellarum multitudinem et velocitatem motus, et omnia ista faciunt ipsum priorem nobilitate et substantia.»

does not follow the natural necessity, then the order of the stars is produced by a voluntary arranger. Since the order of the stars does not follow | a natural necessity, because the sun is the noblest star in light, size, and power of generation and is the giver of life, as the senses testify, then it naturally befits the noblest of the spheres. And the noblest of the spheres is the highest sphere or the first mobile, which is nobler than the other [spheres], as the senses testify.

§ 4.4.2 Then it remains that the order of the stars was produced by a voluntary arranger who intended the final purpose, and this is what was intended. The first sphere is nobler than the others, as the Philosopher explains in *On the Heavens* 2, text. 68,[a] where he states: "It is appropriate to know that the first sphere is the principle of potentiality and the cause of life for every living being, more than the rest of the spheres," and as the Philosopher explains in *Metaphysics* 12, text. 44,[b] where he states: "It is clear, then, that there are substances and that one of them is first and another second, according to the order of the stars." And Averroes explicates: "For it is quite clear that this substance, which moves all of them, surpasses everything, because every one of them is intended for this great motion, which is prior to the rest in nature, place, size, number of stars, and speed of motion. And all of these make it prior in rank and in substance."

---

[a] 44] emend. Copp.; 99 b; 44 L.

[a] *Cael.* 2.12.292b–293a.   [b] Cf. *Metaph.* 12.8.1073b.

§ 4.4.3 And Averroes explains the same in *The Incoherence of the Incoherence* 3, eighteenth investigation.[a] And it becomes clear from all this that the order of the stars and also the stars themselves are not eternal. It therefore follows that the spheres are also not eternal, because the stars are necessarily part of the spheres; because, if so, one of two [cases] would be unavoidable, and this is so: if the stars were bodies existing between one [sphere] and another sphere, then (1) a vacuum would necessarily exist between the sphere and its neighbour, or (2) they [i.e., the stars] would be fixed within the body of the sphere. And according to this, it would follow that one of two [things would be true]: either (a) that the bodies of the sphere were void in those places in which the stars would be embedded, or (b) that a body was penetrating another body, and these two are impossible. And Aristotle explains the same thing in *On the Heavens* 2, text. 41:[b] | "We said that apart from the aforementioned [things], it follows that we say that every star is [part] of the body of that sphere in which it will move." And Aristotle explains the same in the name of the Ancients: "They said about them that the stars are igneous. They only say this because they think that the upper body is igneous." And Averroes explains his words: "This sentence is contrary to the given proposition that it is necessary that the whole [has to] be of the nature of the part. And anyone who agrees with this also agrees with the contrary sentence."

§ 4.5.1 Third, it becomes clear that the spheres are not [pre]eternal in this way: because the mover of the first sphere is a voluntary mover. If so, then it follows that its propulsion is not [pre]eternal and it therefore follows that the spheres moved by its force are also not [pre]eternal.

§ 4.5.2 And the consequence is evident, because the eternal thing has no true agent, least of all a voluntary agent, as is self-evident, and Averroes explains this in *On the Heavens* 4, text. 1.

§ 4.5.3 The [antecedent] premise—in which we said that the first mover is a voluntary mover—becomes clear in this way: because every motion will be either natural or voluntary or necessarily violent. And the motion by which all the spheres that are below him [i.e., the first mover] are moving is not natural to them, because every one of them has a natural motion designated for it, different from [i.e., contrary to] the motion of the diurnal [motion] in time and in the direction towards which it will move. And it

---

[a] Cf. *Incoherence* 138–139.   [b] *Cael.* 2.7.289a.

§ 4.4.3 וזה בעצמו באר אבן רשד בספר הפלת ההפלה מאמר ג׳ חקירת י״ח. וכאשר התבאר מכל אלה שסדר הכוכבים וכן הכוכבים הם בלתי קדמונים יתחייב מזה שגם הגלגלים הם בלתי קדמונים כי הכוכבים הם בהכרח חלקי הגלגלים כי אם לא היה זה לא ימלט מאחת משתים וזה אם שהכוכבים הם גשמים עומדים בין גלגל לגלגל ואם כן היה ריקות נמצא בהכרח בין שאר הגלגל ושכנו או שהם קבועים בגרם הגלגל ולזה יתחייב אחת משתים אם שיהיו גשמי הגלגלים חסרים באותם המקומות אשר בם הכוכבים משוקעים או שיכנס גשם בגשם ושתי אלה נמנעות. וזה בעצמו באר ארסטו׳ בספר השמים מאמר ב׳ פרק מ״א באמרו: | "נאמר שמלבד הנזכר לעיל צריך שנאמר שכל כוכב הוא מגרם אותו הגלגל אשר בו יתנועע" עכ״ל וזה בעצמו באר שם ארסטו׳ בשם הקדמונים באמרו: "אותם שאמרו שהכוכבים הם אשיים לא אמרו זה אלא מפני שחשבו שהגשם העליון הוא אשיי. ודבריו אלה באר אבן רשד באמרו: "הנה זה משפט מתהפך עם ההנחה האומרת[a] שראוי הוא שיהיה הכל מטבע החלק ומי שיסכים בזה יסכים גם כן במשפט המתהפך עמו."

§ 4.5.1 שלישית יתבאר שהגלגלים הם בלתי קדמונים באופן זה כי אמנם מניע הגלגל הראשון הוא מניע רצוני. אם כן יתחייב שהנעתו היא בלתי קדמונית ומזה יתחייב שגם הגלגלים המתנועעים מכחו הם בלתי קדמונים.

§ 4.5.2 התולדה אמנם היא מבוארת כי הדבר הקדמון אין לו פועל באמת כל שכן פועל רצוני כאשר הוא מבואר בעצמו ובארו אבן רשד בספר השמים והעולם מאמר ד׳ פרק א׳.

§ 4.5.3 אמנם ההקדמה אשר אמרנו בה שהמניע הראשון הוא מניע רצוני יתבאר באופן זה כי כל תנועה תהיה או טבעית או רצונית או בהכרח מכרחת והנה התנועה אשר בה יתנועעו כל הגלגלים שתחתיו אינה טבעית להם כי אמנם לכל אחד מהם יש תנועה טבעית מיוחדת אליו נבדלת מתנועת היומי בזמן ובצד אשר אליו יתנועע ומן הנמנע

---

[a] האובדת; [a corr] האומרת.

§ 4.4.3 Et idem apertius habetur ab eodem Aven R. in lib. Destructionis D., disputatione III, dubio 18, cum autem ex dictis pateat, stellas non fuisse ab eterno, sequitur quidem, ut neque orbes habuissent esse ab eterno. Stelle, enim, sunt necessario horum orbium partes. Alias, enim, vel essent corpora inter duos orbes posita, et sic daretur de necessitate in residuo vacuum, vel essent corpora orbibus infixa, et tunc sequeretur alterum duorum, vel scilicet ut orbium corpora deficerent in illis locis ubi ipse stelle infixe sunt, vel daretur corporum penetratio. Quorum utrumque est inconveniens. Et idem habetur a Phylosopho in lib. *De Celo* II t.c. 41 ubi dicit: «Dicamus igitur quod oportet nos preter ea que diximus superius ponere quamlibet stellarum ex illo corpore in quo moventur etc.» et idem infert ibidem antiquorum auctoritate ubi dicit: «Dicentes quod stelle sunt ignee non dicebant hoc nisi quia corpus altissimum ponebant igneum» ubi Aven R. exponens ait: «Hec est concessio conversionis istius propositionis, scilicet, quod totum debet esse nature sue partis, et qui hoc concedit concedit etiam conversam.»

§ 4.5.1 Tertio arguitur sic nulla actio voluntarie facta habuit esse ab eterno. Primi orbis motio est huiusmodi. Ergo huiusmodi motio non habuit esse ab eterno. Et per consequens neque corpora[a] mobilia habuerunt esse ab eterno consequentia patet.

§ 4.5.2 Similiter et antecedens quoad primam partem, qua scilicet dicitur quod nulla actio voluntarie facta habuit esse ab eterno. Quia voluntarie agens habet necessario secundum tempus precedere ad suum actum, ut supra. Quare Aven Ro. in commento lib. *De Celo* IV t.c. 1 ait: «Quod universum, quia ab eterno non habet vere agens.»

§ 4.5.3 Quo autem ad secundam antece | dentis partem, qua scilicet dicitur quod primi mobilis motio qua scilicet inferiora mobilia movet, est huiusmodi, probatur quia quilibet motus non naturalis vel est voluntarius vel violentus, sed sic est, quod motus diurnus omnibus mobilibus infra primum existentibus est his non naturalis, quia quodlibet horum habet naturalem motum primo contrarium, ergo

§ 4.4.3 And Averroes explicates this in *The Incoherence of the Incoherence* 3, eighteenth doubt,[a] where it becomes clear that the stars are not eternal, and it would also follow that the spheres are not eternal. The stars are necessarily part of the spheres, and then either they would be bodies existing between two spheres, which would mean that there would necessarily be a void, or they would be fixed within the body of the sphere. Therefore, two different instances would follow, either that the bodies of the spheres were void in those places in which they are embedded or that there would be a penetration of bodies, and both possibilities are incongruous. The Philosopher explains this in *On the Heavens* 2, text. 41,[b] where he states: "We say that it follows that we state that each star consists of the upper body in which it moves, etc.," and the same [Aristotle] explains in the name of the Ancients, when he states: "They say that the stars are igneous, and they say this thing because they place an igneous body as the upper body." And Averroes explicates [this]: "This sentence is the contrary of this proposition; namely, that the whole has to be of the nature of its part. And anyone who agrees with this also agrees with the contrary sentence."

§ 4.5.1 Third, I would argue that no voluntary action is [pre]eternal. The motion of the first sphere is a voluntary activity; therefore, its motion is not [pre]eternal. And consequently, mobile bodies are also not [pre]eternal.

§ 4.5.2 The consequence is evident and the first part of the antecedent, in which we said that voluntary activity is eternal, is proved because a voluntary agent is necessarily prior to its act, as mentioned above, as Averroes explicates in the Commentary on *On the Heavens* 4, text. 1, where he states: "An eternal thing does not have a true agent."

§ 4.5.3 The second part of the ante|cedent, in which we said that the motion of the first movable moves inferior movables, is proved because every motion that is not natural is either voluntary or violent. And if so, diurnal motion is the first [motion] of all existing movables, and it is not natural because their natural motion is contrary to the first movable; therefore, diurnal motion is either voluntary or

---

[a] corpora] b[corr]; tempora b; הגלגלים a.

[a] Cf. *Incoherence* 138–139.   [b] *Cael.* 2.7.289a.

is impossible that it could occur that they move in a diurnal motion caused by the thrusting [i.e., the contrary circular movement] of the upper sphere, which thrusts the spheres that are below it, insofar as they are in contact with each other. For if this were true, it would then be necessary that every single one of the lower spheres would move in [agreement with] every motion of the spheres above them. And sense [perception] testifies the contrary of this. It therefore remains, then, that the [differentiated] diurnal motion for all the spheres that are below the diurnal [sphere] would either be violent or voluntary. And since every violent motion is [caused] by the motion of a voluntary mover, who moves either immediately or mediately, it is then self-evident, and al-Ġazālī explains, as Averroes quotes in his name in *The Incoherence of the Incoherence* 13, first investigation, that it follows that the [afore]mentioned [designated] diurnal motion in the spheres below the [afore]mentioned diurnal [sphere] occurs through the power of a voluntary mover.[a] And this is what we wanted to explain. And since the aforementioned motion occurs through the power of a voluntary mover, it therefore follows that it is not [pre]eternal, as mentioned above. It follows, then, that the spheres moving by this motion are also not [pre]eternal, because if they were [pre]eternal, despite having a non-[pre]eternal diurnal motion, it would therefore follow that they would have been without that motion for an infinite time, and after that—without any cause—they would have possessed the [afore]mentioned motion. And this is incongruous.

19ᵛ § 4.6 We answer, if so, to dispel [any] doubt about the [afore]mentioned thesis, by saying that the heavens are not [pre]eternal; instead, they have an existence after non-existence and absolute nothingness through the power of a creator, who intends [them] for a final purpose.

§ 4.7.1 And to the opponent's arguments, which say first that corruption [lit. privation] does not occur to an existent that has no contrary and that since no existent is contrary to the heavens—there is no motion contrary to circular [motion]—it follows that corruption [lit. privation] does not occur to them, we answer that there are two kinds of corruption [lit. privation]. One is corruption [lit. privation] that occurs "from form to form," and this will be [the case] when the substrate undergoes an essential alteration by which the form that was in it in potentiality is actualised. And Aristotle's and Averroes's arguments in *On the Heavens* 1, text. 124[b] and 137[c] are correct

---

[a] Cf. *Incoherence* 285–287.   [b] *Cael.* 1.12.282b.   [c] *Cael.* 1.12.283b.

horum huiusmodi motus scilicet diurnus eidem superveniens est voluntarius vel violentus. Huiusmodi autem violentia non contingit fieri nisi, vel per accidens ratione contactus secum ducentis, vel ratione voluntariji moventis huiusmodi violentiam inferentis, sed sic est, quod non ratione contactus, quia si sic, idem contingeret soli per motum superiorum quare deviaret quandoque ab ecliptica per diversitatem polorum superiorum cuius contrarium testantur eclipses. Restat ergo, ut fiat per voluntarium motorem violentiam inferentem, mediatum scilicet vel immediatum, sicut habetur auctoritate Algazelis in lib. *Destructionis D.*, disputatione XIII, dubio 1, quod est intentum. Cumque huiusmodi motio a voluntario motore emanans non habuisset esse ab eterno ut supra. Sequitur quidem ut neque mobilia eadem motione mota habuissent esse ab eterno, alias, enim, sequeretur, ut ab eterno habuissent esse sine huiusmodi motu deinde eisdem supervenisset huiusmodi motio sine causa, quod est inopinabile.

§ 4.6 Ad dubium ergo respondetur: quod non ab eterno habuit esse celum, immo habuit produci per Creatorem finem intendentem.

§ 4.7.1 Ad argumenta vero ex primo quoad primum. Respondetur quod duplex est corruptio. Alia, enim, est illa, que fit de forma ad formam per substantialem subiecti alterationem, cui alia supervenit forma, que sibi potentialiter inerat et de huiusmodi corruptionis genere procedunt rationes Phylosophi et Aven R. in lib. *De Celo* Iprimi t.c. 137

violent. Violent [motion] is only produced by chance, and this is either by accident, by means of contact with itself, or by will, and the motion itself causes the violence. And if this is true, then there is no reason to have contact, because if it were so, it would happen that the sun would be moved according to the motion of the upper movables when it undergoes an eclipse, thanks to the difference of the superior poles. And the contrary of this is testified by the occurrence of eclipses. It therefore remains that motion is produced by a voluntary mover who causes the violence mediately or immediately, as al-Ġazālī explicates in *The Incoherence of the Incoherence* 13, first doubt,[a] and this is what was intended. Whenever a motion emanating from a voluntary mover is [pre]eternal, as mentioned above, it follows that no movables moved by this motion are [pre]eternal, because if they were [pre]eternal, then their motion would occur without a cause, and this is incongruous.

§ 4.6 To dispel any doubt, I would argue that the heavens are not [pre]eternal; on the contrary, they were produced by a creator who intends their final purpose.

§ 4.7.1 In response to the first argument, I will reply: there are two kinds of corruption. One of them is made from form to form by the substantial alteration of the substrate; the other is according to the form that is potentially [inherent] in the substrate. And with regard to this kind of privation, Aristotle and Averroes prove this in the book *On the Heavens* 1, text. 137,[b] because in order to arrive at corrup-

---

[a] Cf. *Incoherence* 285–287.   [b] *Cael.* 1.12.283b.

about this kind of corruption [lit. privation], because for this kind of corruption [lit. privation], it is necessary that there is a disposition for corruption [lit. privation] in the affected thing that is not in the existents that do not have contrariety, because their substrate is not affectable and not alterable. And since the heavens do not have contrariety and therefore alteration does not occur to them and [there is] no corruption [lit. privation] of form that will be in them in potentiality, it follows that this kind of corruption [lit. privation] has never occurred to them and will never occur to them. But the second kind of corruption [lit. privation]—which is from existence to absolute non-existence—already occurred to the heavens before their creation. And it is not impossible that this could have occurred to them through the will of their creator, because, as their existence is not by means of a potentiality existing in a substrate, but through the power of a wise and voluntary creator, without the existence of any substrate that is disposed to a certain form, he brings forth the substrate and the predicate, too. It is not impossible that they will also be corrupted into absolute non-existence by that wisdom that brought them forth after absolute non-existence and gave them perpetuity of their existence, as it says (Nehemiah 9:6): "You preserve them all," and as Averroes explains in [the Commentary on] *On the Heavens* 4, text. 1, and others. And this is perhaps what Plato wanted [to say], what Averroes grasped of it in [the Commentary on] *On the Heavens* 1, text. 124,[a] saying that it is not impossible for there to be an existent for which corruption [lit. privation] is possible [but] which will never occur to it. And this is correct when corruption [lit. privation] is understood as occurring not through the potentiality of any substrate, but through the power of a creator *ex nihilo* or [a maker] *ab novo*.

§ 4.7.2 And this is what the Poet says in Psalm 104(:5): "He established the earth on its foundations, so that it shall never totter." And this is understood to be the first kind of corruption [lit. privation]. But when he says in Psalm 102(:26–27), "Of old You established the earth; and the heavens are the work of Your hands. They shall perish, but You shall endure," it is understood that the second kind of corruption [lit. privation] is possible for them, as mentioned above.

---

[a] Cf. *Cael.* 1.12.282b.

quia ad huiusmodi corruptionem agendam habet corruptibilitas necessario inesse patienti, et talis non habet inesse his quibus non inest contrarietas, et per consequens neque alterabilitas sive potentia ad forme privationem, horum enim subiectum non est alterabile, quare celo cui nulla inest contrarietas numquam in preterito contingit huiusmodi corruptionis genus. Alia est corruptio ab esse ad purum non esse ad quam nulla requiritur alteratio, neque nova subiecti forma, sicut ad productionis genus huiusmodi corruptioni oppositum et talis est creatio nullum requiritur subiectum et per consequens neque potentia in eodem subiecto existens. Et huiusmodi corruptionis sive privationis genus contigit quidem et fortasse continget celo per eandem sapientissimam voluntatem et virtutem per quam post purum non esse productum est ut supra. Et idem fortasse sensit Plato in lib. *De Celo* primi t.c. 124 ab Aven Ro. accusatus, cum scilicet dixerit quod possibile est ut aliquid habeat potentiam ad corruptionem quod tamen numquam | corrumpatur. Intelligens scilicet de illo corruptionis genere, quod non per subiecti naturam sed per voluntatem eiusdem producentis sive creantis virtutem tantum contingere posset.

§ 4.7.2 Et idem videtur in Sacris Scripturis doceri, ubi scilicet in Psalmo 103ᵃ [104:5] ait: «fundavit terram super dispositiones suas non vacillabit in seculum seculi» et hoc dixit intelligens de primo corruptionis genere illud, enim numquam continget terre saltem secundum totum in Psalmo vero 101 [102:26–27] ait: «tu Domine terram fundasti et opera manuum tuarum celi. Ipsi peribunt tu autem remanebis.» Et hoc dixit intelligens de secundo corruptionis genere.

tion, the corruptibility of a passive thing is necessary, and this [does not happen] in those things in which there is no contrariety. Consequently, there is neither alteration nor privation in potentiality according to the form, because its substrate is not alterable. The heavens do not have contrarieties and will never be subject to this kind of corruption. The other kind of corruption is from existence to absolute nothingness, which does not require alteration or a new form in a substrate. This kind of production is the opposite of corruption. This is the creation that does not need a substrate, or consequently, something existing in potentiality in the substrate. This kind of corruption or privation happens to those things, and perhaps it happens to the heavens through the wisest will and power that produced them after absolute nothingness, as mentioned above. And perhaps Plato meant this in the book *On the Heavens* 1, text. 124,[a] when Averroes reproaches him for saying that it is possible that something may have the potential for corruption | even if it is not corruptible. This kind of corruption is not natural in the substrate, but could only happen through the will of the maker or through the power of the creator.

§ 4.7.2 As Psalm 103 (104:5) teaches: "He set the foundations of the earth, and it will never be moved," meaning that according to the first kind of corruption, nothing can ever happen to the earth, at least with respect to the whole. As Psalm 101 (102:26–27) teaches: "Of old you laid the foundation of the earth, and the heavens are the work of thy hands. They will perish, but you remain," this is the second kind of corruption.

---

[a] 103] emend. Copp.; 105 b; 104 M; 103 V.

[a] *Cael.* 1.12.282b.

§ 4.8.1 To the argument brought by the opponent that says that if the heavens were created, it would follow that there would have been a vacuum in their space before their creation, we answer: their space was created together with their motions and the time following them together with the creation of the heavens. And therefore, there does not have to be a vacuum at all, and also, it does not follow that the heavens are predestined [to exist] for an infinite time.

§ 4.8.2 The Torah of our God explains all of these by *revealing His powerful deeds*,[a] and it says that He "created" the heavens and their centre—which is the earth—which they surround (Genesis 1:1). Regarding the luminaries and the rest of the stars, it says: "And He made" (Genesis 1:16), because they as a whole are part of the spheres or the heavens, whose creation [*ex nihilo*] has already been described. And therefore, it does not refer to their "creation," [but] only [to their] "making," and this is that He brought them forth from some parts of the spheres into a round shape and a light-giving form. And this is proven in its saying (Genesis 1:17–18): "And God set them in the expanse of the heavens to shine, etc., to dominate, etc., and to separate [light from darkness]. And God saw that this was good"; that is to say, the place of the luminaries in the firmament, which is not proper according to the nature of their rank, as mentioned above, tells [us] that they are not in this place by nature, but through the intention of an intender (Genesis 1:18): "To shine and to dominate and to separate [light from darkness]." And this is so because God saw (ibid.) "that it was good"; that is to say, He intended the "good" by this, and this is the proper final purpose of His [afore]mentioned action, which is the derivation of His wisdom. And therefore, it follows that the luminaries are not [pre]eternal. And therefore, it also becomes clear that the heavens are not [pre]eternal, but created through the power of a creator, not from a thing prior [to them, but] without a substrate prior to them, as mentioned above.

§ 4.9.1 And Isaiah explains the same (40:26): "Lift high your eyes and see: Who created these? He who sends out their host by count, Who calls them each by name: Because of His great might and vast power, Not one fails to appear"; that is to say, it becomes clear that God—may He be praised—created the spheres first, since their hosts—and these are the stars—exist in them in a number that is not limited according to the spheres and their number, but limited according to the role of the stars and their activities. This is so because many stars exist in the first of the

---

[a] Cf. Ps 111:6.

§ 4.8.1 אמנם על הטענה אשר טען החולק באמרו שאם היו השמים נבראים היה מתחייב שהיה במקומם ריקות קודם הבריאה. נשיב שיחדיו עם בריאת השמים נברא מקום עם תנועותם והזמן הנמשך להם ובכן לא יתחייב ריקות כלל וגם כן לא יתחייב שיהיו השמים מֻגבלים זמן בלתי בעל תכלית.

§ 4.8.2 ‏‏*ואת* כל אלה בארה תורת אלהינו בהגיד כח מעשיו, ואמרה ש"ברא" השמים ומרכזם והוא הארץ אשר יקיפו עליה (בראשית א' א'). אמנם על המאורות ושאר הכוכבים[a] אמר: "ויעש" (בראשית א' ט"ז) כי היו בכלל חלקי הגלגלים או השמים אשר כבר ספר בריאתם ולזה לא הזכיר להם ‹בריאה› רק ‹עשיה›, וזה שהמציא אותם ממקצת חלקי הגלגלים על תמונה כדורית וצורה מאירה והודיעה[b] זה במופת באמרה: "ויתן אותם אלהים ברקיע השמים להאיר וגו' ולמשול וגו' ולהבדיל וגו' וירא אלהים כי טוב" (בראשית א' י"ז-י"ח), כלומר כי אמנם מקום המאורות ברקיע אשר לא יאות לטבע מעלתם כנזכר לעילא יורה על היותם במקום ההוא לא בטבע אבל בכונת מכוין: "להאיר ולמשול ולהבדיל" (שם שם י"ח). וזה כי ראה "אלהים כי טוב" (שם), כלומר שכיון בזה אל ה‹טוב›, והוא התכלית הנאות לפעלו הנזכר אשר גזרה חכמתו וממה יתחייב שאין המאורות קדמונים וממה התבאר שהשמים גם כן בלתי קדמונים אבל מחודשים בכח בורא לא מדבר קודם מבלי אין נושא קודם להם כנזכר לעיל.

§ 4.9.1 ‏‏*וזה* בעצמו באר ישעיהו באמרו "שאו מרום עיניכם וראו מי ברא אלה? המוציא במספר צבאם לכלם בשם יקרא מרוב אונים ואמיץ כח איש לא נעדר" (ישעיהו מ' כ"ו), כלומר כי אמנם יתבאר שהאל יתברך ברא הגלגלים ראשונה בהיות צבאם. והם הכוכבים נמצאים בהם על מספר בלתי שומר יחס הגלגלים ומספרם אבל שומר ענין הכוכבים ופעולתם. וזה כי בגלגל הראשון להם נמצאו כוכבים רבים מאד ובגלגל אשר מיד תחתיו לא נמצא כי אם כוכב אחד וכן

---

[a] הכוכבים] coni. Dunk.; כוכבים a. [b] והודיעה] coni. Dunk.; והודיע a.

§ 4.8.1 Ad secundum vero argumentum respondetur: quod simul cum celo tam locus quam tempus habuerunt per creationem produci, quare non sequitur vacuum neque infinitum tempus ab eodem celo terminari.

§ 4.8.2 Quare Sacrum Genesis Documentum cap. primo [Gen 1:1] docet primo, creationem qua habuit esse celum eiusque centrum, solem vero et lunam ceterasque stellas. Docet habuisse esse per factionem Dei iussu factam. Ad necessitatem vel ad melius intentam, prout ibidem infert cum dicit: «et vidit Deus quoniam bonum.» Et idem demonstrative docet per luminarium loca que nonnisi finem intendentis nutu contigit fuisse ut supra. Et hoc infert ubi [Gen 1:17–18] dicit: «et posuit ea Deus in orbe celorum ut illuminarent super terram et preessent diei et nocti etc.» Quasi dicat quod cum posita sint extra loca sibi naturaliter competentia patet, quod non contigit fuisse nisi ad illuminandi super terram sub quadam intenta mensura, et per consequens nonnisi ad huiusmodi finem intendentis nutum, ad quod sequitur ut celum cuius ipse stelle sunt partes fuisset ab eodem fine intendente productum et hoc per creationem ut supra.

§ 4.9.1 Quare Esaias cap. 40 [40:26] docens celum fuisse creatum illud demonstrative ostendit dicens: «*levate in excelsum oculos vestros et videte quis creavit hec qui educit in numero exercitum eorum omnes nomine vocat a multitudine virtutum et fortis roboris unus non defuit etc.* Quibus infert quod patet et Deum creasse orbes primo scilicet per hoc quod videmus sydera sub quodam limitato numero non naturali. Itaque primus orbis abundat tot stel-

§ 4.8.1 In response to the second argument, I will reply: the heavens, place, and time were created together with creation, and the existence of the vacuum does not follow from this, nor does an infinite time after which the heavens will end [i.e., that the heavens will exist forever].

§ 4.8.2 Then the Holy Book of Genesis (1:1) teaches that Creation was the creation of the heavens and their centre; the sun, moon, and other stars were created by the action of God for a universal necessity according to the best intention, [for it] says: "And God saw that it was good." And [Genesis] teaches that the place of the luminaries was created only through the intention of the intender, saying (Genesis 1:17–18): "And God set them in the firmament of the heavens to give light on the earth, to rule over the day and over the night, etc." Likewise, it says that the place of the luminaries is not properly in accordance with the nature of their rank, because the luminaries shine over the earth through an intended measurement, and consequently through the intended purpose of the intender, and consequently, it would follow that the heavens, which include the stars, were created for an intended purpose, and this was by creation, as mentioned above.

§ 4.9.1 Then Isaiah 40 (40:26) explains the same, that the heavens were created, saying: "Lift up your eyes on high, and see who has created these things, who brings out their host by number; He calls them all by name, by the greatness of His might and the strength of His power; not one is missing, etc." From these [words], it is clear that God created the spheres first and that through them, we see a limited number of stars, which is not natural. Because the first of the spheres has many stars, and the sphere that

spheres, and in the sphere that is just below, there are none, except for a single star, and so it is in every single one of the spheres below it. And therefore, he [Isaiah] analyses that the difference that is between them in this [case] is not due to a difference in their natures, ranks, or place, for since the stars are noble parts in them [i.e., the spheres], as Averroes explains in the Commentary on *On the Heavens* 2, text. 41,[a] the spheres' relative rank to each other is in accordance with their place, size, and proximity to the first [i.e., the sphere of the fixed stars], as Aristotle and Averroes explain in *Metaphysics* 12, text. 44,[b] as mentioned above. It would [therefore] follow that in each upper [sphere] that is nobler than the others below it, there would exist a greater number of stars than in the sphere below it. But sense [perception] testifies the contrary of this in existing reality. And therefore, it follows that the apparent difference between the spheres does not exist in them due to a difference in their nature, but thanks to the activity of a voluntary intending creator, who brought forth the stars in a limited number according to need or to the higher good.

§ 4.9.2 And in some way, this seems to be in accordance with what the Philosopher considers in *On the Heavens* 2, text. 67:[c] "We now want to dispel the second doubt, why there are many stars in the eighth sphere, which is next to the first; and in every one of the rest of the spheres, which have one motion, there is only one star. We say, then, that this is right because it is necessary to know that the first sphere is the principle of potentiality and the cause | of the life of all living beings more than the rest of the spheres. And therefore, it is the mover of many bodies, and every single one of the others moves one star only." From these words, it follows that there is doubt about the difference in the number of the stars that is not congruent with the natural relationship to the spheres, necessitating with it that it [i.e., the difference] exists for a final purpose, and this is only possible through the will of a voluntary agent intending the final purpose while the congruence of their natures is not achieved.

§ 4.9.3 And apart from this, the Prophet brings a second proof (Isaiah 40:26): "Who calls them each by name." By this, he means that the stars that are in one and the same sphere are different from each other by name, informing [us] about the form and the agent designated to that star, named with the name that is designated for it. Because since they are noble parts, which are the same in a single sphere, congruent in [their] light and spherical shape, it is

---

[a] Cf. *Cael.* 2.7.289a. [b] *Metaph.* 12.8.1073b. [c] *Cael.* 2.12.292b.

lis, orbis vero immediate sequens ab ipso adeo differt ut eidem una tantum insit stella, et idem indifferenter contigit omnibus inferioribus orbibus ut scilicet horum singulo una tantum in est stella. Quare patet quod huiusmodi differentia qua primus orbis ab alijs differt non contingit ab orbium natura, qua scilicet nobilitate vel loco ab invicem differant: quorum orbium ipse stelle nobiliores partes sicut habetur ab Aven R. in comento *De Celo* II t.c. 41 quia huiusmodi nobilitas ut Phylosophus et Aven Ro. dicunt *Metaphysicorum* XII t.c. 44 consideratur penes eorum locorum et magnitudinem. Quare si ab huiusmodi nobilitate causaretur differentia numeri stellarum inter primum orbem et reliquos idem contingeret cuiuslibet sequentium orbium respectu inferioris illo ut, scilicet, pluribus vigeret stellis, quam reliqui orbes ipso inferiores tanquam ipsis nobilior, cuius | oppositum patet sensu. Quibus sequitur, ut huiusmodi differentia qua scilicet primus orbis a reliquis orbibus quoad stellarum numerum adeo differt non ex orbum nature diversitate contingit sed a voluntario agente, vel producente huiusmodi limitatum numerum ad necessitatem vel ad melius intendente emanare.

§ 4.9.2 Et idem videtur Philosophum quodamodo sensisse in lib. *De Celo* II t.c. 67 ubi dicit: «Volumus modo dissolvere secundam questionem quare in octavo orbe propinquo orbi primo, sint plures stelle non numerate, et in uno quoque aliorum orbium habentium unum motum est una stella tantum[a] etc.» Quibus videtur dubitare de causa huiusmodi diversitatis non proportionale orbium naturis nullo pacto attribuende. Ubi idem Phylosophus subdit dicens: «Dicamus igitur quod recte hoc fuit. Sciendum igitur est quod primus orbis principium est potentie et vite cuiuslibet vivi plusquam alij orbes. Qua propter primus orbis movet plura corpora et unusquisque ceterorum[b] movet unam stellam tantum etc.» Quibus inferri videtur: stellarum numerum esse ad finem qui nonnisi ab agente finem intendente esse contingit.

§ 4.9.3 Secundo probat propheta idem per diversitatem naturarum et actionum stellarum eodem orbe existentium. Quia cum eidem insint orbi cuius ipse stelle sunt nobiliores partes, deberent harum nature et actiones saltem genere convenire, nec deberent ab invicem differre

is below it is different from it, having only a single star, and the same happens with each inferior sphere, which is different, having a single star, then it is clear that the difference between the first sphere and the others does not pertain to the nature of the spheres, because they are each different from the others in general through the nobility of their rank, because the stars are the noblest part of these spheres, as Averroes explicates in the Commentary on *On the Heavens* 2, text. 41.[a] Because, as the Philosopher and Averroes explain in *Metaphysics* 12, text. 44,[b] nobility is connected to their size and their place. And if so, nobility is the cause of the difference in the numbers of stars between the first sphere and the others; this is also the case for the sphere that is below and the inferior spheres, because many stars prosper in it [i.e., the first sphere] compared to the rest of the inferior spheres, just because it is nobler than them. But the contrary | seems to be evident. It would follow that the difference between the first sphere and the rest of the spheres concerning the number of stars is not due to the different nature of the spheres, but to the will of an agent: and then the intended producer emanates the stars in a certain number either out of necessity or for the good.

§ 4.9.2 And the Philosopher explains this in *On the Heavens* 2, text. 67,[c] where he states: "We now want to dispel the second doubt, why there are so many stars in the eighth sphere, which is next to the first, while in each of the rest of the spheres, which have only one motion, there is only one star. And it seems that there is doubt regarding the cause of the difference, which is not proportional to the nature of the sphere." And the Philosopher continues: "We say that this is correct, because it is necessary to know that the first sphere is the principle of potentiality and the cause of all living beings, more than the rest of the spheres. And therefore, the first sphere moves all bodies and every single one of the others moves one star only." From these [words], it seems that the number of the stars exists for a final purpose, and this is possible only through an agent who intends the final purpose.

§ 4.9.3 Second, this is proved by the prophet (Isaiah 40:26) according to the difference in the nature of the stars and the difference in their activities in every sphere. Hence, the stars are the noblest part of these spheres, and they are congruent in nature and in kind of activity, but they are

---

[a] tantum] emend. Copp.; tautum b; tantum L. [b] ceterorum] emend. Copp.; cetetorum b; ceterorum L.

[a] *Cael.* 2.7.289a. [b] Cf. *Metaph.* 12.8.1073b. [c] *Cael.* 2.12.292b.

necessary that they are congruent in nature and in kind of activity. And the experience of astronomers and stargazers has testified the contrary of this over a long period of time and many generations.

§ 4.9.4 And the same becomes clear in *The Incoherence of the Incoherence*, quoting al-Ġazālī, 3, twenty-sixth investigation: "Out of the same existing sphere of the fixed stars exist around 1,022 [stars] and they differ from each other in size and shape and position and nature and activities, which come into this world like good influence and evil influence, which is obvious in generations and other [events]."[a] And since they are different from each other in actions, it therefore follows that they are different in forms, by which difference the actions that follow them will be different, as explained above. And since this difference between them is not caused by differences in their substrate—because they are parts of one and the same sphere—it follows that this occurs thanks to the intention of an agent who brings them forth by intention together with this variety according to need or for the higher good, without a substrate prior to them that would make it possible to think that they were created from it. It follows that their [afore]mentioned forth-bringer created them not from a prior substrate, but through this creation. And this is what the prophet wanted to explain.

§ 4.9.5 And apart from this, the prophet brings a third proof, saying (Isaiah 40:26): "Because of His great might and vast power, [etc.]," because by saying "because of His great might," he points to the eighth sphere, in which there are many stars of different powers. And by saying "vast power," he points to the sun, which has more power than any other star. [And this is] to say: when we look at the rank of the eighth sphere, which is the noblest of all the rest of the spheres, and at the rank of the sun, which is nobler than all the rest of the stars, although they are not congruent in place, it becomes clear that this order does not exist because of their nature, but by the will of a forth-bringer who intended this order for a final purpose through wisdom according to need or the higher good. And therefore, it also follows that their existence occurs thanks to the will of a forth-bringer who intended this order, bringing them necessarily forth by means of creation. And he says (Isaiah 40:26): "Not one fails to appear," meaning that they are not corruptible by their nature, proving that their existence is through creation, because the [type of] creation that exists thanks to the movement of generation is not without a material substrate, which is necessarily corruptible.

---

[a] Cf. *Incoherence* 149.

nisi secundum magis et minus, cuius oppositum docet longa astronomorum experientia.

§ 4.9.4 Quare in lib. *Destructionis D.*, disputatione III, dubio 26 Algazelis auctoritate hoc idem habetur, ubi dicit: «Ab eo namque[a] procedit res stellarum fixarum que 1022 sere reperiuntur numero, et differunt ab invicem magnitudine et in figura et in situ et in colore et in actionibus ab eisdem in hoc mundo venientibus, ut bona et mala natura earum in nativitatibus et alijs etc.» Cum autem ab invicem differant actionum genere. Sequitur quidem ut differant formis a quibus habent diversa actionum genera emanare. Et hec docet ibidem propheta [Isa 40:26] dicens: «omnia nomine vocat.» Propria, enim, nomina proprias formas annotare videntur, ad quarum diversitatem diversificantur scilicet specie. Cum autem huiusmodi diversitas inter stellas eiusdem orbis contingentes non a diversa subiectorum natura procedere contingat, cum sint omnes eiusdem orbis partes ut supra. Sequitur quidem ut contingat per voluntarium agentem huiusmodi diversitatem ad necessitatem vel ad melius intendentem. Cum autem non detur subiectum his tempore prius a quo productas fuisse contingat. Sequitur quidem ut horum productio fuisset per creationem. Quod est prophete intentum.

§ 4.9.5 Tertio probat propheta [Isa 40:26] idem ubi dicit: «A multitudine virtutum, et fortis roboris.» Ubi per «multitudinem virtutum» intelligit octavum orbem, cui quam plurime insunt stelle virtutibus diverse, pro fortem roboris vero intelligit solem, qui scilicet virtute ceteris preest sideribus. Quasi dicat quod considerata octavi orbis et solis nobilitate, quibus tamen non correspondet locorum ordo. Patet quidem ut huiusmodi or | do non perveniat ab eorum natura, sed a voluntario ordinante, et per consequens producente per huiusmodi ordinem finem nonnullum intendentem ad necessitatem vel ad melius sua sapientia ordinante, et per consequens producente et creante ut supra. Per hoc autem quod [Isa 40:26] dicit: «*unus non defuit.*» Probatur per eorum immortalitatem quod non habuerunt produci nisi per creationem, generatio enim non fit nisi in potentiali subiecto, quare genitum est necessario quid corruptibile.

§ 4.9.4 As al-Ġazālī explains in the book *The Incoherence of the Incoherence* 3, twenty-sixth doubt, in which he states: "For out of it there emanates the sphere of the fixed stars, in which there are a thousand and twenty-odd stars, 'different in magnitude, shape, position, colour,' and influence, be it of ill omen or auspicious according to their nature, etc."[a] Now, since they are different from one another in the kinds of [their] actions, it would follow that they are different in forms, from which different kinds of action are emanated. And the prophet teaches (Isaiah 40:26) this when he says: "Who calls them each by name"; in fact, the proper appellation seems to designate the proper forms by which they are diversified according to the difference in the species. Now, since the differences between the stars and their spheres do not occur because of the different nature of the substrate, because the stars are part of the sphere, as mentioned above, it would follow that this occurs thanks to a voluntary agent and that the difference occurs out of necessity or for a higher good, because there was no substrate before them, and then it would follow that their production was by creation. That is also what the prophet intended.

§ 4.9.5 Third, this is proved by the prophet (Isaiah 40:26), saying: "Because of His great might and vast power, not one fails to appear." "His great might" means the eighth sphere, in which there are many stars with different powers, and "vast power" means the sun, which has more power than the rest of the stars. For if we say that the eighth sphere and the sun can be considered nobler than the others, then the order of place does not depend on them, because | the order does not come from their nature, but from the voluntary arranger. And consequently, the maker intends the final purpose through his wisdom out of necessity or for the higher good and then through production or by creation, as mentioned above. When the prophet says: "Not one is missing," Isaiah proves that they are immortal because they are only produced by creation. Generation only exists in a potential substrate that is created, and it is necessarily corruptible.

---

[a] namque] emend. Copp.; nanque b; namque DD.

[a] Cf. *Incoherence* 149.

§ 4.10 And the prophet | explains the same in his fourth proof (Isaiah 48:12–13): "I am He. I am the first and I am also the last. My own hand founded the earth and My right hand spread out the heavens. I call unto them, let them stand up together"; that is to say, it becomes clear that "I am the first and the last" because I gave a foundation to the earth in the lowest [part] of existence in the way that it is in the centre of existence, remote in equal [distance] from each side of the surrounding [sphere]. And this will only be so since the roundness of the sphere is exceptionally equal from each side in a way that man could not produce with his hands, as the Philosopher explains in *On the Heavens* 2, text. 32.[a] And it also becomes clear that "I am the first and the last" because "My right hand spread out the heavens"; which is to say: I brought forth the spheres and I spanned them to a limited quantity, in such a way that "they stand up together." And they do not hinder each other from motion and also there is no vacuum between them. And since the limitation in quantities is [as exact as] a hair's breadth, it is incongruous that it should occur in every single sphere by chance; rather, this will necessarily occur thanks to the intention of an intender who brought it forth. It follows, then, that "I am the first" who brought forth and [who is] prior in time, as is necessary for every voluntary agent, as explained above. And by saying "I am also the last," it seems that he [Isaiah] wanted to say that for everything besides Him—may He be praised—it is possible to be corrupted. And this [will occur] thanks to the second kind of corruption, as explained above, and it [will occur] thanks to the will of His wisdom by which they all exist from absolute nothingness. And the prophet explains this in a broader commentary (Isaiah 51:6): "Raise your eyes to the heavens and look upon the earth beneath: Though the heavens should melt away like smoke, and the earth wear out like a garment, and its inhabitants die out as well, My victory shall stand forever."

---

[a] *Cael.* 2.4.287b.

§ 4.10 Et idem[a] probat propheta capitulo 48 [48:12–13] ubi dicit: «sic dicit Dominus etc. Ego ipse primus et ego novissimus manus quoque mea fundavit terram et dextera mea mensa est celos ego vocabo eos et stabunt simul etc.» Quasi dicat patet quidem me esse primum et novissimum per hoc quod fundavi terram, itaque ipsa terra est respectu celi undequaque quasi fundum in infima parte sua, quod scilicet non contingit nisi per summam celi rotunditatem qualis non fieret manibus, sicut Phylosophus id sentiens aperte docet in lib. *De Celo* II t.c. 32 similiter per hoc [Isa 48:13] quod «manus mea mensa est celos» illos scilicet statuens sub quodam limitata mensura qua se invicem non impediant a moto neque detur inter eos vacuum ut supra. Quia cum non contingat talis limitatio in omnibus occurrisse casu sed per voluntarium agentem illam intendentem sequitur quidem me esse tempore primum qui illos vocans sive sapienter nutu creans feci illos actu existere simul se invicem non impedientes. Per hoc autem quod [Isa 48:12] dicit: «et ego novissimus» videtur docere quod reliqua omnia sunt corruptibilia saltem secundo corruptionis modo ut supra. Iubente scilicet eadem sapientia per quam habuerunt esse post purum non esse. Et idem apertius docet idem propheta cap. 51 [Isa 51:6] ubi dicit: «Levate ad celos oculos vestros et aspicite terram deorsum quia celi sicut fumus consumentur, et terra sicut vestimentum inveterabitur et inhabitantes eam similiter morientur, salus autem mea in sempiternum erit.»

§ 4.10 And the prophet proves this in chapter 48 (48:12–13), where he says: "And the Lord says, etc. I am the first and I am the last as well, and my hand laid the foundation of the earth, and My right hand hath measured the heavens: I call unto them, and they shall stand together, etc.," which means that "I am the first and I am the last" by which "I laid the foundation to the earth"; the earth is then compared with the heavens, which are situated in the lowest part, because it would not have been possible to produce the great roundness of the heavens by hand, as the Philosopher explains in *On the Heavens* 2, text. 32.[a] And "My hand spread the heavens" means that there is a limited quantity so that the spheres would not prevent each other from moving and so that there is no vacuum between them, as mentioned above. Hence, this limitation does not happen by chance, but is rather produced by a voluntary agent, who intends the final purpose. And then by saying "I am the first," the arranger calls them or wisely creates them, accordingly bringing forth an act without the spheres hindering each other. And by saying: "I am also the last," it seems to teach that everything is corruptible, at least according to the second kind of corruption, as aforementioned. And this [will be] by the will of His wisdom, by which they all exist from absolute nothingness. And the prophet clearly teaches this in chapter 51 (Isaiah 51:6), where he says: "Raise your eyes to the heavens, and look upon the earth beneath: though the heavens should melt away like smoke, and the earth wear out like a garment, and its inhabitants die out as well, My victory shall stand forever."

---

[a] idem] coni. Copp.; idem.4 b.

[a] *Cael.* 2.4.287b.

§ 5 Fifth:
It is appropriate to inquire whether motion is [pre]eternal.

And it seems at the beginning of the investigation that it is indeed [pre]eternal.

§ 5.1.1 And additionally, it seems that anyone who says the contrary is either crazy or joking, as the Philosopher explains in *Physics* 8, text. 14.[a] And this is so because, as Averroes, ibid., text. 15, explains, when we said that motion was not [pre]eternal, it seems that two incongruities and contrarieties to nature would follow. (1) First, that it would then follow that the motion in the substrate would be possible for an infinite time and would later actualise; yet not only would there be no motion, but one could [also] not avoid either (a) that there would be a [state of] rest concerning the mobile necessarily [enacted] through violence for an infinite time, or (b) that there would now be a motion concerning the mobile necessarily [enacted] through violence for an infinite time. And in any case, these two [cases] are incongruous, because the thing that is in potentiality in any existent would necessarily be actualised an infinite amount of times in an infinite time.

§ 5.1.2 (2) Second, if | this was true [i.e., that motion was not [pre]eternal], it would be necessary that the mover and the mobile had already existed for an infinite time without motion, and after this, the same mover would have begun to move without a cause, which would necessarily be there then and not have been there before. And the answer of Empedocles and his partisans, who say that it is not appropriate to ask for a "why" with regard to principles, is not sufficient, for as Averroes explains in the aforementioned place, this proposition is only correct for an eternal being, not for a [newly] created one. And the answer of the Mutakallimun [Muslim theologians], who say that the created comes to be by the power of the eternal will, would also not suffice, because, as Averroes explains, ibid.: "It is incongruous that there could be a thing newly created by an eternal will unless [it was created] intermediately by an [eternally] created thing, because the will does not postpone doing something that it wants to do, unless something were created in an intended [thing] that did not exist in it at the time of the will." And in [the context of] that explanation, it is necessary that there would be a specific time for the action and then doubt would arise regarding the creation of this specific time, because the voluntary

---

[a] *Phys.* 8.1.252a.

§5 Quinto Dubitatur

Utrum motus habuisset esse ab eterno.

Et videtur quod sic.

§ 5.1.1 Immo videtur ut sermo dicens motum habuisse esse postquam nullus fuisset motus sit similis stultorum vel fingentium sermoni. Sicut Phylosophus expresse ait in lib. *Physicorum* VIII t.c. 14. Nam sicut ibidem, t.c. 15 Aven R. infert ad huiusmodi sermonem duo videntur sequi inconvenientia et nature contraria. Quorum primum est ut per infinitum tempus fuisset motus possibilis deinde provenisset ad actum. Quia dum non erat motus vel erat quies in mobili per infinitum tempus violenta, vel[a] nunc in eodem mobili est infinitus motus violentus, quorum utrumque est inconveniens. Potentia, enim, illius[b] in quo est potentia exit ad actum in tempore infinito vicibus infinitis necessario.

§ 5.1.2 Secundum autem inconveniens est ut detur movens et mobile fuisse tempore | infinito sine motu, deinde idem movens incepisset movere sine causa quare illa hora et non ante. Nec valet ratio Empedoclis et sequacium dicentium quod de principijs non est querendum[c] quare nam sicut Aven R. ibidem ait hoc non verificatur nisi de eternis non autem de nova factione. Nec valet illa loquentium ratio qui scilicet dicunt quod ex antiqua voluntate emanavit nova factio. Quia sicut Aven R. ibidem dicit: «Impossibile videtur ut nova factio dependeat ab antiqua voluntate nisi sit antiqua actio media, voluntas enim non postponit facere illud quod intendit nisi propter existentiam[d] alicuius intentionis in re intenta que non erat tempore voluntatis.» Et tale in propositio haberet esse saltem tempus ad illud proportionatum[e] quare tunc insurgeret questio de huiusmodi temporis sic proportionati factione. Motor,

§5 Fifth,

it may be inquired whether motion is [pre]eternal.

And it seems to be so.

§ 5.1.1 On the contrary, it seems that the discussion about motion, since there is no motion at all, is like a discussion held by fools or fabricators, as the Philosopher explains in *Physics* 8, text. 14,[a] and Averroes explicates in *Physics* 8, text. 15.[b] It seems that two incongruities and [opinions] that contradict nature [contraries to nature] follow from this discussion. First: there would be a potential motion for an infinite time and afterwards it would be actualised, because in the meantime, there would be no motion; thus, either the mobile would stay at rest through a violent [motion] for an infinite time or there would be an infinite violent motion in the mobile. Both of these possibilities are incongruous. According to the definition of potentiality, something in potentiality will necessarily move in order to be actualised for an infinite time in infinite successions.

§ 5.1.2 Second: if a mover and a mobile existed for an infinite time | without motion, then the mover would begin to move without a cause, which would necessarily be there then and would not have been there before. And the argument of Empedocles and his partisans about these principles is invalid, since Averroes states that this is only true for an eternal being and not for a newly created one. Likewise, the argument of the Mutakallimun [Muslim theologians], who say that a new creation is emanated from an eternal will, is not sufficient, because Averroes states: "It seems impossible that a new creation can depend on an eternal will, unless there is an eternally created thing as an intermediary. The will does not postpone doing something that it intends to do, unless [this is] for the sake of something intended in an intended thing that was not there at the time of the will." And according to this statement, a specific [period of] time would exist, and then a question would arise regarding the creation of this specific time,

---

[a] vel] b[corr]; vei b.   [b] illius] b[corr]; ilus b.   [c] querendum] coni. COPP.; quereudum b.   [d] existentiam] emend. COPP.; essentiam b; existentiam L.   [e] proportionatum] coni. COPP.; proportionatu b.

---

[a] *Phys.* 8.1.252a.   [b] *Phys.* 8.1.252a.

mover moves at the beginning of the willed thing or of its imagination, which exists in the [faculty of] imagination of the agent or the mover.

§ 5.2.1 But the contrary of this—namely, that motion is necessarily not [pre]eternal—becomes clear in this way: because for every single kind of motion, it necessarily follows that the mover, the mobile, and the disposition to motion precede it in time. If this is so, it necessarily follows that no kind of motion is [pre]eternal. The consequence is evident, since it is necessary that something will be temporally prior to it—and this is contrary to the definition of "[pre]eternal"—therefore, it is impossible that it could be [pre]eternal.

§ 5.2.2 The [antecedent] premise becomes clear in this way. First, regarding what we said—that the mobile and the disposition for motion are necessarily temporally prior to the motion—this becomes clear from Aristotle's proofs in *Physics* 8, text. 4:[a] "Thus, we say that motion is the action of the existent which is capable of motion, etc." And Averroes explains these words: "As already became clear in the third book of *Physics*, one of the definitions of motion [i.e., entelechy] is that it is the actualisation of a mobile thing when it is a mobile thing in potentiality. And the actualisation of an existent that is capable of moving [in short: the entelechy], if so, necessitates that the movable things exist prior to the [actualisation of] motion in every kind of motion. And since the movable thing is prior to motion, the capability for motion is prior to motion. It is therefore necessary to understand that the movable thing is temporally prior to motion for two reasons, as mentioned." And the Philosopher continues to explain all of this, ibid., in a second proof:[b] "Apart from this definition, everyone agrees that it does not follow that only an existent that is able to move will move. And this is necessary for all kinds of motion, because nothing changes apart from the thing that is able to change, and nothing moves by locomotion apart from a thing that is disposed for moving by locomotion. If so, it follows that a thing is burnable before it is burnt, and [capable] of burning before it burns." And what we said—that the mover is necessarily temporally prior to the movement—will become clear in this way: because every agent is temporally prior to its activity, and the mover is the agent of the movement. If so, the mover is temporally prior to the movement.

---

[a] *Phys.* 8.1.251a. [b] *Phys.* 8.1.251a.

הרצוניי יתנועע תחלה מן הדבר הנרצה או מתמונתו אשר בדמיון הפועל או המניע.

§ 5.2.1 אמנם הפך זה רצוני לומר שהתנועה היא בהכרח בלתי קדמונית יתבאר באופן זה. כי אמנם לכל אחד ממיני התנועה יתחייב בהכרח שיקדם קדימה זמנית המניע והמתנועע וההכנה אל התנועה. אם כן יתחייב בהכרח שאין שום מין ממיני התנועה קדמון. הנה חיוב התולדה הוא מבואר כי בהיות מן ההכרח שיהיה איזה דבר קודם לו בזמן וזה הפך לגדר הקדמון אם כן מן הנמנע שיהיה הוא קדמון.

§ 5.2.2 אמנם ההקדמה הנה תתבאר באופן זה: ראשונה מה שאמרנו שהמתנועע וההכנה אל התנועה הם בהכרח קודמים בזמן לתנועה יתבאר במופת ארסטו׳ בספר השמע מאמר ח׳ פרק ד׳ באמרו: »נאמר אם כן שהתנועה היא פעל הנמצא המוכן אל התנועה« עכ״ל. ודבריו אלה באר אבן רשד: »כי כבר התבאר בשלישי מספר השמע שאחד מגדרי התנועה הוא שהוא פעל המתנועע כאשר הוא מתנועע בכח ופעל הנמצא המוכן להתנועע אם כן יתחייב שהדברים המתנועעים יהיו נמצאים קודם לתנועה בכל אחד ממיני התנועה ובהיות המתנועע קודם לתנועה הנה ההכנה אל התנועה היא קודמת לתנועה. וראוי להבין מזה שהמתנועע קודם בזמן לתנועה על שני פנים כנזכר« עכ״ל. והוסיף הפילוסוף לבאר כל זה שם במופת שני באמרו: »ובלעדי זה הגדר הנה כל אדם יסכים בזה שלא יתחייב שיתנועע זולתי הנמצא שיכול | להתנועע וזה הוא הכרחי בכל מיני התנועה כי לא ישתנה זולתי הדבר שיוכל להשתנות ולא יתנועע תנועה מקומית זולתי הדבר המוכן להתנועע תנועה מקומית. אם כן יתחייב שיהיה הדבר מוכן להשרף קודם שישרף ולשרוף קודם שישרוף« עכ״ל. אמנם מה שאמרנו שהמניע קודם בזמן לתנועה בהכרח, יתבאר באופן זה כי אמנם כל פועל קודם בזמן לפעלתו. והנה המניע הוא פועל את התנועה אם כן המניע קודם בזמן לתנועה.

enim, voluntarius movetur prius a voluntato[a] vel ab eius imaginatione sine postpositione, ut supra.

§ 5.2.1 Ad oppositum vero arguit sic: ad quodlibet motuum genus habet necessario secundum tempus precedere motor et mobile et potentia ab ipsum motum actu fiendum que mobilitas et motivitas dicuntur ergo nullum motuum genus habuit esse ab eterno. Consequentia patet quia ex quo ad eius esse requiritur quid tempore prius que requisitio repugnat eternorum diffinitioni non datur fuisse ab eterno.

§ 5.2.2 Antecedens vero probatur et primo quoad primam partem qua scilicet dicitur quod mobile et mobilitas et motivitas habent necessario precessisse secundum tempus ad ipsum motum. Rationibus et auctoritate Phylosophi *Physicorum* VIII t.c. 4 ubi dicit: «Dicamus igitur quod motus est actus eius quod innatum est moveri etc.» ubi Aven R. exponens ait: «Dicamus igitur quod quia declaratum est in tertio istius quod altera diffinitionum motus est endelechia eius quod natum est moveri, et endelechia moti secundum quod est motum, necesse est ut res mobiles sint ante motum in unoquoque generum et cum res mobiles fuerint ante motum tunc potentia ad motum erit ante motum. Et intelligendum est ex hoc quod motum est prius tempore motu duobus modis etc.» et idem affirmat Phylosophus ibidem dicens: «Et sine hac diffinitione omnes homines credunt quod non est necesse moveri nisi illud, quod potest moveri et hoc est necesse in unoquoque motuum, verbi gratia quod non alteratur nisi illud quod potest moveri et hac est necesse in unoquoque motuum v.g. non alteratur nisi illud quod inatum est alterari nec transfertur nisi illud quod inatum est transferri in loco necesse est, ergo ut res sit innata comburi antequam comburatur et comburere antequam comburat etc.» Quod autem et motor habeat necessario ad ipsam motionem secundum tempus precedere probatur sic omne agens habet necessario precedere ad suam actionem secundum tempus. Motor est motionis agens, ergo habet ad ipsam motionem secundum tempus precedere.

because the voluntary mover would move at the beginning according to the will or according to his imagination without postposition, as mentioned above.

§ 5.2.1 On the contrary it is to argue that any kind of motion temporally precedes the mover and the mobile and the potentiality that is produced by the motion in actuality, called mobility and movability, and thus no kind of motion is [pre]eternal. The consequence is evident, because something that was temporally prior to motion would be required and this is contrary to the definition of eternity; therefore, it is impossible that it could be [pre]eternal.

§ 5.2.2 The antecedent is proved, as the first part of it—in which we said that the mover, the mobile, mobility, and movability [i.e., the disposition for the motion] temporally precede the motion—is proved, as the Philosopher explains in *Physics* 8, text. 4,[a] where he states: "We said that motion is the actualisation of what is capable of motion [i.e., movable], etc." And Averroes explicates: "As already became clear in the third book of *Physics*, one of the other definitions of motion is 'entelechy,' which is the actualisation of what is capable of motion, the entelechy of a mobile as a mobile. It is necessary that mobile things exist prior to the motion in every species, and if the mobile things existed before the motion, then the potentiality also existed before the motion. It is necessary to understand according to this definition that the mover is temporally prior to motion, for two reasons." And then the Philosopher continues: "And apart from the definition, everyone would admit that what is in motion must be that which is capable of movement in the particular sense of the word in question—if it is a movement of modification, then the modifiable; if it is of transference, then that which is capable of changing its place—so that there must be something [that is] combustible before there can be combustion and something that can burn before there can be burning, etc."[b] Now, since it has been proven that the mover is necessarily temporally prior to its motion, every agent is then necessarily temporally prior to its activity, and the mover is the agent of motion and the mover is temporally prior to its motion.

---

[a] voluntato] b[corr]; voluntate b.

[a] *Phys.* 8.1.251a.   [b] *Phys.* 8.1.251a.

§ 5.2.3 This consequence is self-evident. And the [antecedent] premise becomes clear in this way: because if the instant in which the agent exists in actuality does not exist, it is impossible that there may exist a first instant in which the beginning of the time of the activity lies. And there is undoubtedly a [period of] time between two indivisible instants, as was explained above. And apart from this, it is self-evident that if no agent existed at the beginning of the time of the activity, then the time of that activity would not exist, [and the activity] would [also] not occur. Because if [it happens] in time, then it will become clear from all of this that the agent will be temporally prior to the beginning of its activity, [and] all the more so will it be temporally prior to the activity that follows at the end of the [period of] time. And the Philosopher explains this in *Metaphysics* 12, text. 32:[a] "The existent in actuality is prior." And Averroes explains his words: "It becomes clear in other places that the disposition [i.e., potentiality] is temporally prior to the individuals that are generated. And a thing that exists in actuality is absolutely prior to the potentiality, because a thing does not actualise from potentiality except by means of a thing that exists in actuality." And Averroes explains the same in [his Commentary on] *Metaphysics* 9, text. 13: "And in general, since potentiality is non-being and actuality is being, it follows that being will be prior to non-being and that the agent will temporally precede the actuality." And Aristotle explains the same in the aforementioned book, [*Metaphysics*]12, text. 16:[b] "And the causes that move things are the preceding things." And Averroes explains his words: "Because the agent [i.e., efficient cause] and the mover are prior to the thing affected and moved by it. And the formal and the material causes are brought forth together with the created thing." And Averroes explains this in the [Commentary on] *Posterior Analytics* 2, text. 11:[c] "The causes that exist by way of an acting cause [i.e., agent] are things that are prior to the effects in movement and in time."

§ 5.2.4 And what we said—that the mover is the agent of the motion—is self-evident. And the Philosopher explains this in *Physics* 3, text. 18:[d] "A mover is the mover of a thing that is capable of movement. And it is a mover, insofar as it is acting." And Averroes explains his words: "The activity of a mover is to make others than itself move." And therefore, Averroes says in *Metaphysics* | 9, text. 13:[e] "Everything moved is moved in potentiality, prior to which exists a mover in activity." One cannot say that it is appropriate to discriminate between the motion—which in its entirety

---

[a] *Metaph.* 12.6.1072a. [b] *Metaph.* 12.4.1070a. [c] Cf. *An. post.* 2.11.95a.
[d] *Phys.* 3.3.202a. [e] Cf. *Metaph.* 9.9.1049b.

§ 5.2.3 Consequentia patet et antecedens probatur primo, scilicet, ratione quia non dato instanti in quo agens habeat actu existere non datur primum actionis instans in quo actio habeat incipi ab agente actu existente nedum ad actionis finem, inter que diversa instantia datur necessario | tempus ut supra. Quia cum habeat necessario esse tempore prius ad actionis principium multo maius habet precedere ad actum provenientem in fine actionis. Cuius processus non fit nisi in tempore quare Phylosophus *Metaphysicorum* XII t.c. 32 ait: «Quoniam vero actus est prior etc.» ubi Aven R. exponens ait: «Determinatum est enim in alijs locis quod potentia precedit tempore ad individuum generatum, actus vero precedit simpliciter cum nihil exeat de potentia ad actum nam sive pro aliquid actu» et ibidem habetur ratione et auctoritate Aven R. in comento *Metaphysicorum* IX t.c. 13 ubi dicit: «Et universaliter quia potentia est non ens et actus est ens necesse est ut esse precedat ad non esse et agens precedat tempore actum» et idem habetur ab eodem Phylosopho *Metaphysicorum* XII t.c. 16 ubi dicit: «Et cause moventes sunt que precedunt» ubi Aven R. exponens ait: «Quia agens et movens precedit ad quod agitur et movetur, formalis autem et finalis sunt cum generatione» et idem habetur ab eodem Aven R. *Posteriorum* II t.c. 11 ubi dicit: «Quia cause que sunt secundum modum agens sunt res precedentes causata in investigatione et in tempore etc.»

§ 5.2.4 Quo autem ad secundam antecedentis partem qua scilicet dicitur quod motor est agens qui agit motionem sive motum patet sensu. Et habetur a Phylosopho *Physicorum* III t.c. 18 ubi dicit: «Motor est motor eius quod potest ad motum et movet secundum quod agit» ubi Aven R. exponens ait: «Actio enim motoris est facere motum in alium» quare idem Aven R. in comento *Metaphysicorum* IX t.c. 13 ait: «Et omne quod movetur, movetur a motore in actu ante ipso existente.» Cavillosus autem et absurdus videretur sermo quo diceretur quod aliud est considerare motum prout est quid totale aggregatum ex pluri-

§ 5.2.3 The consequence is evident and the antecedent is proved because [since] there is no instant in which the agent will exist in actuality, [then] there is no first instant of actuality in which the activity will start from the agent's activity, still less after the end of the activity, because between two different instants, there is necessarily | a [span of] time, as aforementioned. Because it is necessary that something is temporally prior to the beginning of the activity, and still more that it will be prior to the activity of what comes at the end of the activity, and its process is only produced in time, as the Philosopher explains in *Metaphysics* 12, text. 32,[a] where he states: "But that actuality is prior," and Averroes explicates: "It has been shown elsewhere that potentiality is temporally prior to the generated individual and that actuality is absolutely prior to potentiality, because nothing passes from potentiality into actuality except through the action of something actual." And [this is] according to the argument and authority of Averroes in the Commentary on *Metaphysics* 9, text. 13,[b] where he states: "And in general, since potentiality is non-being and actuality is being, it is necessary that existence will be prior to non-existence and that the agent will be temporally prior to the activity," as the Philosopher explains in *Metaphysics* 12, text. 16,[c] where he states: "Moving causes are causes in the sense of pre-existent things," and Averroes explicates: "The efficient and moving cause precedes that which it produces and moves, whereas the formal cause and the material cause are simultaneous with the production." And Averroes explicates the same in *Posterior Analytics* 2, text. 11,[d] where he states: "Because the causes that are by way of an agent are things prior to the caused in invention [i.e., discovery] and in time, etc."

§ 5.2.4 The second part of the antecedent, in which we said that the mover is an agent who enacts motion without movement, is testified by the senses, as the Philosopher explains in *Physics* 3, text. 18,[e] where he states: "A mover is the mover of a thing that is capable of movement, and it moves as it is acting," and Averroes explicates: "The activity of the mover is to make things other than itself move," and in the Commentary on *Metaphysics* 9, text. 13,[f] where he states: "Everything that is moved is moved by a mover in activity existing prior to it." Therefore, it seems that it would be captious and incongruous to say that one has to distinguish between motion as an entire combination

---

[a] *Metaph.* 12.6.1072a. [b] *Metaph.* 9.3.1047a. [c] *Metaph.* 12.4.1070a. [d] Cf. *An. post.* 2.95a. [e] *Phys.* 3.3.202a. [f] *Metaph.* 9.9.1049b.

is combined of particular movements [belonging] to the past, the future, and infinity—and every particular movement that [is part of] that combination. And it is incongruous to say that a thing that is combined of created parts that approach each other is [pre]eternal, although every part of that combination is created in any case. And this is so because that combination imagined by us is nothing other than all the parts combined in our imagination, and every single one of them is created. And in the absence of every part of them, or when the absence of all of them is imagined, no combination of them may be imagined, still less may it be imagined that [this combination] is [pre]eternal. And therefore, it becomes clear that a movement that is combined of many movements is not [pre]eternal. And this is what we wanted to explain.

§ 5.2.5 And apart from this, if it were true that what is composed out of these movements, each one coming after the other, was [pre]eternal—although none of its parts was [pre]eternal—it would follow that this composite would not fit the definition given to each of its parts; and especially not the definition given by the Philosopher by which it follows that an existent is temporally prior to the movement. And therefore, two incongruities would follow. (1) First, it would follow that there would be a new definition that would fit the composite which is not in agreement with the definition of each of its parts, and therefore, for the whole and the part, the name "movement" would only be said by equivocation. (2) Second, although a composite is nothing other than created parts that approach each other in such a way that by the approaching of those parts, nothing [else] would remain in any case, a composite of them would be [pre]eternal. But this is undoubtedly a statement that combines two contradictory parts; namely, that one and the same thing will be created, according to all [its] parts, and [also] [pre]eternal, [i.e.,] not created, according to its whole, which is nothing but all of its parts. And the Philosopher explains the contrary of this in *On the Heavens* 1, text. 19:[a] "What we say about the part and about the whole is one and the same thing."

§ 5.3.1 Second, what we said—that motion is not [pre]eternal—becomes clear in this way: because if motion was [pre]eternal, it would not avoid one of two [consequences]: either (1) that we say that the existence of the act is acquired at the end of the movement, and that it would also be [pre]eternal, or (2) that we say that it is not [pre]eternal. And if we say that it is also [pre]eternal, it would therefore follow that the movement of the

---

[a] *Cael.* 1.3.270a.

bus motibus tam preteritis quam futuris et aliud est considerare quamlibet eiusdem aggregati partem, itaque dicatur quod licet quelibet eiusdem aggregati pars habuisset esse quid novum. Aggregatum tamen ex huiusmodi partibus successive compositum habuisset esse ab eterno. Diffinitio, enim, non partibus competit inquantum tales immo principaliter et proprie competit universali particularibus vero eiusdem partibus competit inquantum participant tantum, preterea patet quod illud universale ex partibus aggregatum nisi aliud est quam huiusmodi partes per actum intellectus simul sumpte. Quibus destruuctis vel nobis non representatibus nullum esse universale imaginari contigit nedum ut de eo dicatur ut fuisset ab eterno. Et per consequens motus in universali ex successivis motibus compositus non habuit esse ab eterno, quod est intentum.

§ 5.2.5 Preterea si idem universale ex pluribus successivis motibus aggregatum habuisse esse ab eterno quamvis nulla eiusdem partium fuisset talis sequere ut eidem universali cum sit qui eternum non competat eadem diffinitio que competit suis partibus cum sint quid corruptibile. Presertim illa Phyilosophi diffinitio qua, scilicet, datur necessarie quid ipse prius ad ipsum motum. Quare duo sequerentur inconvenientia: primo, scilicet, ut oporteat novam indagare diffinitionem eidem universali competentem. Secundo ut equivoce dicatur motus de universali similium | partium et eiusdem particularibus partibus. Cuius oppositum docet ratio et Phylosophi auctoritas in lib. *De Celo* primo t.c. 19ᵃ ubi dicit: «Sermo, enim, toto et partibusᵇ idem est.»

§ 5.3.1 Secundo arguitur sic: si motus habuisset esse ab eterno vel ergo similiter habuisset esse actus per motum acquisitus vel non. Si primum tunc sequeretur ut numquam in eodem mobili habuit secundum tempus preesse

of many movements, in the past as well the future, and motion as parts of the combination, and for this reason, we say that the parts of this combination are newly created, and consequently, according to the parts of the combination, the combination of movements is [pre]eternal. The definition [of combination] does not absolutely and properly pertain [to the definition] of the parts; [the definition of combination] pertains [to the definition] of the whole, and it pertains [to the definition] of its particular parts, because parts share something [with the whole]. Moreover, it is clear that the whole is nothing more than the combination of parts, in which the parts are assumed through an intellectual activity, considering that we cannot imagine a whole, and for this reason, we say that it is [pre]eternal. And consequently, motion as a whole is composed of a succession of movements and it cannot be [pre]eternal, and this is what was intended.

§ 5.2.5 But if the whole that is composed of a succession of particular movements is [pre]eternal, though its parts are not [pre]eternal, it would follow that the whole, while it is eternal, did not pertain to the same definition that pertains to its parts, which are corruptible, especially according to the definition given by the Philosopher, by which it has to be temporally prior to its movement. And therefore, two incongruities follow. First: one would need to reformulate the definition of the universal [whole]. Second: one would speak of the universal movement | and the movement of its particular parts by equivocation. And the Philosopher explains the contrary of this in *On the Heavens* 1, text. 19,ᵃ where he states: "The same argument applies to the whole and the part."

§ 5.3.1 Second, I would argue that if motion is [pre]eternal, then either there is an activity that is acquired by the movement, or not. If the first case was true, then it would follow that nothing in the mobile would precede the motion

---

ᵃ 19] emend. Copp.; 29 b; 19 L.   ᵇ partibus] emend. Copp.; pertibus b; partibus L.

ᵃ *Cael.* 1.3.270a.

sphere would not temporally precede the actualisation of that which comes by it at the end of the movement, so that both of them would be [pre]eternal. And therefore, it would follow that there would be together in one and the same substrate: (a) the duration of the movement, in which the perfection of the intended [thing] exists only in potentiality, and (b) the end of the movement, in which the [afore]mentioned intended [thing] is actualised. And this statement combines two contradictory parts, because the potentiality is the manner of a still non-existent perfection and the actualisation is perfection originating from the movement, which then [no longer] exists. And Averroes explains this in *On the Heavens* 3, text. 29:[a] "It is not correct [to say] that a substrate will be in potentiality | with respect to any thing, except when it is not in it in actuality." If so, if we said that the existence of perfection acquired at the end of movement is eternal in the sphere, [then] it would follow that we had stated one of two incongruities. These are either (1) that we said that the existence of perfection acquired at the end of the movement is also in the sphere, without any movement preceding it, while it [i.e., the sphere] is [pre]eternal; [then] this statement would contain two contradictory parts, because perfection acquired at the end of a movement is necessarily preceded by a movement that is temporally prior to it, or (2) that we said that in the sphere, the movement and the perfection that is acquired at its end exist at one and the same time, because they are both [pre]eternal and one does not precede the other in the sphere by temporal precedence. And this is also a statement that necessarily contains two parts of a contrary, as explained above. And the contrary of this becomes clear from Aristotle's proof in *Metaphysics* 9, text. 5.[b]

23r

§ 5.3.2 And apart from this, if it were true that both were [pre]eternal—that is, the [afore]mentioned motion and the perfection—it would follow that we would state one of two things: either (1) that we would say that it was always so that both things were in the sphere at one [and the same] time [and] the whole time, while one of them did not precede the other, and [that they] were in one substrate under the law of their eternity, and therefore, it would follow that this was also [the case] today, and this is an evident fault [and] its contrary is testified by sense [perception]; or (2) that we would say that this thing was not always so and that the nature of the motion was created afterwards to [be] what it is now; namely, that the motion is temporally prior to the perfection that is acquired at its end. And, if so, doubt[s] would arise: When was it created, and why

---
[a] Cf. *Cael.* 3.2.302a.   [b] *Metaph.* 9.3.1047a.

motum in fieri ad factum esse sive ad actum per motum productum in eodem mobili et per consequens ab eterno habuit esse motus actu non tardius motu in fieri immo sibi coeternus. Et per consequens simul tempore habuit mobile esse motum in fieri et in facto esse, quod implicat contradictionem. Potentia, enim, nil aliud est quam via ad actum nondum existentem et motus actum nil aliud est quam perfectio eveniens per motum in fieri ad ipsum precedentem. Quare Aven R. in comento lib. *De Celo* III t.c. 29 ait: «Hoc enim subiectum positum non est in potentia nisi in quantum non est in actu.» Si ergo dicatur ut mobile ab eterno fuisset actu motum sequeretur necessario alterum duorum inconvenientium, vel ut actus in mobile ab eterno existens habuisset in eo esse sine precedente motione a quo fieret, vel saltem ut simul tempore habuisset idem motus esse actum cum motione a qua causaretur. Quorum utrumque implicat contradictionem ut supra. Et cuius oppositum habetur ratione et auctoritate Phylosophi Contra Gariconem *Metaphysicorum* IX t.c. 5.

until its end and nothing in the mobile would precede the act produced by the motion, and consequently, the motion would be [pre]eternal and the movement in actuality would not be later in respect of the end of the movement, but rather they would be co-eternal, and consequently, the mobile would simultaneously be at the beginning and the end [of the motion], and this implies a contradiction. Potentiality is nothing more than a manner of still non-existent [perfection] in actuality, and movement is nothing more than the perfection acquired by the activity preceding the movement, as Averroes explicates in the Commentary on *On the Heavens* 3, text. 29,[a] where he states: "This substrate is in potentiality except when it is actualised." If we said that a mobile is [pre]eternal through a motion in actuality, then two incongruities would necessarily follow: either the actualisation in the substrate would be [pre]eternal without any movement prior to it, or the movement and actualisation would be caused by motion[s] which existed at the same time. Both of these imply a contradiction, as mentioned above. And the opposite of this is according to the argument and authority of the Philosopher in *Metaphysics* 9, text. 5, *Against Garicon*.[b]

§ 5.3.2 Preterea si hoc ab eterno contigisset ut non prius fuisset moto in primo mobili quam motum esse actu cum ambo fuisset ab eterno, vel ergo sic semper perseveraret ut, scilicet, daretur actus simul tempore cum sua potentia quod patet esse falsum, vel ut natura mutasset ordinem et tunc surgeret questio de quando et quare tunc et

§ 5.3.2 Moreover, if [the actualisation] is [pre]eternal, then either the motion in the first movable is not prior because the motion would be in actuality and it would consequently be [pre]eternal, since it would continue forever, and the actuality would also be in potentiality at the same time, and this seems to be false, or nature changes the order, and then a question would arise about time, whether

---

[a] Cf. *Cael.* 3.2.302a.   [b] *Metaph.* 9.3.1047a.

was it created then and not before? If so, from all of what we said, it follows that we would say that the existence of perfection acquired at the end of motion is not [pre]eternal in the sphere. And therefore, it follows that the motion in it is also not [pre]eternal, because if it was [pre]eternal while the existence of the perfection acquired by it was not [pre]eternal, it would follow that there was motion in the sphere for an infinite time prior to the existence of the perfection acquired by it. And doubt would arise: How was the aforementioned perfection achieved then and not before? It follows, if so, that motion is also not [pre]eternal, just as the perfection acquired by it is not [pre]eternal. And this is what we wanted to explain.

§ 5.4 We answer, if so, to dispel [any] doubt about the [afore]mentioned thesis, that motion is not [pre]eternal, because the mover and the mobile, the disposition [i.e., potentiality] of the agent for the action, and the disposition of the passive [thing] for the effect temporally precede it. And this is by a priority that is measured as a difference between two temporal instants, by which they differ by species—no need to say "by individuality." And they are: (1) the instant in which all the [afore]mentioned preceding [things] exist [in actuality], without which the existence of the beginning of the activity [i.e., the motion] would be impossible, and (2) the instant that is the beginning of the number of movement.

§ 5.5.1 To the opponent's arguments, we answer, in general, that they are correct for the true time that, since it is the measure of the movement, has a finite or infinite quantity belonging to it. And by this, "before" and "after" are measured, which are first measured in quantity, as the Philosopher explains in *Physics* 4, text. 99:[a] "Because 'before' and 'after' exist in quantity, they necessarily also exist in motion like they do in quantity." But these proofs are not correct for that supposed instant of time, since there was not yet motion prior to the creation of the world, because then there was no substrate for the quantity and therefore there was neither quantity nor time, as we say now that outside of the heavens there is none of these, as the Philosopher explains in *On the Heavens* 1, text. 99:[b] "There is no place outside the heavens, no plenum and no vacuum, and there is no time there." And he continues: "Time is the number of motion, and there is no motion without a natural body." And since, moreover, no motion exists, there is also no quantity and no time. If so, there is also no existence of finite and infinite measure, because measure is likewise [found] in the category of quantity.

---

[a]*Phys.* 4.11.219a.   [b]*Cael.* 1.9.279a.

non ante. Restat ergo ut dicatur ut primum mobile non ab eterno habuisset esse actu motum. Et per consequens neque motio in fieri a qua factus est habuit esse ab eterno. Si, enim, ipsa motio in fieri habuisset esse ab eterno sequeretur ut per infinitam motionem habuisset mobile moveri antequam devenisset ad actum, quod est inconveniens et penitus inopinabile. Quibus sequitur ut neque motio in fieri neque motus in facto esse habuit esse ab eterno quod est intentum.

§ 5.4 Ad dubium ergo respondetur quod non ab eterno habuit esse motum immo habuerunt necessario tam motor quam mobile et potentia ad motum tam activa quam passiva ad ipsum motum in fieri sive ad motionem secundum tempus precedere. Prioritate scilicet considerata penes instantium diversitatem qua scilicet habuerunt specie nedum numero ab invicem differre. Illud scilicet instans in quo habuerunt premissa omnia actu existere ad hoc ut daretur principium motus differens ab illo instanti quod habuit esse numerationis motus principium licet nulla consideretur temporis quantitas tunc inter ea currens.

§ 5.5.1 Ad argumenta vero universaliter respondetur quod bene procedunt de vero tempore, cui tanquam mensura motus competit quantitas finita vel in | finita, similiter prius et posterius. Que primo insunt quantitati sicut habetur a Phylosopho *Physicorum* IV t.c. 99 ubi dicit: «Et quia prius et posterius sunt in quantitate necesse est ut prius et posterius sint in motu etiam secundum quod ilic etc.» Sed non procedunt argumenta de duratione considerata dum motus non erat scilicet ante universi creationem. Tunc, enim, nullum erat quantitativum vel qualitas. Et per consequens neque tempus sicut nunc extra celum nullum horum dicitur esse, prout habetur a Phylosopho in lib. *De Celo* primo t.c. 99 ubi dicit: «Et nullus locus extra celum neque plenus neque vacuus neque tempus» subdit ibidem dicens: «Tempus etiam est numerus motus et motus non est sine corpore naturali.» Cumque dum non erat motus nulla fuisset quantitas neque tempus nulla ergo erat finitas vel infinitas que sunt proprie quanti passiones.

it was produced then and not before. Therefore, there remains [one possible case]: that the first mobile is not eternal, but rather exists according to a movement in actuality; consequently, the end of the motion is not [pre]eternal either, because if motion in actuality is [pre]eternal, then the mobile would be moved by an infinite motion before being in actuality, and this is incongruous and erroneous. From these [words], it would follow that neither motion in actuality nor the end of the movement is [pre]eternal, and this is what was intended.

§ 5.4 To dispel any doubt, I will reply: motion is not [pre]eternal, but a mover and a mobile, and a potentiality for motion, both active and passive with respect to the movement in actuality, are necessarily prior [to the motion]. And this [happens] by priority, which is given in the difference of the instants by which they differ from each other in species—not to mention in [individual] number. There is an instant in which all the aforementioned things exist in actuality and in which the beginning of the motion is different from the beginning of the number of the movement, if one considers the quantity of time that elapses between them.

§ 5.5.1 In response to the general argument, I will reply: since they proceed correctly with respect to true time, therefore the measurement of the motion pertains to a finite or | infinite quantity, and similarly the "before" and "after" that are in the first quantity, as the Philosopher explains in *Physics* 4, text. 99,[a] where he states: "And since 'before' and 'after' exist in quantity, therefore 'before' and 'after' also exist in motion, etc." But this argument is not verified according to quantity, because there was no motion before creation, and consequently, there were no quantities or qualities and therefore no time, because outside of the heavens, there is none of these, as the Philosopher explains in *On the Heavens* 1, text. 99,[b] where he states: "There is no place outside the heavens, no plenum and no vacuum and no time," and he continues: "Time is the number of motion, and there is no motion without a natural body." Moreover, if there was no motion, then there was no quantity or time; therefore, nothing was finite or infinite because these pertain to the category of quantity.

---

[a] *Phys.* 4.11.219a.   [b] *Cael.* 1.9.279a.

§ 5.5.2 And therefore, when the opponent is questioning and saying that if motion was not [pre]eternal, it would therefore follow that the disposition for motion in the mobile would be [there] for an infinite time, we answer that this does not follow at all, because, if motion does not exist, then the mobile also does not exist, and nor does the time to which the measure of either finite or infinite applies, because the motion and the time are created together with the mobile. And Plato seems to have thought the same, which Aristotle stresses in contrast to his words in *Physics* 8, text. 10:[a] "Time is not at all created, but Plato creates it when he says that it is created together with the heavens, and that the heavens were also created."

§ 5.5.3 And also, when the opponent is questioning [this] by saying that if we said that the motion was created, it would therefore follow that the voluntary agent would delay [doing] the thing he wanted for no reason, we answer: this does not follow at all, because, in addition to motion not existing, time, by which [temporal] priority and posteriority are measured, would also not exist. And therefore, it becomes clear that the Creator—may He be praised—creates a mobile without temporal delay together with the disposition for motion, and [He does] this in an instant in which they necessarily exist prior to the beginning of the motion that only exists thanks to their actual existence.

§ 5.6.1 And He—may He be praised—also declares in the Torah of the Holy One, as it testifies (Exodus 24:12): "Which I have inscribed to instruct them," and it declares first how the sphere and the centre were created without time. And it says this (Genesis 1:1): "In the beginning He created," as mentioned, because the first instant, which is the beginning of time, was the absolute beginning. And after this, it says that that centre, which is called "earth" in [the account of] creation, | was a thing composed of prime matter and the first form, called "Tohu and Bohu," because in it, all the bodies that we call "elements" were in proximate disposition. And it says that afterwards, there was motion (Genesis 1:2)—"a spirit from God sweeping"—meaning, by saying "a spirit from God," that separate substance that swept and moved the sphere, which surrounded the centre, which then moved the dark air, which surrounded the water, which was then covering the earth, as explained above. And this mover was the intellect of the sphere or its soul, which are substances not mixed with the body, and they are called "the spirit of God," as it says (Psalm 104:4): "He makes [the] spirits [or: winds] His messengers."

---
[a] *Phys.* 8.1.251b.

§ 5.5.2 ולכן כאשר הקשה החולק ואמר: כי אם לא היתה התנועה קדמונית היה מתחייב מזה שהיתה ההכנה אל התנועה במתנועע משך זמן בלתי בעל תכלית. נשיב ונאמר שלא יתחייב זה כלל כי בעוד שלא היתה תנועה נמצאת הנה אז המתנועע גם כן לא היה נמצא ולא גם כן הזמן אשר עליו יפול שיעור היותו בעל תכלית או בלתי בעל תכלית כי אמנם התנועה והזמן נתחדשו יחדיו עם המתנועע. וזה בעצמו נראה שהרגיש אפלטון אשר התאמץ ארסטו׳ לסתור דבריו בספר השמע מאמר ח׳ פרק י׳ באמרו: "אמנם הזמן אינו מחודש אפס כי אפלטון מחדש אותו באמרו שנתחדש עם השמים ושהשמים גם כן מחודשים."

§ 5.5.3 וכן כאשר הקשה החולק באמרו שאם אמרנו שהתנועה מחודשת יתחייב מזה שהפועל הרצוני איחר את הדבר הנרצה ממנו בלתי סבה הנה נשיב ונאמר שלא יתחייב זה כלל כי בעוד שלא היתה תנועה נמצאת לא היה נמצא גם כן זמן שישוער בו קדימה ואיחור ובזה יתבאר שהבורא ית׳ חדש בלתי איחור זמניי את המתנועע עם הכנה אל התנועה וזה ברגע אשר בו נמצאו בהכרח קודמים להתחלת התנועה אשר לא תהיה זולתי במציאותם בפעל.

§ 5.6.1 וכן הורה הוא ית׳ בתורת קדשו כאשר יעד באמרו: "אשר כתבתי להורותם" (שמות כ״ד י״ב) והודיע ראשונה איך הגלגל ומרכזו נבראו בלתי זמן וזה באמרו: "בראשית ברא" (בראשית א׳ א׳), כנזכר כי אמנם הרגע הראשון אשר היה ראשית הזמן הוא היה ראשית במוחלט ואחר כך אמר שאותו המרכז אשר נקרא ›ארץ‹ בבריאה | היה דבר מורכב מחומר ראשון וצורה ראשונה קראו ›תהו ובהו‹ כי בו היו בכח קרוב כל הגשמים הנקראים אצלנו ›יסודות‹ ואמר שאחר כך היתה התנועה באמרו: "ורוח אלהים מרחפת" (שם שם ב׳), רצה באמרו: "רוח אלהים" אותו העצם הנבדל המרחף ומניע את הגלגל סביב המרכז אשר הניע אז את האויר החשוך סביב המים אשר היו אז מכסים הארץ כמבואר לעיל וזה המניע הוא שכל הגלגל או נפשו שהם עצמים בלתי מעורבים עם גשם ונקראים ›רוח אלהים‹ באמרו: "עושה מלאכיו רוחות" (תהלים ק״ד ד׳).

§ 5.5.2 Quare cum primo arguitur dicendo, quod nisi fuisset ab eterno sequeretur ut mobilitas habuisset per infinitum tempus in esse mobili, negatur consequentia. Quia dum motus non erat nullum erat mobile, cui mobilitas inesset, neque erat tempus in quo finitas vel infinitas consideraretur. Motus, enim, et tempus simul cum mobili producta sunt et idem videtur sensisse Platonem cui Phylosophus contradicere conatur *Physicorum* VIII t.c. 10 ubi dicit: «Quia tempus non est generatum, Plato vero generat ipsu, dicit enim ipsum generari cum celo et quod celum est generatum et novum.»

§ 5.5.3 Similiter cum arguitur quod ad novum motum sequeretur ut voluntarius agens postposuisset suum voluntatum per infinitum tempus sine causa negatur consequentia. Quia dum motus non erat nihil temporis erat in quo daretur postpositio vel retardatio. Quare patet quod Creator sine temporali postpositione sive retardatione produxit mobile cum potentia ad motum que scilicet potentia devenit ad actum sine temporali postpositione. Dato scilicet illo instanti in quo habuit necessario motor et mobile et potentia ad actualem motione actualiter existere ut supra quibus patet quod volens nullo pacto postposuit suum voluntarium neque illud pro aliquod tempus retardavit, cum nullum tunc fuisset tempus in quo daretur retardatio ut supra.

§ 5.6.1 Quare Sacrum Genesis Documentum cap. primo [1:1] docet quod primo fuit creatio orbis eiusque centri sine tempore cum scilicet dicit: «In principio creavit Deus.» Per «principium» intelligens absolute primum temporis instans ante quod ut sic nihil erat temporis. Deinde dicit quod huiusmodi centrum sive terra ut prefertur creata erat quid mixtum sive Chaos cui potentialiter inerant illa que nunc sensibilium elementa appellamus. Et hoc infert ubi [Gen 1:2] dicit: «Terra autem erat etc.» Subsequenter docet quod habuit deinde esse localis orbium motus, et hoc ubi [1:2] dicit: «et Spiritus Dei ferebat sive circumvehebat super aquam.» Ubi per «Spiritum Dei» intelligit orbis motorem vel eiusdem animam eundem orbem centro circumvehentem, que scilicet anima dicitur esse quid corpori immixtum

§ 5.5.2 In response to the first argument, I will reply: if [motion] was [pre]eternal, it would follow that mobility would be in a mobile for an infinite time, and this inference is not correct, because if there is no motion, then there is no mobile in which mobility exists and there is no time in which it is possible to measure the finitude or infinitude. Motion and time are created together with the mobile, as Plato seems to have felt, and the Philosopher confutes this in *Physics* 8, text. 10,[a] where he states: "Time has no origin. Plato alone assigns an origin to time, for he says that it came into existence simultaneously with the universe, and he assigns an origin to that."

§ 5.5.3 Similarly, I will reply: When a new motion occurred, it would follow that a voluntary agent would delay [doing] something according to his will for an infinite time without a particular reason, and the inference is not correct, because if there is no motion, then there was no time in which postposition or delay existed. Therefore, it is clear that a creator, without postposition or delay, created the mobile together with the potency for motion because potentiality is an activity without temporal postposition. And then there would be an instant in which the mover and the mobile and the potentiality for an actual motion were actualised, as mentioned above. From these [things], it is evident that a voluntary [agent] would never postpone [doing] something according to its will, nor would it slow down time according to its will, because there would be no time in which the postposition [lit. delay] existed, as mentioned above.

§ 5.6.1 The Holy Book of Genesis (Genesis 1:1) teaches that in the beginning, there was the creation of the sphere and its centre without time, saying: "In the beginning God created," and "the beginning" means the absolute first instant of time before time, because there was no time. Afterwards, (Genesis 1:1) records that before the creation of the centre, or the earth, there was a "compound" or "chaos" that contained all things in potential which we call the sensible elements, continuing: "And the earth was, etc." It would immediately follow that the locomotion of the spheres was created, saying (Genesis 1:2): "And the Spirit of God moved over the waters." "Spirit of God" means the mover of a sphere or the soul of the sphere that moved over the centre, which is called "soul" because it is unmixed with a body.

---

[a] *Phys.* 8.1.251b.

§ 5.6.2 And it seems that the Philosopher's words in *Metaphysics* 12, text. 36,[a] concern this substance: "And it moves in the way the desired thing moves." And Averroes explains his words: "Therefore, it becomes clear that these bodies have a soul and that the only faculty among the faculties of the soul that they have is the faculty that desires to move [by] locomotion." And it becomes clear in this way, as it becomes clear in *Physics* 8, that there is a mover of these bodies, and he continues: "We say, if so, that they are moving only because they understand from their substance that their essential perfection is through motion." And Averroes speaks about this kind of soul in *On the Soul* 3, text. 5, and in the *Treatise on the Substance of the Celestial Sphere*, ch. 4, saying that it is a form not mixed with a substrate.[b] And also in *The Incoherence of the Incoherence* 13, first investigation,[c] he speaks about the aforementioned soul referring to al-Ġazālī: "Al-Ġazālī said, referring to the Philosopher, that the sphere is a living being, and that its soul is attributed to its body as our souls are to our bodies, because just as our soul moves by will towards what is desired, the celestial bodies move to hear to the voice of God—may He be praised—and His grandeur."

§ 5.6.3 "And a spirit from God sweeping over the water"; that is to say that the mover moved the darkness [through] a circular motion "over the water," which at that point was surrounding the sphere of the earth. [This is said] to explain two things. First, that this motion was not natural, but was intended by a voluntary agent, because a circular motion is not appropriate for nature, because indeed nature, as al-Ġazālī explains, only moves by locomotion if it is moving towards an appropriate place. And this is not achieved by circular motion, because by this motion, the movable reaches neither any place nor any position in which it will be situated at a certain time. And the second is: since the voluntary mover and the mobile and others necessarily precede the voluntary motion in time, as explained above, it follows that the motion of the sphere, which was the first [motion], is not [pre]eternal. And therefore, it follows that motion is absolutely not [pre]eternal. And this is what the Torah wanted to explain.

---

[a] *Metaph.* 12.7.1072.   [b] Cf. *Sub. orb.* 112–113.   [c] Cf. *Incoherence* 285.

§ 5.6.2 De qua videtur Phylosophus intendere *Metaphysicorum* XII t.c. 36ᵃ ubi Aven R. exponens ait: «Ex hoc apparet bene hec corpora esse animata et quod non habent de | virtutibus nisi intellectivam et desiderativam virtutem qua moventur in loco et hoc declarabitur ex his. Dictum est, enim, in VIII *Physicorum* quoniam moventes hec corpora etc.» subdit ibidem dicens: «Dicamus igitur quod non moventur nisi quia intelligunt quod perfectio est substantie eorum in motu» et de eadem facit mentionem Algazelis auctoritate in lib. *Destructionis D.*, disputatione XIII, dubio primo ubi dicit: «Ait Algazel dicunt Peripatetici quod celum est animal et comparatio ipsius anime ad eius corpus est comparatio nostrarum animarum ad nostrum corpus eo quod sicut anima voluntarie movetur versus partem desideratam similiter corpora coelestia moventur ad obedientiam et reverentiam gloriosi Dei etc.»

§ 5.6.3 Huiusmodi autem orbis motorem sive animam merito Sacrum Genesis Documentum appellat *Spiritum Dei* cum sit intellectiva substantia corpori imixta ut supra. De cuius substantie genere intelligit Psalmus 103ᵇ [104:4] ubi dicit: «Fecit angelos suos spiritus.» Quod demonstrative dicit prefatum Genesis Documentum [Gen 1:2] cum dicit: «et Spiritus Dei circumferebat super aquam.» Id est circumvehebat orbem super aquam que tunc terram circumquaque cooperiebat, per quem circularem motum duo ostendere videtur. Primo scilicet quod huiusmodi motor non est naturalis imo est voluntarius finem intendens, et per consequens est quid intellectuale et hoc quia non contingit ut natura circulariter moveat. Natura enim sicut habetur ab Algazele ibidem, non movet localiter nisi ad locum mobili competentem, quod non contingit fieri per circularem motum per quem scilicet mobile nullum acquirit locum neque situm in quo per tempus maneat. Secundo vero ostendit quod cum ad voluntatum motum habeat necessario volens et mobile et alia ut supra secundum tempus precedere patet quidem ut orbium motus qui dicitur esse omnium primus non habuit esse ab eterno et per consequens neque motus absolute habuit esse ab eterno quod est intentum.

§ 5.6.2 And the Philosopher explains this in *Metaphysics* 12, text. 36,ᵃ and Averroes explicates: "From this, it appears in all clarity that these celestial bodies have souls and that of the faculties of the soul, they have only | the intellect and the faculty of desire; I mean [the faculty] that imparts locomotion to them. This appears from what I say: it is explained in the eighth book of *Physics* that the mover of these celestial bodies is without matter and a separate form, etc.," and he continues: "Their motion [i.e., of the stars] is not for the sake of letting these forms pass from potentiality into actuality because this is their first entelechy, but because it is a corollary of their first entelechy." And al-Ġazālī explains [this] in *The Incoherence of the Incoherence* 13, first doubt,ᵇ where he states: "The philosophers also say that heaven is an animal and possesses a soul that has the same relationship to the body of the heavens as our souls [have] to our bodies, and just as our bodies move by [our] will to their ends through the moving power of the soul, the heavens act [in the same way]. And the aim of the heavens in their essential movement is to serve God, etc."

§ 5.6.3 For this reason, in the Holy Book of Genesis, the mover of the sphere or the soul is called "the Spirit of God," because [the Spirit of God] is an intellectual substance unmixed with the body, as Psalm 103 (104:4) intended [to say]: "He makes His angel spirits." And this is what the Holy Book of Genesis teaches, saying: "And the spirit of God moved over the waters," which means that He moved the sphere surrounding the circumference of the earth over the water in a circular motion. And this seems to show two things. First: the mover is not natural, but is rather intended by a voluntary agent, and is consequently an intellectual being, because nothing in nature moves circularly. Indeed, nature, according to al-Ġazālī, only moves by locomotion when moving towards a proper place, because this is not achieved by circular motion, since through this movement, the movable reaches neither any place nor any position in which it remains for a certain time. Second: the voluntary [mover] and the mobile and other things, as mentioned above, are necessarily prior to the voluntary motion, and this is clear because the movement [motion] of the sphere, which we say is first to all motion, is not [pre]eternal, and consequently, motion is absolutely not [pre]eternal, and this is what was intended.

ᵃ 36] emend. Copp.; 6 b; 36 L.   ᵇ 103] emend. Copp.; 105 b; 104 M; 103 V.

ᵃ *Metaph.* 12.7.1072a.   ᵇ Cf. *Incoherence* 285.

§ 6 Sixth:

We will inquire whether it is appropriate to say that there is creation *ab novo* | or creation *ex nihilo*, by which the substrate and its form are created and [by which] the [first] composed existent was entirely [created] after absolute non-existence, or not.

And it seems, at the beginning of the inquiry, that it is incongruous that this can be [the case].

§ 6.1 [This is so,] as Averroes explains citing al-Ġazālī in *The Incoherence of the Incoherence* 1, twenty-first investigation: "Al-Ġazālī says: 'The philosophers' fourth thesis is that it necessarily follows that matter is prior to everything created anew, because everything created anew is undoubtedly created anew from matter. And therefore, it follows that matter cannot be created anew in any case.'" And Averroes explains his words: "We say that the meaning of these words is that everything that is created anew is possible before it is [actually] created anew, and that therefore this possibility necessarily needs a thing to which it is predicated; namely, a receiving substrate." And he continues: "The generation of one existent is the corruption of another. And moreover, the corruption of one [thing] is the generation of another, because nothing is generated out of nothing."[a]

§ 6.2.1 Second, this becomes clear because it is impossible that there may be a created body, and therefore, it follows that the separate substance is also not created, and it then follows that nothing is created. The consequence follows because the material substance is not created. And therefore, it follows that the sphere was not created and also that it was not generated from another body, such that it filled the space of the first body, since the existence of a [so-called] sixth body is impossible, as Aristotle explains in *On the Heavens* 1, text. 23.[b] It then follows that the heavens were not generated in any way.

§ 6.2.2 And therefore, it follows that their movers, which we call "the separate substances," were not created. And apart from this: if the separate [substances] were created—and the bodies were not separate—it would follow that the first bodies were nobler than the separate substances with regard to eternity and perpetuity. And this is incongruous, because the separate [substances], since they are simpler, are more suited to perpetuity and to eter-

---

[a] Cf. *Incoherence* 58–60. [b] *Cael.* 1.3.270b.

§6. Sexto Dubitatur

Utrum detur creatio qua scilicet tam subiectum et formam quam totum compositum habuissent esse post purum non esse.

Et videtur quod non.

§6.1 Ratione et auctoritate Algazelis de mente phylosophorum, quam Ave. R. refert in libro *Destructionis D.*, disputatione prima dubio 21ª ubi dicit: «Ait Algazel quarta auctoritas Phylosophorum hec est, oportet necessario ut materia precedat quodlibet inovatum quelibet enim innovatio in quadam proculdubio materia intervenit, unde sequitur ut materia nullatenus innovat» et ubi Aven R. exponens ait: «Quod sentencia horum verborum est quod quodlibet inovatum est possibile antequam innovetur et quod possibilitas exigit rem in qua substentetur scilicet subiectum recipiens etc.» subdit ibidem dicens: «Generatio enim cuiuscunque est alterius corruptio, et eius corruptio est generatio alterius | nihil enim ex nihilo fit.»

§6.2.1 Secundo arguitur sic: nullum corpus habuit esse creatum. Ergo neque incorporea substantia et per consequens nihil habuit esse creatum. Consequentia tenet quia cum corpora sint increata ergo et celum est increatum cum sit corpus immo neque productum ex alio corpore in cuius loco succederet cum non detur sextum corpus sicut habetur ratione et auctoritate Phylosophi in lib. *De Celo* primo t.c. 23. Quare patet ut celum sit nullo pacto productum. Et per consequens neque eius motores[b] quorum substantias dicimus esse abstractas.

§6.2.2 Preterea si diceremus abstracta esse creata, corpora vero increata. Sequeretur ut prima corpora non ex alio precedente producta preessent abstractis quoad eternitate quod est inconveniens; abstracta, enim, cum sint simpliciora sunt ad semper esse aptiora. Quare Phyloso-

§6 Sixth,

it may be inquired whether there is a creation in which the substrate and [its] form as well as its compound are after absolute nothingness.

And it does not seem to be so.

§6.1 [First, I would argue] according to the argument and authority of al-Ġazālī in the name of the philosophers that Averroes reports in *The Incoherence of the Incoherence* 1, twenty-first doubt, where he states: "Al-Ġazālī says that the fourth thesis of the philosophers is that it necessarily has to be [the case] that matter is prior to everything that is created anew, because everything that is created anew undoubtedly comes from matter. And therefore, it has to be the case that matter is by no means created anew." And Averroes explicates: "We say that the meaning of these words is that everything that is created anew [i.e., renewed] is possible before it is created anew [i.e., renewed], and therefore that possibility necessarily needs a thing on which it may be predicated; namely, a receiving substrate," and he continues: "The generation of the one existent is the corruption of the other, and the corruption of the one is the generation of the other, because | nothing is generated out of nothing."[a]

§6.2.1 Second, I would argue that a body was not created, and therefore also an incorporeal substance [was not created], and consequently, creation is impossible. The consequence is evident, for bodies were not created, and therefore the heavens were not created, because they are a body. Indeed, the heavens were not generated from another body that succeeded them in another place, because there is no sixth body, according to the argument and authority of the Philosopher in *On the Heavens* 1, text. 23;[b] it is clear that the heavens were not generated in any way. And consequently, their movers, which are called "separate substances," were also not generated.

§6.2.2 Moreover, if we said that the separate [i.e., abstract] substances were created and that bodies were not created, it would follow that the first bodies, which were not generated from another preceding existent, would have existed before the separate [i.e., abstract] substances from eternity, and this is incongruous. The separate [i.e., abstract] substances, since they are simpler, are always in act, as the

---

[a] 21] emend. Copp.; 1 b; 21 DD.   [b] motores] coni. Copp.; motorens b.

[a] Cf. *Incoherence* 58–60.   [b] *Cael.* 1.3.270b.

nity, as Aristotle explains in *On the Heavens* 1, text. 100:[a] "Nothing beyond the last movement can undergo change or affection. If so, they [i.e. separate substances] have an enduring and perpetual life."

§ 6.2.3 Regarding what we said in the [antecedent] premise—that it is impossible that there can be a created body—this becomes clear from Aristotle's proofs in *On the Heavens* 3, text. 29:[b] "It is impossible that there can be a created body if there exists no vacuum." And he continues: "The space in which a body now exists was void before." And since it is impossible that a vacuum in which there will be a space disposed for a body can exist, as is evident from Aristotle's proofs in *Physics* 4, text. 76 and others,[c] it then follows that it is impossible that there can be any created body.

§ 6.3.1 However, the contrary of this—namely, that it is necessary that there is a creation | by which a newly created [thing] will exist after absolute non-existence—will become clear after we lay down that the forms of the four elements were the first [forms] immediately [impressed] in prime matter. And this [is so] because no part of the elements is [pre]eternal. And therefore, every single one of them was created anew, as explained above. And since some of their parts do not undergo corruption while they exist, therefore we cannot say that the now existent [parts] were created anew from other parts in a recurring process. And moreover, they were not created anew from prime, simple matter that was temporally prior to them, because then this prime matter would have been devoid of all form at a certain time, and this is incongruous, as explained above. It would then follow that their creation was not from a substrate, but by creation [out of nothing]. Regarding what we said—that some parts of the elements do not undergo corruption while they exist—this becomes clear from those parts of fire that are [next] to the concavity of the sphere and from those parts of the earth that are [situated] around the centre [of the earth], as explained above in the investigation of the elements.[d] And therefore, it becomes clear that those parts which are necessarily created to be corruptible by nature, as explained above, were created by creation [out of nothing]. And this is what we wanted to explain.

25r

---

[a] *Cael.* 1.9.279a. [b] *Cael.* 3.2.302a. [c] *Phys.* 4.8.215b. [d] Cf. § 2.2.3.

---

6. בריאה

באמרו: »אין דבר חוץ למתנועע האחרון שיהיה בו השתנות ולא התפעלות אם כן יש להם חיים קיימים נצחיים« עכ״ל.

§ 6.2.3 אמנם מה שאמרנו בהקדמה שהוא מן הנמנע שיהיה איזה גוף נברא יתבאר בראיית ארסטו׳ בספר השמים מאמר ג׳ פרק כ״ט באמרו: »מן הנמנע הוא שיהיה שום גוף נברא אם לא ימצא ריקות«. והוסיף ואמר כי »המקום אשר בו נמצא הגוף עתה היה בו ריק קודם לכן« עכ״ל. ובהיות מן הנמנע שימצא ריקות אשר בו יהיה מקום מוכן לגוף כמו שמבואר במופתי ארסטו׳ בספר השמע מאמר ד׳ פרק ע״ו וזולתו התחייב אם כן שהוא מן הנמנע שיהיה שום גוף נברא.

§ 6.3.1 **אמנם** הפך זה רצוני לומר שמן המחוייב שהיתה איזו בריאה אשר בה נמצא איזה מחודש אחר אפיסות מוחלט. הנה יתבאר אחר שנניח שצורות הד׳ יסודות הן ראשונות בחומר הראשון בלתי אמצעי. וזה כי אמנם כל אחד מחלקי היסודות הוא בלתי קדמון ובכן כל אחד מהם מחודש כמבואר לעיל. ובהיות שקצת חלקיהם לא קרה להם הפסד מעת שנמצאו ובכן לא נאמר שהנמצאים עתה התחדשו מחלקים אחרים בחזרת חלילה. וגם כן לא התחדשו מחומר ראשון פשוט קודם להם קדימה זמנית כי אם כן היה החומר הראשון באיזה זמן מופשט מכל צורה וזה לא יתכן כמבואר לעיל. יתחייב אם כן שהיה חדושם לא מנושא אבל היה בבריאה. אמנם מה שאמרנו שקצת חלקי היסודות לא קרה להם הפסד מעת שנמצאו הנה זה התבאר מאותם חלקי האש אשר במקוער הגלגל ומאותם חלקי הארץ אשר סביב המרכז כמבואר לעיל בחקירת היסודות. ומזה יתבאר שאותם החלקים אשר הם מחודשים בהכרח להיותם נפסדים בטבע כמבואר לעיל היה חדושם על ידי בריאה וזה הוא מה שרצינו לבאר.

phus in lib. *De Celo* primi t.c. 100 ait: «Nullum extrinsecum ab ultimo motu potest alterari et transmutari omnino sed semper est permanens non transmutabile neque passibile, vita est ergo eis semper manens perpetua etc.»

§ 6.2.3 Antecedens vero quo dicitur quod nullum corpus habuit esse creatum probatur ratione et auctoritate Phylosophi in lib. *De Celo* tertij t.c. 29 ubi dicit: «Impossibile est ut aliquid corpus fiat nisi vacuum sit etc.» subdit dicens: «Locus in quo corpus est fuit vacuum necessario etc.» Cum autem non detur vacuum in quo deinde habeat locari corpus prout habetur rationibus et auctoritate[a] Phylosophi *Physicorum* IV t.c. 64 et t.c. 76 et alijs, sequitur ergo ut non detur aliquod corpus creari quod est intentum.

§ 6.3.1 Ad oppositum vero presuposito scilicet ut quatuor forme corporum que dicimus esse prima mortalium elementa sint prime forme immediate in materia prima impresse, prout Phylosophus inferre videtur. Arguitur ergo sit: nulla elementorum pars habuit esse ab eterno. Ergo harum quedam habuit esse post purum non esse. Quare patet ut detur creatio sive esse post purum non esse consequentia tenet. Quia cum in quibusdam huiusmodi partium non detur reciprocatio scilicet in[b] illis terre partibus que sunt[c] circa centrum similiter de illis ignis partibus que sunt circam orbem prout superius in dubio de elementis probatum est, a nullo ergo subiecto his tempori priori potuerunt produci, quia neque per reciprocationem habuit subiectum tempore preesse, neque materia prima in qua dicuntur immediate imprimi habuit ad ea secundum tempus precedere. Quia si sic habuisset quandoque ipsa materia prima esse a quale forma denudata existere, cuius contrarium[d] habetur ab Aristotele in lib. *De Generatione* II t.c. 6 et idem habetur rationibus et auctoritate Aven R. in comento lib. *De Celo* III t.c. 29 quare patet quod habuerunt esse sine subiecto tempore priore. Cum ergo verificatum sit quod nulla elementorum pars habuisset esse ab eterno prout superius rationibus et auctoritate probatum est.

Philosopher explains in *On the Heavens* 1, text. 100,[a] where he states: "Nothing beyond the last movement can change or be entirely affected, but it exist forever, without change or affection, and therefore they [the separate substances] will have an enduring and permanent life, etc."

§ 6.2.3 The antecedent, in which we said that bodies were not created, is proved according to the argument and authority of the Philosopher in *On the Heavens* 3, text. 29,[b] where he states: "It is impossible that there can be a created body if there is no vacuum, etc.," and he continues: "The space in which a body now exists was void before." Since there is no void from whence there will be space for a body, as the Philosopher explains in *Physics* 4, text. 64[c] and text. 76[d] and others, it would follow that there are no created bodies, which is what was intended.

§ 6.3.1 On the contrary it is to argue that there are four forms of bodies, which are called the first of the mortal elements, and these were the first forms immediately impressed in prime matter, according to what the Philosopher seems to conclude. Therefore, I would argue that no part of an element is [pre]eternal, and therefore, every single one of their parts takes its being out of absolute nothingness. Indeed, it is evident that there is creation or an existence that takes place out of absolute nothingness. The consequence is evident, because there is no movement of generation from those parts of earth that are around the centre and from those parts of fire that are near the sphere, as is proved in the aforementioned *quaestio* on the elements.[e] Therefore, they [the parts of the elements] could not be produced by a substrate that was temporally prior to them, because there was no substrate that was temporally prior in terms of the movement of generation, and there was no prime matter—which we said was immediately impressed—that was temporally prior to them, because if so, prime matter would have existed devoid of all form, and the Philosopher explains the contrary of this in *On Generation and Corruption* 2, text. 6,[f] and Averroes explicates [it] in the Commentary on *On the Heavens* 3, text. 29.[g] And therefore, it is clear that [the parts of the elements] exist without a substrate that is temporally prior to them. This is verified because no part of an element is [pre]eternal, as is rationally demonstrated above.

---

[a] auctoritate] coni. COPP.; auctoritatem b.   [b] in] coni. COPP.; i b.   [c] sunt] coni. COPP.; sut b.   [d] contrarium] coni. COPP.; contrariu b.

[a] *Cael.* 1.9.279a.   [b] *Cael.* 3.2.302a.   [c] *Phys.* 4.8.214b.   [d] *Phys.* 4.8.215b.   [e] Cf. § 2.2.3.   [f] *Gen. corr.* 2.1.329a.   [g] Cf. *Cael.* 3.2.302a.

§6.3.2 And when we say that the elements were generated from a first compound that preceded them and [that] this [generation happened] through the corruption of that compound, as Scripture testifies (Genesis 1:2), "And the earth was Tohu and Bohu," as was explained above, then this will become clearer, because that first compound that was corrupted [through the generation of the elements generated from it] was necessarily not [pre]eternal, and therefore, it itself was created. And it was not created from an existent that was temporally prior to it, since its first form was within prime matter, which cannot exist devoid of all form, as explained above. And therefore, it becomes clear that its existence and its creation came about by means of creation [out of nothing]. And this is what we wanted to explain.

§6.4.1 Second, that there was necessarily the creation of something becomes clear after we lay down three postulates, which are acceptable as commonly known to someone who is able to comprehend. First, that something that exists in one manner in many things cannot possibly be in all of them by chance, and this is self-evident and also becomes clear from proofs made by Aristotle in *Physics* 2, text. 48,[a] and *On the Heavens* 2, text. 45.[b]

§6.4.2 Second, that the final purpose appearing in a thing shows the same substantial evidence of a voluntary agent in that thing as movement shows of a mover. And this is self-evident, and Averroes explains it in the *Treatise on the Substance of the Celestial Sphere*, ch. 2.[c]

§6.4.3 Third, that every single one of the spheres has a certain quantity, necessarily determined exactly by a hair's breadth, [to allow] for the possibility of their movement. And moreover, there are kinds of exactly determined qualities in the elements that maintain equibalance. And in all of them, there is a final purpose, which is evident from their activities and their continuity and which is not achieved without the maintenance of balance and [afore]mentioned determination. And therefore, it becomes clear that since they are the activity of a voluntary agent, who intends | the final purpose, they are [made] with wisdom, which exists in the determination and in the [afore]mentioned balance. And they exist in one manner in many existents, by which it becomes clear that they do not exist by chance, but [rather] through the intention of a voluntary intending agent, as mentioned above. And the agent, particularly a voluntary [agent], is necessarily tem-

---

[a] *Phys.* 2.4.196b; cf. §1.6, proposition 8.   [b] *Cael.* 2.8.289b; cf. §1.6, proposition 8.   [c] Cf. §1.6, proposition 5.

§ 6.3.2 Sequitur quidem ut prefate saltem partes habuisset de novo produci post purum non esse, quod est intentum. Si vero teneatur ut habuissent produci ex primo chaos ut supra habetur sequitur quidem ut illud chaos cum fuisset eandem[a] corruptum fuisset quid non eternum, cumque illud tanquam primum non habuisset | ab alio produci sequitur fuisse corpus creatum quod est intentum.

§ 6.4.1 Secundo probatur idem: Tribus primo presuppositis et probatis. Primo, scilicet, quod illud quod est ut in pluribus observatum non dicitur fieri casu prout per se patet et habetur superius in preambuli presuppositorum 8 ratione et auctoritate probatum.

§ 6.4.2 Secundo quod finis in re apparens significat eiusdem rei voluntarium agentem significatione propria, sicut motus significat motorem prout per se patere videtur, et ibidem superius in 5 presuppositione ratione et auctoritate probatum est.

§ 6.4.3 Tertio quod tam in celestium orbium figuris et quantitatibus ad unguem in omnibus opportune observatis, quam in elementorum proportionali contrarietatum equalitate sensu apparente significatur artificium ad finem intentum sine quo impedirentur eorum operationes, neque eorum substantia permaneret, et per consequens habuit esse a voluntario agente finem huiusmodi intendente ut supra. Et hoc tam ratione finis per ipsum artificium apparentis quam ratione eiusdem artificii in tot numero observati. Cumque agens saltem voluntarius

§ 6.3.2 It would at least follow that the aforementioned parts were produced anew out of absolute nothingness, which is what was intended. If it is true that the parts of the elements were generated from a first chaos, as proved above, it would at least follow that this chaos, which was corrupted, was not [pre]eternal and that it was produced from another being, and then it follows that this body was created, | which is what was intended.

§ 6.4.1 Second, I would argue in three postulates, which are already proposed and proved. First, that something observed in many things does not exist by chance, as is evident according to the argument and authority that is demonstrated in the eighth proposition[a] in the prologue.

§ 6.4.2 Second, that the purpose appearing in a thing indicates [the presence of] a voluntary agent in that thing, since movement indicates a mover, as is evident according to the argument and authority that is demonstrated in the fifth proposition.[b]

§ 6.4.3 Third, that that which is precisely observed in the shapes and quantities of the celestial spheres, as well as in the proportional equality of contrary elements, which is evident, signifies an activity intended towards a final purpose, without which their operations would be impeded and their substance would not persist. Consequently, it exists through a voluntary agent who intended the final

---

[a] eandem] emend. COPP.; tandem b[corr]; andem b.

[a] Cf. § I.6: *Cael.* 2.8.289b and *Phys.* 2.4.196b.   [b] Cf. § I.6: *Metaph.* 2.2.994b and *Sub. orb.*, ch. 2.

porally prior to its activity, as explained above. And it also becomes clear that no substrate is temporally prior to the celestial bodies, or to the elements, or to the first compound from which they are generated through its corruption, as explained above.

§ 6.4.4 And it then follows that the agent who intends the final purpose in them brought forth the heavens and the elements or their first substrate from absolute non-existence and total privation. And this is only possible by way of creation [out of nothing]. And therefore, it follows that creation [out of nothing] and a creator exist. And this is what we wanted to explain.

§ 6.5.1 Third, the same becomes self-evident after laying down four assumptions. (1) First, that an actual substance can only be a cause of the existence of another substance by way of an efficient cause. And this is in one of two [ways]. (a) First, [if] its substrate changes from a certain form to another form that was in it in potentiality, and this is by generation and corruption.

§ 6.5.2 (b) Second, [if] it brings forth an existent from formlessness to a certain form, without movement and without any prior substrate, and this is creation [out of nothing], which brings forth an existent after absolute non-existence. And therefore, it follows that every substance that does not have the potentiality of a creator does not have the potentiality of an agent unless there is a certain substrate that is disposed to be affected by it. And therefore, it follows that it does not have a form that pertains to an agent unless we were to imagine that it owns it in vain. And due to the absence of the form, it would follow that it does not exist in that way. And therefore, the very same can be said about things that are affected by affected forms. And therefore, their substances do not exist in this way unless there is an agent exists who is disposed and designated to actualise them.

בפרט רצוניי יקדם בזמן לפעלתו בהכרח כמבואר לעיל. והתבאר גם כן שאין נושא קודם בזמן לגרמים השמימיים ולא גם כן ליסודות או למורכב ראשון אשר ממנו נתהוו בהפסדו כמבואר לעיל.

§ 6.4.4 יתחייב אם כן שהפועל אשר כיון התכלית בהם הוא המציא את השמים ואת היסודות או נושאם הראשון אחר אפיסות מוחלט והעדר גמור וזה בלתי אפשר זולתי בבריאה ומזה יתחייב שנמצאו בריאה ובורא וזה הוא מה שרצינו לבאר.

§ 6.5.1 שלישית יתבאר זה בעצמו אחר הקדמת ארבע הנחות. ראשונה שלא יהיה שום עצם בפעל סבה למציאות עצם זולתו זולתי על דרך סבה פועלת וזה על אחד משני פנים. האחד הוא בשנותו את הנושא מאיזו צורה אל צורה אחרת אשר היתה בו בכח זה בתנועת הויה והפסד.

§ 6.5.2 והשני הוא בהמציאו נמצא בלתי תנועה ובלתי נושא קודם מלא צורה אל איזו צורה. וזו היא הבריאה הממציאה את הנמצא אחר אפיסות מוחלט. ומזה יתחייב שכל עצם אשר אין לו כח בורא לא היה לו שום כח פועל לולא היה במציאות איזה נושא מוכן להתפעל ממנו. ומזה יתחייב שלא היתה לו אותה הצורה הפועלת אם לא שנצייר שהיתה בו לריק. ובהעדר הצורה יתחייב שלא היה לו זה המציאות. ובכן בעצמו נאמר על המתפעלים של צורות המתפעלות ובכן לעצמותם לא היה זה המציאות לולא שקרה שהיה במציאות איזה פועל מוכן ומיוחד לפעול בהם.

6. DE CREATIONE

habeat necessario ad suum actum secundum tempus precedere, prout superius in presuppositorum tertio probatum est. Et cum hoc non detur subiectum celestibus vel elementis tempore prius ex quo habuisset voluntarius agens huiusmodi artificiata producere, prout ibidem preseuppositorum 10 ratione et auctoritate patuit.

§ 6.4.4 Preterea quia si daretur tale subiectum fuisset necessario et illud quid corruptibile cum fuisset substantialiter transmutatum, et per consequens fuisset quid productum, et sic procederetur ad infinitum, quod est inconveniens prout habetur a Phylosopho *Metaphysicorum* 11 t.c. 5. Quare deveniendum est ad primum alterabile ad artificiata intentum quod non habuisset ab alio priori produci. Sequitur ergo ut ipse agens habuisset eadem artificiata vel horum subiectum si detur quid tempore prius post purum non esse producere, et per consequens creare. Quare datur creatio et Creator quod est intentum.

§ 6.5.1 Tertio probatur idem principale quatuor presuppositis. Primo scilicet quod nihil penitus datur vel imaginatur produci ab agente nisi altero duorum modorum, vel scilicet per motum in subiecto quod substantialiter alteretur a forma ad formam, et talis est generatio, vel scilicet ut tam subiectum et forma quam totum compositum producatur ad esse post purum non esse, et talis est creatio.

§ 6.5.2 Secundo presupponitur quod agens in subiecto non quamlibet formam in quolibet subiecto introducere potest sed illam tantum quae fuerit eidem subiecto proportionata. Quare sequitur ut nullus agens non creativus potest aliquid agere nisi dato subiecto eidem actioni proportionato, et per consequens ut tali subiecto non dato neque habeat eandem activam formam esse,[a] et per consequens neque habeat eandem substantiam esse.[b] Et idem dicendum est de passivis subiectis, quod scilicet horum passibilis forma, | et per consequens horum substantia non habeat esse nisi dato agente eorum passibilitati proportionato.

41ᵛ
[42]

purpose in such a way as is mentioned above, and this is observed in the evident purpose of the activity as well as in the activity itself in such a great number [of cases]. Therefore, the purposive agent was necessarily prior to his act, as is proven in the third proposition.[a] And therefore, there is no substrate that was prior to the celestial bodies or to the elements through which a voluntary agent produced artefacts, according to the argument and authority of the tenth proposition.[b]

§ 6.4.4 Moreover, because if it were [composed] of such a substrate, it would necessarily be corruptible because it would be able to change entirely and consequently, it would be something generated and this would continue *ad infinitum*, and this is incongruous, as the Philosopher explains in *Metaphysics* 2, text. 5.[c] And therefore, from altered beings, we arrive at the first intention of artefacts that is not generated by another existent. And if there is something temporally prior, it would follow that the agent would have generated those artefacts or their substrate from absolute nothingness, and would consequently have created [them]. And then there would be creation and also a creator, which is what was intended.

§ 6.5.1 Third, I would argue in four assumptions. First, that there are only two different ways in which it is possible to imagine that something may be generated by an agent [i.e., there is nothing that exists or that is imagined to be generated by an agent except in these two ways]: either something in a substrate changes substantially from form to form through movement, which is generation, or the substrate and form along with the composite occur out of absolute nothingness, which is creation.

§ 6.5.2 Second, that this agent in a substrate cannot introduce all forms into all substrates, but can only introduce a form that is designated for this substrate. It would follow that no non-creative agent could act unless it were given a subject that was designated for its action. Consequently, if there is no such substrate, a creating thing cannot have an active form, and consequently cannot have a substance. We can say the same thing about passive substrates, because their passive form—and consequently their substance—only exist if there is an agent that can introduce a form | designated for their passivity.

41ᵛ
[42]

---

[a] esse] b^corr; om. b. [b] esse] b^corr; om. b.

[a] Cf. § 1.6: cf. *Metaph.* 9.3.1048a and *An. post.* 2.95a. [b] Cf. § 1.6: *Cael.* 1.3.270b. [c] *Metaph.* 2.2.994b.

§ 6.5.3 (2) Second, that everything that occurs to any existing substance cannot avoid either (a) that it will come to be by a voluntary agent who intends this thing to occur to that substance, or (b) that it will come to be without the intention of any intender, and this means that it will happen by chance, as is self-evident. And Aristotle explains this in *Physics* 2, text. 51.[a]

§ 6.5.4 (3) Third, that the things that are made by chance are not necessary and exist only rarely, as is self-evident. And the Philosopher explains this in *Physics* 2, text. 48.[b]

§ 6.5.5 (4) Fourth, that an existent that is uncaused is eternal and [its] existence is necessary, insofar as it is impossible that an uncaused thing will not have existence. And this is also self-evident and Aristotle explains it in *On the Heavens* 1, text. 124.[c]

§ 6.5.6 And after laying down the aforementioned four assumptions, we say that sense [perception] testifies that there is a great number of kinds of affected substrates. Every single one of them is disposed to be affected, yet not by every agent, but by the activity of an agent designated for it, | because it is not [the case] that a thing may be generated from any substrate and [this] is not [possible] through the power of every efficient cause, but it is generated because there is an agent designated for the affected [thing]. And therefore, it is inevitable either (1) that we say that this order in every single one of them is intended by a certain voluntary, intending agent, and it therefore becomes clear that all the forms that they enact are intended and exist thanks to that [same] intender, and without any substrate prior to all of them, it follows that the aforementioned intender who willed their existence brought them forth after absolute non-existence and [that it did] this through a creator's power. And therefore, it becomes clear that a creator exists, who has necessarily created.

§ 6.5.7 Or (2) [it is inevitable] that we say that those agents and their designated affected [things] cannot have existence—nor can their activity or their affection or their designation or their correlation—through the intention of any intender. And if so, it would be by mere chance that there existed such a great number of affected [things], every single one of which was disposed and designated for the activity of an agent designated for it. And this means that if this chance had not occurred, then the agents' possible activities would have been without substrates desig-

---

[a] *Phys.* 2.5.197a.   [b] *Phys.* 2.4.196b.   [c] *Cael.* 1.12.282b.

§ 6.5.3 שנית שכל מה שיקרה לאיזה עצם נמצא לא ימלט אם שיבואהו מצד פועל רצוני מכוין שיקרה אותו הדבר לעצם ההוא. אם שיבואהו בלתי כוונת שום מכוין. וזה יאמר לו במקרה כאשר הוא מבואר בעצמו ובארו ארסטו' בספר השמע מאמר ב' פרק נ"א.

§ 6.5.4 שלישית שהדברים ההווים במקרה אינם הכרחיים ולא ימצאו רק על המעט. כמו שהוא מבואר בעצמו ובארו הפילוסוף בספר השמע מאמר ב' פרק מ"ח.

§ 6.5.5 רביעית שהנמצא אשר הוא בלתי מסובב הוא קדמון ומחוייב המציאות עד שהוא מן הנמנע שאותו הבלתי מסובב לא יהיה במציאות וזה גם כן מבואר בעצמו ובארו ארסטו' בספר השמים מאמר א' פרק קכ"ד.

§ 6.5.6 ואחר שהקדמנו את הד' הנחות הנזכרות נאמר כי אמנם זה יעיד החוש שנמצאו מיני נושאים מתפעלים רבים במספר וכל אחד מהם מוכן להתפעל לא מכל פועל אבל בפעולת פועל מיוחד אליו. | כי לא יתהווה כל דבר מכל דבר נושא ולא בכח כל סבה פועלת אבל יתהווה בהיות הפועל מיוחד למתפעל. ובכן לא ימלט אם שנאמר שהיה זה הסדר בכל אחד מהם מכוון מאיזה פועל רצוני מכוין. ומזה יתבאר שכל צורותיהם אשר בהם יפעלו הן[a] מכוונות ונמצאות מאתו המכוין ומבלי אין נושא קודם לכלם יתחייב שהמכוין הנזכר אשר רצה מציאותם המציאם אחר אפיסות מוחלט וזה בכח בורא. ומזה התבאר שיש נמצא בורא שברא בהכרח.

§ 6.5.7 ואם שנאמר שמציאות אותם הפועלים והמתפעלים המיוחדים להם לא נמצאו הם ולא פעלתם והתפעלותם ולא ייחודם ויחסם בכוונת שום מכוין. ואם כן מקרה הוא שקרה שימצאו כל כך מתפעלים רבים במספר כל אחד מהם מוכן ומיוחד לפעלת פועל מיוחד לו. באופן כי לולא זה המקרה לא היו פעלות הפועלים

---

[a] הן] coni. Dunk.; הם a.

§ 6.5.3 Secundo presupponitur quod illud cuius substantia sive forma ab extra evenit non autem per se eternorum more, vel sibi evenit a voluntario agente huiusmodi adventum ad finem intendente, vel evenit preter alicuius intentum, et tunc dicitur fieri casu prout per se patet, et habetur a Phylosopho *Physicorum* II t.c. 51.

§ 6.5.4 Tertio presupponitur quod illa quae casu contingunt non sunt necessaria prout per se patere videtur, et habetur a Phylosopho *Physicorum* II t.c. 48.[a]

§ 6.5.5 Quarto presupponitur quod quicquid est incausatum est, quid per se necessarium inesse itaque impossibile est ut non sit, prout per se patere videtur et habetur ratione et auctoritate Phylosophi in *De Celo* I t.c. 124. His autem presuppositis.

§ 6.5.6 Arguo sic: huiusmodi scilicet inventio qua tot active substantie inveniunt tot idem passiva subiecta suis actionibus proportionata ad horum esse necessaria ut supra, vel fit ab aliquo voluntario agente finem intendente, vel non si dicatur quod non. Tunc sequitur ut tam activa quam passiva sibi invicem preter intentum proportionata habuissent esse casum, cuius oppositum superius in octava propositione probatum est. Restat ergo ut habeant esse ab aliquo agente finem intendente, et per consequens nihil horum habuit esse incausatum vel per se necessarium.

§ 6.5.7 Cum autem in entibus sit necessario deveniendum ad quoddam primum saltem penitus incausatum, est ergo illud in sua actione non indigens subiecto sue actioni pro-

§ 6.5.3 Second, [otherwise], a thing that comes forth out of its substance or its form would not follow the rule of the eternal existents. Either it comes forth from a purposive agent and it is intended towards a final purpose, or it comes forth without intention, and then we say that it is made by chance, as is evident, as is explained by the Philosopher in *Physics* 2, text. 51.[a]

§ 6.5.4 Third, that things made by chance are not necessary, as is evident, as the Philosopher explains in *Physics* 2, text. 48.[b]

§ 6.5.5 Fourth, that an uncaused thing is absolutely a necessary existent and it is impossible that it may not exist, as is evident according to the argument and authority of the Philosopher in *On the Heavens* 1, text. 124.[c]

§ 6.5.6 After these assumptions, I will argue that this invention, by which a great number of active substances find a great number of passive substrates designated to their actions [that are] necessarily fit for their existence, as mentioned above, is either made by a purposive agent that intends to reach a final purpose, or not. If not, it would follow that both the active [substances] and the passive [substrates], which are mutually disposed, are made by chance without intention. The opposite of this is proved in the eighth proposition.[d] It remains that they exist via a purposive agent intended to reach the final purpose, and consequently, none of them is uncaused or necessary in itself.

§ 6.5.7 And therefore, it is necessary to arrive at the first of the uncaused existents, which does not need a particular [designated] substrate in order to perform its activity,

---

[a] 48] emend. COPP.; 45 b; מ״ח a; 48 L.

[a]*Phys.* 2.5.197a. [b]*Phys.* 2.4.196a. [c]*Cael.* 1.12.282b. [d]Cf. *Cael.* 2.8.289b and *Phys.* 2.4.196b.

nated for them on which they could act, and therefore their forms would be missing or existing in vain. And therefore, it follows that none of the aforementioned agents needs a substrate for their activity that is necessary for the existing reality and not one among them is uncaused. And it is necessary that the order of existing reality will lead to a first uncaused cause, because otherwise it means that the thing would proceed until infinity, and this is incongruous, as explained above. And it necessarily follows that this necessary cause is an existent that does not need a substrate on which it acts for its activity. And this is congruous only for creation, which brings forth the substrate [together] with its form after absolute non-existence. And therefore, the existence of creation and of a creator necessarily becomes clear. And this is what we wanted to explain.

§ 6.6.1 Fourth, in this way, it becomes clear that existents exist by virtue of creation through the power of a creator: because every [successive] order of caused things necessarily has to be traced back to a first cause, as mentioned above. And this is an active existent and a forth-bringer through self-intellection, as becomes clear. And that existent is a simple substance and every simple thing either is entirely known or cannot be known at all. It necessarily follows that its aforementioned intellection lies within an indivisible instant. And therefore, it follows that the bringing-forth of existents that exist through that intellection lies within an indivisible instant. And if so, it is without time and without movement. And if so, it is without the affection of a substrate, but is [moved] from formless[ness] to form and from non-existence and absolute privation to existence, between which there is no medium. And this bringing-forth is creation [out of nothing], which we wanted to explain, because the activity that is without time is undoubtedly creation [out of nothing], | as mentioned above. And regarding what we said—that the first cause acts through its self-intellection—this becomes clear from proofs made by Aristotle in *Metaphysics* 12, text. 51,[a] saying that the first cause—namely, the existent that arranges the order of existing reality and unifies it—necessarily knows all the existents, as the order and the aforementioned conjunction attest. And this will become clear to us below in a broader explanation.

§ 6.6.2 It then follows that the knowledge of this arranger of order in existents comes about by one of two means: either (1) it is caused by the aforementioned existents that are caused by it, or (2) it is not caused by them. And if we say that its [i.e., the arranger of order's] aforementioned

---

[a] *Metaph.* 12.8.1074b.

portionato, et talis est Creator ad cuius actionem quae est creatio nullum requiritur subiectum, cum sit productio tam subiecti quam forme, quod est intentum.

§ 6.6.1 Quarto probatur idem principale sic arguendo: omnia causata habent mediate vel immediate a prima causa causari per illam intellectionem qua se ipsam intelligit. Huiusmodi autem intellectio fit in instanti, ergo huiusmodi causatio entium saltem in immediate facti, habuit esse in instanti scilicet sine tempore, et per consequens sine motu, et sic ex non forma ad formam inter quae non datur medium, et talis est creatio quod est intentum. Consequentia patet, et antecedens probatur ratione et auctoritate Phylosophi *Metaphysicorum* XII t.c. 51. Ubi infert, quod cum prima causa sive universi ordinator et colligans illa omnia sciat prout ipse ordo ipsaque colligatio satis docere videntur et apertius infra in suo docebitur loco. Eius ergo scientia de entibus habita vel dependet ab entibus ab eadem causatis, vel non. Non primum: quia si sic sequeretur ipsam causam perfici ab entibus ab eadem causatis quae sunt quid ea ignobilius quod est inconveniens, causa enim | habet esse quid suis causatis nobilius.

§ 6.6.2 Preterea si ipsa prima causa per sua causata perficeretur, sequeretur ut saltem mediate causaret se ipsam, substantie enim perfectio saltem in abstractis est quid idem

and this is the creator for whose activity, which is creation, no substrate is needed, because this is a generation of substrate as well as form, which is what was intended.

§ 6.6.1 Fourth and principal [argument]: I would argue that all things are caused by a mediate or immediate first cause through self-intellection [i.e., an intellection that understands itself]. This intellection creates in an instant; therefore, the cause of existents also creates immediately. Then the creation occurs in an instant—that is, outside of time—and consequently, it is without motion, and also without [a change] from form to form in which there is no medium, and this is creation, which is what was intended. The consequence is evident, and the antecedent is proved according to the argument and authority of the Philosopher in *Metaphysics* 12, text. 51,[a] where he states that the first cause or the arranger and joiner of the universe necessarily knows all existents. It seems that order and connection attest to this, and this will be clearly attested below in this explanation. Therefore, his intellectual knowledge of the existents either depends on existents that are caused | by it, or not.

§ 6.6.2 The first case is not correct [i.e., that knowledge depends on existents], because then it would follow that the first cause had acquired perfection from existents that were caused by it and that were less noble than it, and this is incongruous, because the cause is nobler than the existents that are caused by it. Moreover, if the first cause

---

[a] *Metaph.* 12.8.1074b.

knowledge is caused by the existents, two incongruities would therefore follow: the first [would be] (a) that perfection would then be acquired by a thing that is inferior to it in rank, and this is incongruous, because the perfecting cause is nobler than that which is perfected, and secondly, (b) it would follow that this [first] existent would perfect itself through its [own] existence, at least mediately. And therefore, it would follow that it would be a cause of the existence of its [own] substance, because the perfection of the [first] existent, especially in the separate substances, is its true substance. And therefore, it would follow that the aforementioned first cause would be concurrently in potentiality and in actuality with regard to its perfection and the existence of its substance, and this is incongruous and unthinkable.

§ 6.6.3 It then remains that its knowledge is not caused by the existents, and therefore it follows that the existents are caused by its [i.e., the first cause's] knowledge, since we already said that its knowledge is not caused by the existents. If we then also said that the existents were not caused by its knowledge, then it would not have knowledge of the existents by any means. And the contrary becomes clear from the order of the existents and their conjunction. It then follows that the existents are caused by its knowledge, by which it knows itself, and that its knowledge is the efficient cause of all the existents, as will become clear to us below in the [appropriate] place [in this book] from a broader explanation.

§ 6.6.4 Its intellection, by which it knows itself, is the intellection of an absolute simple substance. And every simple thing [either] will necessarily be entirely [i.e., perfectly] known or will be entirely [i.e., perfectly] unknown. It then follows that it [i.e., the intellection] will lie within an indivisible instant. And therefore, it follows that the existence of the existents [emanated] from it within an indivisible instant and without movement, because movement does not [take place] without time. And a thing that comes to be without time and without movement will only exist by creation [out of nothing], as explained above. And this is what we wanted to explain.

§ 6.6.5 And therefore, when Averroes understood this kind of knowledge that brings forth existents by way of its intellection, he was very much astonished, as he explained in his Commentary on *On the Soul* 3, text. 36:[a] "The existents have an existence only through the existence of the knowledge of God—may He be exalted—and also, the causes of

---

[a] Cf. *De an.* 3.7.431b.

הנזכרת מסובבת מן הנמצאות הנה לזה יתחייבו שתי נמנעות האחת שאם כן יהיה קונה שלמות בדבר שהוא למטה ממנו במעלה וזה לא יתכן כי אמנם הסבה המשלמת היא יותר נכבדת מן המושלם. שנית יתחייב שזה הנמצא ישלים עצמו במציאותו לפחות על ידי אמצעי ומזה יתחייב שיהיה הוא סבה למציאות עצמותו כי אמנם שלמות הנמצא ובפרט בעצמים הנבדלים הוא עצמותו ממש ומזה יתחייב שהסבה הראשונה הנזכרת תהיה בכח ובפעל יחד לשלמותו ומציאות עצמותו וזה נמנע לא יעלה על לב.

§ 6.6.3 ישאר אם כן שידיעתו אינה מסובבת מהנמצאות ומזה יתחייב שהנמצאות הן[a] מסובבות מידיעתו כי אחרי שאמרנו שידיעתו אינה מסובבת מהנמצאות אם נאמר גם כן שהנמצאות הם בלתי מסובבות מידיעתו לא תהיה לו אם כן ידיעה בנמצאות בשום אופן והפך זה התבאר מסדר הנמצאות וקשרם יתחייב אם כן שהנמצאות הם מסובבות מידיעתו אשר בה הוא יודע את עצמו ושידיעתו היא סבה פועלת לכל הנמצאות כמו שיתבאר לפנינו במקומו בביאור יותר רחב.

§ 6.6.4 ובהיות שהשכלתו אשר בה ידע את עצמו היא השכלת עצם פשוט בתכלית הפשיטות וכל דבר פשוט יהיה בהכרח נודע מכל וכל או נעלם מכל וכל יתחייב אם כן שתהיה ברגע בלתי מתחלק ובכן יתחייב שמציאות הנמצאות מאתו הוא ברגע בלתי מתחלק ובלתי תנועה כי התנועה לא תהיה בלתי זמן והנה ההווה בלתי זמן ובלתי תנועה לא יתהווה כי אם בבריאה כמבואר לעיל. וזה הוא מה שרצינו לבאר.

§ 6.6.5 ולזה כאשר הבין אבן רשד אופן זאת הידיעה הממציאה את הנמצאות בהשכלתה השתומם מאד כמו שבאר בביאורו לספר הנפש מאמר ג׳ פרק ל״ו באמרו: »הנמצאות אין להם מציאות כי אם מציאות

---

[a] הן] coni. Dunk.; הם a.

cum ipsa substantia cuius est perfectio, et sic haberet ipsa prima causa simul et semel esse actu et potentia quo eandem perfectionem et substantiam quod est inconveniens et penitus inopinabile.

§ 6.6.3 Restat ergo ut eiusdem prime cause scientia non dependeat a causatis entibus. Vel ergo ipsa entia dependent ab ipsa scientia, vel non. Non secundum quia cum ipsa scientia non dependeat ab entibus, ut supra, si similiter ipsa entia non dependerent ab ipsa scientia nullo pacto contingeret ipsa primam causam habere scientiam de entibus, cuius contrarium testantur ordo et colligantia in his entibus apparentes ut supra. Sequitur ergo ut entium esse habeat dependere ab eiusdem prime cause scientia, qua scilicet se ipsam intelligit tanquam veram entium causam, prout plenius infra in suo patebit loco.

§ 6.6.4 Cum autem huiusmodi intellectio sit simplicissime substantie cognitio ergo de ipsa, vel penitus sciri, vel penitus ignorari contingit. Sequitur ergo ut huiusmodi prime cause de se ipsa intellectio vel cognitio habeat in instanti fieri et per consequens entium productio ab ipsa intellectione immediate emanans habuit esse in instanti, productio autem in instanti facta non datur esse nisi creatio ut supra. Quibus patet ut detur necessario Creator et creatio quod est intentum.

§ 6.6.5 Quare Aven R. huiusmodi active scientie genus et entium emanationem merito miratur in comento lib.ᵃ De Anima tertij t.c. 36ᵇ ubi dicit: «Entia enim aliud sunt quam scientia eius scilicet Dei neque cause entium aliud sunt

achieved perfection from something that he had caused, it would follow that at least [the first cause] had caused itself mediately; in fact, the perfection of the substance, especially in the separate substances, would be the same as the perfection of itself. Therefore, the first cause would be concurrently in actuality and in potentiality with regard to its perfection and its substance, and this is incongruous and absurd.

§ 6.6.3 Therefore, it remains that the knowledge of the first cause does not depend on caused existents and that the existents either depend on knowledge, or [they do] not. The second [inference] is not possible, because knowledge does not depend on existents, as proved above. Similarly, if these existents do not absolutely depend on knowledge, the first cause will not have knowledge of existents, and the contrary of this is verified from the order and conjunction [i.e., joining] of existents, as proved above. It follows that one existent depends on knowledge of the first cause, which knows itself, because it is the true cause of existents, as will become clear below [in this book].

§ 6.6.4 This intellection is the knowledge of the simplest substances. Therefore, either it knows the substances perfectly, or it does not know the substances perfectly. It would follow that the intellection or knowledge of the first cause was made in the same instant as itself [i.e., the first cause], and consequently, the generation of existents, which are immediately emanated from intellection, occurred in the same instant, and also generation made in the same instant only occurred through creation, as proved above. From these [things], it is clear that there is necessarily a creator and creation, which is what was intended.

§ 6.6.5 And therefore, Averroes observes the origin of active knowledge and the emanation of existents in his Commentary on *On the Soul* 3, text. 36,ᵃ where he states: "The existents are nothing other than knowledge—namely, God's knowledge—and also the causes of the existents

---

ᵃ lib.] coni. Copp.; libr. b.   ᵇ 36] bᶜᵒʳʳ; 136 b; 36 L.   ᵃ Cf. *De an.* 3.7.431b.

the existents only have an existence through His knowledge. And how wondrous is this order, and how [wondrous] is this kind of existence." And therefore, he says in *The Incoherence of the Incoherence* 12, second investigation: "It is not appropriate to draw any | comparison between divine and human knowledge, because divine [knowledge], insofar as it does not grasp anything except itself, is uncaused, and insofar as it enacts [everything] besides it, since it is a first cause, it is efficient knowledge."[a] And it seems that the Poet was astonished by this (Psalm 104:24): "How many are the things You have made, O ha-Shem! You have made them all with wisdom," which means: their existence comes from the knowledge of God and His wisdom, and God's knowledge of them does not come from them, and therefore, it is wondrous in his eyes.

27r

§ 6.7.1 We answer, if so, to permit the aforementioned thesis, that it is necessary that there is a creator who created and brought forth the existents after non-existence and absolute nothingness.

§ 6.7.2 It seems that the same is necessary in the opinion that Averroes reports, citing Aristotle, in [the Commentary on] *Metaphysics* 7, text. 31:[b] "Aristotle held the opinion that there is a mover that is separate from matter. [This is] what he recognises from the existence of intellectual powers, since the intellectual powers [i.e., faculties], for him, are separate from matter. And therefore, it follows that a thing that is unmixed with matter is generated in this way from a thing that is absolutely unmixed with matter, as it is necessary that everything mixed with matter is generated from a thing mixed with matter." And he [i.e., Averroes] says the same in *The Incoherence of the Incoherence* 3, eighteenth investigation.[c] And since the substance of the separate things only has an intellectual form—and therefore it is an absolutely simple substance that does not inform a substrate that acquires a form through the movement of generation—[it is] clear that the production [i.e., creation] of this substance can only be creation [out of nothing], and therefore, it becomes clear that a creator and creation exist. And this is what we wanted to explain.

§ 6.8 However, to the opponent's arguments, saying first that nothing is generated out of nothing and that it therefore follows that there could not be existence after absolute non-existence, we answer: this does not have to be so at all, because [we] also [say that] nothing is generated out of nothing, because in the existing reality, there is not [even] a part of something that does not entirely exist in

---

[a] Cf. *Incoherence* 280. [b] *Metaph.* 7.10.1034b. [c] Cf. *Incoherence* 126–127.

quam scientia eius. Et quam mirabilis est iste ordo et quam extraneus est iste modus essendi etc.» Quare idem in lib. *Destructionis D.*, in disputatione XII, dubio 2 ait: «Nulla debet fieri comparatio inter scientiam divinam et humanam. Quoniam enim alia non intelligit est impassibilis et in quantum alia efficit est scientia agens etc.»

§ 6.7.1 Ad dubium ergo respondetur: quod datur necessario creatio et per consequens Creator dans scilicet esse post purum non esse.

§ 6.7.2 Et idem videtur sequi ad opinionem Phylosophi quam Aven R. refert in comento lib. *Metaphysicorum* VII t.c. 31 ubi dicit: «Sed movit Arist. ad ponendum | moventem separatum a materia in factione virtutum intelligentium quia virtutes intellectuales apud eum sunt non mixte cum materia, unde necesse est ut illud quod est non mixtum cum materia generetur quoquo modo a non mixto cum materia simpliciter, quemadmodum necesse est ut omne mixtum cum materia generetur ex mixto cum materia» et idem habetur ab eodem Aven R. in lib. *Destructionis D.*, disputatione tertia dubio 18. Cumque abstractorum substantia sit quid simplicissimum cum sit intellectualis forma tantum ad cuius productionem non datur intervenire subiectum per generationis motum in illa substantia conversum, patet quidem quod huiusmodi substantie productionis nil aliud sit quam creatio. Et per consequens datur creatio et Creator, quod est intentum.

§ 6.8 Ad argumenta vero et primo quoad primum: quo scilicet dicitur quod cum ex nihilo nihil fiat sequitur ut non detur esse post purum non esse. Respondetur negando consequentiam: licet et non. Detur fieri ex nihilo cum nulla detur nihili pars de qua verificetur ly ex et quae possit in

are nothing other than His knowledge. And how wondrous is this order, and how foreign is this mode of being." And he explicates [this] in *The Incoherence of the Incoherence* 12, second doubt, where he states: "It is not appropriate to draw any comparison between divine and human knowledge, because divine [knowledge], insofar as it cannot understand anything except itself, is uncaused, and insofar as it enacts [everything] outside of itself, since it is a first cause, it is efficient knowledge."[a]

§ 6.7.1 To dispel any doubt, I would argue that creation necessarily does exist, and consequently, there is a creator who brings forth out of absolute nothingness.

§ 6.7.2 And the same seems to follow from the opinion of the Philosopher, which Averroes reports in the Commentary on *Metaphysics* 7, text. 31,[b] where he states: "Aristotle is quoted saying that there is | a mover that is separate from matter in the act of the creation of the intellectual powers, because the intellectual faculties, for him, are separate from matter. And therefore, it has to be the case that a thing that is unmixed with matter is generated from a thing that is absolutely unmixed with matter, as it is necessary that everything mixed with matter is generated from a thing mixed with matter," as Averroes explicates in *The Incoherence of the Incoherence* 3, eighteenth doubt.[c] Since the substance of the separate existents is simple, because it is only an intellectual form of generation in which there is no substrate that acquires a form through the movement of generation, it is clear that the production of this substance is nothing other than creation. Therefore, it becomes clear that there is creation and a creator, which is what was intended.

§ 6.8 In response to the first argument, I will reply: nothing is produced from nothing, and it would follow that nothing can be after absolute nothingness. I will reply by rejecting the inference: nothing is produced from nothing because there is no part of a thing for which it is possible to verify that it was [produced] out [of nothing] and which is

---

[a] Cf. *Incoherence* 280.   [b] *Metaph.* 7.10.1034b.   [c] Cf. *Incoherence* 126–127.

a way that is described as [being] "[made] out of" [something]. But from [the fact] that change into another thing is possible, it does not necessarily follow that a thing cannot be created out of nothing and without any prior substrate. And this is [possible] through the power of a creator who brings forth the form and its substrate out of nothing, since with regard to the reality of creation, which is the bringing-forth of [something] anew after absolute nothingness, Averroes explains in the Commentary on *Metaphysics* 12, text. 18 [paraphrase][a] that it is not appropriate [to proclaim] a substrate out of which something is newly created by creation [out of nothing], as the aforementioned incongruity would follow, that the words "out of," which proclaim a certain substrate, would be said about the non-existence [of a substrate]. But the contrary is appropriate; that is to say, what is created by creation [out of nothing] is necessarily not created from something, and [it is created] without any substrate, because the existence of the substrate comes to be together with the form in it, and therefore the existence of the whole compound comes to be in the creation.

§ 6.9.1 And to the opponent's argument that if there was a body created [out of nothing], it would then follow that a vacuum would have existed [before this], we answer that this does not have to be so | at all, if we do not assume one incorrect premise by saying the place that body is now occupying existed prior to the body's existence. And this is false, because prior to the body's creation [out of nothing], its place did not exist, neither void nor plenum, as now there is no place at all outside the heavens, as Aristotle explains in *On the Heavens* 1, text. 100,[b] but this place will be created anew together with the body that exists in it now. And this is through the power of a creator who brings both of them forth after absolute non-existence.

§ 6.9.2 And as the Sages of the Nations cannot imagine the possibility of this creation, since it is [absolutely] impossible for them that something can be generated without a prior substrate, as, it seems, Aristotle thought in *Physics* 1, text. 82,[c] and *Metaphysics* 12, text. 12,[d] and Averroes thought in the Commentary on the aforementioned book 12, text. 18, in his endeavour to refute the words of the Mutakallimun [Muslim theologians] while attributing disgraceful words to them. And also, during the ages of the world that came before us, there is no memory of the existence of creation, except in Israel. And therefore, the Creator—may He be exalted—introduces [Himself]

---

[a] Cf. *Metaph.* 12.3.1070a. [b] *Cael.* 1.9.279a. [c] *Phys.* 1.9.192a. [d] *Metaph.* 12.3.1069b.

במציאות חלק דבר שאינו נמצא כלל באופן שיפול עליו הוראת ⟨מן⟩ ושיוכל להתהפך אל דבר אחר לא יתחייב מזה שלא יתחדש דבר לא מדבר ובלתי שום נושא קודם וזה בכח בורא ממציא הצורה ונושאה לא מדבר. כי אמנם למציאות הבריאה אשר היא המצאת מחודש אחר העדר מוחלט כאשר באר אבן רשד בביאור ספר מה שאחר מאמר י״ב פרק י״ח לא יאות נושא אשר ממנו יתהווה מחודש בבריאה באופן שיתחייב הנמנע הנזכר שתיבת ⟨מן⟩ שהיא מורה איזה נושא נאמר[a] אותה על נעדר המציאות אבל יאות בה הפך זה רצוני לומר שהמחודש בבריאה יתחדש בהכרח לא מדבר. ובלתי שום נושא כי אמנם יתהוה בה מציאות הנושא עם הצורה בו ובכן יתהוה בה מציאות כל המורכב.

§ 6.9.1 ועל אשר טען החולק באמרו שאם היה איזה גוף נברא היה מתחייב מציאות ריקות נשיב שלא יתחייב זה | כלל אם לא שנניח הנחה אחת כוזבת ונאמר שקודם מציאות הגוף היה מציאות המקום אשר הוא בו ועתה וזה שקר כי קודם בריאת הגוף לא היה מקומו במציאות לא ריק ולא מלא כמו שעתה חוץ לשמים אין מקום כלל כמו שביאר ארסטו׳ בספר השמים מאמר א׳ פרק ק׳ אבל נתחדש אותו המקום יחדו עם הגוף הנמצא בו עתה וזה בכח בורא שהמציא שניהם אחר העדר מוחלט.

§ 6.9.2 וכאשר לא יכלו חכמי האומות לצייר אפשרות הבריאה בהיות נמנע אצלם שיתהוה דבר בלתי נושא קודם כאשר נראה שחשב ארסטו׳ בספר השמע מאמר א׳ פרק פ״ב ובספר מה שאחר מאמר י״ב פרק י״ב[b] ואבן רשד בביאור הספר הנזכר מאמר י״ב פרק י״ח בהתאמצו לסתור דברי המדברים ויחס להם דברים מגונים. על כן לעולמים אשר היו מלפנינו לא היה זכרון מציאות בריאה כי אם בישראל. ולכן יקרא הבורא יתברך אצלנו בג׳ שמות הקדש בראשונה

---

[a] נאמר] a, coni. Dunk.; לא נאמר a[corr]. [b] י״ב] emend. Dunk.; ל׳ a; 12 b.

aliquid converti, hoc tamen non obstat quin[a] detur aliquid de novo productum non ex aliquo precedente subiecto. Et hoc per creationem ad quam non requiritur subiectum ad ipsam precedens ex quo habeat fieri. Immo creatio prout Aven R. in libris *Metaphysicorum* XII t.c. 18 ait, est quoddam productionis genus per quod non minus subiectum quam forma totumque compositum habent post merum non esse produci. Quare in ea non sequitur illud inconveniens ut aliquid producatur ex eo quod non est, immo creati proprium est produci non ex aliquo per creativam potentiam illud producentem.

§ 6.9.1 Quo autem ad secundum argumentum quo, scilicet, arguitur: quoad corporum creationem sequeretur ut daretur vacuum, negatur consequentia. Ad illam enim presupponitur ut ante huiusmodi corporis productionem habuisset necessario esse eiusdem corporis locus quod est falsum, immo ante corporis creationem nullus habuit esse locus neque vacuus neque plenus sicut nunc extra celum nullus datur locus, prout habetur a Phylosopho in lib. *De Celo* primi t.c. 100, sed habuit ipse corporis locus simul et semel cum ipso corpore per creationem produci.

§ 6.9.2 Cumque Gentilium sapientes nunquam potuissent huiusmodi creationis possibilitatem imaginari habentes pro penitus inconveniens ut detur productio non dato subiecto quod agens deducat de potentia ad actum. Prout videtur Phylosophus opinari *Metaphysicorum* XII t.c. 12 et Aven R. ibidem t.c. 18. Ubi theologis aperte oppugnat illisque plura imputat turpia quae tamen theologorum nonnullis falso attribuit. Ideo superioribus seculis apud Hebreos tantum facta est de creatione vel Creatore aliqua mentio. Quare in Sacris Hebreorum Scripturis Creator

able to change into another thing. However, no difficulty arises, because there is something that is generated anew and [that is] not generated from another substrate that is prior to it; rather, it will be generated through creation, in which a substrate that was prior to it is not required. Indeed, creation, as Averroes explicates in *Metaphysics* 12, text. 18,[a] is a kind of production by which not only the substrate, but also the form and the composite occur out of absolute nothingness. This incongruity does not follow in those things, that something is produced from another thing that did not exist before. Indeed, the essence of a created existent is not produced from nothing, but is produced by creative power, which generates those things.

§ 6.9.1 In response to the second argument, I will reply: from the creation of bodies, it would follow that there was a void. I will reply by rejecting the inference. For it was previously supposed that before the generation of a body, there is necessarily a space for that body, but this is incorrect. Indeed, before the creation of a body, there is no space, whether void or full, just as now there is no space at all outside the heavens, as the Philosopher explains in *On the Heavens* 1, text. 100.[b] Rather, the space for a body is generated by creation together and at the same time as the body.

§ 6.9.2 Therefore, the sages among the Nations [i.e., Gentiles] cannot imagine the possibility of creation, because it is absolutely impossible for them that there would be production but no substrate, because the agent draws out potential into act, as the Philosopher explains in *Metaphysics* 12, text. 12,[c] and Averroes also explicates in the same book 12, text. 18, in which he refutes the opinions of the theologians and attributes disgraceful words to them. In the centuries that came before us, there was no mention of creation or a creator, with the exception of the Jews. For in the Holy Scripture of the Jews, the Creator was mainly called

---

[a] quin] b[corr]; quia b.

[a] Cf. *Metaph.* 12.3.1070a.   [b] *Cael.* 1.9.279a.   [c] *Metaph.* 12.3.1069b.

to us with three holy names. First and substantially, they teach [us] about the truth of the creation [out of nothing] and the necessity of bringing-forth. The first [name] is "Elohim" [God], which teaches [us] that He is a governor and an arranger of the order of existence. And from this order, which appears to be intended for a final purpose, it becomes clear that He brought it forth on purpose. And therefore, it follows that He created it, as was explained above in the second demonstration of this thesis. And the second name for God—may He be exalted—is "Shin-Dalet-Yod'" [Shaddai], [which teaches us] that His existence suffices for the activity designated for Him without [the] existence [of anything] besides Him, as is necessary for a first existent. And therefore, no existent besides Him will boast. And therefore, it follows that He is the Creator, as explained above in the third demonstration of this thesis. The third name for God—may He be exalted—is the special name of four letters [i.e., the Tetragrammaton], which teaches [us] that He brought forth the existence [of the created world] in its entirety after absolute non-existence and provides perpetuity to it, since after He brought it forth, it would not have had an enduring existence if existence did not emanate on it from its forth-bringer, without any foundation of existence besides that which comes from the first efficient cause, which is the forth-bringer and a creator and a provider of perpetuity for existence through His self-intellection. And therefore, it follows that He is a creator, as was explained above in the fourth demonstration of this thesis. And therefore, among us this name is called the "special name," because with all the teachings [bound] to this name, it does not have anything in common with another god. And therefore, in the book of Job—which is said to have been written by Moses—our teacher, peace upon him where he reports the opinions of the sages of the Gentiles, who did not think about the possibility of creation [out of nothing], this special name [i.e., the Tetragrammaton] is not mentioned, but solely the name "Eloha" [i.e., a god]. For they thought that there was a mover and an arranger of order, but they did not know and did not think that the existing reality had a true agent, as was the opinion of Averroes and others, as explained in the Commentary on *On the Heavens* 4, text. 1, and also in *The Incoherence of the Incoherence* 3, eighth and tenth investigations, in his word[s] against those who follow the opinions of Plato.[a]

---

[a] Cf. *Incoherence* 100–101; 103–104.

tribus principaliter appellatur nominibus quorum unum significat ipsum esse | universi Rectorem et Ordinatorem, quo ordine ad finem sensu apparente indicatur ipsum esse eiusdem universi voluntarium efficientem, et per consequens eiusdem Creatorem, prout supra in secunda huius questionis resulutione habetur. Secundum vero nomen quo idem Creator ibidem appellatur, significat quod est ens quoddam quod sufficit, scilicet, ad actionem sibi propriam faciendum secluso quocumque alio ente, et hoc non contingit nisi Creatori ad eius actionem quae est creatio nullum requiritur subiectum, prout supra diffusius in tertia habetur demonstratione. Tertium vero nomen eidem Deo attributum est illud quod quatuor annotatur litteris quod Greci Tetragrammaton dicebant, per quod nomen significatur universi Creator et eiusdem essentie Conservator, universum enim cum sit quid productum ut supra non per se habet essentiam et perdurationem nisi pro quanto eidem ab eodem emanat Creatore, creata enim cum per se non habuissent esse quare non ab eterno sed per essentiam a Creatore emanantem, prout supra; scilicet per benignam eiusdem intellectionis naturam, quae est quid idem cum eo. Patet quod multo minus haberent continuam vel perseverantem essentiam. Quare huiusmodi nomen tanta significans, sibi Creatori proprium dicitur. Quare in originali Hebreorum textu ubi in libri Job dialogo narrantur Gentilium opiniones. Qui scilicet universum putarunt habere conservatorem et ordinatorem non autem Entificantem sive Creatorem aliquid actu producentem post purum non esse, numquam ponitur huiusmodi Dei nomen sed nomen tantum significans ipsum Rectorem Ordinatorem et Conservatorem, qualem tantum ipsum esse perceperunt, sicut et Aven R. opinari videntur in commento lib. *De Celo* IV t.c. 1 et in lib. *Destructio Des.*, disputatione tertia dubio 8 et 10 contra Platonicos sermonem faciens.

by three names. | One of them means that He is the governor of the universe and the arranger [i.e., Elohim] through the order that is manifest towards a final purpose, and it is revealed that He is the voluntary efficient cause of the universe and consequently that He is also its Creator, as was proved above in the second thesis. The second true name by which the Creator is called [i.e., "Shin," "Dalet," "Yod"] means that His essence suffices for His proper activity excluding every other being, and this is possible only for the activity of the Creator, because creation does not require a substrate, as is proved above in the third demonstration. His third true name is a special attribute of God that is written with four letters, which the Greeks called the *Tetragrammaton*. This name means "Creator of the universe and preserver of its essences," because if the universe is generated, as proved above, it does not have essence and perpetuity in itself, but [only] according to what is emanated by the Creator. And then created things do not exist in themselves, and they are not eternal, but they exist by means of the essence that emanates from the Creator, as aforementioned, meaning that this essence is emanated by means of the good nature of His intellection, which is identical with Him, and it is evident that existents have [something that is] far inferior to a continuous or permanent essence. And then in the original book of the Jews, in the [Holy] Book of Job, which narrates the opinions of the Gentiles—who think that the universe has a ruler and an arranger, but do not think that there is a creator of beings or a creator who, through his activity, produced something out of absolute nothingness—the name of God was not specified, but only the name that means "governor, ruler, and arranger," as they perceive this being. Averroes explicates this in the Commentary on *On the Heavens* 4, text. 1, and in *The Incoherence of the Incoherence* 3, eighth and tenth doubts, against those who follow the opinions of Plato.[a]

---

[a] Cf. *Incoherence* 100–101; 103–104.

§ 6.9.3 But the Torah of our God is the only [book] that declares it [i.e., creation out of nothing] with proofs that hint | to the three aforementioned holy names, as explained above. And it adds, to give a proof that teaches [us] that the existing reality has a forth-bringer, a creator (Genesis 2:4): "These are the generations of the heavens and the earth when they were created." That means: through the conjunction of the heavens with the earth, since they are connected and congruent through their act of generation, which is especially mentioned in the story of the third, fifth, and sixth days [of creation], it becomes clear that this [means] "when they were created" through the power of a creator who brought them forth and arranged their order, in such a way that they are connected by [acts of] generation ordered by Him, as it [i.e., the Torah] explains when it continues, saying (Genesis 2:4): "On the day that God, ha-Shem, made earth and heavens." If their creation and their making had not occurred—that is, their existence and their order [had not been] brought forth by an intending forth-bringer—then this would have been mere chance. And it is incongruous that this [i.e., mere chance] could be in so many different things and be continuously [there], as explained above.

§ 6.10 And Moses—our teacher, peace be upon him—explains this very same demonstration (Deuteronomy 4:39): "And know therefore this day and keep in mind that ha-Shem alone is God in the heavens above and on earth below; there is no other," which means that from the conjunction of the higher [realms] and the lower [parts of the world] and the governance of their order, which would be incongruous without the intention of a forth-bringer who brought them forth, it becomes clear that ha-Shem, who generates and gives existence, is Elohim [God], who governs and arranges order. And therefore, it becomes clear that [there is] nothing else, because the existence of more than one creator would be incongruous, as will be explained to us below by proof, and also in Proverbs (3:19), which says: "Ha-Shem founded the earth by wisdom." It [i.e., Holy Scripture] proves the existence of creation [as] in the fourth demonstration explained above in this thesis. And this is so because after it becomes clear from the order that is commonly [known] in existing reality, for which it is incongruous that the existence of this order should happen by chance, it follows that He is the forth-bringer who founded [it] through wisdom and adjusted [it] through understanding. And it is impossible that His wisdom and His understanding of the existents should come to Him from the existents, as explained above, but instead it is by His self-intellection only. And since His self-intellection is timeless, it then follows that His activ-

6. DE CREATIONE

§ 6.9.3 Quare Sacrum Genesis Documentum talia demonstrative docere intendens, ibidem [2:4] ait: «Iste sunt generationes celi et terre quando creati sunt.» Quasi dicat quod per colligatum celestium et terrestrium concursum in generationibus apparentem, in quo tot diversa simul concurrere requiruntur, quare patet non contingere casu sive preter alicuius intentum, sequitur quidem ut illa omnia habuissent esse a quodam finem intendente. Illa scilicet non casu sed voluntarie producente, et per consequens horum Creator cum non detur precedens subiectum ex quo habuissent produci, prout per illud divinum nomen superius dictum ostenditur, quod scilicet in preallegato testu scribitur per quod Entificans sive Creator significatur.

§ 6.10 Et eadem replicatur demonstratio in Sacro Deuteronomij Documento [4:39] ubi dicit: «Scito hodie et cogitato in corde tuo quod Dominus est ipse Deus in celo sursum et in terra deorsum etc.» Quasi dicat quod per ordinem et colligationem inter celestia et terrestria apparentem convenit nos cogitare. Quod non contingit ut omnia huiusmodi colligata et sapienter ordinata habuis|sent esse preter alicuius intentum, ut supra, sed a Domino scilicet ab Entificante sive Creatore ut supra. Qui est ipse Deus scilicet idem quod Rector sive Ordinator ut supra, cuius ordo in omnibus patet.

§ 6.9.3 The Holy Book of Genesis (2:4) teaches the same, saying: "These are the generations of the heavens and the earth, when they were created," which means that this conjunction of heaven and earth is the evident combination in generated things, in which different things need to be combined at the same time, because this does not occur by chance or without intention. It would follow that all existents exist for a purpose; they were not made by chance, but by an intentional producer. Consequently, they were produced by their creator, because there was no prior substrate from which they were produced, as is proved by means of the divine name in this aforementioned chapter, and this is the reason, because a creator of beings is a creator.

§ 6.10 And this demonstration is also explained in the Holy Book of Deuteronomy (4:39), saying: "Know therefore this day and keep in mind that the Lord alone is God in heaven above and on earth below; there is no other, etc.," which means that one must think that there is an order and a conjunction between heaven and earth, because it is impossible that every existent that is connected and wisely ordered should exist without intention, as proved above. Rather, every existent is joined and wisely ordered | by the Lord; that is, by the Maker of beings or the Creator, as mentioned above; that is God, the ruler and the arranger, as aforementioned, whose order appears in them all.

ity when He founded and adjusted [the heavens and the earth] through His aforementioned self-intellection was creation, which alone is a timeless activity. And he [i.e., Solomon] explains this by mentioning the name of the Special One, which tells of a creator and a forth-bringer (Proverbs 3:19): "Ha-Shem founded by wisdom, etc."

כן שפעלתו כאשר יסד וכונן בהשכלתו הנזכרת תהיה בריאה שהיא לבדה פעלה בלתי זמן וזה ביאר בהזכירו שם המיוחד המורה בורא וממציא באמרו: »ה׳ בחכמה יסד וכו׳« (שם).

6. DE CREATIONE

§7 Seventh:
We will inquire whether the creator is a body [i.e., corporeal] or a power in a body, or neither of them [i.e., incorporeal].

And it seems at the beginning of the inquiry that one could not think that an incorporeal principle could exist.

§7.1 [This is so,] because, as Averroes explains citing the [position of the] Sabaean people in the Commentary on *Metaphysics* 12, text. 41,[a] since it is evident for many [people] that the heavens are eternal, it is possible to believe that there is no principle besides them in existing reality, because, as the Philosopher says: "If it is true that the stars are moved | by a certain corporeal power that is necessarily finite, [and] if their motion is therefore finite, it is only correct if we likewise say that the stars are composed of matter and form, and this is wrong. And therefore, it does not follow that their motion is finite, because it is possible that there is a certain finite power, but that likewise its activity will be infinite, because the reason for being finite and having a limit of duration of motion or activity is exhaustion, which happens to an agent or mover when it is affected by motion. But for the power, which would not be affected, it is not impossible that it should enact an infinite activity, as exhaustion does not occur to it."

§7.2.1 But the contrary of this—namely, that the creator does not have a body and is not a power in a body—becomes clear in this way: because everything corporeal only acts in time [and] with movement in an affected substrate, but the creator acts without time and without movement and without a substrate. If so, the creator is incorporeal. The consequence is self-evident and the [antecedent] premise becomes clear in this way. First, regarding what we said—that no corporeal thing can act on an affected substrate without time and without movement—it becomes clear in this way: because every corporeal agent either (1) acts through its matter, and this according to its qualities, by which a substrate changes one quality for another, or (2) it acts through its form—that is, when a substrate undergoes substantial, local, or quantitative change—and all this [happens] after locomotion, when the agent approaches the affected thing. And it follows for all of these [acts] that there is a time in which it [i.e., the agent] acts on the substrate and moves it, either through a certain quality or through a certain corporeal instrument, through one kind of motion, since every form that acts without quality

---
[a] Cf. *Metaph.* 12.8.1073a.

7. DE INCORPOREITATE

§ 7 Septimo Dubitatur
Utrum idem Creator sit quid corporeum vel sit quid incorporeum.

Et videtur quod non.

§ 7.1 Sit deveniendum ad incorporeum principium quia sicut Aven R. ait auctoritate Zabiorum *Metaphysicorum* XII t.c. 41. Cum putetur declaratum quod corpus celeste sit quid immortale et ab eterno. Possibile est existimare ut non sit opus ponere aliud principium illo nobilius. Illa enim qua de mente Aristotelis dicitur: «Propositio, scilicet, quod si stelle moverentur per potentiam finitam sequeretur quod actio esset finita, videtur non vera nisi cum hoc dicatur ut stelle sint composite ex materia et forma, quod omnino negatur, possibile enim est ut potentia sit finita et cum hoc sit infinite actionis. Quia finitas actionis non contingit nisi per alterationem qua motor alteratur a moto, qua propter accidit lassitudo; illud ergo quod non alteratur non est inconveniens ut faciat infinitam actionem, cum scilicet eidem nulla contingat lassitudo.»

§ 7.2.1 Ad oppositum vero arguitur sic nullum corporeum operatur nisi per motum in subiecto. Creator autem operatur sine motu, ergo Creator est quid non corporeum. Consequentia patet, et antecedens probatur, et primo quo ad primam partem. Quia quodlibet corpus vel est animatum vel est non animatum. Si ergo animatum tunc eiusdem anima tamquam corporea virtus nonnisi per corporea organa operatur suis actionibus propria, sicut patet de sensibus. Si enim sine corpore operetur, tunc esset mera forma per se operans nullo indigens corpore, et sic esset quid abstractum et corpori immixtum nullo pacto corporeum, sicut per se patet. Et habetur a Phylosopho in lib. *De Anima* III t.c. 6 ubi dicit: «Si esset mixtum cum corpore tunc esset in aliqua dispositione aut calidum ut frigidum aut haberet instrumentum sicut habet sentiens etc.» Cum autem operans per corporea organa non contingat ut per illa operetur nisi illa moveat in fieri, dum scilicet per illa alteret subiectum, quare neque ante actionis principium neque expleta actione requiritur instrumentum sed in fieri tantum requiritur ab subiectum alterandum, ut eidem nova

§ 7 Seventh,
it may be inquired whether the creator is corporeal or incorporeal.

And it seems he is not [incorporeal].

§ 7.1 Averroes explicates that [the creator] is corporeal, presenting the position of the Sabaeans, in *Metaphysics* 12, text. 41.[a] For if it is shown that a celestial body is immortal and eternal, it may be assumed that it does not need another principle nobler than it in order to exist. It is therefore stated in the name of Aristotle: "The premise that if the stars are moved according to a finite potential if there are potentialities in the star, then these must be finite would be true only if the stars were composed of matter and form. And this is wrong. Consequently, there must be in them powers whose action is infinite, because the finiteness of the imparted motion and the act are merely due to the influence of the moved object on the mover, so that it is bound to grow tired. But that which does not grow tired is not prevented from exerting an infinite action."

§ 7.2.1 On the contrary it is to argue that a corporeal thing acts only by means of movement in a substrate. However, a creator acts without movement, and thus the creator is incorporeal. The consequence is evident, and the first part of the antecedent is proved, because every corporeal body is either animated or not animated. If it is animated, then its soul as well as its corporeal power act only through corporeal instruments according to their specific activities, as is clear from experience. If it [i.e. the soul] acts without a body, then it is a pure form and does not need a body. If this is true, then it is separate and it is never mixed with a body. This is clear and the Philosopher explains this in *On the Soul* 3, text. 6,[b] where he states: "If it [i.e. the intellectual soul] were to be mixed with a body, it would become somehow qualitative, e.g., hot or cold, or would even have organs, as the sensitive faculty has, etc." Therefore, it would only occur that it was acting through corporeal instruments if it were to move them into coming-to-be, while it affects the substrate through them. For neither the beginning nor the end of an activity needs an instrument, but only in coming-to-be does it need an affected substrate so

---

[a] Cf. *Metaph.* 12.8.1073a.   [b] *De an.* 3.4.429a.

or corporeal instrument is incorporeal, but is undoubtedly a separate substance, as Aristotle explains in *On the Soul* 3, text. 6:[a] "If the intellect was mixed with matter, it would then have a certain quality, such as warmth or coldness, or it would have a corporeal instrument, as the senses have."

§ 7.2.2 But what we said—that the creator is an agent without time and without movement—becomes clear in this way: because there is no medium between being and non-being, since they are two parts of a contradiction, because one of two things is necessarily correct for everything: either (1) it exists, or (2) it does not exist. And since creation [out of nothing] is creation of being after absolute non-being, it necessarily follows that it will be without a prior substrate and without time. And therefore, it also follows that there will be no movement, because there cannot be movement without a time in which the substrate moves from the place in which it is to the place in which it will be, and this is self-evident. And Aristotle explains this in *Physics* 4, text. 129:[b] "It is clear that every change and every movement is temporal, because swiftness and slowness exist in every change." And therefore, | it becomes clear that creation cannot be the activity of any corporeal existent. And therefore, it follows that the creator is an incorporeal existent. And this is what we wanted to explain.

§ 7.3.1 Second, what we said—that the creator is incorporeal—becomes clear in this way: since the mover of the first sphere is necessarily incorporeal, the creator is incorporeal. This consequence becomes clear in this way: because there are many kinds of existents that have order and perpetuity through the movement of that mover, as testified by sense [perception]. It follows that this mover produces it [i.e., order and perpetuity] in one of two ways: either (1) he produces it through his intention for and his investigation into the perpetuity of these species and their order, like an agent who seeks the perpetuity of his actions and their order, and therefore, it follows that this mover is creating them, and, if so, he himself is the creator, or (2) he produces it since he was created by the creator and orderly arranged through the aforementioned creator in order to [give] the aforementioned perpetuity that is intended by the one who is their creator and who seeks their perpetuity and the perpetuity of their order. Because if there was not some kind of aforementioned mover, one of these two, it would follow that it occurred by chance to the creator and to every single kind of his creatures that—without any intending endeavour—there was a mover who arranged

---
[a] *De an.* 3.4.429a. [b] *Phys.* 4.14.222b.

היא בלתי גשמית אבל היא עצם נבדל בלי ספק כמו שביאר ארסטו' בספר הנפש מאמר ג' פרק ו' באמרו: »אם היה השכל מעורב בחומר היה אז באיזו תכונה בחום או בקור או היה לו כלי גשמי כמו שיש לחושים« עכ"ל.

§ 7.2.2 אמנם מה שאמרנו שהבורא הוא פועל בלתי זמן ובלתי תנועה הנה יתבאר באופן זה כי אמנם בין המציאות והעדרו לא יפול שום אמצעי להיותם שני חלקי הסותר כי על כל דבר יצדק בהכרח אחת משתים אם שימצא ואם שלא ימצא ובהיות שהבריאה היא חדוש מציאות אחר העדר גמור יתחייב בהכרח שתהיה בלתי נושא קודם ובלתי זמן ומזה יתחייב גם כן שתהיה בלי תנועה כי לא תהיה שום תנועה זולת זמן אשר בו יתנועע הנושא מגבול מה שממנו לגבול מה שאליו וזה מבואר בעצמו. וביאר אותו ארסטו' בספר השמע מאמר ד' פרק קכ"ט[a] באמרו: »דבר ברור הוא שכל השתנות וכל תנועה יהיו בזמן כי המהירות והאיחור נמצאים בכל השתנות« עכ"ל ומזה יתבאר[b] שהבריאה לא תהיה פעולת שום נמצא גשמי ומזה יתחייב שהבורא הוא נמצא בלתי גשמי וזה הוא מה שרצינו לבאר.

§ 7.3.1 שנית יתבאר זה שאמרנו שהבורא הוא בלתי גשמי באופן זה כי אמנם מניע הגלגל הראשון הוא בהכרח בלתי גשמי אם כן הבורא הוא בלתי גשמי הנה חיוב זאת התולדה יתבאר באופן זה. כי בהיות מיני נמצאים רבים מאד שיש להם סדר וקיום בתנועת אותו המניע כאשר יעיד החוש יתחייב שאותו המניע יעשה זה על אחד משני פנים: אם שיעשה בכוונה ועיון מאתו לקיום אותם המינים וסדרם כמו פועל חפץ בקיום פעליו וסדרם ומזה יתחייב שאותו המניע הוא חדש אותם ואם כן הוא עצמו הבורא, או שיעשה זה בהיותו מחודש מהבורא ומסודר מאת הבורא הנזכר לקיום המכוון מאתו שהוא הבורא

---
[a] קכ"ט] emend. Dunk.; קכ"ד a; 129 b; 129 L. [b] באמרו] a^{corr}; באדו a.

7. DE INCORPOREITATE

introducatur forma. Sequitur ut nullum corporeum operetur nisi per motum, quo scilicet res agenda existit in fieri, prout in prima antecedentis parte dictum est.

§ 7.2.2 Quo autem ad secundam eiusdem partem qua scilicet dicitur quod Creator non operatur per motum probatur primo scilicet quia motus non habet esse nisi in fieri in creatione au|tem nullum datur fieri quia inter purum esse et purum non esse, sive inter aliquid esse et nihil esse patet quod nullum datur medium, et per consequens in illa non datur fieri, quare neque motus qui scilicet habet esse in fieri tantum. Secundo probatur idem quia ad quemlibet motum requiritur tempus prout habetur ratione et auctoritate Phylosophi *Physicorum* IV t.c. 129 ubi dicit: «Manifestum est quod omnis transmutatio et omnis motus fit in tempore, velocius enim et tardius inveniuntur in omni transmutatione etc.» Cum autem creatio sit aliquid esse post purum non esse inter que non datur tempus in quo scilicet non affirmetur alterum contradictorium, patet ergo quod in creatione non datur motus. Quibus patet quod creatio non fit corporei actio,[a] et per consequens Creator est quid non corporeum, quod est intentum.

§ 7.3.1 Secundo arguitur sic: motor primi mobilis est necessario quid incorporeum, ergo et Creator. Consequentia tenet, quia cum omnia reliqua corpora moveat ordinet et conservet, vel hoc contingit casu sive preter alicuius intentum, scilicet sibi motori ut haberent esse tot corpora ab eodem movenda, sine quo casu fuisset quid frustratorium et actione privatum. Similiter casu contigit tot corporibus motis conservatis et ordinatis ut habuisset esse huiusmodi motor sine quo casu fuissent sine huiusmodi motu,

that a new form may be introduced in it. It follows that a corporeal thing acts only through movement, through which an affected thing exists in coming-to-be, according to what was said in the first part of the antecedent.

§ 7.2.2 Then the second part of the antecedent, in which it is said that the creator does not act by motion, is proved, first because in creation, movement only exists in coming-to-be. | Moreover, nothing exists between absolute being and absolute non-being, or in between, because there is no intermediary [i.e., no medium]. Consequently, in creation, nothing exists, because there is no movement in coming-to-be. Second, because time is necessary for any movement according to the argument and authority of the Philosopher in *Physics* 4, text. 129,[a] where he states: "It has become clear that all changes and everything that moves are conditioned by time. For it is a patent fact that every change may be quicker or slower, etc." Now, since creation takes place out of absolute nothingness in which there is no time, it is consequently not possible to affirm one of these contradictions. Therefore, it is clear that no movement is detected in creation. For these reasons, it is evident that creation is not a power in a body, and consequently, the creator is not corporeal, which is what was intended.

§ 7.3.1 Second, I would argue that the mover of the first mobile spheres is necessarily incorporeal; therefore, the creator [is incorporeal]. The consequence is evident, because if [the creator or the first mover] moved, ruled, and perpetuated all [the rest of the] bodies and this happened by chance—namely, without someone's intention—to the mover himself, there would be a mover moving all bodies without a cause, which is something futile and unproductive. Similarly, it would have happened by chance to the bodies that are moved, preserved, and ordered that there exists a mover. Without this, they would have been

---

[a] corporei actio] b[corr]; corpore in actu b.

[a] *Phys.* 4.14.222b.

their order and their perpetuity, which without him would not be orderly arranged or perpetual. And it would also be necessary that it would occur to the mover by chance that a certain potential matter existed that was disposed for recurring generation, without which the act of this movement would not be possible, because the matter would run out, as mentioned above. And this is not possible by any means. And especially, if we were to say that they existed without the intention of an intending agent, it would follow that they were eternal. If so, their existence would be self-necessary, and this is the contrary of the aforementioned necessity, according to which it is necessary that if no chance occurs, then the existence of their action is impossible. And through the impossibility of their action, their forms would also be impossible or [would exist] futilely [and] would not act.

§7.3.2 And then it would follow, as we said, that for the first mover, one of two cases would be applicable: either (1) that he himself is the creator who created the orderly arranged existents by himself, and therefore, as will be explained to us below, the aforementioned mover is incorporeal, and what we wanted to explain—namely, that the creator is incorporeal—becomes clear; or (2) if we say that the mover is created by the Creator—may He be praised—and orderly arranged by him, then it would also follow that the Creator was incorporeal. Since something [that is] separate [from matter] is indivisible, therefore time and movement and a substrate that changes from one form to another, all of which are necessary for the action of a corporeal agent, do not apply to its creation, as mentioned above.

§7.3.3 It follows that the creator who created this incorporeal mover is also incorporeal. And this is what we said: that the creation of an incorporeal existent can only be [achieved] by an incorporeal creator. Averroes also explains this, referring to Aristotle in [the Commentary on] *Metaphysics* 7, text. 31:[a] "This led Aristotle to say that there is a mover separate from matter who has intellectual powers, since intellectual powers [i.e., faculties] are [found] | in the [things] that are separate from matter. And therefore, it follows that what is not composed of matter is generated from a[nother] thing that is not composed of matter, as it is necessary that every compound containing matter is generated from an existent that is composed of matter."

---

[a] Cf. *Metaph.* 7.10.1034b.

7. DE INCORPOREITATE

ordine, et conservatione et necessaria in mortalibus reciprocatione in tot diversis diversimode observata quod est inopinabile. Quoniam illud quod in pluribus observatur non contigit fuisse casu, preterea quia ut sic habuisset esse non producta sed sic ab eterno, quare non haberent potentiam ad non esse immo ad semper per se esse, quare frustratoria esset conservatoris et ordinatoris operatio.

§ 7.3.2 Restat ergo ut idem motor sit horum omnium productor vel a productore ordinatum et productum. Cum ergo patuerit infra ipsum primum motorem esse quid incorporeum habetur intentum. Nam si idem motor est mobilium productor et per consequens Creator ut supra, patet intentum principale, quod scilicet Creator sit incorporeum, si vero dicatur quod primus motor sit quid productum et ordinatum a mobilium producente sive Creatore, non minus patebit idem intentum, quia cum de eodem motore patuerit ut infra ut sit incorporeum, et per consequens quid indivisibile ad cuius productionem non datur tempus neque motus neque alterabile subiectum, que omnia necessario requiruntur ad corporei actionem ut supra.

§ 7.3.3 Sequitur quidem ut dato eiusdem motoris productore idem productor sive Creator habeat esse quid incorporeum. Quare Aven R. in commento lib. *Metaphysicorum* VII[a] t.c. 31 ait: «Sed movit Aristotelem ad ponendum monens separatum a materia in factione virtutum intelligentium, quia virtutes intellectuales apud eum sunt non mixte cum materia unde necesse est ut illud quod non est mixtum cum materia generetur quoquomodo a non mixto cum materia simpliciter etc.»

without motion, order, and preservation, which is necessarily observed in the reciprocal action of different species of mortal beings, and this would be incongruous. What is observed in many things does not occur by chance, because if something is not produced, then it is eternal, since there would be no potential for non-being, and consequently, it would exist forever, and the action of the order and the arranger would be futile.

§ 7.3.2 It remains either that this mover is the producer of all those things or that [this mover] was ordered and created by a producer. And then, as will be made clear below, one must demonstrate that the first mover is incorporeal, and, for instance, that the mover is the producer of the mobile spheres and is consequently the creator, as mentioned above. It is also clear that our principal aim is [to prove that] the creator is incorporeal. If this is true, one would say that the first mover was created and ordered by the producer of the mobiles; that is, the creator. Moreover, our principal aim is evident, because it is clear that the mover is incorporeal, as proved below, and consequently, he is inseparable from his production, such that there is neither time nor movement nor an affected substrate, because all these things necessarily require a corporeal action, as mentioned above.

§ 7.3.3 It would follow that if the mover of the first mobiles is incorporeal, then the producer or the creator will [also] be incorporeal, as Averroes explicates in the Commentary on *Metaphysics* 7, text. 31,[a] where he states: "Aristotle asserts that there is a mover that is separate from matter in the act of the creation of the intellectual powers, because for him, the intellectual faculties are separate from matter. And therefore, it has to be the case that a thing that is unmixed with matter is generated from a thing that is absolutely unmixed with matter, etc."

---

[a] VII] emend. COPP.; XII b; VII L.

[a] Cf. *Metaph.* 7.10.1034b.

§7.3.4 The [antecedent] premise, in which we said that the first mover is incorporeal, becomes clear from Aristotle's proof in *Physics* 8, text. 85,[a] "It is necessary that it will always [either] thrust or draw," and Averroes explains his words: "Aristotle wants to explain that through the power by which the celestial movement is continuously acting in one and the same way, it becomes clear that the mover is incorporeal." And he continues: "The corporeal mover moves either by thrusting or by drawing or by both of these. And drawing and thrusting will not be [found] together in the approach to and distancing from the moving [thing] at the beginning of the movement and at its end. It then follows that its movement will not be one [and the same] at its beginning and at its end, and therefore the movement will not be continuous." If so, if the movement of the sphere continues in one and the same manner as it is [currently moving], it will not be through the power of any corporeal mover. It follows that the mover of the sphere is an incorporeal existent. And this is what we wanted to explain.

§7.4 We answer, then, to dispel [any] doubt about the aforementioned thesis, that it is necessary that the creator is an incorporeal existent.

§7.5 To the opponent's arguments, we answer that the incorrect opinion of the Sabaean people already became clear through Aristotle's aforementioned proof, which instructs [us] that the movement of the sphere is continuous in one manner, as is evident from sense [perception]. And this is impossible for a corporeal mover, as explained above. It necessarily follows that the mover is an incorporeal existent that is capable of this. And if so, it is a principle and a cause nobler than the heavens and prior to them. And furthermore, it becomes clear from the proofs explained above that the heavens have an incorporeal agent who is their creator. And therefore, it follows that He is prior to them in rank and in cause, as it says (Deuteronomy 33:26): "Rider of the heavens."

§7.6.1 And [Holy] Scripture (Deuteronomy 4:15–16) instructs this: "Be most careful—since you saw no image [of God at Mount Horeb]—not to act wickedly and make for yourselves a sculptured image in any likeness whatever," to remind [us] that we must not err and think that God—may He be praised—is corporeal and make an image depicting Him. And it continues (Deuteronomy 4:19): "And lest you look up to the heavens and behold the sun and the

---

[a] *Phys.* 8.10.267b.

§7.3.4 אמנם ההקדמה שאמרנו בה שהמניע הראשון הוא בלתי גשמי התבאר במופת ארסטו' בספר השמע מאמר ח' פרק פ"ה באמרו: "מן ההכרח הוא שלעולם ידחה או ימשוך כו'." ודבריו אלה באר אבן רשד באמרו: "רצה ארסטו' לבאר שממך התמדת התנועה השמימית על אופן אחד בעצמו יתבאר שהמניע הוא בלתי גשמי." והוסיף ואמר כי "המניע הגשמי בהיות שלא יניע כי אם בדחייה או במשיכה או בשתיהן ועניין המושך והדוחה לא יהיה על אופן אחד מקורבה וריחוק ביחס אל המתנועע בראשית התנועה ובסופה אם כן שתנועתו לא תהיה על עניין אחד בתחלתה ובסופה ואם כן התנועה לא תהיה מתמדת" עכ"ל יאמר אם כן שבהיות תנועת הגלגל מתמדת על עניין אחד אשר כמוהו לא יהיה בכח שום מניע גשמי יתחייב שמניע הגלגל הוא נמצא בלתי גשמי וזה הוא מה שרצינו לבאר.

§7.4 **נשיב** אם כן להתיר ספק החקירה הנזכרת שמן ההכרח הוא שיהיה הבורא נמצא בלתי גשמי.

§7.5 **אמנם** לטענות החולק נשיב שכבר התבאר שקר דעת אנשי הצבא במופת ארסטו' הנזכר המורה שבהיות תנועת הגלגל מתמדת על עניין אחד כמבואר בחוש והיא בלתי איפשרית למניע גשמי כמבואר למעלה יתחייב בהכרח שיהיה המניע נמצא בלתי גשמי יכול על זה ואם כן הוא התחלה וסבה יותר נכבדת מן השמים וקודמת להם ויותר מזה התבאר במופתים המבוארים למעלה המורים שיש לשמים פועל בלתי גשמי הוא בוראם ומזה יתחייב שהוא קודם להם במעלה ובסבה באמרו: "רוכב שמים." (דברים ל"ג כ"ו)

§7.6.1 **וזה** הורה הכתוב באמרו: "ונשמרתם מאד לנפשותיכם כי לא ראיתם כל תמונה וכו'[a] פן תשחיתון ועשיתם לכם פסל תמונת כל סמל" וכו'[b] (דברים ד' ט"ו-ט"ז), להזהיר שלא נטעה ונחשוב שהאל יתברך הוא גשמי ונעשה תמונה מורה עליו. והוסיף ואמר: "ופן תשא עיניך השמימה וראית את השמש ואת הירח" וכו'[c] (דברים ד'

---

[a] וכו'] a corr; כנ"ז a.   [b] וכו'] coni. Dunk.; כנ"ז a.   [c] וכו'] coni. Dunk.; כנ"ז a.

7. DE INCORPOREITATE

§ 7.3.4 Antecedens vero quo scilicet dicitur quod motor primi mobilis est quid incorporeum probatur ratione et auctoritate Phylosophi in libro *Physicorum* VIII t.c. 85[a] ubi dicit: «Necesse est ut semper expellat vel attrahat etc.» ubi Aven R. exponens ait: «Vult declarare quod ex ipsa continuatione motus sequitur quod iste motor non sit corpus etc.» ubi subdit dicens: «Motor enim corporeum cum non moveat nisi expellendo vel attrahendo vel utrumque agendo. Attrahens vel expellens non eodem modo se habent circa illud quod movetur in principio expulsionis vel attractionis et in eius fine, scilicet in propinquitate et remotione. Motor ergo qui est corpus non est consimilium dispositionum apud illud quod movetur. Motus ergo ab illo non est continuus etc.» Quibus, scilicet, infert: quod cum motus primi mobilis sit continuus et uniformis qualis non datur fieri per corporeum motorem, sequitur ut eiusdem motionis motor sit quid incorporeum, quod est intentum.

§ 7.4 Ad dubium ergo respondetur quod Creator sive Entificans est necessario quid incorporeum.

§ 7.5 Ad argumentum vero respondetur: quod huiusmodi Zabiorum opinio reprobatur, et penitus redarguitur per preallegatam Phylosophi rationem. Qua scilicet per continuationem et uniformitatem motus sensu apparentis probatur, quod illius motor est necessario quid incorporeum et celo nobilius, cum possit continue et uniformiter movere, quod scilicet non possit idem celum neque virtus in eo cum sit quid corporeum ut supra. Et idem patet preallegatis rationibus et auctoritatibus quibus scilicet patuit, quod datur celi agens vel creans quod est proculdubio incorporeum et celo nobilius.

§ 7.6.1 Quare Sacrum Deuteronimij Documentum cap. 4 [4:15–16] ait: «Custodite valde animas vestras quoniam non vidistis aliquod simulacrum in die qua locutus est Dominus vobis in Horeb a medio ignis, ne faciatis vobis sculptum similitudinem, aut imaginem masculi vel femine etc.» Quibus monet ne quis deceptus putans Deum esse quid corporeum faciat aliquam imaginem ad illum representandum. Subdit paulo post dicens [4:19]: «Ne forte levatis oculis ad celum videas solem et lunam et omnia astra celi

§ 7.3.4 The antecedent, in which it was said that the mover of the first mobile spheres is incorporeal, is proved according to the argument and authority of the Philosopher in *Physics* 8, text. 85,[a] where he states: "It is necessary that it always thrusts or draws," and Averroes explicates: "He explains that the motion proceeds from this continuity; therefore, the motor is incorporeal." He continues: "The corporeal mover can only move either by thrusting or by drawing or by [doing] both of these. The drawing and thrusting are not to be found in the same manner in relation to a moving thing at the beginning of the motion and at its end; that is, in a state of thrusting or drawing. And then the mover that is a body will not have the same disposition in relation to a moving thing. Movement will not be continuous, etc." With these [words], it is explained that the movement of the first mobiles is continuous and uniform and that it was not produced by a corporeal mover. Therefore, it would follow that the mover of the mobiles is incorporeal, and this is what was intended.

§ 7.4 To dispel any doubt, I would argue that the creator—namely, "the creator of beings"—is necessarily incorporeal.

§ 7.5 In response to the arguments, I will reply: the opinion of the Sabaeans is refuted by the Philosopher [and] proved by the continuity and uniformity of the motion, as the senses testify. The mover is necessarily incorporeal and nobler than the heavens, because he can move infinitely and uniformly, and this would not be possible if the creator were corporeal, as is the case for the heavens and his power, as mentioned above. It is clear from the aforementioned arguments that there is an agent of the heavens, or a creator who is incorporeal and nobler than the heavens.

§ 7.6.1 Therefore, the Holy Book of Deuteronomy 4 (4:15–16) states: "So for your own sake, therefore, be most careful, since you saw no shape when the Lord your God spoke to you at Horeb out of the fire, not to act wickedly and make for yourselves a sculptured image in any likeness whatever: the form of a man or a woman, etc." With these [words], [Deuteronomy] reminds us that we must not err and consider God to be corporeal, making an image to represent Him. And then (4:19): "Beware so that you do not lift up your eyes to the heavens and see the sun and the moon and

---

[a] VIII t.c. 85] emend. Copp.; V, 55 b; VIII, 85 L.

[a] *Phys.* 8.10.267b.

moon," to remind [us] that we will fall into the same error as the Sabaeans, who thought that the celestial bodies were nobler [than everything] that exists and that there was no principle besides them in existing reality, and therefore, we [would] think that it was appropriate to worship them.

§ 7.6.2 And it [i.e., Holy Scripture] gives proof of the error of their thought (Deuteronomy 4:19): "Ha-Shem your God allotted these to all nations," which means: because of the order that appears in the hosts of the heavens, who serve the many nations in their different | orbits as they need it. And it does not come to mind that this is in all of them by chance, but [rather] by the order of an intending agent. And therefore, it becomes clear that He brings all of them forth after absolute non-existence, and this is necessarily through the power of an incorporeal creator, who is necessarily prior to them in rank and in cause, as we explained above. It is appropriate, if so, that we do not worship anybody besides Him and that we do not make an image to depict Him and to remind us of Him, because He is incorporeal, as mentioned before. And this is indicated by mentioning the "special name" [i.e., the Tetragrammaton], which instructs [us] that the whole of existing reality was generated by Him and that this is only possible through the power of a creator who cannot possibly be corporeal, as we have explained.

י״ט), להזהיר שלא נטעה בטעות אנשי הצבא החושבים שהגרמים השמימיים הם היותר נכבדים שבמציאות ושאין למציאות התחלה זולתם ולזה נחשוב שראוי לעבדם.

§ 7.6.2 ונתן מופת על שבוש מחשבתם באמרו: »אשר חלק ה׳ אלהיך אותם לכל העמים,« (שם) כלומר כי הסדר הנראה בצבא השמים המשרתים לעמים רבים באופנים | מתחלפים כפי המצטרך להם ולא יעלה על לב שהיה זה בכלם במקרה אבל בסדר פועל מכוין. ומזה יתבאר שהוא המציא את כלם אחר העדר מוחלט. וזה בהכרח בכח בורא בלתי גשמי הוא בהכרח קודם להם במעלה ובסבה כאשר בארנו למעלה. ראוי אם כן שלא נעבוד לזולתו ולא נעשה תמונה להורות עליו ולהזכירו לנו בהיותו בלתי גשמי כנזכר. וזה הורה בהזכירו ‹השם המיוחד› המורה היות כל מציאות הווה מאתו וזה לא יתכן זולתי בכח בורא אשר הוא מן הנמנע היותו גשמי כמה שבארנו.

7. DE INCORPOREITATE

et errore deceptus adores ea et colas quae divisit Dominus Deus tuus in ministerium cunctis populis etc.»

§ 7.6.2 Ubi postquam monuisset cavere errorem putantium Deum esse quid corporeum. Monet ut neque incurramus Zabiorum opiniones putantium scilicet ut celestia sint omnium entium nobilissima et merito colenda. Deinde ostendit utriusque opinionis errorem dicens [Deut 4:19]: «Que divisit Dominus Deus tuus in ministrum etc.» Quasi dicat quod per tot gentium ministerium quod scilicet fit tanto celestium ordine de quo patet quod non contigit casu scilicet preter alicuius intentum, sequitur quidem illud fieri cuiusdam id intendentis iussu et ordine, de quo ordinante inopinabile est ut casu invenisset tot ordinanda ad | suum huiusmodi finem consequendum disposita. Quare sequitur ut illa produxisset, cum autem huiusmodi productio non contigit fuisse nisi per creationem, sequitur quidem ut idem productor sit quid incorporeum et celo nobilius tanquam Creator sive Entificans quod per ly Dominus Hebraice significatur. Quare neque imagines corporea presentantes neque celestia colere convenit, sed idem entificans tantum sive Creator incorporeus scilicet et omnium nobilissimus colendus est.

the stars, all the vast army of the heavens, so that you are not lured away and do not bow down to them and worship them—things that the Lord your God has allotted to all the nations under all the heavens., etc."

§ 7.6.2 Afterwards, [Deuteronomy] reminds us to pay attention to the errors of one who thinks that God is corporeal and reminds us not to adopt the opinion of the Sabaeans, who think that the celestial bodies are nobler than all other beings and worship them for this reason. After that, [Deuteronomy] shows us the errors of both opinions, saying (4:19): "The Lord your God has allotted to all, etc.," which means that the service of all the nations as well as the order in the hosts of the heavens does not occur by chance, but by someone's intention. Indeed, it would follow that what is produced by His order | and will cannot occur by chance, since every ordered thing proceeds from His purpose. Since He produced everything, this kind of production only occurs through creation. Then, it would follow that the producer is incorporeal and nobler than the heavens and that the "Creator" or "Creator of beings" means "Lord" for the Jews. Moreover, it is not appropriate to adore corporeal images or celestial images, but rather we must worship only the "Creator of beings," or the Creator who is incorporeal and nobler than all beings.

§ 8 Eighth:
We will inquire whether there exists only one creator or a great number of creators.

And it seems at the beginning of the inquiry that there are many.

§ 8.1 And the proof of this is an argument made by many of the Ancients that Averroes recounts in *Metaphysics* 12, text. 52,[a] that since it is necessary that contraries have contrary principles, the good and the evil, which appear in reality as contraries, it is necessary to think that there are at least two principles and agent causes in reality, one of whom created the good things and the other of whom created the evil things, because sense [perception] testifies that although there are many [things] that are good amongst the natural things, there are also some that are undoubtedly evil. And therefore, it seems that they are two [creators] who bring forth and create, and two governments.

§ 8.2 But the contrary of this becomes clear; that is to say that there is only one creator and there is no creator besides him who is equal to him, first from Aristotle's proof in *Metaphysics* 10, text. 7:[b] "In affections and in qualities and in [all] kinds of quantity and in [all] kinds of movement, there is one." And Averroes explains his words: "In the kinds of affections, qualities, quantities, and movements; in every one of them, there exists one, which is the principle of number of this kind." And he continues: "And what is connected to this is what became clear in the natural sciences [i.e., physics], and this is that there is a first eternal mover who is absolutely separate from all matter. And it became clear that he is a principle not as a mover only, but also as form and end [i.e., final purpose]. It also became clear that he is the existent who is the principle of the substance." With these words, they explain that it becomes clear from research that in every species, things come to one existent, which is the principle of this species. [It is] appropriate that this is also [the case] in the category of substance, which come | to one, which is the principle of the category of substance, and this is the first mover. And the same seems to result from their words in *Metaphysics* 12, text. 39.[c] And since it was already made clear above [either] (1) that the creator himself, who is only one, is the first mover, or (2) that he is a nobler existent than the first mover and that he created the aforementioned mover, which, since he is indivisible, is possible only through one alone [and] through the power of a creator, as mentioned

---

[a] Cf. *Metaph.* 12.10.1075a. [b] Cf. *Metaph.* 10.1.1052b. [c] *Metaph.* 12.7.1072b.

---

§ 8 שמינית נחקור אם נמצא במציאות בורא אחד בלבד או ימצאו בוראים רבים במספר

ונראה בתחלת העיין שיהיו רבים.

§ 8.1 והראיה על זה היא טענת[a] רבים מהקדמונים אשר ספר אבן רשד בספר מה שאחר מאמר י״ב פרק נ״ב באמרו שבהיות שלהפכים ראוי שתהיינה התחלות הפכיות והטוב והרע הנראים במציאות הם הפכיים הנה ראוי לחשוב שתהיינה לפחות שתי התחלות וסבות פועלות במציאות אחת מהן מחדשת הטובות והשנית מחדשת הרעות כי אמנם יעיד החוש על זה שאף על פי שבדברים הטבעיים נמצאו רבים שהם טובים הנה ימצאו גם כן קצתם רעים בלי ספק. ומזה נראה שהם שני ממציאים בוראים ושתי רשויות.

§ 8.2 **אמנם** יתבאר הפך זה רצוני לומר שבורא הוא אחד בלבד ואין בורא זולתו שוה אליו. ראשונה בראיית ארסטו׳ בספר מה שאחר מאמר י׳ פרק ז׳ באמרו: »בהתפעליות ובאיכייות[b] ובמיני הכמות ובמיני התנועה נמצא אחד במספר« עכ״ל. ודבריו אלה באר אבן רשד באמרו כי »אמנם במיני ההתפעלות והאיכות והכמות והתנועה נמצא בכל אחד מהם אחד שהוא התחלת מספר אותו המין.« והוסיף ואמר: »וכשנחבר עם זה מה שהתבאר בטבעיות והוא שיש מניע ראשון קדמון נבדל בהחלט מכל חומר. והתבאר שזה הוא התחלה לא כמו מניע בלבד אבל גם כן צורה ותכלית התבאר גם כן שהוא הנמצא אשר הוא התחלת העצם« עכ״ל. הנה בדבריהם אלה בארו שאחרי שהתבאר בחפוש שבכל מין מהנמצאות יעלה הדבר אל נמצא אחד במספר שהוא התחלה לאותו המין ראוי שיהיה זה גם כן במאמר העצם שיעלה | הדבר אל אחד שהוא התחלת מאמר העצם וזה הוא המניע הראשון וזה בעצמו נראה היות עולה מדבריהם בספר מה שאחר מאמר י״ב פרק ל״ט. **ובהיות** שכבר התבאר למעלה שהבורא הוא בעצמו המניע הראשון אשר הוא אחד בלבד או שהוא נמצא יותר נכבד מהמניע הראשון והוא חִדש את המניע הנזכר אשר בהיותו בלתי מתחלק לא היה איפשר התחדשו כי אם על יד אחד בלבד בכח בורא

---

[a] טענת] a[corr]; טעות a. [b] ובאיכייות] coni. Dunk.; ובאביות a.

§ 8 Octavo Dubitatur

Utrum unus tantum detur Creator vel plures dentur creatores eque primi.

Et videtur ut dentur plures uno.

§ 8.1 Ratione et auctoritate antiquorum ab Aven R. relata *Metaphysicorum* XII t.c. 52. inferentium quod cum contrariorum contraria habeant esse principia: bonum vero et malum in universo apparentia sint sibi invicem contraria. Sequitur ut duo saltem dentur principia eque prima quorum alterum sit productor bonorum alterum, vero malorum, sensu enim patere videtur quod in rerum natura cum hoc quod plura sint bona nonnulla tamen sint mala proculdubio apparentia.

§ 8.2 Ad oppositum tamen arguitur ratione et auctoritate Phylosophi *Metaphysicorum* X t.c. 7 ubi dicit: «In passionibus et in quantitatibus et in qualitatibus et in motu est numerus et in omnibus unum aliquod etc.» ubi Aven R. exponens ait: «Cum sit verificatum quod in passionum predicamentis et quantitatum et qualitatum et motus sit numerus, et in omnibus est unum quod est principium illius numeri necesse est secundum hoc ut similiter sit in substantijs scilicet, ut in eis sit unum quod est principium numerorum etc.» subdit ibidem dicens: «Quod intendit quod cum huic iunctum fuerit quod declaratum est in Physicis scilicet hoc esse primum motorem eternum et absolutum ab omni materia et declaravit quod hoc non solummodo est principium tanquam motor sed tanquam forma et finis, declarabitur quod illud est hoc quod est principium substantie etc.» Quibus inferri videtur quod per universalem discursum pateat quod in unoquoque genere sit deveniendum ad quoddam unum quod est illius generis principium dicendum ergo est quod idem est de substantia quod scilicet deveniendum est ad unum substantie principium et talis est primus motor. Cum autem patuisset ut supra quod primus motor vel est idem quod Creator et ipse motor est unus tantum vel est necessario dandum quid ipso motore nobilius eundem motorem producens. Qui motor cum sit quid indivisibile nonnisi ab uno per creationem produci potuit, patet quidem eadem Phyloso-

§ 8 Eighth,

it may be inquired whether there is one creator or many creators at the same time.

And it seems that there are many creators.

§ 8.1 According to the argument and authority of the Ancients in Averroes's Commentary on *Metaphysics* 12, text. 52,[a] if we said that contraries have contrary principles, the good and the evil, which appear in the universe and are contrary to one another, it would follow that there are two principles at the same time, one of them creating the good and the other the evil. The senses testify this because among the natural things, many [of them] appear [to be] good, while others undoubtedly [appear to be] evil.

§ 8.2 On the contrary it is to argue according to the argument and authority of the Philosopher in *Metaphysics* 10, text. 7,[b] where he states: "In the categories of affection, quality, quantity, and movement, there is a number and a one in every case," and Averroes explicates: "This is true because in the category of affection and quality and quantity and movement, there is a number and in all of them there is a one, and this is the principle of numbers, and it is necessary that the same occurs in the category of substance, and in it, there is a one, which is the principle of numbers," and he continues: "And according to what was explained in *Physics*, there is a first eternal mover, absolutely separate from all matter. And it became clear that he is a principle, not as a mover only, but also as a form and an end [i.e., final goal]. It also becomes clear that this is the principle of the substance, etc." By these [words], it seems to explain that it is clear, per a universal discourse, that every species comes down to one [in number], which is the principle of this species, and then this is also in the substance that comes to one principle of substance, and this is the first mover. And it seems to be clear, as aforementioned, that the first mover is either the creator himself and that this mover is one only, or that there is necessarily something nobler than this mover who creates the mover. And since the mover is indivisible, it is only possible that it was generated by creation from a one, and it is

---

[a] *Metaph.* 12.10.1075a.   [b] *Metaph.* 10.1.1052b.

above. The truth of Aristotle's statement becomes clear from this: that it is necessary that it comes to one principle, and this is an existent that is the principle of the substance, and it concurrently becomes clear from this that it is a creator, and therefore, it follows that the creator is one alone. And this is what we wanted to explain.

§ 8.3.1 Second, the same becomes clear from Aristotle's proof in *Metaphysics* 12, text. 52:[a] "There is some good in the community and also in the leader, and it is greater [in the latter]." And Averroes explains these words: "There is good in the army because of its leader and because of its order, but the good that is found in the leader is much better than the good that is found in the order." And Aristotle continues, ibid.: "All the existents are orderly arranged in relation to each other, intended towards an existent that is one." And Averroes explains his words: "It is evident that this is common to all the existents and that they all exist for the sake of one and that the actions of all of them are intended for [i.e., tend towards] that one, and he is the first cause, just as all the things that are in a house are there for the sake of the owner of the house."

§ 8.3.2 And therefore, it is fitting that in the Holy Scripture (Psalm 24:10), the Creator who brings forth and arranges the order of the species of existents is called by the name "*Ha-Shem of hosts*," to instruct [us] that from the common order of the [celestial] hosts and their species, in which there is a connected and single existence, the existence of an arranger of order becomes clear, and that there is only one who intended the unity of [all] existence.

§ 8.4.1 Third, that the creator is only one becomes clear in this way: because if there were many creators, it would be inevitable either that they were equal in rank of capability [i.e., power] of creation, or that they were not equal. And if we say that they are equal, then one of three cases would be inevitable. (1) The first would be to say that every single one of the existents would have been created by one of them only. (2) The second would be to say that every one of them would have been created by all of the creators together. (3) And the third would be to say that one of them would have created some of them and another would have created the others. The second case is impossible, because there is no medium between being and absolute non-being, as was explained above. It is evident that creation occurs in an indivisible instant and without time. And therefore, it becomes clear that the creation of a single existent is only [performed] by virtue of a single one,

---

[a] *Metaph.* 12.10.1075a.

---

§ 8.3.1 **שנית** יתבאר זה בעצמו בראיית ארסטו׳ בספר מה שאחר מאמר י״ב פרק נ״ב באמרו: »אמנם בעיר נמצא איזה טוב ונמצא גם כן טוב בשר הצבא והוא היותר טוב.« ודבריו אלה באר אבן רשד באמרו כי »אמנם הטוב נמצא בצבא בסבת שר הצבא ובסבת סדרו אמנם הטוב אשר בשר הוא יותר מן הטוב אשר בסדר« והוסיף ארסטו׳ שם ואמר כי »כל הנמצאות הן[a] מסודרות זו עם זו מכוונות אל איזה נמצא אחד במספר« ודבריו אלה באר אבן רשד באמרו: »מבואר הוא שזה כולל לכל הנמצאות שכלם הם בשביל אחד ושפעולותם כלם מכוונות לאותו האחד והוא הסבה הראשונה כמו שכל הדברים אשר בבית הם בסבת בעל הבית« עכ״ל.

§ 8.3.2 ובכן יאות שבספרי הקדש נקרא הבורא הממציא ומסדר מיני הנמצאות בשם ›ה׳ צבאות‹ להורות שמן הסדר המפורסם בצבאות ומיניהם[b] אשר היה בו[c] המציאות מקושר ואחד יתבאר מציאות המסדר והיותו אחד בלבד אשר כיון אחדות המציאות.

§ 8.4.1 **שלישית** יתבאר שהבורא הוא אחד בלבד באופן זה כי אם היו בוראים רבים במספר לא ימלט אם שיהיו שוים במעלת היכולת על הבריאה ואם שהם בלתי שוים ואם נאמר שהם שוים הנה לא ימלט מאחד משלשה פנים. האחד הוא שנאמר שכל הנבראים נבראו מאחד מהם בלבד. והשני הוא שנאמר שכל אחד מהם נברא מכל הבוראים יחד. והשלישי שנאמר שאחד מהם ברא קצתם והאחד ברא קצתם. אמנם החלק השני הוא נמנע כי בהיות שבין המציאות והאפיסות מוחלט אין שום אמצעי כמבואר למעלה הוא מבואר שהבריאה היא ברגע בלתי מתחלק ובלתי זמן ומזה יתבאר שכל בריאת נמצא אחד לא תהיה מכח אחד במספר זולתי בכל מה

---

[a] הן] coni. DUNK.; הם a.   [b] ומיניהם] a^corr; מיניהם a.   [c] בו] a^corr; om. a.

phi sententia quod sit deveniendum ad unicum substantie principium, et quod illud sit Creator. Quare sequitur ut unus tantum detur Creator quod est intentum.

§ 8.3.1 Secundo arguitur ratione et auctoritate Phylosophi *Metaphysicorum* XII t.c. 52 ubi dicit: «In civitate enim est bonum et in duce exercituum et ille magis etc.» ubi Aven R. exponens ait: «Bonum enim existit in exercitu propter ducem et propter ordinem suum, sed bonum quod est in duce est maius bono quod est in ordine» ubi Phylosophus subdit dicens: «Omnia enim ordinata sunt ad invicem respectu alicuius» etc. ubi Aven R. exponens ait: «Apparet enim, quod hoc commune est omnibus entibus scilicet quod omnia sunt propter unum, et quod actiones eorum sunt circa illud unum et primam causam, queadmodum omnia que sunt in domo propter dominum domus sunt etc.»

§ 8.3.2 Quare in Sacris Scripturis eadem prima causa scilicet agens sive omnium productor et ordinator merito [Ps 24:10] appellatur: «Dominus exercituum.» Quibus dictionibus docetur quod entium ordo exercituum more apparens fit a Domino scilicet Entificante sive Creante ut supra. Quibus patet ordinatoris et ducis unitas a quo universi unitas intenditur quod est idem quod eiusdem universi productor sive Creator, quod est intentum.

§ 8.4.1 Tertio arguitur sic si essent plures creatores vel essent virtutis creandi equales vel non. Si primum, tunc vel omnia creata habuerunt per horum unum et idem produci, vel unaqueque rerum productarum habuit per omnes creatores simul et semel produci, vel harum altera ab altero eorum altera vero ab horum alio. Non secundum quia cum inter purum esse et purum non esse non detur medium patet quidem quod creatio sit quid indivisibile in instanti scilicet et sine tempore fiendum, quare eius totum ab uno tantum emanare contigit. Si enim contingeret per duos

clear, according to the statement of the Philosopher, that it comes down to one principle of substance, and this is the creator. Then, it would follow that there is one creator, and this is what was intended.

§ 8.3.1 Second, I would argue according to the argument and authority of the Philosopher in *Metaphysics* 12, text. 52,[a] where he states: "Some good exists in the community, and good also exists in the leader of the army, and [there is] more in the latter," and Averroes explicates: "The good exists in the army because of the army's leader and because of its order. But the good that is in the leader is much better than the good that is in the order [of the army]." The Philosopher continues: "All existents are arranged in respect of one being," and Averroes explicates: "It is evident that this is common to all existents: that they all exist for the sake of one, and their activities are turned towards that one. And this is the first cause, just as all things that are in a house are there for the sake of the owner of the house, etc."

§ 8.3.2 Moreover, in the Holy Scripture (Psalm 24:10), the first cause—namely, the agent or Creator of beings or Arranger—is called by the name "the Lord of hosts," to teach us that the order of the hosts that appears in all existence is created by the Lord; namely, the Creator of beings or the Creator, as aforementioned. By these [words], the unity of the arranger or ruler is [the principle] for the unity of the universe, because He is the producer or Creator of the universe. And this is what was intended.

§ 8.4.1 Third, I would argue that if there are many creators, they are either equal in the power of creation, or [they are] not. If the first [instance] is true, then either every produced being was created by one of them, or each and every produced thing was created by all the creators together and at the same time, or one of them created some of them and another created others of them. The second [instance] is impossible, because between absolute being and absolute non-being, there is no intermediary [i.e., medium]; this is clear because creation is indivisible and it is created in an instant and without time, and therefore its whole is emanated from the one. If it were to be

---

[a] *Metaph.* 12.10.1075a.

because in everything that that one makes by [creation], he will undoubtedly make its whole [creation] an indivisible thing and within an indivisible | instant, because if we said that the creation of one existent occurred by virtue of many creators, it would follow that one and the same existent would be generated twice in an indivisible instant, which does not come to mind, and therefore, it becomes clear that an existent is only created by one creator. And the third case is also impossible, because no substrate from which something is generated is needed for creation, nor any time nor any kind of movement that is designated for one of the equal creators rather than its counterpart[s]. There is no reason due to which we [can] say that a certain existent will exist that is designated so that it will be created by one of them rather than by the other[s]. It then follows that all created [things] were created by one creator, and therefore, it follows that the creator of all is one only. And this is what we wanted to explain.

§ 8.4.2 And apart from this, if there are many creators who are equal in their capability [i.e., power] of creation—behold, since the activity of creation is the noblest of all activities, since it comprises [the whole of] reality, and it therefore follows that it is the noblest among the forms—then it follows that those who are equal in their capability [i.e., power] of creation are also equal in form, especially since the form is only differentiated through its activity, as Averroes explains in *The Incoherence of the Incoherence* 6, sixth investigation.[a] And after already had become clear that one who is a creator is necessarily separate from matter, as explained above. And it then becomes clear that it is impossible that there can be an individual difference in something with a similar equality, in such a manner that we can—within this equality—denote a number, as Averroes explains in the Commentary on *Metaphysics* 1, text. 40: "But duality in one thing is because of matter." And the same becomes clear from a proof quoting al-Ġazālī in *The Incoherence of the Incoherence* 5, second investigation, quoting the Philosopher: "If things separate [from matter] were equal in each and every thing, no plurality would apply to them, because the whole would be one, because we say that there [can only] be two identical black visible [things] if they are in two different substrates or [at two different] times. And we say also that blackness and movement are two things because they are different from each other in their substance. But if they are one thing in substance, like two identical black visible [things], then when they are at one and the same time and in one and the same place, undoubtedly no plurality will apply to them. And

---
[a] Cf. *Incoherence* 217.

simul et semel fieri sequeretur ut idem in eodem instantibus[a] fieret quod est inopinabile. Quare patet quod non contingit per plus uno idem creari. Neque dicendum est tertium prefate divisionis membrum, scilicet ut entium quedam per horum unum quedam vero per horum alterum producta sint. Quia cum ad creationem nullum requiratur subiectum per quod consideretur proportio inter ipsum et agentem currens neque tempus neque motuum genus, que magis creantium uni quam horum alteri appropriari contingat nulla daretur causa, quare creandorum quedam magis per creantium alterum quam per horum reliquum creari contigerit. Restat ergo ut omnia fuissent per unum et idem tantum producta, et per consequens unus tam datur ominum Creator quod est intentum.

§ 8.4.2 Preterea si essent plures creatores in virtute creandi equales, tunc cum creatio sit actio omnium nobilissima, et per consequens illa forma a qua provenit huiusmodi actio eque primo habet necessario esse formarum nobilissima, sequeretur ut huiusmodi creatores essent omnino forma similes, forma enim nonnisi per actionem sibi propriam nosci contingit, sicut habetur ab Aven R. in lib. *Destructionis D.*, disputatione VI dubio 6. Cumque iam patuisset quod non datur Creator materie mixtus ut supra. Patet quidem quod nulla individualis detur dif|ferentia inter huiusmodi similes unde contingat dari dualitas vel numeratio. Sicut habetur ab Aven R. in comento Metaphysicorum primi t.c. 40 ubi dicit: «Dualitas in una re est propter materiam» et idem habetur ratione et auctoritate Algazelis relata in lib. *Destructionis Des.*, disputatione V dubio 2 ubi de mente Phylosophorum ait: «Si essent omnino similes nulla esset ibi numeratio neque binitas, due namque nigredines dicuntur quando sunt in duobus subiectis vel non in uno et eodem tempore sed in duobus temporibus. Nigredo, enim, et motus sunt duo quia in substantia different, sed quando in substantia non differunt sicut sunt due nigredines cum unitate temporis et loci tunc sine dubio nulla est numeratio, et si possibile esset ut dentur in uno tempore et in uno subiecto due nigredines, possibile ergo

created by two creators together and at the same time, it would follow that this thing would have been created by them in the same instant, and this is incongruous, because it is clear that nothing has been created by more than one [creator]. The third [instance] concerning the division of members—namely, that one of them created some of them and another created the others—is also impossible, because no substrate is needed for creation by which it is possible to examine the relationship between the substrate and the agent, since neither time nor any kind of movement is designated for one of the creators rather than its counterparts due to something having been created by one of them rather than by the others. It remains that all [created things] were created by only one [creator], and consequently, there is only one creator, and this is what was intended.

§ 8.4.2 Moreover, if there were many creators equal in the power of creation, since creation is the noblest of all activities, [then] the form would have come from this creation. And if so, the first equal activity would necessarily have come from the noblest among the forms, and it would follow that the creators were similar in form, and a form is only differentiated by its activity, as Averroes explains in *The Incoherence of the Incoherence* 6, sixth doubt. Therefore, it becomes clear that the creator is not mixed with matter, as aforementioned, and that there is no individual | difference between similar beings, in such a way that duality or multiplicity could be possible, as Averroes explicates in the Commentary on *Metaphysics* 1, text. 40,[a] where he states: "Duality in one thing exists because of matter,"[b] and according to the argument and authority of al-Ġazālī in the name of the philosophers in *The Incoherence of the Incoherence* 5, second doubt, where he states: "If they were similar, there would be no number or binarities. We say that two black things exist when they have two substrates, or just one, but at different times. And so the blackness and the movement are two at the same time because their substance is separate, but when their substance is not separate, if there are two black things that have unity in time and space, then undoubtedly there is no number, and if it is impossible to say that there are two black things in one substrate and at the same time, then concerning every

---

[a] instantibus] coni. Copp.; instanbis b.

[a] *Metaph.* 1.9.992a.   [b] Cf. *Incoherence* 217.

if—when they are in one substrate and at one and the same time—it were possible to say that they were two black visible [things], it would also be possible to say that every individual of every species would be two, even though we would not recognise that there was a plurality."[a] And therefore, it becomes clear that it is impossible that there can be two equal creators in reality.

§ 8.4.3 And if we said that there are two or more creators, but that they are not equal in [their] capability [i.e., power] of creation, and insofar as they are not equal, plurality applies to them, and according to this, the nobler existents were imputed to the superior [creator] and the inferior [existents] to one [of the other creators] who is inferior to him, then one of two [cases] would be inevitable: either (1) that we would say that the one who is inferior to the superior [creator] | is caused by the superior [creator], created and intended by him, or (2) that we would say that it was not created, but eternal in the eternity of the superior [creator]. But it becomes clear that the second case is impossible in this way: because in the inferior [existents], which are then necessarily related to the activity of the inferior creator, there is government, order, and perpetuity from the noble existents, which are undoubtedly [created by] the activity of the superior [creator]. It would then follow that the activity of the inferior [creator] would be very defective, because in itself it is impermanent and disordered, such that it would not be appropriate to relate it [even] to an artisan—an amateur among amateurs—still less to a separate substance that is considered to be second to God [i.e., a secondary god], may He be praised. If so, the first case remains: that if we perhaps say that there is a creator of an inferior rank to the first and inferior to Him in the activity of creation, although there is no necessity that this will be [so] in reality, [then] he will in any case only be caused by the First [Creator], created and orderly arranged by His intention. And therefore, it becomes clear that he is not equal to the First [Creator] and not eternal in His eternity. And therefore, it becomes clear that the First Creator is not an equal existent to him, as it says (Isaiah 40:25): "To whom, then, can you liken Me; to whom can I be compared?", and that He is one, in an existence separate from all existence besides Him, as it says (Deuteronomy 6:4): "Ha-Shem is one." And this is what we wanted to explain.

§ 8.5.1 And perhaps this is what Plato wanted [to say] in his statement that Averroes mentions in the Commentary on *Metaphysics* 12, text. 44:[b] "This is what Plato said

---

[a] Cf. *Incoherence* 174–175. [b] Cf. *Metaph.* 12.8.1073b.

ואם בהיותם[a] בנושא אחד ובזמן אחד בעצמו היה איפשר לומר שהן שתי מראות שחורות[b] היה גם כן איפשר לומר על כל איש מאישי כל מין שהוא שנים גם שלא[c] נכיר שיהיה שם מספר« עכ״ל ומזה התבאר שהוא מן הנמנע שיהיו במציאות שני בוראים שוים.

§ 8.4.3 ואם נאמר שנמצאו שני בוראים או יותר אבל הם בלתי שוים ביכולת הבריאה ומצד היותם בלתי שוים יפול עליהם מספר ולפי זה ניחס את הנמצאות הנכבדות לגדול והשפלות מהם למי שלמטה ממנו. הנה אז לא ימלט מאחת משתים אם שנאמר שמי שהוא למטה מהגדול | הוא מסובב מהגדול מחודש ומכוון מאתו. או שנית שנאמר שהוא בלתי מחודש אבל קדמון בקדמות הגדול. אמנם שזה החלק השני נמנע הנה יתבאר באופן זה כי בהיות שבשפלים אשר אם כן היה ראוי ליחסה לפעולת הבורא הקטן נמצאת ההנהגה וסדר וקיום מצד הנמצאות הנכבדים שהם פעלת הגדול בלי ספק היה מתחייב אם כן שפעולת הקטן היתה חסורה מאד מצד עצמה בלתי קיימת ובלתי מסודרת באופן שלא היה ראוי ליחסה לאומן הדיוט שבהדיוטים כל שכן לעצם נבדל אשר היה נחשב שני לאל יתברך ישאר אם כן החלק הראשון שאם אולי נאמר שיש בורא למטה מהראשון וקטון ממנו בפעולת הבריאה אף על פי שאינו מחוייב שיהיה זה במציאות לא יהיה בשום פנים זולתי מסובב מהראשון מחודש ומסודר בכוונה מאתו ובכן התבאר שאינו שוה לראשון ולא קדמון בקדמותו ובכן התבאר שהבורא הראשון אין נמצא שוה לו כאמרו: »ואל מי תדמיוני ואשוה?«)ישעיהו מ׳ כ״ה(ושהוא אחד במציאות נבדל מכל מציאות זולתו באמרו: »ה׳ אחד«)דברים ו׳ ד׳(וזה הוא מה שרצינו לבאר.

§ 8.5.1 ואולי זה רצה אפלטון במאמרו אשר הביא אבן רשד בביאור ספר מה שאחר מאמר י״ב פרק מ״ד באמרו: »אמנם זה שאמר

---

[a] בהיותם] a[corr]; בהיועצם a. [b] שחורות] emend. Dunk.; שחתרות a; nigredines b. [c] שלא] emend. Dunk.; שלוא a; que ... non b.

esset de quolibet individuo dicere quod sunt duo licet ibi numeratio non cognosceretur etc.»

§ 8.4.3 Si vero dicatur tertium divisionis membrum, scilicet, ut plures sit creatores creandi tamen virtute inequales, per quam inequalitatem detur inter eos numeratio, et ut sic haberent productarum rerum nobiliores, creantium maiori attribui, ignobiliores vero horum minori. Tunc vel huiusmodi minor est quid a maiori causatum et ad huiusmodi ignobiliora entia producenda ordinatum, vel non. Non secundum quia cum infima entia eidem minori ut sic attribuenda nonnisi per nobiliora regantur ordinentur et conserventur. Sequeretur ut eiusdem minoris actio esset per se quid vanum.[a] Cum entia per illam producta essent per se impermanentia et inordinata adeo ut neque artificium vilissimo competeret, nedum enti adeo nobili ut deus secundus quodammodo reputaretur. Restat ergo primum ut si detur Creator primo minor (licet non necessario) sit quid ab ipso primo causatum et ordinatum, et per consequens intentum et productum non eque primum, quod est intentum.

§ 8.5.1 Et fortasse id voluit Plato in sermone ab Aven R. allegato in comento *Metaphysicorum* XII t.c. 44 ubi dicit:

individual [being], it would be possible to say that it is two, even if we do not recognise numeration there, etc."[a]

§ 8.4.3 If so, we say that there is a third form of division, in such a way that there are many creators with unequal power of creation, insofar as this inequality produces numeration between them. And according to this, the nobler created things would imputed to the greater [creator] and the lower ones would be imputed to the inferior [creator]. And then either a lower [thing] would have been generated by a greater [creator], and it would have been ordered according to the lower existents, or not. The second [instance] cannot be [the case], because if lower beings, which are imputed to an inferior creator, were ruled, ordered, and perpetuated only in accordance with a greater creator, then the activity of the lower creator would have been futile. Also, because the created beings would be impermanent and disordered, it would not be appropriate to relate them to a lower artisan, or to a noble being that is considered a secondary god. Thus, the first [instance] remains: if there is a creator below the first, even though this is not necessary, then it would have been caused and ordered by the first, and consequently, it would have been intended and produced with a status not equal to the first, and this is what was intended [to be explained].

§ 8.5.1 And this is probably what Plato wanted [to explain] in the speech that Averroes quotes in the Commentary on *Metaphysics* 12, text. 44,[b] where he states: "This is what

---

[a] vanum] emend. COPP.; vanne b.

[a] Cf. *Incoherence* 174–175.   [b] Cf. *Metaph.* 12.8.1073b.

in his obscure statements, [i.e.,] that the Creator created the angels with His hands and afterwards He gave them the order that they should create the generables and corruptibles, and He remained at rest. It is not appropriate to understand it literally." And perhaps he mentioned Plato in order to consider this: the opinion of some later [philosophers], who said that it is appropriate that the first substance should be simple with absolute simplicity, and that from a simple unity [lit. one] nothing may be generated except [another] unity [lit. one]. However, since this opinion is not demonstrative, but only the opinion of Avicenna and, besides him, of other later [philosophers], as Averroes explains in *The Incoherence of the Incoherence* 3, twelfth investigation,[a] it seems that it is not relevant here, because the existents caused by the creator are not generated by him via a way of [generating] a thing from something that is similar [to it] in substance, but are generated by way of creation by an intellectual creator, who necessarily wills this through wisdom intended for a final purpose. And therefore, it is congruous that different existents are generated by him according to the purpose-related differentiations that are intended by him. And since this first simple substance—and this is the Creator, may He be praised—creates noble existents after absolute nothingness, as explained above, it becomes clear, if so, that He can [also] create what is less noble than them. And since by His strength and His modesty and His good[ness], He preserves and gives perpetuity to the less noble existents and arranges their perceivable order mediately or immediately, as explained above, it is congruous that He creates them [out of nothing] immediately, not [mediately], and that He does not detest their lowliness.

§ 8.5.2 And from all of this, it becomes clear that there is no existent in reality that is created by them [i.e., the angels or any intermediators] mediately or immediately. Better is the view | of the wise Simonides [of Ceos] in his statement that Aristotle mentions in the Introduction to *Metaphysics*:[b] "For God alone is this glory," that He is the cause and is by no means caused. And therefore, it seems that the Poet agrees, saying (Psalm 24:10): "Ha-Shem of hosts, He is the King of glory!"

§ 8.6 And we answer, then, to dispel [any] doubt about the aforementioned thesis, by saying that the creator is necessarily only one and that there is no existent besides him that will, by its substance, have the capability [i.e., power] to create and bring forth an existent after absolute non-existence.

---

[a] Cf. *Incoherence* 105–109. [b] *Metaph.* 1.2.982b.

«Hoc autem quod Plato dixit in suis verbis obscuris, quod Creator creavit angelos manu, deinde praecepit eis creare alia mortalia et remansit ipse in quiete sine labore, non est intelligendum ad litteram etc.» Et hoc fortasse putavit Plato ductum illa modernorum ratione ab Aven R. ibidem relata, qua, scilicet, dicitur quod: «Prima substantia habet esse una et simplex in fine, quoque ab uno et simplici non provenit nisi unum.» Sed huiusmodi ratio non bene videtur in hoc concludere, quoniam entia non procedunt a Creatore per modum derivationis, ita ut habeant esse eidem necessario similia, immo procedunt per modum productionis ab intelligente substantia talia sapienter volente et finem intendente. Quare habet suos actus diversificare iuxta intentorum finium diversitatem. Cumque ipsa Prima Substantia sive Creator imediate produxisset entia nobilia post purum non esse ut supra. Quare patet quod non minus potuit ignobiliora et minoris entitate[a] producere que tandem dignata est mediate vel immediate conservare, merito dicendum videtur ut eadem ignobiliora produxisset et creasset preter, quam frustra diversi dentur creatores ad ignobiliora scilicet creanda.

Plato said in his obscure words: the creator created the angels with his hands, and afterwards he ordered them to create the mortal beings, and he remained at rest without working. It is not appropriate to understand this literally." And this is probably what Plato thought, according to what Averroes explains considering the position of some modern philosophers who say that the first substance is one and absolutely simple, because one comes from the one and the simple. But this argument seems to an incorrect demonstration, because beings do not come from the creator by derivation, meaning that they would necessarily be similar. On the contrary, beings come forth through generation from an intellectual substance, who wills it by wisdom, intending it for a purpose. And therefore, he differentiates his activity according to the differentiation of the final purpose. Since either this first substance or the creator created immediately noble [i.e., superior] existents after absolute nothingness, as aforementioned, it becomes clear that he can also create less noble [i.e., inferior] existents. Moreover, through his nobility, he perpetuates the less noble [i.e., inferior] existents mediately and immediately, and for this reason, it seems that he generated and created the less noble [i.e., inferior] existents, as it would be incongruous that different creators would create less noble beings.

§ 8.5.2 Cumque his pateat quod nihil preter primam substantiam detur esse quin ab ipsa substantia intendatur et ab eadem saltem mediate causetur et producatur. Merito ergo Phylosophus Symonides[b] auctoritate in *Metaphysicorum* preambulo [I t.c. 2] ait: «Quod solus Deus hunc habet honorem quod scilicet sit causa et nullo pacto causatus» Et idem videtur inferre Psalmus 23 [24:10] dicens: «Quis iste est rex honores sive glorie, Dominus exercituum ipse est rex glorie» intendens de praefato honore sive gloria qua nihil preter eum dignus est ut supra.

§ 8.5.2 It is clear that nothing exists except the first substance, nothing exists without being intended by the first substance, and nothing is mediately created or generated by it. This is in accordance with what Simonides explained in the introduction to *Metaphysics*,[a] where he states: "For God alone is this glory," because He is the cause and is by no means caused. And therefore, it seems that Psalm 23 (24:10) explained the same, saying: "Who is the King of glory? The Lord of Heavens' Hosts—he is the King of glory," since one would say that the aforementioned "honour" or "glory" means that nothing is appropriate except Him, as mentioned above.

§ 8.6 Ad dubium ergo respondetur quod unus tantum datur Creator per se scilicet habens virtutem dandi esse post purum non esse.

§ 8.6 To dispel any doubt, I would argue that there is only one creator who has the power to bring forth from absolute nothingness.

---

[a] entitate] b[corr]; entitati b. [b] Symonides] coni. COPP.; Sinoidis b; סינואידוס a.

[a] *Metaph.* 1.2.982b.

§ 8.7 But to the opponent's arguments, we answer by saying: "evil" may be said of [something] in many ways. First, in terms of what is evil in relation to a particular existent, but good in relation to another one. And this is not said [to be] an "absolute evil," because it is good in a certain way, such as when it occurs through the punishment of an evildoer [who behaves] in an evil way towards the other created beings, so that although the punishment [means] destruction and "evil" in relation to the punished [person], it is indeed good in relation to the other[s]. And therefore, it is appropriate that [this] should come from the creator of the good [things] mediately or immediately, insofar as it is good and necessary for the perpetuity of another, as it says (Sanhedrin 71b): "The death of the evildoer is beneficial to them and beneficial to the world." And 'evil' is also said of the evil [things] that human beings do by freedom [of choice] to one another or that one of them [does] to himself. And this kind of evil is not related to the Creator—may He be praised—at all, because the freedom [of choice] is given to man by Him—may He be praised—for a good final purpose, because by it, man will be in the "*likeness of God*"[a] when he walks before Him and will be perfect, as explained above, and this will become clear to us below in a more extensive commentary. And "evil" is also said of what necessarily occurs in a material existent: the matter from which it is taken. And this is so because its matter is by nature disposed for its actualisation, just like what happens in the corruption of the generables and corruptibles. And this kind of evil is nothing but a privation of the goodness of perpetuity [i.e., immortality]. And therefore, among the number of existents, there is nothing for which we need to introduce a [new] cause designated for creating the evil.

§ 8.8.1 And this oneness, which is particular to the Creator—may He be praised—is explained by proof in His Torah, saying (Deuteronomy 4:39): "And know therefore this day and keep in mind that ha-Shem alone is God in the heavens above and on earth below; there is no other"; that is to say, His government and His perceivable order in the superior and inferior [things] is hinted at by the term "Elohim" [God], making it known that He is ha-Shem, [the] Creator and Generator. And therefore, it is made known that there is "no other," because it is impossible that there can be a second eternal creator alike to His eternity or equal to Him, as explained above. And this is so because from the perceivable order in which the generables "on the earth below" are generated and from the intermediation of [celestial] bodies, which are "in the heavens above,"

---

[a] Gen 5:1.

§ 8.7 Ad argumentum vero respondetur: quod malum dicitur vel de illo quod est tale respectu alicuius tantum et illud non est absolute malum immo alicuius respectu et ex parte finis et summopere bonum. Sicut accidit de male factoris pena que scilicet intenditur ad patrie salutem respectu cuius est quid penitus bonum. Et tale non est inconveniens ut a bonorum principio vel a Creatore mediate vel immediate emanet huiusmodi bonum intendente, scilicet ut reliqui conserventur, vel dicitur malum de illo quod a libero hominis arbitrio turpiter procedit. Quod, scilicet, arbitrium ab ipso bonorum Creatore intenditur ut homo reddatur beatitudine dignus, prout infra apertius patebit. Vel dicitur malum de illo quod fit ex necessitate materie passionibus disposite, sicut accidit de mortalium corruptione, que scilicet nil aliud est quam inmortalitatis privatio, et talis non est de numero entium ad quod non est opus novum dare principium a quo producatur.

§ 8.8.1 Quare Sacrum Deuteronomij Documentum cap. 4 [4:39] Creatoris unitatem demostrative docere intendens ait: «Scito ergo hodie et cogitato in corde tuo quod Dominus ipse est ille Deus in celum sursum et in terra deorsum et non est alius.» Quasi dicat quod per illum colligatum

§ 8.7 In response to the first argument, I will reply: evil can only be said either to exist in relation to a particular existent only, and this is not absolute evil, because it could be good in relation to another existent, such as the punishment of an evildoer that is intended for public safety, and this is good. And therefore, it is appropriate that [something should be called good if it was] emanated from the principle of good or from the creator who intends the good, mediately or immediately, meaning that the rest of the beings are perpetuated. Alternatively, a thing is called evil if it comes from human free choice, because free choice is intended by the creator of good things and a worthy man could attain beatitude, as will be explained below, or a thing that is necessarily produced by material affection, such as the corruption of a mortal thing, is called evil, and this is nothing other than the privation of immortality, and it is not in accordance with the number of existents, which needs to give a new principle from which evil is produced.

§ 8.8.1 Moreover, the Holy Book of Deuteronomy (4:39) conclusively teaches the unity of the Creator, saying: "Know therefore this day, and consider it in thine heart, that the Lord He is God in heaven above and upon the earth beneath: there is none else" [Know therefore this day and keep in mind that the Lord alone is God in heaven above and on earth below; there is no other], which means that we know that the government of them all and their order comes from one governor who intended this whole order. And therefore, it follows that He Himself brought them forth, because it is incongruous that it could have happened to an arranger of order by chance that he found all these existents that were not intended by him which had no | order although they were disposed for an order and an intended connection now [given] by him. And therefore, it follows that He created them after absolute nothingness, because it would be incongruous that there should be [a] matter or substrate prior to them from which it is considered that they were generated, as mentioned above. If so, it becomes clear that He is the Creator who is indicated by the "special name" and that He is one alone, in the way that there is no existent like Him.

§ 8.8.2 And the prophets teach us the same when they say (Psalm 24:10): "Ha-Shem of hosts," as if to say that from the commonly known connection between the hosts of creatures above and the hosts of creatures below in a wondrous order—like the order existing in every army, whose individuals form a unit through the intention of the leader of the army—the oneness of a creator and a generator who is indicated by the "special name" becomes clear, as explained above. Indeed, the name of the divine [i.e., God] in the Holy Scripture is [found] in many expressions. For the most part, it teaches [us] that He is—in a certain way—all beings, as it says (Isaiah 6:3): "His presence fills all the earth!" And this is so because through His efficient knowledge, which is His substance—may He be praised—the existence of all existents is and will come to be, along with their government and their order and their perpetuity, as became clear and will become clear to us below with the help of ha-Shem, may He be praised. And Averroes explains this citing the Philosopher in [the Commentary on] *Metaphysics* 12, text. 24:[a] "Everything natural is produced from a thing that is similar to it, and the artificial form—which is [produced] by virtue of the formative power of an artisan—creates the artificial form outside the soul." And he continues, ibid.: "The disposition of the first [i.e., last] mover is somewhat like the disposition of the proximate mover." Since the first mover moves the substrates to bring forth all forms in them, it becomes clear that the form of the first mover is somehow all forms. And he explains this in the Commentary on *On the Soul* 3, text. 36:[b] "The existents are nothing other than divine knowledge. And this order is highly remarkable, and this manner of being is very strange." And he explains this in *The Incoherence of the Incoherence* 12, second investigation: "This

---

[a] *Metaph.* 12.5.1070b. [b] Cf. *De an.* 3.7.431b.

ordinem inter superiora et inferiora sensu apparentem. Quo, scilicet, patet omnia ab uno et eodem mediate vel immediate regi et ordinari, et per consequens ab eodem produci. Cum non casu sive preter eiusdem intentum eidem contigisset posse hec facere, et per consequens patet ut illa post purum non esse produxisset, cum non detur subiectum his tempore prius ex quo fierent ut supra, patet quidem unum tantum esse omnium Creatorem. Qui scilicet per ly Dominum Hebraice significatur ut supra, quod est intentum.

§ 8.8.2 Et idem docent prophete omnes eundem universi Creatorem «Dominum Exercituum» appellantes [Ps 24:10]. Quo nomine inferre videntur quod per unitatem inter celestes et terrestres exercitus apparentem qua scilicet colligato ordine exercituum more concurrunt ad ducis intentum exequendum ostenditur. Quidem eiusdem Domini unitas cuius ordine colligatur et unitur universum. Cum autem ly Deus Hebraice sub plurali exprimatur dictione divinitus quidem inferri videtur illum quodammodo esse omnia entia sive om|nium forma et finis, et hoc cum per suam activam scientiam qua se ipsum intelligit mirabiliter creavit quam plurima entia et illa conservat tanquam omnium formalis et finalis forma, prout infra apertius dicetur. Et idem videtur Aven R. inferre de mente Phylosophi *Metaphysicorum* XII t.c. 24 ubi exponens ait: «Cum quodlibet non fiat nisi a convenientit ut homo generat hominem in rebus naturalibus et forma artificialis facit aliam formam etc.» subdit dicens: «Et quia dispositio ultimi moventis omnia est aliquo modo, sicut dispositio moventis propinqui et primus movens movet ad omnes formas, manifestum est quod forma primi moventis est quodammodo omnes forme.» et idem habetur ab eodem Aven R. in lib. *De Anima* III t.c. 36 ubi dicit: «Entia nil aliud sunt nisi scientia Dei neque cause entium nihil aliud sunt nisi eius scientia et quam mirabile est iste ordo et quam extraneus est iste modus essendi etc.» Et idem habetur ab eodem in lib. *Destructionis D.*, disputatione XII, dubio 2 ubi dicit:

the order of interconnection between superior and inferior is evident, because it is clear that all things are ruled and governed mediately or immediately by one [principle] and they were consequently produced from this one, because production does not happen by chance or without intention, and consequently, it is clear that they were produced after absolute nothingness, because there is no substrate prior to them from which they were generated, as aforementioned, and it is clear that there is only one creator of everything—that is, the Lord of the Jews—and this is what was intended.

§ 8.8.2 And the prophets teach us the same, calling the Creator of the universe (Psalm 24:10) "the Lord of Hosts." This name means that the unity of the celestial and terrestrial hosts is evident, and this connection is shown through the order existing in an army, which follows the intention of the leader of the army. The unity of the Lord by means of His order connects and unifies the universe. In Hebrew, the name of God has a plural form, meaning that in a certain way, He is all beings or the | formal and final [cause] of all beings, because through His actual knowledge, He knows Himself, as He creates the most and a great number of beings, just as he preserves every formal and final cause, as aforementioned. And Averroes explains this in the name of the Philosopher in *Metaphysics* 12, text. 24,[a] where he states: "Everything is produced only according to an appropriate [form], as in nature, man generates man and the artificial form is produced from another form," and he continues: "Because the disposition of the last mover is in a certain manner similar to the disposition of the proximate mover. Since the first mover moves every form, it becomes clear that the form of the first mover is in a certain way all forms." Averroes explains this in *On the Soul* 3, text. 36,[b] where he states: "Existents are nothing other than the knowledge of God, just as the cause of the existents is nothing other than His knowledge, and what is so remarkable is this order, and what is strange is this manner of being, etc.," and in *The Incoherence of the Incoherence* 12, second doubt, where he

---

[a] *Metaph.* 12.5.1070b.   [b] Cf. *De an.* 3.7.431b.

is what many of the Ancients said, that God—may He be praised—is all."[a] And our Rabbanan also said (*Sukkah* 53a): "If I am here, everyone is here." And therefore, in the book of Job, in which Moses our teacher—peace be upon him—wrote the opinions of the wise men of the Gentiles, who did not think this, "Eloha" [i.e., a god] is written, in most cases, as a singular term only.

הוא הכל" עכ"ל. וכן אמרו רבותינו ז"ל "אם אני כאן הכל כאן." (סוכה נ"ג א) ולזה הנה בספר איוב אשר בו כתב משה רבינו ע"ה דיעות חכמי הגוים אשר לא השכילו זאת נכתב על הרוב ‹אלוה› בלשון יחיד בלבד.

---

[a] Cf. *Incoherence* 281.

«Et hoc est quod dicebant aliqui antiquorum quod Deus est omne.» Quare in libro Job ubi Gentilium opiniones hec ignorantium[a] narrantur, ly Deus nonnisi sub singulari exprimitur numero.

states: "This is what many of the Ancients said: that God is all,"[a] and in the [Holy] Book of Job, in which are attested the opinions of the Gentiles, the name of God is written in the singular form only.[b]

---

[a] ignorantium] b[corr]; ignorantur b.

[a] Cf. *Incoherence* 281. [b] Hebrew "Eloha." The name of the God of the Jews, "Elohim," is expressed in Hebrew as a *pluralis maiestatis*.

§9 Ninth:
We will inquire whether the sole creator of whom we speak knows everything [i.e., is omniscient], or not.

And it seems at the beginning of the inquiry that he does not know everything.

§9.1 First, from proofs that the Philosopher cites referring to the Ancients in | *Metaphysics* 12, text. 51,[a] where it says that if the first [existent] was to think something besides itself, then it would be inevitable either (1) that that object of intellection was nobler than the first thinking [existent], and then doubt would arise about that object of intellection as to whether it is something that thinks and knows, and moreover the thing would proceed to infinity, or (2) that this object of intellection was something inferior to the thinking [existent], and then, since the object of intellection is the perfection of the thinking [existent], it would therefore follow that the thinking creator would acquire perfection from a thing that was inferior to him. And this is incongruous, because [the thing in] perfection is necessarily nobler than the thing that is perfected by it. And apart from this, since the creator brings forth the existents, if we [then] say that he acquires intellectual perfection through the things that are created by him, it would follow that this was the cause of his own existence. And this is so because the object of intellection becomes a substance and will become one thing with the substance of the perfected intellect. And therefore, it would follow that it would be [both] cause and caused, in actuality and in potentiality with respect to the existence of its substance, and this is incongruous. And apart from this, if we say that the creator was intellecting something other than himself, it would follow that he would be actualised by this, and if so, he would need an[other] agent to actualise him. And the aforementioned doubt would also arise about that agent regarding whether it knew something other than itself, and the thing would proceed to infinity.

§9.2.1 Second, this becomes clear from al-Ġazālī's proof, which Averroes cites in *The Incoherence of the Incoherence* 12, first investigation,[b] saying that all philosophers agree on this: that God—may He be praised—does not know individuals, so that Avicenna, who thinks that God—may He be praised—knows existents apart from Himself, also explicitly says that He knows them in a universal way, without the interference of time. Because through the change in the known, the knowledge about it [also] changes, and through the diversity and change in the knowledge, the

---

[a] *Metaph.* 12.8.1074b.   [b] Cf. *Incoherence* 275–279.

§9 Nono Dubitatur
Utrum idem unicus creator omnia sciat, vel non.

Et videtur quod non[.]

§9.1 Primo rationibus a Phylosopho relatis Caldeorum auctoritate quos patres appellat *Metaphysicorum* XII t.c. 51. Scilicet, quod si illud quod est omnium primum aliquid preter se ipsum intelligeret, vel intelligere quid eo nobilius et tunc surgeret questio de eodem nobiliora et fieret processus ad infinitum. Vel intelligeret quid eo ignobilius et tunc cum intellecta sint intellectus perfectio, sequeretur ut perficeretur per quid eo ignobilius, quod est inconveniens. Preterea cum sit reliquorum entium causa, si ergo per suos causatos perficeretur, sequeretur ut idem esset sui ipsius causa, et sic simul esset causa et causatum et potentia et actu quod est inconveniens, preterea si aliud intelligeret illud faceret, exiens de potentia ad actum quare indigeret motore ad actum deducente a quo pateretur, et de illo surgeret questio et fieret processus ad infinitum.

§9.2.1 Secundo arguitur ratione et auctoritate Algazelis relata in lib. *Destructionis Destructionis* disputatione XII, dubio primo, dicentis quod omnes Phylosophi conveniunt in hoc quod Deus ignorat particularia. Itaque etiam Avicenna qui opinatus est ut Deus sciat se et alia entia preter se, expresse tamen dicit quod illa scit universali modo nullo tempore indigente, quia mutato scibili mutatur scientia de eo, et mutata scientia mutatur sciens,

§9 Ninth,
it may be inquired whether the sole creator knows everything [i.e., is omniscient] or not.

And it seems he does not.

§9.1 First, I would argue, as the Philosopher explains in the name of the Chaldeans, whom he calls "fathers" in *Metaphysics* 12, text. 51,[a] that certainly, if that which is the first of all existents understood [thought] something besides itself, then either [the first of all existents] would understand [think] something nobler than itself and therefore a question would arise about things nobler than it and it would proceed to infinity; or [the first of all existents] would understand [think] something less noble [i.e., lower] than itself and then—since the objects of intellection are the perfection of the intellect—it would follow that [perfection] might be acquired by something lower than it, and this is incongruous. Moreover, it [the first of all existents] is the cause of all beings, and if it acquired perfection through things that are caused by it, it would then be the cause of itself, and at the same time cause and caused, in potentiality and in actuality, and this is incongruous. Moreover, if it understood [thought] something and made [something], departing from potentiality to actuality, for which a[nother] motor was required to bring [it] to fruition by which it would be affected, then the aforementioned question would arise again, and it would proceed to infinity.

§9.2.1 Second, I would argue according to the argument and authority of al-Ġazālī in *The Incoherence of the Incoherence* 12, first doubt,[b] by saying that all philosophers agree on this, that God ignores particulars, and also that Avicenna thinks that God knows Himself and existents besides Himself, explicitly saying that He knows them in a universal way, without the interference of time, because a known thing changes, the knowledge of it changes, and through the change in the knowledge, the knower changes.

---

[a] *Metaph.* 12.8.1074b. [b] Cf. *Incoherence* 275–279.

knower changes. And therefore, it follows that the individuals of the species, like Reuven and Shimon, who are different [i.e., separate] from each other only in sense [perception] and not in [cognition by the] intellect, do not fall under God's knowledge at all.

§ 9.2.2 And this seems to be the opinion that Job wanted [to express] (Job 10:4–6): "Do You have the eyes of flesh? Is Your vision that of mere men? Are Your days the days of a mortal, Are Your years the years of a man, that You seek my iniquity and search out my sin?"; that is to say, since individuals are only apprehended by sense [perception] and are subject to time, they do not fall under divine knowledge at all. And if so, he [i.e. the god of the philosophers] has providence neither over them nor over their iniquities, as Averroes thought according to what is explained in his Commentary on *Metaphysics* 12, text. 37.[a]

§ 9.3 Third, it becomes clear that the creator does not know anything apart from himself in this way: because for contingent future things and those that fall under free will, it seems that it is impossible for them to fall under divine knowledge at all. And it also seems that it is impossible that he could know them after their generation if knowledge was not created for him. It then follows that he does not know anything apart from himself. This consequence is self-evident and the premise becomes clear | in this way: because if the creator knew the future before its generation—[and] behold, since his knowledge cannot be denied, it would follow that the future thing would in any case be as it was in the prior knowledge of God, may He be praised—and if this was correct, there would exist neither contingency nor free will, and this is incongruous. And if we say that He only knows them after their generation, it would therefore follow that His knowledge of them is generated insofar as they are individuals of the existents that are only apprehended by sense [perception]. And it seems that this is entirely incongruous, as we explained above.

§ 9.4 Fourth, the same becomes clear from Averroes's proof, which explains in [his Commentary on] *Metaphysics* 12, text. 51,[b] that since the individuals are of an infinite number, they do not fall under knowledge in any case. And therefore, it follows that the Creator—may He be praised—does not know them.

---

[a] Cf. *Metaph.* 12.6.1072a.   [b] Cf. *Metaph.* 12.8.1074b.

9. DE SCIENTIA

quare | individua sicut sortes et alias qui ab invicem per sensum tantum distinguuntur non autem per intellectuum Deus proculdubio ignorat.

§ 9.2.2 Et idem videtur inferri in libro Job cap. 10 [10:4–6] esse antiquorum Gentilium opinionem, ubi scilicet narrat Job, Deum arguentem dixisse: «Nunquid oculi carnei tibi sunt, sicut videt homo et tu videbis, nunquid sicut dies hominis dies tui sunt, et anni tui sicut humana tempora, ut queras iniquitatem meam et peccatum meum scruteris etc.» Quasi dicat, quod cum individua sint sensuum obiecta et habeant sub tempore percipi nullo pacto habent a Deo cognosci, et per consequens neque de illo etc. peccati habere sollicitudinem sive curam sicut et Aven R. *Metaphysicorum* XII t.c. 37 opinari videtur.

§ 9.3 Tertio arguitur sic: futura contingentia et arbitraria videtur necessario ignorare antequam sint omnino. Immo videtur quod etiam post quam fuerit non habeat illa scire nisi novam acquirat scientiam et quodammodo patiatur ut supra quod est inconveniens. Quibus sequitur ut non omnia sciat, quod autem talia ignoret antequam sint omnino patet, quia si illa tunc sciret cum eius scientia habeat esse semper vera et infallibilis sequeretur ut necessario haberent illa sic se, et sic negaretur natura contingentis, et liberi arbitrij, quod est inconveniens.

§ 9.4 Quattuor[a] arguitur ratione Aven R. *Metaphysicorum* XII t.c. 51 ubi dicit: «Quod cum individua sint numero infinita non habent scientia determinari» quare sequitur ut neque Deum illa scire contingat.

Therefore, God ignores all | individual species and other things that are separated from each other only in the senses, but not in the intellect.

§ 9.2.2 And it seems that this can be shown in the [Holy] Book of Job (10:4–6), in which there are the opinions of the Ancients among the Gentiles, when Job says to God: "Do you have eyes of flesh, or do you see as a human being sees? Are your days like the days of a mortal, or your years like the years of a mortal, that you must search out my iniquity, and inquire about my sin, etc.?" This means that individuals are the object of the senses and are subject to time and do not fall under divine knowledge at all, and consequently, He does not have providence or care over their sins, as Averroes explicates in *Metaphysics* 12, text. 37.[a]

§ 9.3 Third, I would argue that it seems that he [i.e. the god of the philosophers] necessarily completely ignores future things, which are contingents and under free will, before they are; indeed, it seems that he can only understand things after their existence, and he would acquire new knowledge if he was affected by them in a certain manner, as mentioned above, and this is incongruous. From these [words], it would follow that he does not know everything, because it is clear that he ignores such [things] completely before they are, because if he knew those things—and his knowledge is always right and perfect—it would follow that he necessarily knew them. And this would deny the nature of the contingent and free will might be denied, and this is incongruous.

§ 9.4 Fourth, I would argue according to what Averroes explicates in *Metaphysics* 12, text. 51,[b] where he states that since individuals are infinite in number, they do not fall under knowledge in any case, and it would follow that God does not know them.

---

[a] Quattuor] coni. Copp.; Quinto b.

[a] *Metaph.* 12.8.1074b.   [b] Cf. *Metaph.* 12.8.1074b.

§ 9.5 Fifth, the same becomes clear from al-Ġazālī's proof, which says, citing the Philosopher, as explained in *The Incoherence of the Incoherence* 11, first investigation: "According to the opinion of the philosophers, who deny the creation of the world, it follows that the things that are caused by the first cause are caused by it by necessity or naturally, and not by will, but in the manner that warmth is caused by fire, and light by the sun, and that neither of the two knows itself, still less so that it knows something apart from itself. And it is not impossible that many existents who know themselves and things apart from themselves are caused—at least mediately—by an existent which does not know itself. And it would not follow from this that the caused thing was nobler than its cause."[a] Because, as it appears from al-Ġazālī's opinion, which is explained in the aforementioned book 10, third investigation: "[As] nature has providence over us and gives us senses with which to apprehend the individuals, [so that] we can protect ourselves from the damage that comes from them, while it is not thought to be a deficiency of God—may He be praised—that He does not have the aforementioned senses, since He does not need them, it is also not incongruous that—although knowledge of the universals of the existents is thought to exist for our sake, [namely,] for [our] perfection, because by their knowledge we are protected from damage and acquire a life in the world after death—in any event, its absence is not seen as a deficiency with respect to the Creator—may He be praised—since He does not need all these [things]."[b]

§ 9.6.1 But the contrary of this opinion, which is that God—may He be praised—also knows everything apart from Himself, becomes clear in this way: because every arranger of order necessarily knows the existents that are orderly arranged by him, so that he will order them in such a way that the final purpose intended by this order will be achieved, and the Creator is an arranger of order of existents. If so, it follows that He knows the existents.

§ 9.6.2 The consequence is self-evident and so is the [antecedent] premise, in which we said that the arranger of order necessarily knows the | existents that are orderly arranged by him, because the order is nothing other than the interconnection of existents and their unity. Through that unity—together with the preservation of their ranks and their mutual relationships—a certain intended final purpose is to be achieved. And therefore, it follows that the arranger of order knows the orderly arranged things; not only their existence, but also their ranks and relationships.

---

[a] Cf. *Incoherence* 270. [b] Cf. *Incoherence* 266.

9. DE SCIENTIA

§ 9.5 Quinto arguitur ratione Algazelis de mente physicorum in lib. *Destructio des.* relata disputatione XI, dubio primo ubi dicit: «Quia secundum Phylosophos negantes mundi novitatem sequitur ut illa que a prima producuntur causa habeant per necessitatem vel naturam ab eadem procedere sicut calor procedit ab igne et lumen a sole, quorum neuter se ipsum nedum extrinseca noscit, nec est inconveniens ut ab eo qui se ipsum ignorat procedant saltem mediate plura que se ipsa et alia sciat, neque ad hoc sequitur ut causatum sit nobilius sua causa» quia sicut videtur Algazelis ratione ibidem disputatione X, dubio 3 inferri: «Quemadmodu natura nobis providit de sensibus ut percipiamus individua, quorum lectiones[a] cavere possemus, Deo tamen cum his non indigeat non imputetur defectus hoc scilicet ut huiusmodi sensus non habeat, sic non est inconveniens ut quamvis nobis sit perfectio habere scientiam de universalibus, que scientia nobis requiritur ad gloriam post mortem consequendum, Deo tamen cum his non indigeat non imputetur defectus huiusmodi universalium ignorantia.»

§ 9.5 Fifth, I would argue as al-Ġazālī explicates in the name of the physicians in *The Incoherence of the Incoherence* 11, first doubt, where he states: "According to the opinion of the philosophers, who deny the creation of the world, it would follow that things caused by the first cause are caused by it by necessity or naturally, in the way that warmth is caused by fire and light by the sun, but neither of the two knows itself, still less does it know something apart from itself. And it is not impossible that many existents who know themselves and things apart from themselves were caused—at least mediately—by an existent that does not know itself, and it would follow that the caused was nobler than its cause."[a] And al-Ġazālī explains this in the above-mentioned book 10, third doubt, where he states: "As nature has providence over us according to the senses by which we apprehend individuals [and] protect ourselves from damage that comes from them, and as it is not thought to be a deficiency of God that He does not have the aforementioned senses, since He does not need them, it is also not incongruous that perfection may be for us to have knowledge of the universals, and that through knowledge, we can achieve a life after death. In any case, this ignorance about the universals is not seen as a deficiency with respect to God, since He does not need all these [things]."[b]

§ 9.6.1 Ad oppositum arguitur primo sic: quodlibet ordinator habet necessario scire sua ordinanda ad hoc ut illa ad ordinis finem consequendum | opportune ordinet. Creator est entium ordinato, ergo Creator habet necessario ipsa entia ab eo adeo sapienter ordinata penitus scire.

§ 9.6.1 On the contrary it is to argue, first: any arranger necessarily knows all the things that are ordered by him because he orders them in accordance with the final purpose | proper to the order. The creator is the arranger of the existents; therefore, the creator necessarily knows those existents that are wisely ordered by Him.

§ 9.6.2 Consequentia patet similiter et antecedens, quoad primam partem qua scilicet dicitur quod ordinator habet necessario sua ordinanda scire. Ordo enim nil aliud esse videtur quam ordinandorum gradus consideratio qua ad intentum finem consequendum ordinata, quare habeat necessario ipsa ordinanda horumque gradus ab horum ordinatore cognosci sive sciri.

§ 9.6.2 The consequence is evident and the first part of the antecedent is proved when we say that the arranger necessarily knows his ordered things, because it seems that order is nothing more than the contemplation of the rank of ordered existents following the intended final purpose, because ordered things and their rank are recognised—that is: known—by their arranger.

---

[a] lectiones] emend. Copp.; lesiones b; lectiones DD.

[a] Cf. *Incoherence* 270. [b] Cf. *Incoherence* 266.

§ 9.6.3 Indeed, what we said—that the creator is an arranger of order of existents—becomes clear in this way: because between the upper parts of [all] existence and the lower parts of it—[as] became clear—there is a certain order of interconnection[s] by which there is a unity of existence, as sense [perception] proves. And Aristotle explains this in *Metaphysics* 12, text. 52.[a] Regarding this order, it follows that we think about one of two [alternatives]: either (1) that this order comes from the Creator—may He be praised—who brought forth the existents mediately or immediately, or (2) that this order comes not from Him, but from an arranger of order other than Him.

§ 9.6.4 But it is incongruous that this could be through an arranger of order apart from him, because then it would follow that [it had happened] by chance that the arranger of order had found such existents that were intended to receive his order without his intention or his endeavour and also that the existence of some of them was necessary for the existence of some of the others. And if this chance had not occurred, then this arranger of order would not exist; if not, he would perhaps be useless [if he did] not have any activity. And also, it would follow that it happened by chance to all the existents that [this] arranger of order existed. And if there had not been the aforementioned chance, then the existents would have come from the creator who brought them forth, [but] without any order, although we see a certain portion of quantity and quality that is intended for the aforementioned order in every single one of the existents. And it would be incongruous that all these [things] could have occurred by chance in such a large number of things, because there are only a few things that exist by chance, as is self-evident. And Aristotle explains this in *Physics* 2, text. 48,[b] and *On Generation and Corruption* 2, text. 39.[c] And regarding this, he says in *On the Heavens* 2, text. 45:[d] "If this was [the case] for the property of only one or two stars, then it would not be so very impossible that this could have happened by chance, but since all the planets share one [same] property, then this is an absurd statement."

§ 9.6.5 And apart from this, if we were to say that the order [that is] evidently [present] in the existents was intended by an arranger of order besides the creator who brought them forth, it would therefore follow that he brought them forth without any order or any sort of perpetuity, if there had not occurred a chance that was unintended by him that a certain arranger of order existed who arranged the

---

[a] *Metaph.* 12.10.1075a. [b] *Phys.* 2.4.196b. [c] *Gen. corr.* 2.6.333b. [d] *Cael.* 2.8.289b.

§ 9.6.3 אמנם מה שאמרנו שהבורא הוא המסדר את הנמצאות יתבאר באופן זה כי אמנם בין חלקי המציאות העליונים וחלקיו התחתונים התבאר שיש איזה סדר התקשרות אשר בו היה אחדות המציאות כמו שיעיד החוש ובאר זה ארסטו' בספר מה שאחר מאמר י"ב פרק נ"ב. והנה על זה הסדר יתחייב שנחשוב אחת משתים אם שנאמר שהיה זה הסדר מאת הבורא יתברך הממציא הנמצאות באמצעי או בלתי אמצעי או שנאמר שלא היה זה הסדר מאתו אבל היה ממסדר זולתו.

§ 9.6.4 אמנם לא יתכן שהיה זה ממסדר זולתו כי אם כן יתחייב שמקרה הוא קרה למסדר בלתי כוונתו והשתדלותו שמצא כל כך נמצאות מוכנות לקבל סדרו עם היות מציאות קצתם הכרחי למציאות קצתם ושאם לא היה זה המקרה לא היה זה המסדר נמצא אם לא היה אולי בטל בלתי שום פעולה וכמו כן יתחייב שמקרה הוא קרה לכל הנמצאות שנמצא איזה מסדר ושלולא המקרה הנזכר היו הנמצאות מאת הבורא הממציאם בלי סדר עם היות שאנחנו רואים בכל אחת מהנמצאות קצבת מה מכמות ואיכות מוכנת אל הסדר הנזכר וזה לא יתכן שיקרו כל אלה במקרה בכל כך רבים במספר כי הדברים אשר במקרה לא יהיו כי אם על המעט כמו שהוא מבואר בעצמו ובאר אותו ארסטו' בספר השמע מאמר ב' פרק מ"ח ובספר ההויה וההפסד מאמר ב' פרק ל"ט ולזה אמר בספר השמים מאמר ב' פרק מ"ה ש"אם היה על תכונת מה כוכב אחד או שנים בלבד לא היה כל כך נמנע שיקרה זה במקרה אבל בהיות כל כוכבי לכת על תכונה אחת הנה זה מאמר בטל."

§ 9.6.5 ובלעדי זאת אם נאמר שהסדר המבואר בנמצאות היה מכוון ממסדר זולת הבורא הממציאם יתחייב מזה שהוא המציא אותם בלי סדר ואופן קיום לולי קרה מקרה בלתי מכוון מאתו שנמצא איזה

§ 9.6.3 Quo autem ad secundam partem qua scilicet dicitur, quod Creator est entium ordinator probatur. Quia in universi partibus tam superioribus quam inferioribus patet esse colligationis ordo quo scilicet fit universi unitas prout percipitur sensu et habetur a Phylosopho *Metaphysicorum* XII t.c. 52. Huiusmodi autem entium ordo vel fit ad eorum Creatoris nutum vel non.

§ 9.6.4 Non secundum, quia ut sic sequeretur ut casu sive preter agentis intentum contigisset ordinatori ut invenisset entia suo ordini disposita. Sine quo casu habuisset ipse ordinator esse quid ociosum, hisque ordinatis casu contigisset ut habuisset esse huiusmodi ordinator sine quo casu fuissent sine ordine. Quamvis in singulis pateat esse quantitatum et qualitatum gradus huiusmodi ordini oportunus quod est inopinabile, illa enim que casu et preter alicuius intentum contingunt nonnisi de raro et in paucis fiunt prout habetur a Phylosopho *Physicorum* II t.c. 48 et *De Generatione* II t.c. 39 quare in lib. *De Celo* II t.c. 45 ait: «Si igitur una stellarum aut due essent huiusmodi, non esset inopinabile tantum scilicet ut casu et preter agentis intentum contigisset sic esse. Cum autem omnes stelle scilicet planete, sint huiusmodi iste sermo est fabulosus etc.»

§ 9.6.5 Preterea sequeretur ut Creator huiusmodi entia sic tandem ordinata producens fecisset opus per se confusum et sine ordine quare et impermanens[a] nisi per ordinatorem preter eiusdem Creatoris intentum ordinarentur, quod

§ 9.6.3 The second part of the antecedent, in which we said that the creator is the arranger of the existents, is proved because the order of interconnections in both the upper and lower parts of the universe produces the unity of the universe, as the senses testify and as the Philosopher explains in *Metaphysics* 12, text. 52.[a] Regarding the order of existents, it is either produced by the creator's command, or not.

§ 9.6.4 The second [inference] cannot be [true] [namely, that the order is not produced by the creator's command], because it would follow that if it occurred by chance or without the intention of the agent that the existents were disposed on his order, then the arranger would not exist because he would be an idle essence. And if it had occurred by chance to the ordered existents that such an arranger existed, they would have existed without order had this chance not occurred, although it is clear that the rank of quantity and quality is necessary for the order of every single one of the existents. This is incongruous. Only a few rare things exist by chance or without intention, as the Philosopher explains in *Physics* 2, text. 48,[b] and in *On Generation and Corruption* 2, text. 39.[c] Moreover, the Philosopher explains this in *On the Heavens* 2, text. 45,[d] where he states: "If only one or two stars were [moving] in this way, it would not be that impossible. But since all the stars are [moving] in this way, this statement is absurd."

§ 9.6.5 Therefore, it would follow that the creator, who produces ordered existents, had generated something confused and without order and that the ordered things would have been ordered by an order without the will of the cre-

---

[a] impermanens] b[corr]; permanens b; בלי סדר ואופן קיום a.

[a] *Metaph.* 12.10.1075a. [b] *Phys.* 2.4.196b. [c] *Gen. corr.* 2.6.333b. [d] *Cael.* 2.8.289b.

order of his creatures and gave them perpetuity by his order. And this would be disgraceful with respect to every agent, also to that which was inferior and minor, and this is even more incongruous with respect to the Creator, He who is nobler than all existents. If so, what necessarily remains is that this evident order in the upper and lower parts of [all] existence and their connection, and the evident [order] in the parts of every composed [thing] that possesses [appropriate] instruments [or organs], is intended by the Creator—may He be praised—and is generated by Him, mediately or immediately. And this is what we wanted to explain. | And it seems that Aristotle explains this in *Metaphysics* 12, text. 52,[a] saying: "All existents are orderly arranged in respect of one existent." And Averroes explains his words, saying: "It is evident that this thing is common to all existents: that they all exist for the sake of one and their activities are turned towards that one—and this is the first cause—just as all things that are in a house are [there] for the sake of the owner of the house."

§ 9.7.1 Second, the same becomes clear in this way: because every agent who intends that a certain final purpose will be achieved by his activity necessarily has to know the thing by which that final purpose will be achieved. And the Creator—may He be praised—intends that a certain final purpose will be achieved through the existents that He created. If so, He necessarily knows the existents. And since all the existents that are besides Him are caused by Him mediately or immediately, it follows that the aforementioned Creator knows all the existents.

§ 9.7.2 The consequence is evident and the [antecedent] premise becomes clear, first, when we say that the agent who intends that a certain final purpose will be achieved by his activity necessarily knows that activity. This becomes clear in this way: because the final purpose is the thing intended by the agent, who mediately or immediately enacts this activity in order to achieve that final purpose. And this is self-evident, and Aristotle explains it in *Physics* [2], text. 49:[b] "Some of the existents exist for the sake of a certain final purpose and some others do not, because some exist by intention and by will and by free choice, and some others do not." In these words, he explains that the things that exist for the sake of a final purpose are made by knowledge and free choice through which the remote or proximate agent intends the final purpose that will be achieved by means of the activity. And therefore, it follows that he will know that activity.

---

[a] *Metaph.* 12.10.1075a. [b] *Phys.* 2.5.197a.

מסדר שסדר את ברואיו וקיים אותם בסדרו וזה היה מגונה בחוק כל פועל גם שיהיה פחות ונקלה כל שכן שזה נמנע בחק הבורא שהוא נכבד מכל הנמצאים. אם כן ישאר בהכרח שזה הסדר המבואר בחלקי המציאות העליונים וחלקיו התחתונים וקשרם והמבואר בחלקי כל מורכב בעל כלים הוא מכוון מאת[a] הבורא יתברך והווה מאתו באמצעי או בלתי אמצעי וזה הוא מה שרצינו לבאר. | וזה נראה שבאר ארסטו' בספר מה שאחר מאמר י"ב פרק נ"ב באמרו: »כל הנמצאות הם מסודרות בהבטה אל נמצא אחד.« ודבריו אלה באר אבן רשד באמרו כי: »אמנם הוא מבואר שזה דבר כולל לכל הנמצאות שכלם הם בשביל אחד ושפעולותם פונות אל אותו האחד והוא הסבה הראשונה כמו שכל הדברים שבבית הם בשביל בעל הבית.« עכ"ל.

§ 9.7.1 **שנית** יתבאר זה בעצמו באופן זה כי אמנם כל פועל המכוון שיושג איזה תכלית בפעלתו יתחייב בהכרח שידע אותו הדבר אשר בו יושג אותו התכלית והנה הבורא יתברך הוא מכוון בנמצאות אשר חדש שיושג בהם איזה תכלית אם כן הוא בהכרח יודע את הנמצאות ובהיות שכל הנמצאות אשר זולתו הם מסובבות מאתו באמצעי או בלתי אמצעי יתחייב הבורא הנזכר יודע את כל הנמצאות.

§ 9.7.2 הנה חיוב התולדה הוא מבואר. וההקדמה תתבאר ראשונה באמרנו שהפועל המכוון אל שיושג איזה תכלית בפעלתו הוא בהכרח יודע אותה הפעולה הנה יתבאר באופן זה כי אמנם התכלית הוא הדבר המכוון מפועל אשר יפעל באמצעי או בלתי אמצעי איזו פעלה להשיג אותו התכלית וזה הוא כמבואר בעצמו ובארו ארסטו' בספר השמע מאמר ב'[b] פרק מ"ט באמרו: »הנמצאות קצתם יש להם מציאות בשביל איזה תכלית וקצתם אינם לתכלית כי קצתם יש להם מציאות בכוונה וברצון ובבחירה וקצתם אינם כן« עכ"ל הנה בדבריו אלה ביאר שהדברים אשר מציאותם לתכלית הם נעשים בידיעה ובחירה אשר בה הפועל הקרוב או הרחוק מכוין אל התכלית אשר יושג באמצעות הפעולה ומזה יתחייב שהוא יודע אותה הפעלה.

---

[a] מאת] מאתו a[corr]. [b] מאמר ב'] emend. Dunk.; om. a; 2 b.

esset quid turpe etiam artificum vilissimo, nedum Creatori entium scilicet nobilissimo. Restat ergo primum scilicet quod huiusmodi ordo tam in universi partibus quam in cuiuslibet compositi organis apparens ab eorundem entium creatori mediate vel immediate fiat et principaliter intendatur, et idem videtur inferri ratione et auctoritate Phylosophi *Metaphysicorum* XII t.c. 52 ubi dicit: «Omnia ordinata sunt respectu alicuius etc.» ubi Aven R. exponens ait: «Apparet enim quod hoc commune est omnibus entibus scilicet, quod omnia sunt propter unum, et quod actiones eorum sunt erga illud unum, et est prima causa, quemadmodum que sunt in domo sunt propter dominum domus.»

§ 9.7.1 Secundo arguitur sic. Quilibet agens intendens finem ad suam actionem sequendum habet necessario scire illud ad quod finem sequi intendit, Creator est huiusmodi quoad entia scilicet quod intendit fine sequi ad entia per ipsum producta. Ergo Creator habet necessario ipsa entia scire. Cumque omnia entia preter ipsum Creatorem sint ab eodem Creatore producta ut supra. Sequitur quidem ut idem Creator omnia sciat.

§ 9.7.2 Consequentia patet, et antecedens probatur, et primo quoad primam partem qua scilicet dicitur quod agens ad finem habet necessario scire illud quod finaliter intendit. Quia finis nil aliud est quam illius quod agens mediate vel immediate intendit ut sequatur ad eiusdem actionem, sicut per se patet, et habetur a Phylosopho *Physicorum* II t.c. 49, ubi dicit: «Ea que sunt quedam sunt propter aliquid et quedam non, quedam enim sunt per cogitationem, vel voluntatem, et electionem, et quedam non.» Ex quibus inferre videtur, quod oportet ut illa que sunt propter aliquid fiant per cogitationem qua scilicet agens immediate vel saltem mediate illa intendit sicut res se habet in artificialibus ut scilicet artifex cogitet finem ab huiusmodi actum sequendum, et per consequens habet ipse agens necessario scire suum actum ad quem habet intentum finem sequi.

ator, and this is disgraceful for every agent and impossible for the creator, who is nobler than all existents. Then, there remains the first [inference] that the order in the upper parts of the universe, as well in every composed thing that possesses organs, was intended by the creator and was generated by him mediately or immediately, according to the argument and authority of the Philosopher in *Metaphysics* 12, text. 52,[a] where he states: "All existents are arranged in respect of one being." And Averroes explicates: "It is evident that this is common to all existents: that they all exist for the sake of one, and their activities are turned towards that one. And this is the first cause, just as all things that are in a house are there for the sake of the owner of the house."

§ 9.7.1 Second, I would argue that every agent intending a final purpose necessarily knows everything following its activity from which the final purpose follows. The creator has this nature because he intends the final purpose of the existents that were created by him; therefore, a creator necessarily knows every existent. Every existent, except the creator, was generated by the creator, as mentioned above. Therefore, it would follow that the creator knows everything.

§ 9.7.2 The consequence is evident, and the antecedent is proved in the first part in which we said that the agent of the final purpose necessarily knows the outcome, because the final purpose is nothing more than something that an agent intends mediately or immediately following his activity. This is evident, as the Philosopher explains in *Physics* 2, text. 49,[b] where he states: "Some existents exist for the sake of a certain purpose and some others do not, because some have an existence through knowledge, will, and free choice, and some others do not." With these [words], Aristotle explains that things are produced by the knowledge by which the agent knows those things, immediately or at least mediately, and this is the case for artificial things because the artisan thinks of the final purpose, from which his activity follows, and consequently, the agent necessarily knows his activity, which follows from the intended final purpose.

---

[a] *Metaph.* 12.10.1075a.   [b] *Phys.* 2.5.196b.

§ 9.7.3 [Second:] And what we said, that the Creator—may He be praised—intends that a certain purpose will be achieved through the existents that He created, becomes clear in this way: because in the composition of the composed existents—especially those that possess [appropriate] instruments [or organs]—and in their order, there are many characteristics that are made by wisdom, intended for the need of a certain necessary or beneficial good, depending on what is most appropriate. Without these characteristics, that good will not be achieved. It is evident that all [these things] do not exist by chance, but are necessarily intended by a certain proximate or remote agent that intended the achieved final purpose. And it is incongruous that this intender could be anyone other than the first [being] who brought them forth mediately or immediately, as mentioned above. And the same becomes clear from Aristotle's proofs in *Physics* 2, text. 77, and others,[a] in which he cites a proof of the preservation of the intention for the final purpose in many species. And this informs us about the intention of the remote or proximate agent who intended that final purpose, as became clear in the definition of the final purpose, which Aristotle explains | in *Metaphysics* 2, text. 9.[b] And regarding this, Averroes writes in the *Treatise on the Substance of the Celestial Sphere*, ch. 2, that the final purpose provides essential information about the agent, just as a motion informs us about the mover.[c]

§ 9.7.4 And therefore, it becomes clear, as Aristotle says in *Physics* 2, text. 86,[d] that nature does not intend a final purpose. It is necessarily understood that nature is acting under the command of a remote agent that is nobler than it. And it [the agent] is the intender for this final purpose, as Averroes explains in the Commentary on *Metaphysics* 12, text. 18:[e] "In this way, it is appropriate that it is understood from our words that nature enacts a certain thing in perfection and in order, although it does not understand [anything], whereas the active powers, which are nobler than it, which are called 'separate intellects,' are governing it." And he explains the same in *The Incoherence of the Incoherence* 10, second investigation: "And when the philosophers saw that the natural activities were proceeding as in the [same] way as the artificial activities, they drew from this [the conclusion] that the natural powers are generated by the same intellect, and it gives an order to all existents."[f] From all these [words], it becomes clear that the First [Being] is the arranger of order of all existents, medi-

---

[a] *Phys.* 2.8.198b.   [b] *Metaph.* 2.2.994b.   [c] Cf. *Sub. orb.* 85.   [d] *Phys.* 2.8.199b.
[e] Cf. *Metaph.* 12.3.1070a.   [f] Cf. *Incoherence* 262.

§ 9.7.3 Quo autem ad secundam antecedentis partem, qua scilicet dicitur quod Creator est huiusmodi probantur. Quia cum plura appareant in entium compositione et ordine ad necessitatem vel ad bene esse oportuna, sine quibus non sequeretur illud bonum quod inde sequitur, patet quidem quod non casu sive preter alicuius intentum fuisse contingit, sed a quodam mediato vel immediato agente finem intendente observata sunt. Et talis est omnium necessario primus, illa scilicet ut supra mediate vel imediate producens, et per consequens idem producens sive creans habuit finem intendere. Et idem infertur rationibus Phylosophi *Physicorum* II t.c. 77 et sequentibus, ubi per bonum apparens in pluribus probat esse ad intentum finem sive propter aliquid gestum, quod non contingit esse nisi sit ab agente mediato vel immediato intentum, sicut per se satis patet, et habetur per finis diffinitionem a Phylosopho traditam *Metaphysicorum* II t.c. 9 quare Aven R. in *Tractatu de Substantia Orbis* cap.2 ait: «Quod finis significat agentem significatione propria sicut motus significat motorem.»

§ 9.7.4 Cum ergo Phylosophus *Physicorum* II t.c. 86 inferat quod non est inconveniens ut natura agat ad finem preter eiusdem nature cogitationem, intelligit necessario ut natura illud agat nutu cuiusdam nobilioris mediate agentis, huiusmodi finem intendentis. Prout habetur ab Aven R. in comento *Metaphysicorum* XII, t.c. 18 ubi dicit: «Secundum hoc igitur est intelligendum que natura facit aliquid perfecte et ordinate quamvis non intelligat, quasi esset memorata a virtutibus agentibus nobilioribus ea que dicuntur intelligentie etc.» et idem infert in lib. *Destructio Des.* disputatione X, dubio 2, ubi dicit: «Et quia viderunt (scilicet Phylosophi) opera naturalia modo artificialium currentia, iudicarunt quod ab eodem intellectu virtutes naturales procedunt, et ille est qui entibus omnibus ordinem dat etc.» Ex quibus sequitur, ut primus ens reliqua

§ 9.7.3 The second part of the antecedent, in which we said that the creator has this nature, is proved. Because many things are apparent in the composition and order of existents that exist out of necessity or convenience [and] a good thing does not follow without these [characteristics]. It is clear that this does not occur by chance or without the intention of an agent, but [necessity and good] are observed in what occurs thanks to a purposive agent who intends them mediately or immediately for a final purpose. It is necessary that this [agent] is the first of all existents, who produces them mediately or immediately. Consequently, that which produces or creates must intend a final purpose. And this becomes clear according to the Philosopher's explanation in *Physics* 2, text. 77,[a] and others, where the good observed in many things proves that there is a final purpose by means of an action, and this only happens if the intention is produced by an agent mediately or immediately, as is evident from the definition of the final purpose. The Philosopher explains this in *Metaphysics* 2, text. 9,[b] and Averroes explicates it in the *Treatise on the Substance of the Celestial Sphere*, ch. 2, where he states that "the final purpose" signifies the agent, in the same way that "motion" signifies the mover.[c]

§ 9.7.4 Therefore, the Philosopher explains in *Physics* 2, text. 86,[d] that it is not incongruous that nature should act for the final purpose without nature itself thinking. One must understand that nature necessarily acts mediately by the command of a purposive agent who is nobler than itself, as Averroes explicates in the Commentary on *Metaphysics* 12, text. 18,[e] where he states: "In this way, it is appropriate to understand that nature produces something in perfection and in order, although it does not understand, as it is inspired by active powers that are nobler than it, which are called 'intellects,' etc." And he explains this in *The Incoherence of the Incoherence* 10, second doubt, where he states: "When they—i.e., the philosophers—saw that the natural activities were proceeding in the same way as the artificial activities, they drew from this that the natural powers are generated by the same intellect, and he gives an order to all existents."[f] With these [words], it would follow that the first being, ordering all | existents mediately or

---

[a] *Phys.* 2.8.198b. [b] *Metaph.* 2.2.994b.   [c] Cf. *Sub. orb.* 85.   [d] *Phys.* 2.8.199b.
[e] Cf. *Metaph.* 12.3.1070a.   [f] Cf. *Incoherence* 262.

ately or immediately. He enacts and makes [things] in an intended artificial manner, and therefore, it follows that He knows all of them. And this is what we wanted to explain.

§ 9.8 Third, this very same [thing] becomes clear in this way: because many existents who know themselves and [who know things] besides themselves were generated by the first cause. If so, the first cause—and this is the Creator, may He be praised—knows Himself and what is beside Himself. The premise is evident from sense [perception] and the consequence becomes clear from Averroes's proof, which explains in *The Incoherence of the Incoherence* 11, first investigation: "Regarding what al-Ġazālī says, that it is possible that living beings may be generated by a non-living being and that a knower may be generated by a non-knower, and, if so, that there would be no other rank for the First [Being] than for him to be the principle of what is beside himself, we say: it is an evident falsehood that if it was possible that life could be generated from a non-living being, it would therefore necessarily be possible that existence would also be generated from a non-being and that [therefore] everything would be generated from everything. And this is an evident falsehood."[a]

§ 9.9 We answer, then, to dispel a doubt about the aforementioned thesis, that the first existent, who brought forth the [other] existents and created them, knows itself and the rest of the existents. Indeed, there is no acquisition of knowledge from the existents, but rather it knows them through that knowledge by which it knows itself, by which it necessarily knows that it is their forth-bringer and their creator for an intended final purpose. And this seems to be what Averroes considers in *The Incoherence of the Incoherence* 3, eighteenth investigation: "God, from the reality of His essence, understands existents in the noblest way in which it is possible for them to exist. And it is through His understanding that [the] intellect is the cause of all the existents."[b] | And he explains the same in ibid., 10, second investigation: "And the philosophers agree that this intellect, when it intellects itself, intellects [all] the other existents. And because it intellects itself, it is indeed the intellect, and all the existents are known."[c]

§ 9.10.1 So, to the opponent's arguments, we answer, after having laid down one premise and what follows from it [i.e., a corollary]. And the premise is that our knowledge is caused by the existents that are in actuality outside of the intellect. But the knowledge of the creator, to which no existent is prior, is necessarily contrary to our knowledge,

---

[a] Cf. *Incoherence* 273.   [b] Cf. *Incoherence* 129.   [c] Cf. *Incoherence* 262.

הנמצאות באמצעי או בלתי אמצעי פעל ועשה על דרך מלאכותיי מכוין ומזה יתחייב שהוא יודע את כלם וזה הוא מה שרצינו לבאר.

§ 9.8 שלישית יתבאר זה בעצמו באופן זה כי מן הסבה הראשונה נתהוו נמצאים רבים שיודעים עצמם וזולתם אם כן הסבה הראשונה והוא הבורא יתברך יודע עצמו וזולתו. ההקדמה הנה היא מבוארת בחוש וחיוב התולדה אמנם יתבאר בראיית אבן רשד אשר באר בספר הפלת ההפלה מאמר י״א חקירה א׳ וזה לשונו: »אמנם זה שאמר אלגזיל שהוא איפשר שהחיים יתהוו ממנצא בלתי חי ושיתהוה יודע מבלתי יודע ואם כן אין לראשון מעלה אחרת אלא שהוא התחלה לזולתו נאמר שהוא שקר מבואר שאם היה איפשר שהנמצא בלתי חי יתהווה חיות היה מתחייב מזה שיהיה איפשר גם כן שיתהוה מציאות מבלתי נמצא ושכל דבר יתהוה מכל דבר וזה שקר מבואר.«

§ 9.9 נשיב אם כן להתיר ספק החקירה הנזכרת שהנמצא הראשון אשר המציא את הנמצאות וברא אותם הוא יודע את עצמו ואת שאר הנמצאות אמנם לא בידיעה קנויה מאת הנמצאות אבל יודע אותם באותה הידיעה שיודע את עצמו אשר בה ידע בהכרח שהוא ממציאם ובוראם לתכלית מכוין וזה נראה שחשב אבן רשד בספר הפלת ההפלה מאמר ג׳ חקירה י״ח באמרו: »מה שהאל מבין ממציאות עצמו הם נמצאות על אופן יותר נכבד שאיפשר שימצאו וזה בהבינו שהוא שכל סבה לכל הנמצאות« עכ״ל. | *וזה* בעצמו באר שם מאמר י׳ חקירה ב׳ באמרו: »והסכימו הפילוסופים שזה השכל בהשכילו את עצמו ישכיל שאר הנמצאות. וזה כי השכילו את עצמו הוא אמנם השכל וידוע את כל הנמצאות.«

§ 9.10.1 אמנם לטענות החולק נשיב אחר שנקדים הקדמה אחת עם הנמשך ממנה. ההקדמה היא אמנם שידיעתנו היא מסובבת מן הנמצאות אשר הם בפעל חוץ לשכל. אבל ידיעת הבורא אשר לא קדם לה שום נמצא היא בהכרח הפכית לידיעתנו כי לא תהיה

49ʳ om|nia mediate vel immediate ordinans habuisset artificialium more horum finem intendere, et per consequens habet illa omnia scire quod est intentum.

§ 9.8 Tertio arguitur sic: a prima causa plura procedunt que se ipsa et alia sciunt, ergo et ipsa Prima Causa sive Creator habet[a] se ipsam et alia scire. Consequentia tenet ratione et actoritate Aven R. in lib. *Destructiones dest.*, disputatione XI, dubio primo, ubi dicit: «Sed illud quod dicit Algazel scilicet quod vita potest procedere ab eo quod vivum non est, et sciens a non sciente, et ideo prerogativa primi principij est inquantum est principium tantum, dicimus quod sunt verba falsissima, si enim possibile esset quod ab eo quod vitam non habet procederet vita sequeretur ut entitas procederet ab eo quod non est ens, et tandem quodlibet a quolibet quod est falsum.»

§ 9.9 Ad dubium ergo respondetur: quod entium primum reliqua scilicet entificans sive creans scit se ipsum et alia entia. Non tamen per scientiam ab ipsis entibus dependentem, sed per illam qua se ipsum scit, per quam necessario scit se ipsum esse omnium entium entificantem sive creantem ad intentum finem. Et idem videbitur sensisse Aven R. in lib. *Destructio dest.* disputatione III,[b] dubio 18, ubi dicit: «Id quod intelligit de se ipso sunt entia sub nobiliori modo quo fieri possit, scilicet sciens quod ipse intellectus qui omnium entium est causa.» et idem infert ibidem disputatione x, dubio 2, ubi dicit: «Et concluserunt, scilicet, Phylosophi, quod ipse intellectus intelligendo se ipsum intelligit omnia alia entia, idest quod se ipsum intelligere idem est quod intelligere entia.»

§ 9.10.1 Ad argumenta vero respondetur presupponendo unam propositionem et unum corollarium.[c] Propositio autem[d] est ista, nostra scientia causatur necessario ab entibus extra anima existentibus, Creatoris vero scientia ad quam nullum entium habuit esse prius, est necessario nostre scientie opposita, non modo enim non causatur

§ 9.8 Third, I would argue that many existents that proceed from a first cause know themselves and others; therefore, the first cause—namely, the creator—knows himself and the other existents. The consequence is evident according to the argument and authority of Averroes, explained in *The Incoherence of the Incoherence* 11, first doubt, where he states: "Regarding what al-Ġazālī said, that it is possible that living beings may be generated by a non-living being and that a knower may be generated by a non-knower, if this was so, then there would be no other choice for the first of the first beings because he is only the first of them. We say that this is an evident falsehood, because if it was possible that living beings could be generated from a non-living being, it would therefore be necessarily possible that an existent would also be generated from a non-existent, and this is an evident falsehood."[a]

§ 9.9 To dispel any doubt, I would argue that the first of all existents, who is the Creator of beings or the Creator, knows himself and the other existents. He knows not only through the knowledge that depends on those existents, but also through the knowledge by which He knows Himself, by which He necessarily knows the intended final purpose of all beings, as Averroes explains in *The Incoherence of the Incoherence* 3, eighteenth doubt, where he states: "What He knows from Himself are the existents in the noblest way that is possible, and it is by His understanding [that He knows] that the intellect is the cause of all the existents."[b] And he explains this in ibid., 10, second doubt, where he states: "And the philosophers agree that this intellect, when it intellects itself, intellects the other existents, and because it intellects itself, it is indeed the intellect, and the known are all existents."[c]

§ 9.10.1 In response to this argument, I will reply after laying down one premise and a corollary. The premise is that our knowledge is necessarily caused by existents that exist outside of the soul [intellect]. But the knowledge of the creator, to whom no existent is prior, is necessarily the contrary to our knowledge, because it is not only caused by

---

[a] habet] b^corr; habetur b.   [b] III] emend. Copp.; 8 b; 'ג מאמר a.   [c] corollarium] coni. Copp.; correlarium b.   [d] autem] coni. Copp.; aute b.

[a] Cf. *Incoherence* 273.   [b] Cf. *Incoherence* 129.   [c] Cf. *Incoherence* 262.

because it is not caused by the existents, but its manner is the contrary to this; namely, that the existents are indeed necessarily caused by the creator's knowledge. And what follows from this is that the word "knowledge" is only said of the creator's knowledge and of our knowledge by equivocation, as Averroes explains in the Commentary on *Metaphysics* 12, text. 51.[a] And regarding this, he says in *The Incoherence of the Incoherence* 12, second investigation: "We say that all these many words, which are said based on the [supposed] similarity between divine knowledge and human knowledge, are nonsense. Indeed, according to the truth, they do not agree in definition, but are only [similar] by equivocation, because human apprehension is through the senses—that is, the intellection of the individuals—and the apprehension of the universals of the existents is received by the intellect. And therefore, there is no doubt that this [human] apprehension follows the changes in the objects of apprehension."[b] And He—may He be praised—testifies so, as it says (Isaiah 55:8): "For My thoughts are not your thoughts, nor are My ways your ways."

§ 9.10.2 And after having laid down these [words], behold, to what the opponent argues and says—that if the Creator—may He be praised—knew [something] besides Himself, it would follow that He would change and become perfected by things that are below Him—we answer by saying that this would follow if divine knowledge were caused by the existents, as is the case with human knowledge. However, since divine knowledge is the contrary of this, because it is not caused by the existents, but rather causes them, this does not have to be so at all, because it will then not change as a result of a change in the existents and will not become perfected by their existence, because it is not caused by them. And so, when the opponent argues by saying that individual existents will only be apprehended by the senses and will therefore not fall under divine knowledge, we answer by saying: this is indeed correct for human apprehension, since it only exists in the material or potential intellect, because since it is not perfect according to the second perfection, it has no way to apprehend existents besides the experience that is acquired from the apprehended things, which will be apprehended one after the other by sense [perception]. But this is not correct for the knowledge that the separate substances have, since it receives its existence from a perfect intellect in actuality. It has no need of something like experience, because the relationship between the perfect separate intellect | and the intelligibles of the existents is like the relationship

36ʳ

---

[a] Cf. *Metaph.* 12.8.1074b.   [b] Cf. *Incoherence* 280.

מסובבת מהנמצאות. אבל יהיה עניינה בהפך זה שהנמצאות הןᵃ בהכרח מסובבות מידיעת הבורא. והנמשך ממנה הוא שמלת ‹ידיעה› תאמר על ידיעת הבורא ועל ידיעתנו בשתוף השם בלבד כאשר באר אבן רשד בביאור ספר מה שאחר מאמר י״ב פרק נ״א ולזה אמר בספר הפלת ההפלה מאמר י״ב חקירהᵇ ב׳ וזה לשונו: «נאמר אנחנו שכל אלה הדברים המרבים הבל נאמרו על יסוד מדמה הידיעה האלהית לידיעה האנושית והן לפי האמת בלתי מסכימות בגדר אבל בשתוף השם בלבד כי ההשגה האנושית היא אמנם מהחושים רצוני לומר השכל האישים והשגת כוללי הנמצאות המקובלות בשכל. ולכן אין ספק שאותה ההשגה היא הולכת אחר השתנות המושגים» עד כאן לשונו. וכן העיד הוא יתברך באמרו: «כי לא מחשבותי מחשבותיכם ולא דרכיכם דרכי» (ישעיהו נ״ה ח׳).

§ 9.10.2 ואחר שהקדמנו את אלה הנה על מה שטען החולק ואמר שאם הבורא יתברך ידע זולתו יתחייב שישתנה וישלם בדבר שהוא למטה ממנו. נשיב ונאמר שזה אמנם יתחייב אם היתה הידיעה האלהית מסובבת מהנמצאות כמו העניין בידיעה האנושית. אבל בהיות הידיעה האלהית על הפך זה. כי אמנם אינה מסובבת מהנמצאות אבל היא מסבבת אותם לא יתחייב זה כלל. כי היא אם כן לא תשתנה בהשתנות הנמצאות ולא תשלם במציאותם בהיותה בלתי מסובבת מהם. וכן כאשר טען החולק ואמר שאישי הנמצאות לא יושגו כי אם בחושים ובכן לא יפלו תחת ידיעה אלהית. נשיב ונאמר שזה אמנם יצדק על ההשגה האנושית בהיות מציאותה בשכל היולאני או כוחיי בלבד כי בהיותו בלתי שלם כפי השלמות השני אין לו דרך להשיג הנמצאות זולתי בנסיון קנוי מן המושגים אשר יושגו בחוש פעם אחר פעם. אבל לא יצדק זה בידיעת העצמים הנבדלים אשר בהיות מציאותה בשכל שלם בפועל לא תצטרך לכמו זה הנסיון כי אמנם יחס השכל הנבדל השלם | אל מושכלי הנמצאות הוא כמו יחס כח הראות

36ʳ

ᵃ הן] coni. Dunk.; הם a.   ᵇ חקירה] coni. Dunk.; חקירת a.

ab entibus, verum etiam opposito se habet modo, scilicet quod ipsa entia causantur ab eiusdem Creatoris scientia. Corollarium[a] vero ad hoc sequens est hoc scilicet, equivoce tantum dicitur scientia de divina que, scilicet, est Creatoris, et de scientia nostra, scilicet, humana; prout habetur ab Aven R. *Metaphysicorum* XII t.c. 51. Quare idem in libro *Destructio Des.*, disputatione XII, dubio 2 ait: «Dicimus nos quod omnes iste ambages sunt, et oriuntur assimilando divinam scientiam humane scientie, que secundum veritatem non conveniunt nisi equivoce. Comprehensio enim humana est comprehensio a sensibilis, scilicet comprehensio individuorum, et comprehensio universalium entium que sciuntur ab intellectu, et ideo non est dubium quod comprehensio imitatur comprehensorum multitudinem etc.»

§ 9.10.2 Cum ergo primo arguitur quod si alia preter se ipsum intelligeret, sequeretur ut transmutaretur et perficeretur per quid eo ignobilius, respondetur quod illud sequeretur si illa scientia haberet esse eo modo quo habet esse humana | scientia. Que, scilicet, habet dependere ab entibus, sed non sequitur de ipsa divina scientia, opposito modo se habente. Cum, scilicet, sit scientia activa a qua entia causantur, quare non habet per scita entia transmutari neque per ignobilia perfici. Similiter cum arguitur de individuis quod, scilicet, cum non habeant nisi sensu percipi non habent sub scientia comprehendi. Respondetur quod hoc verificatur de illa scientia tantum que habet originem ab entibus, et talis est humana scientia, que cum habeat fieri per potentialem intellectum. Qui, scilicet, est quoad secundum actum imperfectum, nullo pacto percipit entia nisi per discursum a pluribus sensatis perceptum. Sed non verificatur de abstractorum scientia, que cum fiat per intellectum actu perfectum non indiget huiusmodi discursu. Qui, scilicet, potentiali inquantum talis est requiritur, talis enim est proportio intellectus actu perfecti ad intelligibilia omnia qualis est proportio potentie visive ad

49ᵛ [58]

the existents, but its manner is the contrary of this; namely, that existents are necessarily caused by the knowledge of their creator. The corollary would follow: the word "knowledge" is said of the knowledge of the creator and of our knowledge by equivocation only, as Averroes explicates in the Commentary on *Metaphysics* 12, text. 51.[a] And he explains this in *The Incoherence of the Incoherence* 12, second doubt, where he states: "We say that all these many words are ambiguous, and they are said on the basis of the similarity of divine knowledge to human knowledge. Indeed, according to the truth, they do not agree in definition, but are only [similar] by equivocation, because human apprehension is made by the senses—namely, the intellection of the individuals—and the apprehension of the universals made by the existents is received by the intellect. And therefore, there is no doubt that this apprehension follows the changes in the objects of apprehension."[b]

§ 9.10.2 In response to the first argument that if the creator knows other things besides himself, it would follow that he would be changed and that he would be perfected by existents lower than himself, I will reply: it would follow that if this knowledge exists with this prerogative, this would be the case for | human knowledge, which depends on existents. But it is not the case with divine knowledge, which is the contrary of this, because active knowledge is caused by existents, and it cannot be changed by knowledge of existents or perfected by existents that are lower than him. Similarly, in response to the argument about individuals—namely, that if something is only apprehended by the senses, it could not be comprehended by knowledge—I will reply: this is only true for the knowledge that is generated from existents, and this is the case for human knowledge, which is generated by the potential intellect, since it is not perfect according to the second perfection, and thus it can only know existents through the perception of sensible things. But this is not true for the knowledge of the separate substances, which results from a perfect intellect in act and does not require the same inference. Such a thing does not need something in potentiality, like the rela-

49ᵛ [58]

---

[a] Corollarium] coni. COPP.; Correlarium b.

[a] Cf. *Metaph.* 12.8.1074b.   [b] Cf. *Incoherence* 280.

between the power of sight and the sight of the objects seen in actuality, and like the relationship between the human intellect and the first intelligibles, which are self-evident for it [i.e., the human intellect] in such a way that there is no need for it to actualise [them] in order to know them, and still less so is the aforementioned premise incorrect about divine knowledge. It is not enough that it is not generated from the existents, because the existence of the existents and their order and their perpetuity are also generated by the aforementioned divine knowledge, and therefore it follows that divine knowledge contains the knowledge of all the existents, but [also] that it knows them in a nobler way than anyone else, [and it is nobler] still than the human species by virtue of its [i.e. the human species'] aforementioned imperfect intellect.

§ 9.11.1 And the prophet [Jeremiah] informs us about this in his statement (Jeremiah 23:24): "'If a man enters a hiding place, Do I not see him?'—says ha-Shem. 'For I fill both the heavens and earth'"; that is to say, there is no existence for them besides what continuously emanates from My existence, which is My knowledge. And so, when the opponent argues by saying that if God—may He be praised—knew the future and arbitrary [things], then it [i.e., His knowledge] would fall under the nature of contingency and the nature of free choice, we answer: even though this follows for human knowledge, because since it is generated from the existents, then if there were no necessary existents, there would be no way for it to apprehend them, yet this is not necessary for divine knowledge, because since it is not generated from the existents whose existence is outside of the intellect, it is not required that the known thing be necessary in order to it [i.e., divine knowledge] to be capable of apprehending it, because the relationship between this knowledge and all the existents is indeed like the relationship between the power of sight and the visibles that are in front of it [i.e., sight], because it undoubtedly apprehends them, be they of the necessary kind or of the contingent kind. And therefore, divine knowledge extends to the contingent things as well as to the necessary things, and to the generables in actuality that are present in front of us.

§ 9.11.2 And so, when the opponent argues that since the individuals are of an infinite number, no knowledge can encompass them and therefore no knower can know them, we answer by saying: this is correct for every knower who acquires his apprehension from the existents, because since they are infinite, his knowledge of them can never be perfected. But this is not correct for divine knowledge, which is not generated from the existents, because through this knowledge, by which God—may He be praised—

illa que actu videt, et sicut se habet humanus intellectus ad propositiones primas et per se notas. Quare non indiget exitu de potentia ad actum a fortiori, quod non verificatur de divina scientia cuius cognitio de entibus est pro quanto habent entia ab eadem divina scientia mediate vel immediate emanare. Quare non habet per ipsa scita transmutari neque per ignobiliora perfici ut supra.

§ 9.11.1 Et idem docet Yeremias propheta cap. 23 [23:24] dicens: «Numquid lateat homo in latibulo et ego non videam eum dicit Dominus non ne celum et terram ego impleo» quasi dicat quod nihili entium habet esse nisi quantum a mea entitate continue emanet et conservetur, que est qui idem cum mea scientia, quam illa necessario scit sed nobiliori modo. Quam ille, quo nos ipsa entia percipimus. Similiter cum arguitur quod si sciret futura auferretur natura contingentis, et liberi arbitrij. Respondetur quod argumentum concluderet de humana scientia que scilicet habet ab entibus dependere, quare nisi essent quid per se necessaria nullo pacto haberent per humanam scientiam presciri, non tamen sequitur de divina scientia. Illa enim cum non dependeat ab entibus extra animam existentibus sibi non requiruntur scitorum necessitas, immo uniformiter se habet ad omnia tam presentia quam futura et tam contingentia quam necessaria, sicut se habet visiva potentia ad visibilia sibi presentia, quorum non minus illaque sunt in se contingentia quam illa que sunt in se necessaria vere percipit, et nihil de ipsis dubitat, quare ipsa divina scientia non minus ad futura contingentia quam ad necessaria et presentia se extendere convenit.

§ 9.11.2 Similiter cum arguitur quod particularia cum sint infinita non habent sub scientia comprehendi. Respondetur quod illud verificatur de illa scientia que habet ad entibus dependere que entia cum sint infinita non contigit pervenire ad horum totalem numerum quo omnia comprehendantur. Sed non verificatur de divina | que non habet ab ipsis entibus dependere, immo una et eadem scientia

tionship of the power of vision to the sight of the objects seen in actuality; and human knowledge, according to the first propositions [i.e., intelligibles], which are self-evident, does not require a transition from potentiality to actuality. But this is not true for divine knowledge. This knowledge is not generated from existents, because existents are generated mediately or immediately from divine knowledge, and divine knowledge will not change through knowledge of existents, nor could it be perfected by the lower existents, as mentioned above.

§ 9.11.1 And the prophet Jeremiah teaches this in chapter 23 (23:24), saying: "Can anyone hide himself in secret places so that I shall not see him? Says the Lord: Do I not fill the heavens and the earth?" This means that there is no existence besides what is continuously emanated and conserved from My existence; that is, My knowledge that knows everything in the nobler way by which we perceive existents. Similarly, in response to the argument that if [God] knows the future existents, then [His knowledge] falls under the nature of the contingent and the nature of free choice, I will reply, as a conclusive argument concerning human knowledge, that human knowledge depends on the existents, except for existents that are necessary in themselves and which are foreknown by human knowledge. It would follow that divine knowledge does not depend on existents that are outside the soul [intellect], because they are not necessary for knowledge. Indeed, [divine knowledge] uniformly knows everything in the present as well as in the future, contingent things as well as necessary things, like the relationship of the power of sight to the seen objects that are in front of it. Divine knowledge apprehends not only existents that are contingent, but also existents that are necessary, and divine knowledge does not doubt them because divine knowledge knows not only future contingent things, but also necessary and present things.

§ 9.11.2 Similarly, in response to the argument about particular existents, which are infinite—namely, they cannot be understood by knowledge—I will reply: this is true for the knowledge that depends on existents, because existents are infinite and human science cannot know the total number of them. But this is not true for divine knowledge, | which does not depend on existents. Indeed, this is the only knowledge by which God knows. Every exis-

knows Himself [and] by which He knows that He gives existence and perpetuity to every existent by intention and will, He necessarily knows the existents that are generated and given perpetuity by Him intentionally and voluntarily, and also that they are individuals and numerically infinite. And therefore, Averroes says in *The Incoherence of the Incoherence* 12, second investigation: "I say that all these words are false, because the word 'knowledge' is an equivocation. And therefore, the true philosophers | did not attribute to God—may He be praised—[any] knowledge of the particulars and the universals, because knowledge that has these conditions is undoubtedly the knowledge of a passive intellect, which is caused. But the first intellect is pure act and cause. And one cannot draw an analogy between divine [knowledge] and human knowledge, because divine knowledge, insofar as it does not understand anything besides itself, is not passive, and, insofar as it brings forth the existents, insofar as it is a first intellect, it is active knowledge. And that is the Philosopher's opinion, because he already explained with proof that God—may He be praised—does not understand anything besides Himself." And he continues, saying: "And therefore, it follows that since divine knowledge is nobler than our knowledge, [its knowledge] of the existents will be nobler than our knowledge of them. And therefore, it follows that there will be two kinds of existence for the existents: one of them noble, one of them lower. And this is what some of the Ancients said: that God—may He be praised—is the whole."[a] And it seems that this becomes clear from the name "Elohim," which is attributed to God—may He be praised—because it indicates a governor and an arranger of order of existents by the commonly known intention of the intellect, by the testimony of sense [perception]. It becomes clear that He necessarily has knowledge of them, as became clear above.

§ 9.12.1 And Isaiah the prophet explains all these [things] and says (Isaiah 29:15–16): "Ha! Those who would hide their plans deep from ha-Shem! Who do their work in dark places and say: 'Who sees us, who takes note of us?' How perverse of you! Should the potter be accounted as the clay? Should what is made say of its Maker: 'He did not make me'; and what is formed say of Him who formed it: 'He did not understand'?" And in these words, he informs us, first, about the opinion of those who think that God does not know the individuals, let alone their activities. And this is so, first, insofar as they are individuals that we can only apprehend via the senses, which are not attributed to God, may He be praised. And the

[a] Cf. *Incoherence* 280–281.

qua Deus scit se esse entium omnium efficientem sive producentem et conservantem, scit necessario omnia illa per ipsum producta et conservata quantumcumque fuerit particularia individua et infinita. Quare Aven R. in lib. *Destructio Des.*, disputatione XII, dubio 2 ait: «Dico quod omnia ista sunt soffistica[a] verba. Nomen enim scientie equivocum, est etc.» subdit ibidem dicens: «Unde veri phylosophi non attribuunt Deo Benedicto scientiam in particularibus neque in universalibus, scientia enim que tales habet conditiones est proculdubio intellectus passibilis[b] qui est causatus, sed primus intellectus est purus actus et causa, quare nulla habet fieri comparatio inter divinam scientiam et humanam, quoniam enim alia non intelligit est impassibilis, et in quantum alia entia efficit prout ipse est primus est scientia agens, et declaratio phylosophorum in hoc talis est. Declaratum est enim ab eis demostrative quod ipse Deus non intelligit nisi se ipsum, ergo est intellectus etc.» subdit ibidem dicens: «unde si Dei scientia nobilior est nostra, ergo dependet ab ente nobiliori modo quam nostra scientia dependeat ab ente, et si sic ens duas habet entitates, una nobilis alia vero vilis, et hoc est quod dicebant aliqui antiquorum quod Deus est omne.»

§ 9.12.1 Quare Esays propheta cap. 29 [29:15–16] premissa demnstrative docens ait: «Vae[c] qui profundi estis ut a Domino abscondatis consilium quorum sunt in tenebris opera, et dicunt quis videt nos et quis novit nos, perversa est hec cogitatio vestra, quasi si luteum vas contra figulum cogitet et dicat opus factori suo, non fecisti me, et figmentum dicat factori suo ut non intellexisset etc.» Quibus succinte docet opinionem putantium Deum ignorare saltem individua, nedum eorum opera, et hoc primo ratione individuatis, quia videntur ut individua nonnisi a sensibus percipi contingat, qui scilicet sensus non sunt aliquo pacto Deo attribuendi, et hoc inferebant cum scilicet dice-

tent that is caused is generated and conserved. He necessarily knows every universal existent generated and conserved by Him even if they are particular individuals [i.e., finite] or infinite, as Averroes explains in *The Incoherence of the Incoherence* 12, second doubt, where he states: "I say that all these words are false [i.e., like the words of a sophist], because the word 'knowledge' is an equivocation, etc.," and he continues: "Therefore, the true philosophers did not attribute knowledge of the particulars and the universals to the Blessed God, because that knowledge, which has these conditions, is undoubtedly the knowledge of the passive intellect, which is caused. But the first intellect is pure act and cause. And one does not draw a comparison between divine and human knowledge, because it does not understand anything besides itself, and it is not passive, and insofar as it brings forth beings it is first, active knowledge. The opinion of the philosophers is this, because it is already explained by reason that God does not understand anything besides Himself." He continues: "And therefore, if divine knowledge is nobler than our knowledge, it depends on a being nobler than our knowledge of them. Therefore, if there are two kinds of existence for existents, one of them is noble, one of them is lower. And this is what some of the Ancients said, that God is the whole [everything]."[a]

§ 9.12.1 As Isaiah the prophet teaches us in chapter 29 (29:15–16), saying: "Ah [Ha], you who hide deep from the Lord your counsel, whose deeds are in the dark, and who say, 'Who sees us? Who knows us?' You turn things upside down! Shall the potter be regarded as the clay, that the thing made should say of its maker, 'He did not make me'; or the thing formed say of him who formed it, 'He has no understanding'?" With these [words], [Isaiah] teaches us about the opinion of those who think that God does not know individuals, still less their activities. First, through the concept of indivisibility, because it seems that individual existents, which are only apprehended by the senses, are not attributed to God, saying, "Who sees us?" Second,

---

[a] soffisitica] coni. Copp.; suffistica b; sophisticalia DD.   [b] passibilis] emend. Copp.; possibilis b; passibilis DD.   [c] Vae] emend. Copp.; vel b; veh b[corr]; vae V.

---

[a] Cf. *Incoherence* 280–281.

prophet informs us about this in his saying (ibid.): "And they say: 'Who sees us?'" Second, because insofar as they are contingent and insofar as they are infinite, no knowledge applies to them. And he informs us about this by saying (ibid.): "Who takes note of us?" And to the contrary of their opinions and views, the prophet brings demonstrative proof and experience, saying (ibid.): "How perverse of you! Should the potter be accounted as the clay?"; that is to say, the proof indicates the contrary of your opinions and views, even if the Creator's relationship to you was not nobler than the potter's relationship to the clay—which is a falsehood, because the potter does indeed act on the substrate, [but] does not bring it forth, and God, the Creator, also brought the substrate forth. In any case, the contrary of your opinion becomes clear, which is [i.e., the opinion] that God—may He be praised—does not know the existents, which you [indeed] do know. And it follows that the contrary is [the case], because divine knowledge is the cause of your knowledge and is nobler than it. It follows that whatever you know, He knows in a nobler way. And he explains the same afterwards [as derived] from experience by an example, saying (ibid.): "Should what is made say of its Maker: 'He did not make me'?"; that is to say, your role in this is like that of an earthen vessel whose former made it through artificial wisdom saying to his maker: "He did not make me | in the way of a true agent, in that his activity was intentional and voluntary, but I was generated by him without his intention and without his wisdom, like warmth and light are generated from the sun or from fire." Doubtless, this statement about the vessel is evidently false, because the wisdom of artistry visible in the vessel testifies the contrary of this statement, and this is incongruous *per se*. It would follow, according to the opinion of those who say that God—may He be praised—does not know individuals, that according to their words, He does not know the individuals of the spheres and the individuals of the celestial hosts, since they are individuals, and still less does He know the particulars of the generables and corruptibles. And the order and wisdom of artistry that are found in them testify the contrary of this.

§ 9.12.2 Second, he gives a proof of the contrary of their opinion, as it says (ibid.): "Who takes note of us?" This means: it is impossible, regarding us, that God—may He be praised—may know our deeds, since they are [performed] by free choice. And if so, they are contingent, and in addition to this, they are infinite. And therefore, they say that knowledge will not encompass them. And to the contrary of this, he brings a proof, saying (ibid.): "And [does] what is formed say of He who formed it: 'He did not understand'?"; that is to say, if it is so that the formed, which is an earthen

bant: «Quis videt nos.» Secundo ratione infinitatis et contingentie, quia cum humana opera sint infinita et contingentia, videtur ut non possint sub determinata scientia contineri, quare dicebant: «Quis novit nos.» Quorum opiniones horumque rationes reprobat propheta ratione et exemplo, dicens: «perversa est hec vestra cogitatio.» Quasi dicat econverso et oppositum eius quod vos putatis indicat ratio, vos enim putatis Deum ignorare individua que vos tamen scitis, cuius oppositum esse convenit, divina enim scientia cum sit nobilior vestra et sit causa a qua ipsa vestra scientia causatur, habet illa que vos quoquomodo percipitis nobilius scire. Et hoc ostendit exemplo dicens: «Quasi si luteum vas contra figulum cogitaret etc.» Quasi dicat quod casu quo luteum vas putaret ut | figulus ignoraret ipsum vas. Patet quod stulte putaret illud. Quia, ut sic sequeretur ut ipsum vas processisset a figulo eodem figulo inscio, sicut calor procedit ab igne, cuius oppositum[a] testatur eiusdem vasis artificium. Quod nonnisi a voluntario figulo sapienter factum esse contingit et idem sequeretur inconveniens ad opinionem qua putaretur Deum ignorare individua. Quare et celum eiusque sydera nedum mortalium individua haberet ut sic ignorare, cuius oppositum testatur artificium et ordo in his omnibus apparens.

through the concept of infinity and contingency, because it seems that human activities are infinities and contingents, and it seems that they could not be held under determined knowledge, saying: "And who knows us?" And to the contrary of their opinions, the prophet brings us a proof by means of an example, saying: "You turn things upside down!", which means the contrary and the opposite of your opinion; you think that God ignores particulars that you yourself know. The contrary of this is proved by divine knowledge, which is nobler than our knowledge, and it is the cause by which our knowledge is caused, and for that reason, He knows what we perceive in a nobler way. Isaiah teaches us by means of an example [i.e., metaphor], saying: "Shall the potter be regarded as the clay, etc.?", which means that a clay vessel thinks that the | potter ignores this vessel, yet it is clear that [the clay vessel] is foolish to think so, because it would follow that this vessel had been generated by a potter without being known by him, as warmth is generated by fire. The contrary of this is verified by the artistry visible in the vessel, because it is generated by a voluntary potter by means of wisdom, and it would follow that the opinions of those who say that God ignores particulars are incongruous, because according to their opinions, God ignores the heavens and their stars and human individuals, but the contrary of this is verified by the artistry and order that are visible in every one of them.

§ 9.12.2 Secundo reprobat propheta rationem dicentium quod Deus habet ignorare hominum opera cum sint arbitraria et per consequens contingentia et numero infinita saltem successive, et hoc reprobat rationali exemplo dicens: «et figmentum dicat fictori suo non intelligit.» Quasi dicat quod si contingeret figmento casu quo aliquid

§ 9.12.2 Second, the prophet rejects the opinions of he who says that God ignores the activities of man because activities are arbitrary and are consequently contingent and numerically infinite. He rejects those opinions by means of an example, saying: "Or the thing formed say of him who formed it, 'He has no understanding'?" This means that if it happens that something understands [thinks]—that is,

---

[a] oppositum] coni. Copp.; appositum b.

vessel, made by the hands of a former, understands a certain thing through the power of the former who gave it the disposition for that thing, then if that vessel thinks that its former does not understand that thing, there is no doubt that he who thinks so errs, because no one who understands can be generated from someone who does not understand, just as no existent can be generated from a non-existent, as became clear above. And God's knowledge enacts [i.e., brings forth] all the existents and gives perpetuity to those that are without existence in themselves besides their generation by the Creator—may He be praised—after absolute non-existence. And from many species of existents, there are [many] species of knowable [things]. It necessarily follows that God—may He be praised—knows everything knowable of His creatures that can be known, including the contingent and the infinite [creatures], because it is incongruous that this knowledge of them could exist if they did not have perpetuity and existence from the Creator, may He be praised. But He—may He be praised—knows them in a nobler way than the kind of knowledge that His aforementioned creatures possess. And therefore, the word "knowledge" only applies to two aforementioned [ways of] apprehension by equivocation, as became clear above.

בכח היוצר שנתן בו הכנת אותו הדבר הנה אז אם היה אותו הכלי חושב שיוצרו לא היה מבין אותו הדבר אין ספק שהיה חושב תועה כי אמנם לא יתהוה מבין מבלתי מבין כמו שלא יתהוה נמצא מבלי נמצא כמו שהתבאר למעלה. ובהיות שידיעת האל פועלת לכל הנמצאות ומקיימת אותם מבלי אין להם בעצמם מציאות זולתי ההווה להם מאת הבורא יתברך אחר אפיסות מוחלט. ומכלל מיני הנמצאות הם מיני הידיעות יתחייב בהכרח שהאל יתברך ידע כל הנודע אצל ברואיו גם האיפשריים והבלתי בעלי תכלית במספר כי לא יתכן שיהיה מציאות אותה הידיעה בהם אם לא היה להם קיום ומציאות מהבורא יתברך אמנם הוא יתברך ידעם על אופן יותר נכבד מאופן הידיעה אשר לברואיו הנזכרים ובכן על שתי ההשגות הנזכרות תפול מלת ‹ידיעה› בשתוף השם בלבד כאשר התבאר למעלה.

intelligeret vel sciret et cum hoc putaret ut figulus a quo eius scientia dependeret illud ignoraret ut stulte proculdubio cogitaret. Quia non datur ut procedat sciens a non sciente sicut neque ens a non ente ut supra. Quare cum Dei scientia sit entium agens tam scientiarum quam reliquorum entium ut supra et illa successive conservet, cum nihil per se habeant entitatis, sed illud tantum quod a Creatore acquirunt post purum non esse, habet ergo ipsa divina scientia omnia a suis creatis cogitata necessario scire tam contingentia quam necessaria et tam finita quam infinita nobiliori scilicet modo quam sua causata sciant ut supra, de cuius causa et causatorum cognitione equivoce tantum dicitur scientia.

knows—and consequently thinks that the potter on whom his knowledge depends does not know him, [it] is foolish to think so, because there is no knower that proceeds from a non-knower, or an existent from a non-existent, as mentioned above, because the knowledge of God pertains to the existents who know as well as the existents who do not know, as mentioned above, and He preserves them because nothing exists of themselves, but rather they can only be generated by a creator after absolute nothingness. Therefore, this divine knowledge necessarily knows every known thing among His creatures, the contingent ones as well as the necessary ones, the finite as well as the infinite, in a nobler way than that of the caused existents, as mentioned above. The word "knowledge" is only applied to the cause and the caused of apprehension by equivocation.

§ 10 Tenth:
We will inquire whether the creator is a voluntary agent or not.

And it seems at the beginning of the inquiry that he is not a voluntary agent.

§ 10.1 [This is so,] because a voluntary agent is moved to its activity by imagining the existence of the thing that it wants to achieve, as Averroes explains in [the Commentary on] *Physics* 8, text. 15,[a] and this does not happen to the creator at all, because prior to creation, | nothing existed that could have made it possible for us to think that something or the imagination of it had prompted the creator to [undertake] the activity of creation. If so, it would follow that the creator did not bring things forth by intention or by will.

§ 10.2 Second, this becomes clear from what al-Ġazālī says referring to the philosophers, which Averroes quoted in *The Incoherence of the Incoherence* 9, third investigation: "And there is no doubt that the philosophers deny the [existence of the] differentiating will,"[b] as if to say that the philosophers indeed deny that God—may He be praised—has a free will by which He differentiates one contrary from another and arbitrates. And he explains the same in ibid., 11, first investigation: "The philosophers deny that the creator has a will."[c]

§ 10.3.1 But the contrary of this becomes clear in this way: since every agent is either natural or voluntary, and the creator is not a natural agent, then he is a voluntary agent. This consequence is evident and so is the [antecedent] premise, as we said, that every agent is either natural or voluntary, because a violent agent is undoubtedly connected to a voluntary agent, as Averroes explains referring to al-Ġazālī in *The Incoherence of the Incoherence* 13, first investigation,[d] saying: "Because a mover through constraint is a body [either] moved through will or moved through constraint. In this way, one will arrive in any case at a voluntary agent." That the creator is a non-natural agent becomes clear in this way: because there is no natural agent that enacts two contraries, and the Creator—may He be praised—enacts and brings forth contraries. If so, He is not a natural agent.

§ 10.3.2 This consequence is evident and the [antecedent] premise becomes clear from experience of what can be perceived in many natural agents: that there is not even a

---

[a] Cf. *Phys.* 8.1.252a. [b] Cf. *Incoherence* 248. [c] Cf. *Incoherence* 270. [d] Cf. *Incoherence* 285.

---

10. רצון

§ 10 עשירית נחקור אם הבורא הוא פועל רצוניי אם אין

ונראה בתחלת העיון שאינו פועל רצוניי.

§ 10.1 כי הפועל הרצוניי יתנועע אל הפעלה מתמונת מציאות אותו הדבר אשר ירצה להשיג, כמו שבאר אבן רשד בספר השמע מאמר ח' פרק ט"ו ובהיות שלבורא לא קרה זה כלל כי אמנם קודם הבריאה לא היה שום דבר נמצא באופן שנוכל לחשוב שאיזה דבר או תמונתו העיר את הבורא לפעולת הבריאה אם כן יתחייב שהבורא לא המציא דבר בכוונה וברצון.

§ 10.2 **שנית** יתבאר זה ממה שאמר אלגזיל בשם הפילוסופים אשר הביא אבן רשד בספר הפלת ההפלה מאמר ט"א חקירת ג' באמרו »ואין ספק שהפילוסופים יכחישו הרצון המבדיל«, כלומר שהפילוסופים אמנם יכחישו שהאל יתברך יהיה לו רצון בחיריי בו יבדיל אחד מההפכים מחבירו ויבחרהו וזה בעצמו ביאר שם מאמר י"א חקירת א' באמרו: »שהפילוסופים יכחישו היות לבורא רצון.«

§ 10.3.1 **אמנם** הפך זה יתבאר באופן זה כי אמנם כל פועל הוא אם טבעי ואם רצוניי והנה הבורא אינו פועל טבעי אם כן הוא פועל רצוניי הנה חיוב התולדה הוא מבואר וכן ההקדמה כמה שאמרנו שכל פועל או הוא טבעי או הוא רצוניי כי אמנם הפועל המוכרח יעלה בלי ספק אל פועל רצוניי כאשר באר אבן רשד בשם אלגזיל בספר הפלת ההפלה מאמר י"ג חקירת א' באמרו: »כי המניע בהכרח הוא אמנם איזה גשם מתנועע ברצון או מתנועע בהכרח באופן שיעלה הדבר על כל פנים אל פועל רצוניי.« אמנם מה שהבורא הוא פועל בלתי טבעי יתבאר באופן זה כי אין שום פועל טבעי שיפעל שני הפכים והנה הבורא יתברך פעל והמציא ההפכים אם כן אינו פועל טבעי.

§ 10.3.2 הנה חיוב התולדה הוא מבואר וההקדמה תתבאר בנסיון המוחש בפועלים טבעיים רבים שאין גם אחד מהם שיפעל זולתי על

---

[a] ט'] emend. Dunk.; ט' a, 10 b, 9 dd.

10. DE VOLUNTATE

§ 10 Decimo Dubitatur
Utrum idem Creator sit voluntarius agens vel non.

Et videtur quod non.

§ 10.1 Quia voluntarius agens habet primo moveri ab imaginatione illius rei quam intendit, prout per se patet et habetur ab Aven R. *Physicorum* VIII t.c. 15. Cum autem Creatori non habuisset hoc contingere, quia ante creationem, nihil habuit esse a cuius presentia vel imaginatione habuisset ad creandum moveri, ergo Creator nihil produxit voluntarie.

§ 10.2 Secundo arguitur auctoritate Algazelis de mente Phylosophorum relata in lib. *Destructio Des.*, disputatione IX[a] dubio tertio ubi dicit: «Et non est dubium quod Phylosophi negant distinguentem voluntatem alterum contrariorum ab alio distinguentem.» et idem habetur eiusdem auctoritate ibidem disputatione XI dubio primo ubi Phylosophos alloquens ait: «Sed vos qui removetis ab eo voluntatem et mundi innovationem totaliter negatis et opinamini quod illud quod procedit ab eo procedit de necessitate vel natura etc.»

§ 10.3.1 Ad oppositum arguitur sic: quilibet agens vel est naturalis vel est voluntarius. Creator est agens non naturalis ergo est agens voluntarius | consequentia patet, similiter et antecedens. Quia quilibet agens non naturalis vel est voluntarius vel violentus qui tandem reducitur ad voluntarium, ut per se patere videtur. Et habetur ratione et auctoritate Algazel in lib. *Destructio Des.*, disputatione XIII, dubio primo ubi dicit: «Id itaque quod violenter movet aut est aliud corpus mobile voluntate vel violenter, itaque oportet ut perveniat in fine ad voluntarium etc.» Quo autem ad secundam partem probatur sic, nullus naturalis agens facit duo contraria, Creator agit sive producit quam plurima sibi invicem contraria, ergo Creator est agens non naturalis.

51[r]
[61]

§ 10.3.2 Consequentia patet et antecedens habetur per discursum a sensibus sumptum et Phylosophi auctoritate *Physicorum* II t.c. 85[b] ubi dicit: «Res naturales semper

§ 10 Tenth,
it may be inquired whether the creator is a voluntary agent or not.

And it seems he is not.

§ 10.1 First, I would argue that a voluntary agent is moved by the imagination of the thing that he wants to achieve, as Averroes explicates in *Physics* 8, text. 15.[a] Now, since this does not happen to a creator, because prior to creation there was nothing that could cause the activity of creation by means of its image or representation, therefore the creator did not create voluntarily.

§ 10.2 Second, I would argue as al-Ġazālī explains in the name of the philosophers in *The Incoherence of the Incoherence* 9, third doubt, where he states: "And there is no doubt that the philosophers deny a will that differentiates one of the contraries from the others [there is no doubt that philosophers do not admit a differentiating will]."[b] And he also explains this in ibid., discussion 11, first doubt, where he states: "But you [the philosophers], who deny his will and completely deny the creation of the world, have supposed that this thing proceeds from him by necessity or by nature, etc."[c]

§ 10.3.1 On the contrary it is to argue that every agent is either natural or voluntary. The creator is not a natural agent; therefore, he is a voluntary agent. | The consequence is evident, as is the antecedent, because any unnatural agent is either voluntary or violent, which at least traces back to a voluntary [agent], according to the argument and authority of al-Ġazālī in *The Incoherence of the Incoherence* 13, first doubt,[d] where he states: "Because [the mover] that moves something through constraint is a body either moved through will or through constraint. Therefore, it is necessary that we finally arrive at a voluntary [mover]." Therefore, the second part of the antecedent is proved; an unnatural agent enacts two contraries, the creator enacts or creates many contraries, and therefore, the creator is an unnatural agent.

51[r]
[61]

§ 10.3.2 The consequence is evident and so is the antecedent, as the senses also testify and the Philosopher explains in *Physics* 2, text. 85,[e] where he states: "The natural things

---

[a] IX] emend. COPP.; X b; IX DD.   [b] 85] emend. COPP.; 45 b; 85 L.

[a] Cf. *Phys.* 8.1.252a.   [b] Cf. *Incoherence* 248.   [c] Cf. *Incoherence* 270.   [d] Cf. *Incoherence* 285.   [e] *Phys.* 2.8.199b.

single [agent] that does not always act in one way alone. And Aristotle explains in *Physics* 2, text. 85:[a] "The natural things always proceed in one way, if nothing hinders them." And he explains the same in ibid., [2], text. 80:[b] "This is very common for living beings whose activities are not the outcome of art." And Averroes explains his words, saying: "If they were doing this by means of intention, they would carry [i.e., move] themselves from one thing to another." And he explains the same in *The Incoherence of the Incoherence* 3, first investigation: "We find that the agents that give form are divided into two kinds. The first is that which essentially performs only one activity, such as warmth, which produces warmth, and coldness, which produces cold. And the agents that are like this are called 'natural agents.' And the second kind is that which sometimes performs one activity and sometimes its opposite. And the agents of this kind are called | 'voluntary' and 'selective' by the philosophers. And when the agent is like this, it undoubtedly acts with understanding and with deliberation."[c] From all these [words], it becomes clear that the creator, who brought forth things that are different and contrary to each other, necessarily brings things forth voluntarily, acting by intention and will, as was explained above, in a way nobler than the way of the will that is in man, as Averroes explains in the aforementioned place.

§10.4.1 Second, the same becomes clear in this way: since every agent [acting] for a final purpose is undoubtedly voluntary, and the creator is an agent for a final purpose, then the creator is a voluntary agent. The consequence is evident and so is the [antecedent] premise, as we said, that the agent for a final purpose is necessarily voluntary, because the final purpose is nothing other than a good thing that is intended by the intending agent, as is self-evident. And Aristotle explains this in *Metaphysics* 2, text. 9.[d]

§10.4.2 So, what we said in the [antecedent] premise—that the creator is indeed an agent [acting] for a final purpose—becomes clear in this way: because in all existents, especially when they possess life, there is a final purpose intended by their measurements, appearances, order, and organs. And the final purpose informs [us] about the existence of the agent who intends that final purpose, as becomes clear above. Indeed, that this intender for the aforementioned final purpose is God—may He be praised—becomes clear in this way: because if this intender was someone other than the creator, it would there-

---

[a] *Phys.* 2.8.199b. [b] *Phys.* 2.8.199a. [c] Cf. *Incoherence* 88. [d] *Metaph.* 2.2.994b.

sunt in eodem cursu nisi abscindatur etc.» et idem videtur Aven R. docere ibidem t.c. 80 ubi Phylosophus dicit: «Et hoc apparet multum in animalibus que agunt non propter artem etc.» ubi Aven R. exponens ait: «Quoniam si agerent hoc propter cogitationem tunc transferrentur de aliquo in aliquid etc.» et idem apertius docet in lib. *Destructio Des.*, disputatione tertia dubio primo ubi dicit: «Nos enim invenimus agentia et imprimentia duobus modis divisa, quorum unius una tantum est eius actio per se, ut calor agit calorem, et frigus frigiditatem, et talia agentia naturalia nuncupantur. Secundus vero modus est quo quis quandam interdum agit actionem et interdum eius oppositum et talia agentia vocantur a phylosophis volentia et eligentia, quandocumque agens fuerit huiusmodi agit proculdubio cum deliberatione et meditatione etc.» Quibus omnibus patet quod Creator cum diversa produxerit sibi invicem contraria est necessario voluntarius producens cum cogitatione et deliberatione ut supra, licet nobiliori modo quam ille quo de humana dicitur voluntate, prout idem Aven R. inferre videtur.

§ 10.4.1 Secundo arguitur sic omnis agens ad finem est proculdubio voluntarius, Creator est huiusmodi, ergo Creator est agens sive producens voluntarius. Consequentia patet, similiter et antecedens, quoad primam partem qua, scilicet, dicitur quod agens ad finem est voluntarius. Quia finis nil aliud est quam ultimum bonum ab agente voluntario intentum, prout per se patet et habetur a Phylosopho *Metaphysicorum* II t.c. 9.

§ 10.4.2 Quo autem[a] ad secundam antecedentis partem qua, scilicet, dicitur quod Creator est agens ad finem probatur quia in omnibus entibus presertim in animatis apparet intentus finis in horum quantitatibus ordine et organis significans agentem ipsum finem intendentem ut supra. Quod autem huiusmodi finem in entibus apparentem intendens sit idem Creator probatur. Quia si fuisset

always follow their movement, if nothing hinders, etc." And Averroes explicates this in *Physics* 2, text. 80,[a] where the Philosopher states: "This is very common for the animals, whose activities are not the outcome of art," and Averroes explains: "If they were doing this by means of intention, they would move themselves from one thing to another, etc." And he explains this in *The Incoherence of the Incoherence* 3, first doubt, where he states: "We find that the agents [and those] who give forms are divided into two kinds. The first is the one who exclusively performs one activity essentially, such as warmth, which gives heat, and coldness, which gives cold. And these kinds of agents are called 'natural agents.' And the second kind is that which sometimes performs one activity and sometimes its opposite. And the agents of this kind are called 'voluntary' and '[freely] choosing' [selective] by the philosophers. And when the agent is of this kind, it undoubtedly acts out of deliberation and meditation [i.e., selection]."[b] From these [words], it is clear that the creator creates different contrarieties, and it is necessary that he creates voluntarily out of reflection [i.e., meditation] and deliberation, as mentioned above, in a way nobler than the human will, as Averroes explains.

§ 10.4.1 Second, I would argue that every agent intending to attain a final purpose is undoubtedly voluntary. The creator is an agent intending to attain a final purpose, and therefore the creator is a voluntary agent or producer. The consequence is evident, as is the first part of the antecedent, in which we said that an agent intending to attain a final purpose is voluntary, because the purpose is nothing other than the final good intended by a voluntary agent, as the Philosopher explains in *Metaphysics* 2, text. 9.[c]

§ 10.4.2 The second part of the antecedent, in which we said that the creator is an agent attaining the final purpose, is proved because in every being, and particularly in living beings, there is an intended final purpose in the order of their quantities and organs, because "agent" signifies an intended final purpose, as aforementioned. And the intended final purpose that exists in living beings is the creator, because if the intender was someone different

---

[a] autem] coni. COPP.; aotem b.

[a] *Phys.* 2.8.199a. [b] Cf. *Incoherence* 88. [c] *Metaph.* 2.2.994b.

fore be necessary that a chance would have occurred to this intender that existents existed that he did not bring forth and that they did not have that appearance and those organs, insofar as they had existence. And nonetheless, he would have ordered and measured the measurements of their quantities, appearances, and organs for a final purpose.

§ 10.4.3 And it would also have occurred to him that a prime matter that was necessarily common to the existents existed for the possibility of the generation of the recurring generables and corruptibles, because without the nature of this matter, there would be no perpetual movement of generation because the matter would be annihilated, as Averroes explains in [the Commentary on] *Metaphysics* 12, text. 33.[a] And according to this: if this chance had not occurred, then that intending existent would be useless and without any [adequate] activity. Also, it would follow that this chance had occurred to every one of those orderly arranged existents: that there existed an existent that was preserving the dimensions of their measurements and their order. And if that chance had not occurred, then the existents would have been without an essential and adequate activity. And therefore, it would follow that they would not be in accordance with the form from which that activity had come. And therefore, it would follow that the one who had brought the existents forth after absolute non-existence, whose activity informs [us] that he is the noblest [being] in all existence, had made all of their activities without being good, without a final purpose, and without ordering [them], as far as his activity is concerned. And all these [things] are incongruities, which is inconceivable.

§ 10.4.4 It follows then that the creator is the one who brings forth the organs and their appearances | and the measurements of their quality, by which the stated final purpose is achieved in every one of them. And the existence of the final purpose informs [us] about the existence of the intender, as became clear above. And Averroes also explains this in the *Treatise on the Substance of the Celestial Sphere*, ch. 2.[b] And as only a voluntary agent can intend, it necessarily follows that the forth-bringer of the existents is a voluntary agent, and He is the Creator, may He be praised. And this is what we wanted to explain.

§ 10.5 Third, this becomes clear from Averroes's proof, which explains in *The Incoherence of the Incoherence* 11, first investigation: "It has been explained that the philoso-

---

[a] Cf. *Metaph.* 12.6.1072a.   [b] Cf. *Sub. orb.* 84–85.

quid aliud ab eo, sequeretur ut casu sive preter alicuius intentum contigisset eidem finem intendenti, ut habuissent esse entia non ab eo producta, que tamen habuisset ipse ad finem mensurare et ordinare.

§ 10.4.3 Similiter casu contigisset ut habu|isset esse prima materia his omnibus communis, in qua daretur eorum reciprocatio ad eorum successionem necessaria ad hoc ut non consumatur materia, prout habetur ab Aven R. *Metaphysicorum* XII t.c. 33. Sine quo casu fuisset idem finem intendens ociosius. Similiter casu contigisset singulo entium ut habuisset esse quoddam ens mensurans et ordine componens, sine quo casu essent ipsa entia sine suis oportunis mensura et ordine, et per consequens sine recta actione sibi propria, et per consequens non essent sub illa forma a qua ispa recta actio nunc emanat, et per consequens horum productor nihil boni fecisset, que omnia sunt inopinabilia.

§ 10.4.4 Preterea patet quod ipsa animatorum organa nonnisi ab eorum productore facta esse contingit, in his enim apparet finis per eundem organicum intentus, finis autem significat agentem significatione propria prout per se patet et habetur ab Aven R. in *Tractatu De Substantia Orbis* capitulo secundo 2 ubi dicit: «Finis significat agentem significatione propria sicut motus significat moventem etc.» Et hoc quoniam finis nil aliud est quam illud ultimum quod intenditur per actiones, prout habetur a Phylosopho, ut supra. Quod scilicet intentum nonnisi a voluntario agente illud intendente fieri contingit. Quare sequitur ut entium productor sit voluntarius agens, et talis est Creator ut supra, quod est intentum.

§ 10.5 Tertio arguitur ratione et auctoritate Aven R. in lib. *Destructio Destructionum*, disputatione XI dubio primo ubi dicit: «Patet ergo quod Phylosophi conveniunt cum istis

from him, it would follow that the purpose was by chance or without intention, because beings would not be created by him; nevertheless, he would have ordered and measured for a final purpose.

§ 10.4.3 Similarly, it could happen that | there was a prime matter common to every existent in which their movement of generation necessarily existed according to their succession, because matter cannot be annihilated, as Averroes explicates in *Metaphysics* 12, text. 33.[a] And if this was not possible, then the intended end would be pointless. Similarly, it could happen to one of the beings, that there would be a certain essence that preserves [their] measurement and order. And if this was not possible, those beings would be without measurements and an order that would be suitable for them, and consequently without their own adequate activity, and consequently, they would not be in accordance with their form from which the adequate activity is emanated, and consequently, their producer would have created them without good, and all of these hypotheses are incongruous.

§ 10.4.4 Moreover, it is clear that the organs of living beings can only be created by their producer, because their intended end is evident through their organs, because "purpose" signifies an agent, as Averroes explains in the *Treatise on the Substance of the Celestial Sphere*, ch. 2, where he states that "purpose" signifies an agent just as "motion" signifies a mover.[b] And the final purpose is nothing more than the purpose that is intended in relation to the activities, according to the Philosopher, as mentioned above. Moreover, the intention is only produced by a voluntary agent who intends it, and then it would follow that the producer of beings is a voluntary agent, and the creator is a voluntary agent, as mentioned above. And this is what we wanted to explain.

§ 10.5 Third, I would argue according to the argument and authority of Averroes in *The Incoherence of the Incoherence* 11, first doubt, where he states: "It is clear that the philosophers agree with these in attributing will to

---

[a] Cf. *Metaph.* 12.6.1072a.   [b] Cf. *Sub. orb.* 84–85.

phers agree with these [theologians] in attributing a will to God—may He be praised. And therefore, this makes what al-Ġazālī says citing the philosophers—that the things that are generated by Him are generated by Him in a natural way—a falsehood. Because those who follow the opinions of the Mutakallimun [Muslim theologians] say, in accordance with the truth, that the existents are generated by Him in a way [that is] nobler than natural generation, and nobler than the means of generation by human will." And he continues, saying: "And the proof of this is: because it is evident that he knows two contraries. If so, if he made all that he knows, then he would enact two contraries at once. And this is false. It then follows that he enacts one of the two contraries by free choice and will."[a]

§10.6 We answer, then, to dispel any doubt about the aforementioned thesis, that the creator brings everything forth by intention and will and orderly arranges it and provides perpetuity to all; indeed, through a will nobler than the human will.

§10.7.1 Indeed, to the opponent's arguments, first, saying that it follows that before the voluntary agent enacts his activity, the imagining of the thing that he wants to enact moves him to [enact] it, and that it therefore would follow that a certain existent existed prior to the activity of the voluntary agent and that this is incongruous for the creation of the world and its creation [out of nothing], we answer: although this is also correct for the human will, it is not correct for the divine will, because the principle of human knowledge is [what comes] from the existents that exist in potentiality or in actuality outside the soul. It follows that the will, which has a principle [coming] from that knowledge, is generated from the aforementioned existents. And the contrary of this occurs regarding the divine will, because it is indeed different from the human will in rank and in species. It is generated from divine knowledge, which is God—may He be praised—Himself, and it is not generated from existents that exist outside of Him, as Averroes explains in *The Incoherence of the Incoherence* 9, third investigation.[b] And apart from this, we answer: because it is indeed congruous that the divine will [should come] from the imagination of the existents that are one and the same thing in the divine substance. And therefore, it is congruous that the case of the divine will is comparable to the case of the will of [someone] who brings forth | a new [kind of] artistry by which the agent is moved to its activity by imagining the thing that is in its thought in order to bring [it] forth, while it also never existed outside the soul.

---

[a] Cf. *Incoherence* 271–272. [b] Cf. *Incoherence* 248–249.

in attribuendo Deo voluntatem, et id quod dixerat scilicet Algazel, Phylosophorum nomine, videlicet quod illud quod procedit ab eo scilicet primo procedit per modum nature, falsum est. Immo dicunt Peripatetici loquentes secundum veritatem quod entia procedunt ab eo altiori modo quam sit natura, et quam sit humana voluntas etc.» ubi subdit dicens: «Et probatio quam vult hec est notum est quod ipse scit duo contraria quare si ipse quantum scit faceret, ageret quidem duo contraria simul, quod est falsum, oportet ergo ut faciat unum contrariorum voluntate.»

§10.6 Ad dubium ergo respondetur quod Creator omnia voluntarie produxit, ordinavit et conservavit nobiliori tamen voluntate quam sit humana voluntas.

§10.7.1 Ad argumenta vero et primo quoad primum quo dicitur: quod voluntarius agens habet primo moveri a presentia illius rei quam vult. Vel ab eius imaginatione, et per consequens datur necessario quid presens, vel imaginabile ad ipsam voluntariam actionem precedens, quod non datur data universi productione vel creatione. Respondetur quod licet hec verificentur de humana voluntate que dependet ab entibus presentibus, vel cogitatis. Non tamen verificantur de divina voluntate que nullo pacto dependet ab entibus extra animam existentibus. Divina, enim, voluntas nobilitate et genere ab humana differens habet[a] divina scientia que est quid | idem cum ipso Deo ab eodem[b] necessario dependere non autem ab entibus extra illam existentibus. Sicut habetur ab Aven R. in lib. *Destructio Des.*, disputatione ix dubio 3. Preterea respondetur quod non est inconveniens ut divina voluntas habuisset esse per creandorum imaginationem factam per eiusdem scientiam que est quid idem cum ipso Deo. Quare non est inconveniens ut de eadem divina volontate quodammodo contingat, sicut de voluntate artificis aliquid novi excogitantis. Que scilicet fit per imaginationem illius nuper excogitati in eiusdem artificis anima existentis, licet illud numquam habuisset extra animam esse.

God. And therefore, what al-Ġazālī says, quoting some philosophers—that the things emanated by him are emanated by him in a natural way—is a falsehood. Because those who follow the opinions of the Peripatetics say, according to the truth, that existents are emanated in a way other than through nature or through human will." And he continues: "And the proof of this is that he would know two contrary things, and then he could enact two contraries together, and this is false. Therefore, it is necessary that he produces one of the two contraries through his will."[a]

§10.6 To dispel any doubt, I would argue that the creator creates, orders, and preserves all beings voluntarily; indeed, through a will nobler than human will.

§10.7.1 In response to the first argument, when we said that a voluntary agent is moved by the existence of a thing that he wills or by his imagination, it is necessary that something exists or is imagined prior to this voluntary activity, and then the generation of the universe or creation would not be possible, I will reply: this is correct in terms of the human will, which depends on existents or beings, but it is not correct for the divine will, which never depends on beings existing outside the soul. Therefore, the divine will is different from the human will in rank and genus. Divine knowledge, which is | necessarily God Himself, never depends on beings that exist outside of Him, as Averroes explains in *The Incoherence of the Incoherence* 9, third doubt.[b] Moreover, I will reply: it is incongruous that the divine will should exist through the imagination of existents that are created by his knowledge, which is God Himself. Furthermore, it is incongruous that the divine will should be in a certain manner similar to the will of an artisan inventing anew, meaning that something is produced by the imagination inventing anew in the artisan's soul while it also has no existence outside the soul.

---

[a] habet] b[corr]; habeat b.   [b] ab eodem] b[corr]; om. b.

[a] Cf. *Incoherence* 271–272.   [b] Cf. *Incoherence* 248–249.

§10.7.2 And to what the opponent argues [related] to the statement of the philosophers, who deny that God—may He be praised—has a will, we answer: this is correct for the will that is generated by an incorrect opinion, as happens with the human species in many cases, because for the Creator—may He be praised—[possessing] a will like this is not proper in any case. And we say: it is true that the Creator does not have a will of this kind at all, but He has a will that is generated from a correct intellect, which intends a proper final purpose through wisdom. And this indeed is attributed to the Creator—may He be praised—as Averroes explains in *The Incoherence of the Incoherence* 9, third investigation: "And therefore, al-Ġazālī errs in this place in the understanding of the intended, when we say that the agent designates a certain property for a certain existent, because this differentiation of which the philosophers speak is not similar to the differentiation of which the Mutakallimun [Muslim theologians] speak. Because the Mutakallimun intend by this that the agent differentiates a thing from a[nother] thing that is similar to it, or from its contrary, without the wisdom letting the agent incline more towards one of the similar or contrary things than towards its neighbour[s]. But the philosophers mean by this differentiation that through the activity, the wisdom brings into effect the property that it [i.e., the certain existent] has in its nature, and [thereby] it is the final cause. Because among the philosophers, [the opinion is that] there is neither a quantity nor a quality in any being that is not due to its wisdom. And therefore, one of two things is inevitable: either (1) that this property is necessary for the nature of that existent's activity, or (2) that it is according to the greater good, so that if there was a certain quantity or quality not generated by that wisdom in the existents, it would follow that something that it is not proper to attribute [even] to the worst of the artisans would be attributed to the creator or the first agent. Because there is no doubt that every activity that is performed by the hand of a certain artisan is loved by that artisan and done with discernment, and therefore, when wisdom is removed from the activities of nature, the cause of all activities is also removed. And this is against the philosophers' principles and their conclusions. If so, it is evident that the world has a perspicacious and wise agent from whom the order of all the existents is generated."[a] And he explains this in the aforementioned book 11, first investigation: "Since the creator knows two contraries, although he makes only one of them, it follows that he chooses to make it intentionally and voluntarily."[b]

§10.7.2 ועל מה שטען החולק ממאמר הפילוסופים המכחישים שיהיה לאל יתברך רצון. נשיב כי זה יצדק על הרצון ההווה מסברה בלתי ישרה כאשר יקרה למין האנושי ברבים מעניינו כי רצון כזה לא יאות בשום פנים לבורא יתברך ונאמר באמת שאין לבורא רצון מזה המין כלל אמנם יש רצון הווה משכל ישר מכוין בחכמה לתכלית נאות. וזה אמנם מיוחס[a] לבורא יתברך כמו שבאר אבן רשד בספר הפלת ההפלה מאמר ט׳ חקירת ג׳. באמרו: »ולכן טעה אלגזיל בזה המקום בהבנת המכוון באמרנו שהפועל מיחד איזו תכונה לאיזה נמצא. כי אמנם זה הייחוד אשר אמרו הפילוסופים אינו דומה ליחוד אשר אמרו המדברים. כי אמנם המדברים כיוונו בזה שהפועל יבדיל דבר מדבר דומה לו או מהפכו לא שהחכמה תטה את הפועל אל אחד מהדומים או מהההפכיים יותר ממה שיטהו לחברו. אבל הפילוסופים מכוונים בזה הייחוד שהחכמה תתן בפעולה[b] התכונה אשר לה בטבעה וזו היא הסבה התכליתית כי אמנם אצל הפילוסופים אין שום כמות ולא איכות בשום נמצא שלא תהיה מצד חכמתו. ולזה לא ימלט מאחת משתים אם שהתכונה ההיא הכרחית לטבע פעולת אותו הנמצא או שהוא על צד היותר טוב שאם היה בנמצאים איזה כמות או איכות בלתי הווה מאותה החכמה היה מתחייב שנייחס לבורא או לפועל הראשון מה שאין ראוי שייוחס לפחות שבבעלי המלאכות. כי אין ספק שכל פעולה שנעשתה על יד איזה אומן היא נאהבת מאותו האומן ונעשית מידו בהבחנה. ולזה כשתוסר החכמה מפעולות הטבע תסור גם כן הסבה מכל הפעולות וזה הוא נגד שרשי הפילוסופים והסכמותיהם אם כן מבואר הוא שיש לעולם פועל נבון וחכם אשר מאתו הווה סדר כל הנמצאים« עד כאן לשונו. וזה בעצמו ביאר בספר הנזכר מאמר י״א חקירת א׳ באמרו: »שבהיות שהבורא יודע שני ההפכים. ועם זה הוא עושה אחד מהם בלבד יתחייב שבחר לעשותו בכוונה וברצון.«

---

[a] Cf. *Incoherence* 248–249.   [b] Cf. *Incoherence* 272.

[a] מיוחס] coni. Dunk.; מוחס a.   [b] בפעולה] בפעולת a[corr]; a.

§10.7.2 Quo autem ad secundum argumentum quo, scilicet, arguitur phylosophorum auctoritate negantium huiusmodi voluntatem inesse Deo respondetur. Quod etiam secundum eorum mentem distinguendum est de voluntate, quedam enim est absoluta nulla recta ratione ducta et talis merito negatur inesse Deo, quedam vero est voluntas sapienter et recte finem intendens et talis proculdubio est divina. Et idem videtur Aven R. inferre in lib. *Destructionis dest.*, disputatione nona dubio 3 ubi dicit: «Unde Algazel erravit hoc loco in intentione nominis appropriationis, quia appropriatio de qua locuti sunt Phylosophi dissimilis est appropriationis loquentium, loquentes enim intendunt per hoc ut distinguatur res a suo simili vel a suo contrario non quod sapientia indicet unum ipsorum similium vel oppositorum magis quam alterum. Sed phylosophi in hoc loco intendunt per dictam appropriationem ut sapientia inferat in effectu id quod habet de sua natura, et hec est causa finalis, apud phylosophos enim nulla est quantitas neque qualitas in aliquo entium que non sit propter suam sapientiam, quare non evadit quin sit unum duorum videlicet quia aut necessarium de natura actus illius entis, aut quia est secundum bene esse. Si enim in creatis esset aliqua quantitas vel qualitas ab illa sapientia non producta, sequeretur attribuere primo Creatori illud quod non haberet attribui alicui vilissimo artifici. Nam nullum est dubium quod quilibet effectus ab aliquo artifici factus diligitur, et cum provisione ab eodem magistro fit, et ideo remota sive separata sapientia a nature operibus removetur et finalis causa ab omnibus effectibus nature, quod est contra omnes phylosophorum radices et conclusiones. Patet ergo ut mundus habeat unum efficientem sagacissimum a quo entia cuncta seriatim ministrentur» et ideo docet idem Aven R. in eodem libro disputatione XI, dubio primo ubi ut supra. Per hoc quod ipse Creator necessario scit utrumque contrariorum quorum tamen alterum tantum facit probat quod illud facit voluntarie.

§10.7.2 In response to the second argument, in which the position of the philosophers who deny that God has a will is described, I will reply: according to their positions, there should be a distinction between the [different] kinds of will. One kind is led by a wrong opinion, and such a will does not belong to God. The other is wisely and rightly striving for a final purpose, and such a will is the divine will, as Averroes explains in *The Incoherence of the Incoherence* 9, third doubt, where he states: "And therefore al-Ġazālī errs in this place in the interpretation of what was intended, because the particular interpretation that the philosophers infer is different from the interpretation of the Mutakallimun [Muslim theologians]. The Mutakallimun [Muslim theologians] mean by this that a thing is differentiated from that which is similar to it or from its contrary without wisdom indicating one of the similar or contrary [things] more than the other. But the philosophers in this context, according to this particular interpretation, mean that wisdom brings into effect what it [a thing] has in its nature, and [thereby] it is the final cause. For philosophers, there is no quantity or quality in any being that is not due to wisdom, [and] therefore one of two things is inevitable: because either it is necessary in the nature of the act of this being, or it is according to the good [principle of superiority]. Therefore, if a quantity or a quality in created beings is not determined by wisdom, it would follow that it would attribute to the first creator something that it is not proper to attribute to the worst artisan. Because there is no doubt that every activity that is performed by a certain artisan is loved and performed by this master with discernment. And therefore, a wisdom that is remote or separated is removed from the activities of nature, and the final cause of all activities is also removed. And this is against the principles of the philosophers and their conclusions. Moreover, it is evident that the world has one perspicacious agent, from whom all existents are supplied."[a] And Averroes explains this in the aforementioned book, discussion 11, first doubt, where he states: "Since the creator knows necessarily two contraries, although he makes only one of them, it proves that he chooses to make it voluntarily."[b]

---

[a] Cf. *Incoherence* 248–249. [b] Cf. *Incoherence* 272.

§10.8.1 And this same proof seems to be what [Holy] Scripture explains, as it says (Genesis 1:4–5): "And God saw that the light was good, and God separated the light from the darkness. God called the light 'day,' and the darkness He called 'night.'" And this is so, because after it [Holy Scripture] explains the power of the deed of ha-Shem—for He is great—that He brought forth existents after absolute nothingness, as it says (Genesis 1:1): "In the beginning God | created," [Holy Scripture] explains by proof that He is a voluntary agent and created both intentionally and voluntarily. And this is so because He is the forth-bringer of two contraries, and these are light and darkness. And He determined a limited time for one of them and called it "day," and for [the other] one He determined a limited time, which He called "night"—without solar motion, because there was no motion of the sun then; [only] by the fourth day [of creation]. And therefore, it explains, in short, that the creator is a voluntary agent and [it] provides three proofs:

§10.8.2 (1) First, because [He is] the forth-bringer of contraries, which can only be brought forth by a voluntary agent, not a natural agent, as Averroes explains in *The Incoherence of the Incoherence* 3, first investigation.[a]

§10.8.3 (2) Second, because He assigns different times for each of two contraries, so that one of them does not disturb the activity of its contrary. And all this is necessarily by will and arbitrary consent, because in saying "darkness," He was not merely seeking the privation of light, since separation can only apply to two existents, and ["darkness"] is not the privation of everything, but He sought dark air.

§10.8.4 (3) Third, [Holy Scripture] explains this with regard to the final purpose that is seen in the existents, from which it becomes clear that the agent's activity is voluntary. And it [i.e., Holy Scripture] informs [us] of this when it says in this place [in the text], and for the rest of the existents: "And God saw that it was good"; that is to say that He brought forth all the existents for an intended final purpose, which is proper, so He called it "good," as the Philosopher explains in *Metaphysics* 2, text. 8.[b]

---

[a] Cf. *Incoherence* 187–188. [b] *Metaph.* 2.2.994b.

§10.8.1 וזה המופת בעצמו נראה שבאר הכתוב באמרו: »וירא אלהים את האור כי טוב ויבדל אלהים בין האור ובין החושך ויקרא אלהים לאור ‹יום› ולחשך קרא ‹לילה›« (בראשית א׳ ד׳-ה׳). וזה כי אחר שבאר כח מעשה ה׳ כי נורא הוא שהמציא נמצאות אחר אפיסות מוחלט באמרו: »בראשית ברא | אלהים« (שם א׳ א׳). באר במופת שהוא פועל רצוניי וברא בכוונה וברצון. וזה בהיות שהמציא שני ההפכים והם האור והחושך וקבע לאחד מהם זמן מוגבל קראו ‹יום› ולאחד קבע זמן מוגבל קראו ‹לילה› בלתי תנועה שמשית כי לא היתה אז תנועת שמש עד היום הרביעי. ובזה ביאר בקצור שהבורא הוא פועל רצוניי ונתן ג׳ ראיות:

§10.8.2 ראשונה בהיות שהמציא ההפכים אשר לא ימציאם זולתי פועל רצוניי לא פועל טבעי כמו שבאר אבן רשד בספר הפלת ההפלה מאמר ג׳ חקירת א׳.

§10.8.3 שנית בהיות שקבע לכל אחד משני ההפכים זמנים מתחלפים שלא יבלבל אחד מהם את פעולת הפכו. וכל זה בהכרח ברצון והסכמה בחיריית כי אמנם באמרו ‹חשך› לא רצה העדר האור בלבד כי ההבדל לא יפול זולתי בין שני נמצאים. ואין ההעדר מכללם אבל רצה האויר החשוך.

§10.8.4 שלישית ביאר זה מצד התכלית הנראה בנמצאות אשר בו יתבאר היות פעולת הפועל רצוניית. וזה הורה באמרו בזה המקום ובהיות שאר הנמצאות[a] »וירא אלהים ... כי טוב« (בראשית א׳ ד׳), כלומר שכל הנמצאות המציא לתכלית מכוון אשר מן הראוי לקראו ‹טוב› כמו שביאר הפילוסוף בספר מה שאחר מאמר ב׳ פרק ח׳.

---

[a] הנמצאות] coni. Dunk.; הנמאות a.

§ 10.8.1 Et eande demonstrationem videtur inferre Sacrum Genesis Documentum capitulo 1 [1:4–5] ubi dicit: «Et vidit Deus lucem quod esset bona, et distinxit lucem a tenebris appellavit que lucem dem et tenebras noctem etc.» Postquam enim docuisset summam Dei potentiam qua scilicet produxit celum et terram post purum | non esse et hoc ubi [Gen 1:1] dixit: «In principio creavit Deus etc.» demostrative ostendit ipsum Deum esse voluntarium agentem sive productorem per hoc quod duo produxit contraria scilicet lucem et tenebras, quorum alterum in aliquo terminato tempore tantum statuit ministraturum quod diem appellavit; reliquum vero in alio statuit tempore quod noctem appellavit. Quibus succinte ostendit eiusdem Dei actionem esse voluntariam, tribus, scilicet, medijs.

§ 10.8.2 Primo per hoc, quod produxit contraria que non dantur fieri, per naturalem agentem sed per voluntarium tantum prout supra patuit, et habetur ab Aven R. in lib. *Destructio Des.*, disputatione tertia, dubio primo.

§ 10.8.3 Secundo vero probat idem per hoc: quod eisdem contrarijs diversa deputavit tempora eisdem limitata quibus se invicem non impedirent quoad effectus ab illis intentos quare patet voluntaria agentis electio sive deliberatio. Per lucem enim et tenebras lucidum, scilicet, aerem eiusque oppositum necessario intelligit non autem merum lumen eiusque privationem inter que non est opus divisionis vel distinctionis actu.

§ 10.8.4 Tertio ostendit idem per finem in omnibus entibus apparentem, quo patet actionem esse voluntariam. Et hoc ubi ibidem et in sequentibus [Gen 1:10] ait: «Et vidit Deus quod esset bonum» inferens illa omnia fecisse[a] intendens finem inde sequentem quod merito dicitur bonum, prout ut habetur a Phylosophi *Metaphysicorum* 11 t.c. 8 et *Physicorum* 11 t.c. 31.

§ 10.8.1 The Holy Book of Genesis (1:4–5) teaches us this, saying: "And God saw the light, that it was good. And God separated the light and the darkness. And God called the light 'day' and He called the darkness 'night.'" After this, Genesis explains the highest power of God, by which He created beings in the heavens and on earth after absolute nothingness, saying: "In the beginning God created." Genesis explains by means of demonstration that God is the voluntary agent or producer by reason of the fact that He created two such contrary things, which are light and darkness, and he determined a limited time for one of them and called it "day," and for the other he determined another time and he called it "night." With these [words], Genesis shows that the activity of God is voluntary by three proofs.

§ 10.8.2 First, because He created contrary existents that are not produced by a natural agent, but only by a voluntary agent, as Averroes explains in *The Incoherence of the Incoherence* 3, first doubt.[a]

§ 10.8.3 Second, because he assigned different limited times to each of these contraries, so that one of them would not impede the activity of its contrary; moreover, it is clear that this occurs through the will and deliberation of the agent: "light" and "darkness" mean "transparent air" and necessarily "its contrary," not only because light is the absolute privation of darkness in which there is no distinctive or separate activity.

§ 10.8.4 Third, the final purpose, which is seen in every existent, is a voluntary activity, and Genesis states here and in other places: "And God saw that it was good," which means that every being is made for an intended purpose which is called "good," as the Philosopher explains in *Metaphysics* 2, text. 8,[b] and in *Physics* 2, text. 31.[c]

---

[a] fecisse] coni. COPP.; feeisse b.

[a] Cf. *Incoherence* 87–88.   [b] *Metaph.* 2.2.994b.   [c] *Phys.* 2.2.195a.

§11 Eleventh:

We will inquire whether the creator has providence over the individuals of the generables and corruptibles, insofar as they are individuals, or not.

And it seems, at the beginning of the inquiry, that he does not have providence over them.

§11.1 First, according to the opinion of some of the First [i.e., the ancient philosophers], which Averroes explains in [the Commentary on] *Metaphysics* 12, text. 52,[a] as they said that there are many evil things in existence, from which it is appropriate that the Wise [i.e., God] stays away, and among them is the corruption that occurs in the individuals of the existents.

§11.2 Second, the same becomes clear in this way: because it is a deficiency for the Noblest [i.e., God] to exert His providence over very lower things, and the individuals of the generables and corruptibles are the lowest of all existents. If so, there would be a deficiency for God, the Creator, who is the Noblest of all existents, that He would have providence over the individuals of the corruptibles. And therefore, it seems that the statement of Averroes in [the Commentary on] *Metaphysics* 12, text. 37[b] is correct: "Indeed, providence over individuals in a manner | that somebody else will not have a part in that providence is not fitting for the divine goodness."

§11.3.1 Indeed, the contrary of this becomes clear after laying down some premises. First, that every man by nature also desires to know the divine [things], especially when he is awakened from his sleep [to strive] for this perfection, at least by an awakener, and when desires for pleasure and other impediments do not hinder him, as sense [perception] testifies and the Philosopher explains in his foreword to *Metaphysics*.[c] And this yearning is called among our Rabbanan—of blessed memory—"good inclination."

§11.3.2 Second, that this wish to know is a yearning for the perfection of the intellectual soul, because knowledge is the perfection of the intellectual soul only, and nothing besides it.

---

[a] Cf. *Metaph.* 12.10.1075a. [b] Cf. *Metaph.* 12.6.1072a. [c] *Metaph.* 1.1.980a.

11. DE SOLLICITUDINE

§ 11 **Undecimo Dubitatur**
Utrum idem Creator habeat sollicitudinem sive curam de mortalium individuis vel non.

Et videtur quod non.

§ 11.1 Primo ratione et auctoritate antiquorum quas Aven R. refert *Metaphysicorum* XII t.c. 52 dicentium quod cum multa in mundo sint mala debet sapiens illa dimittere de quorum numero videntur esse corruptiones.

§ 11.2 Secundo arguitur sic ratione, scilicet, quod turpe videtur nobilissimo ut minimis et vilissimis adhibeat curam, mortalium individua sunt entium vilissima. Ergo quid turpe videretur Creatori omnium nobilissimo ut huiusmodi vilissimis adhibeat curam, quare Aven R. in comento *Metaphysicorum* XII t.c. 37. Merito dixisse videtur sollicitudo autem circa individuum tali modo ut nullus habeat communicationem cum eo, hoc non est fas divine bonitati.

§ 11.3.1 Ad oppositum vero arguitur quibusdam presuppositis: primo, scilicet, quod omnes homines natura scire desiderant saltem cum fuerint ad illud excitati et non impediantur a lascivis, prout sensu patet et habetur a Phylosopho in *Metaphysicorum* primo.

§ 11.3.2 Secundo presupponitur quod per huiusmodi desiderium nil aliud petitur quam intellective anime perfectio. Scientia | enim nonnisi eiusdem intellective anime est perfectio.

§ 11 **Eleventh,**
it may be inquired whether the creator has providence or care over human beings or not.

And it seems that he does not.

§ 11.1 First, I would argue according to the argument and authority of Averroes in the name of the Ancients in *Metaphysics* 12, text. 52,[a] where he states that there are many evil things in the world, from which the Wise [i.e., God] should stay away, including the corruption of individual existents.

§ 11.2 Second, I would argue that it seems that it is inappropriate that the most noble [existent] should have providence over lower and less noble existents. Human beings are lower existents, and therefore it seems that the most noble, the creator, does take care of the lower existents, as Averroes explicates in the Commentary on *Metaphysics* 12, text. 37,[b] where he states: "Providence over an individual, in which nobody else shares, is something that the divine bounty does not necessitate."

§ 11.3.1 On the contrary it is to argue by laying down some assumptions, first: that all men by nature desire to know, at least when they are aroused by this desire and are not hindered by lustful things, as the senses testify and as the Philosopher explains in *Metaphysics* 1, text. 1.[c]

§ 11.3.2 Second: that this desire is for nothing other than the perfection of the intellectual soul, | because knowledge is nothing other than the perfection of the intellectual soul.

---

[a] Cf. *Metaph.* 12.10.1075a.   [b] Cf. *Metaph.* 12.6.1072a.   [c] *Metaph.* 1.1.980a.

§ 11.3.3 Third, that the nature of this intellectual soul is its first perfection, which is a certain power for the second perfection, in which it is perfected, as is evident from experience. And the Philosopher explains this in *On the Soul* 3, text. 4,[a] and 5.[b]

§ 11.3.4 Fourth, that this second perfection is not achieved by all humans, nor by the majority of them. And those who achieve it do not achieve it in one manner, and not through the activity of nature, as occurs in the perfection of the other powers; they achieve it through individual free choice, as experience testifies, because if an individual human being does not agree to investigate and to inquire through his [own] free choice, he will never rise to the rank of the perfection of this power.

§ 11.3.5 Fifth, that nature is acting for a final purpose, as is evident from the Philosopher's proofs in *Physics* 2, text. 77, and others.[c]

§ 11.3.6 Sixth, that the activity performed for a final purpose is necessarily caused by a certain intellect intending that final purpose, as is evident from the definition of the final purpose, which is the final [good] intended by the activity of the prior [things], as is self-evident. And Aristotle explains this in *Physics* 2, text. 31,[d] and *Metaphysics* 2, text. 8[e] and 9.[f] And since the intention of the final purpose necessarily comes from an intellect, and this is because the aforementioned intention is undoubtedly an intellectual activity, it therefore follows that since nature acts for a final purpose without thought and consideration, as Aristotle explains in *Physics* 2, text. 86,[g] then the intention of the final purpose is necessarily ascribed to a certain intending intellect, as Averroes explains in [the Commentary on] *Metaphysics* 12, text. 18:[h] "And in this way, it will be understood that nature makes a thing in perfection and in order, even if it does not understand, because it makes it under the governance of active powers that are nobler than it and called 'separate intellects.'" And in addition to this, the connection of [all] existence, by which it is one, testifies the existence of an existent that orderly arranges all existence. And this is the first of all existents, as becomes clear from Aristotle's proof in *Metaphysics* 12, text. 52.[i] It follows, then, that the whole order of existence and the intention of the final purpose in the existents may be attributed to that first one [existent].

---

[a] *De an.* 3.4.429a18–20. [b] *De an.* 3.4.429a21–24. [c] *Phys.* 2.8.198b. [d] *Phys.* 2.2.195a. [e] *Metaph.* 2.2.994b. [f] *Metaph.* 2.2.994b. [g] *Phys.* 2.9.200a. [h] Cf. *Metaph.* 12.3.1070a. [i] *Metaph.* 12.10.1075a.

§ 11.3.3 שלישית שטבע זאת הנפש השכלית הוא היות שלמותה הראשון כח מה אל השלמות השני אשר בו תשלם כמו שהוא מבואר בנסיון ובאר אותו הפילוסוף בספר הנפש מאמר ג' פרק ד' וה'.

§ 11.3.4 רביעית שזה השלמות השני לא ישיגוהו כל בני האדם ולא רובם והמשיגים לא ישיגוהו על אופן אחד ולא ישיגוהו בפעלת הטבע כאשר יקרה בשלמות שאר הכחות אבל ישיגוהו בבחירה אישיית כאשר יעיד הנסיון כי אם האיש האנושי לא יסכים בבחירתו לחקור ולעיין לא יעלה לעולם למדרגת שלמות זה הכח.

§ 11.3.5 חמשית שהטבע יפעל לתכלית כמבואר בראיות הפילוסוף בספר השמע מאמר ב' פרק ע"ז וזולתו.

§ 11.3.6 ששית שהפעולה הנעשית לתכלית תהיה בהכרח מסובבת מאיזה שכל מכוין אל התכלית. כמבואר מגדר התכלית שהוא האחרית אשר היה מכוון בפעולת הקודמות כאשר הוא מבואר בעצמו ובאר אותו ארסטו' בספר השמע מאמר ב' פרק ל"א ובספר מה שאחר מאמר ב' פרק ח' וט'. ובהיות שכוונת התכלית תהיה בהכרח מאיזה שכל. וזה כי אמנם הכוונה הנזכרת היא פעולה שכלית בלי ספק. ומזה יתחייב שבהיות שהטבע פועל לתכלית בלתי מחשבה ועיון כאשר ביאר ארסטו' בספר השמע מאמר ב' פרק פ"ו תיוחס בהכרח כוונת התכלית אל איזה שכל מכוין כמו שבאר אבן רשד בספר מה שאחר מאמר י"ב פרק י"ח באמרו: «בזה האופן יובן שהטבע עושה דבר בשלמות ובסדר גם שהוא לא יבין כי זה יעשה בהנהגת כחות פועלות נכבדות ממנו הנקראות ›שכלים נבדלים‹» עד כאן לשונו. ועם זה הנה קשר המציאות אשר בו הוא אחד יעיד על היות איזה נמצא מסדר כל המציאות והוא הראשון לכל הנמצאות כאשר התבאר במופת ארסטו' בספר מה שאחר מאמר י"ב פרק נ"ב. הנה יתחייב אם כן שנייחס כל סדר המציאות וכוונת התכלית בנמצאות אל אותו הראשון.

§ 11.3.3 Tertio presupponitur quod de natura huiusmodi intellective est, ut habeat potentiam ad secundum actum quo perficiatur, prout experientia docet, et habetur a Phylosopho in libro *De Anima* III t.c. 4 et t.c. 5.

§ 11.3.4 Quarto presupponitur quod huiusmodi perfectio non acquiritur per commune hominum arbitrium quod, scilicet, omnes participant, sed acquiritur per illud particulare individui arbitrium. Quo fit merita diligentia ad huiusmodi perfectionem acquirendam, quare non contingit huiusmodi perfectionem fieri in omnibus humani generis individuis neque in maiori eorum parte, sicut de reliquarum naturalium virtutum effectu contingit quod, scilicet, fit saltem in maiori individuorum parte prout experientia aperte docet.

§ 11.3.5 Quinto presupponitur quod natura semper operatur ad finem, prout habetur ratione et auctoritate Phylosophi *Physicorum* II t.c. 77 et sequentibus.

§ 11.3.6 Sexto presupponitur quod finis nil aliud est quam ultimum bonum propter quod precedentes operationes fiunt, prout per se patet et habetur a Phyilosopho *Physicorum* II t.c. 31 et *Metaphysicorum* II t.c. 8. Cumque prefata diligentia ad perfectionem acquirendam nonnisi per intellectualem cognitionem et deliberationem fieri contingat, eius ergo finis qui, scilicet, est ipsa perfectio habet necessario a quodam intellecto intendi, quare cum natura operetur ad finem ut supra que tamen non intendit finem, prout in quibusdam patet sensu, et habetur a Phylosopho *Physicorum* II t.c. 86 necesse est ut ipsa natura regatur a quodam intelligentia huiusmodi finem intendente. Quare Aven R. in comento *Metaphysicorum* XII t.c. 18 ait: «Hoc igitur modo est intelligendum quod natura facit aliquid perfecte et ordinate, quamvis non intelligat quasi esset memorata a virtutibus agentibus nobilioribus ea que dicuntur intelligentie etc.» Cumque universi colligatio qua unitur et fit quid unum doceat quod est quoddam eiusdem universi ordinator, et talis est omnium entium primum, prout habetur ratione et auctoritate Phylosophi *Metaphysicorum* XII t.c. 52. Huiusmodi ergo universi ordo et finis intentio est eidem primo attribuenda.

§ 11.3.3 Third: that the nature of this intellectual soul is that its first perfection is a certain power for the second perfection by which it is perfected, as experience teaches and as the Philosopher explains in *On the Soul* 3, text. 4[a] and text. 5.[b]

§ 11.3.4 Fourth: that perfection is not achieved by the communal [i.e., shared] free choice that is shared by all men, but is acquired by individual free choice, which is produced by "good selection," from which perfection is acquired, since this kind of perfection is not equally produced in all human beings, nor in their majority, but occurs to the few through the effect of natural powers, which are produced in at least the majority of human beings, as experience teaches.

§ 11.3.5 Fifth: that nature always acts for a final purpose, according to the argument and authority of the Philosopher in *Physics* 2, text. 77,[c] and others.

§ 11.3.6 Sixth: that the final purpose is nothing other than the final good by which the aforementioned activities are produced, which is evident, as the Philosopher explains in *Physics* 2, text. 31,[d] and *Metaphysics* 2, text. 8.[e] However, the aforementioned care, acquired through perfection, is produced only by intellectual knowledge and choice, and then its final purpose, which is the same perfection, is necessarily intended by an intellect, because nature acts for a final purpose, as aforementioned, without understanding the purpose, as is evident and as the Philosopher explains in *Physics* 2, text. 86.[f] It is necessary that nature is guided by a certain intellect for an intended final purpose, as Averroes explicates in the Commentary on *Metaphysics* 12, text. 18,[g] where he states: "In this way, it is appropriate to understand that nature produces something in perfection and in order, although it does not understand, as it is inspired by active powers that are nobler than it, which are called 'intellects.'" Moreover, the connection [i.e., conjunction] of the universe, by which it is one and produces unity, testifies that there is an arranger of the universe, who is the first of all existents, according to the argument and authority of the Philosopher in *Metaphysics* 12, text. 52.[h] And then the order of the universe and the intention of the final purpose are attributed to this first existent.

---

[a]*De an.* 3.4.429a18–20. [b]*De an.* 3.4.429a21–24. [c]*Phys.* 2.8.198b. [d]*Phys.* 2.2.195a. [e]*Metaph.* 2.2.994b. [f]*Phys.* 2.8.199b. [g]Cf. *Metaph.* 12.3.1070a. [h]*Metaph.* 12.10.1075a.

§ 11.3.7 Seventh, that everyone | who intends a final purpose necessarily has providence over the only means by which the final purpose will be achieved, and nothing besides them. And he will oppose those who resist in order to impede the achievement of the final purpose, because otherwise, his wish [to achieve] the final purpose would be without perfect consideration. And it is not appropriate to attribute [this] to the First Wise [i.e., God].

§ 11.4.1 And after having laid down the aforementioned premises, we will explain what is intended in this way: since there is an arranger of the order of existence who desires the perfection of the intellectual soul, and this can only be achieved by individual free choice when it consents, and this perfection will be impossible when individual free choice does not consent, it follows, then, that the aforementioned arranger of order will have providence over those who choose the aforementioned perfection to aid them and will also have providence over the individuals who choose the contrary to oppose them. And God—may He be praised—informs [us] about this with a proof (Exodus 20:5–6): "Visiting the guilt of [...] of those who hate Me, but showing kindness to [...] those who love Me," because human love and hatred can only reach God—may He be praised—in this way: that He calls those who endeavour to do His will and reach His desire to [achieve the] final purpose by perfecting human intellect "lovers," and calls those who stand up against and oppose His will "haters."

§ 11.4.2 And apart from this, since human individual free choice will improve some of the generable and corruptible existents and provide perseverance by being right[eous] and will destroy some of them by being the contrary of this, it is not proper for the Wise, the Forth-bringer [i.e., God], to disregard all of these and not to have providence over anything, [consequently] making His will like our will. If so, it follows that the First of all existents, the Wisest of all, and the Lover of his action, as is appropriate for every wise agent, will have providence over individual free choice and will endeavour to bring His will to the final purpose intended by Him. And this is what we wanted to explain.

§ 11.5 We answer, if so, to dispel [any] doubt about the aforementioned thesis, that the First of all existents, who is the Creator, necessarily has providence over every individual of the human species. Yet over the rest of the generables and corruptibles, for which the intended [final purpose] is achieved in their species and not only in [a single] individual of them, it is appropriate that the providence of the arranger of order will be [exerted] over them according to the species only.

11. השגחה

§ 11.3.7 שביעית שכל | מכוון אל תכלית הוא בהכרח משגיח אל האמצעיים אשר באמצעותם בלבד יושג התכלית ולא זולתם ויתקומם נגד המתקוממים למנוע השגת התכלית כי באופן אחר היה בקשו התכלית בלתי עיון שלם וזה אין ראוי שייוחס אל החכם הראשון.

§ 11.4.1 ואחר שהנחנו ההקדמות הנזכרות הנה נבאר המכוון באופן זה כי בהיות שמסדר המציאות חפץ בשלמות הנפש השכלית וזה לא יושג זולתי בבחירה אישיית בהיותה נאותה ויהיה זה השלמות נמנע כאשר תהיה הבחירה האישיית בלתי נאותה יתחייב אם כן שזה המסדר הנזכר ישגיח על הבוחרים בשלמות הנזכר לעזור אותם ולהשגיח גם כן על האישיים הבוחרים הפך זה להתקומם כנגדם וזה הורה האל יתברך במופת באמרו: «פוקד עון ... לשונאי ועושה חסד ... לאוהבי» (שמות כ׳ ה׳-ו׳), כי אמנם לא תפול אהבה ושנאה אנושית על האל יתברך זולתי באופן זה שיקרא ‹אוהבים› את המשתדלים לעשות רצונו ולהביא חפצו אל תכלית בהשלים השכלית האנושית ויקרא ‹שונאים› את המתנגדים ומתקוממים נגד רצונו זה.

§ 11.4.2 וּבלעדי זאת הנה בהיות שהבחירה האנושית האישיית תתקן ותקיים קצת מהנמצאות ההוות ונפסדות בהיותה ישרה ותסתור קצתם בהיותה הפך זה לא יאות לחכם הממציא שיתעלם מכל אלה ולא ישגיח לדבר מזה לעשות רצונו כרצונו. אם כן יתחייב שהראשון לכל הנמצאות החכם מכלם ואוהב פעלו כראוי לכל פועל חכם ישגיח על הבחירה האישיית[a] וישתדל להביא רצונו אל התכלית המכוון מאתו וזה הוא מה שרצינו[b] לבאר.

§ 11.5 נשיב אם כן[c] להתיר ספק החקירה הנזכרת שהראשון לכל הנמצאות אשר הוא הבורא הוא בהכרח משגיח על כל איש מאישי המין האנושי. אמנם על שאר ההווים ונפסדים אשר המכוון מהם יושג במיניהם[d] לא באיש זולת איש מהם ראוי שתהיה השגחת המסדר עליהם כפי המין בלבד.

---

[a] האישיית] coni. Dunk.; האשיית a. [b] שרצינו] coni. Dunk.; שרצנו a.
[c] כן] add. Dunk.; om. a. [d] במיניהם] coni. Dunk.; במינהם a.

§ 11.3.7 Septimo presupponitur quod quilibet finem intendens habet necessario curare de his que possent suum effectum perturbare eisdem pro viribus resistendo, similiter habet curare de his que suo intento assistunt, alias enim negligenter intenderet huiusmodi finem quod esset quid turpe sapienti.

§ 11.4.1 Tunc arguo sic ipse omnium ordinator intendit humane intellective perfectionem. Sed illam non consequitur nisi per individualem deliberationem ad ipsam perfectionem consequendum precedentem. Ergo habet de illo individuali processu et per consequens de ipsis individuis inquantum individua curare sive sollicitudinem habere. Quare hoc divinitus ostendes in Sacro Exodi [Exod 20:5–6] testu «benefactores Dei amicos» appellat tanquam eiusdem intento assistentes, malefactores vero | «inimicos» appellat tanquam eiusdem intentum perturbantes. Quare ibidem merito, monet individualiter circa illos curam exhibiturum.ᵃ

§ 11.4.2 Preterea cum per individuorum hominum arbitrium et deliberationem bonam vel malam eiusdem creatoris ordo et opus saltem circa mortales conservatur vel perturbatur, et pro parte destruitur, prout sensu patet. Turpe videretur eidem talia producenti ut non curaret de ipsis individuis intento assistentibus, vel perturbantibus pro eiusdem operis conservatione. Assistentibus, scilicet, iuvando. Perturbantibus vero resistendo. Cum autem huiusmodi negligentia nullo pacto eidem Creatori tanquam sapientissimo et suum opus diligenti competat, sequitur ergo ut eisdem humanis individuis horumque actionibus adhibeat sollicitudinem sive curam quod est intentum.

§ 11.5 Ad dubium ergo respondendum quod entium primus sive horum Creator habet immediate sollicitudinem sive curam de unoquoque humano individuo. De reliquis vero mortalium generibus quorum intentus finis per horum genera tantum habetur non autem per individua, merito decet ipsam primam naturam ordinantem de horum generibus tantum habere curam.

§ 11.3.7 Seventh: that anyone who intends a final purpose necessarily has providence over beings who impede his work, resisting them by all means. But he also necessarily takes care of beings who facilitate his intention, as otherwise he would inattentively strive for the final purpose, and this is not appropriate for the Wise.

§ 11.4.1 I would argue that the arranger of all existents desires human intellectual perfection, and this is only achieved through individual choice, which follows this perfection. It would follow that he has providence or care over individuals because they are individual existents. This is divinely proved in the Holy Book of Exodus (20:5–6), in which those who help his intention are called "lovers" and | those who interfere with his intention are called "enemies" [i.e., haters]. In these [assumptions], the providence over them is demonstrated.

§ 11.4.2 Moreover, through individual free choice and a right or wrong decision, the creator's order over and behaviour towards a mortal individual could be preserved or troubled or destroyed, as is evident. And it would not be proper for the arranger not to have providence over the individuals who help his intention or over individuals who impede his preservation, supporting those who help him and resisting those who trouble him. However, indifference is never proper for the creator, who is the most wise and whose behaviour corresponds to his intention, and it would follow that he has providence or care over individual human activities. This is what was intended.

§ 11.5 To dispel any doubt, I would argue that the first of the existents—namely, their creator—necessarily has providence or care over every individual human, but over the rest of the generated species whose intended final purpose is achieved in their species, [his providence] is not individual. It is appropriate that the providence of the arranger of order is over them according to their species only.

ᵃ exhibiturum] coni. Copp.; exibiturum b.

§ 11.6 However, to the opponent's arguments, first, saying that it is not appropriate that evil things should be under the governance of a wise arranger of order, we answer that it is appropriate to oppose this [argument] and to say that evil things are (1) partially evil in relation to a certain existent only, like the perdition of sinners, which is evil concerning the corrupted [sinner], but indeed good concerning those who are freed from the harms of his sin, (2) that some evil things are generated by human free choice, and it is not appropriate to attribute this kind of evil thing to the arranger of order, because he orders the aforementioned free choice according to the good, because the human intellectual soul is perfected by it, as becomes clear to us below with the help of ha-Shem, and the evil things that are consequent upon it [i.e., the free choice] are not | intended by Him at all, and (3) that some are evil things that occur because of the deficiency of the matter, which does not reach a good state because of this, like the kinds of corruption that happen to the corruptibles, and like those [evil things], it is good for them that the arranger of order orders them according to the good that is [at least] possible through them.

§ 11.7 Indeed, to the opponent's second argument, which says that it is not appropriate for the absolutely Noble [i.e., God] that He will have providence over the absolutely low [things]—and these are the individuals of the generable and corruptibles—we answer, first, that this is indeed correct for every noble whose power is finite. And this is so because through his providence over the lower things, he becomes passible and weary to some degree, and his providence over the nobler things will necessarily decrease. [But] this is not correct for the First Noble [i.e., God], because His power is infinite and impassible. And therefore, weariness does not occur to Him, which would be a miserliness in Him if He were to close Himself to the providence of all, *from the horns of wild oxen to the eggs of lice*.[a] And the Poet explains this, as it says (Psalm 145:9): "He-Shem is good to all."

§ 11.8 Second, we answer: because it is not correct for the providence over the individuals of the human species that this should be a providence over lower existents. And this is so because every one of them has an intellectual soul, which is a separate, incorruptible substance, especially when it is perfected in cognition and action, as becomes clear. Noble [individuals have the ability to] think and are worthy of divine providence, especially when they are right[eous], to reflect the will of their Creator. And Israel is

---

[a] *'Abod. Zar.* 3b.

§ 11.6 Ad argumenta vero et primo quo ad primum respondetur: distinguendo de malis. Quedam enim sunt talia respective tantum, sicut malefactorum perditio, que scilicet licet patientis sic perditi respectu sit proculdubio malum patrie tamen respectu est quid optimum quare per hoc nullum malum est ordinatori imputandum. Quedam vero contingunt per humanum arbitrium facta, que similiter non sunt ordinatori imputanda, cum fiant preter eiusdem sensum, arbitrium enim ab ipso ordinatore est ad bonum tantum ordinatum et intentum, ad hoc, scilicet, ut per ipsum arbitrium intellective perfectio acquiratur ut infra patebit. Quare divina sapientia non habet illud aliquo pacto dimittere, immo ipsam decet inquantum est quid bonum principaliter intendere, neque per hoc mala inde sequentia sunt sibi imputanda. Quedam vero videntur absolute mala sicut corruptionum genera naturaliter contingentia, et talia fiunt ex materie natura non pervenientis ad immortalem gradum quo inde composita magis consequatur boni, et talia non habent dici mala, sed potius diminutio ab ulteriori bono, immo horum est ut pro quanto merentur ad ipsa extendatur divina sollicitudo.

§ 11.7 Quo autem ad secundum argumentum quo, scilicet, arguitur: quod non est fas divine bonitati omnium nobilissime ut minimis et vilissimis adhibeat curam et talia sunt mortalium individua respondetur. Distinguendo de nobili, vel, enim, dicitur de illo cuius virtus est finita et passibilis, et de tali verificatur prefata propositio. Qua cum non equebene sufficiat ad plura sicut ad pauciora, turpe esset divertere sive subtrahere a nobilioribus eiusdem virtutis curam eandem ignobilioribus applicando. Vel dicitur propositio de nobili cuius virtus est infinita et impassibilis, et | tunc negatur propositio huiusmodi, enim, virtus cum sit infinita et impassibilis quare nulla sibi accidit lassitudo. Sufficit ad hoc ut tam nobilioribus quam ignobilioribus et tam pluribus quam paucioribus se simul et semel eque bene extendat. Quare Psalmus 144 [145:9] idem inferens ait: «Bonus est Dominus universis.»

§ 11.8 Preterea respondetur negando ut humanum individuum dicatur esse quid vile, quia cum eidem insit intellectiva anima, que, scilicet, est quid abstractum et immortale ut infra ostendetur. Merito reputatur quid nobile et divina sollicitudine dignum. Cura vero circa reliqua mortalium

§ 11.6 In response to the first argument, I will reply by making a distinction according to the definition of evil things. Some of them are only [evil] in relation to certain existents, such as the perdition of sinners, which is evil in relation to a corrupt man, but good in relation to one who is freed from this perdition. For this reason, no evil can be attributed to the arranger. Others are produced by human free choice, and it is not possible to attribute them to the arranger, because these kinds of evil things are generated by the senses. On the contrary, free choice is ordered and intended for the good by the arranger, because intellectual perfection is acquired by free choice, as will be clear below. And this is never appropriate for divine knowledge, which is always good, and it is not possible that evil things could follow from Him. Some of them are absolute evil, like the corruption that is proper to contingent species, and some of them are produced from matter and could not attain the good according to the immortal rank, such as the composed beings. This kind of thing is not called evil, but we say that there is a deficiency in relation to the supreme good. Indeed, divine providence serves the good, which is increased by it.

§ 11.7 In response to the second argument, I will reply: it is not appropriate for divine goodness, which is the noblest [being], to have care over the lower and less noble existents, and human individuals are lower existents. I will reply by making a distinction according to the definition of noble existents. Either we say in respect of the noble existents that their power is finite and passible, and this is true according to the aforementioned assumption, because the power does not provide the same good for the majority as it does for the minority of existents, because it is not appropriate that providence should be applied to ignoble existents by [its] turning away or withdrawing power from the nobler existents; or we say in respect to noble existents that their power is infinite and impassible, | and then the [aforementioned] assumption is refuted, because if the power is infinite and impassible, then there is no weariness; the power provides for the nobler existents as well for the ignoble ones, for the majority no less than for the minority, because powers increase together and at the same time equally well, as Psalm (145:9) explains, saying: "The Lord is good to all."

§ 11.8 Moreover, I refute the assumption in which it is said that mortal individuals are lower existents because they have an intellectual soul, which is separate and immortal, as will be shown below. For this reason, we can consider man a noble existent and worthy of divine providence. And it seems that He [i.e. God] has care over the rest of

more right[eous] [and worthy] of this, and they are bearers of His covenant. The Creator—may He be praised—is called "the God of Israel"; that is to say, He who has providence over their [the Israelites'] individuals. And this is so because the providence over the particulars of their individuals in this world is even greater than that over the particulars of the individuals of the Nations, who are not right[eous] [enough] to worship Him, except for a minority of a minority, until He makes *the Nations pure of speech, so that they all invoke ha-Shem by name and Him with one accord*,[a] and then undoubtedly *He will be called "God of all the earth."*[b] Indeed, the common providence in the rest of the species of corruptibles, as is evident, is [consequent upon] the wisdom of artistry of their composition, although they are lower things, yet it [i.e., the providence] is over their species only, insofar as they are parts of the world. Even though their portion in existence is very small, it is appropriate for an agent who encompasses existence to have providence over them, in order that his activity will be complete [i.e., perfect].

§ 11.9 And apart from these [words], we will answer after having laid down two assumptions: (1) first, that the whole of the rest of the corruptibles exist for the needs of the human race and for its sake, as experience testifies for some of them, and this becomes clear from Aristotle's opinion in *Politics* [1, text. 6]:[c] "It is appropriate to think this about all generables and corruptibles, because the plants exist for the sake of living animals and the living animals exist for the sake of the human species"; (2) second, that there is [something] incorruptible in the human species that is perfected by means of and by the aid of corruptible powers, as becomes clear to [us] with ha-Shem's help.

§ 11.10 And therefore, to the opponent's argument, saying that if the creator had providence over the generables and corruptibles, it would therefore follow that the noblest of the existents would have providence over the lowest of the existents, which is disgraceful, we answer and say: the providence | that applies to a low and corruptible existent could be [found] in one of two cases. (1) First, it could be that providence will be over the lower existent for its own sake, and in this case, we might think that it is disgraceful that the providence of the noblest should apply to the lowest corruptible, and (2) second, [it could be] that providence will be over the corruptible insofar as it is for the needs of the perfection of the human intellectual soul—which is indeed a noble thing—which is incorruptible, as men-

---

[a] Zeph 3:9.   [b] Isa 54:5.   [c] *Pol.* 1.3.1256b.

genera ut videtur adhibita, prout artificium in his apparens satis docet. Quamvis sint per se vilia eisdem tamen adhibetur ipsa cura tanquam universi partibus quantum cumque minimis ad eiusdem universi perfectionem, sicut accidit artifici aliquod limitatum componenti. Quod non diceretur suum opus perfectum si quid eius quantuncunque minimum deficeret, quare oportet ut de quacunque eius parte quantunque minimum deficeret, quare oportet ut de quacumque eius parte quantunque minima curet.

§ 11.9 Preterea respondetur duobus presuppositis. Primo, scilicet, quod omnia mortalia preter humanum genus habent esse ad eiusdem generis humani oportunitatem tanquam eorum nobilissimi, prout de quibusdam eorum experientia satis docere videtur, et idem habetur ratione et auctoritate Phylosophi Polyticorum primi ubi dicit: «Similiter est de genitis quoque existimandum plantasque animantium esse gratia, cetera vero animantia hominum causa etc.» Secundo presupponitur quod humano generi inest quoddam[a] inmortale quod, scilicet, habet mortalium auxilio perfici, prout infra diffusius Deo dante explicabitur.

§ 11.10 Quare cum arguitur quod si Creator omnium nobilissimus adhiberet curam mortalibus sequeretur ut omnium nobilissimus de vilissimis curaret quod videtur quid turpe, respondetur distinguendo de cura talibus adhibita. Alia, enim, est cura qua huiusmodi vilia quis respiceret illa tantum intendens, et talis non est divina cura de illis, alia vero est cura qua huiusmodi vilia quis respiceret pro quanto sunt oportuna ad intellective anime perfectionem que, scilicet, est quid inmortale et nobile ut supra. Cui

the human species, as is evident from the wisdom of the artistry in them; although they are lower in themselves, nevertheless providence contributes to reaching perfection in every part of the universe, even for the lowest. And therefore, if the artistry seems to be limited [to the lower existents], because we cannot say that his activity is perfect if it lacks something, however small, then it is appropriate to say that he has providence over every part, even the lowest.

§ 11.9 I will reply by laying down two assumptions. First [assumption]: that all mortal existents, except the human species, are a convenience for the human species, being the noblest among them, as experience testifies and according to the argument and authority of the Philosopher in *Politics* 1, text. 6,[a] where he states: "It is appropriate to think this about all generable existents, because plants exist for the needs of living animals and living animals for the needs of the human species." Second [assumption]: that the human species is immortal because it is perfected by means of aid emanated from God, as we will explain below.

§ 11.10 In response to this argument, I will reply: if the creator, who is the noblest among the existents, has providence over mortals, then the noblest among the existents will have providence over the lower existents, which is incongruous. I will reply by making a distinction according to the definition of providence that is given over existents. One kind is the providence over the lower existents for its own sake, which is not appropriate for divine providence. The other is the providence over the lower existents according to what is convenient for the perfection of the intellectual soul, which is immortal and noble, as afore-

---

[a] quoddam] coni. Copp.; quddam b.

[a] *Pol.* 1.3.1256b.

tioned above. And in this way, this [kind of] providence does not apply to the lower things for their own existence's sake, but applies to them for the needs of the perfection of that incorruptible thing, which is considered to be a noble thing, to which it is appropriate that there is divine providence over it. And due to this, [divine providence] will be over the corruptibles, whose existence is for its [i.e., the human intellectual soul's] sake and need.

§ 11.11.1 And the Poet, who speaks about the opinions of the deniers of divine providence among the individuals of the human species, explain this, saying (Psalm 94:7): "And they say: 'Ha-Shem does not see [it], the God of Jacob does not pay heed.'" And he answers them, saying (Psalm 94:9): "Shall He who implants the ear not hear, He who forms the eye not see?"; that is to say, the artistry of the model, which is seen in the composition of the eye and the ear, informs [us] about the providence of the artisan who made them, because it is strong in the species of corruptibles, necessarily coming from the forth-bringer, the first arranger of order, and generated by him mediately or immediately.

§ 11.11.2 And he continues, saying (Psalm 94:10): "Shall He who disciplines nations not punish?" And by this, he teaches [us] through a proof that divine providence is necessarily [exerted] over the individuals of the human species. And this is so for two reasons. First, for the perpetuity of existence, so that some part of it shall not be corrupted by the free choice of some individuals of the human species, and therefore, it follows that He sometimes rebukes some of them, so that some part of existence will not be corrupted by a harm that comes from their free choice. And he informs [us] about this, saying (ibid.): "Shall He who disciplines nations not punish?"; that is to say, He who gives the nations an ethical standard depending on choice to give perpetuity to order, which is necessary for the human species, shall He not rebuke some who, by their deviation from that ethical standard, cause a corruption of the aforementioned order, against His will and order? And [second,] he continues, saying (Psalm 94:10): "He who instructs men in knowledge"; that is to say, it is known that they are the first intelligibles that He put in each and every individual of man by nature. And from them, all inquirers begin, through their free choice to pursue the knowledge of various sciences, to perfect their intellectual soul. It becomes clear that He—may He be praised—has providence over the individuals of man[kind] and therefore He examines disruptions and the stupidity of the opinions of the deniers of providence, saying (Psalm 94:7): "Ha-Shem does not see [it]," as mentioned above.

לעיל. וזאת ההשגחה בזה האופן לא תפול על הפחותים לסבת מציאות עצמם אבל תפול עליהם לצורך שלמות אותו הבלתי נפסד הנחשב דבר נכבד ראוי שתהיה עליו השגחה אלהית ובגללו[a] תהיה בנפסדים אשר מציאותם בעבורם ולצרכו.

§ 11.11.1 וזה ביאר המשורר המספר דעות כופרי ההשגחה האלהית באישי המין האנושי באמרו: »ויאמרו: ›לא יראה יה ולא יבין אלהי יעקב.‹« (תהלים צ״ד ז׳). ועליהם השיב באמרו: »הנוטע אזן הלא ישמע אם יוצר עין הלא יביט« (שם שם ט׳), כלומר שמלאכת התבנית הנראית בהרכבת העין ואזן תורה על השגחת אומן שעשאם כי רבה היא על מיני הנפסדים הבאה בהכרח מן הממציא המסדר הראשון והווה מאתו באמצעי או בלתי אמצעי.

§ 11.11.2 והוסיף ואמר: »היוסר גויים הלא יוכיח?« (שם שם י׳). ובזה הורה במופת שההשגחה האלהית תהיה בהכרח על אישי המין האנושי. וזה לשתי סבות ראשונה לקיום המציאות שלא יפסד קצתו בבחירת קצת אישי המין האנושי. ולזה יתחייב שלפעמים ייסר את קצתם למען לא יפסד קצת המציאות בנזק הבא בבחירתם וזה הורה באמרו: »היוסר גויים הלא יוכיח?« (שם), כלומר מי שנתן בגויים מוסר בחיריי לקיום המדינות ההכרחי למין האנושי הלא יוכיח את קצתם בסורם מאותו המוסר להפסיד המדינות הנזכרות נגד רצונו וסדרו? והוסיף ואמר: »המלמד אדם דעת?« (שם), כלומר שמהדעת שהם המושכלות הראשונות אשר שם בכל איש מאישי האדם בטבע. ומהם יקחו כל המעיינים התחלה בבחירתם לידיעת חכמות מתחלפות לשלמות נפשם השכלית. התבאר שהוא יתברך משגיח באישי[b] האדם ובזה יבחן שבושי וסכלות דעת כופרי ההשגחה באמרם: »לא יראה יה« (תהלים צ״ד ז׳) כנזכר למעלה.

---

a. ובגללו] a^{corr}; ובגלגלו a.   b. באישי] coni. Dunk.; באיש a.

merito divina adhibentur cura ut supra, et talis est divina cura de brutis quorum existentiam et conservationem respicit pro quanto sunt ad intellective perfectionem oportuna.

§ 11.11.1 Quare Psalmus 93 [94:7] Gentilium opinionem narrans, qua scilicet negabant Deum scire mortalium individua, nedum ut eisdem adhiberet sollicitudinem sive curam, et hoc ubi dicit: «Et dixerunt non videt Dominus neque intelligit etc.» illos ibidem redarguit ubi subdit dicens: «Qui plantat aurem nonne audietur, qui format oculum nonne aspiciet» quasi dicat quod per artificium in aure et oculo apparens, quod nonnisi per quandam abstractam intelligentiam huiusmodi mortalis individui oportunitatem intendentem fieri contingit, patet divinam curam ad mortalium individua mediate vel immediate extendi. Huiusmodi enim intelligentia vel est quid idem cum ipso Deo universi ordinatore vel est quid ab eo ordinatum.

⟨§ 11.11.2⟩

§ 11.12 | Esaias vero cap. 40 [40:27] succinte quidem narrat rationem dicentium Deum non curare de mortalium individuis, et hoc quia illa tanquam sensus obiecta ignorat. Et quia dedignaretur de his minimis curare licet illa sciret, et hoc ubi dicit: «Quare dicis Jacob et loqueris Israel abscondita est via mea a Domino et a Deo meo iudicium meum transibit» inferens, quod illud probant duobus medijs. Primo quod cum individua per sensus tantum percipi videantur Deus ergo cum non percipiat per sensus nullum pacto habet illa scire nedum de illis curare, et hoc infert ubi dicit: «Abscondita est via mea a Domino.» Secundo idem probabant dicentes quod dato ut illa sciat non tamen habet eisdem tamquam minimis adhibere curam, et hoc infert ubi dicit: «Et a Deo meo iudicium meum transibit» quasi dicat quod dato ut individua sciat, habet tamen iudicium de illis ab eodem transire sive pretermitti tanquam minimum et divina cura indignum.

mentioned. This is appropriate for divine providence, as aforementioned. Divine providence takes care of the existence and conservation of the lower existents, which exist for the need of the intellectual soul.

§ 11.11.1 Psalm 93 (94:9) teaches [us] about the opinion of the Gentiles [Nations] who deny God's knowledge of mortal individuals and deny that He has providence or care over them, saying: "And they have said: The Lord shall not see," and he [the psalmist] refutes them, saying: "He who planted the ear, does he not hear? He who formed the eye, does he not see?" This means that the artistry in the ears and eyes is evident because the excellence of the human individual is generated only by means of separate intellects, and it is clear that divine providence reaches out over mortal individuals, mediately or immediately, because the separate intellect either coincides with God, who is the arranger of the universe, or is ordered by Him.

⟨§ 11.11.2⟩

§ 11.12 Isaiah (40:27) explains about those who say that God does not have providence over mortal individuals, that He also ignores the objects of the senses, and that He disdains to take care of the lower existents, although He could know them, and states: "Why do you say, O Jacob, why declare, O Israel, 'My way is hid from the Lord, My cause is ignored by my God'?" This means that we can prove this in two inferences. First [inference]: it seems that individuals perceive through their senses only, and if God does not perceive through His senses, then He cannot know them or have providence over them, and hence the saying, "My way is hid from the Lord." Second [inference]: also, if He knows them, He does not have necessary providence over lower things, hence the saying, "My cause is ignored by my God," which means that He knows individuals, but He passes over them or He ignores the judgement of them, because the lower existents are not worthy of divine providence.

§ 11.12 And Isaiah explains the same when he describes the opinions of those who deny the Creator's knowledge of the individuals of the human species, let alone that He would not have providence over them. And he provides proofs of the contradiction of their opinions, and he says this (Isaiah 40:27): "Why do you say, O Jacob, why declare, | O Israel: 'My way is hid from ha-Shem, my cause is ignored by my God'?"; that is to say that those who do not believe in the Creator's knowledge and in His providence over the individuals of the human species give a reason for their words [here]: (1) first, because the individuals of the species are not apprehended by the intellect, but are apprehended by sense [perception], then for the Creator, to whom senses are not attributed, it would be impossible to know them, and they explain this, saying (ibid.): "My way is hid from ha-Shem"; (2) second, because even if He does know them, it is appropriate that He, the Noblest of all existents, does not turn to them, because they are absolute lowliness and corruption, and they explain this, saying (ibid.): "My cause is ignored by my God."

§ 11.13.1 To these two arguments, the prophet answers, saying (Isaiah 40:28): "Do you not know? Have you not heard? Ha-Shem is God from of old, Creator of the earth from end to end"; that is to say: Did you not know that every agent of an activity that is limited in quality and quantity, even if that agent is very noble, necessarily needs to have providence over every part of it, even a minor and inferior part? And this is so because without that inferior part, the agent's activity would not be perfect within the boundaries that he wanted for it.

§ 11.13.2 [Second:] And he continues to answer, saying (Isaiah 40:28): "He never grows faint or weary"; that is to say, although it is not appropriate for a powerful figure with a final purpose who experiences weariness through his efforts to exert providence over lower things—because he would need to reduce his providence over the noble things—yet God—may He be praised—"never grows faint or weary" (ibid.), and therefore He does not let His eyes derogate from the noble things and also has providence over the lower things. It would be a miserliness in Him, as [in the case of] someone who keeps a good [thing] away from his companions, if he were to disregard the providence over the lower things.

§ 11.13.3 [Third:] And he continues (Isaiah 40:28): "His understanding cannot be fathomed." And by this, he responds to the argument that they gave that the individuals are only apprehended by the senses, which are not ascribed to the Creator, may He be praised. And he says

§ 11.12 וזה בעצמו באר ישעיהו כאשר ספר דעות הכופרים ידיעת הבורא באישי המין האנושי כל שכן שלא ישגיח בהם והביא מופתים על סתירת דעותם. וזה באמרו: «למה תאמר יעקב ותדבר | ישראל: 'נסתרה דרכי מה' ומאלהי משפטי יעבור'»? (ישעיהו מ' כ"ז), כלומר שהכופרים ידיעת הבורא והשגחתו באישי המין האנושי נותנים טעם לדבריהם ראשונה כי אמנם אישי המין לא נשיגם בשכל אבל נשיגם בחוש. ואם כן הבורא אשר לא ייוחסו אליו חושים אי איפשר שידע אותם. וזה בארו באמרם: «נסתרה דרכי מה'» (שם). שנית כי גם שידעם ראוי שהוא הנכבד מכל הנמצאות לא יפנה אליהם בהיותם בתכלית הפחיתות וההפסד. וזה בארו באמרם: «ומאלהי משפטי יעבור» (שם).

§ 11.13.1 והנה על שתי אלה הטענות השיב הנביא באמרו: «הלא ידעת? אם לא שמעת? אלהי עולם ה' בורא קצות הארץ» (ישעיהו מ' כ"ח), כלומר הלא ידעת שכל פועל פעולה מוגבלת באיכות וכמות עם היות הפועל נכבד מאד יצטרך בהכרח שישגיח על כל חלק ממנה עם היותו אותו החלק מעט ופחות מאד? וזה כי אמנם זולת אותו החלק הפחות לא תהיה פעולת הפועל שלמה על הגבול אשר רצה בו.

§ 11.13.2 והוסיף להשיב ואמר: «לא ייעף ולא יגע» (שם), כלומר אף על פי שלא יאות לבעל כח אשר לו תכלית אשר בהתפעלותו יקרה לו ליאות להשגיח על הפחותים וזה כי היה צריך למעט השגחתו על הנכבדים הנה האל ית' ש«לא ייעף ולא יגע» (שם) ובכן לא יגרע עינו מהנכבדים גם שישגיח על הפחותים היה זה צרות עין בחוקו כמונע טוב מבעליו אם היה מתעלם מהשגיח על הפחותים.

§ 11.13.3 והוסיף ואמר «אין חקר לתבונתו» (שם). ובזה השיב על הטענה אשר אמרו שהאישים לא יושגו זולתי בחושים אשר לא ייוחסו לבורא יתברך. ואמר שאף על פי שהאדם לא ישיג את המושכלות

11. DE SOLLICITUDINE

§ 11.13.1 Quas rationes redarguit propheta ibidem [Isa 40:28–29] dicens: «Nunquid nescis aut non audisti Deus sempiternus Dominus qui creavit terminos terre non lassabitur neque laborabit, non est inquisitio sapientie sue. Dat lasso virtutem et illi cui non sunt fortitudines roborem multiplicat etc.» Quibus succinte redarguit prefatas negantium rationes, et primo illam qua dicunt Deum non curare de mortalium individuis propter illorum ignobilitatem. Huiusmodi autem rationem redarguit dicens quod licet sint in se quid ignobile habet tamen Deus de illis curare tanquam de integralibus partibus orbis terre ab eodem Deo sub limitato termino facti, sine quibus partibus quantumcunque minimis esset sua terminatio imperfecta, et hoc infert ubi dicit: «Qui creavit terminos terre.»

§ 11.13.2 Secundo redarguit eandem rationem dicens quod licet illis nobilibus quorum virtus est finita non competat curare de minimis, quoniam per huiusmodi minimorum curam diverteretur necessario vel subtraheretur saltem aliquid cure a nobilibus, et hoc cum fit quid passibile. Quare oportet ut tandem lassetur et deficiat, convenit tamen divine virtuti que cum fit quid impassibile neque lassatur neque deficit et per consequens non minus sufficit[a] plurimis quam sufficiat paucioribus, quare illam ut sic ad omnia eque bene sufficientem. Decet quidem tanquam non avaram non minus ignobilibus quam nobilibus adhibere curam, et hoc infert ubi [Isa 40:28] dicit: «Non deficiet et non laborabit.»

§ 11.13.3 Tertio redarguit propheta illam rationem qua dicebant quod impossibile est Deum habere cognitionem de mortalium individuis nedum de ipsis curare, et hoc cum sint numero infinita et per consequens incomprehensibilia, et quia sunt sensu tantum perceptibilia, et nullo pacto intellectus obiectum, et hoc redarguit propheta

§ 11.13.1 The prophet (Isaiah 40:28–29) refutes these opinions, saying: "Do you not know? Have you not heard? The Lord is God from of old, Creator of the earth from end to end, He never grows faint or weary, His wisdom cannot be fathomed. He gives strength to the weary." With these [words], the prophet refutes the aforementioned positions. First, the opinion of those who said that God does not have providence over individuals because of their inferiority. The prophet refutes them by saying that although they are inferiors, God also has providence over them, as the integral parts of the sphere of the earth, which were produced by God with limitation. Without these parts, no matter how small, its final purpose would be imperfect, and this he states by saying: "Creator of the earth from end to end."

§ 11.13.2 Second, the prophet refutes this opinion about the noble existents, [because] we said that their power is finite and that it is not sufficient that He [i.e. God] should have providence over the lower existents, because this would necessarily distract from the providence over the lower existents, or it would at least reduce the providence over the noble existents. This is because power is passible, and consequently, it becomes weary and deficient, but this is inappropriate for divine power, which is impassible, and "He never grows faint or weary." Consequently, it is not only sufficient for the many, but also for the few, because it is equally sufficient for all things. It is inappropriate to ascribe miserliness to providence, because there is providence over the lower as well as the nobler existents, hence the saying: "He never grows faint or weary."

§ 11.13.3 Third, the prophet refutes the opinion of those who said that it is impossible that God knows mortal individuals and that He does not have providence over them, and this is because they are infinite in number and consequently, they are incomprehensible, because they can only be perceived by the senses and they are never an object

---

[a] sufficit] coni. COPP.; sefficit b.

that although man can only apprehend the intelligibles via sense [perception], this is not proof that the Creator—may He be praised—cannot apprehend them without sense [perception], because indeed "it cannot be fathomed" (ibid.) and [there is] no method of research [that can enable someone] to draw an analogy from our knowledge to His knowledge and from the way of our apprehension to His apprehension [that may be used] as a proof. And this is so, because the term[s] "understanding" and "apprehension" are only said of His understanding and our understanding by way of equivocation.

§ 11.13.4 [Fourth:] And he continues to answer the argument they gave—that it is not appropriate for a noble [being] to have providence over the lower [being]—saying (Isaiah 40:29): "He gives power to the weary, fresh vigour to the spent"; that is to say, there is a faculty[a] in the individuals of man[kind] that is a separate substance. And he informs [us] that it gives fresh vigour to the spent; that is to say [those who are] in the[ir] old age, as it says (Shabbat 152a): "As scholars grow older, wisdom is increased in them." And therefore, it becomes clear that this faculty does not become old, and therefore, it follows that it is incorruptible. If so, it is not correct [to say] of it that it is a lower thing that is not worthy for divine providence, as the opponent thinks, saying: "My cause is ignored by my God." And he continues [with] proof of the rank of this faculty [or: power], saying (Isaiah 40:30–31): "Youths may grow faint and weary, and young men stumble and fall; but they who trust in ha-Shem shall renew their strength, etc."; that is to say, he also testifies that this power is immaterial and incorruptible. | Indeed, the material [i.e., corporeal] powers, even in the time of their youth, when they act and are affected, become weary and faint. But for this power, the more it acts, the more it grows in strength, as it says (Berakhot 40a): "If you listened to the old, you will listen to the new."

⟨§ 11.14⟩

---

[a] In Hebrew, the same term is used for "power."

dicens quod licet hec verificarentur de humano intellectu cuius scientia dependet ab entibus extra animam existentibus, non tamen verificantur de divina intelligentia cuius scientia non dependet a reliquis entibus, immo reliqua entia de|pendent ab ipsa divina scientia et hoc infert ubi [Isa 40:28] dicit: «Non est inquisitio sapientie sue» quasi dicat quod nulla est inquisitio qua consideremus quantum divina scientia fit humana nobilior, et hoc quia non comprehenduntur sub eodem genere, quare nulla datur inter eas comparatio, et per consequens neque ab harum altera ad reliquam arguendum est.

§ 11.13.4 Quarto redarguit propheta illam rationem qua dicebant negantes quod cura de humanis individuis est quid vile quare non competit Deo, et hoc redarguitur negando ut humanum individuum sit quid vile, immo eidem inest virtus quedam que tanquam corpori non mixta, neque lassatur, neque deficit sive senescit, et per consequens est quid immortale, quare non est quid vile et divina cura indignium, et hoc infert ubi [Isa 40:29] dicit: «Qui dat lasso virtutes et cui non sunt fortitudines robur multiplicat» quibus ostendit huiusmodi virtutis nobilitatem. Cum, scilicet, deficienntibus corporeis virtutibus apud senectutem. Illa quidem virtus, scilicet, intellectiva multiplicat robur tanquam minus impedita, et nullo pacto senescens, et per consequens est quid immortale et corpori non mixtum. Quare ibidem subdit propheta [Isa 40:30–31] dicens: «Current pueri et lassabuntur et iuvenes delabentur, qui vero sperant in Domino etc. Currunt et non laborant ambulant et non lassantur etc.» quasi dicat quod huiusmodi virtus que in his qui in Deo sperant vigere solet, talis est quod currens non laborat, id est quod non lassatur per hoc quod se exerceat ad quoddam forte intelligibile percipiendum, ita ut non possit alia faciliter intelligere, immo illa deinde facilius intelligit, cuius oppositum accidit corporeis virtutibus.

§ 11.14 Quare Phylosophus in lib. *De Anima* III t.c. 7 ait: «Sensus enim non potest sentire post forte sensatum v.g. post sonos maximos aut post colores fortes aut post odores fortes, intellectus autem cum intellexerit aliquod forte intelligibilium, tunc non minus intelligit illud quod est sub primo, sentiens enim non est extra corpus iste autem est abstractus etc.» Cum autem his pateat quod huiusmodi humana virtus scilicet intellectiva sit quod corpori non mixtum, et sit quid immortale patet ergo quod curare de[a] illo similiter de his que ad eius perfectionem requiruntur non est quid vile quod est prophete intentum.

of the intellect. The prophet refutes them, saying that this is true for the human intellect, whose knowledge depends on existents that exist outside of the soul, but it is not true for divine knowledge, which does not depend on the rest of the existents. Indeed, the rest of the existents | depend on divine knowledge, as it is said: "His wisdom cannot be fathomed," because one considers divine knowledge to be nobler than human [knowledge], and this is because we cannot understand them to be of the same species; no comparison is possible between them and consequently, the remainder cannot be compared with any of the others.

§ 11.13.4 Fourth, the prophet refutes the position of the deniers, who stated that providence over human individuals is lowly and does not concern God. He refuted them by saying that human individuals are lower, but that there is a faculty in them that is not mixed with the body and that does not grow faint or weary or age. Consequently, this faculty is immortal, and for this reason, it is not base or unworthy of divine providence, saying (Isaiah 40:29): "He gives strength to the weary, fresh vigour to the spent," which shows something about the nobility of this faculty. Corporeal power becomes lacking due to senility, but intellectual powers increase their strength, never grow old, and are consequently immortal and unmixed with the body. And afterwards, the prophet (Isaiah 40:30–31) states: "Youths may grow faint and weary, and young men stumble and fall; [...] They shall run and not grow weary, they shall march and not grow faint," which means that the faculty normally flourishes in those who believe in God, saying "they shall run and not grow weary," and that this faculty will "not grow faint," because it increases itself, perceiving strong intelligibles, in such a way that it cannot easily understand, but will understand more easily. The opposite of this occurs with corporeal powers.

§ 11.14 [This is] as the Philosopher explains in *On the Soul* 3, text. 7,[a] where he states: "The sense cannot sense after it has sensed a strong sensible thing; for example, after loud sounds or vivid colours or strong smells. But if the intellect understands strong intelligibles, then it will not understand less of what is below the first. Perception is not outside the body, but it is separate." From these [words], it is clear that human power is intellectual, not mixed with a body, and immortal. It is clear that its is appropreate [for Him] to have providence over existents which are similar to Him and which need His perfection, as this is the prophet's intention.

---

[a] de] coni. COPP.; oe b.

[a] *De an.* 3.4.429a29–b5.

§ **11.15.1** And to the aforementioned opponent's arguments, saying that divine providence is impossible for the individuals of the corruptibles, because it is impossible for the Separate One [i.e., God], who does not have senses, to apprehend them, and also because of the inferiority of the corrupt, which is not worthy for a noble one to have providence over it, the Poet answers (Psalm 113:5–6): "Who is like ha-Shem our God, who, enthroned on high, sees what is below?"; that is to say, these analogies are not correct for the knowledge of God and His providence. There is no similarity and no comparison between His knowledge and the way of His apprehension and the knowledge and apprehension of every other existent, as became clear above.

§ **11.15.2** And therefore, what Averroes says in *The Incoherence of the Incoherence* 12, second investigation, corrects this: "We say that these many words are nonsense, only founded on the [illusive] imagination that divine knowledge resembles human knowledge, which—according to the truth—are only in agreement by equivocation."[a] And the prophet teaches us this, as it says (Isaiah 46:5): "To whom can you compare Me or declare Me similar? To whom can you liken Me, so that I seem comparable?"

---

[a] Cf. *Incoherence* 279–281.

---

§ **11.15.1** **וְעַל** טענות החולק הנזכר באמרו היות ההשגחה האלהית נמנעת באישי הנפסדים הן מצד היות ההשגה בהם נמנעת לנבדל אשר אין לו חושים הן לסבת פחיתות הנפסד אשר אין ראוי לנכבד להשגיח עליו השיב המשורר באמרו: «מי כה' אלהינו המגביהי לשבת המשפילי לראות?» (תהלים קי״ג ה׳-ו׳), כלומר שאלה ההיקשים לא יצדקו על ידיעת הבורא והשגחתו מבלי אין דמיון וערך בין ידיעתו ואופן השגתו לידיעת והשגת כל נמצא זולתו כמו שהתבאר למעלה.

§ **11.15.2** **וְלָזֶה** היטיב דבר אבן רשד בספר הפלת ההפלה מאמר י״ב חקירת ב׳ באמרו: «נאמר אנחנו כי אלה הדברים המרבים הבל נוסדו יחד על דמיון שידמו את הידיעה האלהית לידיעה האנושית אשר לפי האמת אינם מסכימים זולתי בשתוף השם בלבד» עכ״ל. וזה הורה הנביא באמרו: «למי תדמיוני ותשוו? ותמשילוני ואדמה?»[a] (ישעיהו מ״ו ה׳).

---

[a] ואדמה] a; ונדמה M.

§ 11.15.1 Quare Psalmus 112 [113:5–6] considerans difficultatem que videtur contingere in hoc, ut divina cura se extendat ad minima mortalium individua ait: «Quis est similis Domino Deo nostro qui in altis habitat et humilia respicit» quasi dicat quod hoc contingit per illam excellentiam qua Deus a ceteris cunctis differt, quare eius cura non est ceteris equiparanda neque est eidem per reliquas arguendum.

§ 11.15.2 Quare Aven R. in lib. *Destructio Des.*, disputatione XII dubio 2 ait: «Dicimus nos quod omnes iste ambages sunt et oriuntur assimilando divinam scientiam humane scientie quod secundum veritatem non comunicant nisi equivoce.»

§ 11.15.1 [This is] as Psalm 112 (113:5–6) teaches that divine providence may include the lower mortal individuals, saying: "Who is seated on high, who looks far down," which means that the superiority of God is different from the rest, because His providence cannot be compared with the rest.

§ 11.15.2 [This is] as Averroes explains in *The Incoherence of the Incoherence* 12, second doubt, where he states: "We say that all these words are ambiguous because they originate in the assimilation of divine knowledge with human knowledge, which, according to the truth, only agree by equivocation."[a]

---

[a] Cf. *Incoherence* 279–281.

§ 12 Twelfth:
We will inquire whether the human intellectual soul, by which man is essentially rational, is incorruptible [i.e., immortal] or not.

And it seems at the beginning of the inquiry that it is corruptible.

§ 12.1.1 First, because every form of a corruptible is corruptible, and the human intellectual soul is a form of a corruptible. If so, it is corruptible. The necessity of the consequence is evident, [and] so is the [antecedent] premise: first, as we said, that every form of a corruptible is corruptible, since the form of the corruptible—through its designation by which the substrate is designated—[this] is what essentially generates a certain compound that exists in actuality. But for the incorruptible, which by its essence is a substance existing in actuality that still exists after the corruption of every corruptible [thing], it does not seem to be congruous that it is a form of a corruptible. It is incongruous for a thing that exists in actuality, as long as it is in actuality, that it will take on another essential form, because if it was possible that a second essential form could inform it, | it would necessarily follow that there would be two essential forms for one existent at the same time. And therefore, it would follow that with regard to the first form, this existent will be the same as it was before the coming of the second form, and with regard to the second form, it would follow that it was a different existent from the first. And therefore, it would follow that one thing was at the same time the same existent that it was before and simultaneously something different from the existent that it was before, which is unthinkable. And Aristotle explains the same in *Metaphysics* 1, text. 17,[a] and 2, text. 7,[b] and in *Physics* 1, text. 71,[c] in the name of the Ancients.

§ 12.1.2 Regarding what we said in the [antecedent] premise—that the human intellectual soul is a form of a corruptible (and this is man)—[this] becomes clear from the activity designated for man, which is only attributed to his form alone, because the activities of man are intellectual, and therefore, they are different from the activities of all non-rational living beings. So, the kinds of forms of the existents will be examined by their activities, as Averroes explains in *The Incoherence of the Incoherence* 6, sixth investigation: "It is explained that the philosophers proved the [existence of a] substrate by [its] affections, just as they

---
[a] *Metaph.* 1.8.989b. [b] *Metaph.* 2.2.994a. [c] *Phys.* 1.8.191a.

§12 Duodecimo Dubitatur

[70] Utrum intellectiva hominis anima qua substantialiter dicitur rationalis sit quid immortale vel non.

Et videtur quod non.

§12.1.1 Sic primo arguendo: nulla mortalium forma est immortalis, intellectiva hominis anima est huiusmodi, ergo non est immortalis. Consequentia patet, et antecedens probatur, et primo quo ad primam partem qua dicitur quod nulla mortalium forma est immortalis, quia mortalium forme sunt ille per quarum unamquaque cum suo subiecto fit quid unum substantialiter actu existens, ex immortali autem non datur quid aliud fieri. Ergo nullum immortale habet esse mortalis forma. Immortale enim cum sit quid idem actu semper existens etiam post mortalium omnium corruptionem, non datur quid aliud cum alio fieri substantialiter, quamvis daretur cum alio coniungi. Compositio enim ad hoc facta ut inde fiat quid novum substantialiter unum, novam proculdubio requirit formam. Cum ergo ingrederetur quid immortale semper idem existens, sequeretur ut huiusmodi compositum simul et semel duabus divesis informaretur formis, per quarum unam esset idem quod prius, per reliquam vero esset non idem quod prius, et sic idem esset in eodem instanti idem et non idem, quod implicat contradictionem. Et idem habetur a Phylosopho *Metaphysicorum* I t.c. 17 et eiusdem II t.c. 7,[a] et ab eodem antiquorum auctoritate *Physicorum* I t.c. 71.

§12.1.2 Quo autem ad secundam eiusdem antecedentis partem qua scilicet dicitur quod intellectiva hominis anima est mortalis forma, scilicet, probatur per propriam[b] hominis actionem a sua propria forma necessario emanantem. Propria, enim, hominis actio qua a brutis differt est rationalis sive intellectualis. Entium enim formas per suas proprias venamur actiones, prout habetur ab Aven R. in lib. *Destructio Des.*, disputatione VI, dubio 6 ubi dicit: «Patet quod ipsi scilicet Phylosophi sumpserunt signum subiecti

---

[a] 7] emend. Copp.; 17 b; 7 L. [b] propriam] coni. Copp.; propiziam b.

§12 Twelfth,

it may be inquired whether the human intellectual soul, by which man is essentially called rational, is immortal [i.e., incorruptible] or not.

And it seems that it is not [immortal].

§12.1.1 First, I would argue that no form of a mortal thing is immortal, that the human intellectual soul is of this kind, and that therefore, it is not immortal [i.e., it is corruptible]. The consequence is clear, and the antecedent is proven, and first of all in relation to the first part, in which it is said that no form of a mortal thing is immortal. Indeed, the forms of mortal things are those through which something existing in actuality essentially becomes one with its substrate, but it is not possible that something else may be generated from an immortal being. Therefore, no immortal being has the being of a mortal thing as a form. Indeed, it is not possible that an immortal being—since it always remains the same in actuality, even after the corruption of all mortal things—may essentially become something else together with another thing, although it is possible that [the immortal being] may be conjoined with something else. A compound is made in order to produce something substantially new, [and] so it requires a new form. If something immortal, which always remains the same, entered [the compound], it follows that such a compound would be formed together and at the same time by two different forms: through one of them, it would be the same as before, and through the other, it would be different from before. If so, then the same thing would be simultaneously identical and not identical. This implies a contradiction. The same is affirmed by the Philosopher in *Metaphysics* 1, text. 17,[a] *Metaphysics* 2, text. 7,[b] and in the name of the ancient philosophers in *Physics* 1, text.71.[c]

§12.1.2 In relation to the second part of the antecedent, in which it is said that the human intellectual soul is a mortal form, this is proven thanks to the specific human activity that necessarily emanates from its specific form. The specific human activity through which he differs from the beasts is rational or intellectual. One will pursue the forms of beings through their specific actions, in accordance with what Averroes explains in *The Incoherence of the Incoherence* 6, sixth doubt, where he says: "It is evident that the philosophers proved [the existence] of a substrate through

---

[a] *Metaph.* 1.8.989b. [b] *Metaph.* 2.2.994a. [c] *Phys.* 1.8.191a.

proved the [existence of the] form by [its] activities."[a] And the same is clear from the definition of man that Porphyry and Averroes explain in *Isagoge* 4.[b]

§ 12.2.1 Second, it is clear that the aforementioned intellectual soul is corruptible as follows. If it was incorruptible, it would necessarily have to be a separate substance, as became clear above. And therefore, one of two cases would be inevitable: first, that that soul would be one [that was] common to the whole human species, or second, that it would be as numerous as the number of individuals of the human species. And if we said that they were as numerous as the number of human individuals, then every single one of them would be a substance [that is] separate from matter. It would follow that many separate substances would exist equal to the number of individual humans, and then one of two [sub-cases] would be inevitable. Either (1) we would say that they were not equal in rank and therefore, it would follow that they were different from one another in form. Therefore, it would follow that they were different in activity, which results from the form. However, sense [perception] testifies the contrary of this. Moreover, it would therefore follow that each individual human being would be different from the others in species and in their activities, which result from their specific form. And therefore, it would follow that the word "man" was only correct for all of them by equivocation.

§ 12.2.2 And sense [perception] testifies the contrary of all of this, because all individual human beings share and have in common the rational faculty and the first intelligibles, which are in every individual by nature, like the form that is common to the whole species. Alternatively, (2) we would say that they are separate substances that totally resemble each other, and therefore, it would follow that they were different from each other in individual number | only, as is a rule for the individuals of the whole of the rest of the species. And this would be incongruous, because when they are substances separate from matter—especially after the death of the individual body, since then they are not different from each other insofar as there is no substrate and no time, and additionally to this, they resemble [each other] entirely in the rank of the[ir] form—there is no difference left between them by which an individual number would be applicable to them. And this is self-evident, and Averroes explains it in [the Commentary on] *Metaphysics* 1, text. 40:[c] "The number two can [only] apply to one thing due to matter." And the same becomes clear

---

[a] Cf. *Incoherence* 217. [b] Cf. Porphyry, *Introduction*, trans. Jonathan Barnes (Oxford: Clarendon Press, 2003), 8–11. [c] Cf. *Metaph.* 1.9.992a.

ex passionibus, sicut signum forme recipiunt ex actionibus» et idem patet per diffinitionem eiusdem hominis a Porphyrio et Aven R. in lib. *Predicabilium* cap. IV tradita.

§ 12.2.1 Secundo arguitur sic: si ipsa humana intellectiva esset quid immortale et per consequens abstracta substantia actu existens ut supra, vel ergo esset una tantum numero toti humano generi communis, vel plures essent substantie ad individuorum numerum dinumerabiles. Si plures, tunc cum essent tot substantie actu a materialibus subiectis separabiles, sequeretur ut tot essent substantie quot sunt humana individua, talia autem vel differret ab invicem gradu, et per consequens forma, et per consequens actione ab eadem forma emanante, et sic equivoce tantum diceretur hoc nomen homo de diversis humanis individuis.

§ 12.2.2 Cuius oppositum testatur sensus quod | scilicet conveniunt actionibus a rationalitate emanantibus tanquam a communi speciei forma. Vel huiusmodi forme essent omnino similes, et tunc cum essent quid abstractum nulla daretur inter eas numeratio. Ad numerationem enim requiritur diversitas, vel quoad subiectum, vel quoad formam, vel quoad tempus, in abstractis ergo cum non detur diversitas in subiecto neque in tempore nisi ergo detur diversitas forme, inopinabile est ut detur in eis numeratio. Quare Phylosophus *Metaphysicorum* I t.c. 40 ait: «Et non est numerus unus iteratus» ubi Aven R. expo-

the affections, just as they proved [the existence] of the forms through the activities."[a] The same thing is clear from the definition of man that Porphyry and Averroes report in book 4 of the *Isagoge*.[b]

§ 12.2.1 Second, I would argue that if the intellectual human [soul] is immortal [i.e., incorruptible] and consequently a separate substance existing in actuality, as aforementioned, either there would necessarily be one [intellectual soul] for all the individual human beings or there would be as many [separate] substances as the number of individual human beings. And if there are many substances, then since there would be as many substances in actuality [that are] separable from the material substrates, it would follow that the number of the substances would also be the [same as the] number of individual human beings. Therefore, either (1) they would be different from each other in rank, and consequently in form, and consequently in the activity emanating from their form, and so the name "man" would be said of every different individual human being by equivocation.

§ 12.2.2 But the contrary of this is proven by the senses, because | [the individual human beings] share activities that are emanated from the rational faculty, as well as from the form that is common to their species. Or (2) [alternatively], the forms would be entirely similar, and consequently, they would be separate [substances]; then, there would be no numeration among them, since for [the concept of] numeration, the [concept of] difference is required with respect to the substrate, the form, or the time. Therefore, since there is no difference in the separate substances in the substrate or in time, if there is then no difference in the form, it would be unthinkable for numeration to be present in them. For this reason, the Philosopher says in *Metaphysics* 1, text. 40,[c] "It is impossible to reiterate the number one," and Averroes explains:

---

[a] Cf. *Incoherence* 217. [b] Cf. Porphyry, *Introduction*, trans. Jonathan Barnes (Oxford: Clarendon Press, 2003), 8–11. [c] *Metaph.* 1.9.992a.

in *The Incoherence of the Incoherence* 5, second investigation, citing al-Ġazālī: "To things separate from matter that resemble [each other] entirely, number is not applicable, because—as an example—it is [only possible] to say of two black things that they are two because they are in two substrates or at two different times. And it is rightly said that the blackness and the movement are also two when they are [only] in one substrate and at one time, as they are essentially separate. But when there are two things that are not essentially separate, such as when they are [both] black visible things, and, in addition to this, they are in one place and at one time, then doubtlessly no number [applies]. And if it was possible that there could be two black things in one and the same time and place, it would also be possible to state about every single individual that it is two, even if we do not recognise any duality in it."[a]

§ 12.2.3 And if we said that the human intellectual soul was only one shared by the whole human species—as it seems was Averroes's opinion in his Commentary on *On the Soul* 3, text. 5,[b] and as also seems to have been the opinion of some Ancient [philosophers], as told by al-Ġazālī's words with reference to Plato and others among the Ancients in *The Incoherence of the Incoherence* 1, eighth investigation,[c] and 4, seventh investigation[d]—then it would have to be necessary that everything understood and apprehended by a certain human individual would be understood and apprehended by every individual of the aforementioned species—at least [by] those individuals who were equal to that understanding [individual] in the mode of investigation [i.e., speculation] and who were jointly investigating with it using one intelligible or various intelligibles. And experience testifies the contrary of this. It is evident that this would have to be so, because the relationship between the intellect and the intelligibles is like the relationship between sense [perception] and the sensibles, as Aristotle explains in *On the Soul* 3, text. 3.[e] And if it was possible that many individuals with equal understanding were all seeing and watching with the power of one eye common to all of them and that that eye was able to see various things, [then] there would be no doubt that everything that that eye saw would be equally perceived by every one of the individuals of the species who were seeing with the power of that eye, because there would be no decisive reason by which one of them should perceive those things that were sensible to the aforementioned eye [a little] more [or less] than [any of] the others. Likewise, if many individuals that were equal in perfection of investigation were

---

[a] Cf. *Incoherence* 174–175. [b] Cf. *De an.* 3.4.429a21–24. [c] Cf. *Incoherence* 15. [d] Cf. *Incoherence* 169. [e] Cf. *De an.* 3.4.429a15–18.

nens ait: «Dualitas enim in una re est propter materiam» quare in lib. *Destructio Des.*, disputatione v, dubio 2 Algazelis auctoritate ait: «Due enim nigredines dicuntur quando sunt in duobus subiectis vel uno, sed in diversis temporibus. Nigredo enim et motus in uno tempore sunt duo quia in substantia differunt, sed quando in substantia non differunt, si sunt due nigredines cum unitate temporis et loci tunc sine dubio nulla est numeratio, et si possibile esset dicere quod in uno tempore et uno subiecto essent due nigredines possibile ergo esset de quolibet individuo dicere quod sint duo licet ibi nulla numeratio cognoscatur etc.»

§ 12.2.3 Si autem dicatur ut ipsa intellectiva sit una tantum toti humano generi communis sicut Aven R. tenere videtur in commento lib. *De Anima* III t.c. 5 et eadem videtur esse nonnullorum antiquorum opinio, prout Algazel ait auctoritate Platonis et aliorum, prout habetur in lib. *Destructio Dest.*, disputatione I, dubio 8 similiter ibidem disputatione IV, dubio 7. Tunc sequeretur ut quicquid contingeret aliquem humanum individuum percipe, illud per omnes humani generis individuos saltem equales perfectionis existentes (et idem vel diversa simul tempore speculantes) uniformiter intelligeretur, cuius oppositum docet experientia. Quod autem hoc sequatur patet, quia sicut Phylosophus ait *De Anima* III t.c. 3 sicut se habet sensus ad sensibilia sic se habet intellectus ad intelligibilia. Sed sic est, quod dato ut per eundem oculum diversa visibilia percipientem plures eidem equaliter proportionati simul tempore intuerentur, certum est, quod quicquid contingeret in ipso oculo esse perceptum per suos scilicet radios ad unum vel diversa directos, uniformiter ab unoquoque illorum sic intuentium necessario perciperetur, quia nulla esset ratio quare magis unum visibilium in eodem oculo, scilicet, perceptorum magis ab altero intuentium quam a reliquis perciperetur. Eodem ergo modo, si plures indivi-

"The number of two only applies to one thing by reason of [its] matter," [and] as he states according to the authority of al-Ġazālī in *The Incoherence of the Incoherence* 5, second doubt: "We said that two blacknesses exist when they have two substrates, or one, but in a different time. Indeed, a blackness and a movement [that exist] at the same time are two because they differ in substance, but when they do not differ in substance, if there are two blacknesses that have unity in time and space, then undoubtedly, there is no numeration. If it were possible to say that there were two blacknesses in one substrate at the same time, then it would be possible to say concerning every individual [being] that it was two, even if in that case, no numeration is recognised, etc."[a]

§ 12.2.3 If we say that the intellectual soul is only one common to all individual human beings—as seems to be the opinion of Averroes in the Commentary on *On the Soul* 3, text. 5,[b] and some of the ancient philosophers seem to be of the same opinion, as affirmed by al-Ġazālī with reference to Plato and other philosophers, as found in *The Incoherence of the Incoherence* 1, eighth doubt,[c] and discussion 4, seventh doubt[d]—then it would occur that an individual human being would perceive something that would be understood in the same way by all individual human beings who were equal in perfection and who were simultaneously looking at identical or different things. However, the opposite is testified by experience, as the Philosopher says in *On the Soul* 3, text. 3:[e] "The sense faculty is related to sensible objects, as the intellectual faculty is related to intelligible objects." But it is the case that if many [observers] who were equally proportioned [to perceive] were to simultaneously observe different visible things through the same eye, it is certain that anything perceived in that same eye through its rays, which would point towards one [thing] or towards different things, would necessarily be perceived in the same way by each of the observers. Indeed, there is no reason why one of the seeing—that is, perceiving [beings]—should perceive more [through the same eye] than the others. Likewise, if many individual human beings who were equal in per-

---

[a] Cf. *Incoherence* 174–175. [b] Cf. *De an.* 3.4.429a21–24. [c] Cf. *Incoherence* 15. [d] Cf. *Incoherence* 169. [e] Cf. *De an.* 3.4.429a15–18.

to jointly investigate one thing or various things using an intellect that was the same for everyone [and] common to all, it would follow that every one of the aforementioned individuals would equally apprehend all the intelligibles apprehended by that intellect.

§ 12.2.4 For this kind of apprehension of the individuals is nothing other than the reception of the intelligibles by that intellect that is common to all individuals of the human species due to its conjunction with the individuals of the aforementioned species, as Averroes explains in his Commentary on *On the Soul* 3, text. 5,[a] where he doubts this, saying: "According to this opinion, the conjunction of the material intellect with every single one of the [human] individuals existing in actuality at a certain time in the absolute perfection that is possible for them ought to be one and the same; for there is no reason that the relation of the conjunction of one individual should be different from the conjunction of another. And according to this, it follows that if you apprehended one particular intelligible, I would also apprehend the very same intelligible. And this is impossible."

§ 12.2.5 And if we say that the same common [material] intellect would acquire a plurality via various individuals who possess imaginative power[s], as seems to be Averroes's opinion in the aforementioned place: "Indeed, if we say that an intelligible [i.e., imaginable] that is in me and an intelligible [i.e., imaginable] that is in you are many in a substrate [i.e., subject], insofar as the intelligible [i.e., imaginable] is true, and it is the form of the imagination, and is one [thing] in a substrate [i.e., subject], insofar as it is intellect, and it is the material intellect, we will dispel all these doubts," then we will answer and say, if so, [then] one of two cases is inevitable. Either (1) we say that this truth [of the intelligible], which is acquired by intellection, will remain within the material intellect by which it will be perfected and a second perfection will be acquired, as seems to be the opinion of Aristotle in the aforementioned book, 3, text. 3[b] and 5. Or (2) we say that that truth acquired by intellection will pass to the imaginative power and will remain within it and not in the material [intellect]. But the second way [i.e., inference] is not correct, because according to this, the imaginative power would be the recipient of the intelligibles and our knowledge would be in it, although it is a power in matter and corruptible.

---

[a] Cf. *De an.* 3.4.429a21–24.   [b] *De an.* 3.4.429a15–18.

בשלמות העיון יעיינו יחדו בדבר אחד או בדברים מתחלפים בכח שכל אחד בעצמו משותף לכלם היה מתחייב שכל המושכלות באותו השכל באיזה ענין ישיגום בשוה כל אחד מהאישים הנזכרים.

§ 12.2.4 כי אמנם השגת האישים לפי זה לא היה דבר אחר זולתי קבלת המושכלות באותו השכל המשותף לכל אישי המין האנושי בהדבקו אל אישי המין הנזכר כמו שביאר אבן רשד בביאורו לספר הנפש מאמר ג׳ פרק ה׳ בהיותו מסופק בזה באמרו וזה לשונו: »אמנם לפי זה הדעת הנה דבקות השכל ההיולאני עם כל אחד מהאישים הנמצאים בפעל באיזה זמן בתכלית[a] השלמות האיפשר להם ראוי שיהיה אחד בעצמו כי אין סבה שתבדיל בין יחס הדבקות של אחד מהאישים ליחס דבקות האחר ולפי זה יתחייב שכשתשיג אתה איזה מושכל אשיג אני גם כן אותו המושכל בעצמו וזה הוא נמנע« עכ״ל.

§ 12.2.5 ואם נאמר שאותו השכל המשותף יקנה רבוי בהתחלפות האישים בעלי כח כמדמה כמו שנראה היות דעת אבן רשד במקום הנזכר וזה לשונו: »אמנם כאשר נאמר שהמושכל אשר אצלי והמושכל אשר אצלך הם רבים בנושא מצד מה שהמושכל אמתי והיא צורת המדמה ושהוא אחד בנושא מצד מה שהוא שכל נמצא והוא השכל ההיולאני נתיר כל אלה הספקות« עד כ״ל. הנה אז נשיב ונאמר שאם כן לא ימלט מאחד משני פנים וזה אם שנאמר שאותו האמת הקנוי בהשכלה נשאר בשכל ההיולאני אשר בו ישלם ותקנה שלמות שני כמו שנראה היות דעת ארסטו׳ בספר הנזכר מאמר ג׳ פרק ה׳ או שנאמר שאותו האמת הקנוי בהשכלה יעבור אל הכח המדמה וישאר בו ולא ישאר בהיולאני. אמנם לא יצדק זה האופן השני כי אמנם לפי זה האופן יהיה הכח המדמה הוא המקבל המושכלות ובו תהיה ידיעתנו עם היותו כח בחומר ונפסד.

---

[a] בתכלית] coni. Dunk.; בתכלי a.

§ 12.2.4 Necesse esset ut omnia intelligibilia in eodem intellectu quovis modo tunc recepta essent uniformiter ab horum unoquoque intellecta et equaliter percepta, quia huiusmodi intellectio ut sic nil aliud esset quam individui continuatio cum materiali intellectu facta, in quo, scilicet, intellectu sunt intelligibilia actu recepta. Nam | sicut in lib. *De Anima* III t.c. 5 Aven R. ubi circa hoc dubitare videtur expresse quidem ait: «Continuatio intellectus materialis cum hominibus existentibus in actu in aliquo tempore in eorum perfectione postrema debet esse eadem continuatio; nihil enim facit alietatem proportionis continuationis inter hec duo continua, quare si hoc est ita, necesse est ut cum tu acquisiveris aliquod intellectum ut ego acquiram illud intellectum quod est impossibile etc.»

§ 12.2.5 Quod si dicatur ut idem quod per unicum materialem intellectum perceptum est, acquirat multitudinem per diversitatem imaginativarum eidem continuatarum et ab eodem recipientium, sicut videtur Aven R. ibidem respondere ubi ibidem dicit: «Cum igitur posuerimus rem imaginabilem que est apud me et apud te multa in subiecto, secundum quod est vera scilicet forma imaginationis, et unum subiecto secundum quod intellectus est ens et est intellectus materialis, dissolvuntur iste questiones perfecte etc.,» tunc arguitur sic: quia vel illa intelligibilium veritas per intellectionem acquisita remanetur in ipso materiali intellectu per quam intellectionem pervenit ad secundum actum, sicut videtur Philosophum tenere in lib. *De Anima* III t.c. 5, vel ipsa veritas transfertur ab ipso materiali intellectu ad nostram imaginativam sibi continuatam, et in ipsa remanet non autem in ipso materiali. Non secundum, quia sequeretur ut ipsa imaginativa esset illa virtus que proprie et permansive recipit intelligibilia et per illa perficitur cum hoc quod sit quid mortale et materie mixtum.

§ 12.2.4 It would be necessary that every intelligible in the same intellect would be received, understood, and perceived by each of them in the same way. Indeed, this intellection would be nothing more than the conjunction [i.e., continuation] of an individual being with the material intellect in which the intelligibles were received in actuality. In fact, | in the book *On the Soul* 3, text. 5,[a] where Averroes seems to doubt this, he clearly says: "The conjunction of the material intellect with men existing in actuality at a certain time in their last perfection ought to be the same conjunction, because nothing in a proportional union produces plurality among two things that are together; if so, it would be necessary that if you acquired an intelligible [i.e., intellect], I would also acquire that intelligible [i.e., intellect], and this is impossible."

§ 12.2.5 If we say that something perceived through the common material intellect acquires plurality thanks to the difference in the imaginative powers that are conjoint with it [the material intellect] and received by it, as Averroes seems to answer, where he says: "Indeed, if we say that an imaginable thing that is in me and in you is many things in a subject, insofar as it is true, namely, a form of the imagination, and is one thing in a subject, insofar as the intellect is a being, and it is the material intellect, all these doubts are perfectly dispelled," then it is argued in the following way. The truth of the intelligibles acquired by the intellection will either remain in the material intellect, and will, through that intellection, reach the second act [i.e., perfection], as the Philosopher seems to believe in *On the Soul* 3, text. 5;[b] or that truth will be transferred from the material intellect into our imaginative power conjoint with it [the material intellect] and it will remain in the imagination, but not in the material intellect. The second inference is impossible because it would follow that the imaginative power would be the power that specifically and permanently receives the intelligibles, and that by them, it would be perfected, although it is mortal and mixed with matter.

---

[a] Cf. *De an.* 3.4.429a21–24.   [b] Cf. *De an.* 3.4.429a21–24.

§12.2.6 And the natural desire in us to know the divine intelligibles, and the power in us to know them, even if knowledge of them is of no benefit in the generables and corruptibles, testify the contrary of this. Likewise, the proofs of Aristotle testify [it], as will become clear to us below. And likewise, it seems that Averroes explains [this] against Abu Bakr ibn al-Saigh in the Commentary on the aforementioned book, 3, text. 5.[a] If so, the first case remains, and this is that the knowledge of the truths of the intelligibles remains within the material [intellect], and through it, we imagine them and know them. And therefore, it follows that if this material [intellect] is only one common to the whole human species, it must follow that an intelligible that is apprehended by one | of those who have an equal rank in investigation investigating together is like an object of vision apprehended by an eye that is shared by the many who are seeing. If that [one] eye were equally close to every one of them, everyone would undoubtedly apprehend that object of apprehension equally, as became clear above. And perhaps even if the opponent insisted and said that there have never been two beings [that are] equal in understanding and conjunction in any event, it would follow that one of the investigators who was more disposed to and conjoined with that common intellect would apprehend all the intelligibles that are apprehended by that intellect, although they were transmitted from many imaginative powers [belonging to many investigators].

§12.2.7 And this seems to happen to the [faculty of] common sense, because different sensible objects are transmitted to it from different senses. And although the transmitted [sensible objects] are different, the human individual who has that common sense apprehends all the sensible objects of apprehension through that sense and collects them and imagines a relationship between them, as experience testifies. And Aristotle explains this in *On the Soul* 2, text. 145.[b]

⟨§12.2.8⟩

---

[a] Cf. *De an.* 3.4.429a21–24. [b] *De an.* 3.2.426b.

§12.2.6 והנה על הפך זה יעיד הכוסף הטבעי אשר בנו לדעת את המושכלות האלהיות והכח אשר בנו לדעת אותם עם היות הידיעה בהם בלתי מועלת בדברים ההוים ונפסדים וכמו כן יעידו מופתי ארסטו' כאשר יתבאר לפנינו וכמו שנראה שביאר אבן רשד נגד אבובכר[a] בן אלצאיג בביאור הספר הנזכר מאמר שלישי פרק חמישי ישאר אם כן האופן הראשון והוא שידיעת אמתות המושכלות נשארת בהיולאני ובו נציירם ונדעם ומזה יתחייב שאם זה ההיולאני אחד בלבד משותף לכל המין האנושי היה מתחייב שיהיה ענין המושכל המושג אצל אחד | מהמעיינים יחדו השוים במדרגת[b] העיון כמו שהיה ענין הנראה המושג בעין משותף למביטים רבים כאשר יקרב העין ההוא לכל אחד מהם יחדו בשוה שאותו המושג בלי ספק ישיגהו[c] כל אחד מהם בשוה כאשר התבאר למעלה. וגם אם אולי יתעקש החולק ויאמר שלא ימצא לעולם שווי בהכנה ודבקות בין שני מעיינים מכל מקום יתחייב שאותו האחד מן המעיינים אשר הוא יותר מוכן ודבק עם אותו השכל המשותף ישיג כל המושכלות אשר הושגו באותו השכל אף על פי שהובלו מכחות מדמות רבות.

§12.2.7 וזה נראה שקרה לחוש המשותף כי אמנם יובלו אליו מוחשות מתחלפות מחושים מתחלפים ועם היות המובילים מתחלפים הנה האדם האישיי אשר לו אותו החוש המשותף משיג את כל המוחשות המושגות באותו החוש ומרכיב אותם ומשער יחס קצתם לקצתם כאשר יעיד הנסיון וביאר זה ארסטו' בספר הנפש מאמר ב' פרק קמ"ה.

⟨§12.2.8⟩

---

[a] אבובכר] emend. Dunk.; אבוכפר a; Abubacher b. [b] במדרגת] coni. Dunk.; במדרדת a. [c] ישיגהו] coni. Dunk.; ישגהו a.

§ 12.2.6 Cuius oppositum docet naturale desiderium ad divina sciendum et naturalis potentia ad illud per primas propositiones nobis naturaliter infusas, quamvis prefata divina nihil quoad mortalia prosint, et idem oppositum videtur idem Aven R. docet in commento lib. *De Anima* III t.c. 5 contra Abubacher arguens. Restat ergo primum, quod, scilicet, intellectiva cognitio acquisita remaneat in ipso materiali intellectu. Si ergo esset quid unum tantum nobis omnibus commune, per cuius continuationem tantum imaginaremur et sciremus, sequeretur ut quicquid esset in ipso materiali tunc perceptum ab omnibus saltem equalis perfectionis et per consequens continuationis simul tempore contemplantibus uniformiter perciperetur. Diversitas enim imaginativarum saltem si fuerint equalis perfectionis nedum maioris nullo pacto habet deteriorare continuationem per quam tantum ut sic sit nobis cognitio.

§ 12.2.7 Preterea patet idem experimento, quia sicut se habet sensus ad sensibilia, sic se habet intellectus ad intelligibilia, ut supra. Sed sic quod communis sensus licet a diversis sensibus sibi presentantibus diversa recipiat sensata, sicut experientia docet et habetur a Phylosopho *De Anima* II t.c., 145,[a] imaginative tamen memorative et reminiscentive virtutes per eiusdem sensus communis copulationem omnia in eodem recepta uniformiter recipiunt.

§ 12.2.8 Sicut | experientia docet et habetur a Phylosopho in *De Memoria et Reminiscentia*, eodem ergo modo haberet contigere se intelligibilibus. Si daretur huiusmodi intellectus materialis omnibus communis, ut scilicet quicquid in eo esset receptum, licet fuisset eidem a diversis presentatum imaginativis, ab omnibus tamen uniformiter saltem eidem simul tempore continuatis et equaliter copulatis uniformiter reciperetur, et sic sequeretur ut quicquid unus simul tempore contemplantium et perfectione equalium ab eodem communi intellectu reciperet, uniformiter omnes reciperet, cuius oppositum docet experientia. Quare patet ut nullo pacto detur huiusmodi materialis intellectus omnibus communis quod est intentum.

§ 12.2.6 The opposite is testified by the natural desire to know divine things and by the natural power thanks to the first propositions naturally infused in us, even if the aforementioned divine things are of no benefit for mortals. The opposite of this seems to be testified by Averroes himself in the argument against Abubaker in the Commentary *On the Soul* 3, text. 5.[a] Then, there remains the first inference; namely, that the acquired intellectual knowledge remains in the material intellect. If there was something [that was] common to all of us, and only through the conjunction with it we would imagine and know, it would follow that something perceived in the material intellect by all the individual human beings [who were] equal in perfection, and therefore equally conjoint [and] observing at the same time, would be perceived in the same way [by all of them]. A difference in the imaginative powers, if they are equal in perfection and not more, cannot lead to the deterioration of the conjunction, which is the sole means through which we have knowledge.

§ 12.2.7 Moreover, the same is clear from experience, since just as the sense faculty pertains to the sensible objects, the intellectual faculty pertains to the intelligible objects, as aforementioned. However, the common sense collects different sensible objects, though from different senses presenting to it, as experience teaches [us] and as is affirmed by the Philosopher in *On the Soul* 2, text. 145.[b] Therefore, through the union with the common sense, the imaginative, memorative, and reminiscent powers uniformly collect all the objects that have been received by it [the common sense].

§ 12.2.8 As | experience testifies, and as is affirmed by the Philosopher in *On Memory and Recollection*, the same will then occur for the intelligibles. If there were a material intellect common to all, so that every thing received by the material intellect, even if brought by different imaginative powers, would nevertheless be uniformly received by all those who were uniformly conjoint and equally united with it [the material intellect] at the same time— if this were so—then one of those who were observing at the same time and who were equal in perfection would receive something from the common intellect and would also receive all things uniformly, but experience teaches the opposite of this. Therefore, it is clear that there is no common material intellect, which is what was intended [to be explained].

---

[a] 145] emend. Copp.; 142 b; 145 L.

[a] Cf. *De an.* 3.4.429a21–24.   [b] *De an.* 3.2.426b.

§12.2.9 And apart from this, if the material intellect is only one and incorruptible, one of two cases is inevitable. And these are: either (1) that we say that it is in potentiality for a perfection that it will never achieve, and, if so, that potentiality will be in it in vain, or (2) that we say that it is possible that it will achieve the aforementioned perfection, and, if so, in such a long stretch of time that has [passed] before us, it has necessarily already achieved what can be achieved by its potentiality in such way that it is now no longer in potentiality at all, but completely in actuality. And if so, it follows that due to its conjunction, every intelligible that can possibly be apprehended by its conjunction is now [actually] apprehended. From all this, it becomes clear that it is impossible that the human intellect could be one common to many individuals. If so, what remains is that it multiplies, matching the number of the individuals of the species that are similar in form. And in connection with this, since an individual number is not applicable to separate things that are completely similar to each other, it follows that the human intellect accounted for is not separate, and therefore, it follows that it is not immortal.

§12.3 Third, it becomes clear that the intellectual soul that is designated for an individual of the human species is not an immortal thing, because it is not a thing existing in actuality. If so, it is not immortal. The necessity of the consequence becomes clear as follows: because an immortal [thing] is a thing that will exist forever, as is self-evident, and Aristotle explains this in *On the Heavens* 1, text. 124.[a] If so—if the aforementioned intellectual [soul] were immortal—it would necessarily exist after the corruption of that individual for which it was designated, and therefore, it would follow that it was a thing existing in actuality [after the individual's corruption] at that time. If so, when it became clear that it was not existing in actuality [before the individual's corruption], it would follow that it was not immortal. But the premise, by which we said that the intellectual [soul] is not a thing existing in actuality, becomes clear from a proof made by Aristotle in *On the Soul* 3, text. 5,[b] saying: | "The human intellect does not have

---

[a] *Cael.* 1.12.282b. [b] *De an.* 3.4.429a21–24.

§ 12.2.9 Preterea si daretur huiusmodi materialis intellectus, et per consequens et agens illum ad actum perducens, tunc vel huiusmodi actio fit ad eiusdem materialem intellectum perficiendum, vel ad mortalium tantum commoditatem. Non primum, quia ut sic debuisset in tot lapsis seculis devenisse ad perfectionem, si sit quid finitum; si vero infinitum, viderentur vano laborare. Restaret ergo secundum, ut scilicet horum duorum immortalium adeo nobilium actio, et per consequens horum forma et esse, penitus esset ad vilissimam mortalium oportunitatem intenta, quod est inconveniens et quodammodo absurdum.

§ 12.3 Tertio arguitur sic: nullum genitum est quid immortale, intellectiva hominum anima est huiusmodi, ergo intellectiva hominum anima non est quid immortale. Consequentia patet et antecedens probatur, et primo quo ad primam partem, qua scilicet dicitur quod nullum genitum est immortale, hoc ratione et auctoritate Phylosophi in lib. *De Celo* I t.c. 124 ubi dicit: «Si enim esset perpetuum, esset potentia ut semper esset ens et semper non ens, quod est impossibile.» Quo autem ad secundam partem, qua scilicet dicitur, quod intellectiva hominum anima sit quid genitum, probatur Phylosophi ratione et auctoritate in lib. *De*

§ 12.2.9 Moreover, if there were to be such a material intellect, and consequently also an agent who was to bring it to actuality, either this [agent's] action would have been produced to perfect the material intellect or it would have been produced to be of benefit for mortal beings. The first inference is not [correct], because if so, it would have reached perfection after such a long time, if it was finite; and if it was infinite, then it would seem that it had striven in vain. The second inference remains; namely, that the activity of these two immortal and noble beings [the intellect and the agent], and consequently also their form and their essence, is intended for the most futile benefit of humankind, and this is incongruous and impossible.

§ 12.3 Third, I would argue that nothing generated is immortal and the human intellectual soul is generated; therefore, the human intellectual soul is not immortal. The consequence is clear and the antecedent is proven, first with respect to the first part, in which it is said that nothing generated is immortal, according to the argument and authority of the Philosopher in *On the Heavens* 1, text. 124,[a] where he says: "If it were perpetual, then it would have the potentiality to exist forever and to not exist forever, and this is impossible." With respect to the second part, in which it is said that the human intellectual soul was generated, this is proven according to the argument and authority of the Philosopher in *On the Soul* 3, text. 5,[b] where

---

[a] *Cael.* 1.12.282b.   [b] *De an.* 3.429a21–24.

any nature except that it is potential. If so, this part of the soul that is called 'the intellect'—that is to say, that thing by which we differentiate and think—is not an existent in actuality before it contemplates." And also, [if] we say that after it contemplated [and] became a thing existing in actuality, as it seems from the words of the aforementioned Philosopher, in any event, it therefore follows that it would be a corruptible thing, since it is a created thing, as is evident from the proof given by Aristotle in *On the Heavens* 1, text. 121[a] and 124,[b] saying: "We say that a thing that is an immortal existent is not generated and not corruptible." And he continues, saying: "A thing that is generable and corruptible is not an immortal existent, because if it was an immortal existent, it would have a potential to exist forever and a potential not to exist forever. And this is impossible."

§12.4 Fourth, it becomes clear that the aforementioned soul is not immortal as follows: because it is not an intellectual substance, but an imaginative power. And therefore, it follows that it is a material power. If so, it is not immortal. The necessity of this consequence is evident, because every power in matter is necessarily corruptible through the corruption of the material substrate. And the [antecedent] premise—in which we said that the aforementioned soul is not an intellectual substance—becomes clear as follows: the activity of the intellect is always right, while the activity of the aforementioned soul is not always right. If so, it is not an intellectual substance. What we said—that the activity of the aforementioned soul is not always right—is evident because errors often occur to it. And also, what we said—that the activity of the intellect is always right—is evident because the intellect's activity is always the examination of the truth and its apprehension, and this activity is always right. And therefore, it follows that errors may only occur to it via the imaginative power. And Aristotle explains the same in *On the Soul* 3, text. 51:[c] "Every activity of the intellect is right, but the appetite and the imagination are sometimes right and sometimes not."

§12.5.1 But the contrary of this—namely, that the human intellectual soul is immortal—becomes clear as follows: everything that is not mixed with matter, which is called "a separate substance," is immortal, and the aforementioned soul is a substance that is not mixed with matter. If so, it is immortal. The necessity of the consequence is self-evident and the [antecedent] premise—by which we said that every separate substance is immortal—is also evident, because every separate [thing] is simple, and every simple [thing] is essentially incorruptible, and therefore, it is

---

[a] *Cael.* 1.12.282a. [b] *Cael.* 1.12.282b. [c] *De an.* 3.10.433a26–30.

Anima III t.c. 5 ubi dicit: «Et si non habet aliam naturam nisi istam, scilicet, quod est possibilis, illud igitur de anima, quod dicitur intellectus, et dico illud per quod cogitamus et distinguimus, non est in actu aliquod entium antequam intelligat.»

§ 12.4 Quarto arguitur sic: intellectiva hominis anima vel est purus intellectus, et per consequens materie immixtus, vel non est talis, sed potius virtus in corpore, et per consequens quid mortale. Sed non est purus intellectus, ergo est virtus in corpore, et per consequens quid mortale. Consequentia patet et antecedens quo ad primam partem, quo autem ad secundam, quod dicitur quod non sit purus intellectus probatur, quia intellectus huiusmodi actio habet esse semper recta, intellective vero anime actio non est semper recta, immo contingit sepe ut erret, ergo non est purus intellectus. Quod autem puri intellectus actio sit semper recta patet, quia eius est ve|ritatem tantum affirmare et falsum negare quod est quid semper rectum, et idem habetur a Phylosopho in lib. *De Anima* III t.c. 51[a] ubi dicit: «Omnis ergo intellectus actio est recta, appetitus vero et imaginationes quandoque sunt recte et quandoque non.»

§ 12.5.1 Ad oppositum arguitur sic: quodlibet materie immixtum sive abstractum est quid immortale, intellectiva hominis anima est huiusmodi, ergo intellectiva hominis anima est quid immortale. Consequentia patet, et antecedens probatur, et primo quo ad primam partem, qua scilicet dicitur quod quodlibet abstractum est immortale sive

he says: "And if it does not have any other nature besides this one—namely, that it is potential—then this part of the soul, which is called the intellect—I mean the one by which we think and differentiate—is not something that exists in actuality before it understands."

§ 12.4 Fourth, I would argue that the human intellectual soul is either a pure intellect, and that consequently, it is unmixed with matter, or that it is not a pure intellect, but rather a bodily power, and consequently mortal. But the intellectual soul is not a pure intellect, thus it is a bodily power, and consequently, it is mortal. The consequence is clear, and the antecedent with respect to the first and second parts, in which it is said that the intellectual soul is not pure intellect, is proven, because the activity of the intellect must always be right and the activity of the intellectual soul is not always right; on the contrary, it often happens that it errs. Therefore, it is not a pure intellect. It is clear that the activity of the pure intellect is always right, since the | pure intellect asserts only the truth and denies the false, so that it is always right, as is affirmed by the Philosopher in the book *On the Soul* 3, text. 51,[a] where he says: "Every activity of the intellect is right, but appetite and imagination are sometimes right and sometimes not."

§ 12.5.1 On the contrary it is to argue that everything that is not mixed with matter—namely, separate—is immortal, that the human intellectual soul is not mixed with matter, [and] that therefore the human intellectual soul is immortal. The consequence is clear and the antecedent is proven, first, with respect to the first part, in which it is said that every separate substance is immortal; namely, incorrupt-

---

[a] t.c. 51] b[corr]; om. b; פרק נ״א a.

[a] *De an.* 3.10.433a26–30.

immortal. If so, it follows that every separate [thing] is immortal. The necessity of this consequence is self-evident and so is the [antecedent] premise, by which we said that a simple [thing] is incorruptible, because corruption is caused by the antagonism of contraries that exist in a single substrate, since they rise up against each other and cause each other's corruption, as the Philosopher explains in | *On the Heavens* 1, text. 20:[a] "Generation and corruption necessarily exist in contraries." And apart from this, a simple [thing] that is not mixed with matter is necessarily incorruptible, because corruption only happens to it due to the composition of matter and form, as Aristotle explains in *Metaphysics* 12, text. 12.[b] And Averroes explains the same in his Commentary on *On the Soul* 3, text. 4:[c] "The passive, changeable things are the material forms." And he explains this in *The Incoherence of the Incoherence* 2, sixth investigation: "A simple [thing] does not change and is not altered into another substance. And therefore, Hippocrates said: 'If man was created from one thing alone, he would never have undergone change, but would have forever been incorruptible and unalterable.'"[d] But what we said—that the aforementioned intellectual soul is not a power in a body and that it is separate from matter—becomes clear from a proof given by Aristotle in *On the Soul* 3, text. 4:[e] "It follows, since it understands and apprehends everything, that it will not be mixed with matter, as Anaxagoras said. For if it was [mixed] with matter, this would be an impediment for any other form." And Averroes explains his words: "If this intellectual power had a proper form, like the material things [do], that form would impede the substance of the aforementioned intellectual power from receiving many other foreign forms."

§ 12.5.2 And apart from this, this becomes clear because this power judges future events for which there is no power in the body that is able to apprehend them. And if so, this judgment can be only attributed to a separate power, as Aristotle explains in *On the Soul* 3, text. 53:[f] "The intellect compels us to resist for the sake of the future, and the appetite compels us for the sake of present pleasures." And apart from this, it becomes clear from a proof made by Averroes in the [Commentary on the] aforementioned book 3, text. 5:[g] "The reason why this intellect apprehends and understands while prime matter does not apprehend or understand is that prime matter receives individual forms. And this power [i.e., the intellect] receives univer-

---

[a] *Cael.* 1.3.270a. [b] *Metaph.* 12.3.1069b. [c] Cf. *De an.* 3.4.429a18–20. [d] Cf. *Incoherence* 83. [e] *De an.* 3.4.429a18–20. [f] *De an.* 3.10.433b5–10. [g] Cf. *De an.* 3.4.429a21–24.

incorruptibile, quia ad corruptionem requiritur contrarietas in eodem subiecto existens, unde contraria se invicem insurgant et corrumpatur complexio, quare Phylosophus in lib. *De Celo* I t.c. 20 ait: «Generatio et corruptio necessario existunt[a] in contrariis etc.» Preterea patet idem, quia cum abstractum sit quia inmateriale habet necessario esse quid immortale sive incorruptibile, quia corruptio non contingit nisi ratione materie in illo quod compositum est ex materia et forma, sicut habetur a Phylosopho *Metaphysicorum* XII t.c. 12, similiter ab Aven R. in lib. *Destructio Des.*, disputatione II, dubio 6 ubi aperte dicit: «Simplex non permutatur neque ad aliam substantiam convertitur, ideo ait Ypocrates: si homo ex una re sola constitutus esset nunquam aliquam passionem passus esset, immo esset semper incorruptibilis et impermutabilis.» Quo autem ad secundam partem antecedentis, qua scilicet dicitur quod ipsa anima intellectiva est huiusmodi, scilicet quod est quid abstractum et materie immixtum, probatur ratione et auctoritate Phylosophi in lib. *De Anima* III t.c. 4 ubi dicit: «Oportet igitur, si intelligit omnia, ut sit non mixtum sicut dixit Anaxagoras, si enim in eo appareret impediret alienum,» ubi Aven R. exponens ait: «Si enim haberet formam propriam rerum, tunc illa forma impediret eum a recipiendo alias formas diversas extraneas, quia sunt alia ab ea.»

§ 12.5.2 Preterea patet idem per hoc quod de futuris iudicat, ad quorum iudicium fiendum nullam virtutem in corpore videtur habere medium, quare huiusmodi iudicium nonnisi abstracte substantie est attribuendum. Quare Phylosophus in lib. *De Anima* III t.c. 53[b] ait: «Intellectus cogit nos ad prohibendum propter rem futuram, et appetitus propter rem presentis voluptatis.» Preterea patet idem ratione et auctoritate Aven R. ibidem t.c. 5 ubi dicit: «Et causa propter quam ista natura est distinguens, prima autem materia neque distinguens neque cognoscens est, quia prima materia recipit formas diversas, scilicet, individuales, ista autem recipit formas universales»; subdit ibidem

ible. Indeed, in a substrate, we need contraries for corruption; hence, contraries rise up against each other and a combination is corrupted, as the Philosopher explains in *On the Heavens* 1, text. 20:[a] "Generation and corruption necessarily exist in contraries." Moreover, the same is clear because since the separate substance is immaterial, it is consequently necessarily immortal or incorruptible, since corruption in a substance that is composed of matter and form only occurs because of matter, as is affirmed by the Philosopher in *Metaphysics* 12, text. 12,[b] and also by Averroes in *The Incoherence of the Incoherence* 2, sixth doubt, where he clearly says: "The simple does not change and is not altered into another substance; therefore, Hippocrates says: 'If man had been created from one thing alone, he would never have been affected by any passion, but he would have been always incorruptible and unchangeable.'"[c] With respect to the second part of the antecedent, in which it is said that the human intellectual soul is of this kind—namely, that it is separate and not mixed with matter—this is proven according to the argument and authority of the Philosopher in *On the Soul* 3, text. 4,[d] where he says: "It is correct that if it understands everything, it is not mixed with matter, as Anaxagoras said, because if it were [mixed] with matter, it would be prevented from [assuming] any other form." Averroes, explaining this, says: "For if it had the proper form of things, then this form would prevent it from receiving different extraneous forms, because they would be different from the [proper] form."

§ 12.5.2 Moreover, the same is evident from judgements about the future: there is no power in a body that seems to have the possibility to make a judgement about the future, since such a judgement can only be attributed to a separate substance, as the Philosopher says in *On the Soul* 3, text. 53:[e] "The intellect compels us to resist for the sake of future [things], and the appetite [compels us to motion] for the sake of present pleasures." Moreover, this is clear according to the argument and authority of Averroes in the aforementioned book, text. 5,[f] in which he explains: "The reason why this nature is separate, while prime matter is not separate and has no knowledge, is because prime matter receives different individual forms, but this [separate nature] receives universal forms." And he continues:

---

[a] existunt] emend. Copp.; sistunt b; existunt L. [b] 53] emend. Copp.; 55 b; 53 L.

[a] *Cael.* 1.3.270a. [b] *Metaph.* 12.3.1069b. [c] Cf. *Incoherence* 83. [d] *De an.* 3.4.429a18–20. [e] *De an.* 3.10.433b5–10. [f] Cf. *De an.* 3.4.429a21–24.

sal forms." And he continues, saying: "And therefore, it follows that this nature, which is called 'intellect,' receives the forms in a way that is different from the way by which these matters are receiving the forms." And he continues, saying: "And therefore it does not have to be necessary that it will be of the same kind as those matters that include prime matter, because, if this was so, the manner of receiving the forms in these would be of the same kind, because the difference of the nature of the received is the cause of the difference of the nature of the receiver. And this moved Aristotle to speak of the existence of this nature, which is different from prime matter, and from the nature of form, and from the nature of every composed [being]."

§12.5.3 With all these [words], he teaches [us] that prime matter and the material powers receive only individual sensible forms and that the intellectual power | receives universal intelligible forms. It follows that the nature of this power is different from the nature of matter and material things, which are composed of matter and form, and that it is also different from the nature of the form. And therefore, it follows that it is separate from all matter.

§12.5.4 And the same seems to become clear from the proof given by Aristotle in *On Generation and Corruption* 2, text. 45:[a] "It would be incongruous [to say] that the soul is generated from the elements, because [then] the activities of the soul would come to it from nothing." And Averroes explains his words: "For it is impossible to state that the elements are a cause of the activities of the soul and the kinds of its activities." And he continues, saying: "Not a single one of its activities can be related to corporeal activities."

§12.5.5 And the same becomes clear from a proof given by Aristotle in *On the Soul* 3, text. 6:[b] "And therefore, it does not follow that this power is in a body, because if it was a power in a body, it would have a quality—either hot or cold—or it would have a corporeal instrument, as is the case with the senses. Yet this is not so." And Averroes explains his words: "If it was a power in a body, then it would [either] have another disposition and another quality or it would be related to coldness or heat—namely, to the combination insofar as it is a combination—or to a certain quality [existing] in a combination only [and] added to the combination, as is the case for the sensible soul and those that are similar to it. And if this was correct, it would have a corporeal instrument. And since it does not have a quality related to heat or coldness, and also does not have a corporeal instrument, it is not a power in a body."

---

[a] *Gen. corr.* 2.6.334a.   [b] *De an.* 3.4.429a24–29.

מקבל צורות כלליות» והוסיף ואמר: «ולכן יתחייב שזה הטבע הנקרא 'שכל' יקבל הצורות באופן אחר נבדל[a] מהאופן אשר בו מקבלים הצורות אלו החמרים.». והוסיף ואמר: «ולכן לא יתחייב שיהיה ממין אלו החמרים אשר אחד מהם החומר הראשון כי אם כן היה כן הנה אופן קבלת הצורות בהם היה ממין אחר בעצמו כי אמנם התחלפות טבע המקובל הוא סבה להתחלפות טבע המקבל וזה הביא ארסטו' לומר מציאות זה הטבע אשר הוא נבדל מטבע החומר הראשון ומטבע הצורה ומטבע כל המורכב» עכ"ל.

§12.5.3 הנה מכל אלה הורה שבהיות שהחומר הראשון והכחות החומריים מקבלים צורות אישיות מוחשות בלבד וזה הכח השכלי | מקבל הצורות הכלליות המושכלות יתחייב שטבע זה הכח הוא נבדל מטבע החומר והחמריים והם המורכבים מחומר וצורה ושהוא נבדל גם כן מטבע הצורה ומזה יתחייב שהוא נבדל מכל חומר.

§12.5.4 וזה בעצמו נראה שיתבאר בראית ארסטו' בספר ההוייה וההפסד מאמר ב' פרק מ"ה באמרו: «לא יתכן שהנפש תתהוה מהיסודות כי פעולות הנפש מאין יבואו אליה.». ודבריו אלה ביאר אבן רשד באמרו: «כי היה נמנע לתת סבה לפעולות הנפש ומיני התפעלותה שיהיו מן היסודות.» והוסיף ואמר: «אין ליחס שום אחת מפעולותיה לפעולות הגשמיים» עכ"ל.

§12.5.5 וזה בעצמו יתבאר במופת ארסטו' בספר הנפש מאמר ג' פרק ו' באמרו: «ולזה יתחייב שזה הכח לא יהיה כח בגוף כי אם היה כח בגוף היה לו איזו תכונה מחום או קור או היה לו איזה כלי גשמי כאשר יש לחושים ואמנם זה אינו כן.». ודבריו אלה ביאר אבן רשד באמרו: «אם היה כח בגוף הנה אז היה לו תכונה אחרת ואיכות אחר או היה מתיחס אל הקור או החום כלומר אל המזג באשר הוא מזג או לאיזה איכות במזג בלבד נוסף על המזג כמו שהוא העניין בנפש המרגשת והדומים לה ואם כן היה לו איזה כלי גשמי ובהיות שאין לו איכות שיתיחס אל חום או אל קור ואין לו גם כן כלי גשמי אם כן אינו כח בגוף» עכ"ל.

---

[a] נבדל] a[corr]; om. a.

dicens: «Et ideo necesse est ut ista natura que dicitur intellectiva re|cipiat formas modo alio ab eo secundum quem iste materie recipiunt formas»; subdit ibidem dicens: «Et ideo non est ut sit de genere materiarum istarum in quibus prima est inclusa, quoniam si ita esset tunc receptio in eis esset eiusdem generis, diversitas enim nature recepti facit diversitatem nature recipientis. Hoc igitur movit Aristetolem ad ponendum hanc naturam que est alia a natura materie et a natura forme et a natura totius aggregati etc.»

§ 12.5.3 Quibus inferre videtur, quod cum materia et materiales virtutes suscipiant formas individuales scilicet sensibilium tantum, intellectiva vero universales et intelligibiles tantum recipiat, sequitur ut ipsa intellectiva sit diversa a natura materie et materialium formarum, similiter a natura compositorum, et per consequens est nature abstractorum materie scilicet immixtorum.

§ 12.5.4 Et idem videtur inferri ratione et auctoritate Phylosophi in lib. *De Generatione* II t.c. 45 ubi dicit: «Inconveniens est anima ex elementis, alterationes enim anime quomodo erunt etc.,» ubi Aven R. exponens ait: «Inopinabile enim est reddere causam actionum anime et passionum eius ex elementis,» subdit ibidem dicens: «Sed non videtur aliqua actio attribui actionibus corporum etc.»

§ 12.5.5 Et idem habetur ratione et auctoritate Phylosophi in lib. *De Anima* III t.c. 6 ubi dicit: «Ideo necesse est ut sit non mixtum cum corpore, quoniam si mixtum esset cum corpore, esset cum aliqua dispositione aut calidus aut frigidus aut haberet instrumentum, sicut habet sentiens. Modo non est ita etc.,» ubi Ave R. exponens ait: «Si esset virtus in corpore, tunc esset alia dispositio et alia qualitas, aut attribueretur calido vel frigido scilicet in eo quod est complexio, aut esset qualitas existens in complexione tantum addita complexioni, sicut est de anima sensibili et sibi similibus, et sic haberet instrumentum corporale, sed non habet qualitatem attributam calido vel frigido neque habet instrumentum corporale ergo non est mixtum cum corpore etc.»

"Therefore, it is necessary that this nature, which is called 'intellectual,' | receives the forms in a way other than the one by which these matters are receiving the forms." He continues by saying: "Therefore, it does not belong to the kind of matters in which prime matter is included, because if it was so, then the reception of them would be of the same kind; indeed, the difference in the nature of the received [thing] produces the difference in the nature of the receiver. This brings Aristotle to establish this nature, which is different from the nature of the matter and the nature of the form and the nature of every composed being, etc."

§ 12.5.3 From these [words], we can infer that since matter and material powers only receive individual forms, meaning sensible ones, and the intellectual soul only receives universal and intelligible [forms], it follows that the intellectual soul is different from the nature of matter and [that] of material forms, and also from the nature of compounds. Consequently, it has the nature of the matter of separate substances, which is unmixed.

§ 12.5.4 The same seems to be implied according to the argument and authority of the Philosopher in *On Generation and Corruption* 2, text. 45,[a] where he says: "It is not possible that the soul is generated from the elements; in fact, how do the alterations of the soul come about, etc.?" And Averroes explains: "Indeed, it is impossible to give a reason for the activities of the soul and their affections from the elements," and he adds: "It seems that no activity could be attributed to the activities of bodies."

§ 12.5.5 The same is explained according to the argument and authority of the Philosopher in *On the Soul* 3, text. 6,[b] where he says: "Therefore, it is necessary that it is not mixed with a body, because if it were to be mixed with a body, it would become somehow qualitative, hot or cold, or it would have some organs, as the sensitive faculty has. Indeed, this is not correct." Averroes, explaining this, says: "If it were a power in a body, then it would have another disposition and another quality: it would either be related to coldness or heat, because there would be a combination, or it would be a quality existing in the combination only and added to the combination. This is the case for the sensible soul and those that are similar to it, and so it would have a bodily instrument. However, it does not have a quality related to coldness or heat, nor does it have a bodily instrument; consequently, it is not mixed with a body, etc."

---

[a] *Gen. corr.* 2.6.334a.   [b] *De an.* 3.4.429a24–29.

§ 12.6 Second, it becomes clear that this intellectual power is an immortal substance from a proof given by Aristotle, which he explains in *On the Soul* 1, text. 65:[a] "It seems that the intellect is a substance, which is a thing in actuality, and that it is incorruptible, because if it was corruptible, it would be more appropriate that it was corrupted by weariness, which is [found] in old age." And he explains the same thing in the aforementioned book 1, text. 66:[b] "However, the intellect is worthy of being accounted a divine thing and impassible." And with this, he also explains that it does not become old. And therefore, it follows that it does not corrupt, because old age means being affected by the movement of [becoming] defective, which leads to corruption, as becomes clear from sense [perception]. And Averroes explains this in [the Commentary on] *On Generation and Corruption* 1, text. 44. And apart from this, since this power is impassible, it follows that it is incorruptible, because corruption is what follows after the affection that is produced by the movement of corruption.

§ 12.7 Third, what we said—namely, that the human intellectual power is an incorruptible thing—becomes clear from a proof given by Aristotle in *On the Soul* 3, text. 7:[c] "The privation of affection in the senses and in the activity of formation through the intellect are not similar. This is evident from sense [perception], because the senses do not sense after they have sensed a strong sensible thing, for example, after hearing a loud sound | or smelling a strong smell. But when the intellect understands a strong intelligible, it will not lessen in the understanding of what is below the first, but will understand it more. And this is so because sense [perception] is not outside the body, but this power [i.e., the intellect] is separate." And Averroes explains his words: "And by this, we know that it will not be affected and that this intellectual power will not be changed by a strong intelligible." And from all this, it is evident that this power is impassible. It becomes clear that it is incorruptible. And therefore, it follows that it is immortal. And this is what we wanted to explain.

§ 12.8.1 We answer, if so, to dispel any doubt about the aforementioned thesis, that the human intellectual soul, by which it is said that man is essentially a rational living being, is an immortal substance and that plurality is applicable to it, as is the number of the individuals of the human species, and that it has its origin in the potential nature shared by the whole human species, which emanates from the higher separate [intellects], as it says

---

[a] *De an.* 1.4.408b.   [b] *De an.* 1.4.408b.   [c] *De an.* 3.4.429a29–b5.

§ 12.6 Secundo probatur idem principale quod scilicet intellectiva hominis anima sit quid immortale ratione scilicet et auctoritate Phylosophi in lib. *De Anima* I t.c. 65 ubi dicit: «Intellectiva autem videtur esse substantia aliqua que est in re et non corrumpitur, si enim corrumperetur, magis dignum esset ut corrumperetur in fatigatione que est apud senectutem»; et idem habetur auctoritate eiusdem ibidem 66 ubi dicit: «Intellectus autem dignus est ut sit aliquod divinum et impassibile etc.» Quibus infert quod sit quid incorruptibile, corruptio enim nil aliud est quam passio per motum ad corruptionem facta et talis est senectus.

§ 12.7 Tertio arguitur ratione et auctoritate Phylosophi in libro *De Anima* III t.c. 7 ubi dicit: «Quoniam autem privatio passionis in sentiente et in formatione per intellectum non est similis, manifestum est sensu. Sensus enim non potest sentire post forte sensatum v.g. post maximos sonos[a] aut post odores fortes, intellectus autem cum intellexerit aliquod forte intelligibilium, tunc non minus intelligit illud quod est sub primo, immo magis. Sentiens enim non est extra corpus, iste autem abstractus»; ubi Aven R. exponens dicit: «Unde scimus quod non patitur neque transmutatur scilicet intellectus a forte intelligibile etc.» Cum autem his pateat ut humanus intellectus sive intellectiva sit quid impassibile. Patet ergo ut sit quid incorruptibile sive immortale quod est intentum.

§ 12.8.1 Ad dubium ergo respondetur, quod intellectiva hominis anima qua scilicet homo dicitur substantialiter rationalis est quid immortale, ad individuorum numerum dinumerabile, et hoc quia producitur a quadam spirituali natura a superis sive abstractis intelligentiis emanante, quibus ipsa potentialiter inest, que, scilicet, natura est humano generi communis. Prout videtur Aven R. de

§ 12.6 Second, the same—namely, that the human intellectual soul is immortal—is proven according to the argument and authority of the Philosopher in the book *On the Soul* 1, text. 65,[a] where he says: "It seems that the intellectual soul is a substance that is in a thing and that it is incorruptible, because if it were corruptible, it would be more appropriate that it would be corrupted by the tiredness that comes with senility." The same results from his authority in the aforementioned book, text. 66,[b] where he says: "Indeed, it is appropriate that the intellect is a divine thing and impassible, etc." From those words, it seems that the intellectual soul is incorruptible, because corruption is nothing more than an affection through the movement that leads to corruption, and this is the nature of senility.

§ 12.7 Third, I would argue according to the argument and authority of the Philosopher in *On the Soul* 3, text. 7,[c] where he says: "The privation of the affection in the perceiver and in the formation through the intellect are not similar, as is testified by the senses. Indeed, the senses cannot sense after they have sensed a strong sensible thing, for example, after loud sounds or strong smells, but the intellect, when it understands a strong intelligible, will not understand less of what is below the first; on the contrary, it will understand more. Perception is not outside a body, but this [i.e., the intellect] is separate." Averroes explains this, saying: "From this, we know that the intellect will not be affected, nor will it be changed by a strong intelligible, etc." Then, it is clear that the human intellect or the intellectual soul is impassible, and therefore, the intellect is incorruptible or immortal, which is what was intended.

§ 12.8.1 To dispel the doubt, I will reply: the human intellectual soul, by which man is essentially called rational, is immortal, and its number is the [same as the] number of the individual human beings. Indeed, it is produced by a spiritual nature that emanates from higher or separate intellects in which the spiritual nature is potentially present, and this nature is common to all individual human beings. As Averroes explains in the name of

---

[a] sonos] emend. Copp.; senos b; sonos L.

[a] *De an.* 1.4.408b18–24. [b] *De an.* 1.4.408b18–24. [c] *De an.* 3.4.429a29–b5.

(Genesis 1:26): "Let us make man in our image." And our Masters, of blessed memory, said: "He consults with the ministering angels" (Sanhedrin 38b); that is to say that He provided them with the power for this emanation. And therefore, perhaps Aristotle had an awakening, according to what Averroes explains, citing him in *Metaphysics* 7, text. 31,[a] that the intellectual power was generated by the separate [intellects]. And he also explains in the aforementioned book, 12, text. 18,[b] citing Plato, that the human soul is emanated from the secondary gods and [that] the relationship of this emanating nature to the human individual forms is like the relationship of prime matter to the individuals of the substrates of the sensibles that exist in actuality. And it seems that Aristotle says of this nature in *On the Soul* 3, text. 5:[c] "No thing exists in actuality before it contemplates." And this nature is made a substance that exists in actuality after it has emanated on the individual substrate designated for it.

§ 12.8.2 And it is made the form of that individual substrate onto which that nature emanated. For then, it is able to contemplate by means of the corporeal powers that exist in that individual substrate when the imaginations of the sensibles are transmitted to it from the imaginative faculty that is in that substrate. And therefore, it [i.e., the intellect] will strive to attain the second perfection, because then it will be able to perform its activities though the aforementioned imaginations, which are limited to it [alone], to abstract them [from matter] and receive them. And it is also able to command the instruments of the material powers that are in that substrate, and to order them to perform selective activities by means of free will, which is given to it by the divine will—*it is marvellous in our sight*.[d] And this substance that exists [based] on the first perfection that is in it is man, who potentially contemplates before he [actually] contemplates and attains the second perfection. It seems that Aristotle wanted [to explain this] in *On the Soul* 3, text. 14,[e] saying that "it [i.e., the intellect] does not [achieve] the [second] perfection until it understands," and he continues: "And it is like a blackboard that is disposed for images, but is completely blank." And about this substance, it seems that he says in the aforementioned book, 2, text. 21:[f] "And only this can be separate, as immortal is separate from mortal." And so he says in the [afore]mentioned book, | 1, text. 45:[g] "It seems that the intellect is a substance existing in actuality and [that

[a] Cf. *Metaph*. 7.10.1034b.   [b] Cf. *Metaph*. 12.3.1070a.   [c] *De an*. 3.4.429a21–24.   [d] Ps 118:23.   [e] *De an*. 3.5.429b29–430a2   [f] *De an*. 2.2.413b.   [g] *De an*. 1.3.406b26–407a2.

mente Phylosophi inferre *Metaphysicorum* VII t.c. 31 quod scilicet virtus intellectiva tanquam quid abstractus habet ab abstractio quodammodo produci. Et idem Platonis auctoritate infert *Metaphysicorum* XII t.c. 18 ubi dicit: «Animam intellectivam fieri a Deis secundis.» Huiusmodi ergo nature proportio ad actuales hominum individuorum formas talis est qualis est proportio materie prime ad actuales hominum individuorum subiecta, de qua, scilicet, natura videtur Philosophum intelligere in lib. *De Anima* III t.c. 5 ubi dicit: «Quod non est actu aliquod entium antequam intelligat,» est enim potentialis tantum, que tamen fit actualis substantia cum primum a superis emanans cum individuo sibi proportionato copuletur, cuius sit tunc actualis forma, cum scilicet eiusdem individui virtutibus mediantibus possit suas proprias agere actiones.

§ 12.8.2 Et hoc quia, cum eiusdem individui imaginationes eidem spirituali nature presententur, potest illas a materia extrahere, et intellectualiter recipere, illisque receptis primas propositiones, que sibi naturaliter insunt, applicare, et ad ulteriora procedens, recte iudicare, organicisque eiusdem individui virtutibus percipere, ut agant actiones ad libitum fiendas per liberum arbitrium tunc eidem divinitus infusum et mirabiliter exhibitum. De qua potentiali natura sic per individui copulationem ad primum actum ducta, antequam ad secundum deveniat, quo, scilicet, actu intelligat, videtur Philosophum intelligere in lib. *De Anima* III t.c. 14 ubi dicit: «Perfectio autem non est donec[a] intelligat» subdit ibidem dicens: «Et est sicut tabula aptata picturis non picta in actu omnino,» et de eadem natura videtur eundem Philosophum intelligere in lib. *De Anima* II t.c. 21 ubi dicit: «Et iste solus potest extrahi sicut sempiternum ex|trahitur a corruptibili,» similiter ibidem lib. I t.c. 45[b] ubi dicit: «Intellectus autem videtur esse substantia aliqua que

the Philosopher in *Metaphysics* 7, text. 31,[a] the intellectual power, just like a separate thing, is generated from a separate substance. Moreover, he infers the same according to the authority of Plato in *Metaphysics* 12, text. 18,[b] where he says: "The intellectual soul comes from the secondary gods." Hence, the relationship of the spiritual nature to the actual forms of the individual human beings is like the relationship of prime matter to the actual substrates of the individual human beings. It seems that the Philosopher makes reference to this in *On the Soul* 3, text. 5,[c] where he says: "No thing exists in actuality before it understands," but only in potentiality, and it becomes a substance in actuality when it is first emanated from a higher [intellect] [and] is joined with an individual substrate that is proper to it of which it is the form in actuality; namely, when it is able to act by means of the powers of the individual form.

§ 12.8.2 When the imaginations of the individual are presented to the spiritual nature, [the intellectual soul] is able to extract them from matter, receive them intellectually, join the first propositions—which are naturally in it—with the received images, judge rightly, and perceive with the sensitive powers and instruments of the individual so that they act by means of free will, which is divinely instilled and miraculously revealed to it. It seems that the Philosopher is thinking about this potential nature, which comes from the conjunction of the individual with the first act [perfection] before it reaches the second act [perfection]—namely, before understanding in actuality—in *On the Soul* 3, text. 14,[d] where he says: "There is no perfection [for it] until it understands." Moreover, he adds: "It is like a slate that is disposed for images, but has not [yet] been painted on at all." It seems that the Philosopher explains the same nature in *On the Soul* 2, text. 21,[e] where he says: "And only this can be extracted [i.e., separated], as the immortal | is extracted [i.e., separated] from the corruptible." Again, in the aforementioned book 1, text. 45, [he says]:[f] "It seems that the intellect is a substance in a

---

[a] est donec] quousque L.   [b] 45] emend. COPP.; 65 b; 45 L.

[a] Cf. *Metaph.* 7.10.1034b.   [b] Cf. *Metaph.* 12.3.1070a.   [c] *De an.* 3.4.429a21–24.   [d] *De an.* 3.5.429b29–430a2.   [e] *De an.* 2.2.413b.   [f] *De an.* 1.3.406b26–407a2.

it] is incorruptible." And with regard to this substance, it seems that his words are uttered with doubt in *Metaphysics* 12, text. 17:[a] "It is perhaps impossible that this substance—namely, the intellect—will corrupt."

§12.8.3 So, it has already become clear that although the [spiritual] nature that emanates exists only in potentiality before it comes to rest on the individual substrate, it will not exist among the number of the existents in actuality, as became clear above. It is generated to exist in actuality and to join with an individual substrate designated for it, and this is the individual human being, as happens to matter, especially to prime matter, if it is possible that it may exist devoid of all form. Because then, it would be an existent in potentiality only and it would not exist in the number of the existents in actuality until the individual form came onto it. For when the form comes onto the matter, the matter will then be part of a compound existing in actuality.

§12.8.4 And since this [spiritual] form—which is the human intellectual soul—is a thing unmixed with the body, the relationship of this form to the individual substrate whose form it is like the relationship of the sphere's soul to the sphere whose form it is. For it is unmixed with the body of the sphere, although it is its individual form, as Averroes explains in [the Commentary on] *On the Soul* 3, text. 5:[b] "If animate beings do exist whose perfection is a separate substance, as one thinks of the substance of the sphere, etc." And so he explains in the *Treatise on the Substance of the Celestial Sphere*, ch. 4: "It is necessary that this power, which is neither light nor heavy, will be in a simple body, and that it will neither have a substrate nor a contrary, and that the soul will be unmixed with matter, but a soul of an immortal body, in such a way that this soul is not separated from its body, although it is separate from it [in another way]."[c] And it seems that this is what the prophet testified in his [i.e., Ezekiel's] saying (Ezekiel 1:20): "For the spirit of the creatures was in the wheels."

§12.9 And so, it seems that [Holy] Scripture teaches [us about this], saying (Exodus 24:10): "And under His feet there was the likeness of a pavement of sapphire, like the substance of the heavens for purity." And this is so because the earth is compared to His footstool, as it says (Isaiah 66:1): "And the earth is My footstool." And the final purpose of the earth—and the noblest [being] in it is the human species, as it says (Psalm 115:16): "And the earth He gave over to man." And the final purpose of man—and the noblest [being] in him is the substance of the intellectual soul

---

[a] *Metaph.* 12.3.1070a.   [b] Cf. *De an.* 3.4.429a21–24.   [c] Cf. *Sub. orb.* 112–113.

עצם נמצא בפעל והוא בלתי נפסד« עכ"ל. ועל זה העצם נראה שהיו דבריו כמסופקים בספר מה שאחר מאמר י"ב פרק י"ז באמרו: »שהוא אולי נמנע שאותו העצם אשר הוא שכל יפסד.«

§12.8.3 הנה כבר התבאר שעם היות שזה הטבע השופע הוא נמצא בכח בלבד קודם שינוח על הנושא האישיי. ואז אינו במספר הנמצאות בפעל כאשר התבאר למעלה הוא אמנם מתהוה נמצא בפעל בהתאחדו עם נושא אישיי מיוחד אליו והוא האיש האנושי כמו שיקרה לחומר בפרט לחומר הראשון אם היה איפשר שימצא מופשט מכל צורה כי אז היה נמצא בכח בלבד ולא היה במספר הנמצאות בפעל עד בוא אליו הצורה האישיית כי אמנם בבוא הצורה בחומר יהיה החומר אז חלק מורכב נמצא בפעל.

§12.8.4 ובהיות שזאת הצורה אשר היא הנפש האנושית השכלית היא דבר בלתי מעורב עם הגוף. הנה יחס זאת הצורה אל הנושא האישיי אשר היא צורה לו כיחס נפש הגלגל אל הגלגל אשר היא צורה לו כי היא אמנם בלתי מעורבת עם גוף הגלגל עם היותה לו צורה אישיית. כמו שבאר אבן רשד בספר הנפש מאמר ג' פרק ה' באמרו: »אם נמצאו בעלי חיים אשר שלמותם היא[a] עצם נבדל כאשר יחשב על עצם הגלגל.« וכן באר בספר עצם הגלגל פרק ד' באמרו: »היה בהכרח שזה הכח שהוא בלתי קל ובלתי כבד יהיה בגשם[b] פשוט ושאין לו נושא ולא הפכי ושיהיה נפש בלתי מעורב עם חומר אבל הוא נפש של גשם נצחי באופן שזאת הנפש אינה מופשטת מן הגשם שלה ועם זה היא נבדלת ממנו.« וזה נראה שהעיד הנביא באמרו: »כי רוח החיה באופנים.« (יחזקאל א' כ')

§12.9 וכן נראה שהתורה[c] הכתוב באמרו: »ותחת רגליו כמעשה לבנת הספיר וכעצם השמים לטהר« (שמות כ"ד י'). וזה כי בהיות הארץ נמשלת להדום רגליו באמרו: »והארץ הדום רגלי« (ישעיהו ס"ו א'). ותכלית הארץ והנכבד בה הוא המין האנושי באמרו: »והארץ נתן לבני אדם« (תהלים קט"ו ט"ז). ותכלית האדם והנכבד בו היא[d] עצם הנפש

---

[a] היא] coni. Dunk.; הוא a.   [b] בגשם] emend. Dunk.; בגשם a; in corpore b.   [c] שהורה] a[corr]; שהתרה a.   [d] היא] coni. Dunk.; הוא a.

est in re et non corrumpitur» et idem videtur inferre *Metaphysicorum* XII t.c. 17.

§ 12.8.3 Quibus ergo patet quod quamvis huiusmodi spiritualis natura sit quid potentiale tantum antequam individuo sibi proportionato copuletur, quare ut sic non est de numero entium actu existentium ut supra, fit tamen actu ens, cum primum huiusmodi individuo sibi proportionato copuletur, sicut accideret de materia prima. Si daretur actu existens nuda a qualibet forma privata, tunc enim esset quid potentiale tantum, quare non esset de numero entium que tamen fieret actu ens sive actualis individui pars per individualem formam sibi advenientem.

§ 12.8.4 Cum autem huiusmodi spiritualis forma que est intellectiva anima sit quid corpori non mixtum, sic ergo se habet ad humanum individuum cum quo copulatur, sicut se habet anima motiva cuiuslibet orbium ad illum orbem cuius est propria anima, que scilicet est quid non mixtum eiusdem orbis corpori, quamvis sit eiusdem individualis anima, prout habetur ab Aven R. in conmento *De Anima* III t.c. 5 ubi dicit: «Si sunt quedam animata quorum perfectio sit substantia separata, sicut extimamus de corpore celesti etc.» Et idem habetur ab eodem Ave R. in *Tractatu de Substantia Orbis* cap. 4 ubi dicit: «Necesse est ut hec virtus que neque gravis neque levis sit in corpore simplici, et ipsam non habere subiectum neque contrarium, et ut sit anima necessario non admixta materie, sed anima corporis eterni, ita quod ista anima sit non admixta corpori suo, et cum hoc non separata ab ipso.»

§ 12.9 Et idem docetur in libro Exodi cap. 24 [24:10] ubi dicit: «Et viderunt Deum Israelis et sub pedibus suis quasi opus zapiri, scilicet, albi et quasi substantia celi quoad munditiem etc.» Quibus inferre videtur quod illi Deum quodammodo videntes, sive spiritualiter speculantes, noverunt quid esse quasi sub pedibus suis sive quid ei propinquum, et talis est intellectiva hominis anima, quam

§ 12.8.3 From those [words], it is clear that the spiritual nature is in potentiality only before it is joined with an individual proportioned to it, since it does not belong to the number of beings existing in actuality, as aforementioned. Nonetheless, it becomes a being in actuality when it is joined with an individual proportioned to it, as occurs to prime matter. If an existent in actuality [that was] devoid of all forms were to exist, then it would be in potentiality only, since it would not exist among the number of the existents, because the existent in actuality or the actual part of an individual is produced by the individual form coming to it.

§ 12.8.4 Since the spiritual form, which is the intellectual soul, is unmixed with the body, it is to the individual human being with which it is united as the moving soul of the spheres is to the sphere of which it is the proper soul; meaning, the moving soul is unmixed with the body of the sphere, although it is its individual soul. Averroes explicates this in the Commentary on *On the Soul* 3, text. 5:[b] "If animated things whose perfection is a separate substance do exist, as we consider the celestial bodies to be, etc." Averroes asserts the same in the *Treatise on the Substance of the Celestial Sphere*, ch. 4: "It is necessary that this power, which is neither light nor heavy, will be in a simple body, and that it will not have a substrate or a contrary, and that the soul will be necessarily unmixed with matter, but will be the soul of an immortal body, so that this soul is not mixed with its body, although it is not separate from it."[c]

§ 12.9 The [Holy] Book of Exodus 24 (24:10) teaches the same, saying: "And they saw the God of Israel: under His feet there was the likeness of a pavement of sapphire; namely, white, like the substance of the heavens in its clearness." This means that those who saw God or comprehended Him in a spiritual manner knew that there was something under His feet or next to Him. This is the human

---

[a] *Metaph.* 12.3.1070a.   [b] Cf. *De an.* 3.4.429a21–24.   [c] Cf. *Sub. orb.* 112–113.

with [its] free choice, as it says (Genesis 1:26): "Let us make man in Our image, after Our likeness." He said that "under His feet" exists [something] "like a pavement of sapphire" (Exodus 24:10), which is devoid of any colour and receives every colour due to its colourlessness, | because the human intellectual soul, which is disposed for the reception of the form of the perfection of every intelligible, is like this. And adding to this, he said that it is "like the substance of the heavens for purity" (ibid.) due to its deprivation of all material inmixing, because the soul of the heavens, which is their substance and their form by which they move [and] also a separate substance not mixed with the body of the heavens, is the same as the intellectual soul of man: [it] is also his form, by which he will be perfect and will be "man," as it says (Ezekiel 34:31): "You are man," but it is [also] a separate substance, not mixed with the matter of man at all. And it seems that Averroes thought similarly about these [things] in [his Commentary on] *On the Soul* 3, text. 5:[a] "It is appropriate to think that this thing is a fourth kind of being, because as the sensible, intellectual[b] essence [lit. existence] is divided into matter and form, so is the intellectual essence [lit. existence] divided in a way similar to this; namely, so that it contains a thing similar to form and a thing similar to matter."

§ 12.10.1 And to the opponent's arguments, saying that every form of a corruptible is corruptible, we answer that we have to make a distinction: there is a form of a corruptible that is mixed with matter, and for that form, it is correct that it will necessarily corrupt by the corruption of the compound. But there is a[nother] form for the corruptible that is unmixed with matter, and this is the human intellectual [soul], and it is like the souls of the spheres. And likewise, it is not correct that they will corrupt through the corruption of the substrate or the individual for which they are the form.

§ 12.10.2 And to the opponent's argument, saying that [for] a thing that exists in actuality, it is impossible that—while being in actuality—it will change into a substantially different existent, we answer: this is correct when two existents in actuality remain in their first manner after their composition, but it is not correct when a change occurs to the first forms [i.e., the elements] when they are combined, as occurs in the generation of the things composed of the elements, as Aristotle explains in *On Generation and Corruption* 1, text. 84,[c] and in 2, text. 48,[d] [and] in Averroes['s Commentary on] *On the Heavens* 3, text. 67.

---

[a] Cf. *De an.* 3.4.429a21–24. [b] Sforno adds "intellectual" here in his translation of the original Latin quotation. [c] *Gen. corr.* 1.10.327a. [d] *Gen. corr.* 2.7.334b

noverunt esse quid simile albo zaphiro, in hoc quod est quolibet colore privatum, idem enim contingit de intellectiva hominis anima antequam contempletur, est enim tanquam tabula rasa picturis privata ut supra. Preterea noverunt eandem substantiam esse quid simile substantie celi, sive eiusdem anime quoad munditiam, qua, scilicet, est quid corpori immixtum et hoc quia sicut celi anima, cum hoc quod sit substantialis individui perfectio, est tamen eiusdem corpori immixta, sic et humana anima, cum hoc quod sit substantialis hominis perfectio, est tamen eiusdem corpori immixta. Quare Aven R. in conmento lib. *De Anima* III t.c. 5 merito videtur dixisse: «Opinandum est quod istud est quartum genus essentie. Quemadmodum enim sensibile dividitur in formam et materiam, sic intellectuale esse oportet dividi in consimilia his duobus, scilicet, in aliquod simile | forme et aliquod simile materie»

intellectual soul, which they knew to be similar to a white sapphire, since it has no colour. Indeed, the same happens to the human intellectual soul, which, before it contemplates, is like a slate deprived of images, as aforementioned. Moreover, they knew that there is a substance that is similar to the celestial substance or to their soul, and this is "in its clearness"; namely, in this [substance], there is something unmixed with the body. This is because just as the soul of the heavens is unmixed with the body, even though it is the perfection of the individual substance, in the same way, the human soul is unmixed with the body, even though it is the perfection of the human substance, as Averroes explains in the Commentary on *On the Soul* 3, text. 5:[a] "It is appropriate to think that this is the fourth kind of essence. Indeed, any sensible [essence] is divided in matter and form, so any intellectual [essence] is also divided into two; namely, into something similar | to form and something similar to matter."

§ 12.10.1 Ad argumenta vero et primo quoad primum respondetur, distinguendo de forma, quedam enim est forma materie mixta et de tali procedit argumentum, talis enim forma necessario perit ad sui compositi corruptionem, qualis non est intellectiva hominis anima. Alia vero est forma non mixta eiusdem subiecti materie, et tales sunt intellectiva hominis et celestium anima, et de talibus negatur ut habeant corrupti ad harum subiecti corruptionem.

§ 12.10.1 In response to the first argument, I will reply by making a distinction about the form. Indeed, there is a form that is mixed with matter, and the argument deals with this kind [of form], and this form is necessarily destroyed by the corruption of its compound, but this is not the human intellectual soul. The other form is unmixed with the matter of its substrate, and these are the forms of the human intellectual soul and the form of the celestial soul, and it is denied that they are destroyed when their substrate is corrupted.

§ 12.10.2 Ad probationem vero, qua ratione et auctoritate probatur, quod ex eo quod est quid actu non datur quid aliud fieri prima forma remanente, respondetur: quod hoc habet verificari quando post secunde forme adventum restat prima sub pristino esse nullo pacto alterata sive remissa, sed non verificatur quandocumque prima forma per secunde forme adventum remittitur vel refragatur,[a] sicut de mixtis ex elementis contingere patet experimento, et habetur a Phylosopho in lib. *De Generatione* I t.c. 84 et eiusdem II t.c. 48, et apertius ab Aven R. in lib. *De Celo* III t.c. 67.

§ 12.10.2 To the proof in which it is demonstratively proven that nothing can be produced from something existing in actuality if the first form [from the compound] remains, I will reply: this is true when, after the coming of the second form, the original form remains in the former being and is not changed nor removed. However, it is not true whenever the first form is removed or resists by means of the coming of the second form, as occurs with the combination of the elements. This is affirmed by the Philosopher in *On Generation and Corruption* 1, text. 84,[b] and 2, text. 48,[c] and by Averroes in the book *On the Heavens* 3, text. 67.

---

[a] refragatur] coni. COPP.; refragitur b.

[a] Cf. *De an.* 3.4.429a21–24.   [b] *Gen. corr.* 1.10.327b.   [c] *Gen. corr.* 2.7.334b.

§ 12.10.3 And therefore, when the intellectual form comes [upon the substrate], the kind of the first form, in which there is an animal appetite, will be removed. It is congruous that from the substrate whose kind of form is removed and from the intellectual form that will rest on it, a substantially [new] existent will be generated. And moreover: that intellectual form, which before it rests on that individual substrate exists only potentially, will become the form of a certain individual existing in actuality, like [prime] matter, which only exists potentially and will become a substrate for a certain existent in actuality.

§ 12.11.1 And to this argument of the opponent, which says that if this intellectual power [i.e., the intellectual soul] was a separate substance that existed in actuality, it would be incongruous that it would be a form common to all the individuals of the [human] species, we answer that since the nature of this power, which before it rests on an individual among the individuals of the [human] species | exists only potentially, as has become clear in this way, it is congruous to say that it is only one that is common to the whole [human] species. And therefore, it seems that this is the intention of the Poet in his saying (Psalm 24:4): "Who has not lifted up My soul unto vanity," for anyone who receives this nature, which is common to us all, and does not strive to perfect it has received it from the emanator unto vanity. And moreover, it is congruous that [the same] number should apply to it as [the] number of the individuals of the existents in actuality, since it is correct that we say about this nature that it is one, insofar as there are no individual differences in it by which it becomes multiple. And insofar as it has no reality in actuality in such a way that there would be truly one, it is correct that we say about it that it is common and that it becomes multiple when many forms existing in actuality are generated in it, as happens to prime matter, as Averroes explains in [the Commentary on] *Metaphysics* 12, text. 14:[a] "It is appropriate to explain how it is possible that one in number may exist in many [things], because this does not come to mind for a thing that exists in actuality. But for a thing existing only potentially, it is correct that it is [numerically] one and common [to many things], because there are no individual differences by which the individuals are different from each other, insofar as individual differences do not exist in it. And therefore, it is the lack of forms by which the plurality in number exists that makes it correct that we say about it that it is one. And insofar as it lacks the [individual] form because of which we say about a thing that it is one in number, it is correct that it is common to

---

[a] Cf. *Metaph.* 12.3.1070a.

§ 12.10.3 Quare cum per adventum intellective forme remittatur saltem pristina subiecti forma, que sibi inerat inquantum animal, in qua irrationalis appetitus tantum vigebat, convenit quidem ut ex ipso subiecto, in quo est prima forma remissa simul cum ipsa rationali forma superveniente,[a] fiat quid novum ex eis substantialiter compositum, presertim cum ipsa intellectiva anima, antequam cum eodem subiecto copuletur, sit quid potentiale tantum habens potentiam ad hoc[b] ut sit actu huiusmodi subiecti forma, sicut et materia prima est quid potentiale habens potentiam ad hoc ut fiat sensibilis individui subiectum.

§ 12.11.1 Ad secundum vero argumentum respondentur: quod ex quo huiusmodi natura, antequam humano individuo copuletur, est quid potentiale tantum, non est inconveniens ut tunc sit quid commune toti humano generi, quod tamen, postquam cum diversis individuis copuletur, sit ad horum numerum numerabile, et hoc quia, antequam cum individuis copuletur, pro quanto caret tunc individualibus differentiis, quibus actu plurificetur, habet quodammodo dici quid unum, et pro quanto caret tunc actu, quo proprie dicatur esse quid unum, dicitur esse quid commune per diversos actus plurificabile, sicut de materia prima contingere videtur, prout habetur ab Aven R. *Metaphysicorum* XII t.c. 14 ubi dicit: «Demonstrandum est quomodo unum numero potest inveniri in pluribus, hoc enim non intelligitur in eo quod est actu, in eo autem quod est potentia dicendum est quod est unum numero pluribus commune, quia non habet differentias quibus differunt singuli individuorum ab invicem, et quia differentie individuales absunt et caret formis quibus inveniatur pluralitas in numero. Dicitur quod est quid unum, et quia

§ 12.10.3 Therefore, when the original form of the subject is removed by the coming of the intellectual form, in which, insofar as it is an animal, the irrational appetite alone rules, it is appropriate that from the same substrate in which the first form is removed together with the rational form, a substantially new compound is produced. In fact, the intellectual soul, before the conjunction with the substrate, is in potency only, but it possesses the potentiality to be the substrate's form in actuality, as prime matter is in potency only, but possesses the potentiality to become the substrate of the sensible individual being.

§ 12.11.1 In response to the second argument, I will reply: the nature [of the intellectual soul] is in potency only, before the union with the individual human being. Moreover, it is not inappropriate that it [the intellectual soul] should be common to the entire human species; after it [the intellectual soul] is joined with different individual beings, it is numerable according to their number. This is because before it is joined with an individual, insofar as it [the intellectual soul] is deprived of the different individual beings according to which it is multiplied in actuality, it has something that is called "one." Indeed, insofar as it is deprived of actuality, for which it is properly called "one," we say that it is common and it becomes multiple through different acts, as happens to prime matter. Averroes states this in *Metaphysics* 12, text. 14,[a] where he says: "It must be demonstrated how it is possible that one in number may exist in many things, because this is not clear from the fact that it is in actuality, but from the fact that it is in potentiality, it is possible to say that it is numerically one, common

---

[a] superveniente] coni. Copp.; fuperveniente b.   [b] hoc] coni. Copp.; hec b.

[a] *Metaph.* 12.3.1070a.

many things in number, [but] not that it has a common form, as is the case in a genus. It is therefore correct that it is one, insofar as it does not contain differences of individual forms, [but] not because it has an individual form. And insofar as it does not have an individual form in actuality, it is common to many things."

§ 12.11.2 However, although this [spiritual] nature exists before it emanates onto the individuals of the species, it does not imply the same contradiction that would follow if prime matter existed prior to the initiation of a form on it [i.e., devoid of form]. And this is so: indeed, prime matter, due to its potential existence, does not emanate from another existent. So, if it existed prior to the initiation of form on it, it would follow that it existed in actuality. And since its existence is only potential, it—with regard to its substance—does not exist in actuality. And two contradictory things would apply to it, which is not possible, as Averroes explains in *On the Heavens* 3, text. 29.[a] But this intellectual nature, which emanates from the [higher] intellects, is worthy of a potential existence through the emanator before it emanates in actuality. And it will only emanate in actuality when a substrate designated for it and disposed for its reception is brought forth. And then, the existence and the form will be in actuality for that substrate, because just as it will happen that a shiny body will not emit | its light except through a transparent body that is disposed for the reception of its light, likewise, this intellectual nature will only emanate onto an individual of the species that is disposed for its reception in such a way that this intellectual nature will be a form in actuality for the aforementioned individual. And therefore, the aforementioned nature will become multiple according to the number of the individuals onto which it will emanate.

§ 12.12.1 And to the opponent's third argument, saying that this [spiritual] nature is not an existent in actuality and [that] it therefore is not correct [to say] that it will be an immortal existent, we answer: it is not an existent in actuality prior to its emanation onto one of the individuals of the species, but it exists in the emanator only potentially. And therefore, it would not be correct [to say] either that it was immortal or that it was corruptible. However, it acquires existence in actuality when it emanates onto one of the individuals of the species that is designated for it, since it is a form in actuality for the aforementioned individual disposed for acting, because it is able to enact the activities that are designated for it by the powers of the aforementioned individual [substrate], as became clear above.

---

[a] Cf. *Cael.* 3.2.302a.

יצדק עליו שהוא משותף לדברים רבים במספר לא שתהיה לו צורה משותפת כמו שהוא העניין בסוג. אם כן יצדק עליו שהוא אחד מצד מה שאין בו הבדלי הצורות האישיות לא מפני שתהיה לו צורה אישית. ומצד מה שאין לו צורה אישית בפעל הוא משותף לדברים רבים« עכ״ל.

§ 12.11.2 אמנם עם היות זה הטבע נמצא קודם שישפע על אישי המין לא תתחייב אותה הסתירה אשר היתה מתחייבת אם היה החומר הראשון נמצא קודם שתחול עליו צורה. וזה כי אמנם החומר הראשון בהיות מציאותו הכוחי בלתי שופע מנמצא זולתו הנה אם היה נמצא קודם שתחול עליו צורה היה מתחייב מזה שהיה לו מציאות בפעל. ועם זה בהיות מציאותו בכח בלבד הוא מצד עצמו בלתי נמצא בפעל. ויצדקו עליו שני חלקי הסותר אשר לא יתכן כמו שבאר אבן רשד בספר השמים מאמר ג׳ פרק כ״ט אבל זה הטבע השכלי השופע מן השכלים ראוי שיהיה לו מציאות בכחי במשפיע קודם שישפע בפעל. ולא ישפע בפעל זולתי בהמצא נושא מיוחד אליו ומוכן לקבלו. ויהיה אז מציאות וצורה בפעל לאותו הנושא. כי כמו שיקרה לגשם המאיר שלא יגיח | אורו זולתי בגשם ספיריי מוכן לקבלת אור כמו כן לא ישפע זה הטבע השכלי זולתי על איש מהמין שיהיה מוכן לקבלו באופן שיהיה זה הטבע השכלי צורה בפעל לאיש הנזכר. ובכן יתרבה זה הטבע הנזכר כמספר האישים אשר ישפע עליהם.

§ 12.12.1 ועל טענת החולק השלישית באמרו שזה הטבע אינו נמצא בפעל ובכן לא יצדק עליו שיהיה נמצא נצחי. נשיב שעם היות שקודם שישפע על איש מאישי המין הוא בלתי נמצא בפעל אבל בכח במשפיע[a] בלבד ובכן לא יצדק עליו שיהיה נצחי ולא שיהיה נפסד. אמנם הוא קונה מציאות בפעל בהיותו שופע על איש מאישי המין המיוחד[b] לו בהיותו צורה בפעל לאיש הנזכר מוכנת לפעול כי אמנם תוכל לפעול בכחות האיש הנזכר את הפעולות המיוחדות לה. כמו

---

[a] במשפיע] coni. Dunk.; כמשפיע a. [b] המיוחד] coni. Dunk.; מיוחד a.

caret forma qua ens dicitur | esse quid unum numero, dicitur esse communis rebus pluribus, non quia habet formam communem sicut in genere. Dicendum igitur quod quia caret differentiis formarum individualium est unum numero, non ut habeat formam individualem, et secundum quod caret forma individuali in actu est communis pluribus rebus etc.»

to many things. In fact, it does not have the differences by which the individuals [particulars] differ from each other, and there are no individual differences or forms for which plurality in number exists. We say that it is one and that it is deprived of form, for which [reason] we say | that it is numerically one. We say that it is common to many things, not because it has a common form, as in the species; in fact, we say that since it does not have different individual forms, it is numerically one, and this is not because it has an individual form. Therefore, since it does not have an individual form in actuality, it is common to many things."

§ 12.11.2 Et tamen de ipsa spirituali natura quamvis, antequam humano individuo copuletur, habeat quodammodo esse scilicet potentiale, non tamen sequitur illa contradictionis implicatio, que sequitur ad sermonem dicentium ut detur materia prima existens a qualibet forma denudata, quia in quantum materia tantum est quid potentiale tantum, et pro quanto actu existeret, esset quid actu ens, quod implicat contradictionem sicut Aven R. docet in commento lib. *De Celo* III t.c. 29.ᵃ Et quia ipsa intellectiva sive spiritualis natura a superis sive Deis secundis emanans ut supra, non influitur ab eis actu nisi dato subiecto sibi proportionato et eiusdem capaci, cuius sit actu forma, sicut accidit de lucido, a quo non emanat actualis lux nisi dato diaphano eidem luci proportionate. Quare huiusmodi spiritualis natura habet suum potentiale esse in his secundis Deis antequam influant. Suum vero actuale esse acquirit postquam ab eis in subiecto sibi disposito influxa fuerit cum fiat actualis illius forma et per consequens plurificatur ad individuorum numerum ad quos emanare contingit.

§ 12.11.2 Similarly, regarding the spiritual nature, even though it is in potentiality before being joined with the individual human being, this does not imply the contradiction that follows from the speech of those who say that there is a prime matter [that is] devoid of form. Indeed, insofar as it is only matter, it is in potency only, and if it were to exist in actuality, then it would be a being in actuality, and this implies a contradiction, as Averroes explains in the Commentary on *On the Heavens* 3, text. 29.ᵃ Since the intellectual or spiritual nature is emanated from higher or secondary gods, as aforementioned, it does not flow from them [from the secondary gods] in actuality if there is no proportioned and appropriate substrate whose form in actuality it is. The same occurs to a luminous body, which only emanates light in actuality if there is a transparent body that is proportioned to its light. Likewise, the spiritual nature is in potency only before being emanated from the secondary gods. The spiritual nature acquires actuality only after it has been instilled in a substrate [that is] appropriate to it, when it becomes its actualised form, and consequently, it is multiplied according to the number of individuals onto which it emanates.

§ 12.12.1 Quo autem ad tertium argumentum respondetur: quod quamvis antequam in individuis emanet non sit quid actu, immo sit quid potentiale tantum in superioribus intelligentiis existens, ut supra, et per consequens neque per se est mortale neque quid immortale, fit tamen quid actu per hoc quod influitur in subiecto sibi proportionato cuius fit individualis et activa forma, cum scilicet per eiusdem subiecti virtutes possit agere actiones sibi proprias,

§ 12.12.1 In response to the third argument, I will reply: although [the spiritual nature], before it is emanated onto the individual human beings, does not exist in actuality—indeed, it exists in the superior intellects in potency only, as aforementioned, and consequently, [the human intellectual soul] is not mortal or immortal in itself—however, it becomes something in actuality when it is instilled in a substrate appropriate to it, of which it becomes the individual and active form; namely, when it is disposed to enact specific activities through the powers of the substrate, as aforementioned. Therefore, the first propositions

---

ᵃ 29] emend. Copp.; 24 b; 29 L.

ᵃ Cf. *Cael.* 3.2.302a.

And then it will naturally contain the first intelligibles, as sense [perception] testifies. And Averroes explains this in [the Commentary on] *On the Soul* 3, text. 36.[a] And that intellectual form will connect to the first intelligibles, as is appropriate, so that it will produce the activity of intellection, which is its proper activity. And by divine decree, it will then also have free will, by which it will be able to contemplate as it wishes and to command the powers of those who possess corporeal instruments. And this is its first perfection by which it is able to achieve various ranks of perfection.

§ 12.12.2 And the first perfection is like a slate that is disposed to receive images while there is yet no image on it, as Aristotle explains in *On the Soul* 3, text. 14.[b] And so our Masters—of blessed memory—taught us, saying (Shabbat 152b): "A parable of a king who distributed royal garments to his servants. The wise ones folded them and placed them in a box, [whereas] the foolish ones went and worked in them. After a period of time, the king demanded his garments [be returned to him]. The wise ones returned them to him pressed, [but] the foolish ones returned them dirty. The king was happy to greet the wise ones and angry to greet the foolish ones." And the form of this first perfection is not impeded from receiving the forms of the acquired intelligibles, as Averroes explains in the Commentary on *On the Soul* 3, text. 5,[c] saying: "The statement saying that it is not possible that the recipient may have a certain thing in actuality from what it receives is not said absolutely, but conditionally. Because indeed, it is not necessary that it [i.e., the recipient] is not a thing existing in actuality at all, but rather it is necessary that it is not a thing [in actuality] from what it receives."

§ 12.12.3 And if an opponent were to argue that since this [intellectual] substance is a newly created thing—after having not existed [before]—and is also immortal, it would therefore follow that an incorruptible newly created thing would exist. However, the contrary of this becomes clear in a proof given by Aristotle in *On the Heavens* 1, text. 124,[d] as became clear above. We answer, saying: it is appropriate to differentiate between [two] kinds of creation,[e] because there is a [kind of] creation that brings

---

[a] Cf. *De an.* 3.7.431b. [b] *De an.* 3.4.429b29–430a2 [c] Cf. Aristotle, *De an.* 3.4.429a21–24. [d] *Cael.* 1.12.282b. [e] Cf. § 4.7.1 and § 6.5.1–§ 6.6.1.

ut supra. Et tunc in eandem spiritualem virtutem divinitus infunduntur prime propositiones que sibi naturaliter inesse videntur, prout sensu patet et habetur ab Aven R. in commento *De Anima* III t.c. 36. Quibus bene applicatis, fit intellectio que est eiusdem spiritualis nature propria actio, et eidem tunc divinitus datur liberum arbitrium, quo potest ad libitum actu intelligere et organicis virtutibus ad libitum percipere. Huiusmodi autem perfectio tunc sibi divinitus data merito dicitur primus eiusdem actus, quo, scilicet, potest diversos acquirere perfectionis gradus.

§ *12.12.2* Et hoc quia per ipsum primum actum redditur quid simile tabule rase picturis aptate, in qua tamen nihil est depictum, prout habetur Phylosophi auctoritate in lib. *De Anima* III t.c. 14 et idem habetur seniorum auctoritate dicentium, quod idem contingit de beatis animabus et de damnatis. Quod contingit de regalibus vestibus diversis servitoribus a rege traditis, quorum quidam illas | poliunt et ad ulteriorem ducunt perfectionem, quidam vero illas contaminant, his scilicet intelligentes, quod primum actum cum libero arbitrio datum quibus potest ad libitum contemplari et primas propositiones debite applicare. Sancti quidem viri immortalia principaliter intendentes ad illa percipienda intellectivam animam sub primo actu existentem applicant, quibus perceptis ipsa anima moribus et intellectione Deo quodammmodo similis facta devenit ad suam secundam perfectionem, qua redditur quid immortale et beata substantia, illam vero et converso applicantes reddunt eam contaminatam et damnatam. Nec obstat primus actus, quin ei superveniat nova et perfectior forma intelligibilia per contemplationem recipiendo, sicut habetur ratione et auctoritate Aven R. in lib. *De Anima* III t.c. 5 ubi dicit: «Propositio autem dicens quod recipiens nihil debet habere actu non dicitur simpliciter, sed cum conditione, scilicet quod non est necesse ut recipiens non sit aliquid actu omnino, sed ut non sit aliquid in actu ex eo quod recipit.»

§ 12.12.3 Cum autem arguatur quod ad hoc ut huiusmodi substantia sit quid productum et cum hoc sit immortale, sequeretur ut detur quid genitum quod numquam corrumpatur, cuius oppositum habetur ratione et actoritate Phylosophi in lib. *De Celo* I t.c. 124 ut supra. Respondetur distinguendo de productione: alia enim est productio que fit

[i.e., intelligibles], which seem to naturally belong to the substrate, are divinely emanated, as the senses testify and as Averroes affirms in *On the Soul* 3, text. 36.[a] When the first propositions [i.e., intelligibles] are properly connected, intellection is produced, which is the specific activity of the spiritual nature, and the free will with which it is able to comprehend and to freely command the instrumental powers is assigned to it by the divine intellect. Such divinely given perfection is called the first act [i.e., perfection], thanks to which it is able to achieve various ranks of perfection.

§ *12.12.2* This is because thanks to the first act [i.e., perfection], it is like a clean slate, which is disposed for images, but has not yet been painted on at all, as affirmed by the Philosopher in *On the Soul* 3, text. 14.[b] A similar idea is explained by the wise men who say that this is what happens to the souls of the blessed and the damned. This occurs to royal garments [that are] given to different servants by the king: some of them | wash the garments, attaining an ulterior perfection, and other servants ruin them. By these [garments] are meant the intellectual souls, because one can contemplate the first act [perfection] given together with free will *ad libitum* and one must [rightly] apply the first propositions [i.e., intelligibles]. The pious men, who primarily intend to contemplate immortal things, apply the intellectual soul existing under the first act. Having perceived them [the immortal things], the soul, which is made similar to God in manners and intellection, can attain the second perfection, from which it returns immortal and a beatific substance. Those who do the contrary of this make their souls impure and damned. The first act [perfection] is not an obstacle; in fact, a new and more perfect form arrives, receiving intellectual things through contemplation, as is affirmed by Averroes in *On the Soul* 3, text. 5,[c] where he says: "The statement that says that the recipient must not be in actuality cannot be said absolutely, but only conditionally. Indeed, it is not necessary that the recipient is not in actuality at all, but [it is necessary] that it is not in actuality from what it receives."

§ 12.12.3 If one were to argue that such a substance was created and immortal, it would follow that there would be something generated that could not be corrupted, but the Philosopher proved the contrary of this in *On the Heavens* 1, text. 124,[d] as aforementioned. I will reply by making a distinction between the definitions of creation [lit. production].[e] One is the creation [lit. production] pro-

---

[a] Cf. *De an.* 3.7.431b.   [b] *De an.* 3.4.429b29–430a2.   [c] Cf. *De an.* 3.4.429a21–24.   [d] *Cael.* 1.12.282b.   [e] Cf. § 4.7.1 and § 6.5.1–§ 6.6.1.

49ʳ into being through the movement of generation, | by which the matter is moved at a certain time from one form to another. And in the substrate of this kind of creation, there is necessarily a certain potentiality and a disposition to be corruptible and non-existing. And for this kind of creation, Aristotle's aforementioned proof is correct. And there is another kind of creation that brings into being without [moving matter from] one form to another, and this kind of creation is called "creation [out of nothing]," as Averroes explains in [the Commentary on] *Metaphysics* 12, text. 18.[a] There is no substrate required that creation [out of nothing] brings from potentiality to actuality. And the thing that is newly created in this way is—with regard to its substance—incorruptible, except if—by the will of its creator—it returns to nothing, as it was before creation [out of nothing]. And it also seems that this is the opinion of Plato, which states that it is possible that there can be a newly created [thing] that will not corrupt, according to what becomes clear in [Averroes's] Commentary on *On the Heavens* 1, text. 124.[b] And the creation of this intellectual substance is therefore of the second kind, which is from actual non-existence to existence. And therefore, [Holy] Scripture uses the term "creation [out of nothing]" for the creation of this power (Genesis 1:27): "And God created man in His image." And therefore, it is congruous that it is like the rest of those created [beings] that are incorruptible with regard to their substance.

§ 12.13[c] And to the opponent's fourth argument, claiming that the activity of this intellectual power is not always correct and that it therefore follows that it is not a separate intellectual substance, but a material power, we answer: it is false [to say] that its activity is not correct. And to the proof that the opponent brings for this from an occurring error, we answer that the error is not [caused] by the activity of the intellect, but sometimes occurs due to the lack of its activity, when it neglects consideration by its free choice. And then man will not judge by intellect, but will follow the imaginations of the imaginative faculty. And sometimes the error occurs from false propositions that are transmitted to it by the imagination, from which a false consequence is necessarily [drawn]. And those transmitted propositions do not come from the activity of the intellect, but from the activity of the imaginative faculty.

---

[a] Cf. *Metaph.* 12.3.1070a.   [b] Cf. *Cael.* 1.12.282b.   [c] Cf. *LG* § 12.14.1.

per motum generationis et in tempore, et hoc in subiecto actu existente, illud de forma ad formam deducendo. In huiusmodi enim subiecto est necessario potentia ad non semper esse illud novum ad quod per generationis motum deducitur, et de hoc tali, quod hoc productionis modo producitur, procedit Phylosophi ratio. Alia vero est productio que fit per modum creationis scilicet ex non forma ad formam sicut describitur ab Aven R. *Metaphysicorum* XII t.c. 18 et in tali productione nullum datur subiectum de potentia ad actum deducendum. Quare de illo, quod hoc productionis modo producitur, non procedit Phylosophi ratio. Immo est quid per se incorruptibile, cum ad eius productionem nulla concurrat materia, cuius potentialitate habeat procedere ad corruptionem. Et hoc fortasse sensit Plato dicens quod datur genitum incorruptibile, cuius opinionem conatur Aven R. respuere in commento lib. De Celo I t.c. 124. Cum autem intellectiva hominis anima sub secundo productionis modo producatur ut supra, merito dicendum est quod sit incorruptibilis et omnino immortalis ut supra. Quare Sacrum Genesis documentum 1 [1:27] de huiusmodi intellective nature productione loquens ait: «Et creavit Deus hominem ad imaginem suam etc.» Quibus docet huiusmodi intellectivam substantiam, quam «Dei imaginem» appellat, esse quid divinum et per consequens quid immortale, sicut contigit de reliquis per modum creationis productis ut supra.

duced by the motion of generation and in time, and this [happens] in a substrate existing in actuality by bringing it from form to form. In such a substrate, there is necessarily the potentiality to not always be something new, to which it is brought by the movement of generation, and this kind of creation [lit. production] was demonstrated by the Philosopher. The other one is creation [lit. production] without a movement from form to form, which Averroes describes in *Metaphysics* 12, text. 18.[a] In this kind of creation [lit. production], a substrate is not brought from potentiality to actuality, and the Philosopher does not demonstrate this [kind of creation]. On the contrary, it is *per se* incorruptible, because there is no matter in this kind of creation [lit. production] and there is no potentiality for corruption. Perhaps this is what Plato means when he says that there exists something [both] generated and incorruptible; but the contrary of his position is explained by Averroes in the Commentary on *On the Heavens* 1, text. 124.[b] Since the human intellectual soul is created according to the second kind of creation [lit. production], as aforementioned, for this reason, we say that [the intellectual soul] is incorruptible and immortal, as aforementioned. The Holy Book of Genesis (1:27), speaking about the creation [i.e., production] of the intellectual nature, says: "And God created man in His image." This means that the intellectual substance, which is called the image of God [*imago Dei*], is divine and consequently immortal. Something similar occurs to the other beings that are generated through creation, as aforementioned.

§*12.13* Ad quartum vero argumentum respondetur: negando secunda antecedentis partem, qua scilicet dicitur quod intellectiva non semper recte agit, et ad probationem qua scilicet probatur per errorem contingentem respondetur: quod error non contingit per eiusdem intellective actionem, immo contingit quandoque ex eiusdem actionis absentia, et hoc vel ratione arbitrarie negligentie sive pigritie nihil considerantis, quare tunc non sequitur homo intellective rationem, sed sensum et appetitum tantum. Quandoque vero decipitur per falsas propositiones sibi ad imaginativa presentatas, a quibus rationabiliter falsa ori-

§*12.13*[c] In response to the fourth argument, I will reply by denying the second part of the antecedent, in which it is said that the human intellectual soul does not always act rightly. Furthermore, to the proof in which this is demonstrated through an accidental error, I will reply: this error does not depend upon intellectual activity; on the contrary, it sometimes depends upon the absence of its activity. This happens because of voluntary negligence or laziness in non-consideration, since man does not follow the reason of the intellectual [soul], but only the senses and the appetites. Sometimes, one is deceived by false propositions [i.e., intelligibles] when they are revealed to the imaginative faculty. From false propositions [i.e., intelligi-

---

[a] Cf. *Metaph.* 12.3.1070a.   [b] *Cael.* 1.12.282b.   [c] Cf. *OA* §*12.14.1*, first part.

§ 12.14.1[a] And this happens because this intellectual power is only potentially for the second perfection, and therefore, it lacks the separate intellect, which is an intellect in actuality, as it says (Psalm 8:6): "You have made him little less than divine," because although it is an intellect in actuality concerning the first intelligibles, which are naturally in it, as we explained above, it is, however, only potential concerning the rest of the intelligibles, which it acquires only after the particulars of the sensibles are transmitted to it and it abstracts them, receives them, and connects the first intelligibles with them. And therefore, when false imaginations are transported to this intellectual power, the intellectual judgement will be false, but this falseness will not occur because the activity of the intellect was not correct—that is to say that it would produce a distorted judgement—rather, it will occur due to a testimony of false witnesses that is transmitted to it, as happens to a right[eous] judge when false witnesses testify before him, so that although he is right[eous], he undoubtedly produces an incorrect judgement. | And therefore, some contingencies would happen to this intellectual substance insofar as it is, in a certain sense, an intellect in actuality although it is deficient and inferior to the separate intellects, which are intellect[s] fully in actuality. And some contingencies happen to it, insofar as it is an existent which is only potential, concerning the second perfection. And in this way, it will be called "deficient" with regard to the separate intellects, which are intellect[s] in perfect act. And some contingencies apply to it, insofar as it is both; namely, insofar as it is an intellect in potentiality and insofar as it is an intellect in actuality. However, insofar as it is an intellect in actuality, it will find that there is no need for any material instrument in the activities that are designated for it, as Aristotle explains in *On the Soul* 3, text. 6:[b] "If this power was mixed with matter, then it would have a certain quality of heat or cold, or it would have material instruments, like those that the senses have." Yet its activities are the contemplation of the first intelligibles and the abstraction and reception of the intelligibles and the combination of the first intelligibles with the intelligibles acquired by abstraction, as Averroes explains in [the Commentary on] *On the Soul* 3, text. 36:[c] "And we lay down these two principles; namely, that the intellect, which is in us, has two activities, and they are (1) that it is the receptor of the intelligibles and (2) that it brings them

---

[a] Cf. *LG* §12.13.   [b] *De an.* 3.4.429a24–29.   [c] Cf. *De an.* 3.7.431b.

tur conclusio, que tamen vere ad huiusmodi propositiones sequitur, et hoc eidem intellective contingit pro quanto est quodammodo potentialis, scilicet quo ad actum secundum, quare dicitur diminutus scilicet a puro intellectu, qui semper actu intelligit. Et hoc quia licet ipsa intellectiva anima sit actu intellectus quoad primas propositiones que sibi naturaliter insunt, ut supra, est tamen quid potentiale tantum quoad reliqua intelligibilia, que nonnisi imaginata extrahendo recipiendo et primas propositiones debite applicando percipere potest. Cum ergo sibi false propositiones presentatur merito sequitur falsum intellective iudicium, et hoc non fit per non rectam intellective actionem, qua scilicet male videlicet,ᵃ sed ex falsis testimoniis sibi presentatis sicut accidit iustissimo iudici per falsos testes male informato qui licet sit in se iustus tunc tamen male procul dubio diudicat. Quare eidem intellective quedam contingunt inquantum est aliqualiter intellectus et tales sunt prime propositiones. Quedam vero eidem contingunt inquantum est quid potentiale tantum scilicet quoad actum secundum quare dicitur esse quid diminutum respectum intelligentiarum semper puro actu existentium.

bles], a false conclusion is originated that correctly follows from these propositions [i.e., intelligibles]. This happens to the intellectual soul insofar as it is potentiality, namely, with regard to the second act [i.e., perfection]; hence, it is considered deficient with regard to the pure intellect, which always comprehends in actuality. This is because even though the intellectual soul is an intellect in actuality with regard to the first propositions [i.e., intelligibles] that naturally belong to it, as aforementioned, it is nevertheless in potency only with respect to the rest of the intelligibles, which the intellectual soul is able to perceive only by extracting images [and] receiving and correctly applying the first propositions [i.e., intelligibles]. Therefore, when false propositions [i.e., intelligibles] are presented, a false judgement of the intellectual [soul] follows. However, this is not produced by a false activity of the human intellectual soul, due to which it judges in the false way, but from the false witnesses presented to it, such as occurs to a right[eous] judge [who is] wrongly informed by false witnesses, who even though he is right[eous], nonetheless makes an incorrect judgement. Hence, some things occur to the human intellectual soul insofar as it is an intellect, and these are the first propositions [i.e., intelligibles]. Other things occur to the intellectual soul insofar as it is in potency only, meaning with respect to the second act [i.e., perfection]. Therefore, the intellect is considered to be deficient with regard to the separate intellects, which are always in actuality.

§ 12.14.1 Quare Psalmus 8 [8:5–6] hoc intendens ait: «Quid est homo ut memor sis eius? et comminuisti eum paulo minus ab angelis.» Quedam vero eidem intellective anime contingunt in quantum utrumque participat, et tales sunt arbitrarie actiones ut infra. Quod autem prime propositiones sibi contingat in quantum intellectiva patet, quia in his considerandis nullum sibi requiritur materiale instrumentum, quare patet esse quid immixtum materie. Sicut habetur a Phylosophi in lib. *De Anima*ᵇ III t.c. 6 ubi dicit: «Si esset mixtus cum corpore tunc esset in aliqua dispositione aut calidus aut frigidus aut haberet instrumentum sicut habet sensus etc.» Similiter nullum sibi requiritur instrumentum ad actiones sibi proprias scilicet ad extrahenda sensata a materia et ad illa intellectualiter recipienda. Quare Aven R. in commento *De Anima* III t.c. 36 ait: «Et cum hec duo fundamenta sint posita scilicet quod intellectus qui est in nobis habet duas actiones, scilicet comprehendere intellecta et facere ea, intellecta autem duobus

§ 12.14.1 Psalm 8 (8:5–6) explain this, saying: "What is man, that you are mindful of him? [...] You made him to a little lower than the angels." Some other things occur to the intellectual soul insofar as it participates in both, and these are arbitrary actions, as will be explained. It is clear that it reaches the first propositions [i.e., intelligibles], insofar as it is an intellectual [soul], since no material instrument is required when considering them. Hence, it is evident that it is unmixed with matter. In *On the Soul* 3, text. 6,ᵃ the Philosopher says: "If it were to be mixed with a body, it would become somehow qualitative, hot or cold, or it would have some organs, as the senses have, etc." Similarly, no instrument is required for their specific activities, meaning the abstraction of sensible things from matter and their intellectual reception. Averroes explains this in the Commentary on *On the Soul* 3, text. 36:ᵇ "When we lay down these two principles; namely, that the intellect, which is in us, has two activities, and they are to understand the intelligibles and to bring forth the intelligibles.

ᵃ videlicet] coni. Copp.; diuidicet b.   ᵇ Amina] bᶜᵒʳʳ; animas b.

ᵃ *De an.* 3.4.429a24–29.   ᵇ Cf. *De an.* 3.7.431b.

forth by abstraction, since the intelligibles are of two kinds: (1) some of them are in it by nature, and these are the first intelligibles, of which we do not know when, whence, and how they exist for us, and (2) some of them exist for us through free will, and these are the intelligibles acquired from the first intelligibles."

§ 12.14.2 And some things will happen to this intellectual power insofar as it is an incomplete intellect—namely, that it has to begin from the transmitted sensibles—and moreover, only in some [cases] does it apprehend through [strong] effort[s] from things that are evident by nature. And this is so because its relationship to them is like the relationship between a bat and the daylight, as Aristotle explains in *Metaphysics* 2, text. 1.[a] And the contrary of this is necessarily the case for the separate intellects, which do not make use of senses at all, since the relationship of the separate [intellects] to the intelligibles is like the relationship of the eye to the visibles, and like the relationship of our intellect to the first intelligibles. And the intellect that is in us lacks knowledge of the things that it is possibly able to apprehend, since it does not contemplate [them] appropriately. And therefore, it will remain in its first perfection, so that it is able to contemplate and to know, but it is devoid of the second perfection, which is knowledge in actuality. And likewise, error and fault occur to it. And this is so through the faults of the [material] powers, which transmit false imaginations to it, as mentioned above. And some contingencies happen to the intellect that is in us with regard to its perfection and with regard to its defect; namely, the ability of arbitrary and voluntary activities, by which one of two contraries will be chosen and enacted, [and] it will also know that it is able to do its contrary, as the Philosopher explains in [Nicomachean] *Ethics* 5, text. 13,[b] saying: "I say: 'will' is when the agent has free choice and knows this." And | Averroes explains his words, saying: "And this means: when one knows that the thing is reliant upon one['s free choice]. And therefore, it happens that activities that are not correct come forth from the man who intellects."

§ 12.14.3 And this is [possible] in one of three ways. (1) The first is by way of the activities that come to be, insofar [as there is] a defect of the intellect that is in us, when false imaginations are transmitted to it via the inappropriate [material] powers that are needed for the intellection by which the intelligibles will be acquired, as mentioned. And therefore, it will experience error and fault. And this

---

[a]*Metaph.* 2.1.993b. [b]*Eth. nic.* 5.8.1135a.

modis fiunt, aut naturaliter*a* et sunt prime propositiones quas nescimus quando extiterint et unde et quo|modo, aut sunt voluntarie et sunt intellecta acquisita ex primis propositionibus etc.»

§ 12.14.2 Quod autem eidem intellective quedam contingant, inquantum est intellectus diminutus, et quodammodo potentialis, patet quia indiget origine a sensibus sibi presentata. Preterea quia nonnisi difficulter percipit illa que sunt nature ceteris manifestiora, ad que ipsa intellectiva sic se habet, sicut verspetilio ad lucem solis, prout habetur a Phylosopho *Metaphysicorum* II t.c. 1 cuius oppositum contingere convenit abstractis intelligentiis, quibus sensus nullo modo ministrat, quare sic se habent ad intelligibilia sicut se habet sensus ad sensibilia, et sicut se habet intellectus humanus ad primas propositiones. Quare eidem humano intellectui pro quanto est diminutus contigit error privationis sive ignorantie, et hoc ex non sufficienter contemplando, quare remanet sub primo eiusdem actu, similiter eidem contigit error habitus propter defectum sive vitium materialium virtutum interdum falsa sibi presentatium, ut supra. Quod autem eidem humane intellective quedam contingant inquantum utrumque participat, patet per suas arbitrarias actiones quandoque non rectas, quibus, scilicet, alterum oppositum eligit sciens se reliquum indifferenter posse, sicut sensu patet et habetur a Phylosopho *Ethicorum* v t.c. 13*b* ubi dicit: «Dico autem voluntatem quando quis in sua potestate existens sciens etc.» ubi Aven R. exponens ait: «Et videtur quod facere illud in eo est etc.»

§ 12.14.3 Quare tripliciter contingit operationes non rectas a sapiente sive rationali homine procedere, et hoc vel ratione parvitatis vel minutionis sui intellectus, cum, scilicet, presentantes virtutes ad suam intellectionem necessarie non recte ministrent quare contingit error ut supra.

The intelligibles are of two kinds: natural, like the first propositions [i.e., intelligibles], about which we do not know when and from where | and how they exist for us; or voluntary, like the intelligibles acquired from the first propositions [i.e., intelligibles], etc."

§ 12.14.2 It is clear that some things occur to the human intellectual soul insofar as it is an incomplete intellect and somehow in potentiality, since it needs an origin coming from the senses; and also since the intellect has difficulty perceiving things that are evident for the rest of nature, with respect to which the human intellectual soul is like the relationship of a bat to sunlight, as is affirmed by the Philosopher in *Metaphysics* 2, text. 1.[a] The contrary of this happens to the separate intellects, which do not use the senses at all. Hence, their relationship to the intelligibles is like the relationship of the sense faculty to the sensible objects, and like the relationship of the human intellect to the first proposition [i.e., intelligibles]. So, an error due to privation or ignorance happens to the human intellect insofar as it is deficient, and this is because it does not contemplate rightly, since it remains under the first act [i.e., perfection]. Likewise, an error occurs to it because of a lack or fault of the material powers, which present it with false imaginations, as mentioned above. That some things occur to the human intellectual soul insofar as it participates in both is clear from its arbitrary activities whenever they are not right, from which it chooses one contrary while knowing that it could indifferently be the other one, as is clear from the senses and as the Philosopher affirms in *Nicomachean Ethics* 5, text. 13:[b] "I say that the will is when the agent has its free choice and knows this." On this point, Averroes says: "It seems that a thing is made in it, etc."

§ 12.14.3 Erroneous operations from a wise and rational man appear in three ways. First, through the deficiency or insufficiency of his intellect; namely, when the powers that are necessary for intellection rule in the wrong way and consequently, an error occurs, as aforementioned.

---

a naturaliter] *b*corr; naturalem.   *b* 13] emend. Copp.; 12 b; 13 L.

a Metaph. 2.1.993b.   *b Eth. nic.* 5.8.1135b.

defect will be remedied by free choice of investigation and contemplation to acquire the aforementioned second perfection, as it says (*Avot* 4:13): "Be careful in study, for an error in study counts as deliberate sin." (2) And the second way is by freely selected indolence; namely, when the intellect that is in us is indolent and will not withstand the corporeal appetitive power, most of whose desires are not right, and will not overcome its strength and its power by which it hinders it from apprehending [the intelligibles], as would be appropriate, as it says (Sukkah 52b): "If this scoundrel accosted you, drag it to the study hall. If it is [like] a stone, it will be dissolved; if it is [like] iron, it will be shattered." And the unjust activity that occurs in this way is not the activity of this intellectual power, but [results] from the rejection of this activity. (3) And the third way is when the intellect that is in us becomes wise and brings forth behaviours by which the appetitive faculty will achieve a certain wrong purpose that it desires and the intellect does not resist it when it is indolent in intellecting and does not think about its consequence[s]. Then, the activity of the intellect, which is bringing into existence, is not right: although it is [performed] by intellectual and right understanding, it is evil and disgusting because of the disgusting purpose that the appetitive faculty will achieve by means of it, as it says (Jeremiah 4:22): "They are clever at doing wrong." And Aristotle explains this in *Physics* 8, text. 8:[a] "Sometimes, the wise [man] sins when he makes use of his wisdom to do evil." And the intellect knows that the desire of the appetitive faculty is disgusting and harmful and that it would have been possible to resist the aforementioned desired [thing] and to prevent it. And since it will cease to resist it many times, it is evident that this free choice is miraculously provided to it by divine will. And therefore, it can be called a "voluntary agent."

§ 12.15.1 And it teaches [us] this (Genesis 1:26): "And God said: 'Let us make man in Our image, after Our likeness.'" And this is so because in existence, there are no absolute voluntary agents except God—may He be praised—and the human species. But God—may He be praised—selects in a nobler way [and selects] only the good through intention and will, as Averroes explains in *The Incoherence of the Incoherence* 11, first investigation: "But the rest of the beings are all natural agents, which act by nature only, or by decree of God—may He be praised—and by His order," as Averroes explains in the aforementioned book 3, eighteenth investigation: "Every being seeks its purpose by a movement; namely, it moves towards it with the desire for the purpose. But man does this voluntarily, while the rest

---

[a] *Phys.* 8.1.251a–b.

Et huiusmodi defectui gradatim resistimus, prout gradatim procedimus ad arbitrariam contemplationem, qua huiusmodi intellective perfectio acquiritur et sic melius semper gradatim evitat errorem. Vel per secundo per arbitrariam[a] negligentiam, qua scilicet abstinet a resistendo corporali appetitui sepius non recta petenti, licet sciat se posse illi resistere et eundem remittere et moderare, et tunc non fit intellective actio, immo contingit eiusdem privatio. Vel tertio contingit eiusdem sapientis peccatum, cum, scilicet, sapienter sive astute investiget et excogitet modos quibus iniquus appetitus turpia quedam per ipsam intellectivam virtutem turpiter tolerata consequatur. Et tunc illa intellective actio que, scilicet, est huiusmodi investigatio non est falsa conclusio neque est per se non recta, immo est intellectualis et recta consideratio, sed est mala ratione suis finis, quem iniquus appetitus per huiusmodi investigationem consequi posse intenditur. Quare Phylosophus *Physicorum* VIII t.c. 8 ait: «Sciens peccat[b] quandoque quando utitur sua scientia perverse etc.» Cum quo ipsa intellectiva noscat appetitive sive concupiscientie virtutis desideria esse obnoxia sive mala, et se posse ille resistere, cui tamen sepius non resistit. Patet quidem | mirabile sibi inesse arbitrium divinitus traditum quo proprie dicitur voluntarie agens.

§ 12.15.1 Quare Sacrum Genesis Documentum 1 [1:26] hoc docens ait: «Deum fecisse hominem quasi ad eius similitudinem,» nullum enim entium agit voluntarie preter quam Deus et humanum genus. Deus tamen nobilissimo modo, scilicet, optima tantum volens, prout habetur ab Aven R. in lib. *Destructio Des.*, disputatione XI, dubio 1 ubi dicit: «Reliqua enim entium preter Deum et hominem naturaliter tantum vel Dei iussu eiusque ordine operantur.» Quare idem Aven R. ibidem disputatione III,[c] dubio 18 ait: «Et quodlibet entium appetit suum finem per motum scilicet prout erga cum movetur desiderans finem, homo tamen

Similarly, we gradually withstand deficiency, as we gradually proceed to the arbitrary contemplation with which the intellectual perfection is acquired; thus, by gradually [proceeding] one always better avoids the error. Second, through the arbitrary lassitude by which he refrains from resisting the corporeal appetite, which often seeks erroneous things, even though it knows that it is possible to resist them, in order to diminish and moderate it; nonetheless, the intellectual activity does not happen; on the contrary, the privation of it occurs. Third, from the sin of a wise man who wisely and cleverly investigates and finds ways so that the unjust appetite may obtain shameful things that are tolerated by the intellectual power. Therefore, the intellectual action, which is this investigation, does not lead to a false conclusion, nor it is wrong *per se*; on the contrary, the consideration is rational and right, but it is wrong because of the purpose that the corporeal appetite aims to reach through this investigation, as the Philosopher says in *Physics* 8, text. 8:[a] "A wise man sins when he makes use of his wisdom to do evil." The human intellectual soul knows that the desires of the appetitive or concupiscent faculty are guilty and evil and that it is possible to resist them; nonetheless, on many occasions, it does not resist them. It is evident | that there is a miraculous and divinely produced faculty of choice, for which reason it is called a voluntary agent.

§ 12.15.1 Genesis (1:26) teaches us by saying: "And God makes man *quasi* in His likeness." In fact, no being except God and the human species acts voluntarily. Indeed, God desires in the noblest way, meaning always the good way, as Averroes explains in *The Incoherence of the Incoherence* 11, first doubt, when he says: "The rest of the beings except God and man act by nature only or by the decree of God and by His order." In the same book, discussion 3, eighteenth doubt, he says: "Every being seeks its purpose through a movement, which means: one who desires a purpose is moved. But man does this voluntarily and the rest

---

[a] secundo per arbitrariam] b[corr]; per secundo arbitrarium b.   [b] peccat] b[corr]; beccat b; peccat L.   [c] III] emend. Copp.; 5 b; III L.

[a] *Phys.* 8.1.251a.

of the beings do it naturally."[a] And Aristotle was astonished about this in [*Nicomachean*] *Ethics* | 7, text. 3,[b] and wondered how it may happen that sometimes the wise may go astray from the law of moral conduct. And there, Averroes says: "There are indeed two opinions [lit. intentions] that are naturally in conflict with each other; namely, the universal opinion [lit. intention], which is due to the intellect, and the particular, which is due to the desire." By these words, it seems that he is referring to what Aristotle says in *On the Soul* 3, text. 53:[c] "The intellect compels us to resist for the sake of the future, and the appetite [compels us] for the sake of present pleasures."

§ 12.15.2 And [Holy] Scripture teaches [us] this, as it says (Genesis 1:26): "Let us make man in Our image, after Our likeness." Because, as it says (ibid.) "in Our image," this teaches [us] about the human intellect, which is the intellectual soul, about which it says that it is the "image of God," declaring that it is a separate nature, and therefore, it is immortal. And also, it is declared that through the knowledge of the nature of this intellect—which we come to know by its activities—we are able to reach some knowledge about God—may He be praised—and about the separate substances.

§ 12.15.3 And when it says (ibid.) "after Our likeness," it declares that there is an agent [acting] with knowledge and cognition, and therefore, it becomes similar to God—may He be praised—and His angels. And it is not true that this will happen to the other active existents merely naturally, because the likening is coming-to-be by form, and the form is known through the actions that follow from it. But it says (ibid.) "after Our likeness," together with the [letter] "Kaf of resemblance,"[d] in order to teach [us] that the likening is not [a] complete [similarity]. And this is so because man, by his actions, is different in a certain way from God—may He be praised—although he is similar to God—may He be praised—with regard to free will. And this is so because the free choice of God—may He be praised—is always for the good, since the good is in accordance with the final purpose. However, there is no nobler final purpose than the coming into being of His will, may He be praised. But man, although he also arbitrates, sometimes has a final purpose that is not good, for he inclines [to deviate] from the aforementioned divine will, as it says (Ezekiel 18:29): "Are My ways unfair, O House of Israel? It is your ways that are unfair!" And in a certain way, he is different from the angels due to his actions: although he is similar to them, since he

---

[a] Cf. *Incoherence* 138. [b] *Eth. nic.* 7.3.1046b. [c] *De an.* 3.10.433b5–10. [d] In Latin: *quasi*.

voluntarie, et talia entia naturaliter etc.» Quod merito miratur Phylosophus *Ethicorum* VII t.c. 3[a] ubi,[b] scilicet, dubitat de sciente quomodo sit incontinens. Ubi Aven R. ait: «Due ergo opiniones sibi invicem contradicentes sunt naturaliter, intendo[c] opinionem universalem que est ex parte intellectus et particularem que est ex parte concupiscentis etc.» Quibus videtur inferre illud quod Phylosophus docet in lib. *De Anima* III t.c. 53[d] ubi dicit: «Et intellectus cogit nos ad prohibendum propter futurum et appetitus propter rem presentis voluptatis.»

§ 12.15.2 Et hec sapienter docet Sacrum Genesis Documentum 1 [1:27] cum dicit: «Deum creasse hominem ad eiusdem imaginem quasi ad eius similitudinem,» ubi per divinam imaginem intelligit intellectum quo intelligibilia imaginamur, quem dicit esse divine nature et per consequens est quid immortale, et cum hoc docet quod per eiusdem intellective nature cognitionem, quam per suam propriam actionem percipimus, nonnullam de Deo nedum de reliquis abstractis possumus habere cognitionem. Cum, scilicet, huiusmodi naturam Dei imaginem appellet, inferens quod sit quodammodo divine nature, ad quod sequitur ut per eiusdem intellective nature cognitionem ad aliqualem de Deo cognitionem pervenire possumus.

⟨*§ 12.15.3*⟩*q.v. *infra*

of the beings do it naturally."[a] However, the Philosopher is astonished about this, as is explained in [*Nicomachean*] *Ethics* 7, text. 3,[b] in which he doubts that a wise [man] can be immoderate. On this matter, Averroes explains: "There are indeed two opinions naturally in conflict with each other; I mean the universal opinion, which is due to the intellect, and the particular one, which is due to the desire." Similarly, the Philosopher taught this in *On the Soul* 3, text. 53:[c] "The intellect compels us to resist for the sake of future [things], and the appetite [compels us to motion] for the sake of present pleasures."

§ 12.15.2 The Holy Book of Genesis teaches (1:27) this when it says: "God makes man in His image *quasi* in His likeness." The "image of God" means the intellect by which we imagine the intelligibles; [this intellect] possesses a divine nature and is consequently immortal. Similarly, it teaches that through the knowledge of the intellectual nature, which we know through its proper action, we can have some knowledge about God and the rest of the separate intellects. When [Scripture] calls the nature "the image of God," meaning that it is somehow divine, it follows that through knowledge of the intellectual nature, we can reach some knowledge about God.

⟨*§ 12.15.3*⟩*q.v. *infra*

---

[a] 3] emend. Copp.; 5 b; 3 L. [b] ubi] b[corr]; dbi b. [c] intendo] b[corr]; inunedo b; intendo L. [d] 53] emend. Copp.; 52 b; 53 L.

[a] Cf. *Incoherence* 138. [b] Cf. *Eth. nic.* 7.3.1146b–1147a. [c] *De an.* 3.10.433b5–10.

is an agent [acting] with knowledge and cognition, yet the actions of the angels, although they have knowledge and consciousness, are not [performed] by their free choice, because they are an intellect forever in actuality without the opposition of an appetitive faculty. Their action will forever be correct, and sin, which occurs in the actions of man as caused by the appetite and [through] the intellect's negligence in resisting not being an intellect [that is] forever in actuality, will not happen to them, as the Poet testifies (Psalm 148:2, 6): "Praise Him, all His angels, etc., and He made them endure forever, establishing an order that shall never change." And as it says (Psalm 119:91): "They stand this day to [carry out] Your rulings, for all are Your servants." But the actions of man are arbitrarily and voluntarily chosen by him to do the will of His Master and its contrary, as it says (Deuteronomy 10:12): "What does ha-Shem your God demand of you? Only this: to fear, etc., and to love […] ha-Shem, your God." And it says (Berakhot 33b): "Everything is in the hands of [the] heavens except for the fear of [the] heavens." And by this, it teaches [us] that man is in [the] second perfection due to his actions. | And if so, it is also so with regard to his form, by which these actions are nobler than the whole of the rest of the natural existents, although some of them are eternal, like the heavens and all their hosts, as it says (Deuteronomy 10:14–15): "Mark, the heavens to their uttermost reaches belong to ha-Shem, your God, the earth and all that is on it! Yet it was to your fathers that ha-Shem was drawn in [His] love for them, etc."

§ 12.15.4 Indeed, it says (Gen. 1:26): "Let Us make man," as though He was consulting His "family," which are the words of our Masters of blessed memory. It seems that this teaches [us] that God—may He be praised—decreed at that point that the creation of the intellectual power and its emanation onto man would be from His separate servants or from one of them, and then He gave a separate [intellect] power to emanate it, as has become clear above. And this is perhaps what Plato wanted [to say] in his statement that Averroes cites in the Commentary on *Metaphysics* 12, text. 44:[a] "God created the angels Himself and commanded that they should create the corruptible things. And He remained inactive."

---

[a] Cf. *Metaph.* 12.8.1073b.

⟨§ 12.15.4⟩ *q.v. *infra*

§ 12.15.5 Some of what [Holy] Scripture teaches [us] in the two terms mentioned above [i.e., image and likeness] seems [to be] what Averroes teaches [us] in many words in [the Commentary on] *On the Soul* 1, text. 2:[a] "Know that the support [lit. benefit] of the science (of knowledge) of the soul for (the knowledge of) the rest of the sciences is of three kinds." And he continues: "An investigator of the divine things [i.e., a metaphysician] receives the substance of his subject from this science, because it will become clear from it that the separate forms are intelligences and also many other things concerning the knowledge of dispositions consequent upon the separate intellect, insofar as it is separate." And he explains the same in the aforementioned book 3, text. 5:[b] "And if this kind of beings, which we know about through the knowledge [i.e., science] of the soul, did not exist, then we would not be able to understand the plurality in the separate substances, just as if we did not know the nature of the intellect, we would not know that the moving powers ought to be intellect[s]."

[§ 12.15.4]

[§ 12.15.3]

---

[a] Cf. *De an.* 1.1.402a. [b] Cf. *De an.* 3.4.429a21–24.

§ 12.15.5 **וקצת** מזה שהורה הכתוב בשתי תיבות הנזכרות לעיל נראה שהורה אבן רשד ברב דברים בספר הנפש מאמר א׳ פרק ב׳ באומרו: »ודע שתועלת חכמת ידיעת הנפש לידיעת שאר החכמות ימצא על שלשה פנים,« והוסיף ואמר: »אמנם החוקר באלהיות יקבל מזאת החכמה את עצם הנושא שלו כי בה יתבאר שהצורות הנבדלות הם משכילות וכאלה רבות מידיעת תכונות מחוייבות לשכל הנבדל כאשר הוא נבדל« עכ״ל. זה בעצמו ביאר בספר הנזכר מאמר[a] ג׳ פרק ה׳ באמרו: »ואם לא היה זה המין מן הנמצאות שאנו יודעים בידיעת הנפש לא היינו יכולים להבין רבוי בעצמים הנבדלים כמו שאם לא היינו יודעים טבע השכל לא היינו יודעים שהכחות המניעות ראוי שתהיינה שכל.«

[§ 12.15.4]

[§ 12.15.3]

---

[a] מאמר] coni. Dunk.; מאמג a.

§ 12.15.5 Quare Aven R. in commento lib. *De Anima* I, t.c. 2 ait: «Et debes scire quod iuvamentum scientie de anima ad alias scientias invenitur tribus modis etc.» subdit ibidem dicens: «Divinus autem sive metaphysicus suscipit ab ea substantiam subiecti sui, hinc enim declaratur quoniam forme abstracte sunt intelligentes et alia multa de cognitione dispositionum consequentium intelligentiam, in eo quod est intelligentia et intellectus etc.» Et idem videtur inferre ibidem III, t.c. 5 ubi dicit: «Et nisi esset hoc genus entium quod scimus per scientiam anime non possemus intelligere multitudinem in rebus abstractis quemadmodum nisi[a] sciremus naturam intellectus non possemus intelligere quod virtutes moventes debeant esse intellectus etc.»

§ 12.15.4 Cumque[b] prefatus Genesis Textus ibidem [1:26], scilicet, circa humanam productionem tamen non autem circa reliquas dicat: «Et dixit Deus faciamus,» quibus videbatur quodammodo angelos alloqui. Docet quidem huiusmodi intellectivam naturam ab eisdem angelis Dei iussu emanare ut supra, et hoc quia tunc Deus dedit eis potentiam influendi huiusmodi naturam quam Dei imaginem appellat ab eodem Deo tunc creatam. Quare sequitur [Gen 1:27] dicens: «Et creavit Deus | hominem ad imaginem suam etc.» Et fortasse hoc voluit Plato dicens quod Deus iussit angelis ut crearent mortalia prout Aven R. refert in commento *Metaphysicorum* XII, t.c. 44.

§ 12.15.3 Cumque idem Genesis Documentum ibidem [1:26] dicat: «quasi ad similitudinem nostram» videtur inferre arbitrariam voluntatem, qua fit quodammodo Deo similis et angelis per quanto est agens cum cognitione, cuius oppositum accidit naturali agenti. Similitudo non per formam, formam vero per actiones consideramus. Merito tamen ponitur ly quasi, inferens quod non est omnimoda similitudo; ab angelis, enim, differt in suis actionibus quoad arbitrium, a Deo vero quoad arbitrii nobilitatem. Quibus demonstrative docet eiusdem Dei imaginis immortalitatem, et hoc quia, cum sit quid divine nature et per consequens presit corporeis etiam celestibus, licet sint quid immortale, a fortiori quidem sequitur ut ipsa Dei imago his prestantior habeat esse quid immortale.

§ 12.15.5 Averroes says in the Commentary on *On the Soul* 1, text. 2:[a] "You must know that the support of the science on the soul for the other sciences is provided in three ways," and he continues: "Indeed, the divine man or metaphysician obtains the substance of his subject from it, since it is clear that the separate forms are intelligences and many other things among the knowledge of the dispositions that are consequent upon intelligence, considered as intelligence and intellect." He explains the same in the same book 3, text. 5,[b] where he says: "If this kind of beings, which we know thanks to the science of the soul, did not exist, then we could not understand the plurality in the separate substances, and if we did not know the nature of the intellect, we could not understand that the moving powers must be intellects."

§ 12.15.4 Then the aforementioned [Holy] Book of Genesis (1:26) teaches us about the creation of man, and not about the creation of the other creatures: "And God said: Let us make," which is a reference to the angels. It teaches indeed that the intellectual nature is emanated according to God's order from the angels, as aforementioned, because God gave them the ability to emanate the nature that is called "the image of God" and it was created from God; hence, [the Scripture] continues: "God created | man in His image." Perhaps this is what Plato intended when he said that the angels created mortal beings by the commandment of God, as Averroes reports in the Commentary on *Metaphysics* 12, text. 44.[c]

§ 12.15.3 Then the same [Holy] Book of Genesis says (1:26): "*Quasi* to our likeness," which seems to be a reference to the "arbitrary will" thanks to which man was created to be similar to God and the angels, insofar as [man] is a voluntary agent; namely, the contrary of a natural agent. The "likeness" is not a similarity of form; indeed, we contemplate the form according to the actions. Consequently, "quasi" is said, meaning that there is no complete similarity; there is a difference from the angels in their actions with respect to the will, and there is a difference from God with respect to the nobility of the choice. This proves the immortality of the image of God, because, since it comes forth from the divine nature and is consequently superior to the bodies, also to the celestial [bodies]—even though they are immortal—still more does it follow that the image of God is more perfect and is an immortal thing.

---

[a] nisi] emend. Copp.; nissi b; nisi L.   [b] Cumque] b[corr]; cumquo b.

[a] Cf. *De an.* 1.1.402a.   [b] Cf. *De an.* 3.4.429a21–24.   [c] Cf. *Metaph.* 12.8.1073b.

§12.16 And all the proofs that we gave concerning the immortality of the intellectual soul are briefly explained by the Poet, when he exclaims (Psalm 119:9): "How can a man keep his way pure?" To be happy, [as it is said] right at the beginning [of his sayings] (Psalm 1:1): "Happy is the man." He says that this happiness is attained by moral perfection and by the perfection of the intelligibles. Moral perfection means (Psalm 1:1): "Who has not followed the counsel of the wicked," and they are those who sin in mutual relations between humans. And the contrary of their way is to do righteousness and justice, as it says (Ezekiel 18:5): "Thus, if a man is righteous and does what is just and right." And he continues, saying (Psalm 1:1): "And has not taken the path of sinners," and they are those who sin in mutual relations between man and his Former, as it says (Genesis 13:13): "And very wicked sinners against ha-Shem." And he continues, saying (Psalm 1:1): "And who did not join the company of the insolent," and they are those who follow the desires. And thereby, they are impeded in the intellection of the truth and the perfection of the intelligibles, as it says (Proverbs 20:1): "Wine is a scoffer, strong drink a roisterer; he who is muddled by them will not grow wise." And he continues, saying (Psalm 1:2): "Rather, the Torah of ha-Shem is his delight." And he said this about the entire investigative portion [of God's Torah], which teaches [us] the truths of the Creator and His greatness and His goodness, from which truly comes love for Him and the fear of Him, which is the intended final purpose of the entire Torah. But the portion of action is called "commandment," as He—may He be praised—explains (Exodus 24:12): "And the Torah and commandments which I have inscribed to instruct them."

§12.17.1 And the Poet gives intellectual proofs | for the happiness and immortality of the aforementioned individual by giving a proof about the nature of the intellectual power by which the individual remains happy and immortal. First, he says (Psalm 1:3): "He is like a tree planted beside streams of water"; that is to say that like a tree planted beside streams of water, he will not need someone to till the soil to come to it from the outside in order to bring forth its fruit from potentiality to actuality. So, this intellectual power does not need its [i.e. a material instrument's] activities; namely, the abstraction and reception of anything outside of it, as was explained above. And the contrary of this occurs to the material powers, all of which need material instruments, and this will teach [us] about the being of this immaterial power. And therefore, it follows that it is a simple and immortal substance.

⟨§12.16⟩

§12.17.1 Et idem succinte et demonstrative docet primus [1:3] Psalterii Psalmus beatitudinem promittens viro lascivam vitam evitanti et contemplative se semper tradenti. Cum scilicet in doctrina Dei die noctuque meditetur, dicit enim huiusmodi virum: «Esse similem harbori circa rivos acque plantate etc.,» inferens diversas considerationes circa huiusmodi similitudinem, quarum prima est quod potest reddere fructum sine agricole mediis, sub qua consideratione assimilatur contemplativus vir huiusmodi arbori, cum fuerit perfectus, cum scilicet ad suam propria actionem non requirantur materialia organa, prout supra patuit, cuius oppositum contigit corporeis virtutibus, quare patet huiusmodi contemplativam virtutem esse quid corpori immixtum, et per consequens quid immortale.

⟨§12.16⟩

§12.17.1 The first Psalm of the Psaltery (1:3) teaches us by promising beatitude to the man who avoids a lustful life and devotes himself to a contemplative life. When he meditates day and night on God's teaching, it says that "this man is like a tree which is planted near the running waters, etc.," suggesting different considerations about this analogy. First: it can produce fruit without husbandry; according to this interpretation, a contemplative man is like this tree, since he is perfect, because he does not need any material instruments for his activity, as is explained above. The contrary occurs to the bodily powers. Hence, it is clear that the contemplative power is unmixed with the body and is consequently immortal.

§ 12.17.2 Second, as he says (Psalm 1:3): "Which yields its fruit in season," [that is to say] that it is like someone who judges [well] and knows the future needs of the descendants of man who will be there at that time. And as this intellectual power judges future things, and since no material power is in any way concerned with future things at all, it becomes clear that this power is immaterial. And therefore, it follows that it is an immortal substance, as has become clear.

§ 12.17.3 Third, he says (Psalm 1:3): "Whose foliage never fades"; that is to say that it will not grow old. And also, this power will not become weak, but will become stronger in old age, as they—of blessed memory—say (Shabbat 152a): "As scholars grow older, wisdom is increased in them." And in this way, he examines that it is immortal, because everything that does not become old is undoubtedly incorruptible.

§ 12.17.4 Fourth, he says (Psalm 1:3): "And whatever it produces thrives," and by this, it teaches [us] that this power is separate from all material powers in two [ways]. First, that this power, as it continues to enact the activity of intellection designated for it, will continue to understand and have the ability to acquire intelligibles besides those apprehended by first intellection, as it says (Berakhot 40a): "If you listened to the old, you will listen to the new." And the contrary of this happens to material powers; they will all, when they act and are in actuality, become weary and tired, as became clear above. And in this way, he examines that this power is immaterial. And in this way, he examines that it is immortal, as became clear above. Second, he explains, as it says (Psalm 1:3): "And whatever it produces thrives," that all the activities of this power are right, as became clear. And the contrary of this is the case for every material power, because many of its activities are not right.

§ *12.18* And this is the same as what Isaiah seems to explain (Isaiah 40:29, 31): "He gives power to the weary, fresh vigour to the spent, etc., but they who trust in ha-Shem shall renew their strength." And this is so, because he says (Isaiah 40:29): "He gives power to the weary." He explains that in old age, which is [the age] of powerlessness for the body, this same power increases, as it says (Shabbat 152a): "Wisdom is increased in them, etc." And he continues, saying (Isaiah 40:30, 31): "Youths may grow faint and weary, etc. But they who trust in ha-Shem shall renew their strength; as eagles grow new plumes: They shall run and not grow weary"; that is to say that the material powers, even if their strength is like [that of the] young ones, cannot escape weariness and tiredness, especially because of the plural-

§ 12.17.2 Secunda vero consideratio de huiusmodi similitudine est, [Ps 1:3:] «quod fructum suum datur in tempore suo,» scilicet, in tempore nutriendis opportuno, quasi previdens futuram nutriendorum oportunitatem, et idem contigit de contemplativa virtute. Quod scilicet iudicat de futuris, cuius oppositum contingit de materialibus virtutibus, que nonnisi circa sensatorum imagines versantur. Quare similiter significatur ipsam contemplativam virtutem esse quid materie immixtum et per consequens quid immortale sive beatum.

§ 12.17.3 Tertia vero huiusmodi similitudinis consideratio est [Ps 1:3]: «quod folium eius non defluit,» quare non videtur crescere[a] vel senescere, cui ipsa contemplativa virtus videtur assimilari in hoc quod non senescit ut supra, quare sequitur ut sit quid immortale.

§ 12.17.4 Quarta vero eiusdem similitudinis consideratio est [Ps 1:3]: «quod quantumcumque faciet prosperabitur,» cui contemplativa virtus[b] est similis in hoc duplice modo. Primo quod semper agit recte ut supra. Secundo quod post plura per ipsam gesta non minus feliciter se gerit et nullo pacto lassatur, hoc autem sibi contingit tanquam impassibili et per consequens incorruptibili sive immortali. Quibus concludit quod cum huiusmodi vir lasciva evitans se perfecerit per Dei doctrine contemplationem, se proculdubio reddet quid immortale et beatum quod est intentum.

§ 12.18 Et idem videtur Esayam dicere 40 [40:30–31] ubi dicit: «Deficient pueri et lassabuntur et iuvenes delapsu delabuntur, qui autem sperant in Deo mutabunt fortitudines, assument pennas sicut aquile, current et non lassabuntur, ambulabunt et non deficient etc.» Quibus demonstrative docere videtur excellentiam intellective virtutis de qua paulo ante fecit mentionem ut supra. Qua, scilicet, virtute sperantes in Deo preceteris utuntur, presertim in noscendo Dei potestatem eiusque benignitatem. Quare in eodem merito sperant, et de eadem virtute demonstrative hoc docet illam comparando corporeis virtutibus, quibus proculdubio contingit labor et lassitudo propter suam passibilitatem, ita ut tandem contingit defectio delapsus et

§ 12.17.2 Second (Psalm 1:3): "Its fruit is given at the right time"; this is the time that is suitable for the ones who need to be nourished [i.e., the offspring], in view of the future benefit of those who need to be nourished. This occurs to the contemplative power—namely, that it contemplates future things—but the contrary occurs to the material powers, which are directed to the images of the [present] sensible objects. Therefore, the contemplative power is unmixed with matter, and consequently, it is immortal or blessed.

§ 12.17.3 Third (Psalm 1:3): "The leaves [of the tree] do not fall," because it seems that they do not grow or become old, like the contemplative power, because it does not grow old, as aforementioned, and is consequently immortal.

§ 12.17.4 Fourth (Psalm 1:3): "Whatever happens, it will be prosperous," and this is similar to the contemplative power in two ways. First, the contemplative power always acts rightly, as aforementioned. Second, after many actions, the contemplative power acts with no less success and it does not grow faint. This [only] happens to an impassible thing, and consequently, [it is] incorruptible and immortal. In conclusion, when a man avoids lustful things and perfects himself in the contemplation of the knowledge of God, he makes himself immortal and blessed, [and] this is what was intended.

§ 12.18 Furthermore, Isaiah chapter 40 (40:30–31) says: "Youths may grow faint and weary, and young men stumble and fall; but they who trust in the Lord shall renew their strength as eagles grow new plumes: they shall run and not grow weary, they shall march and not grow faint." This proves the quality of the intellectual power, as aforementioned, since men who hope in God make use of the intellectual power in knowing the strength and the grace of God. Hence, they hope in Him with good reason. It [the Scripture] teaches this about the intellectual power by comparing the intellectual power with the corporeal powers; effort and lassitude occur to the latter because of its passibility, so that in the end, the weakness of decline

---

[a] crescere] coni. COPP.; arescere b.   [b] virtus] b[corr]; virus b.

ity of their activities. But this [intellectual] power will not attain weariness and will not become weak even after difficult and challenging activities, because through its multiple [acts] of intellecting and its [act of] intellecting a strong intelligible, it will gain strength and will change into a power that is more perfect. And these two [arguments] teach [us] that this power is immaterial | and impassible, and therefore, it follows that it is immortal [and] incorruptible. And this is what the prophet wanted to explain.

בהרבותם פעולתם אמנם זה הכח גם מן הפעולה החזקה במרוצה לא ישיגהו ליאות ויגיעה כי אמנם בהרבותו להשכיל ובהשכילו מושכל חזק יוסיף אמץ ויחליף כח יותר שלם. ושתי אלה יורו שזה הכח הוא בלתי גשמי | ובלתי מתפעל ומזה יתחייב שהוא נצחי בלתי נפסד. וזה הוא מה שרצה הנביא לבאר.

casus per senectutem. Cuius oppositum contingit huiusmodi contemplative virtuti, quod scilicet neque senescit neque lassatur per exercitium sibi proprium quantumcumque forte fuerit, immo fortificatur ut supra. Quibus scilicet ostendit huiusmodi virtutem esse quid impassibile et per consequens immortale. Quare patet quod cum quis fuerit per divinam doctrinam moribus et divina cognitione ornatus reddet se quid immortale et beatum quod est prophete intentum.

and fall occurs because of ageing. The contrary occurs to the contemplative power, which never grows old or weary through its own exercise, even if [it is exercised] strongly; on the contrary, it will be even stronger, as aforementioned. From these [words], it is clear that the intellectual power is impassible and consequently immortal. Hence, it is clear that the one who follows the customs through divine teaching and the knowledge of God makes himself immortal and blessed, and this is the intention of the prophet.

§13 Thirteenth:
We will inquire whether morality, by which man intends [to do] good deeds, contributes to the perfection of this intellectual soul.

And it seems, at the beginning of the inquiry, that it is not at all an issue in the perfection of the [afore]mentioned intellectual soul

§13.1 And this is so because the perfection of the intellectual soul, insofar as it exists in potentiality, is the actualisation of what it potentially is, and it is the activity of intellection by which it actually intellects. And this activity may only be achieved by the abstraction of perceptibles from matter and by their reception [by the intellect]. And morality, since its concern is the activities of generables and corruptibles, seems to be neither an activity of intellection nor in any way close to it. If so, it follows that it does not add [anything] at all to the perfection of the intellectual soul, but that its proper concern is solely for the perfection of the governance of the city, as Averroes explains in the Commentary on *Metaphysics* 2, text. 14:[a] "The perfection of human beings will not occur outside of a community. And the community will be perfected by good morals, because good morals are necessary for them. But knowledge of the truth is not necessary for them."

§13.2.1 However, the contrary of this becomes clear in this way: since, when a thing is more similar to God—may He be praised—who is the most perfect existent in existence, it is true that it is more perfect than all existents that are inferior to it with respect to this similarity. And as the intellectual soul, in which the aforementioned morality is located, is more similar to God—may He be praised—than any other intellectual soul that is lacking the aforementioned morality, even if it is equal in everything apart from this, then the intellectual soul that possesses morality will be more perfect. And therefore, it follows that a certain perfection is acquired through morality. If so, it follows that morality necessarily adds to the aforementioned perfection of the intellectual soul.

§*13.2.2* And this consequence is evident and so is the premise, in which we said that everything that is more similar to the most perfect among the existents than anything else (and this is the Creator, may He be praised) is more perfect than everything that is inferior to it with respect to this similarity, because everything by which the Creator—may He be praised—is described is one with

---

[a] Cf. *Metaph.* 2.2.994b.

§13 שלש עשרה נחקור אם מעלת המדות אשר בה יכוין האדם אל המעשים הטובים תכנס בשלמות זאת הנפש השכלית

ונראה בתחלת העיון שאין לה ענין בשלמות הנפש השכלית הנזכרת כלל.

§13.1 וזה כי אמנם שלמות הנפש השכלית מצד מה שהיא כוחית הוא צאתה מן הכח אל אותו הפועל אשר היא כוחית עליו והוא פעל ההשכלה אשר בו תהיה משכלת בפעל. וזה הפעל לא תשיגהו זולתי בהפשטה המוחשות מן החומר ובקבלה אותם. והנה מעלת המדות בהיות ענינה כל בפעולות הוות ונפסדות נראה שאינה פעל ההשכלה ולא דרך אליה אם כן יתחייב שלא תכנס כלל בשלמות הנפש השכלית. אבל יהיה ענינה נאות לשלמות הנהגת המדינה בלבד כמו שבאר אבן רשד בביאור ספר מה שאחר מאמר ב' פרק י״ד[a] באמרו: »שלמות בני האדם לא יהיה זולתי בקבוץ והקבוץ ישלם בטוב המדות כי טוב המדות הוא הכרחי להם אמנם ידיעת האמת היא בלתי הכרחית« עד כאן לשונו.

§13.2.1 **אמנם** הפך זה יתבאר באופן זה כי אמנם בהיות איזה דבר יותר דומה לאל ית׳ אשר הוא השלם שבמציאות יצדק עליו שהוא יותר שלם מכל נמצא שהוא למטה ממנו בזה ההדמות. והנה הנפש השכלית אשר בה מעלת המדות הנזכרת היא יותר דומה לאל ית׳ מנפש השכלי אחרת[b] אשר תהיה נעדרת מעלת המדות הנזכרת גם שתהיינה שוות בכל מה שזולת זה. אם כן הנפש השכלית בעלת מעלת המדות היא יותר שלמה. ומזה יתחייב שתקנה איזה שלמות בסבת מעלת המדות. אם כן יתחייב שמעלת המדות תכנס בהכרח בשלמות הנפש השכלית הנזכרת.

§13.2.2 הנה חיוב זאת התולדה הוא מבואר. וכן ההקדמה במה שאמרנו שכל מה שהוא יותר דומה מזולתו אל השלם שבנמצאות והוא הבורא ית׳ הוא יותר שלם מכל מה שלמטה ממנו בזה ההדמות. כי אמנם כל מה שנתאר בו הבורא ית׳ הוא דבר אחד עם עצמו אשר

---

[a] י״ד] emend. Dunk.; ב״י a; 14 b; 14 L.   [b] אחרת] a[corr]; אחרית a.

13. DE MORALITATE

§ 13 Tertio-decimo Dubitatur
Utrum moralitas qua, scilicet, pia opera intenduntur requiratur ad intellective hominis anime perfectionem,

et videtur quod non.

§ 13.1 Quia intellective perfectio nil aliud videtur esse quam proprius eius actus ad quem habet potentiam; et talis est intellectio per quam ipsa intellectiva fit actu intelligens sive sciens: qui, scilicet, actus nonnisi imaginata extrahendo et illa extracta recipiendo fieri videtur, et talia sunt universalia tantum. Morale autem cum sit intentio ad quedam particularia, scilicet, pia opera fienda. Patet quidem quod non est intellectio et per consequens non requiritur ad eiusdem intellective anime perfectionem, sed potius requiritur ad civile regimen tantum. Quare Aven R. in comcto *Metaphysicorum* II t.c. 14 ait: «Complementum hominum non completur nisi per congregationem, et congregatio per bonitatem, esse ergo boni est eis necessarium et non est necessarium eis scire veritatem.»

§ 13.2.1 Ad oppositum arguitur sic: cum Deus sit omnium entium perfectissimus, quidquid ergo fuerit eidem Deo ceteris similius, erit proculdubio his omnibus perfectius. Sed sic est quod intellectiva moribus dotata est huiusmodi, ergo illa sic dotata est ceteris perfectior, et per consequens moralitas habet concurrere ad eiusdem anime intellective perfectionem.

§ 13.2.2 Consequentia patet similiter et antecedens quoad primam partem, quo autem ad secundam partem qua, scilicet, dicitur quod intellectiva moribus dotata est huius-

§ 13 Thirteenth,
it may be inquired whether morality, through which good deeds are intended, is required for the perfection of man's intellectual soul.

And it seems that it is not.

§ 13.1 Because intellectual perfection seems to be nothing other than a particular activity for which one possesses potentiality, and this is the intellection by which the intellectual [i.e., intellect] produces actual understanding or knowledge, that is to say, the activity is only produced by the abstraction of imagined things and their reception, which are universals only. Therefore, morality is produced by a particular intention aiming at good deeds. It is evident that morality is not an intellectual activity; consequently, morality is not a prerequisite for the perfection of the intellectual soul. Rather, morality is necessary for the governance of a city, as Averroes explicates in the Commentary on *Metaphysics* 2, text.14,[a] where he states: "The perfection of human beings exists only in a community, and the perfection of a community exists in terms of the good. Thus, the good is necessary for them [i.e., for human beings], but the knowledge of truth is not necessary."

§ 13.2.1 On the contrary it is to argue: since God is the most perfect of all beings, then whatever is similar to God will, without doubt, be the most perfect of all beings. But since it is the case that the intellectual [soul], [which is] endowed with moral behaviours, is like this [i.e., similar to God], therefore whatever is endowed [with moral behaviours] will also be perfect, and consequently, morality coincides with the perfection of the intellectual soul.

§ 13.2.2 Similarly, the conclusion is clear, according to the first part of the premise. The second part, in which it is said that the intellectual soul is endowed with moral

---

[a] *Metaph.* 2.2.994b.

His substance, which is perfect by absolute perfection. | Indeed, what we said—that this intellectual [soul], which has morality, is more similar to God, may He be exalted, than to what is inferior to it with respect to this rank—becomes clear in this way: because the existence of the existents does not add any perfection to the existence of the Creator—may He be praised—and does not remove [anything] from Him. It follows that their existence, their order, and their perpetuity are generated by Him—may He be praised—mediately or immediately, when it becomes clear that they can only come to be from Him through His compassion, which is one with His substance, as it says (Psalm 89:3): "I declare, 'Your steadfast grace is confirmed forever.'" And the final purpose of their existence is to gain the favour of His compassion, which is the highest kind of final purpose, as [the Rabbanan] say (Avot 6:11): "Whatever the Holy Blessed One created in His world, He created only for His glory, as it is said: (Isaiah 43:7): 'All who are linked to My name, whom I have created, formed, and made for My glory.'"

§ 13.2.3 And al-Ġazālī explains this in his statement, which Averroes cites in his name in *The Incoherence of the Incoherence* 5, fourth investigation: "And when the philosophers say that God—may He be praised—is good, they mean by this that the beings are generated by Him through absolute compassion, not for hope of a reward and not for His own needs, but through His absolute goodness."[a] And since morality intends good deeds, it is a property in the intellectual soul through which it intends to perform deeds that are similar to the deeds of God—may He be praised—for the sake of resembling Him as far as possible in order to do His will without hope of a reward and without fear of punishment, but out of love for His goodness and fear of His greatness. And it becomes clear that whoever rises towards this rank will add to his soul the property of intellectual perfection, [thereby] aiming at the final purpose that is also intended by God. And therefore, he will be similar to Him. And therefore, it follows that this rank will add to the perfection of the intellectual soul. And this is what we wanted to explain.

§ 13.2.4 And therefore, al-Ġazālī agrees in his statement, which Averroes cites in *The Incoherence of the Incoherence* 14, first investigation: "When a man wears the garbs of morality and proficiency in the sciences, he will then be closer to God—may He be praised—than the rest of the human beings."[b] And therefore, it seems that Aver-

---

[a] Cf. *Incoherence* 184. [b] Cf. *Incoherence* 293–294.

modi probatur, quia cum Deus nullo reliquorum entium indigeat, | horum ergo ordo regimen et conservatio mediate vel immediate ad eodem emanantes ut supra. Non nisi ab eiusdem benignitate emanare contingit, que, scilicet, benignitas est quid idem cum eo tanquam eius perfectio, ad cuius satisfactionem talia gerit.

§ 13.2.3 Quare in lib. *Destructio des.*, disputatione quinta, dubio quarto, Algazelis auctoritate ait: «Aven R. et quando dicunt Deum esse bonum, scilicet, phylosophi intendunt dicere quod entia omnia ab eo pura miseratione non premiali intentione neque more indigentie immo summa benignitate etc.» Cum ergo moralitas pia opera intendens nonnisi benignitas esse videatur quia, scilicet, non nobis sed Deo vel saltem proximo rem gratam facere intendimus. Quisquis ergo fuerit huiusmodi benignitate ornatus erit quid Deo similius ceteris omnibus, scilicet, illa non ornatis et per consequens his perfectius quod est intentum.

§ 13.2.4 Quare in prefato *Destructio des.*, lib. [disputatione] XIV, dubio primo Algazel auctoritate dicit: «Quando, enim, homo se induit vestibus moralium et scientijs, divino Deo propinquior quam alij homines etc.» Et idem videtur Aven R. quodammodo inferre cum ibidem dicit quod celi

behaviours, is proved because God does not need other beings, thus | their order, management, and conservation is a direct or indirect emanation from Him, as mentioned above. The emanation occurs through His goodwill only, and the goodwill is indistinguishable from Him, and from His perfection, by which He carries all existents to fulfilment.

§ 13.2.3 In *The Incoherence of the Incoherence* 5, fourth doubt, in the passage quoted by Averroes, al-Ġazālī explains: "And when the philosophers say that God is good, they mean that all beings were created from Him by absolute compassion and not out of anticipation of reward, or for His own need, but through His highest goodwill."[a] And thus morality, aiming at good deeds, corresponds to the goodwill according to which we do not intend to seek forgiveness from ourselves, but rather from God, or at least from the being closest to Him. Therefore, anyone who is adorned with goodwill will be more similar to God than the other existents that are not adorned [with it], and this being will be more perfect than them, which is what was intended [to be explained].

§ 13.2.4 Al-Ġazālī explicates this in the introduction to *The Incoherence of the Incoherence* 14, first doubt, where he states: "When a man puts on garments of morality and science, he will be closer to God than the rest of the human beings."[b] Therefore, it seems that Averroes agrees when he

---

[a] Cf. *Incoherence* 184.   [b] Cf. *Incoherence* 293–294.

roes agreed in this place when he said that the spheres are likened to the Creator—may He be praised—since they give life to the lower existents.

§ 13.3.1 Second, this becomes clear because the property of morality by which good deeds are intended is the property of contemplating a universal with right judgement, and every contemplation and intellection will therefore undoubtedly add to the perfection of the intellectual soul. If so, the aforementioned morality will add to the perfection of the intellectual soul.

§ 13.3.2 This consequence is evident and so is the second part of the aforementioned [antecedent] premise, because the perfection of the intellectual soul—and this is the activity of intellection, which it is potentially—is necessarily [achieved] through the contemplation of universals with right judgement, which is only [possible] through the activity of the intellect. The first part of it [i.e., the premise], in which we said that the property of morality is | a property of contemplation with right judgment, becomes clear in this way, because the aforementioned contemplation is nothing but contemplation by the intellect that apprehends this universal: man likens [himself] to the Creator—may He be praised—through his endeavour for good deeds, and this likening will fit him [to gain] favour before ha-Shem. And this is called "doing [something] for its own sake" among the Rabbanan of blessed memory. And when he recognises and contemplates this, he will command the material instruments to do good deeds and will withstand the appetitive faculty, which demands material pleasures that are opposed to his aforementioned intention, as is evident from sense [perception]. And the Philosopher explains this in *On the Soul* 3, text. 53:[a] "The intellect compels us to resist for the sake of future [things], and the appetite [compels us to motion] for the sake of present pleasures." And therefore, Averroes agrees in [the Commentary on *Nicomachean*] *Ethics* 7, text. 5:[b] "They, if so, are two contradictory intentions in nature; namely, the universal intention, which is on the part of the intellect, and the particular [intention], which is on the part of the appetite."

§ 13.4 We answer, to dispel [any] doubt about the aforementioned thesis, that morality adds to the perfection of the intellectual soul, and [it does] this since its final purpose is to become similar to God—may He be praised—by

---

[a] *De an.* 3.10.433b5–10. [b] Cf. *Eth. nic.* 7.5.1048b–1049a.

13. DE MORALITATE

conantur assimilari Creatori per motum dando vitam inferioribus.

§ 13.3.1 Secundo arguitur sic: mortalitas qua pia opera intenduntur, est proculdubio habitus intellectualis considerationis universalia recte considerando factus. Quodlibet tale habet ad intellectiva perfectionem concurrere, ergo huiusmodi mortalitas habet ad intellective perfectionem concurrere.

§ 13.3.2 Consequentia patet similiter et antecedens quoad secundam partem, quia quodlibet intellectualis habitus habet necessario in eandem intellectivam addere perfectionem. Quo autem ad primam antecedentis partem probatur, quia huiusmodi moralis habitus nil aliud est quam scientifica consideratio: qua, scilicet, noscit se pijs operibus reddere quid Deo similius et idem gratius, similiter noscit lasciva esse quid huic oppositum. Quare hec noscens iubet pia fieri, et resistit appetitui lascivas voluptates turpiter potenti tanquam intento penitus oppositas.[a] Prout experientia docere videtur, et habetur a Phylosopho in lib. *De Anima* III, t.c. 53[b] ubi dicit: «Intellectus cogit nos ad prohibendum propter rem futura et appetitus[c] propter rem presentis voluptatis» quare Aven R. in comento lib. *Ethicorum* VII t.c. 5 ait: «Due ergo sunt opiniones sibi invicem contradicentes naturaliter intendendo. Opinio, scilicet, universalis que fit ex parte intellectus et particularis que est ex parte concupiscentie.»

§ 13.4 Ad dubium ergo respondetur: quod ad intellective hominum anime perfectionem concurrit moralitas. Que, scilicet, est cognitio qua pia opera intendimus ad hoc ut Deo assimilemur considerantes hoc esse quid optimum et

says that the heavens can be likened to the creator through the motion that gives birth to the lower existents.

§ 13.3.1 Second, I would argue that the morality by which good deeds are intended is without any doubt an intellectual property by which universals are contemplated, employing right judgement. Any such things contribute to intellectual perfection; therefore, morality also contributes to intellectual perfection.

§ 13.3.2 The consequence is evident, according to the second part of the antecedent, because any intellectual property is necessarily acquired through intellectual perfection. The first part of the antecedent is proved because the moral property is nothing more than systematic [i.e., scientific] contemplation. Through knowledge, it is possible to recognise good deeds, which make us better and more similar to God. Similarly, this knowledge recognises that material pleasures are the contraries of this, since this acknowledgement arranges the performance of good deeds and resists the material pleasures produced by the appetitive faculty, which are completely at odds with the intention. This is what experience teaches and what the Philosopher explains in *On the Soul* 3, text. 53,[a] where he states: "The intellect compels us to resist for the sake of future [things], and the appetite [compels us to motion] for the sake of present pleasures." Therefore, Averroes explicates this in the Commentary on *Ethics* 7, text. 5,[b] where he states: "They are two contradictory intentions in nature: the universal intention resulting from the intellect and the particular [intention] resulting from the appetite."

§ 13.4 To dispel any doubt, I will reply: morality carries the perfection of the intellectual soul of human beings, meaning the knowledge by which one intends good deeds, making us similar to God. With this truth in mind, this is some-

---

[a] oppositas] b[corr]; opposito b.   [b] 53] emend. COPP.; 52 b; 53 L.   [c] appetitus] b[corr]; eppetitus b; appetitus L.

[a] *De an.* 3.433b5–10.   [b] Cf. *Eth. nic.* 7.5.1148b–1149a.

walking in His ways to satisfy the desire of His will aiming at its perfection, as is appropriate for every agent who wishes for the perfection of its activity.

§ 13.5 And to the opponent's arguments, we answer that although some good deeds are not *per se* intellectual thing[s] by which the intellectual soul may be perfected, nevertheless, the character of the desire for them in order to [do] the will of its Creator by which He commanded the intellect to perform them, as we explained, is intellectual. And it is necessary, from what this intellect knows and recognises, that this deed is approved by the Creator. And therefore, it is appropriate and fitting and will necessarily contribute to the perfection of the intellectual soul insofar as it is intellectual perfection and insofar as it is the [process of] becoming similar to the Creator, may He be exalted.

§ 13.6 And the deeds that follow the rules [of this property], which are favourable before God—may He be praised— are undoubtedly appropriate to multiply [the soul's] happiness and the light of the king's face in eternal life, as is appropriate for those who love the king [and] who endeavour to gain His favour, as it says (Exodus 20:6): "Showing kindness to [...] those who love [Me]," and as it says (*Avot* 3:15): "And everything is in accordance with the preponderance of works," and to convey and teach the intention of the commandments and the Torah in its entirety, that man shall become as much like his Former as possible, which is the intention of his Creator, as is testified (Genesis 1:26): "Let us make man in our image, after our likeness."

§ 13.7 He warns [us] against [doing] anything else, which the whole, or [at least] many [verses], of the Torah explains (Leviticus 19:2): "You shall be holy, for I, ha-Shem, your God, am holy."

§ 13.8 And it says (Leviticus 11:44): "You shall sanctify yourselves and be holy, for I am holy." And He explains that this is the intention of the whole Torah and its final purpose, as it says (Deuteronomy 11:22): "Keep all these commandments that I command you, loving ha-Shem, your God, walking in all His ways, and holding fast to Him." And therefore, it testifies that the intention of the commandments is (1) to enlighten us to the love of God—may He be praised—and [it does] this by letting us know | His grace and His goodness towards the whole of existence in general, and towards Israel in particular, through an intellectual demonstration; (2) to lead us "walking in all His ways" (ibid.), so that we will resemble Him as far as possible, and the final purpose of all this is so that we shall conjoin with

Deo gratissimum tamquam opifici sui operis perfectionem volenti. Quare moralitas huiusmodi tamquam intellectualis cognitio et divine nature assimilatio merito habet ad intellective anime perfectionem concurrere.

§ 13.5 Ad argumenta vero respondetur: quod quamvis ipsa pia opera in quantum opera non sint quid intellectuale. Moralis tamen habitus illa fienda iubens, est proculdubio quid intellectuale et divine nature simile. Et per consequens habet ad intellective[a] anime perfectionem merito concurrere, ipsa vero pia opera tanquam Deo grata sunt proculdubio meritoria et ad immortalis vite felicitatem conferentia, ad opera vero his opposita oppositum merito sequi videtur.

⟨§ 13.6⟩

§ 13.7 Quare Sacrum Levitici Documentum 19 [19:2], bonos mores sanctamque vitam docens, reddit rationem quare merito observentur dicens, quod per huiusmodi moralitatem reddimus nos Deo quodammodo similes, et hoc infert ubi dicit: «Sancti estote quoniam Sanctus sum ego Dominus Deus vester.»

§ 13.8 Et idem docetur in libro Deuteronomij cap.11 [11:13] ubi dicit: «Ut diligatis Dominum Deum vestrum et ambuletis in omnibus vijs suis et adhereatis ei.» Quasi dicat ut amore Dei ducti (et hoc nonnisi per eiusdem excellentie et benignitatis cognitionem) eiusdem sequamur vestigia sive mores. Quibus eidem Deo aliquali nobilitatis gradu adheremus tanquam ceteris eidem similiores et per consequens perfectiores ut supra.

thing good and most pleasing to God, just as an artisan desires the perfection of his work. Since morality has this nature, the intellectual knowledge and the resemblance to the divine nature contribute to the perfection of the intellectual soul.

§ 13.5 In response to this argument, I will reply: good deeds *per se*, insofar as they are merely activities, are not intellectual. Nevertheless, the moral property that enjoins [us] to perform good deeds is without doubt something comparable to the intellectual and divine nature. Consequently, the moral property necessarily contributes to the perfection of the intellectual soul. Nonetheless, good deeds and the grace of God are undoubtedly meritorious, and they lead to the happiness of immortal life. The opposite of this seems to occur when one follows the contrary activities.

⟨§ 13.6⟩

§ 13.7 Therefore, the Holy Book of Leviticus (19:2), teaching good behaviours and a saintly life, demonstrates the same thing. When good deeds are observed according to moral principles, we make ourselves similar to God, when it says: "Be you Holy, because I, the Lord, am holy."

§ 13.8 And Deuteronomy 11 (11:13) teaches the same: "Which I command that you love the Lord your God and serve Him with all your heart and with all your soul." This means that when one is led by the love of God, and this happens thanks to the merit and knowledge of His goodwill, one follows His footsteps and His behaviours. Through these [things], one participates in God's nobility to the same degree, because we are more similar to Him than the other beings, and consequently, we are more perfect too, as mentioned above.

---

[a] intellective] b[corr]; intellectiue b.

Him in perpetual happiness, which is appropriate to everyone who is similar to Him in the aforementioned way, as it says (Psalm 65:5): "Happy is the man You choose and bring near." And this is testified at the beginning of the giving of the Torah, as it says (Exodus 19:5–6): "If you will obey Me faithfully, etc., you shall be Mine, etc., and a holy nation," and also at the end of the Torah, it is said (Deuteronomy 26:18–19): "And ha-Shem has affirmed this day that you are His treasured people, etc., and that you shall be a holy nation." Because He did not promise us the holiness of the fear of sin, which is only reached by free will, but [rather] He promised immortality, which is absolute holiness, as it says (Sanhedrin 92a): "Just as the Holy One exists forever, so too will they exist forever," and it is also testified (Leviticus 11:45): "And you shall be holy, for I am holy." And this is so because He commanded that by likening [ourselves] to our Creator through morals and intelligibles, we shall make ourselves holy, because He is holy. And therefore, we shall be holy in perpetual happiness, as it says (ibid.): "And you shall be holy." And therefore, our Rabbanan—of blessed memory—enlightened us, saying (Yoma 39a): "A person who sanctifies himself a little, they sanctify him greatly. [If a person sanctifies himself] below, they sanctify him above. [If a person sanctifies himself] in this world, they sanctify him in the World-to-Come."

באמרו: »אשרי תבחר ותקרב« (תהלים ס״ה ה׳). וזה ייעד בראשית מתן תורה באמרו: »אם שמוע תשמעו וכו׳ אתם תהיו לי וכו׳ וגוי קדוש« (שמות י״ט ה׳-ו׳). וכן בסוף התורה באמרו: »וה׳ האמירך היום להיות לו לעם סגלה וכו׳ ולהיותך עם קדוש« (דברים כ״ו י״ח-י״ט). כי אמנם לא נדר לנו קדושת יראת חטא אשר לא תושג זולתי בבחירה בלבד. אבל נדר הנצחיות אשר הוא קדושה בהחלט באמרם: »מה קדוש לעולם קיים אף הם לעולם קיימים« (סנהדרין צ״ב א). וכן ייעד באמרו: »והייתם קדושים כי קדוש אני« (ויקרא י״א מ״ה). וזה כי צוה שנתקדש בהדמות לבוראנו במדות ובמושכלות כי קדוש הוא ובכן יקדשנו באישור נצחי באמרו: »והייתם קדושים« (שם). ולזה העירו רז״ל באמרם: »אדם מקדש עצמו מעט מקדשין אותו הרבה למטה מקדשין אותו למעלה בעולם הזה מקדשין אותו לעולם הבא« (יומא ל״ט א).

13. DE MORALITATE

§ 14 Fourteenth:
We will inquire whether the second perfection of the aforementioned human intellectual soul is attained only by human power and not by divine or natural power in any case.

And it seems, at the beginning of the inquiry, that this is impossible.

§ 14.1 [This is so,] because there is nothing that may be attained by a small power that a bigger and stronger power is not able to attain. And see: natural power, and all the more so divine power, is greater and stronger than human power. If so, it follows that this perfection that can possibly be attained by human power is necessarily [even] more fitting to be potentially attained by divine or natural power.

§ 14.2 Second, it seems that it is incongruous that the perfection of the intellectual soul may be attained by human power. And this is so because every natural activity—still more a divine one—is absolute perfection, [and does] not lack anything that is required for its existence, and the intellectual soul is a divine or natural activity. If so, it follows that it does not require an additional perfection that would be attained by human power. The necessity of this consequence is evident and so is the second part of the [antecedent] premise. The first part of it becomes clear from experience of what sense [perception] testifies about the majority of natural activities. And Aristotle explains this in *On the Soul* 3, text. 45:[a] "Nature does not do anything | in vain. And it enacts necessary things with perfection, except by way of monstrosity." And he explains the same in *Politics* 1 [text. 8]:[b] "Nature does nothing imperfect." From all this, it seems to become clear that the intellectual soul, since it is a divine or natural activity, is necessarily perfect. And therefore, it follows that it does not require any perfection that would be attained by a power besides this.

§ 14.3.1 And the contrary of all of this becomes clear in this way: because the things that happen to the few are not related to a natural power, still less to a divine power, and the second perfection of the intellectual soul is [only achieved] by a few. If so, it is not related to a natural power, still less to a divine power.

---

[a] *De an.* 3.12.434a31.   [b] *Pol.* 1.3.1256b.

§14 Quarto-decimo Dubitatur

Utrum intellective anime perfectio per humanam virtutem tantum acquiri contingat. Non autem per divinam vel naturalem virtutem,

et videtur quod non.

§14.1 Quia nihil datur fieri per debiliorem virtutem quin maius per fortiorem fieri possit, sed sic est quod tam Dei quam nature virtus est humana fortior, ergo intellectiva perfectio cum possit per humanam virtutem acquiri, fortius per naturalem nedum per divinam acquiri potest.

§14.2 Secundo arguitur sic: quilibet nature nedum Dei effectus est quid perfectum nihil, scilicet, deficiens horum que ad eius esse requiruntur. Intellectiva hominis anima est huiusmodi, ergo habet esse quid perfectum et per consequens non habet per humanam virtutem perfici. Consequentia patet similiter et antecedens quo ad secundam partem. Quo autem ad primam partem probatur discurrendo per plures nature effectus. Quare Pyilosophus in lib. *De Anima* tertij t.c. 45 ait: «Natura nihil facit ociosum et perfecte operatur in necessarijs sit in rebus monstruosis» et idem habet ab eodem in lib. *Polyticorum*, 1 ubi dicit: «Natura, enim, nihil fecisset imperfectum etc.» Adque sequi videtur ut intellectiva virtus cum sit Dei vel nature opus nulla indigeat ulteriori perfectione. Quare nullo pacto habet per humanam virtutem perfici.

§14.3.1 Ad oppositum vero arguit sic: que contingunt ut in paucioribus non sunt nature nedum Dei virtuti attribuenda. Intellective perfectio quo ad secundum actum est huiusmodi, ergo non est Dei vel nature virtuti attribuenda.

§14 Fourteenth,

it may be inquired whether the perfection of the intellectual soul can be attained by human power alone and not by divine or natural power.

And it seems that it cannot.

§14.1 Because nothing can be produced by a weaker power that cannot be produced by a stronger power. But in fact, it is true that divine power as well the power of nature are both stronger than human power. Therefore, intellectual perfection, which can be attained by the human faculties, can be attained in a stronger way by natural power, and even more so by divine power.

§14.2 Second, I would argue that every natural activity, and even more so every divine [activity], is perfect, meaning that there is nothing lacking that is required for its existence. The human intellectual soul is a such [a kind of activity]; therefore, it is perfect, and consequently, the intellectual soul does not require human power to be perfected. The consequence is evident and so is the second part of the antecedent. Moreover, the first part of the antecedent is proved in accordance with the majority of natural activities, as the Philosopher explicates in *On the Soul* 3, text. 45,[a] where he states: "Nature does not do anything in vain and it acts perfectly in the necessary things—except in the monstrous things," and similarly in *Politics* 1, [text. 8],[b] where he states: "Nature does nothing imperfect, etc." Furthermore, it seems to follow that the intellectual faculty, since it is a divine or natural activity, does not need additional perfection, and consequently, the intellectual soul does not require the human power to be perfected.

§14.3.1 On the contrary one argues that something that occurs infrequently may not be attributed to a natural force, all the more so with regard to divine power: The intellectual perfection that is [achieved by] the second act is of this kind. Therefore, it is not attributed to natural or divine power.

---

[a] *De an.* 3.12.434a31.   [b] *Pol.* 1.3.1256b.

§14.3.2 The consequence is evident, and so is the second part of the aforementioned [antecedent] premise, because there are [only a] few human individuals who perfect their intellectual soul through the perfection that is possible for it. The first part of this becomes clear in this way: because when the agent always acts in one way—and nothing hinders him—all his activities are [performed] in one way. If so, nature—or divine power—acts [in all] the individuals of every species in one way and nothing hinders [it], at least for the majority. It follows that its activities [i.e., of nature or divine power] are in one way at least for the majority, not only the few. And Aristotle explains this in *Physics* 2, text. 77:[a] "These organs and all the naturally generated [things] always exist the way they [usually] are, or at least in the majority [of cases]." And he explains the same ibid., [2], text. 78:[b] "And when he [i.e., the agent] is capable of doing that, he always does it, if nothing hinders him."

§14.4 Second, this becomes clear from the testimony of experience, because we have not heard until now, and it is not stated in the Scriptures of the Elders who came before us, that any individual human has attained the aforementioned perfection by divine or natural power without an endeavour of free will. If so, it seems to be incongruous that this perfection could be attained by divine or natural power, because if this was possible, it would be inconceivable that divine or natural power would be so miserly as to not grant this attainment to any of the human individuals in such a way that it would be transmitted to the [next] generation.

§14.5 And we answer, if so, to dispel [any] doubt about the aforementioned thesis, that the second perfection of the human intellectual soul is only attained by the power of human free will. And this is as follows: When he intends to liken himself to the Creator through cognition and action, and when a human individual does this to gain God's favour—may He be praised—then his soul will become perfect, in a certain way similar to God—may He be praised—and worthy of favour before Him, by serving [Him] out of love. And therefore, its portion of life will be approved, *like one who finds favour*;[c] like a judgement, *which sees the king's face*.[d] They find favour in His eyes, *those sitting first in the kingdom*.[e]

---

[a]*Phys.* 2.8.198b.   [b]*Phys.* 2.8.198b.   [c]Song 8:10.   [d]Est 1:14.   [e]Est 1:14.

§14.3.2 הנה חייוב התולדה הוא מבואר וגם כן החלק השני מההקדמה הנזכרת כי הנה מעט הם אישי האדם אשר תשלם נפשם השכלית בשלמות האפשר לה. אמנם החלק הראשון ממנה יתבאר באופן זה כי אמנם כשהפועל יפעל תמיד באופן אחד ולא יהיה לו מונע תהיינה כל פעולותיו באופן אחד אם כן בהיות הטבע או הכח האלהי פועל אישי כל מין על אופן אחד ואין לו מונע לפחות על הרוב יתחייב שתהיינה פעולותיו לפחות על הרוב באופן אחד לא על המעט בלבד וזה ביאר ארסטו' בספר השמע מאמר ב' פרק ע״ז[a] באמרו: »אלו האברים וכל הדברים ההווים בטבע נמצאים תמיד על הענין אשר הם בו או על הרוב.« וזה בעצמו ביאר שם פרק ע״ח באמרו: »וכאשר הוא מוכן לעשות כן הוא עושה תמיד אם לא יהיה לו מונע.«

§14.4 **שנית** יתבאר זה בעדות הנסיון כי אמנם לא שמענו עד כה ואין מגיד בכתבי ראשונים אשר היו לפנינו שאיזה איש מאישי האדם השיג את השלמות הנזכרת בכח אלהי או טבעי בלתי השתדלות בחיריי אם כן נראה שהוא נמנע שזה השלמות יושג בכח אלהי או טבעי כי אם היה איפשר זה לא יעלה על הדעת שהכח האלהי או הטבעי יהיו כל כך צרי עין שלא נתנו זאת ההשגה לשום איש מאישי האדם באופן שיסופר לדור.

§14.5 **נשיב** אם כן להתיר ספק החקירה הנזכרת שהשלמות השני לנפש השכלית האנושית לא יושג זולתי בכח אנושי בחיריי וזה כשיתכוין להדמות לבורא בעיון ובמעשה וכאשר יעשה זה איזה איש מאישי האדם להפיק רצון האל יתברך אז תהיה נפשו שלמה דומה בצד מה לאל יתברך וראויה שתהיה לרצון לפניו בעובדת מאהבה ובכן יאושר חלקה בחיים כמוצאת[b] שלום כמשפט רואי פני המלך המוצאים[c] חן בעיניו היושבים ראשונה במלכות.

---

[a]ע״ז] emend. Dunk.; כ״ז a; 77 b.   [b]במוצאת [כמוצאת a[corr]; [c]המוציאים [המוצאים a[corr];

§ 14.3.2 Consequentia patet similiter et antecedens quoad secundam partem. Quod autem ad primam partem probatur, quia discurrentes per plurima nature opera, invenimus: illam in horum | singulis saltem non impeditam (ut sepius) perfecte et uniformiter procedere, nedum divine virtutis opera que[a] nunquam impeditur, et per consequens illa que in paucioribus tantum fiunt non sunt nature nedum divine virtuti attribuenda. Quare in lib. *Physicorum* II, t.c.[b] 77 ait: «Ista enim membra et omnia que sunt facta per naturam sunt in eo que sunt ut semper aut in maiori parte etc.» et ibidem t.c. 78 ait: «Et sicut natus est ut agat agit nisi impediatur.»

§ 14.4 Secundo arguitur sic: nullus hucusque retulit quendam apparuisse. Qui huiusmodi intellective perfectionem scilicet quo ad actum secundum per nature vel Dei virtutem preter arbitrariam hominis diligentiam consecutum fuisse. Ergo non datur per divinam vel naturalem virtutem consequi. Consequentia tenet quia si hoc esset possibile inopinabile esset ut essent adeo avare ut non alicui saltem hoc esse concessum sentiremus.

§ 14.5 Ad dubium ergo respondetur: quod intellective perfectio nonnisi per arbitrarium hominis diligentiam consequi contingit. Qua, scilicet, quis Deo quodammodo assimilari intendens scientia in divinis et moralitate munitur. Quibus Deum respiciens eidem Deo tanquam benigno rem gratam facere intendendo. Redditur ipsa intellectiva Deo quodammodo similis et per consequens perfectior, et eidem Deo gratior[c] et per consequens felicior.

§ 14.3.2 The consequence is evident, as is the second part of the antecedent. Thus, the first part of the antecedent is proved because according to the majority of the activities in nature, we discovered | that what is not hindered, at least only in individual cases, frequently proceeds perfectly and uniformly, and even more so in the activity of divine power, which is never hindered, and consequently, those [activities] that occur in [only a] few cases may not be attributed to natural power, still less to divine power, as the Philosopher explains in the book *Physics* 2, text. 77,[a] where he states: "These organs and all things that are naturally generated are always the way they are, or [at least] in the majority [of cases], etc.," and similarly in *Physics* 2, text. 78,[b] where he states: "And like something which born to act it acts unless something hinders it."

§ 14.4 Second, it is argued: no one, until now, has been found to report of anyone who could attain intellectual perfection, meaning the second act [perfection], through divine or natural power without free will; therefore, intellectual perfection is not attained through divine or natural power. The consequence is evident, because if this was possible, then it would be inconceivable that divine and natural power would be so miserly that we would not have encountered anyone who had received this [perfection].

§ 14.5 To dispel any doubt, I will reply: intellectual perfection can only be attained by human free will. This occurs when someone intends to be assimilated to God through morality and through knowledge of the divine things. With this, someone who serves God will intend to seek forgiveness from the good Lord, and then his intellectual soul will seek to be similar to God and consequently, [he will be] more perfect, grateful to God, and consequently happier.

---

[a] que] coni. Copp.; qne b.   [b] II, t.c.] emend. Copp.; om. b; מאמר ב׳ פרק ע״ז a.   [c] gratior] b[corr]; grata b.

[a] *Phys.* 2.8.198b.   [b] *Phys.* 2.8199a.

§14.6 And to the opponent's argument, first, saying that all that is possible for a weak power is undoubtedly possible for a strong power, we answer: this assumption is correct for those actions for which nothing is required besides strength of the efficient power, because then the consideration of the power is with regard to its greatness or smallness. It will necessarily follow that the aforementioned assumption about the power of that first intelligible, which says that the whole is greater than the part, from which [it] necessarily follows that the whole includes the quantity of the part and more, is correct. And so: in the quality of the greater power, there exists an amount of the quality of that power that is smaller than it and more. And therefore, it follows that when the action is possible thanks to the amount of the quality of a small power, it will be more appropriate that it will be possible thanks to the power that is greater than it, which includes the [afore]mentioned [smaller] amount and more. But for the actions that require a limited proportion between the agent and the affected, this assumption is not correct. For when we say that one amount of heat will [suffice for] cooking something limited, it therefore does not follow that double the amount of heat would [suffice for] cooking the same [quantity] or [even] more, because perhaps they will melt or burn it or it will not cook at all due to the lack of a limited proportion that is necessary for the action of that cooking. And also, the perfection of the intellectual soul requires a property of morality that aims at good deeds in order to resemble the Creator, may He be praised. It therefore follows that all of this happens through individual free will and not through a necessitating divine or natural power. Therefore, it is not correct—as it is in this aforementioned premise in the way that we explained—that the attainment of the aforementioned perfection of the soul that is possible for the human individual power would be even more possible for a divine or natural power, for this combines two parts of a contradiction, which cannot both be correct at once. And this is because, insofar as the attained is the perfection that is willed by God—may He be praised—it needs to be [attained] through [human] free will, and if it was [something] attained by divine or natural power, it would not occur through [human] free will. And this is incongruous.

§14.7 And to the second argument that the opponent brings—that if perfection of the intellectual soul was attained by a human individual power adding to the first perfection [of the soul] that is already [in man], it would follow that the natural or divine power that brought forth [the soul] would have performed a deficient action—we answer: a lack in the aforementioned soul could be stated

§14.6 ועל טענת החולק ראשונה באמרו שכל מה שיוכל עליו הכח החלוש יוכל עליו יותר בלי ספק הכח החזק ממנו. נשיב שזאת ההנחה תצדק באותן הפעולות אשר לא יבוקש בהן זולתי חוזק הכח הפועל. כי אז בהיות הבחינה על הכח אצל רב גדלו ומיעוטו יתחייב בהכרח שתצדק ההנחה הנזכרת מכח אותו המושכל ראשון שיאמר בו שהכל גדול מן החלק אשר ממנו יתחייב שבכל יהיה כמות החלק ויותר ממנו. וכן באיכות הכח הגדול נמצא שיעור איכות הכח הקטן ממנו ויותר. ומזה יתחייב שכאשר תהיה הפעולה איפשרית בשיעור איכות הכח הקטן יהיה יותר ראוי שתהיה איפשרית בכח הגדול ממנו אשר בו השיעור הנזכר ויותר. אמנם בפעולות אשר יבוקש בהן יחס מוגבל בין הפועל והמתפעל לא תצדק ההנחה הנזכרת. כי אמנם כשנאמר שמעלה אחת בחום תבשל איזה בישול באיזה דבר מוגבל. לא יתחייב מזה ששתי מעלות בחום יבשלו בו אותו הבשול או יותר כי אולי יתיכוהו או ישרפוהו ולא יבשלוהו כלל להעדר היחס המוגבל הצריך לפעלת אותו הבשול. וכמו כן בהיות שלשלמות הנפש השכלית תבוקש תכונת מעלות המדות מכוונת אל המעשים הטובים להדמות לבורא ית׳. ובכן יתחייב שיהיה כל זה בבחירה אישיית לא בכח אלהי או טבעי מכריח לזה לא תצדק בכמו זה ההנחה הנזכרת באופן שנאמר שבהיות השגת שלמות הנפש הנזכרת איפשרית בכח אנושי אישיי תהיה איפשרית יותר בכח אלהי או טבעי כי אמנם היה זה מקבץ שני חלקי הסותר אשר לא יצדקו יחדיו בשום פנים. וזה כי מצד היות המושג הוא השלמות הנרצה לאל יתברך יתחייב שיהיה בחיריי. ומצד היותו מושג בכח אלהי או טבעי היה בלתי בחיריי וזה לא יתכן.

§14.7 ועל הטענה השנית שטען החולק באמרו שאם יושג שלמות לנפש השכלית בכח אנושי אישיי נוסף על אשר מקודם יתחייב שהכח הטבעי או האלהי אשר המציא אותה עשה פעולה חסרה. נשיב כי אמנם החסרון בנפש הנזכרת יאמר על אחד משני פנים. ראשונה על

§ 14.6 Ad argumenta vero et primo quo ad primum respondetur: quod propositio qua dicitur quod quicquid potest debilior virtus idem et fortius habet virtus illa fortior posse. De his actionibus tantum verificatur ad quas virtutis fortitudo tantum requiritur. Tunc enim cum huiusmodi virtutis posse secundum maius et minus tantum consideretur, sequitur quidem prefate propositionis verificatio—per illam maximam qua dicitur quod totum est maius sua parte—et per consequens ipsum totum cui pars inest habet necessario posse quicquid potest sua pars et aliquid ultra. Remissior enim virtus in intensiori tanquam eiusdem pars contineri videtur. Quare cum detur aliquid posse per remissiorem virtutem fieri idem necessario et ultra per intensiorem fieri posset. Sed non verificatur de illis actionibus in quibus requiritur limitata proportio inter agentem et patientem currens. Quare non sequitur ut cum aliquis caloris gradus aliquod coquendum perfecte coquat, ut calor illo intensior sive fortior idem perfectius coquat, immo contingit ut tanquam improportionato nullo pacto illud coquat, sed potius comburat. Quare idem contingit de illa moralitate[a] que habet ad intellective perfectionem concurrere, illa enim habet per nos sponte fieri nullo pacto ut ducti tali enim nos Deo sponte benefactori et benigne facienti quodammodo assimilabimur. Quare de tali actione non verificatur illa propositio ut cum possit fieri per humanam virtutem similiter et fortius[b] possit fieri per divinam vel naturalem tanquam intensiores, immo per illas nul|lo pacto fieri contigit. Quia deesset illa conditio que principaliter requiritur, que, scilicet, est: ut sponte operemur, vel opus sponte et benigne intendamus quo tantum Deo sponte benefactori assimilari possumus.

§ 14.7 Ad secundum vero argumentum quo, scilicet, dicitur: quod si intellectiva haberet per humanam virtutem perfici sequeretur ut Dei vel nature opus hac perfectione[c] indigens esset quid imperfectum. Respondetur quod du-

§ 14.6 In response to this argument, I will reply: the assumption in which we said that whatever is possible for a weaker power is also possible for a stronger power has been proven. This is true when [we take into account] the actions for which nothing is required besides efficient power. Therefore, since the force of the power is considered in terms of more and less, it would follow that the aforementioned assumption is true, in accordance with the statement "the whole is greater than the part," and consequently, the whole includes its part and the whole will necessarily be its parts and something more. Therefore, it seems that a weaker power will be included in a stronger power because it is a part of it. Therefore, if something has been produced by a weaker power, it can necessarily be produced by a stronger power. But this is not true with respect to actions for which a limited analogy [lit. proportion] between the agent and the recipient is required. Therefore, it does not follow that every level of heat, when it cooks something, will cook perfectly, [or] that a more intense or stronger heat will cook more perfectly than the other level of heat. However, it might happen that a disproportionate level of heat does not cook, but rather burns. And the same occurs with the immortality [of the soul], which corresponds to the perfection of the intellect. Immortality can never be achieved by means of free will alone. It only occurs when our free will is led by the goodwill of God and by morality. Nevertheless, this assumption is not true with respect to some actions: something that is possible for human power can be possible at the same or to a greater degree for divine or natural power because these [powers] are greater than it. Indeed, it cannot be limited to just them, | because the principle precondition is missing: either we act through free will, or we intend the action as something free and good because we can become similar to the good Lord.

§ 14.7 In response to the second argument, saying that if the intellectual soul can be perfected by human power, it would follow that the divine or natural action lacks perfection and will thus be imperfect, one should reply: there is a

---

[a] moralitate] b[corr]; immortalitate b.   [b] fortius] coni. COPP.; fortuis b.
[c] perfectione] coni. COPP.; perfectone b.

in one of two cases. First, a lack of its first perfection, and it not correct [to assert] this kind of lack in regard to it at all, since in the first perfection, it is absolutely as perfect as possible in order to be disposed for the second perfection. Second, a lack insofar as it lacks the second perfection. And this is indeed correct for it, but it is not related to a lack in the action of the agent, because the agent's intention is such that it [i.e., the human intellectual soul] is entirely disposed for the attainment of the second perfection, which cannot be attained by something other than individual free will, as became clear.

§ 14.8.1 And this teaches [us] (Leviticus 19:2): "You shall be holy, for I, ha-Shem, your God, am holy"; that is to say, they are sanctified by magnificent actions through [human] free will, | such as: "I am holy"—[and] by magnificent actions through [divine] free will, which are compassion and truth, as it says (Psalm 25:10): "All ha-Shem's paths are compassion and truth." And this is so that you will liken yourselves to Me in a certain way.

§ 14.8.2 And this teaches [us] (Deuteronomy 10:12): "What does ha-Shem your God demand of you? Only this: to fear ha-Shem, your God, to walk only in His paths and to love [Him]"; that is to say, it is not in His hands, since He wills that all of this is up to your free will [alone], as it says (Berakhot 33b): "Everything is in the hands of [the] heavens except for the fear of [the] heavens." And it continues and says (Deuteronomy 10:13) "for your good"; that is to say, see what His request is in all these, for His request is not for His own necessity, but it is because He wants what is good for you. And if so, it is appropriate that you too will do all this to gain His favour, as it says (Avot 2:4): "Do His will as though it were your will."

plex est actus. Primus, scilicet, quo prime insunt propositiones et liberum arbitrium divinitus situm. Secundus vero est ille actus qui mediante primo acquiritur. Quo ergo ad primum actum qui Deo vel nature spectat est quidem quid perfectum. Ad secundum vero actum nonnisi per liberi arbitrij diligentiam pervenire contingit ut supra.

§ 14.8.1 Quare Sacrum Levitici Documentum cap. 19 [19:2] hoc demostrative docens ait: «Sancti estote quia ego sanctus sum etc.» Quibus precipiens docet: quod nobis convenit moralia ibidem precepta observare, ut eidem Deo Sancto et sponte benefactori quodammodo nos similes reddamus.

§ 14.8.2 Et idem docet in lib. Deuteronomij cap. 10 [10:12] ubi dicit: «Et nunc Israel quid Dominus Deus tuus petit a te nisi ut timeas Dominum Deum tuum et ambules in vijs suis etc.» inferens quod hoc non contingit nisi per te sponte fieri, quare: «a te petit» ut id sponte facias, ubi subdit dicens [Deut 10:13]: «ut bene sit tibi» inferens quod cum pateat quod finis per huiusmodi petitionem intentus nil aliud sit quam: «ut bene sit tibi» tanquam benigne tuam perfectionem volens ipse enim nullo pacto indiget tibi.[a] Cui ergo eiusdem vestigia sequenti ut eidem quodammodo simil eris convenit quidem ut benigne in tuis actionibus te geras. Quibus eidem Deo rem gratam facias tuam perfectionem benigne volenti.

two-fold action. First, the earlier propositions and the free will are divinely placed; second, the action is acquired in virtue of the first proposition only. Furthermore, the first action is due to God or nature and it is perfect; the second activity is due to free will, as mentioned above.

§ 14.8.1 Moreover, the Holy Book of Leviticus (19:2) teaches [the same thing] by means of demonstration, saying: "You shall be holy because I am Holy, etc." Prescribing those things that the [Holy] Book teaches: it is better for us to observe moral commandments when we seek to assimilate ourselves to Holy God.

§ 14.8.2 And the [Holy] Book of Deuteronomy (10:12) teaches the same thing, saying: "And now, Israel, what does the Lord God require of you, but that you fear the Lord your God, and walk in His ways, etc.," which means that this only occurs through free will, since "He requires [it] of you," which means that you will choose freely. Afterwards, [it says] (10:13): "That it may be well with you [...] for your good," which means that the intended end is nothing more than "that it may be well with you," since He desires your perfection even if He does not require you. Furthermore, you should follow in his footsteps, for you will be similar to Him, and you should comport yourself kindly in your actions. Through these things, you will attain the goodwill of God, who desires your perfection.

---

[a] tibi] b[corr]; tui b.

§15 Fifteenth:
We will inquire whether the celestial bodies exist for the sake of the inferior existents; namely, the generables and corruptibles.

And it seems that this is not at all conceivable.

§15.1 [This is so] as Averroes explains in *The Incoherence of the Incoherence* 14, first investigation:[a] "If the first intention of the movement of the spheres was for the benefit of the inferior existents, it would follow then that the noble [existents] existed for the sake of the abominable [existents]. And this is false," because the celestial bodies are—according to all the Sages—nobler than all the rest of the bodies. And therefore, it is not suitable [to say] that they exist for the sake of the abominable [bodies] among them.

§15.2.1 Second, it becomes clear in this way that it is incongruous: if the celestial bodies existed for the sake of the generables and corruptibles—while the generation of every single individual among them means the corruption of another of their individuals, and accordingly the corruption of every single individual among them means the generation of another individual among them, as sense [perception] testifies and as Aristotle explains in *On Generation and Corruption* 1, text. 21[b]—[then] it would follow that the forth-bringer and creator of existence as a whole, who is absolutely wise, as testified by his activities, intended a very low and futile purpose, and this would be incongruous. But that this follows is evident, because none of the corruptible things is permanent in any case, not even for a single hour. And this is so because immediately upon arriving at the purpose, its growth will immediately turn into decline and corruption, as sense [perception] testifies for many of them, especially for the species of plants and the species of animals.

§15.2.2 And although the movement of generation is recurringly performed in order that the genders and species will endure by it, this does not at all pertain | to the existence of existents outside the soul, because genders and species only exist within the soul, in no way outside it, as Aristotle explains in *Metaphysics* 1, text. 26,[c] 27,[d] and 44.[e] And in this way, it therefore follows that God—may He be praised—who is nobler than all besides Him, would—God forbid!—in His works resemble a potter who always makes a certain vessel perfectly and immediately breaks it and makes another form from its matter, then immediately

---

[a] Cf. *Incoherence* 293. [b] *Gen. corr.* 1.3.319a. [c] *Metaph.* 1.9.990b.
[d] *Metaph.* 1.9.990b. [e] *Metaph.* 1.9.992a–b.

§15 Quinto-decimo

Dubitatur Utrum orbium et siderum corpora habeant esse ad mortalium opportunitates, scilicet, ad genitorum reciprocationes et conservationes fiendas.

Et videtur quod non.

§15.1 Ratione et auctoritate Aven R. in lib. *Destructio des.*, disputatione XIV, dubio primo ubi dicit: «Si enim prima huius motus intentio fuisset pro inferiorum utilitatibus tunc esset nobilius pro viliori, quod est falsum» quia celi iuxta omnes sapientes nobiliores corporibus reliquis sunt quare non decet ut sint pro vilioribus.

§15.2.1 Secundo arguitur sic: si orbes essent ad mortalium opportunitates, quorum unius generatio est alterius corruptio, prout sensu patet et habetur a Phylosopho in lib. *De Generatione* primi t.c. 21. Sequeretur ut horum nobilium agentis vel illorum ordinatoris sive Creatoris intentus finis esset quid vilissimum et penitus vanum: quod est inopinabile. Quod autem hoc sequatur patet, quia nihil mortalium est permanens, itaque neque | per tempus permanet in eadem dispositione, immo cum primum ad augumenti finem pervenerit statim incipit procedere ad corruptionem per declinationem tunc incipientem, prout in pluribus eorum saltem animatorum sensu patet.

§15.2.2 Neque horum reciprocatio quicquam conserit[a] alicui eorum que extra animam existunt, genera enim et species que dicuntur permanere nihil sunt eorum que extra anima existunt. Immo non habent esse nisi per operationem intellectus, prout habetur a Phylosopho *Metaphysicorum* primi t.c. 26 et t.c. 27 et t.c. 44. Quare videtur ut horum nobilium agentis vel ordinatoris sive productoris finis in tali opere intentus et per consequens in tota universi machina, esset quid simile operi figuli semper testatea vasa perfecte facentis, et illa statim destruentis et ex illorum materia alia vasa facientis, et sic semper et circula-

§15 Fifteenth,

it may be inquired whether the planets and the stars exist for the benefit of human beings; that is, for the cycles of generation and activities of conservation.

And it seems that they do not.

§15.1 [First, I would argue] according to the argument and authority of Averroes in *The Incoherence of the Incoherence* 14, first doubt,[a] where he states: "If the first intention of this movement [of the spheres] was for the benefit of the inferior existents, the noble beings would exist for the sake of the lower beings, which is false." Because according to all the sages, the heavens are nobler than the rest of the bodies, and it is not appropriate to say that they [the celestial bodies] exist for the benefit of the lower beings.

§15.2.1 Second, I would argue: if the spheres existed for the benefit of human beings, therefore the generation of one of them would correspond to the corruption of the other. As the senses testify and as the Philosopher explains in *On Generation and Corruption* 1, text. 21,[b] it would follow that the intended purpose of the agent of the noble things, who is their arranger or creator, would be something most base and extremely vain, which is incongruous. Consequently, nothing mortal is permanent, therefore nothing | remains in the same disposition over time; indeed, when there is an increase, there is therefore also a corruption through deterioration, as the senses testify for many beings, especially the animals.

§15.2.2 Moreover, their alternation brings together something existing outside the soul; in fact, genera and species, which are said to endure forever, do not exist outside the soul. Indeed, this kind of being exists only by means of intellectual operation, as the Philosopher explains in *Metaphysics* 1, text. 26,[c] text. 27,[d] and text. 44.[e] It seems that in this kind of activity, and consequently in the whole machinery of the universe, the intended purpose of the agent of the noble things or their arranger or producer would resemble the activity of a potter who always created perfect vessels out of clay, but immediately destroyed them and created other vessels from their matter, with this

---

[a] conserit] coni. COPP.; consert b.

[a] Cf. *Incoherence* 293.   [b] *Gen. corr.* 1.3.319a.   [c] *Metaph.* 1.9.990b.
[d] *Metaph.* 1.9.990b.   [e] *Metaph.* 1.9.992a–b.

breaks the second [vessel] and uses the matter for the third form. And a maker like this would undoubtedly be considered a fool and a stupid person. God forbid! [to say] about God—may He be praised—that something like this may come from Him, because all His ways are justice and all His works, through their form and their shape and their order and their perpetuity, tell [us] about [His] elevated wisdom, which is wondrous in our eyes.

§ 15.3.1 But the contrary of this—that is to say that the existence of the celestial bodies is intended for the sake of the existence of lower generables and corruptibles—becomes clear in this way: because the celestial bodies exist for the sake of their movements, and their movements are for the sake of the movement of generation and corruption. If so, the celestial bodies exist for the sake of the movement of generation and corruption, which is [intended] for the existence of the generables and corruptibles. And therefore, it follows that the aforementioned celestial bodies exist for the sake of the generables and corruptibles. The necessity of the conclusions is evident.

§ 15.3.2 And the [antecedent] premise—in which we said that the spheres exist for the sake of their movements—becomes clear from a proof made by Averroes, which he brings in the *Treatise on the Substance of the Celestial Sphere*, ch. 2: "Some of the agents are temporally prior to their activity. And every agent that is [located] in the [sublunary] globe of this existence is [of] this [kind]. And some of them are prior to their activity temporally and naturally. And this is [so in case of] the [highest celestial] sphere, to which time is subsequent; and [also for] the agent of the sphere, which created it with the properties that are necessary to achieve the final purpose for the sake of which it exists. And many who do not know that this is the opinion of Aristotle say about this that he did not say 'efficient cause,' but only 'moving cause.' And this is highly disgraceful. And there is no doubt that the forth-bringer [i.e., its efficient cause] is [also] its mover, because whoever moves it by a movement designated for it is [also] the one who bestowed upon it the dispositions prior to it, by which it achieves the movement designated for it,"[a] and he explains the same, ibid., ch. 4: "The sphere exists for the sake of its movement. And if the heavens were destroyed, then the movement of the lower existents would also be destroyed."[b] With all these words, he explains that the spheres, and also the stars, which are part of the spheres, exist for these movements and that the

---

[a] Cf. *Sub. orb.* 85–86. [b] Cf. *Sub. orb.* 117.

בחמרו צורה שלשית. והנה יוצר כזה היה נחשב לאויל ומהביל בלי ספק חלילה לאל יתברך שתצא כזאת מלפניו כי כל דרכיו משפט וכל מעשיו בצורתם ותבניתם וסדרם וקיומם יורה על חכמה מאד נעלה היא נפלאת בעינינו.

§ 15.3.1 אמנם הפך זה רצוני לומר שמציאות הגרמים השמיימים הוא מכוון לתכלית מציאות השפלים ההוים ונפסדים יתבאר באופן זה. כי אמנם מציאות הגרמים השמיימים הוא לתכלית תנועתם והנה תנועותם הם לתכלית תנועת ההויה וההפסד. אם כן מציאות הגרמים השמיימים הוא לתכלית תנועת ההויה וההפסד ההוה למציאות ההוים ונפסדים. ומזה יתחייב שמציאות הגרמים השמיימים הנזכרים הוא לתכלית מציאות ההוים ונפסדים. הנה חיוב התולדות הוא מבואר.

§ 15.3.2 וההקדמה במה שאמרנו שמציאות הגלגלים הוא לתכלית תנועותם יתבאר בראיית אבן רשד אשר הביא בספר עצם הגלגל פרק ב׳ באמרו: »קצת מן הפועלים קודם לפעולתו בזמן. וזה הוא כל פועל אשר בכדור זה המציאות. וקצתם קודם לפעולתו בזמן ובטבע וזה הוא הגלגל אשר ימשך אליו הזמן. ופועל הגלגל רצוני לומר אשר העשה אותו בתכונות הכרחיות להשיג התכלית אשר בעבורו נמצא ורבים אשר לא ידעו שזה דעת ארסטו׳ אמרו עליו שלא אמר ‹סבה פועלת› אבל אמר ‹הסבה המניעה› בלבד וזה היה מגונה מאד. ואין ספק שהממציא אותו הוא המניע אותו כי המניע אותו בתנועה המיוחדת לו הוא אשר נתן לו קודם ההכנות אשר בם הוא משיג את התנועה המיוחדת לו עד כאן לשונו.« וזה בעצמו באר שם פרק ד׳ באמרו: »הגלגל הוא נמצא בשביל תנועתו. ואם השמים היו אובדים גם כן תנועת הנמצאים השפלים« עד כאן לשונו. הנה בכל דבריו אלה באר שהגלגלים וכמו כן הכוכבים שהם חלקי הגלגלים נמצאים בשביל התנועות וכי מציאות התנועות הוא תכלית מציאות הגלגלים וחלקיהם ועל זה הביא ראיה מהכונתיהם ההכרחיות אל התנועה אשר מהם התבאר שמציאותם הוא בשביל התנועה. כי אמנם יעידו

riter reciprocantis; qui, scilicet, figulus demens proculdubio et penitus insanus reputaretur. Cuius oppositum apparet in singulis eiusdem ordinatoris sive Creatoris operibus, in quorum artificio ordine et conservatione summa eiusdem apparet sapientia.

§ 15.3.1 Ad oppositum arguitur sic: orbium et syderum corpora habent esse ad suos proprios motus tanquam ad finem, sed sic est quod ipsi motus ad mortalium opportunitates fiunt tanquam ad finem. Ergo orbium et syderum corpora habent esse ad mortalium opportunitates tanquam ad finem.

§ 15.3.2 Consequentia patet et antecedens probatur. Et primo quo ad primam partem, ratione et auctoritate Aven R. in *Tractatu de Substantia Orbis* cap. 2 ubi dicit: «Sed in genere agentium quoddam est prius tempore actu, et est omne quod est in sphera huius mundi. Quoddam est prius naturaliter et tempore et est orbis quem sequitur tempus et agens orbem scilicet faciens[a] ipsum in dispositionibus necessarijs in inveniendo finem propter quem fiunt. Et cum ignoraverunt hoc quidam de opinione Aristotelis, dixerunt ipsum non dicere causam agentem sed moventem et illud fuit valde absurdum. Et non est dubium in hoc quod agens ipsum est movens ipsum, quod enim movet illud motu proprio illi est illud quod largitur illi dispositiones per quas acquirit motum eidem proprium etc.» et idem infert ibidem cap. 4 ubi dicit: «Celum est propter suum motum, et si celum destrueretur motus entium inferiorum destrueretur etc.» Quibus aperte docet quod orbes et per consequens sidera que sunt eorundem orbium partes, habent esse propter suos motus fiendos tanquam ad finem,

happening constantly and perpetually. Without a doubt, one would consider this potter foolish and deeply stupid, but the contrary seems to be evident in the activities of the [divine] arranger or the creator; his highest wisdom is evident in every activity concerning the order and conservation [of his creatures].

§ 15.3.1 On the contrary it is to argue that the bodies of the spheres and the stars exist for their own movements, which is for a final purpose: the movements exist for the benefit of human beings, which is the final purpose. Therefore, the bodies of the spheres and the stars exist for the benefit of human beings, which is the final purpose.

§ 15.3.2 The consequence is evident and the first part of the antecedent is proved according to the argument and authority of Averroes in the *Treatise on the Substance of the Celestial Sphere*, ch. 2, where he states: "But in the class of agents, a certain one is temporally prior to the activity, and this is the agent that is in the sphere of the world. And another agent is naturally and temporally prior and this is the agent of the sphere, to which time is subsequent, and the agent of the sphere, which made it with dispositions that are necessary to achieve the purpose for whose sake it exists. And many who do not know that this is Aristotle's opinion say about this: he did not say 'efficient cause,' but only 'moving cause,' which is incongruous. And there is no doubt that this agent is also the mover, because [the one] who moves it through a specified [designated] movement is also [the one] who grants the dispositions by which it achieves the movement."[a] And he also explains this in ibid., ch. 4, where he states: "The heavens exist for the sake of their movement. And if the movement of the heavens was destroyed, the movement of the lower existents would also be destroyed, etc."[b] With these [words], [Averroes] teaches [us] that the spheres and consequently the stars, which are part of the spheres, exist for the sake of their own move-

---

[a] faciens] b^{corr}; feciens b.

[a] Cf. *Sub. orb.* 85–86. [b] Cf. *Sub. orb.* 117.

existence of these movements is the final purpose of the existence of the spheres and their parts. And he brought a proof of this [derived] from their necessary dispositions for movement, by which it became clear that they exist for movement because their shape | and the measurements of their quantity testify this, as they are determined by a hair's breadth in such a way that they touch each other, but do not prevent each other from movement. And there is no vacuum and no other body between them. And al-Ġazālī and Averroes seem to explain the same thing, according to what seems to be Averroes's statement in *The Incoherence of the Incoherence* 9, third investigation: "We say that it is appropriate to wonder about the words of this man—al-Ġazālī—because he referred to the Philosopher when he said that they [i.e., the [materialist] philosophers] cannot state [that there is] an agent besides the celestial body, because they would have to answer by one principle, which they refute. And this is so because the spheres are determined by specific measurements by a differentiating cause, although it is possible that they could have measurements of quantity other than these." And he continues, saying, ibid.: "Indeed, the philosophers in this place, by the issue of this determination, intend [to declare] that wisdom bestows upon the existent everything that is in it by its nature. And that is the 'final cause,' because among the philosophers, there is no quality and no quantity in any existent whose existence is not generated from the aforementioned wisdom, because if there was a quality or a quantity whose existence was not [generated] from the aforementioned wisdom in the created [things], it would follow that [something] was attributed to the first creator that is not appropriate to be attributed to an inferior material artisan." And he continues, saying, ibid.: "It is evident, if so, that existence has a wise and understanding agent from which the existents receive their order."[a] These words of his inform [us] that the measurements of the determined quantities that exist in the celestial bodies inform [us] about a final purpose that is intended by a certain intending agent. And since there is no activity that is subsequent to the measurements of the quantity and shapes of the spheres besides the movement, it becomes clear, if so, that the final purpose intended by the measurements of their quantity and shape is the movement. And therefore, it follows that the spheres and their stars exist for the sake of the movement. And this is what we wanted to explain.

---

[a] Cf. *Incoherence* 248–249.

et hoc videtur probari per illorum dispositiones ad motus necessarios, et per consequens ad illorum esse intentas, huiusmodi autem dispositiones sunt sicut horum quantitates et figure punctualiter[a] limitate, itaque sunt contigui et non impediunt se invicem a motu neque inter eos habet esse vacuum vel aliud corpus. Et idem videtur Algazalem et Aven R. sentire in lib. *Destructio destru.*, disputatione IX, dubio 3 ubi Aven R. ait: «Dicemus nos quod verba huius hominis sunt ad|miranda ipse enim obijcit phyosophis quodam argumento dicens, quod ipsi nequeunt asserere efficiens preter corpus celeste, quia indigent responsione cuiusdam radicis quam ipsi negant, videlicet quod celi appropriantur in proprijs mensuris ratione et causa appropriantis licet alias magnitudines habere possent etc.» subdit ibidem dicens: «Sed phylosophi in hoc loco intendunt per dictam appropriationem, quod sapientia inferat in effectu illud quod habet de sua natura et hec est causa finalis, apud phylosophos enim nulla est quantitas neque qualitas in aliquo entium que non sit propter suam sapientiam etc.» Quibus inferre videtur quod limitate celestium quantitates sint ad finem ab efficiente intentum. Cum autem nullam videatur actionem ad orbium quantitates horumque figuras sequi preter motum, sequitur quidem ut finis per horum quantitates et figuras intentus sit ipse motus quod est intentum.

ment, which is their final purpose. Therefore, this seems to be proved by their necessary dispositions to movement and consequently to their existence, because the dispositions are their measurements and their shapes, which are precisely limited. They are therefore in contact with each other and do not prevent each other from movement, and between them, there is no vacuum and no other body. And al-Ġazālī and Averroes explain this in *The Incoherence of the Incoherence* 9, third doubt, where Averroes states: "We say that it is appropriate to wonder about the words of this man, because | he cites the Philosopher when he said that they refuse to state [that there is] an agent besides the celestial body, because they will have to answer with a single principle, which they refute. And this is so, because the heavens are endowed with determined measurements by a determinative cause, although it is possible that they could have other measurements of quantity, etc.," and he continues: "Indeed, in this place, the philosophers, by the issue of this determination, are intending [to declare] that the wisdom bestows upon the existent all that is in it by its nature. And that is the 'final cause,' because among the philosophers, there is no quality and no quantity in any existent whose reality is not generated from the mentioned wisdom, etc."[a] With these [words], Averroes explains that the limited quantities of the celestial [bodies] exist for an intended final purpose through an efficient cause. Since there is no activity that is subsequent to the measurements of the quantity of the sphere and their shapes besides the movement, it would follow that the intended final purpose of their quantities and shapes is their movement. And this is what we wanted to explain.

---

[a] punctualiter] coni. COPP.; punctualitar b.

[a] Cf. *Incoherence* 248–249.

§15.3.3 But the second part of our aforementioned antecedent [premise], where we said that the movement of the spheres is intended for the need[s] of the inferior corruptibles, becomes clear in this way: because movement is an imperfect activity, progressing step by step towards perfection, which is generated by it. And this is the case in the [Aristotelian] category of substance, as in the category of quantity, quality, and place, as Averroes explains in [the Commentary on] *Physics* 3, text. 4,[a] and others. And since the generation of any perfection in all of these [categories] is not be achieved in the celestial bodies through the movement of the spheres, it follows that its final purpose is to achieve a certain perfection in them in the inferior generables and corruptibles. And therefore, it follows that they exist for the need[s] of the generables and corruptibles. And this is what we wanted to explain.

§15.3.4 But what we said—that the movement of the spheres does not cause any of the aforementioned perfections in the celestial bodies—is evident, because neither a change in substance nor in quality nor in quantity nor in place will occur to them, because neither according to whole nor to the part will [anything] be moved from the place in which they have been remaining ever since.

56ᵛ §15.4.1 Second, what we said—that the final purpose of the existence of the celestial bodies is the existence of the inferior corruptibles—becomes clear in this way: because for the generation of the species of the corruptibles, especially those that contain many different organs, material dispositions designated for the forms of those species are needed, [as well as] for the generation of those dispositions that require determined measurements [lit. degrees] of heat generated by the movements of the celestial bodies. If so, the celestial bodies, which exist for the sake of their movement, as has become clear above, exist for the sake of the existence of the inferior corruptibles.

§15.4.2 The consequence is evident, because if the aforementioned bodies did not exist for the need[s] of the aforementioned generated [things] by the order of an intending agent, [then] it would therefore follow that no intention existed regarding the corruptibles and their forthbringer, [and] that the matter that is common to all of them would obtain dispositions in the form of designated measurements in accordance with the need[s] of every single species of corruptibles. And this, if so, would happen by chance, as Aristotle explains in *Physics* 2, text. 51,[b]

---

[a] Cf. *Phys.* 3.1.200b.   [b] *Phys.* 2.5.197a.

§15.3.3 אמנם החלק השני מהקדמתנו הנזכרת באמרנו שתנועת הגלגלים מכוונת לצורך השפלים הנפסדים יתבאר באופן זה כי אמנם התנועה היא פעלה בלתי שלמה מתנהלת חלק אחר חלק אל השלמות אשר יתהווה בה. וזה, במאמר העצם או במאמר הכמה או באיכות[a] או במקום כאשר ביאר אבן רשד בספר השמע מאמר ג׳ פרק ד׳ וזולתו ובהיות שבתנועת הגלגלים לא יושג הוויית איזה שלמות מכל אלה בגרמים השמימיים יתחייב שתהיה תכליתה להשיג איזה שלמות מהם בשפלים ההווים ונפסדים ומזה יתחייב שמציאותם הוא לצורך ההווים ונפסדים וזה הוא מה שרצינו לבאר.

§15.3.4 אמנם מה שאמרנו שתנועת הגלגלים לא תסבב שום אחד מהשלמויות הנזכרים בגרמים השמימיים הוא מבואר כי אמנם לא יקרה בהם השתנות בעצם ולא באיכות ולא בכמות ולא במקום כי לא כפי הכל ולא כפי החלק יתנועע אל המקום אשר ינוחו בו זמן מה.

56ᵛ §15.4.1 **שנית** יתבאר זה שאמרנו שתכלית מציאות הגרמים השמימיים הוא מציאות השפלים הנפסדים ויתבאר באופן זה. כי אמנם להוויית מיני הנפסדים בפרט אותם אשר בהם כלים מכלים שונים יצטרכו הכנות חמרים מיוחדות לצורות אותם המינים ולהוויית אותם ההכנות יצטרכו מדרגות חום מוגבלות מתהוות בתנועות הגרמים השמימיים. אם כן מציאות הגרמים השמימיים אשר הוא לתכלית תנועותיהם כמו שהתבאר למעלה הוא לתכלית מציאות השפלים הנפסדים.

§15.4.2 הנה חיוב התולדה הוא מבואר כי אם לא היה מציאות הגרמים הנזכרים לצרכי ההוויות הנזכרות בסדור פועל מכוין לזה היה מתחייב שבלתי שום כוונה היתה זאת לנפסדים ולממציא שהחומר המשותף לכלם ישיג הכנות בשעורים מיוחדים כפי צורך כל אחד ממיני הנפסדים. וזה אם כן קרה במקרה כמו שביאר ארסטו׳ בספר

---

[a] באיכות] coni. Dunk.; באכות a.

§ 15.3.3 Quo autem ad secundam antecedentis partem qua scilicet dicitur quod orbium motus sunt ad mortalium oportunitates probatur sic arguendo: motus est actus imperfectus procedens ad illam perfectionem que per ipsum fit pars post partem in substantia scilicet vel in quantitate vel in qualitate vel in loco. Prout habetur ab Aven R. *Physicorum* III t.c. 4 et alibi, sed sic est quod celestium motus ad nihil huiusmodi perfectionum in superiora neque in ipsa celestia corpora inferendum procedit sed in mortalia tantum. Ergo huiusmodi motus habet esse ad aliquid harum perfectionum in mortalia tantum inferendum. Et per consequens ipsi celestium motus, habent esse ad mortalium oportunitates tantum quod est intentum.

§ 15.3.4 Quod autem celestium motus nihil huiusmodi perfectionum in ipsa celestia inferant patet, quia neque in quantitate neque in qualitate neque in substantia transmutari videntur. Neque in loco secundum totum omnino, neque secundum partem transferuntur ad locum vel situm quo per tempus morentur.

§ 15.4.1 Secundo arguitur sic: ad inferiorum species presertim organicas requiruntur dispositiones illis proprie. Ad huiusmodi autem dispositiones necessario requiruntur limitate caloris mensure celestius motibus facte. Ergo celestium motus et per consequens horum corpora ad horum motus ut supra intenta habent esse ad inferiorum oportunitates intenta.

§ 15.4.2 Consequentia tenet quia nisi ipsa celestia habuissent esse ad huiusmodi inferiorum sive mortalium oportunitates ordinata ab agente scilicet illa intendente sequeretur ut preter alicuius intentum et cognitione contigisset ipsis mortalium singulis horumque agenti, ut materia his omnibus communis a celestibus oportune disponeretur sub diversis mensuris quarum unaqueque alicui tantum mortalium speciei appropriaretur, et per consequens diceretur horum omnium singulis contigisse casu tantum. Prout habetur a Phylosopho *Physicorum* II t.c. 51 itaque

§ 15.3.3 The second part of the antecedent, in which we said that the movements of the sphere exist for the benefit of human beings, is proved in the following way. Movement is an imperfect activity, which proceeds towards perfection that is produced by it part after part, in substance, quantity, quality or place, and Averroes explicates this in *Physics* 3, text. 4,[a] and in other chapters. But since this is true, the celestial movement does not proceed to bring about perfection in the higher beings or the celestial bodies, but only in human beings. Therefore, the movement exists only to bring about perfection in humans, and consequently, celestial movement exists for the benefit of human beings, and this is what we wanted to explain.

§ 15.3.4 Moreover, celestial movement does not bring about perfection in the celestial beings, and this is clear because no change is seen in [their] substance, quality, or quantity. Nothing changes in the place either in the whole or in the part, because they remain in the same place from that point.

§ 15.4.1 Second, I would argue: the inferior species, especially those with organs, necessitate proper dispositions [for themselves], while dispositions necessarily need limited measurements of heat generated by the movement of the celestial bodies. Therefore, the movement of celestial beings, and consequently their bodies, which are intended for their movement, as mentioned above, exist for the benefit of the inferior beings.

§ 15.4.2 The consequence is evident because if the celestial bodies did not exist for the benefit of inferior and human beings ordered by an agent who intended them, it would follow that there was no intention or knowledge with respect to the human beings and their agent that the matter that was common to all celestial bodies should be adequately disposed according to different measurements, each of which is appropriate for only a particular mortal species. And consequently, we say that it would only happen by chance, as the Philosopher explains in *Physics* 2,

---

[a] Cf. *Phys.* 3.1.200b.

in a way that, had this chance not happened and had it not been [there] continuously, then the forth-bringer would exist in vain, and so would the prime matter, which is necessary by its commonality for the existence of the species of the corruptibles and for their recurring generation.

§ 15.4.3 Because none of this would be actualised without the celestial bodies and their movements, as became clear. And all this is inconceivable. And apart from this: in such a forth-bringing of dispositions [consisting] in limited measurements, which are generated from limited measurements of heat, every single one of them is determined for a necessarily determined disposition for a certain form determined for it. So, anyone who says that all this is by chance, without the intention of any intender, is like a person who has undoubtedly been led astray, as Aristotle explains in *On the Heavens* 2, text. 45:[a] "If perhaps only one or two stars were like this, it would not be so improbable as to be a coincidence. But since all the stars move in this way, this statement is fallacious." From all these [words], it follows that the existence of the spheres and their stars, which exist for the sake of the movement, as explained above, is for the need[s] of the existence of the inferior corruptibles. And this is what we wanted to explain. But what we said—[namely, that] in order that the species of the corruptibles may exist, it necessarily follows that the aforementioned dispositions exist in limited measurements, as testified by sense [perception], especially in many of the species of plants, which are subsequent in their forms and their quantity and their quality to the variety of the movements of the celestial bodies—also becomes clear from the proofs made by Averroes, who brings [them] in his Commentary on *Physics* 8, text. 46: "If there had not been a certain disposition for every form that was designated for it alone, it would follow that everything would be generated from everything. And sense [perception] testifies the contrary of this." And therefore, he writes in the Commentary on *Metaphysics* 12, text. 18:[b] "The kinds of heat that are generated from the heat | of the stars, which generate every species, and the species of the animals, have specific measures." And he continues, saying: "And these measures come from the divine intellectual craftsmanship."

§ 15.5 And we answer, if so, to dispel [any] doubt about the aforementioned thesis, that the celestial bodies exist for the need[s] of inferior corruptibles and that this is through the intention and will of an agent who intended to bring them and their order forth for this.

---

[a] *Cael.* 2.8.289b. [b] Cf. *Metaph.* 12.3.1070a.

§ 15.4.3 כי לא היה יוצא לפעל דבר מכל זה לולי הגרמים השמימיים ותנועותיהם כאשר התבאר וכל זה לא יעלה על לב. ובלעדי זאת הנמצא כל כך הכנות על שיעורים מוגבלים מתהוות משיעורי חום מוגבלים כל אחד מהם מיוחד להכנה הכרחית לאיזו צורה מיוחדת לה. הנה מי שיאמר שכל זה היה במקרה בלתי כוונת שום מכוין יהיה כמתעתע בלי ספק כמו שבאר ארסטו׳ בספר השמים מאמר ב׳ פרק מ״ה באמרו: »אם אולי כוכב אחד או שנים בלבד היו על זה האופן לא היה כל כך רחוק שיהיה מקרה אבל בהיות כל כוכבי לכת על זה אופן זה. הנה זה המאמר הוא מאמר מתעתע« עכ״ל. הנה מכל אלה יתחייב שמציאות הגלגלים וכוכביהם אשר הוא בשביל התנועה כמבואר לעיל הוא לצורך מציאות השפלים הנפסדים. וזה הוא מה שרצינו לבאר. **אמנם** מה שאמרנו שלמציאות מיני הנפסדים יתחייב בהכרח מציאות ההכנות הנזכרות על שעורים המוגבלים יעיד עליו החוש בפרט ברבים ממיני הצמחים הנמשכים בצורותם וכמותם ואיכותם אחר התחלפות תנועות הגרמים השמימיים ויתבאר גם כן בראיות אבן רשד אשר הביא בביאורו לספר השמע מאמר ח׳ פרק מ״ו באמרו: »שאם לא היתה לכל צורה איזו הכנה מיוחדת לה לבדה היה מתחייב שיתהוה כל דבר מכל דבר ועל הפך זה יעיד החוש.« ולזה כתב בביאור בספר מה שאחר מאמר י״ב פרק י״ח וזה לשונו: »מיני החום המתהוים מחום | הכוכבים המהוים כל מין ומין ממיני בעלי חיים יש להם מדות מיוחדות.« והוסיף ואמר: »ואלו המדות באות ממלאכה אלהית שכלית.«

§ 15.5 **נשיב** אם כן להתיר ספק החקירה הנזכרת שמציאות הגרמים השמיימיים[a] הוא לצורך השפלים הנפסדים וזה בכוונת וברצון פועל מכוין שהמציאם וסדרם לזה.

---

[a] השמיימים] coni. Dunk.; השממיים a.

nisi contigisset | huiusmodi casus, et nisi ad conservationem perseveraret, tam agens quam materia prima (que sua communitate tot diversis speciebus harumque reciprocationi necessaria est) fuissent quid ociosum.

§ 15.4.3 Cum, scilicet, nihil horum effectuum resultare potuisset: quod est inopinabile. Preterea quia cum in tot diversis fiant limitate dispositiones et calorum mensure quarum unaqueque alicui generabilium specierum tantum appropriatur, fabulosum videtur dicendum ut casu preter alicuius intentum contingant. Quare Phylosophus in lib. *De Celo* II t.c. 45 ait: «Si igitur una stella aut due essent huiusmodi non esset inopinabile tantum, cum autem omnes stelle sint huiusmodi iste sermo est fabulosus etc.» Restat ergo ut celestium motus et per consequens horum corpora (gratia cuius sunt ut supra) habent esse ad mortalium oportunitates intenta quod est intentum. Quod autem ad mortalium species requirantur huiusmodi dispositionum limitationes et calorum mensure patet sensu, presertim in diversis vegetabilium formis quantitatibus, et qualitatibus celestium motuum diversitatem aperte sequentibus, et idem habetur ratione et auctoritate Aven R. in lib. *Physicorum* VIII t.c. 46 ubi dicit: «Quod nisi cuilibet forme requiratur materia sibi propria, sequeretur ut quodlibet fieret ex quolibet cuius oppositum testatur sensus.»

§ 15.5 Ad dubium ergo respondetur: quod celestia corpora sunt ad mortalium oportunitates intenta et ordinata ab agente illud sapienter intendente.

text. 51.[a] And if this did not happen | by chance and continuously, then the agent as well as prime matter, which is necessary for the unity of different species and for their reciprocation, would be futile, because there would be no effect at all, and this is incongruous.

§ 15.4.3 Moreover, in such dispositions of limited measurements generated from the measurement of heat, every single one of them is determined only for a certain species of generable beings, and it seems impossible to say that this happens by chance without the intention of any intender. And the Philosopher explains this in *On the Heavens* 2, text. 45,[b] where he states: "If only one or two stars were [moving] in this way, it would not be that impossible. But since all the stars are [moving] in this way, this statement is absurd." It remains that celestial movement, and consequently the celestial bodies [which exist for the sake of movement, as mentioned above], are intended for human events, and this is what we wanted to explain. But the human species needs a limited disposition and measurement of heat, as the senses testify, especially in different species of plants, which in their forms, quantity, and quality follow a variety of movements of the celestial bodies, according to the argument and authority of Averroes in *Physics* 8, text. 46,[c] where he states: "If not every form needed a matter that was specified [i.e., determined] for it alone, it would have to be [the case] that everything would be generated from everything. And the senses testify the contrary of this."

§ 15.5 To dispel any doubt, I would argue that the celestial bodies exist for the benefit of human beings according to the intention of an agent, who wisely intends and orders them.

---

[a] *Phys.* 2.5.197a. [b] *Cael.* 2.8.289b. [c] Cf. *Phys.* 8.6.258b.

15. תכלית כל גשמי

§ 15.6.1 **ולטענות** החולק נשיב אחר שנקדים שלש הנחות ראשונה שתכלית כל ההווים ונפסדים הוא המין האנושי שהוא הנכבד מכלם כמו שביאר ארסטו׳ בספר הנהגת המדינה באומרו: »וכמו כן ראוי לחשוב גם בהווים ונפסדים שהצמחים הם בשביל הבעלי חיים ושאר הבעלי חיים הם בשביל המין האנושי קצתם שהם בני תרבות הנה הם לתועלתו ואשר אינם בני תרבות לעשות מהם מלבושים וכלים אחרים גם שלא יצדק זה על כלם ובהיות שהטבע לא עשה דבר בלתי שלם ולא דבר לבטלה יתחייב שעשה כל אלה בשביל המין האנושי.«

§ 15.6.2 שנית שהנפש האנושית השכלית היא בלתי שלמה בשלמות השני ותשיג אותו בפעולה אנושית בחיריית כמבואר לעיל.

§ 15.6.3 שלישית שהנפש השכלית הנזכרת היא עצם נבדל אשר בהיותו בשלמותו השני הוא יותר דומה מכל נמצא לאל יתברך.

§ 15.6.4 ואחר שהקדמנו אלו השלש הקדמות אשר הם מבוארות במופת ממה שקדם נאמר[a] שמכל אלה יתחייב שהנפש האנושית בהיותה עצם נבדל היא נכבדת מן הגרמים השמיימים ולזה כאשר טען החולק באמרו שאם היה מציאות הגרמים השמיימיים[b] לצורך השפלים הנפסדים היה מתחייב שיהיה מציאות הנכבד לצורך מה שלמטה ממנו. נשיב שזה היה מתחייב אם היה מציאות הנפסדים הוא התכלית האחרון אמנם בהיות מציאות הנפסדים לצורך שלמות עצם נבדל מן הגרמים השמיימיים[c] לא יתחייב שום נמנע וזה כי אמנם בהיות הנפש האנושית השכלית[d] עצם נבדל הנה היא יותר נכבדת מכל עצם גשמי ובהיות שלא יושג שלמות זה העצם בלתי פעולה אנושית בחיריית ולא יתכן מציאות זאת הפעולה באופן שלם בלתי מציאות ההווים ונפסדים אם כן ראוי שיהיה מציאות גרמים שמיימיים[e] לצרכי ההווים ונפסדים אשר מציאותם הכרחי לשלמות העצם הנזכר.

---

§ 15.6.1 And we will answer the opponent's arguments after laying down three assumptions. (1) First, that the final purpose of all generables and corruptibles is the human species, which is nobler than all of them, as Aristotle explains in *Politics* [1, text. 6]:[a] "And it is also appropriate to think regarding the generables and corruptibles that plants exist for the sake of animals and the rest of the animals exist for the sake of the human species. Some, which are domesticable, are [there] for its usage, and those which are not domesticable are [there so that one can] make clothes and other useful things out of them, although it is not true for all of them. And since nature does nothing imperfect and nothing in vain, it follows that it made all of these for the sake of the human species."

§ 15.6.2 (2) Second, that the human intellectual soul is not perfect in the second perfection and achieves it [only] through human activity from free choice, as explained above.

§ 15.6.3 (3) Third, that the aforementioned intellectual soul is a separate substance, which in its second perfection is more similar to God—may He be praised—than any other existent.

§ 15.6.4 And after laying down these three assumptions, which are evident from the preceding proof, we say that from all these, it follows that the human soul, since it is a separate substance, is nobler than the celestial bodies. And therefore, when the opponent argues by saying that if the celestial bodies existed for the need[s] of the inferior corruptibles, it would follow that the existence of what is noble would be for the need[s] of what is below it, we answer: this would follow if the existence of the corruptibles was the final purpose, but since the corruptibles exist for the need[s] of the perfection of a separate substance, which is nobler than the celestial bodies, nothing incongruous follows. And this [is so] because, since the human intellectual soul is a separate substance, it is nobler than all the material substances. And since the perfection of this substance is not achieved without human activity from free choice—and [since] it is incongruous that the activity should exist in a perfect way without the existence of the generables and corruptibles—then it is necessary that the celestial bodies exist for the needs of the generables and corruptibles, whose existence is necessary for the perfection of the aforementioned substance [i.e., the human intellectual soul].

---

[a] *Politics* 1.3.1256b.

a. השממיים] coni. Dunk.; השמימיים   b. השממיים] coni. Dunk.; השמימיים   a. ואמר] a[corr]; נאמר   a. השכלית] coni. Dunk.; השכלית   c. השממיים] coni. Dunk.; השמימיים   a. השממיים] coni. Dunk.; שמיים[e]

15. DE CELESTIBUS

§15.6.1 Ad argumenta vero respondetur tribus presuppositis: primo quod omnium mortalium finis est humanum genus tanquam horum omnium nobilissimum, sicut habetur a Phyilosopho *Polyticorum* primo ubi dicit: «Similiter est de genitis quoque existimandum plantasque animalium esse gratia, et cetera animalia hominum causa. Mansneta quidem propter utilitatem, fera vero et si non omnia ut vestes et alia instrumenta ex illis fiant, si ergo natura nihil neque imperfectum neque frustra facit, necessarium est illa hominum gratia fecisse naturam etc.»

§15.6.2 Secundo presupponitur quod intellectiva hominum anima est quid imperfectam, quod, scilicet, habet per arbitrariam hominum diligentiam quoad secundum actu perfici.

§15.6.3 Tertio presupponitur quod ipsa intellectiva presertim cum fuerit in secundo actu perfecta itaque reddatur quid ceteris Deo similius, ut supra, et est quid abstractum et Deo gratissimum.

§15.6.4 Quibus presuppositis tanquam plene superius probatis, sequitur ut huiusmodi intellectiva sit quid orbium corporibus nobilius. Quare cum arguitur quod si celestia essent ad mortalium oportunitatem sequeretur ut quid nobile haberet esse propter eo vilius. Respondetur: quod hoc sequeretur si ipsa mortalium oportunitas esset quid ultimum a celestibus intentum, sed cum ultimum ab eis intentum sit ultima intellective perfectio que tunc est quid abstractum et Deo preceteris simile negatur consequentia. Celestia enim cum sint corpora sunt proculdubio abstractis inferiora quare merito operantur circa | mortalia ad huiusmodi intellectiva in perfectionem consequendam que nonnisi mortalibus medijs consequi contingit ut supra.

§15.6.1 In response to the first argument, I will reply by laying down three assumptions. First, the final purpose of [all] mortal beings is the human race, which is the noblest of all of the existents, as the Philosopher explains in *Politics* [1, text. 6],[a] where he states: "And it is also appropriate to think that plants exist for the sake of animals and that the other animals exist for the sake of the human species. Some, which are domesticated, were created for its usage, and the wild animals, though not all of them, were created so that clothes and other useful things could be made out of them. And since nature does nothing imperfect and nothing in vain, it has to be [the case] that it made all these for the sake of the human species."

§15.6.2 Second, the intellectual soul of man is imperfect because [the soul] is perfected only by human free choice, which is the second act [perfection].

§15.6.3 Third, the intellectual soul is perfected only in its second act [perfection], and it renders us more similar to God than the other existents, as aforementioned, and the intellectual soul is separate and closest to God's goodwill.

§15.6.4 According to these assumptions, which are accurately proven [in chapter 14] above, it would follow that the intellectual soul is nobler than the celestial bodies. To the [first] argument [of the opponent] that if the celestial bodies existed for the benefit of human beings, any nobler beings would exist for [the sake of] inferior ones, I will reply: this would follow if the final purpose of the celestial bodies was the benefit of mortal beings; nonetheless, since their final purpose is the final perfection of the intellectual soul, which is separate and which make us more similar to God than any other existents, the consequence is not correct. Since the celestial beings are bodies that are undoubtedly inferior [and] separate, it is therefore appropriate that they should work to accomplish the intellectual perfection of corruptibles, which can only be accomplished by corruptibles, as mentioned above.

---

[a] *Pol.* 1.3.1256b.

§ 15.6.5 And so, when the opponent argues, second, by saying that if the celestial bodies existed for the needs of the corruptibles, it would follow that the corruptibles were the final purpose of the intender of the existence of the whole sensible [world]—and this is disgraceful and complete nonsense—we answer: although correct, this would follow [only] if the existence of the corruptibles was the final purpose. But this is not correct. Instead, they exist | for the need[s] of the perfection of the aforementioned intellectual soul, which through its perfection will be an existent more similar to God—may He be praised—and nobler than the whole of the rest of the existents, especially the material existents.

§ 15.7 And this seems to be what [Holy] Scripture teaches [us], as it says (Deuteronomy 10:12, 14–15): "And now, O Israel, what does ha-Shem your God demand of you? Only this: to fear ha-Shem, your God, to walk only in His path, etc. Mark, the heavens to their uttermost reaches belong to ha-Shem, your God, the earth and all that is on it! Yet it was to your fathers that ha-Shem was drawn in [His] love for them, etc."; that is to say, God—may He be praised—wishes for your freely chosen perfection. And this is so that you will fear Him, which only occurs through the intellect, and know Him, and walk in His ways, which are compassion and truth. And therefore, you will become similar to Him to a certain degree. And all this is a wish that will be [fulfilled] by your freedom of choice, therefore He "demand[s] of you" (ibid.) that you do so, without this [decision] being in His hands, as explained above, and as it says (Berakhot 33b): "Everything is in the hands of [the] heavens except for the fear of [the] heavens." And it is made known that it is beloved in His eyes, more than the heavens and the earth, as it says (Deuteronomy 10:14–15): "The heavens belong to ha-Shem, your God, etc. Yet it was to your fathers that He was drawn in [His] love for them."

§ 15.8 And Isaiah explains this, as it says (Isaiah 66:1–2): "Thus said ha-Shem: 'The heavens [are] My throne and the earth is My footstool, etc. All this was made by My hand, and thus it all came into being,' declares ha-Shem. 'Yet to such a one I look: to the poor and broken-hearted, who is concerned about My word.'" He explains that although the heavens are the throne of God—may He be praised—and the earth is His footstool, the righteous and anyone who is concerned with His word are more beloved in His eyes—may He be praised—than the heavens and the earth. As it says (Ketubot 5a): "The handiwork of the righteous is greater than [the creation of the] heavens and [the] earth." And to convey and teach [us] why this [is so] and for what [reason], the aforementioned prophet said (Isaiah 49:3):

§ 15.6.5 Similiter cum arguitur quod si celestia essent, ad mortalium oportunitates ordinata, sequeretur ut tota universi machina esset ad mortalium oportunitates vel horum reciprocationes intenta quod esset quid vilissimum et penitus vanum. Respondetur: quod hoc quidem sequeretur si illud mortalium esset quid ultimum ab ordinatore intentum, sed cum intendatur quid ulterius et penitus nobile, et tale est intellective perfectionem consequendum ut supra. Negatur consequentia, huiusmodi enim consequendum cum sit quid abstractum et Deo ceteri similius, et per consequens gratius est proculdubio celestibus corporibus nobilius.

§ 15.7 Et idem videtur inferre Sacrum Deuteronomij documentum cap. 10 [10:2] ubi dicit: «Et nunc Israel quid Dominus Deus tuus petit a te nisi ut timeas Dominum Deum tuum et ambules in vijs suis etc.» subdit ibidem [10:14–15] dicens: «En Domini Dei tui celum est et celum celi terra et omnia que in ea sunt et tamen patribus tuis conglutinatus est et amavit eos etc.» Quasi dicat quod cum homo tantum possit per suam arbitrariam virtutem hoc facere, scilicet, ut fiat ceteris Deo similius, et per consequens quid omnium saltem corporeum nobilissimum et Deo gratissimum. Quod tamen non contigit ut Deus per se faciat propter contradictionis implicationem ut supra. Ideo ab ipso homine «petit ut faciat,» et ideo licet celestia et terrestria sua sint tuis tamen patribus tantum conglutinatus est amore tanquam celestibus et terrestribus nobilioribus et merito his omnibus gratioribus.

§ 15.8 Et idem docet Esaias cap. 66 [66:1–2] ubi dicit: «Hec dicit Dominus celum est sedes mea et terra est scabellum pedum meorum etc.» subdit ibidem [66:2] dicens: «Omnia hec manus mea fecit et facta sunt universa ista dicit Dominus, ad quem autem respiciam nisi ad pauperculum et contritum spiritu et tremens ob sermones meos etc.» Quibus aperte docet quod Dei verbum timentes et per consequens eiusdem mores sequentes, quales non dantur nisi post eiusdem Dei cognitionem pro viribus habitam, sunt celestibus terrestribusque Deo gratiores, et hoc cum sint his omnibus Deo similiores et per consequens nobiliores, ut supra. Et idem Esaias cap. 49 [49:1] docens ait: «Dominus ab utero vocavit me etc.» ubi subdit dicens [49:3]: «Et dixit

§ 15.6.5 In response to the other argument that if the celestial beings were ordered for the benefit of human beings, it would follow that the machinery of the universe was intended either for the benefit of human beings or for their reciprocation, which is incongruous and complete nonsense, I will reply that this would follow if the human beings were the last intended purpose of the divine arranger, but something is intended that is additionally and completely noble, as is the case for intellectual perfection, as aforementioned. The consequence is therefore not correct, since what is aimed at [i.e., intellectual perfection] is something separate and more similar to God than the other existents, and consequently, it is more beloved and nobler than the celestial bodies.

§ 15.7 It seems that the Holy Book of Deuteronomy (10:12) teaches this, saying: "And now, Israel, what does the Lord your God demand of you but that you fear the Lord your God and walk in all His ways, etc.," continuing (10:14–15): "To the Lord your God belong the heavens, even the highest heavens, the earth and everything in it. Yet the Lord set His affection on your fathers and loved them, etc." This means that a man can only do something through his own free choice—namely, he will become more similar to God than any other existent—and consequently nobler than other bodies and closest to God's goodwill. It is not possible that God's act may involve a contradiction, as explained above. For this reason, from man, "He demands, that he should do," and for this reason, His celestial and terrestrial beings are closely joined to your fathers, and through this love, we are nobler than the other celestial and terrestrial beings and closer to goodwill than the rest of the existents.

§ 15.8 And Isaiah (66:1–2) teaches the same thing, saying: "This is what the Lord says: Heaven is my throne, and the earth my footstool," and he continues: "My hand made all these things, and all these things were made, said the Lord. These are the ones I look on with favour: those who are humble and contrite in spirit, and who tremble at my word." With these [words], the prophet teaches us that those who fear the word of God and consequently follow His customs, which are only given to us after the knowledge of God, are closer in goodwill to God than the other celestial and terrestrial beings, and consequently, he is more similar to Him than the other existents and consequently nobler, as aforementioned. And Isaiah (49:1) says: "The Lord has called me from the womb," and he continues

"And He said to me: 'You are My servant, Israel in whom I glory'"; that is to say that God—may He be praised—will glory in the righteous, just as the artisan will glory in the perfect activity that is among his activities.

§15.9 And therefore, He will glory in Israel, because man is the species that resembles its maker more than [any of] the rest of the existents, as it says (Genesis 1:26): "Let us make man in our image, after our likeness," and among man[kind], Israel is [the] part that resembles God—may He be praised—the most and is close[est] to Him, since it recognises its Lord and holds fast in His covenant. And it is intentionally designed *to serve Him with one accord*,[a] more than the rest of the human species, who have only either their bodies or their pride for their imaginations, as it says (Psalm 20:8): "They [call] on chariots, they [call] on horses, but we call on the name of ha-Shem, our God." And it is said (*Avot* 3:14): "Beloved is man for he was created in the image [of God], etc. Beloved are Israel in that they were called 'children to the All-Present.'" It is appropriate, if so, that He will be glorified in Israel, which is a choice of His works. *He, the Most High, will preserve it*,[b] *that the deliverance of Israel might come from Zion!*[c]

---

[a] Zeph 3:9. [b] Ps 87:5. [c] Ps 14:7.

לי: »עבדי אתה ישראל אשר בך אתפאר« (ישעיהו מ״ט ג׳). כלומר שהאל ית׳ מתפאר בצדיקים כמו שיתפאר האומן בפעולה השלמה שבפעולותיו ולזה יתפאר בישראל.

§15.9 כי אמנם בהיות האדם הוא המין הדומה ליוצרו יותר משאר הנמצאים באמרו: »נעשה אדם בצלמנו כדמותנו« (בראשית א׳ כ״ו). ובמין האדם הנה ישראל חלק ממנו יותר דומה לאל יתברך וקרוב אליו בהיותו מכיר את רבונו ומחזיק בבריתו. ומתכוין לעבדו שכם אחד יותר מכל שאר המין האנושי אשר אין לפניהם בלתי אם גויתם וגאות דמיוניהם. באמרו: »אלה ברכב ואלה בסוסים ואנחנו בשם ה׳ אלהינו נזכיר« (תהלים כ׳ ח׳). ובאמרם: »חביב אדם שנברא בצלם ... חביבין ישראל שנקראו ›בנים למקום‹« (אבות ג׳ י״ד). ראוי אם כן שיתפאר בישראל אשר הוא מבחר מעשיו הוא יכוננגו עליון, יתן מציון תשועת ישראל.

mihi servus meus es tu Israel qui in te gloriabor etc.» et hoc quia cum Israel dicatur esse hominum genus quod preceteris Deum noscit eiusque sequitur mores. Quare est pre ceteris Deo similius et per consequens nobilius ut supra; merito dicit Deus se in Israel gloriari prout opificem in eiusdem operum nobilissimo gloriari decet.

⟨§ 15.9⟩

(49:3): "You are my servant Israel, for I glory in your will," and this is so, because we say that Israel is the people that knows God more than other people, and Israel follows His customs, and for this reason, Israel is more similar to God than the other peoples, and consequently nobler, as aforementioned. It is appropriate that he says that God is to be glorified in Israel, as it is proper that the artisan is glorified in His noblest work.

⟨§ 15.9⟩

§16 [Summary]

All these [investigations] will bear witness when an intelligent [man] looks at them.

§16.1 And they examine the words of the Torah scholars and the Sages of the Nations, because both *a path and a way*[a] is described in concise words in order to dispel the aforementioned doubts and to achieve true opinions through them. Are they not very divergent ways that are full of difference[s]? And when an investigator looks at the two contraries at once, he will easily judge which one is true, this one or that one, as the Philosopher [explains] in *On the Heavens* 2, text. 40.[b]

§16.2 For the philosophers who saw that there was an agent and affected [things] in [all] the sensible [objects] knew that the affected [things] pertain to the matter and that the agent pertains to the form. And therefore, they knew that the sensible [world] is composed of a form and its substrate, and they founded their opinions on assumptions that they thought necessary.

§16.3.1 Now, these [assumptions] are: first, that it is impossible that something may be generated out of nothing. And this assumption is indeed undoubtedly true, because, by its contrary, a thing and its opposite would be stated [at once]. And this is so, because when we say of a thing that it does not exist at all, we undoubtedly say that the existent has no matter, because if the existent had matter, it would have been part of it. However, it is not correct [to say about it] that it does not exist at all, but rather the contrary is correct, and we say that it undoubtedly exists. And as they thought that it was also incongruous that something could be generated without having been generated from another existing thing, without proceeding to infinity, as has been explained perfectly, they say that it is necessary that a certain kind of material is a first substrate to all substrates. And since it is incongruous that this substrate may be generated from another substrate that is prior to it, and since it is prior to all of them, and [since] it is incongruous among them that it could have been created from anything else, they say that it is necessarily uncreated. And if so, it has existed ever since and is called "[pre]eternal."

---

[a] Isa 35:8. [b] *Cael.* 2.6.288b.

[כלל העולה]

הן כל אלה יתנו עדיהם בהשקיף עלימו משכיל.

§16.1 ויבחנו דברי תופשי התורה וחכמי הגויים כי יספר[a] בקוצר מלין מסלול ודרך שניהם להתיר הספקות הנזכרים ולהשיג בהם דעות אמתיות הלא הם דרכים שונים רב ההבדל ביניהם? ובהביט המעיין אל שני ההפכים יחד ישפוט על נקלה. איזה יכשר הזה או זה כמו שאמר הפילוסוף בספר השמים והעולם מאמר ב' פרק מ'.

§16.2 כי אמנם הפילוסופים אשר ראו היות במוחשים פעל והתפעלות נודע אצלם היות ההתפעלות מצד החומר והפעל מצד הצורה ובכן ידעו היות המוחש מורכב מצורה ונושאה ויסדו דעותם על הנחות אשר חשבו הכרחיות.

§16.3.1 הן הנה היו: ראשונה שהוא מן הנמנע שיתהוה יש מאין וזאת ההנחה אמנם אמתית בלי ספק כי בהפכה יאמר דבר והפכו וזה כי באמרנו על דבר שהוא בלתי נמצא כלל אמרנו בלי ספק שאינו חומר לדבר נמצא כי אם היה חומר לנמצא היה חלק ממנו ולא יצדק עליו שאינו נמצא אבל יצדק עליו סותר זה ונאמר שהוא נמצא בלי ספק ובחשבם היות כמו כן נמנע שיתהוה דבר בלתי שיתהוה מדבר אחר נמצא ולא ילך זה אל לא תכלית כמבואר לעילא אמרו היות מן ההכרח שיהיה איזה מין מן החמרים נושא ראשון לכל הנושאים ובהיות מן הנמנע שיתהוה אותו הנושא מנושא אחר קודם לו בהיותו ראשון לכלם וזה מן הנמנע אצלם שיתחדש לא מדבר אחר אמרו שהוא בהכרח בלתי מחודש ואם כן היה מעולם ונקרא ›קדמון‹.

---

[a] יסופר; A. ›יספר‹

§16 [Sumarium]

§16.1 Cum autem huius opusculi fructus facilime per plures degustari intendam, succinte pro viribus ostendere conabor diversitatem, qua maxime dif|ferat processus Sacre Scripture Documenti ad veritatem demonstrandam circa questiones in preambulo positas et in libello disputatas ab illo processu quo Gentilium Phylosophii ad idem procedere videntur; paucis, scilicet, utrumque successive narrans, quibus iuxta se positis facilius horum verior discernatur, prout habetur a Phylosopho in libro *De Celo* II t.c. 40.

§16.2 Phylosophii enim huiusmodi considerantes sensibilibus, in quantum sensibilia sunt, inesse necessario materiam, et in quantum activa eisdem inesse formam, cui ipsa materia est proculdubio subiectum,

§16.3.1 ducti scilicet primo illa propositione qua, scilicet, dicitur quod ex nihilo nihil fit. Cuius oppositum implicaret contraditionem, quia cum penitus dicatur de aliquo quod non est, aperte negatur ut habeat esse alicuius subiectum, putantes esse uniformiter impossibile, ut aliquid sit productum non ex aliquo subiecto. Arguerunt quod cum non sit in subiectis procedendum ad infinitum, sit ergo deveniendum ad quoddam subiectum omnium primum. Cumque illud non habuisset esse ex alio subiecto illo priori, cum presupponatur devenisse ad subiectorum primum. Et cum hoc habuissent pro penitus inconvenienti ut detur aliquid productum non ex aliquo sive post purum non esse, oportuit eos necessario dicere ut huiusmodi primum subiectum sit quidnunquam productum, et per consequens ut habuisset esse ab eterno.

§16 [Summary]

§16.1 Since I want the fruit of this treatise to be tasted by the majority of people in the simplest way, I shall try, according to my strength, to briefly prove the difference between the way the Holy Scripture demonstrates the truth about the questions presented in the introduction and discussed throughout this pamphlet and the way in which the philosophers among the Gentiles [i.e., Nations] proceed, reporting both [positions] in a few words, one following the other. In this manner, it will be easier to establish which of them is truer, as the Philosopher explains in *On the Heavens* 2, text. 40.[a]

§16.2 These philosophers—when they considered that matter necessarily belongs to what is perceived by the senses, insofar as they are sensible objects, and that form belongs to them, insofar as they are in actuality, and that matter is necessarily the substrate of that form—

§16.3.1 [They] were led first by that proposition in which it is said that "nothing is generated from nothing." The opposite of this would imply a contradiction, because if one were to say that something did not exist, it would be denied that it has the substrate of a certain being. They [the philosophers] thought that it was impossible that something could have been generated that did not come from another substrate. Moreover, they argued that it is impossible to proceed to infinity in the chain of substrates; therefore, one must arrive at a first substrate for everything, and this substrate would not have received existence from another substrate prior to it if one had to suppose that it was the first of all substrates. Since they considered it incongruous that there could be something [that was] not produced from anything else or from pure nothingness, then [the philosophers] necessarily stated that the first substrate is something that was not generated from anything and consequently [that it] is [pre]eternal.

---

[a] *Cael.* 2.6.288b.

§ 16.3.2 And as they saw that all the sensible [objects; i.e., the mortal species] change into others mediately or immediately, and [since] it is impossible that a thing that exists in actuality, while existing in actuality, may change into a thing other than itself—because, if so, it would bear two forms at once, and it would correctly [bear] its own name and the name of the other, which does not come to mind—

§ 16.3.3 they [then] said that this first substrate is a matter existing in potentiality and not in actuality. And therefore, it follows that nothing ever exists without form. And among them, it is called "prime matter."

§ 16.3.4 And as they thought that since the forms of the first elements are [the basis] for all forms of the sensible [objects] generated immediately in prime matter, it follows among them that the elements are also [pre]eternal.

§ 16.4.1 Second, as they thought that movement was necessarily [pre]eternal, they came to state that someone who says the contrary of this is undoubtedly a fool or a stupid person. | And it is, as they say, incongruous that a thing may be created without a motion that moves the creator to create that thing. And if it is so, as we said, that the motion is created, [then] we said that it is necessarily created by a prior motion, and this would proceed to infinity.

§ 16.4.2 And therefore, it follows for them that movement is [pre]eternal. And since the existence of movement is impossible without a mover and a mobile, they say that it follows that the mover and the mobile are [pre]eternal and those are, for them, the spheres and their movers.

§ 16.4.3 And as they thought that from the existence of the elements and the movements of the spheres, which are necessary for the existence of generation and corruption, then generation and corruption necessarily exist, it follows, for them, that the movement of generation and corruption is [pre]eternal. And it is incongruous for them that

§ 16.3.2 וכאשר ראו שכל המוחשים משתנים מזה לזה באמצעי או בלתי אמצעי ומן הנמנע שיהיה דבר נמצא בפעל בעודו מתהפך לדבר אחר זולתו כי אם כן היה מתלבש שתי צורות יחד ויצדק עליו שם עצמו ושם זולתו אשר לא יעלה על לב.

§ 16.3.3 אמרו שאותו הנושא הראשון הוא חומר נמצא בכח לא בפעל ובכן התחייב שלא נמצא לעולם בלי צורה והוא הנקרא אצלם ‹חומר ראשון›.

§ 16.3.4 וכאשר חשבו היות צורות היסודות ראשונות לכל צורות המוחשים הוות בחומר הראשון בלתי אמצעי התחייב אצלם שיהיו היסודות גם כן קדמונים.

§ 16.4.1 **שנית** בחשבם היות התנועה קדמונית בהכרח עד שאמרו שמי שיאמר הפך זה הוא בלי ספק סכל או מתעתע. | וזה באמרם שהוא מן הנמנע שיתחדש דבר בלתי תנועה שתניע המחדש לחדש אותו הדבר. ואם כן באמרנו שהתנועה התחדשה נאמר בהכרח שהתחדשה בתנועה קודמת וילך הדבר אל לא תכלית.

§ 16.4.2 ולכן התחייב אצלם שתהיה התנועה קדמונית. הנה בהיות מן הנמנע המצא תנועה בלתי מניע ומתנועע אמרו שזה יתחייב שימצא מניע ומתנועע קדמונים והם אצלם הגלגלים ומניעיהם.

§ 16.4.3 ובחשבם שבהמצא היסודות ותנועות הגלגלים המחוייבים למציאות ההוויה וההפסד נמצאו אז בהכרח ההוויה וההפסד התחייב אצלם היות תנועת ההוויה וההפסד קדמונית. ובהיות נמנע אצלם היות

§ 16.3.2 Cumque percepissent, quod mortalium genera in se invicem mediate vel immediate convertantur, presupponentes, ut ex nullo actu existente, dum actu existit, detur quid aliud substantialiter fieri, quia ut sic sequeretur ut illud inde productum esset simul et semel duabus diversis formis substantialiter impressum, per quorum alteram esset idem quod prius per reliquam vero econverso, quod est inconveniens.

§ 16.3.3 Dixerunt huiusmodi primum subiectum esse quid potentiale tantum omnes mortalium formas successive recipiens. Quod, scilicet, potentiale materiam primam appellarunt.[a] Que, scilicet, numquam habuit esse denudata a qualibet forma, quia si hoc contigisset sequeretur ut per se habuisset actu existere, et per consequens fuisset quid actu non quid potentiale tantum, quod est contra presuppositum et probatum ut plenius supra habetur.

§ 16.3.4 Cumque putassent elementorum formas esse omnium mortalium primas in huiusmodi prima materia immediate existentes, habuit necessario apud eos sequi, ut similiter elementa habuissent esse ab eterno.

§ 16.4.1 Secundo ducti illa propositione quam putarunt ad eo manifestam ut eius oppositam dixerunt esse similem stultorum vel fingentium sermoni, qua, scilicet, dicunt motum habuisse esse ab eterno. Et hoc dicunt habentes pro inconveniente ut aliquid sit quod producatur sine motu, quo saltem productor moveatur ad illud novum producendum, quare si motus esset quid productum | habuisset per alium motum produci, et sic fieret in motibus processus ad infinitum.

§ 16.4.2 Habuit apud eos sequi ut mobile et motor sine quibus non datur motus habuissent similiter esse ab eterno, et tales dicunt esse celestium orbes et sydera horumque motores, ad quorum motus videntur reliquos sequi et non econtra, et per consequens huiusmodi celestia habuerunt esse ab eterno.

§ 16.4.3 Cumque putassent ut datis elementis celestibusque motibus ad genitorum generationem concurrentibus tanquam agentibus et patientibus bene dispositis et ad invicem proportionatis, habuissent necessario simul esse generationes et corruptiones. Inde habuit apud eos sequi

---

[a] appellarunt] coni. Copp.; appellaverunt b.

§ 16.3.2 Therefore, the philosophers conceived that the corruptible species change into one another mediately or immediately. [They] proposed that it is not possible that something may be substantially generated from anything existing in actuality while it exists in actuality, since this would imply that the produced thing would be substantially impressed by two different forms together and at the same time: according to one of them [one of the two forms], it would be the same as before, but according to the other, it would be the opposite, and this is incongruous.

§ 16.3.3 The philosophers indicated that the first substrate is in potency only, receiving all corruptible forms in a successive moment. For that reason, they called this potential thing "prime matter," which never exists without a form, because if so, it would exist in actuality, and consequently, it would be something in act and not only in potency; and the opposite [position] is what we have broadly proposed and proved above.

§ 16.3.4 The philosophers thought that the forms of the elements are the first forms of all corruptible things existing immediately in prime matter, and consequently, for them, the elements are also [pre]eternal.

§ 16.4.1 Second, the philosophers are led by an assumption [i.e., proposition] that they consider so obvious that they say that the opposite [position], in which they say that movement is [pre]eternal, is meaningless and ridiculous. They state that it would be incongruous to think that something could be created without a motion by which the producer was moved to produce something new, because if a motion is created, then | it would necessarily have been created by another motion, and this would run until infinity for every kind of motion.

§ 16.4.2 It follows that for the philosophers, the movable thing and the mover, without whom there is no motion at all, are also eternal; and they said that the celestial spheres, the stars, and their movers are also eternal. It seems that the other beings also follow their motions and not the opposite, [and] consequently the celestial beings are eternal.

§ 16.4.3 However, they supposed that given that the elements and the celestial bodies take part in the generation of generated things and that they act and are affected while being rightly disposed and mutually proportioned, therefore there would necessarily be generation and corruption

there may be any form among the forms that is not in matter that is disposed for it. And if so, man would have come to be only from the semen of man, and likewise also for the rest of the species.ᵃ It would follow that man and the rest of the species have existed ever since. For them, the movement of the spheres is [pre]eternal [and] ceaseless, and they thought that this was only possible thanks to a ceaseless mover. And moreover, they observed that the movement of the spheres is absolutely equal. They said that from these [things], it follows that the mover is a simple existent, without a body, and not a power in a body either, because of the equality of the movement, which is impossible for a material mover, or because of the permanence of the movement, which for them is incongruous that it exists thanks to a force in matter, which is indeed finite. Nonetheless, regarding the second proof, the Sabaean people disagreed.

§16.4.4 And they said that the mover of the sphere is a power in a body, and although it [i.e., the body] is finite [i.e., in spatial dimensions], it is not impossible that it is a permanent mover, because that force is not affected by the movement and therefore does not become tired and weary, and this is sufficient for them [to state] that there is a permanent mover, as Averroes describes in [the Commentary on] *Metaphysics* 12, text. 41.ᵇ And as the aforementioned philosophers explain, [given] that the aforementioned mover is not a power in a body, for them it follows that it necessarily is one, because number does not apply to [things] separate from matter, which [i.e., matter] is the cause of number in the particulars, except for those which are different in species.

§16.5 Third, it is commonly [known] that it is impossible that an infinite number of existents may exist at one time since the existents for which it is correct [to state] that they all exist at one time are undoubtedly finite, because it is not correct [to suppose a] limit that encompasses what is infinite. And therefore, it follows for them that every individual human soul is corruptible. And this is so because they say that the human species has existed ever since for an infinite time. If the soul of man was an incorruptible thing, there would be an infinite number of ancient human souls at one time, and therefore, it would follow for them that they would state [either] one of two [things]: either (1) that the soul of man was corruptible, or (2) that there was a separate immortal intellect, | numerically one, common to the whole human species, [and] there would not

59ʳ

ᵃ Cf. *Metaph.* 12.3.1070a.   ᵇ Cf. *Metaph.* 12.8.1073a.

צורה מן הצורות זולתי בחומר מוכן אליה ואם כן לא היה אדם כי אם מזרע אדם. וכן שאר המינים התחייב שלעולם נמצאו אדם ושאר המינים. ובהיות אצלם תנועת הגלגלים קדמונית לבלי תכלית וחשבו היותה בלתי אפשרית זולתי בכח מניע בלתי בעל תכלית וגם ראו היות תנועת הגלגלים בתכלית השווי אמרו משאלה יתחייב שיהיה המניע נמצא פשוט בלתי גוף ובלתי כח בגוף הן בסבת שווי התנועה אשר היא בלתי איפשרית למניע חמרי הן בסבת נצחיות התנועה אשר הוא נמנע אצלם שתמצא על ידי כח בחומר אשר הוא אמנם בעל תכלית. אפס כי על הראייה השנית חלקו אנשי הצבא.ᵃ

§16.4.4 ואמרו היות מניע הגלגל כח בגוף. ועם היותו בעל תכלית לא ימנע היותו מניע נצחי כי הכח ההוא לא יתפעל מהתנועה ולכן לא ייעף ולא ייגע וזה מספיק אצלם אל שיהיה מניע נצחי כמו שספר אבן רשד בספר מה שאחר מאמר י״ב פרק מ״א. וכאשר ביארו הפילוסופים הנזכרים היות המניע הנזכר בלתי כח בגוף התחייב אצלם בהכרח היותו אחד במספר כי המספר לא יפול על נבדלים מחומר אשר הוא סבת המספר בפרטים זולתי בהיותם נבדלים במין.

§16.5 **שלישית** בהיות מן המפורסם שאי איפשר שימצאו נמצאים בלתי בעל תכלית במספר בזמן אחד. כי הנמצאים אשר יצדק עליהם שהם כלם בזמן אחד הנה יש להם תכלית בלי ספק כי מה שאין תכלית לו לא תצדק עליו הגבלה מקפת בכל. לכן התחייב אצלם שתהיה כל נפש אדם פרטי נפסדת. וזה כי באמרם שלעולם היה מין האדם נמצא בזמן בלתי בעל תכלית אם היתה נפש האדם דבר בלתי נפסד היו נפשות בני אדם קדומות בזמן אחד בלתי בעלת תכלית במספר. ומזה התחייב אצלם שנאמר אחת משתים אם שתהיה נפש האדם נפסדת. ואם שתהיה שכל נבדל | נצחי אחד במספר משותף לכל המין האנושי לא שיהיו שכלים רבים נבדלים כמספר בני האדם. ומזה

59ʳ

ᵃ הצבא] coni. Dunk.; הצאב a.

ut generationes et corruptiones habuissent esse ab eterno. Et quia nulla mortalium forma videtur inesse nisi in materia sibi propria, quare homo verbi gratia «Nonnisi ex hominis semine generatur non autem ex semine equi etc.,» inde habuit apud eos sequi ut ab eterno habuisset esse homo similiter[a] alie genitorum species. Cumque ad celestem motionem quam putarunt fuisse ab eterno ut supra putassent requiri virtus motiva infinita et per consequens incorporea. Preterea cum huiusmodi motus sit continuus et uniformis qualis non contingeret fieri per corpoream virtutem, inde habuit apud eos sequi, ut celi motor sit quid incorporeum, et hoc tam ratione uniformitatis et continuatis eiusdem motus quam ratione eiusdem infinitatis, cuius tamen infinitatis rationem reprobant Sabii, ut supra.

§16.4.4 Cumque declarassent huiusmodi motorem esse incorporeum inde habuit apud eos sequi, ut unus tantum esset primi mobilis motor, et hoc quia cum ratione motus continuitatis et uniformitatis pateat esse quid incorporeum ut supra. Patet quidem ut sit quid unum tantum, quia non datur numeratio omnino similium nisi ratione materie ut supra.

§16.5 Tertio ducti illa propositione que videtur adeo manifesta ut eius opposita videatur inopinabilis, qua, scilicet, dicitur quod non dantur numero infinita simul actu existentia, et hoc quia illa que habent simul et semel actu existere habent contineri sub quodam toto, extra quod nihil horum existat. Cuius oppositum contigit de numero infinitis, prout per se patet et habetur a Phylosopho Physicorum III t.c. 62, ideo habuerunt necessario dicere quod impossibile est ut humane anime ad individuorum numerum dinumerabiles sint immortales, et hoc quia apud eos ab eterno habuit esse homo ut supra, et per consequens infiniti habuerunt esse homines, successive existentes. Si ergo horum individuales anime essent immortales sequetur ut omnes simul tempore actu existerent, et per consequens darentur numero infinita simul actu existentia quod est inopinabile ut supra. Quare oportuit eos alterum duorum dicere, vel scilicet ut quelibet humana anima sit penitus quid mortale, prout videtur Alexandrum de mente Aristotelis sentire; vel ut dicant ut illa intellectiva que putatur immortalis | rationibus ut supra a Phylosopho assignatis non sit ad individuorum numerum dinumerabilis, sed sit

at the same time. Consequently, for the philosophers, generation and corruption are [pre]eternal. Since any form of corruptible being belongs only to its specific matter, for example, "a man is generated from the sperm of a man and not from the sperm of a horse, etc.,"[a] then it follows for them that man and the other species of generated beings are eternal. They thought that the motion of the celestial bodies, which they considered [pre]eternal, as mentioned above, requires an infinite and incorporeal power of motion. Moreover, since the motion is continuous and uniform, it could not be produced by a corporeal power, [and] therefore it follows that for them, the mover of the heavens is incorporeal because of the uniformity and continuity of their motion, as well as its infinity. The Sabaeans refuted the idea of infinity, as proved above.

§16.4.4 They said that the mover is incorporeal and so there is only one mover of the first mobile, because the motion is continuous and uniform. Therefore, it is evident that it is incorporeal, as mentioned above. It is clear that it is only one, because number can only be applied to matter, as mentioned above.

§16.5 Third, [the philosophers were] led by the assumption [i.e., proposition] that seemed to be so obvious that its opposite was considered unthinkable; namely, that no numerically infinite beings exist simultaneously in actuality, because beings existing in actuality together and at the same time are encompassed in a whole; besides them, nothing exists. The opposite occurs to the numerically infinite beings, as is evident and as the Philosopher explains in *Physics* 3, text. 62.[b] The philosophers necessarily said that it is impossible that the human souls, [which are] countable according to the number of the individual beings, may be immortal, because they consider man to be eternal, as aforementioned. Consequently, men are infinite, and they exist in a successive series [of generations]. If the individual souls were immortal, it would follow that they would all exist in actuality together and at the same time, [and] then there would be infinite beings existing in actuality at the same time, but this is incongruous, as aforementioned. Therefore, it is necessary that they say one of two different [things]: either the human soul is mortal, according to Alexander [of Aphrodisia] [and] supported by Aristotle; or the intellectual soul, which is considered to be immortal | for the reasons given by the Philosopher, as aforementioned, is not countable according to the number of the

---

[a] similiter] b[corr]; similem b.

[a] *Metaph.* 12.3.1070a. [b] *Phys.* 3.6.206b.

be so many separate intellects equal to the number human beings. And therefore, it would follow that after death, there would be no difference between the righteous man and the sinner, [between] the servant of God and everyone who does not serve Him. And according to this, nature would have given us in vain the desire for knowledge of the truth in the divine things that are not needed for the political community, [but] which every man yearns to know,[a] at least when they wake him up for it, *and he awoke as from sleep, shaking off wine*.[b]

§ 16.6 Fourth, they said that an eternal and permanent thing does not truly have an agent, and this assumption is true and self-evident. And there is no doubt about this, because the agent undoubtedly temporally precedes its activity. And a thing that is eternal [and] ceaseless has nothing prior to it. And therefore, it follows for them that there was no agent in the whole of existence. For them, the heavens and the earth [lit. world] are eternal; namely, the celestial bodies and the elements, the movement of generation and corruption, and the existence of the prime matter, as mentioned above. And they saw that there is an order of and a connection between things in existence, especially through the movement of the first mover. And thanks to the aforementioned interrelationship, there exists only one existence as a whole. And it follows, therefore, that there is an existent who intended the aforementioned interrelationship, and they say that there is doubtlessly an arranger of order. And according to this, for them, his activity would be for the sake of the order and connection of the existents of whom he is not the forth-bringer. And therefore, according to their opinion, it [would be] a coincidence [that it occurred] to the existents that there was a permanent arranger of order who ordered and linked them together, because otherwise there would be no order or linking. And [it would be] a coincidence that the existents that were arranged and linked together by the arranger of order existed, because otherwise, he would be in vain and not acting. And, if so, in this activity, he would resemble *a partridge hatching what she did not lay*.[c] And as this is not incongruous among them, it follows that they also bring forth a demonstrative proof of the first mover being one and without a body. [However,] from this, it does not follow that there is not another separate intellect besides Him who is equal to Him in rank, who arranges the order of existence and links it together. And number does apply to them because of differences in their activities, which informs [us] about the difference of their form

---

[a] Cf. Averroes on *Metaph.* 2, text. 14 (cf. *Metaph.* 2.2.994b). [b] Cf. Ps 78:65.
[c] Jer 17:11.

יתחייבו שלא יהיה אחר המות הבדל בין צדיק לרשע בין עובד אלהים לאשר לא עבדו. ולפי זה חנם שם בנו הטבע תאות ידיעת האמת בדברים האלהיים הבלתי צריכים לקבוץ המדיני אשר כל אדם נכסף לדעת אותם לפחות כאשר העירוהו עליו, ויקץ כישן מתרונן מיין.

§ 16.6 *רביעית* באמרם שהדבר הקדמון ונצחי אין לו פועל באמת וזאת ההנחה אמתית ומבוארת בעצמה. אין ספק בה כי הפועל יקדם בזמן לפעלו בלי ספק. והדבר אשר היה לעולם בזמן בלתי בעל תכלית לא היה דבר קודם לו. לכן התחייב אצלם שאין לכלל המציאות פועל בהיות אצלם השמים והעולם קדמונים היינו הגרמים השמימיים והיסודות ותנועת ההוויה וההפסד ומציאות החומר הראשון כנזכר לעיל. וכאשר ראו היות במציאות סדור והתקשרות קצתו בקצתו בפרט בתנועת המניע הראשון ובהתקשרות הנזכרת היה המציאות בכללו אחד במספר והתחייב מזה שיש נמצא מכוין ההתקשרות הנזכרת אמרו שיש מסדר בלי ספק. ולפי זה יהיה פעלו אצלם לסדר ולקשר נמצאות אשר הוא לא המציאם. ובכן לפי דעתם זה מקרה הוא היה לנמצאות שימצא מסדר נצחי שסדרם ויקשרם כי זולתו היו בלתי סדר וקשר. ומקרה הוא היה למסדר שימצאו נמצאות יסדרם ויקשרם כי זולתם היה בטל ובלתי פועל. והוא אם כן בפעלתו זאת דומה לקורא אשר דגר ולא ילד. וכאשר היה זה אצלם בלתי נמנע התחייב שגם שיביאו ראיה מופתית על היות המניע הראשון אחד ובלתי גוף לא יתחייב מזה שלא ימצא זולתו שכל נבדל שוה לו במעלה שיהיה מסדר המציאות ומקשרו ויפול מספר עליהם בסבת הבדל פעלם המורה על הבדל צורתם בו יהיו נבדלים במין כאשר באר

quid unum numero tantum toti humano generi commune, et per consequens post corporis mortem nullo pacto differt iustus ab iniusto, neque sapiens ab ignaro vel stulto. Immo et durante hac vita apud eos nihil refert esset iustum vel sapientem, nisi pro quanto convenit civili congregationi, et per consequens natura frustra nobis intulit desiderium ad divina scienda et potentiam ad illa que, scilicet, ad humanam congregationem nullo pacto sunt oportuna, prout per se patet et habetur ab Aven R. *Metaphysicorum* II t.c. 14 que in saltem excitati naturaliter scire desideramus.

§ *16.6* Quarto ducti illa propositione qua, scilicet, dicitur, quod non datur quid eternum habere agentem. Que, scilicet, per se nota videtur, cum, scilicet, vere agens habeat necessario secundum tempus precedere ad suum actum. Habuerunt necessario dicere ut universum quod putarunt fuisse ab eterno ut supra nunquam habuisset vere agentem. Cumque vidissent ordinem in ipso universo observatum, quo ordine eiusdem universi partes ad invicem colligantur et sic sit quid unum, oportuit eos necessario dicere ut universum habeat ordinatorem, quo ordine conservatur, et ut sic huiusmodi ordinatoris ordo versatur circa ordinanda et conservanda, que, scilicet, non sunt ab ipso ordinatore producta. Cumque ut sic habuissent ipsa ordinata esse preter eiusdem ordinatoris intentum, sequitur ergo ut casu contigisset eidem ordinatori ut habuissent esse ordinanda, sine quibus sensisset ipse ordinator ociosus. Quoque casu contigisset ordinandis ut habuissent esse ordinator, sine quo casu habuissent esse sine ordine et sine conservatione, et per consequens per se apta nata corrumpi, cum hoc quod dicant ut habuissent esse ab eterno, et per consequens ut numquam habuissent potentiam ad non esse ut supra. Preterea ut sic sequeretur ut eidem gubernatori idem contingat quod perdici, quam dicunt *aliena calefacere ova* [cf. Jer 17:11]. Que tamen omnia videntur inopinabilia. Cumque non habeant hec omnia pro inconvenienti, licet ergo probent primum motorem esse quid abstractum et per consequens quid unum tantum ut supra patuit. Non tamen esset inconveniens ut darentur substantie numero plures quamvis abstracte et eque prime, et hoc cum essent actionis genere differentes et per consequens forma, itaque illarum altera esset quid movens reliqua vero

individual beings, but is only one in number [and is] common to the whole of the human species. Therefore, after bodily death, there would be no difference between the righteous [man] and the sinner, [or between] the wise men and the ignorant or stupid men. On the contrary, for them in this life, being righteous or wise, or just enough as is convenient for the community in political life, does not make a difference. Consequently, nature in vain gave us the desire to know divine things, as well as the ability to [to] things that are not useful for the social community, as Averroes explicates in *Metaphysics* 2, text. 14,[a] saying that men naturally desire to know.

§ *16.6* Fourth, the philosophers are led by an assumption [lit. proposition] according to which something that is eternal does not have an agent. This is evident because a true agent is necessarily temporally prior to its activity. They necessarily stated that the universe, which they supposed to be eternal, as mentioned above, does not truly have an agent. However, they saw that an order is observed in the universe. By this order, the parts of the universe are mutually connected, and so it is one. Moreover, they necessarily say that the universe has an arranger who conserves the order and that the order of the arranger resides in the order and in the conservation of beings that were not produced by it. Therefore, since the ordered things exist without the intention of the arranger, it follows that it would happen to the arranger by chance that there were things to be ordered, and without them, the arranger would be pointless. It would also happen by chance that the ordered things had an arranger, because without the arranger, the things would exist without order and conservation, and consequently, they would naturally be disposed to be corrupted, even though they say that these ordered things are eternal, and as a consequence, they do not have the potency of non-being, as mentioned above. Therefore, the governor [arranger] would resemble [a partridge] hatching foreign eggs.[b] All these things seem to be incongruous. However, they do not consider all these things incongruous, even though they proved that the first mover is a separate substance and that it is consequently only one, as mentioned above. However, it would not be incongruous that there were several substances in number, though separate and equally first. And since they are different in kind of activity and consequently in form, therefore one of them

---

[a] *Metaph.* 2.2.994b.   [b] Cf. Jer 17:11.

by which they are separate in species, as Averroes explains in *The Incoherence of the Incoherence* 5, second investigation.[a] And according to this, it follows that the name of divinity applies to both of them equally, or that not only one of them will be God. And they made effort[s] to convey and teach the contrary of this—namely, that there is only one God—as was explained in *Metaphysics* 12, text. 39,[b] 49,[c] and elsewhere.

§16.7.1 Fifth, they saw that the achievement of knowledge among us takes place in one of two ways: (1) the first through the senses, and this is [knowledge] of the particulars of the sensible [objects], which are only perceived by the senses, and (2) the second through the intellect, and this is [knowledge] of the kinds of the intelligibles that are devoid of matter. They say that it is incongruous that divine knowledge should apply to the particulars of the sensible [objects] as Job thought, as it says (Job 10:4): "Do You have the eyes of flesh?", and moreover—as is evident | among them—that divine providence does not apply to them.

§16.7.2 Averroes explains this in [the Commentary on] *Metaphysics* 12, text. 37.[d] And therefore, it follows that God—may He be praised—does not discriminate between a righteous man and a sinner, or [between] a wise man and a fool, not in their lifetime and not after their death, since they are particulars of the sensible [objects] to which His knowledge, let alone His providence, are not applicable. And when they say that there is individual providence in the corporeal organs of every living being, which are undoubtedly intended for the necessary benefit of this particular [being], they say that all this is the activity of nature, and since everything is intended for a final purpose, it is undoubtedly an intellectual power. And the power that formed the organs of the living beings formed them without a material instrument, which is not appropriate for a power in matter, as Averroes says in the name of Aristotle in [the Commentary on] *Metaphysics* 7, text. 31.[e] If this is correct, it follows that the nature acting for a final purpose without a material instrument is either (1) an intending separate intellect, or (2) its instrument, as Averroes says in the [Commentary on] the aforementioned book, 12, text. 18.[f] And therefore, it follows that this separate intellect has providence over the particulars. And the doubt of those who say that it is not appropriate for a separate intellect to know particulars, still less to have providence over them, remains.

---

[a] Cf. *Incoherence* 174–175. [b] *Metaph.* 12.7.1072b. [c] *Metaph.* 12.8.1074a.
[d] Cf. *Metaph.* 12.6.1072a. [e] Cf. *Metaph.* 7.10.1034b. [f] Cf. *Metaph.* 12.3.1070a.

אבן רשד בספר הפלת ההפלה מאמר ה' פרק ב'. ולפי זה יתחייב שיפול שם אלהות על שניהם בשוה או שלא יהיה אחד מהם אלוה. והנה הם מתאמצים להבין ולהורות הפך זה היינו שאין אלוה כי אם אחד במספר כמבואר בספר מה שאחר מאמר י״ב פרק ל״ט ומ״ט וזולתם.

§ 16.7.1 חמישית בראותם היות השגת ידיעה אצלנו על אחד משני פנים האחד בחושים וזה בפרטי המוחשים אשר לא נשיגם כי אם בחושים. והשני בשכל וזה במיני המושכלות המופשטות מחומר אמרו שהוא מן הנמנע שתפול ידיעה אלהית על פרטי המוחשים כמו שחשב איוב באמרו: «העיני בשר לך? וכו'» (איוב י' ד'). וכל שכן שהוא כמבואר | אצלם שלא תפול עליהם השגחה אלהית,

§ 16.7.2 כמו שביאר אבן רשד בספר מה שאחר מאמר י״ב פרק ל״ז ומזה יתחייב שלא יבדיל האל יתברך בין צדיק לרשע בין חכם לכסיל לא בחייהם ולא אחר מותם להיותם פרטי מוחשים אשר לא תפול ידיעתו עליהם כל שכן השגחתו ובהיותם רואים היות ההשגחה פרטית באיברי כל חי מכוונים בלי ספק לתועלת הכרחי לפרטי ההוא אמרו היות כל זה פעלת הטבע ובהיות שכל מכוין לתכלית הוא כח שכלי בלי ספק והיה הכח המצייר הכלים בבעלי חיים מציירם בלתי כלי חמרי אשר לא יאות לכח בחומר כאשר הורה אבן רשד בשם ארסטו' בספר מה שאחר מאמר ז' פרק ל״א הנה אם כן יתחייב שיהיה הטבע הפועל לתכלית בלי כלי חמרי אם שכל נבדל מכוין ואם כלי לו כמו שהורה אבן רשד בספר הנזכר מאמר י״ב פרק י״ח ומזה יתחייב שיהיה אותו השכל הנבדל משגיח בפרטים וישאר הספק אשר אמרו שלא יאות לשכל נבדל לדעת פרטים כל שכן להשגיח עליהם.

quid ordinans,ᵃ et per consequens vel nullus daretur Deus vel plures darentur eque primi. Cuius oppositum conatur Phylosopho docere *Metaphysicorum* XII t.c. 39 et ibidem, t.c. 52 ubi infert quod omnia in universo sunt propter unum horum omnium primum.

§ 16.7.1 Quinto considerantes quod cognoscibilium duo sunt apud nos genera: sensibilium, scilicet, que sensibus tantum percipi videntur, et intelligibilium que non sensibus sed intellectu tantum percipiuntur. Ideo habuerunt pro inconvenienti, ut divinus intellectus habeat sensibilium individua perci|pere cum sint sensuum tantum obiectum, nedum ut ipse divinus intellectus habeat de ipsis individuis curare sive de illis habere sollicitudinem.

§ 16.7.2 Quare Aven R. *Metaphysicorum* XII t.c. 37 ait: «Sollicitudo circa individuum tali modo, quod nullus habeat communicationem cum eo, hoc non est fas divine bonitati etc.» Ad quod aperte sequitur ut secundum eos nulla sit cura apud Deum de iusto vel iniusto neque in eorum vita neque post eorum mortem. Cumque in cuiuslibet individui organis individuale appareat artificium, et per consequens cura sive sollicitudo ab aliquo intellectu proculdubio emanans, que quidem omnia nature attribuunt, sequitur ut ipsa natura sit quoddam intellectuale abstractum individui oportunitatem sapienter curans, vel ut sit corporea virtus que tamen cum more intellectuali procedat, scilicet, ad intentum finem et sine materiali instrumento, prout sensu patet et habetur ab Aven R. Phylosophi auctoritate in commento *Metaphysicorum* VII t.c. 31. Habet quidem necessario regi ab aliqua, scilicet, abstracta intelligentia huiusmodi organa sub proportionali mensura individuo eiusque sexui oportuna sapienter intendenti, prout videtur Aven R. fateri *Metaphysicorum* XII t.c., 18. Et sic non minus imminet eadem difficultas qua, scilicet, dicunt quod individua cum sint sensuum obiecta non habent ab abstractis percipi, nedum ut abstractum dicatur habere de illis sollicitudinem sive curam, cuius oppositum ut sic experimento patere videtur.

[the separate substances] would be the mover of the rest, the true arranger. Consequently, there would either be no god or several gods [that were] equally first. The opposite of this was proven by the Philosopher in *Metaphysics* 12, text. 39,ᵃ and 12, text. 52,ᵇ in which Aristotle states that all things in the universe are caused by one who is the first of them.

§ 16.7.1 Fifth, the philosophers say that there are two kinds of knowable objects for us: the sensible objects, which seem to be known by the senses only; and the intelligibles, which are perceived not through the senses, but through the intellect only. Therefore, they consider it incongruous that the divine intellect should perceive particulars among sensible beings, | which are objects of the senses only, and that the divine intellect should have providence or care over these particular beings.

§ 16.7.2 [This is] as Averroes explicates in *Metaphysics* 12, text. 37,ᶜ where he states: "Providence for an individual, in which nobody else shares, is something that the divine bounty does not necessitate, etc." Therefore, it follows for them that God has no providence over the righteous [man] or the sinner, either in their lifetime or after death. However, artifice is visible in the individual organs of every particular being, and consequently providence or care that is emanated from an intellect. The philosophers attributed all these things to nature. It follows that this nature would be intellectual and separate, taking care of the benefit of a particular being; alternatively, it would be a corporeal power, which, however, proceeds in an intellectual way; namely, towards an intended purpose and without a material instrument, as the senses testify and Averroes explicates in the Commentary on *Metaphysics* 7, text. 31.ᵈ It must be [the case] that the organs are necessarily ruled by a separate intellect, which wisely and proportionately takes care of what is appropriate to the individual and its genus, as Averroes explicates in *Metaphysics* 12, text. 18.ᵉ So, the same problem arises no less, because [the philosophers] claimed that since the individual beings are objects of the senses, they are not perceived by the separate intellects, and consequently, this separate intellect has no providence and care over them, but the opposite of this seems to be evident according to experience.

ᵃ quid movens reliqua vero quid ordinans] bᶜᵒʳʳ; quid ordinans b.

ᵃ *Metaph.* 12.7.1072b.   ᵇ *Metaph.* 12.10.1075a.   ᶜ *Metaph.* 12.7.1072a.
ᵈ *Metaph.* 7.10.1034b.   ᵉ Cf. *Metaph.* 12.3.1070a.

§ **16.8.1 Yet:**
The Torah of our God teaches one who understands true opinions through correct proofs, and in order to dispel the aforementioned doubts [i.e., questions], it established a path and a way for us that differs greatly from the way of the aforementioned philosophers, by which everyone who investigates will come to recognise our Lord—He may be praised—[to be] the intellect who is known [by the] wonders from His Torah.

§ **16.8.2** And this is so because it is already clear to everyone who investigates by searching [their] experience until [they reach] a first intelligible, [which tells us] that the existent thing that persists in many existents did not come to them by [mere] chance, unintended by any voluntary or natural agent, as is evident in *On the Heavens* 2, text. 45,[a] and *Physics* 2, text. 48.[b] But this necessarily occurs [either] through the activity of a voluntary agent intending a certain end or through the activity of a natural agent under the command and produced by the rule and government of an intellectual being, who undoubtedly intends [it], as Averroes explains in [the Commentary on] *Metaphysics* 12, text. 18.[c]

§ **16.9.1** Second, it becomes clear that in every single one of the spheres whose movements are known from sense [perception]—of which there are at least eight—there exists a [accurately] limited quantity. If it was larger or smaller by even a hair's breadth, there would be a vacuum between them or they would prevent each other from moving. And from the aforementioned limitation that exists in every single one of them, everyone who investigates will come to know that their aforementioned limited quantity and the substance that bears the quantity are necessarily intended by a voluntary agent or by the activity of a natural agent who brought them forth by the government and commandment of an aforementioned voluntary intending agent.

§ **16.9.2** And Isaiah teaches [us] this, as it says (Isaiah 48:13): "My right hand spread out the heavens. I call unto them, let them stand up together"; that is to say, I spread them out and measured them in such a way that they are able to stand together and will not hinder each other in the activity of their movement.

---

[a] *Cael.* 2.8.289b.   [b] *Phys.* 2.4.196b.   [c] Cf. *Metaph.* 12.3.1070a.

§ 16.8.1 **Sacra vero**

Scriptura veras opiniones circa premissas questiones tenendas demonstrative docens Phylosophorum quidem processui modo quodam aliqualiter opposito procedere videtur.

§ 16.8.2 Illa enim merito habens pro per se noto, ut illud, ad quod optatus quidam sequitur effectus et fit frequenter et in plurimis, non contingat fieri casu,[a] scilicet, preter intentum alicuius agentis huiusmodi effectum finaliter intendentis, sicut habetur a Phylosopho in lib. De Celo II t.c. 45 et Physicorum II t.c. 48. Immo oportet ut sit actus voluntarii agentis finem intendentis inmediate, scilicet, vel saltem mediate, pro habetur ab Aven R. *Metaphysicorum* XII t.c. 18.

§ 16.9.1 Secundo presupponit prout sensu patere videtur, quod in quolibet celestium orbium quorum motus percipitur sensu et tales sunt saltem octo, est quidem quantitas ad unguem limitata, qua maiori vel minori data daretur inter eos necessario vacuum vel novum corpus, aut se invicem impedirent a motu, per quam limitationem sic ad unguem apparentem competit per modum finis sequitur effectus. Patet quidem ut horum quantitates sic in omnibus limitate, et per consequens horum corpora quibus huiusmodi quantitates insunt habuerunt esse ab agente sive producente voluntario mediato scilicet vel immediato finem huiusmodi intendente ut supra.

69ᵛ
[98] § 16.9.2 Et hoc docuit Esaias cap. 48 [48:13] ubi dicit: «Dextra mea mensa est celos, vocabo eos et stabunt simul» quasi dicat constitui orbes sub quadam mensura adeo limitata ut possint simul contiguit stare nullo pacto se invicem a motu impedientes ut supra.

§ 16.8.1 **However:**

The Holy Scripture, demonstratively teaching the true opinions to be held concerning the aforementioned *quaestiones*,[a] seems to take an opposite approach in comparison to that of the philosophers.

§ 16.8.2 [The Holy Scripture] rightly considers it self-evident that a thing from which the desired effect follows and that occurs frequently and in several things does not happen by chance—namely, without the intention of an agent finally aiming at this effect—as the Philosopher explains in *On the Heavens* 2, text. 45,[b] and in *Physics* 2, text. 48.[c] This is the activity of a voluntary agent, who aims at an end immediately, or at least mediately, as Averroes explicates in *Metaphysics* 12, text. 18.[d]

§ 16.9.1 Second, it proposes, as seems to be evident to the senses, that in every celestial sphere whose movement is perceived by the senses—and there are at least eight of them—there is a very accurately limited quantity, and if [the quantity] is [too] great or small, then an empty or a new body will necessarily exist between them, or they will impede each other from moving. From this limitation, which is most accurate, as is apparent, the effect follows as [their] final purpose. It is clear that their quantities are limited in every existent; therefore, their bodies, to which the quantities belong, exist, mediately or immediately, thanks to a voluntary agent or a producer who aims at a purpose, as aforementioned.

§ 16.9.2 This is what Isaiah teaches in chapter 48 (48:13), saying: "My right hand hath measured the heavens: I call unto them, and they shall stand together," which is like saying: I established the spheres according to a limited measurement, so that the celestial bodies would be able to stand together and not impede each other from movement, as aforementioned.

69ᵛ
[98]

---

[a] casu] bᶜᵒʳʳ; cau b.

[a] Cf. *OA* § 16.8, in which Sforno employs the term *safeq* (*dubium*). [b] *Cael.* 2.8.289b. [c] *Phys.* 2.4.196b. [d] *Metaph.* 12.3.1070a.

§ 16.10.1 Third, it becomes clear from sense [perception] that in the formation of the corruptibles that have corporeal organs, there exist many organs with different shapes, and the individual has an evident benefit from every single one of them, which it will not obtain if it does not have that shape. And therefore, it becomes clear that they are intended by a voluntary agent, or a natural [agent] under the government of an aforementioned voluntary intending [agent].

§ 16.10.2 The Poet teaches us the same thing, as he says (Psalm 94:9): "Shall He who implants the ear not hear, He who forms the eye not see?", meaning: Shall He not know and have providence? The statement of the unbelievers is the contrary, saying (Psalm 94:7): "Ha-Shem does not see it, the God of Jacob does not pay heed." And he continues [with] proof of this that He necessarily has providence over the individuals of the human species, insofar as morals and the first intelligibles naturally exist in the individuals of the aforementioned [human] species, as it says (Psalm 94:10): "Shall He who disciplines nations not punish, He who instructs men in knowledge?" And this is so because they have only [those kinds of] instruments [or: organs] for the perfection of intelligibles that are acquired by individual free will. Because of [one's] morality, one yearns for knowledge of the truth, and also [the truth] in the divinity, which is not necessary for the [benefit of the] political community, and [he yearns for knowledge] of the first intelligibles. [This] will only be possible for him through individual free will. And therefore, it follows that there is [divine] providence over individual free will.

§ 16.11.1 Fourth, it becomes clear from experience that the existence of the nature of prime matter, without which things would not be generated from each other and matter would be annihilated most of the time, is necessarily required for the activities of the [recurring] generation of the corruptibles, as Averroes explains in [the Commentary on] *Metaphysics* 12, text. 33,[a] and [moreover] the existence of the straight motion of the diurnal sphere and the existence of the oblique motions of the planets [are required], especially the oblique motion of the sun and the existence of the light of the sun and the stars and their heat, as is evident from sense [perception]. And Averroes explains this in the Commentary on the aforementioned book, ibid., text. 18. And from the need for the aforementioned [recurring] generation, [i.e.,] so that every one of these [necessary things] will exist and will [also] be [in] a relationship

---

[a] Cf. *Metaph.* 12.6.1072a.

§ 16.10.1 שלישית התבאר מן החוש שביצירת הנפסדים בעלי האיברים נמצאו איברים רבים במספר על תמונות שונות ובכל אחת מהן תועלת מבואר לפרטי ההוא אשר לא היה משיגו זולתי בתמונה ההיא. ומזה התבאר היותם מכוונים מפועל רצוני או טבעי בהנהגת רצוני מכוין כנזכר.

§ 16.10.2 כמו שהורה המשורר באמרו: »הנוטע אזן הלא ישמע אם יוצר עין הלא יביט?« (תהלים צ״ד ט׳), כלומר הלא ידע וישגיח? הפך מאמר הכופרים באמרם: »לא יראה יה[a] ולא יבין אלהי יעקב« (שם שם ז׳). והוסיף מופת על היותו בהכרח משגיח באישי המין האנושי מצד המוסר והמושכלות הראשונות אשר נמצאו בטבע באישי המין הנזכר באמרו: »היוסר גויים הלא יוכיח המלמד אדם דעת?« (שם שם י׳). וזה כי אמנם הם אינם כלים לשלמות מושכלות נקנות בבחירה אישיית כי במוסר יכסוף לידיעת האמת גם באלהיות הבלתי הכרחיית לקבוץ המדיני ובמושכלות הראשונות יהיה איפשר לו זה בבחירה אישיית לא זולתה. ומזה יתחייב שתהיה ההשגחה על הבחירה האישיית.

§ 16.11.1 רביעית התבאר בנסיון שלפעלות תולדות הנפסדים יצטרך בהכרח מציאות טבע החומר הראשון אשר זולתו לא יתהוו זה מזה ויכלה החומר ברב הזמן כאשר באר אבן רשד בספר מה שאחר מאמר י״ב פרק ל״ג ומציאות תנועת הגלגל היומי הישרה ומציאות תנועות הכוכבים המעוותות בפרט תנועת השמש המעוותת ומציאות אור השמש והכוכבים וחומם כמבואר בחוש ובארו אבן רשד בביאור הספר הנזכר מאמר הנזכר פרק י״ח ובהיות צורך התולדות הנזכר שיהיה כל אחד מאלה עם יחס מיוחד לכל תולדה ותולדה נודע

---

[a] יה] emend. Dunk.; om. a; dominus b; יה M.

§ 16.10.1 Tertio presupponit quod mortalium organizatis organa insunt numero plura sub diversis figuris, in quorum singulis est manifesta utilitas per figuras situm,[a] et alia ad illius individui cui inest necessitatem, vel saltem comoditatem, sine qua figura non consequeretur huiusmodi proficuum. Quibus patet quod ipsa organa sunt sic intenta a quodam mediate vel inmediate agenti voluntarie, scilicet finem huiusmodi intendente.

§ 16.10.2 Et hoc docet Psalmus 93 [94:9] ubi dicit: «Qui plantat aurem nonne audiet. Anqui fixit oculum non perspiciat,» quasi dicat quod inopinabile est ut ille, qui mediate vel immediate tanto artificio formavit mortalium organa, non habeat de illis cognitionem nedum sollicitudinem, sicut putabant Gentiles, quorum opiniones paulo ante retulit dicens: «Et dixerunt non videbit Dominus neque intelligit Deus Jahacob etc.,» inferentes quod Deus de mortalium individuis, que sensuum tantum videntur esse obiecta, nullam habet cognitionem.

§ 16.11.1 Quarto presupponit prout experientia docere videtur, quod ad genitorum reciprocationem habent necessario quatuor concurrere. Primo, scilicet, materie prime natura, sine qua non possent ab invicem fieri et per consequens non daretur horum successiva reciprocatio, quia consumeretur materia et sic non daretur generationum perseveratio. Secundo requiritur motus diurnus rectus. Tertio requiritur motus planetarum obliquus, presertim solis. Quarto requiritur lumen solis et syderum horumque calores diversimode proportionati, prout habetur ab Aven R. *Metaphysicorum* XII t.c. 18. Cum autem huiusmodi concursus per tot fiendus simul et proportiones diverse secundum diversorum oportunitatem non contingat, ut

§ 16.10.1 Third, it proposes that the organs of the corruptible beings are many in number [and] organised according to different shapes; the function of their shape is evident in each of them, and other organs in some individual beings are placed in them for necessity or at least for convenience, and without them, the shape would not achieve any benefit. From these [words], it is clear that the organs are, mediately or immediately, produced by a voluntary agent who aims at a purpose.

§ 16.10.2 Psalm 93 (94:9) says: "He who planted the ear, does he not hear? He who formed the eye, does he not see?", which is like saying that it is incongruous that the one who mediately or immediately formed the organs of the corruptible beings by artifice does not have knowledge or care about them, as the Gentiles thought. Then, the Psalmist (94:7) replied to their opinions: "Yet they say, the Lord shall not see, neither shall the God of Jacob understand." [The Gentiles] concluded that God ignores the corruptible individual beings, which are only objects of the senses.

§ 16.11.1 Fourth, it proposes, as experience seems to show, that four things concur in the movement of the reciprocation of generated beings. First, the nature of prime matter, without which nothing would be generated from one another, and consequently, there would be no successive reciprocation, because matter would be completely consumed and so there would be no continuation of the generation. Second, a straight diurnal motion is required. Third, the oblique motion of the planets, and especially of the sun, is required. Fourth, the light of the sun and the stars and their differently proportioned [amounts of] warmth are required, as Averroes explicates in *Metaphysics* 12, text. 18.[a] Since the participation in the production of different proportions at the same time according to the benefit of

---

[a] situm] b^corr; suum b.

[a] Cf. *Metaph.* 12.3.1070a.

that is specific for each and every generation, it is undoubtedly known that they are all in agreement with the activity of generation not by chance, but necessarily through the intention of a voluntary or natural agent, as mentioned, who causes their agreement and their existence mediately or immediately for the final purpose of the activity of the aforementioned generation.

§ 16.11.2 And Isaiah teaches [us] this, as he says (Isaiah 45:7): "Who forms light and creates darkness, and who makes peace and who creates evil: I ha-Shem make all these things"; that is to say: (1) from the existence of "peace," which is [concluded] between the opposite motions of the spheres who are in this agreement with each other in [the case of] the aforementioned activity of generation, and (2) from the existence of prime matter, which is called "evil" by many of the Ancients, as mentioned above, it will become clear that "I, ha-Shem" (ibid.) means: [I am] a generator following absolute non-existence, as he said (ibid.): "I make all these things." And this is so because they were certainly not generated from a prior substrate, [but were generated] without a substrate prior to prime matter and [prior] to the aforementioned spheres | and their motions. And if so, it becomes clear that their existence is thanks to the power of My [i.e., God's] free will.

§ 16.12.1 Fifth, this becomes clear from sense [perception], because the existence of the species of animals cannot endure without the species of plants by which they live. And the existence of human beings is not pleasant without the species of plants and some of the species of land animals, especially the domesticated [animals], which serve them for the harvest in [various] ways. And it is evident that it is not by coincidence that for each and every single species of animal, there are species of plants that are necessary for the perpetuity of some or most of them [and] that are designated for a [particular] species rather than for [another particular] species. And it is not by coincidence that for the human species, species of plants exist that are designated for its perpetuity, and [also] species of land animals that are designated for serving it. Yet it follows that the existence of all of them is intended by a voluntary agent, or a natural agent ordered by the will of a voluntary agent, who intended it for a final purpose, as mentioned, as the Poet explains when he says (Psalm 104:14): "You make the grass grow for the cattle, and herbage for man's labour that he may get food, etc."

in omnibus fiat casu, patet quidem quod habent necessario[a] fieri per voluntarium mediate vel immediate agentem, inde finem intendentem prout supra.

§ 16.11.2 Et hoc docet Esayas cap. 45[b] [45:7] ubi dicit: «Faciens pace et creans malum ego Dominus faciens omnia hec etc.» quasi dicat quod per illam pacem, que apparet inter oppositos celestium motus et oppositas elementorum qualitates, et hoc cum ab generationes concurrant[c] et sibi invicem conveniant, et per naturam materie prime, quam antiquorum nonnulli malum appellabant ut supra, que similiter necessario concurrit ad easdem generationes fiendas, patet me Dominum, scilicet, dans esse sive Creatorem hec omnia fecisse secundum totum. Et hoc cum pateat illa omnia ad generationes penitus necessaria non concurrisse casu, sed iussu mei voluntarie agentis, et per consequens illorum producentis, cum scilicet inopinabile sit ut horum omnium esse horumque concursum habuissent casu tantum preter alicuius intentum existere, et per consequens | patet me esse Creatorem, cum nec materia prima neque celestia contingat ut habuissent esse a subiecto his priori ut supra.

70ʳ
[99]

§ 16.12.1 Quinto presupponitur prout sensu patere videtur, quod animalium genera non sustentantur sine diversis vegetabilium generibus his diversis diversimode proportionatis, neque humanum genus bene se habere preter vegetabilium genera sibi proportionata, et nisi haberent esse animalium genera saltem mansueta eiusdem servitiis non mediocriter oportuna. Cumque pateat, quod non casu contigisset animalibus, ut haberent esse tot diversa vegetabilium genera eisdem animalibus diversimode et oportune proportionata per que sustentarentur. Neque humano generi casu contigisset, ut ultra vegetabilium genera sibi proportionata haberent esse tot animalium genera sue servituti disposita, patet quidem quod horum omnium esse a quodam facta sunt voluntarie agente huiusmodi finem intendente ut supra. Et hoc docet Psalmus 103 [104:14] ubi dicit: «Producens senum iumento et herbam serviti homini ut educat panem a terra.»

each thing does not occur by chance, it is clear that they are necessarily produced mediately or immediately by a voluntary agent who aims at a purpose, as mentioned above.

§ 16.11.2 Isaiah teaches this in chapter 45 (45:7), saying: "He, who makes peace and who creates evil: I the Lord that do all these things," which is like saying that from "peace," which is evident between opposite motions of the celestial bodies and the opposite qualities of the elements— and this is because they concur with the generation and fit with each other—and from the nature of prime matter, which some of the ancient philosophers called "evil," as mentioned above, and which also concurs with the generation of beings, it is clear that I am the Lord, who bestows being, or the Creator, who generates everything according to the whole. This is because it is clear that all the things necessary for generation do not concur by chance; rather, everything happens according to My commandment as a voluntary agent, and consequently also as their producer. Indeed, it is impossible that their existence and participation should only occur by chance without any intention. As a consequence, it is clear | that I am the Creator, because neither prime matter nor celestial bodies come forth from a substrate that is temporally prior to them, as mentioned above.

70ʳ
[99]

§ 16.12.1 Fifth, it is proposed, as seems evident from the senses, that the animal species cannot survive without different vegetal species proportioned to them in different ways, nor does the human species receives good [things] besides [i.e., without] the vegetal species proportionate to it, and without some animals, especially the domesticated ones, which are necessary to serve it. Thus, it is clear that it does not happen to the animals by chance that there are so many different vegetal species [that are] conveniently and differently proportioned [i.e., designated] to them, which are necessary for the survival of animals. Also, it does not happen to the human species by chance that besides the species of plants proportioned [i.e., designated] to them, there are so many species of animals arranged to serve them; and it is clear that all of them are generated by a voluntary agent who aims at a goal, as aforementioned. Psalm 103 (104:14) teaches: "He causes the grass to grow for the cattle and herb for the service of man, that they may bring forth food, etc."

---

[a] necessario] coni. Copp.; neeesario b.   [b] 45] emend. Copp.; 43 b; 45 M; 45 V.   [c] concurrant] coni. Copp.; concurcant b.

§ 16.12.2 And as it becomes clear from all these and other [words] above—every single thing is in its place—the existence of the spheres and their stars and their motions, and the existence of prime matter, are necessarily the activity of a voluntary agent; it brought them forth for a final purpose, and this w necessarily by way of creation without a prior substrate, as mentioned. And it becomes clear that the existence of the generation of the corruptibles cannot occur without the activity of the spheres and the activity of their planets [or: stars] and the activity of their motions and the affection of prime matter. Then, it becomes clear that the existence of all of them and their government and their conjunction are thanks to the activity of a voluntary agent, which brought them forth and led them,

§ 16.12.3 as it says (Genesis 1:1): "In the beginning God created." And this is the name that informs [us] about a "leader" and an "arranger of order"; that is to say, His government and His order are [found] in the existents, which teaches us that He created them all. And it [i.e., Holy Scripture] continues to explain the proof, as it says (Genesis 2:4): "These are the generations of the heavens and the earth when they were created on the day God, ha-Shem, made earth and heavens"; that is to say, the aforementioned generations are the "generations of the heavens and the earth," because they would not exist without the existence of the substance of the heavens and the existence of their stars and the existence of their motions and their light and their heat, which acts in material [things], and the existence of the earthly matter that is affected by them. It is inconceivable that all those things that are necessary for the generations should exist by chance, but their existence teaches [us] that this is the activity of a voluntary agent, who brought them forth and created them. And together with this, it becomes clear that the agreement of all of them in an agent and in affection is necessary for generation. If so, they teach [us] that their agreement is [made] by the activity of an intender for a certain final purpose. And therefore, it follows that the existence of every existent is [caused] by their creation by ha-Shem, who intended and created [them] after absolute non-existence. And their [mutual]

§ 16.12.2 וכאשר התבאר מכל אלה וזולתם לעיל איש על מקומו שמציאות הגלגלים וכוכביהם ותנועותיהם ומציאות החומר הראשון היו בהכרח פעלת פועל רצוני שהמציאם לתכלית וזה בהכרח דרך בריאה מבלי אין נושא קודם כנזכר והתבאר שמציאות תולדות הנפסדים לא יהיה בלתי פעלת הגלגלים ופעלת כוכביהם ופעולת תנועותיהם והתפעלות החומר הראשון הנה התבאר היות מציאות כלם והנהגתם וקשרם מפעולת[a] פועל רצוני הוא ממציאם ומנהיגם,

§ 16.12.3 באמרו: »בראשית ברא אלהים« (בראשית א׳ א׳). והוא השם המורה ‹מנהיג› ו‹מסדר› כלומר שהנהגתו וסדרו בנמצאות מורים שהוא ברא את כלם והוסיף לבאר המופת באמרו: »אלה תולדות השמים והארץ בהבראם ביום עשות ה׳ אלהים ארץ ושמים« (שם ב׳ ד׳), כלומר שבהיות תולדות הנזכרות »תולדות השמים והארץ« (שם), כי לא תהיינה בלתי מציאות עצם השמים ומציאות כוכביהם ומציאות תנועותיהם ואורם וחומם הפועלים בחמרים ומציאות החומר הארציי המתפעל מהם אשר לא יעלה על לב שנמצאו כלם הכרחיים לתולדות במקרה אבל יורו היותם פעלת פועל רצוני שהמציאם ובראם ועם זה התבאר היות הכרחית לתולדות הסכמת כלם בפעל והתפעלות הנה אם כן יורו היות הסכמתם פעולת מכוין בה לתכלית מה ובכן התבאר שמציאות כל הנזכר בהבראם היה מאת ה׳ המהווה ובורא אחר אפיסות מוחלט והסכמתם יחד בתולדות היתה

---

a. מפעולת] a[corr]; לפעולת a.

§ 16.12.2 Cum autem ex omnibus premissis et aliis ut supra in suis habetur locis pateat, quod tam celestia quam prima materia habuerunt esse ab agente finem intendente et per consequens a creante post purum non esse producente, et hoc quia non datur subiectum illis aliquo pacto prius, similiter pateat quo ad mortalium generationes habent necessario concurrere actiones orbium et siderum luminis caloris et motus et prime materie passio. Patet quidem quod horum omnium esse horumque regimen et concursus emanat a quodam mediate vel immediate agente illa omnia voluntarie ad finem producente illaque omnia ad idem intentum finem colligante.

§ 16.12.3 Et hoc docet Sacrum Genesis Documentum [2:4] ubi dicit: «Iste sunt generationes celi et terra quando creati sunt etc.» intelligens de mortalium generationibus, de quibus paulo ante fecerat verbum. Quasi dicat quod cum huiusmodi generationes nonnisi per celum et terram simul facte sint, et hoc quia non dantur fieri preter naturam prime materie, que est terrestribus communis, cum, scilicet, sit per celestia ad generationes disposita, inopinabile quidem est ut omnia illa sic necessario ad idem concurrentia habuissent sic esse casu, quare patet ut habuissent esse per voluntarium producentem illa omnia creantem. Quare ibidem subdit dicens: «Quando creati[a] sunt,» inferens quod his satis patet de eorum creatione, et ideo ibidem sequitur dicens: «In die qua fecit Dominus Deus terram et celum,» quasi dicat quod similiter per colligationem celestium et terrestrium in generationibus apparentem patet quidem illa omnia esse eiusdem voluntarii agentis finem intendentis actum. Dicit ergo quod cum ad ipsas generationes requirantur presentie celestium et terrestrium, quare inopinabile est ut illa omnia sic ad idem necessario concurrentia habuissent esse casu, sed penitus per agentem finem intendentem significatur horum omnium creatio. Quodque per horum colligationem | in eisdem generationibus apparentem significatur eorundem ordinem ab eodem creatore emanare, et hoc cum nullum detur subiectum his terrestribus vel celestibus prius, ex quo subiecto contingat ut agens illa fecisse. Sequitur quidem ut tam eorum subiecta quam eorundem forme sint producta post eorum purum non esse, et hoc nonnisi per illum productionis modum quem Sacra Scriptura creatio-

§ 16.12.2 From all these aforementioned premises, here and in other places, it is clear that the celestial bodies as well as prime matter came forth from a voluntary agent who aims at a purpose, and consequently, from a creator who generated them after absolute nothingness. This occurred because there was no substrate prior to them. Similarly, it is clear that the actions of the spheres, the heat of the stars' light, the movement, and the affection of prime matter necessarily concur with the generation of corruptible beings. The existence of all of them, their order, and their conjunction [i.e., joining] is emanated, mediately or immediately, from a voluntary agent who produces them for a purpose and connects them for the same intended purpose.

§ 16.12.3 The [Holy] Book of Genesis (2:4) teaches this, saying: "These are the generations of the heavens and the earth, when they were created," meaning the generation of corruptible beings, which were mentioned a little earlier, as if to say that since these generations were simultaneously produced by the heavens and the earth—and this because they could not be produced aside from the nature of prime matter, which is common to all terrestrial elements, because it was ordered for generation by the celestial bodies—it would be incongruous that all these things necessarily participating in the same thing had been produced by chance. Therefore, it is clear that they received their being from a voluntary producer, who created all of them. Hence, Genesis (2:4) says: "When they were created," which means that their creation is evident, and it continues: "In the day that the Lord God made the heavens and the earth," as if to say that from the connection between celestial and terrestrial beings appearing in the generations, it is clear that a voluntary agent who aims at a purpose produced them. Therefore, it says that since the existence of celestial and terrestrial beings is necessary for the generation of mortal beings, it would hence be incongruous that all these things necessarily participating in the same thing were produced by chance. On the contrary, "an agent who aims at a purpose" means "the creation of all things." Furthermore, the connection appearing in | the generations means that their order was emanated from the creator. This is because there was no substrate that was prior to the terrestrial or celestial beings out of which the agent produced these things. Therefore, it follows that their substrates, as well as their forms, came out of absolute nothingness, and this only by way of a production that the Holy Scripture calls "creation" in which the

---

[a] creati] coni. Copp.; ereati b.

agreement, in addition to the generation, was thanks to His activity, since He is God, who arranges order and rules; He, who after He created, made and ordered [the] earth and [the] heavens to agree to the activities intended by Him, may He be praised.

§ 16.12.4 And apart from these, it becomes clear that every activity of an agent, except that of creation [out of nothing], necessarily requires a certain substrate that exists so that the agent may enact his action on it, | and also the affection needs an affectable [thing] so that an agent may exist to act in it. And if so, it follows that not a single one of them may exist without the existence of its neighbour, if [its] existence were not to have been in vain.

§ 16.12.5 Second, it becomes clear that the existence of the substance of the agent does not follow from the existence of the substrate; and also that the existence of the substance of the substrate does not follow from the existence of the agent, unless we say that every single one of them is a cause of the existence of the other. But if we say so, it follows that every single one of them is a cause of the existence of its [i.e., the other's] substance, which cannot be imagined. And this is so because it cannot be imagined that the existence of a substance is necessary from the existence of something else, except by way of cause and caused. It follows, if so, that the existence of anyone of them is not necessary from the existence of the other, but in it, the other's existence can only be a contingency. And therefore, it follows that the possibility of the activity of the agent, and also the possibility of the affected [thing], are contingent, because if this possibility had not happened to the agent, insofar as the affected [thing] is uncaused by it, its activity would not be possible. And also, the affection of the agent would not be possible if it had not happened that there existed an[other] agent that acted on it. And therefore, it follows that the existence of the agent and the affected thing is contingent, not necessary *per se*. Because from the absence of the possibility of the agent and the affected thing would follow the absence of the forms from which the agents and their affection follow, unless we were to say that there were forms without any potentiality [for actuality]. And this is inconceivable. And therefore, it follows that not a single one of them is eternal, but [it] succeeds to the activity of an intending agent, because the eternal [thing] is necessary by existence *per se*, without any need for the existence of another existent, as is evident from the proof given by Aristotle in *On the Heavens* 1, text. 124.[a]

---

[a] *Cael.* 1.12.282b.

nem appellat, qua, scilicet, tam producti subiectum quam eiusdem forma producuntur, prout habetur ab Aven R. *Metaphysicorum* XII t.c. 18 et de eodem productionis modo intendit Sacrum Genesis documentum cap. primi [1:1] ubi dicit: «In principio creavit Deus,» quasi dicat in illo instanti quod fuit temporis principium, quo nihil temporis habuit esse prius, et per consequens neque motus, quo productor moveretur ad producendum vel quo subiectum alteraret, sicut nunc «extra celum neque motus datur neque tempus,» quare non valet argumentum dicentis quare tunc et non ante ut supra.

§ 16.12.4 Preterea ipsa Sacra Scriptura duo quidem presupponere videtur. Primo, scilicet, quo ad quamlibet actionem (dempta creatione) requiritur necessario subiectum in quod agens agat, quare non dato subiecto non datur agens, nisi fortasse ociosum sub forma nullius actionis de qua ut sic equivoce tantum diceretur forma.

§ 16.12.5 Secundo quod non datur ut alicuius substantie essentia sequatur ad essentiam alterius substantie nisi per modum cause agentis causatum producentis, non autem sicut accidens v.g. sequitur ad esse substantie[a] vel econverso. Cum ergo agens et subiectum, quamvis horum unius existentia non detur sine alterius essentia, prout supra patuit, non tamen habent ab invicem causari, quia si sic, sequetur ut agens causaret se ipsum, quod est inopinabile, patet, quidem ut horum unius essentia nullo pacto fiat per alterius essentiam sed contingenter tantum accidit horum uni ut habeat alterum esse, quod, scilicet, est eidem uni pro sua actione necessarium ut supra. Cum autem non dato huiusmodi contingente non detur horum essentia, sequitur quidem ut horum esse sit quid non per se necessarium et per consequens non ab eterno, illud, enim, quod ab eterno est, habet esse quid per se secluso quocunque alio necessario, cum non possit non esse. Sicut habentur ratione Phylosophi in lib. *De Celo* I t.c. 124, ex quibus sequitur ut nulla natura preter Creantem habuit esse ab eterno.

substrate along with its form are created, as Averroes explicates in *Metaphysics* 12, text. 18.[a] Genesis (1:1) explains the same, saying: "In the beginning God created," which is like saying that that instant was the beginning of time. Therefore, time did not exist before and consequently, there was no motion by which a producer was moved to generate or by which the substrate changed, as now "there is no motion nor time beyond the heavens." Thus, the argument saying "why then and not before?" is not valid, as aforementioned.

§ 16.12.4 Furthermore, the Holy Scripture postulated two assumptions. First, that a substrate is necessary for every activity in which an agent acts except creation. If there is no substrate, there is no agent, unless it is inactive under the form of no activity, which, if so, we call "form" only by equivocation.

§ 16.12.5 Second, that it is not possible that the essence of one substance follows the essence of another substance, unless [it is] according to the mode of causality of an agent who produces a caused thing, so, for instance, an accident does not follow the being of a substance and vice versa. Indeed, since the agent and the substrate (even though one does not exist without the existence of the other, as aforementioned) do not mutually cause each other—because if this were so, it would follow that the agent would cause itself, and this is incongruous—it is clear that the essence of one of them is never produced by the essence of another. Hence, it occurs only by contingency that one of them exists and the other exists as well, and this is necessary for one of them for [performing] its activity, as mentioned above. Moreover, if there is no contingency, they do not exist, [and] therefore their existence is not necessary and it is consequently not eternal; only something eternal exists *per se* and cannot be non-existing, as the Philosopher explains in *On the Heavens* 1, text. 124.[b] From these [words], it follows that nothing besides the creator is eternal.

---

[a] substantie] b[corr]; suo stantie b.

[a] Cf. *Metaph.* 12.3.1070a.   [b] *Cael.* 1.12.282b.

§16.13 And the *Guide to Justice*[a] [God]—may He be praised—informs [us] about all these [things], as He said (Genesis 17:1): "I am El Shaddai. Walk before Me and be perfect"; that is to say, I alone exist, which is enough for My existence, for the activity designated to Me. And this is creation [*ex nihilo*]. And this is not possible for any existent other than Me; namely, that its own existence is sufficient for it alone for the activity designated to its form. If so, it [i.e., any other existent] will not be as perfect as My perfection is. And therefore (ibid.): "Walk before Me," [meaning:] walk in My ways to acquire the perfection of My deeds, and you will be perfect according to your species.

§16.14 And just as it becomes clear that it is impossible that creation is an activity of any material existent or power in a body, it [also] becomes clear that the creator is one only and nothing else. And this is so because plurality is not applicable to the [things] that are perpetual [and] entirely separate from matter, and neither is number, as has become clear from the demonstration above.

§16.15 And it is necessary that there is an eternal existent, because otherwise, the thing would proceed until infinity. So, it is necessary that there is an existent, a creator out of nothing, who is the only eternal existent whose activity is creation. But it is | incongruous that creation should be the activity of a material [or: corporeal] agent or a power in a body. This becomes clear in this way: because creation brings a thing forth after absolute nothingness and total non-existence. And between existence and total non-existence, there is no intermediary at all, [and] so two contradictory things would be [true]. It follows that creation only [happens] in an indivisible instant, as it [i.e., Holy Scripture] testifies, saying (Genesis 1:1): "In the beginning God created"; that is to say, at the beginning of time, which is necessarily an indivisible instant. And therefore, it teaches [us] that prior to creation, there was no time at all. And therefore, there is no motion by which the agent is moved to act that the philosophers thought to be necessary and eternal. And there is no time between the beginning of the creation and its end. And therefore, it follows that motion is not applicable to it, nor any material instrument. And it has already become clear that in every activity of a power in a body, time and motion and a material instrument are necessarily [involved] between the beginning of the activity and its end. If so, it therefore follows that the

---

[a] Cf. Joel 2:23.

§16.13 ואת כל אלה הורה המורה לצדקה יתברך באמרו: »אני אל שדי התהלך לפני והיה תמים« (בראשית א׳ י״ז), כלומר אני לבדי נמצא אשר די במציאותי לפעולה המיוחדת לי והיא הבריאה וזה לא יתכן לשום נמצא זולתי היינו שיספיק מציאות עצמו לבדו לפעולה המיוחדת לצורתו אם כן אין שלם כשלמותי ובכן »התהלך לפני« (שם) ללכת בדרכי למען תקנה שלמות מעשי ותהיה שלם במינך.

§16.14 וכאשר יתבאר היות מן הנמנע שתהיה הבריאה פעולת שום נמצא גשמי או כח בגשם הנה יתבאר היות הבורא אחד בלבד ואין זולתו וזה כי אמנם בנבדלים מחומר המתמדים לגמרי לא יפול רבוי ולא מנין כאשר התבאר לעיל במופת.

§16.15 ובהיות מן ההכרח שימצא איזה נמצא קדמון כי באופן אחר ילך הדבר אל לא תכלית הנה מן ההכרח שיהיה איזה נמצא בורא מבלי אין קדמון זולתי הנמצא אשר פעלו הבריאה. אמנם היות | מן הנמנע שתהיה הבריאה פעלת פועל גשמי או כח בגוף הנה יתבאר באופן זה. כי בהיות הבריאה המצאת דבר אחר האפיסות המוחלט וההעדר הגמור ובין המציאות וההעדר הגמור אין אמצעי כלל להיותם שני חלקי הסותר. הנה יתחייב שלא תהיה הבריאה כי אם ברגע בלתי מתחלק כאשר העיד באמרו: »בראשית ברא אלהים« (בראשית א׳ א׳), כלומר בראשית הזמן אשר היה מן ההכרח רגע בלתי מתחלק ובזה הורה שקודם הבריאה לא היה זמן כלל ובכן לא היתה תנועה שינוע בה הפועל לפעלו אשר חשבו הפילוסופים היותה הכרחית וקדמונית ובהיות כי אין זמן בין תחלת הבריאה וסופה ומזה התבאר שלא תפול בה תנועה ולא כלי חמרי וכבר התבאר שבכל פעולת כח בגוף יהיה בהכרח זמן ותנועה וכלי חמרי בין תחלת הפעלה וסופה אם כן יתחייב

§ 16.13 Et hec omnia succinte docet Sacrum Genesis Testamentum cap. 17 [17:1] ubi dicit: «Ego Deus Omnipotens ambula coram me et esto perfectus,» per ly «Omnipotens» inferendo quod potest operari sine subiecto. Et apertius idem docetur in originali Hebreorum testu ibidem dicente: «Ego Deus qui sufficit,» quasi dicat ego tantum sum talis qui possum per me ipsum[a] secluso quocumque alio ente facere actionem mihi propriam, et talis est creatio, ad quam non requiritur alterius entis existentia. Quare sequitur dicens: «Ambula coram me et esto perfectus,» id est sequere vestigia mea ut mihi omnium perfectissimo pro viribus assimileris, ad hoc ut sis ceteris perfectior.

⟨§ 16.14⟩

§ 16.15 Cumque pateat quod in entibus sit tandem deveniendum ad quoddam eternum, scilicet, incausatum, et per se necessarium, alioquin fieret processus ab infinitum, patet | ergo ut sit deveniendum necessario ad naturam creantem per se necessariam nullo alio ente indigentem. Cum ergo patuisset huiusmodi naturam esse quid abstractum, quoque in abstractis omnino similibus non datur numeratio sive pluralitas, prout supra ratione et auctoritate patuit, sequitur quidem ut unus tantum numero sit creans, ut ipse tantum habuisset esse ab eterno.

Quod autem natura creans sit necessario quid abstractum patet, quia inter purum esse non esse non datur medium. Quare in creatione que, scilicet, est dare esse post purum non esse non datur medium sive tempus in quo detur fieri, et per consequens neque motus, et per consequens neque materiale instrumentum, que omnia requiruntur in fieri tantum, et sunt ad corporearum virtutum actiones necessaria. Ex quibus sequitur ut Creator in cuius

§ 16.13 The Holy Testament in Genesis (17:1) succinctly teaches all these things, saying: "I am God, the Almighty: Walk before me and be perfect." "Almighty" means that He can act without a substrate. The same thing is taught more clearly in the original Hebrew text: "I am God, who is enough" [El Shaddai], which is like saying: I am the only one able to enact my own action by myself without another being, as is the case of creation, which does not need the existence of another being. Therefore: "Walk before me and be perfect"; namely, by following my traces, you will become similar to Me, the most perfect being, and you will be more perfect than other beings.

⟨§ 16.14⟩

§ 16.15 It is evident that among the beings, it is necessary to arrive at something eternal, meaning uncaused and necessary, otherwise it would run until infinity. Therefore, it is clear that it | is necessary to arrive at a creating nature [that is] necessary by itself and that does not need another being to exist. Moreover, since it is clear that this nature is separate, there is also no numeration or plurality in separate substances that are completely similar, as is proven above according to the argument and authority [of Aristotle and Averroes]. Thus, there is only one creator in number, and only He is eternal. It is evident that the creating nature is necessarily separate, because between absolute existence and nothingness, there is no intermediary. Therefore, in creation, which was out of nothingness, there was no intermediary or time, and consequently no motion or material instrument. All these [things] are only required in production, and they are necessary for the activities of the corporeal potencies. From these [words], it follows that the

---

[a] ipsum] b[corr]; ipsam b.

creator acts apart from all these [things]. He is not a power in a body, still less an inanimate body that truly has no activity. So it [i.e., Holy Scripture] teaches [us] (Deuteronomy 4:15): "Be most careful—since you saw no image."

§ 16.16 And since intellectual providence is commonly [known] to exist, at least in the corruptibles with organs, which through their compositeness have instruments and many different organs that are intended for the final purpose of the activity of that particular [thing] in which those particular organs are found; and [since] the aforementioned providence is undoubtedly intended by the Creator—may He be praised—mediately or immediately, because if it was not intended by Him, it would have occurred accidentally, as mentioned above, it therefore follows that the Creator—may He be praised—has providence over their species and their particulars, as part of the species, mediately or immediately, as he [i.e., the Poet] teaches [us] (Psalm 94:9): "Shall He who implants the ear not hear?"

§ 16.17 And there exists a certain power in the human species to acquire intelligibles that are not useful for the political community, together with a natural desire to achieve them, which teaches [us] that their achievement is intended by an arranger of order, by intention and will. In addition to this, their achievement is only gained through individual free will, and this [only] by single [individuals] who choose to contemplate and to acquire [it] in different ways, and their achievement will be of different ranks. And many other single [individuals] [will become] fatigued in achieving [it] or will [even] reject or oppose the intention of the aforementioned arranger of order. It follows that the providence of the aforementioned arranger of order, who wills the aforementioned human perfection that is intended by Him, will be [exerted only] individually, especially in man, insofar as they are individuals, not insofar as they are parts of the species only. But individual providence is over every single one of the individuals. [There are] some whom the intention of the arranger of order brought to the final purpose and some who reject it or oppose it, as it says (Psalm 94:11–12): "Ha-Shem knows the thoughts of men, etc. Happy is the man, etc.," because otherwise, His endeavour would lack what is appropriate to strive for the wish to bring what He intended | towards the final purpose, as it says (Psalm 94:14): "For ha-Shem will not

מזה שהבורא הפועל בלעדי כל אלה אינו כח בגוף כל שכן שאינו גוף בלתי חי אשר אין לו פעלה באמת וכן הורה באמרו: »ונשמרתם מאד לנפשותיכם כי לא ראיתם כל תמונה« (דברים ד׳ ט״ו).

§ 16.16 ובהיות במציאות השגחה שכלית מפורסמת לפחות בנפסדים בעלי כלים אשר בהרכבתם נמצאו אברים וכלים מכלים שונים מכוונים לתכלית פעלת אותו הפרטי אשר בו האברים הפרטיים ההם וההשגחה הנזכרת היא בלי ספק מכוונת מאת הבורא ית׳ באמצעי או בלתי אמצעי כי אם לא היתה מכוונת מאתו היתה מקרית כנזכר לעיל הנה התחייב מזה שהבורא ית׳ משגיח במיניהם ובפרטיהם כמו חלקי המין באמצעי או בלתי אמצעי כאשר הורה באמרו: »הנוטע אזן הלא ישמע?« (תהלים צ״ד ט׳).

§ 16.17 ובהיות במין האנושי כח מה להשיג מושכלות בלתי מועילות לקבוץ המדיני עם תאוה טבעית להשיגם מורה על היות השגתם מכוונת מאת מסדר בכוונה וברצון ועם זה לא תמצא השגתם כי אם בבחירה פרטית זה ביחידים בוחרים להתבונן ולהשיג בדרכים שונים ותהיה השגתם על מעלות שונות ויחידים זולתם רבים נרפים מהשיג או מואסים או מתקוממים לכוונת המסדר הנזכר. הנה התחייב שהשגחת המסדר הנזכר החפץ בשלמות האנושי הנזכר המכוון ממנו תהיה פרטית בפרטי האדם באשר הם פרטים לא באשר הם חלקי המין לבד אבל תהיה השגחה פרטית על כל אחד מהפרטים אשר קצתם מביא כוונת המסדר אל תכלית וקצתם מואס בה או מתקומם עליה באמרו: »ה׳ יודע מחשבות אדם וכול׳ אשרי הגבר וכו׳« (תהלים צ״ד י״א-י״ב), כי אמנם זולת זה היה השתדלותו חסר מן הראוי למשתדל החפץ להביא מכוונו אל | תכלית באמרו: »כי לא יטוש ה׳ את עמו« (שם שם י״ד). וכן הורה באמרו: »ואך את דמכם לנפשותיכם אדרוש«

actione non datur aliquid istorum sit proculdubio quid non corporeum.

§ 16.16 Cumque intellectualis cura et sollicitudo in universi ordine apparens non minus in quolibet mortalium genere saltem organicorum apparere videatur, prout horum organa organorumque ordines et alia singulorum actionibus horumque substentationi competentia sapienter in eidem facta testari videantur. Patet quidem quod eiusdem Creatoris sollicitudo sive cura a quo universi ordo emanat ad mortalium saltem organicorum genera non mediocriter extendatur.

§ 16.17 Cumque humano generi naturaliter insit arbitrium et potentia ad divina contemplanda, et tandem scienda cum desiderio ad illud; quoque finis inde intentus tanquam eiusdem potentie actus non per omnes humani generis individuos immo per rarissimos tantum habeatur. Per reliquos vero eidem intento potius repugnari videatur. Necesse est ut divina sollicitudo talia ordinans et huiusmodi finem intendens ad humanos individuos intentum exequentes extendatur, quorum impeditis individualiter assistat,[a] similiter extendatur ad reliquos humani generis individuos turpiter prefato eiusdem intento repugnantes, quibus merito individualiter resistat, aliter enim adeo nobile intentum negligenter curare videretur, quod est inopinabile.

Quare Sacrum Exodi Documentum cap. 20 [20:5–6] talia succinte et ratione docens Illos quidem qui huius-

creator acts apart from them, and he is undoubtedly not corporeal.

§ 16.16 Moreover, the intellectual providence and care in the order of the universe is no less evident, and it also seems so in every species of corruptible being and even the organic ones, because their organs, the order of their organs, and all the things relevant to the actions of the individuals and to their sustenance testify that they are wisely made. It is clear that the providence or care of the creator, from which the order of the universe emanates, is extended to the corruptible species and even the organic ones.

§ 16.17 Moreover, free will and the power to [attain through] contemplation of the divine things, together with a natural desire to know, naturally belong to the human species. The intended goal and the activity of the power do not apply to every individual of the human species, but only to a few. It seems, in fact, that the rest cannot reach it. It is necessary that divine providence, which orders these things and aims at a purpose, spreads over human individuals who are equal to the intended purpose. Divine providence individually takes care of those who are incapable [of attaining the contemplation of the Divine]. Similarly, divine providence is spread over the other individuals of the human species who shamelessly reject the intended purpose: [providence] rightly opposes them, otherwise it would seem that divine providence was neglecting the noble aim, and this would be incongruous, as the Holy Scripture explains in the [Holy] Book of Exodus 20 (20:5–6), saying that those who follow the intention of God are

---

[a] assistat] b[corr]; assistant b.

forsake His people," and it also teaches [us] (Genesis 9:5): "But for your own life-blood I will require a reckoning," to convey and teach His individual providence in the human species for the reason of his [i.e., man's] divine soul, as it continues to explain (Genesis 9:6): "For in His image did God make man."

§16.18 His [i.e., God's] knowledge is not caused by the existents, since it is prior to the existents, and [it is instead] their cause, and it is impossible that an existent may bring itself forth. And the contrary of this is the case for the human intellect, because it only has knowledge if it is caused by the existents [in such a way that] their image is transmitted to it via the senses, [and] after [that, it] abstracts them from matter and gains universals from them. And therefore, the term "knowledge" is only correctly said about the knowledge of the Creator and our knowledge by equivocation. It then follows that knowledge of the human intellect [alone] does not apply to the existents that do not [fulfil certain] conditions; namely, that the [existents] are (1) necessary, (2) universals, which are abstract from matter, [and] (3) numerically infinite, because knowledge of the human intellect is only applicable to the [existents] under the aforementioned conditions. And [it is] not applicable to (1) multiple [things] that are not numerically finite, (2) contingent things, and (3) particulars, because man cannot apprehend one of these except by the senses, not by intellectual apprehension. If so, for divine knowledge, which is undoubtedly uncaused by the existents, as mentioned above, it follows that there is no difference between one existent and [another] existent. And therefore, it is appropriate that it should apply to multiple numerically infinite [things] as well as to finite [things], and to the particulars as well as to the universals, and to contingent things as well as to necessary things, and to material [things] as well as to [things] devoid of matter, and to the future as well as to the present, especially as existence is not possible for every single [thing] apart from His existence—may He be praised—which is one thing with His knowledge. And it also teaches [us] this (Genesis 18:14): "Is anything too wondrous for ha-Shem?" And the prophet teaches [us] this through the aforementioned demonstration, as it says (Jeremiah 23:24): "'If a man enters a hiding place, Do I not see him?'—says ha-Shem. 'For I fill both the heavens and earth.'"

§16.19 And since the Creator—may He be praised—brought forth contraries, which no natural agent may bring forth, and [since] by every single contrary, a final purpose is brought forth for which it is inconceivable that it is not intended by a voluntary agent, it becomes clear that the

(בראשית ט׳ ה׳), להבין ולהורות היות השגחתו פרטית במין האנושי לסבת נפשו האלהית כאשר הוסיף לבאר באמרו: »כי בצלם אלהים עשה את האדם« (שם שם ו׳).

§ 16.18 ובהיות ידיעתו בלתי מסובבת מהנמצאות להיותה קודמת לנמצאות וסבה להם ומן הנמנע לנמצא שימציא את עצמו והפך זה יקרה לשכל האנושי כי אמנם לא תהיה לו ידיעה כי אם מסובבת מהנמצאות וציורם המובל אליו מן החושים אחר אשר יפשיטם מחומר ויעשה מהם כללים. ובכן לא יאמר שם ›ידיעה‹ באמת על ידיעת הבורא וידיעתנו כי אם בשתוף השם. אם כן יתחייב שאע״פ שלא תפול ידיעת שכל אנושי על הנמצאות בלתי תנאים בהם היינו שיהיו הכרחיים כלליים מֻפשטים מחומר בלתי בעלי תכלית במספר כי רק בהיותם על התנאים הנזכרים תפול עליהם ידיעת שכל אנושי. ולא תפול על רבים אין תכלית למספרם ולא על מקרים ולא על פרטים כי אמנם לא ישיג האדם אחד מאלה כי אם בחושים לא בהשגה שכלית. אם כן אצל הידיעה האלהית אשר היא בלי ספק בלתי מסובבת מהנמצאות כנזכר לעילא יתחייב שלא יהיה הפרש בין נמצא לנמצא ולכן ראוי שתפול על רבים אין תכלית למספרם כמו על בעלי תכלית ועל הפרטים כמו על הכללים ועל המקרים כמו על הדברים ההכרחיים ועל החמרים כמו על המופשטים ועל העתיד כמו על ההווה בפרט כאשר לא יהיה איפשרות מציאות כל אחד מהם זולתי ממציאותו ית׳ שהוא דבר אחד עם ידיעתו וכן הורה באמרו: »היפלה מה׳ דבר?« (בראשית י״ח י״ד). וזה הורה הנביא במופת הנזכר באמרו: »»אם יסתר איש במסתרים ואני לא אראנו? נאם ה׳. הלא את השמים ואת הארץ אני מלא««‹ (ירמיהו כ״ג כ״ד).

§ 16.19 ובהיות שהבורא יתברך המציא הפכים אשר לא ימציאם פועל טבעי ובכל אחד מההפכים נולד תכלית אשר לא יעלה על לב היותו בלתי מכוון מפועל רצוני הנה התבאר היות הבורא פועל רצוני

modi Dei intentum exequuntur eiusdem Dei amicos appellat, quibus dicit se auxiliaturum Repugnantes vero ostes appellat, quos minatur puniturum.

§16.18 Cumque eiusdem Creatori scientia non dependeat ab entibus, cum ipse sit horum causa agens, et non habeat causare se ipsum sicut plenius supra. Cuius opportunum contigit humane scientie. Quamvis ergo humane scientie requirantur sciendorum entium conditiones, quibus ipsa scienda humano intellectui proportionentur ad hoc ut ab eodem percipiantur, scilicet, ut sint in se necessaria et abstrahantur a materia. Quare humanus intellectus necessaria tantum et universalia scire potest, et hoc per discursum ab entibus sumptum, sensu, scilicet, prius | perceptis et per operationem intellectus abstractis. Quare individua et contingentia tanquam eidem humano intellectui non proportionata nonnisi sensibus percipere valemus.ᵃ Non tamen hoc habet contingere Divine scientie que, scilicet, nullo pacto ab entibus dependet. Quare nulla eidem requiritur sciendorum entium conditionum quibus habeant eidem proportionari, et per consequens non minus ad individua quam ad universalia, nec minus ad contingentia, quam ad necessaria, neque minus ad futura, quam ad presentia habet se merito et indifferenter extendere.

§16.19 Cumque idem Creator produxisset contraria in quorum singulo intentus apparet finis. Talis autem contrariorum actionis finisque intentio nonnisi a voluntario agente emanare contingat. Patet quidem ut idem Creator sit agens

called His friends and He will help them; those who reject His intention are called enemies, and He threatens to punish them.

§16.18 Moreover, the Creator's knowledge does not depend upon the existent beings because He is their agent cause and He does not cause Himself, as is proven at length above. The opposite of this befalls human knowledge. Although human knowledge requires the conditions of the beings that are to be known, by which the things to be known are proportioned to the human intellect so that they are perceived by it, meaning that they are necessary and separate from matter, hence, the human intellect can only know necessary and universal things, and this is because of the knowledge taken from the beings that are initially perceived | by the senses and afterwards are abstracted by the intellectual operation. We are not able to perceive individual or contingent things that are not proportioned to the human intellect if not through the senses. Nonetheless, this does not occur to divine knowledge, which never depends upon existent beings. No condition of the beings that are to be known is required by Him, by which they are proportioned to Him, and consequently, divine knowledge includes knowledge of particulars as well as universals, accidents as well as necessary things, and future things as well as present ones.

§16.19 Moreover, the Creator also produces contraries, and [also in that case] the intended purpose is evident in every single one of them. The intention of the activity and of the aim of the contraries only occurs if it emanates from a voluntary agent. It is clear that the Creator is the voluntary

---

ᵃ valemus] bᶜᵒʳʳ; valimus b.

Creator is a voluntary agent, as he teaches [us], saying (Isaiah 45:7): "Who forms light and creates darkness, and who makes peace and who creates evil: I ha-Shem make all these things."

§ 16.20 And since the Creator is perfect and exalted above all existents, it becomes clear that every existent that is similar to Him is nobler and more perfect than the rest of the existents.

§ 16.21 And the perfection of the Creator, His wisdom, and His compassion are known to us through His actions, as it says (Psalm 104:24): "You have made them all with wisdom." And as he [i.e., the Poet] says (Psalm 145:17): "And faithful | in all His works." And since He enacts [things] well without obligation and without need, it becomes clear that when He wills man to be as similar to the Creator—may He be praised—as possible, it is necessary that He is wise and compassionate, still more that He is just.

§ 16.22 And since the compassion of the Creator and His righteousness come from Him by will and free choice, [which] is not necessary [at all], since He is a voluntary agent, as mentioned, He knows [both of] two contraries and He is capable [of doing both] of them equally and to choose the best of them, although He knows that He is able to do the [other] contrary; it follows that the act of goodness that comes from a man who is similar to his Creator will come from him by will and absolute free choice [and will] not [be] necessary at all. Moreover, He knows that He is able to do the contrary, as it says (Deuteronomy 30:19): "Choose life."

§ 16.23 And this kind of freedom of choice is impossible in the created [beings] if it is in an imperfect intellect that is sometimes not intellecting in actuality. And then it will not stand up to overcome the evilness of the appetitive power, which gives commands to material powers that are not correct, as happens to non-rational animals. And as it says (Psalm 49:13): "He is like the beasts that perish," [meaning:] He also knows that he is able to oppose Him when he walks with God, since he is intellecting in actuality. And therefore, [this] kind is the human intellectual soul called "the image of God," which has the power of free choice and will, which is called by [Holy] Scripture: "Likeness of God" (Genesis 5:1). And this does not occur to any other [creature], as Averroes explains in *The Incoherence of the Incoherence* 3, eighteenth investigation.[a] And it is said that

---

[a] Cf. *Incoherence* 138.

וכן הורה באמרו: »יוצר אור ובורא חשך עושה שלום ובורא רע אני ה׳ עושה כל אלה« (ישעיהו מ״ה ז׳).

§ 16.20 וּבִהְיוֹת הבורא שלם ומעולה מכל הנמצאות התבאר שכל נמצא הדומה לו הוא יותר נכבד ושלם מיתר הנמצאות.

§ 16.21 וּבִהְיוֹת ששלמות הבורא חכמתו וחסדו נודע אצלנו מצד מעשיו באמרו: »כלם בחכמה עשית« (תהלים ק״ד כ״ד). ובאמרו: »וחסיד | בכל מעשיו« (שם קמ״ה י״ז). וזה בהיותו מטיב בלתי חייב ובלתי צריך הנה התבאר שכשירצה האדם להדמות לבורא יתברך כפי האיפשר יצטרך היותו חכם וחסיד כל שכן שיהיה צדיק.

§ 16.22 וּבִהְיוֹת חסד הבורא וצדקו באים מאתו ברצון ובחירה בלתי מוכרחת כלל בהיותו פועל רצוני כנזכר יודע שני הפכים ויכול עליהם בשוה ובוחר בטוב מהם עם היותו יודע שיוכל לעשות הפכו הנה התחייב שפעלת הטוב אשר תבוא מאת האדם הדומה לבוראו תהיה מאתו ברצון ובחירה מוחלטת בלתי מוכרחת כלל עם שידע היותו יכול לעשות הפכה באמרו: »ובחרת בחיים« (דברים ל׳ י״ט).

§ 16.23 וּבִהְיוֹת זה המין מן הבחירה נמנע בנבראים כי אם בשכל בלתי שלם אשר לפעמים הוא בלתי משכיל בפעל. ובכן לא יתקומם להעביר את רעת[a] הכח המתאוה המצוה לכחות הגשמיות דברים אשר לא כן כמו שיקרה לבעלי חיים בלתי מדברים. באמרו: »נמשל כבהמות נדמו« (תהלים מ״ט י״ג). גם שידע שיוכל להתקומם עליו ברצותו עם אלהים. וזה בהיותו משכיל בפעל. ומזה המין היא הנפש האנושית השכלית הנקרא ›צלם אלהים‹ אשר לו כח בחירה רצונית הנקרא בכתוב »דמות אלהים« (בראשית ה׳ א׳). ולא יקרה זה לזולתו כמו שבאר אבן רשד בספר הפלת ההפלה מאמר ג׳ חקירת י״ח.

---

[a] רעת] emend. Dunk.; דעת a; רעת A.

voluntarius, non autem naturalis tantum, sicut nonnulli turpiter putasse videtur.

§ 16.20 Cumque idem Creator sit quid omnium nobilissimum, prout actio eidem propria aperte testatur, quicquid ergo reliquorum entium fuerit eidem similius erit necessario hic reliquis nobilius.

§ 16.21 Cumque eiusdem Creatori nobilitas et perfectio per scientiam et benignitatem in suis operibus apparentem nobis pateat. Nobis ergo pro viribus eidem assimilari intendentibus, scientia quidem Sue quodammodo similis requiritur, que, scilicet, habet versari circa cognitionem de Eo pro viribus habendam, et benignitatem sive moralitatem. Qua pia et benigna intendamus opera eiusdem Creatoris operibus pro viribus similia, qui, scilicet, cum nihil indigeat entium, illa tantum benigne produxit, substentat et quotidie benefacit.

§ 16.22 Cumque eiusdem Creatoris opera nonnisi a libera eiusdem emanent voluntate utrumque contrariorum sciente et indifferenter potente, horum tamen melius benigne eligente, nobiliori, scilicet, modo quam nos eligere contingat. Moralitas ergo qua eidem Creatori quodammodo assimilari intendamus habet necessario similiter a nostra libera voluntate emanare, qua, scilicet, scientes nos posse oppositum, illud tamen eligimus quod Deo gratius et per consequens melius esse consideramus.

§ 16.23 Cumque huiusmodi arbitrium non contingat inesse alicui intellectui semper actu intelligenti preterquam Creatori. Et hoc quia relique omnes intelligentie semper actu intelligentes nunquam nisi recte operantur. Et per consequens nonnisi rem Deo (cui omnes tenentur) gratam operari contingit, quare non datur inesse liberum ad utrumque contrariorum arbitrium nisi Deo nobilissimo modo, et humano generi ignobili modo. Et hoc quia Deus qui nulli entium tenetur, illud operari convenit quod sibi satisfacit, quo nihil datur prestantius. Humano vero generi tanquam diminutio et non semper intelligenti datur inesse arbitrium ignobili tamen modo. Et hoc quia excitatur a

agent and not only the natural one, as someone disgracefully supposed.

§ 16.20 Moreover, the Creator is the noblest being, as His activity clearly proves. Any of the other beings that are similar to Him are necessarily nobler than the other ones.

§ 16.21 The nobility of the Creator and His perfection is clear to us through the knowledge and goodwill appearing in His actions. Thus, if we intend with all our might to be similar to Him, we require a similar kind of knowledge. [This kind of knowledge] has to be dedicated to the knowledge of Him that we need to have and to goodwill and morality. Indeed, we consider good and charitable deeds to be the actions that are similar to the actions of the Creator, who, since He does not require the existence of any other beings, produced them through His grace, supports them, and blesses them every day.

§ 16.22 Moreover, the Creator's activity is emanated from His free will, which knows two contraries and can [act] indifferently and with goodness, choosing the best among them, a nobler way of choosing than ours. Thus, the morality by which we intend to be similar to the Creator is emanated by way of our free will, since we are able to understand the contrary; nonetheless, we choose what is graceful to God and consequently what we consider better.

§ 16.23 Moreover, except for the Creator, the choice does not belong to an intellect that always comprehends in actuality, because all the other intellects, which always comprehend in actuality, always act rightly. Consequently, it enacts only a thing dear to God, to whom everything is bound, since there is a choice open to any of the contraries only in the noblest way for God and in an ignoble way for men. This is because God, who is not bound by any being, chooses to act in a way to satisfy Himself, and there is nothing more excellent than His choice. To the human species, which is so deficient and which is not always intelligent, choice is given in an ignoble way. This is because it is

not one of the existents has free choice except man alone, because the others besides him act through [their] nature alone. If so, it follows that there is only free choice for (1) the Creator—may He be praised—in a noble and exalted way, and (2) for man in an inferior way, as Averroes teaches [us] in the aforementioned book 11, first investigation. If so, the Creator's wish is to bring forth an existent similar to Him, as far as possible, which will necessarily be a selection of the existents. And their final purpose is necessarily that He will create man in His likeness and in His image, as testified by the activity at the end of the work of creation. [And] it says (Genesis 1:26): "Let us make man in our image, after our likeness," and He commanded us to do what is possible for us in order to resemble Him, as it says (Deuteronomy 8:6): "Walk in His ways" and (Leviticus 11:44): "You shall sanctify yourselves and be holy, for I am holy."

§16.24 And the intellectual soul knows that it is able to resemble its Creator by cognition and action, and that therefore the Creator—may He be praised—achieves His wish and His intention, which is not necessarily achieved by divine power. For if there was no free choice of will by which the intellectual soul chooses the better of two contraries without being compelled to tend to [one of] them, the likeness that is intended by Him would not occur at all. And therefore, it is not appropriate that the Creator will actualise the potential of man without the agreement and will of his intellectual soul, as it says (Deuteronomy 10:12): "What does ha-Shem, your God, demand of you, etc.?" And it says (Berakhot 33b): "Everything is in the hands of [the] heavens except for the fear of [the] heavens." If so, the human soul will decide and bring itself and others closer to resembling | the Creator, for the sake of achieving their Creator's wish, to be undoubtedly like a son who serves his father out of love, as it says (Deuteronomy 14:1): "You are sons of ha-Shem your God."

§16.25 And the Creator—may He be exalted—is more perfect than all the existents. And by Him, all perfection and every power is generated, since He is *a master, who can produce anything*[a] mediately or immediately, as becomes clear, saying (1 Chronicles 29:11): "Yours, ha-Shem, are greatness, might, etc., all that is in [the] heavens and on earth belong to You, ha-Shem, etc." Especially because He is compassionate, as explained above, still more because He is righteous, as it says (Psalm 145:17): "Ha-Shem is righteous in all His ways." It becomes clear that His righteousness

---

[a] Prov 26.10.

materiali appetitu sepius non recta petenti, cui humanus intellectus quandoque non resistit quamvis sciat se posse, et hoc negligentia ductus, scilicet, a resistendo vel ab hoc ut | malum inde resultans consideret. Quia ad hoc ut recte consideret, indiget virtute ad actum deducente, cum non sit semper actu intelligens, cum autem ipsum liberum ad utrumque contrariorum arbitrium Deo tantum insit nobilissime, humane quoque intellective licet ignobilior. Merito Sacra Genesis Scriptura dicit hominem esse ad Dei similitudinem factum, et hoc cap. 1 [1:26] ubi dicit: «Et dixit Deus faciamus hominem ad imaginem nostram quasi ad similitudinem nostrum,» ubi per imaginem intelligit intellectivam virtutem, per similitudinem vero arbitrariam, quo Deus tantum et homo gaudent. Dicit tamen quasi ad similitudinem quia Deus nobilissime, homo autem ignobiliter ut supra. Creator ergo ens quoddam sibi Deo pro viribus simile producere intendens, tanquam operum perfectissimum et merito reliquorum, finem habuit necessario facere hominem ad eiusdem imaginem et similitudinem. Prout idem in prefato Genesis documento cap. primo fecisse testatur.

§ 16.24 Cumque ipsa hominis intellectiva sciat[a] se posse per voluntariam contemplationem cum piis moribus se Deo quodammodo similem reddere. Et hoc eidem Deo sui operis perfectionem merito volenti esse quid gratum. Quod tamen nonnisi per eiusdem intellective arbitrium fieri contingit, quia non dato huiusmodi libero arbitrio non daretur intenta Dei similitudo suo libero arbitrio facientis ut supra. Ille ergo qui in seipsum vel alios induxerit huiusmodi similitudinis perfectionem ad hoc ut Creator per illam suum consequatur intentum faciet effectum Creatori gratissimum, quem propter prefatam contradictionis implicationem ipse Creator nonnisi per meram hominis electionem consequi contingit ut supra.

§ 16.25 Cumque idem Creator sit adeo benignus ut, quamvis nihilo teneatur, cunctis tamen etiam non benemeritis benefacere dignetur, a fortiori habet benefacere his qui rem adeo gratam eidem Creatori et ad eiusdem satisfactionem fecerint, eosdem scilicet tanquam gratissimos remunerans. Cumque filiorum officium fit ut tanquam patrem merito diligentes rem eidem gratam facere curent. Illi ergo

excited by the material appetite, which often desires the wrong things and which the human intellect sometimes does not resist, even though it recognises that it is possible to resist, and, led by negligence, this happens because the human intellect understands something incorrectly. | Indeed, in order for the human intellect to understand something correctly, a power [capacity] is needed that follows an act, since the human intellect does not always understand in actuality because the choice open to any of the contraries belongs only to God in the noblest way, and also to human intellectual [nature], even though in an ignoble way. As the Holy Scripture explained in Genesis (1:26), men are created similar to God, saying: "And God said: Let us make man in our image, as our likeness," which means that the "image" corresponds to the intellectual power and the likeness to free will, which is a prerogative attributed to God and to men only. Nonetheless, it says "as our likeness" because God chooses in the noblest way and men [choose] in an ignoble way, as aforementioned. The Creator, wanting to produce a being similar to Him, the most perfect being of His works, necessarily had the aim of creating man in His image and likeness, as is proven in the above-mentioned text from Genesis.

§ 16.24 Therefore, the human intellectual soul knows that it can become similar to God through voluntary contemplation and through good deeds. This is something [that is] dear to God, who wants the perfection of His work. This only happens through the choice of the intellectual [soul]. Without free will, there is no likeness to God, who acts with His free will, as mentioned above. Then, thanks to the likeness, the intellect human soul, led by perfection, attains the final purpose. The one who induces the perfection of this similarity in himself or in others so that God may reach His purpose produces an effect that is very dear to God; indeed, because of the above-mentioned implication of the contradiction, the Creator only achieves [His purpose] through man's mere choice, as mentioned above.

§ 16.25 Therefore, the Creator is so benevolent that even though He has no obligation, He deigns to do good to everyone, even to those who perform no good deeds. Even more so, He does good to those who do things very dear to God and for His satisfaction, so He rewards them. Hence, the obligation of the sons is, as much as they love their father, to take care to do something [that is] dear to him.

---

[a] sciat] b[corr]; sicut b.

and the kinds of reward that are necessary from His aforementioned righteousness are bigger and better than all the rewards that are [granted] by the rest of the existents. And therefore, it follows that goodness is undoubtedly rewarded in the doers of His will who intend that He should achieve His wish by the power of their free choice, *as a father delights in his son.*[a] As it says (*Avot* 2:4): "Do His will as though it were your will, so that He will do your will as though it were His." And these [people] are called "sons," as mentioned (see above, Deuteronomy 14:1). Indeed, those who do this out of fear of punishment or in the hope of a reward are called "servants." And the reward for servants *who serve the master in the expectation of receiving a reward*[b] is appropriate for them. But the entirely righteous [people] are sometimes called "servants" in relation to the angels, who are called "sons of God," since a righteous [person] is inferior to them in intellection, especially in this [sensible] world. And also, it follows that God judges by His righteousness and punishes indolent [people] through the activities of His will and His requests, especially by letting them recognise that He is able to do what He [wants to] do, still more that He will punish the [people] who reject [Him], still more the [people] who resist [Him] and those who hinder the actualisation of the intended [purpose] and [those] who destroy the "corner [stone] of His intention" and His final purpose in existence, as it says (Jeremiah 33:25): "As surely as I have established My covenant with day and night, the laws of [the] heavens and earth." And therefore, indolent [people] are called "beasts," as it says (Psalm 49:13): "He is like the beasts that perish." And the rejectors and resistors are called "criminals," "enemies," "haters," and "adversaries," as it says (Psalm 139:21): "O ha-Shem, do I not hate those who hate You, and loathe Your adversaries?" And the Creator—may He be praised—is called "vengeful," as it says (Nahum 1:2): "Ha-Shem is vengeful and fierce in wrath," and this is [said] against the [people] who stand against His intention and His wish, and who use the power of His image to stand against Him. And therefore, they are called "adversaries," as it says (Nahum 1:2): "Ha-Shem takes vengeance on His adversaries."

§16.26 And the intellectual soul is an immortal thing, as became clear from the demonstration above, and the nature of its activities, working without material instrument[s], testifies this. And since it does not become weary through the intellection of a strong intelligible and does not become old, because of which it is called the "image

---

[a] Prov 3:12. [b] *Avot* 1:3.

homines qui prefatum effectum tanquam rem Deo gratam facere intenderint merito in Sacris Dei Scripturis Dei filii [cf. Deut 14:1] et eiusdem amici appellantur, licet et quamquam in hac vita servi, angelorum, scilicet, respectu dicantur. Illi autem qui spe vel metu ducti prefatum effectum faciunt eiusdem Dei servi tantum absolute dicuntur. Illi vero homines quod pigritia vel ignorantia ducti eiusdem Dei intentum contrafaciunt, merito in eisdem Sacris Scripturis [cf. Ps 49:13] bestiales stulti et ignari appellantur. Respuentes vero et presumptuose Dei intento repugnantes[a] et illud perturbantes eiusdem Dei inimici emuli et in eundem insurgentes dicuntur [cf. Ps 139:21]. Quare eundem Deum tanquam Sapientissimum et Omnipotentem ad eiusdem universi conservationem et regimen iuste procedentem et finem inde intentum consequi proculdubio volentem eisdem sibi adversariis condignas solvere penas et tanquam quodammodo lesus de lesione huiusmodi merito ulcisi decet. Quare in eisdem Sacris Scripturis idem Deus zelotes iracundus et ultor non immerito dicitur.

§16.26 Cumque intellectiva hominis anima a qua huiusmodi effectus boni vel mali emanant sit quid immortale, prout eiusdem natura Deique imago ut supra appellata docere videtur. Et hoc quia tanquam corpori immixta nulla indiget materiali instrumento ad actiones sibi proprias,

Therefore, those men who long for the above-mentioned effect as much as to do something [that is] dear to God are called "sons of God" and His friends in the Holy Scripture (cf. Deuteronomy 14:1), even though they are sometimes called "servants"[a] in relation to the angels. Those who produce the above-mentioned effect out of hope or fear are only called "servants of God." Those who, led by laziness or ignorance, do something contrary to the will of God are called "stupid and brutish beasts" in the Holy Scripture (cf. Psalm 49:13). Those who reject and conceitedly oppose the will of God and bother Him are called "enemies of God, rivals and rebels against Him" (cf. Psalm 139:21). Hence, it is proper that the wise and omniscient God—who keeps and rules the universe and who wishes to achieve the intended purpose—should pay the price appropriate for His enemies, and He, offended, deservedly avenges. Hence, in the Holy Scripture, God is also called "jealous," "angry," and "vengeful."

§16.26 Thus, | the human intellectual soul, from which the effects of good and evil emanate, is immortal. This is because its nature is the image of God, as was explained before. The human intellectual soul is not mixed with the body and does not need a material instrument for its

---

[a] repugnantes] coni. Copp.; repugnants b.

[a] 1 Chr 6:49; 2 Chr 24:9; Neh 10:29; Dan 9:11.

of God," it is not appropriate for any intellectual person to think that its reward or punishment will be a corruptible thing. And therefore, when the Torah explains the reward intended for the intellectual soul by the Creator—may He be praised—it testifies that the Creator—may He be praised—sanctifies it to convey and teach that accomplished immortality will be bestowed upon it, as it says (Exodus 19:6): "But you shall be to Me a kingdom of priests and a holy nation," and it also says (Deuteronomy 26:18–19): "And ha-Shem has affirmed to you, etc., that you shall be a holy nation, etc." And it also teaches us (Genesis 17:7): "I will maintain My covenant, etc., an everlasting covenant, | to be God to you and to your offspring to come," because the intention of a good governor is the perpetuity of the existents through His government and His order towards the good, which is in the characteristics according to the possibility of those who receive it. God—may He be praised—is the governor who intends this without intermediary. The perpetuity through His government will be permanently [aimed] towards the good that is in the received characteristics, as far as possible. And therefore, for the intellectual soul, which is incorruptible by its nature, as mentioned above, His covenant will be an eternal covenant that gives it completion, [i.e.,] its immortality [based] on the goodness that is [achieved] through [its] characteristics, according to the rank of its perfection. And therefore, when the Torah explains the punishment that is appropriate for it, it says (Leviticus 19:8; Genesis 17:14): "The soul shall be cut off" (Leviticus 23:30) "and I will cause that soul to perish."

§ 16.27 If so, when He testifies about the corruptible good and evil [things] in the Torah, the intention is to give His servants [a hint about] the necessity of serving Him, as it says (Psalm 105:44–45): "He gave them the lands of nations, etc.; they might keep His laws and observe His teachings, etc.," and that He will bring to His enemies evil [things] that hinder them from resistance against Him and from the interruption of His intention. And so it [i.e., Holy Scripture] testifies, as it says (Deuteronomy 6:24–25): "Ha-Shem commanded us to observe [all these laws], etc., for our lasting good and for our survival, as is now the case. It will therefore be to our merit."

⟨§ 16.28⟩

שיהיה גמולה או עונשה דבר נפסד ולזה כאשר בארה התורה את הגמול המכוון לנפש השכלית מאת הבורא ית׳ העידה שהבורא ית׳ יקדש אתה להבין ולהורות שיתן לה נצחיות מוצלח. באמרו: »ואתם תהיו לי ממלכת כהנים וגוי קדוש« (שמות י״ט ו׳), וכן באמרו: »וה׳ האמירך כו׳ ולהיותך עם קדוש כו׳« (דברים כ״ו י״ח-י״ט), וכן הורה באמרו: »והקימותי את בריתי כו׳. ברית עולם. להיות לך לאלהים לזרעך אחריך« (בראשית י״ז ז׳). כי בהיות כוונת המנהיג הטוב לקיים הנמצאים בהנהגתו וסדרו על הטוב שבתכונות כפי אפשרות המקבלים. הנה בהיות האל יתברך הוא המנהיג בלתי אמצעי המכוון זה יהיה הקיום בהנהגתו נצחית על הטוב שבתכונות כפי אפשרות המקבלים. ובכן לנפש השכלית הבלתי נפסדת בטבעה כנזכר לעיל. יהיה בריתו ברית עולם נותן לה הצלחה להיות נצחייותה על הטוב שבתכונות כפי מדרגת שלמותה. ולזה כאשר בארה התורה את העונש הראוי לה אמרה: »ונכרתה הנפש« (ויקרא י״ט ח׳; בראשית י״ז י״ד), »והאבדתי את הנפש« (ויקרא כ״ג ל׳).

§ 16.27 אם כן כאשר ייעד בתורה הטובות והרעות הנפסדות היתה הכוונה שיתן לעובדיו הצריך להם לעבודתו באמרו: »ויתן להם ארצות גוים כו׳ בעבור ישמרו חקיו ותורותיו כו׳« (תהלים ק״ה מ״ד-מ״ה). ושיביא על אויביו רעות מונעות אותם מהתקומם נגדו ומהפר כוונתו. וכן העיד באמרו: »ויצונו ה׳ אלהינו לעשות כו׳. לטוב לנו כל הימים לחיותנו כהיום הזה וצדקה תהיה לנו כו׳« (דברים ו׳ כ״ד-כ״ה).

⟨§ 16.28⟩

neque perturbetur per fortissima intelligibilia prius[a] considerata quin postea possit alia eque bene percipere, neque senescit, prout supra diffusius patuit. Incompetens quidem videretur ut mortalibus felicitatibus vel penis remuneraretur vel puniretur, quare Deus in suis Sacris Scripturis condignam docens ad remunerationem per ipsum benigne intentam se sanctitatem ait exhibiturum,[b] intelligens sanctitatem eternam et beatam vitam. Prout habetur in lib. Exodi cap.19 [19:6] et Deuteronomii cap.26 [26:18–19] ubi Dei mandata observantes in gentem sanctam ait facturum et gloriose constituturum. Condignam vero penam qua rebelles ait puniturum docet quidem ubi dicit Et minatur animam perditurum et illam suam iniquitatem passuram prout in lib. Levitici cap.20 et in lib. Numeri cap.15 habetur; cum ergo idem Deus in Suis Sacris Scripturis quedam mortalia promittere et quibusdam similiter mortalibus minari videantur, prout in Sacris sepius habetur.

⟨§16.27⟩

§16.28 Commoditates tantum intelligit ipsum colentibus exhibiturum, illasque a delinquentibus ablaturum, malaque impedimenta illaturum presertim his qui Dei imagine ad iniqua indaganda mediaque ad effectus Dei intento oppositos excogitanda turpiter utuntur. Quandoque tamen ad stimulum excitandi ad penitentiam nonnullas mortales infelicitates minatur missurum, prout in lib. Levitici cap. 23[c] [23:30] aperte habetur.

actions, nor is it bothered by stronger intelligible [powers] [that are] more considered [than it]; it is able to perceive existents in the right way and it does not become old, as mentioned at length above. It seems insufficient to be recompensed or punished with mortal prosperities or punishments, hence in His Holy Scripture, God teaches the appropriate remuneration for one who makes himself holy, meaning eternal holiness and a blessed life. In fact, the ones who observe the commandments of God will be included and placed among the holy people, according to Exodus 19 (19:6) and Deuteronomy 26 (26:18–19). He teaches the appropriate punishment with which He says that the rebels will be punished, where it says: "And He threatens that the soul will be destroyed and that it will suffer its own iniquity," according to Leviticus chapter 19 (19:8) and Numbers 15 (15:30–31). In His Holy Scripture, God promises some men [that they will achieve eternal life] and threatens others [with not achieving it], as is often said in Scripture.

⟨§16.27⟩

§16.28 He means the advantages that will be reserved for those who serve Him, and He knows the advantages that will be taken away from those who commit crimes, as well as the evil obstacles that will be especially inflicted on those who use the image of God to investigate unsuitable things and to find instruments for effects contrary to God's intention. Sometimes, He threatens that He will send mortal misfortunes to exhort them to repent, as is written in Leviticus 23 (23:30).

---

[a] prius] b[corr]; plus b.   [b] exhibiturum] coni. Copp.; exibiturum b.   [c] 23] emend. Copp.; 36 b.

§ 16.29 Indeed, everyone turned to look and found pleasant words and details of all that is mentioned in the extensive work by signs and proofs. Are they not found above, each in its place? And by it, one will know and find a fountain of their spring and *the hole of the pit*[a] in Holy Scripture and the scriptures of the philosophers. Then, he will understand the fear of ha-Shem and the knowledge of the holy [things] that are next to Him. He will be sanctified by His dignity.

⟨§ 16.30⟩

§ 16.29 אמנם כל סר לראות ומצא דברי חפץ. ופרטי כל הנזכר במאמר רחב באותות ומופתים הלא אתם ימצא לעיל איש על מקומו? ובו ידע וימצא מקור מבועם ומקבת בורם בספרי הקדש וספרי הפילוסופים אז יבין יראת ה' ודעת קדושים הנגשים אליו ונקדש בכבודו.

⟨§ 16.30⟩

---

[a] Isa 51:1.

§16.29 Premissorum vero singula diffusius apertiusque ostensu cum citatione locorum ubi in Sacris Scripturis et in profanis Phylosophorum libris diffuse tractantur. In huius opusculi questionibus facillime in suis invenientur locis.
    Ad laudem Dei.

§16.30 Finis libri Lumen Gentium nuncupati quo demostrative docetur contra nonnullas Peripateticorum opiniones religionis fundamentis aperte repugnantes, qui scilicet liber nuper editus est pro Servadeum Sphurnum[a] medicum hebreum Bononie moram trahentem.

§16.29 Every single premise is abundantly and clearly exposed, together with the quotations from the places in the Holy Scripture and in the profane books of the philosophers where they are diffusely treated.
    For the Glory of God.

§16.30 This is the end of the book called *Light of the Nations*, in which by means of demonstration is taught against some of the Peripatetics' opinions that clearly oppose the principles of religion. And this book was recently edited for Servadio Sforno, a Jewish physician living in Bologna.

---

[a] Sphurnum] b[corr]; Sphurmon b.

⟨§17⟩

[Imprimatur]

§ 17 Ego frater Tomasmaria Beccadellus Bononiensis inquisitor consentio ut hic liber possit imprimi.

[Imprimatur]

§ 17 I, Brother Tomasmaria Beccadellus from Bologna, inquisitor, consent that this book may be printed.

כלל העולה לאור עמים: MS IOM B 169,3

§ 16 | הן כל אלה יתנו עדיהם בהשקיף עלימו משכיל

§ 16.1 | ויבחנו דברי תופשי התורה וחכמי הגויים | כי יסופר בקצר מלין מסלול ודרך שניהם להתיר הספקות הנז(כרים) ולהשיג בהן דעות | אמתיות הלא הם דרכים שונים רב ההבדל ביניהם ובהביט המעיין אל שני | ההפכים יחד ישפוט על נקלה איזה יכשר הזה או זה כמו שאמ(ר) הפילוסוף בספ(ר) השמי(ם) |⁵ והעולם מאמר ב פ(רק) מ.

§ 16.2 | כי אמנם הפילוסופי(ם) כאשר ראו היות במוחשים פועל והתפעלות ונודע אצלם | היות ההתפעלות מצד החמר והפעל מצד הצורה אמרו שהמוחש מורכב מחמר | וצורה בלי ספק ובכן יסדו דעות על הנחות אשר חשבו אמתיות ומוכרחות.

§ 16.3.1 | הן הנה היו ¹⁰| ראשונה שהוא מן הנמנע שיתהוה יש מאין וזאת ההנחה היא אמתית | בלי ספק וזה כי בהפכה ויאמר דבר וסותרו כי אמנם באמרנו על דבר שהוא בלתי נמצא | כלל אמרנו בלי ספק שאינו חומר לדבר נמצא כי אם היה חומר לו היה חלק ממנו | וימצא החלק בהמצא הכל ולא יצדק עליו שאינו נמצא כלל אבל יצדק עליו סותרו | ונאמר שהוא נמצא באמת ובחשבם שיהיה כמו כן נמנע שיתהוה דבר לא מדבר |¹⁵ אבל יתחייב אצלם שכל מתחדש יתהוה מנושא נמצא ומן השקר שילך זה אל בלתי | תכלית כמבו(אר) לעיל אמרו היות מן ההכרח שיהיה איזה מין מהחמרים נושא ראשון | לכל הנושאים ובהיות מן הנמנע שהתחדש אותו הנושא מנושא נמצא קודם לו | בהיותו ראשון לכלם והיה מן הנמנע שיתחדש לא מנושא קודם כנ(זכר) לעי(ל) | אמרו שהוא בהכרח בלתי מחודש ואם כן היה מעולם ונקרא קדמון.

§ 16.3.2 |²⁰ וכאשר | ראו שכל המוחשים ישתנו זה לזה באמצעי או בלתי אמצעי וחוזרי(ם) | חלילה ומן | הנמנע שיהיה דבר נמצא בפועל בעודו בפועל והפך לדבר זולתו כי אם | כן היה מתלבש בשתי צורות יחד ויצדק עליו שם עצמו ושם זולת(ו) | זה לא יעלה על | לב.

§ 16.3.3 | אמרו שאותו הנושא הראשון הוא חמר נמצא בכח לא בפועל ובכן התחייב | שאותו הנושא לא נמצא לעולם בלתי צורה והוא הנק(רא) אצלם חומר ראשון.

§ 16.3.4 |²⁵ וכאשר חשבו היות צורות היסודות ראשונות לכל צורות מוחשות הוות בחמר הראשון | בלתי אמצעי התחייב אצלם שיהיו היסודות ג(ם) כ(ן) בלתי מחודשים וא(ם) כ(ן) הם קדמונים.

§ 16.4.1 | שנית בחשבם היות התנועה קדמונית בהכרח עד שאמרו שמי שיאמר הפך זה הנה | הוא סכל או מתעתע וזה באמרם היות מן הנמנע שיתחדש דבר בלתי תנועה | תניע המחדש לחדש אתו הדבר ואם כן נאמר שהתנועה התחדשה יתחייב שהתחדשה |⁵ בתנועה קודמת ויפול הספק על הקודמת כמו כן וילך הדבר אל בלתי תכלית § 16.4.2 עד | בואין אל תנועה קדמונית בהכרח ובהיות מן הנמנע המצא תנועה בלתי | מניע ומתנועע אמרו שמזה יתחייב שימצאו מניע ומתנועע קדמונים.

§ 16.4.3 | ובחשבם שבהמצא היסודות ותנועות הגלגלים ההכרחיים למציאות ההוייה | וההפסד | הנה התחייב אצלם היות תנועת ההויה וההפסד קדמונית ובהיות נמנע ¹⁰| אצלם שתהיה צורה מן הצורות זולתי בחמר מוכן אליה ואם כן לא היה מעולם | כי אם מזרע אדם המוכן להיות אדם התחייב אצלם שלעולם היה אדם וכן שאר | המינים בפרט מיני בעלי חיים וצמחי(ם) | ובהיות אצלם תנועת הגלגלים קדמונית | ובלתי נעדרת וא(ם) כ(ן) היא בלתי בעלת תכלית ונצחית וחשבו היות תנועה כזאת | בלתי אפשרית זולתי לכח מניע בלתי בעל תכלית ואמרו היות מן הנמנע שיהיה |¹⁵ כח כזה בגוף גם ראו היות תנועת הגלגלים בתכלית השווי בכל זמן אשר | לא יאות היותה על ידי כח אשר לא תהיה הוויתו שוה בראשית ההוויה

ובסופה אמרו שמאלה יתחייב שיהיה המניע נמצא פשוט בלתי גוף ובלתי | כח בגוף אמנם על הראיי(ה) הראשונה חלקו אנשי הצבא.

§ 16.4.4 ואמרו שמניע הגלגל | הוא כח בגוף וגם כי מזה יתחייב היותו בעל תכלית לא ימנע מזה היותו נצחי |²⁰ בהיותו בלתי מתפעל כי התפעלות המניע היא הסבה להגיעת המניע ולהפסק התנוע(ה) | כמו שספר אבן רשד כשאמ(ר) בס(פר) שמע מה שאחר מאמר יב פ(רק) מא וכאשר בארו | היות המניע כח נפרד מחמר אמרו שמזה יתחייב היותו אחד במספר לא יותר | וזה כי המספר לא יפול על שנים בצורה נבדלים מן החמר אשר הוא אמנם | סבת המספר הפרטי.

§ 16.5 |²⁵ שלישית בהיות מן המפורסם שאי איפשר שיהיו נמצאים אין תכלית למספרם בזמן אחד | כי הנמצאים אשר יצדק עליהם שהם כלם בזמן אחד הנה יש להם תכלית בלי ספק | כי מה שאין לו תכלית לא תצדק עליו הגבלה מקפת בכל לכן התחייב אצלם שתהיה | נפש האדם הפרטית נפסדת וזה כי באמרם שלעולם היה אדם נמצא בזמן | בלתי בעל תכלית והנה אם היתה נפש האדם הפרטית דבר בלתי נפסד היו |⁵ נפשות בני אדם קיימות בזמן אחד בלתי בעל תכלית במספר ומזה התחייב | שיאמרו על נפש האדם השכלית אחת משתים וזה אם שתהיה נפסדת ואם | שתהיה שכל נבדל נצחי אחד במספר משותף לכל המין האנושי לא שיהיו | שכלים נבדלים רבים כמספר בני האדם ומזה יתחייב שלא יהיה אחר המות | הבדל בין צדיק לרשע בין עובד אלו(הים) לאשר לא עבדו ולפי זה חנם שם שם בנו |¹⁰ הטבע תשוקת ידיעת האמת בדברים האלהיים הבלתי צריכים לקבוץ המדיני | אשר כל אדם נכסף לדעת אותם לפחות כאשר יעירוהו עליו וייקץ כישן | מתרונן מיין.¹

§ 16.6 רביעית באמרם שהדבר אשר הוא קדמון ונצחי אין לו פועל באמת וזאת | הנחה אמתית מבוארת בעצמה אין ספק בה כי הפועל יקדם בזמן |¹⁵ לפעלו בלי ספק והדבר הקדמון אשר אין לקדמותו תכלית לא היה דבר | קורה לו בזמן. לכן התחייב אצלם שאין לכלל המציאות פועל וזה בהיות | אצלם כלל המציאות קדמון היינו הגרמים השמימיים והיסודות ותנועת | ההוייה וההפסד ומציאות החמר הראשון כנז(כר) לע(יל) וכאשר ראו היות במציאות סדור | והתקשרות קצתו בקצתו בפרט בתנועת המניע הראשון ובתולדות החווים |²⁰ ונפסדים ובהתקשרות הנז(כרת) היה המציאות בכללו אחד במספר והתחייב מזה שיש | נמצא מסדר ₣ מכוין להתקשרות הנז(כרת) וקיומו אמרו שיש מסדר בלי ספק | ולפי זה יהיה פעלו אצלם ממציאות לסדר ולקשר ולקיים נמצאות אשר | הוא לא המציאם ובכן היה לדעתם ובכן היה מקרה קרה לנמצאות שימצא מסדר | נצחי יסדרם ויקשרם כי זולתו היו בלתי סדר וקשר ומקרה קרה למסדר | שימצאו נמצאות יסדרם ויקשרם כי זולתם היה בלתי פועל או פועל בטל | והוא בפעלתו זאת לדעתם דומה לקורא אשר דגר ולא ילד וכאשר | היה כל זה אצלם בלתי נמנע. התחייב אם כן שגם שיביאו ראיה מופתית | על היות המניע אחד ובלתי גוף לא יתחייב מזה שלא יהיה זולתו שכל נבדל |⁵ שוה לו שיהיה מסדר המציאות ומקשרים ויפול מספר עליהם בסבת הבדל פעלם | בו יהיו נבדלים במין כאשר באר אבן רשד בס(פר) הפלת ההפלה מאמר ה פ(רק) ב | ולפי זה יתחייב שיפול שם אלהות על שניהם בשוה או שלא יהיה אחד מהם אלוה | והנה הם מתאמצים להבין ולהורות הפך זה היינו שאין אלוה כי אם אחד במספר | כמבו(אר) בספ(ר) מה שאחר מאמר יב פ(רק) לט ומט וזולתם.

§ 16.7.1 |¹⁰ חמשית בראותם היות השגת ידיעה אצלנו על אחד משני פנים האחד בחושים זה | בפרטי המוחשות אשר לא נשיגם כי אם בחושים והשני בשכל זה במיני המושכלות | המופשטות מחמר אמרו שהוא מן הנמנע שתיפול ידיעה אלהית על פרטי המוחשים | כמו שחשב איוב באמרו העיני בשר לך כו'² וכל שכן שהוא כמבואר אצלם שאי איפשר שתיפול | עליהם השגחה אלהית.

---

1 Ps 78:65.
2 Job 10:4.

§ 16.7.2 כמו שאמר אבן רשד בס(פר) מה שאחר מאמ(ר) יב פ(רק) לז ומזה יתחייב שלא יבדיל האל ית(ברך) בין צדיק לרשע בין חכם לכסיל | לא בחיים ולא במות להיות פרטים אשר לא תפול ידיעתו עליהם כל שכן | השגחתו וכאשר ראו היות השגחה פרטי(ת) באיברי בעלי חי מכוונים בלי ספק | לתועלת הכרחי לפרטי ההוא אמרו היות כל זה פעלת טבע ובהיות כל מכוין | לתכלית כח שכלי בלי ספק והיה הכח המצייר בב(עלי) ח(יים) מציירם בלתי כלי חמרי | [20] אשר לא יאות לכח בחמר כאשר הורה אבן רשד בשם ארסטו' בס(פר) מה שאחר מאמ(ר) | ז פ(רק) לא הנה א(מ)כ(ן) יתחייב שיהיה אותו בטבע הפועל לתכלית ובלתי כלי חמרי | שכל נבדל מכוין לתכלית הוא שיהיה בטבעו בעצמו ואם שיהיה הטבע | אמצעי אשר בו יפעל השכל המכוין כאשר הורה אבן רשד בס(פר) הנז(כר) מאמ(ר) יב | פ(רק) יח ומזה יתחייב שיהיה אותו השכל הנבדל משגיח בפרטים ובכן | [25] ישאר הספק אשר אמרו שלא תפול ידיעת שכל נבדל על פרטי(ם) כל שכן השגחתו.

§ 16.8.1 אמנם | תורת אלהינו אשר תודיע במופתים נכוחים למבין דעות אמתיות ולהתיר | כל הספקות הנז(כרות) כוננה עלינו מסלול ודרך רב ההבדל מדרן הפילוסופי(ם) הנז(כרים) | בו יבוא כל מעיין להכיר רבונו יתהלל השכל וידוע נפלאות מתורתו.

§ 16.8.2 | [5] וזה כי התבאר אצל כל מעיין בחפרש הנסיון עד היותו כמושכל ראשון שכל דבר | מתמיד בנמצאים רבים במספר לא יפול בהם במקרה היינו בלתי מכוון | לתכלית כמבוא(ר) בס(פר) שמע טבעי מאמר ב פ(רק) מח ובס(פר) השמים מאמר ב פ(רק) מה | אבל יהיה מפעלת פועל רצוניי מכוין לתכלית מה או פעולת פועל טבעי מצווה | ועושה במצות והנהגת משכיל מכוין כמו שבאר אבן רשד בס(פר) מה שאח(ר) מאמר יב פ(רק) יח.

§ 16.9.1 | [10] שנית התבאר שבכל אחד מהגלגלים אשר נודעה תנועתם בחוש שהם לפחות שמנה | נמצאת קצבת כמות מוגבלת אשר אם היתה יותר או פחות כחוט השערה | היה ביניהם ריקות או היו מונעים זה את זה מן התנועה ומן ההגבלה הנז(כרת) | הנמצאת בכל אחד מהם נודע אצל כל מעיין היות כמותם המוגבל כנז(כר) | וכמו כן העצם הנושא אותו הכמות בהכרח מכוונים מפועל רצוני או הם | [15] פעלת פועל טבעי המציאם בהנהגת ומצות פועל רצוני מכוין כנז(כר).

§ 16.9.2 | וזה אמנם הורה ישעיה באמרו וימיני טפחה שמים קורא אני אליהם | יעמדו יחדו[3] כלומ(ר) טפחתי ומדדתי שמים על כמות מוגבל בכל גלגל | מהם בו יוכלו לעמוד יחדו ולא ימנעו זה את זה מה מפעלת תנועתם.

§ 16.10.1 | שלישית התבאר מן החוש שביצירת הנפסדים בעלי האיברים נמצאו איברי(ם) | [20] רבים במספר על תמונות שונות ובכל אחת מהן תועלת מבואר לפרטי ההוא | אשר לא היה משיגו זולתי בתמונה ההיא ומזה התבאר היותם מכוונים מפועל | רצוני או היותם פעלת פועל טבעי בהנהגת רצוני מכוין כנז(כר).

§ 16.10.2 | וזה אמנם הורה משורר המזמור באמרו הנוטע אזן הלא ישמע אם יוצר | עין הלא יביט כלומר מי שכיון לתמונת האזן והעין אשר בהם תחבולה רבה | יראה ממנה תכלית לתועלת הפרטי הלא ישגיח בפרטים הפך מאמר הכופרי(ם) | באמרם לא יראה י(ה) ולא יבין כו'.

§ 16.11.1 | רביעית התבאר בנסיון שלפעלת תולדות הנפסדי(ם) יצטרך בהכרח ראשונ(ה) מציאות | [5] טבע החמר הראשון אשר זולתו לא יתהוו זה ויכלה החמר כאשר באר אבן | רשד בס(פר) מה שאחר מאמר יב פ(רק) לג שנית מציאות תנועת הגלגל היומי הישרה | שלישית מציאות תנועת כוכבי לכת המעוותת בפרט תנועת השמש רביעית | מציאות אור השמש והכוכבי(ם) וחומם כמבו(אר) בחוש ובארו אבן רשד בס(פר) הנז(כר) | מאמר

---

3 Isa 48:13.

הנז(כר) פ(רק) יח ובהיות צורך התולדות הנז(כר) לכל אחד מאלה עם בייחס עצמו ומיוחד⁴ לכל
ו?–? וא?–? ¹⁰ | נודע בלי ספק שלא הסכימו כלם לפעלת התולדות הנז(כרות) במקרה אבל
בכוונת פועל | רצוני או טבעי בהנהגה⁵ רצוני כנז(כר) מסבב הסכמתם וממציאה לתכלית
פעלת התולדות | הנז(כרת).

§ 16.11.2 | וזה אמנם הורה ישעיהו באמרו עושה שלו(ם) ובורא רע אני ה' עושה כל אלה⁶ |
כלומר שמתוך מציאות השלו(ם) אשר בין תנועות הגלגלים המתנגדות והם ¹⁵ | עם זה
מסכימות יחד בפעלת התולדות הנז(כרת) וכמו כן מתוך מציאות טבע | החמר הראשון
נקר(א) רע אצל רבים מהקדמוני(ם) התבאר כי אני ה' ר(צוני) ל|(ומר) מהווה | אחר אפיסות
מוחלט באמרו עושה כל אלה כלומר כי אין ספק אלה לא התהוו | מנושא קודם מבלי אין נושא
קודם לחמר הראשון גם לא לגלגלים ותנועותיה(ם) | כמב(ואר) לע(יל) ובכן התבאר שהיה
מציאותם מכח בריאתי.

§ 16.12.1 |²⁰ חמישית התבאר בחוש כי מציאות מיני בעלי חיים לא יהיה בלתי מיני הצמחי(ם) |
אשר בם יחיו וכי מציאות האדם לא ייטב בלתי מיני הצמחים ומיני | הבהמות לפחות הביתיות
העובדות אותו במיני האסיף ומן המבוא(ר) שלא היה | זה מקרה קרה לכל מיני בעלי חיים
שימצאו מיני צמחים הכרחיים לקיומם | כל אחד מהם ולא מקרה קרה לאדם שימצאו מיני
הצמחים לקיומו ומיני | הבהמות לעבודתיו אבל התחייב שהיה מציאות כלם בלתי מכוון
מפועל רצוני או | טבעי בהנהגת רצוני המכוין תכלית כנז(כר). | וזה אמנם באר המשורר
באמרו מצמיח חציר לבהמה ועשב לעבודת האדם להוצי(א) לחם.⁷

§ 16.12.2 | וכאשר התבאר מכל אלה וזולתם לע(יל) איש על מקומו שמציאות הגלגלים
וכוכביהם |⁵ ותנועותיהם ומציאות החמר הראשון היו בהכרח פעולת פועל רצוני המציאם
לתכלית | על ידי בריאה מבלי אין נושא קודם שיוכל לעלות על הדעת שהתהוו ממנו והתבאר
שמציאות תולדות הנמצאים הנפסדי(ם) | לא יהיה בלתי מציאות פעלת הגלגלים | ומציאות
פעלת כוכביהם בתנועותיהם ומציאות אורם וחמם ומציאות | התפעלות החמר הראשון הנה
התבאר היות מציאות כלם והנהגתם וקשרם פעלת |¹⁰ פועל רצוני הוא ממציאם ומנהיגם.

§ 16.12.3 | באמרו בראשית ברא אלו(הים)⁸ והוא השם המורה | מנהיג ומסדר כלומר שהנהגתו
וסדרו מורים על בריאתו והוסיף לבאר המופת | באמרו אלה תולדות השמים והארץ בהבראם
ביום עשות ה' אלו(הים) ארץ ושמים⁹ | כלומר שבהיות תולדות הכוכבים הנ(זכרות) תולדות
השמים והארץ כי לא יתכן | היותם בלתי מציאות עצם השמים וכוכביהם ותנועותיהם
הפועלים | בחמרים ובלתי מציאות החמר הארצי המתפעל מהם כי לא יעלה | על לב שעם היות
מציאות כל אחד מהם הכרחי לתולדות ועם היות כלם | נועדים בפעלת התולדות הנ(זכרות)
יפול כל זה במקרה בלתי כוונת מכוין אבל¹⁰ | יורו היותם פעלת פועל רצוני המציאם וברא
ובכן המציא הסכמתם | והועדם בפועל והתפעלות הכרחי לתולדות הנה אם כן התבאר
שמציאות |²⁰ כל הנז(כר) היה בהבראם היינו על יד ממציא אחר אפיסות מוחלט והסכמתם |
והועדם יחד בתולדות היה ג(ם) כ(ן) מפעלתו וסדרו באשר הוא אלו(הים) מסדר ומנהיג |
שאחר שברא עשה וסדר ארץ ושמים נכונים לפעלת מכוונת מאתו יתב(רך).

§ 16.12.4 | ובלעדי אלה הנה התבאר שלכל פעולת פועל חוץ מן הבריאה יצטרך בהכרח היות
נושא | נמצא שבו יפעל הפועל פעלו וכמו כן להתפעלות מתפעל יצטרך בהכרח פועל יפעל
בו |²⁵ ואם כן לא יהיה כי מציאות אחד מהם בלתי מציאות חבירו אם לא שהיה מציאות בטל.

---

4 ומיוחד] emend. Dunk.; ומיחד a; ?–?ומיו A.
5 בהנהגה] coni. Dunk.; בהנהגת A.
6 Isa 45:7.
7 Ps 104:14.
8 Gen 1:1.
9 Gen 2:4.
10 אבל] emend. Dunk. ex a; אבל אבל A.

§ 16.12.5 | שנית התבאר שממציאות הנושא לא יתחייב מציאות עצם הפועל וכן | ממציאות הפועל לא יתחייב מציאות עצם הנושא כי אמנם | לא יצוייר שיהיה עצם מתחייב למציאות עצם זולתו כי אם על דרך עלה | ועלול ואם היה זה בפועל ובמתפעל שיהיה עצם אחד מהם סבה ועלה לעצם |⁵ חבירו הנה יתחייב שיהיה סבה ועלה למציאות עצמו אחד שלא יתכן | מציאות האחד בלתי מציאות חבירו הנז(כר) וזה לא יתכן ומזה יתחייב | שאין מציאות אחד מתחייב למציאות חבירו ואם כן מקרה הוא בלתי | מחוייב קרה לכל אחד מהם שימצא חבירו ובכו התחייב שלא היה אחד | מהם קדמון כי אמנם הקדמון הוא מחוייב המציאות בעצמו בלתי שיצטרך |¹⁰ על תנאי במציאותו כמבו(אר) במופת ארסטו בס(פר) השמים והעולם מאמר א פ(רק) קכד.

§ 16.13 | ואת כל אלה הורה המורה לצדקה באמרו אני אל שדי¹¹ התהלך לפני והיה תמים¹² כלו(מר) אני לבדי | נמצא אשר די במציאותי לפעלה המיוחדת לי והיא הברוא(ה) וזה לא יתכן לשום נמצא | זולתי א(ם) כ(ן) התהלך לפני(י) והיה תמים בלכתך בדרכי אחר שאין שלם¹³ בשלימותי.

§ 16.14 | וכאשר התבאר לעיל במופת שבנפרדים המתדמים לא יפול רבוי ומספר הנה |¹⁵ כאשר יתבאר שפעלת הברוא(ה) נמנעת לגוף או בכח בגוף יתבאר | שאין בורא כי אם אחד.

§ 16.15 | וכאשר התבאר היות מחוייב שיהיה איזה נמצא קדמון הנה מחוייב שיהיה איזה נמצא בורא | אמנם היות מן הנמנע שתהיה הבריאה על ידי גוף או כח בגוף הנה | התבאר באופן זה כי אמנם בין המציאות והאפיסות המוחלט אין |²⁰ אמצעי להיותם שני חלקי הסותר א״ב ומזה יתחייב שלא יהיה זמן בין | תחלת הבריאה וסופה אבל תהיה בעתה שאמרו בראשית ברא אלו(הים)¹⁴ וזה הוא | הוא רגע בלתי מתחלק אשר הוא ראשית הזמן כי לא היה זמן קודם לו ומזה יתחייב שלא היתה תנועה שיונע בה והפועל לפעלו אשר חשבו הפילוסופים¹⁵. | ומבלי אין זמן בבריאה יתחייב שלא תפול בה תנועה ולא כלי חמרי | כי לא יהיו רק בזמן בין תחלת הפעלה וסופה ובהיות שבכל פעלת | פועל גופני או כח בגוף יתחייב בהכרח זמן ותנועה וכלים | חמריים הנה התחייב מזה שיהיה הבורא בלתי גוף ובלתי | כח בגוף. | וכן הורה באמרו כי לא ראיתם כל תמונה.¹⁶

{lac}

§ 16.16 |⁵ ובהיות במציאות ההשגחה שכלית לא בכללים בלבד אבל גם | בפרטי כל מין ומין בפרט מהמינים הכלים אשר בכל פרטי מהם | כלים מכלים שונים במדה וצורה פרטית נאותה והכרחית למציאות | הפרטי ההיא ובלעדי מציאות הפרטים לא יהיה מציאות הכללים | הנה יתחייב שתהיה ההשגחה¹⁷ הפרטית ההיא מאת מסדר הכללים באמצעי |¹⁰ או בלתי אמצעי לפחות כמו חולק מהמי כאשר הורה באמרו הנוטע אזן הלא ישמע.¹⁸

§ 16.17 | ובהיות במין האדם כח מה להשיג מושכלות בלתי מחוייבות למדינות | עם תאוה טבעית להשיגם מורה על היות השגתם מכוונת | מאת המסדר ועם זה אמנם לא תמצא השגתם כי אם | בבחירה פרטית זה ביחידים בוחרים להשיג בדרכים שונים |¹⁵ איש איש כפי בחירתו הפרטית ורבים זולתם מואסים כונת | או בוחרים ברע ובזה מתקוממים לכונת המסדר הנ(זכר) הנה | הנה התחייב שתהיה השגחת המסדר החפץ בתכלית המכוון ממנו |

---

11 שדי] emend. Dunk ex a; ?–? ש A.
12 Gen 17:1.
13 שלם] coni. Dunk.; סלם A.
14 Gen 1:1.
15 שלא ... הפילוסופים] emend. Dunk. ex a; ?–? חשבו ?–? לפעלו ?–? בה וה ?–? תנועה ?–? שלא A (text is partially hidden in the fold).
16 Deut 4:15.
17 ההשגחה] coni. Dunk.; ההשגחת A.
18 Ps 94:9.

משגיח בפרטי האדם באשר הם פרטים לא חלקי המין בלבד | אבל השגחה פרטית על כל פרטי מביא כוונת המסדר אל תכלית | או מואס בה או מתקומם עליה באמרו ה׳ יודע מחשבות אדם |⁵ כו׳ אשרי הגבר אשר תיסרנו וכו׳¹⁹ *כי אמנם זולת זה ?— היה השתדלותו חסר שהראוי להביא מכוונו אל תכלית באמרו כי לא יטוש ה׳ את²⁰* | עמו וכו׳²¹ וכן הורה באמרו ואך את דמכם לנפשותיכם אדרוש²² להבין | ולהורות היות השגחתו פרטי(ת) במין האדם לסבת נפשו כאשר השלים לפרש כלומר | כי בצלם אלו(הים) עשה את האדם*.²³

§ 16.18 |¹⁰ ובהיותו ידיעתו בלתי מסובבת מהנמצאות להיותה קודמת לנמצאות | וסבה להם והפך זה יקרה לשכל האנושי כי אמנם | לא תהיה ידיעתו כי אם מסובבת מהנמצאות המובלות אליו מן החושי(ם) | אחר אשר יפשיטם מחמר ויעשה מהם כלליים ובכן לא יאמר | שם ידיעה באמת על ידיעת הבורא וידיעתנו כי אם בשתוף |¹⁵ השם אם כן יתחייב שאע״פ שלא תפול ידיעה | שכל אנושי על נמצאות בלתי תנאים בהם היינו | שיהיו הכרחיים כלליים מופשטים מחמר בלתי בעלי תכלית | במספר כי רק בהיותם על²⁴ התנאים הנז(כרים) תוכל להסתבב | מהם ידיעה לשכל האנושי ולכן ולא תפול על רבים אין תכלית |²⁰ למספרם ולא על מקרים ולא על פרטים כי לא ישיג אלה | האדם רק בחוש לא בהשגה שכלית הנה אצל הידיעה | האלהית אשר היא בלתי מסובבת | מהנמצאות יתחייב שלא יהיה הפרש בין נמצא לנמצא ולכן ראוי שתפול על | רבים אין תכלית למספרם כמו על בעלי תכלית ועל הפרטי(ם) | כמו על הכלליים | ועל המקרים כמו על הדבר(ים) ההכרחי(ים) ועל החמריים כמו על הנבדלים מחמר | ועל העתיד כמו על ההווה וכן הורה באמרו היפלא מה׳ דבר.²⁵

§ 16.19 |⁵ ובהיות שהבורא המציא הפכים אשר לא ימציאם פועל טבעי הפועל לעולם | על ענין אחד כמבואר מהיסודות ינשאו ההפכיות האיכיות הראשונות | ובכל אחד מהההפכים נודע תכלית אשר לא יחשב היותו כי אם מכוון | מפועל רצוני הנה התבאר שהבורא הוא פועל רצוני לא טבעי כאשר | אמרו רבי(ם) מדוברי עתק. וכן הורה באמרו יוצר אור ובורא חשך כו׳ אני |¹⁰ ה׳ עושה כל אלה.

§ 16.20 | ובהיות הבורא שלם ומעולה מכל הנמצאות התבאר שכל נמצא אשר יהיה | דומה לבורא יותר נכבד משאר הנמצאות הוא בלי ספק נכבד ומעולה מהם.

§ 16.21 | ובהיות ששלמות הבורא ומעלתו נודעו אצלנו מצד חכמתו וחסדו הנראים | במעשיו באמרו כלם בחכמה עשית²⁶ ובאמרו וחסיד בכל מעשיו²⁷ **התבאר** זה התבאר בהיותו מטיב ובלתי צריך |¹⁵ שכשירצה האדם להדמות לבורא כפי האפשר ישתדל להיות חכם וחסיד | וכל שכן שיהיה צדיק.

§ 16.22 | ובהיות חסדי הבורא באים מאתו ברצון ובחירה בלתי מוכרחת כל זה התבאר | בהיותו פועל רצוני כנ(זכר) יודע שני ההפכים ויכול עליהם בשוה ובוחר הטוב מהם עם | היותו יודע שיוכל לעשות הפכו הנה התחייב שפעולות הטוב אשר תבוא |²⁰ מאת האדם המתדמה לבורא תהיה מאתו ברצון ובחירה מוחלטת בלתי | מוכרחת כלל עם שידע היותו יכול לעשות הפכה באמרו ובחרת בחיים.²⁸

§ 16.23 | בהיות זה המין ᵈהבחירה נמצע בנבראים כי אם בשכל בלתי שלם אשר הוא | לפעמים בלתי משכיל בפועל ובכן לא יתקוממו להעביר את רעת הכח המתאוה | המצוה לכחות הגופניות דברים אשר לא כן כמו שיקרה לבעלי חיים בלתי | מדברים באמרם אדם ביקר ולא יבין נמשל כבהמות נדמו²⁹ ויהיה שיחדל | להתקומם גם שידע שיוכל להתקומם ולנצח ברצותו עם אלו(הים) היינו בהיותו |⁵ משכיל בפועל ובמבין לאשרו ומזה המין היא הנפש האנושית השכלית הנקר(א) | בכתוב צלם אלו(הים)³⁰ אשר לו כח בבחירה רצוניות הנק(רא) דמות אלו(הים)³¹ וזה כי כמו | שכתב אבן רשד בס(פר) הפלת ההפלה מאמ(ר) ג פ(רק) יח לא תמצא לאחד מהנמצאי(ם) | הטבעיים בחירה כי אם לאדם לבדו אבל האחרים זולתו יפעלו בטבע | בלבד הנה התחייב אם כן שלא תמצא בחירה לשום נמצא זולתי לבורא |¹⁰ יתע(לה) באופן נכבד ומעולה ולאדם אמנם באופן שפל כאשר הורה אבן | רשד בס(פר) הפלת ההפלה מאמר יא פ(רק) א. אם כן כאשר חפץ הבורא | להמציא נמצא דומה לו כפי האיפשר אשר יהיה בהכרח מבחר הנמצאות | בפרט הגשמיים ותכליתם היה מן המחויב שיברא האדם בדמותו | בצלמו כאשר העיד באמרו נעשה אדם בצלמנו כדמותנו³² ובכן |¹⁵ צונו לעשות האיפשר אצלנו להדמות אליו באמרו והלכת בדרכיו³³ | ובאמרו והתקדשתם והייתם קדושים כי קדוש אני.³⁴

§ 16.24 | וכאשר תדע הנפש השכלית הנ(זכרת) שתוכל להדמות לבוראה בעיון ובמעשה | ושבזה ישיג הבורא חפצו וכוונתו אשר לא תושג בכח אלהי מכריח | כי אמנם אם לא תהיה הבחירה רצונית בוחרת בחכמה הטוב משני |²⁰ חלקי הסותר בלתי מכריח שיטהו אליו לא יהיה כלל הדמות המכוון מאתו | יתע(לה) ובכן לא יכון שיוציא הבורא כח האדם לפועל בלתי הסכמת | ורצון נפשו השכלית באמרו מה ה' אלו(היך) שואל מעמך וכו'³⁵ ואמרו הכל | בידי שמים חוץ מיראת שמים³⁶ ואם כן כאשר תבחר ותקרב הנפש | השכלית עצמה וזולתה להדמות לבורא למען ישיג הבורא חפצו | תהיה אז בלי ספק כבן עובד מאהבה באמרו בנים אתם לה' אלוהיכ(ם).³⁷

§ 16.25 | ובהיות הבורא שלם מכל הנמצאים וממנו הווה כל שלמות וכל כח להיותו | מחולל כל באמצעי או בלתי אמצעי כמבו(אר) לע(יל) |⁵ לך ה' הגדולה והגבורה והתפארת כו'³⁸ בפרט כי בהיותו חסיד באשר התבאר להיותו מטיב בלתי חייב ובלתי צריך כל שכן שהוא צדיק באמרו צדיק ה' בכל דרכיו³⁹ הנה התחייב שיהיה | צדקו ומיני הגמול הבאים מאת צדקו הנז(כר) גדולי(ם) וטובי(ם) מכל אשר | בשאר הנמצאות ובכן התחייב שיגמול טוב בלי ספק לעושי רצונו | אשר ברצונם ובכח בחירתם השיג הוא חפצו וכאב את בן ירצה |¹⁰ באמרם עשה רצונו כרצונך כדי שיעשה רצונך כרצונו⁴⁰ ואלה | יקראו בנים כנז(כר) אמנם העושים אלה מיראת שכר ᵉⁿᵘˢʰ או לתקות | גמול יקראו עבדים ולהם יאות הגמול הראוי לעבדים המשמשים | את הרב על מנת לקבל פרס אמנם הצדיקי(ם) גמורי(ם) יקראו עבדי(ם) בערך | אל המלאכים לבד הנקראי(ם) בני האלוהי(ם)⁴¹ ובכן התחייב שישפוט בצדקו |¹⁵ ויענוש הנרפים מעשות רצונו ומבוקשו בפרט בהכירם שיוכלו לעשותו | כל שכן שיעניש המואסי(ם) כל שכן המתקוממים ומונעי(ם) יציאת כוונתו ותכליתו במציאות | לפועל והורסים פנת כוונתו ותכליתו במציאות באמרו אם לא | בריתי יומם ולילה חקות שמים וארץ לא שמתי⁴² ובכן יקראו הנרפים | בהמות

באמרו נמשל כבהמות נדמו⁴³ והמואסים והפושעים נקראים פושעים |²⁰ אויבים שונאים
וצרים באמרו הלא משנאיך ה׳ אשנא ובתקוממיך אתקוטט⁴⁴ | ועל זה הדרך יקרא הבורא
נוקם באמרו נוקם ה׳ ובעל חמה⁴⁵ וזה נגד המתקוממי(ם) | לכוונתו ומשתמשים בכח צלמו
להתנגד לרצונו הנקראים צרים באמרו | ונקם ישיב לצריו.⁴⁶

§ 16.26 | ובהיות הנפש השכלית דבר בלתי נפסד כאשר התבאר במופת לעי(ל) <u>אשר לזה</u>
<u>נקרא(ת)</u>⁴⁷ ויורה עליו טבע פעלתו | הנעשית בלתי כלי חמרי והיותה בלתי עיפה⁴⁸ בהשכלת מושכל חזק ובלתי
מזקת אשר לזה נקראת⁴⁹ צלם אלו(הים)⁵⁰ לא יאות לכל משכיל להעלות על לב בשום אופן שיהיה
גמולה או | ענשה דבר נפסד ולזה כאשר בארה התורה את הגמול המכוון לה מאת האל
ית(ברך) העידה שהוא יקדש אתה להודיענו שיתן לה נצחיות מוצלח ומאושר באמרו | ואתם
תהיו לי ממלכת כהנים וגוי קדושי⁵¹ וכן באמרו וה׳ האמירך כו׳ לתתך | עליון על כל הגויים
כו׳ ולהיותך עם קדוש⁵² † וכאשר הזכירה את העונש הראוי | לנפש הנז(כר) אמרה ונכרתה
הנפש⁵³ והאבדתי את הנפש.⁵⁴

§ 16.27 | אם כן כאשר יעד | בתורה הטובות והרעות הנפסדות היתה הכוונה שיתן לעובדיו את
הצריך להם |¹⁰ לעבודתו באמרו ויתן להם ארצות גויים כו׳ בעבור ישמרו חקיו ותורותיו כו׳⁵⁵ |
ושיביא על אויביו רעות מונעות אותם מלהתקומם נגדו ומהפר כוונתו וכן | העיד באמרו ויצונו
כו׳ לטוב לנו כל הימים לחיותנו כו׳ וצדקה תהיה לנו כו׳.⁵⁶

⟨§ 16.28⟩

§ 16.29 | אמנם כל סר לראות ומצא דברי חפץ ופרטי כל הנז(כר) במאמר רחב באותות |
ומופתים הלא אותם ימצא איש על מקומו לע(יל) ובו ידע מקור |¹⁵ מבועו ומקבת בורם בספרי
הקדש וספרי הפילוסופ(ים) | אז יבין יראת ה׳ | ודעת קדושים הנגשים אליו ונקדש בכבודו.

{lac}

† וכן הורה באמרו והקימותי את בריתי כו׳ ברית עולם להיות לך לאלו(הים) | לזרעך אחריך⁵⁷ |
וזה כי בהיות כוונת המנהיג הטוב לקיים הנמצאי(ם) | בהנהגתו וסדרו על הטוב שבתכונות
כפי יכלתו וכפי איפשרות המקבלים הנה בהיות האל ית(ברך) הוא המנהיג בלתי אמצעי |²⁰
המכוון זה יהיה בהכרח הקיום בהנהגתו נצחי על הטוב שבתכונות כפי אפשרות | המקבלים
ובכן מה לנפש השכלית הבלתי נפסדת בטבעה כנז(כר) לע(יל) | יהיה בהנהגתו נצחיות על
הטוב שבתכונות כפי מדרגת שלימותה.

---

43 Ps 49:13.
44 Ps 139:21.
45 Nahum 1:2.
46 Deut 32:43.
47 Erased text below the following four words in this line.
48 עיפה] emend. Dunk. ex a; עיף A.
49 נקראת] emend. Dunk. ex a; נק–? A.
50 Gen 1:26.
51 Ex 19:6.
52 Deut 26:18–19.
53 Lev 19:8.
54 Lev 23:30.
55 Ps 105:44–45.
56 Deut 6:24–25.
57 Gen 17:7.

Signs

(...)	Abbreviated word(s); extension in round brackets
דבר עצם	Interlinear text (superscript)
דבר עצם	Text in the margin of the page
?; ?–?	One unreadable letter; an uncountable series of unreadable letters
אשר	Uncertain reading
{lac}	Lacuna left by the author
ממציאות	Text erased by the author
20|	Line separator with line indicator
|155ᵛ|	Folio
†	Sigla for addition of text by the author (text written at the bottom of the page to be inserted at the position of the †)
דבר	Addition by a later hand (author or other scribe)

Abbreviations in the apparatus:
- **a** — *Or ʿAmmin* (Bologna, 1537)
- **A** — MS IOM B 169,3
- DUNK. — Dunklau, Florian (editor)

The manuscript has almost no punctuation. The full stops at the end of each paragraph have been added by the editor.

ESSAY

From Nothing Comes Nothing: The Theory of Primordial Chaos in Sforno's Writings

Giada Coppola

The aim of *Light of the Nations*, which is presented as a *summa*, is to demonstrate the errors and mistakes that result from the philosophical positions of the Gentiles. In order to contradict these positions, Sforno adopted both the Christians' method and their arguments, and the *quaestio disputata*, the expression *par excellence* of the Christian tradition, became the instrument by which he was to refute the Aristotelian system on which they relied. In light of this fact, it is not surprising that scholars have considered this text to be a work of *Religionphilosophie*[1] ("philosophy of religion"), given Sforno's arguments regarding the examination of philosophical issues involved in central questions of the religious tradition. His main aim was to explain the philosophical doctrines in order to dispel any doubts that might arise from ignorance of the "true" knowledge that is found in the Torah. However, it is only possible to understand the ontological, metaphysical, and theological issues that Sforno attempts to relate to the account of creation by comprehending the physical phenomena in the sublunary and superlunary realms.

The creation of the world is the key to Sforno's philosophical system, and his exegetical readings, which are integrated into *Light of the Nations*, constitute the strongest point of his methodology when examining Aristotle's and Averroes's doctrines. He explains his *modus operandi* in the section that he calls the *ordo*/סדר, which consists of seven points (eight in *Lumen Gentium*) that can be summarised as follows: 1) the fundamental principles of the Jewish religion (עקרים, meaning the Jewish "dogmas"); 2) the Aristotelian position and its confutation; 3) following on from this, a presentation of the opinion (דעת) of Aristotle and his interpreters; 4) an argument that will confute the abovementioned opinions; 5) the philosophers' objections in respect of their own positions, meaning the incoherence of these positions; 6) the confutation of the philosophers; and 7) (8 in the Latin version) the biblical explanation that will resolve the philosophical questions. The Latin version contains an additional seventh point which is included before the biblical interpretation: "Septimo ut Sacrarum Loca ostendamus […] inseruntur sepe etiam eundem [secundum] Latinam translationem que scilicet in plurimis proculdubio deficit, quare omnia in originali Hebreorum textu rectius apertiusque fulgere patet."

Sforno translated the biblical verses into Latin himself, offering an innovative interpretation that differs from the Vulgate translation, because, as he stated, the Vulgate does not follow the original meaning that seems to be evi-

---

1 Julius Fürst, *Bibliotheca Judaica: Bibliographisches Handbuch der gesammten jüdischen Literatur mit Einschluss der Schriften über Juden und Judenthum und einer Geschichte der jüdischen Bibliographie nach alfabetischer Ordnung der Verfasser*, vol. 3 (Leipzig, 1863), 319: "אור עמים 'ס oder eine ausführliche Religionsphilosophie, worin über Gott und dessen Wesen, über Einheit, Allmacht, Vorsehung, über die Seele, über Atheisten, Epikuräer u. Läugner des Gesetzes usw."

dent (*rectius apertiusque fulgere patet*) in the Hebrew Bible. Even though his Latin translation is verbatim, it nevertheless reflects his exegetical activities. Sforno appealed to the Torah in order to find a "rational" solution, as in his view, philosophy was insufficiently equipped to answer his questions; in order to impose reason on these questions, biblical authority replaces the opinions of the philosophers. As the questions are always resolved in accordance with the Bible, it is not surprising that in *Lumen Gentium*, Sforno employed expressions such as "in Sacris Dei Scripturis demonstrative probatum, demonstrative ostendit, demonstrative docere intendens, quod demonstrative dicit, etc.," to confer a scientific value on the Holy Scriptures.

Sforno also presented twenty-seven propositions, *praesuppositiones* or הנחות (§ 1.6), which are in harmony with the Jewish principles of faith; these are opinions found in Aristotle's and Averroes's works that are not in opposition to the Torah. These propositions follow a similar scheme based to the twenty-six Maimonidean propositions in the introduction to part 2 of the *Guide of the Perplexed*. Sforno considered these propositions to be postulates, and he employed them as the principal positions in his argumentation. In my opinion, the philosophical assumptions that Sforno introduces in *Light* also have a particular function, which is that they enable him to avoid having to deal with certain philosophical difficulties in detail. Sforno was acquainted with philosophical notions—particularly with the Aristotelian/Averroeian system—and he was certainly able to develop a complex philosophical argument, but he deliberately chose to skirt the obstacle by giving the correspondent definition without further explanation.[2] To my mind, this is due to the fact that he was above all a rabbi and an exegete and therefore that he felt more comfortable with the biblical expositions; in light of this, his explanation in the last part of the *quaestio*—that is, the solution—is fluid and clear in both the Hebrew version and its Latin translation.

1 The Function of the Prologue and the Fifteen *Quaestiones*

The *prologus*/הקדמה is the first part of the general introduction. Here, Sforno presents the genealogy of wisdom and science from the ancients (הקדמונים) down to Aristotle and his commentators. The main idea found in this genealogy is based on the concept of *translatio studiorum*. For Sforno, this idea is synonymous with "lost wisdom,"[3] because in his view, the Torah represents the origin of all science and knowledge, while philosophy is considered to be a kind of corruption of this original wisdom. This position can be qualified as a radical form of anti-Aristotelianism—confirmed by the use of strong expressions such as "the error of those who think that the Holy Scripture teaches many easy answers and doubtful opinions, which is a point of derision for the Philosopher." (§ 1.4.2)—which echoes other Jewish thinkers, such as Judah Halevi[4] and

---

2 See the section on "Sforno's Incompleteness."
3 Cf. Giuseppe Veltri, *Alienated Wisdom: Enquiry into Jewish Philosophy and Scepticism* (Berlin: De Gruyter, 2018).
4 See Judah Halevi, *Kitab al Khazari*, trans. Hartwig Hirschfeld (London: Routledge; New York: Dutton, 1905), 1.63 (p. 53): "There is an excuse for the Philosophers. Being Grecians, science and religion did not come to them as inheritances. They belong to the descendants of Japheth, who inhabited the north, whilst that knowledge coming from Adam, and supported by the

Abba Mari of Lunel,[5] who also believed that the Greek philosophers had stolen knowledge and science from the Jews.

Sforno's attitude was antithetical to the spirit of the Renaissance supported by thinkers such as Menachem of Recanati, Judah Abravanel, David ben Judah Messer Leon, and Johanan Alemanno, in which wisdom was considered to be the result of an encounter between the two cultures, Hebrew and Greek, as attested, for example, by the anecdote according to which Plato studied with the prophet Jeremiah. Similarly, in the Christian Humanist environment, the idea of original wisdom was presented, with reference to the Platonic and Neoplatonic traditions, as *philosophia perennis/prisca theologia*.[6] The genealogy of knowledge was considered to stretch from the origin of the world to Plato, in order not only to conciliate philosophy and religion, but also to integrate Plato into the Aristotelian system. From my perspective, Sforno was undoubtedly familiar with the Christian sources, especially those of the church fathers. He probably ignored contemporary debates and was therefore not interested in presenting kabbalistic or exoteric elements in his genealogy of wisdom, because, as is evident from his writings, he had no interest in Kabbalah whatsoever.

The first wise men mentioned by Sforno are Enoch and Noah before the Great Flood and Eber and Abraham, the wisest of the Chaldeans, after it. In this context, Sforno's *excursus* on the origin of the "Jews" is noteworthy, as he traces it to Eber and Abraham (§ I.1.2). In my opinion, Sforno follows what Flavius Josephus presents in *Jewish Antiquities*,[7] in which the Hebrews and the Chaldeans are both mentioned. In his *Book of the Khazar (The Kuzari)*,[8] Judah Halevi mentions Eber twice. Nonetheless, Sforno's reference seems to be associated with a Christian interpretation, such as Augustine's reference in *The City of God*.[9]

---

divine influence, is only to be found among the progeny of Shem, who represented the successors of Noah and constituted, as it were, his essence. This knowledge has always been connected with this essence, and will always remain so. The Greeks only received it when they became powerful, from Persia. The Persians had it from the Chaldaeans. It was only then that the famous [Greek] Philosophers arose, but as soon as Rome assumed political leadership they produced no philosopher worthy the name."

5   Cf. Abba Mari of Lunel, *Sefer Minḥat Kena'ot* (Pressburg, 1838).
6   I would like to maintain the distinction between *prisca theologia* and *philosophia perennis*, considering that the latter "makes wisdom originate in a very ancient time, often applying the same genealogy of the transmission of *sapientia* like the *Prisca theologia*, but it also puts emphasis on the continuity of valid knowledge through all periods history." See Charles Schmitt, quoted in Wouter Hanegraaff, *Esotericism and the Academy: Rejected Knowledge in Western Culture* (Cambridge: Cambridge University Press, 2012), 7.
7   *A.J.* 10.10.2.
8   Halevi, *Kuzari* 1.49 (p. 50): "They feared magic and astrological arts, and similar snares, things which, like deceit, do not bear close examination, whereas the divine might is like pure gold, ever increasing in brilliancy. How could one imagine that an attempt had been made to show that a language spoken five hundred years previously was none but Eber's own language split up in Babel during the days of Peleg; also to trace the origin of this or that nation back to Shem or Ham, and the same with their countries?"; ibid., 2.68 (124–125): "The whole is traced back to Eber, Noah and Adam. It is the language of Eber after whom it was called Hebrew, because after the confusion of tongues it was he who retained it. Abraham was an Aramaean of Ur Kasdim, because the language of the Chaldaeans was Aramaic. He employed Hebrew as a specially holy language and Aramaic for everyday use. For this reason, Ishmael brought it to the Arabic speaking nations, and the consequence was that Aramaic, Arabic and Hebrew are similar to each other in their vocabulary, grammatical rules, and formations."
9   Augustine, *Civ.* 16.3: "Cainan genuit Sala, Sala genuit Heber. Non itaque frustra ipse primus est nominatus in progenie ueniente de Sem et praelatus etiam filiis, cum sit quintus nepos,

Sacra testatur Scriptura post illam vero fuerunt Heber et Abraham, Caldeorum sapientissimus, eiusdem Heberis doctrinam sequens quare Hebreus dicebatur prout in libro Genesis 14:13 habetur [...] scilicet prefatam Heberis doctrinam et opiniones sequentes merito Hebreorum nomine appellati sunt.[10]	ואחר המבול עבר ואברהם ‹אב› בחכמה מכל הכשדים אשר למד מפי עבר והחזיק בדעותיו ולכן נקרא ‹עברי› כמו שנאמר: «ויגד לאברם העברי» (בראשית י״ד י״ג) [...] ובכן בחר בעמו יודעי שמו כמשפט כאשר באר משה רבינו עליו השלום באמרו: «ה׳ אלהי העברים» (שמות ג׳ י״ח), כלומר המחזיקים בדעות עבר אשר היו אז מפורסמות.[12]

According to Sforno's chronology, after many centuries, the wisdom of the Chaldeans vanished; however, their knowledge was transmitted to the Greeks, as attested by Aristotle, who called them "fathers."[11] Sforno attributes the idea of a chain of transmission to Aristotle, who mentioned the position of the ancients in *Metaphysics* 12.8.1074b:

> A tradition has been handed down by the ancient thinkers of very early times, and bequeathed to posterity in the form of a myth, to the effect that these heavenly bodies are gods, and that the Divine pervades the whole of nature.[12]

Averroes interpreted the passage as referring to the Chaldeans:

> As he was the first among the men of his time to have perceived this principle and nobody had preceded him in this theory, he wants to take as witness for his theory the ancient saying inherited from the Chaldeans, of whom it is thought that Wisdom was already professed among them.[13]

However, Sforno writes that the holders of such wisdom were the *Coelicolarum et Zabiorum*/העובדים לצבא השמים, respectively the "worshippers of heaven"[14] and the "Sabaeans" (*Zabiorum*/אנשי הצבא)[15]

---

nisi quia uerum est, quod traditur, ex illo Hebraeos esse cognominatos, tamquam Heberaeos; cum et alia possit esse opinio, ut ex Abraham tamquam Abrahaei dicti esse videantur; sed nimirum hoc uerum est, quod ex Heber Heberaei appellati sunt, ac deinde una detrita littera Hebraei, quam linguam solus Israel populus potuit obtinere, in quo dei ciuitas et in sanctis peregrinata est et in omnibus sacramento adumbrata."

10   *Light of the Nations* § I.1.2–3.
11   Sforno mentions this anecdote twice in *Lumen Gentium*, in § I.1.2 and again in § 9.1 ("relatis Caldeorum auctoritate quos patres appellat Metaphysicorum XII, 51"). Cf. also Agostino Steuco, *De perennis philosophia* (Ludguni, 1540), 1.3: "Ipsi Chaldei, genitorum Deum."
12   Aristotle, *Metaphysics, Volume 2: Books 10–14. Oeconomica. Magna Moralia.* trans. Hugh Tredennick and G. Cyril Armstrong (Cambridge, MA: Harvard University Press, 1935), 163.
13   Cf. Averroes, *Ibn Rushd's* Metaphysics: *A Translation with Introduction of Ibn Rushd's Commentary on Aristotle's* Metaphysics, *Book Lām*, trans. Charles Genequand (Leiden: Brill, 1984), 188.
14   Between the seventeenth and eighteenth centuries, two dissertations dealing with the history of the Jews and the *coelicoli* were published: see Ernst Cregel and Gottfried Saltzmann, *Disputationem circularem ad tit. Cod. IX. lib. I. cum seq. de Judaeis coelicolis, & ne Christianum mancipium &c.* (Altdorf, 1673) and Johann A. Schmidt, *Historiam coelicolarum ad tit. Codicis de Iudaeis & coelicolis* (Helmstedt, 1704).
15   As Warren Zev Harvey has suggested to me, Sforno's explanation of the term "Sabaeans" is

It is impossible to precisely identify the *Coelicolarum*; nonetheless, in both the *Codex Theodosianus*[16] and Augustine,[17] they are presented as a heretical sect. The opinions of the Sabaeans are mentioned on three occasions in *Light of the Nations*. Sforno's reference is connected to Averroes's commentary on *Metaphysics* 12, text. 41: "But if there is a body eternal in its substance, it may be thought that its moving power must impart motion eternally. Concerning this passage, the Sabaeans and their scholars were mistaken."[18] The Sabaeans believed that the heavenly bodies were immortal and eternal (*immortale* and *ab eterno*/קדמונים) and for them, there was no principle nobler than the heavens. At the end of this passage, Averroes quotes a verse from the Quran in order to contextualise the Sabaeans:[19] this reference only appears in the original Arabic, not in the Latin version.[20] In addition to this, Averroes refers to the Sabaeans in his *Epitome of the Metaphysics*[21] and part 2 of *The Incoherence of the Incoherence*.[22]

---

related to the exegetical interpretation of the prophetic ה' צבאות (cf. Zechariah, 1 Samuel, Isaiah, Jeremiah, Malachi, Amos, Haggai, and Psalms); furthermore, I would suggest that, as in the case of Abraham Farissol in *Magen Avraham*, Sforno deduces their positions from Maimonides's *Guide*: see David B. Ruderman, *The World of a Renaissance Jew: The Life and Thought of Abraham ben Mordecai Farissol* (Cincinnati: Hebrew Union College Press, 1981), 74.

16 *Cod. Theod.* 16.8.19, "De Judaeis, Coelicolis et Samaritanis" (in Jakob Gothofredus and Antoine de Marville, eds., *Codex Theodosianus*, vol. 6.1 [Lipsiæ, 1743], 257): "Coelicolarum nomen, inauditum quodammodo novum crimen superstitionis vinidicavit. Hi nisi infra anni terminois ad Dei cultum venationemque Christianam conversi fuerint, his legibus, quivus praecipimus haereticos adstringi, se quoque noverint adtiniendos."

17 Augustine, *Epistola ad Eleusium* 6.13. "Iam enim miseramus ad Maiorem Coelicolarum quem audieramus novi apud eos baptismi institutorem extitisse, et multos illo sacrilegio seduxisse, ut cum illo, quantum ipsius temporis patiebantur angustiae, aliquid loqueremur."

18 Averroes, *Ibn Rushd's* Metaphysics, 164: "This idea is very obscure and as a result this passage has been a stumbling-block for scholars. For if it is shown that this body is eternal in its substance, it may be assumed that it does not need, in order to exist, another principle distinct from it and nobler than it, because it may be thought that our principle that 'every power in a body is finite' is not true, except in the case of material bodies subject to generation and corruption. But if there is a body eternal in its substance, it may be thought that its moving power must impart motion eternally. Concerning this passage, the Sabians and their scholars were mistaken. This is the meaning to which the quranic passage alludes: 'we showed Abraham the kingdom of the heavens and the earth so that he may be one of the firm believers etc.'"

19 Cf. introduction to Averroes, *Ibn Rushd's* Metaphysics, chapter 4, "The Prime Mover," 46: "Ibn Rushd then reasserts the validity of the principle that 'every power in a body is finite,' even if that body is not subject to generation and corruption. The eternal motion of the heaven points to the existence of an immaterial mover. This is where the mistake of the Sabians resides. The stars themselves are not gods: they are only signs of the deity. This is also the meaning of the coranic verses VI, 75 sqq.: God does not show Abraham the heavens so that he may believe in them, but only in the God whom they reveal."

20 Qu'ran 6:75.

21 Cf. Averroes, *On Aristotle's "Metaphysics": An Annotated Translation of the So-Called "Epitome,"* trans. Rüdiger Arnzen (Berlin: De Gruyter, 2010), 177: "Si autem aliquod aeternum est in sua substantia, existimatum erit, quod necesse est potentiam eius manentem esse eternae motionis. Et in hoc loco erravertunt Zabii, et sapientes eorum. Et Aristo sustentatus est in hoc super duas propositiones: quarum una est, quod omnis potentia in materia finita est; secunda autem est, quod actio infinita non fit ex potentia finita: unde provenit quod faciens motum infinitum est potentia non in materia. Et ipse laborabat in declaratione istarum duarum propositionum in Octavo Physicorum."

22 Cf. Averroes, *Tahafut al-tahafut* (*The Incoherence of the Incoherence*), trans. Simon van den Bergh, repr. ed. (Oxford: Oxbow Books, 2012), 359: "Bodily resurrection is also affirmed in

The Sabaeans, also known as the Sabaeans of Harran, are identified as the ancient nation that lived during the Abbasid rule,[23] and they are also mentioned in the Quran. Their religion and beliefs were fundamentally based on worshipping the heavenly bodies, since they believed that agricultural success depended on this worship of the stars and spheres,[24] which they considered the most perfect beings. In the Bible, the Sabaeans are explicitly mentioned by Isaiah[25] and in the book of Job,[26] but in both cases, the name "Sabaeans" has no connection with the orthography (צאביה) used in the later Jewish tradition; Maimonides referred to them as a religious sect[27] that believed in the eternity of the world and in the divinity of the heavenly bodies. In view of this fact, they were considered idolaters.[28] As Leo Strauss suggests, according to the Maimonidean interpretation, the Sabaeans are remembered as idolaters who perpetuated corporealism.[29]

---

the New Testament and attributed by tradition to Jesus. It is a theory of the Sabaeans, whose religion is according to Ibn Hazm the oldest."

23 Cf. François de Blois, "The 'Sabians' (Sabi'un) in Pre-Islamic Arabia," *Acta Orientalia* 56 (1995): 41 n. 8; Sarah Stroumsa, "Sabéens de Harran et Sabéens de Maïmonide," in *Maimonide: Philosophe et savant*, ed. Tony Lévy and Roshdi Rashed (Louvain: Peeters, 2004), 335–352.

24 Moses Maimonides, *The Guide of the Perplexed*, ed. Shlomo Pines, 2 vols. (Chicago: University of Chicago Press, 1963), 3.30 (2:522): "Their men of knowledge, as well as the ascetics and the men of piety among them, preached this to the people and taught them that agriculture, on which the existence of man depends, can only be perfected and succeed according to wish if you worship the sun and the stars."

25 Isa 45:14: "So said the Lord, 'The toil of Egypt and the merchandise of Cush and the Sabaeans, men of stature, shall come over to you and shall be yours; they shall follow you; they shall come over in chains, and they shall prostrate themselves before you, they shall pray to you, 'Only in you is God and there is no other god'"/כה אמר יהוה יגיע מצרים וסחר/ כוש וסבאים אנשי מדה עליך יעברו ולך יהיו אחריך ילכו בזקים יעברו ואליך ישתחוו אליך יתפללו אך בך אל ואין עוד אפס אלהים

26 Job 1:15: "When Sabaeans attacked them and carried them off, and put the boys to the sword; I alone have escaped to tell you"/ותפל שבא ותקחם ואת הנערים הכו לפי חרב ואמלטה/ רק אני לבדי להגיד לך

27 Cf. Maimonides, *Guide* 3.29 (2:514–515): "It is well known that Abraham our Father, peace be on him, was brought up in the religious community of the Sabians, whose doctrine it is that there is no deity but the stars. When I shall have made known to you in this chapter their books, translated into Arabic, which are in our hands today, and their ancient chronicles and I shall have revealed to you through them their doctrine and histories, it will become clear to you from this that they explicitly asserted that the stars are the deity and that the sun is the greatest deity. No one is antagonistic to him or ignorant of his greatness except the remnants of this religious community that has perished, remnants that survive in the extremities of the earth, as for instance the infidels among the Turks in the extreme North and the Hindus in the extreme South. These are the remnants of the religious community of the Sabians, for this was a religious community that extended over the whole earth."

28 Maimonides, *Guide* 1.63 (1:153): "You know that in those times the teachings of the Sabians were generally accepted and that all except a few men were idolaters. I mean by this that they believed in spirits, that they believed that those spirits can be made to descend among men, and that they made talismans"; and 3.29 (2:518–519): "The most important book about this subject is 'The Nabatean Agriculture' translated by Ibn Wahshiyya. In a future chapter I shall let you know why the Sabians treated their doctrines and agriculture in the same work. This book is filled with the ravings of the idolaters and with notions to which the souls of the vulgar incline and by which they are captivated—I mean the actions of talismans, practices with a view to causing spirits to descend, demons, and ghouls living in deserts. In this book are also included extraordinary ravings laughed at by the intelligent, which are thought to depreciate the manifest miracles through which the people of the earth know that there is a deity governing the people of the earth."

29 Leo Strauss, "How to Begin to Study *The Guide of the Perplexed*," in Maimonides, *Guide*, 1:

Maimonides discussed the Sabaeans' beliefs in both the *Guide of the Perplexed*[30] and the *Treatise on the Resurrection*.[31] Nonetheless, I suspect that Sforno's reference to the Sabaeans is drawn from Averroes's works rather than from those of Maimonides, because in the Hebrew version, he does not employ the expression "אמונת הצאבה," which appears in Ibn Tibbon's translation of Maimonides's *Guide*, but rather "אנשי הצאבא," the "Nation of the Sabaeans," even if he was undoubtedly aware of the corresponding passage in the *Guide*. Sforno explains that the transmission of ancient wisdom continued through Abraham's offspring, who followed the beliefs of Eber/the Hebrews. This is shown by the fact that when Moses received the Torah during the revelation at Sinai, he said: "Ha-Shem, the God of the Hebrews" (Exod 3:18). The knowledge revealed in the Torah—namely, the existence of one God, eternal, incorporeal, and omniscient—was denied by the Gentiles. From this point onwards (§ 1.2), the genealogy of wisdom follows the Aristotelian "historical order" presented in book 1 (alpha) of *Metaphysics*, or, more accurately, in Averroes's commentary on *Metaphysics* 1, text. 5. According to Sforno, the "first philosophers" included Anaximander,[32] Empedocles, Democritus, Heraclitus,[33] Pythagoras,[34] Socrates, Plato, and finally Aristotle.[35]

2 Sforno's Incompleteness

The most complicated challenge in understanding the complexity of Sforno's philosophical interpretation is related to the "incompleteness" of his argumentation. In my view, Sforno cherrypicks particular passages in order to

---

xlii: "Maimonides marks a progress even beyond the post-Mosaic prophets in so far as he combines the open depreciation of the sacrifices with a justification of the sacrificial laws of the Torah, for his depreciation of the sacrifices does not as such mean a denial of the obligatory character of the sacrificial laws. He is the man who finally eradicates Sabianism, i.e., corporealism as the hidden premise of idolatry, through the knowledge of Sabianism recovered by him." See also: "He [Maimonides] never forgot the power of what one may call the inverted Sabianism that perpetuates corporealism through unqualified submission to the literal meaning of the Bible and thus even outdoes Sabianism proper (I 31); nor did he forget the disastrous effect of the exile (I 7, II 11): 'If the belief in the existence of God were not as generally accepted as it is not the religions [i.e., Judaism, Christianity, and Islam], the darkness of our times would even be greater than the darkness of the times of the sages of Babylon' (III 29). This it to say nothing of the fact that Sabianism proper was not completely eradicated and could be expected to have a future" (ibid.).

30 Maimonides, *Guide* 1.63; 1.70; 2.23; 2.39; 3.29–31; 3.37; 3.45–50.

31 Moses Maimonides, *Ma'amar Teḥiyyat ha-Metim* [*Treatise on the Resurrection of the Dead*], in Maimonides, *Book of Letters and Responsa* (ותשובות אגרות ספר) (Jerusalem, 1978), ix: "At that time (nearly) all of mankind belonged to the sect of Sabians who believed in the eternity of the world and who considered the Almighty to be the spirit of the planets as we have explained in *The Guide of the Perplexed*. And they deny the transmission of prophecy from God to mankind."

32 Probably confused with Anaxagoras.

33 Cf. Introduction.

34 § 1.2.2 "Pitagora et aliorum Italorium."

35 It is worth noting that in this section of the book, a copy of *Or 'Ammim* owned by the German theologian and humanist Johann Albrecht Widmannstetter (d. 1557) contains handwritten notes, presumably made by Widmannstetter himself (Munich, Bayerische Staatsbibliothek, Res/4 A.hebr. 310). Widmannstetter is also known to have possessed a notable collection of manuscripts in Hebrew, Arabic, and Syriac. We cannot discount the possibility that Reuchlin recommended that he read or study Sforno's work or that he meet Sforno when he was in Bologna.

present and resolve a question, which implies that he employed only one or two ideas from an extremely complex discussion. Thus, as Warren Zev Harvey has suggested, this indicates that he did not receive a thorough philosophical education. When explaining the reasoning behind his argumentation, Sforno leaves aside concepts that are fundamental to understanding the problem in its entirety. In his introduction, the twenty-seven propositions are conceived as postulates of some concepts that he does not really address in his discussion. However, in order to interpret and above all to understand his philosophical position, we need to comprehend what Sforno intended to demonstrate even though he did not possess all the tools to decipher the most complicated questions found in Aristotelian works and Averroes's commentaries on them.

As a result, Sforno's arguments raise queries about the *quaestiones* that he presents, since he does not fully explain his reasoning. In contrast, in the places where he explains the conclusion he draws on the basis of his biblical exegesis, his discourse is fluid and comprehensive. His exegesis became his philosophical instrument for understanding Averroes's and Aristotle's thought. However, when he deals with difficult notions, he does not always give a full and comprehensive explanation of the problem; rather, he resorts to offering quotations from philosophical sources rather than philosophical explanations. The chains of quotations (from Averroes and Aristotle, naturally) build arguments that include one (or more) premise(s) and a conclusion, but Sforno does not furnish further clarifications of his own in order to explain the process that allows us to understand the final statement by means of "philosophical evidence," instead basing his findings on the exegetical interpretation.

3 Sforno's Sources

Sforno's erudition encompasses the Jewish, [Arabic],[36] and Scholastic traditions. Nonetheless, his philosophical enquiry is founded on Aristotelian and Averroean texts and argumentations. The only two philosophical authorities that are explicitly quoted in the whole treatise—which in the Latin version are always introduced with the formula "ratione et auctoritate"—are Aristotle and Averroes,[37] while the other Greek and Arabic thinkers that Sforno mentions in the text are mediated through Averroes's works.

The almost complete absence of Maimonides from Sforno's work,[38] as noted by Alessandro Guetta, is perfectly in line with the Averroistic tendency of his time. However, the pamphlet's rationalistic structure was undoubtedly inspired

---

36 I prefer to place the Arabic sources in brackets because Sforno did not read the original works and his knowledge of Arabic thinkers was mediated by translations of Averroes.

37 With some exceptions: §6.1; §8.4.2; §9.2.1; §10.3; "ratione et auctoritate Algazelis." It is worth mentioning that Sforno only employs the expression *auctoritate* to refer to other thinkers: proposition 26, "Avicenne auctoritate"; §2.5.1, "Anaximandri auctoritate"; §4.4.3; §12.1.1, "antiquorum auctoritate"; §5.6.2; §10.2; §12.2.2; §13.2.3; §13.2.4, "Algazelis auctoritate"; §7.1, "auctoritate Zabiorum"; §8.5.2, "philosophus Symonides auctoritate"; §9.1, "Caldeorum auctoritate"; §12.8.1, "Platonis auctoritate"; §12.12.2, "seniorum auctoritate."

38 Sforno mentions Maimonides's *Guide of the Perplexed* in *Or 'Ammim*, introduction (*Guide* 2.22; cf. §1.3.3) and chapter 4 (*Guide* 3.13; cf. §4.3.1); he also refers to *Sefer ha-Maddaʿ*.

by him,[39] since the philosophical design that Sforno adopts in *Light of the Nations* belongs to the Aristotelian-Averroean-Maimonidean system. In addition to this, the omnipresence of Maimonides in his biblical commentaries—and also Reuchlin's attitude towards Maimonides, in light of Sforno's teachings[40]—testify to his essential role in Sforno's philosophy. The influence of the *Guide of the Perplexed* in Sforno's *Light of the Nations* can be detected in many passages in the disputed questions. For example, in all of the discussions on God's providence, the first chapters of section 3 (especially 3.16 and 17) of the *Guide of the Perplexed* must be considered to be the underlying matter of Sforno's assumptions. Levi Gersonides is the second extremely significant Jewish authority in Sforno's philosophical analysis, and there is also a demonstrable influence from Joseph Albo and his *Book of Principles*. On the other hand, it is difficult to prove any influence from Albo's teacher Hasdai Crescas, not least because *Light of the Lord* was not printed until 1555.[41] However, Sforno was reasonably well acquainted with the classical Jewish philosophical corpus (Judah Halevi, Saadia Gaon, Abraham ibn Daud, Abraham ibn Ezra, Baḥya ibn Paqudah, Shem Ṭov Falaquera, and Flavius Josephus), and we may suppose that he was also familiar with the works of his contemporaries such as Isaac and Judah Abravanel and Calo Calonimus.[42]

Concerning the Averroean corpus, besides the Long Commentaries, *The Incoherence of the Incoherence*, and the *Treatise on the Substance of the Celestial Sphere*, it is evident that Sforno was aware of the *Kitāb al-Kašf ʿan Manāhiǧ al-Adilla*: two partial versions of the treatise had been translated by Abraham de Balmes and Calo Calonimus, with the latter's work being the most likely way for Sforno to have come across some passages of it.[43] He read the *Incoherence of the Incoherence* and the *Treatise on the Substance of the Celestial Sphere* thanks to Agostino Nifo's editions, as I will explain below.

Readers could access the Aristotelian commentators, Alexander of Aphrodisias, John Philoponus, and Themistius, through Averroes or Nifo's commentaries.[44] Sforno could not read Greek, and although Latin editions of Themis-

---

39   Cf. Alessandro Guetta, "Renaissance Maimonideanism," in *Encyclopedia of Renaissance Philosophy*, ed. Marco Sgarbi (Cham: Springer, 2015), https://doi.org/10.1007/978--3--319--02848--4_161--1.

40   Cf. Saverio Campanini, "Roman Holiday: Conjectures on Johann Reuchlin as a Pupil of Obadiah Sforno," in *The Literary and Philosophical Canon of Obadiah Sforno*, ed. Giuseppe Veltri et al. (Leiden: Brill, 2023).

41   However, as Warren Zev Harvey emphasises, there are some elements that may indicate that Hasdai Crescas influenced Sforno's thought, as the affirmation at the beginning of *Light of the Nations* in which he asserts that there is no commandment to believe seems to reflect Crescas's arguments. It may be possible that Sforno was taking into account Josef Albo's explanation in *Book of Principles*, 1.26: "This is also the opinion of my teacher Rabbi Hasdai Crescas, that all these as well as creation are true doctrines which every one professing the Law of Moses should believe, but they are not principles of this law, derivative or primary, general or special" (David J. Bleich, *With Perfect Faith: The Foundations of Jewish Belief* [New York: Ktav, 1983], 66).

42   Calo Calonimus, *Liber de mundi creatione physicis rationibus probata egregij doctoris Calo Calonymos hebrei Neapolitani ad reuerendissimum dominum dominum Egidium cardinalem litterarum patrem* (Venetiis, 1527).

43   Silvia di Donato, "Il 'Kasf'an manahig' di Averroè: Confronto fra la versione latina di Abraham de Balmes e le citazioni di Calo Calonimo nel 'De mundi creatione,'" *Materia giudaica* 9 (2004): 241–248.

44   Cf. Agostino Nifo, *Commentationes in librum Averrois De substantia orbis* (Venetiis, 1508), fol. 2.

tius were available,[45] we cannot rule out the possibility that he read the Hebrew translation. He also explored particular Presocratic positions concerning the origin of the world, and we may conjecture that given that he had no direct access to the original sources, as mentioned above, he reported opinions that he came across in Aristotle's texts.

Even if Sforno is considered to be part of the Jewish Scholastic movement, he was not acquainted with its sources. I have not found any "hidden" references to Judah Messer Leon, his son David Messer Leon, Abraham Bibago, or Elijah Del Medigo in Sforno's work. Nonetheless, it is evident that he was involved in contributing to the Latin debate in the Late Scholastic period, and also that he was interested in a dialogue with the Christian intellectual milieu.

We cannot reject the possibility that Sforno approached the *quaestiones* regarding Aristotle by following several commentaries composed in Paduan philosophical and academic circles. His *modus operandi* resembles the methodology of Paul of Venice, Gaetano da Thiene, and Agostino Nifo (and consequently, he was presumably also familiar with the interpretation of Averroes's partisans, first and foremost Jean de Jandun). This particular approach could indicate that he was not a complete outsider to the Paduan Averroist school.

Thomas Aquinas is Sforno's principal source for the Scholastic tradition, as attested in Elijah of Butrio's commentary on *Or 'Ammim*, in which Sforno's pupils mention him several times,[46] and Sforno certainly had knowledge of the opinions of the church fathers through Aquinas's writings. He probably also had the opportunity to examine some Augustinian works, as some of his original ideas seem to echo Augustine's. In addition, Butrio explicitly refers to Boethius's *Consolation of Philosophy* in his commentary on two occasions. Sforno was also extremely familiar with Robert Grosseteste's oeuvre, especially with his theological treatise *Hexaemeron*,[47] and it is evident that he was also interested in Grosseteste's philosophical arguments.

4   The Account of Genesis in *Light of the Nations* and Sforno's Biblical Commentaries

The first six *quaestiones* describe the account of creation given in the book of Genesis, in which Sforno offers an all-comprehensive view of the creation of the universe according to the philosophical exposition found in Aristotle's works and in Averroes's commentaries on them. His theories display an original approach to the physical phenomena, which are analysed not only through a scientific and philosophical approach, but also according to the Bible. This is the strong point of Sforno's analysis.

Scholars have not stressed the philosophical aspects of Sforno's approach, although they have identified the original ideas in his biblical commentaries. Norbert Samuelson considers Sforno to be one of the major rabbinic commentators alongside Rashi, Ibn Ezra, and Nahmanides, a status suggested by the fact

---

45   Themistius, *Libri paraphraseos Themistij: Peripatetici acutissimi. In posteriora Aristotelis. In physica. In libros de anima. In commentarios de memoria & reminiscientia. De somno & vigilia. De insomnijs. De diunatione per somnium*, trans. Ermalao Barbaro (Venetia, 1527).
46   See Parma, Biblioteca Palatina, MS 2624.
47   The term *hexaemeron* generally refers to particular theological works in which the account of Genesis is described and explained.

that his commentary is included in the *Rabbinic Bible* (מקראות גדולות), and he defines him as "an excellent representative of how a committed and informed rabbinic Jew of the Italian Renaissance interpreted creation in the light of the entire tradition of classical rabbinic commentaries."[48] Samuelson notes that Sforno's interpretation is "closer to the implicit physics of the biblical text" than those of the other interpreters, emphasising the fact that he seems to refer to the "pneuma" and the Stoics (Gen 1:2).[49] The same principle applies when exploring Sforno's philosophical approach to the entire account of creation, which includes discussions of the doctrines of other ancient philosophers.

As mentioned above, *Light of the Nations* is founded on the Aristotelian system, and to my mind, the Neoplatonic elements that emerge from the text are not linked to Neoplatonic sources, though they are mediated by Aristotle, Averroes, and Neoplatonic influences on the Jewish tradition.

5 Outline of the First Six Disputed Questions

Utrum motus generationis et corruptionis habuisset esse ab eterno?   ראשונה אם תנועת ההויה וההפסד קדמונית

Outline of *quaestio* 1

§1	Statement of the issue under discussion: the eternity of the movement of generation and corruption.
§1.1.1–§1.3	Definition of "substance": *Metaphysics* 8, text. 12, *On Generation and Corruption* 2, text. 24; locomotion is continuous and eternal: *On Generation and Corruption* 2, text. 55; the causes: *On Generation and Corruption* 2, text. 59.
§1.4.1–§1.9 *Or 'Ammim*	Temporal priority; whatever is generated or destructible is not eternal: *Metaphysics* 9, text. 5; potency precedes the
§1.4.1–7 **Lumen Gentium**	act: *Physics* 8, text. 4, *Metaphysics* 9, text. 5; the agent precedes the act: *Metaphysics* 2, text. 8 and 9, *Physics* 2, text. 89, *Physics* 6, text. 26, *Metaphysics* 12, text. 18, *Treatise on the Substance of the Celestial Sphere* 2; on efficient causality: *Physics* 2, text. 26, 48, 51, 77, and 86; dispositions and powers: *Physics* 8, text. 46; priority of locomotion: *On Generation and Corruption* 2, text. 55, *Physics* 7, text. 57; matter (*Or 'Ammim* only): *Physics* 8, text. 46, *Metaphysics* 2, text. 5.
§1.10	Solution: the movement of generation and corruption is not eternal.
§1.11–12	Philosophical conclusions: the elements and heavenly bodies were generated by an agent.
§1.13–14	Exegetical conclusions: Genesis 1:2/*Metaphysics* 2, text. 8 and 9, *The Incoherence of the Incoherence* 9.

---

[48] See Norbert M. Samuelson, *Judaism and the Doctrine of Creation* (Cambridge: Cambridge University Press, 1994), 113.

[49] Samuelson, *Judaism and the Doctrine of Creation*, 144 n. 242.

Utrum prima mortalium elementa habuissent esse ab eterno אם הגרמים הנקראים יסודות ראשונות לכל המוחשים הם קדמונים

Outline of *quaestio* 2

§ 2	Statement of the issue under discussion: the eternity of the elements.
§ 2.1	Different kinds of creation: creation *ex nihilo*; creation from an actualised being; creation from a potential being: *Physics* 1, text. 77, *On the Heavens* 3, text. 29, *Physics* 1, text. 82, *Metaphysics* 8, text. 12.
§ 2.2–3	Anything that is generated or perishable is not eternal: *On the Heavens* 1, text. 19, 124, and 137, *On the Heavens* 2, text. 45, *On the Heavens* 3, text. 52, *On the Heavens* 4, text. 1, *On Generation and Corruption* 2, text. 37, *Physics* 2, text. 51; the elements change into their contraries: *On Generation and Corruption* 1, text. 54 and 87, *Metaphysics* 8, text. 14, *Physics* 8, text. 46.
§ 2.4	Solution: the elements are not eternal
§ 2.5/§ 2.7	Philosophical conclusions: the elements were created: *On the Heavens* 1, text. 100, *Metaphysics* 12, text. 18, *Physics* 1, text. 32.
§ 2.6	Exegetical conclusions: Genesis 1:1, Genesis 1:2; Psalms 104:4/*Physics* 7, text. 46, *On the Heavens* 2, text. 42, *Physics* 1, text. 32 (*Lumen Gentium*).

Utrum materia prima habuisset esse ab eterno שלישית אם החמר הראשון קדמון

Outline of *quaestio* 3

§ 3	Statement of the issue under discussion: the eternity of prime matter.
§ 3.1	Prime matter is incorruptible and ungenerated: *Physics* 1, text. 82; *Metaphysics* 12, text. 12.
§ 3.2–4	Potentiality and actuality: *On the Heavens* 3, text. 29, *On Generation and Corruption* 2, text. 6, *Metaphysics* 1, text. 17, *Metaphysics* 2, text. 7, *Metaphysics* 9, text. 5 and 13, *Physics* 2, text. 48, *Physics* 4, text. 129, *Physics* 8, text. 4, *Treatise on the Substance of the Celestial Sphere* 2; *Posterior Analytics* 2, text. 11; prime matter is the substrate for contraries: *Physics* 1, text. 42, *Physics* 8, text. 46, *On Generation and Corruption* 2, text. 6, *On Generation and Corruption* 2, text. 87; no part of the elements is eternal: *On the Heavens* 1, text. 23 and 124, *On Generation and Corruption* 2, text. 6.
§ 3.5	Solution: prime matter is not eternal.
§ 3.6/§ 3.8	Philosophical conclusions: prime matter was created: *Metaphysics* 12, text. 18.

(cont.)

Outline of *quaestio* 3

§ 3.7	Exegetical conclusions: Genesis 1:1, Genesis 1:2, Psalms 104:4, Isaiah 45:7; *On the Heavens* 2, text. 42, *Metaphysics* 12, text. 54, *On Generation and Corruption* 1, text. 2 and 87.

Utrum celi habuisset esse ab eterno	רביעית אם השמים קדמונים

Outline of *quaestio* 4

§ 4	Statement of the issue under discussion: the eternity of the heavens.
§ 4.1–2	Incorruptible substances are eternal: *On the Heavens* 1, text. 20 and 137; the problem of the void: *On the Heavens* 3, text. 29, *Physics* 4, text. 86.
§ 4.3–5	The agent precedes everything: *On the Heavens* 2, text. 45, *The Incoherence of the Incoherence* 3 and 9, *Treatise on the Substance of the Celestial Sphere* 2; the voluntary agent: *Physics* 8, text. 15, *Metaphysics* 12, text. 44, *On the Heavens* 2, text. 41 and 68, *The Incoherence of the Incoherence* 3, text. 18; no activity is eternal: *On the Heavens* 4, text. 1, *The Incoherence of the Incoherence* 13.
§ 4.6	Solution: the heavens are not eternal.
§ 4.7/§ 4.8	Philosophical conclusions: corruption of matter: *On the Heavens* 1, text. 124 and 187, *On the Heavens* 2, text. 32, 41 and 67, *Metaphysics* 12, text. 44, *The Incoherence of the Incoherence* 5.
§ 4.9/§ 4.10	Exegetical conclusions: Psalms 104:4, Psalms 102:25–26, Genesis 1:1, Genesis 1:17–18, Isaiah 40:26, 48:12–13, 51:6.

Utrum motus habuisset esse ab eterno	חמישית אם התנועה קדמונית

Outline of *quaestio* 5

§ 5	Statement of the issue under discussion: the eternity of movement.
§ 5.1	Actuality and potentiality: *Physics* 8, text. 14 and 15.
§ 5.2–3	Priority of the agent, mereological questions: *Physics* 8, text. 4, *Metaphysics* 12, text. 32, *Metaphysics* 9, text. 13, *Metaphysics* 12, text. 16 and 32, *Posterior Analytics* 2, text. 11, *Physics* 3, text. 18, *Metaphysics* 9, text. 13, *On the Heavens* 1, text. 19; the first mobile: *On the Heavens* 3, text. 29, *Metaphysics* 9, text. 5.
§ 5.4	Solution: movement is not eternal.
§ 5.5	Philosophical conclusions: time and motion: *Physics* 4, text. 99, *On the Heavens* 1, text. 100, *Physics* 8, text. 10.

(cont.)

Outline of *quaestio* 5

§ 5.6	Exegetical conclusions: Genesis 1:1, Genesis 1:2, Psalms 104:4, *Metaphysics* 12, text. 36, *The Incoherence of the Incoherence* 14.

Utrum detur creatio qua scilicet tam subiectum et formam quam totum compositum habuissent esse post purum non esse. Utrum detur creatio qua scilicet tam materia et forma quam totum compositum habuisset esse post merum non esse?	ששית אם יש נמצא קדמון בורא וממציא יש אחר האפיסות המוחלט והוא עשה אינו ישנו ששית נחקור אם ראוי שנאמר שהיה חדוש

Outline of *quaestio* 6

§ 6	Statement of the issue under discussion: creation from absolute nothingness.
§ 6.1–2	*Creatio ex novo*: *The Incoherence of the Incoherence* 1; bodies are not created: *On the Heavens* 1, text. 23 and 100, *On the Heavens* 3, text. 29, *Physics* 4, text. 64 and 76.
§ 6.3–6	The elements: *On Generation and Corruption* 2, text. 6, *On the Heavens* 3, text. 29; nothing is created by chance; the final goal: *On the Heavens* 2, text. 45, *Physics* 2, text. 48, *Metaphysics* 2, text. 8 and 9, *Treatise on the Substance of the Celestial Sphere* 2, *Metaphysics* 9, text. 13, *Posterior Analytics* 2, text. 11, *On the Heavens* 1, text. 23, *Metaphysics* 2, text. 5; creation from form to form: *Physics* 2, text. 45 and 51, *On the Heavens* 1, text. 124; the first cause: *Metaphysics* 12, text. 51, *On the Soul* 3, text. 36, *The Incoherence of the Incoherence* 12.
§ 6.7	Solution: *Metaphysics* 7, text. 31, *The Incoherence of the Incoherence* 3.
§ 6.8	Philosophical conclusions: *Creatio ex nihilo*: *Metaphysics* 12, text. 18, *On the Heavens* 1, text. 100, *Metaphysics* 12, text. 12 and 18, *On the Heavens* 4, text. 1, *The Incoherence of the Incoherence* 3.
§ 6.8.3–§ 6.9	Exegetical conclusions: Genesis 2:4, Deuteronomy 4:39.

6 Creation and Generation

In summary, an overview of Sforno's approach to the account of creation in *Light of the Nations* clearly shows that all the arguments offered in the first part of his *summa* are aimed at presenting a rational explanation for the creation of the world. As previously stated, Sforno builds his arguments in order to confirm that all kinds of rational proofs may be found in the Torah. He saw the Torah as confirmation of the validity of some of the philosophical positions expressed by Aristotle and the philosophers, not the opposite, and therefore considered it to be the foundation of all kinds of knowledge, which the philosophers merely confirm. This approach, as Warren Zev Harvey has suggested, may indicate a possible connection to Hasdai Crescas, who emphasised the difference between the Torah's approach and philosophical speculation in the preface to *Light of the Lord*, which states that philosophy corroborates what is found in the Scriptures.

The main issue lies in the ontological distinction between creation out of nothingness (or *creatio ex nihilo*), which is ascribed to the intellectual action of God, and generation or production. Sforno offers a clear definition of creation in § 6.5.1: creation in the strict sense is a creation from nothing, meaning that the compound of primaeval matter (which is always in potency) and forms (which are in actuality) comes to exist from nothing in a single instant, while generation, in contrast, is a substantial movement that results in a transformation from one form to another. There is a Maimonidean assumption underlying Sforno's thesis—namely, that there is an existent that necessarily exists in respect of its own essence[50]—which takes for granted other philosophical postulates that are discussed in each disputed question according to different arguments.[51] Sforno's discussion follows the classical Jewish and Scholastic tradition in which the notion of Aristotelian efficient causation is combined with the Neoplatonic view, meaning that beings are produced by a series of emanations that emerge from God's will.[52] Sforno does not explicitly refer to the incorporeal or separate intelligences in his account of creation, and for this reason, I would suggest that his position is not completely reflective of the Maimonidean opinion, but is instead closer to Aquinas's (or Avicenna's) approach. In light of this fact, we may also comprehend the distinction that Sforno makes in the statement in *quaestio* 7: *Utrum data creatione et per consequens Creatore* [*etc.*]. I would read this as an implicit reference to the Thomistic discussion in *Summa Theologica* 1.3.4, which implies that God, as the "creator of beings," has no reciprocal relationship with them: creatures depend on God, but God in no way depends on creation.[53] However, since God knows all things (past, present, and future), it follows that everything is emanated,[54] either mediately or immediately,[55] from His self-intellection.[56]

7   *Ex nihilo nihil fit*

The point of departure for Sforno's reflection on the account of creation is the Parmenidian assumption *ex nihilo nihil fit*. This formula is a paraphrase of one of the positions of the Presocratic thinkers that attempted to explain the first

---

50   Cf. Maimonides, *Guide* 2.1 (2:248).
51   § 3.6, § 4.7.1, § 4.8, § 4.9.3, § 5.6.1, § 6.3.1, § 6.8.1, § 6.8.2, § 7.2.2, § 8.4.1, § 10.1, § 10.7.1, § 12.12.3.
52   Sforno uses the expression *emanare*, which corresponds to the Hebrew שוף, נמשך, השפע, יצא.
53   Cf. David B. Burrell, "The Act of Creation with Its Theological Consequences," in *Creation and the God of Abraham*, ed. David B. Burrell, Janet Soskice, and Carlo Cogliati (Cambridge: Cambridge University Press, 2010), 40–52; cf. Burrell and Isabelle Moulin, "Albert, Aquinas, and Dionysius," *Modern Theology* 24 (2008): 642.
54   Cf. Tamar M. Rudavsky, *Divine Omniscience and Omnipotence in Medieval Philosophy: Islamic, Jewish, and Christian Perspectives* (Dordrecht: D. Reidel Publishing Co., 1985).
55   As Sforno always specifies.
56   Cf. § 6.6.1 and § 6.8.2.

principles of the cosmos, which Aristotle evaluated in his works.[57] Nevertheless, the maxim *ex nihilo nihil fit* was well known in the Scholastic tradition[58] in relation to Aristotle's interpretation of the ontological and metaphysical issue concerning the impossibility of generation from a non-existent, as he stated in *Physics* 1.4.187a, "common to all the Physicists, that 'nothing can come out of what does not exist.'"[59] Aristotle confutes the idea that something may be created from nothing, and consequently, things are created out of something which had not previously been actual, but they cannot be created out of pure nothingness. The discussion is developed in *On Generation and Corruption*, *On the Heavens*, and above all in book 9 of *Metaphysics*, with all occurrences being linked to the nature of the motion that takes place in substantial change, as I will explain in the following paragraphs.

Similarly, Sforno presents this statement in different sections of his *Light of the Nations*.[60] The main idea is to refute creation out of pure nothingness, and he therefore develops his argumentation by means of two different ideas. As well as the principle that nothing can be produced from nothing, he postulates the impossibility of the existence of a void ("There is no place outside the heavens, no plenum and no vacuum and no time"),[61] following Aristotle's arguments in *On the Heavens* 4.7[62] and *Physics* 4.9.[63] This argument follows the classical interpretation of the ancient commentators on Aristotle such as Philoponus and Simplicius.[64] As Herbert Davidson emphasises, they argued that "a

---

57 Cf. also *Phys*. 4.12; 5.5; 8.7 and 8.
58 Cf. Aristotle, *Auctoritates Aristotelis et aliorum philosophorum* (Koln, 1498).
59 Aristotle, *Physics, Volume 1: Books 1–4*, trans. P.H. Wicksteed and F.M. Cornford (Cambridge, MA: Harvard University Press, 1957), 43.
60 § 2.1.1, § 2.5.1, § 2.5. 2, § 3.1, § 3.6, § 6.1, § 6.8.1.
61 Proposition 9: "Extra celum non datur tempus neque locus neque plenus neque vacuus. Hoc autem habetur a Philosopho in lib. De Celo I, 99" and "שאין חוץ לשמים זמן ולא מקום
    לא מלא ולא ריק וזה באר ארסטו' בספר השמים מאמר א' פרק ק"
62 *Phys*. 4.7.213b (Aristotle, *Physics*, 337): "To determine whether the void exists or not, we must know what they who use the word really mean by it. The current answer is, 'a place in which there is nothing.' But that is in the mouths of people who consider that nothing 'exists' except material substances; so they mean that a body must be in a place, but a place in which there is not a body must be absolutely empty; so that wherever there is not 'body' there is vacancy. Again, they regard all corporeal substances as 'tangible'; and this they regard as identical with 'possessed of gravity or levity.' Thus, we may logically expand their definition of the void as 'that in which there is nothing that is either heavy or buoyant.' For this, as we have just said, is implicit in their actual words; but no one could suppose them to mean that a point is a void, though it complies with the definition just given. We must add that in defining a void as a place they assign to it dimensionality as of a tangible body."
63 *Phys*. 4.9.217b (Aristotle, *Physics*, 371): "Our conclusion is that the void does not exist either in separation (whether considered by itself or as implicated in tenuous substances) or even potentially; unless anyone should choose to call that which causes local movement 'vacancy.' For in that case the material components of the heavy and buoyant would, as such, be vacancy, for the dense and rare under that aspect are the causes of movement, whereas under their aspect of hard and soft they are the cause of readiness or unreadiness to yield, and so of qualitive modification rather than of local movement. Let this stand then as our conclusion about how the void does or does not exist."
64 Cf. Panayiotis Tzamalikos, *Anaxagoras, Origen, and Neoplatonism: The Legacy of Anaxagoras to Classical and Late Antiquity* (Berlin: De Gruyter, 2016), 481: "The theory that generates things from the incorporeal involves a void separate from any body, because everything that comes to be, it comes to be in *something*, and that in which its coming to be takes place must be either incorporeal or corporeal: if corporeal, there will be two bodies in the same place at once, namely, that which is in the process of formation and that

vacuum is impossible. Consequently, the generation of something from nothing is impossible, and matter must be eternal."[65] In Islamic and Jewish Kalam, the Aristotelian tradition embraces the Platonic conception of creation from a pre-existent matter in order to avoid the need to posit a vacuum. However, like Maimonides and Averroes, Sforno considers these positions to be insufficient from a theological and rational point of view. He assumes that the position adopted by those Kalam thinkers who cannot conceive of creation from nothing differs from that of creation *ex nihilo* and that these two different kinds of creation are both called "creation" only by equivocation.[66] His position is that creation takes places out of nothingness according to God's will through self-intellection and that the compound of matter and forms is created in the same instant of God's creation. Therefore, there is no pre-existent and eternal matter.

Sforno's philosophical system is based on Aristotelian assumptions, and it therefore seems to be evident that his position results from Maimonides's interpretation of God as the only necessary being, embodying Aristotle's idea of a purely intellectual deity, and also from Aquinas's position in the *Summa Theologica*, which makes it clear that creation is an activity unique to God:[67] "Since there is no process of change in creation, a thing is simultaneously being created and is created."[68]

8   Creation as Generation: On the Movement of Generation and Corruption

Sforno's opening *quaestio* confutes the eternity of the movement of generation and corruption; namely, the movement of coming-to-be and passing-away. This question can be considered the premise of the following chapters in which he refutes the eternity of the world and the physical sublunary elements, which undergo a continuous process of change. Likewise, in Averroes's system, the movement of generation and corruption serves the function of introducing the account of creation.[69] The discussion of the movement of generation and corruption leads into a discussion of the notion of divine causality, which concludes that God's action creates the world, but does not need "direct" contact[70] with the physical creation or a pre-existent matter, because God does not require anything outside Himself in order to create.

---

which was there before; if incorporeal, there must be a separate void. However, earlier he had argued that generation *ex nihilo* demands a 'separate' void and that this generation is impossible. In short, elements are generated from one another, because it is impossible for generation to take place either from the incorporeal or from any other body. Hence, in the ensuing chapter, he argues that his Presocratic predecessors, such as Democritus Empedocles, as well as Plato, who spoke of 'generation out of one another,' got it wrong, since they actually spoke of 'a *semblance* of generation out of one another.'"

65   Cf. Herbert A. Davidson, *Proofs for Eternity, Creation and the Existence of God in Medieval Islamic and Jewish Philosophy* (Oxford: Oxford University Press, 1987), 27.
66   Likewise, the distinction between divine and human knowledge; cf. proposition 21.
67   Thomas Aquinas, *Summa Theologica* 1.45.2.
68   Thomas Aquinas, *Summa Theologiae*, ed. and trans. Thomas Gilby O.P. (Cambridge: Cambridge University Press, 2006), 8:33.
69   Cf. Cristina Cerami, *Génération et substance: Aristote et Averroès entre physique et métaphysique* (Berlin: De Gruyter, 2015), 285–286.
70   Cf. William Wallace, *The Elements of Philosophy: A Compendium for Philosophers and Theologians* (New York: Alba House, 1977), 140.

Or 'Ammim presents two different formulations of the disputed question:

Or 'Ammim, introduction	*Or 'Ammim*, "On the Movement of Generation"
ראשונה אם סדר ההויה וההפסד קדמון	ראשונה אם תנועת ההויה וההפסד קדמונית

In the introduction, the term "order" (סדר) is employed instead of "movement" (תנועה). I would suggest that Sforno chose to use a "familiar" term in the preface to *Or 'Ammim*, which is also employed in exegetical contexts. For example, in his commentary on Ecclesiastes (1:6),[71] Abraham Farissol (1451–1525) uses the term סדר to discuss the relationship between the order of nature and the seasons. Similarly, in *Genesis Rabbah* 3:7,[72] the expression indicates the order of time in relation to day and night, and in both cases, it is used as a synonym for circular movement. Gersonides, in his supercommentary on Averroes' Middle Commentary on *On the Heavens*, employed סדר to indicate the regular order in circular motions resulting from the movement of generation and corruption.[73]

ר״ל שלא יפסידו אחד מהם חברו בכללו וזה אמנם ישלם בתנועות רבות | כמו שקדם עד שיהיה ההויה וההפסד בהם שומר סדר ואולם אי זה תמונה היא תמונת זה הגרם הנה כבר יחויב שיהיה כדורי כמו שקדם

In *Wars of the Lord* (5.2.1), he highlighted a similar idea, which is also found in *On Generation and Corruption* 2.10.336b5–15, and stressed that the influence of the heavenly bodies on the terrestrial elements should be considered an "ordered" process.

9 Locomotion and the Movement of Generation and Corruption

Locomotion (*motus localis*/*tenu'ah maqomit*), following the definition in Aristotle's *On Generation and Corruption* 2.10.336a and Averroes's commentary thereon,[74] is continuous and eternal. Therefore, the movement of generation

---

71 Cf. Eccl 1:6: הולך אל דרום וסובב אל צפון סובב סבב הולך הרוח ועל סביבתיו שב הרוח; Farissol commentary: ובזה הפסוק כולל חלקים רבים מתחכמת התכונה והטבע והוא באור סדר ההויה וההפסד כי בארבע תקופות השנה סבות גוברות על ארבע יסודות (Abraham Farissol, *Be'ur le-Sefer Qohelet*. ed. Simḥah Bamberger [Jerusalem: Defus Eretz Yisrael, 1938], 13).

72 Cf. *Ber. Rab.* 3:7: "Rabbi Judah ben Simon said: 'Let there be evening' is not written here, but 'and there was evening': hence we know that a time-order existed before this" (Harry Freedman, *Midrash Rabbah: Genesis*, in *Midrash Rabbah*, vols. 1–2, trans. Harry Freedman and Maurice Simon, 3rd ed. [London: Soncino Press, 1961], 23).

73 Cf. ספר השמים והעולם, 91 ב.

74 Cf. Aristotle and Averroes, *De coelo; De generatione et corruption; Meteorologicorum; De plantis*, vol. 5 of *Aristotelis Stagiritae omnia quae extant opera* (Venetiis, 1550; republished 1562 and 1574), 309ᵛ: "Declaratum autem est in naturalibus quod motus localis est continuus et eternus. Quapropter et generatio est continua et eterna quoniam motus generat faciendo appropinquare generantem generando. Et hoc rectum est inquantum iste motus est primus omnibus trasmutabilibus ut ostensum est. Et etiam apparet quod illud quod movetur isto motu est ens et illud quod generatur per ipsum est non ens et quod est maxime ens est causa non entis semper."

and corruption is also continuous and eternal, since the movement produces generation by bringing the "generator" (i.e., the sun) closer to the matter out of which that which is generated comes to be (the four elements). In that sense, Gad Freudenthal's interpretation[75] of the movement of the sun is key to understanding Sforno. Freudenthal explains that because of its double movement (daily and seasonal), the sun causes the four elements to constantly transform, taking on one another's properties, and thus it brings about the regular generation and corruption of the sublunary substances. Hence, generation and corruption can go on—and indeed have occurred and will continue to occur—eternally.

Sforno's argument confronts us with an ontological problem that concerns the definition of being and non-being (or existence and non-existence), which is also presented in *Physics* 1.7,[76] in order to explain substantial generation: generation and corruption pertain to what is capable of being and non-being. Naturally, non-being is the privation of something: it is not absolutely "nothing," but is rather a relative non-being, the non-existence of a particular possibility. However, the possibility itself exists and therefore does so in something else.

In *On Generation and Corruption* 2.9.335a–b, Aristotle asserts:

> Now cause in the sense of matter for things which are of a nature to come-to-be is "the possibility of being and not-being." For some things exist of necessity, for example, the things which are eternal, and some things of necessity do not exist; and of these two classes it is impossible for the first not to be, while for the second it is impossible to be, because they cannot be other than they are in violation of the law of necessity. Some things, however, can both be and not be. This is the case with that which can come-to-be and pass-away; for at one moment it exists, at another it does not exist. So coming-to-be and passing-away must occur in the sphere of what can-be-and-not-be. This, then, is the cause, in the sense of material cause, of things which are of a nature to come-to-be, whereas cause, in the sense of their "end in view," is their shape and form; and this is the definition of the essential nature of each of them.[77]

Moreover, in *The Incoherence of the Incoherence*, Averroes explains:

> The philosophers do not believe that the possibilities of a thing's existence and of its non-existence are equivalent at one and the same time; no, the time of the possibility of its existence is different from the time of the possibility of its non-existence, time for them is the condition for the production of what is produced, and for the corruption of what perishes. If the time for the possibility of the existence of a thing and the time for the possibility of its non-existence were the same, that is to say in its proximate matter, its existence would be vitiated, because of the possi-

---

75 Gad Freudenthal, "(Al-)Chemical Foundations for Cosmological Ideas: Ibn Sînâ on the Geology of an Eternal World," in *Physics, Cosmology and Astronomy, 1300–1700: Tension and Accommodation*, ed. Sabetai Unguru (Dordrecht: Kluwer, 1991), 47–73.
76 Cf. Cerami, *Génération et substance*, 372.
77 Aristotle, *On Sophistical Refutations. On Coming-to-be and Passing Away. On the Cosmos*, trans. E.S. Forster and D.J. Furley (Cambridge, MA: Harvard University Press, 1955), 307–308.

bility of its non-existence, and the possibility of its existence and of its non-existence would be dependent only on the agent, not on the substratum.[78]

To paraphrase Thomas Aquinas, generation is a change from non-existence to existence—from matter and privation to form—while corruption, conversely, is a change from existence to non-existence.[79] In his commentary, Averroes explained that "what is moved by this motion is being, and what is generated from it is non-being, and the supreme being is the cause for what is always non-being."[80]

In his commentary on book 8 of *Physics*, Thomas Aquinas interpreted *maxime ens* ("supreme Being or the super-excellence of Being,"[81] which, in a sense, should be identified as non-being) as God, who is the cause of all existents.

> Nor, moreover, is this in keeping with the intention of Aristotle who in *Metaphysics* 11 proves that the supremely true and the Supreme Being is the cause of being for all existents. Hence the being which prime matter has—i.e., a being in potency—is derived from the first principle of being which is in a supreme way a being. Therefore, it is not necessary to presuppose for its action anything not produced by it.[82]

This distinction introduces a Neoplatonic theme concerning the difference between being and non-being according to Dionysius's idea of God as non-being, transcendent being, and the cause of being.[83] The relationship between existence and goodness is a Neoplatonic idea that is also developed by Scholastic thinkers, such as Boethius and Aquinas, and in Kalam philosophy, particularly that of Avicenna[84] and al-Ġazālī. Sforno undoubtedly introduces this idea in order to support a belief that there is a universal order of beings that cor-

---

78   Averroes, *Incoherence* 1.31 (68).
79   Cf. Thomas Aquinas, *De principiis naturae* 1.7: "Generatio vero et corruptio simpliciter non sunt nisi in genere substantiae; sed generatio et corruptio secundum quid sunt in aliis generibus. Et quia generatio est quaedam mutatio de non esse vel ente ad esse vel ens, e converso autem corruptio debet esse de esse ad non esse, non ex quolibet non esse fit generatio, sed ex non ente quod est ens in potentia."
80   Averroes, *Commentary on On Generation and Corruption* 2, text. 55: "Quod illud movetur isto motu est ens, et illud quod generatur per ipsum est non ens et quod est maxime ens est causa non entis semper."
81   Cf. Pseudo-Dionysius, *Corpus Dionysiacum I: De divinis nominibus*, ed. Beate Regina Suchla (Berlin: De Gruyter, 1990); Pseudo-Dionysius, *Corpus Dionysiacum II: De coelesti hierarchia. De ecclesiastica hierarchia. De mystica theologia. Epistulae*, ed. Heil Günter and Adolf Martin Ritter (Berlin: De Gruyter, 2012).
82   Thomas Aquinas, *Physics* 8, lectio 2, 974: "Nec hoc etiam est secundum intentionem Aristotelis. Probat enim in 11 *Metaphysics*, quod id quod est maxime verum et maxime ens, est causa essendi omnibus existentibus: unde hoc ipsum esse in potentia, quod habet materia prima, sequitur derivatum esse a primo essendi principio, quod est maxime ens. Non igitur necesse est praesupponi aliquid eius actioni, quod non sit ab eo productum" (English translation taken from Aquinas, *Commentary on Aristotle's* Physics, trans. Richard J. Blackwell, Richard J. Spath, and W. Edmund Thirlkel [New Haven, CT: Yale University Press, 1963], 395).
83   Cf. Fran O'Rourke, *Pseudo-Dionysius and the Metaphysics of Aquinas* (Leiden: Brill, 1992).
84   Maimonides, for example, mentions Avicenna's position in his "Letter to Samuel ibn Tibbon": "Avicenna in the discussion of causality states: 'The metaphysicians do not intend by

responds to the order of the beings' degrees of perfection and goodness, an order that is proportionate to their capacity to have knowledge of or imitate God.

10 Divine Causation

The argument on divine causation is presented according to Aristotle's position in *On Generation and Corruption* 2.10, in which the movement of generation and corruption is continuous. Hence, we face an evident contradiction if we compare this statement to what he claims in *Metaphysics* 3.4: that something that is continually moving is necessarily eternal, but this does not occur in the case of the movement of generation and corruption:

> Again, if nothing is eternal, even generation is impossible; for there must be something which becomes something, i.e. out of which something is generated, and of this series the ultimate term must be ungenerated; that is if there is any end to the series and generation cannot take place out of nothing. Further, if there is generation and motion, there must be limit too. For no motion is infinite, but every one has an end [...]. But if this is impossible, there must be something, the shape or form, apart from the concrete whole.[85]

The movement of generation and corruption involves a substantial change, which means that in every instance of such change, there is something that changes and something that persists. This movement is continuous, and since it is produced by a substantial change (which involves a substrate), it cannot be eternal, because it is generated from something else.

Aristotle suggests the theory of "what is better" in *Generation of Animals* 2.1.731b–732a (and *Metaphysics* 7.7) by explaining:

> I have already said that the male and the female are "principles" of generation, and I have also said what the sexes is their *dynamis* and the *logos* of their essence. As for the reason why one comes to be formed, and is, male, and another female, in so far as this results from necessity, i.e., from the proximate motive cause and from what sort of matter, our argument as it proceeds must endeavour to explain; in so far as this occurs on account of what is better, i.e., on account of the final cause (the Cause "for the sake of which"), the principle is derived from the upper cosmos what I mean is this. Of the things which are, some are eternal and divine, others admit alike of being and not-being, and the beautiful and the divine acts always, in virtue of its own nature, as a cause which produces that which is better in the things which admit of it; while that which is not eternal admits of

---

the agent (the efficient cause) the principle of movement only, as do the natural philosophers, but also the principle of existence and that which bestows existence, such the Creator of the world'"; see Alexander Marx, "Texts by and about Maimonides," *Jewish Quarterly Review* 25 (1935): 379–380.

85 Aristotle, *Metaphysics, Volume 1: Books 1–9*, trans. Hugh Tredennick (Cambridge, MA: Harvard University Press, 1933), 123–125 (*Metaph.* 3.4.999b5–16).

being ⟨and not-being⟩, and of acquiring a share both in the better and in the worse; also, Soul is better than body, and a thing which has Soul in it is better than one which has not, in virtue of that Soul; and being is better than not-being, and living than not living. These are the causes on account of which generation of animals takes place, because since the nature of a class of this sort is unable to be eternal, that which comes into being is eternal in the manner that is open to it. Now it is impossible for it to be so numerically, since the "being" of things is to be found in the particular, and if it really were so, then it would be eternal; it is, however, open to it to be so specifically.[86]

Sforno stresses the origin of the movement by emphasising that material, efficient, and final causes in the movement of generation and corruption are produced by the same "agent." Nonetheless, he does not explicitly identify the agent as God, but refers to Him as an "efficient cause," because He is considered to be the agent who is acting for an end. In this regard, the efficient cause corresponds to the final cause, which is always God. Sforno uses several names and epithets for God: *Artifex*/בעל מלאכה, *Creator-Creante*/בורא, *Deus*/אל, *Dominus*/אלהים, *Ordinator*/מסדר, *Productor*/ממציא—מסודר, *Rector*/מנהיג, *Conservator*, which translates the Tetragrammaton, and *Entificans* (only in *Lumen Gentium*). Therefore, it is evident that in his philosophical system, "God" transcends the theological dimension and is identified as the agent of the universe.

In my opinion, this idea—namely, the recognition of God as the agent and "administrator" of the universe—was common in the Bolognian academic environment. In light of this, Julius Caesar Scaliger opens his *Exotericae Excercitationes*[87] with the question "An Deus sit efficiens Mundi causa secundum Arist." (ex. 3) ("Whether God is the efficient cause of the world according to Aristotle"). Scaliger confutes Cardano and the other interpreters who understood God not as the creator of the world, but as its administrator.[88]

According to Aristotle, it is possible to reduce the four causes to two, one involving matter and the other involving form. In this sense, the efficient cause can be viewed as the initiator of the development of the form, the formal cause as the process of the form's actualisation, and the final cause as the goal of the process, the form's actualisation.[89] The actualisation of matter (*materie actus*/החומר הראשון לפועל) attests that matter cannot be eternal because it is passive, existing in potency only (*materia sit quid passivum potentia tantum ens*/החומר דבר מתפעל נמצא בכוח בלבד), and that it can only be brought from potency to actuality (*de potentia ad actum*/מן הכוח אל הפועל) by an active power (*per virtutem activam*/בכוח פועל). Therefore, the efficient cause is the primary source of the change or rest[90] and it is always prior to the caused things in time

---

86 Aristotle, *Generation of Animals*, trans. A.L. Peck (Cambridge, MA: Harvard University Press, 1942), 129–131.
87 Julius Caesar Scaliger, *Exotericarum exercitationum liber XV, de subtilitate, ad Hieronymum Cardanum* (Paris, 1557).
88 Cf. Kuni Sakamoto, *Julius Caesar Scaliger, Renaissance Reformer of Aristotelianism: A Study of His* Exotericae Exercitationes (Leiden: Brill, 2016), 16.
89 Cf. Jan Klein and Normal Klein, eds., *Solitude of a Humble Genius—Gregor Johann Mendel. Volume 1: Formative Years* (Berlin: Springer, 2013), 20.
90 *Phys.* 2.3.194b30.

and existence, as Aristotle affirms in *Posterior Analytics* 1.2.71b31.[91] It is worth noting that Sforno also mentions Averroes's Middle Commentary on *Posterior Analytics*—which is the only case in the entire book where he uses a Middle Commentary—though he amended the text: instead of "quia que sunt secundum viam agentis, sunt res precedentes causata **in existentia** et in tempore," he wrote "quia que sunt secundum viam agentis, sunt res precedentes in tempore et **in inventione**."[92]

The final cause in the movement of generation and corruption is understood as the ultimate goal of the movement itself, meaning that a thing that is affected by the movement of generation and corruption aims to approach the noblest being, which corresponds to its final cause and also to its formal and efficient cause. The beings' proximity to the agent is determined by their goodness and perfection. Hence, this discussion is linked to Neoplatonic themes, according to which the Supreme Being creates beings through emanation and those existents furthest from the Supreme Being are the most imperfect and inferior.

The distinction between nobler and inferior existents and the principle that it is impossible for a nobler being to act on an inferior being are central topics in Sforno's philosophy.[93] The nobler being is always "better" than the inferior one, and the more closely beings approach the noble existent, the more they are perfected, as Gersonides explained in detail in *Wars of the Lord*.[94]

Sforno anticipates the discussion of the "final cause" by underlining that beings are moved towards a goal and that this goal is God, as Aristotle also explains in this passage (which curiously does not appear in the argument):

> As has already been remarked, coming-to-be and passing-away will take place continuously, and will never fail owing to the cause which we have given. This has come about with good reason. For nature, as we maintain, always and in all things strives after the better; and "being" (we have stated elsewhere the different meanings of "being") is better than "not-being," but it is impossible that "being" can be present in all things, because they are too far away from the "original source." God, therefore, following the course which still remained open, perfected the universe by making coming-to-be a perpetual pro-process; for in this way "being" would acquire the greatest possible coherence, because the continual coming-to-be of coming-to-be is the nearest approach to eternal being.[95]

Every activity that is performed for a purpose is preceded by the existence of the agent, which has active powers and also passive powers that are actualised

---

91 "[Things are] prior, inasmuch as they are causative" (Aristotle, *Posterior Analytics. Topica*, trans. Hugh Tredennick and E.S. Forster [Cambridge, MA: Harvard University Press, 1960], 31).
92 In *Or 'Ammim*, Sforno does not mention *in inventione*, but only time.
93 Cf §15.1.
94 See Levi Gersonides, *The Wars of the Lord, Volume 3. Book Five: The Heavenly Bodies and Their Movers, the Relationship amongst These Movers, and the Relationship between Them and God; Book Six: Creation of the World*, trans. Seymour Feldman (Philadelphia: Jewish Publication Society of America, 1999).
95 Aristotle, *Coming-to-be*, 317 (*Gen. corr.* 2.10.336b).

by the movement (*kinesis*), since sensible substances involve both actuality (*energeia*) and potentiality (*dunamis*).[96] There is an efficient cause prior to its operation, which is the efficient cause in potentiality, and there is also an efficient cause in operation, which is the efficient cause in actuality.[97] In light of this definition, the central issue of Sforno's argument concerns the role of the efficient cause in the process of generation and corruption.

The distinction between potentiality (*dunamis*) and actuality (*energeia*) is discussed in book 9 (theta) of *Metaphysics*,[98] in which Aristotle discusses the concept of actuality and potentiality as a property of beings. Sforno called this chapter *Contra Gariconem*/נגד גאריקו, though the original Greek is Μεγαρικοί; namely, "the Megarians." At the beginning of the third chapter of book 9, Aristotle writes: "εἰσὶ δέ τινες οἵ φασιν, οἷον οἱ Μεγαρικοί" ("there are some, such as the members of the Megaric school, etc."). The correct translation in the Latin version is found, for example, in the Junta edition: "Ut quidam, ut Megarici, etc." Averroes naturally examined this passage in his Long Commentary, and it should be recalled that the Megarian school appears only twice throughout the whole of *Metaphysics*.

The Megarians rejected the idea of potentiality altogether, considering it to be prior to act by supposing that it only exists in conjunction with it;[99] there is no power apart from its operation, and therefore, only actual beings exist, while potentiality does not (*Metaphysics* 9.1046b). Charlotte Witt[100] summarises this position by saying that

> Aristotle draws on the same modal connection between *dunamis* and possibility to argue for the ontological priority of eternal substances in relation to perishable substances. Aristotle's rejection of the Megarian position that only what is actual exists introduces the conceptual connection that he draws upon in his later argument.[101]

For Aristotle, existence and non-existence are not in contradiction, because existence can be either actual or potential.[102]

In the Jewish, Arabic, and Scholastic contexts, the relationship between actual existence and possible existence is directly linked to the idea of creation, meaning the possibility of creation out of nothingness. Following Aristotle, Sforno explains that potentiality temporally precedes act. For example, the disposition for generation precedes the movement of generation, because, as proved in the first counterargument, the movement of generation is the actualisation of the disposition for generation.

---

96 Cf. Stephan Menn, "Aristotle's Concept of *Energeia*: *Energeia* and *Dunamis*," *Ancient Philosophy* 14 (1994): 73–114.
97 Cf. Arthur Hyman, "Maimonides on Causality," in *Maimonides and Philosophy*, ed. Yirmiyahu Yovel and Shlomo Pines (Dordrecht: Nijhoff, 1986), 157–158.
98 See *Metaph*. 9.3.1.
99 Cf. Averroes, *Incoherence* 1.
100 Charlotte Witt, *Ways of Being: Potentiality and Actuality in Aristotle's* Metaphysics (Ithaca, NY: Cornell University Press, 2003); Witt, "Powers and Possibilities: Aristotle vs. the Megarians," *Proceedings of the Boston Area Colloquium in Ancient Philosophy* 11 (1995): 249–266.
101 Cf. Witt, *Ways of Being*, 10.
102 Josep Puig Montada, "Ibn Rushd versus Al-Ghazali: Reconsideration of a Polemic," *Muslim World* 82 (1992): 127.

This distinction is articulated in *Physics* 8.4 (202a), which contains the definition of motion; however, although the statement is clear, *Lumen Gentium* presents a problematic issue:

Physics, Scot Venice, 1496	*Physics*, Mantino Venice, 1550	*Lumen Gentium* § 1.5.2	*Or ʿAmmim* § 1.5.2
Dicamus igitur quod motus est actus eius quod **innatum** est moveri secundum quod **innatum** est moveri. Necesse est igitur illa esse in quorum potentia est moveri unoquoque motuum. Et sine hac diffinitione omnes homines concedunt quod non est necesse moveri nisi illud quod post moveri; et hoc necesse est in unoquoque motuum v.g. [verbi gratia] quod non alteratur nisi illud quod **innatum** est alterari nec transfertur nisi illud quod **innatum** est transferri in loco. Necesse igitur ut res sit **innata** comburi prius antequam comburatur, et comburere antequam comburat.	Dicamus igitur quod motus est actus eius quod **innatum** est moveri secundum quod **innatum** est moveri. Necesse est igitur illa esse in quorum potentia est moveri unoquoque motuum. Et sine hac definitione omnes homines concedunt quod non est necesse moveri nisi illud, quod post moveri; et hoc necesse est in unoquoque motuum verbi gratia quod non alteratur nisi illud, quod **innatum** est alterari nec transfertur nisi illud, quod **innatum** est transferri in loco. Necesse est igitur ut res sit innata comburi prius, antequam comburatur, et comburere antequam comburat.	Dicamus igitur quod motus est actus eius quod **innatum** est moveri secundum quod **innatum** moveri, necesse est igitur illa esse in quorum potentia est moveri unoquoque motuum et sine hac diffinitione omnes homines concedunt quod non est necesse moveri nisi illud quod post moveri; et hoc necesse est in unoquoque motuum v.g. [verbi gratia] quod non alteratur nisi illud quod natum est alterari nec transfertur nisi illud quod **natum** est transferri in loco, necesse igitur est quod res sit **nata** comburi antequam comburatur, et comburere antequam comburat ergo	נאמר אם כן שהתנועה היא פעל **הדבר המוכן** להתנועע מצד מה שהוא **מוכן** להתנועע אם כן יתחייב שתהיה נמצאת בדברים אשר בהם כוחיות להתנועע. וזה בכל אחד ממיני התנועה ובלעדי הגדר הזה הכל מודים שלא יתחייב שיתנועע אלא הדבר שיוכל להתנועע וזה הוא הכרחי בכל אחד ממיני התנועה. המשל בזה שלא ישתנה אלא **הדבר המוכן** להשתנות ולא יתנועע ממקום למקום אלא **הדבר המוכן** להתנועע תנועה מקומית אם כן יתחייב שיהיה **הדבר מוכן** להשרף קודם שישרף. ולשריף קודם שישרוף

Both the Latin editions (by Scot and Mantino) use the expression *innatum/rei innata*, as does *Or ʿAmmim* (הדבר המוכן). However, in *Lumen Gentium*, Sforno follows the original quotation by using *innatum* in the first part of the sentence, while in the second part, he uses *natum* and *res nata*. One might suspect a typographical error in the Latin print, because in the Hebrew version, the term is correctly translated. However, the same phenomenon occurs in a quotation from *Metaphysics* 9.3.1048b:

Metaphysics, Mantino Venice, 1550	*Lumen Gentium* § 3.2.2	*Or ʿAmmim* § 3.2.2
Illud enim quod est principium potentie, est **illud quod innatum** est esse actu ab aliquo, quod est in actu	Illud enim quod est principium potentie, est **illud quod natum** est esse actu ab aliquo, quod est in actu	הדבר אשר הוא ראשית הכוחיות הוא **הדבר אשר הוא מוכן** להיות נמצא בפעל על ידי דבר שהוא נמצא בפעל

Nonetheless, in other places in *Lumen Gentium*, Sforno employed the term *innatum* (§ 5.2.2). It is therefore impossible to identify the reason for this choice.

Motion implies change and transition from potentiality to actuality according to "natural dispositions"[103] because "powers and dispositions are abilities that an object has to enact or to suffer a change."[104]

The debate on divine causality and the nature of the agents continued, as proven by the works of Landolfo Carracciolo,[105] Jacopo (Giacomo) Nacchiante (*quaestio prima*: *De creatione rerum*),[106] Giovanni Jacopo Pavesi (*Peripateticae Disputationes*),[107] Pietro Pomponazzi,[108] who considered God to be the effective (and efficient) cause "per similitudinem,"[109] and Alessandro Achillini (*De Intelligentiis*).[110]

---

103   *Phys.* 1.7; 4.211b31–33; *Met.* 7.7.1032b29–1033a22; 12.1–2.1069b8–16.

104   Cf. Witt, "Powers and Possibilities," 249.

105   Cf. William Duba, "Masters and Bachelors at Paris in 1319: The *lectio finalis* of Landolfo Caracciolo, OFM," in *Schüler und Meister*, ed. Thomas Jeschke and Andreas Speer (Berlin: De Gruyter, 2016), 315–365.

106   Jacopo Nacchiante, *Jacobi Naclanti, Clugiensis episcopi operum [tomi duo], id est enarrationes in D. Pauli epistolas ad Ephesios et Romanos [...] Sacrae scripturae medulla [...] Tractatus item decem et octo, in quibus varia [...] Rerum argumenta tractantur [...]* (Venetiis, 1567), 671: "Ad haec brevibus respondetur: et ad primum negatur antecedens, imo dicimus quod apud Aristotelem datur agens, sive producens, non tantum per transmutationem et motum, sed et per emanationem simplicem: cuius rei multiplex testimonum assero. Siquidem hoc habetur a Commentatore 1 Coeli com. 2 ubi dicit, quod generatio alicuius est duplex, scilicet, ex aliquot et ex nullo et quod primo modo generatio sumitur secundum famositatem, et quod talem Arist. Removit a coelo, non generationem quae est ex nullo. Haec Commentator, licet loco praepositionis ex, utuatur praepositine, ab, ut consideranti patet. Item Commentator 4 De Coelo, com. 1 et 12 Metaph. Com. 44 ponit duplex agens: alterum quod appellat verum, et est agens per transmutationem, reliquum quod vocat secundum similitudinem, et est quod nos dicimus agens per emanationem simplicem. Aristot. Quoque 9 Metaph. Text."

107   Giovanni Jacopo Pavesi, *Peripataticae disputationes in prima Aristotelis philosophia* (Venetiis, 1566), cap. 16, *Quo pacto caelestia, quo ad eorum substantiam, a Deo dependeant*, p. 122ᵛ: "Habet autem dubium, nam cum dicimus ex uno non ordinatur nis unum, est verum de agente, in quantum est agens tantum, non inquantum est forma, et finis, quoniam forma et finis dicuntur agentia quodammodo similitudinis. Ex quibus quo pacto caelestia efficentem causam habeant, planum fit, nempe corpora haec, a propriis formis, esse et permanentiam aeternam habent et sunt id quod sunt; igitur cun esse a forma consequantur, ideoeorum forma, agens quoquomodo dicitur, est enim forma agens secundum similitudinem, nam agens dicitur, quatenus esse largitur, et hoc est id, quod Arist. secundo Methaph. Docuit, ibi enim de principiis ommnibus caelestium corporum, et non tantum de Deo loquitur, nam plurali numero utitur, quae causae agentes dicuntur, non quoniam, ea de potentia ad actum transferunt, vel quoniam, per simplicem emantionem ipsa producant, sed quatenus cum sint propriae formae, causae sunt, quibus animalia divina, sunt id, quod sunt."

108   "Per hoc patet ad auctoritatem Commentatoris, comm. primo, IV De caelo, quod in abstractis non est efficiens nisi secundum similitudinem, id est efficiens producens, quod non praesupponit materiam, quod est per simplicem emanationem": see Vittoria Perrone Compagni, "La teologia di Pomponazzi: Dio e gli dei," in *Pietro Pomponazzi: Tradizione e dissenso. Atti del congresso internazionale di studi su Pietro Pomponazzi, Mantova, 23–24 ottobre 2008*, ed. Marco Sgarbi (Florence: Olschki, 2010), 118.

109   Cf. Bruno Nardi, *Studi su Pietro Pomponazzi* (Florence: Le Monnier, 1965).

110   Alessandro Achillini, *De intelligentiis*, in Achillini, *Opera omnia in unum collecta* (Venetiis, 1568), p. 17ʳ (Quodlibetum secundum, III): "Agens est duplex scilicet verum et est productium rei. Aliud secundum similitudinem et est forma dans esse patet distinction Quattro Coeli comm. Primo. Coelum habet agens secundum similitudinem, quia formam dantem esse scilicet intelligentiam, quae est anima eius, et apud Aristo non habet ceolun efficiens verum, ut pater etc. Accedamus ad veritatem, et dicamus omnem intellectum citra primo esse creatum. Ex hoc sequitur quod non omni agenti aliquid subiicitur in agendo. Secundo quod non potentia activa est transmutans. Tertio quod non omnia actio est idem passioni. Quarto quod ex nihilo tranquam termino a quo ex nihilo tanqua, ex subiecto aliquid fieri

11   Agent and Goal

In the first part of *Light of the Nations*, Sforno expounds on the relationship between the agent and the goal, whereby the agent (or the generator) brings forth generable things from potentiality to actuality according to his own intention, which is to achieve the goal. The definition of "goal"—meaning the final cause—and subsequently that of the agent—meaning the efficient cause—is one of the postulates that Sforno presents in the introduction. The assumption is presented on several occasions in *Light of the Nations* (§ 3.2.3; § 4.3.4; § 9.7.3; § 10.4.3; § 15.3.2).

---

5. Finis significat agentem significatione propria sicut motus significat motorem. Hoc autem sequitur ad eiusdem finis diffinitionem a Philosopho traditam Metaphysicorum II, 9 et aperte habetur ab Aven R. in Tractatu de Substantia Orbis cap. 2.	שמציאות התכלית מורה על מציאות הפועל הוראה עצמית כמו שהתנועה מורה על מציאות המניע וזה יתבאר מגדר התכלית אשר באר אריסטו׳ בספר מה שאחר מאמר ב׳ פרק ט׳ ובמאמר רחב הורה זה אבן רשד בספר עצם הגלגל פרק ב׳.

This quotation is found in Averroes's *Treatise on the Substance of the Celestial Sphere*. Nonetheless, in the original source, we read "finis significat agentem significatione propria sicut motus significat movens." The Hebrew מניע can translate both Latin terms, *movens* and *motor*. As Averroes's assertion was well known in Scholastic and Jewish philosophy, it is impossible that Sforno could have made a mistake in his Latin translation, especially because the statement occurs on three occasions in the book (§ 1.6; § 6.4.2; § 9.7.3).

I do not think that Sforno read Avicenna's *Metaphysics*, where we find the idea of *motor* in substantial changes. His knowledge is probably based on al-Ġazālī's assertion as quoted in *The Incoherence of the Incoherence*, as the last quotation in the chapter also suggests to us. In his *Metaphysics*, Avicenna argues that natural agents produce the "form," which is then actually introduced from outside effect. The substantial form is the efficient cause of self-motion, and the *motor coniunctus* is conceived to be the natural form in order to explain the continuation of motion in a body; namely, the *motor coniunctus* explains how bodies, once generated, can naturally move in the absence of the *generans*.[111] I would suggest that the definition of *motor* in this context is related to the definition given by Aristotle in *Metaphysics* 9, text. 13: "Omne, enim, quod generatum movetur a motore ante ipsum." In light of this explanation, motion and mover are two sides of the same coin: the movement is produced by a mover, who is, ultimately, the first mover.

---

potest et consequenter aliqua est actio sine transmutatione, quia ipse prius non erat et nunc est. Quinto ponendum est annuhulationem esse possibilem, neque oportet sequi aliquod illorum quae pro inconvenientibus ibi riliquuntur. Patet minorando corpus ad non quantum uniformiter non dixi uniformiter proportionabiliter. Sexto conceditur quod idem in numero reveretur et his fundamentis rationes in oppositum solvitur. Neque inconvenit ponere aliquam productionem terminari ad substantia quae non fit generatio immo necesse eam dari ut pater spiratione spiritus sancti."

111   Cf. James A. Weisheipl, *Nature and Motion in the Middle Ages*, ed. William E. Carroll (Washington, DC: Catholic University of America Press, 1985), 113–114.

The agent and the goal are described in accordance with the definition of the goal itself: the goal is nothing other than the intention by which the agent brings something forth from potentiality to actuality. Therefore, the agent's intention is the beginning of any activity, and in light of this principle, Sforno presents the "Aristotelian" statement according to which "finis in cogitatione est principum operationis" (שתכלית המחשבה הוא ראשית הפעולה). This is the Averroean interpretation of what Aristotle explains at the end of the second book of *Physics*; namely, "principius in cogitatione est finis in operatione, et finis in cogitatione est principium in operatione."

The "statement" in *Light of the Nations* seems to suggest an alternative interpretation: in fact, Aristotle asserted that the commencement in the agent's mind is the goal of the activity and the goal in the agent's mind is the commencement *in* the activity. Sforno employed the formula *principum operationis*—literally, the commencement *of* the activity—and this formula suggests that the activity in the agent's mind corresponds to his intellectual activity.

In order to explain the priority of the agent and the goal, Sforno quotes *Metaphysics* 2, text. 8[112] and 9,[113] which are undoubtedly connected to the discussion in *Metaphysics* 9, text. 13, according to which every generated thing is moved by a mover prior to it (*omne enim quod generatum movetur a motore ante ipsum*/כל מתהווה מתנועע על ידי מניע קודם) and the agent is prior to its activity, because an act cannot be temporally prior to the matter and the agent. Sforno references *Metaphysics* 1, text. 17, and 2, text. 7, which are directly connected to the discussion of the generation of the elements and their substantial principles: because there is only one matter for all sensible bodies (*corporibus sensibilium*/הגשמים המוחשים), this matter is not separable (*non separabilem*/בלתי נפרד), but is always related to contraries inhering in it (*semper cum contrarietate*/תמיד עם איזה הפכיות).

Sforno's discussion continues with a quotation of a passage from the *Treatise on the Substance of the Celestial Sphere* in which Averroes explains the nature of celestial bodies, whose matter has no potentiality:

> For it has been shown concerning the matter of the celestial body that it possesses no potentiality at all, for everything in which there is a potentiality, by which I mean a potentiality which is in a substance, is [in] potentiality in respect to two contradictories [...] the celestial body functions as matter for this incorporeal form, but it is a matter that exists in actuality. The celestial bodies, therefore, possess something resembling matter only insofar as they have an underlying matter for the reception of form. Therefore, the term subject is more truly applied to them than the term matter. The reason is that the sublunary matter is called by that name inasmuch as it is potentially the form that comes to be in it; but it is called "subject" inasmuch as it sustains the form and inasmuch as it is a part of the composite made up by it and the form.[114]

---

112 An agent will not begin an activity unless it intends an ultimate end.
113 The ultimate end is intended for activities; without it, the activity would be in vain.
114 Averroes, *De substantia orbis: Critical Edition of the Hebrew Text with English Translation and Commentary*, trans. Arthur Hyman (Cambridge, MA: Medieval Academy of America; Jerusalem: Israel Academy of Sciences and Humanities, 1986), 74, 82.

Matteo Di Giovanni's work[115] explains Averroes's approach, according to which celestial bodies and stars are said to possess matter only by equivocation.[116] Following Aristotle's distinction (and Themistius's interpretation), one type of matter is responsible for substantial change—that is, generation and corruption—and the other accounts only for spatial change, locomotion: because locomotion does not entail substantial change, a matter that is the substrate of locomotion but not of other forms of change can exist and, therefore, celestial bodies are composed of this kind of matter.[117] However, Sforno does not consider this section of the *Treatise on the Substance of the Celestial Sphere*. Instead, he quotes a specific passage in which Averroes offers a distinction between two kinds of agents: one that acts in the terrestrial world and one that acts in the celestial world. Sforno mentions only the first part of the passage, and his argument is naturally incomplete:

Sforno, *Lumen Gentium* §1.5.5	Nifo, *Commentationes in librum Averrois de substantia orbis* (1508)	Sforno, *Or ʿAmmim* §1.5.5	Hyman, *De substantia orbis* (Hebrew)
Sed in genere agentium quoddam est prius tempore acto, **et est omne quod fit in sphera huius mundi et istius agentis et acti quoddam est prius naturaliter et tempore et est orbis**	Sed in genere agentium quoddam est prius tempore acto, **et omne, quod fit in sphaera istius mundi, est istius agentis, et istius acti, quoddam est prius natura, sicut est dispositio temporis cum orbe,** [et agentis cum orbe, scilicet facientis ipsum in dispositionibus necessariis in inveniendo finem, ob quem fuit]	אמנם מהפועלים ימצאו שני מינים המין האחד הוא שהפועל קודם לפעולתו בזמן ומזה המין הוא כל פועל ופעולה אשר תחת גלגל העולם הזה והמין השני הוא פועל קודם **לפעולה בטבע ובזמן** ומזה המין הוא הגלגל	אלא שזה הפועל והפעול ממנו מה שהפועל קודם בזמן על פעולו והוא מה שיתפרש בכדור העולם, ומזה הפועל **ופעולו מה שהוא קודם בטבע על הזמן**, והוא הגלגל, [אשר הזמן נמשך לו ומשיג ממשיגיו, והפועל, ר״ל המיוחד לו בתכונות והתארים ההכרחיים במציאות התכלית אשר נמצאת בעבורם]

The activity of the agent is prior in terms of both nature and time, and *naturaliter* and *tempore* have the same adverbial function as בטבע ובזמן in the Hebrew edition. Sforno's interpretation is faithful to the original source, and it is worth comparing it with Hyman's edition in relation to the expression ופעולו מה שהוא קודם בטבע על הזמן. *Or ʿAmmim* respects the original Averroean position: time is subsequent to the celestial body and to the celestial agent, and this agent cannot be temporally prior to that upon which it acts; that is, the celestial agent is contemporaneous with the celestial body. Most of the Latin translations read *prius natura*, thus indicating that the priority of the celestial agent to the celestial body is a priority "according to nature," not "according to time."[118] *Prius naturaliter* is employed instead of *prius natura*, and it is therefore

---

115 Cf. Matteo di Giovanni, "Averroes on the Species of Celestial Bodies," *Miscellanea mediaevalia* 33 (2006): 438–466.
116 Cf. di Giovanni, "Averroes on the Species of Celestial Bodies," 442.
117 Di Giovanni, 440.
118 Cf. Hyman, in Averroes, *De substantia orbis*, 85 n. 40.

From Nothing Comes Nothing

evident that Sforno wanted to stress the idea that an agent is always temporally prior to its activity.

In *Or 'Ammim*, the term כדור העולם ("terrestrial sphere") is rendered with תחת גלגל העולם ("beneath the sphere of the world"), which calls to mind an expression found in Maimonides's *Guide of the Perplexed* 2.10:

Hyman, *De substantia orbis* (Hebrew)	*Or 'Ammim* §1.5.5	Maimonides, *Guide of the Perplexed* 2.10
אלא שזה הפועל והפעול ממנו מה שהפועל קודם בזמן על פעולו והוא מה שיתפרש **בכדור העולם**	אמנם מהפועלים ימצאו שני מינים המין האחד הוא שהפועל קודם לפעולתו בזמן ומזה המין הוא כל פועל ופעולה אשר **תחת גלגל העולם**	ואמנם אמרם שה׳מלאך׳—שליש העולם—והוא אמרם ב׳בראשית רבה׳ בזה הלשון "שהמלאך—שלישו של עולם"—הוא מבואר מאוד וכבר בארנו זה בחבורנו הגדול בתלמוד. כי הנבראות כולם—שלשה חלקים השכלים הנפרדים—והם ה׳מלאכים׳—והשני—גופות הגלגלים והשלישי—החומר הראשון—רצוני לומר הגופות המשתנות תמיד אשר **תחת הגלגל**

The same quotation from the *Treatise on the Substance of the Celestial Sphere* occurs in § 15.3.2, with some differences:

Lumen Gentium § 15.3.2	*Lumen Gentium* § 1.5.5	*Or 'Ammim* § 15.3.2	*Or 'Ammim* § 1.5.5	Hyman, *De substantia orbis* (Hebrew)
Sed in genere agentium quoddam est prius tempore actu, et est omne quod est in sphera huius mundi. **Quoddam est prius naturaliter et tempore** et est orbis quem sequitur tempus et agens orbem scilicet faciens ipsum in dispositionibus necessariis in inveniendo finem propter quem fiunt. Et cum ignoraverunt hoc quidam de opinione Aristotelis, dixerunt ipsum non dicere causam agentem sed moventem et illud fuit valde absurdum. Et non est dubium in hoc quod agens ipsum est movens ipsum,	Sed in genere agentium quoddam est prius tempore acto, et est omne quod fit in sphera huius mundi **et istius agentis et acti** quoddam est prius naturaliter et tempore et est orbis	קצת מן הפועלים קודם לפעולתו בזמן. וזה הוא כל פועל אשר בכדור המציאות. וקצתם קודם לפעולתו **בזמן ובטבע** וזה הוא הגלגל אשר ימשך אליו הזמן. ופועל הגלגל רצוני לומר העושה אותו בתכונות הכרחיות להשיג התכלית אשר בעבורו נמצא ורבים אשר לא ידעו שזה דעת אריסטו׳ אמרו עליו שלא אמר סיבה פועלת אבל אמר הסיבה המניעה בלבד וזה היה מגונה מאד. ואין ספק שהממציא אותו הוא המניע אותו כי המניע אותו בתנועה המיוחדת לו הוא אשר נתן לו קודם ההכנות אשר בם הוא משיג את התנועה המיוחדת לו עד כאן לשונו. וזה בעצמו ביאר	אמנם מהפועלים ימצאו שני מינים המין האחד הוא שהפועל קודם לפעולתו בזמן ומזה המין הוא כל פועל ופעולה אשר תחת גלגל העולם הזה והמין השני הוא פועל קודם לפעולה **בטבע ובזמן** ומזה המין הוא הגלגל	אלא שזה הפועל והפעול ממנו מה שהפועל קודם בזמן על פעולו והוא מה שיתפרש **בכדור העולם**, ומזה הפועל ופעולו מה שהוא קודם **בטבע על הזמן**, והוא הגלגל, אשר הזמן נמשך לו ומשיג ממשיגיו, והפועל, ר״ל המיוחד לו בתכונות והתארים ההכרחיים במציאות התכלית אשר נמצאת בעבורם. ולמה שסכלו זה בני אדם מסברות אריסטו אמרו שהוא לא יאמר בסבה פועלת לו הוא המניע לו. וזה אשר יניעהו התנועה המיוחדת לזה הכח הוא אשר השנה עליו אריסטו בזולת זה המקום בספרו בהשמים והעולם. ויראה שהוא יותר גבוה מהשמים וייותר עליון

(cont.)

Lumen Gentium §15.3.2	Lumen Gentium §1.5.5	Or 'Ammim §15.3.2	Or 'Ammim §1.5.5	Hyman, De substantia orbis (Hebrew)
quod enim movet illud motu proprio illi est illud quod largitur illi dispositiones per quas acquirit motum eidem proprium etc.		שם פרק ד' באמרו הגלגל הוא נמצא בשביל תנועתו. ואם השמים היו אובדים היתה אובדת גם״ כן תנועת הנמצאים השפלים עד כאן ״לשונו		

A comparison between Sforno's *Or 'Ammim* and Hyman's edition reveals that Sforno does not use Hebrew sources, but instead, like his contemporaries,[119] employs Nifo's edition of *The Incoherence of the Incoherence*, which contained the translation by Calo Calonimus (1497 or 1508).[120] We can identify which edition Sforno used from two details. The first concerns the section titles, which correspond to the opinions of al-Ġazālī and Averroes. In *Lumen Gentium*, Sforno labels the paragraphs of the discussion as *dubia*: *Destructio Destructionum, Disputatione* [...] *Dubio* [...]. In the Hebrew, we find two different formulations, the more common [...] ספר הפלת ההפלה מאמר [...] חקירה and the alternative form [...] ספר הפלת ההפלה מאמר [...] פרק. In the first case, Sforno calls the *dubia* "questions," while in the second, they are called "paragraphs." Another peculiarity that leads us to suspect that Sforno was using Nifo's edition consists in the inversion of the last two discussions:[121] in fact, discussion 13 corresponds to discussion 14, and discussion 14 to discussion 15.

The passage in Sforno's Latin translation recalls Jean de Jandun's interpretation of Averroes, which appears in two different works:

Gaietanus super libros De anima [...]. *Item De substantia orbis Joannis de Gandano cum questionibus eiusdem* (Venetiis, 1493)[122]	*Opera latine cum commentariis Averrois, recensuit Nicolatus Vernia* (Venetiis, 1483)	Or 'Ammim
Sed de numero agentium quoddam est prius tempore actu, et est omne quod fit in sphere istius mundi et	Sed in genere agentium quoddam est prius tempore acto, et est omne quod fit in sphera istius mundi et istius agents	קצת מן הפועלים קודם לפעולתו בזמן. וזה הוא כל פועל אשר בכדור זה המציאות. וקצתם קודם לפעולתו בזמן ובטבע וזה

---

119 Edward P. Mahoney noted that this edition was cited by Elijah Del Medigo: see Mahoney, "Giovanni Pico della Mirandola and Elia del Medigo, Nicoletto Vernia and Agostino Nifo," in *Giovanni Pico della Mirandola: Convegno internazionale di studi nel cinquecentesimo anniversario della morte (1494–1994)*, ed. Gian Carlo Garfagnini (Florence: Olschki, 1997), 2:127–156.

120 Agostino Nifo, *Eutyci Augustini Niphi Philothei Suessani in librum destructio destructionum Auerrois commentarii* (Venezia, 1498); Nifo, *Destruciones destructionum Averroiis cum Agostino Niphi de Sessa expositione* (Venezia, 1497).

121 See Moritz Steinschneider, *Die hebraeischen Übersetzungen des Mittelalters und die Juden als Dolmetscher* (Berlin, 1893; repr. Graz: Akademische Druck- und Verlagsanstalt, 1956), §186 (p. 331).

122 Gaetano da Thiene, *Super libros de anima. Questiones de sensu agente et de sensilibus com-*

(cont.)

Gaietanus super libros De anima [...]. Item De substantia orbis Joannis de Gandano cum questionibus eiusdem (Venetiis, 1493)	*Opera latine cum commentariis Averrois, recensuit Nicolatus Vernia* (Venetiis, 1483)	*Or 'Ammim*
istius angentis et acti quoddam est prius naturaliter tempore et est orbus scilicet faciens ipsum in dispositionibus necessariis inveniendo finem propter quem fuit. Et cum hoc ignoraverunt quidam esse de opinione Aristotelis, dixerunt ipsum non dicere causam agentem tantum sed moventem et istud fuit valde absurdum. **Et non est dubium** in hoc quod agens ipsum est movens ipsum, quod enim motum ipsum motu proprio, est illud quod largitur ei primo dispositiones per quas acquirit motum proprium.	et acti, quoddam est prius naturaliter et tempore et est orbis quem sequitur tempus et cui accidit et agens orbem scilicet faciens ipsum in dispositionibus necessariis in inveniendo finem propter quem fiunt. Et cum ignoraverunt hoc quidam esse de opinione Aristotelis, dixerunt ipsum non dicere causam agentem tantum sed moventem et illud fuit valde absurdum. **Et non est dubium** in hoc quod agens ipsum est movens ipsum, quod enim motum ipsum motu proprio illi est illud quod largitur illi primo dispositiones per quas acquirit motum proprium.	הוא הגלגל אשר ימשך אליו הזמן. ופועל הגלגל רצוני לומר העושה אותו בתכונות הכרחיות להשיג התכלית אשר בעבורו נמצא ורבים אשר לא ידעו שזה דעת אריסטו' אמרו עליו שלא אמר סיבה פועלת אבל אמר הסיבה המניעה בלבד וזה היה מגונה מאד. **ואיו ספק** שהממציא אותו הוא המניע אותו כי המניע אותו בתנועה המיוחדת לו הוא אשר נתן לו קודם ההכנות אשר בם הוא משיג את התנועה המיוחדת לו עד כאן לשונו. וזה בעצמו ביאר שם פרק ד' באמרו הגלגל הוא נמצא בשביל תנועתו. ואם השמים היו אובדים היתה אובדת גם כן תנועת הנמצאים השפלים עד כאן לשונו

In this passage, Sforno emphasised two ideas: (1) the priority of the existence of an agent that produces the movement in the spheres (because the agent is the efficient cause) and (2) the ultimate goal of the movement of the spheres (which corresponds to the final cause).

The influence of the spheres on the sublunary world is empirical evidence that "man is begotten by man and by the sun" (*Phys.* 2.2.194b13).[123] The sun is the efficient cause of generation in human beings because, as Aristotle suggests in *On Generation and Corruption* 2.2.338b and *On the Heavens* 2.3.286a, its cyclical movement produces the seasons and the seasons provide living things with the nutrients required for generation and growth.[124] Similarly to the fifteenth *quaestio*, Sforno's position stresses the idea that the stars and planets exist for the sake of things in the sublunary world and that they were designed for the benefit of sublunary existence.

This argument was employed by some authors in the Middle Ages and the Renaissance in order to attest to the effect of the spheres in the inferior world. Paul of Venice illustrates the process by paraphrasing Averroes's and Aristotle's positions and gives a complete explanation of the influence of the heavenly bodies in the sublunary world:

> Quartum inconveniens est quod unum in actu secundum quod est unum in actu dependet a dubobus agentibus non subordinatis. Quod istud sit

---

munibus: Ac de intellectu. Item de substantia orbis Ioannis de Gandavo cum questionibus eiusdem [Venice], 1493, unpaginated.
123 ἄνθρωπος γὰρ ἄνθρωπον γεννᾷ καὶ ἥλιος.
124 Cf. David Ebrey, *Theory and Practice in Aristotle's Natural Science* (Cambridge: Cambridge University Press, 2015), 87.

> inconveniens patet, quia eo facto quod effectus est unus in actu non habet nisi unum agens, quia, si habet plura agentia, oportet quod illa sint subordinata, iuxta illud Philosophi, secundo Phisicorum: "Sol et homo generant hominem ex materia." Et quod illud sequatur manifestum est, quia tam homo quam equus, qui est unus effectus in actu, secundum quod huiusmodi necessario dependet ab agente materiali generante subiectum et ab agente immateriali generante formam. Et quod ista agentia non sint subordinata, secundum illos, patet, quia, si essent subordinata, aut ambo generarent subiectum aut ambo generarent formam—quod negat ista opinio.[125]

Sforno abandoned this argument in order to introduce the notion of chance by saying that every activity is performed for a goal and that since there is a goal, nothing happens by chance. Sforno was probably recalling the discussion in the *Guide of the Perplexed* (2.20 and 2.4)[126] and Gersonides's *Wars of the Lord* (5.2 and 5.5).[127] Among the twenty-seven propositions, two deal with the definition of chance:

125 Cf. Gabriele Galluzzo, *The Medieval Reception of Book Zeta of Aristotle's* Metaphysics, *Volume 2: Pauli Veneti*, Expositio in duodecim libros metaphysice Aristotelis, *liber VII* (Leiden: Brill, 2013).

126 Cf. Maimonides, *Guide* 2.20 (2:312–313): "Aristotle demonstrates regarding all natural things that they do not come about by chance—his demonstration being, as he has stated it: the fortuitous things do not occur either always or in the majority of cases; the natural things, however, occur either always or in the majority of cases. Thus the heavens and all that is in them remain always in certain states that do not change, as we have explained, either in their essence or through change of place. As for the natural things that are beneath the sphere of the moon, some of them occur always and others in the majority of cases. Instances of what occurs are the heating action of fire and the falling-down of a stone, while instances of what occurs in the majority of cases are the shapes and acts of the individuals of every species. All this is clear. Now if the particular things of the world are not due to chance, how can the whole of it be due to chance? This is a demonstration proving that these beings are not due to chance. Here is the text of the statement of Aristotle in his refutation of those of his predecessors who believed that this world has happened to come about by chance and spontaneously, without a cause. He says: other people have thought that the cause of these heavens and all these worlds is to be sought in their spontaneity. They say that revolution and motion that has differentiated and constituted all things according to this order were due to their spontaneity. Now this is a point arouses strong astonishment; I mean the fact that they say concerning animals and plants that they do not come about and are not produced by chance, but have a cause, which is either nature or intellect or some other similar thing … and they say of the heavens and of the bodies that alone are divine among all the visible bodies, that they have come into being spontaneously and that they have no cause at all such as is possessed by the animals and the plants. But it is not clear to me that Aristotle believes that, because these beings have not come into being spontaneously, it follows necessarily that they have come into being in virtue of the purpose of one who purposed and the will of one who willed. For to me a combination between existing in virtue of purpose and will—a combination uniting these two—comes near to a combination of two contraries"; *Guide* 2.4 (2:258): "Thus He burns by means of a fire, and this fire is moved by means of the motion of the sphere, and the sphere in its turn is moved by means of a separate intellect. […] There are separate intellects that are in no way a body. All of them overflow from God, may He be exalted, and they are the intermediaries between God and all these bodies."

127 Gersonides, *Wars of the Lord* 3, 5.2 (p. 91): "Or, perhaps he means by this that in the case of the separate intellect its activity is [identical with] itself, i.e., cognition, since cognition is its proper activity; whereas in the case of this form [that generates animate creatures] its activity is different from itself, i.e., [its activity produces] a generated corporate form. That [the activity] of this form is not identical with the form itself is evident; for this form employs a corporeal organ in its operation and a body is the recipient of this activity. The

6. Quecumque sunt preter voluntatem et cognitionem dicuntur fieri casu. Hoc autem habetur a Philosopho Physicorum II, 51.	ו׳ שכל מה שנעשה בלתי כוונה ורצון יאמר עליו שנעשה במקרה וזה באר ארסטו׳ ספר השמע מאמר ב׳ פרק נ״א
8. Quicquid est in pluribus observatum non habet esse casu. Hoc autem infertur a Philosopho in lib. De Celo II, 45 et Physicorum II, 48.	ח׳ שכל מה שיהיה בדברים רבים לא יפול בהם במקרה, וזה יתבאר מדברי אריסטו׳ בספר השמים והעולם מאמר ב׳ פרק מ״ה ובספר השמע מאמר ב׳ פרק מ״ח.

Living beings possess instruments (*organa*[128]/כלים) that enable them to perform these activities, and such instruments are mediately or immediately produced by an agent's will or thought (*preter cogitationem et voluntatem*/בכוונת מכוין הפועל)[129] that is aimed toward a goal.[130] Things that are produced without intention or will are produced by chance, as the Philosopher stresses in *Physics* 2.5, and yet the instruments of what is created are not produced by chance because instruments are produced by an agent for an identifiable goal. The empirical proof is based on the Aristotelian idea that fortuitous things do not occur either always or in the majority of cases (*Physics* 2, text. 48).

Sforno's discussion continues along the lines of Averroes's commentary on *Metaphysics* 12, text. 18,[131] which states that activities are produced by a divine mind (*ab arte divina intellectuali*/במלאכה אלהית שכלית) and that nature, *quasi*

---

first of these interpretations seems more likely, [since] it is consistent with Averroes' views on this topic in his commentary on Book XII of the *Metaphysics*."

128 It is also interesting that Sforno uses the term *organa* instead of *instrumenta*.
129 Cf. §1.5.7.
130 A similar idea is offered by Paul of Venice in his commentary on *Metaphysics*: "*There might be some doubts concerning* Aristotle's text and Averroes's comments. For it might seem that the animals that are not generated from seed, but by putrefaction, are not generated by chance. A casual effect comes about rarely and besides the intention of the agent, as Aristotle says in *Phys.*, Book II. The animals that do not come from seed, by contrast, are generated frequently and in accordance with the intention of the heavenly body generating them. *It should be replied* that it is not inappropriate for some event to be casual with respect to one cause and non-casual with respect to another. Therefore, if the generation without seed of some animals is understood in relation to the power of the heaven, it is not casual, because the heaven is the principal agent of generation, which has in view the generation of this or that animal. If, by contrast, generation without seed is understood in relation to the putrefying heat of the containing body, which does not have in view the generation of this or that animal, then it is casual and accidental. 'Causal' is here understood not strictly, as Aristotle takes it in the Physics, but in a broad sense so as to cover every effect which comes about besides the intention of the agent": see Galluzzo, *Medieval Reception of Aristotle's* Metaphysics, 621.
131 Averroes, *Ibn Rushd's* Metaphysics, 111: "As for the heats generated by the heats of the stars, which produce each distinct species of animals and which are potentially that species of animal, the power presents on the amount of the motions of the stars and their reciprocal proximity or remoteness; this power originates from the work of the divine mind which I like the single form of the single commanding arts are subordinated. Accordingly, one must understand that nature, when it produces something very highly organized without itself being intelligent, is inspired by active powers which are nobler than it and are called 'intellect' (intelligences)."

esse memorata,[132] is inspired by active powers that are called *intelligentie*/שכלים נבדלים, or "separate intellects" in the Hebrew translation. Like Maimonides and Gersonides, he suggests that the motions of the heavenly bodies are the result of incorporeal movers, "the separate intellects," and that the heavenly bodies are moved by virtue of their apprehension (ציור) of God, the First Intellect.[133]

Sforno stresses the priority of the agent, the ultimate goal, the substrate, and its disposition in order to demonstrate that the movement of generation and corruption is not eternal. He affirms that the movement of generation and corruption does not occur in the first instant, because the first instant involves only creation. Therefore, the movement of generation is not eternal. Similarly, he holds that everything naturally follows the ultimate finality and that a deficit therefore indicates the absence of perfection and, consequently, the ultimate goal, which is the highest perfection. His interpretation follows Maimonides's explanation in *Guide of the Perplexed* 3.3:

> I shall return to the subject of this chapter, namely, to the discussion of final end. I say then: Aristotle has made it clear that in natural things the agent, the form, and the final end are one the same thing […]. Regarding the ultimate finality of every species, all those who discourse on nature deem that it is indispensable, but very difficult to know; all the more is this so of the finality of what exists as a whole. What appears to result from the discourse of Aristotle is that, according to him, the ultimate finality of these species consists in the permanence of coming-to-be and passing-away […]. For the ultimate purpose consists in bringing about perfection […] according to the doctrine of the eternity. On the other hand […] the finality of all that exists is solely the existence of the human species so it should worship God, and that all that has been made has been made for it alone so that even the heavenly spheres only revolve in order to be useful to it and to bring into existence that which is necessary for it […]. Necessarily and obligatorily the argument must end with the answer being given that the final end is: God has wished it so, or His wisdom has required to this to be so.[134]

12 Generation *in fieri*

Sforno, like Thomas Aquinas and other Scholastic thinkers, outlines the central issue in accordance with an ontological distinction between creation and generation (meaning change). The movement of generation and corruption is a change or alteration of the substrate. In the process of creation, there is no alteration of the substrate; instead, a thing comes into existence from God's act.

In this first counterargument on the movement of generation and corruption, Sforno maintains that nothing that is necessarily preceded in time by something else is eternal, and therefore a generated being necessarily has a cause that is prior to it. Generation is actualised (Hebrew: ההויה לפועל) in a process within time, which means a process that actualises the potency of a

---

132 *Rememorata* in the original Latin translation.
133 See Gersonides, *Wars of the Lord 3*, 240 n. 4.
134 Maimonides, *Guide* 3.3 (2:451–452).

substrate. While in *Or 'Ammim*, he uses the expression "actualisation of generation," meaning "generation as the process of actualisation of potentiality," in *Lumen Gentium*, we find *generatio in fieri*. *Generatio in fieri* does not translate the same concept: it concerns the idea of the actualisation of movement in the account of creation, following Aquinas's definition: *generatio autem significat ut in fieri, sed paternitas significat complementum generationis*.[135] In the Scholastic tradition, the distinction between *generatio in fieri* and *generatio in facto* is employed in order to account for and describe not only the process of creation, but also the nature of the Eucharistic conversion.[136]

I will underline this aspect of Sforno's philosophical system. Here, he transfers an idea that does not belong to the "pure" Aristotelian and Averroistic tradition into the Latin-Jewish context; nonetheless, in the Paduan and Bolognian academic milieu, the definition of *generatio in fieri* appears in two commentaries on Aristotle, Nifo's *Expositiones in Aristotelis libros metaphysices*[137] and Ludovico Boccadiferro's *In duos libros Aristotelis de generatione et corruptione doctissima commentaria*.[138] This last work undoubtedly played an important role in Sforno's thought: taking into account Guido Bartolucci's suggestion,[139] I will assume that Sforno developed the idea of *generatio in fieri* through this tradition.

Josep Puig Montada[140] writes that for Averroes, the distinction between *generatio in fieri* and *generatio in facto* is inaccurate. Averroes presented this definition in order to describe the idea of relative and absolute generation. The discussion differs from the Scholastic tradition because in Averroes, the distinction between the two kinds of generation does not concern creation, but rather the nature of motion. If there is a movement that is prior to *generatio in fieri*, then *generatio in fieri* is not eternal, and this is also what Sforno aims to demonstrate: that the notion of priority is in contradiction to the definition of eternity.

The origin of the ambiguity is found in the Aristotelian text. The Greek term *entelekia* is translated as "actualisation," which in Aristotle is "the actualization of that which is potentially."[141] Aryeh Kosman[142] claims that "actualisation" may refer either to a process or to the result of a process[143] and that the ambiguity in the Aristotelian lexicon is due to this double meaning. *Energeia*, which normally translates the term "actuality," is also used by Aristotle to define the movement of generation in *On Generation and Corruption*. For Chen Chung-Hwan,[144] *energeia* is the expression that designates the movement of generation from potentiality to actuality, since it expresses two different concepts at the same time, "being actualised" and "being perfect." However, naturally, this kind of movement is intended as *entelechia*: as Aristotle asserts in *Metaphysics*

---

135 Aquinas, *Summa Theologica* 1.33.2.2.
136 Cf., for instance, Alexander of Hales, *Summa fratris Alexandri*, ed. Bernardini Klumper, 4 vols. (Rome: Collegii S. Bonaventurae, 1924–1948).
137 Nifo, *Expositiones in Aristotelis libros Metaphysices*, 1.113.
138 Cf. index and p. 24.
139 Cf. Guido Bartolucci, "Elijah of Nola and Moshe Finzi: Medicine and Aristotelianism in Sixteenth-Century Bologna," in Veltri, *Literary and Philosophical Canon*.
140 Cf. Josep Puig Montada, "Aristotle and Averroes on *Coming-to-be and Passing-Away*," *Oriens* 35 (1996): 1–34.
141 William David Ross, *Aristotle*, 5th rev. ed. (London: Methuen & Co., 1949), 81.
142 Aryeh L. Kosman, "Aristotle's Definition of Motion," *Phronesis* 14 (1969): 40–62.
143 Kosman, "Aristotle's Definition of Motion," 40.
144 Chen Chung-Hwan, "Different Meanings of the Term *Energeia* in the Philosophy of Aristotle," *Philosophy and Phenomenological Research* 17 (1956): 56–65.

9.8.1050a21–23, "For the activity is the end, and the actuality is the activity; hence the term 'actuality' [*energeia*] is derived from 'activity' [*ergon*], and tends to have the meaning of 'complete reality' [*entelecheia*]."[145] The *entelechia* is the completeness and perfection that pertains to the movement itself.

The idea of perfection corresponds to the idea of being. As mentioned above, "being" is better than "non-being"; therefore, it is impossible that *generabilium materia simul tempore esse actu et potentia, sub esse perfecto et imperfecto, quod est quid absurdum*/ומזה יתחייב שהחומר ההוא הכולל היה בזמן אחד בעצמו שלם ובלתי שלם נמצא בכח ונמצא בפעל.[146] In the Aristotelian system, perfection is only possible if there is an achievement that corresponds to the final end of the action and if there is a generated being that is predisposed for the movement that leads to perfection. Nonetheless, a generated being is nothing more than the result of an actualisation that comes from the generation; therefore, there is something that precedes the activity and which is prior to the movement of generation and corruption. The general discussion of the movement of generation and corruption is undoubtedly connected to Gersonides's interpretation, which stresses the importance of the relationship between heavenly bodies and terrestrial elements.[147]

13   The Elements and Prime Matter

In introducing the question of the movement of generation and corruption, Sforno presupposes the reader's acquaintance with some philosophical definitions. The first argument in favour of the eternity of the movement of generation and corruption is connected to the idea of the eternity of the elements: if the elements are eternal, then the movement of generation and corruption is also eternal.

The central issue in book 8 (eta) of *Metaphysics* deals with the definition of substance (*substratum*). I will assume that Sforno introduces the "elements" as part of an understanding of substance, in the same way that Aristotle presents the definition of substance, meaning in accordance with the definition of elements at the end of book 7 of *Metaphysics*,[148] which is related to the discussion in *Metaphysics* 8, text. 12 (8.4.1044b).[149]

---

145   Aristotle, *Metaphysics 1*, 459.
146   Cf. §1.4.3.
147   Gersonides, *Wars of the Lord 3*, 32: "Aristotle says in *On Generation and Corruption* that the regular order obtaining in the generation and destruction of sub-lunar phenomena is consequent upon the motions of the sun along the inclined circle; and that the duration of any existent thing in the sub-lunar world is determined by the circular motion [of the sun], such that the number of rotations by virtue of which the growth of something is determined is equal to the number of rotations determining its decay and destruction."
148   *Metaph.* 7.1028b (Aristotle, *Metaphysics 1*, 313–315): "Substance is thought to be present most obviously in bodies. Hence we call animals and plants and their parts substances, and also natural bodies, such as fire, water, earth, etc., and all things which are parts of these or composed of these, either of parts of them or of their totality; e.g. the visible universe and its parts, the stars and moon and sun. [...] We must consider, then, with regard to these matters, which of the views expressed is right and which wrong; and what things are substances; and whether there are any substances besides the sensible substances, or not; and how sensible substances exist; and whether there is any separable substance (and if so, why and how) or no substance besides the sensible ones."
149   *Metaph.* 8.5.1044b (Aristotle, *Metaphysics 1*, 419): "But in the case of substances which

Sforno retains the distinction offered by Averroes, according to which philosophers talk about "matter" and "form" and theologians talk about "substratum" and "quality in the mind." The philosophers accept causality and the existence of the effect, while the theologians admit the possibility of "signs."[150]

Sforno's first argument in the first disputed question (§1.1.1) begins by postulating the existence of the "elements" and their eternity. Nonetheless, he does not offer a definition of the elements—which is given in the second question—though he does introduce the notion of eternal substances such as the heavenly bodies. Hence, Aristotle explains that substances—for instance, the heavenly bodies—have no matter and are therefore eternal.[151] Averroes's commentary here (on *Metaphysics* 8, text. 12)[152] deals with the distinction between "whole" and "part" according to the definition of substances that are subject to generation and corruption; namely, the elements. In light of this, if a substance cannot be subject to generation and corruption, then this substance has no matter, because "material" substance has the potency to change. Consequently, a substance that exists in "actuality" only is an eternal substance, and it is not affected by the movement of generation and corruption.[153]

Following this passage, Sforno introduces a significant discussion of mereology, meaning the relationship of part-to-whole that played a noteworthy role in medieval philosophy. Nonetheless, in *Light of the Nations*, this argument is further developed later on, in the chapters "On the Elements,"[154] "On Prime Matter,"[155] "On Creation,"[156] and "On Free Will."[157] In the Western tradition, mereology is part of the study of metaphysics. Boethius of Dacia stresses the study of the "whole" and the "parts" because these concepts are "not peculiar to some specific body of knowledge, but are common to all of them."[158] There-

---

though natural are eternal the principle is different. For presumably some of them have no matter, or no matter of this kind, but only such as is spatially mobile. Moreover, things which exist by nature but are not substances have no matter; their substrate is their substance."

150 Cf. Montada, "Ibn Rushd versus Al-Ghazali," 126.
151 It should be noted that this argument is connected to *Metaph.* 12.1.1069a and 12.9.1075b.
152 *Metaph.* 8.6.1045a.
153 Cf. *Cael.* 1.12.281b–282a (Aristotle, *On the Heavens*, trans. W.K.C. Guthrie [Cambridge, MA: Harvard University Press, 1939], 115): "Hence everything which exists for ever is absolutely indestructible. If it was generated, it will have the power of for some time not being; for just as the destructible is that which formerly was but now is not, or has the possibility of not being at some future time, even so the generated is that which at some time past may not have been. But with that which exists for ever, there is no time during which it may not have been, whether finite or infinite, since of course if it has the power for an infinite time it has it also for a finite. Therefore, the same thing which has the power of always being cannot also have the power of always not being. Nor can it have the contradictory of its own power, i.e. that of not always being. Therefore, it is impossible for a thing both to exist for ever and to be destructible. Similarly, also, it cannot be generated; for if the second of two terms is impossible without the first, and the first is impossible, the second must be impossible also. Thus, if that which exists for ever cannot at any time not be, it is also impossible that it should be generated."
154 §2.2.
155 §3.2–4.
156 §6.3.
157 §14.6.
158 "Non appropriantur alicui scientiae speciali, sed communes sunt omnibus" (Boethius of Dacia, *Modi significandi sive quaestiones super Priscianum maiorem*, ed. John Pinborg and Henry Roos with Severino Skovgaard Jensen [Copenhagen: G.E.C. Gad, 1969], q. 8, dubium, ll. 5–43, pp. 37–38; English translation in Desmond Paul Henry, *Medieval Mereology* [Amsterdam: B.R. Grüner, 1991, 5]).

fore, the study of the relationship of part-to-whole became one of the most important topics in medieval times (in Gilbert of Poitiers, Aquinas, Buridan, Wycliff, and Ockham, to mention only a few) and continued to be discussed in Renaissance philosophy. Paul of Venice devoted the whole of the eighth section of his *Logica Magna* to this question[159] and also addressed it in his commentary on Aristotle's *Metaphysics*.[160] Considering the impact of Paduan Averroism in *Light of the Nations*, especially the influence of Agostino Nifo on some arguments, I cannot rule out the possibility that Sforno was also familiar with the works of Paul of Venice.

Paul of Venice followed the Averroean interpretation and pointed out three different definitions in Aristotle: in *Metaphysics* 5, the element is "the primary constituent of something, which is indivisible into parts specifically different from itself"—meaning prime matter and substantial form. In *Metaphysics* 7, the element is "that into which a thing resolves, and which pre-exists in the thing," which only pertains to matter, whether prime or secondary. In *On the Heavens*, book 3, an element is "a body into which the other bodies are divided, present in them potentially or actually, and not itself divisible into (bodies) of some other species," a definition that exclusively pertains to the four elements.[161]

Sforno discusses the topic of the "whole" and the "part" in several places, and this issue is also reported in three different instances in the introduction (propositions 13, 14, and 15):

13. Cuiuslibet elementi partes conveniunt cum suo toto nomine et diffinitione. Hoc autem habetur a Philosopho et Aven R. in lib. De Celo I, 19.	י״ג שכל אחד מחלקי היסוד מסכים עם הכל שלו בשם ובגדר וזה באר ואריסטוטיליס ואבן רשד בספר השמים מאמר א׳ פרק י״ט.
14. Nulla elementorum pars est incorruptibilis. Hoc autem habetur a Philosopho in lib. De Celo III, 52.	י״ד שאין שום חלק יסוד שיהיה בלתי נפסד. וזה בארו אריסטוטיליס בספר השמים מאמר ג׳ פרק נ״ב.
15. Nullum elementorum habuit esse secundum totum corruptum. Hoc autem habetur ab Aven R. in lib. De Generatione II, 37.	ט״ו שמעולם לא נפסד אחד מהיסודות בכללו. וזה באר אבן רשד בביאור ספר ההויה וההפסד מאמר שני פרק ל״ז.

In the definition of the "whole" and the "part" found in his Epitome of *Metaphysics*—which was translated into Latin by Jacob Mantino in 1523[162]—

---

159 Paul of Venice, *Logica Magna* (Venezia, 1499); cf. also Paul of Venice, *Logica Magna. Part II, Fascicule 8: Tractatus de obligationibus*, ed. E.J. Ashworth (Oxford: Oxford University Press, 1988).
160 Gabriele Galluzzo, "Paul of Venice's Commentary on the *Metaphysics*," in Galluzzo, *Medieval Reception of Aristotle's* Metaphysics, 467–751.
161 Galluzzo, 748–749.
162 Jacob Mantino, *Averroys epithoma totius methaphisices Aristotelis in quattuor secatum tractatus. Interpraete Iacob Mantino* (Bononiæ, 1523).

Averroes defines the whole[163] as *id quod continent omnes partes extra quod nihil invenitur* ("that which contains all parts [of a thing] in such a way that nothing is found outside [that thing]") and *quod non habet partes in actu* ("that which has no parts in actuality"). Averroes offers a definition of a part[164] that pertains to quantity and dimension, on the one hand, and to the "corporal" parts, meaning the parts of a compound, on the other. The "part" is not understood univocally in the Aristotelian works;[165] in fact, "part" can be predicated not only in relation to the elements, but also in relation to matter and form. It is logical to assume that Sforno presents the "elements" in order to introduce the definition of the "substance," meaning a compound of "matter" and "form" such as the "subject" (or substrate) of substantial generation (and corruption). The "whole" is intended to provide the definition of "compound," meaning the matter and the forms—which Aristotle calls *synolon* in *Metaphysics* 7.3.1029a—and can be compared to what he states in *Metaphysics* 5.2.1013b: "Of these [i.e., material causes] some are causes in the sense of substrate: e.g., the parts; and others in each case is a cause in the sense of essence: e.g., the whole, and the composition, and the form."[166]

The arguments offered in the third disputed question, "On Prime Matter," have a similar structure; in fact, Sforno suggests that if a part of one of the first elements were to exist at the same time as prime matter, insofar as this part is corruptible, it would follow that the elements have no potency to exist forever and consequently, they cannot be eternal. And since matter is never deprived of form, the forms are not eternal either. Nothing exists outside the four elements and the celestial bodies, as Aristotle claims in *On the Heavens* 1, text. 23.[167]

---

163 Cf. Averroes, *On Aristotle's "Metaphysics,"* 47: "'Whole' signifies that which contains all parts [of a thing] in such a way that nothing is found outside [that thing]. In general, it is synonymous with what is signified by the first mode of predication of 'complete' (in this way we say of body that it is divisible into 'the whole' of dimensions). In general, 'whole' is predicated in two ways, either of the continuous (i.e. that which has no parts in actuality) or of the discrete. Of the latter there again two types, one in which the parts have positions with respect to one another (as bodily organs), the second in which the parts do not have position with respect to one another (as numbers and letters). However, one marks off the first type which is predicated of the continuous, by the term 'whole' (*totius*), and the second type, which is predicated of the discrete, by the term 'total' (*aggregatum*)."

164 Averroes, 47: "'Parts' is predicated in two ways. Firstly, [it is predicated] in a merely quantitative sense. To this [type] belongs that which measures a thing and that which does not measure [a thing]. To this [latter] belongs that which is in a thing in actuality, that which is so not in actuality, that which is homeomeric, and that which is not homeomeric. Secondly, the term 'part' (*partis*) signifies that into which a thing is divisible with respect to quality and form. In this way we say that bodies (*corpora*) are composed of matter and form and [that] definition is composed of genus and differentia."

165 *Metaph.* 7, 10, 12, 13; *An. Post.* 2.19, *Cael.* 2.1 and 3.1; and *Phys.* 1.2.

166 Aristotle, *Metaphysics 1*, 213.

167 Cf. *Lumen Gentium*, introduction, proposition 10: "Non datur sextum corpus quod scilicet sit quid preter quatuor elementorum et preter celestium corpus [pro ut habetur De Celo I (23)]" (*OA*, introduction, proposition 10: "שלא ימצא גוף ששי היינו גשם מלבד הד' יסודות והגרמים השמימיים וזה באר אריסטו' ואבן רשד במופת בספר השמים מאמר א' פרק כ"ג).".

Averroes, Long Commentary on *Metaphysics* 8, text. 12

Giunta edition (1562–1574)	*Lumen Gentium* § 1.1.1.	*Or ʿAmmim* § 1.1.1
Deinde dicit: in substantiis verum naturalibus, etc. et intedit corpora celestia, et cum dicitur rectum est ut quaedam non habeant materia, non intendit quaedam corporum celestium: omnia enim non habent materiam: sed intendit elementa quae sunt eterna secundum totum et generabilia et corruptibilia secundum partem ut dicitur est in naturalibus [...]. Materia enim in rei veritate cuius esse in potentia non invenitur nisi in substantis generabilibus et corruptibilus. Substantiae vero aeternae, quia in eis non est potentia ad corruptionem, non est in ei materia sed materia eorum est aliquid existens in actu.[168]	Quod intelligit de elementis que sunt eterna secundum totum, quamvis sint generabilia et corruptibilia secundum partem [...]. Materia, enim, secundum veritatem cuius esse est in potentia non invenitur nisi in substantiis generabilibus et corruptibilibus. Substantie, enim, eterne quia in eis non est potentia ad corruptionem non est in eis materia, sed materia eorum est aliquid existens in actu.	שהיסודות קדמונים כפי הכל עם היותם הווים ונפסדים כפי החלק [...] אמנם החומר לא ימצא זולתי בגרמים ההווים ונפסדים אבל הגרמים שהם קדמונים מאחר שאין בהם כוחיות על ההפסד אם כן אין להם חומר אבל הנושא שלהם הוא דבר נמצא לעולם בפעל

Sforno translates *substantia* as גרם, which designates "substance," but also the body,[169] such as the heavenly bodies (גרם השמים). He translates *materia* in two different ways, חומר and נושא. In *Lumen Gentium*, he uses the term *subiectum*—that is, the "material" substrate[170]—instead of *substratum*, which is often employed in the Scholastic lexicon. This shows his familiarity with the topic: taking a "modern" approach, he resolves the ambiguity in the Aristotelian text—in particular that of *Metaphysics* 8.1.1042a, in which Aristotle defines the (sensible) substances; namely, the substances affected by the movement of generation and corruption—according to which the underlying matter (*hyle hypokeimenon*) is also a substance (*ousia*).[171]

Averroes presents the distinction between sensible and non-sensible substances in his commentary on *Metaphysics* 12, text. 5; only the former are affected by the movement of generation and corruption:

---

168 Aristotle and Averroes, *Aristotelis metaphysicorum libri XIIII cum Averrois cordubensis in eosdem commentariis et epitome, Theophrasti metaphysicorum liber editio Juntina prima*, vol. 8 of Aristotle and Averroes, *Aristotelis Stagiritae omnia quae extant opera* (Venitiis, 1552; republished 1562 and 1574), 103.

169 As Warren Zev Harvey has suggested to me, Sforno considers substance in the sense of natural substances or celestial substances (i.e., bodies).

170 Cf. Sheldon Cohen, "Aristotle's Doctrine of the Material Substrate," *The Philosophical Review* 93 (1984): 171–194.

171 *Metaph.* 8.1.1042a (Aristotle, *Metaphysics 1*, 403): "Now these are the sensible substances, and all sensible substances contain matter. And the substrate is substance; in one sense matter (by matter I mean that which is not actually, but is potentially, an individual thing); and in another the formula and the specific shape (which is an individual thing and is theoretically separable); and thirdly there is the combination of the two, which alone admits of generation and destruction, and is separable in an unqualified sense—for of substances in the sense of formula some are separable and some are not. That matter is also substance is evident, etc."

> He [Aristotle] says that there are three substances: sensible substance and non-sensible substance, and sensible substance is divided into two: eternal substance, without generation and corruption, as it has been explained in *Physics*, it is the fifth body. The other substance is subject to generation and corruption and is universally acknowledged: for instance, plants and animals. He says: "the elements of which we must discern." Alexander says: one must not understand by that the substance subject to generation and corruption, but the two substances: sensible and subject to generation, and not subject to generation [etc.].[172]

As Enrico Berti emphasises,

> the division inside the sensible substance, between perishable and eternal substance is due, following Frede, to the fact that eternal substances are the crucial link between the incorruptible and the corruptible; so—he says [Frede]—Aristotle must think that the postulation of such substances is necessary to explain how eternal substances can be the principles of corruptible things.[173]

I believe that Sforno interprets Averroes in the same way as "our" modern interpreters understand Aristotle by considering the eternal substances (and particularly the heavenly bodies) to be a critical point that is midway between the incorruptible and the corruptible. In his discussion of the movement of generation and corruption, there is no real distinction between those substances that are subject to generation and corruption and the eternal substance, as is also indicated in book 12 of *Metaphysics*.[174] Even if celestial bodies have matter, it is not the same as that of the other substances, and therefore they are not subject to generation and corruption. In light of this, Sforno does not focus his discussion on the nature of the heavenly bodies,[175] but instead presupposes

---

172   Averroes, *Ibn Rushd's* Metaphysics, 72.
173   Enrico Berti, "The Program of *Metaphysics* Lambda (Chapter 1)," in *Aristotle's* Metaphysics *Lambda—New Essays*, ed. Christoph Horn (Berlin: De Gruyter, 2016), 77.
174   Cf. *Metaph.* 12.2.1069b19–20 (Aristotle, *Metaphysics 2*, 125–127): "Sensible substance is liable to change. Now if change proceeds from opposites or intermediates—not from all opposites (for speech is not white), but only from the contrary—then there must be something underlying which changes into the opposite contrary; for the contraries do not change. Further, something persists, whereas the contrary does not persist. Therefore, besides the contraries there is some third thing, the matter. Now if change is of four kinds, in respect either of substance or of quality or of quantity or of place, and if change of substance is generation or destruction in the simple sense, and change of quantity is increase or decrease, and change of affection is alteration, and change of place is locomotion, then changes must be in each case into the corresponding contrary state. It must be the matter, then, which admits of both contraries, that change. And since "that which is" is twofold, everything changes from that which is potentially to that which is actually; e.g. from potentially white to actually white. The same applies to increase and decrease. Hence not only may there be generation accidentally from that which is not, but also everything is generated from that which is, but is potentially and is not actually."
175   Cf., for example, Thomas Aquinas's Commentary on *Metaphysics* 8, lectio 1: "He shows how there is matter in natural substances which are eternal, namely, in the celestial bodies. He says that the matter in natural substances which are eternal, namely, in the celestial bodies, is not the same as that in bodies subject to generation and corruption. For perhaps such substances do not have matter, or if they do have matter, they do not have the sort that generable and corruptible bodies have, but only that which is subjected to local motion"

their existence and concentrates on introducing the elements as corporeal substances that are subject to generation and corruption.

The introduction of the statement of the *quaestio* on the elements presents some divergences:

Lumen Gentium, introduction	*Lumen Gentium*, quaestio 2	*Or 'Ammim*, quaestio 2	*Or 'Ammim*, introduction
Utrum corruptibilium elementa habuissent esse ab eterno	Utrum prima mortalium elementa habuissent esse ab eterno (Whether the first elements of perishable things are eternal.)	אם **הגרמים** הנקראים יסודות ראשונות לכל **המוחשים** הם קדמונים (Whether the bodies called "first elements," with regard to the sensible things, are eternal.)	שנית אם היסודות קדמונים

In *Or 'Ammim*, we find the expression גרם הנקרא יסודות הראשונות, meaning "bodies called first elements," and the substantive מוחש ("sensible") instead of *mortalium*. Aristotle identifies the natural bodies as the first elements in *Metaphysics* 7.2 (1028b), according to the definition of substance: "Substance is thought to be present most obviously in bodies. Hence, we call animals and plants and their parts substances, and also natural bodies (*physica somata*), such as fire, water, earth, etc."[176] A similar definition is found in the Epitome of *Metaphysics*: "Elementorum dicitur primo de eo ad quod res resolvitur proprie forme et per hunc modum quattor corpora scilicet ignis aer aqua et terra dicitur esse elementa ceterorum corporum compositum."[177]

In *Lumen Gentium*, Sforno mentions *mortalium* elements, meaning "perishables" or "corruptible substances." This idea is also in agreement with *On the Heavens* (books 3 and 4) and *On Generation and Corruption*. It seems to be evident that the four elements that compose every perishable substance in the sublunary world are themselves perishable. Since the elements were created, they were therefore either created *ex nihilo* or created from something existing in actuality or from a potential being; this kind of discussion is undoubtedly related to the argument against the Megarian school (*Metaphysics* 9, text. 5) examined in the first disputed question. In the Hebrew version, the order is inverted: the first possibility is from an existent in potency or in act; the second is out of nothing.

§ 2.1.1	§ 2.1.1
Quia si fuissent genita vel ex nihilo scilicet post purum non esse, vel ex aliquo actu existente, vel saltem potentia ente.	כי אם היו מחודשים היה התחדשותו מאיזה דבר נמצא בכח או בפועל או מלא דבר ואין

(Aquinas, *Commentary on Aristotle's* Metaphysics, trans. John P. Rowan [Chicago: Henry Regnery Co., 1961], 642).
176 *Metaph.* 7.2.1028b9–12 (Aristotle, *Metaphysics 1*, 313).
177 Cf. Mantino, *Averroys epithoma*, 7ᵛ.

In *Or 'Ammim*, Sforno does not translate *ex nihilo*, but *post [purum] non esse*, literally מלא דבר ואין. In his philosophical work, he employs the expression יש מאין,[178] which translates the Latin formula *ex nihilo*, on only one occasion. In classical Jewish terminology, the expression מלא דבר ואין is attested in Maimonides's *Guide of the Perplexed* (2.13), Gersonides's *Wars of the Lord* (part 6), Crescas's *Light of the Lord* (2.4), and Isaac Abravanel's *New Heavens*.

In line with the principles of the Aristotelian system, Sforno states that it is impossible that the elements were created out of nothing, because *ex nihilo nihil fit*/דבר לא יתהווה דבר כי אמנם מלא דבר התחדשותם שהיה לומר ראוי: "One ought to say that their origination is from nothing, even though nothing can come to be from nothing." It is possible that Sforno had learned of this tradition either through Thomas Aquinas or through contemporary scholars: I would suggest that he might have read Calo Calonimus's *Liber de mundi creatione physicis*,[179] in which we find both formulations, *ex nihilo nihili fit* and *ex non esse puro*.

Calonimus, *Liber de mundi creatione physicis*	Calonimus, *Liber de mundi creatione physicis*	Thomas Aquinas, *On Physics* (lectio 14 191a23–b34)	Thomas Aquinas, *On Physics* (lectio 9 187a27–188a18) *Summa contra Gentiles*, book 2[180]	Ludovico Boccadiferro, *Explanatio libri I. physicorum Aristotelis*
Ideo Aristoteles primo Physicorum tex. comma 34 non	Averroes autem non defecit loqui contra opinantes creationem mundi ex nihilo	Ex nihilo nihil fit.[181]	Ex nihilo nihil fiat.[182]	Ex nihilo nihil fit.

178 Cf. §16.3.1.
179 Calonimus, *Liber de mundi creatione physicis*.
180 Thomas Aquinas, *Summa contra Gentiles*, ch. 16: "Ex hoc autem confutatur error antiquorum philosophorum qui ponebant materiae omnino nullam causam esse, eo quod actionibus particularium agentium semper videbant aliquid actioni praeiacere: ex quo opinionem sumpserunt, omnibus communem, quod ex nihilo nihil fit. Quod quidem in particularibus agentibus verum est. Ad universalis autem agentis, quod est totius esse activum, cognitionem nondum pervenerant, quem nihil in sua actione praesupponere necesse est"; ch. 34: "Communis autem sententia est omnium philosophorum ex nihilo nihil fieri"; ch. 37: "Communis enim philosophorum positio ponentium ex nihilo nihil fieri, ex quo prima ratio procedebat, veritatem habet secundum illud fieri quod ipsi considerabant" and "Et hanc quidem factionem non attigerunt primi naturales, quorum erat communis sententia ex nihilo nihil fieri."
181 Thomas Aquinas, *Commentary on Physics* 1: "Et ad hoc ponendum eos infirmitas intellectus coegit; quia nescierunt hanc rationem solvere, per quam videbatur probari quod ens non generatur. Quia si ens fit, aut fit ex ente aut ex non ente: et utrumque horum videtur esse impossibile, scilicet quod ens fiat ex ente et quod fiat ex non ente. Quod enim ex ente aliquid fieri sit impossibile, ex hoc manifestum est, quia id quod est non fit; nihil enim est antequam fiat: et ens iam est; ergo non fit. Quod etiam ex non ente aliquid fieri sit impossibile, ex hoc manifestum est, quia semper oportet aliquid subiici ei quod fit, ut supra ostensum est, et ex nihilo nihil fit. Et ex hoc concludebatur quod entis non erat generatio neque corruptio."
182 Aquinas, 1: "Duo autem supponebat Anaxagoras, ex quibus procedebat. Quorum primum est quod etiam ab omnibus naturalibus philosophis supponebatur, quod scilicet ex nihilo nihil fiat. Et hoc est quod dicit, quod Anaxagoras ex hoc videbatur opinari esse principia infinita, quia accipiebat communem opinionem omnium philosophorum naturalium esse veram; hanc scilicet, quod id quod simpliciter non est, nullo modo fiat. Quia enim hoc supponebant tanquam principium, ad diversas opiniones processerunt. [...] Dicebat enim quod contraria fiunt ex alterutris: videmus enim ex calido fieri frigidum et e

(cont.)

Calonimus, *Liber de mundi creatione physicis*	Calonimus, *Liber de mundi creatione physicis*	Thomas Aquinas, *On Physics* (lectio 14 191a23–b34)	Thomas Aquinas, *On Physics* (lectio 9 187a27–188a18) *Summa contra Gentiles*, book 2	Ludovico Boccadiferro, *Explanatio libri I. physicorum Aristotelis*
demonstravit quod impossibile sit ut ex nihilo aliquid fiat.[183]	nam 8 Physicorum comma 4 dixit "et hac diffinitione motus apparet bene impossibile esse generationem esse ex non esse puro."[184]			

Sforno quotes *Physics* 1.77 (1.8.191a), "what comes to be must do so either from what is or from what is not, [both of which are impossible],"[185] and observes that if the elements were created from nothing, then there must previously have been a void, but this is impossible: "Generation *ex nihilo* is an impossibility, for it demands a void to hold previously non-existent bodies, and such a void has been disproved in earlier treatises."[186] He argues that it is also impossible that the elements were created from an actual being, because if something exists in act, then something temporally prior to it would have to have existed and the process would be repeated *ad infinitum*. The elements would then have been generated from a potential being, such as prime matter, but in this case too, Sforno argues that this is absurd, basing himself on the definition of matter given by Aristotle in *Metaphysics* 9 and 12,[187] *Physics* 1.9 (192a31–32),[188] *On Generation and Corruption* 1.4 (320a2–3)[189] and 2.6 (334b),[190] and Averroes's commentary on *On the Heavens* 3, text. 29, as indicated in the eleventh proposition:

11. Materia prima nunquam habuit esse denudata forma. Hoc autem habetur a Philosopho in lib. De Generatione II, 6 et ratione et auctoritate Aven R. in lib. De Celo III, 29.	שהחמר הראשון לא היה בשום זמן מופשט מכל צורה

converso. Et ex hoc concludebat quod, cum ex nihilo nihil fiat, quod unum contrariorum praeexistit in altero."

183 Calonimus, *Liber de mundi creatione physicis* 2.4.
184 Calonimus, 2.4.
185 *Si igitur aliquid fuerit ens non est ex non ente.*
186 Cf. *Cael.* 3.2.302a; *Phys.* 4.6, 8, and 9.
187 Cf. Mantino, *Averroys epithoma*, 7ᵛ: "Materia autem dicitur diversimode: nam quaedam est materia prima que est imperceptibilis. Quedam vero hominis forma scilicet ipsa elementa quattuor que sunt materia corporum compositum."
188 Aristotle, *Physics*, 95: "For what I mean by matter is precisely the ultimate underlying subject, common to all the things of Nature, presupposed as their substantive, not incidental, constituent."
189 Aristotle, *Coming-to-be*, 201: "Matter, in the chief and strictest sense of the word, is the substratum which admits of coming-to-be and passing-away."
190 Aristotle, 303: "The other bodies will result from the contraries (that is, from the elements) when mixed together, and the elements will result from the contraries existing somehow potentially—not in the sense in which matter exists potentially."

Averroes explained in his Commentary on *On the Heavens*[191] that prime matter is always devoid of forms and that it is neither a substance nor any of the other ten categories of being. It is therefore pure potency, and it is impossible for it to exist in potency and act at the same time, as proved in the refutation of the Megarian in *Metaphysics* 9, text. 5.

If prime matter were to exist in actuality, it would occupy a space (and following Aristotle's definition, space only exists when bodies exist because of their corporeal quantities), and therefore this space would have previously been void, which is impossible.[192] Therefore, prime matter exists in potency only and is disposed to receive the forms of the elements; no form exists without a matter that is proper to it.

27. Nulla materialis forma datur esse nisi in materia sibi propria. Hoc autem habetur ratione et auctoritate Aven R. in commento Physicorum VIII, 46.	כ״ז שלא תמצא צורה חמרית זולתי בחמר מיוחד אליה. וזה התבאר במופת אבן רשד בביאור ספר השמע מאמר ח׳ פרק מ״ו.

Matter and form are therefore jointly considered the first substrate (*subiectum*/נושא), because matter needs forms in order to become matter in actuality, and forms need matter in order to take on a form. It is therefore impossible to posit the existence of matter devoid of form, because forms are also disposed for a specific matter.

The substrate and the dispositions (*dispositio*/הכנה) that are proper to it temporally precede the movement of generation and corruption, because the generated substance does not exist before a particular instance of matter takes on a specific form. A generated thing attains its specific form only after its qualities have been actualised. As Averroes explained in the Long Commentary on *Physics* 8, text. 46, generation takes place when matter and form are combined in a particular substrate.

In view of the Aristotelian and Averroean arguments, Sforno claims that the movement of generation and corruption is not eternal because the agent, the substrate, its dispositions—meaning the active and passive powers in the substrate—and the ultimate goal are prior to the movement of generation and corruption. He then argues that the elements cannot be eternal because their parts are generable and corruptible (as Aristotle claims in *On the Heavens* 3.6.305a); the argument is that if their parts are corruptible, then their whole would also be corruptible, because the whole is by definition the composite of its parts (*On the Heavens* 1.3.270a).

These assumptions are presented in Sforno's introduction:

---

191 Cf. Aristotle and Averroes, *De coelo* 3, text. 29.
192 Aristotle and Averroes, *De coelo*, 3, text. 29: "Si aliquid in potential fuerit denudatum ab actu illus enim quod est in potentis si denudatum fueri a forma et ab omnimus accidentibus, necessario erunt illic dimensiones abstrace in quibus existet corpus generatum et hoc dicitur vaccum quamvis vacuus esse contingit dicentibus primum corpus generari ex non corpe simpliciter aut non ex corpore in actu."

12. Nullum corruptibile habuit esse ab eterno.
Hoc autem habetur ratione et auctoritate Philosophi in lib. De Celo I, 124.

י״ב שאין שום דבר נפסד קדמון. וזה התבאר במופת אריסטוטולו בספר השמים והעולם מאמר א׳ פרק קכ״ד.

13. Cuiuslibet elementi partes conveniunt cum suo toto nomine et diffinitione.
Hoc autem habetur a Philosopho et Aven R. in lib. De Celo I, 19.

י״ג שכל אחד מחלקי היסוד מסכים עם הכל שלו בשם ובגדר וזה באר אריסטוטיליס ואבן רשד בספר השמים מאמר א׳ פרק י״ט.

14. Nulla elementorum pars est incorruptibilis.
Hoc autem habetur a Philosopho in lib. De Celo III, 52.

י״ד שאין שום חלק יסוד שיהיה בלתי נפסד. וזה בארו אריסטוטיליס בספר השמים מאמר ג׳ פרק נ״ב.

15. Nullum elementorum habuit esse secundum totum corruptum.
Hoc autem habetur ab Aven R. in lib. De Generatione II, 37.

ט״ו שמעולם לא נפסד אחד מהיסודות בכללו. וזה באר אבן רשד בביאור ספר ההויה וההפסד מאמר שני פרק ל״ז.

This is evident if one observes the combination of a simple body that is a compound of two—or more—elements, as a result of which their properties change into contrary properties. This kind of movement is considered a substantial change, because it occurs as a result of the movement of generation and corruption. The argument is clearly connected to that of *Metaphysics* 12.8 (1069 a–b) and *On Generation and Corruption* 2.6 (333b–334b),[193] and it was also discussed in the foregoing *quaestio*. A counterargument to corruptibility is that if the parts of the elements change and perish, then the whole that they

---

[193] Aristotle, *Coming-to-be*, 295, 303: "Further, according to Empedocles, growth, too, would be impossible except by addition: for in his view Fire increases by Fire and 'Earth increases its own body, and ether increases ether,' and these are additions; and it is not generally held that things which increase do so in this way. And it is much more difficult for him to give an account of coming-to-be by a natural process. For the things which come-to-be naturally all come-to-be, either always or generally, in a particular way, and exceptions or violations of the invariable or general rule are the results of chance and luck. What, then, is the reason why man always or generally comes-to-be from man, and why wheat (and not an olive) comes-to-be from wheat? Or does bone come-to be, if the elements are put together in a certain manner? For, according to Empedocles, nothing comes-to-be by their coming together by chance but by their coming together in a certain proportion. What, then, is the cause of this? It is certainly not Fire or Earth; but neither is it Love and Strife, for the former is a cause of 'association' only and the latter of dissociation only. No: the cause is the substance of each thing and not merely, as he says, "a mingling and separation of things mingle"; and chance, not proportion, is the name applied to these happenings: for it is possible for things to be mixed by chance. [...] Is the following a possible solution based on the fact that there are greater and less degrees in hot and cold? When one of them is actually in being without qualification, the other will be potentially in existence; but when neither completely exists but (because they mix and destroy one another's excesses) there is a hot which, for a hot, is cold, and a cold Ih, for a cold, is hot, then the result will be thaI neither their matter nor either of the two contraries will be actually in existence without qualification but an intermediate, and according as it is potentially more hot than cold or, vice versa, it will possess a power of heating greater in proportion—whether double or treble or in some such ratio—than its power of cooling. The other bodies will result

constitute is not completely corrupted, since the whole is never entirely corrupted due to its resistance. This resistance is introduced here in order to avoid the positing of a void so as to account for the movement of the elements.

Dicatur quod horum totum non corrumpitur a contrario propter proportionalem qualitatum equalitatem inter ipsa secundum totum observatam, quare fit resistentia ad totalem corruptionem	ואם יטעון החולק ויאמר שהכל שלהם לא ישתנה מהפכו מפני שווי יחס איכויותיהם אשר בו ימלט הכל שלהם מהיות נפסד בפעולת הפכו

The resistance is produced by the equal proportion of the qualities of the parts of the elements. Sforno does not describe the nature of this process, though he does mention the idea that the complete corruption of the whole is impossible because of *proportionalem equalitatem qualitatum*/שווי יחס איכויותיהם. Aristotle mentions the idea of an "equal ratio of qualities" in connection with the process of generation and corruption in *On Generation and Corruption* 2.1 (329a and sec.) and *Physics* 4.8. However, he did not develop this concept, and his commentators[194] attempted to discern excatly what the "equal measurement of qualities" meant.

In his commentary on Galen's *Elements*, Averroes claims that when these kinds of qualities are associated with different ratios (*proportio*), this can generate a new body. Each prime element is characterised by different qualities: fire is hot and dry, water is cold and wet, air is hot and wet, and earth is cold and dry:[195]

> The matter of the simple bodies is their common component that exists only in potency, as will become clear, while their forms are the four simple qualities, which are at the extreme. (I mean the two of them that are active and passive, for example, the hot and dry that are in fire and in the cold and wet that are in water.)[196]

The corruption is only associated with the parts and does not affect prime matter, which was previously predisposed to receive the forms of the elements. In addition to this, matter cannot be corruptible according to Averroes's own defi-

---

from the contraries (that is, from the elements) when mixed together, and the elements will result from the contraries existing somehow potentially—not in the sense in which matter exists potentially but in the manner already explained."

194 Cf. Philoponus, *in Phys.* 216a; Simplicius, *in Phys.* 225a33.
195 *Gen. corr.* 2.2.331a (Aristotle, *Coming-to-be*, 281): "Air will result from Fire by the change of one quality; for Fire, as we said, is hot and dry, while Air is hot and moist, so that Air will result if the dry is overpowered by the moist. Again, Water will result from Air, if the hot is overpowered by the cold; for Air, as we said, is hot and moist, while Water is cold and moist, so that Water will result if the hot undergoes a change. In the same way, too, Earth will result from Water, and Fire from Earth; for both members of each pair have qualities which correspond to one another, since Water is moist and cold, and Earth is cold and dry, and so, when the moist is overpowered, Earth will result. Again, since Fire is dry and hot, and Earth is cold and dry, if the cold were to pass away, Fire will result from Earth."
196 Jon McGinnis, "Natural Knowledge in the Arabic Middle Ages," in *Wrestling with Nature: From Omens to Science*, ed. Peter Harrison, Ronald L. Numbers, and Michael H. Shank (Chicago: Chicago University Press, 2011), 71.

nition, because natural change is a process of coming-to-be out of potency and potency requires matter. Sforno's position is similar to that of Zabarella: the element is moved *per se* by its own form, as though by an agent, for through that agent, the natural motion in the element itself immediately arises. In other words, an element effects the change proper to it if it is unimpeded. The agent is prior in the *ordine naturae*, and the effect, which arises through the combination of what is acted upon and the resistance that follows from the patient's prior properties, is posterior.[197]

The resistance to the corruption of the whole is never contingent, and consequentially it does not occur by chance, as Aristotle explains in *On the Heavens* 2.8 (289b).[198] Therefore, if it does not occur by chance, it is produced by a voluntary agent for a goal, as proved in the first *quaestio* on the movement of generation and corruption.

6. Quecumque sunt preter voluntatem et cognitionem dicuntur fieri casu. Hoc autem habetur a Philosopho Physicorum II, 51.	ו' שכל מה שנעשה בלתי כוונה ורצון יאמר עליו שנעשה במקרה וזה באר ארסטו' ספר השמע מאמר ב' פרק נ"א.
8. Quicquid est in pluribus observatum non habet esse casu. Hoc autem infertur a Philosopho in lib. De Celo II, 45 et Physicorum II, 48.	ח' שכל מה שיהיה בדברים רבים לא יפול בהם במקרה, זה יתבאר מדברי אריסטו' בספר השמים והעולם מאמר ב' פרק מ"ה ובספר השמע מאמר ב' פרק מ"ח.

On the other hand, if there is no cause, it is therefore produced by chance:[199]

Prout habetur a Philosopho Physicorum II, 51 ubi dicit: «Sed ex causis que sunt sine voluntate et sine cogitatione: et tunc dicuntur quod contingent casu etc.»	שבאר ארסטו' בספר השמע מאמר ב' פרק נ"א באמרו: הסבות אשר הם בלתי כוונה ורצון יאמר עליהם שהיו במקרה

---

[197] James E. McGuire, "Natural Motion and Its Causes: Newton on the 'Vis Insita' of Bodies," in *Self-Motion: From Aristotle to Newton*, ed. Mary Louise Gill and James G. Lennox (Princeton, NJ: Princeton University Press, 1994), 320–321.

[198] Aristotle, *On the Heavens*, 185: "But it is not reasonable to suppose that the speeds of the stars are related to one another as the size of their circles. That the circles should have their speeds proportional to their magnitudes is no absurdity, indeed it is a necessity, but that each of the stars in them should show the same proportion is not reasonable. If it is by necessity that the one which moves in the path of the larger circle is the swifter, then it is clear that even if the stars were transposed into each others' circles, still the one in the larger circle would be swifter, and the other slower; but in that case they would possess no motion of their own, but be carried by the circles. If on the other hand it has happened by chance, yet it is equally unlikely that chance should act so that in every case the larger circle is accompanied by a swifter movement of the star in it. That one or two should show this correspondence is conceivable, but that it should be universal seems fantastic. In any case, chance is excluded from natural events, and whatever applies everywhere and to all cases is not to be ascribed to chance."

[199] §2.2.2.

14 The Role of Chance in the Sublunary World

Sforno's arguments are clearly related to the discussion of divine causality. In this sense, he follows Averroes's position, which suggests that the primary difference between the sub- and superlunary worlds is the impossibility that chance events occur in the superlunary world. Chance is therefore limited to the sublunar realm, and it is manifested in occurrences that are ascribed to an accidental cause. An *accidens* is a phenomenon that is not regularly observed in nature among sensible things, meaning substances composed of matter and form, and it is due to the contingency of the efficient cause. For this reason, Averroes distinguishes between two kinds of agents, one kind that acts in the superlunary world and another that acts in the sublunary world.

In light of this distinction, Sforno mentions a passage from Averroes's Commentary on *On the Heavens*: "The eternal things only have an agent according to likeness."[200] This introduces the idea that there are two different agents, the *agens verum* and the *agens secundum similitudinem*. Sforno did not develop a specific argument in order to explain the existence of two agents, but he offers a few lines in which it is possible to recognise that he was acquainted with this debate. Considering the general context, since philosophers in the Jewish tradition did not focus on this specific issue in relation to the Long Commentary on *On the Heavens*, it is therefore clear that Sforno had read the Scholastic sources.

Jean de Jandun explains Averroes's position in his *Quaestiones super metaphysicam* (book 2, *quaestio* 5)[201] and suggests that eternal substances are not caused "ab agente simpliciter" (or *agens verum*), but rather "ab agente secundum similitudinem." Considering the complexity of the question ("notandum que multe sunt difficultates que quasi habentur pro demonstrationis pro alia parte"),[202] the definition of "agens secundum similitudinem" is presented only in opposition to the "agens simpliciter et proprium": if eternal substances were created by a true agent, which brings something from non-being into being, then there would be an instant in which the eternal substance did not exist, and this is absurd because it would not then be eternal.[203] Therefore, the eternal substances were created by an agent according to resemblance (or likeness),

---

200 "Res enim eterne non habent agens nisi secundum similitudinem neque habent ex quator causis nisi formalem et finalem et si habuerit aliquid quasi agens non erit nisi inquantum est forma illi et perservas ipsum": Averroes, *Commentary on On the Heavens* 4, text. 1.

201 Jean de Jandun, *Quaestiones in duodecim libros metaphysicae* (Venetiis, 1586), 63: "Illud quod conservatur ab aliquo extrinseco qud est nobilius et perfectius eo dependet ab secundum similitudinem quia hoc intelligitur per agens secundum similitudinem ut vult Commentatore 4 Coeli Com. 1 aliquid extrinsecum a quo aliquid dependet in esse et conservati sed substantia aeterna causata dependet ab extrinserco in concersari et in esse ut Deo qui est nobilior omnibus quid autem hoc sit verum patet ex XII huius ubi dicitur ab hoc principio dependet coelum et tota natura."

202 De Jandun, 63.

203 De Jandun, 62: "Si substantia aeterna causata esset ab aliquo vero agente prout agnes distinguitur ab aliis causis tunc simul esset et non esset: hoc est impossibile, quia est contra primam dignitatem. Consequentia patet quia omnis productio ab agente simpliciter est a non esse in esse tunc si producitur substantia eterna a non esse in esse, vel in alio, si in eodem instanti producitur esse in quo non est tunc aliquid simul est et non est et hoc est impossibile. Si in alio instanti habet non esse, tunc inter illa duo instantia esst tempus medium in quo nec esset nec non esset, quod est impossibile quia de quolibet affirmatio vel negatio etc."

which means that they were created from something *ab extrinseco*, which gives them essence and permanence.[204]

15 The Movement of Generation and Corruption and the Compound

In the section *quaestio*, Sforno offers a description of the combination of the elements in the spheres (§ 2.2.3), in which he states that the elements change into those with contrary properties because there is a common matter disposed to receive the forms of the contrary properties. The central issue is the priority of the matter with respect to the dispositions of the forms of the elements. *Lumen Gentium* and *Or ʿAmmim* offer two different descriptions, even though both versions are founded on the same sources, meaning *On Generation and Corruption* 1, text. 54 and 87, *Metaphysics* 8, text. 14, and *Physics* 8, text. 46. According to Averroes's position in *Physics*, the common matter is not immediately disposed for elements, and the different forms of the elements have the same matter as their substrate.

In *Or ʿAmmim*, Sforno explicitly mentions *Guide of the Perplexed* 2.19:[205]

> Thereupon we again put a question to Aristotle, saying to him: Since the mixture of the elements is the cause of the various matters being predisposed to receive the various forms, what is it that prepared this first matter so that a part of it receives the form of fire and part of it the form of earth and that which is intermediate between these two parts is prepared to receive the forms of water and of air, while at the same time the matter of the universe is one and common to all things? Why is the matter of earth more fitted for the form of earth and the matter of fire for the form of fire? Thereupon Aristotle gave an answer to this, saying: This has been made necessary by the differences between the various

---

[204] De Jandun, 65: "Sed tamen dicendum secundum fidem et veritatem quod nihil citra primum est aeternum, sed omnia inceperunt de novo esse et per consequens producta fuerunt a primo principio tanquam ab agente per creationem ex nihilo saltem substantiae abstractae. Et illa creatio non est motus, nec generatio univoce dictus cum motu inferiorum, sed alia productio supernaturalis que non posset convinci ex sensatis et ex naturalibus ex quibus procedunt philosophi naturaliter loquentes, sed tament firmiter hoc credo et scio, non de ratione orta ex sensatis et hos firmiter facit scripture doctoribus reverenter assentire unde ex hoc quid nescio demonstrare ex sensatis nec posset quia est super sensibilia et natura. Tunc simpliciter credendo et fideliter habeo meritum et in hoc est probatur creationis et salvationis excellentia vigoris super agens quolibet naturale."

[205] See Warren Zev Harvey's paper "Averroes & Maimonides in Rabbi Obadiah Sforno's *Lumen Gentium* (1537, 1548)," presented at the "Medieval Jewish Thought & the Italian Renaissance" conference held at the Warburg Institute on 12 April 2021 for an alternative translation: "How astonishing are the words of Maimonides, which he wrote in the *Guide of the Perplexed*, part II, chapter 19, in resolution of this objection. He responded as a defender of Aristotle, and said that the differences in the [four] elements derive from differences in place, whether close to the encompassing celestial sphere or far away from it, as if its place was the cause of the existence of the form. However, sense perception testifies to the contrary. For when the part of an element changes into its contrary form, the part undergoing change is in its place, and does not change its place until after it has changed its form. This is because the form is the cause of a compound thing's being in its place, and not the reverse. Thus, the air [over dry land] is right above the surface of the earth and in the place of water, yet its place does not turn it into water. Furthermore, it is clear that prime matter, whose existence is wholly potential, is in itself nowhere in actuality, so how could its place be a cause of its form?"

places, for these differences have made it necessary for this one matter to have various dispositions. For the part that is near the encompassing sphere, was endowed by the latter with an impress of subtlety and swiftness of motion and nearness to the nature of the sphere. Consequently it received, in virtue of this disposition, the form of fire. And the more distant matter is from the encompassing sphere in the direction of the center of the earth, the thicker and denser and less luminous it becomes, so that it becomes earth. The same cause obtains with regard to water and air. Thus this is necessary; for it is absurd that the matter in question should not be in a place, or that the encompassing sphere should be the center of the earth, and the center of the earth the encompassing sphere. This has been made necessary by particularization of matter by means of various forms; I mean by this the disposition to receive various forms. Thereupon we put a question to him, saying: Is the matter of the encompassing sphere—I mean to say the heavens—the same as the matter of the elements? He said: No. That is another matter and those are other forms. And the term "body," applied to the bodies that are with us and to the heavenly bodies, is equivocal, as has been explained by latter-day thinkers. All this has been demonstrated.[206]

Different elements occupy different places, and Aristotle introduces the notion that they have natural places. He deals with this concept in many passages of his works,[207] particularly *Physics* 8, text. 46, *On the Heavens* (1.8.277b and *passim*),[208] and *Meteorology*. The main idea presented in the Aristotelian system is that the earth is at the centre of the world and that it is surrounded by water, air, and fire (cf. *Or 'Ammim* § 2.3.2).[209] Sforno introduces the notion of the natural place of the elements in the sublunar world in order to explain that they have a common matter. This idea reflects the Avicennian conception of prime matter, yet "prime matter first exists without the form of any of the four elements and [...] then receives a form by virtue of the place it occupies within the sublunary region and the resulting rapidity with which it moves."[210] The common matter is not immediately disposed to receive the elements because the elements maintain their natural place, which is determined by their own properties.

In the *Book of the Khazar*, Judah Halevi presents the opinions of Aristotle and other philosophers,[211] which is that prime matter has neither potential

---

206 Maimonides, *Guide* 2.19 (2:304–305).
207 *Phys.* 4.1–5; *Phys.* 8.7.260a, and *passim*.
208 Aristotle, *On the Heavens*, 79: "It cannot be objected that an external agent is the cause of the elements moving up or down, nor that they are moved by force, the 'extrusion' which some allege. If that were so, a larger quantity of fire would move more slowly upwards, and a larger quantity of earth more slowly downwards; whereas on the contrary the larger quantity of fire or earth always moves more quickly than a smaller to its natural place."
209 As Warren Zev Harvey has suggested to me, Sforno leaves the question open because in the original Aristotelian text, there is no reference to form and place in relation to the elements; in contrast, Maimonides's interpretation of Aristotle's thought connects the form of the elements with their natural place.
210 Cf. Herbert A. Davidson, *Alfarabi, Avicenna, and Averroes, on Intellect: Their Cosmologies, Theories of the Active Intellect, and Theories of Human Intellect* (New York: Oxford University Press, 1992), 78.
211 Halevi, *Kuzari* 5.2 (p. 249): "Philosophers call this object matter, adding that our intelligence grasps its meaning only imperfectly, since imperfection is its nature; that it does not really exist, and therefore cannot claim any predicate, and although it only exists vir-

nor actual existence.[212] Prime matter is only identifiable when it is attached to form. Halevi pursues his argument in a description of the generation of the elements according to the biblical account of creation. Without any doubt, this is another interesting aspect that may confirm Sforno's familiarity with this passage from the *Book of the Khazar*.

Sforno argues that the elements were not brought out of nothing. Instead, they were generated from an actual substrate, which was temporally prior to them. This substrate is a compound in which prime matter and forms are combined together and the elements were in the compound in potency. As I will show later on, in his explanation of the creation account, Sforno interpreted Genesis 1:1 according to this model. The compound that potentially contained the elements was what the "ancients"[213] called *confusum sive chaos*, and Aristotle's explanation includes a reference to Anaximander in *Physics* 3.4 203b6–28. Sforno not only offers a definition of a compound; he also introduces a religious interpretation of a philosophical notion (§ 2.5.1). However, *confusum sive chaos* is the expression that he employs in the explanation of the biblical verse (Gen 1:2), which demonstrates a physical phenomenon, and Sforno, without mentioning the Bible, explicates a similar idea in reference to Anaximander.

Sforno refutes the subsequent argument that creation out of nothingness is impossible (§ 2.5.2). If the elements were created, then they would occupy a place, and the place that they are currently occupying would necessarily have previously been empty. He follows Aristotle's claim in *On the Heavens* 1.9.279a that "there is neither place nor void nor time outside the heaven."[214] The elements were generated together with their place in the same moment of creation, because "creatus est locus in quo habuerunt creata vel producta existere." The "created" is the "place" in which created beings and generated things exist—or in the Hebrew version, ובכן נשיב ונאמר שעם היסודות או נושאם נברא יחדיו אותו המקום אשר הם בו עתה—and this space that they are now occupying was created together with the elements or their substrate. Sforno comprehends the creation as a compound that exists from non-existence.[215]

---

tually, its predicate is corporeal. Aristotle says that it is, so to speak, ashamed to appear naked, and therefore only shows itself clothed in a form. Some people believe that the 'water' spoken of in the biblical account of the creation is an appellation for this matter, and that 'the spirit of the Lord hovering over the surface of the water' only expresses the divine will which penetrates all atoms of matter, with which He does what, how, and when He desires, as the potter with the shapeless clay. The absence of form and order is called darkness and tōhū wabōhū."

212 Cf. Yochanan Silman, *Philosopher and Prophet: Judah Halevi, the Kuzari and the Evolution of His Thought* (Albany, NY: SUNY Press 1995), 31.

213 Cf. the discussion in *Phys.* 1.4, in particular 1.4.187a23 and ff. (Aristotle, *Physics*, 41–43): "The other school, to which Empedocles and Anaxagoras belong, start from the first with both unity and multiplicity; for they assume an undistinguished confusum, from which the constituents of things are sifted out. But they differ in this, that Empedocles supposes the course of Nature to return upon itself, coming round again periodically to its starting-point; while Anaxagoras makes it move on continuously without repeating itself. Moreover, he assumes an unlimited number of distinguishable substances, from the first, as well as an unlimited number of uniform particles in each substance; whereas Empedocles has only his four so-called elements."

214 Aristotle, *On the Heavens*, 91.

215 I would suggest a strange analogy between the compound conceived as the space containing all bodies or a subtle form of materiality in ancient Vedic texts. Cf. Jonathan Duquette and K. Ramasubramanian, "Is Space Created? Reflections on Śaṅkara's Philosophy and Philosophy of Physics," *Philosophy East and West* 60 (2010): 517–533.

16 Matter, the Elements, and the Movement of Generation and Corruption in Sforno's Exegetical Interpretation

Sforno employs biblical verses in order to help him to understand the Aristotelian/Averroean system, providing an original interpretation of the philosophical corpus. A similar phenomenon can be observed in his exegetical works; in other words, his biblical commentaries incorporate elements of philosophy, reflecting analogous ideas exposed in his philosophical pamphlet. He appeals to the Torah in order to find a "rational" solution, as in his view, philosophy was insufficiently equipped to answer the questions he addresses. For this reason, the biblical authority replaces the opinion of the philosophers: these questions are always resolved according to the Bible.

According to Sforno, creation was instantaneous (*creationem fuisse in instante*), meaning that it took place at the absolute beginning of time (*in principio temporis quod idem est quod instans*).

כי אמנם הראשית המוחלט אשר הוא ראשית הזמן הוא רגע בלתי מתחלק אשר אינו
חלק מחלקי הזמן כנזכר לעיל ובזה הודיעה שהיתה הבריאה בלתי זמן

However, Sforno mentions Averroes's commentary: "Those who speak of creation say that the agent brings forth every existent anew, and there is therefore no need for a matter on which he acts, but he creates all."[216] Averroes, following Themistius's interpretation, discerns two schools, one of which supports ongoing creation (*latitatio*) and one of which supports creation and origination (*creatio*). The first believes that things are created eternally and that the agent is only a mover, while the second believes that the agent creates from nothing and that there is no pre-existing matter, which was the position of the Asha'rites (*Loquentibus*), the Christians, and Ioannes Christianus (John Philoponus)[217] in his interpretation of al-Fārābī's "De libro de entibus transmutatis" (*The Changing Beings/al-Mawjudat al-mutaghayyira*).[218] Similarly, in *Guide of the Perplexed* 1.74, Maimonides presents the same distinction in accordance with the Kalam doctrines:[219]

Guide of the Perplexed 1.74

Accordingly its particularization in respect of a certain shape or a certain size or place or accident and a particular time and therewithal the admissibility of all this being different, is a proof of the existence of someone who particularizes, who has freedom of choice, and who has	The third of the premises assumed by the author of this method is that there is no sensible being except substances and accidents, I mean to say the atoms and such of their accidents as he believes in. But if the body is composed of matter and form, as our adversary has demonstrated, it

---

216 *LG* §2.5.2.
217 Cf. John Philoponus, *De opificio mundi* 1–3.
218 Cf. Moritz Steinschneider, "Al Farabi (Alfarabius), des arabischen philosophen Leben und Schriften," *Mémoires de l'Académie impériale des sciences de St. Pétersbourg* 13, no. 4 (1869): 122.
219 Pines supposes that Maimonides also employed the *De libro de entibus transmutatis*; see Maimonides, *Guide*, 1: lxxxv.

(*cont.*)

Guide of the Perplexed 1.74

willed one of two admissible possibilities. Now the fact that the world as a whole or any part of it requires someone who particularizes is a proof of its being created in time. For there is no difference between your saying someone who particularizes or who makes or who creates or who brings into existence or who creates in time or who purposes the universe—all these terms being intended to signify one single notion. They ramify this method into very many subdivisions of a general or a particular nature. Thus they say: the earth's being under the water is not more appropriate than its being above the water. Who therefore has particularized that place for it? And the sun's being circular is not more appropriate than its being square or triangular, as all shapes bear the same relation to the bodies endowed with shapes.[220]

ought to be demonstrated that the first matter and the first form are subject to generation and corruption. If this is done, the demonstration of the coming-into-being of the world in time will be true.[221]

In *Or 'Ammim*, Sforno masterfully connects Averroes's commentary with Ecclesiastes 11:5: "You do not know the work of God, who makes all." A comparison of this verse with his exegetical commentary on Ecclesiastes reveals that he views creation as "absolute creation" because God created not only the compound, but also the matter and the form.

Sforno on Ecclesiastes 11:5	*Or 'Ammim* § 2.5.2
ככה לא תדע את מעשה האלהים שהיא הבריאה אשר יעשה את הכל שבזה המעשה לא המורכב בלבד הוא עושה אבל יעשה את הכל גם החומר והצורה	זה ביאר שלמה בחכמתו בספר קהלת באמרו **ככה לא תדע את מעשה האלהים אשר יעשה את הכל**

In *Lumen Gentium*, the conclusion is introduced by Genesis 1:1 and its explanation, which is exactly the same as the one that Sforno offers in his Bible commentary:

---

220 Maimonides, *Guide* 1.74 (1:218).
221 Maimonides, 1.74 (1:217–218).

Lumen Gentium § 2.6	Sforno on Gen 1:1	
Quare Sacrum Genesis Documentum primo [1:1] docens huiusmodi elementorum productionem, dicit: illa facta esse ex confuso quodam prius creato. Quare dicit Deum in principio, scilicet in instanti, quod scilicet fuit totius temporis tunc futuri principium cuius tamen nulla fuit pars creasse celum et terram.	**In the beginning** that is the beginning of time. This is a first, indivisible moment prior to which there was no time. **Of God's creating.** He made nothing into something. Time is not involved in this at all.	בראשית בתחלת הזמן והוא רגע ראשון בלתי מתחלק שלא היה זמן קודם לו ברא עשה אינו ישנו ובזה לא יפול זמן כלל

Nonetheless, Creation is a creation that occurs in an instant (בראשית), and the elements were generated from a compound that was prior to them. Even though this position seems to have some analogies with the Platonic view of creation from pre-existent matter, as expressed in *Timaeus*, Sforno does not accept Plato's position, as I will explain later on.

The Torah mentions the existence of a compound that contained the elements in potency in the expression *terra autem erat confusum et perplexum*/ והארץ היתה תהו ובהו. The interpretation of "תהו ובהו" ("Tohu and Bohu") corresponds to the idea that everything—meaning the matter and form of the elements—was jumbled together in the compound, which the philosophers also called "chaos." Similarly, Averroes explains in his commentary on *Physics* 8, text. 46, that there is a matter in potency that is disposed to receive the forms of the elements.

In *Lumen Gentium*, Sforno translated the verse according to his own interpretation and the original meaning: *confusum et perplexum* is employed instead of *inanis et vacua*.[222]

Confusum sive chaos cui elementa potentialiter inerant, quamvis interpretes nonnulli ibidem inanis et vacua transtulissent, ex quo confuso diversimode alterationem.[223]

In *Or 'Ammim*, Sforno completes the sentence with reference to Isaiah 34:11, explaining that "תהו" is the form of the first compound and "בהו" the primaeval matter without form:

וזאת היתה צורת המורכב הראשון הנקראת "תהו" אשר נמצאת בחומר הראשון הנקרא "בהו" כמו שהעיד הנביא באמרו: "קו תהו ואבני בהו" (ישעיהו ל"ד י"א). ובאר שאחר כך היה "חשך על פני תהום" (בראשית א' ב') והוא האויר נעדר האור על פני שני היסודות השפלים הנקראים "תהום." והוסיף ואמר: "ורוח אלהים מרחפת" (שם).[224]

---

222 This does not correspond to the gender of the subject, *terra*.
223 LG § 2.6.
224 OA § 2.6.

The same interpretation is offered in his exegetical commentary:

Sforno on Gen 1:2

That earth, which was created, was a compound[225] of primeval matter called Tohu, and the primeval form called Bohu, for it would not be suitable (possible) for primeval to exist without being clothed in some form. This, then, was the first compound perforce, of matter and substance. The Torah is explaining that primeval matter was a totally new creation (there being no "matter" preceding the world's creation). The matter in this initial compound is called Tohu for it possesses potential but not actuality, as it said כי תהו המה—for they are vain (1 Samuel 12:21)—that is, something not existing in reality, only in the imagination. The form of the initial compound is called Bohu, for the Tohu is found in actuality. The prophet calls אבני בהו—stones sunken in the primeval mire (Isaiah 34:11)—any object which does not remain in a given form for an appreciable period of time, just as we call the initial form Bohu which immediately clothed itself in a variety of forms (namely, the four elements).[226]	ואותה הארץ הנבראת אז היתה דבר מורכב מחמר ראשון הנקרא תהו ומצורה ראשונ׳ הנקראת בהו. כי אמנם לא היה נאות לחמר הראשון זולתי צורה אחת היא היתה ראשונה לכל צורות המורכבי׳ בהכרח. ובזה התבאר שהחמר הראשון דבר מחודש. ונקרא החמר של אותו המורכב הראשון תהו להיותו מצד עצמו דבר בכחיי בלבד בלתי נמצא בפעל כאמרו כי תהו המה כלומר בלתי נמצאים בפעל אבל בדמיון בלבד והצורה הנשואה באותו המורכב הראשון נקראת בהו. כי בו בתהו שאמר נמצאת בפעל. וקרא אבני בהו הנושא הבלתי עומד עם צורתו זמן נחשב כמו שקרה לנושא הצורה הראשונה שתכף לבש צורות יסודות מתחלפות

Sforno's position is more radical than those of his predecessors.[227] Rashi interprets "תהו" and "בהו" as insubstantial matter (such as emptiness), Ibn Ezra as a pre-existent matter (which is a clear reference to the Neoplatonic tradition),[228] and Gersonides as form (תהו) and prime matter (בהו). Meanwhile, Nahmanides understands them the other way around; that is, "תהו" as prime matter and "בהו" as first form.[229]

Studies[230] of Philo of Alexandria and his *On Providence* emphasise a particular interpretation concerning *creatio ex materia*. Here, the cosmological

---

225 "Amalgam" in the translation.
226 Obadiah Sforno, *Commentary on the Torah.* Translation and explanatory notes by Raphael Pelcovitz. Complete volume. (Brooklyn: Mesorah Publications, 1997), 5.
227 Samuelson, *Judaism and the Doctrine of Creation*, 140.
228 Cf. *Tim.* 31a–32c.
229 Cf. Warren Zev Harvey, "Rashi on Creation beyond Plato and Derrida," *Aleph* 18 (2018): 27–49. As Harvey has suggested to me, as a good Aristotelian, Sforno rejects the Platonic idea of a pre-existent matter.
230 Cf. Richard Sorbjii, *Time, Creation and the Continuum: Theories in Antiquity and the Middle Ages* (London: Duckworth, 1983), 203–209; James Noel Hubler, "*Creatio ex nihilo*: Matter, Creation, and the Body in Classical and Christian Philosophy through Aquinas" (PhD diss., University of Pennsylvania, 1995).

creation is found in the Creator's mind, a noetic act of creation. In chapter 20, Philo observes:

> Haec Plato a Deo facta fuisse novit; et materiam per se ornatu carentem, in modo cum ornatu ipso prodiisse; hac enim errant primae causae, unde et mundus fuit. Quoniam et Iudaeorum Legisltator Moyses aquam, tenebras, et chaos dixit ante mundum fuisse.[231]

"Chaos" was found at the beginning of the creation of the world, which was created from a timeless and motionless matter.

If we compare Sforno with his contemporaries, it seems that we can establish a direct connection with Abravanel's *Dialoghi D'Amore*:[232]

> Philosophers call it [common matter to all elements] prime matter, and the more ancient call it "chaos" which in Greek means confusion, because all things, potentially and originally, are together in confusion; and everything is made from it, each of itself, separately and successively.[233]

Nonetheless, the reference to a pre-existent matter is linked to doctrines belonging to the Platonic and Neoplatonic traditions, which seem irrelevant to our interpretation of Sforno's philosophical position. I would suggest that Plato's pre-cosmic chaos has to be interpreted in opposition to the cosmological order that occurs together with Creation. Sforno does not consider chaos as a lack of order, but rather as a "physical" compound in which matter—in potency—and forms—not yet actualised—are somehow jumbled together, before movement and change. Therefore, God orders the mover of the sphere to move, as explained by the second part of the verse: *et spiritus Dei circumferebat*/ורוח אלהים מרחפת. This means that a separate substance moves the heavens, as is also confirmed by Psalm 104:4, "He makes His angels spirits." During the movement, the elements change into each other, as Aristotle showed in *On the Heavens* 2.7 (289a), since the elemental fire is inflamed by the air by means of motion because the natural place of air and fire is above the heavy elements, meaning earth and water.

---

231 Philo of Alexandria, *De Providentia*, ed. Mireille Hadas-Lebel (Paris: Editions du Cerf, 1973), 176.

232 Leone Ebreo, *Dialoghi di amore, di Leone Hebreo medico* (Venezia, 1565), dialogue 2, pp. 46–47: "Philo: Vediamo che dell'acqua si fa aere, dell'aere, acqua, et di fuoco aere, et dell'aere fuoco, e così anco la terra. Filone: Ancor questo che dici é vero: ma di quelle cose, che si generano delli elementi gli proprii elementi ne son materia, et fondamento, che resta nella cosa generata da loro, ma tuttu quattro uniti virtualmente: ma quando si genera l'uno dell'altro, non puo essere cosi, che quando il fuco (n.d.r fuoco) si converte in acqua, non resta il fuoco nell'acqua, anzi si corrompe il fuoco e si genera l'acqua, e poi ch'é cosi, bisogna assegnare qualche materia commune a tutti gli elementi, nella qual si possino fare queste lor trasmutazioni, laqual essendo una volonta informata d'aere per sufficiente alterazione, lassando quella forma d'aere piglia la forma dell'acqua e cosi delli altri. Questa chiamano gli filosogi materia prima e gli più antichi la chiamano chaos ch'in greco vuol dir confusione: perche tutte le cose potentialmente et generativamente sono in qualla (n.d.r. quella) insieme et in confususione et di quella si fanno tutte ciascuna per se diffusamente et successivamente."

233 Leone Ebreo, *Dialogues of Love*, trans. Damian Bacich and Rosella Pescatori (Toronto: University of Toronto Press, 2009), 88.

However, two different traditions[234] refer to a creation from "chaos." The first is found in talmudic and midrashic literature.[235] In *Bereshit Rabbah*, "Tohu" and "Bohu" should be interpreted as "chaos":

Bereshit Rabbah 1.5		*Bereshit Rabbah* 1.9	
As Rabbi Yossi Bar Chanina said: One who honors oneself at the expense of one's friend has no share in the World to Come. How much more so with the honor of God! And it says afterward (Psalms 31:20): "How abundant is Your goodness that you have laid up for those who fear You." Those who fear You and not for those who hold Your awe in contempt. When a king builds a palace in a place of sewers, dunghills, and garbage, everyone who says: "This palace is built on chaos, darkness and suffer injury" discredits it. So too, everyone who says the universe was created from nothingness discredits it. Rabbi Hunna in the name of Bar Kafra said: If it were not written, it would be impossible to say it. "In the beginning God created" from what? "And the earth was chaos."	דא״ר יוסי בר חנינא: כל המתכבד בקלון חבירו אין לו חלק לעולם הבא. בכבודו של מקום על אחת כמה וכמה, ומה כתיב אחריו (תהלים לא, כ): ״מה רב טובך אשר צפנת ליראיך, ״ ליראיך ולא לבוזים את מוראך [הרב] אל יהי במה רב טובך, בנוהג שבעולם מלך ב״ו בונה פלטין במקום הביבים, ובמקום האשפה, ובמקום הסריות, כל מי שהוא בא לומר פלטין זו בנויה במקום הביבים ובמקום האשפה, ובמקום הסריות אינו פוגם. כך כל מי שהוא בא לומר העוה״ז נברא מתוך תוהו ובוהו, אינו פוגם, אתמהה. ר' הונא בשם בר קפרא אמר, אילולי שהדבר כתוב אי אפשר לאמרו, ״בראשית ברא אלהים, ״ מנין הן, ״והארץ היתה תהו ובהו.״	A philosopher once asked Rabbah Gamliel and said to him, "Your God is only a great artist because he found great materials that helped him: Chaos, darkness, spirit, water, and the depths." Rabbi Gamliel responded to him: "Your spirit should blow! Regarding all of them, the term 'creation' is written: Chaos, as it says (Isaiah 45:7), 'He makes peace and creates evil'; darkness, 'He fashions light and creates darkness'; water (Psalms 148:5), 'Praise the heavens and the waters'—why?—for 'He commanded and they were created'; spirit (Amos 4:13), 'For behold he fashions mountains and creates spirit'; the depths (Proverbs 8:24), 'When there were no depths, I was created.'"	פילוסופי אחד שאל את רבן גמליאל. אמר ליה: צייר גדול הוא אלהיכם, אלא שמצא סממנים טובים שסייעו אותו: תוהו ובוהו, וחושך, ורוח, ומים, ותהומות. אמר ליה: תיפח רוחיה דההוא גברא! כולהון כתיב בהן בריאה: תוהו ובוהו— שנאמר (ישעיה מה, ז): ״עושה שלום ובורא רע״; חושך—״יוצר אור [ובורא חשך]״; מים—(תהלים קמח, ה): ״הללוהו שמי השמים והמים״ למה ש״צוה ונבראו״; רוח (עמוס ד, יג): ״כי הנה יוצר הרים ובורא רוח״; תהומות (משלי ח, כד): ״באין תהומות חוללתי.״

Similarly, in Talmud *Tamid* 32a (3–4):

Alexander continued to ask questions of the Elders of the Negev. He said to them: Were the heavens created first or was the earth created first? They said: The heavens were created first, as it is stated: "In the beginning God created the heaven and the earth" (Genesis 1:1).	אמר להן שמים נבראו תחלה או הארץ אמרו שמים נבראו תחלה שנא׳ (בראשית א, א) בראשית ברא אלהים את השמים ואת הארץ

---

234 I will not consider the Arabic tradition and some Western positions such as that of Raymund Lull, who wrote a *Liber Chaos* (ca. 1285) in which he offers a definition similar to Sforno's: "Chaos is a composite of prime form and prime matter." Cf. Charles H. Lohr, "The Arabic Background to Ramon Lull's *Liber Chaos* (ca. 1285)," *Traditio* 55 (2000): 159–170.

235 Hubler, "*Creatio ex nihilo*," 94–101.

(cont.)

He said to them: Was the light created first, or was the darkness created first? They said to him: This matter has no solution, as the verses do not indicate an answer. The Gemara asks: But let them say to him that the darkness was created first, as it is written: "Now the earth was chaos, and darkness etc." (Genesis 1:2)	אמר להן אור נברא תחלה או חשך אמרו לו מילתא דא אין לה פתר ונימרו ליה חשך נברא תחלה דכתיב (בראשית א, ב) והארץ היתה תהו ובהו וחשך [.]

In the Christian tradition, the interpretation of "Tohu" and "Bohu" as "chaos" is attested from the church fathers,[236] and it endured in the medieval Scholastic tradition:

Augustine[237]	Honorius[238]	Honorius[239]	Peter Lombard[240]
Sed illud quod dictum est, In principio fecit Deus coelum et terram, coeli et terrae nomine universa creatura significata est, quam fecit et condidit Deus. Ideo autem nominibus visibilium rerum haec appellata sunt, propter parvulorum infirmitatem, qui minus idonei sunt invisibilia comprehendere. Primo ergo materia facta est confusa et informis, unde omnia fierent quae distincta atque formata sunt, quod credo a Graecis chaos appellari.	Sed heac tetra rerum imago chaos vel informis materia cognominatur	In principio creaturarum creavit Deus caelum, id est angelos, et terram, scilicet illam materiam quatuor elementatum adhuc confusam, quae dicta est chaos; et hoc fuit ante omnem diem.	Alii quidem tradiderunt omnia simul in materia et forma fuisse creata; quod Augustinus 1 sensisse videtur.—Alii vero hoc magis probaverunt atque asseruerunt, ut primum materia rudis atque informis, quatuor elenientorum commixtionem atque confusionem tenens, creata sit; postmodum vero per iritervalla sex dierum ex illa materia rerum corporalium genera sint formata secundum species pro prias. Quam sententiam Gregorius, Hieronymus, Beda aliique plures 3 commendant ac praeferunt; quae etiani Scripturae Gene seos, unde prima huius rei ad nos manavit cognitio, magis congruere videtur.

---

236 Cf. Greogorius of Nyssa, *Opera exegetica in Genesim*; Jerome, *Quaestiones hebraicae in Genesim*; Bede, *In Genesim expositio*.
237 *De Genesi contra Manichaeos* 1.5.9.
238 *Hexaemeron* 1.
239 *Summa Sententiarum* 3.1.
240 *Sententiae* 2.12.1.

William of Conches[241]	Thierry de Chartres[242]	Peter Aberald[243]	Petrus Comestur[244]
De Chaos, elementorum confusion quae fuit in principio	Istam quattror elementorum informitatem seu potius paene uniformitatem antiqui philosophi tunc hylen tunc chaos appellavertunt.	Quam quidem confusionem nonnulli philosophorum seu poetarum chaos dixerunt	Eamdem machinam quam terram dixerat, abyssum vocat pro sui confusione et obscuritate. Unde et Graecus eam chaos dixit.

In Sforno's *Light of the Nations*, "Tohu" and "Bohu" are identified as Anaximander's compound (§ 2.7) according to the Aristotelian position in *Physics* 3.4.203b6–28—as aforementioned—and *On Generation and Corruption* 2.5.332a20–25.[245] Sforno returned to Aristotle's report of the natural philosophers—namely, the Presocratic thinkers—in order to identify Anaximander's *apeiron*, and in that regard, the compound corresponds to the idea that the first principle contains the contraries in itself (hot and cold, dry and moist). Sforno therefore interpreted the *apeiron* as the compound in which the matter and the forms of the elements are amalgamated together.[246]

The combination of the forms of the elements follows the movement of generation and corruption, so the elements took up their natural places after their actualisation, as described in Genesis 1:2: "And darkness was upon the face of the deep. And the Spirit of God moved upon the face of the waters" (cf. § 3.7.1). The forms of the elements are arranged in two pairs: the heavy elements, meaning water and earth, and the light elements, meaning air and fire.

"Darkness" (*tenebra*/חשך) means air deprived of light, and the abyss (*abyssy*/תהום) is presented as the combination of the two heavy elements, which move toward the centre and whose natural place is closer to the centre of the Earth than the two lighter elements:

Gen 1:2

וחשך, a reference to the dark air which is emanated from the first compound. על פני תהום, over the expanse of the two heavy elements, which were also emanated from the compound, and they surround one another.	וחשך הוא האויר החשוך הנאצל אז מהמורכב הראשון היה על פני תהום. על פני שני היסודות השפלים שנאצלו אז ג״כ מהמורכב הראשון והיו מקיפי׳ זה את זה

---

241 *Philosophia* 1.11.35.
242 *Tractatus de sex dierum operibus*, ch. 24.
243 *Exposition in Hexaemeron*.
244 *Historia scholastica, liber Genesis 2*.
245 This passage does not correspond to the Latin chapter indicated by Sforno: I would read it as *Gen. corr.* 1.1.
246 This should not be confused with Anaxagoras's primaeval chaos.

Hence, in his biblical commentary, Sforno refers to the Aristotelian discussion in *On the Heavens* 2.13–14. Likewise, in *Light of the Nations*, the picture that is given corresponds to the position of the natural place of the elements in the cosmos, in which earth and water naturally move around the centre and the earth is surrounded by the water. The natural position of air and fire moved upwards, away from the centre, and therefore air surrounds water and fire surrounds air. To explain the physical changes of the elements, Sforno drew on *On Generation and Corruption*,[247] which describes the combination of earth/air and fire: "Smoke becomes fire, while smoke is made up of earth and air."[248]

Sforno interpreted the second part of Genesis 1:2, "And the Spirit of God moved upon the face of the waters," in accordance with Aristotle's position in *On the Heavens* 2.7.289a.[249] The "Spirit of God" (*Spiritum Dei*/רוח אלהים), meaning the separate substance (*abstractas substantias*/עצם נבדל), hovers over the dark air on the surface of the water and generates elementary fire (§ 3.7.1). Hence, the "Spirit of God"—which is read in parallel with Psalm 104:4 (103:4 in the Vulgate), "He makes His angels spirits" (*fecit angelos Suos Spiritus*/ עושה מלאכיו רוחות)—implies the idea that angels, which are separate substances or intellects, move the spheres. In the commentary on the Psalms,[250] Sforno claims that these spirits are evidently the movers of the spheres, which is also suggested by Maimonides in *Guide* 2.4,[251] although in his discussion of the same passage in *Hilkhot Yesodei ha-Torah*,[252] he offered a different interpretation.

The analogy between angels and the separate intellects is found in the classical interpretations of the Jewish, Islamic, and Scholastic traditions.[253] This cosmological picture embodies Neoplatonic elements in the Aristotelian sys-

---

247 *Gen. corr.* 1.10.328a.
248 *Gen. corr.* 2.4.331b.
249 *Cael.* 2.7.289a (Aristotle, *On the Heavens*, 179–181): "The heat and light which they emit are engendered as the air is chafed by their movement. It is the nature of movement to ignite even wood and stone and iron, a fortiori then that which is nearer to fire, as air is. Compare the case of flying missiles. These are themselves set on fire so that leaden balls are melted, and if the missiles themselves catch fire, the air which surrounds them must be affected likewise. These then become heated themselves by reason of their flight through the air, which owing to the impact upon it is made fire by the movement. But the upper bodies are carried each one in its sphere; hence they do not catch fire themselves, but the air which lies beneath the sphere of the revolving element is necessarily heated by its revolution, and especially in that part where the sun is fixed. That is the reason for the heat experienced as it gets nearer or rises higher or stands above our head. Let this suffice for the point that the stars are neither made of fire nor move in fire."
250 Ps 104:4: עושה מלאכיו מניעי הגלגלים.
251 Warren Zev Harvey, "Maimonides and Aquinas on Interpreting the Bible," *Proceedings of the American Academy for Jewish Research* 55 (1988): 59–77; Howard Kreisel, "*Imitatio Dei* in Maimonides' *Guide of the Perplexed*," *AJS Review* 19 (1994): 169–221.
252 Cf. Moses Maimonides, *Hilkhot Yesodei ha-Torah* 2:4: "What is meant by the prophets' statements that they saw an angel of fire or with wings? All these are prophetic visions and parables, as [Deuteronomy 4:24] states: 'God, your Lord, is consuming fire,' though He is not fire and [the description of Him in this manner] is only metaphoric. Similarly, [Psalms 104:4] states: 'He makes His angels as winds ....'" (Maimonides, *Mishneh Torah: Hilchot Yesodei Hatorah*, trans. Eliyahu Touger [New York: Moznaim Publishing, 1997], https://www.chabad.org/library/article_cdo/aid/682956/jewish/Mishneh-Torah.htm).
253 Cf. Tobias Hoffmann, ed., *A Companion to Angels in Medieval Philosophy* (Leiden: Brill, 2012); Yossef Schwartz, "Celestial Motion, Immaterial Causality and the Latin Encounter with Arabic Aristotelian Cosmology," in *Albertus Magnus und der Ursprung der Universitätsidee: Die Begegnung der Wissenschaftskulturen im 13. Jahrhundert und die Entdeckung des Konzepts der Bildung durch Wissenschaft*, ed. Ludger Honnefelder (Berlin: Berlin University Press, 2011), 277–298.

tem.²⁵⁴ Aristotle presented two different pictures in order to explain the movement of the heavenly bodies. On the one hand, in *On the Heavens* 1.2–3 (268b–270b), he postulated a fifth body to remove the need for a separate mover who moves the heavenly spheres (and the elementary bodies), and Sforno includes this as one of his twenty-seven propositions.²⁵⁵ On the other hand, in *Metaphysics* 12.7–8 (1072a–1074b), Aristotle presupposed the existence of a separate mover whose motion was caused by the Prime Mover as an object of desire. Sforno introduces the question by quoting Averroes's interpretation of *Metaphysics* 12, text. 44 (1073b), according to which "Plato said in his obscure words: the creator created the angels himself," and the emblematic *Metaphysics* 12, text. 18: "The intellectual soul comes from the secondary gods." He follows Aquinas's interpretation²⁵⁶ in his *De spiritualibus creaturis*,²⁵⁷ *Summa Theologica* 1.50–64, and *Summa contra Gentiles* 2.91.

In the Neoplatonic tradition,²⁵⁸ the identification of angels as separate intelligible substances in the hierarchy of beings can be traced back to Proclus and was developed by Pseudo-Dionysius in his discussion of the structure of the world. In *On Dreams* 1.4.22, Philo of Alexandria concluded that the heavenly bodies are intelligent and animated. In medieval times, probably thanks to the circulation of the *Book of Causes* and a growing awareness of the Arabic and Jewish traditions,²⁵⁹ this idea became completely integrated into the Scholastic system (with some exceptions, such as Albert the Great and Robert Grosseteste above all).

---

254   Cf. Richard C. Dales, "The De-Animation of the Heavens in the Middle Ages," *Journal of the History of Ideas* 41 (1980): 531–550.

255   Cf. proposition 10 and n. 153.

256   Cf. Gregory T. Doolan, "Aquinas on the Demonstrability of Angels," in Hoffmann, *A Companion to Angels in Medieval Philosophy*, 13–44.

257   Thomas Aquinas, *De spiritualibus creaturis*, articles 6–8, cf. 6: "Sic igitur erit duplex ordo substantiarum spiritualium. Quarum quaedam erunt motores caelestium corporum, et unientur eis sicut motores mobilibus, sicut et Augustinus dicit in III de Trinitate, quod omnia corpora reguntur a Deo per spiritum vitae rationalem; et idem a Gregorio habetur in IV dialogorum. Quaedam vero erunt fines horum motuum, quae sunt omnino abstractae, et corporibus non unitae. Aliae vero uniuntur corporibus caelestibus per modum quo motor unitur mobili. Et hoc videtur sufficere ad salvandum intentionem Platonis et Aristotelis. Et de Platone quidem manifestum est; Plato enim, sicut supra dictum est, etiam corpus humanum non dixit aliter animatum, nisi in quantum anima unitur corpori ut motor. Ex dictis vero Aristotelis manifestum est quod non posuit in corporibus caelestibus de virtutibus animae nisi intellectivam. Intellectus vero, secundum ipsum, nullius corporis actus est. Dicere autem ulterius, quod corpora caelestia hoc modo sint animata sicut inferiora corpora quae per animam vegetantur et sensificantur, repugnat incorruptibilitati caelestium corporum. Sic igitur negandum est corpora caelestia esse animata eo modo quo ista inferiora corpora animantur. Non est tamen negandum corpora caelestia esse animata, si per animationem nihil aliud intelligatur quam unio motoris ad mobile. Et istos duos modos videtur Augustinus tangere in super Gen. ad litteram. Dicit enim: solet quaeri, utrum caeli luminaria ista conspicua corpora sola sint, aut habeant rectores quosdam spiritus suos; et si habent, utrum ab eis etiam vitaliter inspirentur, sicut animantur carnes per animas animalium. Sed licet ipse sub dubio utrumque relinquat, ut per sequentia patet, secundum praemissa dicendum est quod habent rectores spiritus, a quibus tamen non sic animantur sicut inferiora animalia a suis animabus."

258   Cf. Luc Brisson, Seamus O'Neill, and Andrei Timotin, eds., *Neoplatonic Demons and Angels* (Leiden: Brill, 2018).

259   Cf. Albertus Magnus, *Alberti Magni opera omnia. Tomus XVII/1: De unitate intellectus; De XV problematibus; Problemata determinata; De fato*, ed. Bernhard Geyer (Aschendorf: Monasterii Westfalorum, 1975), 48, ll. 25–61 [i.e. *Problemata determinata* 2, ed. James Weisheipl].

In the Jewish tradition, angels are presented as the separate intelligences in the works of Ibn Ezra,[260] Ibn Daud (*The Exalted Faith*),[261] and Judah Halevi (*Book of the Khazar*).[262] In *Guide* 2.4–6 and *Hilkhot Yesodei ha-Torah* 3.9,[263] Maimonides goes into a deeper discussion of the nature of the angels as separate intellects:[264]

וימשך לו גם כן הענין אשר כבר התבאר במופת והוא שהאלוה ית' לא יעשה הדברים בקריבה כי כמו שהוא שורף באמצעות האש והאש יתנועע באמצעות תנועת הגלגל כן הגלגל גם הוא יתנועע באמצעות שכל נבדל ויהיו השכלים הם המלאכים המתקרבים אשר באמצעותם יתנועעו הגלגלים[265]

Similar positions are presented by Gersonides in *Wars of the Lord*[266] and by Abravanel in his commentary on Genesis.[267]

In his biblical commentary, Sforno emphasises the same aspects that emerge from *Light of the Nations*, using a similar explanation:

Genesis 1:2

The angels that moved the sphere who are called 'ruaḥ' as it says "Who makes wind His angels" (Psalm 104:4) moved the dark air over the surface of the water, which then encompassed the foundation of the earth. As a result, the inner part of the dark air close to the sphere overheated through the friction of its movement and that became the element of	ורוח אלהים מניעי הגלגל שנקראו רוח כאמרו עושה מלאכיו רוחות מרחפת על פני המים הניעו אז את האויר החשוך על פני המים הסובבים אז את יסוד הארץ. ובכן היה שהחלק ממנו הסמוך לגלגל התלהב בתנועתו והוא האש היסודיי והחלק ממנו הקרוב

---

260   Cf. Shlomo Sela, *Abraham ibn Ezra on Elections, Interrogations, and Medical Astrology* (Leiden: Brill, 2011), 11.

261   Cf. T.A.M. Fontaine, *In Defence of Judaism: Abraham ibn Daud* (Assen: Van Gorcum, 1990), chapter 7, "The Heavenly Spheres and the Intelligences," 111–136.

262   Halevi, *Book of the Khazar* 5.21 (p. 292): "Every soul has intellect, and this intellect is an angel severed from material substance. They called these intellects, or angels, or secondary causes and other names."

263   Maimonides, *Hilkhot Yesodei ha-Torah* 3.9: "All the stars and spheres possess a soul, knowledge, and intellect. They are alive and stand in recognition of the One who spoke and [thus brought] the world into being" (Maimonides, *Mishneh Torah*, digital edition).

264   Cf. Maimonides, *Guide* 2:6: ב'מלאכים' אשר הם שכלים נפרדים (the angels are the separate intellects).

265   Maimonides, *Guide* 2:4 (1:258): "In this connection Aristotle deals further with a matter that has already been demonstrated, namely, that God, may He be magnified and held sublime, does not do things in a direct fashion. Thus, He burns by means of a fire, and this fire is moved by means of the motion of the sphere and the sphere in its turn is moved by means of a separate intellect. For intellects are the angels, which are near to Him, by means of whom the spheres are moved."

266   Cf. 6.8: "Now, in the beginning of this entire creation God said that there should be a domain of light, i.e., the domain of angels, which are the movers of the celestial spheres" (Gersonides, *Wars of the Lord 3*, 448).

267   Cf. Seymour Feldman, *Philosophy in a Time of Crisis. Don Isaac Abravanel: Defender of the Faith* (London: Routledge, 2003), 65: "Before we leave Abravanel's account of creation we should note the progressive character of his depiction of the making of the heavenly domain. On day one the heavens mentioned in the first verse includes, as we have seen, just the uppermost celestial sphere and the angels, at least those that are the movers of the heavenly bodies."

(cont.)

Genesis 1:2	
fire. While the part of the dark air close to the water was cooled by the water, except for a small portion thereof which became heated, thereby forming sparks which gave forth light.	אל המים קנה אז איזה קור מן המים זולתי חלק מועט ממנו המתחמם במקרה בהתהפכות ניצוצות מאורי האור

For Sforno, the creation of prime matter in the Genesis account is corroborated by Isaiah 45:7, "He, who forms light and creates darkness. And He, who makes peace and who creates evil. I am ha-Shem, who made all of these." He finds a direct connection by comparing Genesis 1:2 and Isaiah 45:7: the creation of light and darkness and the description of the darkness and the abyss that surround the light in Genesis correspond to the philosophical explanation of the description of the creation of the elements in *Light of the Nations*. The verse from Isaiah, "who makes peace and who creates evil," is therefore an explanation that introduces the creation of the primaeval matter in the Genesis account.

Sforno delineates the ontological concept of "evil" by exploring the definition of matter. Matter exists in potency only and is devoid of all form, since it is not actualised, and therefore, if the definition of evil is the privation of good and activities, then prime matter should be considered evil. Following Aristotle's saying in *Metaphysics* 12.10 (1075a34), "The evil in itself is one of the elements,"[268] in reference to the movement of generation and corruption, proceeding from contraries, Averroes explains that "some people posited for all things two principles: the good and the evil which are form and matter."[269] Since matter is "evil," "peace" expresses the actualisation of the elements that change into their contraries, as Aristotle explains in *On Generation and Corruption* 1.10.328a: "Some things, then, namely, those whose matter is the same, 'reciprocate.'"[270] The philosophical picture that Sforno offers in *Light of the Nations* matches his interpretation of the prophet Isaiah:

Isaiah 45:7[271]	
Who forms light: with the luminaries [sun and moon].	יוצר אור במאורות
And creates darkness: the dark air from the first compound.	ובורא חשך האויר החשוך מהמורכב הראשון
Who makes peace: between contraries.	עושה שלום בין ההפכים
And creates evil: the prime matter deprived of the form of good.	ובורא רע החומר הראשון נעדר צורת הטוב
I am ha-Shem who made all of these: meaning to achieve the purpose intended in Creation.	אני ה' עושה כל אלה שאמרתי עתה להשיג התכלית המכוון בבריאה

---

268 Averroes, *Ibn Rushd's* Metaphysics, 203.
269 Averroes, 203.
270 Aristotle, *Coming-to-be*, 259.
271 Obadiah Sforno, *Sefer Yeshaʿyah ʿim perush Sforno*, ed. Moshe Kravetz (Bet-Shemesh: s.n., 2017).

Likewise, in *Lumen Gentium*, evil is presented as prime matter deprived of the good, which corresponds to the explanation of the verses from Isaiah: evil is prime matter deprived of the form of good; that is, *materiam primam per se bono privata*/[272] החומר הראשון נעדר צורת הטוב.

Sforno interpreted the dichotomy in the verse from Isaiah represented by "peace" and "evil" as the two Empedoclean principles of the universe: Strife (*lite*/רע) and Love (*amicitia*/שלום), reflecting Aristotle's report in *On Generation and Corruption* 1.2.315a and 2.6.333b14–15. While Sforno explicitly presents the analogy in *Lumen Gentium* (§ 3.8), this part is omitted from the Hebrew version. Nonetheless, in the Jewish tradition, Solomon ibn Gabirol interprets the Empedoclean principle in analogy with the Kernel (Love) and the Shell (Strife). This idea is based on the interaction between the material grounding element and Love, understood as the desire for the goodness of God.[273] However, in Sforno's case, the Empedoclean principle becomes the key to understanding Isaiah 45:7, following the positions of Aristotle and Averroes in *Metaphysics* 12, text. 54 (12.10.1075b):

> Empedocles' theory is also absurd, for he identifies the Good with Love. This is a principle both as causing motion (since it combines) and as matter (since it is part of the mixture). Now even if it so happens that the same thing is a principle both as matter and as causing motion, still the essence of the two principles is not the same. In which respect, then, is Love a principle? And it is also absurd that Strife should be imperishable; strife is the very essence of evil.[274]

And Averroes explains:

> Some people posited for all things two principles: the good and the evil which are form and matter; if this is so, the evil will exist in all things except one, namely form, and it follows that all composite things, in their entirety, are evil, for one of their two elements, namely matter, is evil. [...] Some of the Ancients believed that the first principle is good, but they did not say in which way good is a principle, whether as final cause of the universe, or as mover, or again as form [...]. Empedocles says concerning the principles is a theory from which absurdity results; for the takes the principle which is the good to be love and the principle which is evil to be strife.[275]

In a figurative sense, the Empedoclean principle represents the foundation of the elements and the prime matter, which is actualised from those forms

---

272 In *Or 'Ammim*, Sforno offers the same explanation, but develops the subject in a different way (§ 3.8.2): החומר הראשון אשר הוא מצד עצמו נעדר כל צורה מצד היותו כחיי פשוט כי הצורה מצד היותה תכלית ההויה בפעל תקרא «טוב» ולכן נקרא החומר הראשון «רע» אצל רבים מהקדמונים
273 Cf. Sarah Pessin, *Ibn Gabirol's Theology of Desire: Matter and Method in Jewish Medieval Neoplatonism* (Cambridge: Cambridge University Press, 2013), in particular chapter 4.3, "A Pseudo-Empedoclean Love Story: Unspecified Being, Matter over Form, and the Kernel of Desire," 46–50.
274 Aristotle, *Metaphysics* 2, 171.
275 Averroes, *Ibn Rushd's* Metaphysics, 203–204.

that change into their contraries in accordance with the movement generated by Love, which unites them such that "the mover (Love) is mixed with the thing moved." This kind of movement is emanated from God and is the intended end of Creation. Sforno's exegetical commentary on Isaiah presents the same idea of divine causality expressed in *Light of the Nations*, "I am ha-Shem who made all of these," which he interprets as the intended end of Creation, and therefore the two principles (evil and peace) symbolise the movement of generation that tends towards the final intended goal, which is God.

17 The Ultimate Goal in Genesis

Sforno also argued that the movement of the generation of the elements is temporally prior to the movement of generation and corruption (*ad mortalium generationes narrat precessisse elementorum productio*/בהגיד שמציאות היסודות קדם בזמן למציאות תנועת ההוויות המתהווה מהם) by using the biblical verse וירא אלהים כי טוב/*et vidit Deus quod esset bonum* ("and God saw that it was good").[276] This idea is correlated with the Empedoclean interpretation of the first principles of the universe, which are moved by Love, the highest good. Sforno understands the statement "it was good" according to the idea that God creates everything for a goal (*finem*/תכלית) and that the purpose reflects His "goodness." This idea is introduced in three different sections of *Light of the Nations* (§ 1.13; § 4.8; § 10.8.4)

In *Metaphysics* 12.7 (1072 b), "the final cause is not only 'the good for something,' but also 'the good which is the end of some action,'"[277] and therefore every being imitates the divine substance; that is, its perfect (eternal and pure) actuality, according to the possibilities inherent in the created being's own essence.[278] Sforno, following the Torah, suggests a similar interpretation of the ultimate goal in the Creator's mind. This goal is temporally prior to the movement of generation and corruption. Therefore, the movement of generation and corruption is not eternal.

Similarly, it is possible to establish a parallel between Sforno's exegetical commentary and *Light of the Nations*:

Genesis 1:4		Genesis 1:7		Genesis 1:10		Genesis 1:16	
And so it was, for God saw that light was good and He chose its existence toward	וירא אלהים את האור כי טוב והי׳ כן כי ראה אלהי׳ ובחר במציאותו	*He causes the clouds to ascend from the end of the earth, He makes lightning for the rain*	יקרא אלהים לרקיע שמים ובהגיע שם האיד הקיטורי הנלהב יוליד רעם וברק	**And God saw that it was good**: He so wanted it, toward the intended end	וירא אלהים כי טוב רצה כן בשביל התכלית שהוא טוב המכוון	**That is was good** i.e. God's intent was for the good which was the proper ulti-	כי טוב כלומר שכיון בזה אל הטוב והוא התכלית הנאות לפועלו

---

276 Cf. Gen 1:10; 1:12; 1:16; 1:21; 1:25; and 1:4.
277 Aristotle, *Metaphysics* 2, 147.
278 Cf. Stephan Herzberg, "God as Pure Thinking. An Interpretation of *Metaphysics* Λ 7, 1072b14–26," in Horn, *Aristotle's* Metaphysics Lambda, 160–161.

(cont.)

Genesis 1:4	Genesis 1:7		Genesis 1:10		Genesis 1:16
the end of the achievement of good, and He brought the light into being through His knowledge which is the efficient cause.	מפני התכלית אשר הוא הטוב שבגללו המציאו בידיעתו הפועלת	(Jeremiah 10:13). Since the element waters, which are denser, are above the light air, this condition is contrary to nature, indicating that is an act performed by God's Will, directed without a doubt toward a good purpose and end, as it says: *the firmament shows His handiworks* (Psalm 19:2)	כאמרו מעלה נשיאים מקצה. הארץ ברקים למטר עשה ובהיות קצת היסוד המימי הכבד למעל׳ מהאויר הקל אשר אצלנו נגד טבעם יורה על פעולת פועל רצוני מכוין תכלית בלי ספק כאמרו ומעש׳ ידיו מגיד הרקיע	which was good.	mate purpose of His act.[279]

This is the same idea that Maimonides presents in *Guide* 3.13:

> He brought every part of the world into existence and that its existence conformed to its purpose. This is the meaning of his saying: *And God saw that it was good* [...] and *good* is an expression applied by us to what conforms to our purpose. About the whole, it says: *And God saw everything that He had made, and, behold, it was very good* (Gen. 1:31). For the production in time of everything that was produced conformed to its purpose, and nothing went wrong.[280]

Similarly, Sforno interprets "and God saw" as an intellectual vision, as Maimonides explicates in *Guide* 1.4:

> Know that the three words *to see* [*ra'oh*], *to look at* [*habbit*], and *to vision* [*ḥazoh*] are applied to the sight of the eye and that all three of them are also used figuratively to denote the grasp of the intellect. As for the verb *to see*, this is generally admitted by the multitude. Thus it says: *And he saw, and behold a well in the field* (Gen 29:2). This refers to the sight of the eye. But it also says: *Yea, my heart hath seen much of wisdom and knowledge* (Eccl 1:16); and this refers to intellectual apprehension.[281]

---

279   This only appears in Raphael Pelcovitz's edition. Moshe Kravetz has suggested to me that Pelcovitz used Gottlieb's annexe without specifying that this part is not in the original text.
280   Maimonides, *Guide* 3.13 (2:452–453).
281   Maimonides, 1.4 (1:27).

Sforno follows Averroes's position in *The Incoherence of the Incoherence*[282] and Aristotle's *Metaphysics* 2, text. 8,[283] *Metaphysics* 12, text. 54,[284] and *Physics* 2, text. 31.[285] If goodness is the ultimate goal of every existent, and only God recognises and knows (*videns-noscens*/ידע הכיר) the goodness in the particular created beings,[286] then the order of the universe must be bestowed by God's will and intellection, since good is the ultimate goal of created beings.

Bibliography

Munich, Bayerische Staatsbibliothek, Res/4 A.hebr. 310
Parma, Biblioteca Palatina 2624

Sforno, Obadiah. *Commentary on the Torah*. Translation and explanatory notes by Raphael Pelcovitz. Complete volume. Brooklyn: Mesorah Publications, 1997.
Sforno, Obadiah. *Kitve Rabbi ʿOvadyah Sforno*. Edited by Zeʾev Gottlieb. Jerusalem: Mossad ha-Rav Kook, 1983.
Sforno, Obadiah. *Lumen Gentium*. Bologna, 1548.
Sforno, Obadiah. *Or ʿAmmim*. Bologna, 1537; repr. Ramat Gan, s.n., 1970.
Sforno, Obadiah. *Sefer Yeshaʿyah ʿim perush Sforno*. Edited by Moshe Kravetz. Bet-Shemesh: s.n., 2017.

---

[282] Averroes, *Incoherence* 9, doubt 3 (328): "For according to them there is neither quantity nor quality in any existent except by divine wisdom. [...] But God forbid that we should believe such a thing of the First Creator; on the contrary, we believe that everything in the world is wisdom, although in many things our understanding of it is very imperfect and although we understand the wisdom of the Creator only through the wisdom of nature. And if the world is one single product of extreme wisdom, there is one wise principle whose existence the heavens and the earth and everything in them need. Indeed, nobody can regard the product of such wonderful wisdom as caused by itself, and the theologians in their wish to elevate the Creator have denied Him wisdom and withheld from Him the noblest of His qualities."

[283] *Metaph.* 2.2.994b (Aristotle, *Metaphysics 1*, 91–93): "The Final cause of a thing is an end and is such that it does not happen for the sake of some thing else, but all other things happen for its sake. So, if there is to be a last term of this kind, the series will not be infinite; and if there is no such term, there will be no Final cause. Those who introduce infinity do not realize that they are abolishing the nature of the Good (although no one would attempt to do anything if he were not likely to reach some limit); nor would there be any intelligence in the world, because the man who has intelligence always acts for the sake of something, and this is a limit, because the end is a limit."

[284] Cf. n. 258; and *Metaph.* 12.10.1072b (Aristotle, *Metaphysics 2*, 147): "But the Good, and that which is in itself desirable, are also in the same series; and that which is first in a class is always best or analogous to the best. That the final cause may apply to immovable things is shown by the distinction of its meanings. For the final cause is not only "the good for something," but also 'the good which is the end of some action.' In the latter sense it applies to immovable things, although in the former it does not; and it causes motion as being an object of love, whereas all other things cause motion because they are themselves in motion."

[285] *Phys.* 2.3.194b (Aristotle, *Physics*, 123): "The 'goal' does not mean any kind of termination, but only the best."

[286] Pines states that Maimonides assimilates the passage in *Incoherence* 9, doubt 3, in order to introduce a peculiar idea, which is the notion of "particularisation," as we read in the introduction to the *Guide*: "The deficiency of man's knowledge necessitates the introduction of the notion of a 'Particularizer' who in His wisdom arranged the celestial (and also sublunar) world the way it is" (*Guide*, cxxx–cxxxi).

Abba Mari of Lunel. *Sefer Minḥat Kena'ot*. Pressburg, 1838.

Achillini, Alessandro. *De intelligentis*. In Alessandro Achillini, *Opera omnia in unum collecta*. Venetiis, 1568.

Albertus Magnus. *Alberti Magni opera omnia. Tomus XVII/1: De unitate intellectus; De XV problematibus; Problemata determinata; De fato*. Edited by Bernhard Geyer. Monasterii Westfalorum: Aschendorf, 1975.

Alexander of Hales. *Summa fratris Alexandri*. Edited by Bernardini Klumper. 4 vols. Rome: Collegii S. Bonaventurae, 1924–1948.

Aquinas, Thomas. *Commentary on Aristotle's* Metaphysics. Translated by John P. Rowan. Chicago: Henry Regnery Co., 1961

Aquinas, Thomas. *Commentary on Aristotle's* Physics. Translated by Richard J. Blackwell, Richard J. Spath, and W. Edmund Thirlkel. New Haven, CT: Yale University Press, 1963.

Aquinas, Thomas. *Opera Omnia*. Leonine edition. Vols. 1–16. Rome: Ex Typographia Polyglotta S.C. de Propaganda Fide, 1882–1948.

Aquinas, Thomas. *Summa Theologiae*. Edited and translated by Thomas Gilby O.P. 61 vols. Cambridge: Cambridge University Press, 2006.

Aristotle. *Auctoritates Aristotelis et aliorum philosophorum*. Koln, 1498.

Aristotle. *Generation of Animals*. Translated by A.L. Peck. Cambridge, MA: Harvard University Press, 1942.

Aristotle. *Metaphysics, Volume 1: Books 1–9*. Translated by Hugh Tredennick. Cambridge, MA: Harvard University Press, 1933.

Aristotle. *Metaphysics, Volume 2: Books 10–14. Oeconomica. Magna Moralia*. Translated by Hugh Tredennick and G. Cyril Armstrong. Cambridge, MA: Harvard University Press, 1935.

Aristotle. *On Sophistical Refutations. On Coming-to-be and Passing Away. On the Cosmos*. Translated by E.S. Forster and D.J. Furley. Cambridge, MA: Harvard University Press, 1955.

Aristotle. *On the Heavens*. Translated by W.K.C. Guthrie. Cambridge, MA: Harvard University Press, 1939.

Aristotle. *Physics, Volume 1: Books 1–4*. Translated by P.H. Wicksteed and F.M. Cornford. Cambridge, MA: Harvard University Press, 1957.

Aristotle. *Posterior Analytics. Topica*. Translated by Hugh Tredennick and E.S. Forster. Cambridge, MA: Harvard University Press, 1960.

Aristotle and Averroes. *Aristotelis metaphysicorum libri XIIII cum Averrois cordubensis in eosdem commentariis et epitome, Theophrasti metaphysicorum liber editio Juntina prima*. Vol. 8 of Aristotle and Averroes, *Aristotelis Stagiritae omnia quae extant opera*. Venitiis, 1552; republished 1562 and 1574.

Aristotle and Averroes. *De coelo; De generatione et corruption; Meteorologicorum; De plantis*. Vol. 5 of *Aristotelis Stagiritae omnia quae extant opera*. Venetiis, 1550; republished 1562 and 1574.

Augustine of Hippo. *Lettres 1–30. Epistulae I–XXX*. Translation and commentary by Serge Lancel, Emmanuel Bermon, and Alois Goldbacher. Paris: Insitut d'Études Augustiniennes, 2011.

Averroes. *De substantia orbis: Critical Edition of the Hebrew Text with English Translation and Commentary*. Translated by Arthur Hyman. Cambridge, MA: Medieval Academy of America; Jerusalem: Israel Academy of Sciences and Humanities, 1986.

Averroes. *Ibn Rushd's* Metaphysics: *A Translation with Introduction of Ibn Rushd's Commentary on Aristotle's* Metaphysics, *Book Lām*. Translated by Charles Genequand. Reprint ed. Leiden: Brill, 1984.

Averroes. *On Aristotle's "Metaphysics": An Annotated Translation of the So-Called "Epitome."* Translated by Rüdiger Arnzen. Berlin: De Gruyter, 2010.

Averroes. *Tahafut al Tahafut (The Incoherence of the Incoherence). Translated from the Arabic, with Introduction*. Translated by Simon van den Bergh. Reprint ed. Oxford: Oxbow Books, 2012.

Bartolucci, Guido. "Elijah of Nola and Moshe Finzi: Medicine and Aristotelianism in Sixteenth-Century Bologna." In *The Literary and Philosophical Canon of Obadiah Sforno*, edited by Giuseppe Veltri et al. Leiden: Brill, 2023.

Berti, Enrico. "The Program of *Metaphysics* Lambda (Chapter 1)." In *Aristotle's Metaphysics Lambda—New Essays*, edited by Christoph Horn, 67–86. Berlin: De Gruyter, 2016.

Bleich, David J. *With Perfect Faith: The Foundations of Jewish Belief*. New York: Ktav, 1983.

Blois, François de. "The 'Sabians' (Sabi'un) in Pre-Islamic Arabia." *Acta Orientalia* 56 (1995): 39–61.

Boethius of Dacia. *Modi significandi sive quaestiones super Priscianum maiorem*. Edited by Jan Pinborg and Henry Roos with Severino Skovgaard Jensen. Copenhagen: G.E.C. Gad, 1969.

Brisson, Luc, Seamus O'Neill, and Andrei Timotin, eds. *Neoplatonic Demons and Angels*. Leiden: Brill, 2018.

Burrell, David B. "The Act of Creation with Its Theological Consequences." In *Creation and the God of Abraham*, edited by David B. Burrell, Janet Soskice, Carlo Cogliati, and William R. Stoeger, 40–52. Cambridge: Cambridge University Press, 2010.

Burrell, David B., and Isabelle Moulin. "Albert, Aquinas, and Dionysius." *Modern Theology* 24 (2008): 633–649.

Calonimus, Calo. *Liber de mundi creatione physicis rationibus probata egregij doctoris Calo Calonymos hebrei Neapolitani ad reuerendissimum dominum dominum Egidium Cardinalem litterarum patrem*. Venetiis, 1527.

Campanini, Saverio. "Roman Holiday: Conjectures on Johann Reuchlin as a Pupil of Obadiah Sforno." In *The Literary and Philosophical Canon of Obadiah Sforno*, edited by Giuseppe Veltri et al. Leiden: Brill, 2023.

Cerami, Cristina. *Génération et substance: Aristote et Averroès entre physique et métaphysique*. Berlin: De Gruyter, 2015.

Chung-Hwan, Chen. "Different Meanings of the Term *Energeia* in the Philosophy of Aristotle." *Philosophy and Phenomenological Research* 17 (1956): 56–65.

Cohen, Sheldon. "Aristotle's Doctrine of the Material Substrate." *The Philosophical Review* 93 (1984): 171–194.

Compagni, Vittoria Perrone. "La teologia di Pomponazzi: Dio e gli dei." In *Pietro Pomponazzi: Tradizione e dissenso. Atti del congresso internazionale di studi su Pietro Pomponazzi, Mantova, 23–24 ottobre 2008*, edited by Marco Sgarbi, 107–129. Florence: Olschki, 2010.

Cregel, Ernst, and Gottfried Saltzmann. *Disputationem circularem ad tit. Cod. IX. lib. I. cum seq. de Judaeis coelicolis, & ne Christianum mancipium &c.: D. XVI*. Altdorf, 1673.

Dales, Richard C. "The De-Animation of the Heavens in the Middle Ages." *Journal of the History of Ideas* 41 (1980): 531–550.

Davidson, Herbert A. *Alfarabi, Avicenna, and Averroes, on Intellect: Their Cosmologies, Theories of the Active Intellect, and Theories of Human Intellect*. Oxford: Oxford University Press, 1992.

Davidson, Herbert A. *Proofs for Eternity, Creation and the Existence of God in Medieval Islamic and Jewish Philosophy*. Oxford: Oxford University Press, 1987.

Di Donato, Silvia. "Il 'Kashf'an manahig' di Averroè: Confronto fra la versione latina di Abraham de Balmes e le citazioni di Calo Calonimo nel 'De mundi creatione.'" *Materia giudaica* 9 (2004): 241–248.

Di Giovanni, Matteo. "Averroes on the Species of Celestial Bodies." *Miscellanea mediaevalia* 33 (2006): 438–466.

Doolan, Gregory T. "Aquinas on the Demonstrability of Angels." In *A Companion to Angels in Medieval Philosophy*, edited by Tobias Hoffmann, 13–44. Leiden: Brill, 2012.

Duba, William. "Masters and Bachelors at Paris in 1319: The *lectio finalis* of Landolfo Caracciolo, OFM." In *Schüler und Meister*, edited by Thomas Jeschke and Andreas Speer, 315–365. Berlin: De Gruyter, 2016.

Duquette, Jonathan, and K. Ramasubramanian. "Is Space Created? Reflections on Śaṇkara's Philosophy and Philosophy of Physics." *Philosophy East and West* 60 (2010): 517–533.

Ebreo, Leone. *Dialoghi di amore, di Leone Hebreo medico*. New corrected ed. Venezia, 1565.

Ebreo, Leone. *Dialogues of Love*. Translated by Damian Bacich and Rosella Pescatori. Toronto: University of Toronto Press, 2009.

Ebrey, David. *Theory and Practice in Aristotle's Natural Science*. Cambridge: Cambridge University Press, 2015.

Farissol, Abraham. *Be'ur le-Sefer Qohelet*. Edited by Simḥah Bamberger. Jerusalem: Defus Eretz Yisrael, 1938.

Feldman, Seymour. *Philosophy in a Time of Crisis. Don Isaac Abravanel: Defender of the Faith*. London: Routledge, 2003.

Fontaine, T.A.M. *In Defence of Judaism: Abraham ibn Daud. Sources and Structures of ha-Emunah ha-Ramah*. Assen: Van Gorcum, 1990.

Freedman, Harry. *Midrash Rabbah: Genesis*. In *Midrash Rabbah*, vols. 1–2, translated by Harry Freedman and Maurice Simon. 3rd ed. London: Soncino Press, 1961.

Freudenthal, Gad. "(Al-)Chemical Foundations for Cosmological Ideas: Ibn Sînâ on the Geology of an Eternal World." In *Physics, Cosmology and Astronomy, 1300–1700: Tension and Accommodation*, edited by Sabetai Unguru, 47–73. Dordrecht: Kluwer, 1991.

Fürst, Julius. *Bibliotheca Judaica: Bibliographisches Handbuch der gesammten jüdischen Literatur mit Einschluss der Schriften über Juden und Judenthum und einer Geschichte der jüdischen Bibliographie nach alfabetischer Ordnung der Verfasser*. Vol. 3. Leipzig, 1863.

Galluzzo, Gabriele. *The Medieval Reception of Book Zeta of Aristotle's* Metaphysics, *Volume 2: Pauli Veneti*, Expositio in duodecim libros metaphysice Aristotelis, *liber VII*. Leiden: Brill, 2013.

Gersonides, Levi. *The Wars of the Lord, Volume 3. Book Five: The Heavenly Bodies and Their Movers, the Relationship amongst These Movers, and the Relationship between Them and God; Book Six: Creation of the World*. Translated by Seymour Feldman. Philadelphia: Jewish Publication Society of America, 1999.

Gothofredus, Jakob, and Antoine de Marville, eds. *Codex Theodosianus*. Vol. 6.1. Lipsiæ, 1743.

Guetta, Alessandro. "Maimonideanism in the Renaissance." In *Encyclopedia of Renaissance Philosophy*, edited by Marco Sgarbi. Cham: Springer, 2015. https://doi.org/10.1007/978--3--319--02848--4_161--1.

Halevi, Judah. *Kitab al Khazari*. Translated by Hartwig Hirschfeld. London: Routledge; New York: Dutton, 1905. https://www.sefaria.org/Kuzari.

Hanegraaff, Wouter. *Esotericism and the Academy: Rejected Knowledge in Western Culture*. Cambridge: Cambridge University Press, 2012.

Harvey, Warren Zev. "Maimonides and Aquinas on Interpreting the Bible." *Proceedings of the American Academy for Jewish Research* 55 (1988): 59–77.

Harvey, Warren Zev. "Rashi on Creation beyond Plato and Derrida." *Aleph* 18 (2018): 27–49.

Henry, Desmond Paul. *Medieval Mereology*. Amsterdam: B.R. Grüner, 1991.

Herzberg, Stephan. "God as Pure Thinking. An Interpretation of *Metaphysics* Λ 7, 1072b14–26." In *Aristotle's* Metaphysics *Lambda—New Essays*, edited by Christoph Horn, 157–180. Berlin: De Gruyter, 2016.

Hoffmann, Tobias, ed. *A Companion to Angels in Medieval Philosophy*. Leiden: Brill, 2012.

Hubler, James Noel. "*Creatio ex nihilo*: Matter, Creation, and the Body in Classical and Christian Philosophy through Aquinas." PhD diss., University of Pennsylvania, 1995.

Hyman, Arthur. "Maimonides on Causality." In *Maimonides and Philosophy*, edited by Yirmiyahu Yovel and Shlomo Pines, 157–172. Dordrecht: Nijhoff, 1986.

Jandun, Jean de. *Quaestiones in duodecim libros metaphysicae*. Venetiis, 1586.

Klein, Jan, and Norman Klein, eds. *Solitude of a Humble Genius—Gregor Johann Mendel. Volume 1: Formative Years*. Berlin: Springer, 2013.

Kosman, Aryeh L. "Aristotle's Definition of Motion." *Phronesis* 14 (1969): 40–62.

Kreisel, Howard. "*Imitatio Dei* in Maimonides' *Guide of the Perplexed*." *AJS Review* 19 (1994): 169–211.

Lohr, Charles H. "The Arabic Background to Ramon Lull's *Liber Chaos* (ca. 1285)," *Traditio* 55 (2000): 159–170.

Mahoney, Edward P. "Giovanni Pico della Mirandola and Elia del Medigo, Nicoletto Vernia and Agostino Nifo." In *Giovanni Pico della Mirandola: Convegno internazionale di studi nel cinquecentesimo anniversario della morte (1494–1994)*, edited by Gian Carlo Garfagnini, 2:127–156. Florence: Olschki, 1997.

Maimonides, Moses. *Guide of the Perplexed*. Translated by Shlomo Pines. 2 vols. Chicago: University of Chicago Press, 1963.

Maimonides, Moses. *Mishneh Torah: Hilchot Yesodei Hatorah*. Translated by Eliyahu Touger. New York: Moznaim Publishing, 1997. Digital edition. URL: https://www.chabad.org/library/article_cdo/aid/682956/jewish/Mishneh-Torah.htm.

Mantino, Jacob. *Averroys epithoma totius methaphisices Aristotelis in quattuor secatum tractatus. Interpraete Iacob Mantino*. Bononiæ, 1523.

Marx, Alexander. "Texts by and about Maimonides." *Jewish Quarterly Review* 25 (1935): 371–428.

McGinnis, Jon. "Natural Knowledge in the Arabic Middle Ages." In *Wrestling with Nature: From Omens to Science*, edited by Peter Harrison, Ronald L. Numbers, and Michael H. Shank, 59–82. Chicago: Chicago University Press, 2011.

McGuire, James E. "Natural Motion and Its Causes: Newton on the 'Vis Insita' of Bodies." In *Self-Motion: From Aristotle to Newton*, edited by Mary Louise Gill and James G. Lennox, 305–330. Princeton, NJ: Princeton University Press, 1994.

Menn, Stephan. "The Origin of Aristotle's Concept of *Energeia*: *Energeia* and *Dunamis*." *Ancient Philosophy* 14 (1994): 73–114.

Montada, Josep Puig. "Aristotle and Averroes on *Coming-to-be and Passing-Away*." *Oriens* 35 (1996): 1–34.

Montada, Josep Puig. "Ibn Rushd versus al-Ghazālī: Reconsideration of a Polemic." *Muslim World* 82 (1992): 113–132.

Nacchiante, Jacopo. *Jacobi Naclanti, Clugiensis episcopi operum [tomi duo], id est enarrationes in D. Pauli epistolas ad Ephesios et Romanos [...] Sacrae scripturae medulla [...] Tractatus item decem et octo, in quibus varia [...] Rerum argumenta tractantur [...]*. Venetiis, 1567.

Nardi, Bruno. *Studi su Pietro Pomponazzi*. Florence: Le Monnier, 1965.

Nifo, Agostino. *Commentationes in librum Averrois de substantia orbis*. Venitiis, 1508.

Nifo, Agostino. *Destruciones destructionum Averroiis cum Agostino Niphi de Sessa expositione*. Venezia, 1497.

Nifo, Agostino. *Eutyci Augustini Niphi Philothei Suessani in librum destructio destructionum Auerrois commentarii*. Venezia, 1498.

Nifo, Agostino. *Expositiones in Aristotelis libros metaphysices*. Venetiis, 1547.

O'Rourke, Fran. *Pseudo-Dionysius and the Metaphysics of Aquinas*. Leiden: Brill, 1992.

Paul of Venice. *Logica Magna*. Venezia, 1499

Paul of Venice. *Logica Magna. Part II, Fascicule 8: Tractatus de obligationibus*. Edited by E.J. Ashworth. Oxford: Oxford University Press, 1988.

Pavesi, Giovanni Jacopo. *Peripataticae disputationes in prima Aristotelis philosophia*. Venetiis, 1566.

Pessin, Sarah. *Ibn Gabirol's Theology of Desire: Matter and Method in Jewish Medieval Neoplatonism*. Cambridge: Cambridge University Press, 2013.

Philo of Alexandria. *De Providentia*. Edited by Mireille Hadas-Lebel. Paris: Editions du Cerf, 1973.

Pseudo-Dionysius. *Corpus Dionysiacum I: De divinis nominibus*. Edited by Beate Regina Suchla. Berlin: De Gruyter, 1990.

Pseudo-Dionysius. *Corpus Dionysiacum II: De coelesti hierarchia. De ecclesiastica hierarchia. De mystica theologia. Epistulae*. Edited by Heil Günter and Adolf Martin Ritter. 2nd ed. Berlin: De Gruyter, 2012.

Ross, William David. *Aristotle*. 5th rev. ed. London: Methuen & Co., 1949.

Rudavsky, Tamar M. *Divine Omniscience and Omnipotence in Medieval Philosophy: Islamic, Jewish, and Christian Perspectives*. Dordrecht: D. Reidel Publishing Co., 1985.

Ruderman, David B. *The World of a Renaissance Jew: The Life and Thought of Abraham ben Mordecai Farissol*. Cincinnati: Hebrew Union College Press, 1981.

Sakamoto, Kuni. *Julius Caesar Scaliger, Renaissance Reformer of Aristotelianism: A Study of His Exotericae Exercitationes*. Leiden: Brill, 2016.

Samuelson, Norbert M. *Judaism and the Doctrine of Creation*. Cambridge: Cambridge University Press, 1994.

Scaliger, Julius Caesar. *Exotericarum exercitationum liber XV, de subtilitate, ad Hieronymum Cardanum*. Paris, 1557.

Schmidt, Johann A. *Historiam coelicolarum ad tit. Codicis de Iudaeis & coelicolis*. Helmstedt, 1704.

Schwartz, Yossef. "Celestial Motion, Immaterial Causality and the Latin Encounter with Arabic Aristotelian Cosmology." In *Albertus Magnus und der Ursprung der Universitätsidee: Die Begegnung der Wissenschaftskulturen im 13. Jahrhundert und die Entdeckung des Konzepts der Bildung durch Wissenschaft*, edited by Ludger Honnefelder, 277–298. Berlin: Berlin University Press, 2011.

Sela, Shlomo. *Abraham ibn Ezra on Elections, Interrogations, and Medical Astrology*. Leiden: Brill, 2011.

Silman, Yochanan. *Philosopher and Prophet: Judah Halevi, the Kuzari and the Evolution of His Thought*. Albany, NY, SUNY Press, 1995.

Sorabji, Richard. *Time, Creation and the Continuum: Theories in Antiquity and the Middle Ages*. London: Duckworth, 1983.

Steinschneider, Moritz. "Al Farabi (Alfarabius), des arabischen philosophen Leben und Schriften." *Mémoires de l'Académie impériale des sciences de St. Pétersbourg* 13, no. 4 (1869): 1–268.

Steinschneider, Moritz. *Die hebraeischen Übersetzungen des Mittelalters und die Juden als Dolmetscher*. Berlin, 1893; repr. Graz: Akademische Druck- und Verlagsanstalt, 1956.

Steuco, Agostino. *De Perennis Philosophia*. Ludguni, 1540.

Strauss, Leo. "How to Begin to Study *The Guide of the Perplexed*." In Moses Maimonides,

The Guide of the Perplexed, translated by Shlomo Pines, 1: xi–lvi. Chicago: University of Chicago Press, 1963.

Stroumsa, Sarah. "Sabéens de Harran et Sabéens de Maïmonide." In *Maimonide: Philosophe et savant*, edited by Tony Lévy and Roshdi Rashed, 335–352. Louvain: Peeters, 2004.

Themistius. *Libri paraphraseos Themistij: Peripatetici acutissimi. In posteriora Aristotelis. In physica. In libros de anima. In commentarios de memoria & reminiscientia. De somno & vigilia. De insomnijs. De diunatione per somnium.* [...]. Translated by Ermalao Barbaro. Venetia, 1527.

Thiene, Gaetano da. *Super libros de anima. Questiones de sensu agente et de sensilibus communibus: Ac de intellectu. Item de substantia orbis Ioannis de Gandavo cum questionibus eiusdem.* [Venice], 1493.

Tzamalikos, Panayiotis. *Anaxagoras, Origen, and Neoplatonism: The Legacy of Anaxagoras to Classical and Late Antiquity*. Berlin: De Gruyter, 2016.

Veltri, Giuseppe. *Alienated Wisdom: Enquiry into Jewish Philosophy and Scepticism*. Berlin: De Gruyter, 2018.

Wallace, William. *The Elements of Philosophy: A Compendium for Philosophers and Theologians*. New York: Alba House, 1977.

Weisheipl, James A. *Nature and Motion in the Middle Ages*. Edited by William E. Carroll. Washington, DC: Catholic University of America Press, 1985.

Witt, Charlotte. "Powers and Possibilities: Aristotle vs. the Megarians." *Proceedings of the Boston Area Colloquium in Ancient Philosophy* 11 (1995): 249–266.

Witt, Charlotte. *Ways of Being: Potentiality and Actuality in Aristotle's* Metaphysics. Ithaca, NY: Cornell University Press, 2003.

Glossary

This glossary contains a selection of key philosophical and scientific terms. The references given do not indicate every occurrence of a term and exclude specifically colloquial usages or inexact renderings (as a consequence of Sforno's revision of the Latin text). *Hebr.* or *Lat.* indicates a specific translation in one of the versions (e.g. "mixed compound" for *Lat.* confusum as Sforno's translation of תהו).

1 Hebrew–Latin–English

Hebrew	Latin	English
אבדן	perditio	perdition (§ 11.6)
אדם	homo	man (§ 12.2.1, § 12.8.1.)
אויר	aer	air (§ 3.8.1)
אומות (pl.)	Gentiles (pl.)	Nations, Gentiles (§ 6.9.2)
אומן	artifex (§ 10.7.2) opifex (§ 15.8)	artisan
אופן	modus	manner (§ 12.5.2)
אור	lumen	light (§ 10.8.3)
אחדות	unitas	unity (§ 8.3.2)
אחרון	ultimus	final (1.6.2 (1.))
אחרית	finis	end (§ 1.5.4)
איבר	membrum (§ 14.3.2) organum (§ 16.16)	organ
איחור	postpositio	retardation, delay, postposition (§ 5.5.3)
איחר (pi.)	postpono (v.)	to postpone (§ 5.5.3)
איכות	qualitas	quality (§ 1.14)
איש	homo	man (§ 9.11.1)
	individuum	individual (§ 9.4)
אישי	individuis (adj.)	individual (§ 11.3.4.)
אל / אלהים	Deus	God (§ 1.3)
שני לאל / אלהים שנים	Deus secundus	secondary god(s) (§ 8.4.3 / § 12.8.1)
אלהי	divinus	divine (§ 14.4)
חוקר באלהייות	Divinus sive metaphysicus	divine man (*Lat.*), investigator of divine things, metaphysician (§ 12.15.5)
אמיתי	verum (adj.)	true (§ 1.3)
אמצעי	medium	middle (§ 6.6.1)
אמצעי / בלתי אמצעי	mediate/immediate	mediately/immediately (§ 1.5.3)
אמת	veritas	truth (§ 12.2.5)
אנושי	humanus	human (§ 14.1)
אפיסות	non esse	non-being (§ 6.4.4)
אפשר	possibile	possible (§ 14.4)
אפשרות	possibilitas	possibility (§ 6.9.2)
אפשרי	possibilis	possible (§ 4.7.1)
	contingens	contingent (§ 9.11.1)
ארץ	terra	earth (§ 5.6.1)

(cont.)

Hebrew	Latin	English
אש	ignis	fire (§ 3.8.1)
אש יסודי	elementalis ignis	elementary fire (§ 3.8.1)
אשי	igneus (adj.)	igneous, fiery (§ 3.8.1)
בהמה	bestia	beast (§ 16.25)
בורא	Creator	Creator (§ 5.5.3)
בחירה	arbitrium (§ 11.3.4.)	choice
	electio (§ 9.7.2)	
	liberum arbitrium	free choice (§ 14.7)
בחר (qal)	eligo (v.)	to choose (§ 12.14.2)
בטל	fabulosus (adj.)	fabulous; in vain (§ 2.2.2)
	ociosus	in vain (§ 9.6.4)
בייתי	mansuetus	domesticated (§ 16.12.1)
בכלל	universale (adv.)	universally (§ 5.5.1)
בעל חיים	animal	living being; animal (§ 16.12.1)
בעל תכלית / בלתי בעל תכלית	finitum/infinitum	finite/infinite (§ 11.7)
בעלי הדתות (pl.)	theologi (pl.)	theologians; adherents of religion (§ 1.5.2)
ברא (qal)	creo (v.)	to create (§ 3.6)
	produco (v.)	to produce, to generate (§ 8.8.1)
בריאה	creatio	creation (§ 6.4.4)
גדר	diffinitio	definition (§ 5.2.5)
גודל	magnitudo	magnitude, size (§ 4.9.4)
גוים (pl.)	Gentiles (pl.)	Nations; Gentiles (§ 8.8.2)
גוף	corpus	body (§ 1.6.2 (10.))
גלגל	orbis	sphere (§ 4.9.1)
גרם	corpus	body (§ 1.6.2 (10.))
גרם שמימי	corpus celestis	celestial body (§ 1.6.2 (10.))
גרם	substantia	substance, substrate (§ 1.1.1)
גשם	corpus	body (§ 4.4.3)
גשם טבעי	corpus naturalis	natural body (§ 5.5.1)
גשמי	corporeus (adj.)	corporeal, material (§ 12.7.1)
דבקות	continuatio	conjunction (§ 12.2.4)
דבר	verbum	word; discourse (§ 6.1)
דברים מזוייפים (pl.)	soffisitica verba (pl.)	sophistic discourse (§ 9.11.2)
דומה	similis (adj.)	similar (§ 12.9)
דחייה	expellens	thrusting (§ 7.3.4)
דין	ius	law; right (§ 1.2.4)
דמות	similitudo	likeness (§ 2.2.3)
דעת	opinio	opinion (§ 7.5)
דרך	medium	way, means (§ 12.5.2); via (§ 3.2.3)
	modus	manner (§ 9.7.4)
דת	religio	religion (§ 1.2.4)
הבדל	differentia	difference (§ 4.9.1)
	diversitas	diversity (§ 5.4)
הבחנה	provisio	discernment, foresight (§ 10.7.2)
הבין (hif.)	intellego/intelligo (v.)	to know, to understand (§ 1.2.4)
הבל	ambages	ambiguity, nonsense (§ 9.10.1)

(cont.)

Hebrew	Latin	English
הבנה	consideratio	consideration; contemplation (§ 12.4.3)
הגבלה	appropriatio	differentiation (§ 15.3.2)
	limitatio	limitation (§ 4.10)
הוברי שמים החוזים בכוכבים (pl.)	astronomi (pl.)	astronomers, stargazers (pl.) (§ 4.9.3)
הוויה	generatio	generation (§ 1.1.2)
הווים ונפסדים (pl.)	mortalia (pl.)	generables and corruptibles, mortal beings (§ 8.5.1), mortals (§ 11.10); human beings (pl.) (§ 15.3.1)
הוראה	significatio	signification, indication (§ 6.4.2)
היקש	comparatio	comparison (§ 11.13.3)
הכחיש (hif.)	nego (v.)	to refute (§ 9.5)
הכיר (hif.)	nosco (v.)	to know, to recognize (§ 8.4.2)
הכנה	dispositio (§ 1.6)	disposition
	motivitas (§ 5.2.1)	
	potentia	potency, potentiality (§ 5.4)
הכרח	necessarium	necessary (§ 2.2.2)
הכרחי	necessarium	necessary (§ 1.14)
	violentus	violent (§ 4.5.3)
המציא (hif.)	emano (v.)	to emanate (§ 6.9.2)
	produco (v.)	to produce, to create, to generate (§ 16.23)
	provenio (v.)	to come forth (§ 8.4.2)
הנאה	voluptas	pleasure (§ 13.3.2)
הנהגת המדינה	civile regimen	governance of the city (§ 13.1)
	Polyticorum [libri]	[Book of] *Politics* (§ 11.9)
הנחה	propositio	proposition, statement (§ 12.13)
	sententia	thesis (§ 1.4.1)
הנעה	motio	motion, propulsion (§ 4.5.1)
תנועה מקומית	localis motio	locomotion (§ 1.6.2 (23.))
הסכמה	conclusio	solution (§ 10.7.2)
	deliberatio	deliberation (§ 10.3.2)
העדר	corruptio	corruption (§ 4.7.1)
	privatio	privation (§ 10.8.3)
הפך	oppositus	opposite, contrary (§ 1.4.1)
	contrarium	contrary (§ 1.1.2)
הפכיות	contrarietas	contrariety (§ 1.1.2)
הפסד	corruptio	corruption (§ 1.1.2)
הפשיט	extraho (v.)	to abstract (§ 12.8.2)
הקדמה	presuppositus	presupposition, assumption (§ 11.9)
הקרבה	appropinquatio	approaching (§ 1.7)
הקריב (hif.)	appropinquo (v.)	to approach (§ 1.7)
הרגיש (hif.)	sentio (v.)	to sense (§ 12.7)
הרכבה	compositio	compound (§ 9.7.3)
השארות	immortalitas	immortality (§ 1.2.4)
השגחה	cura	care; providence (*Hebr.*) (§ 11.10)
	sollicitudo	providence (§ 11.8)

(cont.)

Hebrew	Latin	English
השגיח (hif.)	curo (v.) (§ 11.4.2)	to take care; to exert providence (*Hebr.*)
	adhibeo curam (v.) (§ 11.7)	
	provideo (v.)	to exert providence (§ 9.5)
השיא	transfero (v.)	to transfer (§ 10.3.2)
השיג (hif.)	percipio (v.)	to perceive (§ 11.12)
השכיל (hif.)	intellego/intelligo (v.)	to know, to understand (§ 6.6.1; § 9.7.3)
השכלה	intellectio	intellection (§ 6.6.1)
השלים (hit.)	perficio (v.)	to perfect, to accomplish (§ 11.9)
השפיע (hit.)	emano (v.)	to emanate (§ 12.15.4)
השתנה (hit.)	convertor (v.) (§ 3.8.2)	to change
	permuto (v.) (§ 12.5.1)	
	transmutor (v.) (§ 12.7)	
	altero (v.) (§ 1.5.2)	
השתנות	transmutatio (§ 3.6)	change
	alteratio (§ 2.3.3)	
התאחד (hit.)	concurro (v.)	to unite; to join (§ 8.8.2)
התבונן (hit.)	intellego/intelligo (v.)	to know, to understand (§ 12.8.1)
	percipio (v.)	to perceive (§ 2.12.1)
התהווה (hit.)	educo (v.)	to lead (§ 1.5.3)
	genero (v.)	to create, to produce (§ 6.7.2)
	produco (v.)	to produce, to create, to generate (§ 6.2.1)
	provenio (v.)	to come forth (§ 8.5.1)
התהפך (hit.)	convertor (v.)	to change (§ 3.8.2)
התחדש (hit.)	genero (v.)	to produce, to create (§ 5.5.2)
	innovo (v.) (§ 6.1)	to create anew
	produco (v.) (§ 6.8)	
התחלה	principium	principle (§ 8.1)
התחלף (hit.)	muto (v.)	to change (§ 9.2.1)
התחלפות	diversitas	diversity (§ 4.9.2)
התיחס (hit.)	attribuo (v.)	to attribute; to specify (§ 12.5.5)
התייחד (hit.)	approprio (v.)	to determine (§ 8.4.1)
התמדה	continuatio	continuity (§ 7.3.4)
התנגדות	resistentia	resistance (§ 2.2.2)
התנועע (hit.)	moveo (v.)	to move (§ 1.5.2)
התרשל (hit.)	negligo (v.)	to neglect (§ 12.13)
זמן	tempus	time (§ 5.5.1)
חזרה	reciprocatio	reciprocation (§ 6.3.1)
חום	calor	heat (§ 10.3.2)
חומר	materia	matter (§ 6.1)
חומר הראשון	materia prima	prime matter (§ 2.1.3)
חוץ	extra	outside (§ 5.5.1)
חוקר באלהייות	Divinus sive metaphysicus	investigator of divine things; divine man, metaphysician (§ 12.15.5)
חוש	sensus	sense (§ 12.2.7)
חושך	tenebra	darkness (§ 10.8.3)
חזק	fortis	strong (§ 12.7)
חי	vivus (adj.)	alive (§ 9.8)

GLOSSARY   487

(cont.)

Hebrew	Latin	English
חידוש	factio	creation (§ 5.1.2)
	produ(c)tio	creation (§ 7.3.2)
	generatio	generation (§ 4.9.5)
חידוש העולם	universi produ(c)tio (§ 10.7.1)	creation of the universe
	novitas mundi (§ 9.5)	
חידש (pi.)	genero (v.)	to create, to produce (§ 5.5.2)
	creo (v.)	to create (§ 3.6)
	produco (v.)	to produce, to create, to generate (§ 5.5.3)
חילוף	diversitas	diversity (§ 4.9.1)
חכם	sapiens	wise (§ 11.4.2)
	sciens	knowing, understanding (§ 12.14.3)
חכמה	sapientia	wisdom (§ 4.3.3)
חלק	pars	part (§ 14.6)
חסד	benignitas (§ 13.2.2)	benevolence, compassion
	miseratio (§ 13.2.3)	
חסור	vanus	defective, useless (§ 8.4.3)
חסר (qal)	deficio (v.)	to withdraw, to lack (§ 14.2)
חסרון	defectus	lack, privation (§ 9.5)
	diminutio	decrease (§ 1.12)
חפץ	desiderium	desire; wish (§ 11.3.2)
חקירה	dubium	doubt, i.e. question (§ 1.14)
	questio	question (§ 1.3.3)
חשב (qal)	cogito (v.)	to think (§ 9.12.1)
טבע	natura	nature (§ 4.9.1)
בטבע	naturaliter (adv.)	naturally (§ 1.5.5)
טבעית	naturalis (adj.)	natural (§ 4.5.3)
טוב	bonum	good (§ 1.14)
	bonitas	goodness; benevolence (§ 1.14)
טוביּיות אלהי	Divina bonitas	Divine goodness (§ 11.2)
טענה	argumentum	argument (§ 5.5.1)
יבש	siccus	dry (§ 3.8.1)
ידיעה	cognitio	knowledge (§ 1.4.1)
	scientia	science; knowledge (§ 9.2.1)
ידע (qal)	nosco (v.)	to know (§ 9.5)
	scio (v.)	to know, to understand (§ 9.2.1)
יחוד	appropriatio	differentiation (§ 4.3.3)
יחיד	unicus (adj.)	only (§ 9.1)
יחס	concursus	connection (§ 16.11.1)
	proportio	proportion; relation (§ 9.10.2)
ייחס (pi.)	attribuo (v.)	to attribute; to specify (§ 10.7.2)
יכולת	virtus	power; capability (§ 8.4.1)
יסוד	elementum	element (§ 2.1.3)
	fundamentus	principle (§ 1.6.1)
	radix	root (§ 4.3.3)
ישרה / בלתי ישרה	rectus /non rectus (adj.)	right/non-right (§ 12.14.3)
כבד	gravis (adj.)	heavy (§ 12.8.4)

(cont.)

(cont.)

Hebrew	Latin	English
כדור	sphera	sphere (§ 4.3.4)
כדור הארץ	sphera telluris	earth (§ 1.1.1)
כדוריות	rotunditas	roundness (§ 4.10)
כוונה	intentio	intention (§ 1.10)
	voluntas	will (§ 1.5.7)
בלתי כוונה	preter voluntatem	without will, unintended (§ 1.6.2 (6.))
כוזב	falsus	false (§ 6.9.1)
כוח	potentia	potency, potentiality (§ 1.5.3)
בכוח	in potentia	in potentiality (§ 3.2.1)
כוח	virtus	power (§ 12.5.5)
		faculty (§ 12.5.5)
כוחיות	potentia	potency, potentiality (§ 1.1.1)
בכח אנושי	per humanam virtutem	according to human power (§ 14.1)
בכח אלהי או טבעי	per naturalem vel divinam virtutem	according to divine or natural power (§ 1.5)
כוח בחירי	arbitrarium diligentiam	free will (§ 14.5)
כוח מתאוה	desiderativa virtus	appetite (faculty of desire) (§ 5.6.2)
כוח שכלי	virtus intellectiva	intellectual faculty (§ 12.8.1)
כוכב	stella	star (§ 4.9.1)
כלל	universalis	universal (§ 9.11.2)
כללי	universalis (adj.)	universal, general (§ 9.2.1)
כלי	vas	vessel (§ 9.12.1)
	instrumentum	instrument
כלי חומרי	materialis instrumentum	material instrument (§ 16.26)
כלי גשמי	corporalis instrumentum	corporeal instrument (§ 12.5.5)
כלי	organum	organ (§ 1.5.7)
כלים גשמים (pl.)	corporea organa (pl.)	bodily organs (pl.) (§ 7.2.1)
כמות	dimensio (§ 2.1.3)	quantity
	quantitas (§ 5.5.1)	
לבטלה	frustra (§ 15.6.1)	in vain
	ociosus (§ 14.2)	
לוח נקי	tabula rasa	clean slate (*metaph.* intellect) (§ 12.12.2)
לח	humidus	humid (§ 3.8.1)
ליאות	lassitudo	weakness (§ 7.1)
למטה	ignobilis	ignoble (§ 9.1)
לעולם	semper	for ever (§ 2.2.1)
מאור	luminarium	luminary (sun and moon) (§ 4.8.2)
מאמר	sententia	discourse, statement (§ 8.2)
	sermo	discourse (§ 1.3.5)
מאמרות (pl.)	predicamenta (pl.)	categories (pl.) (§ 2.1.2)
מאמרים סתומים (pl.)	verba obscura (pl.)	obscure discourse (§ 8.5.1)
מגונה	iniquus	disgusting (§ 12.14.3)
מדברי / בלתי מדברי	rationale/non rationale	rational/irrational (§ 12.1.2 / § 12.8.1)
מדברים (pl.)	Loquentes (pl.) (§ 4.3.3) theologi (pl.) (§ 6.9.2)	(Muslim) theologians, Mutakallimun
מדרגה	gradus	degree (§ 9.6.2)
מהווה	generans	creator (§ 1.5.3)

GLOSSARY

(cont.)

Hebrew	Latin	English
מהות	quidditas	quiddity (§ 1.3.5)
מהיר	velox	fast (§ 4.3.2)
מוגבל	limitatus (adj.)	limited (§ 4.9.1)
מוחלט	purum (adj., adv.)	pure, absolute (§ 2.5.2)
מוחש	imaginatus	imagined (§ 13.1)
	sensatus	sensible (§ 12.2.7)
	sensibilium	sensible (§ 12.2.7)
מוכן	proportionatus (adj.)	proportionate, capable, disposed (§ 6.5.2)
מונח	positus	placed, underlying (§ 3.2.1)
מופשט	denudatus (adj.)	devoid (§ 2.1.2)
מורכב	aggregatum (§ 12.5.2)	combination; compound
	compositum (§ 2.5.1)	
מורכב / בלתי מורכב	mixtum/non mixtum	mixed/unmixed (§ 7.3.3)
מושכל	intelligibilis	intelligible (§ 12.7)
מושכלות ראשונות (.pl)	prime propositiones (pl.)	first intelligibles (pl.) (§ 12.14.1)
מותמד	continuus (adj.)	continuous (§ 7.3.4)
מזיק	malum	evil (§ 12.14.3)
מחודש	innovatio	creation (§ 6.1)
	nova factio	new creature (§ 5.1.2)
מחודש / בלתי מחודש	genitus/ingenitus (§ 2.1.3)	generated/ungenerated
	generabilis/non generabilis (§ 4.1.1)	
מחשבה	cogitatio (§ 1.5.3)	thought
	meditatio (§ 10.3.2)	
	mens	mind, reasoning (§ 1.6.2 (4.))
מידה	mensura	measurement (§ 15.3.2)
מיוחד	proportionatus (adj.)	proportionate, proportioned (§ 5.1.2)
	proprius	proper, designated (§ 3.3.4)
מים	aqua	water (§ 2.2.2)
מין	genus	genus (§ 4.7.1)
	species	species (§ 1.5.7)
מין אנושי	humanus genus	human species (§ 12.2.1)
מכוון / בלתי מכוון	intendens/preter intentum	intended/unintended (§ 5.5.6 / § 16.8.2)
מכוון אל תכלית	finem intendentem	intended for a goal (§ 10.4.2)
מכריח	violentus	violent (§ 4.5.3)
מלא	plenus	full (§ 2.5.2)
מלאכה	ars	craft, art (§ 1.5.7)
	artificium	artistry; craftsmanship (§ 9.12.1)
ממציא	producens	producer, creator (§ 4.9.1)
מנהיג	Rector	Arranger (§ 6.9.2)
מנוחה	quies	rest (§ 5.1.1)
במנוחה	in quiete	at rest (§ 8.5.1)
מניע	motor	mover (§ 5.4)
	movens	moving (§ 4.3.4)
מניע ראשון	primum mobilis	first mobile (§ 4.5.3)
מסדר	ordinator	arranger (§ 4.4.1)

(cont.)

Hebrew	Latin	English
מסובב / בלתי מסובב	causatus (adj.)/incausatus	caused/uncaused (§ 6.6.1 / § 6.5.5)
מסודר / בלתי מסודר	ordinatus (adj.)/inordinatus	ordered/disordered (§ 7.3.2)
מספר	numeratio	enumeration (§ 12.2.2)
	numerus	number (§ 12.2.1)
מעורב / בלתי מעורב	mixtus/immixtus	mixed/unmixed (§ 12.9)
מעורר	excitatus (adj.)	stimulated (§ 11.3.1)
מעלה	nobilitas	nobility, rank (§ 4.9.1)
מעלת המדות	moralitas	morality (§ 13)
מעשה	intentio	deed, action
מעשים טובים (pl.)	pia intentio (pl.) (§ 1.6.1)	good deeds (pl.)
	pia opera (pl.)	(§ 13.5)
	opus	work (§ 9.12.1)
מציאות	essentia	essence, reality (§ 1.3)
		existence (§ 16.12.5)
	esse	existence; being (§ 16.12.5)
אפיסות	non esse	non-being (§ 6.4.4)
העדר	non esse	non-being (§ 2.1.1)
מקבל	recipiens	receiving, receiver (§ 12.5.2)
מקובץ	aggregatum	combination (§ 5.2.4)
מקום	locus	place (§ 4.9.1)
מקרה	accidens	accident (§ 2.2.3)
	contingentia	contingent being (§ 16.18)
	casus	chance (§ 1.6.2 (6.))
מרכז	centrum	centre (§ 2.2.3)
משותף	communis (adj.)	common (§ 2.3.3)
משך (qal)	attraho	to attract; to drag together (§ 7.3.4)
משתנה / בלתי משתנה	mutabilis (§ 12.5.1)/ impermutabilis	changeable/unchangeable
	alterabilis (§ 4.7.1)	
מתאווה	concupisciens	concupiscent, appetitive (§ 12.14.3)
מתהווה / בלתי מתהווה	genitus (§ 1.5.7)/ingenitus	generated/ungenerated
	generabilis (§ 1.4.2)/non generabilis	
מתחלק / בלתי מתחלק	divisibilis/indivisibilis	divisible/indivisible (§ 7.3.2)
מתנועע	mobilis	mobile (§ 5.4)
מתפעל	generatus	generated (§ 1.2)
	passivus	passive (§ 5.4)
מתפעל / בלתי מתפעל	passibilis/impassibilis	passible/impassible (§ 11.7)
נאה	voluptas	pleasant thing; pleasure (§ 13.3.2)
נבדל	separatus	separate (§ 6.7.2)
	abstractum	separate (§ 1.6.2 (20.))
נבדל מחומר	incorporeus	incorporeal (§ 7.3.3)
עצם נבדל	substantia abstracta	separate substance (§ 3.8.1)
נברא	creatus (adj.)	created (§ 2.5.2)
נושא	subiectum	subject, substrate (§ 4.7.1)
נכבד	nobilis	noble (§ 11.7)
נכנס (nif.)	penetratio	penetration, penetrating (§ 4.4.3)

(cont.)

Hebrew	Latin	English
נכסף (nif.)	desidero (v.)	to desire (§ 11.3.1)
נמנע	impossibilis	impossible (§ 1.3)
	inopinabilis	unimaginable, inconceivable (§ 12.5.4)
נמצא	existens	existent, existing (§ 12.2.4)
	ens	being (§ 9.2.1)
ראשון לכל הנמצאות	primum entium	first being (§ 11.5)
נמשך ממנה	corollarium	corollary (§ 9.10.1)
נמשכים (pl.)	sequaces (pl.)	partisans, followers (pl.) (§ 1.6.1)
נעדר (v.)	careo (v.)	to lack, to be absent (§ 3.2.1)
נפסד (nif.)	corrumpo (v.)	to corrupt (§ 4.1.1)
נפסד / בלתי נפסד	mortalis/immortalis	mortal/immortal (§ 11.10)
	corruptibile/incorruptibile (§ 2.2.1)	corruptible/incorruptible
נפרד	abstractum	separate (§ 1.6.2 (19.))
נפש	anima	soul
נפש אנושית	anima humana	human soul (§ 1.2.4)
נפש שכלית	anime intellectiva	intellectual soul (§ 11.3.2)
נצחי	immortalis	immortal (§ 12.3)
	perpetuum	perpetual (§ 2.2.1)
	semper	perpetual (§ 2.2.1)
	sempiternum	eternal, immortal (§ 12.8.2)
נצחיות	immortalitas	immortality (§ 1.4.1)
נקודה	punctum	point (§ 1.1.1)
נקי	purus (adj.)	pure (§ 9.11.2)
נקלה	vilis	lower, inferior (§ 15.1)
נשא (qal)	su(b)stineo (v.)	to endure (§ 6.1)
נתן צורה (qal)	imprimo (v.)	to inform, to give a form to (§ 10.3.2)
סברא / סברה	ratio	opinion (§ 1.3.2)
	declaratio	exposition (§ 9.11.2)
סדר	ordo	order (§ 4.4.1)
סוג	genus	genus (§ 15.2.2)
סוף	finis	end (§ 5.2.3)
סיבה	causa	cause
סיבה תכליתית	causa finalis	final cause (§ 4.3.3)
סיבה צורית	causa formalis	formal cause (§ 5.2.3)
סיבה חומרית	causa materialis	material cause (§ 5.2.3)
סיבה פועלת	causa agentis	efficient cause (§ 15.3.2)
סיבובי	circular	circular (§ 4.1.1)
ספק	dubium	doubt (§ 4.3.4)
	questio	question (§ 4.9.2)
נשיב אם כן להתיר ספק	ad dubium ergo respondetur	to dispel any doubt I will reply (§ 4.6)
סתירה	contradictio	contradiction (§ 12.11.2)
עגולה	circulus	circle (§ 1.1.1)
עולם	mundus	world (§ 4.9.4)
חידוש העולם	novitas mundi	creation of the world (§ 9.5)
עומד	permanens	permanent (§ 15.2.1)
עונש	pena	punishment (§ 8.7)

(cont.)

Hebrew	Latin	English
עיון	scientia	science, knowledge (§ 14.5)
עיקר	radix	root, principle (§ 15.3.2)
עליון	superior	higher, upper (§ 9.6.3)
עצם	substantia	substance, substrate (§ 4.4.2)
עצם ראשון	prima substantia	first substance (§ 8.5.1)
עצם נבדל	substantia abstracta	separate substance (§ 3.8.1)
ערך	comparatio	comparison (§ 6.6.5)
	respectus	respect, relation (§ 8.7)
עשן	fumus	smoke (§ 3.3.3)
עת	instans	instant (§ 5.4)
עתיד	futurus	future (§ 9.3)
פֹּעַל	actus	actuality (§ 1.5.3)
	endelechia	entelechy (§ 5.2.2)
בְּפֹעַל	in actu	in actuality (§ 1.1.1)
פוֹעֵל	agens	agent (§ 2.5.2)
	generans	generator (§ 1.5.3)
	opifex	agent (§ 13.4)
פוֹעֵל מכוין	agens intendens	purposive agent (§ 9.7.1)
פוֹעֵל רצוניי	voluntarius agens	voluntary agent (§ 10.8.2)
סבה פועלת		
פחות	vilis	lower, inferior (§ 11.2)
פעולה	actio (§ 8.4.2)	action; activity
	effectus (§ 10.7.2)	
	operatio (§ 12.14.3)	
פעולה מיוחדת	propria actio	specific/designated activity (§ 12.1.2)
פעולת השכל	intellectus actio	intellectual activity (§ 12.4)
פעולות מלאכותיות (pl.)	artificialia (pl.)	artificial beings (pl.) (§ 9.7.4)
פרטי	individuum	individual (§ 16.7.1)
	particulare	particular, individual (§ 9.2.1)
פשוט	simplex	simple (§ 6.2.2)
צדק (qal)	verifico (v.)	to verify (§ 2.5.2)
צורה	forma	form
צורה חומרית	forma materialis	material form (§ 1.6.2 (27.))
צורה מלאכותית	forma artificialis	artificial form (§ 8.8.2)
צורות נבדלות (pl.)	forme abstracte (pl.)	separate forms (pl.) (§ 12.15.5)
צורת הנפסד	mortalium forma	mortal form (§ 12.1.1)
צורה אישיות	forma individuales	individual form (§ 12.5.2)
צורה כלליות	forma universales	universal form (§ 12.5.2)
צורך	indigentia	need (§ 13.2.3)
ציור	pictura	image (§ 12.12.2)
ציור בשכל	formatio per intellectum	formation through the intellect [conceptualisation] (§ 12.7)
צלם	imago	image
צלם אלהים	imago divina	divine image (§ 12.15.2)
קבלה	receptio	reception (§ 12.5.2)
קדימה	prioritas	priority (§ 5.4)

(cont.)

Hebrew	Latin	English
קדמון	eternus	eternal (§ 5.2.5)
קדמונים (pl.)	Antiqui (pl.)	Ancients (philosophers) (§ 1.3.5)
קור	frigiditas	coldness (§ 10.3.2)
קורבה	propinquitas	proximity (§ 7.3.4)
קיבוץ	aggregatum	combination (§ 5.2.4)
	congregatio	community (§ 13.1)
קיבל (pi.)	recipio (v.)	to receive (§ 12.5.2)
	suscipio (v.)	to acknowledge (§ 12.15.5)
קיום	conservatio	endurance, perpetuity (§ 13.2.2)
קיים (pi.)	conservo (v.)	perpetuate, provide endurance (§ 7.3.1)
קיים / בלתי קיים	semper manens/impermanentia	permanent/impermanent (§ 9.2.2 / § 8.4.3)
קצב	mensura	measure, ratio (§ 1.7.5)
קרה (qal)	accido (v.)	to happen, to occur (§ 11.7)
קשר	colligatio	conjunction (§ 6.6.1)
	concursus	conjunction (§ 6.9.3)
ראיה	argumentum	argument (§ 5.5.1)
ראייה	visio	vision, seeing
ראייה חושית	sensuali visione	sensorial vision (§ 1.13)
ראייה שכלית	intellectuali visione	intellectual vision (§ 1.13)
ראשון	primus	first (§ 9.8)
ראשונים (pl.)	Antiqui (pl.)	Ancients, ancient philosophers (§ 12.2.3)
ראשון ואחרון	prius et posterius	before and after [priority and posteriority] (§ 5.5.1)
ראשית	primus, principium	first, beginning (§ 3.2.2); principle (§ 4.9.2)
רב	multus (adj.) (§ 11.1) plures (§ 8)	many
רגע	instans	instant (§ 3.7)
ריחוק	remotio	withdrawal; distancing (§ 7.3.4)
ריק	vacuum	void (adj.) (§ 2.5.2)
ריקות	vacuum	vacuum (§ 2.1.3)
רע	malum	evil (§ 3.8.2)
רצון	voluntas	will (§ 10.2)
רצוני	voluntarius (adj.)	voluntary (§ 10.8.2)
רשות	potestas	mastery; authority (§ 1.6.2 (22.))
שוה / בלתי שוה	equales (adj.)/ inequales	equal/unequal (§ 8.4.3)
שיעור	mensura	measurement (§ 10.4.2)
	quantitas	quantity (§ 10.4.2)
שיתוף		
בשיתוף השם	equivoce (adv.)	equivocally (§ 9.10.1)
שכל	intellectus	intellect (§ 9.2.1)
שכל היולאני	intellectus materialis	material intellect (§ 12.2.5)
שכל היולאני או כוחיי	per potentialem intellectum	material or potential intellect (§ 9.10.2)
שכל מתפעל	intellectus passiblis	passive intellect (§ 9.11.2)
שכלים נבדלים (pl.)	intelligentie (pl.)	separate substances, separate intellects (§ 1.5.7)
שכלי	intellectivus (§ 12.10.1) intellectualis (§ 6.7.2)	intellectual

(cont.)

Hebrew	Latin	English
שלם / בלתי שלם	perfectus/imperfectus	perfect/imperfect (§ 1.4.2)
שלמות	perfectio (§ 11.3.2)	perfection
	actus (§ 11.3.3)	
שלמות ראשון	primus actus	first perfection (§ 12.12.2)
שלמות שני	secundus actus	second perfection (§ 11.3.3)
שם	nomen	name (§ 6.9.2)
שם מיוחד	Tetragrammaton	Tetragrammaton (§ 6.9.2)
שמים	celus	heavens (§ 5.5.1)
שמש	sol	sun (§ 4.4.1)
שנים	dualitas	duality (§ 8.4.2)
שניהם קדמונים	coeternus	coeternal (§ 5.3.1)
שפע (qal)	emano (v.) (§ 12.11.2)	to emanate
	influo (v.) (§ 12.11.2)	
שפט (qal)	discerno (v.)	to distinguish (§ 16.1)
	iudico (v.)	to judge (§ 12.5.2)
שפל	infimus	low, inferior (§ 4.10)
שקר	falsus	false (§ 5.3.2)
שרש	radix	root, principle (§ 10.7.2)
תאווה	appetitus	appetite (§ 12.5.2)
		desire (*Hebr.* § 12.14.3)
תהו	confusum sive chaos	"Tohu," confused, chaos (*metaphorical*: mixed compound) (*Lat.* § 2.6)
תולדה	consequentia	consequence (§ 13.2.2)
תועלת	iuvamen	support, benefit (§ 12.15.5)
	utilitas	advantage (§ 16.10.1)
תחתון	inferior	inferior; lower (§ 8.8.1)
תכונה	dispositio (§ 12.5.5)	disposition
	habitus (§ 13.3.1)	
תכלית	finis	purpose (§ 6.4.2)
תמונה	figura	shape, appearance (§ 4.3.2)
	imaginatio	imagination (§ 4.4.1)
תנאי	conditio	condition (§ 9.11.2)
תנועה	motus	motion, movement (§ 5.5.1)
תנועה סיבובית	motus circularis	circular motion (§ 5.6.3)
תנועה יומית	motus diurnus	diurnal movement (§ 4.5.3)
בלתי תנועה	sine motum	without motion (§ 5.1.2)
תענוג	voluptas (§ 12.5.2)	pleasure
	lascivus (§ 11.3.1)	

2 Latin–Hebrew–English

Latin	Hebrew	English
abstractum	נבדל	separate (§ 1.6.2 (20.))
	נפרד	separate (§ 1.6.2 (19.))
substantia abstracta	עצם נבדל	separate substance (§ 3.8.1)
accidens	מקרה	accident (§ 2.2.3)
accido (v.)	קרה (qal)	to happen, to occur (§ 11.7)
actio	פעולה	action; activity (§ 8.4.2)
propria actio	פעולה מיוחדת	specific/designated activity (§ 12.1.2)
intellectus actio	פעולת השכל	intellectual activity (§ 12.4)
actus	פֹּעַל	actuality (§ 1.5.3)
in actu	בְּפֹעַל	in actuality (§ 1.1.1)
actus	שלמות	perfection (§ 11.3.3)
primus actus	שלמות ראשון	first perfection (§ 12.12.2)
secundus actus	שלמות שני	second perfection (§ 11.3.3)
adhibeo curam (v.)	השגיח (hif.)	to take care; to exert providence (§ 11.7)
aer	אויר	air (§ 3.8.1)
agens	פּוֹעֵל	agent (§ 2.5.2)
agens intendens	פּוֹעֵל מכוין	purposive agent (§ 9.7.1)
voluntarius agens	פּוֹעֵל רצוניי	voluntary agent (§ 10.8.2)
aggregatum	מורכב (§ 12.5.2)	combination
	קיבוץ (§ 5.2.4)	
alterabilis	משתנה	changeable (§ 4.7.1)
alteratio	השתנות	change (§ 2.3.3)
altero (v.)	השתנה (hit.)	to change, to alter (§ 1.5.2)
ambages	הבל	ambiguity, nonsense (§ 9.10.1)
anima	נפש	soul
anima humana	נפש אנושית	human soul (§ 1.2.4)
anima intellectiva	נפש שכלית	intellectual soul (§ 11.3.2)
animal	בעל חיים	living being; animal (§ 16.12.1)
Antiqui (pl.)	קדמונים (pl.) (§ 1.3.5)	Ancients (ancient philosophers)
	ראשונים (pl.) (§ 12.2.3)	
appetitus	תאווה	appetite (§ 12.5.2)
		desire (*Hebr.* § 12.14.3)
appropinquatio	הקרבה	approaching (§ 1.7)
appropinquo (v.)	הקריב (hif.)	to approach (§ 1.7)
appropriatio	הגבלה (§ 15.3.2)	differentiation
	יחוד (§ 4.3.3)	
approprio (v.)	התייחד (hit.)	to determine (§ 8.4.1)
aqua	מים	water (§ 2.2.2)
arbitrium	בחירה	choice (§ 11.3.4.)
arbitrarium diligentiam	כוח בחירי	free will (§ 14.5)
liberum arbitrium	בחירה	free choice (§ 14.7)
argumentum	ראיה (§ 5.5.1)	argument
	טענה (§ 5.5.1)	
ars	מלאכה	craft, art (§ 1.5.7)
artifex	אומן	artisan (§ 10.7.2)
artificialia (pl.)	פעולות מלאכותיות (pl.)	artificial beings (pl.) (§ 9.7.4)

(cont.)

Latin	Hebrew	English
artificium	מלאכה	artistry; craftsmanship (§ 9.12.1)
astronomi (pl.)	הוברי שמים החוזים בכוכבים (pl.)	astronomers, stargazers (pl.) (§ 4.9.3)
attraho	משך (qal)	to attract; to drag together (§ 7.3.4)
attribuo (v.)	התיחס (hit.) (§ 10.7.2) ייחס (pi.) (§ 10.7.2)	to attribute; to specify
benignitas	חסד	benevolence, compassion (§ 13.2.2)
bestia	בהמה	beast (§ 16.25)
bonitas	טוב	goodness; benevolence (§ 1.14)
Divina bonitas	טובייות אלהי	Divine goodness (§ 11.2)
bonum	טוב	good (§ 1.14)
calor	חום	heat (§ 10.3.2)
careo (v.)	נעדר (v.)	to lack, to be absent (§ 3.2.1)
casus	מקרה	chance (§ 1.6.2 (6.))
causa	סיבה	cause
causa finalis	סיבה תכליתית	final cause (§ 4.3.3)
causa formalis	סיבה צורית	formal cause (§ 5.2.3)
causa materialis	סיבה חומרית	material cause (§ 5.2.3)
causa agentis	סיבה פועלת	efficient cause (§ 15.3.2)
causatus /incausatus (adj.)	מסובב / בלתי מסובב	caused/uncaused (§ 6.6.1 / § 6.5.5)
celus	שמים	heavens (§ 5.5.1)
centrum	מרכז	centre (§ 2.2.3)
circular	סיבובי	circular (§ 4.1.1)
circulus	עגולה	circle (§ 1.1.1)
civile regimen	הנהגת המדינה	governance of the city (§ 13.1)
coeternus	שניהם קדמונים	coeternal (§ 5.3.1)
cogitatio	מחשבה	thought (§ 1.5.3)
cogito (v.)	חשב (qal)	to think (§ 9.12.1)
cognitio	ידיעה	knowledge (§ 1.4.1)
colligatio	קשר	conjunction (§ 6.6.1)
communis (adj.)	משותף	common (§ 2.3.3)
comparatio	היקש (§ 11.13.3) ערך (§ 6.6.5)	comparison
compositio	הרכבה	compound (§ 9.7.3)
compositum	מורכב	compound (§ 2.5.1)
conclusio	הסכמה	solution (§ 10.7.2)
concupisciens	מתאווה	concupiscient, appetitive (§ 12.14.3)
concurro (v.)	התאחד (hit.)	to unite; to join (§ 8.8.2)
concursus	יחס	connection (§ 16.11.1)
	קשר	conjunction (§ 6.9.3)
conditio	תנאי	condition (§ 9.11.2)
confusum sive chaos	תוהו	"Tohu," confused, chaos (*metaphorical*: mixed compound) (*Lat.* § 2.6)
congregatio	קיבוץ	community (§ 13.1)
consequentia	תולדה	consequence (§ 13.2.2)
conservatio	קיום	endurance, perpetuity (§ 13.2.2)
conservo (v.)	קיים (pi.)	perpetuate, provide endurance (§ 7.3.1)

(cont.)

Latin	Hebrew	English
consideratio	הבנה	consideration; contemplation (§12.4.3)
contingens	אפשרי	contingent (§9.11.1)
contingentia	מקרה	contingent being (§16.18)
continuatio	דבקות	conjunction (§12.2.4)
continuus (adj.)	מותמד	continuous (§7.3.4)
contradictio	סתירה	contradiction (§12.11.2)
contrarietas	הפכיות	contrariety (§1.1.2)
convertor (v.)	השתנה (hit.) (§3.8.2) התהפך (hit.) (§3.8.2)	to change
corollarium	נמשך ממנה	corollary (§9.10.1)
corporeus (adj.)	גשמי	corporeal, material (§12.7.1)
corpus	גוף גרם	body (§1.6.2 (10.))
corpus celestis	גרם שמימי	heavenly (celestial) body (§1.6.2 (10.))
corpus naturalis	גשם טבעי	natural body (§5.5.1)
corrumpo (v.)	נפסד (nif.)	to corrupt (§4.1.1)
corruptibile/incorruptibile	בלתי נפסד/נפסד	corruptible/incorruptible (§2.2.1)
corruptio	העדר (§4.7.1) הפסד (§1.1.2)	corruption
creatio	בריאה	creation (§6.4.4)
Creator	בורא	Creator (§5.5.3)
creatus (adj.)	נברא	created (§2.5.2)
creo (v.)	ברא (qal) (§3.6) חידש (pi.) (§3.6)	to create
cura	השגחה	care; providence (*Hebr.*) (§11.10)
declaratio	סברה	exposition (§9.11.2)
defectus	חסרון	lack, privation (§9.5)
deficio (v.)	חסר (qal)	to withdraw, to lack (§14.2)
deliberatio	הסכמה	deliberation (§10.3.2)
denudatus (adj.)	מופשט	devoid (§2.1.2)
desiderium	חפץ	desire; wish (§11.3.2)
desidero (v.)	נכסף (nif.)	to desire (§11.3.1)
Deus	אל / אלהים	God (§1.3)
Deus secundus	שני לאל / אלהים שנים	secondary god(s) (§8.4.3 / §12.8.1)
differentia	הבדל	difference (§4.9.1)
diffinitio	גדר	definition (§5.2.5)
dimensio	כמות	quantity (§2.1.3)
diminutio	חסרון	decrease (§1.12)
discerno (v.)	שפט (qal)	to distinguish (§16.1)
dispositio	הכנה (§1.6) תכונה (§12.5.5)	disposition
diversitas	הבדל (§5.4) התחלפות (§4.9.2) חילוף (§4.9.1)	diversity

(cont.)

Latin	Hebrew	English
Divina bonitas	טוביויות אלהי	Divine goodness (§ 11.2)
divinus	אלהי	divine (§ 14.4)
Divinus sive metaphysicus	חוקר באלהיות	divine man (*Lat.*), investigator of divine things, metaphysician (§ 12.15.5)
divisibilis/indivisibilis	מתחלק / בלתי מתחלק	divisible/indivisible (§ 7.3.2)
dualitas	שנים	duality (§ 8.4.2)
dubium	חקירה	doubt, i.e. question (§ 1.14)
	ספק	doubt (§ 4.3.4)
ad dubium ergo respondetur	נשיב אם כן להתיר ספק	to dispel any doubt I will reply (§ 4.6)
educo (v.)	התהווה (hit.)	to lead (§ 1.5.3)
effectus	פעולה	action, activity (§ 10.7.2)
electio	בחירה	choice (§ 9.7.2)
elementum	יסוד	element (§ 2.1.3)
eligo (v.)	בחר (qal)	to choose (§ 12.14.2)
emano (v.)	המציא (hif.) (§ 6.9.2)	to emanate
	השפיע (hit.) (§ 12.15.4)	
	שפע (qal) (§ 12.11.2)	
endelechia	פֹּעַל	entelechy (§ 5.2.2)
ens	נמצא	being (§ 9.2.1)
primum entium	ראשון לכל הנמצאות	first being (§ 11.5)
equales (adj.)/inequales	שוה / בלתי שוה	equal/unequal (§ 8.4.3)
equivoce (adv.)	בשיתוף השם	equivocally (§ 9.10.1)
esse	מציאות	existence; being (§ 16.12.5)
non esse	אפסיות	non-being (§ 6.4.4)
non esse	העדר	non-being (§ 2.1.1)
essentia	מציאות	essence, reality (§ 1.3) existence (§ 16.12.5)
eternus	קדמון	eternal (§ 5.2.5))
excitatus (adj.)	מעורר	stimulated (§ 11.3.1)
existens	נמצא	existent, existing (§ 12.2.4)
expellens	דחייה	thrusting (§ 7.3.4)
extra	חוץ	outside (§ 5.5.1)
extraho (v.)	הפשיט	to abstract (§ 12.8.2)
fabulosus (adj.)	בטל	fabulous; in vain (§ 2.2.2)
factio	חידוש	creation (§ 5.1.2)
nova factio	מחודש	new creature (§ 5.1.2)
falsus	כוזב (§ 6.9.1)	false
	שקר (§ 5.3.2)	
figura	תמונה	shape, appearance (§ 4.3.2)
finem intendentem	מכוון אל תכלית	intended for a goal (§ 10.4.2)
finis	אחרית (§ 1.5.4)	end
	סוף (§ 5.2.3)	
	תכלית	purpose (§ 6.4.2)
finitum/infinitum	בעל תכלית / בלתי בעל תכלית	finite/infinite (§ 11.7)

(*cont.*)

Latin	Hebrew	English
forma	צורה	form
forma materialis	צורה חומרית	material form (§ 1.6.2 (27.))
forma artificialis	צורה מלאכותית	artificial form (§ 8.8.2)
forme abstracte (pl.)	צורות נבדלות (pl.)	separate forms (pl.) (§ 12.15.5)
mortalium forma	צורת הנפסד	mortal form (§ 12.1.1)
forma individuales	צורה אישיות	individual form (§ 12.5.2)
forma universales	צורה כלליות	universal form (§ 12.5.2)
formatio per intellectum	ציור בשכל	formation through the intellect [conceptualisation] (§ 12.7)
fortis	חזק	strong (§ 12.7)
frigiditas	קור	coldness (§ 10.3.2)
frustra	לבטלה	in vain (§ 15.6.1)
fumus	עשן	smoke (§ 3.3.3)
fundamentus	יסוד	principle (§ 1.6.1)
futurus	עתיד	future (§ 9.3)
generabilis / non generabilis	מחודש / בלתי מחודש (§ 4.1.1)	generated/ungenerated
	מתהוה / בלתי מתהוה (§ 1.4.2)	
generans	פּוֹעֵל	generator (§ 1.5.3)
	מהווה	creator (§ 1.5.3)
generatio	הוויה (§ 1.1.2)	generation
	חידוש (§ 4.9.5)	
generatus	מתפעל	generated (§ 1.2)
genero (v.)	התהווה (hit.) (§ 6.7.2)	to create, to produce
	התחדש (hit.) (§ 5.5.2)	
	חידש (pi.) (§ 5.5.2)	
genitus/ingenitus	בלתי מחודש / מחודש (§ 2.1.3)	generated/ungenerated
	בלתי מתהווה / מתהווה (§ 1.5.7)	
Gentiles (pl.)	אומות (pl.) (§ 6.9.2)	Nations, Gentiles
	גוים (pl.) (§ 8.8.2)	
genus	מין	genus (§ 4.7.1)
humanus genus	מין אנושי	human species (§ 12.2.1)
genus	סוג	genus (§ 15.2.2)
gradus	מדרגה	degree (§ 9.6.2)
gravis (adj.)	כבד	heavy (§ 12.8.4)
curo (v.)	השגיח (hif.)	to take care; to exert providence (§ 11.4.2)
habitus	תכונה	disposition (§ 13.3.1)
homo	אדם (§ 12.2.1, § 12.8.1)	man
	איש (§ 9.11.1)	
humanus	אנושי	human (§ 14.1)
humidus	לח	humid (§ 3.8.1)
igneus (adj.)	אשי	igneous, fiery (§ 3.8.1)
ignis	אש	fire (§ 3.8.1)
elementalis ignis	אש יסודי	elementary fire (§ 3.8.1)
ignobilis	למטה	ignoble (§ 9.1)
imaginatio	תמונה	imagination (§ 4.4.1)
imaginatus	מוחש	imagined (§ 13.1)

(cont.)

Latin	Hebrew	English
imago	צלם	image
imago divina	צלם אלהים	divine image (§ 12.15.2)
immortalis	נצחי	immortal (§ 12.3)
immortalitas	נצחיִיות (§ 1.4.1) השארות (§ 1.2.4)	immortality
impossibilis	נמנע	impossible (§ 1.3)
imprimo (v.)	נתן צורה (qal)	to inform, to give a form to (§ 10.3.2)
incorporeus	נבדל מחומר	incorporeal (§ 7.3.3)
indigentia	צורך	need (§ 13.2.3)
individuis (adj.)	אישי	individual (§ 11.3.4.)
individuum	איש (§ 9.4) פרטי (§ 16.7.1)	individuum
inferior	תחתון	inferior; lower (§ 8.8.1)
infimus	שפל	low, inferior (§ 4.10)
influo (v.)	שפע (qal)	to flow into (§ 12.11.2)
iniquus	מגונה	disgusting (§ 12.14.3)
innovatio	מחודש	creation (§ 6.1)
innovo (v.)	התחדש (hit.)	to create anew (§ 6.1)
inopinabilis	נמנע	unimaginable, inconceivable (§ 12.5.4)
instans	עת (§ 5.4) רגע (§ 3.7)	instant
instrumentum	כלי	instrument
materialis instrumentum	כלי חומרי	material instrument (§ 16.26)
corporalis instrumentum	כלי גשמי	corporeal instrument (§ 12.5.5)
intellectio	השכלה	intellection (§ 6.6.1)
intellectivus (adj.)	שכלי	intellectual (§ 12.10.1)
intellective iudicium	משפט השכלי	intellectual judgement
intellectualis (adj.)	שכלי	intellectual (§ 6.7.2)
intellectus	שכל	intellect (§ 6.7.2)
intellectus materialis	שכל היולאני	material intellect (§ 12.2.5)
per potentialem intellectum	שכל היולאני או כוחיי	material or potential intellect (§ 9.10.2)
intellectus passiblis	שכל מתפעל	passive intellect (§ 9.11.2)
intellego/intelligo (v.)	השכיל (hif.) (§ 6.6.1) התבונן (hit.) (§ 12.8.1) הבין (hif.) (§ 1.2.4)	to know, to understand
intelligentie (pl.)	שכלים נבדלים (pl.)	separate substances, separate intellects (§ 1.5.7)
intelligibilis	מושכל	intelligible (§ 12.7)
intendens/preter intentum	מכוון / בלתי מכוון	intended/unintended (§ 6.5.6 / § 16.8.2)
intentio	מעשה	deed, action
pia intentio (pl.)	מעשים טובים (pl.)	good deeds (pl.) (§ 1.6.1)
	כוונה	intention (§ 1.10)
iudico (v.)	שפט (qal)	to judge (§ 12.5.2)
ius	דין	law, right (§ 1.2.4)
iuvamen	תועלת	support, benefit (§ 12.15.5)

(*cont.*)

Latin	Hebrew	English
lascivus	תענוג	pleasure (§ 11.3.1)
lassitudo	ליאות	weakness (§ 7.1)
limitatio	הגבלה	limitation (§ 4.10)
limitatus (adj.)	מוגבל	limited (§ 4.9.1)
locus	מקום	place (§ 4.9.1)
Loquentes (pl.)	מדברים (pl.)	(Muslim) theologians, Mutakallimun (§ 4.3.3)
lumen	אור	light (§ 10.8.3)
luminarium	מאור	luminary (sun and moon) (§ 4.8.2)
magnitudo	גודל	magnitude, size (§ 4.9.4)
malum	מזיק (§ 12.14.3)	evil
	רע (§ 3.8.2)	
mansuetus	ביתי	domesticated (§ 16.12.1)
materia	חומר	matter (§ 6.1)
materia prima	חומר הראשון	prime matter (§ 2.1.3)
mediate/immediate	אמצעי / בלתי אמצעי	mediately/immediately (§ 1.5.3)
meditatio	מחשבה	thought (§ 10.3.2)
medium	אמצעי	middle (§ 6.6.1)
	דרך	way, means (§ 12.5.2); via (§ 3.2.3)
membrum	איבר	organ (§ 14.3.2)
mens	מחשבה	mind (§ 1.6.2 (4.))
mensura	מידה (§ 15.3.2)	measurement, measure, ratio
	קצב (§ 1.5.7)	
	שיעור (§ 10.4.2)	
metaphysicus	חוקר באלהיות	divine man, investigator of divine things, metaphysician (§ 12.15.5)
miseratio	חסד	benevolence (§ 13.2.3)
mixtum/non mixtum	מורכב / בלתי מורכב	mixed/unmixed (§ 7.3.3)
mixtus/immixtus	מעורב / בלתי מעורב	mixed/unmixed (§ 12.9)
mobilis	מניע	mobile
primum mobilis	מניע ראשון	first mobile (§ 4.5.3)
mobilis	מתנועע	mobile (§ 5.4)
modus	אופן (§ 12.5.2)	manner
	דרך (§ 9.7.4)	
moralitas	מעלת המדות	morality (§ 13)
mortalia (pl.)	הווים ונפסדים (pl.)	generables and corruptibles, mortal beings (§ 8.5.1), mortals (§ 11.10); human beings (pl.) (§ 15.3.1)
mortalis/immortalis	בלתי נפסד / נפסד	mortal/immortal (§ 11.10)
motio	הנעה	motion, propulsion (§ 4.5.1)
localis motio	תנועה מקומית	locomotion (§ 1.6.2 (23.))
motivitas	הכנה	disposition (§ 5.2.1)
motor	מניע	mover (§ 5.4)
motus	תנועה	motion, movement (§ 5.5.1)
motus circularis	תנועה יומית	circular motion (§ 5.6.3)
motus diurnus	תנועה סיבובית	diurnal movement (§ 4.5.3)
sine motum	בלתי תנועה	without motion (§ 5.1.2)

(cont.)

Latin	Hebrew	English
movens	מניע	moving (§ 4.3.4)
moveo (v.)	התנועע (hit.)	to move (§ 1.5.2)
multus (adj.)	רב	many (§ 11.1)
mundus	עולם	world (§ 4.9.4)
novitas mundi	חידוש העולם	creation of the world (§ 9.5)
mutabilis/impermutabilis	משתנה / בלתי משתנה	changeable/unchangeable (§ 12.5.1)
muto (v.)	התחלף (hit.)	to change (§ 9.2.1)
natura	טבע	nature (§ 4.9.1)
naturaliter (adv.)	בטבע	naturally (§ 1.5.5)
naturalis (adj.)	טבעית	natural (§ 4.5.3)
necessarium	הכרח (§ 2.2.2)	necessary
	הכרחי (§ 1.14)	
negligo (v.)	התרשל (hit.)	to neglect (§ 12.13)
nego (v.)	הכחיש (hif.)	to refute (§ 9.5)
nobilis	נכבד	noble (§ 11.7)
nobilitas	מעלה	nobility, rank (§ 4.9.1)
nomen	שם	name (§ 6.9.2)
nosco (v.)	הכיר (hif.)	to know (§ 9.5)
	ידע (qal)	
nova factio	מחודש	new creature (§ 5.1.2)
numeratio	מספר	enumeration (§ 12.2.2)
numerus	מספר	number (§ 12.2.1)
ociosus	לבטלה (§ 14.2)	in vain
	בטל (§ 9.6.4.)	
operatio	פעולה	action, activity (§ 12.14.3)
opifex	אומן	artisan (§ 15.8)
	פּוֹעֵל	agent (§ 13.4)
opinio	דעת	opinion (§ 7.5)
oppositus	הפך	opposite, contrary (§ 1.4.1)
opus	מעשה	work (§ 9.12.1)
pia opera (pl.)	מעשים טובים (pl.)	good deeds (pl.) (§ 13.5)
orbis	גלגל	sphere (§ 4.9.1)
ordinator	מסדר	arranger (§ 4.4.1)
ordinatus (adj.)/inordinatus	מסודר / בלתי מסודר	ordered/disordered (§ 7.3.2)
ordo	סדר	order (§ 4.4.1)
organum	איבר	organ (§ 16.16)
	כלי	organ (§ 1.5.7)
corporea organa (pl.)	כלים גשמים (pl.)	bodily organs (pl.) (§ 7.2.1)
pars	חלק	part (§ 14.6)
particulare	פרטי	particular, individual (§ 9.2.1)
passibilis/impassibilis	מתפעל / בלתי מתפעל	passible/impassible (§ 11.7)
passivus	מתפעל	passive (§ 5.4)
pena	עונש	punishment (§ 8.7)
penetratio	נכנס (nif.)	penetration, penetrating (§ 4.4.3)
percipio (v.)	השיג (hif.) (§ 11.12)	to perceive
	התבונן (hit.) (§ 12.12.1)	
perditio	אבדן	perdition (§ 11.6)

(*cont.*)

Latin	Hebrew	English
perfectio	שלמות	perfection (§ 11.3.2)
perfectus/imperfectus	שלם / בלתי שלם	perfect/imperfect (§ 1.4.2)
perficio (v.)	השלים (hit.)	to perfect, to accomplish (§ 11.9)
permanens	עומד	permanent (§ 15.2.1)
permuto (v.)	השתנה (hit.)	to change (§ 12.5.1)
perpetuum	נצחי	perpetual (§ 2.2.1)
pictura	ציור	image, imagination (§ 12.12.2)
plenus	מלא	full (§ 2.5.2)
plures	רב	many (§ 8)
Polyticorum [libri]	הנהגת המדינה	[Book of] *Politics* (§ 11.9)
positus	מונח	placed, underlying (§ 3.2.1)
possibile	אפשר	possible (§ 14.4)
possibilis	אפשרי	possible (§ 4.7.1)
possibilitas	אפשרות	possibility (§ 6.9.2)
postpono (v.)	איחר (pi.)	to postpone (§ 5.5.3)
postpositio	איחור	retardation, delay, postposition (§ 5.5.3)
potentia	הכנה	potency, potentiality (§ 5.4)
	כוח	(§ 1.5.3)
	כוחיות	(§ 1.1.1)
in potentia	בכוח	in potentiality (§ 3.2.1)
potestas	רשות	mastery; authority (§ 1.6.2 (22.))
predicamenta (pl.)	מאמרות (pl.)	categories (pl.) (§ 2.1.2)
prepositio	מושכל	intelligible
prime prepositiones (pl.)	מושכלות ראשונות (pl.)	first intelligibles (pl.) (§ 12.14.1)
presuppositus	הקדמה	presupposition, assumption (§ 11.9)
primus	ראשון (§ 9.8)	first
	ראשית (§ 3.2.2)	
principium	ראשית	first, beginning (§ 3.2.2), principle (§ 4.9.2)
	התחלה	principle (§ 8.1)
prioritas	קדימה	priority (§ 5.4)
prius et posterius	ראשון ואחרון	before and after [priority and posteriority] (§ 5.5.1)
privatio	העדר	privation (§ 10.8.3)
producens	ממציא	producer, creator (§ 4.9.1)
produco (v.)	ברא (qal) (§ 8.8.1)	to produce, to create, to generate
	המציא (hif.) (§ 16.23)	
	התהווה (hit.) (§ 6.2.1)	
	התחדש (hit.) (§ 6.8)	
	חידש (pi.) (§ 5.5.3)	
produ(c)tio	חידוש	creation (§ 7.3.2)
universi produ(c)tio	חידוש העולם	creation of the universe (§ 10.7.1)
propinquitas	קורבה	proximity (§ 7.3.4)
proportio	יחס	proportion; relation (§ 9.10.2)
proportionatus (adj.)	מוכן (§ 6.5.2)	proportioned, capable, disposed
	מיוחד (§ 5.1.2)	

(*cont.*)

Latin	Hebrew	English
propositio	הנחה	proposition, statement (§ 12.13)
proprius	מיוחד	proper, designated (§ 3.3.4)
provenio (v.)	המציא (hif.) (§ 8.4.2)	to come forth
	התהווה (hit.) (§ 8.5.1)	
provideo (v.)	השגיח (hif.)	to exert providence (§ 9.5)
provisio	הבחנה	discernment, foresight (§ 10.7.2)
punctum	נקודה	point (§ 1.1.1)
purum (adj., adv.)	מוחלט	pure, absolute (§ 2.5.2)
purus (adj.)	נקי	pure (§ 9.11.2)
qualitas	איכות	quality (§ 1.14)
quantitas	כמות (§ 5.5.1)	quantity
	שיעור (§ 10.4.2)	
questio	חקירה	question (§ 1.3.3)
	ספק	question (§ 4.9.2)
quidditas	מהות	quiddity (§ 1.3.5)
quies	מנוחה	rest (§ 5.1.1)
in quiete	במנוחה	at rest (§ 8.5.1)
radix	יסוד (§ 4.3.3)	root, principle
	עיקר (§ 15.3.2)	
	שרש (§ 10.7.2)	
ratio	סברא / סברה	opinion (§ 1.3.2)
rationale/non rationale	בלתי מדברי/מדברי	rational/irrational (§ 12.1.2 / § 12.8.1)
receptio	קבלה	reception (§ 12.5.2)
recipiens	מקבל	receiving, receiver (§ 12.5.2)
recipio (v.)	קיבל (pi.)	to receive (§ 12.5.2)
reciprocatio	חזרה	reciprocation (§ 6.3.1)
Rector	מנהיג	Arranger (§ 6.9.2)
rectus (adj.)/non rectus	ישרה / בלתי ישרה	right/non-right (§ 12.14.3)
religio	דת	religion (§ 1.2.4)
remotio	ריחוק	withdrawal; distancing (§ 7.3.4)
resistentia	התנגדות	resistance (§ 2.2.2)
respectus	ערך	respect, relation (§ 8.7)
rotunditas	כדוריות	roundness (§ 4.10)
sapiens	חכם	wise (§ 11.4.2)
sapientia	חכמה	wisdom (§ 4.3.3)
sciens	חכם	knowing, understanding (§ 12.14.3)
scientia	עיון (§ 14.5)	science; knowledge
	ידיעה (§ 9.2.1)	
scio (v.)	ידע (qal)	to know, to understand (§ 9.2.1)
semper	לעולם	for ever (§ 2.2.1)
	נצחי	perpetual (§ 2.2.1)
semper manens/impermanentia	קיים / בלתי קיים	permanent/impermanent (§ 6.2.2 / § 8.4.3)
sempiternum	נצחי	eternal, immortal (§ 12.8.2)
sensatus	מוחש	sensible (§ 12.2.7)
sensibilium	מוחש	sensible (§ 12.2.7)
sensus	חוש	sense (§ 12.2.7)

(*cont.*)

Latin	Hebrew	English
sententia	הנחה	thesis (§ 1.4.1)
	מאמר	discourse, statement (§ 8.2)
sentio (v.)	הרגיש (hif.)	to sense (§ 12.7)
separatus	נבדל	separate (§ 6.7.2)
sequaces (pl.)	נמשכים (pl.)	partisans, followers (§ 1.6.1)
sermo	מאמר	discourse (§ 1.3.5)
siccus	יבש	dry (§ 3.8.1)
significatio	הוראה	signification, indication (§ 6.4.2)
similis (adj.)	דומה	similar (§ 12.9)
similitudo	דמות	likeness (§ 2.2.3)
simplex	פשוט	simple (§ 6.2.2)
sol	שמש	sun (§ 4.4.1)
sollicitudo	השגחה	providence (§ 11.8)
species	מין	species (§ 1.5.7)
sphera	כדור	sphere (§ 4.3.4)
sphera telluris	כדור הארץ	earth (§ 1.1.1)
stella	כוכב	star (§ 4.9.1)
subiectum	נושא	subject, substrate (§ 4.7.1)
substantia	גרם (§ 1.1.1) עצם (§ 4.4.2)	substance, substrate
prima substantia	עצם ראשון	first substance (§ 8.5.1)
substantia abstracta	עצם נבדל	separate substance (§ 3.8.1)
superior	עליון	higher, upper (§ 9.6.3)
suscipio (v.)	קיבל (pi.)	to acknowledge (§ 12.15.5)
su(b)stineo (v.)	נשא (qal)	to endure (§ 6.1)
tabula rasa	לוח נקי	clean slate (*metaph.* intellect) (§ 12.12.2)
tempus	זמן	time (§ 5.5.1)
tenebra	חושך	darkness (§ 10.8.3)
terra	ארץ	earth (§ 5.6.1)
Tetragrammaton	שם מיוחד	Tetragrammaton (§ 6.9.2)
theologi (pl.)	בעלי הדתות (pl.) (§ 1.5.2) מדברים (pl.) (§ 6.9.2)	theologians; adherents of religion
transfero (v.)	השיא	to transfer (§ 10.3.2)
transmutatio	השתנות	change (§ 3.6)
transmutor (v.)	השתנה (hit.)	to change (§ 12.7)
ultimus	אחרון	final (§ 1.6.2 (1.))
unicus (adj.)	יחיד	only (§ 9.1)
unitas	אחדות	unity (§ 8.3.2)
universale (adv.)	בכלל	universally (§ 5.5.1)
universalis	כל	universal (§ 9.11.2)
universalis (adj.)	כללי	universal, general (§ 9.2.1)
utilitas	תועלת	advantage (§ 16.10.1)
vacuum	ריק	void (adj.) (§ 2.5.2)
	ריקות	vacuum (n.) (§ 2.1.3)
vanus	חסור	defective, useless (§ 8.4.3)
vas	כלי	vessel (§ 9.12.1)

(*cont.*)

Latin	Hebrew	English
velox	מהיר	fast (§ 4.3.2)
verbum	דבר	word; discourse (§ 6.1)
verba obscura (pl.)	מאמרים סתומים	obscure discourse (§ 8.5.1)
soffisitica verba (pl.)	דברים מזוייפים (pl.)	sophistic discourse (§ 9.11.2)
verifico (v.)	צדק (qal)	to verify (§ 2.5.2)
veritas	אמת	truth (§ 12.2.5)
verum (adj.)	אמיתי	true (§ 1.3)
vilis	נקלה (§ 15.1)	lower, inferior
	פחות (§ 11.2)	
violentus	מכריח	violent (§ 4.5.3)
	הכרחי	(§ 4.5.3)
virtus	יכולת (§ 8.4.1)	power; capability
	כוח (§ 12.5.5)	power; faculty
per humanam virtutem	בכח אנושי	according to human power (§ 14.1)
per naturalem vel divinam virtutem	בכח אלהי או טבעי	according to divine or natural power (§ 1.5)
desiderativa virtus	כוח מתאוה	appetite (faculty of desire) (§ 5.6.2)
virtus intellectiva	כוח שכלי	intellectual faculty (§ 12.8.1)
visio	ראייה	vision, seeing
sensuali visione	ראייה חושיית	sensorial vision (§ 1.13)
intellectuali visione	ראייה שכלית	intellectual vision (§ 1.13)
vivus (adj.)	חי	alive (§ 9.8)
voluntarius (adj.)	רצוני	voluntary (§ 10.8.2)
voluntas	רצון (§ 10.2)	will
	כוונה (§ 1.5.7)	
preter voluntatem	בלתי כוונה	without will, unintended (§ 1.6.2 (6.))
voluptas	הנאה (§ 13.3.2)	pleasure
	תענוג (§ 12.5.2)	
	נאה (§ 13.3.2)	pleasant thing

Bibliography

Sources

ABRAVANEL, Isaac. *Rosh Amanah*. Edited by Menahem Kellner. Ramat-Gan: Bar-Ilan University Press, 1993.

AMRAM, David Werner. *The Makers of Hebrew Books in Italy*. Philadelphia: Greenstone, 1909.

AQUINAS, Thomas. *Contra Gentiles. Book Three: Providence, Q. 1–83*. Translated by Vernon J. Bourke. Edited by Joseph Kenny, O.P. New York: Hanover House, 1955. https://isidore.co/aquinas/ContraGentiles3a.htm.

AQUINAS, Thomas. *On the Unity of the Intellect against the Averroists*. Translated by Beatrice H. Zedler. Milwaukee: Marquette University Press, 1968.

ARISTOTLE AND AVERROES. *Aristotelis metaphysicorum libri XIIII cum Averrois cordubensis in eosdem commentariis et epitome, Theophrasti metaphysicorum liber editio Juntina prima*. Vol. 8 of *Aristotelis Stagiritae omnia quae extant opera*. Venetiis, 1552; revised and republished 1562 and 1574.

ARISTOTLE AND AVERROES. *Metaphysica*. Vol. 3.1 of Aristotle and Averroes, *Opera latine cum commentariis Averrois, recensuit Nicolatus Vernia*. [Venice], 1483.

ARISTOTLE AND AVERROES. *Metaphysica Aristotelis cum commentariis Averrois*. Lyons, 1529.

AVERROES. *Averroes' Destructio destructionum philosophiae Algazelis in the Latin Version of Calo Calonymos*. Edited by Beatrice H. Zedler. Milwaukee: Marquette University Press, 1961.

AVERROES. *Šarḥ mā baʿd al-ṭabīʿa* (شرح ما بعد الطبيعة). Digital copy of Averroes, *Tafsir ma baʿd at-tabiʿat*, edited by Maurice Bouyges. 3 vols. Beirut: Imprimerie catholique, 1938–1952. Available from Cologne's Digital Averroes Research Environment (DARE), 2014: https://dare.uni-koeln.de/app/fulltexts/FT24/section/1120.

BACHER, Wilhelm. "The Views of Jehuda Halevi Concerning the Hebrew Language." *Hebraica* 8, no. 3 (1892): 136–149.

BADAWĪ, ʿAbd al-Raḥmān. *Averroes (Ibn Rushd)*. Paris: Vrin, 1998.

BASS, Shabbatai. *Sefer Sifte Yeshenim*. Vol. 1. Amsterdam, 1680.

BARTHES, Roland. *Elements of Semiology*. New York: Hill and Wang, 1968.

BELLETTINI, Pierangelo. "La stamperia camerale di Bologna. 1—Alessandro e Vittorio Benacci (1587–1629)." *La Bibliofilia* 90 (1988): 21–53.

BERNS, Andrew. "Ovadiah Sforno's Last Will and Testament." *Journal of Jewish Studies* 68 (2017): 1–33.

BEUGHEM, Cornelius van. *Incunabula typographiae sive catalogus librorum scriptorumque proximis ab inventione typographiae annis, usque ad annum Christi M.D.* Amstelodami, 1668.

BIANCHI, Luca. "Continuity and Change in the Aristotelian Tradition." In *The Cambridge Companion to Renaissance Philosophy*, edited by James Hankins, 49–71. Cambridge: Cambridge University Press, 2007.

BONFIL, Robert. "The Doctrine of the Human Soul and Its Holiness in the Thought of Rabbi Obadiah Seforno" [Hebrew]. *Eshel Beer Sheva* 1 (1976): 200–257.

BONFIL, Robert. "Il Rinascimento. La produzione esegetica di O. Servadio Sforno." In *La lettura ebraica delle Scritture*, edited by Sergio J. Sierra, 261–277. Bologna: Edizioni Dehoniane, 1995.

BUXTORF, Johannes. *De abbreviaturis Hebraicis liber novus [et] copiosus*. Basileae, 1613.

BUXTORF, Johannes. *De abbreviaturis Hebraicis liber novus [et] copiosus [...] editione secunda*. Basileae, 1640.

CALO CALONIMUS. *Liber de mundi creatione physicis rationibus probata egregij doctoris Calo Calonymos hebrei Neapolitani ad reuerendissimum dominum dominum Egidium cardinalem litterarum patrem*. Venetiis, 1527.

CAMPANINI, Saverio. "Un intellettuale ebreo del Rinascimento. 'Ovadyah Sforno a Bologna e i suoi rapporti con i cristiani." In *Verso l'epilogo di una convivenza. Gli ebrei a Bologna nel XVI secolo*, edited by Maria Giuseppina Muzzarelli, 98–128. Florence: Giuntina, 1996.

CAMPANINI, Saverio. "Reuchlins jüdische Lehrer aus Italien," ed. Gerald Dörner, *Reuchlin und Italien*, Stuttgart: Jan Thorbecke, 1999: 69–85.

CAMPANINI, Saverio. "Roman Holiday: Conjectures on Johann Reuchlin as a Pupil of Obadiah Sforno." In *The Literary and Philosophical Canon of Obadiah Sforno*, edited by Giuseppe Veltri et al. Leiden: Brill, 2023.

CAMPANINI, Saverio. "Sforno, 'Ovadyah." *Dizionario biografico degli Italiani* 92 (2018). https://www.treccani.it/enciclopedia/ovadyah-sforno_(Dizionario-Biografico).

COLORNI, Vittore. "Spigolature su Obadià Sforno: La sua laurea a Ferrara e la quasi ignota edizione della sua opera OR'AMIM nella versione latina." *La rassegna mensile di Israel* 28, nos. 3/4 (1962): 78–88.

DAHAN, Eric. "Philosophie et tradition dans le commentaire de *Sforno* sur *Qohelet*." *Yod* 15 (2010): 145–87.

DAVID BEN YEHUDAH MESSER LEON. *Tehillah-le David*. Constantinople, 1577.

DE ROSSI, Giovanni B. *Dizionario storico degli autori ebrei e delle loro opere*. Parma, 1802.

DI NOLA, Annalisa. *Le cinquecentine ebraiche—Catalogo*. Milan: Aisthesis, 2001.

DUBNOW, Simon. *Weltgeschichte des Jüdischen Volkes*. Vol. 6. Berlin: Jüdischer Verlag, 1927.

ELIJAH OF BUTRIO. *Yivkeh be-mar nefesh; La-meqonenot qiru le-'orer qinah*. Edited by Meir Benayahu. In *Sefer Rabbi Yosef Qaro*, edited by Yitzḥaq Raphael, 302–340. Jerusalem: Mossad ha-Rav Kook, 1969.

ENGEL, Michael. *Elijah Del Medigo and Paduan Aristotelianism: Investigating the Human Intellect*. London: Bloomsbury, 2017.

FINKEL, Ephraim. *R. Obadja Sforno als Exeget*. Breslau, 1896.

FOREN, Symon. "'A Fourth Kind of Being': The Legacy of Averroes in Obadiah Sforno's Theory of the Intellect." In *The Literary and Philosophical Canon of Obadiah Sforno*, edited by Giuseppe Veltri et al. Leiden: Brill, 2023.

FOREN, Symon. "Reconciling Philosophy and Scripture in Renaissance Italy: Obadiah Sforno's Hebrew and Latin Versions of the *Light of the Nations*." PhD diss., Oxford University, 2020.

FRANK, Daniel H., and Oliver LEAMAN. "Jewish Philosophy in the Renaissance." In *The Jewish Philosophy Reader*, edited by Charles H. Manekin, 282–299. London: Routledge, 2000.

FRIEDENWALD, Harry. *Jewish Luminaries in Medical History and a Catalogue of Works Bearing on the Subject of the Jews and Medicine from the Private Library of Harry Friedenwald*. New York: Ktav, 1946.

FÜRST, Julius. *Bibliotheca Judaica: Bibliographisches Handbuch der gesammten jüdischen Literatur mit Einschluss der Schriften über Juden und Judenthum und einer Geschichte der jüdischen Bibliographie nach alfabetischer Ordnung der Verfasser*. Vol. 3. Leipzig, 1863.

FÜRST, Julius. "Manuscripte in Brody und einzelne Berichte." *Wissenschaftliche Zeitschrift für Jüdische Theologie* 3 (1837): 282–287.

Geiger, Abraham. *Melo Chofnajim*. Berlin, 1840.

Gersonides, Levi. *Milchamot ha-Schem—Die Kämpfe Gottes*. Leipzig, 1866; repr. Berlin: Lamm, 1923.

Gersonides, Levi. *The Wars of the Lord. Book One: Immortality of the Soul*. Translated by Seymour Feldman. Philadelphia: Jewish Publication Society of America, 1984.

Giglioni, Guido. "*Haec igitur est nostra lex*. Teologia e filosofia nel commento di Agostino Nifo alla *Destructio destructionum* di Averroè." In *L'averroismo in età moderna*, edited by Giovanni Licata, 125–144. Macerata: Quodlibet, 2013.

Giglioni, Guido. "Introduction." In *Renaissance Averroism and Its Aftermath: Arabic Philosophy in Early Modern Europe*, edited by Anna Akasoy and Guido Giglioni, 1–34. Dordrecht: Springer: 2013.

Ginsburg, Louis. *Legends of the Jews*. Translated by Henrietta Szold. 7 vols. Philadelphia: Jewish Publication Society of America, 1909–1942.

Giuditta, Elvio. *Araldica ebraica in Italia. Segue parte II: Stemmi esistenti nell'antico cimitero ebraico di Venezia, lettere dalla ralla Z*. Turin: Società italiana di studi araldici, 2007.

Graetz, Heinrich. *Geschichte der Juden, Bd. 9: Von der Verbannung der Juden aus Spanien und Portugal bis zur ersten dauernden Ansiedelung der Marranen in Holland (1618)*. Leipzig, 1866.

Graetz, Heinrich. *History of the Jews, Volume 4: From the Rise of the Kabbala (1270 C.E.) to the Permanent Settlement of the Marranos in Holland (1618 C.E.)*. Edited and translated by Bella Löwy. Philadelphia, 1894.

Guetta, Alessandro. "Renaissance Maimonideanism." In *Encyclopedia of Renaissance Philosophy*, edited by Marco Sgarbi. https://doi.org/10.1007/978--3--319--02848--4_161--1.

Halevi, Judah. *Kitab al Khazari*. Translated by Hartwig Hirschfeld. London: Routledge; New York: Dutton, 1905.

Harboun, Haïm. "*Or Ha'Amim* de Rabbi Obadia Sforno, XVIe siècle: Édition critique et analyse du manuscrit 435 de la Bibliothèque Nationale." PhD diss., Aix-Marseille 1, 1994.

Harvey, Warren Zev. "Sforno on Intellectual *Imitatio Dei*." In *The Literary and Philosophical Canon of Obadiah Sforno*, edited by Giuseppe Veltri et al. Leiden: Brill, 2023.

Hasse, Dag Nikolaus. *Success and Suppression: Arabic Sciences and Philosophy in the Renaissance*. Cambridge, MA: Harvard University Press, 2016.

Karpeles, Gustav. *Geschichte der Jüdischen Literatur*. 2 vols. Berlin, 1886.

Kellner, Menachem. "Maimonides' True Religion: For Jews, or All Humanity?" *Me'orot* 7 (2008): 1–24.

Klein-Braslavy, Sara. "La méthode diaporématique de Gersonide dans les *Guerres du Seigneur*." In *Les méthodes de travail de Gersonide et le maniement du savoir chez les scolastiques*, edited by Colette Sirat, Sara Klein-Braslavy, and Olga Weijers, 121–128. Paris: Vrin, 2003.

Klein-Braslavy, Sara. "The Solutions of the Aporias in Gersonides' *Wars of the Lord*" [Hebrew]. *Da'at* 50/52 (2003): 499–514.

Klein-Braslavy, Sara. *"Without Any Doubt"—Gersonides on Method and Knowledge*. Translated and edited by Lenn J. Schramm. Leiden: Brill, 2011.

Kravetz, Moshe. "The Footprints and Influence of *Or 'Ammin* in Sforno's Exegetical Works." In *The Literary and Philosophical Canon of Obadiah Sforno*, edited by Giuseppe Veltri et al. Leiden: Brill, 2023.

Kravetz, Moshe. "R. Ovadiah Sforno, his school in Bologna, his disciple R. Elia di Nola, and a study of their relationship through Nola's commentary on the Psalms." PhD diss., Universität Hamburg, 2023.

KREISEL, Howard. "*Imitatio Dei* in Maimonides' 'Guide of the Perplexed.'" *AJS Review* 19 (1994): 169–211.

KUHN, Heinrich C. "Die Verwandlung der Zerstörung der Zerstörung. Bemerkungen zu Augustinus Niphus' Kommentar zur *Destructio destructionum* des Averroes." In *Averroismus im Mittelalter und in der Renaissance*, edited by Friedrich Niewöhner and Loris Sturlese, 291–308. Zürich: Spur, 1994.

LICATA, Giovanni. *Secundum Avenroem. Pico della Mirandola, Elia del Medigo e la "seconda rivelazione" di Averroè*. Palermo: Officina di Studi Medievali, 2022.

LOEB, Isidore. "Liste nominative des Juifs de Barcelone en 1392." *Revue des études juives* 7 (1882): 57–77.

MARENBON, John. *Later Medieval Philosophy (1150–1350): An Introduction*. Paperback ed. London: Routledge, 1991.

MARGOT, Jean-Claude. *Traduire sans trahir. La théorie de la traduction et son application aux textes bibliques*. Lausanne: L'Âge d'homme, 1979.

MELAMED, Yitzhak. "Teleology in Jewish Philosophy: From the Talmud to Spinoza." In *Teleology: A History*, edited by Jeffrey McDonough, 123–149. New York: Oxford University Press, 2020.

MONTADA, Josep Puig. "Eliahu del Medigo, the Last Averroist." In *Exchange and Transmission across Cultural Boundaries: Philosophy, Mysticism and Science in the Mediterranean World*, edited by Haggai Ben-Shammai, Shaul Shaked, and Sarah Stroumsa, 155–186. Jerusalem: Israel Academy of Sciences and Humanities, 2013.

MURANO, Giovanna. "Il manoscritto della *Destructio destructionum* di Averroè appartenuto a Giovanni Pico della Mirandola (Napoli, Biblioteca Nazionale, VIII E 31)." *Bulletin de philosophie médiévale* 60 (2018): 67–80.

NEWMARKT, Peter. *A Textbook of Translation*. London: Prentice Hall International, 1988.

NIDA, Eugene Albert. *Toward a Science of Translating with Special Reference to Principles and Procedures Involved in Bible Translating*. Leiden: Brill, 1964.

NIFO, Agostino. *Commentationes in librum Averrois De substantia orbis*. Venitiis, 1508.

NIFO, Agostino. *Destructio destructionum Averroiis cum Agostino Niphi de Sessa expositione*. Venezia, 1497.

POMPONAZZI, Pietro. *On the Immortality of the Soul*. Translated by William Henry Hay II and John Herman Randall, Jr. Edited by Ernst Cassirer, Paul Oskar Kristeller, and John Herman Randall, Jr. Chicago: University of Chicago Press, 1956.

PROSPERI, Adriano. *L'Inquisizione romana: Letture e ricerche*. Rome: Edizioni di storia e letteratura, 2003.

RIVA, Claudio. "Tracce della presenza del banchiere ebreo bolognese Jacob di Rubino Sforno in Cesena." *Studi Romagnoli* 49 (2018): 397–410.

SAUSSURE, Ferdinand de. *Cours de linguistique générale*. Paris: Payot, 1949.

SCHMITT, Charles B. "Towards a Reassessment of Renaissance Aristotelianism." *History of Science* 11 (1973): 159–193.

SFORNO, Obadiah. *Amar ha-ga'on. Shi'ure R. 'Ovadyah Sforno mi-ketav yad talmido 'al ha-Torah*. Edited by Moshe Kravetz. Bet-Shemesh: s.n., 2017.

SFORNO, Obadiah. *Be'ur 'al ha-Torah*. Edited by Ze'ev Gottlieb. Jerusalem: Mossad ha-Rav Kook, 1980.

SFORNO, Obadiah. *Commentary on Pirkei Avos*. Translation and explanatory notes by Raphael Pelcovitz. New York: Mesorah, 1996.

SFORNO, Obadiah. *Commentary on the Torah*. Translation and explanatory notes by Raphael Pelcovitz. 2 vols. Brooklyn: Mesorah Publications, 1987–1989.

SFORNO, Obadiah. *Kitve R. 'Ovadyah Sforno*. Edited by Ze'ev Gottlieb. Jerusalem: Mossad ha-Rav Kook, 1983.

Sforno, Obadiah. *Lumen Gentium*. Bologna, 1548.

Sforno, Obadiah. *Lumen Gentium*. Reggio Emilia, Biblioteca Panizzi, MSS. Vari E. 5.

Sforno, Obadiah. *Maḥzor ke-fi minhag q"q Roma 'im perush Qimḥa de-avshuna ['a. y. Yoḥanan ben Yosef Ish Ṭrivish] u-masekhet Avot 'im perush [...] ha-Rambam ve-'im perush [...] 'Ovadyah Sforno*. Bologna, 1540.

Sforno, Obadiah. *Megillat Qohelet 'im perush Sforno*. Edited by Moshe Kravetz. Bet-Shemesh: s.n., 2016.

Sforno, Obadiah. *Shir ha-Shirim, Rut 'im perush Sforno ha-mevo'ar*. Edited by Moshe Kravetz. Bet-Shemesh: s.n., 2015.

Sforno, Obadiah. *Opusculum nuper editum contra nonnullas Peripateticorum opiniones demonstratiue docens presertim circa creationem & vniuersi nouitatem & diuinam de mortalibus curam & humanarum animarum immortalitatem. Quas ipsi turpiter respuunt religionis penitus irridentes quare illud merito lumen gentium appello*. Bologna, 1548.

Sforno, Obadiah. *Or 'Ammim*. Bologna, 1537; reprint: Ramat Gan: s.n., 1970.

Sforno, Obadiah. *Perush R. 'Ovadyah Sforno ha-mevu'ar: Perush ha-Torah*. Edited by Moshe Kravetz. Bet-Shemesh: s.n., 2015.

Sforno, Obadiah. *Sifre Shir ha-shirim, Rut 'im perush Sforno*. Edited by Moshe Kravetz. Bet-Shemesh: s.n., 2015.

Sforno, Obadiah. *Sifre Yonah, Ḥavaqquq, Zekharyah 'im perush Sforno*. Edited by Moshe Kravetz. Bet-Shemesh: s.n., 2015.

Shem Ṭov Falaquera. *Sefer ha-Ma'a lot*. Berlin, 1894.

Shine, Chaim. *Adam, Ḥevrah u-mishpat be-haguto shel R. 'Ovadyah. Sforno*. Tel Aviv: Sha'are Mishpat, 2001.

Shine, Chaim. "Diyyuno shel Rabbi 'Ovadyah Sforno 'al ha-hashgaḥah." *Pe'amim* 20 (1984): 77–84.

Swinburne, Richard. "Argument from the Fine-Tuning of the Universe." In *Physical Cosmology and Philosophy*, edited by John Leslie, 154–173. New York: Collier Macmillan, 1990.

Veltri, Giuseppe. *Alienated Wisdom: Enquiry into Jewish Philosophy and Scepticism*. Berlin: De Gruyter, 2018.

Veltri, Giuseppe, and Reimund Leicht, eds. *peshat in Context—A Thesaurus of Pre-Modern Philosophic and Scientific Hebrew Terminology*. https://peshat.org.

Vogelstein, Hermann, and Paul Rieger. *Geschichte der Juden in Rom. Band 2, 1420–1870*. Berlin, 1895.

Walk, Joseph. "'Ovadyah Sforno ha-Parshan ha-humanist." In *Sefer Neiger; Ma'amarim be ḥeker ha-tanakh le-zekher David Neiger z"l'*, edited by Arthur Biram, 277–302. Jerusalem: *Israel Society for* Biblical Research, 1959. Reprint: *As Yesterday: Essays and Reminiscences*, Jerusalem 1997, 183–211.

Waterworth, James, trans. *Canons and Decrees of the Council of Trent. The Fourth Session Celebrated on the Eighth Day of the Month of April, in the Year 1546*. London, 1848. http://www.bible-researcher.com/trent1.html.

Wolf, Johann Christoph. *Bibliotheca Hebraea*. Hamburgi & Lipsiae, 1715.

Zaccagnini, Guido. *Storia dello Studio di Bologna durante il rinascimento: Con quarantadue illustrazioni*. Florence: Olschki, 1930.

Zonta, Mauro. *Hebrew Scholasticism in the Fifteenth Century: A History and Source Book*. Dordrecht: Springer, 2006.

Manuscripts

Bazzano, Biblioteca provinciale Salvatore Tommasi, CINQ. B 245 / b
Berlin, Staatsbibliothek, Or. Fol. 1388
Bologna, Biblioteca Universitaria, A. 5. Tab. 1.F.1 402/3
Cincinnati, Hebrew Union College 729
Jerusalem, National Library of Israel, R8 = FR 889
London, Montefiore Library 415 (formerly Montefiore 29)
Mantua, Comunita Israelitica, MS ebr. 105
Modena, Biblioteca Estense Universitaria, A 017 G 006
Munich, Bayerische Staatsbibliothek, Cod. hebr. 65
Munich, Bayerische Staatsbibliothek, Res/4 A.hebr. 310
New York, Columbia University, X 893 T 67.
New York, Jewish Theological Seminary, MIC PRINT 484
Oxford, Bodleian Library, Mich. 441
Paris, Bibliothèque Mazarine, 4° 15228–2 [Res]
Paris, Bibliothèque Nationale, hebr. 886
Paris, Bibliothèque Nationale, hebr. 887
Paris, Bibliothèque Nationale, hebr. 889
Paris, Bibliothèque Nationale, hébreu 1007
Parma, Biblioteca Palatina 2239
Parma, Biblioteca Palatina 2399
Parma, Biblioteca Palatina 2624
Reggio Emilia, Biblioteca Panizzi, MSS. Vari E. 5
Rome, Biblioteca Apostolica Vaticana, Borgh. 306
Rome, Biblioteca Apostolica Vaticana, R.G. Filos. IV.732
Rome, Biblioteca Apostolica Vaticana, Vat. Ebr. 336
Rome, Biblioteca Apostolica Vaticana, Vat Lat. 2080
Rome, Biblioteca Apostolica Vaticana, Vat. Lat. 2081
Rome, Bibliotheca Casanatense, LL.VIII.33.1
Rome, Biblioteca Casanatense, *L[MIN] II 20
St Petersburg, Institute of Oriental Manuscripts of the Russian Academy of Sciences, B 169
Vienna, Österreichische Nationalbibliothek, 20.K.47

Source Index to the Editions and Translations

Bible

Genesis
1:1	113, 126, 127, 146, 147, 166, 167, 254, 376, 379, 380
1:2	94n, 112, 113, 126, 127, 166, 167, 174
1:4	94, 95, 96, 254, 255
1:5	254, 255
1:16	146
1:17–18	146, 147
1:26	54, 55, 294, 298, 312, 313, 314, 316, 319, 332, 358, 388, 389
1:27	306, 307, 315
2:4	190, 191, 376, 377
3:6	52n
5:1	214n, 386
5:24	54, 55
6:4	56n
6:9	54, 55
9:5	384
9:6	384
13:13	320
14:13	52, 53
17:1	380, 381
17:7	392
17:14	392
24:40	54, 55
39:9	48n
44:16	58n
48:15	54
49:21	64n

Exodus
2:6	55
3:18	54
7:28	52n
19:5–6	334
19:6	392, 393
20:5–6	260, 261, 383
20:6	332
20:18	60n
24:10	296, 297, 298
24:12	320
27:20	50n
28:38	58n
29:43	60n
33:16	46n
33:21	62n
34:10	52n
34:12	166

Leviticus
11:44	332, 388
11:45	334
16:2	56n
18:5	56n
19:2	332, 333, 342, 343
19:8	392, 393
23:30	392, 393
26:16	64n

Numbers
11:26	62n
13:33	50n
15:30–31	393
17:25	66n
22:23	64n
24:3	46n
35:22	62n

Deuteronomy
1:5	46n
4:15	382
4:15–16	200, 201
4:19	200, 201, 202, 203
4:39	50, 67, 68, 190, 191, 214, 215
6:4–5	48, 210
6:24–25	392
7:9	68
8:6	388
10:12	316, 342, 343, 356, 357, 388
10:13	342, 343
10:14–15	316, 356, 357
11:13	333
11:22	56n, 60n, 332
14:1	388, 390, 391
25:2	48n
26:18–19	334, 392, 393
28:32	58n
30:19	386
33:16	50n
33:26	200

Judges
5:16	56n

Ruth
2:2	48n

1 Samuel
2:3	48n
26:4	60n

2 Samuel
14:19	46

2 Kings
9:13	52n

1 Chronicles
6:49	391n
28:19	52n
29:11	388

2 Chronicles
20:12	58n
24:9	391n

Nehemiah
8:8	52n
9:6	144
10:29	391n
13:6	56n

Esther
1:4	48n
1:14	56n, 338n

Job
8:19	48n
10:4	368
10:4–6	222, 223
17:9	60n
22:2	46n
33:30	54n, 58n
34:19	50n
35:16	48n

Psalms
1:1	320
1:2	320
1:3	320, 321, 322, 323
8:5	52, 53, 309
8:6	308, 309
12:3	58n
12:7	64n
14:7	358n
19:2	46n
19:9	50n
20:8	358
22:31	64n
23:3	46n
24:4	300
24:10	206, 207, 212, 213, 216, 217
25:10	342
33:14	56n
36:10	50, 52n, 60n
40:8	50n
41:2	46n
44:23	50n
49:10	60n
49:13	386, 390, 391
65:5	334
65:6	64n
68:11	46n
73:1	64n
77:8	50n
78:36	56n
78:65	366n
87:5	50, 358n
89:3	328
94:7	266, 372, 373
94:9	266, 267, 372, 373, 382
94:10	266, 372
94:11–12	382
94:14	382
102:26–27	144, 145
104:4	112, 113, 126, 127, 166, 169
104:5	144, 145
104:14	374, 375
104:24	184, 386
105:44–45	392
106:33	48n
107:42	46n
111:6	146n
111:9	48n
113:5–6	272, 273
115:16	296
118:23	294n
119:9	46n, 320
119:18	50
119:66	50n
119:91	316
119:172	60
125:5	46n, 62n
126:6	56n
139:21	390, 391
145:9	262, 263
145:17	386, 388
148:2	316
149:2	50

Proverbs
3:12	390n
3:19	190, 192
8:9	62n
8:35	46n
12:28	56n
20:1	320
20:24	46
22:21	62n
26:10	388n
30:5	48n

Ecclesiastes
6:11	58n
9:11	50n
9:12	60n
11:9	110
12:9	56n
12:10	50n, 56n
12:11	62n

Song of Songs
5:9	50
8:20	338n

Isaiah
5:8	48n
5:12–13	60
6:3	216
8:20	46n
10:1	46n
10:18	64n
11:4	50n, 58n
24:14	50n
29:13	46n
29:15–16	238, 239, [240], [241]

Isaiah (*cont.*)
34:11	112
35:8	360n
40:5	46n
40:22	52n
40:25	210
40:26	146, 147, 148, 149, 150, 151
40:27	267, 268
40:28	268, 269, 271
40:29	269, 270, 271, 322
40:30	270, 271, 322, 323
40:31	270, 271, 322, 323
41:1	66n
42:3	64n
42:7	60n
43:7	328
44:18	60n
45:7	126, 127, 128, 374, 375, 386
45:19	60, 68, 69
46:5	272
46:10	48n
48:12–13	152, 153
48:13	370, 371
49:1	357
49:3	356
50:11	64n
51:1	394n
51:4	46n
51:6	152, 153
54:5	264n
54:13	58n
55:8	234
57:20	58n
59:11	50n
59:15	54
63:10	46n
66:1	296
66:1–2	356, 357

Jeremiah
2:8	48n
4:22	312
5:12	54
8:19	58n
9:23	60
10:6–7	50
17:11	366n, 367n
23:24	236, 237, 384
33:25	390
48:38	52n
49:7	54n

Lamentations
2:9	56n
3:1	46n

Ezekiel
1:12	62n
1:20	296
18:5	320
18:29	314
34:31	298

Daniel
2:20	48n
9:11	391n
10:11	46n
12:2	64n

Hosea
4:6	60
8:12	60n

Joel
2:23	48n, 68n, 380n
4:14	46n

Jonah
2:9	60n

Micah
4:11	50

Nahum
1:2	390

Habakkuk
2:2	62n

Zephaniah
3:9	60n, 264n, 358n

Rabbinic Literature

Mishnah
Avot 1:3	390
2:4	342, 390
3:14	358
3:15	332
4:13	50n, 312
6:11	328
Sukkah 5:5	46n

Midrash
Mekhiltah Exodus 20:3	48

Talmud
Avodah Zarah 3b	262n
Berakhot 28b	50
33b	316, 342, 356, 388
40a	270, 322
Ketubbot 5a	356
Sanhedrin 38b	294
71b	214
92a	334
106b	50n
Shabbat 152a	322

Sukkah 52b   312
53a   218
Yoma 39a   334

Philosophical literature

Aristotle
Metaphysics
1.1	52n, 53n, 56n, 57n, 256n, 257n
1.2	212n, 213n
1.8	116n, 117n, 118n, 274n, 275n
1.9	74n, 75n, 277n, 344n, 345n
2.1	310n, 311n
2.2	52n, 70n, 71n, 72n, 73n, 76n, 77n, 84n, 85n, 86n, 87n, 92n, 96n, 97n, 116n, 117n, 118n, 177n, 230n, 231n, 246n, 247n, 254n, 255n, 258n, 259n, 274n, 275n
2.6	56n
7.9	72n, 73n
8.2	106n, 107n
8.6	78n, 79n, 100n, 101n
9.3	72n, 73n, 82n, 83n, 84n, 85n, 116n, 117n, 162n, 163n
10.1	54n, 204n, 205n
12.3	70n, 71n, 92n, 100n, 101n, 114n, 115n, 186n, 187n, 288n, 289n, 296n, 297n, 364n, 365n
12.4	158n, 159n
12.6	158n, 159n
12.7	168n, 169n, 204n, 368n
12.8	54n, 55n, 138n, 139n, 148n, 149n, 180n, 181n, 220n, 221n, 368n
12.10	126n, 127n, 206n, 207n, 226n, 227n, 228n, 229n, 258n, 259n, 369n

Nichomachean Ethics
5.8	76n, 77n, 310n, 311n
7.3	314n, 315n

On Generation and Corruption
1.1	129n
1.3	112n, 344n, 345n
1.7	106n, 107n
1.10	106n, 107n, 118n, 121n, 128n, 129n, 298n, 299n
2.1	74n, 75n, 100n, 101n, 116n, 117n, 118n, 119n, 123n, 173n
2.4	78n, 79n, 118n, 121n
2.6	226n, 227n, 290n, 291n
2.7	298n, 299n
2.10	90n, 91n

On the Heavens
1.3	72n, 73n, 74n, 75n, 102n, 103n, 125n, 130n, 131n, 160n, 161n, 170n, 171n, 177n, 288n, 289n
1.5	70n, 71n
1.9	72n, 73n, 110n, 111n, 164n, 165n, 172n, 173n, 186n, 187n
1.10	62n, 63n
1.12	74n, 75n, 100n, 101n, 102n, 103n, 123n, 130n, 131n, 142n, 143n, 178n, 179n, 284n, 285n, 286n, 304n, 305n, 378n, 379n
2.1	130n
2.3	102n, 103n
2.4	152n, 153n
2.5	62n, 63n
2.6	66n, 67n, 360n, 361n
2.7	112n, 113n, 126n, 127n, 140n, 141n
2.8	72n, 73n, 104n, 105n, 132n, 133n, 174n, 175n, 179n, 226n, 227n, 352n, 353n, 370n, 371n
2.12	138n, 139n, 148n, 149n
3.2	98n, 99n, 130n, 131n, 172n, 173n
3.6	74n, 75n, 102n, 103n
3.7	70n, 71n
4.1	56n, 57n

On the Soul
1.3	294n, 295n
1.4	292n, 293n
2.2	294n, 295n
3.2	282n, 283n
3.3	68n, 69n
3.4	74n, 75n, 195n, 196n, 258n, 259n, 271n, 278n, 279n, 280n, 281n, 284n, 285n, 288n, 289n, 290n, 291n, 292n, 293n, 294n, 295n, 304n, 305n, 308n, 309n
3.5	294n, 295n

On the Soul (cont.)

3.10	286n, 287n, 288n, 289n, 314n, 315n, 330n, 331n
3.12	336n, 337n

Physics

1.4	111n, 112n, 113n
1.5	121n
1.8	98n, 99n, 118n, 274n, 275n
1.9	100n, 101n, 114n, 115n, 186n
2.2	88n, 89n, 116n, 255n, 258n, 259n
2.4	72n, 73n, 88n, 89n, 174n, 175n, 178n, 179n, 226n, 227n, 370n, 371n
2.5	72n, 73n, 88n, 89n, 104n, 105n, 178n, 179n, 228n, 229n, 350n, 351n
2.8	88n, 89n, 230n, 231n, 245n, 246n, 258n, 259n, 338n, 339n
2.9	72n, 258n
3.3	158n, 159n
3.6	70n, 71n, 365n
4.8	172n, 173n
4.9	132n, 133n
4.10	132n
4.11	164n, 165n
4.14	117n, 118n, 196n, 197n
6.3	76n, 77n, 86n, 87n
8	168, 169
8.1	84n, 85n, 116n, 117n, 154n, 155n, 156n, 157n, 166n, 167n, 312n, 313n
8.7	76n, 77n, 92n, 93n
8.10	200n, 201n

Politics

1.3	264n, 265n, 354n, 355n, 336n, 337n

Averroes

Incoherence of the Incoherence

1:8	278, 279
1:21	170, 171
2:6	288, 289
3:1	246, 247, 254, 255
3:8	188, 189
3:10	136, 137, 188, 189
3:12	212
3:18	140, 141, 184, 185, 232, 233, 312, 313, 386
3:26	150, 151
4:6	76, 77
4:7	278, 279
5:2	74, 75, 208, 209, 278, 279, 368
5:4	328, 329
6:6	208, 209, 274, 275
9:3	96, 97, 134, 135, 244, 245, 250, 251, 252, 253, 348, 349
10:2	230, 231, 232, 233
10:3	224, 225
11:1	224, 225, 232, 233, 244, 245, 248, 249, 252, 253, 312, 313
12:1	220, 221
12:2	76, 77, 184, 185, 216, 217, 234, 235, 238, 239, 272, 273
13:1	142, 143, 168, 169, 244, 245
14:1	328, 329, 344, 345

Long Commentary on Metaphysics

1:40	208, 209, 276, 277
2:9	86
2:14	326, 327, 366, 367
7:31	184, 185, 198, 199, 294, 295, 368, 369
8:12	78, 79, 100, 101
8:14	106, 107
9:13	72, 73, 86, 87, 116, 117, 119, 158, 159, 177
10:7	204, 205
12:14	300, 301
12:16	158, 159
12:18	88, 89, 110, 111, 124, 125, 186, 187, 230, 231, 258, 259, 294, 295, 306, 307, 352, 368, 369, 370, 371, 372, 373, 379
12:24	216, 217
12:32	158, 159
12:33	248, 249, 372
12:36	168, 169
12:37	222, 223, 256, 257, 368, 369
12:41	194, 195, 364
12:44	138, 139, 148, 149, 210, 211, 316, 319
12:51	76, 77, 222, 223, 234, 235
12:52	204, 205, 206, 207, 228, 229, 256, 257
12:54	[128], [129]

Long Commentary on On the Heavens

1:19	74, 102, 103
1:23	125
1:37	104, 105
1:124	142, 144, 145, 306, 307
1:137	142, 143
2:1	130
2:8	86
2:13	87
2:41	140, 141, 148, 149
3:19	74, 75
3:29	74, 75, 98, 99, 114, 115, 162, 163, 173, 302, 303
3:61	57
3:67	298, 299

Long Commentary on *On the Heavens* (cont.)
    4:1   72, 104, 105, 140, 141, 144, 188, 189

Long Commentary on *On the Soul*
    1:2   318, 319
    3:4   288
    3:5   168, 278, 279, 280, 281, 282, 283, 288, 289, 296, 297, 298, 299, 304, 305, 318, 319
    3:6   290, 291
    3:7   292, 293
    3:36   182, 183, 216, 217, 304, 305, 308, 309

Long Commentary on *Physics*
    2:48   116, 117
    2:80   246n, 247n
    2:89   84, 85
    3:4   350, 351
    3:18   158
    8:4   156, 157
    8:15   136, 137, 154, 155, 244, 245
    8:46   76, 77, 90, 91, 92, 106, 107, 113, 120, 121, 352, 353
    8:85   200, 201

Long Commentary on Porphyry's *Isagoge*
    4   276, 277

Long Commentary on *Posterior Analytics*
    2:11   72, 73, 118, 119, 158, 159, 177n

Middle Commentary on *On Generation and Corruption*
    1:44   292
    1:54   106, 107
    1:87   106, 107
    2:24   78, 79
    2:37   74, 75, 102, 103
    2:45   290, 291
    2:55   78, 79
    2:59   80, 81

Middle Commentary on *Meteorology*
    3:2   58, 59

Middle Commentary on *Nichomachean Ethics*
    5:13   310, 311
    7:5   330, 331

Short Commentary on *On Memory and Recollection*   283

Treatise of the Substance of the Celestial Sphere
    Chapter 2   72n, 73n, 86, 87, 116, 119, 136, 137, 174, 230, 231, 248, 249, 346, 347
    Chapter 4   168, 296, 297, 346, 347

Ibn Tibbon, Samuel ben Judah
Perush ha-millot ha-zarot
                      13, 20, 28, 68

Maimonides, Moses
Guide of the Perplexed
    2:19   108
    2:22   62
    3:13   132
    3:28   48

Mishneh Torah, Hilkhot Yesode ha-Torah 1 [Book of Knowledge]
                      48

Index of Persons

For Introduction and Essay

Abba Mari of Lunel   410
Abraham ben Ḥayyim "the Dyer"   3
Abravanel, Isaac   23, 34, 451, 465, 471
Abravanel, Judah   410, 416
Achillini, Alessandro   433
Albo, Joseph   416
Alemanno, Johanan   410
Arama, Isaac   33
Aristotle *passim*
Ashkenazi, Israel ben Jehiel   1
Aquinas, Pseudo-Thomas   29*n*159, 33
Aquinas, Thomas   19, 30, 31, 417, 422, 424, 427, 442, 443, 446, 449*n*175, 451, 452, 470
Augustine   412, 417
Averroes   16–17, 19, 21, 24, 28, 30–31, 418, 424–427, 431, 435–436, 438, 443, 445, 447–449, 451, 453, 455, 457, 461, 463, 472–473
Avicenna   427*n*84, 434, 459

Bar Ḥiyya, Abraham   33
Bibago, Abraham   21, 417
Boccadiferro, Ludovico   443, 451, 452
Boethius   29, 33, 417, 427, 445
Butrio, Elijah of (alias Elijah ben Joseph di Nola)   17, 21*n*124, 29*n*159, 30, 33, 34, 417

Calonimus, Calo   416, 438, 451, 452
Carracciolo, Landolfo   433
Crescas, Hasdai   4, 28, 416, 422, 451

Da Pisa, Giulia (second wife of Obadia Sforno)   2
Da Pisa, Isaac   2
Da Thiene, Gaetano   21, 417, 438*n*122
De Balmes, Abraham   416
De' Ramazzotti, Armaciotto ("Lord of Tosignano")   2
Del Medigo, Elijah   16, 21, 30*n*170, 417, 438*n*119
Delmedigo, Josef Solomon   33
Di Nola, Elijah ben Joseph. *See* Butrio, Elijah of
Duran, Tzemaḥ   2

Falaquera, Shem Ṭov   20, 416
Farissol, Abraham   411*n*15, 425
Flavius Josephus   410, 416

Al-Ġazālī, Muhammad   434

Gersonides, Levi   23, 27*n*146, 31, 33, 416, 425, 430, 440, 442, 444, 451, 471
Giaccarelli, Anselmo   5, 6*n*44
Grosseteste, Robert   417, 470

Habillo, Eli   21
Halevi, Judah   20, 28, 409, 410, 416, 459, 460, 471
Henri II (king of France)   2*n*16, 6*n*44, 6*n*45, 24

Ibn Daud, Abraham   416, 471
Ibn Ezra, Abraham   416, 417, 464, 471
Ibn Ezra, Moses   3
Ibn Gabirol, Solomon   473
Ibn Paqudah, Baḥya   416
Ibn Rushd. *See* Averroes
Ibn Sina. *See* Avicenna
Ibn Tibbon, Samuel   13, 17*n*98, 19*n*112, 20, 28, 414

Jandun, Jean de   417, 438, 457, 458

Karo, Joseph   33*n*187

Maimonides, Moses   1, 13, 17*n*98, 19, 20, 24, 27, 28, 30, 31, 32, 33, 34, 409, 411*n*15, 413, 414, 415, 416, 422, 424, 427*n*84, 437, 440*n*126, 442, 451, 458*n*205, 459*n*206, 461, 462*n*220, 462*n*221, 469, 471, 475, 476*n*286
Mantino, Jacob   16, 432, 446
Messer Leon, David ben Judah   23, 410, 417
Messer Leon, Judah   21, 417

Nacchiante, Jacopo (Giacomo)   433
Nahmanides   33, 417, 464
Nifo, Agostino   12, 21, 23*n*126, 29, 33, 416, 417, 436, 438, 443, 446
Norsa, Allegra (first wife of Obadiah Sforno)   2

Pavesi, Giovanni Jacopo   433
Philo of Alexandria   464, 465, 470
Plato   31, 33*n*194, 410, 414, 423*n*64, 463
Pomponazzi, Pietro   27, 433

Rambam. *See* Maimonides, Moses
Recanati, Menachem   3*n*24, 410
Reuchlin, Johann   1, 19*n*112, 28*n*149, 35, 414*n*35, 416
Reuveni, David   1

Saadia Gaon   28, 416
Scot, Michael   10, 432
Sforno (Desforn), Dora   2
Sforno (Desforn), Florio   2
Sforno (Desforn), Hananel   2
Sforno (Desforn), Jacob   2
Sforno (Desforn), Jacob di Rubino   1
Sforno (Desforn), Moses   2
Sforno (Desforn), Obadiah ben Jacob *passim*
Sforno (Desforn), Samuele   1*n*2

Sforno (Desforn), Senton (= Shem Ṭov) 1*n*2
Simplicius 33, 423, 455*n*194

Tzarfati, Samuel 1
Troki, Zeraḥ ben Natan of 33

Venice, Paul of 21, 417, 439, 441*n*130, 446